RISK RATIOS

Short-Term Liquidity Risk

$$\text{Current Ratio} = \frac{\text{Current Assets}}{\text{Current Liabilities}}$$
(Page 295)

$$\text{Quick Ratio} = \frac{\text{Cash and Cash Equivalents} + \text{Short-Term Investments} + \text{Accounts Receivable}}{\text{Current Liabilities}}$$
(Page 296)

$$\text{Operating Cash Flow to Current Liabilities Ratio} = \frac{\text{Cash Flow from Operations}}{\text{Average Current Liabilities}}$$
(Page 297)

$$\text{Accounts Receivable Turnover} = \frac{\text{Sales}}{\text{Average Accounts Receivable}}$$
(Page 297)

$$\text{Inventory Turnover} = \frac{\text{Cost of Goods Sold}}{\text{Average Inventories}}$$
(Page 297)

$$\text{Accounts Payable Turnover} = \frac{\text{Purchases}}{\text{Average Accounts Payable}}$$
(Page 297)

Long-Term Solvency Risk

$$\text{Liabilities to Assets Ratio} = \frac{\text{Total Liabilities}}{\text{Total Assets}}$$
(Page 301)

$$\text{Liabilities to Shareholders' Equity Ratio} = \frac{\text{Total Liabilities}}{\text{Total Shareholders' Equity}}$$
(Page 301)

$$\text{Long-Term Debt to Long-Term Capital Ratio} = \frac{\text{Long-Term Debt}}{\text{Long-Term Debt} + \text{Total Shareholders' Equity}}$$
(Page 301)

$$\text{Long-Term Debt to Shareholders' Equity Ratio} = \frac{\text{Long-Term Debt}}{\text{Total Shareholders' Equity}}$$
(Page 301)

Interest Coverage Ratio
$$= \frac{\text{Net Income} + \text{Interest Expense} + \text{Income Tax Expense} + \text{Net Income Attributable to Noncontrolling Interests}}{\text{Interest Expense}}$$
(Page 303)

$$\text{Operating Cash Flow to Total Liabilities Ratio} = \frac{\text{Cash Flow from Operations}}{\text{Average Total Liabilities}}$$
(Page 304)

9E

Financial Reporting, Financial Statement Analysis, and Valuation

A STRATEGIC PERSPECTIVE

James M. Wahlen

Professor of Accounting

James R. Hodge Chair of Excellence
and Accounting Department Chair

Kelley School of Business
Indiana University

Stephen P. Baginski

Professor of Accounting

Herbert E. Miller Chair in Financial Accounting

J.M. Tull School of Accounting
Terry College of Business
The University of Georgia

Mark T. Bradshaw

Professor of Accounting

Chair, Department of Accounting

Carroll School of Management
Boston College

Australia • Brazil • Mexico • Singapore • United Kingdom • United States

Financial Reporting, Financial Statement Analysis, and Valuation, 9e

James Wahlen, Stephen Baginski, Mark Bradshaw

Vice President, General Manager: Social Science & Qualitative Business: Erin Joyner

Product Director: Jason Fremder

Senior Product Manager: John Barans

Project Manager: Julie Dierig

Content Developer: Tara Slagle, MPS Limited

Product Assistant: Aiyana Moore

Executive Marketing Manager: Robin LeFevre

Marketing Coordinator: Hillary Johns

Senior Content Digitization Specialist: Tim Ross

Senior Content Project Manager: Tim Bailey

Production Service: Cenveo Publisher Services

Senior Art Director: Michelle Kunkler

Cover and Internal Designer: Imbue Design

Cover Image: Ravil Sayfullin/Shutterstock.com

Intellectual Property

Analyst: Reba Frederics

Project Manager: Betsy Hathaway

For product information and technology assistance, contact us at
Cengage Customer & Sales Support, 1-800-354-9706

For permission to use material from this text or product, submit all requests online at **www.cengage.com/permissions**
Further permissions questions can be emailed to
permissionrequest@cengage.com

Library of Congress Control Number: 2017947010
ISBN: 978-1-337-61468-9

Cengage
20 Channel Center Street
Boston, MA 02210
USA

Cengage is a leading provider of customized learning solutions with employees residing in nearly 40 different countries and sales in more than 125 countries around the world. Find your local representative at **www.cengage.com**.

Cengage products are represented in Canada by Nelson Education, Ltd.

To learn more about Cengage platforms and services, register or access your online learning solution, or purchase materials for your course, visit **www.cengage.com**.

Printed in the United States of America
Print Number: 02   Print Year: 2018

For our students,

with thanks for permitting us to take the journey with you

For Clyde Stickney and Paul Brown,

with thanks for allowing us the privilege to carry on their legacy of teaching through this book

For our families, with love,

Debbie, Jessica, Jaymie, Ailsa, Lynn, Drew, Marie, Kim, Ben, and Lucy

PREFACE

The process of financial reporting, financial statement analysis, and valuation helps investors and analysts understand a firm's profitability, risk, and growth; use that information to forecast future profitability, risk, and growth; and ultimately to value the firm, enabling intelligent investment decisions. This process is central to the role of accounting, financial reporting, capital markets, investments, portfolio management, and corporate management in the world economy. When conducted with care and integrity, thorough financial statement analysis and valuation are fascinating and rewarding activities that can create tremendous value for society. However, as the recent financial crises in our capital markets reveal, when financial statement analysis and valuation are conducted carelessly or without integrity, they can create enormous loss of value in the capital markets and trigger deep recession in even the most powerful economies in the world. The stakes are high.

In addition, the game is changing. The world is shifting toward a new approach to financial reporting, and expectations for high-quality and high-integrity financial analysis and valuation are increasing among investors and securities regulators. Many of the world's most powerful economies, including the European Union, Canada, and Japan, have shifted to International Financial Reporting Standards (IFRS). The U.S. Securities and Exchange Commission (SEC) accepts financial statement filings based on IFRS from non-U.S. registrants, and has considered whether to converge financial reporting from U.S. Generally Accepted Accounting Principles (GAAP) to IFRS for U.S. registrants. Given the pace and breadth of financial reform legislation, it is clear that it is no longer "business as usual" on Wall Street or around the world for financial statement analysis and valuation.

Given the profound importance of financial reporting, financial statement analysis, and valuation, and given our rapidly changing accounting rules and capital markets, this textbook provides you with a principled and disciplined approach for analysis and valuation. This textbook explains a thoughtful and thorough six-step framework you should use for financial statement analysis and valuation. You should begin an effective analysis of a set of financial statements with an evaluation of **(1)** the economic characteristics and competitive conditions of the industries in which a firm competes and **(2)** the particular strategies the firm executes to compete in each of these industries. Your analysis should then move to **(3)** assessing how well the firm's financial statements reflect the economic effects of the firm's strategic decisions and actions. Your assessment requires an understanding of the accounting principles and methods used to create the financial statements, the relevant and reliable information that the financial statements provide, and the appropriate adjustments that you might make to improve the quality of that information. Note that in this text we help you embrace financial reporting and financial statement analysis based on U.S. GAAP and IFRS. Next, you should **(4)** assess the profitability, risk, and growth of the firm using financial statement ratios and other analytical tools and then **(5)** forecast the firm's future profitability, risk, and growth, incorporating information about expected changes in the economics of the industry and the firm's strategies. Finally, you can **(6)** value the firm using various valuation methods, making an investment decision by comparing likely ranges of your value estimate to the observed market value. This six-step process forms the conceptual and pedagogical framework for this book, and it is a principled and disciplined approach you can use for intelligent analysis and valuation decisions.

All textbooks on financial statement analysis include step (4), assessing the profitability, risk, and growth of a company. Textbooks differ, however, with respect to their emphases on the other five steps. Consider the following depiction of these steps.

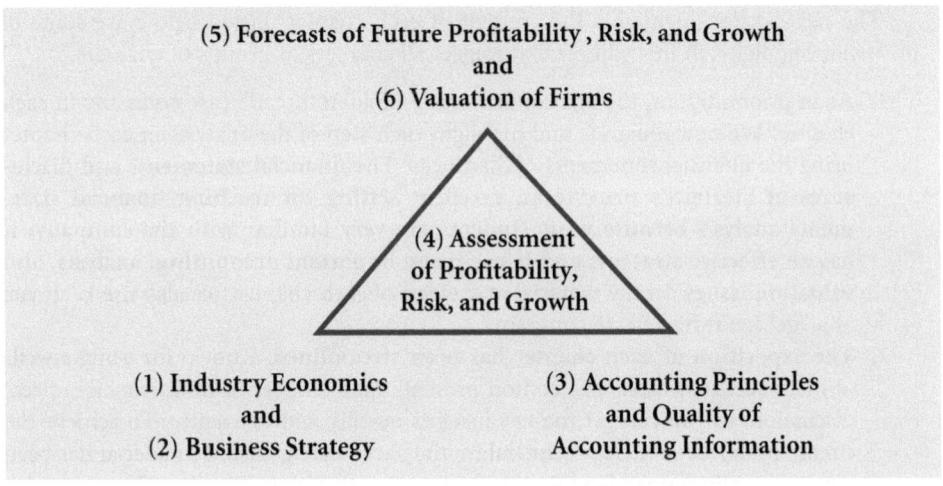

(5) Forecasts of Future Profitability , Risk, and Growth
and
(6) Valuation of Firms

(4) Assessment of Profitability, Risk, and Growth

(1) Industry Economics and
(2) Business Strategy

(3) Accounting Principles and Quality of Accounting Information

Our view is that these six steps must form an integrated approach for effective and complete financial statement analysis. We have therefore structured and developed this book to provide balanced, integrated coverage of all six elements. We sequence our study by beginning with industry economics and firm strategy, moving to a general consideration of GAAP and IFRS and the quality of accounting information, and providing a structure and tools for the analysis of profitability, risk, and growth. We then examine specific accounting issues and the determinants of accounting quality, and conclude with forecasting and valuation. We anchor each step in the sequence on the firm's profitability, risk, and growth, which are the fundamental drivers of value. We continually relate each part to those preceding and following it to maintain this balanced, integrated perspective.

The premise of this book is that you will learn financial statement analysis most effectively by performing the analysis on actual companies. The book's narrative sets forth the important concepts and analytical tools and demonstrates their application using the financial statements of Starbucks. Each chapter contains a set of questions, exercises, problems, and cases based primarily on financial statement data of actual companies. Each chapter also contains an integrative case involving Walmart so you can apply the tools and methods throughout the text. A financial statement analysis package (FSAP) is available to aid you in your analytical tasks (discussed later).

Some of the Highlights of This Edition

In the 9th edition, the author team of James Wahlen, Stephen Baginski, and Mark Bradshaw continues to improve on the foundations established by Clyde Stickney and Paul Brown. Clyde Stickney, the original author of the first three editions of this book and coauthor of the fourth, fifth, and sixth editions, is enjoying his well-earned retirement. Paul Brown, a coauthor of the fourth, fifth, and sixth editions, recently announced his retirement as the president of Monmouth University. Jim, Steve, and Mark are internationally recognized research scholars and award-winning teachers in accounting, financial statement analysis, and valuation. They continue to bring many fresh new ideas and insights to produce a new edition with a strong focus on thoughtful and disciplined fundamental analysis, a broad and deep coverage of accounting issues including IFRS, and expanded analysis of companies within a global economic environment.

The next section highlights the content of each chapter. Listed below are some of the major highlights in this edition that impact all chapters or groups of chapters.

1. As in prior editions, the 9th edition uses a "golden thread" case company in each chapter. We now illustrate and highlight each step of the analysis in each chapter using the financial statements of Starbucks. **The financial statements and disclosures of Starbucks provide an excellent setting for teaching financial statements analysis because most students are very familiar with the company; it has an effective strategy; and it has many important accounting, analysis, and valuation issues.** In the material at the end of each chapter, we also use Walmart as a "golden thread" case company.

2. **The exposition of each chapter has been streamlined.** Known for being a well-written, accessible text, this edition presents each chapter in more concise, direct discussion, so you can get the key insights quickly and efficiently. To achieve the streamlining, some highly technical (mainly accounting-related) material has been moved to online appendices that students may access at www.cengagebrain.com.

3. The chapters include **quick checks**, so you can be sure you have obtained the key insights from reading each section. In addition, each section and each of the end-of-chapter questions, exercises, problems, and cases is **cross-referenced to learning objectives**, so you can be sure that you can implement the critical skills and techniques associated with each of the learning objectives.

4. The chapters on profitability analysis (**Chapter 4**) and risk analysis (**Chapter 5**) continue to provide **disaggregation of return on common equity** along traditional lines of profitability, efficiency, and leverage, as well as along operating versus financing lines.

5. The book's companion website, at www.cengagebrain.com, contains an **updated Appendix D** with descriptive statistics on 20 commonly used financial ratios computed over the past 10 years for 48 industries. These ratios data enable you to benchmark your analyses and forecasts against industry averages.

6. The chapters on accounting quality continue **to provide broad coverage of accounting for financing, investing, and operating activities. Chapter 6** discusses the determinants of accounting quality, how to evaluate accounting quality, and how to adjust reported earnings and financial statements to cleanse low-quality accounting items. Then the discussion proceeds across the primary business activities of firms in the natural sequence in which the activities occur— raising financial capital, investing that capital in productive assets, and operating the business. **Chapter 7** discusses accounting for financing activities. **Chapter 8** describes accounting for investing activities, and **Chapter 9** deals with accounting for operating activities. Detailed examples of foreign currency translation and accounting for various hedging activities have been moved to online appendices.

7. The chapters on accounting quality continue to provide **more in-depth analysis of both balance sheet and income statement quality**.

8. Each chapter includes **relevant new discussion of current U.S. GAAP and IFRS, how U.S. GAAP compares to IFRS**, and how you should deal with such differences in financial statement analysis. **New material includes recent changes in accounting standards dealing with revenue recognition, leasing,**

and investments in securities. End-of-chapter materials contain many problems and cases involving non-U.S. companies, with **application of financial statement analysis techniques to IFRS-based financial statements**.

9. Each chapter provides references to specific standards in U.S. GAAP using the **new FASB Codification system**.

10. The chapters provide a number of **relevant insights from empirical accounting research**, pertinent to financial statement analysis and valuation.

11. The end-of-chapter material for each chapter contains portions of an **updated, integrative case applying the concepts and tools discussed in that chapter to Walmart**.

12. Each chapter contains **new or substantially revised and updated end-of-chapter material, including new problems and cases**. This material is relevant, real-world, and written for maximum learning value.

13. The Financial Statement Analysis Package (**FSAP**) available with this book has been **substantially revised and made more user-friendly**.

Overview of the Text

This section describes briefly the content and highlights of each chapter.

Chapter 1—Overview of Financial Reporting, Financial Statement Analysis, and Valuation. This chapter introduces you to the six interrelated sequential steps in financial statement analysis that serve as the organization structure for this book. It presents you with several frameworks for understanding the industry economics and business strategy of a firm and applies them to Starbucks. It also reviews the purpose, underlying concepts, and content of each of the three principal financial statements, including those of non-U.S. companies reporting using IFRS. This chapter also provides the rationale for analyzing financial statements in capital market settings, including showing you some very compelling results from an empirical study of the association between unexpected earnings and market-adjusted stock returns as well as empirical results showing that fundamental analysis can help investors generate above-market returns. The chapter's appendix, which can be found on this book's companion website at www.cengagebrain.com, presents an extensive discussion to help you do a term project involving the analysis of one or more companies. Our examination of the course syllabi of users of the previous edition indicated that most courses require students to engage in such a project. This appendix guides you in how to proceed, where to get information, and so on.

In addition to the new integrative case involving Walmart, the chapter includes an updated version of a case involving Nike.

Chapter 2—Asset and Liability Valuation and Income Recognition. This chapter covers three topics we believe you need to review from previous courses before delving into the more complex topics in this book.

■ First, we discuss the link between the valuation of assets and liabilities on the balance sheet and the measurement of income. We believe that you will understand topics such as revenue recognition and accounting for marketable securities, derivatives, pensions, and other topics more easily when you examine them with an appreciation for the inherent trade-off of a balance sheet versus income statement perspective. This chapter also reviews the trade-offs faced by accounting standard setters, regulators, and corporate managers who attempt to simultaneously provide both reliable and relevant financial statement information. We also examine whether firms should recognize value changes immediately in net income or delay their recognition, sending them temporarily through other comprehensive income.

- Second, we present a framework for analyzing the dual effects of economic transactions and other events on the financial statements. This framework relies on the balance sheet equation to trace these effects through the financial statements. Even students who are well grounded in double-entry accounting find this framework helpful in visually identifying the effects of various complex business transactions, such as corporate acquisitions, derivatives, and leases. We use this framework in subsequent chapters to present and analyze transactions, as we discuss various GAAP and IFRS topics.

$A_{BEG} =$	L_{BEG}	$+$	CC_{BEG}	$+$	$AOCI_{BEG}$	$+$	RE_{BEG}
$+\Delta A$	$+\Delta L$		$+\Delta Stock$		$+OCI$		$+NI$ $-D$
$A_{END} =$	L_{END}	$+$	CC_{END}	$+$	$AOCI_{END}$	$+$	RE_{END}

[A=Assets, L=Liabilities, CC=Contributed Capital, AOCI=Accumulated Other Comprehensive Income, RE=Retained Earnings, Stock=Common and Preferred Capital Stock Accounts, OCI=Other Comprehensive Income, NI=Net Income, and D=Dividends.]

- Third, we discuss the measurement of income tax expense, particularly with regard to the treatment of temporary differences between book income and taxable income. Virtually every business transaction has income tax consequences, and it is crucial that you grasp the information conveyed in income tax disclosures.

The end-of-chapter materials include various asset and liability valuation problems involving Biosante Pharmaceuticals, Prepaid Legal Services, and Nike, as well as the integrative case involving Walmart.

Chapter 3—Income Flows versus Cash Flows: Understanding the Statement of Cash Flows. Chapter 3 reviews the statement of cash flows and presents a model for relating the cash flows from operating, investing, and financing activities to a firm's position in its product life cycle. The chapter demonstrates procedures you can use to prepare the statement of cash flows when a firm provides no cash flow information. The chapter also provides new insights that place particular emphasis on how you should use information in the statement of cash flows to assess earnings quality.

The end-of-chapter materials utilize cash flow and earnings data for a number of companies including Tesla, Amazon, Kroger, Coca-Cola, Texas Instruments, Sirius XM Radio, Apollo Group, and AerLingus. A case (Prime Contractors) illustrates the relation between earnings and cash flows as a firm experiences profitable and unprofitable operations and changes its business strategy. The classic W. T. Grant case illustrating the use of earnings and cash flow information to assess solvency risk and avoid bankruptcy has been moved to an online appendix.

Chapter 4—Profitability Analysis. This chapter discusses the concepts and tools for analyzing a firm's profitability, integrating industry economic and strategic factors that affect the interpretation of financial ratios. It applies these concepts and tools to the analysis of the profitability of Starbucks. The analysis of profitability centers on the rate of return on assets and its disaggregated components, the rate of return on common shareholders' equity and its disaggregated components, and earnings per share. The chapter contains a section on alternative profitability measures, including a discussion of "street earnings." This chapter also considers analytical tools unique to certain industries, such as airlines, service firms, retailers, and technology firms.

A number of problems and exercises at the end of the chapter cover profitability analyses for companies such as Nucor Steel, Hershey, Microsoft, Oracle, Dell, Sun Microsystems, Texas Instruments, Hewlett Packard, Georgia Pacific, General Mills, Abercrombie & Fitch, Hasbro, and many others. The integrative case examines Walmart's profitability.

Chapter 5—Risk Analysis. This chapter begins with a discussion of recently required disclosures on the extent to which firms are subject to various types of risk, including unexpected changes in commodity prices, exchange rates, and interest rates and how firms manage these risks. The chapter provides new insights and discussion about the benefits and dangers associated with financial flexibility and the use of leverage. This edition shows you how to decompose return on common equity into components that highlight the contribution of the inherent profitability of the firm's assets and the contribution from the strategic use of leverage to enhance the returns to common equity investors. The chapter provides you an approach to in-depth financial statement analysis of various risks associated with leverage, including short-term liquidity risk, long-term solvency risk, credit risk, bankruptcy risk, and systematic and firm-specific market risk. This chapter also describes and illustrates the calculation and interpretation of risk ratios and applies them to the financial statements of Starbucks, focusing on both short-term liquidity risk and long-term solvency risk. We also explore credit risk and bankruptcy risk in greater depth.

A unique feature of the problems in Chapters 4 and 5 is the linking of the analysis of several companies across the two chapters, including problems involving Hasbro, Abercrombie & Fitch, and Walmart. In addition, other problems focus on risk-related issues for companies like Coca-Cola, Delta Air Lines, VF Corporation, Best Buy, Circuit City, The Tribune Company and The Washington Post. Chapter-ending cases involve risk analysis for Walmart and classic cases on credit risk analysis (Massachusetts Stove Company) and bankruptcy prediction (Fly-By-Night International Group).

Chapter 6—Accounting Quality. This chapter provides an expanded discussion of the quality of income statement and balance sheet information, emphasizing faithful representation of relevant and substantive economic content as the key characteristics of high quality, useful accounting information. The chapter also alerts you to the conditions under which managers might likely engage in earnings management. The discussion provides a framework for accounting quality analysis, which is used in the discussions of various accounting issues in Chapters 7 through 9. We consider several financial reporting topics that primarily affect the persistence of earnings, including gains and losses from discontinued operations, changes in accounting principles, other comprehensive income items, impairment losses, restructuring charges, changes in estimates, and gains and losses from peripheral activities. The chapter concludes with an assessment of accounting quality by separating accruals and cash flows and an illustration of a model to assess the risk of financial reporting manipulation (Beneish's multivariate model for identifying potential financial statement manipulators).

Chapter-ending materials include problems involving Nestlé, Checkpoint Systems, Rock of Ages, Vulcan Materials, Northrop Grumman, Intel, Enron, and Sunbeam. End-of-chapter materials also include an integrative case involving the analysis of Walmart's accounting quality.

Chapter 7—Financing Activities. This chapter has been structured along with Chapters 8 and 9 to discuss accounting issues in their natural sequence—raising financial capital, then investing the capital in productive assets, and then managing the operations of the business. Chapter 7 discusses the accounting principles and practices under U.S. GAAP and IFRS associated with firms' financing activities. The chapter begins by describing the financial statement reporting of capital investments by owners (equity issues) and distributions to owners (dividends and share repurchases), and the accounting for equity issued to compensate employees (stock options, stock appreciation rights, and restricted stock). The chapter demonstrates how shareholders' equity reflects the effects of transactions with non-owners that flow through the income statement (net income) and those that do not (other comprehensive income). The chapter then describes the financial reporting for long-term debt (bonds, notes payable, lease liabilities, and troubled debt), hybrid securities (convertible bonds, preferred stock), and derivatives used to hedge interest rate risk (an online appendix provides specific examples of accounting for interest rate swaps). The lease discussion demonstrates the adjustments required to convert operating leases to capital leases in past financial statements and illustrates lease accounting under the new lease standard going forward. Throughout the chapter, we highlight the differences between U.S. GAAP and IFRS in the area of equity and debt financing.

In addition to various questions and exercises, the end-of-chapter material includes problems probing accounting for various financing alternatives, Ford Motor Credit's securitization of receivables, operating versus capital leases of The Gap and Limited Brands, and stock-based compensation at Coca-Cola and Eli Lilly. End-of-chapter cases include the integrative case involving Walmart, a case on stock compensation at Oracle, and long-term financing and solvency risk at Southwest Airlines versus Lufthansa.

Chapter 8—Investing Activities. This chapter discusses various accounting principles and methods under U.S. GAAP and IFRS associated with a firm's investments in long-lived tangible assets, intangible assets, and financial instruments. The chapter demonstrates the accounting for a firm's investments in tangible productive assets including property, plant, and equipment, including the initial decision to capitalize or expense and the use of choices and estimates to allocate costs through the depreciation process. The chapter demonstrates alternative ways that firms account for intangible assets, highlighting research and development expenditures, software development expenditures, and goodwill, including the exercise of judgment in the allocation of costs through the amortization process. The chapter reviews and applies the rules for evaluating the impairment of different categories of long-lived assets, including goodwill. The chapter then describes accounting and financial reporting of intercorporate investments in securities (trading securities, available-for-sale securities, held-to-maturity securities, and noncontrolled affiliates) and corporate acquisitions. The chapter reviews accounting for variable-interest entities, including the requirement to consolidate them with the firm identified as the primary beneficiary. Finally, an online appendix to the chapter addresses foreign investments by preparing a set of translated financial statements using the all-current method and the monetary/nonmonetary method and describing the conditions under which each method best portrays the operating relationship between a U.S. parent firm and its foreign subsidiary.

The end-of-chapter questions, exercises, problems, and cases include a problem involving Molson Coors Brewing Company and its variable interest entities, an integrative application of the chapter topics to Walmart, and a case involving Disney's acquisition of Marvel Entertainment.

Chapter 9—Operating Activities. Substantially revised Chapter 9 discusses how financial statements prepared under U.S. GAAP or IFRS capture and report the firm's operating activities. The chapter opens with a discussion of how financial accounting measures and reports the revenues and expenses generated by a firm's operating activities, as well as the related assets, liabilities, and cash flows. This discussion reviews the criteria for recognizing revenue and expenses under the accrual basis of accounting and applies these criteria to various types of businesses. The revenue recognition discussion is based on a new revenue recognition standard, and an online appendix illustrates some legacy revenue recognition rules that you might encounter in past financial statements. The chapter analyzes and interprets the effects of FIFO versus LIFO on financial statements and demonstrates how to convert the statements of a firm from a LIFO to a FIFO basis. The chapter identifies the working capital investments created by operating activities and the financial statement effects of credit policy and credit risk. The chapter also shows how to use the financial statement and note information for corporate income taxes to analyze the firm's tax strategies, pensions, and other post-employment benefits obligations. The chapter concludes with a discussion of how a firm uses derivative instruments to hedge the risk associated with commodities and with operating transactions denominated in foreign currency, and an online appendix illustrates the hedge accounting.

The end-of-chapter problems and exercises examine revenue and expense recognition for a wide variety of operating activities, including revenues for software, consulting, transportation, construction, manufacturing, and others. End-of-chapter problems also involve Coca-Cola's tax notes and include the integrative case involving Walmart, and a case involving Coca-Cola's pension disclosures.

Chapter 10—Forecasting Financial Statements. This chapter describes and illustrates the procedures you should use in preparing forecasted financial statements. This material plays a central role in the valuation of companies, discussed throughout Chapters 11 through 14. The chapter begins by giving you an overview of forecasting and the importance of creating integrated and articulated financial statement forecasts. It then demonstrates the preparation of projected financial statements for Starbucks. The chapter also demonstrates how to get forecasted balance sheets to balance and how to compute implied statements of cash flows from forecasts of balance sheets and income statements. The chapter also discusses forecast shortcuts analysts sometimes take, and when such forecasts are reliable and when they are not. The Forecast and Forecast Development spreadsheets within FSAP provide templates you can use to develop and build your own financial statement forecasts.

Short end-of-chapter problems illustrate techniques for projecting key accounts for firms like Home Depot, Intel, Hasbro, and Barnes and Noble, determining the cost structure of firms like Nucor Steel and Sony, and dealing with irregular changes in accounts. Longer problems and cases include the integrative Walmart case and a classic case involving the projection of financial statements to assist the Massachusetts Stove Company in its strategic decision to add gas stoves to its wood stove line. The problems and cases specify the assumptions you should make to illustrate the preparation procedure. We link and use these longer problems and cases in later chapters that rely on these financial statement forecasts in determining share value estimates for these firms.

Chapter 11—Risk-Adjusted Expected Rates of Return and the Dividends Valuation Approach. Chapters 11 through 14 form a unit in which we demonstrate various approaches to valuing a firm. Chapter 11 focuses on fundamental issues of valuation that you will apply in all of the valuation chapters. This chapter provides you with a discussion of the measurement of the cost of debt and equity capital and the weighted average cost of capital, as well as the dividends-based valuation approach. The chapter also discusses various issues of valuation, including forecasting horizons, projecting long-run continuing dividends, and computing continuing (sometimes called terminal) value. The chapter describes and illustrates the internal consistency in valuing firms using dividends, free cash flows, or earnings. We place particular emphasis on helping you understand that the different approaches to valuation are simply differences in perspective (dividends capture wealth distribution, free cash flows capture wealth realization in cash, and earnings represent wealth creation), and that these approaches should produce internally consistent estimates of value. In this chapter we demonstrate the cost-of-capital measurements and the dividends-based valuation approach for Starbucks, using the forecasted amounts from Starbucks' financial statements discussed in Chapter 10. The chapter also presents techniques for assessing the sensitivity of value estimates, varying key assumptions such as the cost of capital and long-term growth rate. The chapter also discusses and illustrates the cost-of-capital computations and dividends valuation model computations within the Valuation spreadsheet in FSAP. This spreadsheet takes the forecast amounts from the Forecast spreadsheet and other relevant information and values the firm using the various valuation methods discussed in Chapters 11 through 14.

End-of-chapter material includes the computation of costs of capital across different industries and companies, including Whirlpool, IBM, and Target Stores, as well as short dividends valuation problems for companies like Royal Dutch Shell. Cases involve computing costs of capital and dividends-based valuation of Walmart, and Massachusetts Stove Company from financial statement forecasts developed in Chapter 10's problems and cases.

Chapter 12—Valuation: Cash-Flow Based Approaches. Chapter 12 focuses on valuation using the present value of free cash flows. This chapter distinguishes free cash flows to all debt and equity stakeholders and free cash flows to common equity shareholders and the settings where one or the other measure of free cash flows is appropriate for valuation. The chapter demonstrates valuation using free cash flows for common equity shareholders, and valuation using free cash flows to all debt and equity stakeholders. The chapter also considers and applies techniques for projecting free cash flows and measuring the continuing value after the forecast horizon. The chapter applies both of the discounted free cash flows valuation methods to Starbucks, demonstrating how to measure the free cash flows to all debt and equity stakeholders, as well as the free cash flows to common equity. The valuations use the forecasted amounts from Starbucks' projected financial statements discussed in Chapter 10. The chapter also presents techniques for assessing the sensitivity of value estimates, varying key assumptions such as the costs of capital and long-term growth rates. The chapter also explains and demonstrates the consistency of valuation estimates across different approaches and shows that the dividends approach in Chapter 11 and the free cash flows approaches in Chapter 12 should and do lead to identical value estimates for Starbucks. The Valuation spreadsheet in FSAP uses projected amounts from the Forecast spreadsheet and other relevant information and values the firm using both of the free cash flows valuation approaches.

Updated shorter problem material asks you to compute free cash flows from financial statement data for companies like 3M and Dick's Sporting Goods. Problem material also includes using free cash flows to value firms in leveraged buyout transactions, such as May Department Stores, Experian Information Solutions, and Wedgewood Products. Longers and cases material include the valuation of Walmart, Coca-Cola, and Massachusetts Stove Company. The chapter also introduces the Holmes Corporation case, which is an integrated case relevant for Chapters 10 through 13 in which you select forecast assumptions, prepare projected financial statements, and value the firm using the various methods discussed in Chapters 10 through 13. This case can be analyzed in stages with each chapter or as an integrated case after Chapter 13.

Chapter 13—Valuation: Earnings-Based Approaches. Chapter 13 emphasizes the role of accounting earnings in valuation, focusing on valuation methods using the residual income approach. The residual income approach uses the ability of a firm to generate income in excess of the cost of capital as the principal driver of a firm's value in excess of its book value. We apply the residual income valuation method to the forecasted amounts for Starbucks from Chapter 10. The chapter also demonstrates that the dividends valuation methods, the free cash flows valuation methods, and the residual income valuation methods are consistent with a fundamental valuation approach. In the chapter we explain and demonstrate that these approaches yield identical estimates of value for Starbucks. The Valuation spreadsheet in FSAP includes valuation models that use the residual income valuation method.

End-of-chapter materials include various problems involving computing residual income across different firms, including Abbott Labs, IBM, Target Stores, Microsoft, Intel, Dell, Southwest Airlines, Kroger, and Yum! Brands. Longer problems also involve the valuation of other firms such as Steak 'n Shake in which you are given the needed financial statement information. Longer problems and cases enable you to apply the residual income approach to Coca-Cola, Walmart, and Massachusetts Stove Company, considered in Chapters 10 through 12.

Chapter 14—Valuation: Market-Based Approaches. Chapter 14 demonstrates how to analyze and use the information in market value. In particular, the chapter describes and applies market-based valuation multiples, including the market-to-book ratio, the price-to-earnings ratio, and the price-earnings-growth ratio. The chapter illustrates the theoretical and conceptual approaches to market multiples and contrasts them with the practical approaches to market multiples. The chapter demonstrates how the market-to-book ratio is consistent with residual ROCE valuation and the residual income model discussed in Chapter 13. The chapter also describes the factors that drive market multiples, so you can adjust multiples appropriately to reflect differences in profitability, growth, and risk across comparable firms. An applied analysis demonstrates how you can reverse engineer a firm's stock price to infer the valuation assumptions that the stock market appears to be making. We apply all of these valuation methods to Starbucks. The chapter concludes with a discussion of the role of market efficiency, as well as striking evidence on using earnings surprises to pick stocks and form portfolios (the Bernard-Thomas post-earnings announcement drift anomaly) as well as using value-to-price ratios to form portfolios (the Frankel-Lee investment strategy), both of which appear to help investors generate significant above-market returns.

End-of-chapter materials include problems involving computing and interpreting market-to-book ratios for pharmaceutical companies, Enron, Coca-Cola, and Steak 'n Shake and the integrative case involving Walmart.

Appendices. Appendix A includes the financial statements and notes for Starbucks used in the illustrations throughout the book. Appendix B, available at www.cengagebrain.com, is Starbucks' letter to the shareholders and management's discussion and analysis of operations, which we use when interpreting Starbucks' financial ratios and in our financial statement projections. Appendix C presents the output from FSAP for Starbucks, including the Data spreadsheet, the Analysis spreadsheet (profitability and risk ratio analyses), the Forecasts and Forecast Development spreadsheets, and the Valuations spreadsheet. Appendix D, also available online, provides descriptive statistics on 20 financial statement ratios across 48 industries over the years 2006 to 2015.

Chapter Sequence and Structure

Our own experience and discussions with other professors suggest there are various approaches to teaching a financial statement analysis course, each of which works well in particular settings. We have therefore designed this book for flexibility with respect to the sequence of chapter assignments. The following diagram sets forth the overall structure of the book.

Chapter 1: Overview of Financial Reporting, Financial Statement Analysis, and Valuation		
Chapter 2: Asset and Liability Valuation and Income Recognition	Chapter 3: Income Flows versus Cash Flows	
Chapter 4: Profitability Analysis	Chapter 5: Risk Analysis	
Chapter 6: Accounting Quality		
Chapter 7: Financing Activities	Chapter 8: Investing Activities	Chapter 9: Operating Activities
Chapter 10: Forecasting Financial Statements		
Chapter 11: Risk-Adjusted Expected Rates of Return and the Dividends Valuation Approach		
Chapter 12: Valuation: Cash-Flow-Based Approaches	Chapter 13: Valuation: Earnings-Based Approaches	
Chapter 14: Valuation: Market-Based Approaches		

The chapter sequence follows the six steps in financial statement analysis discussed in Chapter 1. Chapters 2 and 3 provide the conceptual foundation for the three financial statements. Chapters 4 and 5 present tools for analyzing the financial statements. Chapters 6 through 9 describe how to assess the quality of accounting information under U.S. GAAP and IFRS and then examine the accounting for financing, investing, and operating activities. Chapters 10 through 14 focus primarily on forecasting financial statements and valuation.

Some schools teach U.S. GAAP and IFRS topics and financial statement analysis in separate courses. Chapters 6 through 9 are an integrated unit and sufficiently rich for the U.S. GAAP and IFRS course. The remaining chapters will then work well in the financial statement analysis course. Some schools leave the topic of valuation to finance courses. Chapters 1 through 10 will then work well for the accounting prelude to the finance course. Some instructors may wish to begin with forecasting and valuation (Chapters 10 through 14) and then examine data issues that might affect the numbers used in the valuations (Chapters 6 through 9). This textbook is adaptable to other sequences of the various topics.

Overview of the Ancillary Package

The Financial Statement Analysis Package (FSAP) is available on the companion website for this book (www.cengagebrain.com) to all purchasers of the text. The package performs various analytical tasks (common-size and rate of change financial statements, ratio computations, risk indicators such as the Altman-Z score and the Beneish manipulation index), provides a worksheet template for preparing financial statements forecasts, and applies amounts from the financial statement forecasts to valuing a firm using various valuation methods. A user manual for FSAP is embedded within FSAP.

New to the 9th edition of *Financial Reporting, Financial Statement Analysis, and Valuation* is MindTap. MindTap is a platform that propels students from memorization to mastery. It gives you complete control of your course, so you can provide engaging content, challenge every learner, and build student confidence. Customize interactive syllabi to emphasize priority topics, then add your own material or notes to the eBook as desired. This outcomes-driven application gives you the tools needed to empower students and boost both understanding and performance.

Access Everything You Need in One Place

Cut down on prep with the preloaded and organized MindTap course materials. Teach more efficiently with interactive multimedia, assignments, quizzes, and more. Give your students the power to read, listen, and study on their phones, so they can learn on their terms.

Empower Students to Reach Their Potential

Twelve distinct metrics give you actionable insights into student engagement. Identify topics troubling your entire class and instantly communicate with those struggling. Students can track their scores to stay motivated towards their goals. Together, you can be unstoppable.

Control Your Course—and Your Content

Get the flexibility to reorder textbook chapters, add your own notes, and embed a variety of content including Open Educational Resources (OER). Personalize course content to your students' needs. They can even read your notes, add their own, and highlight key text to aid their learning.

Get a Dedicated Team, Whenever You Need Them

MindTap isn't just a tool; it's backed by a personalized team eager to support you. We can help set up your course and tailor it to your specific objectives, so you'll be ready to make an impact from day one. Know we'll be standing by to help you and your students until the final day of the term.

Acknowledgments

Many individuals provided invaluable assistance in the preparation of this book and we wish to acknowledge their help here.

We wish to especially acknowledge many helpful comments and suggestions on the prior edition (many of which helped improve this edition) from Susan Eldridge at the University of Nebraska—Omaha and Christopher Jones at George Washington University. We are also very grateful for help with data collection from Matt Wieland of Miami University.

The following colleagues have assisted in the development of this edition by reviewing or providing helpful comments on or materials for previous editions:

Kristian Allee, Michigan State University
Murad Antia, University of South Florida
Drew Baginski, University of Georgia
Michael Clement, University of Texas at Austin
Messod Daniel Beneish, Indiana University
Ellen Engel, University of Illinois at Chicago
Aaron Hipscher, New York University
Robert Howell, Dartmouth College
Amy Hutton, Boston College
Prem Jain, Georgetown University
Ross Jennings, University of Texas at Austin
J. William Kamas, University of Texas at Austin

Michael Keane, University of Southern California
April Klein, New York University
Betsy Laydon, Indiana University
Yuri Loktionov, New York University
D. Craig Nichols, Syracuse University
Chris Noe, Massachusetts Institute of Technology
Virginia Soybel, Babson College
James Warren, University of Georgia
Christine Wiedman, University of Waterloo
Matthew Wieland, Miami University
Michael Williamson, University of Illinois at Urbana-Champaign
Julia Yu, University of Georgia

We wish to thank the following individuals at Cengage, who provided guidance, encouragement, or assistance in various phases of the revision: John Barans, Julie Dierig, Conor Allen, Tara Slagle, Darrell Frye, and Tim Bailey.

Finally, we wish to acknowledge the role played by former students in our financial statement analysis classes for being challenging partners in our learning endeavors. We also acknowledge and thank Clyde Stickney and Paul Brown for allowing us to carry on their legacy by teaching financial statement analysis and valuation through this book. Lastly, and most importantly, we are deeply grateful for our families for being encouraging and patient partners in this work. We dedicate this book to each of you.

James M. Wahlen
Stephen P. Baginski
Mark T. Bradshaw

James M. Wahlen is the James R. Hodge Chair, Professor of Accounting, Chair of the Accounting Department, and the former Chair of the MBA Program at the Kelley School of Business at Indiana University. He received his Ph.D. from the University of Michigan and has served on the faculties of the University of Chicago, University of North Carolina at Chapel Hill, INSEAD, the University of Washington, and Pacific Lutheran University. Professor Wahlen's teaching and research interests focus on financial accounting, financial statement analysis, and the capital markets. His research investigates earnings quality and earnings management, earnings volatility as an indicator of risk, fair value accounting for financial instruments, accounting for loss reserve estimates by banks and insurers, stock market efficiency with respect to accounting information, and testing the extent to which future stock returns can be predicted with earnings and other financial statement information. His research has been published in a wide array of academic and practitioner journals in accounting and finance. He has had public accounting experience in both Milwaukee and Seattle and is a member of the American Accounting Association. He has received numerous teaching awards during his career. In his free time Jim loves spending time with his wife and daughters, spoiling his incredibly adorable granddaughter Ailsa, playing outdoor sports (biking, hiking, skiing, golf), cooking (and, of course, eating), and listening to rock music (especially if it is loud and live).

Stephen P. Baginski is the Herbert E. Miller Chair in Financial Accounting at the University of Georgia's J.M. Tull School of Accounting. He received his Ph.D. from the University of Illinois in 1986, and he has taught a variety of financial and managerial undergraduate, MBA, and executive education courses at Indiana University, Illinois State University, the University of Illinois, Northeastern University, Florida State University, Washington University in St. Louis, the University of St. Galen, the Swiss Banking Institute at the University of Zurich, Bocconi, and INSEAD. Professor Baginski has published articles in a variety of journals including *The Accounting Review, Journal of Accounting Research, Contemporary Accounting Research, Review of Accounting Studies, The Journal of Risk and Insurance, Quarterly Review of Finance and Economics,* and *Review of Quantitative Finance and Accounting*. His research primarily deals with the causes and consequences of voluntary management disclosures of earnings forecasts, and he also investigates the usefulness of financial accounting information in security pricing and risk assessment. Professor Baginski has served on several editorial boards and as an associate editor at *Accounting Horizons* and *The Review of Quantitative Finance and Accounting*. He has won numerous undergraduate and graduate teaching awards at the department, college, and university levels during his career, including receipt of the Doctoral Student Inspiration Award from students at Indiana University. Professor Baginski loves to watch college football, play golf, and run (very slowly) in his spare time.

Mark T. Bradshaw is Professor of Accounting, Chair of the Department, and William S. McKiernan '78 Family Faculty Fellow at the Carroll School of Management of Boston College. Bradshaw received a Ph.D. from the University of Michigan Business School, and earned a BBA summa cum laude with highest honors in accounting and a master's degree in financial accounting from the University of Georgia. He previously taught at the University of Chicago, Harvard Business School, and the University of Georgia. He was a Certified Public Accountant with Arthur Andersen & Co. in Atlanta. Bradshaw conducts research on capital markets, specializing in the examination of securities analysts and financial reporting issues. His research has been published in a variety of academic and practitioner journals, and he is an Editor for *The Accounting Review* and serves as Associate Editor for *Journal of Accounting and Economics*, *Journal of Accounting Research*, and *Journal of Financial Reporting*. He is also on the Editorial Board of *Review of Accounting Studies* and the *Journal of International Accounting Research*, and is a reviewer for numerous other accounting and finance journals. He also has authored a book with Brian Bruce, *Analysts, Lies, and Statistics—Cutting through the Hype in Corporate Earnings Announcements*. Approximately 30 pounds ago, Bradshaw was an accomplished cyclist. Currently focused on additional leisurely pursuits, he nevertheless routinely passes younger and thinner cyclists.

BRIEF CONTENTS

CONTENTS

Overview of Financial Reporting, Financial Statement Analysis, and Valuation

LO 1-1 Describe the six-step analytical framework that is the logical structure for financial statement analysis and valuation. It is the foundation for this book.

LO 1-2 Apply tools for assessing the economic characteristics that drive competition in an industry, including (a) Porter's five forces framework, (b) value chain analysis, and (c) an economic attributes framework; then identify the firm's specific strategies for achieving and maintaining competitive advantage within that industry.

LO 1-3 Explain the purpose, underlying concepts, and format of the balance sheet, income statement, and statement of cash flows, and the importance of accounting quality.

LO 1-4 Obtain an overview of useful tools for analyzing a firm's profitability, growth, and risk, including financial ratios, common-size financial statements, and percentage change financial statements, as well as how to use this information to forecast the future business activities of a firm, and to value a firm.

LO 1-5 Consider the role of financial statement analysis and valuation in an efficient capital market, and review empirical evidence on the association between changes in earnings and changes in stock prices.

LO 1-6 Review sources of financial information available for publicly held firms.

Chapter Overview

This book has three principal objectives, each designed to help you gain important knowledge and skills necessary for financial statement analysis and valuation:

1. Chapters 1 to 5: To demonstrate how you can analyze the economics of an industry, a firm's strategy, and its financial statements, gaining important insights about the firm's profitability, growth, and risk.

2. Chapters 6 to 9: To deepen your understanding of the accounting principles and methods under U.S. Generally Accepted Accounting Principles (GAAP) and International Financial Reporting Standards (IFRS) that firms use to measure and report their financing, investing, and operating activities in a set of financial statements and, if necessary, make adjustments to reported amounts to increase their relevance and reliability.

3. Chapters 10 to 14: To demonstrate how you can use financial statement information to build forecasts of future financial statements and then use the expected future amounts of earnings, cash flows, and dividends to value firms.

Financial statements play a central role in the analysis and valuation of a firm. Financial statement analysis is an exciting and rewarding activity, particularly when the objective is to assess whether the market is pricing a firm's shares fairly. This text demonstrates and explains many tools and techniques that you can use to analyze the fundamental characteristics of a firm—such as its business strategies; competitive advantages; product markets; and operating, investing, and financing decisions—and then use this information to make informed decisions about the value of the firm.

Security analysts are professionals whose primary objective is to value equity securities issued by firms. Security analysts collect and analyze a wide array of information from financial statements and other sources to evaluate a firm's current and past performance, predict its future performance, and then estimate the value of the firm's shares. Comparisons of thoughtful and intelligent estimates of the firm's share value with the market price for the shares provide the bases for making good investment decisions.

In addition to estimating firm value, you can apply the tools of effective financial statement analysis in many other important decision-making settings, including the following:

- Managing a firm and communicating results to investors, creditors, employees, and other stakeholders.
- Assigning credit ratings or extending short-term credit (for example, a bank loan used to finance accounts receivable or inventories) or long-term credit (for example, a bank loan or public bond issue used to finance the acquisition of property, plant, or equipment).
- Assessing the operating performance and financial health of a supplier, customer, competitor, or potential employer.
- Evaluating firms for potential acquisitions, mergers, or divestitures.
- Valuing the initial public offering of a firm's shares.
- Consulting with a firm and offering helpful strategic advice.
- Forming a judgment in a lawsuit about damages sustained.
- Assessing the extent of auditing needed to form an opinion about a client's financial statements.

LO 1-1

Describe the six-step analytical framework that is the logical structure for financial statement analysis and valuation. It is the foundation for this book.

Overview of Financial Statement Analysis

We view effective financial statement analysis as a three-legged stool, as Exhibit 1.1 depicts. The three legs of the stool in the figure represent effective analysis based on the following:

1. Identifying the *economic characteristics* of the *industries* in which a firm competes and mapping those characteristics into determinants of profitability, growth, and risk.
2. Describing the *strategies* that a *firm* pursues to differentiate itself from competitors as a basis for evaluating a firm's competitive advantages, the sustainability and potential growth of a firm's earnings, and its risks.
3. Evaluating the firm's *financial statements*, including the accounting concepts and methods that underlie them and the quality of the information they provide.

Our approach to effective analysis of financial statements for valuation and many other decisions involves six interrelated sequential steps, depicted in Exhibit 1.2.

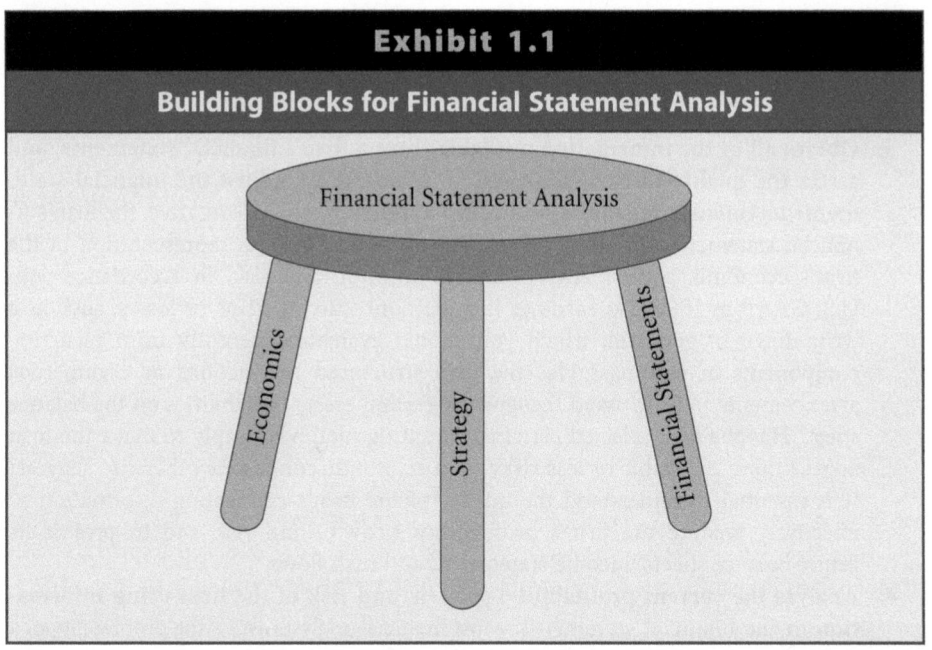

Exhibit 1.1

Building Blocks for Financial Statement Analysis

Financial Statement Analysis

Economics

Strategy

Financial Statements

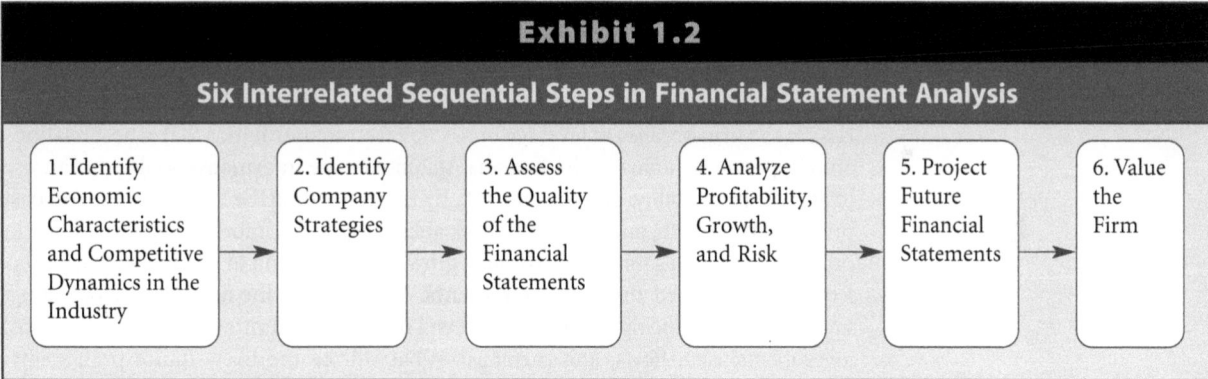

Exhibit 1.2

Six Interrelated Sequential Steps in Financial Statement Analysis

1. Identify Economic Characteristics and Competitive Dynamics in the Industry	2. Identify Company Strategies	3. Assess the Quality of the Financial Statements	4. Analyze Profitability, Growth, and Risk	5. Project Future Financial Statements	6. Value the Firm

1. **Identify the economic characteristics and competitive dynamics of the industry in which a particular firm participates.** What dynamic forces drive competition in the industry? For example, does the industry include a large number of firms selling similar products, such as grocery stores, or only a small number of firms selling unique products, such as pharmaceutical companies? Does technological change play an important role in maintaining a competitive advantage, as in computer software? Understanding the competitive forces in the firm's industry in the first step establishes the economic foundation and context for the remaining steps in the process.

2. **Identify strategies the firm pursues to gain and sustain a competitive advantage.** What business model is the firm executing to be different and successful in its industry? Does the firm have competitive advantages? If so, how sustainable are they? Are its products designed to meet the needs of specific market segments, such as ethnic or health foods, or are they intended for a broader consumer market, such as typical grocery stores and family restaurants? Has the firm integrated backward into the growing or manufacture of raw materials for its products, such as a steel company that owns iron ore mines? Is the firm

diversified across products, geographic markets, or industries? Understanding the firm's strategy and the sustainability of its competitive advantages provides the necessary firm-specific context to evaluate the firm's accounting information; assess profitability, growth, and risk; and project the firm's future business activities.

3. **Obtain all of the information available from a firm's financial statements, and assess the quality of that information. If necessary, adjust the financial statements to enhance reliability and comparability.** To be informative, the firm's financial statements should provide a complete and faithful representation of the firm's economic performance, financial position, and risk, in accordance with U.S. GAAP or IFRS. Do earnings include nonrecurring gains or losses, such as a write-down of goodwill, which you should evaluate differently from recurring components of earnings? Has the firm structured transactions or commercial arrangements so as to avoid recognizing certain assets or liabilities on the balance sheet? Has the firm selected certain accounting methods simply to make the firm appear more profitable or less risky than economic conditions otherwise suggest? It is essential to understand the quality of the firm's accounting information to effectively analyze the firm's profitability, growth, and risk and to project its future balance sheets, income statements, and cash flows.

4. **Analyze the current profitability, growth, and risk of the firm using information in the financial statements.** Most financial analysts assess the profitability of a firm relative to the risks involved. What rate of return is the firm generating from the use of its assets? What rate of return is the firm generating for its common equity shareholders? Is the firm's profit margin increasing or decreasing over time? Are revenues and profits growing faster or slower than those of its key competitors? Are rates of return and profit margins higher or lower than those of its key competitors? How risky is the firm because of leverage in its capital structure? Ratios that reflect relations among particular items in the financial statements are informative tools you can use to analyze profitability, growth, and risk. By understanding the firm's current and past profitability, growth, and risk, you will establish important information you will use in projecting the firm's future profitability, growth, and risk and in valuing its shares.

5. **Prepare forecasted financial statements.** What will be the firm's future operating, investing, and financing activities? What will be the firm's future resources, obligations, investments, cash flows, and earnings? What will be the likely future profitability, growth, and risk and, in turn, the likely future returns from investing in the company? Forecasted financial statements that project the firm's future operating, investing, and financing activities provide the basis for projecting future profitability, growth, and risk, which provide the basis for financial decision making, including valuation.

6. **Value the firm.** What is the firm worth? Financial analysts use their estimates of share value to make recommendations for buying, selling, or holding the equity securities of firms when market price is too low, too high, or about right. Similarly, an investment bank that underwrites the initial public offering of a firm's common stock must set the initial offer price. Also, an analyst in a corporation considering whether to acquire a company (or divest a subsidiary or division) must assess a reasonable range of values to bid to acquire the target (or to expect to receive).

These six steps provide a logical, powerful sequence that will enable you to address very important and difficult questions, such as how to analyze and value a firm. We use these six steps as the analytical framework for you to follow as you develop your skills in analyzing and valuing companies. This chapter introduces each step. Subsequent chapters develop the important concepts and tools for each step in considerably more depth.

How Do the Six Steps Relate to Share Pricing in the Capital Markets?

The extent to which market prices fully reflect the implications of accounting information depends on four links:

1. the accounting system mapping a firm's transactions and events into accounting fundamentals, such as earnings, cash flows, and book value of equity, reported on financial statements;
2. analysts and investors analyzing financial statement information to get a deep understanding of the firm's profitability, growth, and risk;
3. analysts and investors mapping accounting fundamentals into expectations of future earnings and cash flows, and then into estimates of share value; and
4. trading activities mapping share value estimates into stock prices.

Down the left-hand side of Exhibit 1.3 we illustrate these four links. In parallel, down the right-hand side, we illustrate how our six-step analysis and valuation process captures each of those four links.

Beginning in the upper left, the process through which firms create shareholder value is driven by the firm's business activities. The firm executes its strategy to compete in its industry through its financing, investing, and operating activities. Hopefully, these activities enable the firm to create and sustain competitive advantage within the industry, and create shareholder value. On the right side, we illustrate how Steps 1 and 2 of our six-step process focus on analyzing the factors and dynamics of competition within the industry, and then analyzing the firm's competitive strategy and the sustainability of the firm's competitive advantages (if any).

The first link in the share-pricing process involves financial reporting. Through the financial reporting process, the firm's accountants map the firm's business activities to financial statements. The balance sheets, income statements, statements of cash flows, and notes provide the firm a channel of credible communication through which the firm can report fundamentally important information to stakeholders about the firm's financial position and performance. On the right side, in Step 3 of the six-step process, we analyze the accounting information firms report in their financial statements and assess the quality of that information. To what extent do the balance sheets, income statements, cash flows, and notes faithfully represent the firm's underlying financial position and performance?

The second link in the share-pricing process involves financial analysis. In this link, investors and analysts analyze the information in the firm's financial statements to develop a deeper understanding of the firm's profitability, growth, and risk. These are the fundamental drivers of share value. On the right side, in Step 4, we analyze the firm's financial statements using a wide variety of ratios to analyze the firm's profitability, growth, and risk. We analyze how profitability, growth, and risk have changed over time, and how they compare to key competitors in the industry.

The third link in the share-pricing process involves forecasting and valuation. In this link, investors and analysts map the firm's financial statements into expectations of future earnings, cash flows, and dividends, and then map those expectations into share-value estimates. In this link, for example, an analyst or an investor would project the firm's future earnings and cash flows, evaluate the firm's risk, and determine a reasonable range of share values. On the right side, in Steps 5 and 6, we project the firm's future business activities and measure the expected future outcomes with projected future balance sheets, income statements, and cash flows. Next, we use our projected future

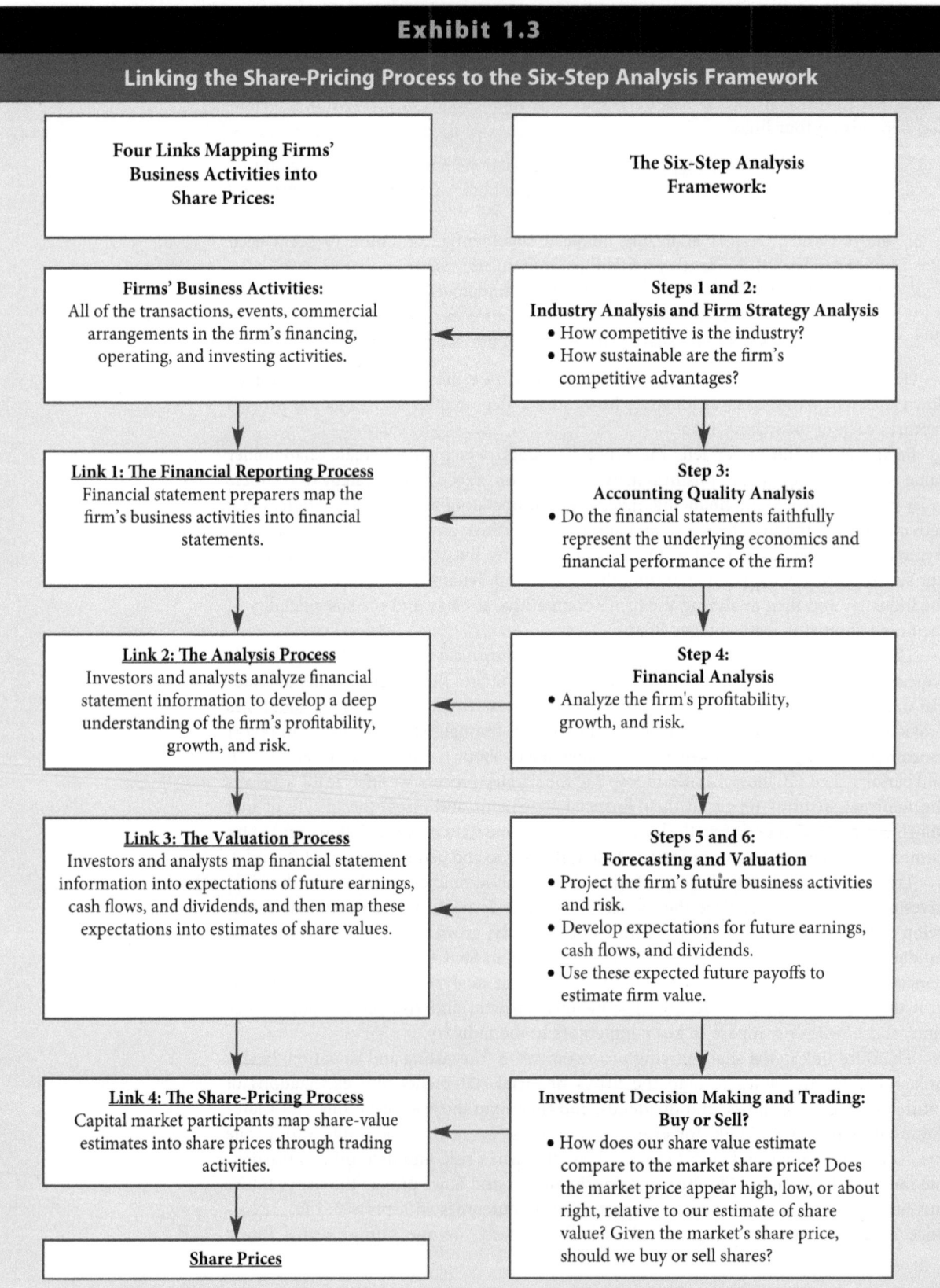

Exhibit 1.3

Linking the Share-Pricing Process to the Six-Step Analysis Framework

Four Links Mapping Firms' Business Activities into Share Prices:

The Six-Step Analysis Framework:

Firms' Business Activities: All of the transactions, events, commercial arrangements in the firm's financing, operating, and investing activities.

Steps 1 and 2: Industry Analysis and Firm Strategy Analysis
- How competitive is the industry?
- How sustainable are the firm's competitive advantages?

Link 1: The Financial Reporting Process Financial statement preparers map the firm's business activities into financial statements.

Step 3: Accounting Quality Analysis
- Do the financial statements faithfully represent the underlying economics and financial performance of the firm?

Link 2: The Analysis Process Investors and analysts analyze financial statement information to develop a deep understanding of the firm's profitability, growth, and risk.

Step 4: Financial Analysis
- Analyze the firm's profitability, growth, and risk.

Link 3: The Valuation Process Investors and analysts map financial statement information into expectations of future earnings, cash flows, and dividends, and then map these expectations into estimates of share values.

Steps 5 and 6: Forecasting and Valuation
- Project the firm's future business activities and risk.
- Develop expectations for future earnings, cash flows, and dividends.
- Use these expected future payoffs to estimate firm value.

Link 4: The Share-Pricing Process Capital market participants map share-value estimates into share prices through trading activities.

Investment Decision Making and Trading: Buy or Sell?
- How does our share value estimate compare to the market share price? Does the market price appear high, low, or about right, relative to our estimate of share value? Given the market's share price, should we buy or sell shares?

Share Prices

financial statements to determine expected future earnings, cash flows, and dividends, and then use those expectations to estimate share value.

In the fourth link in the market's share-pricing process, analysts and investors map their share value estimates into share prices through buying and selling shares. When analysts and investors buy shares at prices that they believe are below the share's fundamental value, the demand for shares should drive price up, toward fundamental value. Similarly, when analysts and investors sell shares at prices that they believe are high relative to fundamental value, that trading should drive prices down. On the bottom right side of the exhibit, we illustrate the culmination of our six-step analysis and valuation process—buying shares at prices that we believe are below fundamental value, and selling shares for prices that we believe are above fundamental value—the old adage, "buy low, sell high."

Note, the four links mapping firms' activities into share prices are not always tight. For example, the financial reporting process and accounting information may not capture all past transactions and events that are value-relevant, and companies differ in the extent to which they face accounting measurement challenges. As such, reported financial statement information may not fully faithfully represent the firm's profitability, growth, and risk (Links 1 and 2). Accounting fundamentals seldom explicitly capture the expected *future* transactions and events that drive firm value, and companies differ in the richness of information available for forecasting these future outcomes (Link 3). Finally, market sentiment, noise trading, and market frictions can lead to temporary departures of price from value even in highly efficient markets, as seen during bubble periods (Link 4). Therefore, the six-step analysis and valuation process enables us to evaluate and analyze the tightness of the four links, and hopefully identify shares that are temporarily overpriced or underpriced.

Introducing Starbucks

Throughout this book, we use financial statements, notes, and other information provided by **Starbucks Corporation** (**Starbucks**; ticker symbol SBUX) to illustrate and apply the six-step analysis and valuation framework. We use **Starbucks** as a "golden-thread" case company throughout the book for three reasons. First, most of you reading this text are likely already familiar with **Starbucks**: they are the world's largest chain of coffee shops. At the end of fiscal 2015 (September 27, 2015), 23,043 **Starbucks** coffee shops were operating in 68 countries around the world. Of those shops, **Starbucks** owned and operated 12,235 shops (53.1%) and licensees owned and operated the other 10,808 shops (46.9%). At the end of fiscal 2015, **Starbucks** had a total of 14,803 shops (64.2%) in the Americas segment; 5,462 shops (23.7%) in the China/Asia Pacific segment; 2,362 shops (10.3%) in the Europe–Middle East–Africa segment; and 416 shops (1.6%) in the "other" segment, which also includes new, developing business.

Our second reason for using **Starbucks** as an illustrative case throughout the book is that **Starbucks** operates a fairly basic business—owning and operating a large chain of coffee shops. This makes it more straightforward for us to understand the industry, **Starbucks'** strategy, and accounting information. Third, **Starbucks** has some pretty interesting accounting. As we will discover, some aspects of **Starbucks'** financial statements reflect very high accounting quality, while other aspects reflect poor accounting quality.

At the end of fiscal 2015, **Starbucks'** shares were trading at a price of $56.84. Is that share price fair? Or is it too high or too low? At a price of $56.84 per share, should we buy or sell SBUX shares? By the end of this book, and after carefully applying all six steps of the analysis and valuation process, we will have a good answer to this difficult but very interesting question.

Appendix A at the end of the book includes the fiscal year 2015 financial statements and notes for **Starbucks**, as well as statements by management and the opinion of the independent accountant regarding these financial statements. Appendix B (which can be found online at the book's companion website at www.cengagebrain.com) includes excerpts from management's discussion and analysis of **Starbucks'** business strategy; it also offers explanations for changes in **Starbucks'** profitability and risk over time.

Appendix C at the end of the book presents the output of the FSAP (Financial Statements Analysis Package), which is the financial statement analysis software that accompanies this book. The FSAP model is an Excel add-in that enables you to enter financial statement data, after which the model computes a wide array of profitability, growth, and risk ratios and creates templates for forecasting future financial statements and estimating a variety of valuation models. Appendix C presents the use of FSAP for **Starbucks**, including profitability and risk ratios, projected future financial statements, and valuation. FSAP is available at www.cengagebrain.com. You can use FSAP in your analysis for many of the problems and cases in this book. (We highlight FSAP applications with the FSAP icon in the margin of the text). FSAP contains a user manual with guides to assist you. Appendix D (also found online at the book's companion website at www.cengagebrain.com) presents tables of descriptive statistics on a wide array of financial ratios across 48 industries.

LO 1-2

Apply tools for assessing the economic characteristics that drive competition in an industry, including (a) Porter's five forces framework, (b) value chain analysis, and (c) an economic attributes framework; then identify the firm's specific strategies for achieving and maintaining competitive advantage within that industry.

Step 1: Identify the Industry Economic Characteristics

The economic characteristics and competitive dynamics of an industry play a key role in influencing the strategies firms in the industry employ; their profitability, growth, and risk factors; and therefore the types of financial statement relations you should expect to observe. Consider, for example, the financial statement data for firms in four different industries shown in Exhibit 1.4. This exhibit expresses all items on the balance sheets and income statements as percentages of revenue. Consider how the economic characteristics of these industries affect their financial statements.

Grocery Store Chain

The products of one grocery store chain are difficult to differentiate from similar products of other grocery store chains, a trait that characterizes such products as *commodities.* In addition, low barriers to entry exist in the grocery store industry; an entrant needs primarily retail space and access to food products distributors. Thus, extensive competition and nondifferentiated products result in a relatively low net income to sales, or profit margin, percentage (3.5% in this case). When this grocery store chain generates one dollar of revenue, it generates a profit of 3.5 cents. Grocery stores, however, need relatively few assets to generate sales (34.2 cents in assets for each dollar of sales). The assets are described as turning over 2.9 times (100.0%/34.2%) per year. (Each dollar in assets generated, on average, $2.90 of revenues.) Thus, during a one-year period, the grocery store earns 10.15 cents (3.5% × 2.9) for each dollar invested in assets.

Pharmaceutical Company

The barriers to entry in the pharmaceutical industry are much higher than for grocery stores. Pharmaceutical firms must invest considerable amounts in research and development to create new drugs. The research and development process is lengthy, with highly

	Exhibit 1.4			
	Common-Size Financial Statement Data for Four Firms **(all figures as a percentage of revenue)**			
	Grocery Store Chain	Pharmaceutical Company	Electric Utility	Commercial Bank
BALANCE SHEET				
Cash and marketable securities	0.7%	11.0%	1.5%	261.9%
Accounts and notes receivable	0.7	18.0	7.8	733.5
Inventories	8.7	17.0	4.5	—
Property, plant, and equipment, net	22.2	28.7	159.0	18.1
Other assets	1.9	72.8	29.2	122.6
Total Assets	34.2%	147.5%	202.0%	1,136.1%
Current liabilities	7.7%	30.8%	14.9%	936.9%
Long-term debt	7.6	12.7	130.8	71.5
Other noncurrent liabilities	2.6	24.6	1.8	27.2
Shareholders' equity	16.3	79.4	54.5	100.5
Total Liabilities and Shareholders' Equity	34.2%	147.5%	202.0%	1,136.1%
INCOME STATEMENT				
Revenue	100.0%	100.0%	100.0%	100.0%
Cost of goods sold	(74.1)	(31.6)	(79.7)	—
Operating expenses	(19.7)	(37.1)	—	(41.8)
Research and development	—	(10.1)	—	—
Interest expense	(0.5)	(3.1)	(4.6)	(36.6)
Income taxes	(2.2)	(6.0)	(5.2)	(8.6)
Net Income	3.5%	12.1%	10.5%	13.0%

uncertain outcomes. Very few projects result in successful development of new drugs. Once new drugs have been developed, they must then undergo a lengthy government testing and approval process. If the drugs are approved, firms receive patents that give them exclusive rights to manufacture and sell the drugs for a number of years. These high entry barriers permit pharmaceutical firms to realize much higher profit margins compared to the profit margins of grocery stores. Exhibit 1.4 indicates that the pharmaceutical firm generated a profit margin of 12.1%, more than three times that reported by the grocery store chain. Pharmaceutical firms, however, face product liability risks as well as the risk that competitors will develop superior drugs that make a particular firm's drug offerings obsolete. Because of these business risks, pharmaceutical firms tend to take on relatively small amounts of debt financing as compared to firms in industries such as electric utilities and commercial banks.

Electric Utility

The principal assets of an electric utility are its power-generating plants. Thus, property, plant, and equipment dominate the balance sheet. Because of the large investments required by such assets, electric utility firms generally demanded a monopoly position in a particular locale, and until recent years, usually obtained it. Government regulators permitted this monopoly position but set the rates that utilities charged customers for electric services. Thus, electric utilities have traditionally realized relatively high profit margins (10.5% in this case) to offset their relatively low total asset turnovers (0.495 = 100.0%/202.0% in this case). The monopoly position and regulatory protection reduced the risk of financial failure and permitted electric utilities to invest large amounts of capital in long-lived assets and take on relatively high proportions of debt in their capital structures. The economic characteristics of electric utilities have changed dramatically in recent years with gradual elimination of monopoly positions and the introduction of competition that affects rates, reducing profit margins considerably.

Commercial Bank

Through their borrowing and lending activities, commercial banks serve as intermediaries in the supply and demand for financial capital. The principal assets of commercial banks are investments in financial securities and loans to businesses and individuals. The principal financing for commercial banks comes from customers' deposits and short-term borrowings. Because customers can generally withdraw deposits at any time, commercial banks invest in securities that they can quickly convert into cash if necessary. Because money is a commodity, one would expect a commercial bank to realize a small profit margin on the revenue it earns from lending (interest revenue) over the price it pays for its borrowed funds (interest expense). The profit margins on lending are indeed relatively small. In contrast, the 13.0% margin for the commercial bank shown in Exhibit 1.4 reflects the much higher profit margins it generates from offering fee-based financial services such as structuring financing packages for businesses, guaranteeing financial commitments of business customers, and arranging mergers and acquisitions. Note that the assets of this commercial bank turn over just 0.09 (100.0%/1,136.1%) times per year, reflecting the net effect of interest revenues and fees from investments and loans of 6–8% per year, which requires a large investment in financial assets.

Tools for Studying Industry Economics

Starbucks competes in the coffee beverage industry. We will begin our analysis of the forces of competition within this industry by using the Porter's five forces framework. We will augment that framework by also evaluating the industry's value chain and by examining an economic attributes framework. The microeconomics literature suggests other analytical frameworks for industry analysis as well.

Porter's Five Forces Framework

Porter suggests that five forces influence the level of competition and the profitability of firms in an industry.[1] Three of the forces—rivalry among existing firms, potential entry, and substitutes—represent horizontal competition among current or potential future firms in the industry and closely related products and services. The other two forces—buyer power and supplier power—depict vertical competition in the value chain, from the suppliers through the existing rivals to the buyers. We discuss each of these forces next and illustrate them within the coffee beverage industry. Exhibit 1.5 depicts Porter's five forces in the coffee beverage industry.

---

[1]Michael E. Porter, *Competitive Strategy: Techniques for Analyzing Industries and Competitors* (New York: Free Press, 1998).

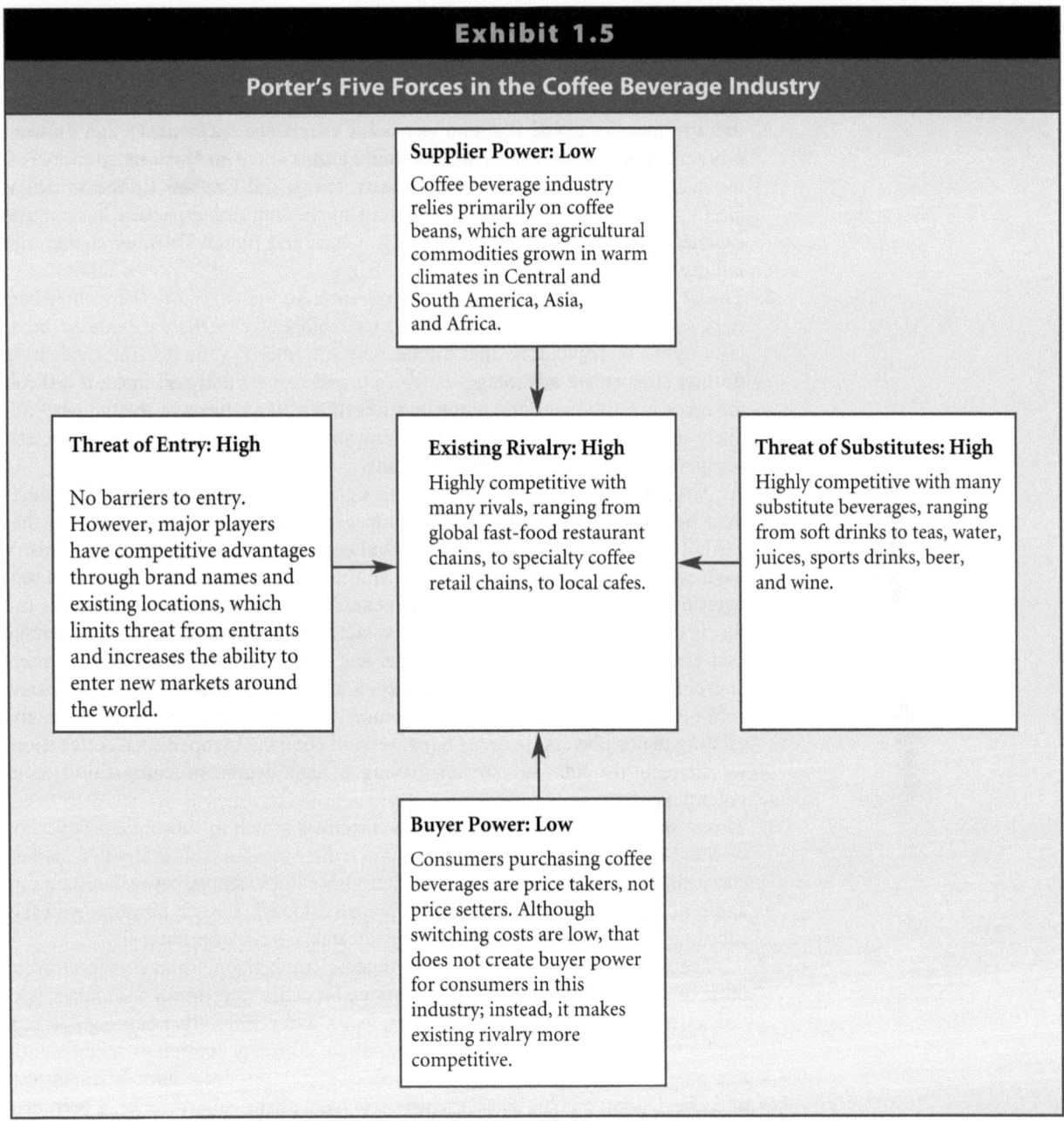

Exhibit 1.5

Porter's Five Forces in the Coffee Beverage Industry

Supplier Power: Low

Coffee beverage industry relies primarily on coffee beans, which are agricultural commodities grown in warm climates in Central and South America, Asia, and Africa.

Threat of Entry: High

No barriers to entry. However, major players have competitive advantages through brand names and existing locations, which limits threat from entrants and increases the ability to enter new markets around the world.

Existing Rivalry: High

Highly competitive with many rivals, ranging from global fast-food restaurant chains, to specialty coffee retail chains, to local cafes.

Threat of Substitutes: High

Highly competitive with many substitute beverages, ranging from soft drinks to teas, water, juices, sports drinks, beer, and wine.

Buyer Power: Low

Consumers purchasing coffee beverages are price takers, not price setters. Although switching costs are low, that does not create buyer power for consumers in this industry; instead, it makes existing rivalry more competitive.

1. **Rivalry among Existing Firms.** Direct rivalry among existing firms is often the first order of competition in an industry. Some industries can be characterized by concentrated rivalry (such as a monopoly, a duopoly, or an oligopoly), whereas others have diffuse rivalry across many firms. Economists often assess the level of competition with industry concentration ratios, such as a four-firm concentration index that measures the proportion of industry sales controlled by the four largest competitors. Economics teaches that in general, the greater the industry

concentration, the lower the competition between existing rivals and thus the more profitable the firms will be.

Starbucks is one of the largest players in the coffee beverage industry worldwide. However, the coffee beverage industry is mature and includes many rivals. The industry includes global fast-food restaurant chains like **McDonald's** and **Subway**; other coffee and donut chains like **Dunkin' Donuts** and **Tim Hortons**; specialty coffee chains like the **Panera Bread Company**, **Peet's**, and **Caribou Coffee**; as well as local cafes. Growth opportunities still exist in the industry, especially in countries experiencing rapid economic growth (e.g., China and India). Thus, we characterize industry rivalry as high.

2. **Threat of Entrants.** How easily can firms enter an industry? Are there entry barriers such as large capital investment, technological expertise, patents or other legal rights, or regulations that inhibit new entrants? Do the existing rivals have distinct competitive advantages (such as brand names) that will make it difficult for other firms to enter and compete successfully? If so, firms in the industry will likely generate higher profits than if entrants can enter the market easily and compete away any potential excess profits.

   The coffee beverage industry has no significant barriers to entry. This is evident by the numerous small coffee shops, fast-food restaurants, and cafes that exist. To be sure, the existing major players within the coffee beverage industry have competitive advantages that reduce the threat of new entrants. Brand recognition by companies such as **Starbucks**, McDonald's and others reduces the threat of potential new competitors. In fact, brand recognition is an advantage that enables companies like **Starbucks** and McDonald's to enter new markets and compete (for example, in fiscal 2015 alone, **Starbucks** opened 1,677 new coffee shops around the world). Because it is easy for a firm (including the existing major players) to enter a market and compete by opening a coffee shop, we characterize this industry as having a high degree of competition from potential entrants.

3. **Threat of Substitutes.** How easily can customers switch to substitute products or services? How likely are they to switch? When there are close substitutes in a market, competition increases and profitability diminishes (for example, between restaurants and grocery stores for certain types of prepared foods). Unique products with few substitutes, such as certain prescription medications, enhance profitability.

   The coffee beverage industry faces intense competition from a wide array of other beverages that consumers can substitute for coffee. Soft drinks, fruit juices, bottled water, sports drinks, teas, milk, beers, wines, and various other beverages serve a similar function to that of coffee. Indeed, in the morning, consumers might substitute caffeinated soft drinks (e.g., Coca-Cola or Pepsi), or orange juice or tea, instead of coffee. During evening social events, consumers might enjoy a coffee, a beer, or a glass of wine. The coffee beverage industry therefore must compete with major global players who offer substitute beverages, including **Coca-Cola**, **PepsiCo**, **Nestlé**, **AB InBev**, **MillerCoors**, **Heineken**, and many others. The threat of substitutes in the coffee beverage industry is high.

4. **Buyer Power.** Within an industry, buyers are extremely important because they purchase the goods and services produced by the industry. However, when analyzing the degree of buyer power, we must examine the relative number of buyers and sellers in a particular industry and the leverage buyers can exert with respect to price and other terms of trade. Are the buyers price takers or price setters? If there are many sellers of a product and a small number of buyers making very

large purchase decisions, such as basic military equipment bought by governments, or automobile parts purchased by automobile manufacturers, or consumer goods purchased by huge retail chains like **Walmart**, the buyer can exert significant downward pressure on prices and therefore on the profitability of suppliers. If there are few sellers and many buyers, as with beverage sales to individual consumers, the buyers can exert less bargaining power.

Buyer power also relates to buyers' price sensitivity and the elasticity of demand. How sensitive are consumers to product prices? If an industry's products are very similar across competitors, consumers may switch to the lowest-priced offering. If consumers view a particular firm's products as unique within an industry, however, they will be less sensitive to price differences. Another dimension of price sensitivity is the relative cost of a product. Consumers are less sensitive to the prices of products that represent small expenditures, such as beverages, than they are to higher-priced products, such as automobiles or homes. However, even though individual consumers may switch easily between brands or between higher- or lower-priced products, they make individual rather than large collective buying decisions, so they are likely to continue to be price takers (not price setters). The ease of switching does not make the buyer powerful; instead, it increases the level of competition between the rivals.

In the coffee beverage industry, buyer power is low. Although there are many rivals and many substitutes creating a very competitive environment, and although switching costs are low, individual consumers buying coffee tend to be price takers rather than price setters. Individual consumers of coffee tend to exhibit relatively low price sensitivity because coffee beverages comprise relatively small-dollar-amount purchases. However, certain buyers (for example, large retail chains such as Walmart purchasing coffee for resale to consumers) make such large beverage purchases on a national level that they can exert significant buyer power.

5. **Supplier Power.** A similar set of factors with respect to leverage in negotiating prices applies on the supply side as well. If an industry is comprised of a large number of potential buyers of inputs that are produced by relatively few suppliers, the suppliers will have greater power in setting prices and generating profits. For example, many firms assemble and sell personal computers and laptops, but these firms face significant supplier power because **Microsoft** is a dominant supplier of operating systems and application software and **Intel** is a dominant supplier of microprocessors. By contrast, if an industry is characterized by many similar suppliers (such as airlines or commercial banks), the suppliers will have limited power to set prices.

Coffee suppliers are farmers who grow green coffee beans. Coffee beans are agricultural commodities, grown around the world. Coffee beans are produced in warmer climates in Central and South America, Asia, and Africa (the top five coffee-producing countries in the world are, in order, Brazil, Vietnam, Colombia, Indonesia, and Ethiopia). As agricultural commodities, green coffee beans are traded daily on the world commodities exchanges. Because of the commodity nature of the product, coffee bean suppliers do not exert much power over the price for coffee.

In summary:

- Competition in the coffee beverage industry is intense among direct rivals and substitutes, and there exists a continual threat of new entrants because there are no barriers to entry.
- The industry faces low buyer power of individual consumers purchasing coffee, but some buyer power among large retail and grocery chains.
- The industry faces low supplier power because the primary input, green coffee beans, are agricultural commodities.

Value Chain Analysis

The value chain for an industry sets forth the sequence or chain of activities involved in the creation, manufacture, and distribution of its products and services. To the extent prices are available for products or services at each stage in the value chain, you can determine where value is added within an industry. You also can use the value chain to identify the strategic positioning of a particular firm within the industry.

As an example, Exhibit 1.6 portrays the value chain for the coffee beverage industry. Coffee beverages begin with farmers growing the green coffee beans. After harvest, the beans are shipped, roasted, and packaged for distribution. The packaged beans are then distributed to retail locations, where they can be sold to consumers. Sales to consumers can occur through two primary channels: retail grocery stores or coffee shops. Grocery stores sell packaged coffee beans directly to consumers, who then brew coffee beverages at home (or at the office). In coffee shops, coffee beverages are prepared for consumers to enjoy, either in the shop or elsewhere.

Because coffee beans are agricultural commodities grown around the world and traded on commodity exchanges, it is difficult for coffee growers to add and capture a lot of the value in this value chain. Similarly, shipping, roasting, packaging, and distribution processes are primarily logistical production activities and do not require sophisticated or advanced technology. As such, these processes do not add the majority of the value in the chain. Instead, the lion's share of value added in the coffee beverage industry occurs in the retail sales of coffee to consumers, through either grocery stores or coffee shops.

Refer to Item 1, "Business," in the 2015 Form 10K for **Starbucks** for a description of **Starbucks'** business segments. **Starbucks** reports four operating segments: (1) Americas (including the U.S., Canada, Mexico, and Latin America); (2) China/Asia Pacific (CAP); (3) Europe, Middle East, and Africa (EMEA); and (4) Channel Development. **Starbucks** reports that the Americas, CAP, and EMEA segments include company-operated and licensed stores. These segments operate in the last stage of the value chain in the coffee beverage industry, which creates and captures the major portion of the value in the industry. **Starbucks** has strategically positioned the largest segments of its business in the highest value-adding stages of the value chain.

Starbucks reports that the Channel Development segment sells **Starbucks**-branded packaged coffee, teas, single-brew products, single-serve products, ready-to-drink beverages (such as Tazo Teas, **Starbucks'** Frappucinos, Doubleshots, and Refreshers), and other branded products through grocery stores, warehouse clubs, specialty retailers, convenience stores, and foodservice accounts.[2] In this segment, **Starbucks** is primarily operating in the third stage of the value chain, distributing packaged products for sale

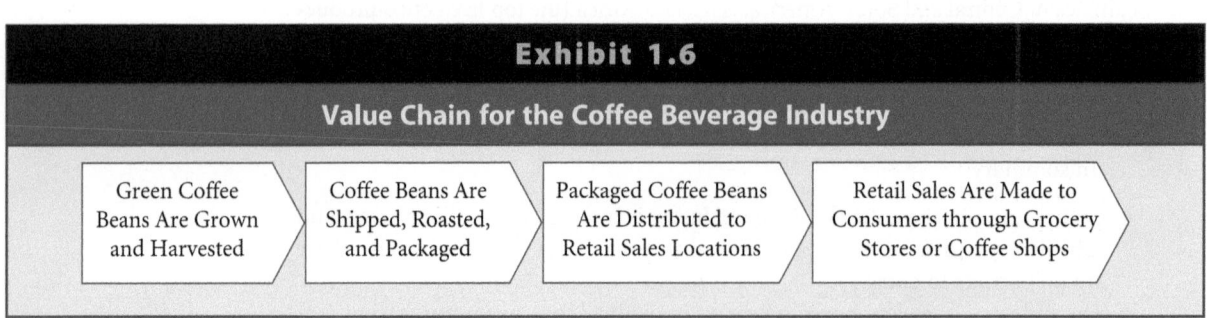

Exhibit 1.6

Value Chain for the Coffee Beverage Industry

| Green Coffee Beans Are Grown and Harvested | Coffee Beans Are Shipped, Roasted, and Packaged | Packaged Coffee Beans Are Distributed to Retail Sales Locations | Retail Sales Are Made to Consumers through Grocery Stores or Coffee Shops |

---

[2]Food service accounts sell food and beverage–related products to food service providers, such as corporate, university, hospital, or government cafeterias, as well as airlines, restaurants, and others.

through retail locations. Although this distribution portion of the value chain does not typically add a majority of value, by distributing **Starbucks'** branded products, **Starbucks** is able to capture a greater portion of the value added here.

Economic Attributes Framework

The following framework can also be useful in studying the economic attributes of an industry.

1. **Demand**
   - Are customers highly price-sensitive, as in the case of automobiles, or are they relatively insensitive, as in the case of soft drinks?
   - Is demand growing rapidly, as in the case of long-term health care, or is the industry relatively mature, as in the case of grocery stores?
   - Does demand move with the economic cycle, as in the case of construction of new homes and offices, or is demand insensitive to business cycles, as in the case of food products and medical care?
   - Is demand seasonal, as in the case of summer clothing and ski equipment, or is it stable throughout the year, as in the case of most grocery store products?

2. **Supply**
   - Are many suppliers offering similar products, or are a few suppliers offering unique products?
   - Are there high barriers to entry, or can new entrants gain easy access?
   - Are there high barriers to exit, as in the case of mining companies or nuclear power plants that face substantial environment cleanup costs?

3. **Manufacturing**
   - Is the manufacturing process capital-intensive (e.g., electric power generation), labor-intensive (e.g., advertising, investment banking, auditing, and other professional services), or a combination of the two (e.g., automobile manufacturing and airlines)?
   - Is the manufacturing process complex with low tolerance for error, as in the case of heart pacemakers and microchips, or relatively simple with ranges of products that are of acceptable quality, as in the case of apparel and nonmechanized toys?

4. **Marketing**
   - Is the product promoted to other businesses, in which case a sales staff plays a key role, or is it marketed to consumers, so that advertising, brand names, and retail distribution locations serve as principal promotion mechanisms?
   - Does steady demand pull products through distribution channels, or must firms continually create demand?

5. **Investing and Financing**
   - Are the assets of firms in the industry relatively short term, as in the case of commercial banks, which require short-term sources of funds to finance them? Or are assets relatively long term, as in the case of electric utilities, which require primarily long-term financing?
   - Is there relatively little risk in the assets of firms in the industry, such as from technological obsolescence, so that firms can carry high proportions of debt financing? Alternatively, are there high risks resulting from short product life cycles or product liability concerns that dictate low debt and high shareholders' equity financing?
   - Is the industry relatively profitable and mature, generating more cash flow from operations than is needed for acquisitions of property, plant, and equipment? Alternatively, is the industry growing rapidly and in need of external financing?

Exhibit 1.7 summarizes the economic attributes of the coffee beverage industry.

Exhibit 1.7

Economic Attributes of the Coffee Beverage Industry Demand

Demand

- Demand is relatively insensitive to price.
- There is low growth in the United States, but more rapid growth opportunities are available in other countries.
- Demand is not cyclical and only slightly seasonal (greater sales in colder seasons).

Supply

- Green coffee bean growers are in warm climates in Central and South America, Asia, and Africa.
- Coffee beans are agricultural commodities, traded on commodities exchanges.

Manufacturing

- The shipping, roasting, packaging, and distribution processes are primarily logistical, and not technologically complex or capital-intensive.
- Final production of coffee beverages from coffee beans is very simple, and can be done by consumers at home or by low-skilled labor at coffee shops.
- Retails sales of coffee beverages to consumers is somewhat capital-intensive, in obtaining high-traffic retail locations for coffee shops and grocery stores.

Marketing

- Brand recognition and established demand pull products through distribution channels, but advertising can stimulate demand to some extent.

Investing and Financing

- Roasting, packaging, and distribution operations are not highly capital-intensive, but they do require some long-term assets, which require some long-term financing.
- Retail sales to consumers, through coffee shops and grocery store chains, requires obtaining and financing retail sales locations, which can be leased.

Step 2: Identify the Company Strategies

Within an industry, firms must strive to establish business strategies to make themselves different from competitors. When a firm creates a strategy that successfully differentiates itself within its industry, it establishes a competitive advantage. The most successful firms create competitive advantages that are sustainable over a long period of time. An industry's economic characteristics affect the flexibility that firms have in designing and executing those strategies to create sustainable competitive advantages. For example, **Starbucks'** size, brand name, and access to distribution channels give it sustainable competitive advantages over smaller, less-known coffee beverage companies. Similarly, the reputation for quality family entertainment provides **Disney** with a sustainable advantage, whereas a reputation for low prices generates advantages for **Walmart**.

In many industries, however, products and ideas quickly get copied. Consider the following examples: cell phones, tablets, and computer hardware; chicken, pizza, and hamburger restaurant chains; and financial services. In these cases, firms may achieve competitive advantage by being the first with a new concept or idea (referred to as *first-mover advantage*) or by continually investing in product development to remain on the leading edge of change in an industry. Such competitive advantages are difficult (but not impossible) to sustain for long periods of time.

Framework for Strategy Analysis

The set of strategic choices confronting a particular firm varies across industries. The following framework dealing with product and firm characteristics helps you identify and analyze the set of trade-offs and choices a firm has made in establishing its strategy within an industry.

1. **Nature of Product or Service.** Is a firm attempting to create unique products or services for particular market niches, thereby achieving relatively high profit margins (referred to as a *product differentiation strategy*)? Or is it offering nondifferentiated products at low prices, accepting a lower profit margin in return for a higher sales volume and market share (referred to as a *low-cost leadership strategy*)? Is a firm attempting to achieve both objectives by differentiating (perhaps by creating brand loyalty or technological innovation) and being price competitive by maintaining tight control over costs?

2. **Degree of Integration in Value Chain.** Is the firm pursuing a vertical integration strategy, participating in all phases of the value chain, or selecting just certain phases in the chain? With respect to manufacturing, is the firm conducting all manufacturing operations itself (as usually occurs in steel manufacturing), outsourcing all manufacturing (common in athletic shoes), or outsourcing the manufacturing of components but conducting the assembly operation in-house (common in automobile and computer hardware manufacturing)?

   With respect to distribution, is the firm maintaining control over the distribution function or outsourcing it? Some restaurant chains, for example, own all of their restaurants, while other chains operate through independently owned franchises. Computer hardware firms have recently shifted from selling through their own salespeople to using various indirect sellers, such as value-added resellers and systems integrators—in effect outsourcing the sales and distribution function.

3. **Degree of Geographical Diversification.** Is the firm targeting its products to its domestic market or integrating horizontally across many countries? Operating in other countries creates opportunities for growth but exposes firms to risks from changes in exchange rates, political uncertainties, and additional competitors.

4. **Degree of Industry Diversification.** Is the firm operating in a single industry or diversifying across multiple industries? Operating in multiple industries permits firms to diversify product, cyclical, regulatory, and other risks encountered when operating in a single industry but raises questions about management's ability to understand and manage multiple and different businesses effectively.

Application of Strategy Framework to Starbucks

To apply this strategy framework to **Starbucks**, we rely on the description provided by **Starbucks'** management (Appendix B). Most U.S. firms include this type of management discussion and analysis in their Form 10-K filing with the Securities and Exchange Commission (SEC).

1. **Nature of Product or Service.** Starbucks' primary strategy is to be the world's leading branded coffee shop chain. Its products are narrowly focused on coffee and related food and beverages. Although one might debate whether its products differ from similar products offered by McDonald's and other competitors (a debate that invariably involves taste), Starbucks relies on brand name to create global recognition and the "Starbucks Experience" to differentiate its products. The "Starbucks Experience" refers to the pleasant service and relaxed atmosphere in its stores. The Starbucks staff enable customers to order and quickly receive a wide variety of different, high-quality coffee beverages customized to each customer's tastes. While the service is quick and efficient, customers can go quickly, or are welcome to stay and relax as long as they wish. Because of differentiation, Starbucks is able to charge a premium price for its products. Because of its brand name recognition, Starbucks is able to grow quickly by opening new stores in mature and new markets around the world, and to distribute branded coffee products in grocery stores and warehouse clubs.

2. **Degree of Integration in Value Chain.** Although Starbucks' primary strategic focus is on the retail sales of coffee beverages to consumers through its chain of coffee shops, Starbucks has vertically integrated its operations. It works closely with green coffee bean farmers in various countries around the world. To control quality and cost, Starbucks often takes delivery of green coffee beans directly from the growers, and then manages the shipping, roasting, packaging, and distribution to all of its coffee shops around the world, as well as to 40,000 grocery stores and warehouse clubs throughout North America.

3. **Degree of Geographical Diversification.** Starbucks has a relatively high degree of geographic diversification. Item 1, "Business," in the 2015 Form 10-K indicates that as of the end of fiscal 2015, Starbucks has 23,043 coffee shops in 68 countries around the world. As noted earlier, as of the end of fiscal 2015, 64.2% of the stores are in the Americas segment, 23.7% of the stores are in the CAP segment, 10.3% of the stores are in the EMEA segment, and 1.6% of the stores are in the "other" segment (which are located in the U.S.). Starbucks' growth strategy in opening new shops is concentrated primarily in the Americas and the CAP segment. Starbucks also has achieved a degree of diversification through licensing shops. At the end of fiscal 2015, Starbucks owned and operated 53.1% of the stores and licensees owned and operated the other 46.9%. Starbucks utilizes licensing arrangements to gain strategic access to key locations (e.g., airports) and to gain local management by licensees in certain international locations (e.g., China, India, and the Middle East).

4. **Degree of Industry Diversification.** Starbucks is concentrated in the coffee beverage industry. It is not diversified across industries. Starbucks does diversify its revenues sources beyond revenues from coffee shops, to some degree by engaging in sales of coffee and other branded products to grocery stores, warehouse clubs, and foodservice accounts through the Channel Development segment.

LO 1-3

Explain the purpose, underlying concepts, and format of the balance sheet, income statement, and statement of cash flows, and the importance of accounting quality.

Step 3: Assess the Quality of the Financial Statements

Firms prepare four principal financial statements to report the results of their activities: (1) balance sheet, (2) income statement, (3) statement of comprehensive income, and (4) statement of cash flows. Firms also prepare a fifth statement, the statement of shareholders' equity, which provides further detail of the shareholders' equity section of the balance sheet. A set of notes that elaborate on items included in these statements is also required. Together, the financial statements and notes provide an extensive set of information about the firm's financial position, performance, and cash flows, and permit users to develop insights about the firm's profitability, risk, and growth.

This section provides a brief introduction to the concept of *accounting quality*. This section also presents a brief overview of the purpose and content of each of the primary financial statements, using the financial statements and notes for **Starbucks** in Appendix A as examples. Understanding accounting concepts and methods and evaluating the quality of a firm's financial statements is a central element of effective financial statement analysis and therefore one of the three central objectives of this book. Chapters 2 and 3 describe the fundamental accounting concepts and methods for measuring and reporting

- assets, liabilities, and shareholders' equity.
- revenues, expenses, and income.
- cash flows associated with operating, investing, and financing activities.

Chapters 6 to 9 describe specific accounting principles and methods in depth, opening with a discussion of accounting quality. In this chapter, we introduce the overall concept of accounting quality by highlighting the key elements of **Starbucks'** financial statements and notes.

What Is *Accounting Quality*?

We frame our discussion of accounting quality by focusing on the following issues that are central to analysis and valuation:

- Accounting information should be a fair and complete representation of the firm's economic performance, financial position, and risk.
- Accounting information should provide relevant information to forecast the firm's expected future earnings and cash flows.

Our notion of accounting quality encompasses the economic information contained in the income statement, the balance sheet, the statement of cash flows, notes to the financial statements, and MD&A (management's discussion and analysis). Each of these financial statements and supplemental disclosures integrates and articulates with the others, and each aids financial statement users in the assessment of profitability, growth, risk, and value.

Our approach to accounting quality is broader and more demanding (and more interesting) than merely asking whether the firm used U.S. GAAP or IFRS and received an unqualified opinion from the independent auditor. We instead apply a rigorous test to reported financial statements to determine whether they provide users with useful information that is relevant and reliable for understanding the firm's financial position, performance, growth, and risk, and that aids the projection of the firm's future earnings and cash flows. It is important to realize that even correctly applied accounting rules may, on occasion, fail to indicate future earnings potential and limit the balance sheet's usefulness in assessing financial position and risk because even the best accounting standards and principles in the world cannot perfectly measure and report each firms' financial position and performance.

Our view of accounting quality is also broader than accounting conservatism, which is sometimes misconstrued as an attribute of reporting quality. Because conservative accounting numbers are biased, they are not, in their own right, high quality for purposes of financial statement analysis and valuation. Conservatism is simply a prudent response by accountants and managers when faced with uncertainty in measuring the economic effects of transactions, events, and commercial arrangements.

Of course, the importance of analyzing firms' accounting quality is further underscored by the rare but dramatic cases in which firms have intentionally misreported financial statement information to mislead users about the firm's profitability, growth, and risk. Sensational cases like **Enron** and **Worldcom** are examples in which firms reported accounting information that misrepresented their underlying economics and earnings potential. We describe accounting quality, and how to assess it, in much more detail in Chapters 6 to 9.

Accounting Principles

U.S. GAAP determines the measurement and reporting methods that American firms use in preparing financial statements. The SEC, an agency of the U.S. government, has the legal authority to specify acceptable accounting principles in the United States (www.sec.gov), but has, for the most part, delegated the responsibility for setting U.S. GAAP to the Financial Accounting Standards Board (FASB), a private-sector body within the accounting profession (www.fasb.org). The FASB is an independent board comprising seven members and a full-time professional staff. The FASB specifies acceptable accounting principles only after receiving extensive comments on proposed accounting standards from various preparers, auditors, and users of financial statements.

The IASB (International Accounting Standards Board) is an independent entity comprising 16 members and a full-time professional staff. The IASB is responsible for developing International Financial Reporting Standards (IFRS; www.ifrs.org). Many countries have dropped their own country-specific accounting rules, formally adopting IFRS as the applicable accounting standards. Beginning in 2005, the financial statements of listed firms in the European Community were required to conform to the pronouncements of the IASB.

The SEC accepts financial statement filings prepared under IFRS from non-U.S. registrants, but it does not yet accept IFRS-based financial statement filings from U.S. firms. The FASB and IASB are working together to harmonize accounting standards and principles worldwide. Although substantial differences must be resolved between the two sets of standards (we will highlight existing differences throughout this book), the two boards have managed to find common ground on many major principles. Now when the two boards propose a new principle or a revision of an existing principle, they typically work jointly to develop the proposed principle and to collect and evaluate comments from various constituencies. They then agree on the final principle, which becomes part of both U.S. GAAP and IFRS. Global harmonization in accounting standards should facilitate better financial statement analysis, enabling analysts to evaluate and compare financial statements from firms across many countries, prepared under similar accounting principles. Accordingly, increasing comparability should make allocation of capital more efficient worldwide.

Balance Sheet—Measuring Financial Position

The balance sheet, or statement of financial position, presents a snapshot of the resources of a firm (assets) and the claims on those resources (liabilities and shareholders' equity) as of a specific date. The balance sheet derives its name from the fact that it reports the following balance, or equality:

$$\text{Assets} = \text{Liabilities} + \text{Shareholders' Equity}$$

That is, a firm's assets are in balance with, or equal to, the claims on those assets by creditors (liabilities) and owners (shareholders' equity). The balance sheet measures and reports the specific resources the firm controls (for example, assets such as cash, inventory, and equipment), the obligations of the entity, and ownership claims on the assets.

The assets portion of the balance sheet reports the effects of a firm's operating activities (principally those day-to-day activities to produce and deliver products and services to customers) and investing activities (principally those activities involving financial assets to generate interest income, dividends, and other returns on investment). Refer to the balance sheets for **Starbucks** as of fiscal year-end 2011 through 2015 in Exhibit 1.8. **Starbucks'** principal operating assets are cash and cash equivalents; receivables; inventories; property and equipment; goodwill; and other assets. **Starbucks'** principal financial assets from investing activities include short-term and long-term investments and equity investments in affiliates.

The liabilities portion of the balance sheet reports obligations that arise from a firm's operating decisions involving obligations to suppliers, employees, and customers, which are reported as accounts payable, accrued liabilities, and deferred revenues. The liabilities portion also reports obligations arising from raising long-term debt capital from banks and other lenders. The shareholders' equity portion of the balance sheet reports equity capital **Starbucks** has raised from investors by issuing common stock (reported as common stock and paid-in capital), and retained earnings.

Under U.S. GAAP, firms are required to report assets and liabilities in descending order of liquidity, so the assets that are closest to cash are listed first, while the assets that are hardest to convert to cash are reported last. Similarly, the liabilities that are likely to be settled soonest are listed first, while the liabilities likely to be settled furthest in the future are shown last.

Formats of balance sheets in some countries can differ from the format used in the United States. Under IFRS, for example, firms can choose to report the balance sheet with assets and liabilities listed in *descending* order of liquidity or they can report the balance sheet with long-term assets such as property, plant, and equipment and other noncurrent assets appearing first, followed by current assets. On the financing side, balance sheets prepared under IFRS may list shareholders' equity first, followed by noncurrent liabilities and current liabilities. Both formats under IFRS maintain the balance sheet equality but present accounts in a different sequence.

In the United Kingdom, for example, the balance sheet commonly takes the following form:

$$\text{Noncurrent Assets} + (\text{Current Assets} - \text{Current Liabilities}) - \text{Noncurrent Liabilities} = \text{Shareholders' Equity}$$

This format takes the perspective of shareholders by reporting the net assets available for shareholders after subtracting claims by creditors. You can always rearrange the components of published balance sheets to the format you consider most informative or comparable with others.

Assets—Recognition, Measurement, and Classification

Which of its resources should a firm *recognize* as assets? How should the firm *measure* these assets? How should it *classify* them in the balance sheet? U.S. GAAP and IFRS establish the principles that firms must use to determine responses to those questions.

Exhibit 1.8

Starbucks Corporation
Consolidated Balance Sheets
(in millions)

	2011	2012	2013	2014	2015
Assets					
Current Assets					
Cash and Equivalents	$ 1,148.1	$ 1,188.6	$ 2,575.7	$ 1,708.4	$ 1,530.1
Short-Term Investments	902.6	848.4	658.1	135.4	81.3
Receivables	386.5	485.9	561.4	631.0	719.0
Inventories	965.8	1,241.5	1,111.2	1,090.9	1,306.4
Prepaid Expenses and Other Assets	161.5	196.5	287.7	285.6	334.2
Total Current Assets	$ 3,564.5	$ 3,960.9	$ 5,194.1	$ 3,851.3	$ 3,971.0
Long-Term Investments	107.0	116.0	58.3	318.4	312.5
Equity and Other Investments	372.3	459.9	496.5	514.9	352.0
Property and Equipment, Gross	6,163.1	6,903.1	7,782.1	8,581.1	9,641.8
Accumulated Depreciation	(3,808.1)	(4,244.2)	(4,581.6)	(5,062.1)	(5,553.5)
Property and Equipment, Net	2,355.0	2,658.9	3,200.5	3,519.0	4,088.3
Deferred Income Taxes, net	230.4	238.7	277.3	317.4	381.7
Other Assets	409.6	385.7	1,427.1	1,375.7	1,765.2
Goodwill	321.6	399.1	862.9	856.2	1,575.4
Total Assets	$ 7,360.4	$ 8,219.2	$ 11,516.7	$ 10,752.9	$ 12,446.1
Liabilities and Stockholders' Equity					
Current Liabilities					
Accounts Payable	$ 540.0	$ 398.1	$ 491.7	$ 533.7	$ 684.2
Accrued Litigation Charge	—	—	2,784.1	—	—
Accrued Liabilities	940.9	1,133.8	1,269.3	1,514.4	1,760.7
Insurance Reserves	145.6	167.7	178.5	196.1	224.8
Deferred Revenue	449.3	510.2	653.7	794.5	983.8
Total Current Liabilities	$ 2,075.8	$ 2,209.8	$ 5,377.3	$ 3,038.7	$ 3,653.5
Long-Term Debt	549.5	549.6	1,299.4	2,048.3	2,347.5
Other Long-Term Liabilities	347.8	345.3	357.7	392.2	625.3
Total Liabilities	$ 2,973.1	$ 3,104.7	$ 7,034.4	$ 5,479.2	$ 6,626.3
Shareholders' Equity					
Common Stock + Paid in Capital	41.2	39.5	282.9	40.1	42.6
Retained Earnings	4,297.4	5,046.2	4,130.3	5,206.6	5,974.8
Accumulated Other Comp. Income/(Loss)	46.3	22.7	67.0	25.3	(199.4)
Total Shareholders' Equity	$ 4,384.9	$ 5,108.4	$ 4,480.2	$ 5,272.0	$ 5,818.0
Noncontrolling Interests	2.4	5.5	2.1	1.7	1.8
Total Equity	$ 4,387.3	$ 5,113.9	$ 4,482.3	$ 5,273.7	$ 5,819.8
Total Liabilities and Shareholders' Equity	$ 7,360.4	$ 8,218.6	$ 11,516.7	$ 10,752.9	$ 12,446.1

Defining what resources firms should recognize as assets is one of the most important definitions among all of the principles established by U.S. GAAP and IFRS:

> Assets are probable future economic benefits obtained or controlled by a particular entity as a result of past transactions or events.[3]

Assets are defined with a forward-looking perspective: resources that have the potential to provide a firm with future economic benefits, such as the ability to generate future cash inflows (as with accounts receivable, inventories, and investments) or to reduce future cash outflows (as with prepaid expenses) or to provide future service potential for operating activities (as with property, equipment, and intangibles). Therefore, asset recognition depends on managers' expectations for future economic benefits. A firm can recognize as assets only those resources for which it

- controls the rights to future economic benefits as a result of a past transaction or event.
- can predict and measure, or quantify, the future benefits with a reasonable degree of precision and reliability.

If an expenditure does not meet *both* criteria, it cannot be capitalized as an asset and must be expensed. A firm should *derecognize* assets (that is, write off assets from the balance sheet) that it determines no longer represent future economic benefits (such as writing off uncollectible receivables or unsalable inventory). Resources that firms do not normally recognize as assets because they fail to meet one or both of the criteria include purchase orders received from customers; employment contracts with corporate officers and employees; and a quality reputation with employees, customers, or citizens of the community.

Assets on the balance sheet are either *monetary* or *nonmonetary*. Monetary assets include cash and claims to future cash flows. **Starbucks'** monetary assets include cash, accounts receivable, and investments in debt and equity securities of other firms. Under U.S. GAAP and IFRS, balance sheets report monetary assets using a variety of measurement attributes intended to enhance the relevance and reliability of reported asset values. Depending on their nature, some monetary assets are reported at current value, others at net realizable value (the amounts the firm expects to collect), others at the present value of future cash flows, and still other assets are typically reported at fair value (the amounts the firm could expect to realize if it sold the assets). Chapter 2 provides more discussion of how accounting is a "mixed attribute" measurement system.

Nonmonetary assets are *tangible*, such as inventories, buildings, and equipment, and *intangible*, including brand names, patents, trademarks, licenses, and goodwill. In contrast to monetary assets, nonmonetary assets do not represent claims to future cash flows. Instead, nonmonetary assets represent benefits from future service potential. Under U.S. GAAP and IFRS, firms report certain types of nonmonetary assets at the amounts initially paid to acquire them (acquisition, or historical, cost) adjusted for the use of the asset over time (accumulated depreciation or amortization), or the amounts currently required to replace them (replacement cost), or the amounts for which firms could currently sell them (net realizable value). Chapter 2 discusses alternative measurement methods and their implications for earnings.

---

[3]Financial Accounting Standards Board, *Statement of Financial Accounting Concepts No. 6*, "Elements of Financial Statements" (1985), par. 25.

The classifications of assets in the balance sheet varies widely in published annual reports. The principal asset categories are as follows:

Current Assets. Current assets include cash and other assets that a firm expects to collect, sell, or consume during the normal operating cycle of a business, usually one year. For example, **Starbucks** reports cash and equivalents; short-term investments; accounts receivable; inventories; and prepayments for expenses such as rent, insurance, and advertising.

Investments. This category includes short-term and long-term investments in the debt and equity securities of other entities. If a firm makes such investments for short-term purposes, it classifies them under current assets. Noncurrent assets include long-term investments and equity investments in noncontrolled affiliates. For these investments in noncontrolled affiliates, the company does not prepare consolidated financial statements; instead, it reports the investments on the balance sheet using the equity method (discussed in Chapter 8).

Property, Plant, and Equipment. This category includes the tangible, long-lived assets that a firm uses in operations over a period of years. Note 7, "Supplemental Balance Sheet Information," to **Starbucks'** financial statements (Appendix A) indicates that property, plant, and equipment includes land; buildings; leasehold improvements; store equipment; roasting equipment; furniture, fixtures, and other; and work in progress. It reports property, plant, and equipment at acquisition cost and then subtracts the accumulated depreciation recognized on these assets since acquisition.

Intangibles. Intangibles include legal or contractual rights to the future use of property. Patents, trademarks, licenses, and franchises are intangible assets. The most troublesome asset recognition questions revolve around which rights satisfy the criteria for an asset. As Chapter 8 discusses in more depth, firms generally recognize the intangibles acquired in external market transactions as assets. For example, in Note 8, "Other Intangible Assets and Goodwill," **Starbucks** details the types and amounts of intangible assets that it has acquired in external market transactions that have indefinite lives (including certain trade names, trademarks, and patents), finite lives (including acquired rights, trade secrets, trade names, trademarks, patents, and licensing agreements), and goodwill. However, firms do not recognize as assets intangibles developed internally by the firm (the **Starbucks** brand name, for example). The rationale for the different accounting treatment is that measurement of value of intangibles acquired in external market transactions is more reliable than the estimates of value of internally developed intangibles.

Liabilities—Recognition, Valuation, and Classification

Under U.S. GAAP and IFRS, firms must report obligations as liabilities if they meet the definition of a liability:

> Liabilities are probable future sacrifices of economic benefits arising from present obligations of a particular entity to transfer assets or provide services to other entities in the future as a result of past transactions or events.[4]

Therefore, liabilities represent a firm's existing obligations to make payments of cash, goods, or services in a reasonably predictable amount at a reasonably predictable future time as a result of a past transaction or event. Liabilities reflect managers' expectations

---

[4]*Ibid.*, par. 35.

of future sacrifices of resources to satisfy existing obligations. Most firms (except banks) classify liabilities in either a current liabilities category, which includes obligations a firm expects to settle within one year, or a noncurrent liabilities category. **Starbucks** reports current liabilities for obligations to suppliers of goods and services (accounts payable and accrued liabilities), insurance reserves, and obligations to customers for deferred revenues (stored-value card obligations). **Starbucks** also reports noncurrent liabilities for long-term debt and other long-term liabilities.

The most troublesome questions regarding liability recognition relate to *executory contracts* and *contingent obligations*. Under U.S. GAAP and IFRS, firms do not recognize executory contracts for labor, purchase order commitments, and some lease agreements as liabilities because the firm has not yet received the benefits from these items and is not yet obligated to pay for them. For example, a firm should not recognize a liability when it places an order to purchase inventory, which is a contingent obligation; the obligation arises only when the firm receives the inventory. Likewise, the firms should not recognize a liability for future wages to employees; instead, it should recognize the liability once the employees have provided services. Notes to the financial statements disclose material executory contracts and other contingent claims. For example, refer to **Starbucks'** Note 10, "Leases" (Appendix A). **Starbucks** reports a large amount of noncancelable operating leases among its executory contracts.

Most liabilities are monetary, requiring future payments of cash. U.S. GAAP and IFRS report those due within one year at the amount of cash the firm expects to pay to discharge the obligation. If the obligations extend beyond one year, U.S. GAAP and IFRS again require firms to use different attributes to measure and report liabilities, depending on their nature. For example, some liabilities are reported at the present value of the required future cash flows. Other liabilities, such as warranties, require delivery of goods or services instead of payment of cash, and the balance sheet reports those liabilities at the expected future cost of providing these goods and services. Other liabilities also involve obligations to deliver goods or services when customers prepay, giving rise to deferred revenue liabilities (such as **Starbucks'** stored-value card liabilities). The balance sheet reports these liabilities at the amount of revenues that have been received from customers and not yet earned.

Shareholders' Equity Valuation and Disclosure

The shareholders' equity in a firm is a residual interest or claim. That is, the owners are entitled to all of the assets that are not required to pay creditors. Therefore, the valuation of assets and liabilities on the balance sheet determines the valuation of total shareholders' equity.[5]

Balance sheets show shareholders' equity separated into

- amounts invested by common shareholders for an ownership interest in a firm (**Starbucks** uses the accounts *Common Stock* and *Additional Paid in Capital*). Some firms may also report amounts invested by preferred shareholders as *Preferred Stock*.
- cumulative net income in excess of dividends declared (**Starbucks'** account is *Retained Earnings*).

---

[5]Bonds with equity characteristics (such as convertible bonds), equity claims with debt characteristics (such as redeemable preferred or common stock), and obligations to be settled with the issuance of equity shares (such as stock options) cloud the distinction between liabilities and shareholders' equity.

- shareholders' equity effects of the recognition or valuation of certain assets or liabilities (**Starbucks'** account is *Accumulated Other Comprehensive Loss*).
- treasury stock (for amounts a firm uses for repurchases of its own shares; **Starbucks** deducts these amounts from *Common Stock*, *Additional Paid in Capital*, and *Retained Earnings*).
- noncontrolling interests, which reflects the amounts of equity capital invested by noncontrolling investors in subsidiaries the firm controls and consolidates (**Starbucks** uses the account *Noncontrolling Interests*).

Assessing the Quality of the Balance Sheet as a Complete Representation of Economic Position

Analysts frequently examine the relation among items on the balance sheet when assessing a firm's financial position and credit risk. For example, when current assets exceed current liabilities, the firm may have sufficient liquid resources to pay short-term creditors. Alternatively, a firm with strong cash flows and bargaining power (like **Walmart** or **Amazon**) can operate with current liabilities in excess of current assets. A relatively low percentage of long-term debt to shareholders' equity suggests that the firm can likely issue new debt financing or use assets to repay debt when it comes due.

However, when analyzing the balance sheet, you must recognize the following:

- Certain valuable resources of a firm that generate future cash flows, such as a patent for a pharmaceutical firm or a brand name for a consumer products firm, appear as assets only if they were acquired from another firm and therefore have a measurable acquisition cost. For **Starbucks**, it has internally developed its brand name, so that does not appear as an asset on the balance sheet.
- Nonmonetary assets are reported at acquisition cost, net of accumulated depreciation or amortization, even though some of these assets may have current market values that exceed their recorded amounts. An example is the market value versus recorded value of land on the balance sheets of railroads and many urban department stores.
- Certain rights to use resources and commitments to make future payments may not appear as assets and liabilities. On the balance sheet of airlines, you generally do not see, for example, leased aircraft or commitments to make future lease payments on those aircraft. **Starbucks**, for example, does not recognize as assets the legal rights to use leased space for the stores it owns and operates, nor does it recognize as liabilities the obligations to make future lease payments.[6]
- Noncurrent liabilities appear at the present value of expected cash flows discounted at an interest rate determined at the time the liability initially arose instead of at a current market interest rate.

For certain firms under these circumstances, the balance sheet reporting may provide incomplete measures of the economic position of the firms. When using the balance sheet, you should consider making adjustments for items that impact balance sheet quality. Chapters 6 to 9 discuss these issues more fully.

---

[6]Lease accounting under U.S. GAAP and IFRS will change in 2019. Under the new lease accounting standard ("FASB Leases," *Topic 842*), lessees will be required to recognize as assets and liabilities any leases that are a year or more in length. We discuss current and future lease accounting in more depth in Chapter 7.

Income Statement—Measuring Performance

The second principal financial statement, the income statement, provides information about the profitability of a firm for a period of time. As is common among analysts and investors, we use the terms *net income*, *earnings*, and *profit* interchangeably when referring to the bottom-line amount on the income statement. Exhibit 1.9 presents the income statements for **Starbucks** for the five years 2011 through 2015.

Exhibit 1.9					
Starbucks Corporation **Consolidated Statements of Earnings** **(in millions, except per-share amounts)**					
	2011	**2012**	**2013**	**2014**	**2015**
Net Revenues:					
Company-operated stores	$ 9,632.4	$ 10,534.5	$ 11,793.2	$ 12,977.9	$ 15,197.3
Licensed stores	1,007.5	1,210.3	1,360.5	1,588.6	1,861.9
CPG, foodservice and other	1,060.5	1,532.0	1,713.1	1,881.3	2,103.5
Total net revenues	**$11,700.4**	**$13,276.8**	**$14,866.8**	**$16,447.8**	**$19,162.7**
Cost of sales (including occupancy costs)	4,915.5	5,813.3	6,382.3	6,858.8	7,787.5
Gross profit*	**$ 6,784.9**	**$ 7,463.5**	**$ 8,484.5**	**$ 9,589.0**	**$11,375.2**
Store operating expenses	3,594.9	3,918.1	4,286.1	4,638.2	5,411.1
Other operating expenses	392.8	407.2	431.8	457.3	522.4
Depreciation and amortization	523.3	550.3	621.4	709.6	893.9
General and administrative expenses	749.3	801.2	937.9	991.3	1,196.7
Gain on property sale	30.2	—	—	—	—
Litigation charges	—	—	2,784.1	20.2	—
Income from equity investees	173.7	210.7	251.4	268.3	249.9
Operating income	**$ 1,728.5**	**$ 1,997.4**	**$ (325.4)**	**$ 3,081.1**	**$ 3,601.0**
Gain on acquisition of JV/Loss on extinguishment of debt	—	—	—	—	329.5
Interest and other income	115.9	94.4	123.6	142.7	43.0
Interest expense	(33.3)	(32.7)	(28.1)	(64.1)	(70.5)
Income before income taxes	$ 1,811.1	$ 2,059.1	$ (229.9)	$ 3,159.7	$ 3,903.0
Provision for income taxes	563.1	674.4	(238.7)	1,092.0	1,143.7
Net income including noncontrolling interest	**$ 1,248.0**	**$ 1,384.7**	**$ 8.8**	**$ 2,067.7**	**$ 2,759.3**
Net income attributable to noncontrolling interest	(2.3)	(0.9)	(0.5)	0.4	(1.9)
Net income attributable to Starbucks	**$ 1,245.7**	**$ 1,383.8**	**$ 8.3**	**$ 2,068.1**	**$ 2,757.4**
Net Income per Share					
Basic	$ 0.83	$ 0.92	$ 0.01	$ 1.37	$ 1.84
Diluted	$ 0.81	$ 0.90	$ 0.01	$ 1.35	$ 1.82

*Gross profit does not appear in Starbucks' Consolidated Statements of Earnings.

Net income equals revenues and gains minus expenses and losses. Revenues measure the inflows of assets and the settlements of obligations from selling goods and providing services to customers. Expenses measure the outflows of assets that a firm consumes and the obligations it incurs in the process of operating the business to generate revenues. As a measure of performance for a period, revenues represent the resources generated by a firm and expenses represent the resources consumed during that period. Gains and losses result from selling assets or settling liabilities for more or less than their book values in transactions that are only peripherally related to a firm's central operations. For example, the sale of a building by **Starbucks** for more than its book value would appear as a gain on the income statement. Chapter 2 describes income measurement in detail, and Chapter 3 contrasts income measurement with cash flows. Chapter 9 describes accounting for operating activities, particularly recognizing revenues and expenses.

Starbucks generates revenues from three principal activities: selling coffee beverages and related products to consumers through company-operated coffee shops; generating royalties and license fees from licensees who operate **Starbucks** coffee shops; and selling **Starbucks'** branded products to grocery stores, warehouse clubs, and foodservice accounts.

Cost of sales includes the costs of producing coffee and coffee beverages (coffee beans, dairy and sugar products, cups and containers, etc.). **Starbucks** also includes occupancy costs, which is primarily rent on company-operated stores. Expenses also include store operating expenses, other operating expenses, depreciation and amortization expenses, general and administrative expenses (including advertising and other promotion costs), interest expense on long-term debt, and income tax expense. **Starbucks** also includes income from equity investees, as well as interest and other income.

When using the income statement to assess a firm's profitability, you should focus on not only its current and past profitability, but also on the likely level of sustainable earnings in the future (Step 5 in our six-step framework). When forecasting future earnings, you must project whether past levels of revenues and expenses will likely continue and grow. In Chapters 6 to 9 we discuss some of the accounting quality factors you should consider when making these judgments. Chapter 10 provides an extensive discussion of forecasting future financial statements.

Accrual Basis of Accounting

Exhibit 1.10 depicts an operating cycle for a typical manufacturing firm. Net income from this series of activities equals the amount of cash collected from customers minus

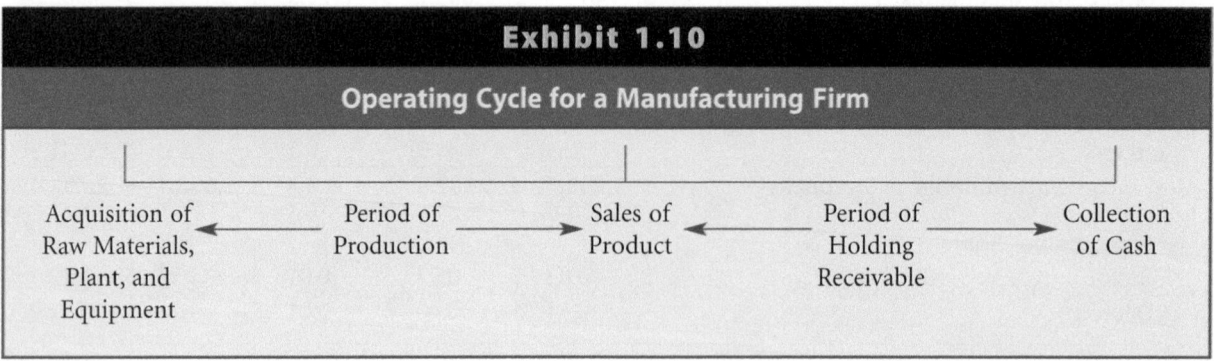

Exhibit 1.10

Operating Cycle for a Manufacturing Firm

Acquisition of Raw Materials, Plant, and Equipment ← Period of Production → Sales of Product ← Period of Holding Receivable → Collection of Cash

the amount of cash paid for raw materials, labor, and the services of production facilities. If the entire operating cycle is complete in one accounting period, few difficulties would arise in measuring operating performance. Net income would equal cash inflows minus cash outflows related to these operating activities. However, firms acquire raw materials in one accounting period and use them in future accounting periods. They acquire buildings and equipment in one accounting period and use them during many future accounting periods. Firms commonly sell goods or services in one period and then customers pay later. Firms often consume resources or incur obligations in one accounting period and pay for those resources or settle those obligations in subsequent periods.

Under a simple cash basis of accounting, a firm recognizes revenue when it receives cash from customers and recognizes expenses when it pays cash to suppliers, employees, and other providers of goods and services. Because a firm's operating cycle usually extends over several accounting periods, the cash basis of accounting provides a poor measure of economic performance for specific periods of time because it focuses on the timing of cash receipt and payment rather than on the underlying economics during the period in which the firm successfully earned resources (revenues) and used resources (expenses) in an effort to generate profits. To overcome this deficiency of the cash basis, both U.S. GAAP and IFRS require that firms use the accrual basis of accounting in measuring performance on the income statement and in measuring assets, liabilities, and equity on the balance sheet.

In Chapters 2 and 9, we describe the principles in the new five-step revenue recognition process (based on satisfying contracts with customers) that the FASB and IASB have adopted, which will become effective in 2017. For our purposes now, it is sufficient to understand that under the accrual basis of accounting, a firm recognizes revenue when it meets the following two criteria:

- **It has completed all or substantially all of the revenue-generating process by delivering products or services to customers.**
- **It is reasonably certain it has satisfied a liability or generated an asset that it can measure reliably.**

Most firms recognize revenue during the period in which they sell goods or render services. Consider the accrual basis of accounting for a manufacturing firm. The manufacturing of product could occur in one period, the sale of product to customers could occur in the next period, and the customer could pay in the following period. The manufacturer would recognize revenue in the period when it sold product to the customer and created the asset (a receivable from the customer). The cost of manufacturing a product would remain on the balance sheet as an asset (inventory) until the time of sale. At the time of sale, the firm recognizes revenue in the amount of cash it expects to collect and recognizes the cost of manufacturing the product as a cost of the goods sold.

Other costs cannot be associated with particular revenues because they are costs of operating the business for a particular period of time (for example, salaries and rent). Therefore, the firm recognizes such costs as expenses on the income statement in the period in which it consumes those resources.

Note that under accrual accounting, a firm should not delay revenue recognition until it receives cash from customers as long as the firm can estimate with reasonable precision the amount of cash it will ultimately receive. The collectible amount will be reported in accounts receivable prior to the receipt of cash. The accrual basis provides a better measure of operating performance than the cash basis because it better captures the economics of a firm's periodic activities and performance than does simply reporting cash flows.[7]

Classification and Format in the Income Statement

Investors commonly assess a firm's value based on the firm's expected future sustainable earnings stream. As Chapter 10 discusses more fully, analysts predict future earnings of a firm by projecting future business activities that will drive future revenues, expenses, profits, and cash flows. To inform analysts and other financial statement users about sustainable earnings, firms often report income from recurring business activities separately from income effects from unusual or nonrecurring activities (such as asset impairments, restructuring, discontinued business segments, and extraordinary events). To provide more predictive information, U.S. GAAP requires that the income statement include separate sections for income from *continuing* operations and income from *discontinued* operations

Income from Continuing Operations

This first section reports the revenues and expenses of activities in which a firm anticipates an ongoing involvement. When a firm does not have any discontinued segments in a particular year, all of its income items relate to continuing operations, so it does not need to use the continuing operations label.

Firms report their expenses in various ways. Most firms in the United States report expenses by their function: cost of goods sold for manufacturing, selling expenses for marketing, administrative expenses for management, and interest expense for financing. Other firms, particularly those in Europe, tend to report expenses by their nature: raw materials, compensation, advertising, and research and development.

Many variations in income statement format appear in corporate annual reports. Most commonly, firms list various sources of revenues from selling their goods and services and then list the cost of goods sold. Some firms (not **Starbucks**) choose to report a subtotal of gross profit (sales revenues minus cost of goods sold), which is an important measure of the inherent profitability of a firm's principal products and services. Firms then subtract the various operating expenses (for example, selling, general, and administrative expenses) and report a subtotal for operating income. The income statement then reports income amounts from investments (interest income and equity income), expenses associated with financing (interest expense), and nonoperating gains and losses (if any). Firms commonly aggregate operating income with the nonoperating income items to report income before income taxes. Firms then subtract the provision for income taxes to compute and report the bottom-line net income.

Many firms, including **Starbucks**, report nonrecurring losses from litigation, restructuring charges, or asset impairment losses in their income statements. Such items often reflect the write-down of assets or the recognition of liabilities arising from changes in economic conditions and corporate strategies. When these nonrecurring losses arise from operating activities, firms often report them in the operating income section of the income statement. If the amounts are material, they appear on a separate

---

[7]Of course, if you define *periodic activities and performance* as the amount of cash collected, then cash flow is an appropriate performance measure. However, investors are primarily interested in the performance of a firm's operating activities, and income statements and balance sheets are the preferred measure based on decades of research, some of which is summarized later in the chapter.

line to distinguish them from recurring income items. Chapters 4 and 6 discuss the benefits and possible pitfalls of segregating such amounts when analyzing profitability.

Income from Discontinued Operations

A firm that intends to remain in a line of business but decides to sell or close down some portion of that line (such as closing a single plant or dropping a line of products) generally will report any income, gain, or loss from such an action under continuing operations. On the other hand, if a firm decides to terminate its involvement in a line of business (such as selling or shutting down an entire division or subsidiary), it will report the income, gain, or loss from operating that line of business in a second section of the income statement, labeled "Income, Gains, and Losses from Discontinued Operations." Income, gains, and losses from discontinued operations appear on the income statement net of any income tax effects. Firms must report the results of discontinued operations separately from continuing operations so financial statement users can assess the portion of earnings that are likely to persist in the future.

Comprehensive Income

The FASB and IASB have determined that the balance sheet is the cornerstone of accounting and that income should be measured by changes in the values of assets and liabilities. To provide relevant and reliable measures of assets and liabilities, U.S. GAAP and IFRS use a variety of measurement attributes, some of which require firms to adjust asset or liability values to reflect changes in net realizable values, fair values, or present values. Valuation adjustments to assets and liabilities usually trigger gains or losses. For example, if a firm determines that it will not collect some of its accounts receivable or will not be able to sell some items of inventory, it should adjust receivables and inventory to their net realizable values and recognize those adjustments as expenses or losses in net income.

The FASB and IASB also have determined that four particular types of valuation adjustments represent unrealized gains or losses that should be reported in a statement of comprehensive income.[8] *Comprehensive income* equals *all* revenues, expenses, gains, and losses for a period, both realized and unrealized. Comprehensive income is measured as *net income* plus or minus the *other comprehensive income* items (if any). The four other comprehensive income items include (1) foreign currency translation adjustments; (2) cash flow hedges, net of tax; (3) certain changes in pension and retiree medical plan obligations, net of tax; and (4) unrealized losses/gains on available-for-sale securities, net of tax (until 2018, when the unrealized gains reporting will be moved to the income statement). Firms that apply IFRS can report a fifth possible other comprehensive income item related to revaluations of property, plant, and equipment. Later chapters discuss the accounting for these items.

Other comprehensive income items are accumulated over time in a special equity account titled Accumulated Other Comprehensive Income or Loss (AOCI). These other comprehensive income items are not recognized in net income until they are realized in an economic transaction, such as when the related assets are sold or the liabilities are settled. The segregation of AOCI acts as a temporary "holding area" for such gains or losses until their ultimate settlement.

Review the consolidated statements of comprehensive income for **Starbucks** in Appendix A. They detail three of the four types of other comprehensive income items

[8]*Accounting Standards Codification 220*, "Comprehensive Income."

that are triggered by the revaluation of assets and liabilities. **Starbucks** includes (1) foreign currency translation adjustments; (2) cash flow hedges, net of tax; and (3) unrealized losses/gains on available-for-sale securities, net of tax. Comprehensive income for **Starbucks** for 2015 is as follows (in millions):

Net income	$2,759.3
Unrealized gains on available-for-sale securities, net of tax	0.9
Unrealized gains on hedging instruments, net of tax	33.5
Foreign currency translation adjustment	(216.7)
Reclassification adjustment for net gains realized in net income	(42.4)
Other comprehensive income items	(224.7)
Comprehensive income	$2,534.6
Comprehensive income (loss) attributable to noncontrolling interests	(29.2)
Comprehensive income attributable to **Starbucks**	$2,563.8

Thus, for fiscal 2015, **Starbucks'** comprehensive income was less than net income, primarily due to a large unfavorable effect from foreign currency translation. Firms may present a single statement of comprehensive income, which includes the standard statement of net income, but continues with other comprehensive income to arrive at comprehensive income. Alternatively, firms may present other comprehensive income as part of a separate statement of comprehensive income, which begins with net income and adds or subtracts various elements of other comprehensive income to compute comprehensive income. **Starbucks** uses the second method of disclosure.

Appendix A indicates that **Starbucks** uses the term *accumulated other comprehensive loss* on its consolidated balance sheet. These cumulative losses amounted to $199.4 million as of September 27, 2015. In addition, **Starbucks** reports the accumulated balances for each component of its other comprehensive income in Note 11, "Equity," to the financial statements.

Assessing the Quality of Earnings as a Complete Representation of Economic Performance

Common stock prices in the capital markets usually react quickly when firms announce new earnings information, indicating that earnings play an important role in the valuation of firms. We provide some striking empirical evidence of the association between earnings and stock returns later in this chapter. In using earnings information for valuation, however, you must be alert to the possibility that reported earnings for a particular period represent an incomplete measure of current period profitability or are a poor predictor of sustainable profitability. For example, reported net income may include amounts that are not likely to recur in the future, such as litigation charges, restructuring or impairment charges, or income from discontinued operations. You may want to eliminate the effects of nonrecurring items when assessing operating performance for purposes of forecasting future earnings. (Chapters 6 and 10 discuss these ideas more fully.)

In some circumstances, some managers might use subtle means to manage earnings upward to meet or beat earnings expectations. For example, a firm might accelerate recognition of revenues, understate its estimate of bad debt expense or warranty expense, cut back on advertising or research and development expenditures, or delay maintenance expenditures as a means of increasing earnings in a particular period. Chapters 6 to 9 discuss the quality of accounting information and illustrate adjustments you might make to improve the quality of earnings.

Statement of Cash Flows

The third principal financial statement is the statement of cash flows. The purpose of the statement of cash flows is important but simple: to inform financial statement users about the sources and uses of cash. This statement is logically organized into its three business activities: operating, investing, and financing. This is an extremely useful statement, but because of the way it is reported by most companies, it can be confusing and misinterpreted. The statement provides useful information to complement the income statement, demonstrating how cash flows differ from accrual-based income. As typically prepared, the statement begins with net income, and effectively "undoes" the accrual accounting procedures to recapture the underlying cash flows.

Even profitable firms—especially those growing rapidly—can sometimes find themselves strapped for cash and unable to pay suppliers, employees, and other creditors in a timely manner. Sometimes firms generate excess cash flows, particularly mature "cash cow" firms. It is important for you to analyze the information in the statement of cash flows to understand how the firm is generating cash and how it is using cash. The information in the statement of cash flows is also useful as a "reality check" on the firm's stated strategy—is the firm using cash in ways that are consistent with its stated strategy?

The statement of cash flows is also helpful in assessing a firm's past ability to generate free cash flows. The concept of free cash flows is first introduced in Chapter 3. As discussed in Chapter 12, free cash flows are central to cash-flow-based valuation models.

Classification of Cash Flows

Cash flows are the connecting link between operating, investing, and financing activities. The statement of cash flows classifies cash flows as relating to operating, investing, or financing activities.

Operating. Selling goods and providing services are among the most important ways a financially healthy company generates cash. Assessing cash flow from operations over several years indicates the extent to which operating activities have provided the necessary cash to maintain operating capabilities (and the extent to which firms have had to rely on other sources of cash).

Investing. The acquisition of long-lived productive assets, particularly property, plant, and equipment, usually represents major ongoing uses of cash. Firms must replace such assets as they wear out. If firms are to grow, they must acquire additional long-lived productive assets. Firms obtain a portion of the cash needed to acquire long-lived productive assets from sales of existing assets. However, such cash inflows are seldom sufficient to cover the cost of new acquisitions.

Financing. A firm obtains cash from short- and long-term borrowing and from issuing preferred and common stock. It uses cash to repay short- and long-term borrowing, to pay dividends, and to reacquire shares of outstanding preferred and common stock.

Exhibit 1.11 presents the consolidated statements of cash flows for **Starbucks** for 2011 through 2015. The statement reveals that cash flow from operating activities exceeded the net cash outflow for investing activities in each year, except fiscal 2014, when **Starbucks** made a huge payment to settle the litigation charges. Also, in every year **Starbucks** used a significant amount of cash for investing activities, and in every year used significant cash for financing activities. These patterns of cash inflows and outflows are typical of a mature, profitable firm.

Exhibit 1.11

Starbucks Corporation
Consolidated Statements of Cash Flows
(in millions)

	2011	2012	2013	2014	2015
Operating Activities:					
Net earnings	$ 1,248.0	$ 1,384.7	$ 8.8	$ 2,067.7	$ 2,759.3
Depreciation and amortization	550.0	580.6	655.6	748.4	933.8
Provisions for impairments/Litigation charge	(85.4)	—	2,784.1	(2,763.9)	—
Deferred income taxes, net	106.2	61.1	(1,045.9)	10.2	21.2
Equity in income of investees	(32.9)	(136.0)	(251.9)	(252.9)	(584.5)
Distributions of income from equity investees	—	86.7	115.6	139.2	148.2
Stock-based compensation	145.2	153.6	142.3	183.2	209.8
Excess tax benefit from exercise of stock options	—	—	(258.1)	(114.4)	(132.4)
Other non-cash items in net earnings	33.3	23.6	23.0	36.2	114.9
Operating assets and liabilities:					
Accounts receivable	(88.7)	(90.3)	(68.3)	(79.7)	(82.8)
Inventories	(422.3)	(273.3)	152.5	14.3	(207.9)
Accounts payable	227.5	(105.2)	88.7	60.4	137.7
Accrued liabilities	(81.8)	23.7	345.7	413.7	212.0
Deferred revenues	35.8	60.8	139.9	140.8	170.3
Other operating assets and liabilities	(22.5)	(19.7)	76.3	4.6	49.5
Net cash provided by operating activities	$ 1,612.4	$1,750.3	$ 2,908.3	$ 607.8	$ 3,749.1
Investing Activities:					
Purchases, sales, maturities of investment securities	(536.0)	47.8	254.3	258.4	52.0
Acquisitions, net of cash acquired	(55.8)	(129.1)	(610.4)	—	(284.3)
Net additions to property, plant, and equipment	(414.5)	(850.9)	(1,151.2)	(1,160.9)	(1,303.7)
Other investments	(13.2)	(41.8)	96.1	84.8	15.7
Net cash used in investing activities	$(1,019.5)	$ (974.0)	$(1,411.2)	$ (817.7)	$(1,520.3)
Financing Activities:					
Net (payments on) proceeds from short-term debt	30.8	(30.8)	—	—	—
Net (payments on) proceeds from long-term debt	—	—	714.5	748.5	238.4
Purchase of noncontrolling interest	(27.5)	—	—	—	(360.8)
Proceeds from issuances of common shares	250.4	236.6	247.2	139.7	191.8
Excess tax benefit from exercise of stock options	103.9	169.8	258.1	114.4	132.4
Repurchases of common equity shares	(555.9)	(549.1)	(588.1)	(758.6)	(1,436.1)
Cash dividends paid	(389.5)	(513.0)	(628.9)	(783.1)	(928.6)
Other	(20.2)	(59.0)	(111.0)	(84.2)	(93.6)
Net cash used by financing activities	$ (608.0)	$ (745.5)	$ (108.2)	$ (623.3)	$(2,256.5)

(Continued)

Exhibit 1.11 (Continued)					
	2011	2012	2013	2014	2015
Effect of exchange rate changes on cash	(90.8)	9.7	(1.8)	(34.1)	(150.6)
Net change in cash and cash equivalents	$ (15.9)	$ 40.5	$ 1,387.1	$ (867.3)	$ (178.3)
Beginning cash	1,164.0	1,148.1	1,188.6	2,575.7	1,708.4
Ending cash	**$ 1,148.1**	**$1,188.6**	**$ 2,575.7**	**$1,708.4**	**$ 1,530.1**

Source: Starbucks, Inc., Forms 10-K for the Fiscal Years Ended 2012–2015.

Firms sometimes engage in investing and financing transactions that do not directly involve cash. For example, a firm might issue common stock upon conversion of long-term debt, or it might acquire a firm with stock rather than cash. Firms disclose these transactions in a supplementary schedule or note to the statement of cash flows in a way that clearly indicates that the transactions are investing and financing activities that do not affect cash.

To help illustrate how the statement of cash flows links to the other financial statements, Chapter 3 describes procedures for preparing a statement of cash flows based only on information on the balance sheet and income statement. Chapter 10 demonstrates techniques for projecting future statements of cash flows from projected balance sheets and income statements.

Important Information with the Financial Statements

A firm's accounting system records the results of transactions, events, and commercial arrangements and generates the financial statements, but the financial statements do not stand alone. To provide more complete information for financial statement users, firms typically provide a lot of important additional information with the financial statements. This section introduces three important elements of additional information: (a) Notes, (b) Management Discussion and Analysis, and (c) Management and Independent Auditor Attestations.

Notes

The notes to financial statements are audited by the firm's independent auditors and are crucial for you to understand the accounting methods and estimates the firm has used to measure assets, liabilities, revenues, expenses, gains, and losses. The first note typically provides a summary of the key accounting principles the firm has used. Because the firm determines each account balance it reports on the financial statements by applying judgments, estimates, and accounting method choices, the notes describe and explain how the firm determined each amount (except those deemed immaterial). For example, the notes explain how the firm is accounting for inventory and the cost methods it used to measure inventory on hand and cost of goods sold. The notes explain how property, plant, and equipment are valued; how they are being depreciated; how much depreciation has been accumulated to date; and what the expected useful lives of the underlying assets are. Notes also provide important details about key financial statement estimates, such as fair values of investment securities, pension and postemployment benefit liabilities, income taxes, and intangible assets.

In its 2015 annual report, **Starbucks** provides a total of 18 notes to explain the accounting principles, methods, and estimates used to prepare the financial statements. Immediately following the financial statements, the notes comprise an additional

36 pages of the annual report. You should read the notes because they provide important information that is useful for understanding the firm's underlying accounting assumptions and assessing its accounting quality.

Management Discussion and Analysis

Many firms accompany the financial statements and notes with extensive narrative and quantitative discussion and analysis from the managers. The Management Discussion and Analysis (MD&A) section of the financial statements provides insights into managers' strategies and their assessments and evaluation of the firm's performance. In some cases, MD&A disclosures provide glimpses into managers' expectations about the future of the company.

In its MD&A (Appendix B), **Starbucks** describes the business as a whole, as well as the operations of the business in each of its segments. In addition to qualitative descriptions, the MD&A section provides valuable details about the financial performance of each division, with managers' analysis comparing results of 2015 to 2014 and 2014 to 2013 for the company as a whole as well as each segment. In addition, **Starbucks'** MD&A section provides important insights into the firm's business risks and the way **Starbucks** is managing them, critical accounting policies **Starbucks** has applied, and **Starbucks'** liquidity and capital resource situation. It also provides valuable glimpses into a few of **Starbucks'** plans for fiscal 2016. For example, **Starbucks** states that it expects revenue growth in excess of 10%, 1,800 net new store openings, a 53rd week in the fiscal year (compared to the normal 52 weeks), an effective tax rate between 34% and 35%, and capital expenditures of roughly $1,400 million. This forward-looking information also will be very helpful when we forecast **Starbucks'** future business activities in 2016 and beyond, as described in Chapter 10. Because the MD&A section provides insights from the managers' point of view, you should read it carefully, but with a bit of skepticism, because it is not audited and managers tend to be optimistic when evaluating the strategies and performance of their own firms.

Management and Independent Auditor Attestation

The design and operation of the accounting system are the responsibility of a firm's managers. However, the SEC and most stock exchanges require firms with publicly traded common stock to have their accounting records and financial statements audited by independent auditors. The independent auditor's attestation as to the fairness and reliability of a firm's financial statements relative to U.S. GAAP or IFRS is an essential element in the integrity of the financial reporting process and the efficiency of the capital markets. Investors and other users can rely on financial statements for essential information about a firm only if they are confident that the independent auditor has examined the accounting records and has concluded that the financial statements are fair and reliable according to U.S. GAAP or IFRS.

In response to some managers' misrepresenting their financial statements and audit breakdowns in now infamous cases involving **Enron**, **Worldcom**, **Global Crossing**, and other firms, Congress passed the Sarbanes-Oxley Act of 2002. This act more clearly defines the explicit responsibility of managers for financial statements, the relation between the independent auditor and the audit client, and the kinds of services permitted and not permitted.[9]

For many years, firms have included with their financial statements a report by management that states its responsibility for the financial statements. The Sarbanes-Oxley Act of 2002 now requires that the management report include an attestation that managers assume responsibility for establishing and maintaining adequate internal control structure and

---

[9]The Sarbanes-Oxley Act of 2002 also created the Public Company Accounting Oversight Board (PCAOB), which has responsibility for setting generally accepted auditing standards, ethics standards, and quality-control standards for audits and is overseen by the SEC.

procedures (referred to as the *Management Assessment Report*). This new requirement now makes explicit management's responsibility not only for the financial statements, but also for the underlying accounting and control system that generates the financial statements. The chief executive officer and the chief financial officer must sign this management report. **Starbucks'** management report appears in Appendix A.

The independent auditor also assesses a firm's internal control system, designs its audit tests in light of the quality of these internal controls, and then forms an opinion about the fairness of the amounts reported on the financial statements based on its audit tests. The independent auditor must now include opinions on the effectiveness of the internal control system (referred to as the *Assurance Opinion*) and the fairness of the amounts reported in the financial statements. This dual opinion makes explicit the independent auditor's responsibility for testing the effectiveness of the internal control system and judging the fairness of the amounts reported. **Starbucks'** management assessment report and independent auditor's assurance opinion (**Deloitte & Touche LLP**) appear at the end of Appendix A. It reads as follows:

> In our opinion, the consolidated financial statements present fairly, in all material respects, the financial position of **Starbucks** Corporation and subsidiaries as of September 27, 2015 and September 28, 2014, and the results of their operations and their cash flows for each of the three years in the period ended September 27, 2015, in conformity with accounting principles generally accepted in the United States of America.

Step 4: Analyze Profitability and Risk

The first three steps of the six-step analytical framework establish three key building blocks in the analysis and valuation process:

- An understanding of the economics of the *industry* in which a firm competes.
- An understanding of the particular strategies that the *firm* has chosen to compete in its industry.
- An understanding of the information contained in the *financial statements* and *notes* that report the results of a firm's operating, investing, and financing activities and an assessment of the quality of the financial statements.

In Step 4, we now use our understanding of the firm's industry, strategy, and financial statement information to evaluate the firm's profitability, growth, and risk. This focus stems from the emphasis of investment decisions on returns and risk. Investors acquire shares of common stock in a company because of the return they expect from such investments. This return includes any dividends received plus the change in the market price of the shares of stock while the investor holds them. A rational investor will demand a higher expected return from higher-risk investments to compensate for the additional risk assumed.

The income statement reports a firm's net income during the current year and prior years. We assess the profitability of the firm during these periods, after adjusting as appropriate for nonrecurring or unsustainable items, as well as growth in revenues and earnings, to determine the drivers of profitability and growth, and to begin gathering information that will help us forecast future profitability. Empirical research has shown a strong association between earnings and stock returns, a point we demonstrate with empirical evidence in the next section and in Chapters 4 and 14.

Financial statements also are useful for assessing the risk of a firm. Empirical research has shown that volatility in reported earnings over time is correlated with stock market–based measures of firm risk, such as market equity beta. In addition, firms that cannot generate sufficient cash flow from operations will likely encounter financial

LO 1-4

Obtain an overview of useful tools for analyzing a firm's profitability, growth, and risk, including financial ratios, common-size financial statements, and percentage change financial statements, as well as how to use this information to forecast the future business activities of a firm, and to value a firm.

difficulties and perhaps even bankruptcy. Firms that have high proportions of debt in their capital structures will experience financial difficulties if they are unable to repay the debt at maturity or replace maturing debt with new debt. Assessing the financial risk of a firm assists the investor in identifying the level of risk incurred when investing in the firm's common stock. Chapter 5 discusses risk analysis.

Tools of Profitability and Risk Analysis

Most of this book describes and illustrates tools for analyzing financial statements. In the next several pages, we simply introduce several of these tools.

Common-Size Financial Statements

One simple but powerful analytical tool is *common-size financial statements*, a tool that is helpful in highlighting relations in a financial statement. Common-size balance sheets express all amounts as a percentage of total assets. Common-size income statements express all items as a percentage of total revenues. Common-size percentages provide an insightful overview of financial position and operating performance.

You must interpret common-size financial statements carefully. The amount for any one item in these statements is not independent of all other items. For example, the dollar amount for an item might increase between two periods, but its relative percentage in the common-size statement might decrease if the dollar amount increased at a slower rate than the total. For example, Starbucks' dollar amounts for receivables increased from $631.0 million in 2014 to $719.0 million in 2015, but the common-size percentages decreased from 5.9% to 5.8%.

The first five columns of Exhibit 1.12 present common-size balance sheets for Starbucks for 2011 through 2015. Note that various common-size percentages for Starbucks remain quite stable while others change over this period. For example, Starbucks experienced a sharp increase in the proportion of assets reflected by goodwill. To better understand the reasons for the increased proportion of goodwill, refer to the investing section of Starbucks' statement of cash flows in Exhibit 1.11. It shows significant cash outflows for several acquisitions during 2011 to 2015. Acquisitions often trigger recognition of significant intangibles, such as goodwill.

The common-size balance sheets also show that the proportion of financing from liabilities rose from 40.4% in 2011 to 53.2% in 2015. Current liabilities remained relatively level, but long-term debt increased significantly. This is consistent with the statement of cash flows in Exhibit 1.11 that show Starbucks increased its long-term borrowing. The common-size balance sheet also reveals that retained earnings decreased as a proportion of total assets, falling from 58.4% in 2011 to 48.0% in 2015. This is also consistent with Starbucks making large cash payments to shareholders for dividends and share repurchases, as seen in the financing sections of the statement of cash flows.

The first five columns of Exhibit 1.13 (page 41) present common-size income statements for Starbucks for 2011 through 2015. Note that net income as a percentage of total revenues (also known as the *net profit margin*) shows that Starbucks was very profitable in all years except 2013. Net income as a percentage of total revenues fell from 10.6% in 2011 to only 0.1% in 2013, and then rebounded to a high of 14.4% in 2015. The common-size income statement for 2013 shows that litigation charges that year amounted to 18.7% of total revenues. Our task, as financial statement analysts, is to understand the implications of these percentages for Starbucks' profitability, growth, and risk, taking into consideration industry economics, company strategies, accounting quality, management's explanations, and the operating results of competitors. Chapter 4 provides a deeper analysis of Starbucks' profitability.

Exhibit 1.12

Common-Size and Percentage Change Balance Sheets for Starbucks
(allow for rounding)

	Common-Size Balance Sheets					Rate of Change Balance Sheets			
	2011	2012	2013	2014	2015	2012	2013	2014	2015
Assets									
Current Assets									
Cash and Equivalents	15.6%	14.5%	22.4%	15.9%	12.3%	3.5%	116.7%	(33.7%)	(10.4%)
Short-Term Investments	12.3%	10.3%	5.7%	1.3%	0.7%	(6.0%)	(22.4%)	(79.4%)	(40.0%)
Receivables	5.3%	5.9%	4.9%	5.9%	5.8%	25.7%	15.5%	12.4%	13.9%
Inventories	13.1%	15.1%	9.6%	10.1%	10.5%	28.5%	(10.5%)	(1.8%)	19.8%
Prepaid Expenses and Other Assets	2.2%	2.4%	2.5%	2.7%	2.7%	21.7%	46.4%	(0.7%)	17.0%
Total Current Assets	**48.4%**	**48.2%**	**45.1%**	**35.8%**	**31.9%**	**11.1%**	**31.1%**	**(25.9%)**	**3.1%**
Long-Term Investments	1.5%	1.4%	0.5%	3.0%	2.5%	8.4%	(49.7%)	446.1%	(1.9%)
Equity and Other Investments	5.1%	5.6%	4.3%	4.8%	2.8%	23.5%	8.0%	3.7%	(31.6%)
Property and Equipment, Gross	83.7%	84.0%	67.6%	79.8%	77.5%	12.0%	12.7%	10.3%	12.4%
Accumulated Depreciation	(51.7%)	(51.6%)	(39.8%)	(47.1%)	(44.6%)	11.5%	7.9%	10.5%	9.7%
Property and Equipment, Net	32.0%	32.3%	27.8%	32.7%	32.8%	12.9%	20.4%	10.0%	16.2%
Deferred Income Taxes, Net	3.1%	2.9%	2.4%	3.0%	3.1%	3.6%	16.2%	14.5%	20.3%
Other Assets	5.6%	4.7%	12.4%	12.8%	14.2%	(5.8%)	270.0%	(3.6%)	28.3%
Goodwill	4.4%	4.9%	7.5%	8.0%	12.7%	24.1%	116.2%	(0.8%)	84.0%
Total Assets	**100.0%**	**100.0%**	**100.0%**	**100.0%**	**100.0%**	**11.7%**	**40.1%**	**(6.6%)**	**15.7%**
Liabilities and Shareholders' Equity									
Current Liabilities									
Accounts Payable	7.3%	4.8%	4.3%	5.0%	5.5%	(26.3%)	23.5%	8.5%	28.2%
Accrued Litigation Charge	0.0%	0.0%	24.2%	0.0%	0.0%	na	na	na	na
Accrued Liabilities	12.8%	13.8%	11.0%	14.1%	14.1%	20.5%	12.0%	19.3%	16.3%
Insurance Reserves	2.0%	2.0%	1.5%	1.8%	1.8%	15.2%	6.4%	9.9%	14.6%
Deferred Revenue	6.1%	6.2%	5.7%	7.4%	7.9%	13.6%	28.1%	21.5%	23.8%
Total Current Liabilities	**28.2%**	**26.9%**	**46.7%**	**28.3%**	**29.4%**	**6.5%**	**143.3%**	**(43.5%)**	**20.2%**

(Continued)

Exhibit 1.12 (Continued)

| | Common-Size Balance Sheets | | | | | Rate of Change Balance Sheets | | | |
	2011	2012	2013	2014	2015	2012	2013	2014	2015
Long-Term Debt	7.5%	6.7%	11.3%	19.0%	18.9%	0.0%	136.4%	57.6%	14.6%
Other Long-Term Liabilities	4.7%	4.2%	3.1%	3.6%	5.0%	(0.7%)	3.6%	9.6%	59.4%
Total Liabilities	40.4%	37.8%	61.1%	51.0%	53.2%	4.4%	126.6%	(22.1%)	20.9%
Shareholders' Equity									
Common Stock + Paid in Capital	0.6%	0.5%	2.5%	0.4%	0.3%	(4.3%)	616.7%	(85.8%)	6.2%
Retained Earnings	58.4%	61.4%	35.9%	48.4%	48.0%	17.4%	(18.2%)	26.1%	14.8%
Accumulated Other Comp. Income/(Loss)	0.6%	0.3%	0.6%	0.2%	(1.6%)	(51.0%)	195.2%	(62.2%)	(888.1%)
Total Shareholders' Equity	59.6%	62.2%	38.9%	49.0%	46.7%	16.5%	(12.3%)	17.7%	10.4%
Noncontrolling Interests	0.0%	0.1%	0.0%	0.0%	0.0%	129.2%	(61.8%)	(19.0%)	5.9%
Total Equity	59.6%	62.2%	38.9%	49.0%	46.8%	16.6%	(12.4%)	17.7%	10.4%
Total Liabilities and Shareholders' Equity	100.0%	100.0%	100.0%	100.0%	100.0%	11.7%	40.1%	(6.6%)	15.7%

Source: Starbucks, Inc., Forms 10-K for the Fiscal Years Ended 2012–2015.

Exhibit 1.13

Common-Size and Percentage Change Income Statements for Starbucks
(allow for rounding)

	Common-Size Income Statements					Rate of Change Income Statements			
	2011	2012	2013	2014	2015	2012	2013	2014	2015
Net Revenues:									
Company-operated stores	82.3%	79.3%	79.3%	78.9%	79.3%	9.4%	11.9%	10.0%	17.1%
Licensed stores	8.6%	9.1%	9.2%	9.7%	9.7%	20.1%	12.4%	16.8%	17.2%
CPG, foodservice, and other	9.1%	11.5%	11.5%	11.4%	11.0%	44.5%	11.8%	9.8%	11.8%
Total net revenues	100.0%	100.0%	100.0%	100.0%	100.0%	13.5%	12.0%	10.6%	16.5%
Cost of sales (including occupancy costs)	42.0%	43.8%	42.9%	41.7%	40.6%	18.3%	9.8%	7.5%	13.5%
Gross profit	58.0%	56.2%	57.1%	58.3%	59.4%	10.0%	13.7%	13.0%	18.6%
Store operating expenses	30.7%	29.5%	28.8%	28.2%	28.2%	9.0%	9.4%	8.2%	16.7%
Other operating expenses	3.4%	3.1%	2.9%	2.8%	2.7%	3.7%	6.0%	5.9%	14.2%
Depreciation and amortization	4.5%	4.1%	4.2%	4.3%	4.7%	5.2%	12.9%	14.2%	26.0%
General and administrative expenses	6.4%	6.0%	6.3%	6.0%	6.2%	6.9%	17.1%	5.7%	20.7%
Gain on property sale	0.3%	0.0%	0.0%	0.0%	0.0%	—	—	—	—
Litigation charges	0.0%	0.0%	(18.7%)	(0.1%)	0.0%	—	—	—	—
Income from equity investees	1.5%	1.6%	1.7%	1.6%	1.3%	21.3%	19.3%	6.7%	(6.9%)
Operating income	14.8%	15.0%	(2.2%)	18.7%	18.8%	15.6%	(116.3%)	(1,046.9%)	16.9%
Gain on acquisition of JV/Loss on extinguishment of debt	0.0%	0.0%	0.0%	0.0%	1.7%	—	—	—	—
Interest and other income	1.0%	0.7%	0.8%	0.9%	0.2%	(18.6%)	30.9%	15.5%	(69.9%)
Interest expense	(0.3%)	(0.2%)	(0.2%)	(0.4%)	(0.4%)	(1.8%)	(14.1%)	128.1%	10.0%
Income before income taxes	15.5%	15.5%	(1.5%)	19.2%	20.4%	13.7%	(111.2%)	(1,474.4%)	23.5%
Provision for income taxes	4.8%	5.1%	(1.6%)	6.6%	6.0%	19.8%	(135.4%)	(557.5%)	4.7%
Net income including noncontrolling interest	10.7%	10.4%	0.1%	12.6%	14.4%	11.0%	(99.4%)	23,396.6%	33.4%
Net income attributable to noncontrolling interest	0.0%	0.0%	0.0%	0.0%	0.0%	(60.9%)	(44.4%)	(180.0%)	(575.0%)
Net income attributable to Starbucks	10.6%	10.4%	0.1%	12.6%	14.4%	11.1%	(99.4%)	24,816.9%	33.3%

Source: Starbucks, Inc., Forms 10-K for the Fiscal Years Ended 2012–2015.

Percentage Change Financial Statements

Another powerful analytical tool is *percentage change financial statements*, a tool that is helpful in highlighting the relative rates of growth in financial statement amounts from year to year and over longer periods of time. These statements present the percentage change in the amount of an item relative to its amount in the previous period or the compounded average percentage change over several prior periods.

The four rightmost columns of Exhibit 1.12 present percentage changes in balance sheet items during 2012 through 2015 for **Starbucks**. Note some of the largest percentage changes in assets occur for goodwill, and some of the largest percentages in liabilities occur for long-term debt, consistent with the preceding observations with respect to the statement of cash flows.

You must exert particular caution when interpreting percentage change balance sheets for a particular year. If the amount for the preceding year that serves as the base is relatively small, even a small change in dollar amount can result in a large percentage change. This is the case, for example, with **Starbucks'** short-term investments in 2015. Short-term investments dropped from $135.4 million to $81.3 million, which is a proportionately large decrease of 40%. A large percentage change in an account that makes up a small portion of total assets is not as meaningful as a smaller percentage change in an account that makes up a larger portion of total assets or total financing.

The four rightmost columns of Exhibit 1.13 present percentage change income statement amounts for **Starbucks**. Note that gross profit grew at faster rates than total revenues in each year from 2013 to 2015, suggesting **Starbucks** had good control over cost of goods sold and/or exhibited strong pricing power during those years. In contrast, the percentage changes in net income show much more volatility over time, particularly due to the litigation charges in 2013. You should carefully investigate the reasons for the volatility in **Starbucks'** profitability.

Financial Statement Ratios

Perhaps the most useful analytical tools for assessing profitability and risk are *financial statement ratios*. Financial statement ratios express relations among various items from the three financial statements. Researchers and analysts have found that such ratios are effective indicators of various dimensions of profitability, growth, and risk and serve as useful signals of future profitability, growth, and risk. Chapters 4 and 5 discuss how to compute and interpret financial statement ratios in depth. The discussion here merely introduces several of them. Appendix D presents descriptive statistics for many of the most commonly used financial ratios across 48 industries over the past 10 years.

Profitability Ratios. Perhaps the most common financial ratio is EPS (earnings per share). Basic EPS equals net income available to the common shareholders (that is, net income minus dividends on preferred stock) divided by the weighted-average number of common shares outstanding. For 2015, basic EPS for **Starbucks** (see Exhibit 1.9) is $1.84 [$2,757.4/1,495.9 shares]. Firms typically report both *basic* and *diluted* EPS on their income statements. As Chapter 14 makes clear, financial analysts often use a multiple of EPS (a price-earnings ratio) to derive what they consider an appropriate price for a firm's common stock.

Another important profitability ratio, which plays a central role in this text, is the *return on common equity* (ROCE). ROCE equals net income available to the common shareholders divided by average common shareholders' equity for the year. ROCE for **Starbucks** for 2015 is 49.7% {$2,757.4/[0.5($5,818.0 + $5,272.0)]}. This is very high relative to most firms. However, we should expect **Starbucks** to generate a high rate of return for its shareholders because it has developed sustainable competitive advantages as a global competitor with the world's largest chain of shops in the coffee beverage industry.

This example illustrates that we must interpret ROCE and other financial ratios with a frame of reference, which we build by first conducting the industry analysis, the strategic analysis, and the accounting quality analysis. For **Starbucks**, their valuable brands lead to higher revenues and earnings, but the value of internally generated brand value does not appear on the balance sheet.[10] Analysts compare ratios to corresponding ratios of earlier periods (*time-series analysis*), to corresponding ratios of other firms in the same industry (*cross-sectional analysis*), and to industry averages to interpret the ratios. Chapter 4 provides an in-depth analysis of **Starbucks'** ROCE and other profitability ratios, including how to adjust reported profitability for unusual or nonrecurring items.

Risk Ratios. A simple method to assess the volatility of a firm's earnings over time and gauge uncertainty inherent in future earnings is to simply calculate the standard deviation in ROCE. Alternatively, to assess the ability of firms to repay short-term obligations, analysts frequently calculate various short-term liquidity ratios such as the current ratio, which equals current assets divided by current liabilities. The current ratio for **Starbucks** at the end of 2015 is 1.19 ($4,352.7/$3,653.5). **Starbucks** appears to have relatively low short-term liquidity risk. As with profitability ratios, this ratio is meaningful only when you perform a time-series and cross-sectional analysis, and interpret it in light of the firm's industry, strategy, and accounting quality.

To assess the ability of firms to continue operating for a longer term (that is, to avoid bankruptcy), you look at various long-term solvency ratios, such the relative amount of long-term debt in the capital structure. The ratio of long-term debt to common shareholders' equity for **Starbucks** at the end of 2015 is 0.40 ($2,347.5/$5,818.0). **Starbucks** has been increasing its leverage, but given **Starbucks'** level of profitability, strong cash flows, and solid short-term liquidity position, bankruptcy risk is low. Chapter 5 provides an in-depth analysis of **Starbucks'** debt-to-equity and other risk ratios.

Step 5: Prepare Forecasted Financial Statements and Step 6: Value the Firm

Each of the six steps in our analysis and valuation framework is important, but the crucial (and most difficult) step is *forecasting* future financial statements. Our forecasts are the inputs into our valuation models or other financial decisions. The quality of our investment decisions rests on the reliability of our forecasts. The primary reason we analyze a firm's industry, strategy, accounting quality, and financial statement ratios is to gather information and insights for our forecasts of future performance. Our forecasted financial statements rely on assumptions we make about the future: Will the firm's strategy remain the same or change? At what rate will the firm generate revenue growth and earnings growth? Will the firm likely gain or lose market share relative to competitors? Will revenues grow because of increases in sales volume, prices, or both? How will its costs change? How much will the firm need to increase operating assets (inventory, plant, and equipment) to achieve its growth strategies? How much capital will the firm need to raise to finance growth in assets? Will it change the mix of debt versus equity financing? How will a change in leverage change the risk of the firm?

Responses to these types of questions provide the basis for forecasting income statements, balance sheets, and statements of cash flows. You can compare financial ratios of

---

[10]Because assets are understated, equity (assets minus liabilities) is also understated, biasing ROCE upwards.

forecasted financial statement items with the corresponding ratios from the reported financial statements to judge the reasonableness of your assumptions. Chapter 10 describes and illustrates the techniques to project future financial statements and applies the techniques to build financial statement projections. Amounts from the forecasted financial statements serve as the basis for the valuation models in Step 6.

Capital market participants most commonly use financial statement analysis to *value* firms. The previous five steps of the framework culminate in a valuation model. Financial statement forecasts—specifically, expected future earnings, dividends, and cash flows—play a central role in firm valuation. To develop reliable estimates of firm value, and therefore to make intelligent investment decisions, you must rely on well-reasoned and objective forecasts of the firm's future profitability, growth, and risk. Forecasts of future dividends, earnings, and cash flows form the basis for the most frequently used valuation models. Thus, the emphasis of this book is to arm you with the knowledge necessary to apply sophisticated and comprehensive valuation models.

In some cases, analysts prefer to assess firm value using the classical dividends-based approach, which takes the perspective of valuing the firm from the standpoint of the cash that investors can expect to receive through dividends (or the sale of their shares). It also is common for analysts to assess firm value using measures of the firm's expected future free cash flows—cash flows that are available to be paid as dividends after necessary payments are made to reinvest in productive assets and meet required debt payments. An equivalent approach to valuation involves computing firm value based on the book value of equity and the earnings of the firm you expect to exceed the firm's cost of capital. In many circumstances, analysts find it necessary or desirable to estimate firm value using valuation heuristics such as price-earnings ratios and market-to-book-value ratios. Chapters 11 to 14 describe the theory and demonstrate the practical applications of each of these approaches to valuation.

LO 1-5

Consider the role of financial statement analysis and valuation in an efficient capital market, and review empirical evidence on the association between changes in earnings and changes in stock prices.

Role of Financial Statement Analysis in an Efficient Capital Market

Security prices represent the aggregate information known by the capital markets about a firm. Market efficiency describes the degree to which the capital market impounds information into security prices. The larger the set of information that is priced and the greater the speed with which security prices reflect new information, the higher the degree of market efficiency. A highly efficient capital market would impound all publicly available value-relevant information (such as an announcement of surprisingly good or poor earnings in a particular period) quickly, completely, and without bias into share prices. In a less efficient market, share prices would react more slowly to value-relevant information. In the U.S. capital markets, the performance of large firms tends to have a wide following of buy-side and sell-side analysts, many institutional investors, and the financial press. The market is more efficient in adjusting the share prices of these large firms than those of smaller market firms, which have no analyst following, no institutional investors, and rare press coverage.

There are differing views as to the benefits of financial statement analysis in the context of market efficiency. One view is that the stock market reacts with a very high degree of efficiency to financial statement information, quickly impounding new financial statement information into security prices, and thus making it nearly impossible for analysts and investors to identify "undervalued" or "overvalued" securities.

By contrast, consider the following:

- Analysts and investors are the capital market participants that actually drive market efficiency. With their expertise and access to information about firms, financial analysts and investors do the analysis and engage in the trading necessary to increase market efficiency. They are agents of market efficiency.
- Research on capital market efficiency aggregates financial data for individual firms and studies the average reaction of the market to earnings and other financial statement information. A finding that the market is efficient *on average* does not preclude temporary mispricing of individual firms' shares.
- Research has shown that equity markets are not perfectly efficient. Anomalies include the tendency for market prices to adjust with a lag to new earnings information, systematic underreaction to the information contained in earnings announcements, and the ability to use a combination of financial ratios to detect under- and overpriced securities.[11]
- The capital markets are economic systems based on human activities (analyzing companies and trading shares). It seems unrealistic to expect that the capital markets price all shares exactly correctly all of the time (human systems rarely work perfectly). It seems much more realistic to expect that shares prices can temporarily deviate from fundamental values (prices become temporarily too high or too low). If so, then financial statement analysis is the process through which analysts and investors can systematically and carefully search to identify share prices that may be temporarily too high or too low. Trading shares accordingly (buying low, selling high) then drives share prices back toward fundamental economic values.
- Financial statement analysis is valuable in numerous settings outside equity capital markets, including credit analysis by a bank to support corporate lending, competitor analysis to identify competitive advantages, and merger and acquisition analysis to identify buyout candidates.

The Association between Earnings and Share Prices

To illustrate the striking relation between accounting earnings and stock returns and to foreshadow the potential to generate positive excess returns through analysis and forecasting, consider the results from empirical research by D. Craig Nichols and James Wahlen.[12] They studied the average cumulative market-adjusted returns generated by firms during the 12 months leading up to and including the month in which each firm announced annual earnings numbers. For a sample of 31,923 firm-years between 1988 and 2001, they found that the average firm that announced an increase in earnings (over the prior year's earnings) experienced stock returns that exceeded market average returns by 19.2%. On the other hand, the average firm that announced a decrease in earnings experienced stock returns that were 16.4% lower than the market average. Their results suggest that merely *the sign* of the change in earnings was associated with a 35.6% stock return differential per year, on average, over their sample period. Exhibit 1.14 presents a graph of their results.

---

[11]For a summary of the issues and related research, see Ray Ball, "The Theory of Stock Market Efficiency: Accomplishments and Limitations," *Journal of Applied Corporate Finance* (Spring 1995), pp. 4–17.

[12]D. Craig Nichols and James Wahlen, "How Do Earnings Numbers Relate to Stock Returns? A Review of Classic Accounting Research with Updated Evidence," *Accounting Horizons* (December 2004), pp. 263–286. The portion of the Nichols and Wahlen study described here is a replication of path-breaking research in accounting by Ray Ball and Philip Brown, "An Evaluation of Accounting Income Numbers," *Journal of Accounting Research* (Autumn 1968), pp. 159–178.

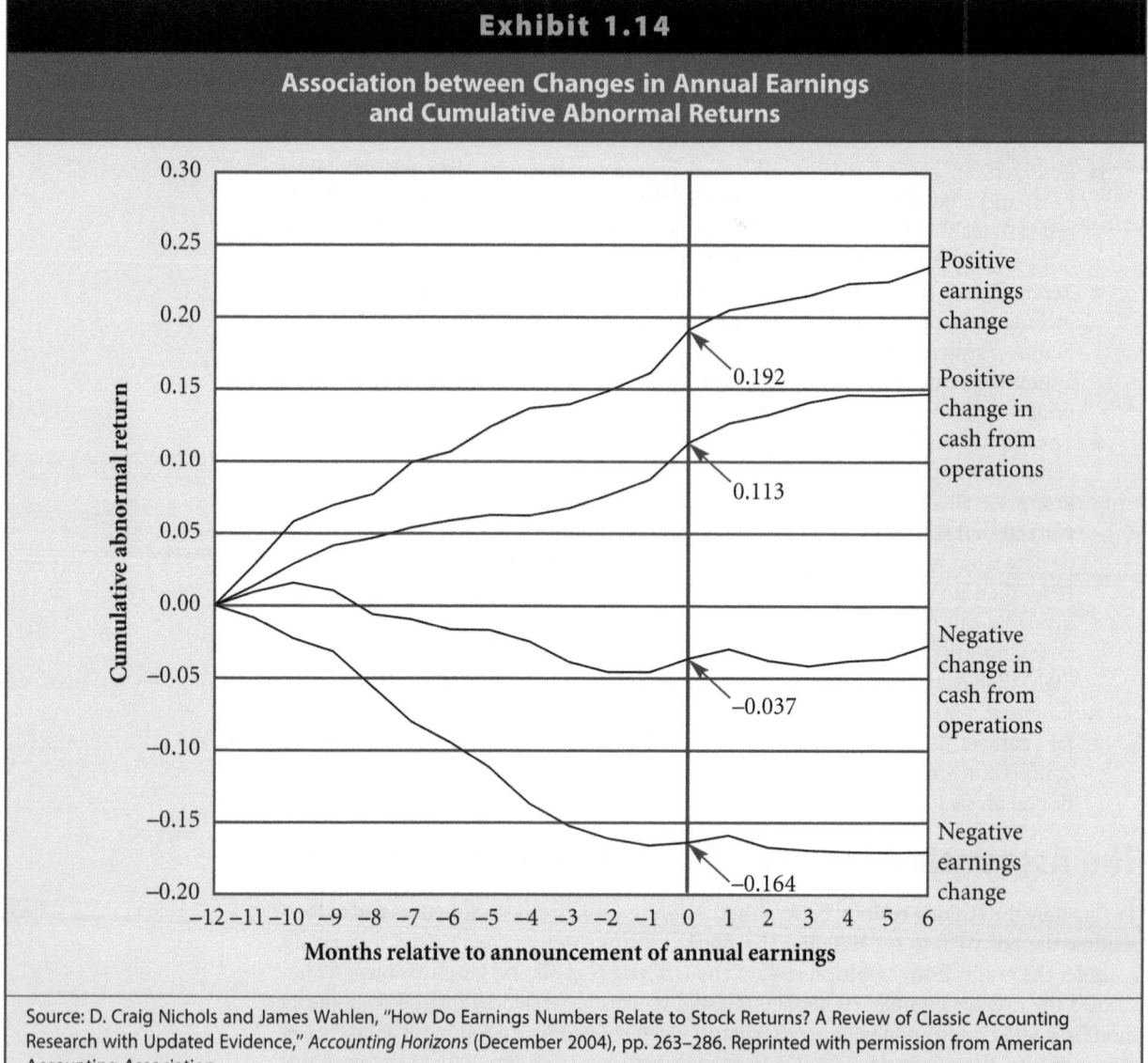

Exhibit 1.14

Association between Changes in Annual Earnings and Cumulative Abnormal Returns

Source: D. Craig Nichols and James Wahlen, "How Do Earnings Numbers Relate to Stock Returns? A Review of Classic Accounting Research with Updated Evidence," *Accounting Horizons* (December 2004), pp. 263–286. Reprinted with permission from American Accounting Association.

The results of the Nichols and Wahlen study indicate how informative accounting earnings are to the capital markets and emphasize the importance of forecasting the changes in earnings one year ahead. We view these results as very encouraging because they imply that being able to simply forecast whether future earnings will be higher or lower than current earnings can yield investment profits. To be sure, Nichols and Wahlen knew with certainty which firms would announce earnings increases or decreases one year ahead. Analysts must forecast earnings changes and take positions in stocks on the basis of their earnings forecasts.

As the graph shows, the study also examined the relation between changes in cash flows from operations and cumulative market-adjusted stock returns. Using the same firm-years, Nichols and Wahlen documented that firms experiencing increases in cash from operations experienced stock returns that beat the market by an average of 11.3%, whereas firms experiencing decreases in cash from operations experienced returns that were lower than the market by an average of 3.7%. These results suggest that the sign of the change in cash from operations was associated with a 15.0% stock return differential per year, on average, during the study period.

This implies that changes in cash flows also are strongly related to stock returns, but they are not as informative for the capital markets as are changes in earnings. This should not be surprising because changes in cash flow are less indicative of a firm's performance in one period than are changes in earnings. For example, a firm experiencing a negative change in cash from operations could be attributable to cash flow distress (bad news) or a large investment of cash in growth opportunities (good news). A negative change in earnings, on the other hand, is almost always bad news. This explains, in part, why analysts, firm managers, the financial press, boards of directors, auditors, and therefore financial statement analysis textbook writers focus so much attention on analyzing and forecasting earnings numbers.

Sources of Financial Statement Information

LO 1-6

Review sources of financial information available for publicly held firms.

Firms whose bonds or common shares trade in public capital markets in the United States typically make the following information available:

- **Annual Report to Shareholders.** The glossy annual report includes balance sheets for the most recent two years and income statements and statements of cash flows for the most recent three years, along with various notes and supporting schedules. The annual report also includes a letter from the chairperson of the board of directors and from the chief executive officer summarizing the activities of the most recent year. The report typically includes management discussion and analysis (MD&A) of the firm's operating performance, financial position, and liquidity. Firms vary with respect to the quality of information provided here. Some firms, such as **Starbucks**, give helpful information about the firm's strategy and reasons for the changes in profitability, financial position, and risk. (See Appendix B.) Other firms merely repeat amounts presented in the financial statements without providing helpful explanations for operating results.
- **Form 10-K Annual Report.** The Form 10-K annual report filed with the SEC includes the same financial statements and notes as the corporate annual report with the addition of supporting schedules required by the SEC. For example, compared to the corporate annual report, Form 10-K often includes more detailed information in the notes. The SEC requires firms to report several key items in the Form 10-K, including
  - a description of the business (Item 1), including its risk factors (Item 1A).
  - a description of company properties (Item 2).
  - the management discussion and analysis (Item 7).
  - the financial statements, notes, and supplemental schedules (Item 8).

  Large firms must file their annual reports with the SEC within 60 days after the end of their annual accounting period; smaller firms must file within either 75 or 90 days.
- **Form 10-Q Quarterly Report.** The Form 10-Q quarterly report filed with the SEC includes condensed balance sheet and income statement information for the most recent three months, as well as comparative data for earlier quarters. Unlike the annual filing of Form 10-K, the financial statements included in Forms 10-Q are not audited.
- **Prospectus or Registration Statement.** Firms intending to issue new bonds or equity shares must file a prospectus with the SEC that describes the offering (amount and intended uses of proceeds). The prospectus includes much of the financial information found in the Form 10-K annual report.

Many firms include all or a portion of their annual reports and SEC filings on their corporate websites. For example, **Starbucks** provides all of the financial data and analysis provided in Appendices A and B on the investor relations page of its website (www .starbucks.com). In addition, many firms provide additional financial data on their sites that are not published in the annual reports. Other useful information in the investor relations section of corporate websites may include (1) presentations made to analysts; (2) press releases pertaining to new products, customer acquisitions, and earnings announcements; and (3) transcripts or archived webcasts of conference calls with analysts.

Firms are required to file reports electronically with the SEC, and filings for recent years are available at the SEC website (www.sec.gov). Numerous commercial online and financial database services also provide financial statement information (for example, **Bloomberg**, **Standard & Poor's**, and **Moody's**).

Summary

The purpose of this chapter is to provide a broad overview of the six-step analysis and valuation framework that is the focus of this book and a logical process for analyzing and valuing companies:

1. Identify the economic characteristics and competitive dynamics of the *industry* in which the firm participates.
2. Identify the strategies that the *firm* pursues to compete in its industry.
3. Assess the quality of the firm's *financial statements*, adjusting them, if necessary, for items lacking sustainability or comparability.
4. Analyze and interpret the *profitability*, *growth*, and *risk* of a firm, assessing the firm's performance and the strength of its financial position.
5. Prepare *forecasted financial statements*.
6. *Value* the firm.

The remaining chapters discuss each step in greater depth.

Questions, Exercises, Problems, and Cases

Questions and Exercises

LO 1-2   **1.1 Porter's Five Forces Applied to the Air Courier Industry**. Apply Porter's five forces to the air courier industry. Industry participants include such firms as **FedEx**, **UPS**, and **DHL**. (Hint: Access Gale's Business & Company Resource Center, Global Business Browser, or Standard & Poor's Industry Surveys to obtain the needed information.)

LO 1-2   **1.2 Economic Attributes Framework Applied to the Specialty Retailing Apparel Industry**. Apply the economic attributes framework discussed in the chapter to the specialty retailing apparel industry, which includes such firms as **Gap**, **Limited Brands**, and **Abercrombie & Fitch**. (Hint: Access Gale's Business & Company Resource Center, Global Business Browser, or Standard & Poor's Industry Surveys to obtain the needed information.)

LO 1-2   **1.3 Identification of Commodity Businesses.** A recent article in *Fortune* magazine listed the following firms among the top 10 most admired companies in the United States: **Dell**, **Southwest Airlines**, **Microsoft**, and **Johnson & Johnson**. Access the websites of these four companies or read the Business section of their Form 10-K reports (www.sec.gov). Discuss the companies' strategies using the framework discussed in the chapter, and describe whether you would view their products or services as commodities. Explain your reasoning.

1.4 Identification of Company Strategies. Refer to the websites and the Form 10-K reports of **Home Depot** (www.homedepot.com) and **Lowe's** (www.lowes.com). Compare and contrast their business strategies.   `LO 1-2`

1.5 Researching the FASB Website. Go to the website of the Financial Accounting Standards Board (www.fasb.org). Identify the most recently issued financial reporting standard and summarize briefly (in one paragraph) its principal provisions. Also search under Project Activities to identify the reporting issue with the most recent update. Describe the issue briefly and the nature of the action taken by the FASB.   `LO 1-3`

1.6 Researching the IASB Website. Go to the website of the International Accounting Standards Board (www.ifrs.org). Search for the International Financial Reporting Standards (IFRS) summaries. Identify the most recently issued international financial reporting standard and summarize briefly (in one paragraph) its principal provisions.   `LO 1-3`

1.7 Effect of Industry Economics on Balance Sheets. Access the investor relations or corporate information section of the websites of **American Airlines** (www.aa .com), **Intel** (www.intel.com), and **Disney** (http://disney.com). Study the business strategies of each firm. Examine the financial ratios below and indicate which firm is likely to be American Airlines, Intel, and Disney. Explain your reasoning.   `LO 1-2`

	Firm A	Firm B	Firm C
Property, plant, and equipment/assets	27.9%	34.6%	62.5%
Long-term debt/assets	18.2%	3.7%	35.7%

1.8 Effect of Business Strategy on Common-Size Income Statements. Access the investor relations or corporate information section of the websites of **Apple Computer** (www.apple.com) and **Dell** (www.dell.com). Study the strategies of each firm. Examine the following common-size income statements and indicate which firm is likely to be Apple Computer and which is likely to be Dell. Explain your reasoning. Indicate any percentages that seem inconsistent with their strategies.   `LO 1-2`

	Firm A	Firm B
Sales	100.0%	100.0%
Cost of goods sold	(82.1)	(59.9)
Selling and administrative expenses	(11.6)	(9.7)
Research and development	(1.1)	(3.1)
Income taxes	(1.4)	(8.9)
All other items	0.2	0.8
Net income	4.1%	19.2%

1.9 Effect of Business Strategy on Common-Size Income Statements. Access the investor relations or corporate information section of the websites of **Dollar General** (www.dollargeneral.com) and **Macy's Inc.** (www.macysinc.com). Study the strategies of each firm. Examine the following common-size income statements and indicate which firm is likely to be Dollar General and which is likely to be Macy's. Explain your reasoning. Indicate any percentages that seem inconsistent with their strategies.   `LO 1-2`

	Firm A	Firm B
Sales	100.0%	100.0%
Cost of goods sold	(70.7)	(60.3)
Selling and administrative expenses	(23.4)	(34.1)
Income taxes	(0.8)	(0.5)
All other items	(4.0)	(0.1)
Net income	1.0%	5.2%

Problems and Cases

1.10 Effect of Industry Characteristics on Financial Statement Relations.

LO 1-2, LO 1-4

Effective financial statement analysis requires an understanding of a firm's economic characteristics. The relations between various financial statement items provide evidence of many of these economic characteristics. Exhibit 1.15 (pages 52–53) presents common-size condensed balance sheets and income statements for 12 firms in different industries. These common-size balance sheets and income statements express various items as a percentage of operating revenues. (That is, the statement divides all amounts by operating revenues for the year.) Exhibit 1.15 also shows the ratio of cash flow from operations to capital expenditures. A dash for a particular financial statement item does not necessarily mean the amount is zero. It merely indicates that the amount is not sufficiently large enough for the firm to disclose it. Amounts that are not meaningful are shown as *n.m.* A list of the 12 companies and a brief description of their activities follow.

A. **Amazon.com**: Operates websites to sell a wide variety of products online. The firm operated at a net loss in all years prior to that reported in Exhibit 1.15.
B. **Carnival Corporation**: Owns and operates cruise ships.
C. **Cisco Systems**: Manufactures and sells computer networking and communications products.
D. **Citigroup**: Offers a wide range of financial services in the commercial banking, insurance, and securities business. Operating expenses represent the compensation of employees.
E. **eBay**: Operates an online trading platform for buyers to purchase and sellers to sell a variety of goods. The firm has grown in part by acquiring other companies to enhance or support its online trading platform.
F. **Goldman Sachs**: Offers brokerage and investment banking services. Operating expenses represent the compensation of employees.
G. **Johnson & Johnson**: Develops, manufactures, and sells pharmaceutical products, medical equipment, and branded over-the-counter consumer personal care products.
H. **Kellogg's**: Manufactures and distributes cereal and other food products. The firm acquired other branded food companies in recent years.
I. **MGM Mirage**: Owns and operates hotels, casinos, and golf courses.
J. **Molson Coors**: Manufactures and distributes beer. Molson Coors has made minority ownership investments in other beer manufacturers in recent years.
K. **Verizon**: Maintains a telecommunications network and offers telecommunications services. Operating expenses represent the compensation of employees. Verizon has made minority investments in other cellular and wireless providers.
L. **Yum! Brands**: Operates chains of name-brand restaurants, including **Taco Bell**, **KFC**, and **Pizza Hut**.

REQUIRED

Use the ratios to match the companies in Exhibit 1.15 with the firms listed above, and explain your reasoning using the strategy framework in the chapter.

1.11 Effect of Industry Characteristics on Financial Statement

LO 1-2, LO 1-4

Relations. Effective financial statement analysis requires an understanding of a firm's economic characteristics. The relations between various financial statement items provide evidence of many of these economic characteristics. Exhibit 1.16 (pages 54–55) presents common-size condensed balance sheets and income statements for 12 firms in different industries. These common-size balance sheets and income statements express various items as a percentage of operating revenues. (That is, the statement divides all amounts by operating revenues for the year.) Exhibit 1.16 also shows the ratio of cash flow from operations to capital expenditures. A dash for a particular financial statement item does not necessarily mean the amount is zero. It merely indicates that the amount is not sufficiently large for the firm to disclose it. The 12 company names and brief descriptions follow.

A. Abercrombie & Fitch: Sells retail apparel primarily through stores to the fashion-conscious young adult and has established itself as a trendy, popular player in the specialty retailing apparel industry.

B. Allstate Insurance: Sells property and casualty insurance, primarily on buildings and automobiles. Operating revenues include insurance premiums from customers and revenues earned from investments made with cash received from customers before Allstate pays customers' claims. Operating expenses include amounts actually paid or expected to be paid in the future on insurance coverage outstanding during the year.

C. Best Buy: Operates a chain of retail stores selling consumer electronic and entertainment equipment at competitively low prices.

D. 3M: Manufactures a wide variety of industrial and consumer products (the firm lists 45 product categories on its website), ranging from home, office, and school products (such as Post-it Notes and Scotch Tape), to wound and skin care (such as Ace bandages), to adhesives for the aerospace and aircraft industries.

E. Hewlett-Packard: Develops, manufactures, and sells computer hardware. The firm outsources manufacturing of many of its computer components.

F. HSBC Finance: Lends money to consumers for periods ranging from several months to several years. Operating expenses include provisions for estimated uncollectible loans (bad debts expense).

G. Kelly Services: Provides temporary office services to businesses and other firms. Operating revenues represent amounts billed to customers for temporary help services, and operating expenses include amounts paid to the temporary help employees of Kelly.

H. McDonald's: Operates fast-food restaurants worldwide. A large percentage of McDonald's restaurants are owned and operated by franchisees. McDonald's frequently owns the restaurant buildings of franchisees and leases them to franchisees under long-term leases.

I. Merck: A leading research-driven pharmaceutical products and services company. Merck discovers, develops, manufactures, and markets a broad range of products to improve human and animal health directly and through its joint ventures.

J. Omnicom Group: Creates advertising copy for clients and is the largest marketing services firm in the world. Omnicom purchases advertising time and space from various media and sells it to clients. Operating revenues represent commissions and fees earned by creating advertising copy and selling media time and space. Operating expenses include employee compensation.

K. Pacific Gas & Electric: Generates and sells power to customers in the western United States.

L. Procter & Gamble: Manufactures and markets a broad line of branded consumer products.

REQUIRED

Use the ratios to match the companies in Exhibit 1.16 with the firms listed above, and explain your reasoning using the strategy framework in the chapter.

Exhibit 1.15

Common-Size Financial Statement Data for Firms in 12 Industries
(Problem 1.10)

	1	2	3
BALANCE SHEET			
Cash and marketable securities	2,256.1%	4.1%	20.1%
Receivables	352.8	2.8	15.2
Inventories	—	2.4	7.9
Property, plant, and equipment, at cost	—	286.8	43.0
Accumulated depreciation	—	(59.8)	(20.4)
Property, plant, and equipment, net	—	227.0%	22.5%
Intangibles	—	36.5	43.4
Other assets	57.3%	7.2	24.0
Total Assets	2,666.2%	280.0%	133.2%
Current liabilities	2,080.8%	37.8%	32.7%
Long-term debt	390.9	69.1	12.7
Other long-term liabilities	92.6	5.6	21.1
Shareholders' equity	101.9	167.5	66.7
Total Liabilities and Shareholders' Equity	2,666.2%	280.0%	133.2%
INCOME STATEMENT			
Operating revenues	100.0%	100.0%	100.0%
Cost of sales (excluding depreciation) or operating expenses[a]	(54.6)	(61.6)	(29.0)
Depreciation and amortization	(2.0)	(9.9)	(4.4)
Selling and administrative	(1.4)	(12.1)	(29.3)
Research and development	(1.6)	—	(12.2)
Interest (expense)/income	9.5	(2.8)	(0.1)
Income taxes	(14.3)	(0.1)	(6.2)
All other items, net	(8.0)	0.1	1.6
Net Income	27.6%	13.6%	20.3%
Cash flow from operations/capital expenditures	n.m.	1.0	4.9

[a]See the problem narrative for items included in operating expenses.

LO 1-2, LO 1-4   **1.12 Effect of Industry Characteristics on Financial Statement Relations: A Global Perspective.** Effective financial statement analysis requires an understanding of a firm's economic characteristics. The relations between various financial statement items provide evidence of many of these economic characteristics. Exhibit 1.17 (pages 56–57) presents common-size condensed balance sheets and income statements for 12 firms in different industries. These common-size balance sheets and income statements express various items as a percentage of operating revenues. (That is, the statement divides all amounts by operating revenues for the year.) A dash for a particular financial statement item does not

Exhibit 1.15 (Continued)

4	5	6	7	8	9	10	11	12
2.0%	10.6%	96.9%	4.1%	2,198.0%	26.0%	4.5%	1.9%	39.3%
8.9	12.0	8.8	4.2	1,384.8	4.0	13.3	2.0	5.1
7.0	2.1	3.0	1.5	—	8.9	4.0	1.3	—
55.4	221.5	33.8	278.8	—	7.8	41.4	61.1	32.9
(32.5)	(132.6)	(22.6)	(52.8)	—	(2.6)	(14.1)	(28.3)	(18.9)
22.9%	88.9%	11.2%	226.0%	—	5.3%	27.3%	32.9%	14.0%
39.8	75.2	40.5	6.0	101.9%	5.0	109.4	8.3	90.9
4.8	19.0	28.3	81.0	208.5	7.2	59.7	11.4	33.3
85.4%	207.9%	188.6%	322.9%	3,893.3%	56.4%	218.2%	57.9%	182.6%
27.7%	26.6%	37.8%	41.7%	2,878.4%	30.0%	20.7%	15.3%	43.4%
31.7	48.2	28.5	172.2	596.1	0.4	38.4	31.6	—
14.6	90.2	15.3	53.8	171.3	4.4	33.9	12.0	9.4
11.3	42.8	107.0	55.1	247.5	21.4	125.3	(1.0)	129.8
85.4%	207.9%	188.6%	322.9%	3,893.3%	56.4%	218.2%	57.9%	182.6%
100.0%	100.0%	100.0%	100.0%	100.0%	100.0%	100.0%	100.0%	100.0%
(58.1)	(40.1)	(36.1)	(56.0)	(73.4)	(85.8)	(59.5)	(75.1)	(26.1)
(2.9)	(15.0)	(1.5)	(10.8)	(5.0)	(1.5)	(5.7)	(4.9)	(2.8)
(23.7)	(27.6)	(27.6)	(19.3)	(5.1)	(2.6)	(27.9)	(7.6)	(33.7)
—	—	(14.6)	—	(7.7)	(5.1)	—	—	(8.5)
(2.5)	(1.9)	1.0	(8.5)	78.4	—	(1.8)	(2.0)	1.3
(3.8)	(3.4)	(4.3)	(2.6)	(16.0)	(1.0)	(2.2)	(2.8)	(4.7)
—	(5.5)	—	2.3	(28.8)	(0.3)	5.2	0.4	—
9.0%	6.6%	17.0%	5.3%	42.3%	3.7%	8.0%	8.0%	25.5%
2.7	1.5	9.8	1.0	n.m.	8.8	1.8	1.6	5.1

necessarily mean the amount is zero. It merely indicates that the amount is not sufficiently large for the firm to disclose it. The names of the 12 companies, the headquarter countries, and brief descriptions follow.

A. Accor (France): World's largest hotel group, operating hotels under the names of Sofitel, Novotel, Motel 6, and others. Accor has grown in recent years by acquiring established hotel chains.

B. Carrefour (France): Operates grocery supermarkets and hypermarkets in Europe, Latin America, and Asia.

Exhibit 1.16

Common-Size Financial Statement Data for Firms in 12 Industries
(Problem 1.11)

	1	2	3
BALANCE SHEET			
Cash and marketable securities	6.7%	23.0%	9.2%
Receivables	13.7	48.4	25.0
Inventories	11.6	9.6	2.9
Property, plant, and equipment, at cost	76.3	101.2	272.3
Accumulated depreciation	(48.2)	(50.9)	(92.8)
Property, plant, and equipment, net	38.1%	50.3%	179.5%
Intangibles	39.1	8.2	—
Other assets	4.1	58.4	60.5
Total Assets	108.1%	197.9%	277.1%
Current liabilities	23.5%	60.0%	51.2%
Long-term debt	28.9	16.5	70.1
Other long-term liabilities	16.8	42.7	88.9
Shareholders' equity	38.8	78.7	66.9
Total Liabilities and Shareholders' Equity	108.1%	197.9%	277.1%
INCOME STATEMENT			
Operating revenues	100.0%	100.0%	100.0%
Cost of sales (excluding depreciation) or operating expenses[a]	(46.1)	(23.4)	(60.7)
Depreciation and amortization	(4.7)	(6.8)	(12.6)
Selling and administrative	(20.4)	(24.1)	—
Research and development	(5.8)	(20.1)	—
Interest (expense)/income	(0.4)	(1.1)	(4.8)
Income taxes	(6.5)	(8.4)	(3.3)
All other items, net	(0.0)	16.7	(10.6)
Net Income	16.1%	32.7%	8.1%
Cash flow from operations/capital expenditures	4.3	5.1	0.8

[a]See the problem narrative for items included in operating expenses.

C. **Deutsche Telekom** (Germany): Europe's largest provider of wired and wireless telecommunication services. The telecommunications industry has experienced increased deregulation in recent years.

D. **E.ON AG** (Germany): One of the major public utility companies in Europe and the world's largest privately owned energy service provider.

E. **BNP Paribas** (France): A multinational bank and financial services company. Offers insurance and banking services. Operating revenues include insurance premiums received, investment income, and interest revenue on loans. Operating expenses include amounts

Exhibit 1.16 (Continued)

4	5	6	7	8	9	10	11	12
Allstate	*P&G*	*✗*	*Kelly*	*A&F*	*Omnicom*	*HSBC*	*McDonalds*	*Hewlett*
362.6%	6.0%	1.1%	1.6%	14.7%	8.3%	27.3%	8.8%	11.6%
47.7	8.9	4.1	15.7	2.7	43.2	697.5	4.0	16.8
—	8.7	10.6	—	10.5	5.0	—	0.5	5.3
10.3	46.4	15.4	6.9	66.1	13.1	3.2	132.4	18.3
(6.7)	(21.8)	(6.1)	(3.7)	(26.6)	(7.7)	(1.3)	(46.3)	(8.5)
3.6%	24.6%	9.3%	3.1%	39.5%	5.4%	1.9%	86.1%	9.8%
2.8	112.8	6.0	2.6	—	55.7	40.9	9.5	34.7
120.7	9.5	4.1	4.7	12.9	12.0	26.7	12.2	22.0
537.5%	170.6%	35.2%	27.8%	80.5%	129.6%	794.3%	121.0%	100.2%
391.7%	39.1%	18.7%	10.3%	12.7%	73.0%	122.1%	10.8%	37.5%
19.4	26.1	2.5	0.9	2.8	22.9	565.5	43.3	12.2
51.3	25.5	3.6	2.7	12.8	7.4	20.2	10.0	15.1
75.1	79.8	10.3	13.9	52.1	26.4	86.5	56.9	35.4
537.5%	170.6%	35.2%	27.8%	80.5%	129.6%	794.3%	121.0%	100.2%
100.0%	100.0%	100.0%	100.0%	100.0%	100.0%	100.0%	100.0%	100.0%
(91.6)	(49.2)	(75.6)	(82.5)	(33.3)	(87.4)	(29.1)	(63.3)	(76.4)
(0.9)	(3.9)	(1.8)	(0.8)	(5.1)	(1.8)	(1.7)	(5.1)	(4.2)
(10.7)	(23.9)	(18.2)	(15.3)	(49.4)	—	(25.0)	(4.9)	(6.0)
—	(2.6)	—	—	—	—	—	—	(2.5)
21.0	(1.7)	(0.2)	—	0.3	(0.6)	(32.7)	(2.2)	(0.6)
(6.9)	(5.1)	(1.5)	(0.5)	(5.0)	(4.1)	(3.7)	(7.8)	(1.5)
4.2	0.7	(0.5)	(0.1)	—	1.2	(3.3)	1.7	(2.1)
15.2%	14.3%	2.2%	0.8%	7.4%	7.5%	4.5%	18.3%	6.7%
18.7	4.6	1.4	1.6	1.3	6.6	100.9	2.8	3.6

actually paid or amounts it expects to pay in the future on insurance coverage outstanding during the year.

F. **Interpublic Group** (U.S.): Creates advertising copy for clients. Interpublic purchases advertising time and space from various media and sells them to clients. Operating revenues represent the commissions or fees earned for creating advertising copy and selling media time and space. Operating expenses include employee compensation.

G. **Marks & Spencer** (U.K.): Operates department stores in England and other retail stores in Europe and the United States. Offers its own credit card for customers' purchases.

Exhibit 1.17

Common-Size Financial Statement Data for Firms in 12 Industries (Problem 1.12)

	1	2	3
BALANCE SHEET			
Cash and marketable securities	2,649.8%	15.8%	21.8%
Receivables	1,754.2	11.9	48.8
Inventories	—	22.4	6.9
Property, plant, and equipment, at cost	83.7	172.5	66.2
Accumulated depreciation	(31.5)	(126.2)	(36.5)
Property, plant, and equipment, net	52.2%	46.3%	29.7%
Intangibles	32.4	1.8	—
Other assets	330.4	29.5	16.2
Total Assets	4,819.1%	127.6%	123.5%
Current liabilities	3,345.8%	30.1%	45.4%
Long-term debt	425.3	27.7	22.8
Other long-term liabilities	706.2	34.2	10.1
Shareholders' equity	241.8	63.2	45.1
Total Liabilities and Shareholders' Equity	4,819.1%	127.6%	123.5%
INCOME STATEMENT			
Operating revenues	100.0%	100.0%	100.0%
Cost of sales (excluding depreciation) or operating expenses[a]	(20.0)	(80.0)	(76.2)
Depreciation and amortization	(4.0)	(5.6)	(5.7)
Selling and administrative	(5.0)	(8.2)	(5.9)
Research and development	—	—	(3.6)
Interest (expense)/income	(45.5)	(0.4)	0.5
Income taxes	(8.1)	(2.6)	(3.5)
All other items, net	(1.0)	(0.3)	0.9
Net Income	16.2%	3.8%	6.5%
Cash flow from operations/capital expenditures	4.2	1.9	2.1

[a]See the problem narrative for items included in operating expenses.

H. Nestlé (Switzerland): World's largest food processor, offering prepared foods, coffees, milk-based products, and mineral waters.

I. Roche Holding (Switzerland): Creates, manufactures, and distributes a wide variety of prescription drugs.

J. Nippon Steel (Japan): Manufacturer and seller of steel sheets and plates and other construction materials.

Exhibit 1.17 (Continued)

4	5	6	7	8	9	10	11	12
4.9%	16.2%	32.7%	151.5%	17.9%	43.4%	4.7%	6.0%	6.5%
12.0	17.0	69.6	14.5	38.8	20.4	6.9	6.6	12.2
2.1	1.3	—	0.6	5.8	12.2	5.9	7.8	8.5
195.3	92.8	23.2	21.9	134.7	62.9	82.6	34.5	42.0
(127.9)	(36.9)	(15.2)	(11.1)	(76.0)	(24.9)	(29.3)	(17.7)	(22.8)
67.4%	55.9%	8.1%	10.8%	58.7%	38.0%	53.3%	16.8%	19.2%
87.5	31.6	46.3	13.3	26.5	32.3	4.4	14.1	34.1
25.9	25.5	17.5	18.7	28.5	12.7	4.9	7.7	16.1
199.7%	147.5%	174.1%	302.8%	176.2%	158.8%	80.1%	59.0%	96.6%
40.3%	70.2%	98.8%	46.4%	40.6%	25.3%	25.5%	32.2%	30.2%
8.8	24.9	25.7	105.6	21.3	6.2	23.4	10.8	5.8
80.7	6.3	14.2	21.8	43.5	15.0	8.1	3.6	10.7
69.9	46.0	35.6	129.0	70.8	112.4	23.2	12.4	50.0
199.7%	147.5%	174.1%	302.8%	176.2%	158.8%	80.1%	59.0%	96.6%
100.0%	100.0%	100.0%	100.0%	100.0%	100.0%	100.0%	100.0%	100.0%
(56.1)	(70.4)	(62.4)	(17.8)	(64.5)	(28.5)	(62.8)	(77.9)	(51.3)
(17.8)	(5.8)	(2.5)	(6.8)	(5.1)	(3.5)	(4.5)	(2.1)	(2.4)
(15.9)	—	(26.4)	(24.4)	(22.7)	(20.5)	(24.7)	(16.3)	(30.2)
—	—	—	(15.6)	—	(18.5)	—	—	(1.8)
(4.0)	(1.1)	(1.7)	(3.1)	(1.4)	0.5	(1.8)	(0.6)	(1.0)
(2.3)	(3.5)	(2.2)	(6.9)	(0.1)	(6.9)	(2.2)	(0.8)	(3.4)
(0.1)	(11.3)	(0.5)	(1.3)	1.1	0.1	1.6	0.1	7.6
3.8%	7.9%	4.2%	24.0%	7.3%	22.6%	5.6%	2.3%	17.3%
2.3	2.0	6.3	7.2	1.7	4.0	2.7	1.8	2.2

K. **Oracle** (U.S.): Offers a comprehensive and fully integrated stack of cloud applications and platform systems. Oracle outsources a majority of its manufacturing.

L. **Toyota Motor** (Japan): Manufactures automobiles and offers financing services to its customers.

REQUIRED

Use the ratios to match the companies in Exhibit 1.17 with the firms listed above, and explain your reasoning using the strategy framework in the chapter.

1.13 Value Chain Analysis and Financial Statement Relations.

Exhibit 1.18 represents common-size income statements and balance sheets for seven firms that operate at various stages in the value chain for the pharmaceutical industry. These common-size statements express all amounts as a percentage of sales revenue. Exhibit 1.18 also shows the cash flow from operations to capital expenditures ratios for each firm. A dash for a particular financial statement item does not necessarily mean the amount is zero. It merely indicates that the amount is not sufficiently large for the firm to disclose it. A list of the seven companies and a brief description of their activities follow.

A. **Wyeth**: Engages in the development, manufacture, and sale of ethical drugs (that is, drugs requiring a prescription). Wyeth's drugs represent primarily mixtures of chemical compounds. Ethical-drug companies must obtain approval of new drugs from the U.S. Food and Drug Administration (FDA). Patents protect such drugs from competition until other drug companies develop more effective substitutes or the patent expires.

B. **Amgen**: Engages in the development, manufacture, and sale of drugs based on biotechnology research. Biotechnology drugs must obtain approval from the FDA and enjoy patent protection similar to that for chemical-based drugs. The biotechnology segment is less mature than the ethical-drug industry, with relatively few products having received FDA approval.

C. **Mylan Laboratories**: Engages in the development, manufacture, and sale of generic drugs. Generic drugs have the same chemical compositions as drugs that had previously benefited from patent protection but for which the patent has expired. Generic drug companies have benefited in recent years from the patent expiration of several major ethical drugs. However, the major ethical-drug companies have increasingly offered generic versions of their ethical drugs to compete against the generic-drug companies.

D. **Johnson & Johnson**: Engages in the development, manufacture, and sale of over-the-counter health care products. Such products do not require a prescription and often benefit from brand recognition.

E. **Covance**: Offers product development and laboratory testing services for biotechnology and pharmaceutical drugs. It also offers commercialization services and market access services. Cost of goods sold for this company represents the salaries of personnel conducting the laboratory testing and drug approval services.

F. **Cardinal Health**: Distributes drugs as a wholesaler to drugstores, hospitals, and mass merchandisers. Also offers pharmaceutical benefit management services in which it provides customized databases designed to help customers order more efficiently, contain costs, and monitor their purchases. Cost of goods sold for Cardinal Health includes the cost of drugs sold plus the salaries of personnel providing pharmaceutical benefit management services.

G. **Walgreens**: Operates a chain of drugstores nationwide. The data in Exhibit 1.18 for Walgreens include the recognition of operating lease commitments for retail space.

REQUIRED

Use the ratios to match the companies in Exhibit 1.18 with the firms listed above, and explain your reasoning using the strategy framework in the chapter.

Exhibit 1.18

Common-Size Financial Statement Data for Seven Firms in the Pharmaceutical Industry (Problem 1.13)

	1	2	3	4	5	6	7
BALANCE SHEET							
Cash and marketable securities	12.5%	1.9%	63.7%	63.7%	12.1%	4.1%	20.1%
Receivables	22.7	5.7	13.8	16.0	18.7	3.9	15.2
Inventories	20.7	7.2	13.8	13.1	3.7	10.7	7.9
Property, plant, and equipment, at cost	34.2	3.9	66.6	73.9	74.2	22.6	43.0
Accumulated depreciation	(13.5)	(2.0)	(27.4)	(24.9)	(27.1)	(5.5)	(20.4)
Property, plant, and equipment, net	20.7%	1.9%	39.2%	49.0%	47.1%	17.1%	22.5%
Intangibles	109.3	6.1	95.5	20.5	5.8	2.3	43.4
Other assets	16.8	2.5	16.9	30.5	8.5	1.6	24.0
Total Assets	202.6%	25.2%	242.9%	192.8%	96.0%	39.7%	133.2%
Current liabilities	30.1%	11.5%	32.6%	30.0%	25.2%	10.7%	32.7%
Long-term debt	100.5	3.3	61.2	47.4	0.0	3.7	12.7
Other long-term liabilities	19.4	1.7	13.3	31.5	5.4	2.6	21.1
Shareholders' equity	52.6	8.8	135.9	84.0	65.4	22.7	66.7
Total Liabilities and Shareholders' Equity	202.6%	25.2%	242.9%	192.8%	96.0%	39.7%	133.2%
INCOME STATEMENT							
Operating revenues	100.0%	100.0%	100.0%	100.0%	100.0%	100.0%	100.0%
Cost of sales (excluding depreciation) or operating expenses	(59.7)	(94.4)	(15.3)	(27.4)	(62.5)	(72.2)	(29.0)
Depreciation and amortization	(8.3)	(0.4)	(7.2)	(4.1)	(3.9)	(1.5)	(4.4)
Selling and administrative	(12.2)	(3.1)	(20.1)	(25.9)	(13.7)	(21.1)	(29.3)
Research and development	(6.2)	0.0	(20.2)	(14.8)	0.0	0.0	(12.2)
Interest (expense)/income	(6.9)	(0.2)	0.2	(0.1)	0.4	(0.1)	(0.1)
Income taxes	(2.7)	(0.5)	(7.0)	(8.4)	(4.3)	(1.8)	(6.2)
All other items, net	0.1	0.0	(2.5)	(0.1)	(5.3)	0.0	1.6
Net Income	4.1%	1.3%	28.0%	19.3%	10.5%	3.2%	20.3%
Cash flow from operations/ capital expenditures	2.3	3.0	8.9	4.4	4.0	2.2	4.9

LO 1-2, LO 1-3, LO 1-4

INTEGRATIVE CASE 1.1

Walmart

The first case at the end of this chapter and numerous subsequent chapters is a series of integrative cases involving **Wal-Mart Stores, Inc. (Walmart)**. The series of cases applies the concepts and analytical tools discussed in each chapter to Walmart's financial statements and notes. The preparation of responses to the questions in these cases results in an integrated illustration of the six sequential steps in financial statement analysis discussed in this chapter and throughout the book.

Introduction

Walmart is a very large chain of retail stores selling consumer goods. As it states in its Form 10-K for fiscal 2015:

> Wal-Mart Stores, Inc. ("Walmart," the "Company" or "we") helps people around the world save money and live better—anytime and anywhere—in retail stores or through our e-commerce and mobile capabilities. Through innovation, we are striving to create a customer-centric experience that seamlessly integrates digital and physical shopping.
>
> Physical retail encompasses our brick and mortar presence in each market where we operate. Digital retail is comprised of our e-commerce websites and mobile commerce applications. Each week, we serve nearly 260 million customers who visit our over 11,500 stores under 63 banners in 28 countries and e-commerce websites in 11 countries.
>
> Our strategy is to lead on price, differentiate on access, be competitive on assortment and deliver a great experience. Leading on price is designed to earn the trust of our customers every day by providing a broad assortment of quality merchandise and services at everyday low prices ("EDLP"). EDLP is our pricing philosophy under which we price items at a low price every day so our customers trust that our prices will not change under frequent promotional activity. Price leadership is core to who we are. Everyday low cost ("EDLC") is our commitment to control expenses so those cost savings can be passed along to our customers. Our digital and physical presence provides customers access to our broad assortment anytime and anywhere. We strive to give our customers and members a great digital and physical shopping experience.

For more detailed discussion of Walmart's stores, products, customers, and business model, visit the company's website: www.corporate.walmart.com.[13]

Financial Statements

Exhibit 1.19 presents comparative balance sheets, Exhibit 1.20 presents comparative income statements, and Exhibit 1.21 (pages 62–63) presents comparative statements of cash flows for Walmart for the three fiscal years ending January 31, 2014, 2015, and 2016. Walmart prepares its financial statements in accordance with U.S. GAAP. For more detail on Walmart financial statements, or to download the fiscal 2015 Form 10-K, you can visit Walmart's investor relations page: www.stock.walmart.com/investors/default.aspx.[14]

REQUIRED

Respond to the following questions relating to Walmart.

---

[13]While more information on Walmart's business may be helpful, it is not necessary to complete this case.

[14]While information on the investor relations page may be helpful, it is not necessary to complete this case.

Exhibit 1.19

Wal-Mart Stores, Inc. Balance Sheets as of January 31
(amounts in millions; allow for rounding)
(Integrative Case 1.1)

	2014	2015	2016
Assets:			
Cash and cash equivalents	$ 7,281	$ 9,135	$ 8,705
Accounts and notes receivable—net	6,677	6,778	5,624
Inventories	44,858	45,141	44,469
Prepaid expenses and other current assets	1,909	2,224	1,441
Current assets of discontinued segments	460	—	—
Current Assets	$ 61,185	$ 63,278	$ 60,239
Property, plant, and equipment—at cost	178,678	182,634	188,054
Accumulated depreciation	(60,771)	(65,979)	(71,538)
Goodwill	19,510	18,102	16,695
Other assets	6,149	5,455	6,131
Total Assets	$204,751	$203,490	$199,581
Liabilities and Equities:			
Accounts payable	$ 37,415	$ 38,410	$ 38,487
Current accrued expenses	18,793	19,152	19,607
Notes payable and short-term debt	7,670	1,592	2,708
Current maturities of long-term debt	4,412	5,078	3,296
Income taxes payable	966	1,021	521
Current liabilities of discontinued operations	89	—	—
Current Liabilities	$ 69,345	$ 65,253	$ 64,619
Long-term debt obligations	44,559	43,495	44,030
Deferred tax liabilities—noncurrent	8,017	8,805	7,321
Redeemable noncontrolling interest	1,491	—	—
Total Liabilities	$123,412	$117,553	$115,970
Common stock + Additional paid-in capital	2,685	2,785	2,122
Retained earnings	76,566	85,777	90,021
Accum. other comprehensive income (loss)	(2,996)	(7,168)	(11,597)
Total Common Shareholders' Equity	$ 76,255	$ 81,394	$ 80,546
Noncontrolling interests	5,084	4,543	3,065
Total Equity	$ 81,339	$ 85,937	$ 83,611
Total Liabilities and Equities	$204,751	$203,490	$199,581

Source: Wal-Mart Stores, Inc. Forms 10-K for the three fiscal years ended January 31, 2014, 2015, and 2016.

Industry and Strategy Analysis

a. Apply Porter's five forces framework to the retail industry.

b. How would you characterize the strategy of Walmart? How does Walmart create value for its customers? What critical risk and success factors must Walmart manage?

Exhibit 1.20

Wal-Mart Stores, Inc.
Income Statements for the Fiscal Years Ended January 31
(amounts in millions; allow for rounding)
(Integrative Case 1.1)

	2014	2015	2016
Revenues	$ 476,294	$ 485,651	$ 482,130
Cost of goods sold	358,069	365,086	360,984
Gross Profit	$118,225	$120,565	$121,146
Selling, general, and administrative expenses	91,353	93,418	97,041
Operating Profit	$ 26,872	$ 27,147	$ 24,105
Interest income	119	113	81
Interest expense	(2,335)	(2,461)	(2,548)
Income before Tax	$ 24,656	$ 24,799	$ 21,638
Income tax expense	8,105	7,985	6,558
Income (Loss) from discontinued operations	144	285	—
Net Income	$ 16,695	$ 17,099	$ 15,080
Net income attributable to noncontrolling interests	(673)	(736)	(386)
Net Income Attributable to Common Shareholders	$ 16,022	$ 16,363	$ 14,694
Other comprehensive income items	(2,409)	(4,172)	(4,429)
Comprehensive Income	$ 13,613	$ 12,191	$ 10,265

Source: Wal-Mart Stores, Inc. Forms 10-K for the three fiscal years ended January 31, 2014, 2015, and 2016.

Exhibit 1.21

Wal-Mart Stores, Inc. Statements of Cash Flows for the
Three Fiscal Years Ended January 31
(amounts in millions; allow for rounding)
(Integrative Case 1.1)

	2014	2015	2016
Net Income	$ 16,695	$ 17,099	$ 15,080
Add back depreciation and amortization expenses	8,870	9,173	9,454
Deferred income taxes	(279)	(503)	(672)
(Increase) Decrease in accounts receivable	(566)	(569)	(19)
(Increase) Decrease in inventories	(1,667)	(1,229)	(703)
Increase (Decrease) in accounts payable	531	2,678	2,008
Increase (Decrease) in income taxes payable	(1,224)	166	(472)
Increase (Decrease) in other current liabilities	103	1,249	1,303
(Income) Loss from discontinued segments	(144)	(285)	—
Other operating cash flows	938	785	1,410
Net Cash Flow from Operating Activities	$ 23,257	$ 28,564	$ 27,389

(Continued)

Exhibit 1.21 (Continued)

Proceeds from sales of property, plant, and equipment	727	570	635
Property, plant, and equipment acquired	(13,115)	(12,174)	(11,477)
Investments acquired	—	—	—
Other investment transactions	(138)	479	167
Net Cash Flow from Investing Activities	**$(12,526)**	**$(11,125)**	**$(10,675)**
Increase (Decrease) in short-term borrowing	911	(6,288)	1,235
Increase (Decrease) in long-term borrowing	2,104	1,270	(4,393)
Share repurchases—treasury stock	(6,683)	(1,015)	(4,112)
Dividend payments	(6,139)	(6,185)	(6,294)
Other financing activities	(982)	(2,853)	(2,558)
Net Cash Flow from Financing Activities	**$(10,789)**	**$(15,071)**	**$(16,122)**
Effects of exchange rate changes on cash	(442)	(514)	(1,022)
Net Change in Cash	**$ (500)**	**$ 1,854**	**$ (430)**
Cash and cash equivalents, beginning of year	$ 7,781	$ 7,281	$ 9,135
Cash and cash equivalents, end of year	$ 7,281	$ 9,135	$ 8,705

Source: Wal-Mart Stores, Inc. Forms 10-K for the three fiscal years ended January 31, 2014, 2015, and 2016.

Balance Sheet

c. Describe how "cash" differs from "cash equivalents."

d. What are Walmart's two largest assets on the balance sheet (in dollar amounts)? How do these assets reflect Walmart's strategy?

e. Walmart reports accounts receivable *net* of an allowance for uncollectible accounts. Why? Identify the events or transactions that cause accounts receivable to increase and decrease. Also identify the events or transactions that cause the allowance account to increase and decrease.

f. How does accumulated depreciation on the balance sheet differ from depreciation expense on the income statement?

g. What is Walmart's largest current liability in dollar amount? What does it represent?

h. What is Walmart's largest liability in dollar amount? In what types of assets did Walmart likely invest this financing?

i. What does Walmart report in accumulated other comprehensive income (loss)? What does this amount represent? When, if ever, will these gains and losses appear in net income?

Income Statement

j. What type of transaction gives rise to the primary source of Walmart's revenues? At the end of each fiscal year, what does Walmart have to estimate to measure total (net) revenues for the fiscal year?

k. What types of expenses does Walmart likely include in (1) cost of goods sold and (2) selling, general, and administrative expenses?

l. Walmart reports interest expense that is much larger than interest income. Why?

Statement of Cash Flows

m. Why does net income differ from the amount of cash flow from operating activities?

n. Why does Walmart add the amount of depreciation and amortization expense to net income when computing cash flow from operating activities?

o. Why does Walmart show increases in inventory as subtractions when computing cash flow from operations?

p. Why does Walmart show increases in accounts payable as additions when computing cash flow from operations?

q. What was the single largest use of cash by Walmart during this three-year period? How does that use of cash reflect Walmart's business strategy?

r. What was Walmart's single largest use of cash for financing activities during this three-year period? What does that imply about Walmart's financial position and performance?

Relations between Financial Statements

s. Prepare an analysis that explains the change in retained earnings from $85,777 million at the end of fiscal 2014 to $90,021 million at the end of fiscal 2015. Do not be alarmed if your reconciliation is close to, but does not exactly equal, the $90,021 million ending balance.

Interpreting Financial Statement Relations

Exhibit 1.22 presents common-size and percentage change balance sheets and Exhibit 1.23 presents common-size and percentage change income statements for Walmart for fiscal years ended January 31, 2014, 2015, and 2106. The percentage change statements report the annual percentage change in each account from fiscal 2013 to 2014, and from fiscal 2014 to 2015.

Exhibit 1.22

Wal-Mart Stores, Inc.
Common-Size and Percentage Change
Balance Sheets as of January 31
(allow for rounding)
(Integrative Case 1.1)

	Common Size			Percentage Change	
	2014	2015	2016	2015	2016
Assets:					
Cash and cash equivalents	3.6%	4.5%	4.4%	25.5%	(4.7%)
Accounts and notes receivable—net	3.3%	3.3%	2.8%	1.5%	(17.0%)
Inventories	21.9%	22.2%	22.3%	0.6%	(1.5%)
Prepaid expenses and other current assets	0.9%	1.1%	0.7%	16.5%	(35.2%)
Current assets of discontinued segments	0.2%	0.0%	0.0%	(100.0%)	na
Current Assets	**29.9%**	**31.1%**	**30.2%**	**3.4%**	**(4.8%)**
Property, plant, and equipment—at cost	87.3%	89.8%	94.2%	2.2%	3.0%
Accumulated depreciation	(29.7%)	(32.4%)	(35.8%)	8.6%	8.4%
Goodwill	9.5%	8.9%	8.4%	(7.2%)	(7.8%)
Other assets	3.0%	2.7%	3.1%	(11.3%)	12.4%
Total Assets	**100.0%**	**100.0%**	**100.0%**	**(0.6%)**	**(1.9%)**
Liabilities and Equities:					
Accounts payable	18.3%	18.9%	19.3%	2.7%	0.2%
Current accrued expenses	9.2%	9.4%	9.8%	1.9%	2.4%
Notes payable and short-term debt	3.7%	0.8%	1.4%	(79.2%)	70.1%
Current maturities of long-term debt	2.2%	2.5%	1.7%	15.1%	(35.1%)

(Continued)

Exhibit 1.22 (Continued)

Income taxes payable	0.5%	0.5%	0.3%	5.7%	(49.0%)
Current liabilities of discontinued operations	0.0%	0.0%	0.0%	(100.0%)	na
Current Liabilities	**33.9%**	**32.1%**	**32.4%**	**(5.9%)**	**(1.0%)**
Long-term debt obligations	21.8%	21.4%	22.1%	(2.4%)	1.2%
Deferred tax liabilities—noncurrent	3.9%	4.3%	3.7%	9.8%	(16.9%)
Redeemable noncontrolling interest	0.7%	0.0%	0.0%	(100.0%)	0.0%
Total Liabilities	**60.3%**	**57.8%**	**58.1%**	**(4.7%)**	**(1.3%)**
Common stock + Additional paid-in capital	1.3%	1.4%	1.1%	3.7%	(23.8%)
Retained earnings	37.4%	42.2%	45.1%	12.0%	4.9%
Accum. other comprehensive income (loss)	(1.5%)	(3.5%)	(5.8%)	139.3%	61.8%
Total Common Shareholders' Equity	**37.2%**	**40.0%**	**40.4%**	**6.7%**	**(1.0%)**
Noncontrolling interests	2.5%	2.2%	1.5%	(10.6%)	(32.5%)
Total Equity	**39.7%**	**42.2%**	**41.9%**	**5.7%**	**(2.7%)**
Total Liabilities and Equities	**100.0%**	**100.0%**	**100.0%**	**(0.6%)**	**(1.9%)**

Source: Wal-Mart Stores, Inc. Forms 10-K for the three fiscal years ended January 31, 2014, 2015, and 2016.

Exhibit 1.23

Wal-Mart Stores, Inc.
Common-Size and Percentage Change
Income Statements for the Three Fiscal Years Ended January 31
(allow for rounding)
(Integrative Case 1.1)

	Common Size			Percentage Change	
	2014	2015	2016	2015	2016
Revenues	100.0%	100.0%	100.0%	2.0%	(0.7%)
Cost of goods sold	(75.2%)	(75.2%)	(74.9%)	2.0%	(1.1%)
Gross Profit	**24.8%**	**24.8%**	**25.1%**	**2.0%**	**0.5%**
Selling, general and administrative expenses	(19.2%)	(19.2%)	(20.1%)	2.3%	3.9%
Operating Profit	**5.6%**	**5.6%**	**5.0%**	**1.0%**	**(11.2%)**
Interest income	0.0%	0.0%	0.0%	(5.0%)	(28.3%)
Interest expense	(0.5%)	(0.5%)	(0.5%)	5.4%	3.5%
Income before Tax	**5.2%**	**5.1%**	**4.5%**	**0.6%**	**(12.7%)**
Income tax expense	(1.7%)	(1.6%)	(1.4%)	(1.5%)	(17.9%)
Income (Loss) from discontinued operations	0.0%	0.1%	0.0%	97.9%	(100.0%)
Net Income	**3.5%**	**3.5%**	**3.1%**	**2.4%**	**(11.8%)**
Net income attributable to noncontrolling interests	(0.1%)	(0.2%)	(0.1%)	9.4%	(47.6%)
Net Income Attributable to Common Shareholders	**3.4%**	**3.4%**	**3.0%**	**2.1%**	**(10.2%)**
Other comprehensive income items	(0.5%)	(0.9%)	(0.9%)	73.2%	6.2%
Comprehensive Income	**2.9%**	**2.5%**	**2.1%**	**(10.4%)**	**(15.8%)**

Source: Wal-Mart Stores, Inc. Forms 10-K for the three fiscal years ended January 31, 2014, 2015, and 2016.

t. The percentage changes in prepaid expenses and other current assets jumped up 16.5% in fiscal 2014 and then fell by 35.2% in fiscal 2015. Did the changes in the dollar amounts of this account have a huge impact on total assets (see Exhibit 1.22)? Explain.

u. During this three-year period, how did the proportion of total liabilities change relative to the proportion of shareholders' equity? What does this imply about changes in Walmart's leverage?

v. How did net income as a percentage of total revenues change from fiscal 2013 to fiscal 2015? Identify the most important reasons for this change.

w. Does Walmart generate high or low profit margins? How do Walmart's profit margins relate to the company's strategy?

LO 1-3, LO 1-4

CASE 1.2

Nike: Somewhere between a Swoosh and a Slam Dunk

Nike, Inc.'s principal business activity involves the design, development, and worldwide marketing of athletic footwear, apparel, equipment, accessories, and services for serious and recreational athletes. Nike boasts that it is the largest seller of athletic footwear and apparel in the world. Nike sells products to retail accounts, through Nike-owned retail stores and Internet websites, and through a mix of independent distributors and licensees throughout the world. Nearly all of Nike's footwear and apparel products are produced in Asia (Vietnam, China, and Indonesia) and elsewhere outside of the U.S., while equipment products are produced both in the U.S. and abroad. For more information, visit Nike's investor relations website page: www.investors.nike.com/Home/default.aspx.[15]

This case uses Nike's financial statements and excerpts from its notes to review important concepts underlying the three principal financial statements (balance sheet, income statement, and statement of cash flows) and relations among them. The case also introduces tools for analyzing financial statements.

Industry Economics

Product Lines

Industry analysts debate whether the athletic footwear and apparel industry is a performance-driven industry or a fashion-driven industry. Proponents of the performance view point to Nike's dominant market position, which results in part from continual innovation in product development. Proponents of the fashion view point to the difficulty of protecting technological improvements from competitor imitation, the large portion of total expenses comprising advertising, the role of sports and other personalities in promoting athletic shoes, and the fact that a high percentage of athletic footwear and apparel consumers use the products for casual wear rather than athletic purposes.

Growth

There are only modest growth opportunities for footwear and apparel in the United States. Concern exists with respect to volume increases (how many pairs of athletic shoes do consumers want) and price increases (will consumers continue to pay prices for innovative athletic footwear that is often twice as costly as other footwear).

---

[15]While information on the investor relations page may be helpful, it is not necessary to complete this case.

Athletic footwear companies have diversified their revenue sources in two directions in recent years. One direction involves increased emphasis on international sales. With dress codes becoming more casual in Europe and East Asia, industry analysts view international markets as the major growth markets during the next several years. Increased emphasis on soccer (European football) in the United States aids companies such as Adidas that have reputations for quality soccer footwear.

The second direction for diversification is sports and athletic apparel. The three leading athletic footwear companies capitalize on their brand-name recognition and distribution channels to create lines of sportswear and equipment that coordinate with their footwear. Team uniforms and matching apparel for coaching staffs and fans have become a major growth avenue.

Marketing

Athletic footwear and sportswear companies sell their products to consumers through various independent department, specialty, and discount stores, as well as through online sales channels. Their sales forces educate retailers on new product innovations, store display design, and similar activities. The market shares of Nike and the other major brand-name producers dominate retailers' shelf space, and slower growth in sales makes it increasingly difficult for the remaining athletic footwear companies to gain market share. The slower growth also has led the major companies to increase significantly their advertising and payments for celebrity endorsements. Many footwear companies, including Nike, have opened their own retail stores, as well as factory outlet stores for discounted sales of excess inventory.

Athletic footwear and sportswear companies have typically used independent distributors to market their products in other countries. With increasing brand recognition and anticipated growth in international sales, these companies have recently acquired an increasing number of their distributors to capture more of the profits generated in other countries and maintain better control of international marketing.

Nike Strategy

Nike targets the serious athlete as well as the recreational athlete with performance-driven footwear, apparel, and equipment. The firm has steadily expanded the scope of its product portfolio from its primary products of high-quality athletic footwear for running, training, basketball, soccer, and casual wear to encompass related product lines such as sports apparel, bags, equipment, balls, eyewear, timepieces, and other athletic accessories. In addition, Nike has expanded its scope of sports, now offering products for swimming, baseball, cheerleading, football, golf, lacrosse, tennis, volleyball, skateboarding, and other leisure activities. In recent years, the firm has emphasized growth outside the United States. Nike also has grown by acquiring other apparel companies, including **Cole Haan** (dress and casual footwear), **Converse** (athletic and casual footwear and apparel), **Hurley** (apparel for action sports such as surfing, skateboarding, and snowboarding), and **Umbro** (footwear, apparel, and equipment for soccer).

To maintain its technological edge, Nike engages in extensive research at its research facilities in Beaverton, Oregon. It continually alters its product line to introduce new footwear, apparel, equipment, and evolutionary improvements in existing products.

The following exhibits present information for Nike:

Exhibit 1.24: Consolidated balance sheets for 2014, 2015, and 2016
Exhibit 1.25: Consolidated income statements for 2014, 2015, and 2016
Exhibit 1.26: Consolidated statements of cash flows for 2014, 2015, and 2016
Exhibit 1.27: Excerpts from the notes to Nike's financial statements
Exhibit 1.28: Common-size and percentage change income statements
Exhibit 1.29: Common-size and percentage change balance sheets

REQUIRED

Study the financial statements and notes for Nike and respond to the following questions.

Exhibit 1.24

Consolidated Balance Sheet for Nike, Inc.
(amounts in millions)
(Case 1.2)

	At Fiscal Year End, May 31:		
	2014	2015	2016
ASSETS			
Current assets:			
Cash and equivalents	$ 2,220	$ 3,852	$ 3,138
Short-term investments	2,922	2,072	2,319
Accounts receivable, net	3,434	3,358	3,241
Inventories	3,947	4,337	4,838
Prepaid expenses and other current assets	818	1,968	1,489
Total current assets	$13,341	$15,587	$15,025
Property, plant, and equipment, net	2,834	3,011	3,520
Identifiable intangible assets, net	282	281	281
Goodwill	131	131	131
Deferred income taxes and other assets	2,006	2,587	2,439
TOTAL ASSETS	$18,594	$21,597	$21,396
LIABILITIES AND SHAREHOLDERS' EQUITY			
Current liabilities:			
Current portion of long-term debt	$ 7	$ 107	$ 44
Notes payable	167	74	1
Accounts payable	1,930	2,131	2,191
Accrued liabilities	2,491	3,949	3,037
Income taxes payable	432	71	85
Total current liabilities	$ 5,027	$ 6,332	$ 5,358
Long-term debt	1,199	1,079	2,010
Deferred income taxes and other liabilities	1,544	1,479	1,770
TOTAL LIABILITIES	$ 7,770	$ 8,890	$ 9,138
Shareholders' equity:			
Common stock at stated value:			
Class A convertible—353 and 355 shares outstanding	—	—	—
Class B—1,329 and 1,357 shares outstanding	3	3	3
Capital in excess of stated value	5,865	6,773	7,786
Accumulated other comprehensive income	85	1,246	318
Retained earnings	4,871	4,685	4,151
TOTAL SHAREHOLDERS' EQUITY	$10,824	$12,707	$12,258
TOTAL LIABILITIES AND SHAREHOLDERS' EQUITY	$18,594	$21,597	$21,396

Source: Nike, Inc., Form 10-K for the Fiscal Year ended May 31, 2016.

Exhibit 1.25

Consolidated Income Statement for Nike, Inc.
(amounts in millions except per share figures)
(Case 1.2)

	For the Fiscal Year Ended May 31:		
	2014	2015	2016
Revenues	$ 27,799	$ 30,601	$ 32,376
Cost of sales	15,353	16,534	17,405
Gross profit	**$12,446**	**$14,067**	**$14,971**
Demand creation expense	3,031	3,213	3,278
Operating overhead expense	5,735	6,679	7,191
Operating Income	**$ 3,680**	**$ 4,175**	**$ 4,502**
Interest (expense) income, net	(33)	(28)	(19)
Other income (expense), net	(103)	58	140
Income before income taxes	**$ 3,544**	**$ 4,205**	**$ 4,623**
Income tax expense	851	932	863
NET INCOME	**$ 2,693**	**$ 3,273**	**$ 3,760**
Earnings per common share:			
Basic	$ 1.52	$ 1.90	$ 2.21
Diluted	$ 1.49	$ 1.85	$ 2.16
Dividends declared per common share	$ 0.47	$ 0.54	$ 0.62

Source: Nike, Inc., Form 10-K for the Fiscal Year ended May 31, 2016.

Exhibit 1.26

Consolidated Statements of Cash Flows for Nike
(amounts in millions)
(Case 1.2)

	For the Fiscal Years Ended May 31:		
	2014	2015	2016
Cash provided by operations:			
Net income	$ 2,693	$ 3,273	$ 3,760
Income charges (credits) not affecting cash:			
Depreciation	518	606	649
Deferred income taxes	(11)	(113)	(80)
Stock-based compensation	177	191	236
Amortization and other	68	43	13
Net foreign currency adjustments	56	424	98

(Continued)

Exhibit 1.26 (Continued)

Changes in certain working capital components and other assets and liabilities:			
Decrease (increase) in accounts receivable	(298)	(216)	60
(Increase) in inventories	(505)	(621)	(590)
(Increase) in prepaid expenses and other current assets	(210)	(144)	(161)
(Decrease) increase in accounts payable, accrued liabilities and income taxes payable	525	1,237	(889)
Cash provided by operations	**$ 3,013**	**$ 4,680**	**$ 3,096**
Cash used by investing activities:			
Purchases of short-term investments	(5,386)	(4,936)	(5,367)
Maturities of short-term investments	3,932	3,655	2,924
Sales of short-term investments	1,126	2,216	2,386
Investments in reverse repurchase agreements	—	(150)	150
Additions to property, plant, and equipment	(880)	(963)	(1,143)
Disposals of property, plant, and equipment	3	3	10
Decrease (increase) in other assets, net of other liabilities	(2)	—	6
Cash used by investing activities	**$(1,207)**	**$ (175)**	**$(1,034)**
Cash used by financing activities:			
Net proceeds from long-term debt issuance	—	—	981
Long-term debt payments, including current portion	(60)	(7)	(106)
(Decrease) increase in notes payable	75	(63)	(67)
Payments on capital lease obligations	(17)	(19)	(7)
Proceeds from exercise of stock options and other stock issuances	383	514	507
Excess tax benefits from share-based payment arrangements	132	218	281
Repurchases of common stock	(2,628)	(2,534)	(3,238)
Dividends—common and preferred	(799)	(899)	(1,022)
Cash used by financing activities	**$(2,914)**	**$(2,790)**	**$(2,671)**
Effect of exchange rate changes on cash and equivalents	(9)	(83)	(105)
Net (decrease) increase in cash and equivalents	**$(1,117)**	**$ 1,632**	**$ (714)**
Cash and equivalents, beginning of year	**$ 3,337**	**$ 2,220**	**$ 3,852**
Cash and equivalents, end of year	**$ 2,220**	**$ 3,852**	**$ 3,138**

Source: Nike, Inc., Form 10-K for the Fiscal Year ended May 31, 2016.

Exhibit 1.27

Excerpts from Notes to Consolidated Financial Statements for Nike
(amounts in millions)
(Case 1.2)

Excerpts from the Summary of Significant Accounting Policies

■ *Revenue Recognition:* Nike recognizes wholesale revenues when title and the risks and rewards of ownership have passed to the customer, based on the terms of sale. This occurs upon shipment or upon receipt by the customer depending on the country of the sale and the agreement with the customer. Retail store revenues are recorded at the time of sale and online store revenues are recorded upon delivery to the customer. Provisions for post-invoice sales discounts, returns and miscellaneous claims from customers are estimated and recorded as a reduction to revenue at the time of sale.

■ *Allowance for Uncollectible Accounts Receivable:* Accounts receivable, net consist primarily of amounts receivable from customers. The Company makes ongoing estimates relating to the collectability of its accounts receivable and maintains an allowance for estimated losses resulting from the inability of its customers to make required payments. In determining the amount of the allowance, the Company considers historical levels of credit losses and makes judgments about the creditworthiness of significant customers based on ongoing credit evaluations. The allowance for uncollectible accounts receivable was $43 million and $78 million at May 31, 2016 and 2015, respectively.

■ *Demand Creation Expense:* Demand creation expense consists of advertising and promotion costs, including costs of endorsement contracts, television, digital and print advertising, brand events and retail brand presentation. Advertising production costs are expensed the first time an advertisement is run.

■ *Inventory Valuation:* Inventories are stated at lower of cost or market and valued on either an average or specific identification cost basis. For inventories in transit that represent direct shipments to customers, the related inventory and cost of sales are recognized on a specific identification basis. Inventory costs primarily consist of product cost from the Company's suppliers, as well as inbound freight, import duties, taxes, insurance and logistics and other handling fees.

■ *Property, Plant and Equipment and Depreciation:* Property, plant and equipment are recorded at cost. Depreciation is determined on a straight-line basis for buildings and leasehold improvements over 2 to 40 years and for machinery and equipment over 2 to 15 years.

■ *Identifiable Intangible Assets and Goodwill:* This account represents the excess of the purchase price of acquired businesses over the market values of identifiable net assets, net of amortization to date on assets with limited lives.

■ *Income Taxes:* The Company accounts for income taxes using the asset and liability method. This approach requires the recognition of deferred tax assets and liabilities for the expected future tax consequences of temporary differences between the carrying amounts and the tax basis of assets and liabilities. Income tax expense includes the following:

(amounts in millions)	2014	2015	2016
Currently Payable	$862	$1,045	$943
Deferred	(11)	(113)	(80)
Income Tax Expense	$851	$ 932	$863

■ *Stock Repurchases:* Nike repurchases outstanding shares of its common stock each year and retires them. Any difference between the price paid and the book value of the shares appears as an adjustment of retained earnings.

Source: Nike, Inc., Form 10-K for the Fiscal Year ended May 31, 2016.

Exhibit 1.28

Common-Size and Percentage Change Income Statements for Nike (Case 1.2)

	Common-Size:			Percentage Change:	
For the Fiscal Year Ended May 31:	2014	2015	2016	2015	2016
Revenues	100.0%	100.0%	100.0%	10.1%	5.8%
Cost of sales	(55.2%)	(54.0%)	(53.8%)	7.7%	5.3%
Gross profit	44.8%	46.0%	46.2%	13.0%	6.4%
Demand creation expense	(10.9%)	(10.5%)	(10.1%)	6.0%	2.0%
Operating overhead expense	(20.6%)	(21.8%)	(22.2%)	16.5%	7.7%
Operating Income	13.2%	13.6%	13.9%	13.5%	7.8%
Interest (expense) income, net	(0.1%)	(0.1%)	(0.1%)	(15.2%)	(32.1%)
Other income (expense), net	(0.4%)	0.2%	0.4%	(156.3%)	141.4%
Income before income taxes	12.7%	13.7%	14.3%	18.7%	9.9%
Income tax expense	(3.1%)	(3.0%)	(2.7%)	9.5%	(7.4%)
NET INCOME	9.7%	10.7%	11.6%	21.5%	14.9%

Exhibit 1.29

Common-Size and Percentage Change Balance Sheets for Nike (Case 1.2)

At Fiscal Year End, May 31:	Common-Size:			Percentage Change:	
ASSETS	2014	2015	2016	2015	2016
Current assets:					
Cash and equivalents	11.9%	17.8%	14.7%	73.5%	(18.5%)
Short-term investments	15.7%	9.6%	10.8%	(29.1%)	11.9%
Accounts receivable, net	18.5%	15.5%	15.1%	(2.2%)	(3.5%)
Inventories	21.2%	20.1%	22.6%	9.9%	11.6%
Prepaid expenses and other current assets	4.4%	9.1%	7.0%	140.6%	(24.3%)
Total current assets	71.7%	72.2%	70.2%	16.8%	(3.6%)
Property, plant and equipment, net	15.2%	13.9%	16.5%	6.2%	16.9%
Identifiable intangible assets, net	1.5%	1.3%	1.3%	(0.4%)	0.0%
Goodwill	0.7%	0.6%	0.6%	0.0%	0.0%
Deferred income taxes and other assets	10.8%	12.0%	11.4%	29.0%	(5.7%)
TOTAL ASSETS	100.0%	100.0%	100.0%	16.2%	(0.9%)

(Continued)

Exhibit 1.29 (Continued)

LIABILITIES AND SHAREHOLDERS' EQUITY					
Current liabilities:					
Current portion of long-term debt	0.0%	0.5%	0.2%	1,429%	(58.9%)
Notes payable	0.9%	0.3%	0.0%	(55.7%)	(98.6%)
Accounts payable	10.4%	9.9%	10.2%	10.4%	2.8%
Accrued liabilities	13.4%	18.3%	14.2%	58.5%	(23.1%)
Income taxes payable	2.3%	0.3%	0.4%	(83.6%)	19.7%
Total current liabilities	**27.0%**	**29.3%**	**25.0%**	**26.0%**	**(15.4%)**
Long-term debt	6.4%	5.0%	9.4%	(10.0%)	86.3%
Deferred income taxes and other liabilities	8.3%	6.8%	8.3%	(4.2%)	19.7%
TOTAL LIABILITIES	**41.8%**	**41.2%**	**42.7%**	**14.4%**	**2.8%**
Shareholders' equity:					
Common stock at stated value:					
Class A convertible—353 and 355 shares outstanding	0.0%	0.0%	0.0%	na	na
Class B—1,329 and 1,357 shares outstanding	0.0%	0.0%	0.0%	0.0%	0.0%
Capital in excess of stated value	31.5%	31.4%	36.4%	15.5%	15.0%
Accumulated other comprehensive income	0.5%	5.8%	1.5%	1,365.9%	(74.5%)
Retained earnings	26.2%	21.7%	19.4%	(3.8%)	(11.4%)
TOTAL SHAREHOLDERS' EQUITY	**58.2%**	**58.8%**	**57.3%**	**17.4%**	**(3.5%)**
TOTAL LIABILITIES AND SHAREHOLDERS' EQUITY	**100.0%**	**100.0%**	**100.0%**	**16.2%**	**(0.9%)**

Income Statement

a. Identify when Nike recognizes revenues. Does this timing of revenue recognition seem appropriate? Explain.

b. Identify the cost-flow assumption(s) that Nike uses to measure cost of goods sold. Does Nike's choice of cost-flow assumption(s) seem appropriate? Explain.

c. Nike reports property, plant, and equipment on its balance sheet and discloses the amount of depreciation for each year in its statement of cash flows. Why doesn't depreciation expense appear among its expenses on the income statement?

d. What does "demand creation expense" represent?

e. Identify the portion of Nike's income tax expense of $863 million for 2016 that is currently payable to governmental entities and the portion that is deferred to future years. Why is the amount currently payable to governmental entities in 2016 greater than the income tax expense?

Balance Sheet

f. Why do accounts receivable (net) appear net of allowance for doubtful accounts? Identify the events or transactions that cause the allowance account to increase or decrease.

g. What is the largest asset (in dollar amount) on Nike's balance sheet? How does this asset relate to Nike's strategy?

h. Identify the depreciation method(s) that Nike uses for its buildings and equipment. Does Nike's choice of depreciation method(s) seem appropriate?

i. Nike includes identifiable intangible assets on its balance sheet. Does this account include the value of Nike's brand name and Nike's "swoosh" trademark? Explain.

Statement of Cash Flows

j. Why does the amount of net income differ from the amount of cash flow from operations?

k. Why does Nike add depreciation expense back to net income when calculating cash flow from operations?

l. Why does Nike subtract increases in accounts receivable from net income when calculating cash flow from operations for 2016?

m. Why does Nike adjust net income by subtracting increases in inventory and adding decreases in inventory when calculating cash flow from operations?

n. When calculating cash flow from operations, why does Nike adjust net income by adding increases and subtracting decreases in accounts payable?

o. Cash flow from operations exceeded net income during fiscal 2015, but not during fiscal 2016. Why? What caused the big drop in cash flows provided by operations from 2015 to 2016?

p. What were Nike's primary financing activities during these three years?

Relations between Financial Statement Items

q. Compute the amount of cash collected from customers during 2016.

r. Compute the amount of cash payments made to suppliers of merchandise during 2016.

s. Reconcile the change in retained earnings during 2016.

Interpreting Financial Statement Relations

t. Exhibit 1.28 presents common-size and percentage change income statements for Nike for 2014, 2015, and 2016. What are some reasons for the increases in the net income/sales revenue percentages for Nike between 2014 and 2015, and between 2015 and 2016?

u. Exhibit 1.29 presents common-size and percentage change balance sheets for Nike at the end of 2014, 2015, and 2016. What is the likely explanation for the relatively small percentages for property, plant, and equipment?

v. What is the likely explanation for the relatively small percentages for notes payable and long-term debt?

Asset and Liability Valuation and Income Recognition

LO 2-1 Describe the mixed attribute measurement model for assets and liabilities, and how it provides relevant and representationally faithful information to financial statement users.

LO 2-2 Explain how changes in valuations of assets and liabilities on the balance sheet are recognized on the income statement and statement of comprehensive income.

LO 2-3 Understand that financial reporting and tax reporting are two different systems, and are linked by permanent differences and deferred tax assets and liabilities.

LO 2-4 Utilize an analytical framework to map business transactions and events to the balance sheet and income statement.

Chapter Overview

To effectively analyze financial statements, you should understand how they are prepared and how they measure and report economic events and transactions. You might question whether it is necessary to understand individual transactions—like purchasing inventory or incurring a specific current liability—if the primary concern is to learn how to analyze financial statements. After all, firms engage in thousands of transactions during the year. Nevertheless, the reasons for the need to understand how specific events and transactions affect the financial statements are twofold:

- First, to be able to make appropriate interpretations about a firm's profitability and risk, you must understand what the balance sheet and income statement tell you about various transactions and events.
- Second, given the complexity of many transactions, effective financial statement analysis requires an ability to deduce how they impact each of the financial statements, especially if your analysis leads you to restate financial statements to exclude the effects of some event or to apply an alternative accounting treatment.

In this chapter, we review basic financial accounting concepts at a high level, focusing primarily on the mixed attribute measurement model. We focus on how and why balance sheets and income statements recognize various transactions and events. Because it is difficult to discuss a line item on one financial statement without referencing another line item or another financial statement, in this chapter we emphasize the articulation of elements in the balance sheet and income statement.[1]

<table>
<tr><td>LO 2-1</td></tr>
</table>

Describe the mixed attribute measurement model for assets and liabilities, and how it provides relevant and representationally faithful information to financial statement users.

The Mixed Attribute Measurement Model

Consider the fundamental accounting identity:

$$\text{Assets} = \text{Liabilities} + \text{Shareholders' Equity}$$

When a firm is formed and receives financing (through equity investments of shareholders and/or debt financing from banks), the balance sheet of a company is simple and the valuation of the assets and liabilities is straightforward. For example, suppose an entrepreneur starts a consulting company by borrowing $1,000,000 from a bank. Initially, the value of the assets would be $1,000,000 in cash, equal to a liability to repay the bank loan in the same amount. However, valuing the company's assets, liabilities, and equity becomes less clear (but more interesting) as the company begins deploying that cash and operating activities commence. The following are a number of challenging examples that might arise, which you will learn to analyze throughout this chapter and the remainder of this text:

1. The entrepreneur purchases an automobile for use in the business. Should the balance sheet reflect this asset at the amount paid by the entrepreneur or at the value the automobile could be sold for in the used car market? If the company also had to pay registration and legal fees, are those fees a part of the value of the automobile?

2. Should the company allocate the cost of the automobile across periods in which it will be used? Or should the entrepreneur periodically reduce the value of the automobile to reflect the wear and tear and associated decline in its value? If so, how would this be measured?

3. If the company acquires a building in which the entrepreneur will work, should the company allocate the cost or periodically adjust the value of the building over time, as it might with the automobile? Unlike an automobile that clearly declines in value over time, the value of a building might increase. Absent a sale of the building, how would someone estimate the value of a specific building?

4. The entrepreneur performs consulting services for 10 clients and bills each client $5,000. The company now has an asset (accounts receivable) reflecting the amount due from each client, totaling $50,000. However, it is statistically probable that some client may not ultimately pay the entire bill. Should the company adjust downward the value of the $50,000 asset to reflect this probability? If so, how much should the value of the asset be reduced? Is the reason for reflecting this amount in the financial statements to value the accounts receivable on the balance sheet appropriately, or is it to ensure that a cost of doing business (that is, selling to people who do not pay) is properly reflected on the income statement, or is it both?

5. The entrepreneur invests some of the remaining cash from the bank loan into a mutual fund. After several months, the value of the mutual fund investment has increased. Should the company adjust the value of this investment on its balance sheet? What should the company do if the investment falls back to the initial

---

[1]After a discussion of asset and liability valuation, the chapter will turn to income recognition. Keep in mind the discussion from Chapter 1 regarding the important difference between *net* income and *comprehensive* income; comprehensive income exists to accommodate various fair value adjustments to balance sheet items.

amount invested? What if the value falls below the initial amount invested? Should the company report each of these adjustments to the balance sheet as a gain or a loss on the income statement?

If these hypothetical questions are prompted by a simple example of a company with limited assets and liabilities, imagine how the valuation of assets and liabilities becomes increasingly complex and interesting when real companies engage in numerous and diverse activities. To provide financial statement users with the most relevant and representationally faithful information about firms' assets, liabilities, and therefore equity, U.S. GAAP and IFRS require firms to use a variety of different approaches to value assets and liabilities in their financial statements. Depending on the nature of the asset or liability, some are measured using historical costs, others are measured at fair values, others at present values of future cash flows, and so on. This variety of approaches to measuring assets, liabilities, revenues, and expenses is the *mixed attribute measurement model.*

The Complementary Nature and Relative Usefulness of the Income Statement and Balance Sheet

Measuring assets and liabilities for the balance sheet will often affect the measurement of revenues and expenses for the income statement as well. The intent of the accounting system is to provide relevant and representationally faithful information about the firm's financial position on the balance sheet and financial performance on the income statement. The two statements are complementary as the balance sheet presents information about financial position *as of* a point in time, whereas the income statement presents information about financial performance *between* two points in time. The *mixed attribute measurement model* is an attempt by standard setters to optimize relevant information given various constraints on the representational faithfulness of measurement. The consequence is an income statement and statement of comprehensive income that report net changes in assets and liabilities as revenues, expenses, gains, and losses.

Academic research has examined the overall relative usefulness of the balance sheet and income statement to explain common stock prices. The evidence supports the notion that over the past several decades, financial statements appear to have become more in line with a balance sheet emphasis relative to an income statement emphasis. Based on data from a study by Collins, Maydew, and Weiss (1997), Exhibit 2.1 shows the incremental power of earnings (income statement emphasis) and book value of equity (balance sheet emphasis) to explain common stock prices over four decades. A decreasing trend line suggests a decline in the ability of a measure to explain security prices relative to the other. Consistent with the claims of many observers, the incremental explanatory power of book values increased relative to earnings over the period. Moreover, the study documented that the overall ability of both book value and earnings has increased over this four-decade period, consistent with increasing usefulness of financial statements.

Asset and Liability Valuation and the Trade-Off between Relevance and Representational Faithfulness

As described in Chapter 1, the balance sheet reports the assets of a firm and the claims on those assets by creditors (liabilities) and owners (shareholders' equity) at a point in

Exhibit 2.1

Relative Explanatory Power of Book Value and Net Income to Explain Market Value from 1953–1993

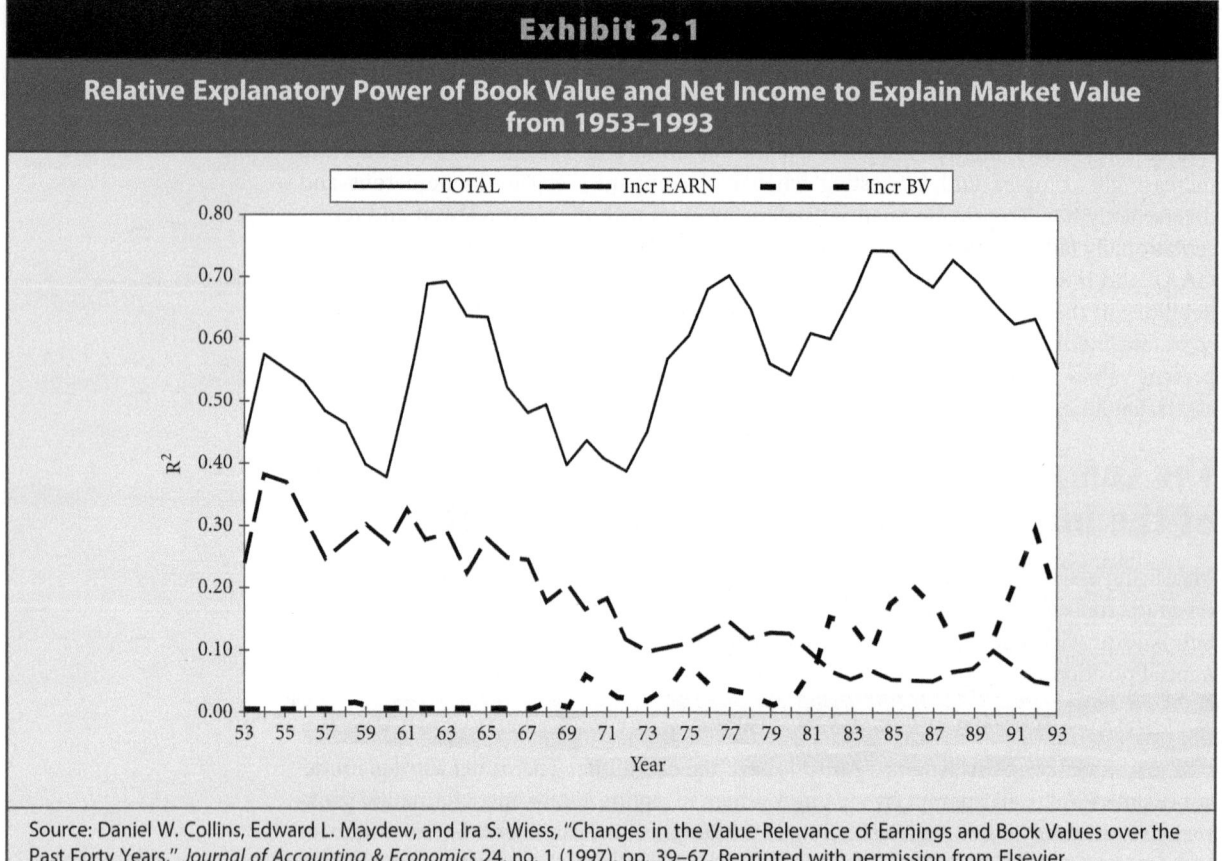

Source: Daniel W. Collins, Edward L. Maydew, and Ira S. Wiess, "Changes in the Value-Relevance of Earnings and Book Values over the Past Forty Years," *Journal of Accounting & Economics* 24, no. 1 (1997), pp. 39–67. Reprinted with permission from Elsevier.

time. Liabilities and shareholders' equity represent the capital contributed by suppliers, lending institutions, and shareholders so that the company can acquire operating assets and fund operations. In this section, we focus on a conceptual understanding of how assets and liabilities should be valued and reported in the financial statements.[2]

Assets provide economic benefits to a firm in the future, and liabilities require firms to sacrifice economic resources in the future. Although assets and liabilities have a future orientation, balance sheet accounting for assets and liabilities under U.S. GAAP and IFRS follows a *mixed attribute measurement model.* Some assets are reported based on original (historic) cost, some are based on current fair values, some are based on realizable values, and so on. Similarly, some liabilities are measured at the initial amount of the incurred liability, whereas others are measured at the current value of the liability based on prevailing interest rates and other factors.

An obvious question is: why aren't all assets and liabilities measured and recorded using the same measurement attribute? Wouldn't that greatly simplify financial statement analysis? For example, it might seem obvious that reporting all assets and liabilities at historical values or all at current fair values would make it easier for users to understand financial statements. The reason most high-quality accounting standards follow a mixed attribute model is because regulators attempt to provide an optimal mix

---

[2]For purposes here, do not become anxious about mastering procedures for analyzing specific assets or liabilities. Such analyses are addressed in subsequent chapters.

of *relevant* and *representationally faithful* information in the financial statements, which helps users better translate the information into assessments of the risk, timing, and amounts of future cash flows.

Relevance and Representational Faithfulness

Financial information is *relevant* if it can influence a user's decision based on the reported financial statements. Making financial information available in a timely manner, for example, is one aspect of relevance. Information is *representationally faithful* if it represents what it purports to represent. The FASB articulates the following in Concepts Statement No. 8:

> Relevant financial information is capable of making a difference in the decisions made by users. Information may be capable of making a difference in a decision even if some users choose not to take advantage of it or already are aware of it from other sources.

> Financial reports represent economic phenomena in words and numbers. To be useful, financial information not only must represent relevant phenomena, but it also must faithfully represent the phenomena that it purports to represent. To be a perfectly faithful representation, a depiction would have three characteristics. It would be complete, neutral, and free from error. Of course, perfection is seldom, if ever, achievable. The Board's objective is to maximize those qualities to the extent possible.[3]

As a consequence of this balancing act to make the overall financial statements as useful as possible to external users, accounting standards require that some assets and liabilities be measured based on more relevant information and others must be based on more representationally faithful information.

Accounting Quality

One way to view financial accounting amounts is that they reflect the following symbolic equation:

$$\text{Financial Accounting Amounts} = f(\text{Economics, Measurement Error, Bias})$$

In words, financial accounting numbers are a function of several features of the financial reporting environment. First, and most importantly, the aim of financial statements is to provide useful information regarding the "true economics" of a firm's financial position or operations. This means that the financial statements measure and report, in an unbiased manner, the underlying economics. Because managers have intimate involvement in and knowledge of the firms' operations and economics, they are responsible for preparing financial statements.

The other two features detract from financial statement quality. Measurement error in reported financial numbers is inevitable because many events and circumstances require estimates. For example, managers must estimate the collectability of accounts receivable, the depreciation of fixed assets, the ultimate liability for postretirement benefits, and so on. Good faith estimates sometimes turn out to be too high, and sometimes

---

[3]Financial Accounting Standards Board, *Statement of Financial Accounting Concepts No. 8*, "Chapter 1, *The Objective of General Purpose Financial Reporting*, and Chapter 3, *Qualitative Characteristics of Useful Financial Information*" (September 2010).

too low. The hope is that, on average, measurement errors cancel each other out. The accounting discretion available to managers in making and reporting accounting estimates, which can lead to measurement error, is granted because this discretion can increase the relevance of the financial statements.

However, managers also can misuse their accounting discretion to bias the reported financial amounts. Managers might bias their estimates in order to help the company appear more profitable or less risky to stakeholders, or for their own personal gain. Managers commonly receive bonus compensation based on reported earnings. The incentive to produce higher earnings, and thus realize higher compensation, can induce a manager to bias earnings upwards. For example, a manager might underestimate the amount of receivables that will ultimately be uncollectible. As a consequence, bad debt expense would be understated in that period, and earnings would be overstated.

Trade-Off of Relevance and Representational Faithfulness

Both measurement error and bias decrease the representational faithfulness of reported financial information. Because these features of reported financial numbers result from discretion available to managers, one might ask, why not remove discretion from managers? The answer pertains to the trade-off of relevance and representational faithfulness already discussed. Without discretion, all firms would have to apply the same accounting principles. For example, accounting rules could remove discretion and stipulate that all firms must recognize a 5% allowance for uncollectible accounts receivable. This would certainly be *representationally faithful* to the extent that it can be mathematically verified, and it would prevent managers from biasing the allowance for bad debts. However, it would probably not be *relevant* for many firms with expected default rates other than 5%.

As accounting standards develop, standard setters are mindful of this trade-off between relevance and representational faithfulness and whether capturing the economics outweighs the potential for measurement error or bias. The result is the mixed attribute measurement model, whereby valuations of assets and liabilities reflect various combinations of historical costs, fair values, and present values of future cash flows. The astute analyst draws advantage from the information available in the mixed attributes of asset and liability measurement.

The remainder of this section provides brief descriptions and examples of the primary valuation alternatives that are most common for balance sheet accounts. This discussion sets the stage for a more detailed understanding of financial statement information in later chapters.

Primary Valuation Alternatives: Historical Cost versus Fair Value

Historical cost is simply the cost the firm originally incurred to acquire an asset or the original (principal) amount of an incurred liability. *Fair value*, on the other hand, reflects the value of the asset or liability based on current market conditions. At the time of an arm's-length transaction, the historical cost of assets and the original amount of liabilities are equal to their fair values.[4]

---

[4]Many market observers have concluded that the FASB and IASB have embarked on an increasing effort to measure assets and liabilities at fair values rather than historical cost, although members of both boards dispute this. Indeed, one interpretation of Exhibit 2.1 is that the increasing ability of book values relative to earnings to explain firm market values is a result of this effort.

Historical Cost

The historical, or acquisition, cost of an asset is the amount paid initially to acquire the asset. Such historical costs include all costs required to prepare the asset for its intended use, but not costs to operate the asset. At the time assets are obtained, acquisition cost valuations are ideal because they are *relevant* insofar as they measure the amounts that firms actually paid to acquire resources, and they are *representationally faithful* because they are unbiased, objective, and verifiable through invoices, canceled checks, and other documents that provide clear support for the valuation.

For example, assume **Mollydooker Wines** buys 10 acres of vineyard land for $100,000, and then spends $10,000 to prepare the land (weeding and tilling) in order to plant grape vines. Mollydooker measures the land's value at $110,000, the historical cost of acquisition and preparation for intended use. Because the land generally does not decrease in value (i.e., using it does not consume it), the asset valuation stays at original historical cost over time.

Is the historical cost valuation relevant to financial statement users? At the time a firm acquires an asset, historical cost valuations are timely and objectively measured, so they are both *relevant* and *representationally faithful* to financial statement users. As time passes, however, the historical cost valuation retains representational faithfulness but can lose relevance if the valuation becomes dated and does not reflect current values.

Adjusted Historical Cost. For some assets, firms adjust historical costs downwards as those assets are consumed. For some assets, the service potential is consumed gradually (like machinery that has a limited life) or immediately (like inventory, which provides all of its benefits when it is sold). As the firm consumes the service potential of an asset, the firm expenses the consumed portion (that is, the asset is reduced and an expense is increased). For machinery, the expense is depreciation; for inventory, the expense is cost of goods sold. Over the life during which a firm enjoys the benefits of an asset, the firm should either derecognize the asset—that is, remove the asset from the balance sheet—when its value has been consumed (for example, inventory) or ratably adjust the acquisition cost downward through systematic depreciation or amortization (for example, machinery).

Like historical costs, adjusted historical costs also involve a trade-off between *relevance* and *representational faithfulness*. For example, consider a firm that acquires computer equipment for $5 million and depreciates it over four years to an estimated salvage value of $1 million. The valuation of the computer equipment at the end of the four years is based on a combination of a representationally faithful acquisition cost ($5 million) and a good faith estimate of the salvage value ($1 million). These estimates attempt to provide valuations that are relevant. Even though the estimates are made in good faith, they relate to uncertain future amounts and may turn out to be inaccurate.

Present Value. Another type of measurement is initial present value. If markets are not sufficiently active to provide reliable evidence of fair value, firms can use the present value of expected cash flows to approximate the fair value of assets and liabilities. Present value methods are often used with receivables and liabilities with payment schedules in excess of one year.

Selling goods or services on account to customers, or lending funds to others, creates a receivable for the selling or lending firm. Purchasing goods or services on account from a supplier or borrowing funds from others creates a liability (for example, accounts payable, notes payable, and bonds payable). Discounting the expected future cash flows under such arrangements to a present value expresses those cash flows in terms of a current cash-equivalent value. When the monetary asset or liability is first entered in the financial statements, the present value computation (if the cash flows span more than one year) uses interest rates appropriate for the particular financing arrangement at that time.

For example, assume **Jordan's Furniture** sells a sofa to a customer on January 1, permitting the customer to delay payment of the $500 selling price for five years. An assessment of the customer's credit standing suggests that 6% per year is an appropriate interest rate for this credit (even though there is no explicitly stated interest rate to the customer). The present value of $500 to be received in five years, when discounted back at 6%, is $373.63. A strict application of the initial present value of cash flows valuation method results in reporting sales revenue and a receivable of $373.63 on January 1 and interest revenue and an increase in the receivable of $22.42 ($0.06 \times 373.63) at December 31. The following year, interest revenue and an increase in the receivable of $23.76 [$0.06 \times (373.63 + 22.42)$] would be recognized, and so on for the next three years, at the end of which the receivable would equal the $500 then due from the customer.

Because financing arrangements between sellers and buyers usually specify the timing and amounts of future cash flows, valuing monetary assets and liabilities at the initial present value of cash flows using historical interest rates is both relevant and representationally faithful. Moreover, for multiyear collection periods, the relevance of the present values (versus nominal values) justifies the extra efforts to discount assets or liabilities to the present value of future cash flows. Some subjectivity may exist in establishing an appropriate interest rate at the time of the transaction. The borrower, for example, might choose to use the interest rate at which it could borrow on similar terms from a bank, whereas the seller might use the interest rate that would discount the cash flows to a present value equal to the cash selling price of the good or service sold. These small differences in interest rates usually do not result in material differences in valuation between the entities involved in the transaction.

Fair Value

Market (or Fair) Value. Because historical costs can lose relevance as valuations become old and outdated and do not reflect current economic conditions, the FASB and IASB have increasingly developed accounting standards that value assets and liabilities using *market* or *fair value approaches*. Both define "fair value" as "the price that would be received to sell an asset or paid to transfer a liability in an orderly transaction between market participants at the measurement date."[5] This definition explicitly characterizes fair value as an "exit value."

Clearly, fair values of assets and liabilities are of interest to financial statement users, particularly in settings where fair values have diverged greatly from acquisition costs of assets or initial present values of liabilities. An obvious example is financial institutions, where we see values of financial assets and liabilities changing immediately with interest rates. Obtaining "the price" at which assets and liabilities can be exchanged can provide extremely relevant and representationally faithful measurements when they are based on observable prices in orderly markets for stocks, bonds, securities, commodities, derivatives, and other items. However, obtaining "the price" can require management estimates when there is no quoted price in an active market for an asset or a liability. Generally, prices are more readily available for financial assets (and commodities) and liabilities than for nonmonetary assets or liabilities, which is why the trend in financial reporting is to employ fair values for most financial assets and liabilities.

---

[5]Financial Accounting Standards Board, *Statement of Financial Accounting Standards No. 157*, "Fair Value Measurements" (September 2006); *FASB Codification Topic 820.*

Even among financial assets and liabilities, however, there is wide variation in the availability of quoted market prices. Accordingly, there is a three-tiered hierarchy within U.S. GAAP and IFRS that distinguishes among different sources of fair value estimates.[6]

Source of Fair Value Estimate	Representational Faithfulness
• **"Level 1" inputs:** readily available prices for identical assets or liabilities in actively traded markets, such as securities exchanges.	High
• **"Level 2" inputs:** quoted prices for similar assets or liabilities in active or inactive markets, other *observable* information such as yield curves and price indexes, and other *observable* data such as market-based correlation estimates.	Medium to High
• **"Level 3" inputs:** a firm's own assumptions about the fair value of an asset or a liability, such as using data about expected future cash flows and discount rates to estimate present values.	Possibly Low

Fair value approaches to valuation for financial assets and liabilities are commonplace within U.S. GAAP and IFRS. Reporting financial assets and liabilities at fair values also is referred to as "mark-to-market" accounting. Although the relevance of fair values is obvious, given the subjective nature of current value estimation along the continuum of representational faithfulness from Level 1 to Level 3 inputs for assets and liabilities, the representational faithfulness of such valuations is sometimes questioned. For example, Level 1 inputs are applicable for most assets traded on active exchanges with published market quotes, whereas Level 3 inputs relate primarily to illiquid investments such as mortgage-backed securities.

Recent rules released by the FASB and IASB allow firms the option to measure and report certain financial instruments at fair value (with subsequent changes to flow through earnings). The decision to use fair value or historical cost must be made at the inception of the financial asset or liability and retained over the life of that financial instrument; however, firms can make different choices for different instruments. The "fair value option" will be most applicable for financial institutions.[7]

Current Replacement Cost. Another type of fair value measurement is *current replacement cost*, which is the amount a firm would have to pay currently to acquire or produce an asset it now holds. By virtue of the term's reference to an external market, this is a special case of applying the fair value approach. However, whereas straightforward fair values generally pertain to financial assets and commodities, current replacement cost generally applies to nonmonetary assets. Current replacement cost valuations

---

[6]These are specified in SFAS No. 157, *FASB Codification Topic 820*, and IFRS No. 7. The International Accounting Standards Board amended IFRS No. 7 to incorporate the Level 1, Level 2, and Level 3 disclosures as well.

[7]Financial Accounting Standards Board, *Statement of Financial Accounting Standards No. 159*, "The Fair Value Option for Financial Assets and Financial Liabilities" (February 2007); *FASB Codification Topic 825*; International Accounting Standards Committee, *International Accounting Standards No. 39*, "Financial Instruments: Recognition and Measurement" (revised June 2005); International Accounting Standards Committee, *International Accounting Standards No. 40*, "Investment Properties" (revised December 2003).

generally reflect greater subjectivity than acquisition cost valuations, but they are the least subjective and most representationally faithful when based on observable market prices from recent transactions in which similar assets or liabilities have been exchanged in active markets. For example, you could obtain reliable measures of current replacement costs of raw commodities by referencing spot prices in commodities markets. However, when active markets do not exist, as is often the case for inventory or equipment designed specifically for a particular firm's needs, the degree of subjectivity increases. Thus, although replacement cost values are more relevant, subjectivity in estimating them in most markets reduces the representational faithfulness of such values. Nevertheless, users of financial statements may find current replacement cost valuations used occasionally and more relevant than out-of-date historical costs.

Net Realizable Value. A hybrid form of historical cost and fair value measurement is the use of *net realizable value*, which is the net amount a firm would receive if it sold an asset (for example, inventory for which current value has declined below cost). Net realizable value is another special case of a fair value approach, but it also shares features of adjusted historical cost valuation because historical cost provides a reference point to determine whether net realizable valuation is applicable. Thus, this is a hybrid approach and the examples that will be discussed exhibit similarities with other valuation approaches (both historical cost and current value). The difference is that rather than estimating the cost of acquiring a similar asset in a hypothetical transaction, the net realizable value approach focuses on the amount a firm is likely to realize given prevailing market conditions, *offset by any pertinent selling costs.*

Contrasting Illustrations of Asset and Liability Valuations, and Nonrecognition of Certain Assets

The previous discussion focused on different approaches to asset and liability valuation. As noted, the differing ability to reliably measure many assets and liabilities results in a mixed approach to asset and liability valuation. Some assets and liabilities are measured at historical cost, whereas others can reliably be measured using relevant fair values. Sometimes measurement is so imprecise that accounting standards preclude recognition of various assets (and sometimes liabilities) altogether. For example, uncertainty is extremely high for the ability to value profitable growth opportunities, internally developed intangibles like brand names and supply chain networks, and other intellectual property such as the value of research and development assets. If every asset and liability could be reliably valued at fair values, the fair value of assets minus the fair value of liabilities would explain well the fair value—or market value—of a firm. Obviously, this is hypothetical because a significant component of the value of many firms is the opportunity to capitalize on future growth options and profitability, for which reliable measurement is nearly impossible.

In this section, we provide balance sheets for two firms with similar market values to highlight the varying ability of measured assets and liabilities to map into book values and market values. Exhibit 2.2 shows the balance sheet for **BlackRock Kelso Capital Corporation** (Nasdaq GS: BKCC), a publicly traded private equity firm that makes investments in middle market firms, those with market valuations between $10 and $50 million. Accordingly, most of the assets on BlackRock Kelso Capital's balance sheet reflect investments explicitly valued at fair value ($1.061 billion out of $1.090 billion in total assets). The remaining recognized assets reflect cash, various short-term receivables, and a small amount of prepaid expenses and other assets, and the reported values of these assets likely also approximate fair value. On the liabilities side of the balance

Exhibit 2.2

BlackRock Kelso Capital Corporation
Consolidated Balance Sheets

	Year 1	Year 2
Assets		
Investments at fair value:		
Non-controlled, non-affiliated investments (cost of $849,028,227 and $959,635,127)	$ 890,691,404	$ 850,511,125
Non-controlled, affiliated investments (cost of $50,983,674 and $59,633,913)	71,035,799	67,750,172
Controlled investments (cost of $137,337,392 and $78,601,629)	87,225,239	143,336,244
Total investments at fair value (cost of $1,037,349,293 and $1,097,870,669)	1,048,952,442	1,061,597,541
Cash and cash equivalents	7,478,904	9,122,141
Cash denominated in foreign currencies (cost of $0 and $300,380)	300,089	—
Unrealized appreciation on forward foreign currency contracts	—	369,417
Receivable for investments sold	2,734,705	504,996
Interest receivable	16,474,871	14,048,248
Dividends receivable	8,493,799	—
Prepaid expenses and other assets	6,740,517	4,375,527
Total Assets	$ 1,091,175,327	$ 1,090,017,870
Liabilities		
Payable for investments purchased	$ 421,597	$ 440,243
Unrealized depreciation on forward foreign currency contracts	1,106,241	—
Debt	343,000,000	346,850,000
Interest payable	5,592,184	5,277,132
Dividend distributions payable	19,040,586	19,196,418
Base management fees payable	5,293,755	5,626,893
Incentive management fees payable	11,878,159	20,277,930
Accrued administrative services	144,625	277,000
Other accrued expenses and payables	3,689,331	4,692,562
Total Liabilities	390,166,478	402,638,178
Net Assets		
Common stock, par value $.001 per share, 200,000,000 common shares authorized, 75,257,888 and 74,636,091 issued and 73,832,381 and 73,210,584 outstanding	74,636	75,258
Paid-in capital in excess of par	983,082,373	917,534,577
Distributions in excess of taxable net investment income	(26,165,703)	(22,291,022)
Accumulated net realized loss	(194,505,823)	(219,270,607)
Net unrealized appreciation (depreciation)	(51,999,958)	20,808,162
Treasury stock at cost, 1,425,507 and 1,425,507 shares held	(9,476,676)	(9,476,676)
Total Net Assets	701,008,849	687,379,692
Total Liabilities and Net Assets	$ 1,091,175,327	$ 1,090,017,870
Net Asset Value Per Share	$ 9.58	$ 9.31

sheet, the largest liability reflects debt ($347 million out of $403 million in liabilities), which likely approximates fair value. Finally, the remaining liabilities are short term and their values are also likely at or near fair values. Thus, given that this firm's assets and liabilities all approximate fair values, the book value of the firm is likely to correspond well to market value (again, ignoring the value of unrecognized growth options). Indeed, the resulting book value of $687 million is quite close to the market of just over $700 million at the end of Year 2.

In contrast to the previous example, where most assets and liabilities are recognized at fair value on the balance sheet, consider Exhibit 2.3, which shows the balance sheet for **Halozyme Therapeutics** (Nasdaq GS: HALO). Halozyme is a biopharmaceutical company that conducts research and development to commercialize products that advance patient care. Like BlackRock Kelso Capital Corporation discussed above, Halozyme also had a market value of approximately $700 million in Year 2. However, reported values of assets and liabilities on the balance sheet of Halozyme diverge substantially from market value. The company has $135 million of assets and $86 million of liabilities, for a net book value of $49 million. What explains the $651 million difference between the net book value and market value?

Most of Halozyme's *recognized* assets likely approximate fair value. For example, $100 million of the total assets of $135 million are cash and cash equivalents. The rest reflect receivables, inventories, prepaid expenses, and property and equipment. It is possible that the depreciated property and equipment have market values above the adjusted historical cost of $3.7 million, but any such difference is unlikely to explain the $651 million difference noted above. The explanation for the divergence between the reported book value and the market value is that Halozyme has assets that the mixed attribute measurement model has not recognized in the financial statements; in other words, such assets are *unrecognized*. Indeed, the company's website indicates that "The company's product portfolio is primarily based on intellectual property covering the family of human enzymes known as hyaluronidases and additional enzymes that affect the extracellular matrix." This intellectual property represents the knowledge acquired from research and clinical trials, patents, and positioning, which will translate into marketable products in the future. In addition, Halozyme likely has the ability to strategically deploy these assets into various opportunities yet to arise. It would be quite difficult to reliably incorporate Halozyme's positioning for future growth into the balance sheet, but the market has attempted to price it at approximately $651 million ($700 market price – $49 million book value).

Unfortunately, important assets like these are not easily recognized under most accounting standards. When companies like Halozyme invest capital and other resources in research and development, those companies are generally required to expense such expenditures rather than recognize "knowledge assets." Clearly, the value of such assets is relevant to financial statement users, but the representational faithfulness of such estimates is so tenuous that standard setters have defaulted towards expensing these amounts rather than potentially contaminating the balance sheet with immense measurement error and/or managerial bias. Thus, investors are left to come up with their own fair values of such assets, with the measurement error in such estimates explaining the higher-than-average stock price volatility of such firms.[8]

---

[8]The fair values of these unrecorded assets are estimated by analysts and investors when they forecast the future cash flows that these assets produce. Clearly, in the case of Halozyme, the investors and analysts are relying heavily on their knowledge and expertise in the company and the industry in forecasting the rate at which Halozyme will transform its intellectual property into future profitable growth. Using company-specific financial statement information combined with industry knowledge to forecast future cash flows, dividends, and earnings and transforming these forecasts into fair value estimates is the dominant theme in this text.

Exhibit 2.3

Halozyme Therapeutics, Inc.
Consolidated Balance Sheets

	Year 1	Year 2
Assets		
Current assets:		
Cash and cash equivalents	$ 52,825,527	$ 99,901,264
Accounts receivable, net	2,262,465	15,703,087
Inventories	567,263	2,670,696
Prepaid expenses and other assets	8,332,242	12,752,888
Total current assets	63,987,497	131,027,935
Property and equipment, net	1,771,048	3,700,462
Total Assets	$ 65,758,545	$ 134,728,397
Liabilities and Stockholders' Equity		
Current liabilities:		
Accounts payable	$ 7,556,859	$ 2,271,689
Accrued expenses	5,615,574	7,783,447
Deferred revenue, current portion	4,129,407	8,891,017
Total current liabilities	17,301,840	18,946,153
Deferred revenue, net of current portion	36,754,583	34,954,966
Long-term debt, net	—	29,661,680
Lease financing obligation	—	1,450,000
Deferred rent, net of current portion	802,006	861,879
Total Liabilities	54,858,429	85,874,678
Stockholders' equity:		
Preferred stock—$0.001 par value; 20,000,000 shares authorized; no shares issued and outstanding	—	—
Common stock—$0.001 par value; 150,000,000 shares authorized; 112,709,174 and 103,989,272 shares issued and outstanding at December 31, 2012 and 2011, respectively	103,990	112,709
Additional paid-in capital	255,817,772	347,314,658
Accumulated deficit	(245,021,646)	(298,573,648)
Total stockholders' equity	10,900,116	48,853,719
Total Liabilities and Stockholders' Equity	$ 65,758,545	$ 134,728,397

Summary of U.S. GAAP and IFRS Valuations

U.S. GAAP and IFRS do not utilize a single valuation method for all assets and liabilities. Instead, they use numerous valuation approaches for different assets and liabilities. U.S. GAAP and IFRS, for example, stipulate that firms use historical values for some assets and liabilities and current, or fair, values for other assets and liabilities. For this reason, U.S. GAAP and IFRS are mixed attribute measurement models. When accounting rules require firms to use fair value for an asset, firms might measure fair value using quoted market prices, current replacement cost, or net realizable value. If markets are not sufficiently active to provide reliable evidence of fair value, firms can use the present value of expected cash flows to approximate fair value. The fair value approach is generally more representationally faithful for financial assets and liabilities that have either observable market prices or contractual future cash flows. Exhibit 2.4 summarizes the use of these valuation methods for various assets and liabilities, which later chapters discuss more fully.

LO 2-2

Explain how changes in valuations of assets and liabilities on the balance sheet are recognized on the income statement and statement of comprehensive income.

Income Recognition

We now turn from the balance sheet to the income statement. The two are integrated: Revenues, expenses, gains, and losses reported on the income statement describe changes in assets and liabilities, and net income from the income statement is transferred into retained earnings on the balance sheet at year-end. The terms *earnings*, *income*, and *profits* are generally used interchangeably among analysts, managers, and investors, and historically refer to *net income*, which is different from *comprehensive income*. As discussed in the previous chapter, comprehensive income equals net income plus other comprehensive income.

In a simple world, net income for a period would equal the net changes in the fair value of the assets and liabilities of a firm (from nonowner sources) during that period. However, as discussed in the previous section, it is commonly very difficult or impossible to measure fair values of certain types of assets and liabilities with much precision. Therefore, financial statement users must wrestle with the mixed attribute measurement

Exhibit 2.4

Examples of Valuation Methods for Various Assets and Liabilities

Historical Cost
- *Acquisition cost:* Land, intangibles with indefinite lives, goodwill, prepayments
- *Adjusted historical cost:* Buildings, equipment and other depreciable assets, intangibles with limited lives, natural resources subject to depletion
- *Initial present value:* Investments in bonds held to maturity, long-term receivables and payables, noncurrent unearned revenue, current receivables and payables (but U.S. GAAP and IFRS ignore the discounting process on the grounds that discounted and undiscounted cash flows do not result in materially different valuations)

Fair Value
- *Market (or fair) value:* Investments in marketable equity securities, investments in debt securities classified as either trading securities or securities available for sale, financial instruments and derivative instruments subject to hedging activities, assets and liabilities of a business acquired using the acquisition method, assets and liabilities of a business to be discontinued

Hybrid of Historical and Fair Values
- *Current replacement cost:* Certain long-lived assets
- *Net realizable value:* Lower of cost or fair value for inventory, net realizable value of inventory, accounts receivable net of an allowance for uncollectible accounts

model, whereby assets and liabilities appear on the balance sheet under different valuation approaches and income recognition sometimes does not reflect all past changes in the economic value of a firm. Further, financial statement users must recognize that financial reporting standards discipline the accounting system and only permit firms to recognize revenues, expenses, and gains and losses that can be reliably measured in terms of changes in assets and liabilities during each period. Therefore, the relevance versus representational faithfulness trade-off impacts the income statement as well. As a result, the income statement might not capture the future value a firm hopes to generate by introducing new products, entering new markets, creating operating efficiencies, and taking other strategic actions.

In an attempt to create useful financial statements, three approaches to income recognition have evolved:

Approach 1. Recognize changes in economic value on the balance sheet *and* income statement when they are *realized* in a market transaction.

Approach 2. Recognize changes in economic value on the balance sheet *and* income statement when they *occur*, even though they are not yet realized in a market transaction.

Approach 3. Recognize changes in economic value on the balance sheet when the value changes *occur* over time, but delay recognition in net income until the value changes are *realized* in a market transaction. Include the delayed value change in "other comprehensive income" and shift it out of other comprehensive income and into net income when it is realized in the market transaction.

Income recognition is based on changes in economic value, not changes in cash. Therefore, before we expand on the three approaches, a brief review of "accrual accounting" is in order.

Accrual Accounting

The ultimate goal of a firm is to create wealth for stakeholders by generating more cash inflows than it incurs as cash outflows. Thus, a very simplistic option for reporting financial performance would be simply to report cash inflows and outflows. However, simply reporting cash inflows and outflows would suffer from timing issues as a measure of firm performance and financial condition. Accrual accounting is the recognition of revenues and expenses based on the underlying economic accomplishments and sacrifices in a particular period rather than when cash inflows or outflows occur. To review this basic premise, consider a stylized example of three transactions under accrual accounting versus cash flow reporting approaches, as presented in Exhibit 2.5.

In this stylized example, a firm purchases supplies (December 31, 2016), uses the supplies to provide services to a customer the next year, and collects cash for the billed services the following year. Under cash flow reporting, income from this transaction appears in three reporting periods in the pattern –$100, $0, and $1,000, whereas under accrual accounting, the net of $900 appears as income in a single period during which the activity occurs. In this example, we see that reporting cash inflows and outflows yields a series of performance measures that vary from negative to zero to positive, whereas accrual accounting measures and reports when and how the value changes are generated. The accrual accounting approach moves the timing of income and expenses to the period in which the real activity occurs (2017). The investment in supplies in 2016 and the collection of the account receivable in 2018 are handled by accruals, which can be thought of as "placeholders" on the balance sheet (assets in this example). Under accrual accounting, the supplies are classified as inventory, which, like many

Exhibit 2.5		
Stylized Example to Demonstrate the Advantages of Accrual Accounting Relative to Cash Flow Reporting		
Date	**Transaction**	
December 31, 2016	Firm purchases supplies for $100	
August 17, 2017	Firm uses supplies to provide services, billed at $1,000	
January 1, 2018	Customer pays $1,000 for services billed	
	2016	**2017**	**2018**
Net cash flow reporting	($100)	$0	$1,000
Accrual accounting	$0	$900	$0
		($1,000 billed − $100 supplies)	

nonmonetary assets, is "an expense waiting to happen." The amount billed for services is classified as a receivable (with the offset being the revenue recorded), which, like many monetary assets, is a "cash inflow waiting to happen."[9]

Although stylized, this example is symbolic of real-world evidence. Noted accounting author Patricia Dechow examined the relative ability of cash flows and accounting earnings to capture firm performance. She predicts and finds that

> ... for firms in steady state (that is, firms with cash requirements for working capital, investments, and financing that are relatively stable), cash flows have few timing and matching problems and are a relatively useful measure of firm performance. However, for firms operating in volatile environments with large changes in their working capital and investment and financing activities, cash flows ... have more severe timing and matching problems. Thus, cash flows' ability to reflect firm performance will decline as the firms' working capital requirements and investment and financing activities increase. Accruals ... mitigate timing and matching problems in cash flows. As a consequence, earnings ... better reflect firm performance than cash flows, in firms with more volatile operating, investment and financing activities .... [Finally], cash flows and earnings ... [are] equally useful in industries with short operating cycles. However, in industries with long operating cycles, cash flows are ... relatively poor measures of firm performance.[10]

In summary, reporting cash inflows and outflows is representationally faithful but is often not relevant for predicting future cash flows. Reporting income under accrual

---

[9]"Accrual accounting" is a general term that captures two distinct situations in which cash flows and economics do not align: accruals and deferrals. Accruals occur when economic activities precede cash flows. The accounts receivable accrual in our example occurred because the economic accomplishment of making a sale preceded the cash inflow from the sale. Deferrals occur when cash flows precede economic sacrifices. The inventory acquisition in our example is an example of a deferred expense. Cash outflow to acquire the inventory preceded the sacrifice of the inventory when sold.

[10]Patricia M. Dechow, "Accounting Earnings and Cash Flows as Measures of Firm Performance: The Role of Accounting Accruals," *Journal of Accounting & Economics* 18 (July 1994), pp. 3–42.

accounting procedures provides a measure of financial performance that is more relevant for users interested in predicting the ultimate payoff of cash flows, albeit with a potential for information to be less representationally faithful.[11]

Approach 1: Economic Value Changes Recognized on the Balance Sheet and Income Statement *When Realized*

The conventional approach to income measurement relies on *realization* as the trigger for recognizing components of income. "Realization" for revenues occurs either when firms receive cash, a receivable, or some other asset subject to representationally faithful measurement from a customer for goods sold or services performed, or when the firm satisfies a liability to a customer by delivering goods or services owed. The receipt of this asset or the satisfaction of the obligation validates the amount of the value change, and accountants characterize the firm as having *realized* the value change. This ensures that the amounts recorded as revenue are both relevant and representationally faithful.

For expenses, the concept of "realization" depends on the consumption of assets or incurrence of liabilities, which often is not as directly observable as an event like a sale to a customer. The conventional way of thinking about recognizing expenses is that they are *matched* to the revenues they help generate, but this convention applies only to certain expenses that can be clearly linked to realization of revenues, such as costs of goods sold or selling commissions.[12] For example, a sale of lumber by **The Home Depot** indicates that revenues have been realized, which then triggers derecognition (that is, removal from the balance sheet) of the inventory and the accompanying recognition of an expense for cost of goods sold. More commonly, expenses are recognized in the particular period in which they are realized by the consumption of resources (such as paying salaries to employees) or the passage of time (such as rent or interest).

As presented in the discussion of asset and liability valuation, delaying the recognition of value changes for assets and liabilities until triggered by some realization (such as a sale or consumption) means that the balance sheet reports assets and liabilities at historical values. When historical values are used, valuation changes in assets and liabilities are not recognized until they are realized, meaning that some event (such as a sale) establishes a reliable basis for measuring and reporting the changes in the assets and liabilities on the financial statements. In this case, realization affects the balance sheet and the income statement simultaneously. For example, a firm that holds land it acquired at $300,000 but is now clearly worth $900,000 does not recognize the $600,000 gain until the land is actually sold.

Note that the receipt or disbursement of cash is *not* a requirement for realization. Because cash flows may precede, coincide with, or follow the value change, the balance

---

[11]The FASB's Conceptual Framework, which is the foundation for U.S. GAAP, is based on observations similar to those documented by Dechow. In *Statement of Financial Accounting Concepts No. 1*, the FASB states, "Information about enterprise earnings and its components measured by accrual accounting generally provides a better indication of enterprise performance than does information about current cash receipts and payments." This will be discussed in more detail in Chapter 3.

[12]As regulators gravitate away from the historical value approaches to assets and liabilities (toward current value approaches), the emphasis and popularity of the matching objective are becoming diminished. However, they remain useful when considering when and how to recognize certain expenses (for example, depreciation).

sheet utilizes various *accruals* and *deferrals* as placeholders for cash flows (such as accounts receivable, accounts payable, or prepayments).

Approach 2: Economic Value Changes Recognized on the Balance Sheet and the Income Statement *When They Occur*

Approach 2 compels firms to revalue assets and liabilities to fair value each period and recognize the *unrealized* gains and losses in net income in that same period. This approach to income recognition aligns well with the current value approach for assets and liabilities because the changes in economic value are reflected on the income statement *even if they are not yet realized.* U.S. GAAP generally does not permit firms to revalue assets upward for value increases, which would recognize the unrealized gain as part of net income. However, certain financial assets receive this treatment. For example, investments a firm makes in marketable equity securities are adjusted to market value each period, with the resulting gain or loss recognized in income of the period. Also, firms must generally write down assets when fair values decrease below book values and recognize the decline in economic value immediately in income.

For example, suppose **Smithfield Foods** has live hog inventory valued at $882 million. Despite the fact that swine flu is not spread by eating properly cooked pork, a swine flu epidemic sends the market price of live hogs down approximately 5% on the Chicago Mercantile Exchange. As a consequence, Smithfield Foods' inventory is overstated by $44 million. This decline in inventory fair value is recognized on both the balance sheet and income statement based on the new market prices. The new value of live hog inventory is $838 million, and this decline in economic value is recognized in income as a lower-of-cost-or-market adjustment for inventory of $44 million. The reason for U.S. GAAP's asymmetric treatment of gains and losses is that the combination of representational faithfulness concerns for the estimated increases in economic value and managers' self-interested incentives to report higher book values and income might lead to poor-quality financial statements (despite the potential for greater relevance). Instead, firms must await the validation of such increases in value through a market transaction (that is, realization) to provide a sound, reliable basis for recognizing the gain.

In contrast, IFRS allows for a number of situations where firms are permitted to increase asset valuations. For example, upon initial adoption of IFRS, firms may elect to value property and equipment at fair value. In addition, firms can record investment property (such as rental property), intangible assets, and some financial assets at fair values even when those fair values rise above carrying values. Note, however, that when firms report unrealized changes in economic value in current earnings under IFRS, additional disclosures must accompany the use of fair values, including the methodology of determining fair value. These additional disclosures are an attempt to increase the transparency of the fair values and therefore the representational faithfulness of these amounts. Also note that under IFRS, if a firm elects to recognize increased fair values of assets, it must do so for entire classes of similar assets (for example, all real estate, not just single properties), and it must continue to revalue such classes of assets thereafter (even if fair values decline). These requirements are meant to discourage firms from cherry-picking which assets to revalue upward and when.

Approach 3: Economic Value Changes Recognized on the Balance Sheet *When They Occur* but Recognized on the Income Statement *When Realized*

The value changes of certain types of assets and liabilities are of particular interest to financial statement users and are measurable with a sufficiently high degree of reliability that U.S. GAAP and IFRS require firms to revalue them to fair value each period. U.S. GAAP and IFRS recognize, however, that the value change is *unrealized* until the firm sells the asset or settles the liability. The ultimate *realized* gain or loss will likely differ from the unrealized gain or loss each period, particularly if the market values of the underlying assets or liabilities are volatile. Therefore, U.S. GAAP and IFRS require firms to delay including the gain or loss in *net income* until realization of the gain or loss occurs. However, such gains or losses do appear as part of *comprehensive income* (as discussed in Chapter 1). The most common types of unrealized gains and losses that receive this treatment (all discussed in Chapters 7–9) include

- foreign currency translation gains and losses.
- fair value gains and losses on revaluations of investments in available-for-sale securities (until rules change for 2018 financial statements).
- fair value gains and losses on derivatives designated as hedges of future cash flows.
- certain adjustments to pension and post-retirement benefit obligations.

As a hybrid of Approaches 1 and 2, Approach 3 attempts to capture the relevant economic value changes recognized for assets and liabilities under Approach 2, using the current value approach for asset and liability valuation. At the same time, Approach 3 incorporates the representational faithfulness feature of Approach 1 by delaying recognition of the economic value change in net income until the change is realized in a market transaction. Instead, such changes appear as part of other comprehensive income on the statement of comprehensive income.

The practice of delaying the recognition of fair value changes in net income under Approach 3 presumes that the investors assign greater relevance to *net income* as the summary measure of performance for a firm, but view amounts recognized as *other comprehensive income* as being of secondary relevance. Indeed, a study of comprehensive income disclosures shortly after they were first required reached the conclusion that investors do not perceive other comprehensive income to be important components of a firm's performance, given net income.[13] However, numerous other studies have demonstrated a strong association between security prices and underlying fair value estimates and between the changes in fair values and stock returns.[14] In addition, the volatility of fair value changes reflected in comprehensive income has been shown to explain numerous measures of risk for commercial banks.[15] Thus, overall it is clear investors view fair value amounts as relevant despite the risk that such amounts might be less representationally faithful than historical valuations.

---

[13]Dan Dhaliwal, K. R. Subramanyam, and Robert Trezevant, "Is Comprehensive Income Superior to Net Income as a Measure of Firm Performance?," *Journal of Accounting & Economics* 26, no. 1–3 (1999), pp. 43–67.

[14]Thomas J. Carroll, Thomas J. Linsmeier, and Kathy R. Petroni, "The Reliability of Fair Value versus Historical Cost Information: Evidence from Closed-End Mutual Funds," *Journal of Accounting, Auditing and Finance* 18, no. 1 (2003), pp. 1–24.

[15]Leslie D. Hodder, Patrick E. Hopkins, and James M. Wahlen, "Risk-Relevance of Fair Value Income Measures for Commercial Banks," *The Accounting Review* 81, no. 2 (March 2006), pp. 337–75.

■ The traditional accounting model relies mostly on historical values for assets and liabilities and delays income recognition until realization (Approach 1). Under this approach
  ● asset and liability valuation directly link to income recognition.
  ● changes in the economic value of assets and liabilities are recognized in net income when some market transaction triggers realization of the economic value changes.
■ The FASB and IASB often require the use of fair values for certain assets and liabilities. Using the fair value approach for assets and liabilities generally translates into Approach 2, which recognizes such economic value changes in income immediately.

■ As a hybrid of these approaches, some economic value changes are recognized on the balance sheet and in comprehensive income before they are recognized in net income on the income statement (Approach 3).
  ● In the intervening time, firms use accumulated other comprehensive income (in shareholders' equity) as a temporary "holding tank" for unrealized gains and losses for which the assets and liabilities have been marked to fair value but the gains and losses are yet to be realized in a market transaction.
  ● When the change in economic value is realized, the firm formally recognizes the gains and losses by removing them from accumulated other comprehensive income and reporting them within net income.

Evolution of the Mixed Attribute Measurement Model

The mixed attribute measurement model does a fairly good job of capturing relevant information about economic events and transactions in a way that maintains the overall representational faithfulness of the financial statements. The FASB, and now the IASB, is constantly monitoring the needs of financial statement users and adapting the financial reporting rules to those needs. The FASB and IASB are actively overhauling the conceptual frameworks upon which the accounting model is based, with the goal of making the accounting for similar events and transactions consistent across firms and across time. However, because of the trade-off between relevance and representational faithfulness, it is unlikely that financial reporting will move toward any extreme, such as full historical values or full fair values. Instead, the evolution of the mixed attribute measurement model reflects a continuous improvement in financial reporting that adapts to the evolving needs of financial statement users. Also, an important fact to keep in mind is that the quality of financial reporting can be enhanced (or offset) by other features of the economic environment, such as managers' voluntary disclosures; corporate governance practices; and shareholder protection, regulation, and enforcement. For example, research demonstrates that the usefulness of accrual accounting is higher in countries with institutional features that protect shareholders (such as common law legal systems and shareholders' rights provisions).[16]

LO 2-3

Understand that financial reporting and tax reporting are two different systems, and are linked by permanent differences and deferred tax assets and liabilities.

Income Taxes

Everyone is aware that taxes are a significant aspect of doing business, but few understand how taxes impact financial statements. The discussion thus far has considered the measurement of assets, liabilities, revenues, gains, expenses, and losses before

---

[16]Mingyi Hung, "Accounting Standards and Value Relevance of Financial Statements: An International Analysis," *Journal of Accounting & Economics* 30, no. 3 (December 2000), pp. 401–20.

considering any income tax effects. The objective of this section is to familiarize you with the basic concepts underlying the treatment of income taxes in the financial statements. Further, analyzing profitability (in Chapter 4) requires that you understand tax effects on profitability, such as the favored treatment of interest expense. Thus, an overview of the required accounting for income taxes under U.S. GAAP and IFRS is necessary.

A complexity in understanding the financial reporting of income taxes arises because the financial reporting of income uses one set of rules (U.S. GAAP, for example), while taxable income uses another set of rules (the Internal Revenue Code, for example). The differences between these sets of rules triggers differences in the timing and amount of tax expense on the income statement and the actual taxes payable to the government, which necessitates recognizing deferred income tax assets and liabilities. These differences are analogous to differences between financial reporting rules and cash basis accounting, which necessitate the use of various accruals such as accounts receivable and accounts payable. Thus, an understanding of financial statement analysis requires the appreciation that there are (at least) three primary methods by which financial performance can be measured, as shown in Exhibit 2.6.

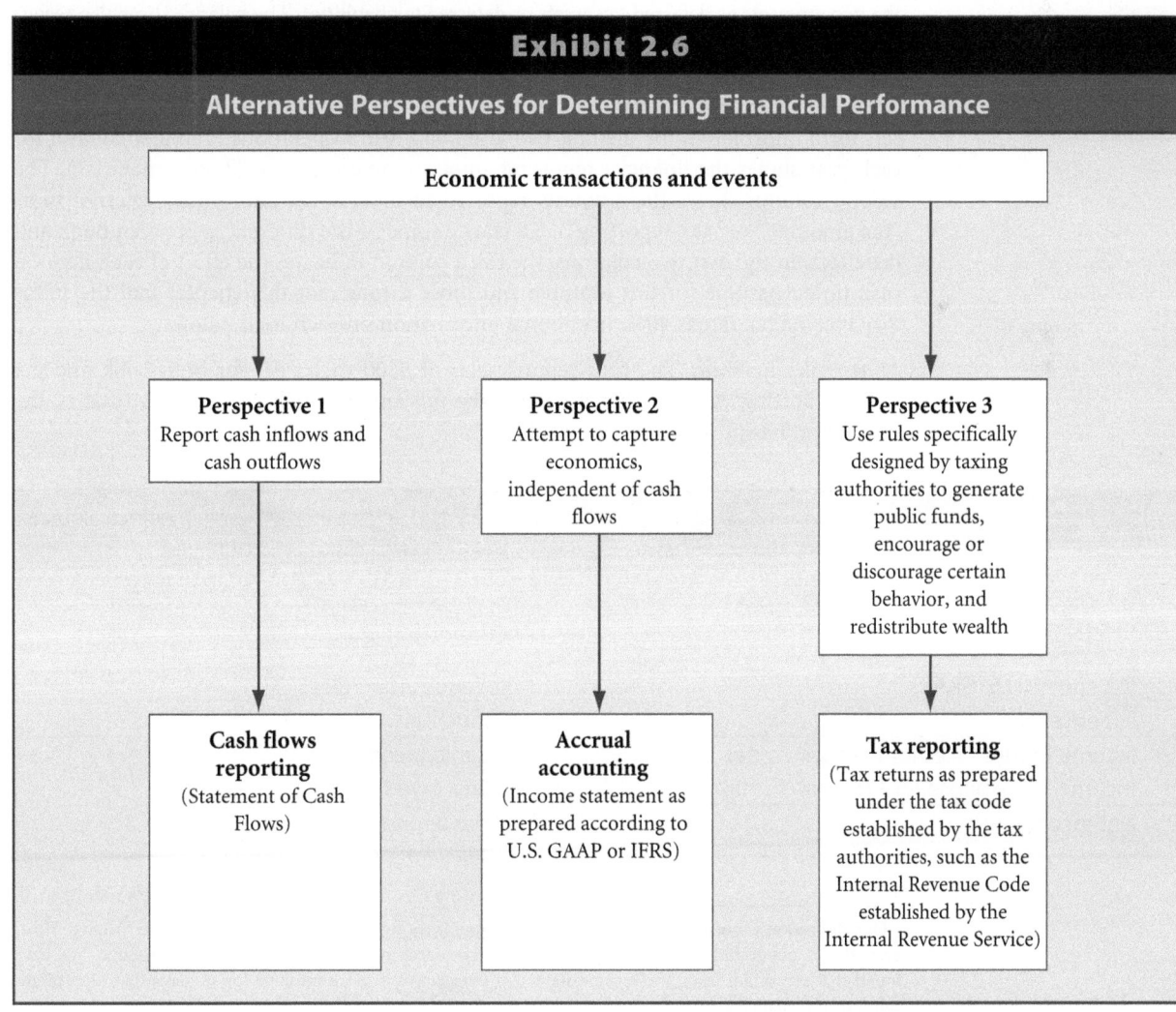

Exhibit 2.6
Alternative Perspectives for Determining Financial Performance

Economic transactions and events

Perspective 1	Perspective 2	Perspective 3
Report cash inflows and cash outflows	Attempt to capture economics, independent of cash flows	Use rules specifically designed by taxing authorities to generate public funds, encourage or discourage certain behavior, and redistribute wealth
Cash flows reporting (Statement of Cash Flows)	**Accrual accounting** (Income statement as prepared according to U.S. GAAP or IFRS)	**Tax reporting** (Tax returns as prepared under the tax code established by the tax authorities, such as the Internal Revenue Code established by the Internal Revenue Service)

Overview of Financial Reporting of Income Taxes

Income taxes significantly affect all of the financial statements and the analysis of a firm's reported profitability (income tax expense is a subtraction in computing net income), cash flows (income taxes paid are an operating use of cash), and assets and liabilities (for accrued taxes payable and deferred tax assets or liabilities). Income tax expense under accrual accounting for a period does not necessarily equal income taxes owed under the tax laws for that period (for which the firm must pay cash). Exhibit 2.7 illustrates the terminology that differs between financial reporting of income taxes in financial statements and elements of income taxes for tax reporting on tax returns.[17]

Both financial reporting and tax reporting begin with revenues, but revenue recognition rules for financial reporting do not necessarily lead to the same figure for revenues as reported for tax reporting. Under tax reporting, firms report "deductions" rather than "expenses." Revenues minus deductions equal "taxable income" (rather than "income before taxes," or "pretax income"). Finally, taxable income determines "taxes owed," which can be substantially different from "tax expense" (often called "provision for income taxes") on the income statement, as highlighted later in this section. The balance sheet recognizes the difference between the two amounts as deferred tax assets or deferred tax liabilities. The balance sheet also recognizes any taxes owed at year-end (beyond the estimated tax payments firms may have made throughout the year) as a current liability for income taxes payable.

A simple example illustrates the issues in accounting for income taxes. Exhibit 2.8 sets forth information for the first two years of a firm's operations. The first column for each year shows the financial reporting amounts (referred to as "book amounts"). The second column shows the amounts reported to income tax authorities (referred to as "tax amounts" or "tax reporting"). To clarify some of the differences between book and tax effects in the first two columns, the third column indicates the effect of each item on cash flows. Assume for this example and those throughout this chapter that the statutory income tax rate is 40%. Additional information on each item follows:

■ *Sales Revenue:* The firm reports sales of $500 each year for both book and tax reporting. Assume that it collects the full amount each year in cash (that is, the firm has no accounts receivable).

Exhibit 2.7

Differences in Terminology for Financial Reporting and Tax Reporting

Financial Reporting	Tax Reporting
Revenues (U.S. GAAP)	Revenues (tax rules)
− Expenses	− Deductions
= Income before taxes (or Pretax income)	= Taxable income
− Income tax expense (or Provision for taxes)	⇒ Taxes owed
= Net income	[no counterpart]

[17]Our discussion proceeds as if accounting for income taxes follows an income statement perspective. However, this is not technically correct, as accounting standards require a balance sheet perspective. We have found that exposition using the income statement perspective is more intuitive for students than the technically correct balance sheet perspective.

■ *Interest Income on Municipal Bonds:* The firm earns $25 of interest on municipal bonds. The firm includes this amount in its book income. The federal government does not tax interest on state and municipal bonds, so this amount is excluded from taxable income.

■ *Depreciation Expense:* The firm purchases equipment for $120 cash, and the equipment has a two-year life. It depreciates the equipment using the straight-line method for financial reporting, recognizing $60 of depreciation expense on its books each year. Income taxing authorities permit the firm to deduct $80 of depreciation of the asset in the first year, and only $40 of depreciation for tax reporting in the second year.

■ *Warranty Expense:* The firm estimates that the cost of providing warranty services on products sold equals 2% of sales. It recognizes warranty expense of $10 (0.02 × $500) each year for financial reporting, which links the estimated cost of warranties against the revenue from the sale of products subject to warranty. Income tax laws do not permit firms to claim a deduction for warranties in computing taxable income until they make cash expenditures to provide warranty services. Assume that the firm incurs cash costs of $4 in the first year and $12 in the second year.

■ *Other Expenses:* The firm incurs and pays other expenses of $300 each year.

■ *Income before Taxes and Taxable Income:* Based on the preceding assumptions, income before taxes for financial reporting is $155 each year. Taxable income is $116 in the first year and $148 in the second year.

■ *Taxes Payable:* Assume for purposes here that the firm pays all income taxes at each year-end.

Exhibit 2.8

Illustration of the Effects of Income Taxes on Net Income, Taxable Income, and Cash Flows

	First Year			Second Year		
	Book Amounts	Tax Amounts	Cash Flow Amounts	Book Amounts	Tax Amounts	Cash Flow Amounts
Sales revenue	$ 500	$ 500	$ 500	$ 500	$ 500	$ 500
Interest on municipal bonds	25	—	25	25	—	25
Purchase of equipment	—	—	(120)	—	—	—
Depreciation expense	(60)	(80)	—	(60)	(40)	—
Warranty expense	(10)	(4)	(4)	(10)	(12)	(12)
Other expenses	(300)	(300)	(300)	(300)	(300)	(300)
Net Income before Taxes ("Book" column) or Taxable Income ("Tax" column)	$ 155	$ 116		$ 155	$ 148	
Income tax expense ("Book" column) or payable ("Tax" column)	(52)	(46.4)	(46.4)	(52)	(59.2)	(59.2)
Net Income or Net Cash Flows	$ 103		$ 54.6	$ 103		$153.8

Income before taxes for financial reporting differs from taxable income for the following principal reasons:

1. **Permanent Differences:** Some revenues and expenses that are part of net income for financial reporting *never* appear on the income tax return. For example, the amount of interest earned on the municipal bond is a permanent revenue difference. Examples of expenses that are not allowed as tax deductions include executive compensation above a specified cap, certain entertainment expenses, political and lobbying expenses, and some fines and penalties.

2. **Temporary Differences:** Some revenues and expenses are part of both net income and taxable income, but in different periods. These timing differences are "temporary" until they "reverse." For example, straight-line depreciation for financial reporting but accelerated depreciation deductions for tax reporting triggers a temporary difference. In the above example, the firm recognizes total depreciation of $120 over the life of the equipment for both financial and tax reporting but in a different pattern over time. Similarly, the firm recognizes a total of $20 of warranty expense over the two-year period for financial reporting. It deducts only $16 over the two-year period for tax reporting. If the firm's estimate of total warranty costs turns out to be correct, the firm will deduct the remaining $4 of warranty expense for tax reporting in future years when it provides warranty services.

A central conceptual question in accounting for income taxes concerns the measurement of income tax expense on the income statement for financial reporting. Should the firm compute income tax expense based on

1. book income before taxes ($155 for each year in Exhibit 2.8)?
2. book income before taxes but excluding permanent differences ($155 – $25 = $130 for each year in Exhibit 2.8)?
3. taxable income ($116 in the first year and $148 in the second year in Exhibit 2.8)?

U.S. GAAP and IFRS require firms to follow the second approach, where tax expense is based on income before taxes minus permanent differences, a number that does not appear on the income statement. For this reason, U.S. GAAP and IFRS require disclosure within the income tax footnote to the financial statements that shows how the firm calculates income tax expense. This disclosure shows that the effective tax rate (income tax expense ÷ pretax income) does not equal the statutory tax rate when permanent differences exist. If a firm does not have any permanent differences, there is no difference between the first and second approaches. Following the second approach results in consistency on the income statement; pretax income is based on accrual accounting, and income tax expense is based on accrual accounting (rather than on tax rules that are relatively close to cash accounting—the third approach).

Continuing the example above, under the second approach, income tax expense is $52 (0.40 × $130) in each year. The impact on the financial statements of recognizing the tax expense, taxes paid, and associated deferred tax accounts is as follows:[18]

---

[18]See the section at the end of this chapter for a formal description of the above framework for analyzing the financial statement impacts of transactions and events.

Assets		=	Liabilities		+	Shareholders' Equity		
						Contributed Capital (CC)	Accumulated Other Comprehensive Income (AOCI)	Retained Earnings (RE)
Cash	(46.4)		Deferred Tax Liability –					Income Tax Expense (52.0)
Deferred Tax Asset –			Depreciation	8.0				
Warranty	2.4							
Income tax expense						52.0		
Deferred tax asset						2.4		
Deferred tax liability							8.0	
Cash							46.4	

The firm recognizes income tax expense of $52.0, which reduces net income, but the firm only pays cash taxes of $46.4. The deferred tax asset measures the future tax saving that the firm will realize when it provides warranty services in future years and claims a tax deduction for the realization of expenses that are estimated in the first year. The firm expects to incur $6 ($10 – $4) of warranty costs in the second year and later years. When it incurs these costs, it will reduce its taxable income, which will result in lower taxes owed for the year, all else equal. Hence, the deferred tax asset of $2.4 (0.40 × $6) reflects the expected future tax savings from the future deductibility of amounts already expensed for financial reporting but not yet deducted for tax reporting. The $8 (0.40 × $20) deferred tax liability measures taxes that the firm must pay in the second year when it recognizes $20 less depreciation for tax reporting than for financial reporting.

The following summarizes the differences between book and tax amounts and the underlying cash flows. The $25 of interest on municipal bonds is a cash flow, but it is not reported on the tax return (it is a permanent difference). Depreciation is an expense that is a temporary difference between tax reporting and financial reporting but does not use cash. The firm recognized warranty expense of $10 in measuring net income but used only $4 of cash in satisfying warranty claims, which is the amount allowed to be deducted on the tax return. Finally, the firm recognized $52 of income tax expense in measuring net income but used only $46.4 cash for income taxes due to permanent and temporary differences. Overall, net income is $103, taxable income is $116, and net cash flows are $54.6. The discrepancy between net income and net cash flows is in large part due to the difference between cash invested in long-term assets relative to periodic depreciation.

In the second year, the impact on the financial statements of the income tax effects is as follows:

Assets		=	Liabilities		+	Shareholders' Equity		
						CC	AOCI	RE
Cash	(59.2)		Deferred Tax Liability –					Income Tax Expense (52.0)
Deferred Tax Asset –			Depreciation	(8.0)				
Warranty	(0.8)							
Income tax expense						52.0		
Deferred tax liability						8.0		
Deferred tax asset							0.8	
Cash							59.2	

As in the first year, income tax is the same, and cash paid for taxes equals the statutory tax rate times taxable income. The temporary difference related to depreciation completely reverses in the second year, so the firm reduces the deferred tax liability to zero, which increases income taxes currently payable by $8. The temporary difference related to the warranty partially reversed during the second year, but the firm created additional temporary differences in that year by making another estimate of future warranty expense. For the two years as a whole, warranty expense for financial reporting of $20 ($10 + $10) exceeds the amount recognized for tax reporting of $16 ($4 + $12). Thus, the firm will recognize a deferred tax asset representing future tax savings of $1.6 (0.40 × $4). The deferred tax asset had a balance of $2.4 at the end of the first year, so the adjustment in the second year reduces the balance of the deferred tax asset by $0.8 ($2.4 − $1.6).

Now consider the cash flow effects for the second year. Cash flow from operations is $153.8. Again, depreciation expense is a noncash expense of $60. The firm recognized warranty expense of $10 for financial reporting but used $12 of cash to satisfy warranty claims. The $2 subtraction also equals the net reduction in the warranty liability during the second year, as the following analysis shows:

Warranty liability, beginning of second year	$ 6
Warranty expense, second year	10
Warranty claims, second year	(12)
Warranty liability, end of second year	$ 4

The firm recognized $52 of income tax expense but used $59.2 of cash for income taxes. The additional $7.2 of cash used to pay taxes in excess of the tax expense reduces the net deferred tax liability position. The $7.2 subtraction also equals the net change in the deferred tax asset ($0.8 decrease) and deferred tax liability ($8 decrease) during the second year, summarized as

Net deferred tax liability, beginning of second year	$ 5.6
($2.4 asset − $8 liability)	
Income tax expense, second year	52.0
Income taxes paid, second year	(59.2)
Negative net deferred tax liability, or net deferred tax asset,	
end of second year ($1.6 asset − $0 liability)	$ (1.6)

At the end of the second year, the totals for net income, cash flows, and tax amounts are as follows:

	First Year	Second Year	Totals
Net income	$103.0	$103.0	$ 206.0
Net cash flows	54.6	153.8	208.4
Taxable income	$116.0	$148.0	$ 264.0
Taxes paid	(46.4)	(59.2)	(105.6)
	$ 69.6	$ 88.8	$ 158.4

The total amounts for net income and net cash flows differ by 2.4, which reflects the following:

Warranty liability for payments not yet made	$ 4.0
Offset by related deferred tax asset	(1.6)
	$ 2.4

The remaining net cash flows associated with the warranty will be the $4.0 cash out-flow, offset by the $1.6 tax expense savings when those warranty payments are deducti-ble. When the warranty liability is finally settled, net income will equal net cash flows. In addition, total net cash flows of $208.4 exceed the net of taxable income and taxes paid of $158.4, a difference of $50.0. This difference reflects the total of permanent dif-ferences across the two years ($25.0 + $25.0). We reconciled net cash flows to net income above, so this additional $50.0 difference reflects a *permanent difference* between what is reported on the tax returns and what appears in the financial statements (both the income statement and statement of cash flows).

Measuring Income Tax Expense: A Bit More to the Story (to Be Technically Correct)

The preceding illustration followed what might be termed an *income statement approach* to measuring income tax expense. It compared revenues and expenses recog-nized for book and tax purposes, eliminated permanent differences, and computed income tax expense based on book income before taxes, excluding permanent differen-ces. However, FASB Statement No. 109 and IAS 12[19] require firms to follow a *balance sheet approach* when computing income tax expense. For example, Statement No. 109 (para. 11) states the following:

> … a difference between the tax basis of an asset or a liability and its reported amount in the [balance sheet] will result in taxable or deductible amounts in some future year(s) when the reported amounts of assets are recovered and the reported amounts of liabilities are settled.

Similarly, IAS 12 states:

> It is inherent in the recognition of an asset or liability that the reporting entity expects to recover or settle the carrying amount of that asset or liability. If it is probable that recovery or settlement of that carrying amount will make future tax payments larger (smaller) than they would be if such recovery or settlement were to have no tax consequences, this Standard requires an entity to recognize a deferred tax liability (deferred tax asset), with certain limited exceptions.

Thus, in the context of the preceding example, the perspective under the balance sheet approach is as follows:

Step 1. In the illustration, the book basis (that is, the amount on the balance sheet) of the equipment at the end of the first year is $60 ($120 cost – $60 accumulated depreciation) and the tax basis (that is, what would appear if the firm prepared a tax reporting balance sheet) is $40 ($120 – $80). Both the book and tax bases are zero at the end of the second year. The book basis of the warranty liability at the end of the first year is $6 ($10 – $4), and the tax basis is zero. (That is, the firm recognizes a deduction for tax purposes when it pays warranty claims and would therefore show no liability if it were to prepare a tax balance sheet.) The book ba-sis of the warranty liability at the end of the second year is $4 ($6 + $10 – $12), and the tax basis remains zero.

---

[19]Financial Accounting Standards Board, *Statement of Financial Accounting Standards No. 109*, "Accounting for Income Taxes" (1992); *FASB Codification Topic 740*; International Accounting Standards Committee, *International Accounting Standards No. 12*, "Income Taxes" (October 1996).

Step 2. After identifying book and tax differences, eliminate those that will not have a future tax consequence (that is, permanent differences). There are no permanent differences in the book and tax bases of assets and liabilities in the example. However, suppose the firm had not yet received the $25 of interest on the municipal bond investment by the end of the first year. It would show an interest receivable on its financial reporting balance sheet of $25, but no receivable would appear on its tax balance sheet because the tax law does not tax such interest; the difference between the book and tax bases is a permanent difference. The firm would eliminate this book–tax difference before moving to the next step.

Step 3. Next, separate the remaining differences into those that give rise to future tax *deductions* and those that give rise to future taxable *income*. Exhibit 2.9 summarizes the possibilities and gives several examples of these temporary differences, as later chapters discuss. The difference between the book basis ($6) and the tax basis ($0) of the warranty liability at the end of the first year means that the firm will have future tax deductions (assuming that the book basis of the estimate is accurate). The difference between the book basis ($60) and the tax basis ($40) of the equipment at the end of the first year gives rise to future taxable income (meaning that depreciation deductions will be lower, which will increase taxable income, all else equal). We multiply these differences by the marginal tax rate expected to apply *in those future periods*. In the example, the future tax deduction for the warranties results in a deferred tax asset at the end of the first year of $2.4 [$0.40 \times$ ($6 book basis – $0 tax basis)]. The future taxable income (due to the lower future depreciation of the equipment) results in a deferred tax liability at the end of the first year of $8 [$0.40 \times$ ($60 book basis – $40 tax basis)].

Exhibit 2.9		
Examples of Temporary Differences		
	Assets	**Liabilities**
Future Tax Deduction *(results in deferred tax assets)*	**Tax basis of assets exceeds financial reporting basis.** *Example:* Accounts receivable using the direct charge-off method for uncollectible accounts for tax purposes exceeds accounts receivable (net) using the allowance method for financial reporting.	**Tax basis of liabilities is less than financial reporting basis.** *Example:* Tax reporting does not recognize an estimated liability for warranty claims (firms can deduct only actual expenditures on warranty claims), whereas firms must recognize such a liability for financial reporting to match warranty expense with sales revenue in the period of sale.
Future Taxable Income *(results in deferred tax liabilities)*	**Tax basis of assets is less than financial reporting basis.** *Example:* Depreciation is computed using accelerated depreciation for tax purposes and the straight-line method for financial reporting.	**Tax basis of liabilities exceeds financial reporting basis.** *Example:* Leases are recognized by a lessee, the user of the leased assets, as a capital lease for tax reporting and an operating lease for financial reporting.

Step 4. Finally, the rules for income tax accounting require managers to assess the likelihood that the firm will realize the future benefits of any recognized deferred tax assets. This assessment should consider the nature (whether cyclical or non-cyclical, for example) and characteristics (growing, mature, or declining, for example) of a firm's business and its tax planning strategies for the future. If realization of the benefits of deferred tax assets is "more likely than not" (that is, the likelihood exceeds 50%), then deferred tax assets equal the amounts computed in Step 3. However, if it is "more likely than not" that the firm will *not* realize some or all of the deferred tax assets, then the firm must reduce the deferred tax asset using a valuation allowance (similar in concept to the allowance for uncollectible accounts receivable). The valuation allowance reduces the deferred tax assets to the amounts the firm expects to realize in the form of lower tax payments in the future (similar to a net realizable value approach). For purposes here, assume that the firm in the preceding illustration considers it more likely than not that it will realize the tax benefits of the deferred tax assets related to warranties and therefore recognizes no valuation allowance.

The result of this four-step procedure for the example is a deferred tax asset and a deferred tax liability at each balance sheet date. The amounts in the preceding illustration are as follows:

	January 1, First Year	December 31, First Year	December 31, Second Year
Deferred tax asset—warranties	$0.0	$2.4	$1.6
Deferred tax liability—equipment	0.0	8.0	0.0

Income tax expense for each period equals:

1. Income taxes currently payable on taxable income
2. Plus (minus) any increases (decreases) in deferred tax liabilities
3. Plus (minus) any decreases (increases) in deferred tax assets.

Thus, income tax expense in the preceding illustration is as follows:

	First Year	Second Year
Income taxes currently payable on taxable income	$46.4	$59.2
Plus (minus) increase (decrease) in deferred liability	8.0	(8.0)
Minus (plus) increase (decrease) in deferred tax asset	(2.4)	0.8
Income tax expense	$52.0	$52.0

The income statement approach illustrated in the first section and the balance sheet approach illustrated in this section yield identical results whenever (1) enacted tax rates applicable to future periods do not change and (2) the firm recognizes no valuation allowance on deferred tax assets. Legislated changes in tax rates applicable to future periods will cause the tax effects of previously recognized temporary differences to differ from the amounts in the deferred tax asset and deferred tax liability accounts. The firm revalues the deferred tax assets and liabilities for the change in tax rates and flows through the effect of the change to income tax expense in the year of the legislated change. A change in the valuation allowance for deferred tax assets likewise flows through immediately to income tax expense.

Reporting Income Taxes in the Financial Statements

Understanding income tax accounting becomes difficult because firms may not include all income taxes for a period on the line for income tax expense in the income statement. Some amounts may appear elsewhere:

- *Discontinued Operations:* Under U.S. GAAP, firms report the results of discontinued operations in a separate section of the income statement, net of the income tax effects. Thus, income tax expense reflects income taxes on income from continuing operations only. IFRS does not permit extraordinary item categorizations, but exceptional or material items may be disclosed separately, including income tax effects.
- *Other Comprehensive Income:* Unrealized changes in the market value of marketable securities classified as "available for sale" (until 2018, when this classification ceases to exist), unrealized changes in the market value of hedged financial instruments and derivatives classified as cash flow hedges, unrealized foreign currency translation adjustments, and certain changes in pension and other post-employment benefit assets and liabilities appear in other comprehensive income, net of their tax effects. These items usually give rise to deferred tax assets or deferred tax liabilities because the income tax law includes such gains and losses in taxable income when realized. Thus, a portion of the change in deferred tax assets and liabilities on the balance sheet does not flow through income tax expense on the income statement.

Income Taxes

Starbucks reports "Income tax expense (benefit)" in its consolidated income statement (see Appendix A). Income tax expense for the year ended September 27, 2015, is $1,143.7 million, and income tax expense for the year ended September 28, 2014, is $1,092.0 million. **Starbucks** reports a tax benefit (a negative income tax expense) of $238.7 million in the year ended September 29, 2013, because it had a net operating loss for the year due to a large litigation charge.

In Note 13 to its financial statements ("Income Taxes"), **Starbucks** provides several other disclosures related to income taxes, most of which we will analyze in detail in Chapter 9. At this point, observe that the second table in that note divides the tax expense reported on the income statement into its current and deferred portions. The income tax expenses for the first two years are primarily current. For example, for the year ended September 27, 2015, total current taxes are $1,123.3 million and total deferred taxes are only $20.4 million, the two of which total to the income statement–reported income tax expense of $1,143.7 million. This does not mean that **Starbucks** has few deferred tax assets and liabilities; it means that the net deferred position (deferred tax assets minus deferred tax liabilities) *changed* very little during the year. In fact, the fourth table in the note shows that, at the end of the most recent reporting period, **Starbucks** had $1,646.3 million in deferred tax assets and $1,137.4 million in deferred tax liabilities. Going back to the second table in the note, the income tax *benefit* reported for the year ended September 29, 2013, was $238.7 million, comprised of a total current tax expense of $806.3 and a deferred tax benefit of $1,045.0. Evidently, the large litigation charge reported on the income statement did not generate a current tax deduction (likely because it had not yet been paid), but will generate a future tax deduction. A future tax deduction generates a future tax savings, which is the definition of a deferred tax asset. The sudden increase in the deferred tax asset reduced **Starbucks** income tax expense to the point where it became negative (an income tax benefit).

Framework for Analyzing the Effects of Transactions on the Financial Statements

LO 2-4

Utilize an analytical framework to map business transactions and events to the balance sheet and income statement.

In each period, firms prepare financial statements that aggregate and summarize the results of numerous transactions. This section presents and illustrates an analytical framework for understanding the effects of various transactions on the financial statements, which is built on basic financial accounting. Understanding the impact of individual transactions is important because financial statement analysis requires an understanding of the composition of current financial statements. Understanding the composition of the current financial statements is necessary for analyzing cash flows (Chapter 3), profitability (Chapter 4), risk (Chapter 5), and especially accounting quality (Chapter 6), all of which help the analyst project future results (Chapter 10) so that the analyst can estimate the value of a firm (Chapters 11–14).

Overview of the Analytical Framework

The analytical framework relies on the balance sheet equation:

$$\text{Assets (A)} = \text{Liabilities (L)} + \text{Total Shareholders' Equity (TSE)}$$

We can expand total shareholders' equity (TSE) into its component parts, which will help identify the sources of changes in shareholders' net investment in a firm:

$$\begin{matrix} \text{Total Shareholders'} \\ \text{Equity} \end{matrix} = \begin{matrix} \text{Contributed} \\ \text{Capital (CC)} \end{matrix} + \begin{matrix} \text{Accumulated Other} \\ \text{Comprehensive Income (AOCI)} \end{matrix} + \begin{matrix} \text{Retained} \\ \text{Earnings (RE)} \end{matrix}$$

Contributed Capital (CC) accumulates net stock transactions with shareholders and includes accounts such as Common Stock, Additional Paid-in Capital, Treasury Stock, and other paid-in capital accounts. Accumulated Other Comprehensive Income (AOCI) is the "holding tank" discussed in Chapter 1, where unrealized gains or losses on certain assets and liabilities are held until realization occurs. Finally, Retained Earnings (RE) is simply the accumulation of all net income minus dividends (and occasionally other transactions, such as share repurchases).

Firms prepare balance sheets at the beginning and end of a period. Thus, for each component of the balance sheet equation, the following equations hold:

$$A_{BEG} + \Delta A = A_{END}$$
$$L_{BEG} + \Delta L = L_{END}$$
$$TSE_{BEG} + \Delta TSE = TSE_{END}$$

where *BEG* and *END* subscripts refer to beginning-of-period and end-of-period balances, respectively, and Δ indicates changes in balances. Changes in assets, liabilities, and total shareholders' equity over a period reflect the net effect of all individual transactions during the period, which is why it is important to understand how individual transactions affect the financial statements. Total shareholders' equity has multiple components, so it reflects the net of stock transactions with owners, the "holding tank" of unrealized gains and losses on certain assets and liabilities, and the accumulation of net income minus dividends in retained earnings. Because of these elements in TSE, it is helpful to partition the change into these components:

$$\Delta TSE = \frac{\text{Stock Transactions}}{(\Delta \text{ Stock})} + \frac{\text{Other Comprehensive}}{\text{Income (OCI)}} + \text{Net Income (NI)} - \text{Dividends (D)}$$

Thus, as a working framework for capturing beginning-of-period and end-of-period balance sheets as well as changes during the period (which include changes due to net income recognized on the income statement), we use the following framework to summarize transactions and events throughout this book:

$A_{BEG} =$	L_{BEG}	$+$	CC_{BEG}	$+$	$AOCI_{BEG}$	$+$	RE_{BEG}
$+\Delta A$	$+\Delta L$		$+\Delta \text{Stock}$		$+OCI$		$+NI$ $- D$
$A_{END} =$	L_{END}	$+$	CC_{END}	$+$	$AOCI_{END}$	$+$	RE_{END}

The following examples demonstrate how to apply this framework to several of the transactions described earlier in this chapter. For the transactions we analyze, we present the analytical framework showing how the transaction affects (decreases shown in parentheses) the categories of the balance sheet. We also present journal entries to show how each transaction will affect specific financial statement accounts.

Example 1—Capital Expenditures

In-N-Out Burger sells land with an acquisition cost of $210,000 for $300,000 in cash. For simplicity, assume that In-N-Out Burger pays taxes immediately at a 40% rate.

Assets		=	Liabilities	+	Shareholders' Equity		
					CC	AOCI	RE
1. Cash	300,000						Gain on Sale of Land 90,000
Land	(210,000)						

Cash			300,000				
Land					210,000		
Gain on Sale of Land					90,000		

Assets		=	Liabilities	+	Shareholders' Equity		
					CC	AOCI	RE
2. Cash	(36,000)						Income Tax Expense (36,000)

Income Tax Expense			36,000		$(0.40 \times [300,000 - 210,000])$		
Cash					36,000		

Note that if you wanted to compute overall changes in balance sheet accounts across a set of transactions, you need only sum the amounts within any partition. For example, the overall impact on assets of the above transactions is a net increase of $54,000, equal to the aggregation of +$300,000, −$210,000, and −$36,000. Similarly, to compute the net impact on income, sum the amounts in the Retained Earnings column. In the above transactions, the impact on *net income* is +$90,000 and −$36,000, or $54,000. Not surprisingly, the change in assets in this example exactly equals the change in retained earnings (because there were no effects on liabilities, contributed capital, or accumulated other comprehensive income).

Example 2—Sale of Inventory

Consider the following three events for **Mollydooker Wines**:

1. The sale of wine for $2,000,000 on account (Accounts Receivable)
2. The derecognition of the wine inventory with an accumulated cost of $1,600,000
3. The immediate payment of income taxes at a 40% rate

	Assets		=	Liabilities	+	Shareholders' Equity		
						CC	AOCI	RE
1.	Accounts Receivable	2,000,000						Sales 2,000,000
	Accounts Receivable			2,000,000				
	Sales					2,000,000		

	Assets		=	Liabilities	+	Shareholders' Equity		
						CC	AOCI	RE
2.	Inventory	(1,600,000)						Cost of Goods Sold (1,600,000)
	Cost of Goods Sold			1,600,000				
	Inventory					1,600,000		

	Assets		=	Liabilities	+	Shareholders' Equity		
						CC	AOCI	RE
3.	Cash	(160,000)						Income Tax Expense (160,000)
	Income Tax Expense			160,000			(0.40 × [2,000,000 − 1,600,000])	
	Cash					160,000		

Summing the increases and decreases in any column indicates the net effect of the wine sale (after taxes). For example, the change in assets as a result of this transaction is $2,000,000 − $1,600,000 − $160,000 = $240,000. Similarly, shareholders' equity increased by the same amount. This transaction has no other effect on Mollydooker's balance sheet. The income effects of this transaction are the sum of any effects reflected under RE that would appear on the income statement, which for this transaction would be +$2,000,000 (Sales), −$1,600,000 (Cost of Goods Sold), and −$160,000 (Tax Expense), for a net impact on income of +$240,000.

Example 3—Inventory Valuation

Smithfield Foods records an inventory write-down for live hog inventory, driven by the drop in market prices of live hogs. Live hog inventory with a book value of $882 million is written down by approximately 5%, or $44 million. Income tax law does not permit Smithfield Foods to deduct the write-down on the live hog inventory until the loss is realized. Thus, the 40% tax effect of the write-down becomes a deferred tax asset until that time. This leads to the recording of the following two effects:

Assets	=	Liabilities	+	Shareholders' Equity		
				CC	AOCI	RE
1. Inventory (44,000,000)						Inventory Write-Down Loss (44,000,000)

Inventory Write-Down Loss	44,000,000
Inventory	44,000,000

Assets	=	Liabilities	+	Shareholders' Equity		
				CC	AOCI	RE
2 Deferred Tax Asset 17,600,000						Income Tax Expense 17,600,000

Deferred Tax Asset	17,600,000
Income Tax Expense	17,600,000 (0.40 × 44,000,000)

The overall impact of the $44 million write-down is to decrease assets by $26.4 million ($44 million write-down offset by $17.6 million deferred tax effect). The same amount flows through to net income as well, reducing retained earnings.

Example 4—External Financing

Petroleo Brasileiro purchases computer equipment from **Sun Microsystems** and signs a five-year note payable in the amount of $998,178 (present value of $250,000 a year for five years at 8%). The purchase, use of the equipment, and first-year principal and interest payment trigger the following events to be recognized (ignore income taxes for this example):

1. Purchase of the computer equipment and signing of the note payable
2. Depreciation of $199,636 ($998,178 ÷ 5) on the computer for the first year based on a five-year useful life
3. Interest expense for the first year of $79,854 (0.08 × $998,178), the cash payment of $250,000, and the reduction in principal of $170,146 ($250,000 – $79,854)

Assets	=	Liabilities	+	Shareholders' Equity		
				CC	AOCI	RE
1. Computer Equipment 998,178		Note Payable 998,178				

Computer Equipment	998,178
Note Payable	998,178

Assets	=	Liabilities	+	Shareholders' Equity		
				CC	AOCI	RE
2. Accumulated Depreciation (199,636)						Depreciation Expense (199,636)

Depreciation Expense	199,636
Accumulated Depreciation	199,636

Assets	=	Liabilities	+	Shareholders' Equity		
				CC	AOCI	RE
3. Cash (250,000)		Note Payable (170,146)				Interest Expense (79,854)

Interest Expense	79,854
Note Payable	170,146
Cash	250,000

Example 5—Other Comprehensive Income

Note: This illustrates the framework if other comprehensive income is affected. The example is correct until 2018, when the gains and losses will be recognized immediately in net income rather than comprehensive income.

Microsoft invests in marketable equity securities. The following events occur:

1. Initial $4,500,000 investment in marketable equity securities
2. Increase in fair value as of December 31 to $4,900,000
3. Deferred tax effect of the unrealized gain (assume 40%)
4. Sale of marketable equity securities in June for $5,000,000
5. Settlement of the tax liability (assume taxes paid immediately after the sale)

	Assets	=	Liabilities	+	Shareholders' Equity		
					CC	AOCI	RE
1.	Marketable Equity Securities 4,500,000 Cash (4,500,000)						

Marketable Equity Securities	4,500,000	
Cash		4,500,000

	Assets	=	Liabilities	+	Shareholders' Equity		
					CC	AOCI	RE
2.	Marketable Equity Securities 400,000					Unrealized Holding Gain 400,000	

Marketable Equity Securities	400,000	
Unrealized Holding Gain		400,000

	Assets	=	Liabilities	+	Shareholders' Equity		
					CC	AOCI	RE
3.			Deferred Tax Liability 160,000			Unrealized Holding Gain (160,000)	

Unrealized Holding Gain	160,000	
Deferred Tax Liability		160,000

	Assets	=	Liabilities	+	Shareholders' Equity		
					CC	AOCI	RE
4.	Cash 5,000,000 Marketable Equity Securities (4,900,000)					Unrealized Holding Gain (400,000)	Gain on Sale of Marketable Equity Securities 500,000

Cash	5,000,000	
Unrealized Holding Gain	400,000	
Marketable Equity Securities		4,900,000
Gain on Sale of Marketable Equity Securities		500,000

	Assets	=	Liabilities	+	Shareholders' Equity		
					CC	AOCI	RE
5.	Cash (200,000)		Deferred Tax Liability (160,000)			Unrealized Holding Gain 160,000	Income Tax Expense (200,000)

Income Tax Expense	200,000		(0.40 × 500,000)
Deferred Tax Liability	160,000		
Unrealized Holding Gain		160,000	
Cash		200,000	

This example demonstrates the mechanics of how other comprehensive income affects the financial statements. At the end of the year, when Microsoft has an unrealized gain of $400,000, the value of the marketable equity securities is written up to its fair value of $4,900,000. Because this increase has not been realized in a market transaction (such as a sale), Microsoft puts this gain in the accumulated other comprehensive income "holding tank" rather than recognize it as part of net income. However, note that Microsoft will be required to present this amount as part of other comprehensive income on the statement of comprehensive income. The amount recognized as other comprehensive income is then closed out to the accumulated other comprehensive income account and labeled as unrealized holding gain or loss. When Microsoft sells the marketable equity securities in June, the $400,000 is removed from the "holding tank" of accumulated other comprehensive income and recognized in income as gain on sale, along with an additional $100,000 that occurred subsequent to December. Of course, the associated tax effects are accumulated and reversed from accumulated other comprehensive income as well. The overall net effect is that Microsoft realizes a $500,000 gain, offset by $200,000 of income tax expense, for an increase in net assets of $300,000.

Summary

This chapter provides a conceptual foundation for understanding the balance sheet and the income statement.

- U.S. GAAP, IFRS, and other major sets of accounting standards are best characterized as mixed attribute measurement models. Assets and liabilities on the balance sheet are valued using various methods based on historical and current values, depending on the nature of the asset or liability.
  - The conventional accounting model uses historical, or acquisition, costs to value assets and liabilities and delays the recognition of value changes until external market transactions validate their amounts. Use of acquisition costs generally results in more *representationally faithful* asset and liability valuations than do current values, but such valuations can lose *relevance*, especially as the time from the initial transactions passes and historical values diverge from current values.
- Recognizing value changes for assets and liabilities still leaves open the question of when the value change should affect net income. Such value changes may affect net income immediately or may affect it later, initially being temporarily held as accumulated other comprehensive income (in shareholders' equity) until validated through an external market transaction.
  - Over sufficiently long time periods, net income equals cash inflows minus cash outflows (excluding cash transactions with owners). Different approaches to asset and liability valuation and to income measurement affect the pattern of net income over time, but not its ultimate amount.
- Almost every transaction affecting net income has an income tax effect. The financial reporting issue is whether firms should recognize the income tax effect when the related revenue or expense affects net income or when it affects taxable income.
  - U.S. GAAP requires firms to measure income tax expense each period based on the pretax income for financial reporting, excluding permanent differences.
- When income tax expense differs from income taxes currently owed on taxable income, firms recognize deferred tax assets and deferred tax liabilities.
  - Deferred tax assets arise when taxable income exceeds book income. Firms prepay taxes now but reduce taxes paid later when the temporary difference reverses and book income exceeds taxable income.
  - Deferred tax liabilities are the opposite, arising when book income exceeds taxable income. Firms delay paying taxes now, but will pay the taxes later when the temporary differences reverse and taxable income exceeds book income.
  - Repeated use of the analytical framework will enable you to become proficient at understanding the link between transactions and events and the financial statements.

Questions, Exercises, Problems, and Cases

Questions and Exercises

LO 2-1

2.1 Relevance versus Representational Faithfulness. "Some asset valuations using historical costs are highly relevant and very representationally faithful, whereas others may be representationally faithful but lack relevance. Some asset valuations based on fair values are highly relevant and very representationally faithful, whereas others may be relevant but lack representational faithfulness." Explain and provide examples of each.

2.2 Asset Valuation and Income Recognition. "Asset valuation and recognition of net income closely relate." Explain, including conditions when they do not.   `LO 2-2`

2.3 Trade-Offs among Acceptable Accounting Alternatives. Firms value inventory under a variety of assumptions, including two common methods: last-in, first-out (LIFO) and first-in, first-out (FIFO). Ignore taxes, assume that prices increase over time, and assume that a firm's inventory balance is stable or grows over time. Which inventory method provides a balance sheet that better reflects the underlying economics, and why? Which method provides an income statement that better reflects the underlying economics, and why?   `LO 2-1`

2.4 Income Flows versus Cash Flows. The text states, "Over sufficiently long time periods, net income equals cash inflows minus cash outflows, other than cash flows with owners." Demonstrate the accuracy of this statement in the following scenario: Two friends contributed $50,000 each to form a new business. The owners used the amounts contributed to purchase a machine for $100,000 cash. They estimated that the useful life of the machine was five years and the salvage value was $20,000. They rented out the machine to a customer for an annual rental of $25,000 a year for five years. Annual cash operating costs for insurance, taxes, and other items totaled $6,000 annually. At the end of the fifth year, the owners sold the equipment for $22,000, instead of the $20,000 salvage value initially estimated. (*Hint: Compute the total net income and the total cash flows other than cash flows with owners for the five-year period as a whole.*)   `LO 2-1, LO 2-2`

2.5 Measurement of Acquisition Cost. United Van Lines purchased a truck with a list price of $250,000 subject to a 6% discount if paid within 30 days. United Van Lines paid within the discount period. It paid $4,000 to obtain title to the truck with the state and an $800 license fee for the first year of operation. It paid $1,500 to paint the firm's name on the truck and $2,500 for property and liability insurance for the first year of operation. What acquisition cost of this truck should United Van Lines record in its accounting records? Indicate the appropriate accounting treatment of any amount not included in acquisition cost.   `LO 2-1`

2.6 Measurement of a Monetary Asset. Assume **Boeing** sold a 767 aircraft to **American Airlines** on January 1, 2016. The sales agreement required American Airlines to pay $10 million immediately and $10 million on December 31 of each year for 20 years, beginning on December 31, 2016. Boeing and American Airlines judge that 8% is an appropriate interest rate for this arrangement.   `LO 2-1`
   a. Compute the present value of the receivable on Boeing's books on January 1, 2016, immediately after receiving the $10 million down payment.
   b. Compute the present value of the receivable on Boeing's books on December 31, 2016.
   c. Compute the present value of the receivable on Boeing's books on December 31, 2017.

2.7 Measurement of a Nonmonetary Asset. Assume **American Airlines** acquires a regional airline in the midwestern United States for $450 million. American Airlines allocates $150 million of the purchase price to landing rights at various airports. The landing rights expire in five years. What type of measurement is applicable to the valuation of the landing rights at acquisition and at the end of each of the five years?   `LO 2-1`

2.8 Fair Value Measurements. The text discusses inputs managers might use to determine fair values of assets and liabilities and identifies different classifications of assets identified in SFAS No. 157. Suppose a major university endowment has investments in a wide array of assets, including (a) common stocks; (b) bonds; (c) real estate; (d) timber investments, which receive cash flows from sales of timber; (e) private equity funds; and (f) illiquid asset-backed securities. Consider how the portfolio manager would estimate the fair values of each of those classes of assets, and characterize the inputs you identify as Level 1, Level 2, or Level 3.   `LO 2-1`

LO 2-3

2.9 Computation of Income Tax Expense. A firm's income tax return shows $50,000 of income taxes owed for 2017. For financial reporting, the firm reports deferred tax assets of $42,900 at the beginning of 2017 and $38,700 at the end of 2017. It reports deferred tax liabilities of $28,600 at the beginning of 2017 and $34,200 at the end of 2017.

a. Compute the amount of income tax expense for 2017.

b. Assume for this part that the firm's deferred tax assets are as stated above for 2017 but that its deferred tax liabilities were $58,600 at the beginning of 2017 and $47,100 at the end of 2017. Compute the amount of income tax expense for 2017.

c. Explain contextually why income tax expense is higher than taxes owed in Part a and lower than taxes owed in Part b.

LO 2-3

2.10 Computation of Income Tax Expense. A firm's income tax return shows income taxes for 2017 of $35,000. The firm reports deferred tax assets before any valuation allowance of $24,600 at the beginning of 2017 and $27,200 at the end of 2017. It reports deferred tax liabilities of $18,900 at the beginning of 2017 and $16,300 at the end of 2017.

a. Assume for this part that the valuation allowance on the deferred tax assets totaled $6,400 at the beginning of 2017 and $7,200 at the end of 2017. Compute the amount of income tax expense for 2017.

b. Assume for this part that the valuation allowance on the deferred tax assets totaled $6,400 at the beginning of 2017 and $4,800 at the end of 2017. Compute the amount of income tax expense for 2017.

Problems and Cases

LO 2-1

2.11 Costs to be Included in Historical Cost Valuation. At a cost of $200,000, assume **In-N-Out Burger** acquired a tract of land for a restaurant site. It paid attorneys $7,500 to conduct a title search and to prepare the required legal documents for the purchase. State real estate transfer taxes totaled $2,500. Building permits totaled $1,200. Compute the acquisition cost of the land.

LO 2-1, LO 2-2

2.12 Effect of Valuation Method for Nonmonetary Asset on Balance Sheet and Income Statement. Assume **Walmart** acquires a tract of land on January 1, 2016, for $100,000 cash. On December 31, 2016, the current market value of the land is $150,000. On December 31, 2017, the current market value of the land is $120,000. The firm sells the land on December 31, 2018, for $180,000 cash.

REQUIRED

Ignore income taxes. Indicate the effect on the balance sheet and income statement of the preceding information for 2016, 2017, and 2018 under each of the following valuation methods (Parts a–c).

a. Valuation of the land at acquisition cost until sale of the land (Approach 1)

b. Valuation of the land at current market value and including market value changes each year in net income (Approach 2)

c. Valuation of the land at current market value but including unrealized gains and losses in accumulated other comprehensive income until sale of the land (Approach 3)

d. Why is retained earnings on December 31, 2018, equal to $80,000 in all three cases despite the reporting of different amounts of net income each year?

LO 2-1, LO 2-2

2.13 Effect of Valuation Method for Monetary Asset on Balance Sheet and Income Statement. Refer to Problem 2.12. Assume that **Walmart** has accounted for the value of the land at acquisition cost and sells the land on December 31, 2018, for a two-year note receivable with a present value of $180,000 instead of for cash. The note bears interest at 8% and requires cash payments of $100,939 on December 31, 2019 and 2020. Interest rates for notes of this risk level increase to 10% on December 31, 2019, resulting in a market value for the note on this date of $91,762.

REQUIRED

Ignore income taxes. Indicate the effect on the balance sheet and income statement of the preceding information for 2018, 2019, and 2020 under each of the following valuation methods.

    a. Valuation of the note at the present value of future cash flows using the historical market interest rate of 8% (Approach 1)

    b. Valuation of the note at the present value of future cash flows, adjusting the note to fair value upon changes in market interest rates and including unrealized gains and losses in net income (Approach 2)

    c. Why is retained earnings on December 31, 2020, equal to $101,878 in both cases despite the reporting of different amounts of net income each year?

2.14 Effect of Valuation Method for Nonmonetary Asset on Balance Sheet and Income Statement. Assume **Southern Copper Corporation (SCCO)** acquired mining equipment for $100,000 cash on January 1, 2016. The equipment had an expected useful life of four years and zero salvage value. SCCO calculates depreciation using the straight-line method over the remaining expected useful life in all cases. On December 31, 2016, after recognizing depreciation for the year, SCCO learns that new equipment now offered on the market makes the purchased equipment partially obsolete. The market value of the equipment on December 31, 2016, reflecting this obsolescence, is $60,000. The expected useful life does not change. On December 31, 2017, the market value of the equipment is $48,000. SCCO sells the equipment on January 1, 2019, for $26,000.

LO 2-1, LO 2-2

REQUIRED

Ignore income taxes.

    a. Assume for this part that SCCO accounts for the equipment using historical cost adjusted for depreciation and impairment losses. Using the analytical framework discussed in the chapter, indicate the effects of the following events on the balance sheet and income statement.

        (1) Acquisition of the equipment for cash on January 1, 2016

        (2) Depreciation for 2016

        (3) Impairment loss for 2016

        (4) Depreciation for 2017

        (5) Depreciation for 2018

        (6) Sale of the equipment on January 1, 2019

    b. Assume that SCCO accounts for the equipment using current fair market values adjusted for depreciation and impairment losses (with changes in fair market values recognized in net income). Using the analytical framework discussed in the chapter, indicate the effect of the following events on the balance sheet and income statement.

        (1) Acquisition of the equipment for cash on January 1, 2016

        (2) Depreciation for 2016

        (3) Impairment loss for 2016

        (4) Depreciation for 2017

        (5) Recognition of unrealized holding gain or loss for 2017

        (6) Depreciation for 2018

        (7) Recognition of unrealized holding gain or loss for 2018

        (8) Sale of the equipment on January 1, 2019

c. After the equipment is sold, why is retained earnings on January 1, 2019, equal to a negative $74,000 in both cases despite having shown a different pattern of expenses, gains, and losses over time?

LO 2-1, LO 2-2 **2.15 Effect of Valuation Method for Monetary Asset on Balance Sheet and Income Statement.** Alfa Romeo incurs direct cash costs of $30,000 in manufacturing a red convertible automobile during 2016. Assume that it incurs all of these costs in cash. Alfa Romeo sells this automobile to you on January 1, 2017, for $45,000. You pay $5,000 immediately and agree to make annual payments of $14,414 on December 31, 2017, 2018, and 2019. Based on the interest rate appropriate for this note of 4% on January 1, 2019, the present value of the note is $40,000. The interest rate appropriate for this note is 5% on December 31, 2017, resulting in a present value of the remaining cash flows of $26,802. The interest rate appropriate for this note is 8% on December 31, 2018, resulting in a present value of the remaining cash flows of $13,346.

REQUIRED

Ignore income taxes.

a. Assume that Alfa Romeo accounts for this note throughout the three years using its initial present value and the historical interest rate (Approach 1). Indicate the effects of the following events on the balance sheet and income statement. For example, the response to (1) would be: Cash decreases $30,000, and inventory increases $30,000, resulting in no change in total assets.
   (1) Manufacture of the automobile during 2016
   (2) Sale of the automobile on January 1, 2017
   (3) Cash received and interest revenue recognized on December 31, 2017
   (4) Cash received and interest revenue recognized on December 31, 2018
   (5) Cash received and interest revenue recognized on December 31, 2019
b. Assume that Alfa Romeo values this note receivable at fair value each year with fair value changes recognized in net income (Approach 2). Changes in market interest rates affect the valuation of the note on the balance sheet immediately and the computation of interest revenue for the next year. Indicate the effects of the following events on the balance sheet and income statement.
   (1) Manufacture of the automobile during 2016
   (2) Sale of the automobile on January 1, 2017
   (3) Cash received and interest revenue recognized on December 31, 2017
   (4) Note receivable revalued and an unrealized holding gain or loss recognized on December 31, 2017
   (5) Cash received and interest revenue recognized on December 31, 2018
   (6) Note receivable revalued and an unrealized holding gain or loss recognized on December 31, 2018
   (7) Cash received and interest revenue recognized on December 31, 2019
c. Why is retained earnings on December 31, 2019, equal to $18,242 in both cases, despite having shown a different pattern of income over time?
d. Discuss the trade-off in financial reporting when moving from Approach 1 in Part a to Approach 2 in Part b.

LO 2-3 **2.16 Deferred Tax Assets.** Components of the deferred tax asset of **Biosante Pharmaceuticals, Inc.,** are shown in Exhibit 2.10. The company had no deferred tax liabilities.

REQUIRED

a. At the end of 2008, the largest deferred tax asset is for net operating loss carryforwards. (Net operating loss carryforwards, also referred to as tax loss carryforwards, are amounts

Exhibit 2.10		
Biosante Pharmaceuticals, Inc. **Income Tax Disclosures (Problem 2.16)**		
	2008	**2007**
Net operating loss carryforwards	$ 23,609,594	$ 17,588,392
Tax basis in intangible assets	403,498	538,819
Research and development credits	3,415,143	2,569,848
Stock option expense	1,462,065	1,017,790
Other	56,063	103,235
Gross Deferred Tax Asset	$ 28,946,363	$ 21,818,084
Valuation allowance	(28,946,363)	(21,818,084)
Net Deferred Tax Asset	$ 0	$ 0

At December 31, 2008, the company had approximately $62,542,000 of net operating loss carryforwards available to reduce future taxable income for a period of up to 20 years. The net operating loss carryforwards expire in 2018–2028. The net operating loss carryforwards as well as amortization of various intangibles, principally acquired in-process research and development, generate deferred tax benefits that have been recorded as deferred tax assets and are entirely offset by a tax valuation allowance. The valuation allowance has been provided at 100% to reduce the deferred tax assets to zero, the amount management believes is more likely than not to be realized. In addition, the company has provided a full valuation allowance against $3,415,143 of research and development credits, which are available to reduce future income taxes, if any, through 2028.

Source: Biosante Pharmaceuticals, Inc., Form 10-K, for the fiscal year ended December 31, 2008.

reported as taxable losses on tax filings. Because the tax authorities generally do not "pay" corporations for incurring losses, companies are allowed to "carry forward" taxable losses to future years to offset taxable income. These future tax benefits give rise to deferred tax assets.) As of the end of 2008, what is the dollar amount of the company's net operating loss carryforwards? What is the dollar amount of the deferred tax asset for the net operating loss carryforwards? Describe how these two amounts are related.

b. Biosante has gross deferred tax assets of $28,946,363. However, the net deferred tax assets balance is zero. Explain.

c. The valuation allowance for the deferred tax asset increased from $21,818,084 to $28,946,363 between 2007 and 2008. How did this change affect the company's net income?

2.17 Interpreting Income Tax Disclosures. The financial statements of ABC   LO 2-3
Corporation, a retail chain, reveal the information for income taxes shown in Exhibit 2.11.

REQUIRED

a. Assuming that ABC had no significant permanent differences between book income and taxable income, did income before taxes for financial reporting exceed or fall short of taxable income for 2013? Explain.

b. Did income before taxes for financial reporting exceed or fall short of taxable income for 2014? Explain.

c. Will the adjustment to net income for deferred taxes to compute cash flow from operations in the statement of cash flows result in an addition or a subtraction for 2013? For 2014?

Exhibit 2.11

ABC Corporation Income Tax Disclosures
(amounts in millions) (Problem 2.17)

For the Year Ended January 31:	2014	2013	
Income before income taxes	$3,031	$2,603	
Income tax expense			
Current:			
Federal	$ 908	$ 669	
State and local	144	107	
Total Current	$1,052	$ 776	
Deferred:			
Federal	$ 83	$ 184	
State and local	11	24	
Total Deferred	$ 94	$ 208	
Total	$1,146	$ 984	

January 31:	2014	2013	2012
Components of deferred tax assets and liabilities			
Deferred tax assets:			
Self-insured benefits	$ 179	$ 143	$ 188
Deferred compensation	332	297	184
Inventory	47	44	56
Postretirement health care obligation	38	42	41
Uncollectible accounts	147	133	113
Other	128	53	166
Total Deferred Tax Assets	$ 871	$ 712	$ 748
Deferred tax liabilities:			
Depreciation	$(1,136)	$ (945)	$ (826)
Pensions	(268)	(218)	(190)
Other	(96)	(84)	(59)
Total Deferred Tax Liabilities	$(1,500)	$(1,247)	$(1,075)
Net Deferred Tax Liability	$ (629)	$ (535)	$ (327)

d. ABC does not contract with an insurance agency for property and liability insurance; instead, it self-insures. ABC recognizes an expense and a liability each year for financial reporting to reflect its average expected long-term property and liability losses. When it experiences an actual loss, it charges that loss against the liability. The income tax law permits self-insured firms to deduct such losses only in the year sustained. Why are deferred taxes related to self-insurance disclosed as a deferred tax asset instead of a deferred tax liability? Suggest reasons for the direction of the change in amounts for this deferred tax asset between 2012 and 2014.

e. ABC treats certain storage and other inventory costs as expenses in the year incurred for financial reporting but must include these in inventory for tax reporting. Why are deferred taxes related to inventory disclosed as a deferred tax asset? Suggest reasons for the direction of the change in amounts for this deferred tax asset between 2012 and 2014.

f. Firms must recognize expenses related to postretirement health care and pension obligations as employees provide services, but claim an income tax deduction only when they make cash payments under the benefit plan. Why are deferred taxes related to health care obligations disclosed as a deferred tax asset? Why are deferred taxes related to pensions disclosed as a deferred tax liability? Suggest reasons for the direction of the change in amounts for these deferred tax items between 2012 and 2014.

g. Firms must recognize expenses related to uncollectible accounts when they recognize sales revenues, but firms claim an income tax deduction when they deem a particular customer's accounts uncollectible. Why are deferred taxes related to this item disclosed as a deferred tax asset? Suggest reasons for the direction of the change in amounts for this deferred tax asset between 2012 and 2014.

h. ABC uses the straight-line depreciation method for financial reporting and accelerated depreciation methods for income tax purposes. Why are deferred taxes related to depreciation disclosed as a deferred tax liability? Suggest reasons for the direction of the change in amounts for this deferred tax liability between 2012 and 2014.

2.18 Interpreting Income Tax Disclosures. Prepaid Legal Services (PPD) `LO 2-3`
is a company that sells insurance for legal expenses. Customers pay premiums in advance for coverage over some specified period. Thus, PPD obtains cash but has unearned revenue until the passage of time over the specified period of coverage. Also, the company pays various costs to acquire customers (such as sales materials, commissions, and prepayments to legal firms that provide services to customers). These upfront payments are expensed over the specified period that customers' contracts span. Exhibit 2.12 provides information from PPD's income tax note.

REQUIRED

a. Assuming that PPD had no significant permanent differences between book income and taxable income, did income before taxes for financial reporting exceed or fall short of taxable income for 2007? For 2008? Explain.

b. Will the adjustment to net income for deferred taxes to compute cash flow from operations in the statement of cash flows result in an addition or a subtraction for 2007? For 2008?

c. PPD must report as taxable income premiums collected from customers, although the company defers recognizing them as income for financial reporting purposes until they are earned over the contract period. Why are deferred taxes related to deferred revenue disclosed as a deferred tax asset instead of a deferred tax liability? Suggest reasons for the direction of the change in amounts for this deferred tax asset between 2007 and 2008.

d. Firms are generally allowed to deduct cash costs on their tax returns, although they might defer some of these costs for financial reporting purposes. As noted above, PPD defers various costs associated with obtaining customers. Why are deferred taxes related to this item disclosed as a deferred tax liability? Suggest reasons for the direction of the change in amounts for this deferred tax asset between 2007 and 2008.

e. Like most companies, PPD uses the straight-line depreciation method for financial reporting and accelerated depreciation methods for income tax purposes. Why are deferred

Exhibit 2.12

Prepaid Legal Services Income Tax Disclosures
(Problem 2.18)

The provision for income taxes consists of the following:

	2008	2007	2006
Current	$36,840	$33,864	$27,116
Deferred	385	(552)	774
Total Provision for Income Taxes	$37,225	$33,312	$27,890

Deferred tax liabilities and assets at December 31, 2007 and 2008, respectively, are comprised of the following:

	2008	2007
Deferred tax liabilities relating to:		
Deferred member and associate service costs	$ 6,919	$ 7,367
Property and equipment	8,693	7,829
Unrealized investment gains	159	131
Total Deferred Tax Liabilities	$15,771	$15,327
Deferred tax assets relating to:		
Expenses not yet deducted for tax purposes	$ 4,028	$ 3,552
Deferred revenue and fees	11,138	11,564
Other	110	101
Total Deferred Tax Assets	$15,276	$15,217
Net Deferred Tax Liability	$ (495)	$ (110)

taxes related to depreciation disclosed as a deferred tax liability? Suggest reasons for the direction of the change in amounts for this deferred tax liability between 2007 and 2008.

f. Based only on the selected disclosures from the income tax footnote provided in Exhibit 2.12 and your responses to Parts d and e above, do you believe that PPD reported growing or declining revenue and profitability in 2008 relative to 2007? Explain.

 2.19 Interpreting Income Tax Disclosures. The financial statements of **Nike, Inc.**, reveal the information regarding income taxes shown in Exhibit 2.13.

REQUIRED

a. Assuming that Nike had no significant permanent differences between book income and taxable income, did income before taxes for financial reporting exceed or fall short of taxable income for 2007? Explain.

b. Did book income before taxes for financial reporting exceed or fall short of taxable income for 2008? Explain.

c. Will the adjustment to net income for deferred taxes to compute cash flow from operations in the statement of cash flows result in an addition or a subtraction for 2008?

Exhibit 2.13

Nike, Inc., Income Tax Disclosures (amounts in millions) (Problem 2.19)

Income before income taxes is as follows:	2008	2007	2006
Income before income taxes:			
United States	$ 713.0	$ 805.1	$ 838.6
Foreign	1,789.9	1,394.8	1,303.0
	$2,502.9	$2,199.9	$2,414.6

The provision for income taxes consists of the following:	2008	2007	2006
Current:			
United States			
Federal	$ 469.9	$352.6	$359.0
State	58.4	59.6	60.6
Foreign	391.8	261.9	356.0
	$ 920.1	$674.1	$775.6
Deferred:			
United States			
Federal	$(273.0)	$ 38.7	$ (4.2)
State	(5.0)	(4.8)	(6.8)
Foreign	(22.6)	0.4	(15.0)
	$(300.6)	$ 34.3	$ (26.0)
Total Provision for Income Taxes	$ 619.5	$708.4	$749.6

Deferred tax assets and (liabilities) are comprised of the following:	2008	2007
Deferred tax assets:		
Allowance for doubtful accounts	$ 13.1	$ 12.4
Inventories	49.2	45.8
Sales returns reserves	49.2	42.1
Deferred compensation	158.4	132.5
Stock-based compensation	55.2	30.3
Reserves and accrued liabilities	57.0	46.2
Property, plant, and equipment	7.9	16.3
Foreign loss carry-forwards	40.1	37.5
Foreign tax credit carry-forwards	91.9	3.4
Hedges	42.9	26.2
Other	40.5	33.0
Total Deferred Tax Assets	$ 605.4	$ 425.7
Valuation allowance	(40.7)	(42.3)
Total Deferred Tax Assets after Valuation Allowance	$ 564.7	$ 383.4

(Continued)

Exhibit 2.13 (Continued)

Deferred tax liabilities:		
Undistributed earnings of foreign subsidiaries	$(113.2)	$(232.6)
Property, plant, and equipment	(67.4)	(66.1)
Intangibles	(214.2)	(97.2)
Hedges	(1.3)	(2.5)
Other	(0.7)	(17.8)
Total Deferred Tax Liability	$(396.8)	$(416.2)
Net Deferred Tax Asset (Liability)	$ 167.9	$ (32.8)

d. Nike recognizes provisions for sales returns and doubtful accounts each year in computing income for financial reporting. Nike cannot claim an income tax deduction for these returns and doubtful accounts until customers return goods or accounts receivable become uncollectible. Why do the deferred taxes for returns and doubtful accounts appear as deferred tax assets instead of deferred tax liabilities? Suggest possible reasons why the deferred tax asset for sales returns and doubtful accounts increased between 2007 and 2008.

e. Nike recognizes an expense related to deferred compensation as employees render services but cannot claim an income tax deduction until it pays cash to a retirement fund. Why do the deferred taxes for deferred compensation appear as a deferred tax asset? Suggest possible reasons why the deferred tax asset increased between 2007 and 2008.

f. Nike states that it recognizes a valuation allowance on deferred tax assets related to foreign loss carryforwards because the benefits of some of these losses will expire before the firm realizes the benefits. Why might the valuation allowance have decreased slightly between 2007 and 2008?

g. Nike reports a large deferred tax liability for intangibles. In another footnote, Nike states, "During the fourth quarter ended May 31, 2008 the Company completed the acquisition of **Umbro Plc** ('Umbro'). As a result, $378.4 million was allocated to unamortized trademarks, $319.2 million was allocated to goodwill and $41.1 million was allocated to other amortized intangible assets consisting of Umbro's sourcing network, established customer relationships and the United Soccer League Franchise." Why would Nike report a deferred tax liability associated with this increase in intangible assets on the balance sheet?

h. Nike recognizes its share of the earnings of foreign subsidiaries each year for financial reporting but recognizes income from these investments for income tax reporting only when it receives a dividend. Why do the deferred taxes related to these investments appear as a deferred tax liability?

i. Why does Nike recognize both deferred tax assets and deferred tax liabilities related to investments in foreign operations?

LO 2-4 **2.20 Analyzing Transactions.** Using the analytical framework, indicate the effect of the following related transactions of a firm.

a. January 1: Issued 10,000 shares of common stock for $50,000.

b. January 1: Acquired a building costing $35,000, paying $5,000 in cash and borrowing the remainder from a bank.

c. During the year: Acquired inventory costing $40,000 on account from various suppliers.

d. During the year: Sold inventory costing $30,000 for $65,000 on account.

e. During the year: Paid employees $15,000 as compensation for services rendered during the year.

f. During the year: Collected $45,000 from customers related to sales on account.

g. During the year: Paid merchandise suppliers $28,000 related to purchases on account.

h. December 31: Recognized depreciation on the building of $7,000 for financial reporting. Depreciation expense for income tax purposes was $10,000.

i. December 31: Recognized compensation for services rendered during the last week in December but not paid by year-end of $4,000.

j. December 31: Recognized and paid interest on the bank loan in Part b of $2,400 for the year.

k. Recognized income taxes on the net effect of the preceding transactions at an income tax rate of 40%. Assume that the firm pays cash immediately for any taxes currently due to the government.

2.21 Analyzing Transactions. Using the analytical framework, indicate the effect of [LO 2-4]
each of the three independent sets of transactions described next.

(1) a. January 15, 2014: Purchased marketable equity securities for $100,000.

 b. December 31, 2014: Revalued the marketable securities to their market value of $90,000. Unrealized changes in the market value of marketable equity securities appear in accumulated other comprehensive income. (This is the correct treatment pre-2018.)

 c. December 31, 2014: Recognized income tax effects of the revaluation in Part b at an income tax rate of 40%. The income tax law includes changes in the market value of equity securities in taxable income only when the investor sells the securities.

 d. January 5, 2015: Sold the marketable equity securities for $94,000.

 e. January 5, 2015: Recognized the tax effect of the sale of the securities in Part d. Assume that the tax is paid in cash immediately.

(2) a. During 2015: Sold inventory on account for $500,000.

 b. During 2015: The cost of the goods sold in Part a is $400,000.

 c. During 2015: Estimated that uncollectible accounts on the goods sold in Part a will equal 2% of the selling price.

 d. During 2015: Estimated that warranty claims on the goods sold in Part a will equal 4% of the selling price.

 e. During 2015: Actual accounts written off as uncollectible totaled $3,000.

 f. During 2015: Actual cash expenditures on warranty claims totaled $8,000.

 g. December 31, 2015: Recognized income tax effects of the preceding six transactions. The income tax rate is 40%. The income tax law permits a deduction for uncollectible accounts when a firm writes off accounts as uncollectible and for warranty claims when a firm makes warranty expenditures. Assume that any tax is paid in cash immediately.

(3) a. January 1, 2015: Purchased $100,000 face value of zero-coupon bonds for $68,058. These bonds mature on December 31, 2019, and are priced on the market at the time of issuance to yield 8% compounded annually. Zero-coupon bonds earn interest as time passes for financial and tax reporting, but the issuer does not pay interest until maturity. Assume that any tax owed on taxable income is paid in cash immediately.

 b. December 31, 2015: Recognized interest revenue on the bonds for 2015.

 c. December 31, 2015: Recognized income tax effect of the interest revenue for 2015. The income tax law taxes interest on zero-coupon bonds as it accrues each year.

    d. December 31, 2016: Recognized interest revenue on the bonds for 2016.
    e. December 31, 2016: Recognized income tax effect of the interest revenue for 2016.
    f. January 2, 2017: Sold the zero-coupon bonds for $83,683.
    g. January 2, 2017: Recognized the income tax effect of the gain or loss on the sale. The applicable income tax rate is 40%, which affects cash immediately.

LO 2-3

INTEGRATIVE CASE 2.1

Walmart

Exhibits 1.19–1.21 of Integrative Case 1.1 (Chapter 1) present the financial statements for Walmart for 2012–2015. In addition, the website for this text contains Walmart's December 31, 2015, Form 10-K. Use this information, especially Note 9, "Taxes," to answer the following questions:

REQUIRED

a. Assuming that Walmart had no significant permanent differences between book income and taxable income, did income before taxes for financial reporting exceed or fall short of taxable income for the year ending January 31, 2016 (hereafter, fiscal 2015)? Explain.

b. Assuming all current taxes are paid in cash, will the adjustment to net income for deferred taxes to compute cash flow from operations in the statement of cash flows result in an addition or subtraction for fiscal 2015?

c. Walmart reports deferred revenue for sales of gift certificates and for Sam's Club membership fees. These amounts are taxed when collected, but not recognized in financial reporting income until tendered at a store. Why does the tax effect of deferred revenue appear as a deferred tax asset?

d. Walmart recognizes a valuation allowance on its deferred tax assets to reflect net operating losses of consolidated foreign subsidiaries. The valuation allowance decreased over the last year. What effect does this have on net income in the most recent year (fiscal 2015)?

e. Walmart uses the straight-line depreciation method for financial reporting and accelerated depreciation for income tax reporting. Like most firms, the largest deferred tax liability is for property, plant, and equipment (depreciation). Explain how depreciation leads to a deferred tax liability. Suggest possible reasons why the amount of the deferred tax liability related to depreciation decreased over the last year.

Income Flows versus Cash Flows: Understanding the Statement of Cash Flows

LEARNING OBJECTIVES

LO 3-1 Identify the purpose of the statement of cash flows and the importance of understanding a firm's cash flows.

LO 3-2 Describe the structure and interpretation of operating, investing, and financing cash flow activities on the statement of cash flows.

LO 3-3 Analyze information in the statement of cash flows to determine where the firm is in its life cycle.

LO 3-4 Understand the relations among the statement of cash flows, the income statement, and the balance sheet.

LO 3-5 Prepare a statement of cash flows from balance sheet and income statement data.

LO 3-6 Examine additional uses of cash flow information.

Chapter Overview

This chapter's focus is on the *statement of cash flows*. In addition to a balance sheet and an income statement, discussed in the previous chapter, U.S. GAAP and IFRS require firms to provide a statement of cash flows each period. First, we explore the partitioning of cash flows into operating, investing, and financing activities; we then examine how various patterns of cash flows reflect various stages of firm life cycles. Second, the chapter illustrates how the balance sheet, income statement, and statement of cash flows are linked. Third, the chapter walks you through the nuts and bolts of preparing the statement of cash flows using information from the balance sheet and income statement. If you understand how to prepare a cash flow statement, you will have a much greater ability to interpret the information in the statement. Finally, the last part of the chapter provides a prelude to how you can use your understanding of the relation between net income and cash flows to draw inferences about earnings quality, liquidity, and credit risk, and calculate free cash flows that you can use in valuations.[1]

---

[1]Analysis of liquidity and credit risk are discussed more fully in Chapter 5; analysis of earnings quality is formally addressed in Chapter 6.

Purpose of the Statement of Cash Flows

The objective of the statement of cash flows is to assist users in understanding the cash *inflows* and *outflows* that arise from a firm's primary activities. Just as the income statement gives you an understanding of how the business performed during the period, the statement of cash flows gives you an understanding of how the business generated and used cash.

Under the frequently used *indirect method* of preparing the statement of cash flows, the statement of cash flows reconciles net income with the net change in cash during the period. Additionally, the statement of cash flows provides numerous insights not available from either the balance sheet or the income statement. The statement of cash flows

- reports all of the sources and uses of cash during a period.
- is logically organized into three sections (*operating* activities, *investing* activities, and *financing* activities), which correspond to the primary activities necessary to support a business and generate profits.
- provides useful information helpful in uncovering accounting discretion.

The accountant's job is to take observed cash flows, along with other events, employ accrual accounting procedures, and prepare the income statement and balance sheet under accrual accounting principles, which do not necessarily align with the timing of cash flows. As discussed in the last chapter, accrual accounting exists to help investors better predict the nature, amount, and timing of future cash flows. In contrast, the statement of cash flows "unravels" the accrual accounting procedures employed in the preparation of the balance sheet and income statement to reveal the underlying cash flows.

The primary purpose of the statement of cash flows is to provide financial statement users with information about a firm's cash receipts and payments that cause the change in the cash balance on the balance sheet. This is accounting in its simplest form:

Beginning Cash + Cash Receipts − Cash Expenditures = Ending Cash Balance

Net cash flows for a period should equal the change in cash for the period. FASB's *Codification Topic 230* and IASB's *International Accounting Standard 7* define cash flows in terms of their effect on the balance of *cash and cash equivalents*. Cash equivalents include highly liquid short-term investments that are readily convertible into cash, including very-short-term Treasury bills, commercial paper, and money market funds. Both U.S. GAAP and IFRS indicate that a maturity date of three months or less would generally qualify short-term investments as cash equivalents. Throughout this book, the term *cash* is used to mean cash and cash equivalents as defined under both U.S. GAAP and IFRS.

On the statement of cash flows, net cash flows equal the (net) sum of cash flows provided by or used for operating, investing, and financing activities. Refer again to **Starbucks'** statement of cash flows in Appendix A. The net cash flow for **Starbucks** during 2015 is the sum of $3,749 million (operations), −$1,520 million (investing), and −$2,257 million (financing), a net change in cash of −$28 million. The balance sheet indicates that cash and cash equivalents declined from $1,708 million to $1,530 million during 2015, a decrease of $178 million. The difference between net cash flows of −$28 million and the actual decrease in cash and cash equivalents of $178 million is $150 million. This reconciling amount is highlighted at the bottom of the statement of cash flows as the effect of exchange rate changes on the measurement of cash and cash equivalents (based on the fair value approach described in Chapter 2). This difference shows that **Starbucks'** cash and cash equivalents experienced negative effects from exchange rate changes, which reduced the U.S. dollar value of **Starbucks'** cash balances at the end of 2015.

Cash Flows versus Net Income

A firm's cash flows will differ from net income each period because

- cash receipts from customers do not necessarily occur in the same period the firm recognizes revenues.
- cash expenditures do not necessarily occur in the same period firms recognize expenses.
- cash inflows and outflows from investing and financing activities do not immediately flow through the income statement.

A primary objective of the income statement is to measure and report profitability under accrual accounting. Accrual accounting measures net income for a period based on the revenues generated that period (the assets created or liabilities satisfied through transactions with customers), minus the expenses incurred in that period (assets consumed or liabilities created through activities in the normal course of business operations). Measurement of net income does not depend on the timing of the inflows and outflows of cash during that period. Nevertheless, it is easy to demonstrate that accrual-based income is more predictive of future cash flows than are cash flows. This point cannot be overemphasized. Scores of finance textbooks criticize accrual-based income as unreliable because it can supposedly be easily manipulated by managers. Consider, however, manipulation of income versus cash flows. If a manager attempts to manipulate income upwards by, say, underestimating bad debt expense, not only will this be subject to scrutiny by auditors, analysts, investors, and regulators, but it will be revealed in future periods when the allowance for bad debts is outpaced by write-offs of accounts receivable. On the other hand, a manager can very easily manipulate cash flows simply by delaying payments to suppliers or selling off assets. In contrast to the auditing and scrutiny of reported income and the timing of revenue and expense recognition, there is no commensurate level of coordinated auditing and scrutiny of the timing of cash flows.

Of course, cash is essential for operating, investing, and financing activities. Accordingly, investors are keenly interested in the inflows and outflows of cash across reporting periods. Thus, it is essential that firms provide a statement of cash flows to report the flows of cash in and out of the firm each period. In addition to providing information on cash inflows and outflows, the statement of cash flows is useful for interpreting information on the balance sheet and income statement, as we will discuss later.

Cash Flows and Financial Analysis

Your understanding of a firm's cash flows will play an important role when you perform the six steps in financial statement analysis discussed in Chapter 1:

- **Identify the Economic Characteristics of a Business:** You will see dramatic differences in the pattern of cash flows from operating, investing, and financing activities among various types of businesses as well as throughout various stages of a firm's life cycle. For example, high-growth, capital-intensive firms generally experience insufficient cash flow from operations to finance capital expenditures (investing activities); thus, they require external sources of capital (financing activities). In contrast, mature companies usually can use cash flows from operations to finance capital expenditures and to repay debt, pay dividends, or repurchase common stock (financing activities).

- **Identify the Strategy of the Firm:** The statement of cash flows will reveal to you the overall strategy of a firm, especially how the firm generates and uses cash to execute its operating, investing, and financing strategies, as well as its growth strategies. For example, a firm opting for organic growth will exhibit large positive cash flows from operations, which it funnels into investing activities. On the other hand, a firm growing by acquiring other firms will report significant cash outflows for corporate acquisitions (investing activities) and, perhaps, large cash inflows from financing activities to raise debt and equity capital to finance the acquisitions.

- **Identify Nonrecurring, Unusual Items and Provide Insight into the Use of Accounting Discretion by Managers:** The cash flow statement provides you with information about the cash versus noncash components of unusual items, such as one-time gains or losses and discontinued operations. In addition, if you choose to eliminate nonrecurring or unusual items from net income to more clearly assess operating profitability, then you also should adjust the relevant parts of the cash flow statement. You also will find that the reconciling adjustments in the operating section, which report the noncash components of revenues and expenses, can sometimes reveal the extent to which managers use accounting discretion to affect reported earnings.

- **Analyze Profitability and Risk:** You learned in Chapter 2 that over sufficiently long periods, net income equals the net cash flows from operating, investing, and nonowner financing activities. Thus, a reality check on reported net income is that it should converge to operating cash flows as a firm matures and transitions into more of a "steady state," although they both will fluctuate from one period to the next. Also, the ability of a firm to generate sufficient cash flow from operations to finance capital expenditures and adequately service debt obligations is a key signal of the financial health of the firm.

- **Prepare Forecasted Financial Statements:** As Chapter 10 will show you, forecasting is the most important part of firm valuation. Forecasting profitability is incomplete without forecasts of all balance sheet items. Together, the forecasted income statement and balance sheet imply a series of cash flows. For example, you may forecast continued growth in net income when you see continued investments in productive assets. However, a key determinant of such forecasts is how the firm will generate the cash necessary to finance future growth, such as internally generated cash flow versus externally obtained financing.

- **Value the Firm:** Chapter 12 discusses firm valuation based on "free cash flows" to equity shareholders, which is cash flow available for distribution to investors after the firm makes necessary reinvestments in operating assets or required payments to debtholders. The statement of cash flows provides information needed to calculate free cash flows.

- The statement of cash flows reveals cash flows relative to reported net income.

- Analyzing the statement of cash flows is an integral part of the six-step process of financial statement analysis.

The Relations among the Cash Flow Activities

LO 3-2

Describe the structure and interpretation of operating, investing, and financing cash flow activities on the statement of cash flows.

The organization of the statement of cash flows partitions a firm's activities into three logical sections: *operating* activities, *investing* activities, and *financing* activities. One intuitive way to think about a firm is that it generates cash inflows and outflows every day from its operating activities, and continually reinvests cash by investing it in long-term productive assets; cash shortfalls trigger the need for new financing, whereas excess cash flows allow a firm to distribute cash by paying off debt or paying dividends to shareholders. The three sections of the statement of cash flows follow this logical progression. The activities to start up a firm, however, occur in reverse order: the firm first obtains cash through financing activities, like issuing equity and debt, then the firm invests the cash in productive assets, followed by generating cash flows from operating activities. Chapters 6, 7, and 8 follow this sequence.

Operating activities include all activities directly involving the production and delivery of goods or services; examples include cash received from customers and cash used to purchase raw materials and to compensate employees. The *investing activities* section chronicles expenditures for and proceeds from dispositions of assets, such as equipment and joint ventures, that are intended to be used to generate cash flows. Also logically included in the investing section are cash flows related to acquisitions and divestitures. The section summarizing *financing activities* of the firm includes cash received from and paid to capital providers such as banks, other lending institutions, and shareholders. The sum of subtotals for net operating, investing, and financing activities' cash flows reconcile with the *net increase* or *decrease* in cash and cash equivalents shown on the balance sheet.

As an example, refer to **Starbucks'** Consolidated Statement of Cash Flows in Appendix A. Note the three activity sections presented in the statement of cash flows. As we will discuss later, **Starbucks** reports the operating activities section using the "indirect method," which unravels the accrual accounting entries that determine net income, which then reveal the underlying cash flows. For all years presented, **Starbucks** generates a great deal of cash from its core operations (as shown in the operating section) and uses much of it to invest in productive assets (shown in the investing section) and to return cash to capital providers (shown in the financing section). For example, in 2015, **Starbucks** generated $3,749 million from operating activities and used $1,520 million for investing activities and $2,257 million for financing activities. For **Starbucks**, the net of operating, investing, and financing activities is a decrease in cash and cash equivalents of $178 million (which includes an adjustment for the effects of exchange rate changes on cash balances).

Note several important line items in **Starbucks'** statement of cash flows for 2015. First, the largest adjustment in the operating section is for the addback of $934 million of depreciation and amortization expense to **Starbucks'** $2,759 million of net income. Second, the next largest adjustment is the addback of $394 million of gains from sales of equity in joint ventures and retail operations. This gain is added back to keep it from being double-counted, as the proceeds from such sales (equal to the book value of the asset *plus* the gain) should appear as cash inflows in the investing activities section. Third, the sum of adjustments for other noncash components of income (from "Litigation charge" through "Other") is $172 million, indicating a net positive adjustment to net income for these items. Fourth, the adjustments for changes in working capital accounts (from "Accounts receivable" through "Prepaid expenses, other current assets and other long-term assets") is $279 million, indicating a decrease of investments in net working capital during 2015. For example, the positive adjustment of $137.7 million for accounts payable reflects a source of cash as the company allowed payables to rise. Fifth, investing cash flows primarily reflects capital expenditures (i.e., "Additions to property, plant and equipment" of $1,304 million). Sixth, the financing section shows that **Starbucks** raised $849 million from issuing long-term debt and repaid $610 million. **Starbucks** also paid cash dividends of $929 million and repurchased common stock totaling $1,436 million.

LO 3-3

Analyze information in the statement of cash flows to determine where the firm is in its life cycle.

Cash Flow Activities and a Firm's Life Cycle

A helpful framework for intuitively grasping the information conveyed through the organization of cash flows involves product life cycle concepts from economics, strategy, and marketing. Individual products (like goods or services) move through four phases: (1) introduction, (2) growth, (3) maturity, and (4) decline. Firms also evolve through these phases, as graphically depicted in Exhibit 3.1, which shows stylized patterns for revenues, net income, and cash flows over the life cycle.

A Firm's Life Cycle: Revenues

The top panel of Exhibit 3.1 shows the pattern of revenues throughout the four phases, which typically follows a period of growth, peaking during maturity, and a subsequent decline as customers switch to new and better alternatives. Obviously, the length of these phases and the steepness of the revenue curve vary by type and success of a product. Products subject to rapid technological change, such as semiconductors and computer software, or driven by fads, such as clothing fashions, move through these four phases in just a few years. Other products, such as venerable staple products like **Coca-Cola** soft drinks, **Advil** pain relievers, **Disney** movies, **Kellogg's** cereal, **Mars'** M&M's, and **Michelin** tires can remain in the maturity phase for many years. Although it is difficult to pinpoint the precise location of a product on its life cycle curve, one can generally identify the phase and whether the product is in the early or later portion of a phase.

A typical firm provides numerous products or services, so the applicability of the theory and evidence for single products is more difficult when firms are diversified across numerous products at different stages of their life cycle. Nevertheless, these

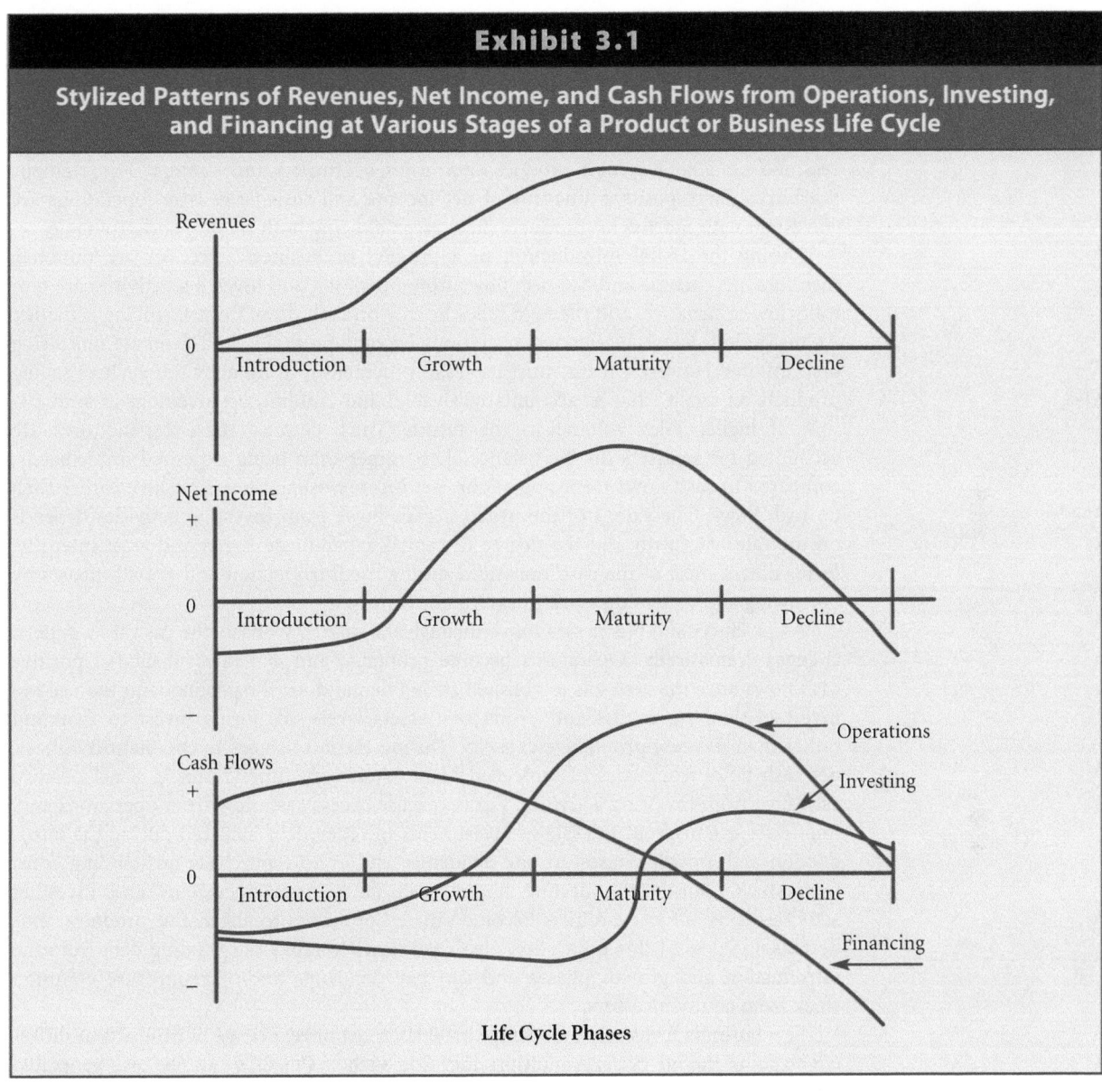

Exhibit 3.1

Stylized Patterns of Revenues, Net Income, and Cash Flows from Operations, Investing, and Financing at Various Stages of a Product or Business Life Cycle

patterns describe firm performance over time as they introduce new products and discontinue older ones.

A Firm's Life Cycle: Net Income

The middle panel of Exhibit 3.1 shows the trend of net income over the life cycle of a product or firm. Net losses usually occur in the introduction and early growth phases because revenues are less than the cost of designing and launching new products. Then, net income peaks during the maturity phase, followed by a decline when revenues decline.

A Firm's Life Cycle: Cash Flows

The lower panel of Exhibit 3.1 shows the cash flows from operating, investing, and financing activities during the four life cycle phases. As with revenues, the length of phases and steepness of the net income and cash flow curves vary depending on the success and sustainability of a product or a firm's operations and strategy. For example, **Starbucks'** large positive amounts of net income and cash flows from operations are consistent with **Starbucks'** products (in aggregate) being both mature and profitable.

During the initial introduction of a product or business, revenues are minimal; therefore, net income and net cash flows from operating and investing activities are typically low or negative, and the firm relies heavily on cash flows from financing activities. As the growth phase accelerates, operations become profitable and generate increasing cash inflows. However, firms must use cash generated to fund activities such as selling products on credit (that is, accounts receivable) and building up inventory in anticipation of higher sales volume in the future. Thus, because these expenditures are accounted for as assets on the balance sheet rather than being expensed immediately, compared to cash flows from operations, net income usually turns positive earlier than do cash flows. The extent of the negative cash flows from investing activities depends on the rate of growth and the degree of capital expenditure needs and asset intensity. Firms obtain most of the cash they need during the introduction and growth phases by borrowing and/or issuing stock to external investors.

As products and businesses move through the maturity phase, the cash flow pattern changes dramatically. Operations become profitable and generate substantial positive cash flows once the firm has established strong demand for the product and the need to invest in working capital and productive assets levels off. Firms invest to *maintain* rather than *increase* productive capacity. During the later stages of the maturity phase, net cash flows from sales of unneeded plant assets sometimes result in a net positive cash flow from investing activities. Firms can use excess cash flow from operations and, to a lesser extent, from the sale of investments to repay debt incurred during the introduction and growth phases, to pay dividends, and/or to repurchase outstanding common stock. During the decline phase, cash flows from operations and investing activities taper off as customers become satiated or switch to alternative products, thus decreasing sales. At this point, firms use cash flows to repay outstanding debt from the introduction and growth phases and can pay dividends and/or repurchase common stock from equity investors.

Few business firms rely on a single product; most have a range of products at different stages of the life cycle. A multiproduct firm such as **PepsiCo** can use cash generated from products in the maturity phase of their life cycle to finance products in the introduction and growth phases and therefore not need as much external financing. Furthermore, the statement of cash flows discussed in this chapter reports amounts for a firm as a whole and not for individual products. For the life cycle concept to assist in analyzing cash flows, you should appreciate how individual products aggregate at the firm level.

Knowledge of competitive industry dynamics and trends can help you assess firm-level cash flows. For example, investor excitement in technology-driven industries such as biotechnology most often peaks during the growth phase. Although such firms may have products in various stages of the product life cycle, the excitement focuses on forecasting the emergence of new technologies that translate into new products that generate large profits and cash flows. A good example is **Tesla** because its electric car technology represents growth potential relative to traditionally powered automobiles.

In contrast, many consumer food companies are characterized as being well into the maturity phase of overall product life cycles. Branded consumer food products can remain in their maturity phase for many years with proper product quality control and promotion, such as **General Mills'** Cheerios.

Companies continually bring new products to the market that replace similar products that are out of favor, but the life cycle of these products tends to be more like products in the maturity phase than introductory products in the growth phase. Certain industries in well-developed economies like the United States, including textiles, appliances, and automobiles, are probably in the early decline phase because of foreign competition, price declines, and/or outdated technology. Some companies in these industries have built technologically advanced production facilities to compete more effectively on a worldwide basis and have, therefore, reentered the maturity phase. Other firms have diversified geographically to realize the benefits of shifts to foreign production, which also prolongs their ability to enjoy the maturity phase of their portfolio of products.

Four Companies: Four Different Stages of the Life Cycle

We conclude this section by surveying excerpts from statements of cash flows for several firms to contrast how these statements capture various stages of the product life cycle (that is, introduction, growth, maturity, and decline).

Atlas African Industries Limited (Introduction Phase)

Atlas African Industries Limited (LON: AAI) is a Kenyan company that operates primarily in Ethiopia and Liberia, providing support services for oil and gas exploration and drilling, mining, and construction. The company was first established in 2012 and initially listed on London's AIM securities market in 2013 under the name Africa Oilfield Logistics Limited. The company then went through several name changes, including Ardan Risk and Support Services and Atlas Development and Support Services, as well as a change in its financial reporting year-end from December 31 to June 30. The company's current mission is to invest in the rapidly growing industrial projects market in Africa. In addition, the company is entering the consumer products markets primarily through investment in glass bottle manufacturing to service the growing beer and beverage industries in Ethiopia.

As is typical of a start-up operation, the company reports losses across years, increasing from a $155,000 loss in 2013 to $9.5 million in 2015. Similarly, cash flows from operating activities are also increasingly negative, with cash flows reaching negative $8.4 million in 2015. Cash flows used in investing activities are negative $8.7 million in 2014 and negative $5.2 million in 2015, largely supported by positive cash flows from financing activities of $6.9 million in 2014 and $17.8 million in 2015. Overall, the statement of cash flows in Exhibit 3.2 clearly paints a picture of a company in the introductory phase of its life cycle.

Ambarella (Growth Phase)

Ambarella (Nasdaq: AMBA) was founded in 2004 and develops video and image products. The company went public in 2012 and has received numerous awards, including the 2009 GSA Start-Up to Watch Award. The company's main products include semiconductor chips used in television broadcasting and various consumer products like security, wearable, and flying cameras. Familiar applications like GoPro cameras and

Exhibit 3.2

Atlas African Industries Limited
Statement of Cash Flows
(amounts in thousands)

	2015	2014	2013
Loss before tax	$ (9,538)	$(1,425)	$ (155)
Net cash used in operating activities	(8,426)	(4,150)	(490)
Net cash used in investing activities	(5,160)	(8,729)	—
Net cash flow from financing activities	17,829	6,856	9,652
Net (decrease)/increase in cash and cash equivalents	4,243	(6,023)	9,162

drones are characterized as being rapidly adopted by consumers, which benefits semi-conductor providers like Ambarella.

The statement of cash flows in Exhibit 3.3 shows typical characteristics of a growth firm. First, profits are increasing at high growth rates, including 51% from $51 million in 2015 to $77 million in 2016. Even more impressive, cash flows from operations increased 136%, from $52 million to $124 million. Cash used for investing activities was approximately $35 million, down slightly from $40 million in 2015. Such large capital expenditures are seen as a signal of management bullishness about future growth. Finally, as is typical of rapidly growing companies, growth in cash flows frequently is not enough to fuel the investments required to sustain growth, so Ambarella realizes substantial inflows of cash from financing activities, which are approximately $9 million and $15 million in 2016 and 2015, respectively. Since going public, the company's stock price has risen from $6 per share to over $60 per share in 2016, reflecting accelerating expectations of future growth.

Cedar Fair L.P. (Maturity Phase)

Founded in 1983 in Sandusky, Ohio, **Cedar Fair L.P.** (NYSE: FUN) is among the largest amusement park companies in the world. The company's statement of cash flows

Exhibit 3.3

Ambarella
Statement of Cash Flows
(amounts in thousands)

	Year Ended January 31,		
	2016	2015	2014
Cash flows from operating activities:			
Net income	$ 76,508	$ 50,571	$25,654
Net cash provided by operating activities	123,561	52,258	34,350
Net cash used in investing activities	(34,796)	(40,061)	(1,688)
Net cash provided by financing activities	9,000	14,700	10,238
Net increase in cash and cash equivalents	97,765	26,897	42,900

Exhibit 3.4

Cedar Fair, L.P.
Statement of Cash Flows
(amounts in thousands)

	2015	2014	2013
Cash flows from operating activities:			
Net income	$ 112,222	$ 104,215	$ 108,204
Net cash from operating activities	342,217	337,103	324,457
Net cash for investing activities	(177,865)	(165,342)	(105,151)
Net cash for financing activities	(174,203)	(155,235)	(178,332)
Net increase (decrease) in cash and cash equivalents (including exchange rate effects)	(9,851)	16,526	40,974

(Exhibit 3.4) exhibits the typically large positive cash flows from operating activities and negative cash flows for both investing and financing activities. The company generates large and persistent net income ($112 million in 2015, up from $104 million in 2014) and enormous cash flows from operating activities ($342 million in 2015). With such large amounts generated by cash flows from operating activities, the company relied very little on external financing; instead, it tended to pay large distributions to partners (the company is a partnership), reflected in the $174 million used for financing activities. Also, Cedar Fair continued to use significant cash for investing activities (a net total of $178 million in 2015). The company believes that annual park attendance is strongly affected by the introduction of new rides and attractions each year, explaining the continuing investment activities. Overall, Cedar Fair exhibits patterns of cash flows typical of a mature firm.

Warner Music Group (Decline Phase)

Exhibit 3.5 shows the statement of cash flows for **Warner Music Group** (NYSE: WMG) during its final years before being acquired by a private company. The company traces its origins back to 1929, and it became one of the world's largest and most influential

Exhibit 3.5

Warner Music Group
Statement of Cash Flows
(amounts in millions)

	2010	2009	2008
Net loss	$(145)	$(104)	$ (51)
Net cash provided by operating activities	150	237	304
Net cash (used in) provided by investing activities	(85)	82	(167)
Net cash used in financing activities	(3)	(346)	(59)
Net increase (decrease) in cash and equivalents (including exchange rate effects)	62	(27)	78

music content companies. It generated revenues from the marketing, licensing, and sale of music through various formats, historically physical formats such as vinyl, cassette, and compact disc. Like other music content companies, Warner Music Group suffered as the music industry experienced a distribution transformation with the development of digital music and other delivery platforms like Internet streaming. As is typical of a firm in decline, Warner Music Group

- reported a string of net losses (increased from $51 million to $145 million between 2008 and 2010).
- generated positive cash flows from operations, but at a substantially decreasing rate (declined from $304 million to $150 million).
- had investing activities that appeared volatile (negative in 2008 and 2010, but positive in 2009 as the company disposed of certain investments).
- had negative cash flows to repay external financing sources, including a large net retirement of debt in 2009.

Subsequently, the company was acquired by a private conglomerate, **Access Industries**.

Quick Check

- The organization of the statement of cash flows into operating, investing, and financing activities helps identify a firm's stage in its life cycle.
- Start-up firms typically have net losses, negative cash flows from operations, negative cash flows for investing activities, but positive cash flows from financing activities.
- Growth firms typically have increasing profits or decreasing losses, positive cash flows from operations, negative cash flows for investing

activities, and positive cash flows from financing activities.
- Mature firms typically have large positive profits, large positive cash flows from operations, stable cash flows from investing activities, and negative cash flows from financing activities.
- Decline firms typically have decreasing profits or increasing losses, declining cash flows from operations, low or positive cash flows for investing activities, and negative cash flows from financing activities.

LO 3-4

Understand the relations among the statement of cash flows, the income statement, and the balance sheet.

Understanding the Relations among Net Income, Balance Sheets, and Cash Flows

As noted in Chapter 2, one alternative to measuring financial performance is simply to measure cash inflows and outflows. If you take this primitive "cash is king" perspective, the statement of cash flows provides fundamental information on the flows of cash in and out of a firm. However, over short horizons such as a fiscal quarter or year, cash inflows and outflows are not very informative with regard to a firm's profitability now or in the future. For example, recall the **Warner Music Group** example highlighted in the prior section, where increasing losses were associated with positive, but declining, cash flows from operations.

One criticism sometimes leveled at accrual accounting is that managers can manipulate reported earnings. However, checks and balances such as accounting standards and principles like U.S. GAAP and IFRS, as well as firms' internal controls, create accounting discipline and govern how firms measure and report income. In addition, auditors, the SEC and other regulators, boards of directors, the press, short sellers, and activist investors scrutinize reported profits, exposing the behavior of managers who attempt to manipulate earnings. Cash flows, on the other hand, are not subject to reporting standards, so managers can much more easily manipulate cash flows relative to their ability to manipulate earnings.

As a simple example, consider the decision to pay a supplier on December 31 versus January 1 of the following year. This decision affects cash flows, but not earnings. Further, the timing of that cash flow would not likely alter any expectations of future performance or cash flows. Thus, whereas accrual accounting has the objective of helping users assess the current financial position and the nature, amount, and timing of future cash flows, the objective of cash flow reporting is to simply track the flows of cash.

Accrual accounting goes beyond measurement of cash flows to measure *economic* inflows and outflows. Economic resources and obligations generate assets and liabilities (the balance sheet), which in turn allow for an improved measure of performance based on economic resources generated and consumed (the income statement). As emphasized above, the statement of cash flows, although quite useful, merely undoes the accrual accounting that transformed cash flows into balance sheets and income statements. Recall Exhibit 1.14, which shows that the difference in stock returns between firms with positive and negative changes in earnings is 35.6%, whereas the change in stock returns between firms with positive and negative operating cash flows is only 15.0%, which indicates periodic earnings are much more associated with changes in stock prices than are cash flows.

To fully interpret and analyze the information in the statement of cash flows, you need to understand the following three relations:

1. The overall relations among the net cash flows from operating, investing, and financing activities.
2. The relation between the change in the cash balance on the balance sheet and the net changes reflected on the statement of cash flows.
3. The specific relation between net income and cash flows from operations.

We discussed the first topic in the previous section that covered four examples of firms in various stages of their life cycle. We discuss the second and third topics next. Because the third relation is most important, we address it in two parts. First, we focus specifically on the operating section of the statement of cash flows, highlighting the types of adjustments necessary to reconcile net income to cash flows from operations; then we discuss the overall relation between net income and cash flows from operations.

The Operating Section

The operating section of the statement of cash flows is arguably the most important because it provides information on a firm's core activities. These activities include cash received from selling goods and services to customers and cash paid to suppliers, employees, governments, and other providers of goods and services. This section also is where you can gather information about the *quality of earnings*. An analysis of the timing of cash flows in the operating section exposes the drivers of reported profitability on the income statement, which can sometimes raise red flags for earnings manipulation.[2]

First, we briefly mention the two formats of the operating section that are permissible under U.S. GAAP and IFRS. Regardless of the format used, a reconciliation of net income to cash flows from operations must be shown, and we will emphasize how to analyze this information. Second, we examine the different types of adjustments to net income that appear in the operating section. Finally, we provide several illustrative examples.

---

[2]As noted at the beginning of the chapter, refer to Chapter 6 for a more complete discussion of how to use the statement of cash flows to assess earnings quality.

The Operating Section: Format Alternatives

Under U.S. GAAP and IFRS, firms may present cash flows from operations in one of two formats: the *direct method* or the *indirect method*. The direct method partitions cash receipts and cash payments into logical categories, such as cash collected from customers, cash paid to suppliers, and cash paid to employees. In contrast, the indirect method does not list cash flows directly, but instead reconciles reported net income to cash flows from operations by "unraveling" noncash (i.e., accrual) components of earnings.

Despite a preference for the direct method by standard setters like the FASB and IASB, almost all companies report cash flows using the indirect method. In 2011, the AICPA surveyed 500 firms and identified only 5 that used the direct method.[3] The reluctance to report under the direct method seems to be based on practicality because the FASB and IASB require that firms using the direct method also provide a separate schedule for the reconciliation between net income and operating cash flows. Thus, a firm that uses the direct method also must report a separate schedule with the indirect method operating section; by contrast, a firm that uses the indirect method is not required to report a separate schedule with a direct method operating section.

Exhibit 3.6 provides a rare example of the direct method for the operating cash flows in the statement for the drugstore chain **CVS Caremark**. Notice that the net operating cash flows are $8,412 million for 2015, which is shown in the top section of the statement. This amount is reported as the result of various direct cash flow amounts, including $148,954 million in cash received from customers, less $122,498 million in cash paid for inventory and prescriptions and $14,162 million paid to other suppliers and employees. Notice also that this same amount is shown at the bottom of the statement in an addendum for the reconciliation of net income to net cash provided by operating activities. Regardless of the method of presentation, net operating cash flows are the same, $8,412 million. The line item descriptions in the direct method are more intuitive than those in the indirect method because the line items all represent cash flows.

In contrast, under the indirect method, not a single line item in the operating section reflects an actual cash flow. Instead, amounts shown are *adjustments* for noncash components of net income. For example, "Cash receipts from customers" is more straightforward than the change in accounts receivable (which includes the allowance for doubtful accounts and effects from acquisitions) shown as a reconciling item in the indirect method (at the bottom of Exhibit 3.6). This chapter later describes how you can compute the more intuitive figures such as cash paid for inventory from information in the balance sheet and income statement.

Under the *indirect method*, firms begin with net income to calculate cash flows from operations. The assumption implicit in starting with net income is that revenues increase cash and expenses decrease cash. However, remember that under accrual accounting, recognition of revenues and expenses does not necessarily coincide with the actual timing of cash receipts or payments. For example, sales to customers on credit trigger recognition of revenues, but this also triggers an increase in accounts receivable because customers have been extended credit and can pay later. Because of differences in the timing of cash flows and income statement recognition, net income must be reconciled to cash flows by adjusting for noncash effects. Again, to contrast the two methods, see CVS Caremark's direct method operating section and compare it to the indirect method reconciliation, at the bottom of Exhibit 3.6.

---

[3]AICPA, *Accounting Trends & Techniques* (2012).

Exhibit 3.6

CVS Caremark
Statement of Cash Flows: Operating Section
under Direct and Indirect Methods
(amounts in millions)

	2015	2014	2013
Cash flows from operating activities:			
Cash receipts from customers	$ 148,954	$ 132,406	$114,993
Cash paid for inventory and prescriptions dispensed by retail network pharmacies	(122,498)	(105,362)	(91,178)
Cash paid to other suppliers and employees	(14,162)	(15,344)	(14,295)
Interest received	21	15	8
Interest paid	(629)	(647)	(534)
Income taxes paid	(3,274)	(2,931)	(3,211)
Net cash provided by operating activities	8,412	8,137	5,783
Cash flows from investing activities:			
Purchases of property and equipment	(2,367)	(2,136)	(1,984)
Proceeds from sale-leaseback transactions	411	515	600
Proceeds from sale of property and equipment and other assets	35	11	54
Acquisitions (net of cash acquired) and other investments	(11,475)	(2,439)	(415)
Purchase of available-for-sale investments	(267)	(157)	(226)
Maturity of available-for-sale investments	243	161	136
Net cash used in investing activities	(13,420)	(4,045)	(1,835)
Cash flows from financing activities:			
Increase (decrease) in short-term debt	(685)	685	(690)
Proceeds from issuance of long-term debt	14,805	1,483	3,964
Repayments of long-term debt	(2,902)	(3,100)	
Payment of contingent consideration	(58)		
Dividends paid	(1,576)	(1,288)	(1,097)
Proceeds from exercise of stock options	299	421	500
Excess tax benefits from stock-based compensation	127	106	62
Repurchase of common stock	(5,001)	(4,001)	(3,976)
Other	(3)		
Net cash provided by (used in) financing activities	5,006	(5,694)	(1,237)
Effect of exchange rate changes on cash and cash equivalents	(20)	(6)	3
Net increase (decrease) in cash and cash equivalents	(22)	(1,608)	2,714
Cash and cash equivalents at the beginning of the year	2,481	4,089	1,375
Cash and cash equivalents at the end of the year	$ 2,459	$ 2,481	$ 4,089

(Continued)

Exhibit 3.6 (Continued)

Reconciliation of net income to net cash provided by operating activities:			
Net income	$ 5,239	$ 4,644	$ 4,592
Adjustments required to reconcile net income to net cash provided by operating activities:			
Depreciation and amortization	2,092	1,931	1,870
Stock-based compensation	230	165	141
Loss on early extinguishment of debt		521	
Deferred income taxes and other noncash items	(266)	(58)	(86)
Change in operating assets and liabilities, net of effects from acquisitions:			
Accounts receivable, net	(1,594)	(737)	(2,210)
Inventories	(1,141)	(770)	12
Other current assets	355	(383)	105
Other assets	2	9	(135)
Accounts payable and claims and discounts payable	2,834	1,742	1,024
Accrued expenses	765	1,060	471
Other long-term liabilities	(104)	13	(1)
Net cash provided by operating activities	$ 8,412	$ 8,137	$ 5,783

Most firms use the indirect method because it reconciles net income with the net amount of cash received from or used for operations, which provides a direct link to the income statement. Critics of the indirect method suggest that the rationale for some of the reconciling items is difficult for less sophisticated users to understand. For example, a *decrease* in receivables is actually associated with an *increase* in cash flows (reflecting cash collected from customers); however, this adjustment is typically labeled as "Decrease in accounts receivable" on the statement of cash flows, which is prone to confuse some users. The equivalent line item under the direct method approach is the much more intuitive "Cash receipts from customers." Although only a moderate amount of effort is required to understand the reconciliation adjustments, certain peculiarities challenge even the most seasoned analysts.

The Operating Section: Adjustments for the Indirect Method

The presentation of cash flows from operations under the indirect method involves two types of adjustments to net income: working capital and other noncash components of income adjustments. Both of these adjustments, explained below, are necessary because of timing differences between income recognition and cash flow realization. Working capital adjustments reflect *changes* in operating working capital accounts during the period, including accounts receivable, inventories, and accounts payable.[4] Common noncash components of income adjustments include depreciation, amortization, deferred taxes, and gains/losses on asset dispositions. These adjustments reflect amounts that affect current period net

---

[4]Working capital means current assets minus current liabilities. Operating working capital accounts generally include all current assets except marketable securities and all current liabilities except short-term loans and the current portion of long-term debt. A later section of this chapter explains the rationale for excluding these items from operating working capital.

income but do *not* affect current period cash flows. Thus, such amounts must be "adjusted out" of the starting point of the statement of cash flows—net income.

Other Noncash Components of Income Adjustments

Depreciation and amortization expense.[5] Depreciation expense reduces net property, plant, and equipment and net income. However, depreciation expense does not require an *operating* cash outflow in the period of the expense. Cash flows paid for depreciable assets are classified as *investing* activities in the year of acquisition. The addback of depreciation expense to net income reverses the effect of the subtraction of depreciation expense when computing net income. Similarly, amortization expense reflects the consumption of intangible assets, and it must be added back to net income in computing operating cash flows. This adjustment is typically the largest in the operating section. For example, in 2015, **Starbucks**' statement of cash flows shows $934 million as the first and largest adjustment to net income of $2,759 million.

Bad debt expense. Like depreciation and amortization expense for fixed and intangible assets, bad debt expense reduces net accounts receivable and net income. However, bad debt expense is a noncash expense, so it must be added back to net income, similar to depreciation and amortization. You will not always see a specific addback for bad debt expense because the amount may be relatively immaterial or may be netted with the working capital accounts receivable adjustment. For example, **Starbucks** does not show an adjustment for bad debt expense (so it is either immaterial or it is included elsewhere). Bad debts are relatively more material for companies that have large receivables from consumers, like **McGrath RentCorp** (Nasdaq: MGRC), which rents modular buildings and storage containers. See Exhibit 3.7, where McGrath shows a $2.1 million addback for bad debt expense (i.e., "Provision for doubtful accounts") in its computation of cash flow provided by operations.

Deferred tax expense. Firms recognize deferred tax assets and/or deferred tax liabilities on the balance sheet when they use different methods of accounting for financial reporting and income tax reporting. The total amount of income tax expense, including current and deferred components, will differ from the amount of income taxes payable for the fiscal year (from the tax return). Thus, firms must add back the deferred portion of income tax expense, which is the excess of income tax expense over income taxes owed for the year (approximated by current tax expense). **Starbucks** shows an addback for deferred income taxes of $21 million in 2015, suggesting that income tax expense exceeds income taxes actually paid for the year. The adjustment for deferred income taxes, however, is a much more complex topic, and it is difficult for investors to uncover the amount of income taxes paid. For this reason, companies are required to provide a supplemental disclosure that specifies the amount of income taxes paid, which for **Starbucks** was $1,072 million; it is shown at the bottom of the statement of cash flows.

---

[5] Adjustments for depreciation and amortization on the statement of cash flows are more complex than implied in this discussion because depreciation is often allocated to the cost of inventory. If the balance of inventory changes during a period, the change may include allocated depreciation to the cost basis of inventory. Thus, the allocation of depreciation (and amortization) to inventory creates a discrepancy between amounts expensed and the addback on the statement of cash flows. Firms handle this discrepancy in a variety of ways, which makes it rare that depreciation expense on the income statement equals the depreciation adjustment on the statement of cash flows. For similar reasons, the change in inventory balances on the balance sheet rarely equals the working capital adjustment for increases or decreases in inventory on the statement of cash flows. This is one of the compelling motivations for requiring a statement of cash flows to be provided by management, who have the information to prepare cash flow statements more precisely than external users can by using approximations from the other financial statements.

Exhibit 3.7

McGrath RentCorp
Income Statement and Statement of Cash Flows Excerpts
(amounts in thousands)

	2015	2014	2013
Cash flows from operating activities:			
Net income	$ 40,470	$ 45,709	$ 43,397
Depreciation and amortization	84,280	81,125	76,849
Provision for doubtful accounts	2,149	1,825	2,144
Share-based compensation	3,399	3,854	3,680
Gain on sale of used rental equipment	(11,902)	(15,368)	(13,091)
Gain on sale of property, plant and equipment	—	(812)	—
Foreign currency exchange loss	488	331	189
Change in:			
Accounts receivable	3,882	(15,469)	2,462
Income taxes receivable	(11,000)	—	—
Prepaid expenses and other assets	12,708	(13,652)	(8,265)
Accounts payable and accrued liabilities	(1,520)	10,662	6,506
Deferred income	7,149	5,136	(2,921)
Deferred income taxes	14,449	19,645	22,693
Net cash provided by operating activities	$144,552	$122,986	$133,643

Stock-based compensation. Stock-based compensation, such as restricted stock and employee stock options, is recognized as an expense on the income statement.[6] This expense reduces net income but increases a shareholders' equity account, and it does not use cash. Because the expense does not use cash, firms add back stock-based compensation expense to net income when computing cash flows from operations. In 2015, **Starbucks** lists an addback of $210 million for "Stock-based compensation" in the operating section of its statement of cash flows.

Gains and losses. Companies that sell an item of property, plant, or equipment report the full cash proceeds from the sale in the investing section on the statement of cash flows. When firms sell assets for amounts that differ from book values, net income includes gains and losses on such sales (that is, sale proceeds minus book value of the item sold). Therefore, the operating section of the statement of cash flows shows an addback for a loss and a subtraction for a gain to offset their effects on net income and to avoid double-counting the gain or loss, given that the investing section includes the full cash proceeds from the asset sale. The absence of a line item for gains or losses on **Starbucks'** statement of cash flows suggests that these amounts either do not exist or are small and likely included in the lines named "Other" in both the operating and investing sections.[7]

---

[6]Stock-based compensation expenses are discussed more fully in Chapter 7.

[7]Starbucks does report an addback for "Gain resulting from acquisition/sale of equity in joint ventures and certain retail operations" totaling $394 million. The logic of this addback follows the discussion for gains on sales of general assets.

Equity method income. Firms holding investments of 20 to 50% of the common shares in another entity generally use the equity method to account for the investment.[8] As an investor, the firm recognizes in net income its share of the investee's earnings each period and increases the balance of the investment account accordingly. It reduces the investment account for any cash dividends received. Therefore, net income reflects the investor's share of the investee's earnings, not the cash received. The statement of cash flows usually shows a subtraction from net income for the investor's share of the investee's earnings (that does not reflect cash) and an addition for the dividends received (which does reflect cash). For example, in the operating section in 2015, **Starbucks** subtracts $190.2 million in "Income earned from equity investees" and then adds $148.2 million in "Distributions received from equity method investees," which represents dividends received from its many investments in various entities such as **Starbucks Coffee Korea, Ltd.**, and **Starbucks Coffee España, S.I.** Sometimes, firms will simply report the net of these two amounts.

Noncontrolling interests. Firms with subsidiaries sometimes own a majority and controlling proportion of shares, but not 100% of the outstanding shares of those subsidiaries. Although the parent controls the operations of the subsidiaries, other investors have a noncontrolling or minority interest. The parent consolidates 100% of the subsidiaries' assets, liabilities, and income but shows deductions for the noncontrolling interests' share of the subsidiaries' net income. For example, **Starbucks** reports "Net earnings including noncontrolling interests" of $2,759.3 million in 2015, but it shows a deduction at the bottom of the income statement for $1.9 million for "Net earnings attributable to noncontrolling interests," leading to "Net earnings attributable to **Starbucks**" of $2,757.4 million. If **Starbucks** began the statement of cash flows with the net earnings of $2,757.3 million, then the $1.9 million earnings attributable to noncontrolling interests is a noncash deduction and would be added back. However, **Starbucks** adopts a common practice and effectively accomplishes this adjustment by beginning the statement of cash flows with net income including noncontrolling interests, totaling $2,759.3 million, which reflects net income before the $1.9 million deduction.

Other comprehensive income. As discussed in prior chapters, other comprehensive income represents noncash adjustments to certain financial securities, foreign currency gains/losses, and various postretirement benefit items. Because firms include these amounts in comprehensive income rather than net income, they do not require adjustments to net income in the statement of cash flows.

Employee-related costs such as pensions. There are two types of pension plans: defined contribution and defined benefit.[9] Defined benefit plans may give rise to large differences between pension expense and actual cash flows, but this is not true for defined contribution plans. This is because defined benefit plans require numerous estimates of future cash payments for benefits in order to compute pension expense, whereas for defined contribution plans, pension expense equals cash contributions under the plans. As a result, companies with defined benefit plans adjust net income for the net difference between recognized pension expense and cash contributions. **Starbucks** has only a defined contribution plan, so it does not require any adjustment for defined benefit pension expenses that differ from contributions. Alternatively,

---

[8]Accounting for investments is more fully covered in Chapter 8.

[9]Pension plans are fully covered in Chapter 9.

companies with large defined benefit plans, like **General Motors**, will make significant adjustments. Exhibit 3.8 shows that General Motors accomplishes this adjustment by adding back pension and other postretirement benefits (OPEB) expense of $321 million, and then subtracting the actual pension contributions and OPEB payments that are much larger, at $1,600 million. The net effect reduces operating cash flows for the payments actually made and removes the effects of the noncash pension expense that was included in net income.

Excess tax benefits from share-based compensation. Companies are required to expense an estimate of the fair value of stock options granted to employees over the vesting period. This expense lowers income, resulting in lower tax expense. When an employee exercises stock options, she will owe taxes on the difference between the stock price at the time of exercise and the amount she has to pay to exercise the option (the strike price). The company is then entitled to a tax deduction equal to the amount the employee realizes as taxable income [that is, total number of shares × (share price − strike price)]. Often, the amount of the tax deduction for compensation is in *excess* of the cumulative compensation expense that has already been recognized. The excess lowers taxes actually paid but does not reduce tax expense recognized on the income statement. Instead, the tax benefit is recognized as a direct credit to paid-in capital in the statement of shareholders' equity. Beginning with fiscal years beginning after December 15, 2016, all tax benefits are to be classified as part of operating cash flows (along with other income tax–related cash flows).

However, the practice prior to then (including most of the cash flow examples provided in this text) was to reclassify the tax benefit from operating cash flows to financing cash flows. **Starbucks'** 2015 statement of cash flows thus shows a $132 million

Exhibit 3.8

General Motors
Operating Cash Flows
(amounts in millions)

	2015	2014	2013
Cash flows from operating activities			
Net income	$ 9,615	$ 4,018	$ 5,331
Depreciation, amortization and impairment charges	8,017	7,238	8,041
Foreign currency remeasurement and transaction losses	829	437	350
Amortization of discount and issuance costs on debt issues	176	181	114
Undistributed earnings of nonconsolidated affiliates and gains on investments	(147)	(301)	(92)
Pension contributions and OPEB payments	(1,600)	(1,315)	(1,458)
Pension and OPEB expense, net	321	439	638
(Gains) losses on extinguishment of debt	(449)	(202)	212
Provision (benefit) for deferred taxes	(2,757)	(574)	1,561
Change in other operating assets and liabilities	(1,754)	244	(1,326)
Other operating activities	(273)	(107)	(741)
Net cash provided by operating activities	$11,978	$10,058	$12,630

deduction of these excess tax benefits from operating cash flows and a simultaneous addback to financing cash flows for the same amount.[10]

Impairment- and restructuring-related charges. Write-offs and write-downs of assets reduce net income through impairment charges, but there are usually no associated cash transactions. Thus, impairment charges must be added back to net income in the computation of operating cash flows. Similarly, restructuring charges are estimated and the associated cash flows generally follow later. Thus, restructuring charges appear as addbacks to income, and the actual cash payments for restructuring appear as subtractions from income in the operating section. Because of continued strong performance, it might not be surprising that **Starbucks** shows no impairment or restructuring charges for 2015. However, Exhibit 3.9 shows that in 2015 **PepsiCo** reports an addback for "Restructuring and impairment charges" of $230 million and a simultaneous deduction for "Cash payments for restructuring charges" of $208 million. Thus, PepsiCo paid less actual cash for restructurings than was expensed, resulting in a net positive adjustment to net income of $22 million ($230 million − $208 million). PepsiCo also shows similar adjustments for restructuring and impairment charges related to transactions with **Tingyi** and Venezuela.

Operating Working Capital Adjustments

The second type of adjustment used to reconcile net income to cash flows from operations involves changes in the working capital (current asset and current liability) accounts. Net income must be adjusted for the cash flows associated with these changes. We discuss the most common of these working capital adjustments.

Accounts receivable and deferred revenue. Revenue recognition is based on the economics of a sale rather than the realization of cash. Unless a customer pays in cash, recognition of revenue increases accounts receivable. An increase in accounts receivable indicates that a firm recognized revenues for which it did not collect cash. Because these revenues are included in net income, a negative adjustment for the change in accounts receivable on the statement of cash flows indicates that a firm collected less cash than it recognized as revenues. Similarly, a decrease in accounts receivable indicates that a firm collected more cash than it recognized as revenues. **Starbucks** shows negative adjustments for accounts receivable in all years, consistent with growth in receivables (i.e., total sales exceed the cash collected from customers in each year).

Deferred revenue is a liability account that reflects the amounts customers have paid in cash in advance of receiving a good or service. The air travel industry is an example where customers pay in advance for services. When customers buy tickets in advance, an airline receives cash and establishes a liability for deferred revenue; when the customer uses the ticket, deferred revenue decreases and revenue is recognized. The adjustments for changes in deferred revenue reflect these timing differences between the receipt of cash and recognition of revenue. Positive adjustments indicate growing deferred revenues, whereas negative adjustments indicate recognition of revenue through reduction in deferred revenue rather than a receipt of cash. **Starbucks** reports a liability for "Stored value card liability," which reflects deferred revenue. The adjustments on the statement of cash flows for stored value card liability are positive in each

---

[10]Both *SFAS No. 95*, "Statement of cash flows," and EITF 00-15 require that all tax benefits from share-based compensation plans should be classified as operating cash flows. *SFAS No. 123(R)*, however, required the excess tax benefits to be shown as financing cash flows, not operating. See *FASB Codification Topic 718* for current guidance, which incorporates FASB Accounting Standards Update 2016-09, released in March 2016.

Exhibit 3.9

PepsiCo
Operating Cash Flows
(amounts in millions)

Fiscal Years Ended:	2015	2014	2013
Operating activities			
Net income	$ 5,501	$ 6,558	$ 6,787
Depreciation and amortization	2,416	2,625	2,663
Share-based compensation expense	295	297	303
Merger and integration charges	—	—	10
Cash payments for merger and integration charges	—	—	(25)
Restructuring and impairment charges	230	418	163
Cash payments for restructuring charges	(208)	(266)	(133)
Charge related to the transaction with Tingyi	73	—	—
Cash payments for restructuring and other charges related to the transaction with Tingyi	—	—	(26)
Venezuela impairment charges	1,359	—	—
Venezuela remeasurement charges	—	105	111
Excess tax benefits from share-based payment arrangements	(133)	(114)	(117)
Pension and retiree medical plan expenses	467	667	663
Pension and retiree medical plan contributions	(205)	(655)	(262)
Deferred income taxes and other tax charges and credits	78	(19)	(1,058)
Change in assets and liabilities:			
Accounts and notes receivable	(461)	(343)	(88)
Inventories	(244)	(111)	4
Prepaid expenses and other current assets	(50)	80	(51)
Accounts payable and other current liabilities	1,692	1,162	1,007
Income taxes payable	55	371	86
Other, net	(285)	(269)	(349)
Net cash provided by operating activities	$10,580	$10,506	$ 9,688

year, indicating that **Starbucks**' customers are increasingly prepaying for coffee through the use of this arrangement.

Inventories. Two features of inventory accounting lead to adjustments to net income in computing operating cash flows. When inventory balances increase, the cash flow statement subtracts this amount because it implies a cash outlay for an inventory build-up, and because the inventory is still on the balance sheet, it has not been sold (so is not included as cost of goods sold, reducing net income). Similarly, when inventory balances decrease, the cash flow statement includes a positive adjustment because the decrease is expensed as cost of goods sold, but some of this amount relates to inventory for which the cash outflow for payment potentially occurred in a prior reporting period. **Starbucks** reports a large negative adjustment for inventories in 2015, consistent with a build-up of inventory (that has yet to flow through cost of goods sold), but the adjustment has been positive in the previous two years, indicating the opposite.

Prepaid expenses. Prepaid expenses are simply cash prepayments for items that will be expensed in the future. Thus, increases in prepaid expenses indicate cash payments in excess of amounts recognized as expenses in computing net income; decreases in prepaid expenses represent amounts that were expensed but for which there was no equivalent simultaneous cash flow. The cash flow statement subtracts increases in prepaid expenses and adds decreases in prepaid expenses to adjust net income back to cash flows.

Accounts payable and accrued expenses. An increase in current liabilities for accounts payable and accrued operating expenses means that a firm did not use as much cash for inventory purchases or other operating expenses as the amounts appearing on the income statement. For example, suppose a firm is invoiced for cleaning services provided at the end of the fiscal year but does not pay the invoices until the following fiscal year. The firm would recognize the services as an expense when provided, which would accompany an increase in an accrued expense liability. The expense reduces net income, but no cash has been paid, so the amount needs to be added back to net income in computing operating cash flows. On the other hand, decreases in accounts payable and accrued expenses would indicate cash payments of such liabilities exceeded expenses that increased those liabilities, implying net cash outflows.

Income taxes payable. Firms typically do not pay all taxes due for a particular year during that year. Some taxes paid within a year relate to taxes due for the preceding year; some taxes due for the current year are paid the following year. Recall from the earlier discussion about adjustments for other noncash components of income that the addition to (or subtraction from) net income for deferred income tax expense (or benefit) converts income tax expense to income taxes currently payable. The adjustment for changes in income taxes payable similarly converts income taxes currently payable to the income taxes actually paid.

Other current assets and liabilities. In addition, there are other current accounts such as marketable securities, short-term investments, commercial paper, and other short-term borrowings. The cash flows pertaining to changes in these items are shown in investing (marketable securities, short-term investments) or financing (commercial paper, short-term borrowings) activities.

Why Do Adjustments Rarely Equal the Changes in Assets and Liabilities on the Balance Sheet?

The reconciling adjustments throughout the statement of cash flows relate to noncash accounts on the balance sheet, but it is rare that changes in the actual balance sheet accounts equal the reconciling adjustments on the statement of cash flows. For example, in 2015, **Starbucks**' balance for accounts and notes receivable increased from $631 million in 2014 to $719 million, an increase of $88 million. However, the adjustment on the statement of cash flows for "Accounts receivable" is −$82.8 million. Similarly, **Starbucks**' balance sheet shows "Accounts payable" increased from $534 million to $684 million, an increase of $150 million. However, the adjustment on the statement of cash flows shows a positive adjustment of $138 million. Why do adjustments on the statement of cash flows rarely match the actual changes in the corresponding line items on the balance sheet?

There are four primary reasons that changes we see on the balance sheet do not match the adjustment on the statement of cash flows:

1. **Acquisitions and divestitures.** If a company acquires another firm for cash, that cash flow appropriately shows up in the investing section of the statement of cash flows. Acquisitions often result in the acquiring company taking over various current assets and liabilities of the acquiree, like receivables, inventory, and payables. These current assets and liabilities will be included in the consolidated balance sheet at the end of the year. However, it would be inappropriate to let the change in the balance sheet totals show up as an adjustment in the operating section of the statement of cash flows, as this would result in double-counting. To illustrate, assume Company X acquired Company Y for $1,000,000 cash, receiving all of Company Y's assets, including $300,000 of its accounts receivable, in the process. Company X will include the additional $300,000 of accounts receivable on its balance sheet. In Company X's statement of cash flows, the acquisition would appear as a $1,000,000 subtraction in the investing section. In the operating section, the $300,000 would not be included in the "Change in accounts receivable" adjustment. Divestitures would have similar effects, but the direction would be the opposite.

2. **Noncash transactions.** Noncash transactions increase or decrease assets, liabilities, or equities but do not involve the exchange of cash. Examples include noncash acquisitions using common stock, the acquisition of assets under lease agreements, asset exchanges, financed asset acquisitions or settlement of liabilities, and debt-for-equity swaps. Similar to the discussion above, for any such line items on the balance sheet, the changes in balances from beginning to end of year would need to be adjusted when preparing the statement of cash flows. For example, reconsider the Company X example, but assume the acquisition of Company Y was accomplished by issuing common shares to Company Y's shareholders rather than paying cash. Significant noncash transactions are supposed to be highlighted separately, along with cash paid for interest and taxes, either as an addendum to the statement of cash flows or in a footnote.

3. **Changes in contra accounts.** Some assets have related contra accounts, such as the bad debt allowance for accounts receivable and accumulated depreciation for property, plant, and equipment. If those assets are shown net of the contra assets on the balance sheet, then changes in the contra accounts also can cause the change on the balance sheet to differ from the adjustments in the operating section of the statement of cash flows. For example, assume that Company Z has the following balances for net accounts receivable:

	2015	2016
Accounts receivable	$500,000	$500,000
Allowance for bad debts	(25,000)	(40,000)
Net accounts receivable	$475,000	$460,000

Assume that during 2016 Company Z worried that changes in the economy will adversely affect the customers who owe the $500,000, so it increases its allowance for bad debts from $25,000 to $40,000. The change in net accounts receivable is −$15,000, which was the result of recognizing noncash bad debt expense of $15,000. The bad debt expense would decrease net income and would typically appear in the operating section of the statement of cash flows separately as an addback to net income or may be netted within other adjustments.

4. **Foreign currency translation.** Global companies have assets and liabilities located in many countries and frequently denominated in various currencies. When these companies prepare consolidated balance sheets, the translation of current assets and liabilities from the local currency into the currency of the consolidated parent can change the balances of assets and liabilities, which is a noncash change. For reasons similar to those discussed for the examples above, the inclusion of foreign currency translation gains or losses within the balances of assets or liabilities would lead to adjustments in the operating section differing from the changes in line item balances from the balance sheet.

On occasion, some firms alert readers of the financial statements that changes in working capital in the operating section of the statement of cash flows do not equal changes in the corresponding accounts on the comparative balance sheet by phrasings in the operating section such as "changes in operating working capital, *excluding effects of acquisitions and dispositions.*" Some of the examples in the next section will show such wording. Note also that this inability to reconcile balance sheet changes perfectly also applies to non–working capital accounts such as property, plant, and equipment; long-term investments; long-term debt; and other liabilities.

The Relation between Net Income and Cash Flows from Operations

What is the general relation between net income and cash flows from operations? When should one exceed the other? Should they be approximately the same over a long time period, and, if so, how long? As you saw in examples presented earlier, net income tends to be primarily below cash flows from operations, but for some firms you will see cash flows from operations less than net income. Not surprisingly, the relation between net income and cash flows depends on numerous factors, including economic characteristics of the industry, the firm, its rate of growth, and even discretionary reporting choices made by managers.

The tendency for operating cash flows to exceed net income is not surprising for several reasons. For example, the largest adjustments to net income in the operating section are generally for other noncash components of income, such as changes in noncurrent assets, noncurrent liabilities, and shareholders' equity accounts, and these are primarily addbacks to net income rather than subtractions. These addbacks include (1) depreciation and amortization expense (noncurrent assets), (2) deferred tax expense (noncurrent liability), (3) share-based compensation (shareholders' equity), and (4) asset impairments and restructuring charges.

Also, rapidly growing firms can reflect various relations between operating cash flows and net income. Growth firms often report substantial adjustments for changes in accounts receivable, inventories, and current operating liabilities. When a firm increases its sales, its working capital accounts tend to increase as well. For example, suppose a firm doubles its sales over several years. It is likely that the company also would increase its sales made on credit (accounts receivable), increase products available for sale (inventory), and increase its own credit with vendors (payables). Most growing firms expand their accounts receivable and inventories (that is, uses of cash) more rapidly than their current operating liabilities (that is, sources of cash). For these firms, the net effect of changes in operating working capital is a subtraction from net income when computing cash flows from operations, which can make cash flows from operations less than net income. Alternatively, if expansions of working capital assets are accompanied by approximately equal increases in working capital liabilities, cash used in the expansion of receivables and inventory can be offset by cash provided by increasing payables. As a result, the primarily positive adjustments for other noncash components of income discussed previously will dominate, leading to operating cash flows greater than net income.

Another factor that may cause cash flow from operations to differ from net income is the length of the operating cycle, which encompasses the period of time from when a firm commences production until it receives cash from customers for the sale of the products. Firms such as construction companies and aerospace manufacturers with relatively long operating cycles often experience a long lag between cash outflows for design, development, raw materials, and labor and cash inflows from customers. Unless such firms receive cash advances from their customers prior to completion and delivery of the products or delay payments to their suppliers, the net effect of changes in operating working capital accounts is a subtraction from net income when computing cash flows from operations. The longer the operating cycle and the more rapid the growth of a firm, the larger the difference between net income and cash flows from operations.

Consider a winery, which must plant vines, cultivate them for years, harvest grapes, ferment the juice, age wine in barrels for months or years, then bottle it, sell it, and ship it. Significant cash outflows are required years before the winery will realize any cash inflows. Firms with short operating cycles, such as restaurants and service firms, experience less of a lag between the creation and delivery of their products and the collection of cash from customers. Thus, for these firms, changes in operating working capital accounts play a relatively minor role in creating a wedge between net income and cash flows from operations.

Exhibit 3.10 shows graphically the relation between net income and cash flows for **Starbucks** from 2010–2015. First, note that cash flows from operations are positive every year, but cash flows from both investing and financing activities are negative each year. This is consistent with the typical pattern for a mature, profitable firm. Second, cash flows from operations exceed net income every year, except for 2014 when **Starbucks** paid a $2,764 million accrued litigation liability that was the primary reason for the low net income in 2013. In all other years, the excess of cash flows from operations over net income is due primarily to the large positive adjustments for other noncash components of income coupled with generally positive but smaller adjustments for working capital. Analysts track patterns in summary amounts like those in this exhibit, and aberrations direct them towards questions that can be answered by examining the detailed line items in the financial statements and the notes to the financial statements.

Exhibit 3.10

Relations among Starbucks' Net Income, Cash Flows from Operations, Cash Flows from Investing Activities, and Cash Flows from Financing Activities

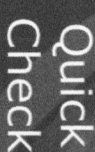

Legend: —— Net income   · ▲ · Operating cash flows   · ◆ · Investing cash flows   ·· ● ·· Financing cash flows

---

- The operating section reconciles net income to cash flows from operations.
- Two options exist for reconciling net income—the indirect or direct method—and most firms use the indirect method.

- Adjustments for working capital and other noncash components of income reflect the reversal of accounting entries recorded to compute balance sheet and income statement line items.

Quick Check

Preparing the Statement of Cash Flows

LO 3-5

Prepare a statement of cash flows from balance sheet and income statement data.

This section illustrates a procedure you can use to prepare an *implied* statement of cash flows using information from the balance sheet and income statement. The implied statement of cash flows assumes that all of the changes in noncash assets, liabilities, and shareholders' equity accounts imply cash flows. For example, an increase in a liability implies borrowing, while a decrease implies payment. Due to the four factors discussed earlier in the chapter for why changes rarely match the actual cash flow adjustments, the implied statement of cash flows that you prepare approximates the amounts the statement of cash flows would report if the analyst had full access to a firm's accounting records. For example, you can assume that all changes in operating working capital accounts are operating transactions even though some of these changes might arise from a corporate acquisition or divestiture, which are investing activities. As a second example, in the absence of information about noncash transactions, the preparation procedure described in this section assumes that the change in each account involves a cash flow that relates to one of the three activities reported in the statement of cash flows. Despite these concerns, the estimated amounts should approximate the actual amounts closely enough to be useful. This procedure is useful in cases when firms might not report a statement of cash flows. More importantly, we will use this approach in Chapter 10 to project implied statements of cash flows from our forecasts of future balance sheets and income statements.

Algebraic Formulation

You know from the accounting equation that

$$\text{Assets} = \text{Liabilities} + \text{Shareholders' Equity}$$

If you subtract the amounts on the balance sheet at the beginning of the period from the corresponding amounts on the balance sheet at the end of the period, you obtain the following equality for changes (Δ) in balance sheet amounts:

$$\Delta \text{ Assets} = \Delta \text{ Liabilities} + \Delta \text{ Shareholders' Equity}$$

You can now expand the change in assets as follows:

$$\Delta \text{ Cash} + \Delta \text{ Noncash Assets} = \Delta \text{ Liabilities} + \Delta \text{ Shareholders' Equity}$$

Rearranging terms,

$$\Delta \text{ Cash} = \Delta \text{ Liabilities} + \Delta \text{ Shareholders' Equity} - \Delta \text{ Noncash Assets}$$

The statement of cash flows explains the reasons for the change in cash during a period. You can see that the change in cash equals the change in all other (noncash) balance sheet amounts. The negative sign on Δ Noncash Assets also explains why increases in noncash assets (acquiring assets) imply decreases in cash, while decreases in noncash assets (selling assets) imply increases in cash.

Refer to Exhibit 3.11, which shows the comparative balance sheet of Footloose Shoe Store for the years ending December 31, Year 2 and Year 1. The balance sheets at the end of Year 1 and Year 2 report the following equalities:

	Cash	+	Noncash Assets	=	Liabilities	+	Shareholders' Equity
Year 1	$13,698	+	$132,136	=	$105,394	+	$40,440
Year 2	12,595	+	129,511	=	85,032	+	57,074

Subtracting the amounts at the end of Year 1 from the amounts at the end of Year 2, you obtain the following:

Δ Cash	+	Δ Noncash Assets	=	Δ Liabilities	+	Δ Shareholders' Equity
$(1,103)	+	$(2,625)	=	$(20,362)	+	$16,634

Exhibit 3.11

Footloose Shoe Store
Balance Sheet

	Year 2	Year 1
ASSETS		
Cash	$ 12,595	$ 13,698
Accounts receivable	1,978	1,876
Inventories	106,022	98,824
Other current assets	—	3,591
Total Current Assets	$120,595	$117,989
Property, plant, and equipment, at cost	$ 65,285	$ 63,634
Less accumulated depreciation	(45,958)	(37,973)
Net property, plant, and equipment	$ 19,327	$ 25,661
Intangible assets	2,184	2,184
Total Assets	$142,106	$145,834
LIABILITIES AND SHAREHOLDERS' EQUITY		
Accounts payable	$ 15,642	$ 21,768
Notes payable	—	—
Current portion of long-term debt	10,997	18,256
Other current liabilities	6,912	4,353
Total Current Liabilities	$ 33,551	$ 44,377
Long-term debt	51,481	61,017
Total Liabilities	$ 85,032	$105,394
Common stock	$ 1,000	$ 1,000
Additional paid-in capital	124,000	124,000
Retained earnings	(67,926)	(84,560)
Total Shareholders' Equity	$ 57,074	$ 40,440
Total Liabilities and Shareholders' Equity	$142,106	$145,834

Rearranging terms,

$$\Delta \text{Cash} = \Delta \text{Liabilities} + \Delta \text{Shareholders' Equity} - \Delta \text{Noncash Assets}$$
$$\$(1,103) = \$(20,362) + \$16,634 - \$(2,625)$$

The decrease in cash of $1,103 equals the decrease in liabilities plus the increase in shareholders' equity minus the decrease in noncash assets.

To link the above decomposition of the balance sheet equation into the format of the statement of cash flows, partition noncash assets and liabilities into working capital and other components. Indicating the components with "WC" and "NWC" subscripts, the equation becomes

$$\Delta \text{Cash} = \Delta \text{Liabilities}_{WC} + \Delta \text{Liabilities}_{NWC} + \Delta \text{Shareholders' Equity}$$
$$- \Delta \text{Noncash Assets}_{WC} - \Delta \text{Noncash Assets}_{NWC}$$

Rearranging terms,

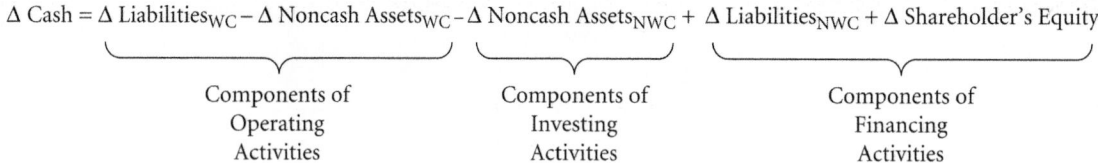

$$\Delta\,Cash = \Delta\,Liabilities_{WC} - \Delta\,Noncash\,Assets_{WC} - \Delta\,Noncash\,Assets_{NWC} + \Delta\,Liabilities_{NWC} + \Delta\,Shareholder's\,Equity$$

| Components of Operating Activities | Components of Investing Activities | Components of Financing Activities |

The rearrangement of the familiar balance sheet equation (and use of simplifying assumptions) yields the intuitive equation above, which *figuratively* maps into the information on the statement of cash flows. The mapping is figurative and is not technically representative, however, because net income is included in Δ Shareholders' Equity above and is an operating activity.

Classifying Changes in Balance Sheet Accounts

To use this approach to prepare an implied statement of cash flows, you must classify the change in each noncash balance sheet account (right side of the preceding equation) into an operating, investing, or financing activity. For some changes in balance sheet accounts, it is obvious which of the three categories is applicable. For example, the change in long-term debt is usually a financing transaction. However, some balance sheet changes (for example, retained earnings) result from the netting of several changes, some of which relate to operations (net income) and some of which relate to financing activities (dividends). You should use whatever information the financial statements and notes provide about changes in balance sheet accounts to classify the net change properly in each account each period.

Exhibit 3.12 classifies the changes in the noncash balance sheet accounts and provides a schematic worksheet for the preparation of the statement of cash flows. The text will refer to this exhibit in walking through the preparation of a statement of cash flows for Footloose Shoe Store and in several exercises at the end of the chapter. The classification of each of these changes is discussed next.

1. Accounts Receivable

Cash collections from customers during a period equal sales for the period plus accounts receivable at the beginning of the period minus accounts receivable at the end of the period, or, alternatively, sales minus the change in accounts receivable.

$$Cash\ Collected\ from\ Customers = Sales - \Delta\ Accounts\ Receivable$$

A decrease in accounts receivable indicates that the firm collected more cash than it recognized in revenues, so the adjustment is an addition, and vice versa for increases in accounts receivable. The change in accounts receivable clearly relates to operations. The amount of sales revenue included in net income adjusted for the change in accounts receivable on line (1) results in the amount of cash received from customers.

2. Marketable Securities

Firms typically acquire marketable securities when they temporarily have excess cash and sell these securities when they need cash. U.S. GAAP and IFRS ignore the reason for the source or use of this cash and classify the cash flows associated with purchases and sales of marketable securities as investing activities. Because net income includes gains or losses on sales of marketable securities, you must subtract gains and add back

	Exhibit 3.12			
	Worksheet for Preparation of Statement of Cash Flows			
Balance Sheet Accounts	**Amount of Balance Sheet Changes**	**Operating**	**Investing**	**Financing**
(INCREASE) DECREASE IN ASSETS				
(1) Accounts receivable	X	X		
(2) Marketable securities	X		X	
(3) Inventories	X	X		
(4) Other current assets	X	X		
(5) Investments in securities	X		X	
(6) Property, plant, and equipment cost	X		X	
(7) Accumulated depreciation	X	X		
(8) Intangible assets	X	X	X	
INCREASE (DECREASE) IN LIABILITIES AND SHAREHOLDERS' EQUITIES				
(9) Accounts payable	X	X		
(10) Notes payable	X			X
(11) Current portion of long-term debt	X			X
(12) Other current liabilities	X	X		
(13) Long-term debt	X			X
(14) Deferred income taxes	X	X		
(15) Other noncurrent liabilities	X	X		
(16) Common stock	X			X
(17) Additional paid-in capital	X			X
(18) Retained earnings	X	X (net income)		X (dividends)
(19) Treasury stock	X			X
(20) Other accumulated comprehensive income				
(21) Cash	X	X	X	X

losses to net income in deriving cash flow from operations. Failure to offset the gain or loss included in earnings results in reporting too much (sales of marketable securities at a gain) or too little (sales of marketable securities at a loss) cash flow from operations.

3. Inventories

Purchases of inventory during a period equal cost of goods sold plus the change in inventory.

$$\text{Purchases of Inventory} = \text{Cost of Goods Sold} + \Delta \text{Inventory}$$

Cost of goods sold is an expense in measuring net income. The change in inventories on line (3) coupled with cost of goods sold included in net income results in the cash flow for purchases for the period. The presumption is that the firm made a cash outflow equal to the amount of purchases. If the firm does not pay cash for all of these purchases, accounts payable will change. You adjust for the change in accounts payable on line (9), discussed later.

4. Other Current Assets

Other current assets typically include prepayments for various operating costs, such as insurance and rent. Unless the financial statements and notes present information to the contrary, the presumption is that the change in other current assets relates to operations. Under this presumption, the related expenses are included in net income, so we must adjust these amounts for any changes in other current assets to convert those expenses into the cash amounts. The logic is the same as that for inventory.

5. Investments in Securities

The Investments in Securities account can change for the following reasons:

Source of Change	Classification in Statement of Cash Flows
Recognition of income or loss using equity method	Operating (subtraction or addition)
Acquisition or sale of investments	Investing (outflow or inflow)
Receipt of dividend from investee	Operating (inflow)
Purchases or sales of securities classified as "trading" securities	Operating (outflow or inflow)

These types of investments are generally disclosed separately. If a firm's balance sheet, income statement, or notes provide information that disaggregates the net change in investments in securities into these separate components, you can make appropriate classifications of the components. Absent such information, however, it is natural to classify the change in investment securities other than trading securities as an investing activity.

6. Property, Plant, and Equipment

Cash flows related to purchases and sales of fixed assets are classified as investing activities. Because net income includes any gains or losses from sales of fixed assets, you offset their effect on earnings by adding back losses and subtracting gains from net income when computing cash flows from operations. You then include the full amount of the proceeds from sales of fixed assets as an investing activity. Impairment charges, if applicable, would be a noncash charge that must be added back to net income in the operating section to appropriately report operating cash flows.

7. Accumulated Depreciation

The amount of depreciation expense recognized each period reduces net income but does not use cash. Thus, add back depreciation expense on line (7). This treatment is appropriate because depreciation expense is not a cash flow (ignoring income tax consequences). If a firm sells depreciable assets during a period, the net change in accumulated depreciation includes both the accumulated depreciation removed from the account for assets sold and depreciation expense for the period. Thus, you cannot assume that the change in the Accumulated Depreciation account relates only to depreciation expense unless disclosures indicate that the firm did not sell any depreciable assets during the year.

8. Intangible Assets

Intangible assets on the balance sheet include patents, copyrights, goodwill, and similar assets. A portion of the change in these accounts represents amortization, which requires an addback to net income when computing cash flows from operations. Unless the financial statements and notes provide contrary information, the presumption is that the remaining change in these accounts is an investing activity. Many firms include another line item on their balance sheets labeled "Other Noncurrent Assets." You should use whatever information firms disclose to determine the appropriate classification of the change in this account.

9. Accounts Payable

Accounts payable are typically due to suppliers from which the firm makes inventory purchases. The cash outflow for accounts payable equals inventory purchases during the period minus the change in accounts payable.

$$\text{Cash Paid to Suppliers} = \text{Purchases of Inventory} - \Delta \text{ Accounts Payable}$$

The amount for inventory purchases of the period was derived as part of the calculations in line (3) for inventories. The adjustment on line (9) for the change in accounts payable converts cost of goods sold that is included within net income to cash payments for purchases and, like inventories, is an operating activity.

10. Notes Payable

Notes Payable is the account generally used when a firm engages in short-term borrowing from a bank or another financial institution. Such borrowings are typically classified as financing activities on the statement of cash flows because the firm might use the proceeds to finance accounts receivable, inventories, or other working capital needs. The presumption underlying the classification of bank borrowing as a financing activity is that firms derive operating cash inflows from their customers, not by borrowing from banks.

11. Current Portion of Long-Term Debt

The change in the current portion of long-term debt during a period equals (a) the reclassification of long-term debt from a noncurrent liability to a current liability (that is, debt that the firm expects to repay within one year of the balance sheet date) minus (b) the current portion of long-term debt actually repaid during the period. The latter amount represents the cash outflow from this financing transaction. The amount arising from the reclassification in connection with line (13) will be considered shortly.

12. Other Current Liabilities

Firms generally use this account for obligations related to goods and services used in operations other than purchases of inventories. Thus, changes in other current liabilities appear as operating activities.

13. Long-Term Debt

This account changes for the following reasons:

- Issuance of new long-term debt.
- Reclassification of long-term debt from a noncurrent to a current liability (current portion of long-term debt).

- Retirement of long-term debt.
- Conversion of long-term debt to preferred or common stock.

These items are clearly financing transactions, but they do not all affect cash. The issuance of new debt and the retirement of old debt do affect cash flows. When long-term debt approaches maturity, the reclassification of long-term debt offsets the corresponding increase in the current portion of long-term debt, and they effectively cancel each other. This is appropriate because the reclassification does not affect cash flow. Likewise, any portion of the change in long-term debt on line (13) due to a conversion of debt into common stock offsets a similar change on lines (16) and (17). You enter reclassifications and conversions of debt on the worksheet for the preparation of a statement of cash flows because such transactions help explain changes in balance sheet accounts. However, these transactions do not appear on the formal statement of cash flows because they do not involve actual cash flows.

14. Deferred Income Taxes

Income taxes currently payable equal income tax expense plus or minus the change in deferred taxes during the period. Thus, changes in deferred income taxes appear as an operating activity.

15. Other Noncurrent Liabilities

This account includes unfunded pension and retirement benefit obligations, long-term deposits received, and other miscellaneous long-term liabilities. Changes in these types of obligations are typically operating activities, absent information to the contrary.

16, 17, and 19. Common Stock, Additional Paid-in Capital, and Treasury Stock

These accounts change when a firm issues new common stock or repurchases and retires outstanding common stock, and they appear as financing activities. The Additional Paid-in Capital account also changes when firms recognize compensation expense related to stock options. This is a noncash expense that, like depreciation, requires an addback to net income to compute cash flows from operations.

18. Retained Earnings

Retained earnings increase by the amount of net income and decrease with the declaration of dividends each period.

$$\text{Ending Retained Earnings} = \text{Beginning Retained Earnings} + \text{Net Income} - \text{Dividends}$$
$$\Delta \text{Retained Earnings} = \text{Net Income} - \text{Dividends}$$

Net income is an operating activity, and dividends are a financing activity.

20. Accumulated Other Comprehensive Income

Recall that accumulated other comprehensive income is a component of shareholders' equity and includes various fair value gains and losses that have not been realized. Examples include gains and losses from foreign currency translation, certain investment securities, derivative instruments, and certain pension items. The change in accumulated other comprehensive income on the balance sheet represents the amount of other comprehensive income for the period, net of any accumulated other comprehensive income items that were realized in cash and therefore recognized in net income during the period. Also recall that

$$\text{Net Income} + \text{Other Comprehensive Income} = \text{Comprehensive Income}$$

Other comprehensive income represents only noncash adjustments (that is, gains and losses that have not been realized). Accumulated other comprehensive income items that are realized in cash are already recognized in net income for the period. Therefore, the change in accumulated other comprehensive income on the balance sheet needs no further recognition on the statement of cash flows because the statement of cash flows starts with net income, not comprehensive income.

Illustration of the Preparation Procedure

Based on the data for Footloose Shoe Store, we illustrate the procedure for preparing the statement of cash flows in Exhibit 3.13. In addition to the balance sheet data shown there, net income was $16,634 for Year 2. The first column of Exhibit 3.14 shows the change in

Exhibit 3.13

Footloose Shoe Store
Worksheet for Statement of Cash Flows
Year 2

Balance Sheet Accounts	Amount of Balance Sheet Changes	Operating	Investing	Financing	Cross-Reference to Statement of Cash Flows in Exhibit 3.14
(INCREASE) DECREASE IN ASSETS					
Accounts receivable	$ (102)	$ (102)	—	—	❶
Inventories	(7,198)	(7,198)	—	—	❷
Other current assets	3,591	3,591	—	—	❸
Property, plant, and equipment	(1,651)	—	$(1,651)	—	❹
Accumulated depreciation	7,985	7,985	—	—	❺
Intangible assets	—	—	—	—	
INCREASE (DECREASE) IN LIABILITIES AND SHAREHOLDERS' EQUITIES					
Accounts payable	$ (6,126)	$ (6,126)	—	—	❻
Notes payable	—	—	—	—	❼
Current portion of long-term debt	(7,259)	—	—	$ (7,259)	❽
Other current liabilities	2,559	2,559	—	—	❾
Long-term debt	(9,536)	—	—	(9,536)	❽
Common stock	—	—	—	—	
Additional paid-in capital	—	—	—	—	
Retained paid-in capital	16,634	16,634	—	—	
Cash	$ (1,103)	$17,343	$(1,651)	$(16,795)	❿

Exhibit 3.14

Footloose Shoe Store
Statement of Cash Flows

	Year 2	Cross-Reference of Year 2 Amounts to Exhibit 3.13
OPERATING		
Net income	$ 16,634	
Depreciation	7,985	❺
(Increase) Decrease in accounts receivable	(102)	❶
(Increase) Decrease in inventories	(7,198)	❷
(Increase) Decrease in other current assets	3,591	❸
Increase (Decrease) in accounts payable	(6,126)	❻
Increase (Decrease) in other current liabilities	2,559	❾
Cash Flows from Operating Activities	$ 17,343	❿
INVESTING		
Sale (acquisition) of property, plant, and equipment	$ (1,651)	❹
Cash Flows from Investing Activities	$ (1,651)	❿
FINANCING		
Increase in notes payable	—	❼
Repayment of long-term debt	(16,795)	❽
Cash Flows from Financing Activities	$(16,795)	❿
Net Change in Cash	$ (1,103)	❿
Cash at beginning of year	13,698	
Cash at End of Year	$ 12,595	

each noncash balance sheet account that nets to the $1,103 decrease in cash for the period. You should observe with particular care the direction of the change. Recall the earlier decomposition of the balance sheet equation. Possible combinations of net changes in cash, liabilities, shareholders' equity, and noncash assets can be described as follows:

Δ Cash	=	Δ Liabilities	+	Δ Shareholders' Equity	−	Δ Noncash Assets
Increase	=	Increase				
Decrease	=	Decrease				
Increase	=			Increase		
Decrease	=			Decrease		
Decrease	=					Increase
Increase	=					Decrease

Changes in liabilities and shareholders' equity have the same directional effect on cash, whereas changes in noncash assets have the opposite directional effect. Bank borrowings increase liabilities and cash; debt repayments decrease liabilities and cash. Issuing common stock increases shareholders' equity and cash; paying dividends or repurchasing outstanding common stock reduces shareholders' equity and cash. Purchasing equipment increases noncash assets and reduces cash; selling equipment reduces noncash assets and increases cash.

You classify the change in each account as either an operating, investing, or financing activity, unless you have other information that more than one activity caused the change in the account. Observe the following inferences for Year 2:

1. Operating activities were a net source of cash for the period. Cash flows from operations approximately equaled net income. Footloose Shoe Store increased its inventories but reduced accounts payable. Most firms attempt to increase accounts payable to finance increases in inventories. The reduced accounts payable suggests a desire to pay suppliers more quickly, perhaps to take advantage of cash discounts, or pressure from suppliers to pay more quickly.
2. Cash flows from operations were more than sufficient to finance the increase in property, plant, and equipment. Note that capital expenditures were small relative to the amount of depreciation for the year, suggesting that the firm is not increasing its capacity.
3. Footloose Shoe Store used the cash derived from operations in excess of capital expenditures to repay long-term debt.

Exhibit 3.14 presents the statement of cash flows for Footloose Shoe Store for Year 2 using the amounts taken from the worksheet in Exhibit 3.13. The far right columns provide cross-references for clarifying how the worksheet is used to prepare the statement of cash flows.

■ Changes in cash are algebraically equal to changes in liabilities and equity minus changes in noncash assets.

■ If you understand how a statement of cash flows is prepared, you will be better able to effectively use the statement of cash flows.

Quick Check

Usefulness of the Statement of Cash Flows for Accounting and Risk Analysis

LO 3-6

Examine additional uses of cash flow information.

Accruals represent the noncash accounting adjustments that are employed to prepare income statements and balance sheets, such as recognizing sales on account, accruing expenses incurred but not paid, and so on. As discussed in the previous chapter, these accounting adjustments involve managerial discretion. For example, revenue recognition often requires managerial judgment about whether the company has surpassed all hurdles for appropriate revenue recognition. Changes in accounts receivable thus reflect discretion by managers. One nice feature of the statement of cash flows is that accruals are captured in its operating section.

As a user of financial statements, you can view the operating section of the statement of cash flows to highlight questions that are informative about managerial discretion. For example, are revenue and income growth mainly driven by accruals for receivables that might reflect aggressive revenue recognition? Are firms delaying recognizing expenses by capitalizing (rather than expensing) costs as assets? Is a persistent excess of net income over statement of cash flows sustainable through growth, or does net income reflect aggressive accruals recognition? Often, it is difficult to distinguish legitimate growth in the business from aggressive managerial discretion over accruals, but the first step is to identify key areas where such discretion might be aggressive.

As a brief prelude to the analysis of accruals to assess earnings quality later in Chapter 6, Exhibit 3.15 shows two versions of the 1998 statement of cash flows for **MicroStrategy, Inc.**: one as originally reported and the other as subsequently restated

Exhibit 3.15

MicroStrategy, Inc.
Statement of Cash Flows for 1998
(amounts in thousands)

	As Originally Reported	Restated
OPERATING ACTIVITIES		
Net income (loss)	$ 6,178	$ (2,255)
Adjustments to reconcile net income (loss) to net cash from operating activities:		
Depreciation and amortization	3,250	3,250
Provision for doubtful accounts, net of write-offs and recoveries	815	815
Net change in deferred taxes	(45)	0
Other	163	1,120
Changes in operating assets and liabilities, net of effect of foreign exchange rate changes:		
Accounts receivable	(17,525)	(10,835)
Prepaid expenses and other current assets	(711)	(3,758)
Accounts payable and accrued expenses, compensation, and benefits	5,948	5,508
Deferred revenue	2,267	3,795
Deposits and other assets	(188)	(188)
Long-term accounts receivable	(2,700)	0
Net Cash Used in Operating Activities	$ (2,548)	$ (2,548)
INVESTING ACTIVITIES		
Acquisition of property and equipment	$ (9,295)	$ (9,295)
Net Cash Used in Investing Activities	$ (9,295)	$ (9,295)
FINANCING ACTIVITIES		
Proceeds from sale of Class A common stock and exercise of stock options, net of offering costs	$ 48,539	$ 48,539
Repayments on short-term line of credit, net	(4,508)	(4,508)
Repayments of dividend notes payable	(5,000)	(5,000)
Proceeds from issuance of note payable	862	862
Principal payments on notes payable	(4,190)	(4,190)
Net Cash Provided by Financing Activities	$ 35,703	$ 35,703
Effect of foreign exchange rate changes on cash	$ 125	$ 125
Net Increase in Cash and Cash Equivalents	$ 23,985	$ 23,985
Cash and cash equivalents, beginning of year	3,506	3,506
Cash and Cash Equivalents, End of Period	$ 27,491	$ 27,491

for changes in the accounting for revenues. MicroStrategy is a provider of software that enables businesses to conduct transaction data through various channels and to examine information about customers, partners, and supply chains. The company aggressively recognized revenue upon signing a contract with customers (and often before that). The restatement announced in March 2000 included revised procedures for recognizing revenues over the contract period or after sales contracts were completed, rather than immediately. The most important point made in Exhibit 3.15 is that regardless of the accounting practices (before or after restatement), *the cash flows do not change*. How could different accounting treatment create or destroy cash flows?

For 1998, software license revenues of $72.721 million were restated downward to $61.635 million and net income was restated downward from a *profit* of $6.178 million to a *loss* of $2.255 million. The restatement affected the balance sheet through decreases in accounts receivable (for revenues recognized premature to the finalization of the contract), increases in deferred revenue (for revenue recognized immediately rather than spread over the contract period), and other miscellaneous adjustments. As Exhibit 3.15 shows, MicroStrategy used $2.548 million of cash for operations, which is unaffected by the restatement of revenues (and associated balance sheet data). As originally reported, adjustments for noncash components of income totaled $4.183 million, which totaled $5.185 million after the restatement; more importantly, working capital adjustments fell from –$12.909 million to –$5.478 million.

Several features of MicroStrategy's original operating section of the statement of cash flows stand out. First, as you have seen in other examples discussed earlier in the chapter, the typical relation of net income being less than operating cash flows is reversed for MicroStrategy. Although net income can legitimately exceed cash flows from operations, especially for growth firms, it can be a red flag for accounting quality issues because of managerial discretion necessary in noncash components of net income. Second, the existence of negative cash flows from operations but positive net income represents a situation in which managers may be keenly interested in reporting profits rather than losses, increasing incentives to adopt aggressive accounting practices. Third, the magnitude of the working capital adjustments exceeds that of adjustments for other noncash components of income, which indicates that the accounting for working capital accounts has an elevated importance for the level of reported earnings. Specifically, accounts receivable and deferred revenues are directly associated with the recognition of revenues.

As originally reported, MicroStrategy showed a negative adjustment for accounts receivable of $17.525 million, indicating that accounts receivable increased (and revenue was recognized); on the other hand, the originally reported change in deferred revenue was relatively smaller, increasing cash flows by $2.267 million (as customers prepaid and MicroStrategy actually deferred revenue). After the restatement, however, the increase in receivables declined to $10.835 million (pushing revenue recognition to future years) and the increase in deferred revenue increased to $3.795 million (deferring even more of the revenues for which customers had prepaid). Both of these changes reflect less aggressive accounting practices in terms of revenue recognition. Finally, the average total assets of MicroStrategy for 1998 were $56.377 million (not shown in Exhibit 3.15), so total accruals are approximately 15.5% of average total assets [{$6,178 − (−$2,548)}/$56,377]. The median value of asset-scaled total accruals for all firms is approximately –0.04. Thus, a value of 0.155 is remarkably high, as will be discussed in more depth in Chapter 6. Higher values of this metric are suggestive of lower earnings quality, which certainly characterized MicroStrategy's originally reported 1998 financial statements.

The restatement was costly to the company's shareholders as the price of Micro-Strategy common shares fell from $227 to $113 over the five days after the announcement of the restatement. Clearly, the financial statements as originally reported contained clues investors could have used to raise concerns about the quality of earnings possibly being low.

In addition to the analysis of accounting quality, the statement of cash flows is useful for liquidity and credit risk analysis. Chapter 5 discusses how you can use information on cash flows to assess a firm's ability to fund its operations and investments and to meet its debt obligations. Also, Chapter 12 discusses how you can use the statement of cash flows to compute free cash flows, which are widely used to estimate firm value.

Quick Check

■ The statement of cash flows is useful in assessing the quality of earnings and elements of the balance sheet.

Summary

As a complement to the balance sheet and the income statement, the statement of cash flows is an informative statement for analysts for the following reasons:

■ The statement of cash flows reveals information about the economic characteristics of a firm's industry, its strategy, and the stage in its life cycle.

■ An understanding of the mechanics of statement of cash flows preparation enables an analyst to better understand the links between the income statement and balance sheet.

■ The statement of cash flows provides information to assess the financial health of a firm. A firm with a healthy income statement is not necessarily financially healthy. Likewise, a firm with healthy cash flows is not necessarily financially healthy. Cash requirements to service debt, for example, may outstrip the ability of operations to generate cash. Or cash flows can be high during periods of value-destroying activities like liquidating productive assets.

■ The statement of cash flows highlights accounting accruals and can be an important tool in analyzing risk and earnings quality, which are necessary for forecasting future profits and valuing the firm.

Questions, Exercises, Problems, and Cases

Questions and Exercises

LO 3-1 **3.1 Need for a Statement of Cash Flows.** "The accrual basis of accounting creates the need for a statement of cash flows." Explain.

LO 3-1 **3.2 Requirement for Managers to Provide a Statement of Cash Flows.** The chapter demonstrates how to prepare a statement of cash flows from information on the balance sheet and income statement. If this is possible, why are managers required to provide a statement of cash flows?

3.3 Structure of the Statement of Cash Flows. "The ordering of the three sections of the statement of cash flows is 'backwards' for start-up firms, but it is more appropriate for businesses once they are up and running." Explain. `LO 3-2`

3.4 Articulation of the Statement of Cash Flows with Other Financial Statements. Describe how the statement of cash flows is linked to each of the other financial statements (income statement and balance sheet). Also, review how the other financial statements are linked with each other. `LO 3-3`

3.5 Classification of Interest Expense. Under U.S. GAAP, the statement of cash flows classifies cash expenditures for interest expense as an operating activity but classifies cash expenditures to redeem debt as a financing activity. Explain this apparent paradox. `LO 3-3`

3.6 Classification of Cash Flows Related to the Cost of Financing. Under U.S. GAAP, the statement of cash flows classifies cash expenditures for interest expense on debt as an operating activity but classifies cash expenditures for dividends to shareholders as a financing activity. Justify this apparent paradox. `LO 3-3`

3.7 Classification of Changes in Short-Term Financing. The statement of cash flows classifies changes in accounts payable as an operating activity but classifies changes in short-term borrowing as a financing activity. Explain this apparent paradox. `LO 3-3`

3.8 Classification of Cash Flows Related to Share-Based Compensation. One reason companies use stock options to compensate employees is to conserve cash. Under current tax law, companies get to deduct compensation when the employees actually exercise options. Explain how the cash flow savings from stock option exercises affect the statement of cash flows. `LO 3-3`

3.9 Treatment of Noncash Exchanges. The acquisition of equipment by assuming a mortgage is a transaction that firms cannot report in their statement of cash flows but must report in a supplemental schedule or note. Of what value is information about this type of transaction? What is the reason for its exclusion from the statement of cash flows? `LO 3-3`

3.10 Computing Cash Collections from Customers. Caterpillar manufactures heavy machinery and equipment and provides financing for purchases by its customers. Caterpillar reported sales and interest revenues of $51,324 million for Year 1. The balance sheet showed current and noncurrent receivables of $15,752 million at the beginning of Year 1 and $18,448 million at the end of Year 1. Compute the amount of cash collected from customers during Year 1. `LO 3-4`

3.11 Computing Cash Collections from Customers. iRobot designs and manufactures robots for consumer, commercial, and military use. For the fiscal year ended January 2, 2016, the company reported the following on its balance sheet and income statement (amounts in thousands): `LO 3-4`

- Accounts receivable, net of allowance of $33 at January 2, 2016, and $67 at December 27, 2014, of $104,679 and $71,056, respectively.
- Revenue for fiscal 2015 (i.e., the year ended January 2, 2016) of $616,778.
- Bad debt expense for fiscal 2015 of $0.

Compute the amount of cash collected from customers during fiscal 2015.

3.12 Computing Cash Payments to Suppliers. Lowe's Companies, a retailer of home improvement products, reported cost of goods sold of $31,729 million for `LO 3-4`

Year 1. It reported merchandise inventories of $7,611 million at the beginning of Year 1 and $8,209 million at the end of Year 1. It reported accounts payable to suppliers of $3,713 million at the beginning of fiscal Year 1 and $4,109 million at the end of fiscal Year 1. Compute the amount of cash paid to merchandise suppliers during Year 1.

3.13 Computing Cash Payments for Income Taxes. Visa Inc., a credit card company, reported income tax expense of $1,648 million for Year 1, comprising $1,346 million of current taxes and $302 million of deferred taxes. The balance sheet showed income taxes payable of $122 million at the beginning of Year 1 and $327 million at the end of Year 1. Compute the amount of income taxes paid in cash during Year 1.

3.14 Interpreting the Relation between Net Income and Cash Flow from Operations. Combined data for three years for two firms follow (in millions).

	Firm A	Firm B
Net income	$2,381	$2,825
Cash flow from operations	1,133	7,728

One of these firms is **Amazon.com**, a rapidly growing Internet retailer, and the other is **Kroger**, a retail grocery store chain growing at approximately the same rate as the population. Identify each firm and explain your reasoning.

3.15 Interpreting the Relation between Net Income and Cash Flow from Operations. Three years of combined data for two firms follow (in millions).

	Firm A	Firm B
Net income	$ 996	$2,846
Cash flow from operations	3,013	3,401

The two firms experienced similar growth rates in revenues during the three-year period. One of these firms is **Accenture Ltd.**, a management consulting firm, and the other is **Southwest Airlines**, a provider of airline transportation services. Identify each firm and explain your reasoning.

3.16 Interpreting Relations among Cash Flows from Operating, Investing, and Financing Activities. Three years of combined data for two firms follow (in millions).

	Firm A	Firm B
Net income	$ 2,378	$ 2,399
Cash flow from operations	7,199	3,400
Cash flow from investing	(6,764)	(678)
Cash flow from financing	570	(2,600)

One of these firms is **FedEx**, a relatively high-growth firm that provides courier services, and the other is **Kellogg Company**, a more mature consumer foods processor. Identify each firm and explain your reasoning.

3.17 Interpreting Relations among Cash Flows from Operating, Investing, and Financing Activities. LO 3-2

Three years of combined data for two firms follow (in millions).

	Firm A	Firm B
Cash flow from operations	$ 2,639	$ 2,759
Cash flow from investing	(3,491)	(1,281)
Cash flow from financing	1,657	(1,654)

One of these firms is **eBay**, an online retailer with a three-year growth in sales of 337.3%, and the other is **TJX Companies, Inc.**, a specialty retail store with a three-year growth in sales of 39.3%. Identify each firm and explain your reasoning.

Problems and Cases

3.18 Interpreting the Statement of Cash Flows. The Coca-Cola Company (Coca-Cola) manufactures and markets a variety of beverages. Exhibit 3.16 presents a statement of cash flows for Coca-Cola for three years. **LO 3-2, LO 3-3**

Exhibit 3.16

**The Coca-Cola Company
Statement of Cash Flows
(amounts in millions)
(Problem 3.18)**

Year Ended December 31,	Year 3	Year 2	Year 1
OPERATING ACTIVITIES			
Net income	$ 5,807	$ 5,981	$ 5,080
Depreciation and amortization	1,228	1,163	938
Stock-based compensation expense	266	313	324
Deferred income taxes	(360)	109	(35)
Equity income or loss, net of dividends	1,128	(452)	124
Foreign currency adjustments	(42)	9	52
Gains on sales of assets, including bottling interests	(130)	(244)	(303)
Other operating charges	209	166	159
Other items	153	99	233
Net change in operating assets and liabilities	(688)	6	(615)
Net Cash Provided by Operating Activities	$ 7,571	$ 7,150	$ 5,957
INVESTING ACTIVITIES			
Acquisitions and investments, principally beverage and bottling companies and trademarks	$ (759)	$(5,653)	$ (901)
Purchases of other investments	(240)	(99)	(82)
Proceeds from disposals of bottling companies and other investments	479	448	640
Purchases of property, plant, and equipment	(1,968)	(1,648)	(1,407)

(Continued)

Exhibit 3.16 (Continued)

Proceeds from disposals of property, plant, and equipment	129	239	112
Other investing activities	(4)	(6)	(62)
Net Cash Used in Investing Activities	$(2,363)	$(6,719)	$(1,700)
FINANCING ACTIVITIES			
Issuances of debt	$ 4,337	$ 9,979	$ 617
Payments of debt	(4,308)	(5,638)	(2,021)
Issuances of stock	586	1,619	148
Purchases of stock for treasury	(1,079)	(1,838)	(2,416)
Dividends	(3,521)	(3,149)	(2,911)
Net Cash Provided by (Used in) Financing Activities	$(3,985)	$ 973	$(6,583)
Effect of exchange rate changes on cash and cash equivalents	$ (615)	$ 249	$ 65
CASH AND CASH EQUIVALENTS			
Net Increase (Decrease) During the Year	$ 608	$ 1,653	$(2,261)
Balance at beginning of year	4,093	2,440	4,701
Balance at End of Year	$ 4,701	$ 4,093	$ 2,440

Source: The Coca-Cola Company, Form 10-K for the Fiscal Year Ended 2008.

REQUIRED

Discuss the relations between net income and cash flow from operations and among cash flows from operating, investing, and financing activities for the firm over the three-year period. Identify characteristics of Coca-Cola's cash flows that you would expect for a mature company.

LO 3-3   **3.19 Interpreting the Statement of Cash Flows.** Texas Instruments primarily develops and manufactures semiconductors for use in technology-based products for various industries. The manufacturing process is capital-intensive and subject to cyclical swings in the economy. Because of overcapacity in the industry and a cutback on spending for technology products due to a recession, semiconductor prices collapsed in Year 1 and commenced a steady comeback during Years 2 through 4. Exhibit 3.17 presents a statement of cash flows for Texas Instruments for Year 0 to Year 4.

REQUIRED

Discuss the relations between net income and cash flows from operations and among cash flows from operating, investing, and financing activities for the firm over the five-year period.

LO 3-2, LO 3-3   **3.20 Interpreting the Statement of Cash Flows.** Tesla Motors manufactures high-performance electric vehicles that are extremely slick looking. Exhibit 3.18 presents the statement of cash flows for Tesla Motors for 2010 through 2012.

REQUIRED

Discuss the relations among net income, cash flows from operations, cash flows from investing activities, and cash flows from financing activities for the firm over the three-year period. Speculate on the reasons for significant adjustments on the statement of cash flows. Describe what stage of life cycle these relations suggest for Tesla Motors. Why are negative operating cash flows less than the net losses? Where is Tesla obtaining cash, and what is it doing with it? What do you think will happen with cash flows in 2013?

Exhibit 3.17

Texas Instruments
Statement of Cash Flows
(amounts in millions)
(Problem 3.19)

	Year 4	Year 3	Year 2	Year 1	Year 0
OPERATIONS					
Net income (loss)	$ 1,861	$1,198	$ (344)	$ (201)	$ 3,087
Depreciation and amortization	1,549	1,528	1,689	1,828	1,376
Deferred income taxes	68	75	13	19	1
Other additions (Subtractions)	(179)	(469)	709	(68)	(2,141)
(Increase) Decrease in accounts receivable					
(Increase) Decrease in accounts inventories	(238)	(197)	(114)	958	(372)
(Increase) Decrease in inventories	(272)	(194)	(39)	482	(372)
(Increase) Decrease in prepayments	134	(183)	191	(235)	56
Increase (Decrease) in accounts payable	(71)	264	(81)	(687)	246
Increase (Decrease) in other current liabilities	294	129	(32)	(277)	309
Cash Flow from Operations	$ 3,146	$2,151	$ 1,992	$ 1,819	$ 2,185
INVESTING					
Fixed assets acquired	$(1,298)	$ (800)	$ (802)	$(1,790)	$(2,762)
Change in marketable securities	145	86	(238)	164	834
Acquisition of businesses	(8)	(128)	(69)	—	(3)
Other investing transactions	—	—	—	—	107
Cash Flow from Investing	$(1,161)	$ (842)	$(1,109)	$(1,626)	$(1,824)
FINANCING					
Increase in short-term borrowing	$ —	$ —	$ 9	$ —	$ 23
Increase in long-term borrowing	—	—	—	3	250
Issue of common stock	192	157	167	183	242
Decrease in short-term borrowing	(6)	(8)	(16)	(3)	(19)
Decrease in long-term borrowing	(429)	(418)	(22)	(132)	(307)
Acquisition of common stock	(753)	(284)	(370)	(395)	(155)
Dividends	(154)	(147)	(147)	(147)	(141)
Other financing transactions	15	260	14	(16)	(290)
Cash Flow from Financing	$(1,135)	$ (440)	$ (365)	$ (507)	$ (397)
Change in Cash	$ 850	$ 869	$ 518	$ (314)	$ (36)
Cash—Beginning of year	1,818	949	431	745	781
Cash—End of Year	$ 2,668	$1,818	$ 949	$ 431	$ 745
Change in sales from previous year	+27.9%	+17.3%	+2.2%	(30.9)%	(1.9)%

Source: Texas Instruments Inc., Form 10-K for the Fiscal Years Ended 2004 and 2002.

Exhibit 3.18

Tesla Motors
Statement of Cash Flows
(amounts in thousands)
(Problem 3.20)

	2012	2011	2010
Cash Flows from Operating Activities			
Net loss	$(396,213)	$(254,411)	$(154,328)
Adjustments to reconcile net loss to net cash used in operating activities:			
Depreciation and amortization	28,825	16,919	10,623
Change in fair value of warrant liabilities	1,854	2,750	5,022
Discounts and premiums on short-term marketable securities	56	(112)	—
Stock-based compensation	50,145	29,419	21,156
Excess tax benefits from stock-based compensation	—	—	(74)
Loss on abandonment of fixed assets	1,504	345	8
Inventory write-downs	4,929	1,828	951
Changes in operating assets and liabilities			
Accounts receivable	(17,303)	(2,829)	(3,222)
Inventories and operating lease vehicles	(194,726)	(13,638)	(28,513)
Prepaid expenses and other current assets	1,121	(248)	(4,977)
Other assets	(482)	(288)	(463)
Accounts payable	187,821	19,891	(212)
Accrued liabilities	9,603	10,620	13,345
Deferred development compensation	—	—	(156)
Deferred revenue	(526)	(1,927)	4,801
Reservation payments	47,056	61,006	4,707
Other long-term liabilities	10,255	2,641	3,515
Net cash used in operating activities	(266,081)	(128,034)	(127,817)
Cash Flows from Investing Activities			
Purchases of marketable securities	(14,992)	(64,952)	—
Maturities of short-term marketable securities	40,000	40,000	—
Payments related to acquisition of Fremont manufacturing facility and related assets	—	—	(65,210)
Purchases of property and equipment excluding capital leases	(239,228)	(184,226)	(40,203)
Withdrawals out of (transfers into) our dedicated Department of Energy account, net	8,620	50,121	(73,597)
Increase in other restricted cash	(1,330)	(3,201)	(1,287)
Net cash used in investing activities	(206,930)	(162,258)	(180,297)
Cash Flows from Financing Activities			
Proceeds from issuance of common stock in public offerings, net	221,496	172,410	188,842
Proceeds from issuance of common stock in private placements	—	59,058	80,000

(Continued)

Exhibit 3.18 (Continued)			
Principal payments on capital leases and other debt	(2,832)	(416)	(315)
Proceeds from long-term debt and other long-term liabilities	188,796	204,423	71,828
Principal payments on long-term debt	(12,710)	—	—
Proceeds from exercise of stock options and other stock issuances	24,885	10,525	1,350
Excess tax benefits from stock-based compensation	—	—	74
Deferred common stock and loan facility issuance costs	—	—	(3,734)
Net cash provided by financing activities	419,635	446,000	338,045
Net increase (decrease) in cash and cash equivalents	(53,376)	155,708	29,931
Cash and cash equivalents at beginning of period	255,266	99,558	69,627
Cash and cash equivalents at end of period	$ 201,890	$ 255,266	$ 99,558

Source: Tesla Motors, Inc., Form 10-K for the Fiscal Year Ended December 31, 2012.

3.21 Interpreting the Statement of Cash Flows. Gap Inc. operates chains [LO 3-3] of retail clothing stores under the names of **Gap**, **Banana Republic**, and **Old Navy**. Exhibit 3.19 presents the statement of cash flows for Gap for Year 0 to Year 4.

Exhibit 3.19					
Gap Inc. Statement of Cash Flows **(amounts in millions)** **(Problem 3.21)**					
	Year 4	Year 3	Year 2	Year 1	Year 0
OPERATIONS					
Net income (loss)	$ 1,150	$ 1,031	$ 478	$ (8)	$ 877
Depreciation	620	675	706	811	590
Other additions and subtractions	(28)	180	166	30	92
(Increase) Decrease in inventories	(90)	385	(258)	213	(455)
(Increase) Decrease in prepayments	(18)	5	33	(13)	(61)
Increase (Decrease) in accounts payable	42	(10)	(47)	42	250
Increase (Decrease) in other current liabilities	(56)	(106)	165	243	(3)
Cash Flow from Operations	$ 1,620	$ 2,160	$1,243	$1,318	$ 1,290
INVESTING					
Fixed assets acquired	$ (442)	$ (261)	$ (308)	$ (940)	$(1,859)
Changes in marketable securities	259	(2,063)	(313)	—	—
Other investing transactions	343	6	(8)	(11)	(16)
Cash Flow from Investing	$ 160	$(2,318)	$ (629)	$ (951)	$(1,875)

(Continued)

Exhibit 3.19 (Continued)

FINANCING

Increase in short-term borrowing	$ —	$ —	$ —	$ —	$ 621
Increase in long-term borrowing	—	85	1,346	1,194	250
Issue of capital stock	130	26	153	139	152
Decrease in short-term borrowing	—	0	(42)	(735)	—
Decrease in long-term borrowing	(871)	(668)	—	(250)	—
Acquisition of capital stock	(976)	—	—	(1)	(393)
Dividends	(79)	(79)	(78)	(76)	(75)
Other financing transactions	—	28	27	(11)	(11)
Cash Flow from Financing	$(1,796)	$ (608)	$1,406	$ 260	$ 544
Change in Cash	$ (16)	$ (766)	$2,020	$ 627	$ (41)
Cash—Beginning of year	2,261	3,027	1,007	380	421
Cash—End of Year	$ 2,245	$ 2,261	$3,027	$1,007	$ 380
Change in sales from previous year	+2.6%	+9.7%	+4.4%	+1.3%	+17.5%

Source: Gap Inc., Form 10-K for the Fiscal Years Ended 2005 and 2003.

REQUIRED

Discuss the relations between net income and cash flow from operations and among cash flows from operating, investing, and financing activities for the firm over the five-year period. Speculate on reasons for the more significant increases and decreases.

LO 3-3

3.22 Interpreting the Statement of Cash Flows. Sirius XM Radio Inc. is a satellite radio company, formed from the merger of Sirius and XM in 2008. Exhibit 3.20 presents a statement of cash flows for Sirius XM Radio for 2006, 2007, and 2008. Sirius XM and its predecessor, Sirius, realized revenue growth of 49% in 2007 and 81% in 2008. The merger was a stock-for-stock merger.

Exhibit 3.20

Sirius XM Radio Inc.
Statement of Cash Flows
(amounts in thousands)
(Problem 3.22)

	2008	2007	2006
CASE FLOWS FROM OPERATING ACTIVITIES			
Net loss	$(5,313,288)	$(565,252)	$(1,104,867)
Adjustments to reconcile net loss to net cash used in operating activities:			
Depreciation and amortization	203,752	106,780	105,749
Impairment loss	4,766,190	—	10,917
Noncash interest expense, net of amortization of premium	(6,311)	4,269	3,107
Provision for doubtful accounts	21,589	9,002	9,370

(Continued)

Exhibit 3.20 (Continued)

Noncash loss from redemption of debt	98,203	—	—
Loss on disposal of assets	4,879	(428)	1,661
Loss on investments, net	28,999	—	4,445
Share-based payment expense	87,405	78,900	437,918
Deferred income taxes	2,476	2,435	2,065
Other noncash purchase price adjustments	(67,843)	—	—
Changes in operating assets and liabilities, net of assets and liabilities acquired:			
Accounts receivable	(32,121)	(28,881)	(1,871)
Inventory	8,291	4,965	(20,246)
Prepaid expenses and other current assets	(19,953)	11,118	(42,132)
Other long-term assets	(13,338)	(729)	(39,878)
Accounts payable and accrued expenses	(65,481)	66,169	26,366
Accrued interest	23,081	(8,920)	1,239
Deferred revenue	55,778	169,905	181,003
Other long-term liabilities	64,895	1,901	3,452
Net Cash Used in Operating Activities	$ (152,797)	$(148,766)	$ (421,702)
CASH FLOWS FROM INVESTING ACTIVITIES			
Additions to property and equipment	$ (130,551)	$ (65,264)	$ (92,674)
Sales of property and equipment	105	641	127
Purchases of restricted and other investments	(3,000)	(310)	(12,339)
Acquisition of acquired entity cash	819,521	—	—
Merger-related costs	(23,519)	(29,444)	—
Purchase of available-for-sale securities	—	—	(123,500)
Sale of restricted and other investments	65,869	40,191	255,715
Net Cash Provided by (Used in) Investing Activities	$ 728,425	$ (54,186)	$ 27,329
CASH FLOWS FROM FINANCING ACTIVITIES			
Proceeds from exercise of warrants and stock options and from share/borrow arrangement	$ 471	$ 4,097	$ 25,787
Long-term borrowings, net of related costs	531,743	244,879	—
Payment of premiums on redemption of debt and payments to minority interest holder	(20,172)	—	—
Repayment of long-term borrowings	(1,146,044)	(625)	—
Net Cash (Used in) Provided by Financing Activities	$ (634,002)	$ 248,351	$ 25,787
Net (Decrease) Increase in Cash and Cash Equivalents	$ (58,374)	$ 45,399	$ (368,586)
Cash and cash equivalents at beginning of period	438,820	393,421	762,007
Cash and Cash Equivalents at End of Period	$ 380,446	$ 438,820	$ 393,421

Source: Sirius XM Radio Inc., Form 10-K for the Fiscal Year Ended December 31, 2008.

REQUIRED

Discuss the relations among net loss and cash flow from operations and the pattern of cash flows from operating, investing, and financing activities during the three years. Speculate on reasons for the more significant increases and decreases.

LO 3-5   **3.23 Interpreting the Statement of Cash Flows.** Sunbeam Corporation manufactures and sells a variety of small household appliances, including toasters, food processors, and waffle grills. Exhibit 3.21 presents a statement of cash flows for Sunbeam for Year 5, Year 6, and Year 7. After experiencing decreased sales in Year 5, Sunbeam hired Albert Dunlap in Year 6 to turn the company around. Albert Dunlap, known in the industry as "Chainsaw Al,"

Exhibit 3.21

Sunbeam Corporation
Statement of Cash Flows
(amounts in millions)
(Problem 3.23)

	Year 7	Year 6	Year 5
OPERATIONS			
Net income (loss)	$ 109.4	$(228.3)	$ 50.5
Depreciation and amortization	38.6	47.4	44.2
Restructuring and asset impairment charges	—	283.7	—
Deferred income taxes	57.8	(77.8)	25.1
Other additions	13.7	46.2	10.8
Other subtractions	(84.6)	(27.1)	(21.7)
(Increase) Decrease in accounts receivable	(84.6)	(13.8)	(4.5)
(Increase) Decrease in inventories	(100.8)	(11.6)	(4.9)
(Increase) Decrease in prepayments	(9.0)	2.7	(8.8)
Increase (Decrease) in accounts payable	(1.6)	14.7	9.2
Increase (Decrease) in other current liabilities	52.8	(21.9)	(18.4)
Cash Flow from Operations	$ (8.3)	$ 14.2	$ 81.5
INVESTING			
Fixed assets acquired	$ (58.3)	$ (75.3)	$(140.1)
Sale of businesses	91.0	—	65.3
Acquisitions of businesses	—	(.9)	(33.0)
Cash Flow from Investing	$ 32.7	$ (76.2)	$(107.4)
FINANCING			
Increase (Decrease) in short-term borrowing	$ 5.0	$ 30.0	$ 40.0
Increase in long-term debt	—	11.5	—
Issue of common stock	26.6	9.2	9.8
Decrease in long-term debt	(12.2)	(1.8)	(5.4)
Acquisition of common stock	—	—	(13.0)
Dividends	(3.4)	(3.3)	(3.3)
Other financing transactions	0.5	(.4)	(.2)
Cash Flow from Financing	$ 16.5	$ 45.2	$ 27.9
Change in Cash	$ 40.9	$ (16.8)	$ 2.0
Cash—Beginning of year	11.5	28.3	26.3
Cash—End of Year	$ 52.4	$ 11.5	$ 28.3

Source: Sunbeam Corporation, Form 10-K for the Fiscal Year Ended 1997.

had previously directed restructuring efforts at Scott Paper Company. The restructuring effort at Sunbeam generally involved firing employees and cutting costs aggressively. Most of these restructuring efforts took place during Year 6. The market expected significantly improved results in Year 7. Reported sales increased 18.7% between Year 6 and Year 7, and net income improved. However, subsequent revelations showed that almost half of the sales increase resulted from fraudulent early recognition of revenues in the fourth quarter of Year 7 that the firm should have recognized in the first quarter of Year 8. Growth in revenues for Years 5, 6, and 7 was −2.6%, −3.2%, and 18.7%, respectively.

REQUIRED

a. Using the information provided and the statement of cash flows for Year 5 in Exhibit 3.21, identify any signals that Sunbeam was experiencing operating difficulties and was in need of restructuring.

b. Using information in the statement of cash flows for Year 6, identify indicators of the turnaround efforts and any relations among cash flows that trouble you.

c. Using information in the statement of cash flows for Year 7, indicate any signals that the firm might have engaged in aggressive revenue recognition and had not yet fixed its general operating problems.

3.24 Interpreting the Statement of Cash Flows. Montgomery Ward   `LO 3-5`
operates a retail department store chain. It filed for bankruptcy during the first quarter of Year 12. Exhibit 3.22 presents a statement of cash flows for Montgomery Ward for Year 7 to Year 11.

Exhibit 3.22					
Montgomery Ward **Statement of Cash Flows** **(amounts in millions)** **(Problem 3.24)**					
	Year 11	**Year 10**	**Year 9**	**Year 8**	**Year 7**
OPERATIONS					
Net income	$(237)	$ (9)	$ 109	$ 101	$ 100
Depreciation	122	115	109	98	97
Other addbacks	13	8	24	25	32
Other subtractions	(197)	(119)	(29)	—	—
(Increase) Decrease in accounts receivable	(32)	(54)	(38)	(9)	9
(Increase) Decrease in inventories	225	(112)	(229)	(204)	(38)
(Increase) Decrease in prepayments	27	(32)	(39)	(58)	36
Increase (Decrease) in accounts payable	(222)	85	291	148	(17)
Increase (Decrease) in other current liabilities	(55)	(64)	(45)	28	(64)
Cash Flow from Operations	$(356)	$(182)	$ 153	$ 129	$ 155
INVESTING					
Fixed assets acquired	$ (75)	$(122)	$(184)	$(142)	$(146)
Change in marketable securities	20	(14)	(4)	(27)	137
Other investing transactions	(93)	27	(113)	6	9
Cash Flow from Investing	$(148)	$(109)	$(301)	$(163)	$ —

(Continued)

Exhibit 3.22 (Continued)					
FINANCING					
Increase in short-term borrowing	$ 588	$ 16	$ 144	$ —	$ —
Increase in long-term borrowing	—	205	168	100	—
Issue of capital stock	3	193	78	1	1
Decrease in short-term borrowing	—	—	—	—	—
Decrease in long-term borrowing	(63)	(17)	(275)	(18)	(403)
Acquisition of capital stock	(20)	(98)	(9)	(11)	(97)
Dividends	(9)	(4)	(24)	(23)	(19)
Other	—	—	1	2	2
Cash Flow from Financing	$ 499	$ 295	$ 83	$ 51	$(516)
Change in Cash	$ (5)	$ 4	$ (65)	$ 17	$(361)
Cash—Beginning of year	37	33	98	81	442
Cash—End of Year	$ 32	$ 37	$ 33	$ 98	$ 81
Change in sales from previous year	(10.0)%	(0.5)%	+17.2%	+3.7%	+2.0%

Source: Montgomery Ward, Form 10-K for the Fiscal Years Ended 1996 and 1994.

The firm acquired **Lechmere**, a discount retailer of sporting goods and electronic products, during Year 9. It acquired **Amoco Enterprises**, an automobile club, during Year 11. During Year 10, it issued a new series of preferred stock and used part of the cash proceeds to repurchase a series of outstanding preferred stock. The "other subtractions" in the operating section for Year 10 and Year 11 represent reversals of deferred tax liabilities.

REQUIRED

Discuss the relations between net income and cash flow from operations and among cash flows from operating, investing, and financing activities for the firm over the five-year period. Identify signals of Montgomery Ward's difficulties that might have led to its filing for bankruptcy.

LO 3-3, LO 3-5   **3.25 Extracting Performance Trends from the Statement of Cash Flows.** The **Apollo Group** is one of the largest providers of private education and runs numerous programs and services, including the **University of Phoenix**. Exhibit 3.23 provides statements of cash flows for 2010 through 2012.

REQUIRED

Discuss the relations between net income and cash flow from operations and among cash flows from operating, investing, and financing activities for the firm, especially for 2012. Identify signals that might raise concerns for an analyst.

LO 3-1   **3.26 Interpreting a Direct Method Statement of Cash Flows.** Aer **Lingus** is an international airline based in Ireland. Exhibit 3.24 provides the statement of cash flows for Year 1 and Year 2, which includes a footnote from the financial statements. Year 2 was characterized by weakening consumer demand for air travel due to a recession and record-high fuel prices. In addition, Year 2 includes exceptional items totaling €141 million, which reflect a staff restructuring program for early retirement (€118 million), takeover defense costs due to a bid by **Ryanair** (€18 million), and other costs (€5 million).

REQUIRED

a. Based on information in the statement of cash flows, compare and contrast the cash flows for Years 1 and 2. Explain significant differences in individual reconciling items and direct cash flows.

b. The format of Aer Lingus' statement of cash flows is the direct method, as evidenced by the straightforward titles used in the operating section. How is this statement different from the presentation that Aer Lingus would report using the indirect method?

Exhibit 3.23			
The Apollo Group **Statement of Cash Flows** **(amounts in thousands)** **(Problem 3.25)**			
	Year Ended August 31,		
	2012	2011	2010
Cash flows provided by (used in) operating activities:			
Net income	$ 417,006	$ 535,796	$ 521,581
Adjustments to reconcile net income to net cash provided by operating activities:			
Share-based compensation	78,705	70,040	64,305
Excess tax benefits from share-based compensation	(1,150)	(4,014)	(6,648)
Depreciation and amortization	178,234	159,006	147,035
Amortization of lease incentives	(15,510)	(18,822)	(13,358)
Amortization of deferred gains on sale-leasebacks	(2,798)	(2,221)	(1,705)
Impairment on discontinued operations	—	—	9,400
Goodwill and other intangibles impairment	16,788	219,927	184,570
Noncash foreign currency (gain) loss, net	(497)	1,662	643
Gain on sale of discontinued operations	(26,678)	—	—
Provision for uncollectible accounts receivable	146,742	181,297	282,628
Litigation charge (credit), net	4,725	(11,951)	177,982
Deferred income taxes	21,850	55,823	(125,399)
Changes in assets and liabilities, excluding the impact of acquisitions and business dispositions:			
Restricted cash and cash equivalents	61,073	64,725	(11,828)
Accounts receivable	(129,773)	(121,120)	(265,996)
Prepaid taxes	9,303	(25,241)	10,421
Other assets	(11,568)	(9,900)	2,183
Accounts payable	12,525	(3,913)	21,624
Student deposits	(58,740)	(70,120)	3,445
Deferred revenue	(39,154)	(79,488)	32,887
Accrued and other liabilities	(109,783)	(44,364)	(528)
Net cash provided by operating activities	551,300	897,122	1,033,242

(Continued)

Exhibit 3.23 (Continued)

Cash flows provided by (used in) investing activities:

Additions to property and equipment	(115,187)	(162,573)	(168,177)
Acquisitions, net of cash acquired	(73,736)	—	(5,497)
Maturities of marketable securities	—	10,000	5,000
Proceeds from sale-leaseback, net	—	169,018	—
Proceeds from dispositions, net	76,434	21,251	—
Collateralization of letter of credit	—	126,615	(126,615)
Other investing activities	(1,694)	—	—
Net cash (used in) provided by investing activities	(114,183)	164,311	(295,289)

Cash flows provided by (used in) financing activities:

Payments on borrowings	(562,269)	(437,925)	(477,568)
Proceeds from borrowings	629,145	410,051	475,454
Apollo Group Class A common stock purchased for treasury	(811,913)	(783,168)	(446,398)
Issuance of Apollo Group Class A common stock	11,949	24,903	19,671
Noncontrolling interest contributions	—	6,875	2,460
Excess tax benefits from share-based compensation	1,150	4,014	6,648
Net cash used in financing activities	(731,938)	(775,250)	(419,733)
Exchange rate effect on cash and cash equivalents	(468)	712	(1,697)
Net (decrease) increase in cash and cash equivalents	(295,289)	286,895	316,523
Cash and cash equivalents, beginning of year	1,571,664	1,284,769	968,246
Cash and cash equivalents, end of year	$1,276,375	$1,571,664	$1,284,769

Source: The Apollo Group, Form 10-K for the Fiscal Year Ended 2012.

Exhibit 3.24

Aer Lingus
Statement of Cash Flows
(amounts in millions)
(Problem 3.26)

	Year 2	Year 1
CASH FLOWS FROM OPERATING ACTIVITIES		
Cash (used in) generated from operations (see Note 27)	€ (8,627)	€ 59,122
Interest paid	(17,684)	(22,437)
Income tax received (paid)	5,046	(4,002)
Net Cash (Used in) Generated from Operating Activities	€ (21,265)	€ 32,683
CASH FLOWS FROM INVESTING ACTIVITIES		
Purchases of property, plant, and equipment	€(114,490)	€(200,604)
Purchases of intangible assets	(5,619)	(4,294)
Proceeds from sale of investment	—	11,374
Disposal of available-for-sale financial assets	—	9,031
(Increase) Decrease in deposits and restricted cash with maturity greater than 3 months	(44,099)	138,066

(Continued)

Exhibit 3.24 (Continued)

Dividends received	—	2,998
Interest received	46,766	60,008
Net Cash (Used in) Generated from Investing Activities	€(117,442)	€ 16,579
CASH FLOWS FROM FINANCING ACTIVITIES		
Costs arising from issuance of ordinary shares	€ —	€ (3,720)
Proceeds from borrowings	186,135	2,090
Repayments of borrowings	(38,695)	(61,104)
Net Cash Generated from (Used in) Financing Activities	€ 147,440	€ (62,734)
Net Increase (Decrease) in Cash, Cash Equivalents, and Bank Overdrafts	€ 8,733	€ (13,472)
Cash, cash equivalents, and bank overdrafts at beginning of year	€ (12,185)	€ (1,226)
Exchange gains on cash, cash equivalents, and bank overdrafts	9,533	2,513
Cash, Cash Equivalents, and Bank Overdrafts at End of Year	€ 6,081	€ (12,185)
Note 27 CASH GENERATED FROM OPERATIONS		
(Loss) Profit before tax	€(119,696)	€ 124,726
Adjustments for:		
Depreciation	69,558	63,664
Amortisation	2,307	5,635
Net movements in provisions for liabilities and charges	(13,084)	(14,690)
Net fair value losses on derivative financial instruments	945	40
Finance income	(60,860)	(65,143)
Finance cost	22,018	22,572
Net exceptional items	140,888	(3,517)
Other (gains) losses	(8,796)	8,880
Changes in working capital		
Inventories	360	(140)
Trade and other receivables	(16,329)	181
Trade and other payables	(25,938)	20,914
Payment to supplemental pension arrangements	—	(104,000)
Cash Generated from Operations	€ (8,627)	€ 59,122

Source: Aer Lingus Group Plc, Annual Report for the Fiscal Year Ended December 31, 2008.

3.27 Identifying Industry Differences in the Statement of Cash Flows. `LO 3-2`

Exhibit 3.25 presents common-size statements of cash flows for eight firms in various industries. All amounts in the common-size statements of cash flows are expressed as a percentage of cash flow from operations. In constructing the common-size percentages for each firm, reported amounts for each firm for three consecutive years were summed and the common-size percentages are based on the summed amounts. This procedure reduces the effects of a nonrecurring item in a particular year, such as a major debt or a common stock issue. Exhibit 3.25 also shows the compound annual rate of growth in revenues over the three-year period. The eight companies are as follows:

■ **Biogen** creates and manufactures biotechnology drugs. Many drugs are still in the development phase in this high-growth, relatively young industry. Research and manufacturing facilities are capital-intensive, although the research process requires skilled scientists.

Exhibit 3.25

Common-Size Statements of Cash Flows for Selected Companies (Problem 3.27)

	1	2	3	4	5	6	7	8
OPERATIONS								
Net income	34.9%	38.6%	40.9%	45.4%	61.2%	62.4%	76.5%	97.6%
Depreciation	47.9	55.2	62.9	37.7	46.0	22.3	38.0	23.3
Other	3.1	24.3	5.1	(5.0)	9.4	11.6	2.3	3.9
(Increase) Decrease in accounts receivable	6.5	(4.8)	(.6)	(12.4)	(34.2)	(7.8)	(6.8)	(8.5)
(Increase) Decrease in Inventories	1.5	(15.1)	(1.2)	(14.4)	(11.9)	(3.1)	(7.4)	(58.4)
Increase (Decrease) in accounts payable	1.5	3.1	(5.6)	12.4	3.0	2.9	12.6	39.9
Increase (Decrease) in other current liabilities	4.6	(1.3)	(1.5)	36.3	26.5	11.7	(15.2)	2.2
Cash Flow from Operations	100.0%	100.0%	100.0%	100.0%	100.0%	100.0%	100.0%	100.0%
INVESTING								
Fixed assets acquired	(37.1%)	(64.0%)	(81.1%)	(165.7%)	(44.7%)	(13.4%)	(39.3%)	(153.4%)
Change in marketable securities	—	—	(2.8)	(75.1)	(14.8)	(3.5)	5.9	(17.5)
Other investing transactions	(7.7)	8.5	16.4	(28.4)	(15.9)	(17.3)	(40.6)	23.2
Cash Flow from Investing	(44.8%)	(55.5%)	(67.5%)	(269.2%)	(75.4%)	(34.2%)	(74.0%)	(147.7%)
FINANCING								
Change in short-term debt	(0.6%)	—	(7.4%)	—	(2.4%)	—	7.9%	—
Increase in long-term debt	19.5	41.4%	8.4	75.7%	—	33.1%	24.0	46.9%
Issue of capital stock	11.2	9.9	—	82.5	17.7	1.7	6.7	13.5
Decrease in long-term debt	(36.0)	(85.0)	(9.1)	(2.7)	(7.0)	(27.6)	(3.1)	(1.2)
Repurchase of capital stock	(18.9)	(1.5)	(0.1)	—	(50.7)	(21.4)	(26.9)	—
Dividends	(29.5)	(10.9)	(29.9)	—	—	(46.1)	(43.5)	(11.5)
Other financing transactions	—	—	(0.2)	—	—	0.6	9.8	1.9
Cash Flow from Financing	(54.3%)	(46.1%)	(38.3%)	155.5%	(42.4%)	(59.7%)	(25.1%)	49.6%
Net Change in Cash	0.9%	(1.6%)	(5.8%)	13.7%	(17.8%)	6.1%	0.9%	1.9%
Growth in Revenues	(3.6%)	5.7%	5.7%	23.0%	18.2%	7.7%	8.6%	28.3%

- **Chevron Texaco** explores, extracts, refines, and markets petroleum products. Extraction and refining activities are capital-intensive. Petroleum products are in the mature phase of their product life cycle.
- **H. J. Heinz** manufactures and markets branded consumer food products. Heinz has acquired several other branded food products companies in recent years.
- **Home Depot** sells home improvement products. Home Depot competes in a new retail category known as "category killer" stores. Such stores offer a wide selection of products in a particular product category (for example, books, pet products, or office products). In recent years, these stores have taken away significant market share from more diversified department and discount stores.
- **Inland Steel** manufactures steel products. Although steel plants are capital-intensive, they also use unionized workers to process iron into steel products. Demand for steel products follows cyclical trends in the economy. Steel manufacturing in the United States is in the mature phase of its life cycle.
- **Pacific Gas & Electric** provides electric and gas utility services. The electric utility industry in the United States has excess capacity. Increased competition from less regulated, more open markets has forced down prices and led some utilities to reduce their capacity.
- **ServiceMaster** provides home cleaning and restoration services. ServiceMaster has recently acquired firms offering cleaning services for healthcare facilities and has broadened its home services to include termite protection, garden care, and other services. ServiceMaster operates as a partnership. Partnerships do not pay income taxes on their earnings each year. Instead, partners (owners) include their share of the earnings of ServiceMaster in their taxable income.
- **Sun Microsystems** creates, manufactures, and markets computers, primarily to the scientific and engineering markets and to network applications. Sun follows an assembly strategy in manufacturing computers, outsourcing the components from other firms worldwide. (Note: The figures in Exhibit 3.25 are prior to Sun's acquisition by Oracle Corporation.)

REQUIRED

Use the clues in the common-size statements of cash flows to match the companies in Exhibit 3.25 with the companies listed here. Discuss the reasoning for your selection in each case.

3.28 Preparing a Statement of Cash Flows from Balance Sheets and Income Statements. **Nojiri Pharmaceutical Industries** develops, manufactures, and markets pharmaceutical products in Japan. The Japanese economy experienced recessionary conditions in recent years. In response to these conditions, the Japanese government increased the proportion of medical costs that is the patient's responsibility and lowered the prices for prescription drugs. Exhibit 3.26 presents the firm's balance sheets for Years 1 through 4, and Exhibit 3.27 presents income statements for Years 2 through 4.

`LO 3-4`

REQUIRED

a. Prepare a worksheet for the preparation of a statement of cash flows for Nojiri Pharmaceutical Industries for each of the years ending March 31, Year 2 to Year 4. Follow the format of Exhibits 3.12 and 3.13 in the text. Notes to the financial statements indicate the following:
   (1) The changes in Accumulated Other Comprehensive Income relate to revaluations of Investments in Securities to market value. The remaining changes in Investments in Securities result from purchases and sales. Assume that the sales occurred at no gain or loss.
   (2) No sales of property, plant, and equipment took place during the three-year period.
   (3) The changes in Other Noncurrent Assets are investing activities.
   (4) The changes in Employee Retirement Benefits relate to provisions made for retirement benefits net of payments made to retired employees, both of which the statement of cash flows classifies as operating activities.
   (5) The changes in Other Noncurrent Liabilities are financing activities.

Exhibit 3.26

Nojiri Pharmaceutical Industries
Balance Sheets
(amounts in millions)
(Problem 3.28)

March 31:	Year 4	Year 3	Year 2	Year 1
ASSETS				
Cash	¥ 6,233	¥ 4,569	¥ 4,513	¥ 5,008
Accounts and notes receivable—Trade	19,003	17,828	19,703	19,457
Inventories	7,693	7,948	8,706	8,607
Deferred income taxes	1,355	1,192	948	824
Prepayments	432	325	640	634
Total Current Assets	¥ 34,716	¥ 31,862	¥ 34,510	¥ 34,530
Investments	3,309	2,356	3,204	4,997
Property, plant, and equipment, at cost	71,792	71,510	71,326	71,018
Less accumulated depreciation	(40,689)	(38,912)	(36,854)	(35,797)
Deferred income taxes	236	1,608	1,481	494
Other assets	4,551	3,904	3,312	3,463
Total Assets	¥ 73,915	¥ 72,328	¥ 76,979	¥ 78,705
LIABILITIES AND SHAREHOLDERS' EQUITY				
Accounts and notes payable—Trade	¥ 10,087	¥ 9,629	¥ 10,851	¥ 10,804
Notes payable to banks	10,360	10,328	9,779	10,023
Current portion of long-term debt	100	200	—	—
Other current liabilities	7,200	6,170	9,779	7,565
Total Current Liabilities	¥ 27,747	¥ 26,327	¥ 30,409	¥ 28,392
Long-term debt	8,140	7,889	6,487	8,147
Deferred income taxes	3,361	—	—	—
Employee retirement benefits	809	905	1,087	1,166
Other noncurrent liabilities	175	174	200	216
Total Liabilities	¥ 40,232	¥ 35,295	¥ 38,183	¥ 37,921
Common stock	¥ 10,758	¥ 10,758	¥ 10,758	¥ 10,758
Additional paid-in capital	15,012	15,012	15,012	15,012
Retained earnings	9,179	11,838	13,697	15,014
Accumulated other comprehensive income	(342)	(490)	(659)	—
Treasury stock	(924)	(85)	(12)	—
Total Shareholders' Equity	¥ 33,683	¥ 37,033	¥ 38,796	¥ 40,784
Total Liabilities and Shareholders' Equity	¥ 73,915	¥ 72,328	¥ 76,979	¥ 78,705

b. Prepare a comparative statement of cash flows for Year 2, Year 3, and Year 4.

c. Discuss the relations among net income and cash flow from operations and the pattern of cash flows from operating, investing, and financing transactions for Year 2, Year 3, and Year 4.

Exhibit 3.27

Nojiri Pharmaceutical Industries
Income Statements
(amounts in millions)
(Problem 3.28)

Year Ended March 31:	Year 4	Year 3	Year 2
Sales	¥ 41,352	¥ 41,926	¥ 44,226
Cost of goods sold	(27,667)	(27,850)	(28,966)
Selling and administrative expenses	(13,396)	(15,243)	(15,283)
Interest expense	(338)	(364)	(368)
Income tax expense	(1,823)	443	34
Net Income	¥ (1,872)	¥ (1,088)	¥ (357)

3.29 Preparing a Statement of Cash Flows from Balance Sheets and Income Statements. Flight Training Corporation is a privately held firm that provides fighter pilot training under contracts with the U.S. Air Force and the U.S. Navy. The firm owns approximately 100 Lear jets that it equips with radar jammers and other sophisticated electronic devices to mimic enemy aircraft. The company recently experienced cash shortages to pay its bills. The owner and manager of Flight Training Corporation stated, "I was just dumbfounded. I never had an inkling that there was a problem with cash." Exhibit 3.28 presents comparative balance sheets for Years 1 through 4, and Exhibit 3.29 presents income statements for Years 2 through 4.

LO 3-4

Exhibit 3.28

Flight Training Corporation
Balance Sheets
(amounts in thousands)
(Problem 3.29)

December 31:	Year 4	Year 3	Year 2	Year 1
CURRENT ASSETS				
Cash	$ 159	$ 583	$ 313	$ 142
Accounts receivable	6,545	4,874	2,675	2,490
Inventories	5,106	2,514	1,552	602
Prepayments	665	829	469	57
Total Current Assets	$ 12,475	$ 8,800	$ 5,009	$ 3,291
NONCURRENT ASSETS				
Property, plant, and equipment	$106,529	$76,975	$24,039	$17,809
Less accumulated depreciation	(17,231)	(8,843)	(5,713)	(4,288)

(Continued)

Exhibit 3.28 (Continued)

Net property, plant, and equipment	$ 89,298	$68,132	$18,326	$13,521
Other assets	$ 470	$ 665	$ 641	$ 1,112
Total Assets	$102,243	$77,597	$23,976	$17,924
CURRENT LIABILITIES				
Accounts payable	$ 12,428	$ 6,279	$ 993	$ 939
Notes payable	—	945	140	1,021
Current portion of long-term debt	60,590	7,018	1,789	1,104
Other current liabilities	12,903	12,124	2,423	1,310
Total Current Liabilities	$ 85,921	$26,366	$ 5,345	$ 4,374
NONCURRENT LIABILITIES				
Long-term debt	$ —	$41,021	$ 9,804	$ 6,738
Deferred income taxes	—	900	803	—
Other noncurrent liabilities	—	—	226	—
Total Liabilities	$ 85,921	$68,287	$16,178	$11,112
SHAREHOLDERS' EQUITY				
Common stock	$ 34	$ 22	$ 21	$ 20
Additional paid-in capital	16,516	5,685	4,569	4,323
Retained earnings	(29)	3,802	3,208	2,469
Treasury stock	(199)	(199)	—	—
Total Shareholders' Equity	$ 16,322	$ 9,310	$ 7,798	$ 6,812
Total Liabilities and Shareholders' Equity	$102,243	$77,597	$23,976	$17,924

Exhibit 3.29

Flight Training Corporation
Income Statements
(amounts in thousands)
(Problem 3.29)

Year Ended December 31:	Year 4	Year 3	Year 2
Sales	$54,988	$36,597	$20,758
Cost of services	$47,997	$29,594	$14,247
Selling and administrative	5,881	2,972	3,868
Interest	5,841	3,058	1,101
Income taxes	(900)	379	803
Total Expenses	$58,819	$36,003	$20,019
Net Income	$ (3,831)	$ 594	$ 739

REQUIRED

a. Prepare a worksheet for the preparation of a statement of cash flows for Flight Training Corporation for each of the years ending December 31, Year 2 through Year 4. Follow the format of Exhibit 3.12 in the text. Notes to the financial statements indicate the following:

(1) The firm did not sell any aircraft during the three-year period.

(2) Changes in other noncurrent assets are investing transactions.

(3) Changes in deferred income taxes are operating transactions.

(4) Changes in other noncurrent liabilities and treasury stock are financing transactions.

(5) The firm violated covenants in its borrowing agreements during Year 4. Therefore, the lenders can require Flight Training Corporation to repay its long-term debt immediately. Although the banks have not yet demanded payment, the firm reclassified its long-term debt as a current liability.

b. Prepare a comparative statement of cash flows for Flight Training Corporation for each of the years ending December 31, Year 2 through Year 4.

c. Comment on the relations among net income and cash flow from operations and the pattern of cash flows from operating, investing, and financing activities for each of the three years.

d. Describe the likely reasons for the cash flow difficulties of Flight Training Corporation.

3.30 Preparing a Statement of Cash Flows from Balance Sheets and Income Statements. **LO 3-4**

BTB Electronics Inc. manufactures parts, components, and processing equipment for electronics and semiconductor applications in the communications, computer, automotive, and appliance industries. Its sales tend to vary with changes in the business cycle because the sales of most of its customers are cyclical. Exhibit 3.30 presents balance sheets for BTB as of December 31, Year 7 through Year 9, and Exhibit 3.31 presents income statements for Year 8 and Year 9.

Exhibit 3.30

BTB Electronics Inc.
Balance Sheets
(amounts in thousands)
(Problem 3.30)

December 31:	Year 9	Year 8	Year 7
ASSETS			
Cash	$ 367	$ 475	$ 430
Accounts receivable	2,545	3,936	3,768
Inventories	2,094	2,966	2,334
Prepayments	122	270	116
Total Current Assets	$ 5,128	$ 7,647	$ 6,648
Property, plant, and equipment, net	4,027	4,598	3,806
Other assets	456	559	193
Total Assets	$ 9,611	$12,804	$10,647

(Continued)

Exhibit 3.30 (Continued)

LIABILITIES AND SHAREHOLDERS' EQUITY

Accounts payable	$ 796	$ 809	$ 1,578
Notes payable to banks	2,413	231	11
Other current liabilities	695	777	1,076
Total Current Liabilities	$ 3,904	$ 1,817	$ 2,665
Long-term debt	2,084	4,692	2,353
Deferred income taxes	113	89	126
Total Liabilities	$ 6,101	$ 6,598	$ 5,144
Preferred stock	$ 289	$ 289	$ —
Common stock	85	85	83
Additional paid-in capital	4,395	4,392	4,385
Retained earnings	(1,259)	1,440	1,035
Total Shareholders' Equity	$ 3,510	$ 6,206	$ 5,503
Total Liabilities and Shareholders' Equity	$ 9,611	$12,804	$10,647

Exhibit 3.31

BTB Electronics Inc.
Income Statements
(amounts in thousands)
(Problem 3.30)

Year Ended December 31:	Year 9	Year 8
Sales	$ 11,960	$ 22,833
Cost of goods sold	(11,031)	(16,518)
Selling and administrative expenses	(3,496)	(4,849)
Interest expense	(452)	(459)
Income tax expense	328	(590)
Net Income	$ (2,691)	$ 417
Dividends on preferred stock	(8)	(12)
Net Income Available to Common	$ (2,699)	$ 405

REQUIRED

a. Prepare a worksheet for the preparation of a statement of cash flows for BTB Electronics Inc. for Years 8 and 9. Follow the format of Exhibits 3.12 and 3.13 in the text. Notes to the firm's financial statements reveal the following (amounts in thousands):

   (1) Depreciation expense was $641 in Year 8 and $625 in Year 9. No fixed assets were sold during these years.

   (2) Other Assets represents patents. Patent amortization was $25 in Year 8 and $40 in Year 9. BTB sold a patent during Year 9 at no gain or loss.

   (3) Changes in Deferred Income Taxes are operating activities.

b. Discuss the relations among net income and cash flow from operations and the pattern of cash flows from operating, investing, and financing activities.

INTEGRATIVE CASE 3.1

Walmart

Exhibit 3.32 presents a statement of cash flows for **Walmart** for fiscal 2015, 2014, and 2013. This statement matches the Walmart statement of cash flows in Appendix A, and is an expanded version of the statement of cash flows for Walmart shown in Exhibit 1.21.

`LO 3-3`

Exhibit 3.32

Walmart Comparative Statements of Cash Flows (amounts in millions) (Case 3.1)

	Fiscal Years Ended January 31,		
	2015	**2014**	**2013**
Cash flows from operating activities:			
Consolidated net income	$ 15,080	$ 17,099	$ 16,695
Income from discontinued operations, net of income taxes	—	(285)	(144)
Income from continuing operations	15,080	16,814	16,551
Adjustments to reconcile income from continuing operations to net cash provided by operating activities:			
Depreciation and amortization	9,454	9,173	8,870
Deferred income taxes	(672)	(503)	(279)
Other operating activities	1,410	785	938
Changes in certain assets and liabilities, net of effects of acquisitions:			
Receivables, net	(19)	(569)	(566)
Inventories	(703)	(1,229)	(1,667)
Accounts payable	2,008	2,678	531
Accrued liabilities	1,303	1,249	103
Accrued income taxes	(472)	166	(1,224)
Net cash provided by operating activities	27,389	28,564	23,257
Cash flows from investing activities:			
Payments for property and equipment	(11,477)	(12,174)	(13,115)
Proceeds from disposal of property and equipment	635	570	727
Proceeds from disposal of certain operations	246	671	—
Other investing activities	(79)	(192)	(138)
Net cash used in investing activities	(10,675)	(11,125)	(12,526)
Cash flows from financing activities:			
Net change in short-term borrowings	1,235	(6,288)	911
Proceeds from issuance of long-term debt	39	5,174	7,072
Payments of long-term debt	(4,432)	(3,904)	(4,968)
Dividends paid	(6,294)	(6,185)	(6,139)

(Continued)

Exhibit 3.32 (Continued)

Purchase of Company stock	(4,112)	(1,015)	(6,683)
Dividends paid to noncontrolling interest	(719)	(600)	(426)
Purchase of noncontrolling interest	(1,326)	(1,844)	(296)
Other financing activities	(513)	(409)	(260)
Net cash used in financing activities	(16,122)	(15,071)	(10,789)
Effect of exchange rates on cash and cash equivalents	(1,022)	(514)	(442)
Net increase (decrease) in cash and cash equivalents	(430)	1,854	(500)
Cash and cash equivalents at beginning of year	9,135	7,281	7,781
Cash and cash equivalents at end of period	$ 8,705	$ 9,135	$ 7,281
Supplemental disclosure of cash flow information:			
Income taxes paid	8,111	8,169	8,641
Interest paid	2,540	2,433	2,362

Source: Walmart, Form 10-K for the Fiscal Year Ended 2012.

REQUIRED

a. Explain why depreciation and amortization appear as an addition when net income is converted to cash flow from operations.

b. For 2016, Walmart shows an adjustment for inventories of negative $703 million. However, on the balance sheet, inventories declined from $45,141 million to $44,469 million, a difference of $672 million. Explain the $703 million adjustment and offer examples of why the adjustment differs from the change in the inventory balance.

c. Estimate the amount of cash received from customers during 2016.

d. Discuss the relation between net income and cash flow from operations for each of the three years.

e. Discuss the relations among cash flows from operating, investing, and financing activities for each of the three years.

CASE 3.2

Prime Contractors

LO 3-2, LO 3-3, LO 3-5

Prime Contractors (Prime) is a privately owned company that contracts with the U.S. government to provide various services under multiyear (usually five-year) contracts. Its principal services are as follows:

Refuse: Picks up and disposes of refuse from military bases.

Shuttle: Provides parking and shuttle services on government-sponsored research campuses.

Animal Care: Provides feeding and veterinary care for animals used in research at government-sponsored facilities.

Prime's sales mix for the years ending September 30, Year 6 to Year 10, is as follows:

	Refuse Services	Shuttle Services	Animal Care Services
Year 6	59.9%	40.1%	—
Year 7	48.5%	31.2%	20.3%
Year 8	20.7%	22.0%	57.3%
Year 9	11.4%	26.9%	61.7%
Year 10	7.1%	22.5%	70.4%

As the sales mix data indicate, Prime engaged in a strategic shift beginning in Year 7. It began to exit the refuse services business and geared up its animal care services business. Exhibit 3.33 presents a statement of cash flows for Prime for Years 6 through 10.

Exhibit 3.33

Prime Contractors
Statement of Cash Flows
(amounts in thousands)
(Case 3.2)

	Year 10	Year 9	Year 8	Year 7	Year 6
OPERATIONS					
Net income	$ 568	$ 474	$ 47	$ 249	$ 261
Depreciation	595	665	827	616	306
Deferred income taxes	(139)	(110)	55	180	159
Loss (Gain) on disposition of fixed assets	(82)	(178)	—	—	20
Other additions and subtractions	(4)	(19)	(52)	(7)	2
(Increase) Decrease in accounts receivable	62	(865)	(263)	(647)	(1,421)
(Increase) Decrease in other current assets	19	(9)	(40)	(26)	(38)
Increase (Decrease) in accounts payable	(174)	(272)	(33)	(177)	507
Increase (Decrease) in other current liabilities	(310)	926	423	100	268
Cash Flow from Operations	$ 535	$ 612	$ 964	$ 288	$ 64
INVESTING					
Fixed assets sold	$ 146	$ 118	$ —	$ —	$ 80
Fixed assets acquired	(15)	(19)	(56)	(911)	(2,003)
Other investing transactions	37	—	—	62	(17)
Cash Flow from Investing	$ 168	$ 99	$ (56)	$ (849)	$ (1,940)
FINANCING					
Increase (Decrease) in short-term borrowing	$ 324	$ 12	$ (127)	$ 276	$ 204
Increase in long-term borrowing	—	—	208	911	1,987
Decrease in long-term borrowing	(960)	(742)	(1,011)	(658)	(423)
Cash Flow from Financing	$ (634)	$ (730)	$ (930)	$ 529	$ 1,768
Change in Cash	$ 69	$ (19)	$ (22)	$ (32)	$ (108)
Cash—Beginning of year	6	25	47	79	187
Cash—End of Year	$ 75	$ 6	$ 25	$ 47	$ 79
Change in sales from previous year	+15.5%	+18.0%	+38.5%	+47.1%	+53.5%

REQUIRED

a. What evidence do you see in Exhibit 3.33 of Prime's strategic shift from refuse services to animal care services?

b. Discuss how Prime's net income could decline between Year 6 and Year 8 while its cash flow from operations increased.

c. Discuss how Prime's net income could increase between Year 8 and Year 10 while its cash flow from operations decreased.

d. What is the likely reason that the adjustment for deferred income taxes when converting net income to cash flow from operations was an addition in Year 6 to Year 8 but a subtraction in Year 9 and Year 10?

e. Explain why gains on the disposition of fixed assets appear as a subtraction from net income when cash flow from operations is computed.

f. Prime increased its long-term debt net in Year 6 and Year 7 but decreased it net in Year 8 to Year 10. What is the likely reason for this shift in financing?

Profitability Analysis

LEARNING OBJECTIVES

LO 4-1 Evaluate firm profitability using techniques such as per-share analysis, common-size analysis, percentage change analysis, segment profitability analysis, and alternative measures of income.

LO 4-2 Understand rate of return analysis as a summary of firm performance, and demonstrate how to interpret the return on assets (ROA) and its components: profit margin and total assets turnover.

LO 4-3 Analyze and interpret return on common shareholders' equity (ROCE) and its components, especially successful use of financial leverage to increase the return to common shareholders.

LO 4-4 Link economic and strategic factors to ROA and ROCE.

LO 4-5 Describe the benefits and limitations of using ratios like ROA and ROCE as part of understanding the historical performance of a company.

Chapter Overview

The value of an equity security depends on the future *profitability* you anticipate relative to the *risk* involved. Valuation is often the ultimate objective of financial statement analysis. However, performance assessment is equally important, and investors and boards of directors examine profitability and risk to understand whether managers are successfully managing shareholder investments. Examining recent profitability of a firm helps you project future profitability and the expected return from investing in the firm's equity securities. Evaluations of risk involve judgments about a firm's success in managing various dimensions of risk in the past and its ability to manage risks in the future.

This chapter describes several financial statement analysis techniques to analyze profitability, and Chapter 5 presents various techniques to assess risk. Both chapters apply these tools of analysis to the financial statements of **Starbucks**, and we recommend that you trace the calculation of each financial ratio discussed in these chapters to the financial statements so that you understand exactly how to do these computations. The analytical tools we discuss provide the framework for subsequent discussions of accounting quality analysis in Chapters 6 through 9 and the forecasting and valuation of firms in Chapters 10 through 14.

As discussed in Chapter 1, financial statement analysis is a three-legged stool (see Exhibit 1.1), which requires you to understand

1. the economics of a firm's industry and markets.
2. the firm's specific strategy within its industry.
3. the information reported in its financial statements.

The analysis of profitability includes, among other things, the analysis of various financial ratios based on numbers from the financial statements. We will discuss many ratios in this chapter. *Ratios are* not *metrics you must memorize,* but are useful tools that you may use to capture information relevant to your particular task. Although we demonstrate the most common and theoretically sound approaches to compute and interpret ratios, some analysts may compute these ratios somewhat differently. For example, in computing certain ratios, analysts may vary whether they include gross or net sales or beginning, average, or ending asset balances. When assessing ratios prepared by others, you must understand how they defined and computed those ratios. Although differences in ratio definitions do not always generate substantive differences in inferences, sometimes they do.

Chapter 1 introduced the economic characteristics of the coffee beverage industry and the strategy of **Starbucks** to compete in this market. We incorporate this information and other information provided by **Starbucks** in its management discussion and analysis (MD&A) into our interpretations of various financial ratios for **Starbucks**. Appendix C, available at www.cengagebrain.com, provides financial data and ratios for **Starbucks** from the FSAP (Financial Statement Analysis Package) available with this book. Finally, Appendix D, also available at www.cengagebrain.com, provides medians across 48 industries for ROA, ROCE, and many other commonly used ratios, which are useful benchmarks for many of the ratios we discuss in this chapter.

LO 4-1

Evaluate firm profitability using techniques such as per-share analysis, common-size analysis, percentage change analysis, segment profitability analysis, and alternative measures of income.

Overview of Profitability Analysis Based on Various Measures of Income

Profitability analysis is a way to evaluate whether managers are effectively executing a firm's strategy. Investors in a firm are keenly interested in how well firm managers are using the capital they have invested to generate returns on that investment. Other stakeholders, such as creditors, employees, suppliers, and customers, are similarly interested in profitability as a measure of the continuing viability of the firm. With this in mind, we view financial statement analysis as a form of hypothesis testing. For example, knowing that **Starbucks** is the most recognized coffee shop chain in the world, we might hypothesize that **Starbucks** is more profitable than the average firm. We can obtain data from the financial statements for **Starbucks** and comparable firms to see if this hypothesis describes **Starbucks'** performance. Because there are numerous tools useful for measuring profitability, it is important to approach them in an organized manner. In this chapter, using **Starbucks** as an example, we discuss the analysis of profitability as a step-by-step examination of different layers of financial performance.

Although firms must report comprehensive income, net income remains the key measure of profitability that is more strongly associated with stock returns.[1] This result is due to net income exhibiting fairly high persistence and other comprehensive income items exhibiting very low persistence. Thus, we focus on net income as our primary measure of profitability, with the caveat that components of other comprehensive income for certain firms can be very important.

---

[1]Dan Dhaliwal, K. R. Subramanyam, and Robert Trezevant, "Is Comprehensive Income Superior to Net Income as a Measure of Firm Performance?," *Journal of Accounting and Economics* 26, nos. 1–3 (January 1999), pp. 43–67.

Exhibit 4.1 provides a diagram of the approaches to analyzing net income. The diagram begins with net income. From net income, two branches represent alternative approaches to obtaining further insight into a firms' profitability. On the left, the approach is to analyze different transformations of net income; on the right, the approach is to compute rate of return analyses. The transformations of net income include per-share analysis, common-size analysis, percentage change analysis, and alternative definitions of profits. These are straightforward approaches to understand profitability. The rate of return analyses include return on assets (ROA) and return on common equity (ROCE), which integrate information from the income statement and the balance sheet. Most of this chapter will focus on understanding how to interpret ROCE and ROA.

As Exhibit 4.1 shows, we can decompose ROA and ROCE into measures of profit margin, turnover, and leverage, which facilitate a deeper understanding of how a firm is generating wealth for its shareholders. The dashed lines for the decomposition of ROCE into profit margin (and leverage) highlight that there are differences in the calculations for ROA and ROCE, which we will discuss later in the section "Relating ROA to ROCE." Finally, the measures of profit margin, turnover, and leverage can be even more deeply analyzed using additional financial ratios prepared from different line items in the financial statements. Note that the two branches of analysis of net income displayed in Exhibit 4.1 are interrelated, especially the use of common-size analysis and alternative definitions of profits. Both of these can be incorporated into rate of return analysis, especially profit margins, as we will do later in the chapter.

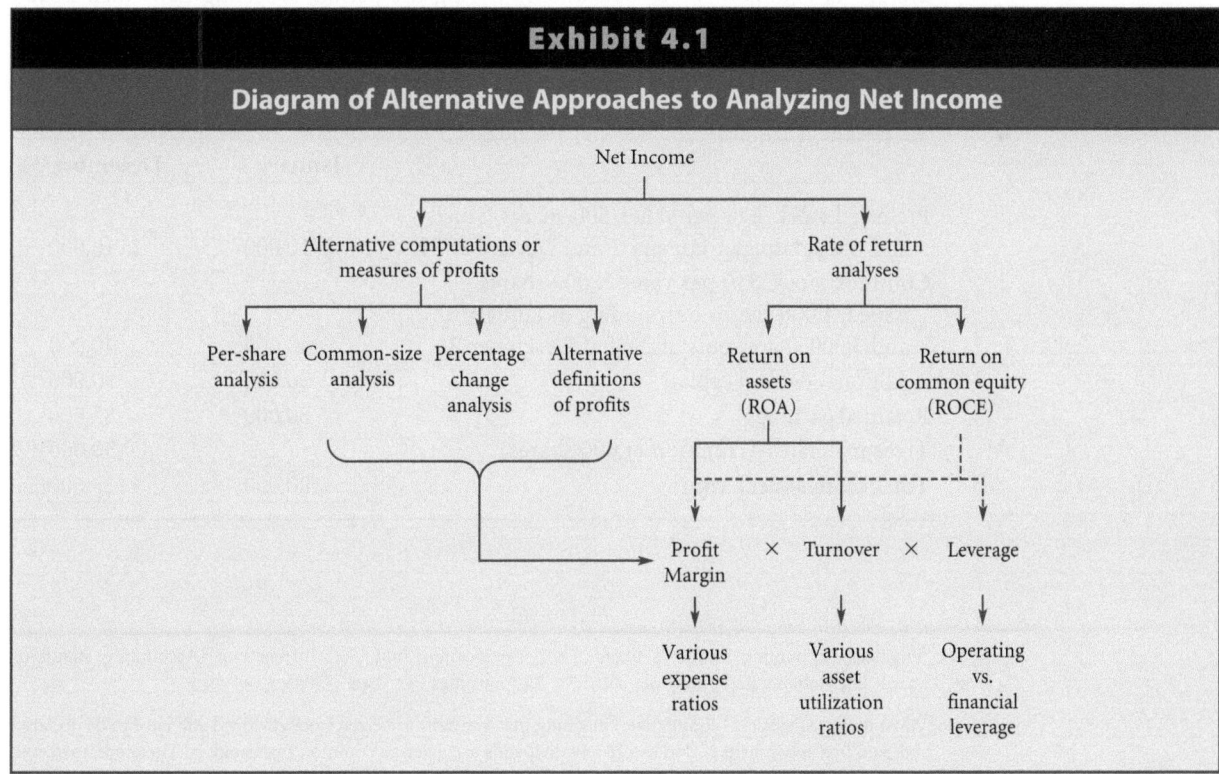

Exhibit 4.1

Diagram of Alternative Approaches to Analyzing Net Income

Earnings Per Share (EPS)

Earnings per share (EPS) is one of the most widely used measures of profitability. Analysts and investors frequently use multiples of EPS, such as price-earnings ratios, to value firms. EPS is the only additional financial ratio that U.S. GAAP and IFRS require firms to disclose on the face of the income statement and is covered explicitly by the opinion of the independent auditor.[2] This section briefly describes the calculation of EPS and discusses some of its uses and limitations.

Calculating Basic EPS

A firm has *simple* capital structure if it has no

- outstanding convertible bonds or convertible preferred stock that holders can exchange for shares of common stock.
- options or warrants that holders can use to acquire common stock.

For such firms, basic EPS is as follows:

$$\frac{\text{Basic EPS}}{\text{(Simple Capital Structure)}} = \frac{\text{Net Income Available to Common Shareholders}}{\text{Weighted-Average Number of Common Shares Outstanding}}$$

Net Income Available to Common Shareholders in the numerator is after deductions for preferred stock dividends and any income attributable to noncontrolling interests.[3] The numerator of basic EPS is adjusted for preferred stock dividends because the denominator includes only common shares outstanding. The denominator is a *weighted average* of common shares outstanding during the period, reflecting new stock issues, treasury stock acquisitions, and similar transactions that occur through the year.

Example 1. Cat Corporation had the following capital structure during its most recent year:

	January 1	December 31
Preferred stock, $20 par value, 500 shares issued and outstanding at January 1 and December 31	$ 10,000	$ 10,000
Common stock, $10 par value, 4,000 shares issued; 4,000 shares outstanding at January 1 and 3,000 shares outstanding at December 31	40,000	40,000
Additional paid-in capital	50,000	50,000
Retained earnings	80,000	85,600
Treasury shares—common (1,000 shares)	—	(30,000)
Total shareholders' equity	$180,000	$155,600

---

[2]Financial Accounting Standards Board, *FASB Codification Topic 260*; International Accounting Standards Board, *International Accounting Standard No. 33*, "Earnings Per Share" (2003).

[3]Most preferred stock is "cumulative," meaning that a missed preferred stock dividend will have to be declared and paid in a subsequent period before any dividends are given to common shareholders. Therefore, preferred stock dividends are subtracted even if they have not been declared or paid.

Retained earnings changed during the year as follows:

Retained earnings, January 1	$80,000
Net income	7,500
Preferred stock dividends	(500)
Common stock dividends	(1,400)
Retained earnings, December 31	$85,600

Assume the preferred stock is not convertible into common stock, the firm acquired 1,000 shares of treasury stock on July 1, and no stock options or warrants are outstanding. The calculation of basic earnings per share for Cat Corporation is as follows:

$$\text{Basic EPS} = \frac{\$7,500 - \$500}{(0.5 \times 4,000) + (0.5 \times 3,000)} = \frac{\$7,000}{3,500} = \$2 \text{ per share}$$

Calculating Diluted EPS with Complex Capital Structure

In contrast to a simple capital structure, firms that have convertible securities and/or stock options or warrants outstanding have *complex* capital structures. Such firms must present two EPS amounts: *basic EPS* and *diluted EPS*. Diluted EPS reflects the dilution potential of convertible securities, options, and warrants. Dilution refers to the reduction in basic EPS that *would* hypothetically result if holders of convertible securities exchanged them for shares of common stock or if holders of stock options or warrants exercised them. Firms include in diluted EPS calculations only those securities, options, and warrants that are exercisable and would reduce EPS. Income and share dilution effects of equity instruments are excluded from both the numerator and denominator if they are not yet exercisable (for example, options that have not yet vested) or if their conversion would *increase* EPS (such securities would be referred to as "out of the money" and their effect on EPS as "antidilutive"). Accordingly, diluted EPS will always be less than (or equal to) basic EPS. This section describes the calculation of diluted EPS in general terms.

$$\frac{\text{Diluted EPS}}{(\text{Complex Capital Structure})} = \frac{\text{Net Income Available to Common Shareholders} + \text{Adjustments for Dilutive Securities}}{\text{Weighted-Average Number of Common Shares Outstanding} + \text{Weighted-Average Number of Shares Issuable from Dilutive Securities}}$$

Adjustments for dilutive securities and the adjustment to weighted-average number of shares outstanding presume that the dilutive securities are converted to common shares *as of the beginning of the year*. To calculate diluted EPS, you assume the conversion of convertible bonds and convertible preferred stock and the exercise of stock options and warrants *only if* their effect would be dilutive. In the numerator, you add back (1) interest expense (net of taxes) on convertible bonds and (2) dividends on convertible preferred stock (that the firm subtracted in computing net income attributable to common shareholders). Consistency suggests that you also add back to net income any compensation expense recognized on the employee stock options. However, U.S. GAAP and IFRS do not stipulate such an addback, but instead require firms to incorporate any unamortized compensation expense on those options into the calculation of the denominator of diluted EPS, as discussed next.

In the denominator of the diluted EPS computation, you increase common shares for the additional shares that are presumed to be issued at the beginning of the year (for conversion of bonds, conversion of preferred stock, and exercise of stock options and warrants). The computation of additional shares due to the exercise of stock options assumes that the firm would repurchase common shares on the open market using an amount equal to the sum of (1) any cash proceeds from such exercise, (2) any unamortized compensation expense on those options, and (3) any tax benefits that would be credited to Additional Paid-in Capital.[4] Only the net incremental shares issued (shares issued under options minus assumed shares repurchased) enter the computation of diluted EPS.

Example 2. Assume that Dawg Corporation has the same capital structure as Cat Corporation, except the preferred stock of Dawg Corporation is convertible into 1,000 shares of common stock. Also assume that Dawg Corporation has stock options outstanding and "in the money," which holders can currently exchange for 300 incremental shares of common stock.[5] The calculation of diluted EPS is as follows:

$$\text{Diluted EPS} = \frac{\$7{,}500 - \$500 + \$500}{[0.5 \times (4{,}000 + 3{,}000)] + [1.0 \times (1{,}000 + 300)]} = \frac{\$7{,}500}{4{,}800}$$
$$= \$1.56$$

The calculation assumes the conversion of the convertible preferred stock into common stock as of January 1. If conversion had taken place, the firm would have had no preferred dividends during the year. Thus, we add back $500 of preferred dividends to the numerator. The weighted-average number of shares in the denominator increases for the 1,000 common shares the firm would issue on conversion of the preferred stock. The weighted-average number of shares in the denominator also increases for the incremental shares issuable under stock option exercises.

Refer to the income statement of **Starbucks** in Appendix A. **Starbucks** reports basic EPS of $1.84 and diluted EPS of $1.82 for fiscal 2015. **Starbucks**' Note 14, "Earnings per Share," shows the calculation of its EPS amounts. For the calculation of diluted EPS, **Starbucks** adds additional common shares assumed to be issued under common stock option and restricted share unit plans, which dilutes EPS by two cents.

Criticisms of EPS

Critics of EPS as a measure of profitability point out that it does not consider the amount of assets or capital required to generate a particular level of earnings. Two firms with the same earnings and EPS are not equally profitable if one firm requires twice the amount of assets or capital to generate those earnings compared to the other firm. Also, the number of shares of common stock outstanding serves as a poor measure of the amount of capital in use. The number of shares outstanding usually reflects a firm's attempts to achieve a desirable trading range for its common stock. For example, suppose a firm has an aggregate market value for its common shares of $10 million. If the firm has 500,000 shares outstanding, the shares would trade around $20 per share. If,

---

[4]Understanding the rationale for including unamortized compensation expense in the computation of the net incremental shares issuable requires an understanding of the accounting for stock options, which is discussed in Chapter 7. Basically, U.S. GAAP and IFRS view the value of stock options, which is expensed over the period of benefit, as a substitute for cash compensation. Assuming unamortized expense leads to repurchased shares presumes that a firm realizes a pseudo cash savings in this amount.

[5]We are simplifying this example with the assumption of 300 *incremental* shares. An actual calculation would require separate computation of the proceeds from exercise, unamortized compensation expense, and associated tax benefits.

instead, the firm has 1 million shares outstanding, the shares would trade around $10 per share. The amount of capital in place is the same in both instances, but the number of shares outstanding (and therefore EPS) is different.

Also, the change in EPS is an ambiguous measure of the change in profitability over time because a change in shares outstanding over time can have a disproportionate effect on the numerator and denominator. For example, a firm could experience a decline in earnings during a year but report higher EPS than it did the previous year if it repurchased a sufficient number of shares early in the period. When assessing earnings performance, you must separate the impact of these two factors on EPS.

Despite these criticisms of EPS as a measure of profitability, it remains one of the focal points of the quarterly earnings announcement season, and analysts frequently use it in valuing firms. The reason for its ubiquity is the direct comparability of a firm's earnings per share to its stock price per share. Chapter 14 discusses the use of EPS in valuation.

Common-Size Analysis

The profitability of two firms can be compared more meaningfully by scaling net income and the individual income statement line items to a common denominator (each firm's total revenues). Common-size analysis converts financial statement line items into percentages of either sales (for line items on the income statement) or total assets (for those on the balance sheet). Through the use of a common denominator, common-size analysis enables you to compare financial statements across firms and across time (for the same firm). Common-size analysis is also a very helpful comparison tool when evaluating financial statements reported using different currencies, or financial statements of firms of different size.

Common-size analysis is a simple but powerful approach to understanding profitability. Common-size income statements provide quick and easy methods to compute firms' profit margins—including gross profit, operating profit, and net profit margins.

Chapter 1 introduced common-size financial statements and presents those for **Starbucks** (Exhibits 1.15 and 1.16). Exhibit 4.2 provides select common size and percentage change information for **Panera**. The 2015 common-size figures suggest that Panera has a more favorable gross profit margin (revenues minus cost of goods sold) of 61.0% of revenues, relative to 59.4% for **Starbucks**. However, operating expenses are significantly higher for Panera, resulting in operating income margin of only 9.0% of revenues relative to 18.8% for **Starbucks**. This difference persists after considering interest, taxes, and other expenses, with **Starbucks** having a net profit margin of 14.4% of revenues compared to 5.6% for Panera.

For example, this analysis suggests that **Starbucks** realizes substantially higher profitability per dollar of sales than Panera. However, to more deeply understand this comparison, you must perform additional analysis to understand the different drivers of revenues and expenses, which we will highlight later in the chapter.

The common-size analysis of profitability across firms can be extended to time-series analysis as well. Examining the time series for each company may suggest the direction in which various expenses are trending. As noted previously, the primary difference between **Starbucks'** and Panera's profitability is due to the lower operating expenses (as a percentage of revenues) for **Starbucks**. Examining the trend in gross profit over the period 2011 through 2015 indicates that **Starbucks'** gross profit fell from 58.0% in 2011 to 56.2% in 2012, but has trended upwards to 59.4% in 2015. Even more compelling, net income has trended steadily up to 14.4% in 2015. In contrast, Panera's

Exhibit 4.2

Select Common-Size and Percentage Change Income Statement Line Items for Panera (allow for rounding)

	Common-Sized Income Statement Line Items					
	2010	2011	2012	2013	2014	2015
Net revenues	100.0%	100.0%	100.0%	100.0%	100.0%	100.0%
Gross profit	62.0%	61.5%	61.8%	61.6%	61.2%	61.0%
Total operating expenses	50.0%	49.4%	48.5%	48.6%	50.3%	52.0%
Operating income	12.0%	12.1%	13.3%	13.0%	10.9%	9.0%
Net income	7.2%	7.5%	8.1%	8.2%	7.1%	5.6%

	Rate of Change Income Statement Line Items					
Net revenues		18.1%	16.9%	12.0%	6.0%	6.0%
Gross profit		17.2%	17.5%	11.6%	5.4%	5.7%
Total operating expenses		16.8%	14.8%	12.2%	9.7%	9.6%
Operating income		19.0%	28.4%	9.5%	(10.9)%	(12.4)%
Net income		21.8%	27.6%	13.1%	(8.6)%	(16.7)%

gross profit exhibits a slight decline, whereas net income has shown no clear trend, but is down significantly in 2015. The different trends suggest that Panera's cost structure is rising at a higher rate than increases in revenue and/or that it is shifting its revenue mix to lower-margin products and markets. Indeed, Panera's MD&A indicates that costs increased due to "food cost inflation and a shift in product mix towards higher ingredient cost products" as well as higher labor and occupancy costs.

When you perform common-size analysis, be aware that percentages can change because of

- changes in expenses in the numerator independent of changes in sales (for example, an increase in employee compensation levels).
- changes in sales independent of changes in expenses (for example, because the expense is fixed for the period).
- interaction effects between the numerator and denominator (an increase in advertising expenses leads to an increase in sales, but possibly at different rates).
- coincident but independent changes in the numerator and denominator (that is, combinations of the other three possibilities).

Thus, although common-size analysis is useful, to fully understand the trends it reveals, you must dig deeper into the economics of the firm's environment, the firm's strategy, and the firm's accounting quality during the period you are analyzing, as well as conduct further financial analysis using finer partitions of data. **That is why the six-step analytical framework of this book begins with an analysis of the firm's economic environment and strategy, followed by an analysis of the firm's accounting quality.** Note that FSAP automatically computes common-size financial statements.

Percentage Change Analysis

Another way to analyze financial data is to compute percentage changes in individual line items, which also can be compared across firms and across time. However, the focus is not on the financial data themselves, but on the *changes* in individual line items through time. Percentage change analysis was also introduced briefly in Chapter 1 along with common-size analysis. Whereas Exhibit 1.15 presents a **Starbucks** common-size analysis for five years, Exhibit 1.16 presents percentage change analysis for only four years because five years of data yield four changes.

In the common-size analysis discussed above, we noted a significant difference in the profitability between **Starbucks** and **Panera**. We can examine whether there are trends in profits as a percentage of revenues for **Starbucks** relative to Panera by comparing the four-year percentage change analyses for **Starbucks** (Exhibits 1.15 and 1.16) and Panera (Exhibit 4.2). **Starbucks**' revenue growth rate shows an increasing trend, from 9.3% in 2011 to 16.5% in 2015. In contrast, Panera's revenue growth rate has declined over the same period from 18.1% in 2011 to 6.0% in 2015. These trends are also evident in operating income and net income, but the differences are even more pronounced. For example, the growth rate of net income for **Starbucks** was 33.4% in 2015, but was −16.7% for Panera in 2015. When forecasting (a focus of Chapter 10), a helpful starting point is to examine prior percentage changes (and common-size data) to identify trends that may persist in the future. With knowledge of the company's strategic plans and recent trends, many changes can be anticipated. However, a limitation of percentage change analysis is that nonrecurring items or changes in "other" categories can be associated with extreme percentage changes; an example is 2013, when **Starbucks** reported a significant litigation charge.

Alternative Definitions of Profits

When you use measures of past profitability to forecast the firm's future profitability, the emphasis is on those items that are expected to persist. If net income in the recent past includes nonrecurring gains from sales of assets or nonrecurring losses from unusual asset impairment or restructuring charges, you might decide to eliminate those items from past earnings when using them as a basis for forecasting future earnings.

For purposes of valuation, the goal is to forecast the sustainable earnings of a firm. The famous investment text by Benjamin Graham and David Dodd refers to this concept of earnings persistence as "earnings power."[6] Sustainable earnings, or earnings power, is the level of earnings and the growth in the level of earnings expected to persist in the future. Nonrecurring gains and losses may occur in future periods, but you cannot anticipate their occurrence, timing, or amount with sufficient precision to include them in sustainable earnings. Thus, a key to developing forecasts that are useful for valuation is to identify components of bottom-line earnings that are recurring.

Segment Profitability

Many firms consist of more than one operating segment. Both U.S. GAAP and IFRS require that companies provide measures of profitability and certain additional

---

[6]Benjamin Graham and David Dodd, *Security Analysis* (New York: McGraw-Hill, 1934).

information for each segment. The definition of segments follows the "management approach," which leaves the identification of operating segments up to managers based on how they manage the operations of the company. For example, **Starbucks** discloses five operating segments (Americas; China/Asia Pacific; Europe, Middle East, and Africa; Channel Development; and All Other). Most often, disclosure of segment profitability data is presented in the footnotes to the financial statements. Given the open-ended management approach to these required disclosures, there is generally wide variation in the details provided by firms, which makes cross-sectional comparisons of segments challenging. However, firms are required to reconcile revenues and other disclosed items presented for segments to the corresponding totals for the firm. It is important to note that firms often do not allocate all general and administrative expenses to individual segments (allocating a portion to the "corporate" segment), so it also is challenging to compare performance of a segment within a multisegment firm to that of a pure-play firm, for which such expenses are included on the income statement.

Comprehensive Income

Financial statement users typically analyze net income as the summary bottom-line measure of performance. However, both U.S. GAAP and IFRS require presentation of comprehensive income, which is defined as

> The change in equity (net assets) of a business entity during a period from transactions and other events and circumstances from non-owner sources. It includes all changes in equity during a period except those resulting from investments by owners and distributions to owners.[7]

Thus, items included as part of "other comprehensive income" are added to or deducted from net income. Such items include certain foreign currency translation items, defined benefit pension plan and other postretirement plan adjustments, certain unrealized gains and losses on investment securities (until 2018) and hedges, and other adjustments.

The overriding objective of reporting items of other comprehensive income is to present an *all-inclusive* picture of a company's economic events during a period, where items included as other comprehensive income are generally more likely to be *temporary* in nature and may likely reverse prior to ultimate realization of the currently recognized gains and losses. Reliance on comprehensive income as a summary measure of performance is generally not emphasized as much as an understanding of the components. The primary interest of analysts in examining the components of other comprehensive income is to assess situations in which certain components are likely to persist. However, because of the volatility and uncertainty surrounding most of these items, they are generally not helpful for predicting future income.

Operating Income, EBIT, EBITDA, and Other Profit Measures

Another factor driving the analysis of different aggregations of income statement line items is that firms have different organizational and capital structures. As a consequence, it is sometimes helpful to examine profitability prior to considering a variety of expenses that vary depending on different organizational or capital structures. Thus, analysts are sometimes interested in analyzing different levels of profitability, such as gross profit, operating income, EBIT, EBITDA, EBITDAR, NOPAT, EBIAT, and

---

[7]*FASB Codification 220-10-20.*

adjusted EBITDA, which can be earnings excluding any number of recognized expenses.[8] The most common of these is EBITDA, which originated as a rough estimate of cash flows. As discussed later in our discussion of earnings quality (Chapter 6), it does not make sense to use EBITDA in lieu of operating cash flows, which are easily found on the statement of cash flows. Each metric identified above can be informative, but none (including net income) should be viewed as the single complete measure of financial performance.

Gross profit is a key component of profitability when comparing **Starbucks** and **Panera**, but the income statement that **Starbucks** actually files with the SEC (in Appendix A) does *not* report a separate line item for gross profit. Similarly, measures of profitability at different levels of the income statement, such as EBITDA, are rarely disclosed on firms' income statements. Thus, you should be adept at reconfiguring income statements to suit different purposes, especially comparisons across companies where you inevitably must use judgment to normalize financial information into the same format.

Pro Forma, Adjusted, or Street Earnings

Managers often discuss specific computations of "earnings" that exclude certain line items and refer to such earnings as "pro forma" or "adjusted" earnings; collectively, such presentations of earnings, which are widely followed on Wall Street, are called "Street" earnings. As director of research at First Call, Chuck Hill commented, "What companies are trying to do is entice analysts into excluding certain charges and value them only on that basis."[9] Suppose a company has revenues of $100 and five expenses (Expense 1–Expense 5) of $10 each. For such a firm, net income equals $50. Consider a manager who argues that Expense 5 is a nonrecurring expense, such as severance payments to workers from a closed plant. The manager would report pro forma earnings of $60 after excluding this charge. Expense 4 might be for an expenditure such as advertising or R&D (research and development); so a manager might claim that these expenditures generate assets and are not relevant for assessing current performance, which would yield pro forma earnings of $70. A scheming manager even might be inclined to argue against including *all* expenses, ending up reporting pro forma earnings equal to revenues.

This may seem far-fetched, but it is what internet firms did during the growth of this sector in the late 1990s. Managers of such firms argued that the key to assessing performance was the level of and growth in revenues, which reflected first-mover advantages to gain market share and growth in customers who would secure the firm's profitability in the future. Needless to say, most market observers agree that the valuation of such firms reached irrational levels and resulted in a subsequent stock market crash, partially attributable to the temporary disregard for operating expenses as a crucial component of profitability.

An empirical research study revealed a significant increase in the trend of managers reporting pro forma earnings higher than bottom-line net income, primarily by excluding certain charges and expenses from reported "pro forma" earnings.[10] Exhibit 4.3

---

[8]The acronyms mentioned are as follows: EBIT = earnings before interest and taxes; EBITDA = earnings before interest, taxes, depreciation, and amortization; EBITDAR = earnings before interest, taxes, depreciation, amortization, and rent; NOPAT = net operating profits after tax; EBIAT = earnings before interest after tax.

[9]Elizabeth MacDonald, "Varied Profit Reports by Firms Create Confusion," *The Wall Street Journal* (August 24, 1999), p. C1.

[10]Mark T. Bradshaw and Richard G. Sloan, "GAAP versus the Street: An Empirical Assessment of Two Alternative Definitions of Earnings," *Journal of Accounting Research* 40, no. 1 (March 2002), pp. 41–66.

Exhibit 4.3

Pro Forma versus U.S. GAAP Annual Earnings per Share (Scaled by Price) for 1985–1999

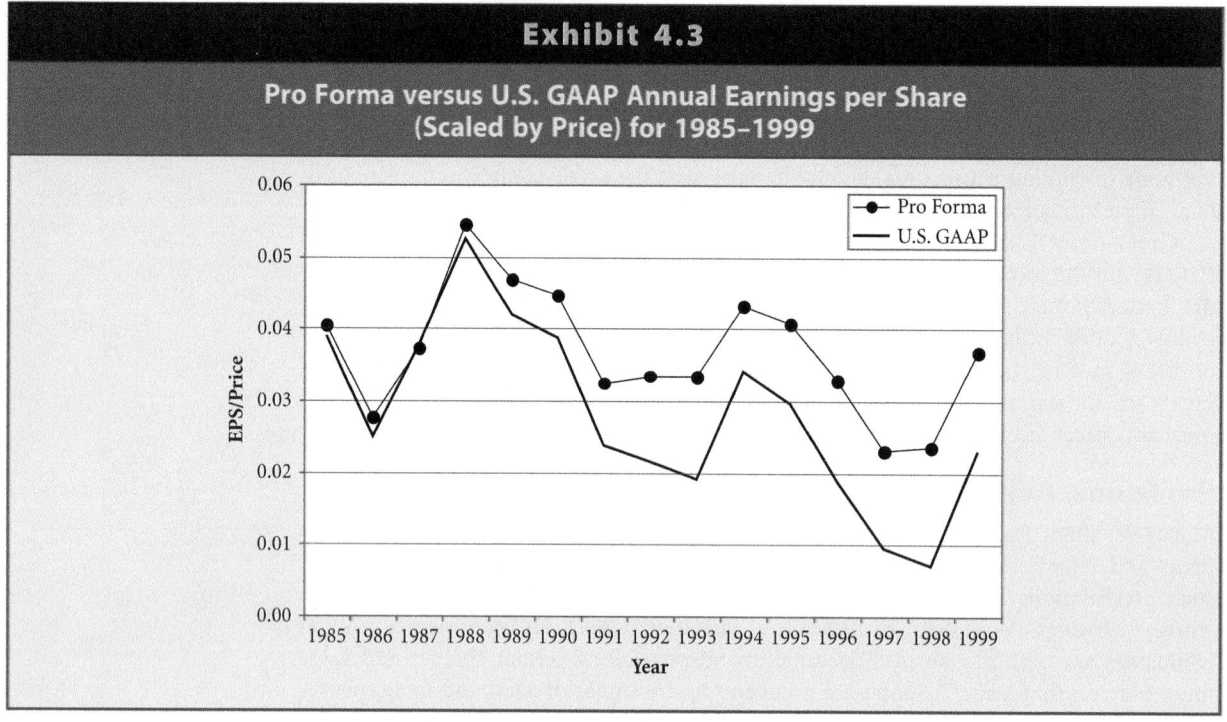

shows results from the study. The widening gap between plots in the graph makes it clear that firms increasingly excluded expenses from reported pro forma earnings beginning as far back as the late 1980s. A study of how managers highlight nonrecurring gains and losses revealed that managers tend to highlight unusual or nonrecurring expenses or losses in the quarter in which they occur, but when that quarter is used as a benchmark for the announcement of the same quarter's earnings in the next year, managers tend not to remind investors that the previous year included an unusual or one-time expense or loss.[11] This makes the earnings announcement at that time appear more favorable in terms of year-to-year improvement in profitability.

In reaction to perceived abuses in the reporting of profits, the U.S. Securities and Exchange Commission (SEC) became concerned that the emphasis placed on pro forma earnings by managers risked misleading the average investor. The SEC issued Regulation G in 2003, which deals with what the SEC calls "non-GAAP" earnings, otherwise known in the investment community as pro forma earnings. Regulation G prohibits firms from placing more emphasis on pro forma earnings relative to bottom-line U.S. GAAP earnings or from identifying an amount as nonrecurring or unusual when such amounts have occurred in the past or are likely to recur in the future. Nevertheless, the reporting of non-GAAP (or pro forma) earnings is not prohibited outright, so investors must be diligent in understanding the composition of alternative measures of profits. Most firms now make it easy for investors to understand how management views non-recurring or unusual charges with separate disclosures. For example, **Starbucks** routinely highlights both "GAAP EPS" and non-GAAP EPS" in quarterly conference calls, where non-GAAP EPS excludes various amounts such as acquisition costs and

---

[11]Catherine M. Schrand and Beverly R. Walther, "Strategic Benchmarks in Earnings Announcements: The Selective Disclosure of Prior-Period Earnings Components," *The Accounting Review* 75, no. 2 (April 2000), pp. 151–177.

adjustments for their 52/53-week fiscal year convention. In accordance with Regulation G, **Starbucks** always presents a reconciliation of GAAP and non-GAAP EPS at the end of its press release.

- Earnings per share is a basic measure of profitability, primarily because it is comparable to price per share.
- Common-size analysis converts financial statement line items to percentages, enabling the comparison of financial results across firms or across time.

- Percentage change analysis is similarly useful for comparing trends across firms and across time.
- Numerous measures of profitability can supplement the analysis of net income, including segment-level profitability, operating income and similar metrics like EBIT and EBITDA, and earnings adjusted for the effects of unusual or nonrecurring items.

Return on Assets (ROA)

LO 4-2

Understand rate of return analysis as a summary of firm performance, and demonstrate how to interpret the return on assets (ROA) and its components: profit margin and total assets turnover.

In Exhibit 4.1, the right branch of the diagram relates to rate of return measures, which assess economic profits relative to the amount of investment. In the analysis of financial statements, the two most common measures of rate of return are ROA and ROCE, or sometimes just ROE (return on equity). Our discussion begins with ROA, followed by ROCE.

ROA measures a firm's success in using assets to generate earnings *independent of the financing of those assets*. This means that a properly calculated ROA will be unaffected by the proportion of debt versus equity financing and the costs of those types of capital. To ensure that financing does not affect the calculation, ROA is defined as

$$\text{ROA} = \frac{\text{Net Income} + \begin{matrix}(1 - \text{Tax Rate}) \times \\ (\text{Interest Expense})\end{matrix} + \begin{matrix}\text{Noncontrolling Interest} \\ \text{in Earnings}\end{matrix}}{\text{Average Total Assets}}$$

The measure of profits pertinent to ROA is net income *before* financing costs, so the numerator of ROA adjusts net income to exclude the effects of any financing costs.[12] Because accountants subtract interest expense when computing net income, you must add it back when computing ROA. However, firms deduct interest expense when measuring *taxable* income. Therefore, the *incremental* effect of interest expense on net income equals interest expense times one minus the marginal statutory tax rate.[13] That is, you add back the amount of interest expense to net income, net of the tax savings from that interest expense.

The tax savings from interest expense depends on the statutory tax rate in the tax jurisdiction where the firm issues debt, and these vary substantially. For example, as of the date this text was written, the statutory federal tax rate is 35% in the United States, 28% in Norway, 25% in China, 20% in the United Kingdom, 12.5% in Ireland, and 0% in the Cayman Islands. In the United States, firms must disclose in a note to the financial statements why the average income tax rate (defined as income tax expense divided by net income before income taxes) differs from the federal statutory tax rate of 35%.

---

[12]If a firm has income from discontinued operations or extraordinary gains or losses, for reasons discussed earlier regarding pro forma earnings, you might exclude those items and start with net income from continuing operations instead of net income if the objective is to measure a firm's sustainable profitability.

[13]The statutory tax rate times interest expense is the *interest tax shield*. An interest tax shield is the reduction in taxes payable for firms that deduct interest expense in the computation of income tax liability.

The statutory federal rate will differ from a firm's average tax rate (computed as income tax expense divided by pretax income) because of

1. the presence of state and local taxes.
2. foreign tax rates that differ from 35% (Chapter 9 provides a discussion of state, local, and foreign tax effects).
3. revenues and expenses that firms include in accounting income but that do not impact taxable income (that is, permanent differences, as described in Chapter 2).

You can estimate the total tax rate that reflects combined statutory federal, state, local, and foreign tax rates using 35% plus or minus these individual rates, but this is only an approximation.[14] To simplify the calculations, we will follow the common practice of using the statutory federal tax rate of 35% in the computations of the tax savings from interest in the numerator of ROA throughout this book.

Because accountants do not subtract dividends on preferred and common stocks when measuring net income, calculating the numerator of ROA requires no adjustment for dividends. However, accountants do subtract the noncontrolling interest in earnings when measuring net income. This subtraction causes an inconsistency in the numerator and the denominator of ROA. The denominator of ROA includes all assets of the consolidated entity, not just the parent company's share. Net income in the numerator, however, represents the parent's earnings plus the parent's share of the earnings of consolidated subsidiaries. Consistency with the inclusion of all of the assets of the consolidated entity in the denominator of ROA requires that the numerator include all of the earnings of the consolidated entity, not just the parent's share. The addback of the noncontrolling interest in earnings accomplishes this objective. Most publicly traded corporations do not disclose the noncontrolling interest in earnings because its amount, if any, is usually immaterial. Thus, you typically make this adjustment only for significant noncontrolling interests. **Starbucks** reports a small amount of noncontrolling interest, so we will make this adjustment in the **Starbucks** computations that follow.

Net income before financing costs in the numerator of ROA represents results for a period of time. To be consistent, the denominator should use a measure of average assets in use during that same period. Using average total assets is not mandatory, however, in the sense that using beginning total assets is not necessarily wrong. (In fact, if total assets have not changed significantly during the period, there will be little difference between the beginning amount and the average.) The use of average total assets is a simple way to account for the changing level of investments in total assets upon which profits are judged. Thus, for a nonseasonal business, an average of assets at the beginning and end of the year is usually sufficient. For a seasonal business, you might use an average of assets at the end of each quarter.

Refer to the financial statements for **Starbucks** in Appendix A. Also refer to the ROA and other ratio computations in the Analysis Spreadsheet of the FSAP presented in Appendix C. The calculation of ROA for fiscal 2015 is as follows:

$$\text{ROA} = \frac{\text{Net Income} + \begin{bmatrix} (1 - \text{Tax Rate}) \times \\ (\text{Interest Expense}) \end{bmatrix} + \begin{matrix} \text{Noncontrolling} \\ \text{Interest in Earnings} \end{matrix}}{\text{Average Total}}$$

$$24.2\% = \frac{\$2{,}757.4 + (1 - 0.35)(\$70.5) + \$1.9}{0.5(\$12{,}446.1 + \$10{,}752.9)}$$

---

[14]Permanent differences usually do not relate to interest expense and therefore should not affect the statutory tax rate applicable to interest expense deductions.

Adjustments for Nonrecurring or Special Items

As noted earlier in this chapter, you should consider whether reported net income includes any nonrecurring or special items that might affect assessments of a firm's ongoing profitability. The notes to the financial statements and the MD&A provide information for making these assessments. **Starbucks** lists two items on its income statement that you might consider unusual or nonrecurring. The first is "Gain resulting from acquisition of joint venture" of $390.6 million; the second is "Loss on extinguishment of debt" of $61.1 million. If the objective is to measure the profitability performance of **Starbucks** in 2015, these items should *not* be excluded, as they impacted **Starbucks**' reported net income. However, if the objective is to measure the sustainable profitability of **Starbucks**, you might decide to exclude the amounts for these items. Collectively, this gain and loss net to a $329.5 million gain, or approximately 8.4% of pretax income.

When deciding whether to eliminate any of these special items as part of assessing sustainable profitability, you should consider whether the event that triggered the gain or loss is likely to persist. Sometimes companies provide forward-looking information that helps you assess the persistence of such amounts, but more often they do not. If an amount is likely to persist, then you should leave it in the reported profitability in the numerator of ROA, but if it is likely to be nonrecurring, then you would remove its effect from the numerator. One could argue that "if it is not one thing, it will be another" and implicitly acknowledge that nonrecurring or unusual charges are more common than the nomenclature implies. A third approach is to leave the special items in earnings but specifically highlight them as nonrecurring when qualitatively analyzing ongoing profitability, which is also a fairly common approach.

Because our ultimate objective is to analyze past profitability and anticipate forecasting future results, we follow the second approach and eliminate two nonrecurring items in 2015 and one in both 2013 and 2014. In Chapter 10, we project future financial statements for **Starbucks** based on the assumption that these charges will not be recurring.

A brief explanation of the two adjustments for 2015 and the one from 2013 follows.

1. **Gain resulting from acquisition of joint venture.** This amount relates to a change in ownership of **Starbucks Japan**. Prior to October 31, 2014, **Starbucks** Japan was a joint venture between **Starbucks** and **Sazaby League, Ltd**. As detailed in Note 2, "Acquisitions and Divestitures," of **Starbucks**' financial statements in Appendix A, when **Starbucks** purchased Sazaby's investment, this triggered a revaluation of **Starbucks**' original investment, which resulted in a $390.6 million gain.

2. **Loss on extinguishment of debt.** As detailed in Note 9, "Debt," of **Starbucks**' financial statements, the company paid $611.1 million to redeem $550 million of debt during 2015. The redemption triggered a charge of $61.1 million.

3. **Litigation charge.** Note 15, "Commitments and Contingencies," in **Starbucks**' financial statements explains a $2,784.1 million charge recognized in 2013 related to arbitration with Kraft Foods. The charge is related to a terminated agreement between the two companies (in which Kraft had been the distributor of all **Starbucks** products to grocery stores and warehouse clubs throughout North America), and reflects legal damages, interest, and attorneys' fees. There is a minor reversal of part of this charge in 2014 of $20.2 million.

In addition to these two adjustments, **Starbucks** defines its fiscal year-end as the Sunday closest to September 30. This means that a fiscal year occasionally will contain 53 weeks. The years 2013 through 2015 all contain 52 weeks, so they are directly comparable.

However, fiscal year 2016 will contain 53 weeks. If we perform an analysis of 2016 profitability in the future, we would also adjust for the extra week in that year to ensure comparability to 52-week years. In addition, in Chapter 10, when we project 2016 revenues and earnings, we will incorporate the 53rd week into our forecasts.

In summary, the gain and loss discussed above are clearly nonrecurring. Thus, we remove their effects from reported profitability for our analyses, which will be a prelude to forecasting in Chapter 10. All adjustments should be net of income tax effects, as we did with the interest adjustment previously. If firms disclose the income tax effect, we could use the reported amounts. Otherwise, we assume that the current marginal statutory federal tax rate applies. It is important to carefully consider the sign of the adjustments in Exhibit 4.4. Income-reducing charges such as losses are *added back* to income before income taxes, and gains are *deducted*.

The adjusted ROA for **Starbucks** for 2015 is as follows:

$$22.3\% = \frac{\$2,543.2 + (1 - 0.35)(\$70.5) + \$1.9}{0.5(\$12,446.1 + \$10,752.9)}$$

We make similar adjustments for the litigation charges in 2014 and 2013. As shown in Exhibit 4.4, adjusted net income is lower than reported net income for 2015 and 2014, but in 2013 adjusted income is significantly higher than reported net income.

Calculations for both unadjusted and adjusted ROA are shown for all three years in Exhibit 4.5. ROA based on reported net income is 24.2%, 18.9%, and 0.3% in 2015, 2014, and 2013, respectively, while ROA based on *adjusted* net income is 22.3%, 18.8%, and 18.6%, respectively. Analyzing the time series of **Starbucks'** ROA based on reported or adjusted net income, performance is trending up and is outstanding in 2015. Refer to the Analysis Spreadsheet in the FSAP model for a five-year time series of these and other ratios computed based on as-reported and adjusted figures (also presented in Appendix C).

Two Comments on the Calculation of ROA

First, some analysts subtract average non-interest-bearing liabilities (such as accounts payable and accrued liabilities) from average total assets in the denominator of ROA, the argument being that these items are sources of indirect financing. An alternative argument for reducing total assets by non-interest-bearing liabilities is that ROA is

Exhibit 4.4			
Adjustments to Reported Net Income for Unusual and Nonrecurring Items for Starbucks (amounts in millions)			
	2015	2014	2013
Net income attributable to Starbucks	$2,757.4	$2,068.1	$ 8.3
Gain resulting from acquisition of joint venture, after tax	(253.9)	—	—
Loss on extinguishment of debt, after tax	39.7	—	—
Litigation charge, after tax	—	(13.1)	1,809.7
Adjusted net income attributable to Starbucks	$2,543.2	$2,055.0	$1,818.0

Exhibit 4.5

Calculations of Unadjusted and Adjusted ROA for Starbucks
(total assets data from Appendix C and archived 2013 Starbucks financial statements; adjusted net income data from Exhibit 4.4)

	2015	2014	2013
Total assets—beginning of year	$10,752.9	$11,516.7	$ 8,219.2
Total assets—end of year	12,446.1	10,752.9	11,516.7
Average total assets	11,599.5	11,134.8	9,868.0
Net income attributable to Starbucks	2,757.4	2,068.1	8.3
Adjusted net income attributable to Starbucks	2,543.2	2,055.0	1,818.0
Interest expense	70.5	64.1	28.1
Net income + (1 − 0.35) × Interest expense + Noncontrolling interest	2,805.1	2,109.4	27.1
Adjusted net income + (1 − 0.35) × Interest expense + Noncontrolling interest	2,591.0	2,096.2	1,836.7
ROA (unadjusted)	24.2%	18.9%	0.3%
ROA (adjusted)	22.3%	18.8%	18.6%

better characterized as a return on *invested* capital when items that are not directly invested capital (such as accounts payable) are deducted from total assets.

Economics suggests that even when liabilities do not provide for *explicit* interest charges, the creditor charges *implicit* interest by adjusting the terms of the contract, such as offering discounts for those who do pay immediately or setting higher prices for those who do not pay immediately. The numerator of the ROA calculation is a measure of income before deducting financing costs; therefore, an alternative approach would be to use total assets in the denominator (i.e., do not subtract non-interest-bearing liabilities) but adjust net income for both explicit and implicit financing costs. Unfortunately, it is quite difficult to reliably estimate the implicit interest charges associated with non-interest-bearing liabilities such as accounts payable and accrued liabilities and to reclassify the implicit increments for financing charges in cost of goods sold and selling, general, and administrative expenses to interest expense (which is added back to net income). Adjusting prefinancing income this way would increase the measure of operating income in the numerator, increasing calculated ROA. (The alternative of reducing the denominator by subtracting non-interest-bearing liabilities from total assets also would increase calculated ROA.) Despite the reasonable arguments for adjusting income in the ROA calculation to account for implicit interest or adjusting total assets for indirectly invested capital, in all but extreme cases such adjustments generally result in only minor changes in time-series or cross-sectional analyses of ROA. Combined with the low degree of precision in estimating such amounts, the examples and problems in this book follow the conventional practice of using average total assets in the denominator of ROA, making no adjustment for non-interest-bearing liabilities.

Second, it is important to note that although we adjusted the numerator of ROA for unusual or nonrecurring items, we did not adjust the denominator. This implicitly assumes the unusual or nonrecurring items are not persistent but that their effects on total assets *are* persistent. For example, consider the gain resulting from the acquisition of **Starbucks Japan** that were added back to net income. This gain increased the carrying value of assets related to this investment. Our adjustment deducted from net income the effect of this gain on the income statement but did not deduct the effects of the gain in the ending balance of total assets, which will be higher because of the increase in asset values. Thus, our adjustment to the numerator (a decrease) was coupled with the impact of the unadjusted balance sheet effects in the denominator (an increase), leading to a slight upward bias in our calculation of adjusted ROA.

The logic behind this seemingly inconsistent treatment is motivated by a desire to compute *sustainable* ROA. The current period gain is unlikely to persist in future periods, but the increased asset value will persist; thus, the adjusted ROA provides a better indicator of the ROA we might expect to observe next period even though it is a biased measure of the current period's ROA. Again, our approach reflects conventional practice, but the astute analyst should understand that blindly ignoring certain items on the income statement but allowing them to affect the balance sheet can affect calculations of adjusted performance.

Disaggregating ROA

You obtain further insight into the behavior of ROA by disaggregating it into profit margin for ROA and total assets turnover (also simply referred to as *assets turnover*) components as follows:

$$\textbf{ROA} = \textbf{Profit Margin for ROA} \times \textbf{Assets Turnover}$$

$$\frac{\begin{array}{c}\text{Net Income} + \text{Interest}\\ \text{Expense (net of taxes)}\\ + \text{Noncontrolling Interest}\\ \text{in Earnings}\end{array}}{\text{Average Total Assets}} = \frac{\begin{array}{c}\text{Net Income} + \text{Interest}\\ \text{Expense (net of taxes)}\\ + \text{Noncontrolling Interest}\\ \text{in Earnings}\end{array}}{\text{Sales}} \times \frac{\text{Sales}}{\text{Average Total Assets}}$$

The profit margin for ROA indicates the ability of a firm to utilize its assets to generate earnings for a particular level of sales. Assets turnover indicates the firm's ability to generate sales from a particular level of investment in assets. The *assets turnover ratio* indicates the firm's *ability to use assets to generate sales*, and the *profit margin for ROA* indicates the firm's *ability to use sales to generate profits*. The product of the two ratios is ROA, indicating the firm's ability to use assets to generate profitability.

The disaggregation of ROA for **Starbucks** for 2015, after adjusting for nonrecurring items, is as follows:

$$\textbf{ROA} = \textbf{Profit Margin for ROA} \times \textbf{Assets Turnover}$$

$$\frac{\$2,591.0}{\$11,599.5} = \frac{\$2,591.0}{\$19,162.7} \times \frac{\$19,162.7}{\$11,599.5}$$

$$22.3\% = 13.5\% \times 1.65$$

Exhibit 4.6 summarizes ROA, profit margin for ROA, and assets turnover for **Starbucks** for 2013 through 2015. **Starbucks'** profit margin for ROA is steadily increasing. In addition, **Starbucks'** assets turnover has fluctuated but is highest in 2015. In the next section, we discuss another measure of profitability—return on common shareholders' equity (ROCE). After that discussion, we explore the economic and strategic factors underlying both measures of profitability.

Exhibit 4.6			
ROA, Profit Margin, and Assets Turnover for Starbucks: 2013–2015 (adjusted data)			
	2015	**2014**	**2013**
ROA	22.3%	18.8%	18.6%
Profit Margin for ROA	13.5%	12.7%	12.4%
Assets Turnover	1.65	1.48	1.51

- Return on assets (ROA) is an overall measure of the profitability of a firm relative to its total assets and is unaffected by how the firm is financed.
- The numerator of ROA is the level of profits before deducting after-tax financing costs.
- ROA can be computed based on the profits reported by a company, or it can be adjusted to exclude the effects of unusual or nonrecurring items, so that the computation yields a better measure of the core or sustainable operations of the company.
- ROA can be disaggregated into profit margin for ROA and assets turnover, which provide insight into the sources of a company's overall profitability.

Quick Check

Return on Common Shareholders' Equity (ROCE)

LO 4-3

Analyze and interpret return on common shareholders' equity (ROCE) and its components, especially successful use of financial leverage to increase the return to common shareholders.

ROA measures the profitability of operations *before* considering the effects of financing. That is, ROA ignores the proportion of debt versus equity financing that a firm uses to finance the assets. ROA is important for analysts interested in the profitability and efficiency of a firm's core operations.

Return on common equity (ROCE), on the other hand, measures the return to common shareholders after subtracting from revenues not only operating expenses (such as cost of goods sold, selling and administration expenses, and income taxes) but also after subtracting the costs of financing debt and preferred stock.[15] The latter includes interest expense on debt and required dividends on preferred stock (if any). Thus, ROCE incorporates the results of a firm's operating, investing, *and financing* decisions.

We calculate ROCE as follows:

$$ROCE = \frac{\text{Net Income Available to Common Shareholders}}{\text{Average Common Shareholders' Equity}}$$

The numerator measures the amount of net income for the period available to the common shareholders after subtracting all amounts allocable to noncontrolling interests

---

[15]Use of ROE is probably more common than ROCE, but we use the latter to emphasize that the construct we want is return on *common* shareholders' equity.

and preferred shareholders. Net income available to common shareholders already reflects subtraction of interest expense on debt, so the numerator of ROCE requires no further adjustment for creditors' claims on earnings (that is, interest expense). However, you must subtract dividends paid or payable on preferred stock from net income to obtain income attributable to the common shareholders.[16]

The denominator of ROCE measures the average amount of total common shareholders' equity during the period. An average of the total common shareholders' equity at the beginning and end of the year is appropriate unless a firm made a significant new common stock issue or buyback during the year. If the latter occurred, you should use an average of the common shareholders' equity at the end of each quarter to better reflect the outstanding common shareholders' equity during the year.

Common shareholders' equity equals total shareholders' equity minus (1) the non-controlling interest in the net assets of consolidated subsidiaries and (2) the par value of preferred stock. Because net income to common shareholders in the numerator reflects a subtraction for the noncontrolling interest in earnings of consolidated subsidiaries, the denominator should exclude the noncontrolling interest in net assets (if any). Firms seldom issue preferred stock significantly above par value, so you can assume that the amount in the additional paid-in capital account relates to common stock.

The calculation of the ROCE of **Starbucks** for 2015, using the *reported* amounts of net income, which is shown on the "Analysis Spreadsheet" of FSAP, is as follows (in millions):

$$\text{ROCE} = \frac{\text{Net Income Available to Common Shareholders}}{\text{Average Common Shareholders' Equity}}$$

$$49.7\% = \frac{\$2,757.4}{0.5(\$5,818.0 + \$5,272.0)}$$

The calculation of the ROCE of **Starbucks** for 2015, using the *adjusted* amounts of net income discussed previously and displayed in Exhibit 4.5, is as follows (in millions):

$$\text{ROCE} = \frac{\text{Adjusted Net Income Available to Common Shareholders}}{\text{Average Common Shareholders' Equity}}$$

$$45.9\% = \frac{\$2,543.2}{0.5(\$5,818.0 + \$5,272.0)}$$

Although **Starbucks** has authorized 7.5 million of preferred stock, none is outstanding (Note 11, "Equity"). The adjusted ROCE of **Starbucks** was 42.1% in 2014 and 37.9% in 2013, consistent with the upward trend in ROA discussed earlier in the chapter.

Benchmarks for ROCE

Having computed ROCE for **Starbucks** of 49.7% (as reported) or 45.9% (adjusted) for 2015, is this "good" or "bad" performance? One benchmark is the average ROCE of other firms (Appendix D includes benchmarking data for many ratios across 48 industries).

---

[16]As discussed later in Chapter 14, for purposes of valuation, you might instead compute ROCE using comprehensive income available to common shareholders, not net income available to common shareholders.

The average ROCE for the cross-section of publicly traded firms in the United States is approximately 10% to 12%, so **Starbucks** is well above the average ROCE; hence, its current ROCE is certainly "good" by this benchmark. Also, the ROCE of a similar firm such as **Panera** can serve as a benchmark. For 2015, Panera had an ROCE of 24.2% (as reported), so **Starbucks** generated a significantly higher ROCE than Panera.

A more direct benchmark against which to judge ROCE is the return demanded by common shareholders for a firm's use of their capital. Because common shareholders are the residual claimants of the firm, accountants do not treat the cost of common shareholders' equity capital as an expense when computing net income. On the other hand, a firm that generates ROCE less than the cost of common equity capital destroys value for shareholders, whereas a firm that generates ROCE in excess of the cost of capital creates value. ROCE measures the return to the common shareholders but does not indicate whether this rate of return exceeds or falls short of the cost of common equity capital.

To illustrate, **Starbucks**' ROCE for 2015 as computed above is 45.9% (adjusted). Chapter 11 provides a discussion of how to compute the cost of equity capital. In that chapter, the cost of equity capital for **Starbucks** is estimated to be 7.2%. Based on this cost of common equity capital, **Starbucks** generated an excess return of 38.7% (45.9% – 7.2%). Compared to most firms, this is an incredibly high excess return.

Conceptually, the cost of common equity capital is the rate of return the common shareholders demand as compensation for delaying consumption and for bearing the risk of investing in a particular firm. Measuring the cost of common equity capital is more difficult than measuring the cost of debt because debt instruments typically specify an interest rate and effective interest rates can be easily determined. The dividend on common stock is not an accurate measure of the cost of common equity capital because managers and boards of directors determine dividend payout policies, whereas equity investors determine the cost of equity capital.

The importance of ROCE is highlighted by its central use in assessing profitability and estimating firm value. As will be shown later in Chapter 13, a measure known as *residual income* (also called *abnormal earnings*) quantifies the profits earned by a company after deducting a charge for the cost of equity capital, calculated as follows:

Residual Income = Net Income Available to Common Shareholders –
(Cost of Equity Capital × Beginning Common Shareholders' Equity)

Residual income is a measure of the wealth a firm generates for its common shareholders in a period beyond the required return on their investment in the firm. In recent years, the financial press and some corporate managers have given considerable attention to similar measures of profits after deducting a charge for the use of capital.[17] The concept behind these refined measures of profits is that a firm does not create value unless it earns more than the cost of all of its capital, including common shareholders' equity capital. As a result, valuations are higher as firms generate future ROCE higher than the cost of equity capital. Thus, the benchmark for ROCE that will be most useful in the remainder of this text is the cost of equity capital.

---

[17]For example, various consulting firms promote similar measures such as Stern Stewart's *economic value added* (EVA)®, HOLT Value Associates' *cash flow return on investment* (CFROI), L.E.K. Consulting's *shareholder value added* (SVA), Marakon's *discounted economic profits* (EP), and KPMG's *earned value management* (EVM).

Exhibit 4.7

Evolution of Future ROCE Conditional on Current ROCE

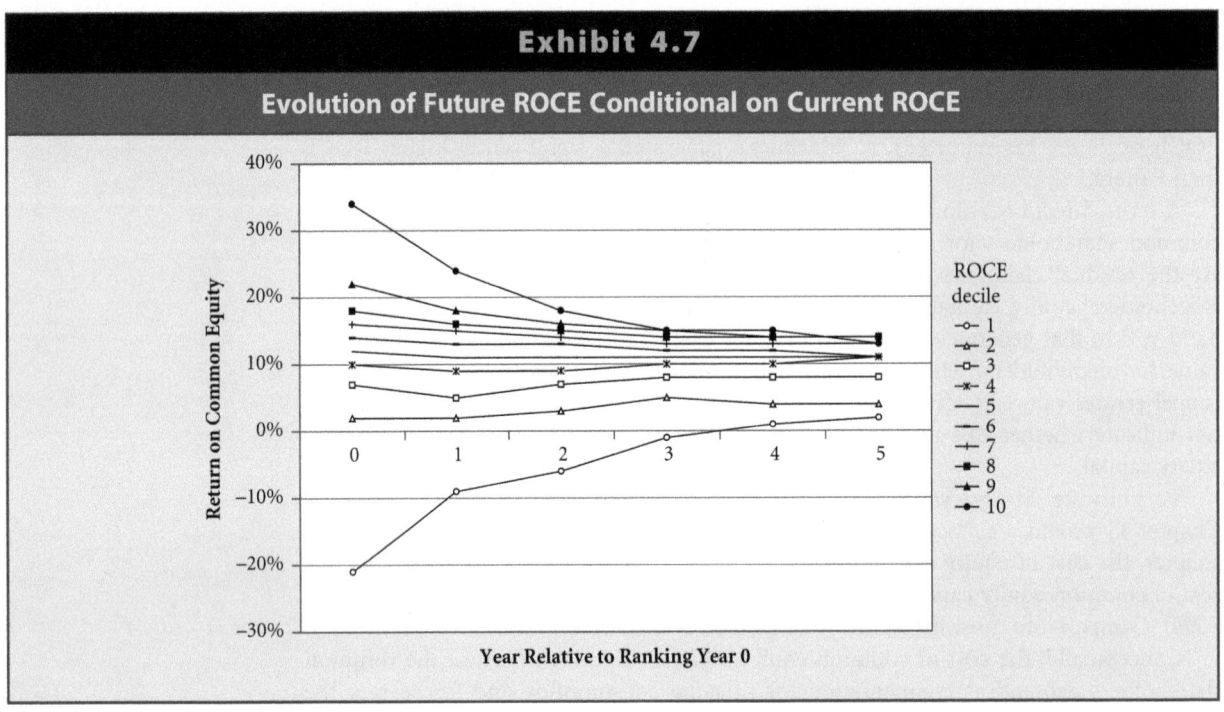

In addition, it is helpful to see how ROCE is subject to the same life cycle and competitive pressures discussed earlier in the chapter. For example, Exhibit 4.7 plots the results from a study of the behavior of ROCE across time.[18] It partitioned firms into deciles based on beginning ROCE and then tracked the average ROCE for each decile over subsequent years. The graph indicates that the initial spread in ROCE is very large, with the most profitable firms generating average ROCE in excess of 30% and the least profitable firms generating average ROCE below negative 20%. However, competitive pressures erode the abnormally high ROCEs of the most profitable firms, and survival (or bankruptcy or an acquisition) results in the poorest performing firms increasing ROCE to positive levels. This does not imply that all firms with above-average ROCEs will realize lower ROCEs in the future, but it is the dominant pattern arising from normal competitive equilibrium conditions. A few companies with sustainable strategic advantages and/or substantial off-balance-sheet assets and equity (such as **Starbucks'** valuable brand and numerous locations) can generate ROCEs well above the average for an extended number of years.

Relating ROA to ROCE

ROA measures operating performance independent of financing, while ROCE explicitly considers the cost of debt and preferred stock financing. Exhibit 4.1 diagrams the relation between ROA and ROCE and shows that both can be broken down into margin,

---

[18]See Victor L. Bernard, "Accounting-Based Valuation Methods, Determinants of Market-to-Book Ratios, and Implications for Financial Statement Analysis." Unpublished manuscript, University of Michigan Business School, Kresge Library (January 1994).

turnover, and leverage (although differences are highlighted with dashed lines). An expanded diagram of the relation between ROA and ROCE is as follows:[19]

Return on Assets		Return to Creditors	Return to Preferred Shareholders	Return to Common Shareholders
$\dfrac{\text{Net Income} + \text{Interest Expense Net of Taxes}}{\text{Average Total Assets}}$	$\rightarrow$	$\dfrac{\text{Interest Expense Net of Taxes}}{\text{Average Total Liabilities}}$	$\dfrac{\text{Preferred Dividends}}{\text{Average Preferred Shareholders' Equity}}$	$\dfrac{\text{Net Income to Common}}{\text{Average Common Shareholders' Equity}}$

This diagram allocates each dollar of prefinancing earnings to the various providers of capital. Creditors receive their return first in the form of interest payments. The cost of this capital to the firm is interest expense net of the income tax benefit derived from deducting interest in calculating taxable income. Many liabilities, such as accounts payable and salaries payable, carry no explicit interest cost.

Preferred stock carries a cost equal to the preferred dividend amount. Historically, firms could not deduct preferred dividends when calculating taxable income, but in recent years, some firms have been successful in structuring preferred stock issues so that they qualify for tax deductibility of dividends paid. In those cases, you should adjust preferred dividends for the related tax savings.

The portion of net income that is *not* allocated to creditors or preferred shareholders is available for the common shareholders, who are the residual claimants. Likewise, the portion of a firm's assets not financed with capital provided by creditors or preferred shareholders represents the capital provided by the common shareholders.[20]

Now consider the relation between ROA and ROCE.

- Under what circumstances will ROCE exceed ROA?
- Under what circumstances will ROCE be less than ROA?

The key to answering these questions lies in understanding how the use of financing from sources other than common shareholders can harm or benefit common shareholders.

ROCE will exceed ROA whenever ROA exceeds the cost of capital provided by creditors and preferred shareholders. Alternatively stated, if common equity holders can rely on lower-cost financing by creditors and preferred shareholders, and use that capital to generate higher rates of return, then they have leveraged such financing for assets that produce a return sufficiently high to pay interest and preferred stock dividends and yield an excess return, which then belongs to the common shareholders.

Common business terminology refers to the practice of using lower-cost creditor and preferred stock capital to increase the return to common shareholders as *financial leverage* or *capital structure leverage*. To clarify the concept, consider the two scenarios shown in Exhibit 4.8.

Under Scenario 1 in Exhibit 4.8, the firm has one common equity investor who invests $100 to generate an ROA of 10%. At the end of the year, income available to the common equity investor is $10, reflecting the ROA and ROCE of 10% ($10 income ÷ $100 investment). Alternatively, in Scenario 2, the single equity investor could have

---

[19]Note that the relation does not appear as an equation. We use an arrow instead of an equals sign to indicate that the return on assets gets allocated to the various suppliers of capital. To accurately express the relation as an equality, you would need to know the weights of each source of financing in the capital structure. Also, note that we assume no noncontrolling interests; if we did, we would also include a term for the return to noncontrolling interests.

[20]If a firm does not own 100% of the common stock of a consolidated subsidiary, the accountant must allocate a portion of the ROA to the noncontrolling shareholders. For such firms (including **Starbucks**), a fourth term would appear on the right side of the arrow: noncontrolling interest in earnings/average noncontrolling interest in net assets.

Exhibit 4.8

ROCE: Example of How Equity Investors Strategically Use Leverage to Increase Their Returns on Investment

	Scenario 1	Scenario 2
Equity investment	$ 100	$ 10
Debt financing	0	90
Total assets	$ 100	$ 100
ROA	10%	10%
After-tax cost of financing	___	5%
Net income available to equity:		
Scenario 1 (10% × $100)	$10.00	
Scenario 2 [$10 – ($90 × 5%)]		$5.50
ROCE:		
Scenario 1 ($10 ÷ $100)	10%	
Scenario 2 ($5.50 ÷ $10)		55%

---

invested only $10 and borrowed $90 to have the same amount to invest ($100) and generate the same return (10%).

Suppose creditors provide the $90 loan at an after-tax interest cost to the firm of 5%. At the end of the year, the firm would have generated the same income of $10, but the after-tax cost of financing would be $4.50 ($90 debt × 5%), leaving income available to the common shareholder of $5.50. *Although the net income is lower in Scenario 2, the ROCE is 55%, much higher, reflecting the strategic use of leverage by the equity investor.* A much smaller investment of $10 (rather than $100) combined with debt financing of $90 enables the common equity investor to realize a substantially higher rate of return. In this case, rather than a 10% return on equity, the equity investor would have realized a 55% return on equity ($5.50 income ÷ $10 investment).

This example demonstrates the advantages of the strategic use of financial leverage to increase returns to equity investors; deploying assets that generate 10% but partially financing them with capital that costs only 5% generates "abnormal" returns. At the same time, increased leverage triggers greater risk, which we will discuss in Chapter 5.

Consider our analysis of **Starbucks**, which generated an adjusted ROA of 22.3% during 2015. The after-tax cost of capital provided by creditors during 2015 was 0.8% $[(1 - 0.35)(\$70.5)/0.5(\$6,628.1 + \$5,480.9)]$.[21] The difference between the 0.8% cost of creditor capital and the 22.3% ROA generated on assets financed with debt capital belongs to the common shareholders. In other words, **Starbucks** has approximately $6 billion in assets financed at a cost of 0.8% (or approximately $48 million), but these assets generate a return of 22.3% (or approximately $1.3 billion).

Starbucks' financial leverage worked to the advantage of its common shareholders from 2013 through 2015 because its ROA exceeded the cost of all non-common equity financing. This resulted in ROCE exceeding ROA in every year (both adjusted): in 2013, 37.9% > 18.6%; in 2014, 42.1% > 18.8%; and in 2015, 45.9% > 22.3%. Next, we explore the possible reasons for the superior returns generated for equity investors when ROCE exceeds ROA.

---

[21]The amounts in the denominator for **Starbucks** equal total assets minus total shareholders' equity, or, equivalently, total liabilities and noncontrolling interest). The after-tax cost of creditor capital seems low, but recall that many liabilities, such as accounts payable and accrued liabilities, do not carry an explicit interest cost.

Disaggregating ROCE

We can analyze ROCE more deeply and gain better insights if we disaggregate it into components, as we did with ROA. The disaggregated components of ROCE are profit margin for ROCE, assets turnover, and capital structure leverage.

$$\text{ROCE} = \text{Profit Margin for ROCE} \times \text{Assets Turnover} \times \text{Capital Structure Leverage}$$

$$\frac{\text{Net Income Available to Common Shareholders}}{\text{Average Common Shareholders' Equity}} = \frac{\text{Net Income Available to Common Shareholders}}{\text{Sales}} \times \frac{\text{Sales}}{\text{Average Total Assets}} \times \frac{\text{Average Total Assets}}{\text{Average Common Shareholders' Equity}}$$

Note that the first distinction between profit margin for ROA and profit margin for ROCE is the different numerator used. The numerator of profit margin for ROCE is net income available to common shareholders, and the numerator for profit margin for ROA is net income with after-tax interest expense and noncontrolling interest added back, which yields a measure of profits before deducting financing costs. The different numerators are aligned with the different denominators (common equity for ROCE and total assets for ROA).

Assets turnover is identical to that used to disaggregate ROA. The additional component in the disaggregation of ROCE is the capital structure leverage ratio, which measures the degree to which a firm strategically utilizes financial leverage to finance assets. The difference between the numerator and the denominator of the capital structure leverage ratio is the amount of liabilities (and preferred shareholders' equity, if any) in the capital structure. The larger the amount of capital obtained from these sources, the smaller the amount of capital obtained from common shareholders and therefore the larger the capital structure leverage ratio. Another way to interpret the capital structure leverage ratio is as follows:

$$\frac{\text{Total Assets}}{\text{Common Shareholders' Equity}} = \frac{\text{Debt} + \text{Preferred Equity} + \text{Common Shareholders' Equity}}{\text{Common Shareholders' Equity}} = 1 + \frac{\text{Debt} + \text{Preferred Equity}}{\text{Common Shareholders' Equity}}$$

Thus, capital structure leverage is simply one plus the debt-to-equity ratio for a firm with no preferred stock or one plus the ratio of debt plus preferred equity to common shareholders' equity for a firm with preferred stock.

Before proceeding with a disaggregation of **Starbucks'** ROCE, we note that there are many more ways to disaggregate ROA or ROCE than are discussed in this chapter. We will describe one alternative method of decomposing ROCE in the next chapter, which highlights the importance of benchmarking returns generated by the firm's assets against the cost of borrowing from creditors. The disaggregation of ROCE for **Starbucks** for 2015 under the basic decomposition discussed in this chapter is as follows:

$$\text{ROCE} = \text{Profit Margin for ROCE} \times \text{Assets Turnover} \times \text{Capital Structure Leverage}$$

$$\frac{\$2{,}543.2}{0.5(\$5{,}818.0 + \$5{,}272.0)} = \frac{\$2{,}543.2}{\$19{,}162.7} \times \frac{\$19{,}162.7}{0.5(\$12{,}446.1 + \$10{,}752.9)} \times \frac{0.5(\$12{,}446.1 + \$10{,}752.9)}{0.5(\$5{,}818.0 + \$5{,}272.0)}$$

$$45.9\% = 13.3\% \times 1.65 \times 2.09$$

	ROCE	=	Profit Margin for ROCE	×	Total Assets Turnover	×	Capital Structure Leverage
Exhibit 4.9							
Disaggregation of ROCE of Starbucks: 2013–2015 (adjusted data)							
2015	45.9%	=	13.3%	×	1.65	×	2.09
2014	42.1%	=	12.5%	×	1.48	×	2.28
2013	37.9%	=	12.2%	×	1.51	×	2.06

Exhibit 4.9 presents the disaggregation of ROCE of **Starbucks** for 2013 through 2015. The increasing ROCE of **Starbucks** results from the net effect of (1) increasing profit margins, (2) fluctuating but increased assets turnover in 2015, and (3) relatively stable capital structure leverage. The increasing profit margin for ROCE mirrors that discussed previously for ROA. The calculation of assets turnover is the same in the decomposition of ROA and ROCE, so it also mirrors the previous discussion about the decomposition of ROA.

The primary mechanical difference between the ROA and ROCE decompositions is the capital structure leverage component, which is relatively unchanged from 2013 through 2015. The stable leverage combined with the increasing profit margin and assets turnover explains the increasing ROCE for **Starbucks**. Thus, **Starbucks** is primarily generating increasing returns to shareholders across years by increasing profit margins.

Companies rarely discuss profit margin for ROCE or total assets turnover directly, but you may glean insight by reading explanations for changes in profits and balance sheet items in the MD&A. **Starbucks** describes increasing profit margins in 2015 as reflecting "sales leverage," which refers to growth in sales exceeding growth in expenses. This is most evident for firms with high fixed costs, like **Starbucks**' significant occupancy costs (rent on stores).

We can gain insight into the change in total assets turnover by examining relative changes in sales (the numerator) and total assets (the denominator). For 2015, sales increased 16.5% while total assets increased 15.7%. The higher growth in sales relative to growth in total assets led to an increase in total assets turnover.

For 2015, capital structure leverage declined from 2014, which was up relative to 2013. **Starbucks**' Note 9, "Debt," indicates that total long-term debt increased during 2015 (from a face value of $2,050 million to $2,350 million). However, this increase of approximately 14.6% was less than the 15.7% increase in total assets, resulting in a decline in capital structure leverage as a portion of total financing.

Quick Check

■ Return on common shareholders' equity (ROCE) is a measure of the profitability of common shareholder investment in a firm, after deducting all costs of financing from other sources (such as debt, preferred equity, and noncontrolling interests).

■ ROCE can be disaggregated into profit margin for ROCE, assets turnover, and capital structure leverage.

■ Like ROA, disaggregation of ROCE reveals insights into the sources of profitability for common shareholders.

Economic and Strategic Determinants of ROA and ROCE[22]

LO 4-4

Link economic and strategic factors to ROA and ROCE.

ROA and ROCE differ across industries depending on their economic characteristics and across firms within an industry depending on the design and implementation of their strategies. This section explores economic and strategic factors that impact the interpretation of the margin and turnover components of ROA and ROCE. (We will discuss the leverage component of ROCE in Chapter 5.) Exhibit 4.10 depicts graphically the 15-year average of the median annual ROAs, profit margins for ROA, and assets turnovers of 23 industries. The two *isoquants* reflect ROAs of 3% and 6%. The isoquants show the various combinations of profit margin for ROA and assets turnover that yield ROAs of 3% and 6%. For instance, an ROA of 6% results from any of the following profit margins for ROA $\times$ assets turnover combinations: 6% $\times$ 1.0, 3% $\times$ 2.0, 2% $\times$ 3.0, 1% $\times$ 6.0.

Financial statement analysis focuses on the ROAs of specific firms (or even segments of specific firms) for particular years (or even quarters). The data for ROA, profit margin for ROA, and assets turnover underlying the plots in Exhibit 4.10 reflect aggregated amounts across firms within industries and across years. What factors explain the

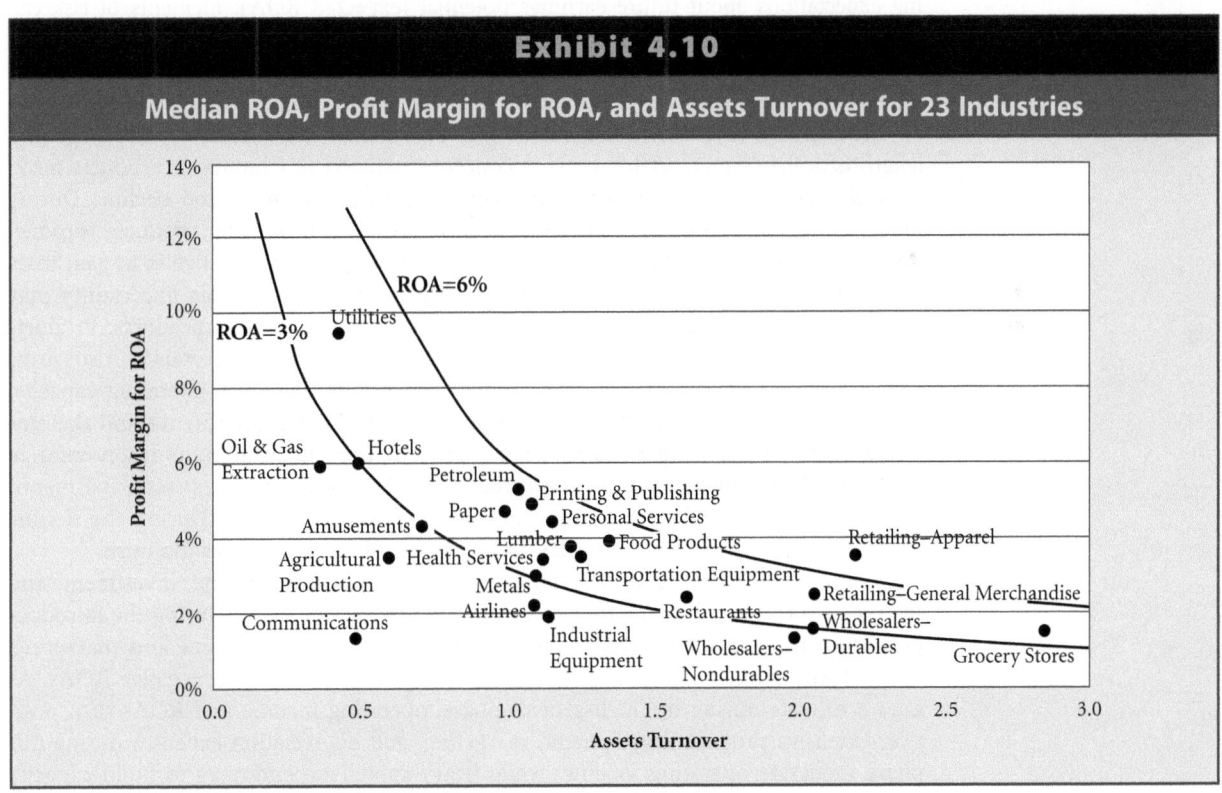

Exhibit 4.10

Median ROA, Profit Margin for ROA, and Assets Turnover for 23 Industries

---

[22]The material in this section draws heavily from Thomas I. Selling and Clyde P. Stickney, "The Effects of Business Environments and Strategy on a Firm's Rate of Return on Assets," *Financial Analysts Journal* (January/February 1989), pp. 43–52.

consistently high or consistently low ROAs of some industries relative to the average of all industries? Further, what explains the fact that certain industries have high profit margins and low assets turnovers while other industries experience low profit margins and high assets turnovers?

The microeconomics and business strategy literature provides useful background for interpreting the behavior of ROA, profit margin, and assets turnover. As a prelude to the discussion that follows, consider the two extreme industries in Exhibit 4.10. Utilities show the highest profit margins, which can be explained by significant barriers to entry (both regulatory and enormous fixed costs). Barriers to entry in this industry permit existing firms to realize higher profit margins due to limited competition, and turnover is lower because of the large asset base required, such as power generation plants and distribution networks. On the other hand, grocery stores show the highest assets turnover. Given lower barriers to entry and significant competition, the firms in this industry survive on the ability to run efficient operations and generate substantial assets turnover, consistent with the perpetual efforts by such companies to generate foot traffic through ever-changing sales and promotions.

Economic theory suggests that higher levels of perceived risk in any activity should lead to higher levels of expected return if that activity is to attract capital from investors. ROAs based on reported financial statement data provide useful information for tracking the past periodic performance of a firm and its segments (realized ROA) and for developing expectations about future earnings potential (expected ROA). Elements of risk can cause realized ROA to diverge from expected ROA. We briefly discuss three elements of risk that are useful in understanding differences in ROAs across firms and changes over time: (1) product life cycles, (2) operating leverage, and (3) cyclicality of sales.

Product Life Cycle. An element of risk that affects ROA relates to the stage and length of a firm's product life cycle, a concept discussed in Chapter 3. Products move through four identifiable phases: introduction, growth, maturity, and decline. During the introduction and growth phases, a firm focuses on developing products (product R&D spending) and building capacity (capital spending). The objective is to gain market acceptance, productive capacity, and market share. Considerable uncertainty may exist during these phases regarding the market viability of a firm's products. Products that have survived into the maturity phase have gained market acceptance. Also, firms have probably been able to cut back capital expenditures on new operating capacity. During the maturity phase, however, competition becomes more intense and the emphasis shifts to reducing costs through improved capacity utilization (economies of scale) and more efficient production (process R&D spending aimed at reducing manufacturing costs through better utilization of labor and materials). During the decline phase, firms exit the industry as sales decline and profit opportunities diminish.

Exhibit 4.11 depicts the behavior of revenues, operating income, investment, and ROA that corresponds to the four phases of the product life cycle. During the introduction and early growth phases, expenditures on product development and marketing, coupled with relatively low sales levels, lead to operating losses and negative ROAs. As sales accelerate during the high-growth phase, operating income and ROAs turn positive. Extensive product development, marketing, and depreciation expenses during this phase moderate operating income, while heavy capital expenditures to build capacity for expected higher future sales increase the denominator of ROA. Thus, ROA does not grow as rapidly as sales. ROA increases significantly during the maturity phase due to benefits of economies of scale and learning curve phenomena and to curtailments of capital expenditures. ROA deteriorates during the decline phase as operating income decreases, but ROA may remain positive or even increase for some time into this phase

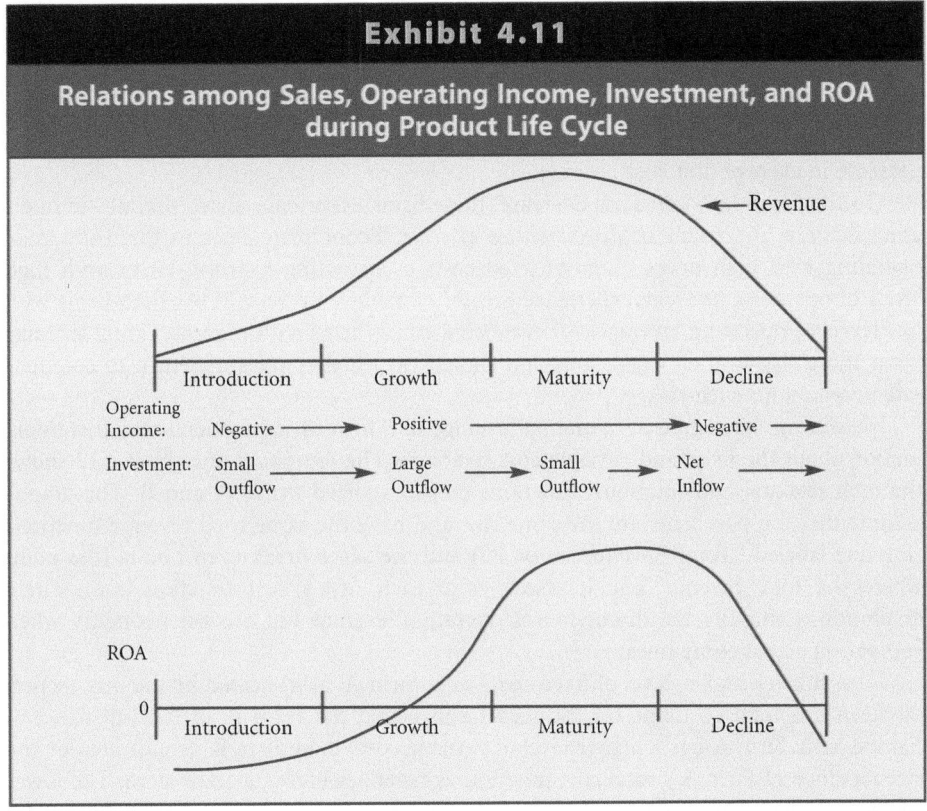

Exhibit 4.11

Relations among Sales, Operating Income, Investment, and ROA during Product Life Cycle

(particularly if the depreciable assets have been largely depreciated). This movement in ROA appears negatively correlated with the level of risk. Risks are probably greatest in the introduction and growth stages, when ROA is low or negative, and least in the maturity phase, when ROA is high.

Note that the product life cycle theory focuses on individual products. We can extend the theory to an industry level by examining the average stage in the product life cycle of all products in that industry. For instance, products in the computer industry range from the introduction to the decline phases, but the overall industry is probably in the maturity phase. The beverage and food-processing industries, the primary markets of **Starbucks**, are mature, although **Starbucks** and its competitors continually introduce new products. We might view the steel industry, at least in the United States, as in the early decline phase, although some companies have modernized production sufficiently to stave off the decline.

In addition to the stage in the product life cycle, the length of the product life cycle also is an element of risk. Products with short product life cycles require more frequent expenditures to develop replacement or new products, thereby increasing risk. The product life cycles of most computer products run just a few years. Most pharmaceutical products experience product life cycles of approximately seven years. In contrast, the life cycles of **Starbucks'** coffee, branded food products, and some toys (for example, Lego® blocks) are much longer.

Operating Leverage. Firms operate with different mixtures of fixed and variable costs in their cost structures. Firms in the utilities, communications, hotel, petroleum, and chemical industries are capital-intensive. Depreciation and many operating costs are more or less fixed for any given period. Most retailers and wholesalers, on the other hand, have high proportions of variable costs in their cost structures. Firms with high proportions of fixed costs experience significant increases in operating income as sales increase, a phenomenon known as *economies of scale*. The increased income occurs because the firms spread fixed costs over a larger number of units sold, resulting in a decrease in average unit cost.

On the flip side, when sales decrease, these firms experience sharp declines in operating income, the result of *diseconomies of scale*. Economists refer to this process of operating with high proportions of fixed costs as *operating leverage*. Firms with high levels of operating leverage experience greater variability in their ROAs than firms with low levels of operating leverage. All else being equal, firms with high operating leverage incur more risk in their operations and should earn higher rates of return to compensate investors for such risk.

Measuring the degree of operating leverage of a firm or its segments requires information about the fixed and variable cost structure. The top panel of Exhibit 4.12 shows the total revenue and total cost functions of two stylized firms, A and B. The graphs assume that the two firms are the same size and have the same total revenue functions (the line labeled "Total Revenue: A or B") and the same break-even points (the point where the total revenue line intersects with each firm's cost function line). These assumptions simplify the discussion of operating leverage but are not necessary when comparing actual companies.

Firm B has a higher level of fixed costs than Firm A, as indicated by the intersection of the firm's total cost line on the *y*-axis above that for Firm A in the top panel of Exhibit 4.12. Firm A has a higher level of variable costs than Firm B, as indicated by the steeper slope of Firm A's total cost function as revenues increase above zero. The lower panel nets the total revenue and total cost functions to derive the operating income function (that is, revenue minus cost). Operating income is equal to the negative of

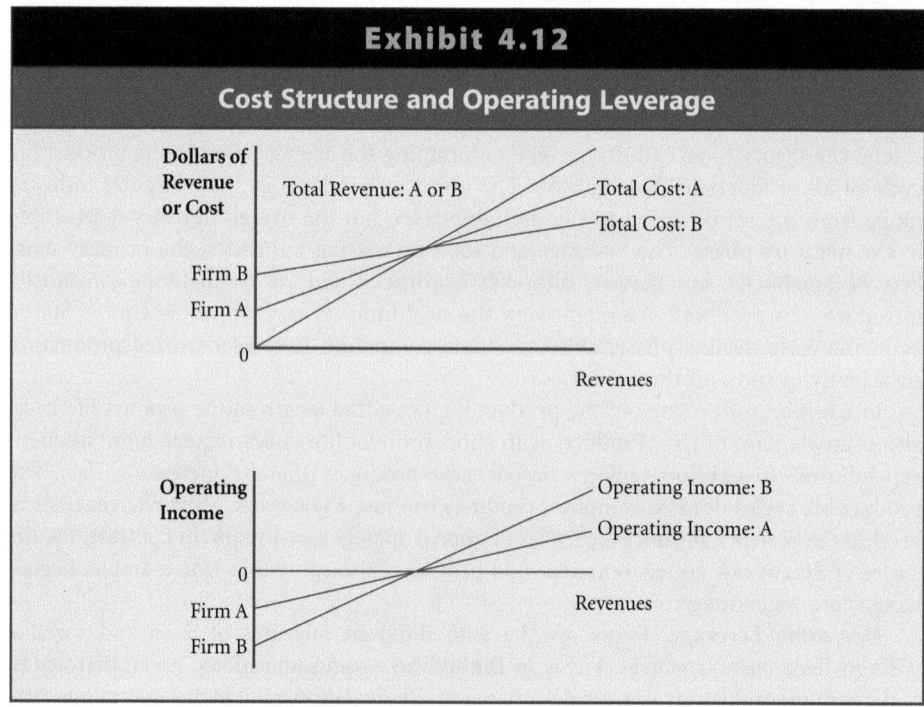

Exhibit 4.12

Cost Structure and Operating Leverage

fixed costs when revenues are zero and operating income is zero when revenues equal the sum of fixed and variable costs (that is, at breakeven). We use the slope of the operating income line as a measure of the extent of operating leverage. Firm B, with its higher fixed costs and lower variable-cost mix, has more operating leverage. As revenues increase, Firm B's operating income increases more rapidly than that of Firm A. On the downside, however, income decreases more rapidly for Firm B as revenues decrease.

Unfortunately, firms do not publicly disclose information about their fixed and variable cost structures. To examine the influence of operating leverage on the behavior of ROA for a particular firm or its segments, you must estimate the fixed versus variable cost structure. For example, **Starbucks** has significant fixed costs related to occupancy costs. A primary component of occupancy costs is rental payments under noncancelable operating leases. Note 10, "Leases," indicates that the minimum rent payments for fiscal 2015 were $1,026.3 million, which is approximately 13.2% of cost of sales including occupancy costs. We might assume that all other costs in this line item are variable costs. In addition, we might estimate that depreciation and amortization ($893.9) and general and administrative expenses ($1,196.7) also are fixed. Together, these three amounts suggest that **Starbucks'** fixed costs are approximately 19.7% of total operating expenses ([$1,026.3 + $893.9 + $1,196.7]/$15,811.6) in 2015. However, each of these estimated amounts likely includes some variable costs as well, so such estimates are approximations.

Another approach to such estimation is to study the various cost items of a firm and attempt to identify those that are likely to behave as fixed costs. Firms incur some costs in particular amounts, referred to as *committed fixed costs*, regardless of the actual level of activity during the period. Examples include depreciation, amortization, and rent. Firms can alter the amount of other costs, referred to as *discretionary fixed costs*, in the short run in response to operating conditions, but in general, these costs do not vary directly with the level of activity. Examples include research and development, maintenance, advertising, and central corporate staff expenses. Whether you should classify these latter costs as fixed costs or as variable costs in measuring operating leverage depends on their behavior in a particular firm. Given sufficient time-series data, you could estimate the level of fixed costs by estimating a regression of an operating expense on a variable that drives the variable component of the operating expense. For example, to estimate the fixed component of cost of goods sold, you could estimate the following regression:

$$\text{Cost of Goods Sold}_t = \alpha + \beta * \text{Sales}_t + \varepsilon_t$$

The estimated intercept, α, would be your best estimate of the fixed component of cost of goods sold, and β would be the estimate of the variable component (as a percentage of sales). Although ideal in theory, you need to use data from past quarters or years, which likely become outdated as the firm changes its strategy and operating structure. As an example of a simpler approach for assessing the relative contribution of fixed versus variable costs—continuing with the cost of goods sold example—you can test for the existence of significant fixed costs by examining the *percent change in cost of goods sold relative to the percent change in sales*. Firms with substantial fixed costs will behave like Firm B in Exhibit 4.12 and show percentage changes in cost of goods sold that are less than the percentage changes in sales. (Chapter 10 provides more discussion of how to estimate fixed versus variable costs and use that information in forecasting future expenses and income.)

Cyclicality of Sales. The sales of certain goods and services are particularly sensitive to conditions in the economy. Examples include construction services, industrial equipment, computers, automobiles, and other durable goods. When the economy is in an upswing (healthy GNP growth, low unemployment, and low interest rates), customers purchase these relatively high-priced items, and sales of these firms grow accordingly. On the other hand, when the economy enters a recession, customers curtail their purchases, and the sales of these firms decrease significantly. Contrast these cyclical sales patterns with those of grocery stores, food processors, non-fashion clothing, and electric utilities. Those industries sell products that most consumers consider necessities. Also, their products tend to carry lower per-unit costs, reducing the benefits of delaying purchases to realize cost savings. Firms with cyclical sales patterns incur more risk than firms with noncyclical sales.

One means of reducing the risk inherent in cyclical sales is to strive for a high proportion of variable cost in the cost structure. Examples of variable-cost strategies include paying employees an hourly wage instead of a fixed salary and renting buildings and equipment under short-term cancelable leases instead of purchasing them. Cost levels should change proportionally with sales, thereby maintaining stable profit margin percentages and reducing risk. Of course, this depends on whether the firm can make timely adjustments to cost structures in response to changes in demand, such as the ability to furlough workers or return leased equipment to lessors.

The nature of the activities of some firms is such that they must carry high levels of fixed costs (that is, operating leverage). Examples include capital-intensive service firms such as airlines and railroads. Firms in these industries may attempt to transform the cost of their physical capacity from a fixed cost to a variable cost by engaging in short-term leases or outsourcing. However, lessors then bear the risk of cyclical sales and demand higher returns (referred to by economists as *rents*). Thus, some firms are especially risky because they bear a combination of operating leverage and cyclical sales risk. A noncyclical sales pattern can compensate for high operating leverage and effectively neutralize this element of risk. Electric utilities, for example, carry high levels of fixed costs. However, their dominant positions in most service areas reduce their operating risks and permit them to achieve stable profitability.

Trade-Offs between Profit Margin and Assets Turnover

Refer again to the average industry ROAs in Exhibit 4.10. The location of several industries is consistent with their incurring one or more of these elements of risk. The relatively high ROAs of the utilities and petroleum industries are consistent with high operating leverage. Paper, petroleum, and transportation equipment experience cyclical sales, and apparel retailers face the risk of their products becoming obsolete. Some of the industry locations in Exhibit 4.10 appear inconsistent with these elements of risk. Oil and gas extraction, agricultural production, and communications are capital-intensive, yet their ROAs are the lowest of the 23 industries. One might view these positions as disequilibrium situations. Generating such low ROAs will not likely attract capital over the longer term.

The ROA locations of several industries appear to be affected by U.S. GAAP. A principal resource of food products firms such as **General Mills** and **Campbell's Soup** is the value of their brand names. Yet U.S. GAAP requires these firms to immediately expense advertising and other costs incurred to develop these brand names. Thus, their asset bases are understated and their ROAs are overstated. Likewise, the publishing industry does not recognize the value of copyrights or authors' contracts as assets, resulting in an overstatement of ROAs. A similar overstatement problem occurs for service firms, for which the value of their employees does not appear as an asset.

In addition to the differences in ROA depicted in Exhibit 4.10, we also must examine reasons for differences in the relative mix of profit margin and assets turnover. Explanations come from the microeconomics and business strategy literature.

Microeconomic Theory. Exhibit 4.13 sets out some important economic factors that constrain certain firms and industries to operate with particular combinations of profit margins and assets turnovers. Firms and industries characterized by heavy fixed capacity costs and lengthy periods required to add new capacity operate under a capacity constraint. There is an upper limit on the size of assets turnover achievable. To attract sufficient capital, these firms must generate a relatively high profit margin. Therefore, such firms operate in the area of Exhibit 4.13 marked Ⓐ. The firms usually achieve high profit margins through some form of entry barrier. The entry barrier may take the form of large required capital outlays, high risks, or regulation. Such factors help explain the profit margin–assets turnover mix of utilities, oil and gas extraction, communications, hotels, and amusements in Exhibit 4.10.

Firms whose products are commodity-like, where there are few entry barriers and where competition is intense, operate under a competitive constraint. There is an upper limit on the achievable level of profit margin for ROA. To attract sufficient capital, these firms must strive for high assets turnover. Therefore, such firms will operate in the area of Exhibit 4.13 marked Ⓒ. Firms achieve the high assets turnovers by keeping costs as low as possible (for example, minimizing fixed overhead costs, purchasing in sufficient quantities to realize discounts, and integrating vertically or horizontally to obtain cost savings). These firms match such actions to control costs with aggressively low prices to gain market share and drive out marginal firms. Most retailers and wholesalers operate in the low profit margin–high assets turnover area of Exhibit 4.10.

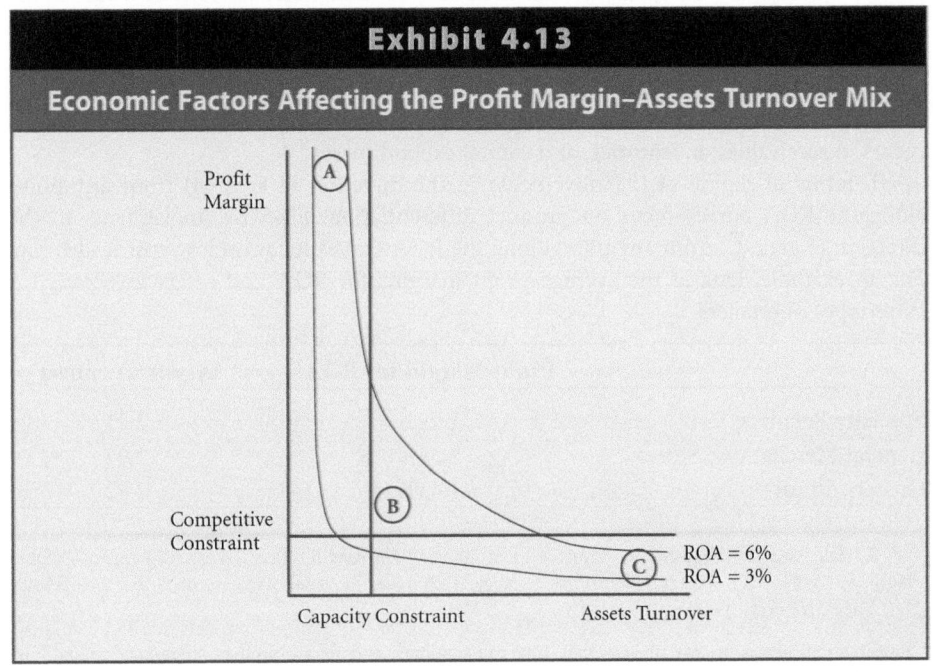

Exhibit 4.13

Economic Factors Affecting the Profit Margin–Assets Turnover Mix

Firms that operate in the area of Exhibit 4.13 marked Ⓑ are not as subject to capacity or competitive constraints as severe as those that operate in the tails of the ROA curves. Therefore, they have more flexibility to take actions that will increase profit margin for ROA, assets turnover, or both to achieve a higher ROA. As already suggested, firms operating in area Ⓐ might attempt to reposition the capacity constraint to the right by outsourcing some of their production. Such an action reduces the amount of fixed assets needed per dollar of sales (that is, increases the fixed assets turnover) but likely will reduce the profit margin for ROA (because of the need to share some of the margin with the outsourcing company). Firms operating in area Ⓒ might add products with a higher profit margin for ROA. Grocery stores, for example, have added fresh flowers, salad bars, fresh bakery products, pharmaceutical prescription services, and home delivery to their product offerings in an effort to increase profit margin for ROA and advance beyond the competitive constraint common for grocery products.

In summary, the economic concepts underlying the profit margin–assets turnover mix are as follows:

Area in Exhibit 4.13	Capital Intensity	Competition	Likely Strategic Focus
A	High	Monopoly	Profit Margin for ROA
B	Medium	Oligopolistic or Monopolistic Competition	Profit Margin for ROA, Assets Turnover, or some combination
C	Low	Pure Competition	Assets Turnover

Business Strategy. Firms have two generic alternative strategies for a particular product: *differentiation* and *low-cost leadership*.[23] The thrust of the product differentiation strategy is to differentiate a product in such a way as to obtain market power over revenues and, therefore, profit margins. The differentiation could relate to product capabilities, product quality, service, channels of distribution, or some other factor. The thrust of the low-cost leadership strategy is to become the lowest-cost producer, thereby enabling the firm to charge the lowest prices and to achieve higher sales volumes. Such firms can achieve the low-cost position through economies of scale, production efficiencies, outsourcing, or similar factors or by asset parsimony (maintaining strict controls on investments in receivables, inventories, and capital expenditures).[24]

In terms of Exhibit 4.13, movements in the direction of area Ⓐ from any point along the ROA curves focus on product differentiation. Likewise, movements in the direction of area Ⓒ from any point along the ROA curves focus on low-cost leadership. For an example, look at the average profit margins for ROA and assets turnovers for three types of retailers.

	Profit Margin for ROA	Assets Turnover
Specialty Retailers	2.97%	2.21
General Merchandise Stores	2.38%	2.02
Grocery Stores	1.43%	2.82

[23]W. K. Hall, "Survival Strategies in a Hostile Environment," *Harvard Business Review* (September–October 1980), pp. 78–85; M. E. Porter, *Competitive Strategy: Techniques for Analyzing Industries and Competitors* (New York: Free Press, 1998).

[24]Research in business strategy suggests that firms can simultaneously pursue product differentiation and low-cost leadership because product differentiation is revenue-oriented (output) and low-cost leadership is more expense-oriented (input).

In the retailing industry, specialty retailers have differentiated themselves by following a niche strategy and have achieved a higher profit margin for ROA than the other two segments. Competition severely constrains the profit margin for ROA of grocery stores, and they must pursue more low-cost leadership strategies. Thus, a firm does not have to be in the tails of the ROA curves to be described as a product differentiator or a low-cost leader. The appropriate basis of comparison is not other industries, but other firms in the same industry.

Remember, however, that the relative location along the ROA curve affects a firm's flexibility to trade off profit margin (product differentiation) for assets turnover (low-cost leadership). More importantly, within an industry, firms are dispersed among the profit margin and asset turnover dimensions. For example, within grocery stores, **Kroger** has higher assets turnover and lower profit margin, whereas **Whole Foods** has higher profit margin but lower assets turnover. Summarizing, differences in the profit margin for ROA–assets turnover mix relate to economic factors external to a firm (such as degree of competition, extent of regulation, entry barriers, and similar factors) and to internal strategic choices (such as product differentiation and low-cost leadership). The external and internal factors are, of course, interdependent and dynamic.

Starbucks' Positioning Relative to the Restaurant Industry

Starbucks is part of SIC code 5812, "Eating places," which is part of the restaurants industry. The median ROA, profit margin for ROA, and assets turnover for this industry and the average amounts for **Starbucks** for 2013 through 2015 are as follows:

	Restaurant Industry	Starbucks
ROA	4.7%	22.3%
Profit Margin for ROA	3.8%	13.5%
Assets Turnover	1.34	1.65

Note that the average ROA of **Starbucks** significantly exceeds that for the restaurant industry because of higher profit margins for ROA. Possible economic or strategic explanations for the higher profit margin for ROA include (1) more value to **Starbucks'** brand name than obtained by other restaurants, (2) greater pricing power because of **Starbucks'** lead position in the retail coffee industry, and (3) greater efficiencies due to **Starbucks'** size or quality of management. The next section explores this higher profit margin for ROA more fully.

Analyzing the Profit Margin for ROA

Profit margin for ROA captures the overall profitability of a firm's operations and is measured as the amount of after-tax profit generated (before financing costs) as a percentage of sales. Thus, the analysis of profit margin focuses on all expenses (other than interest expense) that reduce sales to after-tax profit. ROA for **Starbucks** increased from 2013 through 2015, from 18.6% to 22.3%. The disaggregation of ROA into the profit margin for ROA and assets turnover components in Exhibit 4.6 (using adjusted ROA) reveals that the increase in ROA results from a steady increase in profit margin for ROA and a fluctuating but overall increase in assets turnover.

This disaggregation is like peeling an onion. ROA is the outer layer. Peeling away that layer reveals profit margin for ROA and assets turnover layers. We can peel additional layers by separately examining the components of the profit margin for ROA and the components of assets turnover.

To examine profit margin for ROA, we use common-size analysis, expressing individual income statement amounts as percentages of sales to identify reasons for changes in the profit margin for ROA. Exhibit 4.14 presents these revenue and expense percentages for **Starbucks**. We maintain consistency with our earlier decision to adjust reported amounts for nonrecurring items through an adjustment at the bottom of the exhibit.

Note from Exhibit 4.14 that **Starbucks**' profit margin for ROA increased steadily due to

- decreases in cost of sales relative to sales.
- decreases in store operating expenses relative to sales.
- slight offsetting increases in depreciation and amortization.

It is important to understand that the above summary contains some degree of measurement error relating to the adjustments made earlier, which appear in "Other income/(expense), net" and "Adjustments for nonrecurring items, after tax." The tax effects of adjustments could be separately included in the "Income tax expense/(benefit) line." Thus, because we simplified the presentation of adjustments, it is difficult to interpret some of these amounts in the common-size format.

Your primary task as an analyst is to identify reasons for the changes in the revenue and expense percentages shown in Exhibit 4.14. The MD&A is supposed to provide information for interpreting such changes in these profitability percentages. However, firms vary with respect to the informativeness of these discussions. Some firms give specific reasons for changes in various financial ratios. Other firms simply indicate the amount or rate of increase or decrease without providing explanations for the changes.

Exhibit 4.14

Analysis of the Profit Margin for Starbucks: 2013–2015

	2015	2014	2013
Total net revenues	100.0%	100.0%	100.0%
Cost of sales including occupancy costs	(40.6)	(41.7)	(42.9)
Store operating expenses	(28.2)	(28.2)	(28.8)
Other operating expenses	(2.7)	(2.8)	(2.9)
Depreciation and amortization expenses	(4.7)	(4.3)	(4.2)
General and administrative expenses	(6.2)	(6.0)	(6.3)
Other income/(expense), net	3.2	2.6	(16.2)
Interest expense	(0.4)	(0.4)	(0.2)
Income tax expense/(benefit)	(6.0)	(6.6)	1.6
Add back interest expense, after tax	0.2	0.3	0.1
Adjustments for nonrecurring items, after tax	(1.1)	(0.1)	12.2
Profit margin for ROA	13.5%	12.7%	12.4%

Even when firms provide explanations, you should assess their reasonableness in light of conditions in the economy and the industry, as well as the firm's stated strategy and the results for the firms' competitors.

Below we focus only on the most noticeable changes in components of profit margin and use information provided by **Starbucks** in its MD&A (Appendix B) to identify reasons for changes in the profit margin for ROA.

Cost of Sales including Occupancy Costs

Interpreting changes in the cost of goods sold to sales percentage is often difficult because explanations might relate to sales revenue only, to cost of goods sold only, or to common factors affecting both. Consider, for example, the following possible explanations for a decrease in the cost of goods sold to sales percentage for a firm:

1. An increase in demand for products in excess of available capacity in an industry will likely result in an increase in selling prices. Even though the cost of manufacturing the product does not change, the cost of goods sold percentage will decrease.
2. As a result of product improvements or effective advertising, a firm's market share for its product increases. The firm allocates the fixed cost of manufacturing the product over a larger volume of production, thereby lowering its per-unit cost. Even though selling prices do not change, the cost of goods sold to sales percentage will decrease.
3. A firm lowers the price for its product to gain a larger market share. It lowers its manufacturing cost per unit by purchasing raw materials in larger quantities to take advantage of quantity discounts. Cost of goods sold per unit declines more than selling price per unit, causing the cost of goods sold to sales percentage to decline.
4. A firm sells multiple products with different cost of goods sold to sales percentages. The firm shifts the product mix toward products with higher profit margins, thereby lowering the overall cost of goods sold to sales percentage.

Thus, you must consider changes in selling prices, manufacturing costs, and product mix when interpreting changes in the cost of goods sold percentage. **Starbucks** provides only limited insight into the decrease in cost of sales across years. For the consolidated company results, the 2015 MD&A indicates that from 2014 to 2015, "Cost of sales including occupancy costs as a percentage of total net revenues decreased 110 basis points, primarily driven by sales and operating leverage on cost of sales (approximately 60 basis points), driven by strong sales and initiatives in our supply chain, such as improvements in sourcing, as well as sales leverage on occupancy costs (approximately 40 basis points)." Alternatively stated, the decreases in cost of sales as a percentage of revenues is primarily driven by revenue increases outpacing cost increases. The statement indicates that the primary benefit was due to increasing sales relative to costs of sales, followed closely by increasing sales relative to occupancy costs. In other discussion of segments, **Starbucks** also indicates that certain input costs actually declined, including dairy products. The decrease in cost of sales from 2013 to 2014 is attributed to "lower commodity costs (approximately 80 basis points), mainly coffee, and sales leverage (approximately 40 basis points)."

Store Operating Expenses

There was no change in store operating expenses as a percentage of *total* revenues between 2014 and 2015. However, **Starbucks** provides further insight by noting in the

MD&A that "Store operating expenses as a percentage of company-operated store revenues decreased 10 basis points, primarily driven by sales leverage (approximately 50 basis points) and decreased expenses, largely salaries and benefits, due to the shift to more licensed stores in EMEA [Europe, Middle East, and Africa] (approximately 40 basis points), partially offset by increased investments in store partners (employees) and digital platforms related to in-store initiatives (approximately 100 basis points) in the Americas segment." For the decrease from 2013 to 2014 in store operating expenses as a percentage of total revenues, Starbucks only briefly explains the change as reflecting "decreased 60 basis points, mainly driven by sales leverage (approximately 80 basis points)."

Depreciation and Amortization Expenses

Starbucks attributes the slightly higher depreciation and amortization expenses relative to sales to "the impact of our ownership change in Starbucks Japan (approximately 30 basis points)." As discussed earlier in the chapter where we highlight adjustments to ROA, when Starbucks purchased Sazaby League's investment in Starbucks Japan, the assets of those operations were added to the consolidated balance sheet of Starbucks. This is reflected on the balance sheet, where Property, plant and equipment, net increased from $3,519 million to $4,088 million. The additional fixed assets increase Starbucks' depreciation expense.[25]

Starbucks Segment Data

The aggregate results in the common-size income statements for Starbucks examined in Exhibit 4.14 mask potentially important differences in profitability in different product lines or geographic markets. Fortunately, as highlighted earlier in the chapter, both U.S. GAAP and IFRS require firms to provide financial data for their operating segments, products and services, and major customers.[26] Note 16, "Segment Reporting," of Starbucks' financial statements (Appendix A) presents segment data for 2013 through 2015. Starbucks reports product segment data for five divisions: (1) Americas; (2) China/Asia Pacific (CAP); (3) Europe, Middle East, and Africa (EMEA); (4) Channel Development; and (5) All Other Segments. The Channel Development segment represents branded products (such as Starbucks-branded single-serve products and Tazo® teas) sold in grocery stores, warehouse clubs, and other outlets.

The segment disclosures permit you to examine ROA, profit margin, and assets turnover at an additional level of depth, in effect peeling the onion one more layer. Firms report revenues, operating profits, and other aggregate information by segment. Unfortunately, to avoid disclosure of sensitive information, firms generally do not report cost of goods sold and selling, general, and administrative expenses for each segment. That means we cannot reconcile changes in segment profit margins to changes in the overall levels of these two expense percentages. Firms also report segment data pretax, meaning that the segment ROAs and profit margins exceed those for the overall company to a considerable extent.

---

[25]Note 1, "Summary of Significant Accounting Policies," indicates that depreciation on certain equipment related to production and distribution facilities is included in cost of sales including occupancy costs. This amount is approximately 5% of total depreciation expense. See Chapter 10, where we allocate forecasts of depreciation between cost of sales including occupancy costs and depreciation and amortization expenses.

[26]FASB Codification No. 280; International Accounting Standards Board, International Financial Reporting Standards No. 8, "Operating Segments" (November 2006).

Exhibit 4.15			
Sales Mix Data for Starbucks			
	2015	**2014**	**2013**
Americas	69.4%	72.8%	74.0%
China/Asia Pacific	12.5	6.9	6.2
Europe, Middle East, and Africa (EMEA)	6.3	7.9	7.8
Channel Development	9.0	9.4	9.4
All Other Segments	2.7	3.0	2.6
	100%	100%	100%

Exhibit 4.15 presents sales mix data for **Starbucks**. **Starbucks'** sales mix has shifted away from the Americas towards the China/Asia Pacific market during 2013 through 2015. An important insight that is conveyed by the common-size analysis in Exhibit 4.15 is that the Americas is by far the largest segment, but that the growth is primarily from the China/Asia Pacific segment.

Exhibit 4.16 presents ROAs, profit margins, and assets turnovers for each of **Starbucks'** segments. Note that our methods of computation here differ from those we performed previously for **Starbucks** consolidated because of coarseness in disclosed data. First, we compute segment ROAs and assets turnover using assets at the *end of the period* to simplify the calculations. The difficulty you often encounter with using average segment assets is that firms frequently change their definition of segments over time and firms report the three most recent years of segment asset data in their current annual report. You would need to access asset data for the fourth year back in order to compute average assets for the three years and hope that the firm maintained a consistent definition of segments. Firms that have changed their segment definitions within the last year will not consistently show assets with current segment definitions.

For a stable, mature company such as **Starbucks**, the use of assets at the end of the period instead of the average for the period will affect the level of the ROAs and the assets turnover ratios, but will not likely have a material effect on the trend of these segment ratios over time unless the firm made a significant corporate acquisition or divestiture during one of the years. Second, note that the numerator of our profitability calculations is based on pretax operating profits rather than the usual appropriate measure, net income adjusted for after-tax interest expense. We make this decision because **Starbucks**, like most firms, does not disclose this information at the segment level. Financing policies and activities frequently reside with the corporate division; thus, they are not allocated to operating segments. As with our use of end-of-period total assets, this procedure is not likely to prevent us from gaining objective insight into the relative profitability and efficiency of the segments being analyzed. The primary limitation of these assumptions is that we cannot precisely reconcile the segment calculations with those for the consolidated results of **Starbucks**.

Data availability and practicality frequently drive financial analysis decisions and techniques, which further emphasizes our earlier cautionary note that the astute analyst does not memorize ratios or procedures, but understands the rationale for how to interpret various measures.

Exhibit 4.16

Product Segment Pretax Profitability Analysis for Starbucks

ROA			
	2015	2014	2013
Americas	118.2%	111.4%	101.8%
China/Asia Pacific	22.4%	39.6%	39.9%
Europe, Middle East, and Africa (EMEA)	22.5%	18.0%	12.6%
Channel Development	749.0%	658.6%	465.8%
All Other Segments	(1.4%)	(3.2%)	(4.2%)

	Profit Margin for ROA			Assets Turnover		
	2015	2014	2013	2015	2014	2013
Americas	24.2%	23.4%	21.5%	4.88	4.75	4.73
China/Asia Pacific	20.9%	33.0%	35.0%	1.07	1.20	1.14
Europe, Middle East, and Africa (EMEA)	13.8%	9.2%	5.5%	1.62	1.95	2.27
Channel Development	37.8%	36.0%	29.7%	19.83	18.27	15.68
All Other Segments	(4.7%)	(5.4%)	(8.8%)	0.29	0.60	0.48

The top portion of Exhibit 4.16 indicates that the segment with the highest ROA is the Channel Development segment, followed by the largest segment, the Americas. The lower portion of Exhibit 4.16 shows the breakdown of ROA into profit margin and assets turnover. The profit margins generally mirror the distribution of ROA in the upper portion of Exhibit 4.16, with both Channel Development and the Americas exhibiting the highest profit margins in 2015. Similarly, these divisions also have the highest assets turnovers. The overall higher level of profitability and asset utilization for these two segments is consistent with our discussions of life cycle theory in Chapter 3 (Exhibit 3.1) and earlier in this chapter (Exhibit 4.11). The Channel Development and Americas segments are older and more mature than the other segments, so it is understandable that they are more profitable and efficient. The acquisition of **Starbucks** Japan affects all measures in 2015 for the China/Asia Pacific market, which makes it more difficult to analyze. However, in contrast to the mature Americas segment, the China/Asia Pacific segment appears to be in a growth phase, with decreasing volatile profit margins and asset turnovers. In contrast, the EMEA segment is more mature, with increasing profit margin but decreasing asset turnover, consistent with declining sales and a shift to a higher proportion of licensing agreements. Note that results for both the China/Asia Pacific and EMEA segments are affected by foreign currency translation effects, which for EMEA were unfavorable during 2015 but favorable during 2014.

Growth segments like China/Asia Pacific are not as profitable due to required investments in growing sales volume and refining production and distribution operations to levels comparable to more mature segments. If **Starbucks** proves as successful internationally as it has been in the Americas, profit margins and assets turnovers for these segments should improve in the future. Because of this regularity, segment disclosures are frequently most helpful in the forecasting part of financial statement analysis and valuation, which we will return to in Chapter 10.

A caveat of segment reporting analysis relates to the data used. The information in Note 16 of **Starbucks**' footnotes is the basis of calculations for Exhibits 4.15 and 4.16. Exhibit 4.15 is based on sales that reconcile to the total for consolidated results for **Starbucks**; that is, the total sales of all five segments add up to the total sales for **Starbucks** consolidated. However, Exhibit 4.16 is based on operating profits that do *not* reconcile with consolidated total operating profit for **Starbucks**. The difference between total consolidated operating profit of $3,601.0 million in 2015 and the $4,521.1 million sum of the operating profits of the individual operating segments is caused by unallocated corporate expenses, which are likely included in general and administrative expenses on its income statement but are not allocated to its operating segments when disclosing segment data.

If a large amount of expenses is not allocated to segments in segment disclosures, you must exert caution when interpreting segment profit margins and ROAs. Changes in the amount of expenses allocated versus not allocated to segments, a choice made by management, clearly affect these ratios. The discrepancy between consolidating operating profit and the sum of disclosed segment operating profits can be significantly affected by nonrecurring charges, such as the gain, loss, and litigation charge discussed earlier in the chapter.

Summary of Profit Margin Analysis for Starbucks

We noted at the beginning of this section that **Starbucks**' profit margin for ROA increased from 12.4% to 13.5% from 2013 to 2015. We used common-size analysis to identify the primary contributions to the observed profit margins and analyzed each item to better understand the factors contributing to the overall profit margin for **Starbucks**. The summary of our findings for the analysis of profit margins is as follows:

- Cost of sales including occupancy costs decreased as a percentage of sales due to sales leverage combined with some favorable input price declines.
- Store operating expenses as a percentage of sales were flat from 2014 to 2015, but were down from 2013 to 2014 due to sales leverage.
- Depreciation and amortization expenses increased as a percentage of sales due to **Starbucks**' acquisition of the remaining interest in **Starbucks** Japan, which brought significant fixed assets onto **Starbucks**' consolidated balance sheet.
- Segment analysis suggested that the most profitable divisions are the Americas and Channel Development, with China/Asia Pacific and EMEA segments experiencing lower margins as **Starbucks** invests and grows sales in these segments.

Having examined the first component of ROA—profit margin—we examine next the other component—total assets turnover.

Analyzing Total Assets Turnover

Total assets turnover captures how efficiently the firm utilizes assets to generate revenues. Higher revenues generated with a given level of assets indicates more efficient use of those assets. Exhibit 4.6 showed that **Starbucks'** total assets turnover fluctuated between 2013 and 2015, increasing from 1.51 in 2013 to 1.65 in 2015, after declining slightly to 1.48 in 2014. The first step you might take toward understanding changes in total assets turnover is to be aware of the relative changes in the numerator (sales) and denominator (average total assets) across the years. In 2015, total assets increased 15.7%, but sales increased 16.5%, causing the total assets turnover to improve. Recall that assets increased significantly due to the acquisition of **Starbucks** Japan, but despite this large increase in assets, **Starbucks** generated sales growth at a faster pace. The overall increase in total assets turnover is consistent with **Starbucks'** discussion in the MD&A about significant sales leverage.

Unlike the analysis of profit margin, where we decomposed the numerator by examining different expenses that determined operating profit, the analysis of total assets turnover can best be achieved by decomposing the denominator, total assets. We can gain greater insight into changes in *total* assets turnover by examining turnover ratios for *individual* classes of assets under the logic that turnover ratios for *individual* assets aggregate to *total* assets turnover. The following three turnover ratios are the most popular, largely driven by the important role of each of these assets in the firm's core operating activities:

- Accounts receivable turnover
- Inventory turnover
- Fixed assets turnover

Management's discussion and analysis of operations usually provides detailed explanations for operating profits, but it does not include explanations for changes in individual assets turnovers, so you must search for possible clues through other disclosures. This is unfortunate because small changes in assets turnover can have enormous effects on the overall profitability of a firm (that is, ROA and ROCE).

Accounts Receivable Turnover

The rate at which accounts receivable turn over indicates the average time until firms collect credit sales in cash. You calculate accounts receivable turnover by dividing net *sales on account* by average accounts receivable. Most sales transactions between businesses are on account, not for cash. Except for retailers and restaurants that deal directly with consumers, the assumption that all sales are on account is usually reasonable. However, for companies like **Starbucks**, we should attempt to estimate cash sales versus sales on account. For company-operated stores, we can assume that sales are for cash, but for licensing and consumer packaged goods and food service revenues, we can assume sales are on account. Thus, of the total revenues (in millions) of $19,162.7 for 2015, we conclude that $3,965.4 ($1,861.9 licensed store revenues + $2,103.5 CPG, foodservice, and other) are the net sales on account. The calculation of the accounts receivable turnover for 2015 for **Starbucks** is as follows (in millions):

$$\text{Accounts Receivable Turnover} = \frac{\text{Net Sales on Account}}{\text{Average Accounts Receivable}}$$

$$5.9 = \frac{\$3,965.4}{0.5(\$719.0 + \$631.0)}$$

Starbucks' accounts receivable turnover was 5.8 in 2014 and 5.9 in 2013.

Accounts receivable turnover is often framed in terms of the average number of days receivables are outstanding before firms collect them in cash. The calculation divides 365 days by the accounts receivable turnover.[27] The average number of days that accounts receivable were outstanding was 62.1 days (365/5.9) during 2015, 62.7 days (365/5.8) during 2014, and 62.2 days (365/5.9) during 2013. Thus, receivables turnover was relatively stable across all years.

One also could calculate the days' sales included in the *ending* accounts receivable balance rather than the average, in which case the calculation would be ending accounts receivable divided by average daily sales (sales/365). For 2015, this calculation is $719.0/($3,965.4/365) = 66.2 days. The days outstanding is higher because the ending balance of accounts receivable used in the calculation is higher than the average used in the previous calculation.

The interpretation of changes in the accounts receivable turnover and average collection period also relates to a firm's credit extension policies. Firms often use credit terms to stimulate sales. For example, firms might permit customers to delay making payments on purchases of lawn mowers until after the summer and on snowmobiles until after the winter. Such actions would lead to greater sales but a decrease in the accounts receivable turnover and an increase in the number of days receivables are outstanding. The changes in these accounts receivable ratios would not necessarily signal negative news if the increase in net income from the additional sales exceeded the cost of carrying accounts receivable for the extra time. Firms also can use credit policy to provide implicit financing to support affiliated companies, such as credit extended by automobile manufacturers to dealerships, by producers to closely related distributors, and by restaurant chains to franchisees or licensees.

Retailing firms, particularly department store chains such as **Walmart** and **Target**, offer their own credit cards to customers. They use credit cards to stimulate sales. Interpreting an increase in the number of days accounts receivable are outstanding involves two conflicting signals. The increase might suggest greater risk of uncollectibility, but it also provides additional interest revenues. Some firms price their products to obtain a relatively low gross margin from the sale and depend on interest revenue as a principal source of earnings. Thus, you must consider a firm's credit strategy and policies when interpreting the accounts receivable turnover and days receivables outstanding ratios.

The calculations for accounts receivable turnover for **Starbucks** indicate that customer credit and payment patterns across 2013 through 2015 are relatively stable. Thus, it does not appear that accounts receivable turnover can explain changes in total assets turnover for **Starbucks**. This should not be surprising given that accounts receivable play only a limited role in **Starbucks**' primary operations, representing only 4.9% of total assets at the end of 2015.

Inventory Turnover

The rate at which inventories turn over indicates the length of time needed to produce and sell inventories. You calculate inventory turnover by dividing cost of goods sold by

---

[27]Sometimes you may see the use of 360 days in calculations like this. Although this choice introduces slight measurement error biasing toward faster turnover, as long as it is used consistently in all calculations, it is unlikely to have a significant effect on inferences.

the average inventory during the period. The calculation of inventory turnover for **Starbucks** for 2015 is as follows (in millions):

$$\text{Inventory Turnover} = \frac{\text{Cost of Goods Sold}}{\text{Average Inventories}}$$

$$6.5 = \frac{\$7,787.5}{0.5(\$1,306.4 + \$1,090.9)}$$

Similar to accounts receivable, inventory turnover is often described as the average number of days that inventory is on hand. **Starbucks'** inventory was on hand for an average of 56.2 days (365/6.5) during 2015. **Starbucks'** inventory turnover was 6.2 in 2014 and 5.4 in 2013. In terms of the number of days on hand, **Starbucks** held inventory for an average of 58.6 days in 2014 and 67.3 days in 2013. Thus, inventory turnover increased over the three-year period.

Starbucks does not explain the increased inventory turnover. We can look to Note 5, "Inventories," for more information on inventories, however. Inventories primarily consist of coffee (roasted and unroasted), other merchandise, and packaging supplies. According to **Starbucks**, "Inventory levels vary due to seasonality, commodity market supply and price fluctuations." Inventories totaled $1,306.4 at the end of 2015, up from $1,090.9 and $1,111.2 at the end of 2014 and 2013, respectively. Cost of goods sold increased from $6,382.2 in 2013 to $6,858.8 in 2014 and $7,787.5 in 2015. Thus, cost of goods sold increased 22.0% over the three years, relative to a smaller 17.6% increase in inventories, resulting in increased inventory turnover. The increase in cost of goods sold is largely driven by the increase in sales of 28.9% from 2013 to 2015. Together, these data and the earlier discussions about profit margin indicate that **Starbucks** is realizing economies of scale by rapidly increasing sales at higher margins, while simultaneously maintaining only moderately increasing inventory levels.

If we prepare similar inventory calculations for **Panera**, we obtain inventory turnover of 38.7 in 2015, or an average of 9.4 days (365/38.7) inventory on hand. Compared to **Starbucks**, Panera has a much faster inventory turnover because (a) it has much more emphasis on fresh food and (b) its supply chain is not deeply vertically integrated like that of **Starbucks**.

The interpretation of the inventory turnover figure involves two opposing considerations. A firm would like to sell as many goods as possible with a minimum of capital tied up in inventories. Moreover, inventory is subject to obsolescence or spoilage, especially in the case of food products. An increase in the rate of inventory turnover between periods would seem to indicate more profitable use of the investment in inventory and lowering costs for financing and carrying inventory. On the other hand, a firm does not want to have so little inventory on hand that shortages result and the firm misses sales opportunities. An increase in the rate of inventory turnover in this case may mean a loss of sales opportunities, thereby offsetting any cost savings achieved by a decreased investment in inventory. Firms must make trade-offs in deciding the optimum level of inventory and thus the desirable rate of inventory turnover. For example, the high-end jeweler **Tiffany** typically maintains approximately 500 days' sales in inventory, whereas **Apple** typically maintains only 3 days, indicative of Apple's extremely high inventory turnover relative to Tiffany.

You may gain insight into changes in inventory turnover by examining the changes in relation to changes in the cost of goods sold to sales percentage. Consider the following scenarios and possible interpretations:

- **Increasing cost of goods sold to sales percentage, coupled with an increasing inventory turnover.**
  - The firm lowers prices to sell inventory more quickly.
  - The firm shifts its product mix toward lower-margin, faster-moving products.
  - The firm outsources the production of a higher proportion of its products, requiring it to share profit margin with the outsourcer but reducing the amount of raw materials and work-in-process inventories.
- **Decreasing cost of goods sold to sales percentage, coupled with a decreasing inventory turnover.**
  - The firm raises prices to increase its gross margin, but inventory sells more slowly.
  - The firm shifts its product mix toward higher-margin, slower-moving products.
  - The firm produces a higher proportion of its products instead of outsourcing, thereby capturing more of the gross margin but requiring the firm to carry raw materials and work-in-process inventories.
- **Increasing cost of goods sold to sales percentage, coupled with a decreasing inventory turnover.**
  - Weak economic conditions lead to reduced demand for the firm's products, necessitating price reductions to move goods. Despite price reductions, inventory builds up.
- **Decreasing cost of goods sold to sales percentage, coupled with an increasing inventory turnover.**
  - Strong economic conditions lead to increased demand for the firm's products, allowing price increases. An inability to replace inventory as fast as the firm sells it leads to an increased inventory turnover.
  - The firm implements a just-in-time inventory system, reducing storage costs, product obsolescence, and the amount of inventory held.

Some analysts calculate the inventory turnover ratio by dividing sales, rather than cost of goods sold, by the average inventory. As long as there is a reasonably constant relation between selling prices and cost of goods sold, you can identify changes in the trend of the inventory turnover using either measure. It is inappropriate to use sales in the numerator if you want to use the inventory turnover ratio to calculate the average number of days that inventory is on hand until sale or if you want to compare inventory turnover across firms with different markups and gross profit margins.

The cost-flow assumption (FIFO, LIFO, or weighted-average) for inventories and cost of goods sold can significantly affect both the inventory turnover ratio and the cost of goods sold to sales percentage. Chapter 9 discusses the impact of the cost-flow assumption and illustrates adjustments you might make to deal with these effects.

Fixed Assets Turnover

The fixed assets turnover ratio measures the relation between sales and the investment in property, plant, and equipment. Fixed assets turnover equals sales divided by average fixed assets (net of accumulated depreciation) during the year. The fixed assets turnover ratio for **Starbucks** for 2015 is as follows:

$$\text{Fixed Assets Turnover} = \frac{\text{Sales}}{\text{Average Fixed Assets}}$$

$$5.0 = \frac{\$19,162.7}{0.5(\$4,088.3 + \$3,519.0)}$$

The fixed assets turnover for **Starbucks** was 4.9 in 2014 and 5.1 in 2013. Similar to our findings for accounts receivable turnover, fixed assets turnover is relatively stable across 2013 through 2015, so fixed assets turnover is unlikely to explain changes in **Starbucks'** total assets turnover.

An increasing fixed assets turnover ratio generally indicates greater efficiency in the use of existing fixed assets to generate sales, and lower turnover suggests the opposite. The analysis of fixed assets turnover is also affected by acquisitions and divestitures, particularly if such transactions relate to distinct lines of business with different fixed asset requirements. Like other ratios, you must carefully interpret changes in the fixed assets turnover ratio. Firms invest in fixed assets in anticipation of higher production and sales in future periods. Thus, a temporarily low or decreasing rate of fixed assets turnover may be a positive signal of an expanding firm preparing for future growth. On the other hand, a firm may reduce its capital expenditures if the near-term outlook for its products is poor, which might lead to an increase in the fixed assets turnover ratio.

Other Asset Turnover Ratios

Although turnover ratios are most common for the receivables, inventory, and fixed assets, any asset can be examined as a turnover ratio as long as the appropriate numerator is used in the calculation. For example, firms maintain varying levels of cash, and analysts are often interested in the efficiency with which cash is managed. Thus, an investor can gauge the strategic management of cash balances by a cash turnover ratio. The cash turnover ratio is computed by dividing sales by the average cash balance during the year. The cash turnover ratio for **Starbucks** for 2015 is as follows:

$$\text{Cash Turnover} = \frac{\text{Sales}}{\text{Average Cash and Cash Equivalents}}$$

$$11.8 = \frac{\$19,162.7}{0.5(\$1,530.1 + \$1,708.4)}$$

Thus, **Starbucks** maintains a cash balance of approximately 30.8 days' sales (365/11.8). Calculated with *sales* in the numerator, this implies that **Starbucks** replenishes its cash balance approximately every month. Alternatively, you could view cash as a means of funding other working capital (inventory, for example). With this perspective, you might calculate the cash turnover ratio with cost of goods sold in the numerator. The computations are similar to those above, but the interpretation is different.

Similarly, you might want an overall metric for the efficiency with which *all* current assets are managed (rather than individually). Accordingly, you would compute a current assets turnover ratio by dividing sales by the average current assets during the year. The current assets turnover ratio for **Starbucks** for 2015 is as follows:

$$\text{Current Assets Turnover} = \frac{\text{Sales}}{\text{Average Current Assets}}$$

$$4.5 = \frac{\$19,162.7}{0.5(\$4,352.7 + \$4,168.7)}$$

Thus, **Starbucks** turns over its current assets a little more frequently than once per fiscal quarter. The comparable current asset turnovers for 2014 and 2013 are 3.4 and 3.1, respectively. The current assets turnover ratio conveys information similar to that for individual asset turnover ratios for cash, receivables, or inventory. However, the current assets turnover ratio is often more representative because the volatility of *total* current assets is less than the volatility of any *individual* current asset. For example, stronger-than-expected end-of-year sales might result in ending receivables being temporarily above normal levels and inventory being temporarily below current levels. This would cause the receivables turnover ratio to be deflated but the inventory turnover ratio to be inflated. All else equal, however, the current assets turnover ratio would be less likely to be affected because the volatilities in receivables balances and inventory levels tend to offset each other.

Summary of Assets Turnover Analysis

Starbucks' total assets turnover has increased from 2013 to 2015, but was down slightly in 2014. We first noted the overall increase in total assets turnover is consistent with explanations in **Starbucks'** MD&A about the positive effects on performance from sales leverage. We also examined the three primary asset turnover ratios: accounts receivable, inventory, and fixed assets. The accounts receivable and fixed assets turnover ratios were relatively stable across all years, but inventory turnover increased notably. Accounts receivable make up approximately 5.8% of total assets, and inventories make up approximately 10.5% of total assets. However, fixed assets make up 32.8% of total assets. Thus, one would expect that the pattern in fixed assets turnover would dominate among these three. However, other assets besides receivables, inventories, and fixed assets affect the total assets turnover computation. The utilization of these other assets is sometimes important. For example, the percentage of total assets represented by intangible assets (including goodwill and other intangible assets) rose from 10.5% in 2013 to 16.9% in 2015.

Summary of ROA Analysis

Recalling the analogy of decomposing profitability to peeling back layers of an onion, our analysis of operating profitability involves four levels of depth:

> Level 1: ROA for the firm as a whole
> Level 2: Disaggregation of ROA into profit margin for ROA and assets turnover for the firm as a whole
> Level 3a: Disaggregation of profit margin into expense ratios for various cost items
> Level 3b: Disaggregation of assets turnover into turnovers for individual assets
> Level 4: Analysis of profit margins and asset turnovers for the segments of a firm

Exhibit 4.17 summarizes this analysis for **Starbucks** in a format used throughout the remainder of this book and included in FSAP. **This layered approach to analyzing financial statements provides a disciplined approach that can be applied to any firm.**

Supplementing ROA in Profitability Analysis

ROA uses average total assets as a base for assessing a firm's effectiveness in using resources to generate earnings. For some firms and industries, total assets may be less

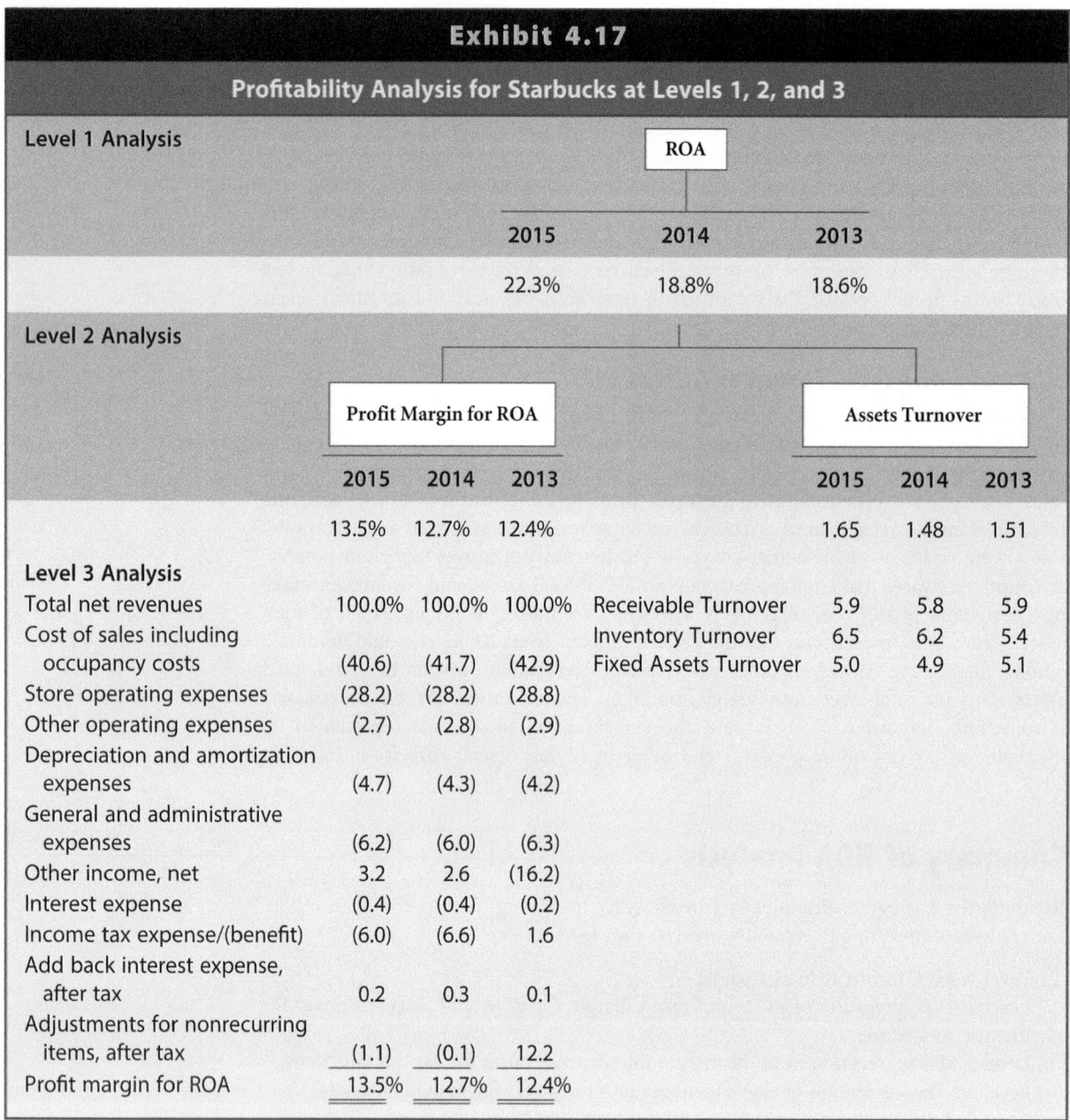

Exhibit 4.17							
Profitability Analysis for Starbucks at Levels 1, 2, and 3							

Level 1 Analysis

ROA

	2015	2014	2013
	22.3%	18.8%	18.6%

Level 2 Analysis

Profit Margin for ROA				Assets Turnover		
2015	2014	2013		2015	2014	2013
13.5%	12.7%	12.4%		1.65	1.48	1.51

Level 3 Analysis

	2015	2014	2013		2015	2014	2013
Total net revenues	100.0%	100.0%	100.0%	Receivable Turnover	5.9	5.8	5.9
Cost of sales including				Inventory Turnover	6.5	6.2	5.4
occupancy costs	(40.6)	(41.7)	(42.9)	Fixed Assets Turnover	5.0	4.9	5.1
Store operating expenses	(28.2)	(28.2)	(28.8)				
Other operating expenses	(2.7)	(2.8)	(2.9)				
Depreciation and amortization							
expenses	(4.7)	(4.3)	(4.2)				
General and administrative							
expenses	(6.2)	(6.0)	(6.3)				
Other income, net	3.2	2.6	(16.2)				
Interest expense	(0.4)	(0.4)	(0.2)				
Income tax expense/(benefit)	(6.0)	(6.6)	1.6				
Add back interest expense,							
after tax	0.2	0.3	0.1				
Adjustments for nonrecurring							
items, after tax	(1.1)	(0.1)	12.2				
Profit margin for ROA	13.5%	12.7%	12.4%				

informative for this purpose because, as Chapter 2 discusses, accounting practices (1) do not assign asset values to certain valuable resources (brand names, technological knowledge, and human capital) and (2) report assets at acquisition costs instead of current market values (forests for forest products companies and land for railroads). To supplement straightforward financial statement analysis, analysts often supplement ROA by relating sales, expenses, and earnings to *nonfinancial* attributes when evaluating profitability. This section discusses techniques for assessing profitability unique to several industries. The discussion is not intended to be exhaustive for all industries, but to provide a flavor for the types of supplemental measures used.

Analyzing Retailers

A key resource of retailers is their retail space. Some retailers own their stores, while others lease their space. You can constructively capitalize the present value of operating lease commitments to ensure that total assets include store buildings under operating leases. An alternative approach when analyzing retailers is to express sales, operating expenses, and operating income on a per-store basis or per square foot of retail selling space. An equally important metric for retail firms is growth in "same store" or "comparable store" sales. Analysts are interested in changes in revenues due to changes in the number of retail stores as well as in changes in revenues due to changes in the average sales per retail store. Thus, a key measure reported by firms in this industry is the change in sales on a comparable store basis (based on the number of stores open throughout the period).

Exhibit 4.18 presents per-square-foot and comparable store data for **Target Corporation** (Target) and **Walmart Stores** (Walmart), as well as profit margin for ROA, assets turnover, and ROA (for 2009). The superior ROA of Walmart results from much higher sales per square foot, which corresponds to its higher assets turnover. However, Target's profit margin is actually higher than that of Walmart. Overall, for this year, Walmart is more profitable in terms of ROA and Walmart actually grew comparable stores sales versus a decline in comparable store sales for Target over the same period.

Analyzing Airlines

Aircraft provide airlines with a fixed amount of capacity during a particular period. The total number of seats *available* to carry passengers times the number of miles flown equals the available capacity. The number of seats *occupied* times the number of miles flown equals the amount of capacity used (referred to as revenue passenger miles). Common practice in the airline industry is to compute the revenues and expenses per available seat mile and per revenue passenger mile flown to judge pricing, cost structure, and profitability.

Exhibit 4.19 presents selected profitability data for **American Airlines**, **JetBlue**, and **Airtran** (for 2008). The first three columns present revenues, expenses, and operating income before income taxes per available seat mile, and the last three columns present the same income items per revenue passenger mile flown.

Exhibit 4.18
Profitability Ratios for Target and Walmart

	Target	Walmart
Per Square Foot:		
Sales	$ 302	$ 454
Cost of goods sold	(205)	(342)
Selling and administrative	(76)	(86)
Operating income	$ 21	$ 26
Profit margin for ROA	4.30%	3.82%
Assets turnover	1.47	2.45
ROA	6.3%	9.4%
Comparable store sales change	(2.9%)	3.5%

Exhibit 4.19

Profitability Ratios for American, JetBlue, and Airtran

	Per Available Seat Mile			Per Revenue Passenger Mile		
	American	JetBlue	Airtran	American	JetBlue	Airtran
Operating revenues	14.53¢	10.44¢	10.72¢	18.04¢	13.00¢	13.47¢
Fuel	(5.51)	(4.17)	(5.02)	(6.84)	(5.19)	(6.30)
Compensation	(4.07)	(2.14)	(1.99)	(5.05)	(2.66)	(2.51)
Other operating expenses	(6.11)	(3.79)	(4.01)	(7.58)	(4.73)	(5.04)
Operating income	(1.16)¢	0.34¢	(0.30¢)	(1.43¢)	0.42¢	(0.38¢)
Profitability decomposition:						
Profit margin for ROA				(8.7%)	2.2%	(8.7%)
Assets turnover				0.68	0.58	1.24
ROA				(5.9%)	1.3%	(10.8%)

Fuel costs were significant for all airlines, but JetBlue had the lowest cost; American had the highest. Compensation costs also were highest at American, as were all other operating expenses. JetBlue had the lowest operating revenue on a per-mile basis, but due to low fuel, compensation, and other costs, it was profitable. The assets turnover for Airtran was highest, which combined with the negative profit margin to yield Airtran's negative ROA. Given similar profit margins, the difference in ROA between Airtran and American is driven by assets turnover differences. The explanation for the higher assets turnover for Airtran relative to American is that in the year shown, Airtran leases 100 of 136 aircraft, versus 220 out of 892 for American (not shown in Exhibit 4.19).

Analyzing Service Firms

Using ROA to analyze the profitability of firms that provide services can result in misleading conclusions because their most important resources, employees who deliver the services, do not appear on the balance sheet as assets under U.S. GAAP. One approach to deal with this omission is to express income on a per-employee basis. However, you must use these data cautiously because of differences among firms in their use of full- versus part-time employees and their mix of direct service providers versus support personnel.

Exhibit 4.20 presents profitability data for three service firms. **VisionChina Media** is one of China's largest mobile TV advertising networks, with extensive coverage in public transportation facilities (<500 employees). **Monster Worldwide** is an online recruitment firm that links employers with people seeking employment (approximately 7,000 employees). **Accenture** is a multinational management consulting firm (>175,000 employees).

VisionChina has the highest operating revenues per employee, followed by Monster, then Accenture, which tracks the total employees at each company. Compensation expense is highest for Accenture, followed by Monster and VisionChina. Administrative and other expenses are highest for VisionChina, which incurs substantial costs for media equipment. The difference in business models leads to lower assets turnover for VisionChina, which maintains substantial investments in assets. Assets turnover is

Exhibit 4.20			
Profitability Data for VisionChina Media, Monster Worldwide, and Accenture			
Per Employee:	**VisionChina Media**	**Monster Worldwide**	**Accenture**
Operating revenues	$ 220,044	$193,328	$130,909
Compensation	(5,619)	(78,168)	(92,259)
Administrative and other expenses	(126,293)	(90,706)	(23,713)
Operating income before income taxes	$ 88,132	$ 24,454	$ 14,937
Profitability decomposition:			
Profit margin for ROA	45.1%	9.4%	7.5%
Assets turnover	0.44	0.67	1.88
ROA	19.8%	6.3%	14.1%

highest for Accenture, which maintains limited fixed assets. Operating revenues and operating income before taxes per employee are lowest at Accenture (with the largest workforce), but Accenture generates a very high ROA due to the high assets turnover.

Per-employee data usefully supplement traditional financial ratios for numerous other industries, including investment banking, temporary help firms, engineering firms, advertising firms, professional sports teams, information technology, and other service firms. The use of per-employee data also supplement the analysis of firms that use fixed assets in the provision of services, such as airlines, health care providers, and hotels.

Analyzing Technology-Based Firms

ROA can be an even more misleading ratio for analyzing technology-based firms than for analyzing service firms if the two most important resources of technology firms do not appear in their assets: (1) their people and (2) their technologies. Employees contribute to the creation of technologies, but the most important resource not recognized is the value of the technologies (unless externally acquired). U.S. GAAP requires firms to expense R&D costs in the year incurred. Thus, both assets and net income are understated during periods in which firms invest heavily in R&D. After R&D has led to the introduction of successful, profitable new products, assets are understated, but income is overstated because the firms have already expensed investments in R&D. Comparisons across firms with different R&D strategies is affected by whether the firm expenses internally developed R&D or purchases it externally and capitalizes it.

- Firms generally trade off profit margin and assets turnover.
- High profit margins tend to reflect high barriers to competitive entry, and low assets turnovers tend to reflect requirements for large capital investments (which can be a barrier to entry).
- Low profit margins tend to reflect low barriers to competitive entry and higher assets turnovers

due to relatively lower requirements for capital investments. Product life cycle theory can be adapted to the profitability of firms during different stages.
- Profit margin for ROA or ROCE can be disaggregated by examining various expense ratios, typically through common-size analysis.
- Assets turnover can be disaggregated by examining various asset turnover ratios.

Quick Check

LO 4-5

Describe the benefits and limitations of using ratios like ROA and ROCE as part of understanding the historical performance of a company.

Benefits and Limitations of Using Financial Statement Ratios

Financial ratios are easy to compute, and there are many sources of financial data that do the computing for investors, including free websites such as Yahoo! Finance and Smartmoney.com. The most important and valuable step, however, is *interpreting and gleaning key insights from a financial ratio.* To do this successfully, you must know how a ratio was computed. For example, was ROA computed correctly such that the numerator includes net profits after taxes but before interest, or is it based on someone else's calculation that simply uses EBIT in the numerator? Differences in computations do not always create significant differences in ratio calculations, but the astute analyst must be aware of the underlying data embedded in ratios.

The second, and most crucial, aspect of interpreting ratios is doing so with an understanding of the firm's economic environment and business strategy. As noted earlier in the chapter, you *must* understand a firm's industry, organizational structure, and strategy to develop hypotheses about what to expect in terms of financial position, profitability, risk, and growth.

Analyzing financial statement ratios is the forensic part of the process of searching for insights and answers to questions about how the firm is performing. In this step, you must dig deep to understand why ratios are what they are. As we saw with **Starbucks**, a company often provides only limited insight into questions raised by your ratio analysis. At a minimum, however, you should discern whether the ratios reflect the economics of the industry and the specific strategy of the firm. Further, using several benchmarks, you should understand whether a firm is performing better or worse than its peers or is performing better or worse through time. Underlying accounting choices also can affect the ratios you construct. In summary, the first three steps of the six-step process discussed in Chapter 1 (that is, (1) identify economic characteristics of the industry, (2) identify company strategies, and (3) assess the quality of the financial statements) link directly to the use of ratios to validate your understanding of the profitability and risk of a firm and to generate new insights not discovered in the first three steps.

You can compare financial ratios for a particular firm with similar ratios for the same firm for earlier periods (time-series analysis), as we did in this chapter for **Starbucks**, or with those of other firms for the same period (cross-sectional analysis), as we did for **Starbucks** and **Panera** and several other sets of firms in this chapter. The next section discusses some of the general issues involved in making such comparisons.

Comparisons with Earlier Periods

You can draw useful insights by comparing a firm with itself over time. We applied this analysis when examining **Starbucks'** ROA decomposition earlier in the chapter. A firm's past financial ratios serve as a benchmark for interpreting its current period financial ratios. You can study the impact of economic conditions (recession and inflation), industry conditions (shift in regulatory status and new technology), and firm-specific conditions (shift in corporate strategy and new management) on the time-series pattern of these ratios.

Some questions you should raise before using ratios of past financial statement data as a basis for interpreting ratios for the current period are as follows:

- Has the firm made a significant change in its product, geographic, or customer mix that affects the comparability of financial statement ratios over time?

- Has the firm made a major acquisition or divestiture?
- Has the firm changed its methods of accounting over time? For example, does the firm now consolidate a previously unconsolidated entity?
- Are there any unusual or nonrecurring amounts that impair a comparable analysis of financial results across years?

Analysts should not use past performance as a basis for comparison without considering the level of past and current performance. For example, prior performance might have been at an unsatisfactory level. Improvement during the current year may still leave the firm at an undesirable level. An improved profitability ratio may mean little if the firm still ranks last in its industry in terms of profitability in all years. Similarly, if the firm's prior performance was exceptional but declined in the current period, the firm still may have performed well in the current period.

Another concern involves interpreting the relative rate of change in a ratio over time. Your interpretation of a 10% increase in profit margin for ROA differs depending on whether other firms in the industry experienced a 15% versus a 5% increase. Comparing a particular firm's ratios with those of similar firms lessens the concerns discussed here. Careful time-series analyses of a firm's financial ratios will not only yield key insights about how and why the firm's profitability has been changing over time, but also will provide valuable information about trends. Chapter 10 discusses techniques for building detailed and careful forecasts of financial statements, and we rely heavily on the information and trends gathered from time-series analysis of ratios. In that chapter, we project future financial statements for **Starbucks** for the next five years, and the information in the current and past financial ratios provides valuable insights to help us make more reliable forecasts.

Comparisons with Other Firms

The major task in performing a cross-sectional analysis is identifying the other firms to use for comparison. The objective is to select firms with similar products and strategies and similar size and age. Few firms may meet these criteria, and no firms will meet these criteria perfectly. For example, although there are numerous obvious competitors that are logical comparisons for **Starbucks**, none are ideal for direct financial comparison because of a lack of data due to being privately held (**Peet's Coffee**) or a wholly owned subsidiary of another company (**Costa Coffee**), or because they are on a sufficiently smaller scale that comparisons would not be meaningful (**David's Tea**). In this chapter, we selected **Panera** as a reasonable comparison but also could have selected **Dunkin' Donuts** or **Tim Horton's**.

Comparable firms are rarely perfectly comparable. Even the comparison of similar firms such as **Coca-Cola** and **PepsiCo** are difficult because Coca-Cola derives all of its revenues from beverages, whereas PepsiCo derives revenues from beverages and food products. Similarly, **Target** and **Walmart** are not directly comparable because Target's operations include a segment for its branded credit card and Walmart's operations include the Sam's Club warehouse store chain. You must accept the fact that cross-sectional comparisons of ratios between firms will require subjective judgment about how the differences across firms in business model, strategy, and accounting affect the ratios.

An alternative approach uses average industry ratios, such as those provided in Appendix D of this text; published by **Moody's**, **Dun & Bradstreet**, and **Robert Morris Associates**; or derived from computerized databases such as **Compustat**. These average industry ratios provide an overview of the performance of an industry, aiming to capture the commonalities across many firms. When using standardized ratios prepared by various databases, you should consider the following issues:

1. **Definition of the industry:** Publishers of industry average ratios generally classify diversified firms into the industry of their major product. **Starbucks**, for example, appears as a "restaurant" company even though it generates most of its sales from coffee. The industry also may exclude privately held and foreign firms if data are not available for those firms. If these types of firms are significant for a particular industry, you should recognize the possible impact of their absence from the published data.

2. **Calculation of industry average:** Industry averages can be a simple average or a weighted average of the ratios of the included firms. Further, it is helpful to know whether summary industry averages are based on the mean or median.

3. **Distribution of ratios around the mean:** To interpret a deviation of a particular firm's ratio from the industry average requires information on the distribution around the mean. You interpret a ratio that is 10% larger than the industry mean differently depending on whether the standard deviation is 5% versus 15% greater or less than the mean. Useful sources of industry ratios give either the quartiles or the range of the distribution.

4. **Definition of financial statement ratios:** As already emphasized, you should examine the definition of each published ratio. For instance, is the rate of ROCE based on average or beginning-of-the-period common shareholders' equity? Are any adjustments made to reported net income, such as for nonrecurring or unusual charges?

Average industry ratios serve as a useful basis of comparison as long as you recognize their possible limitations. To assist the reader, Appendix D presents data on the distribution of the most common financial statement ratios across time for 48 industries.

Summary

This chapter introduced the fourth step of the six-step process of financial statement analysis: analyzing profitability and risk. We examined the two primary summary measures of profitability: ROA and ROCE. Additionally, we examined various financial statement ratios useful for understanding the drivers of ROA or ROCE. Use and interpretation of these financial ratios is important; memorizing them is not. The FSAP  software available with this book facilitates calculation of the ratios and permits you to devote more time to analysis and interpretation. This is a qualitative and intellectual process that requires you to understand the firm's specific strategy in the context of the industry and to be aware of any underlying accounting choices that affect the data used in financial ratios being examined.

We also highlighted alternative methods for examining profitability. The first part of the chapter focused on simple approaches, such as earnings per share, common-size, and percentage change analysis, as well as alternative definitions of profits. However, the majority of the chapter focused on how to interpret different levels of profitability ratios. Exhibit 4.21 summarizes many of the key profitability ratios discussed in this chapter. Profitability analysis proceeds through four levels.

- Level 1 involves measures of profitability for a firm as a whole: the rate of ROA and the rate of ROCE.

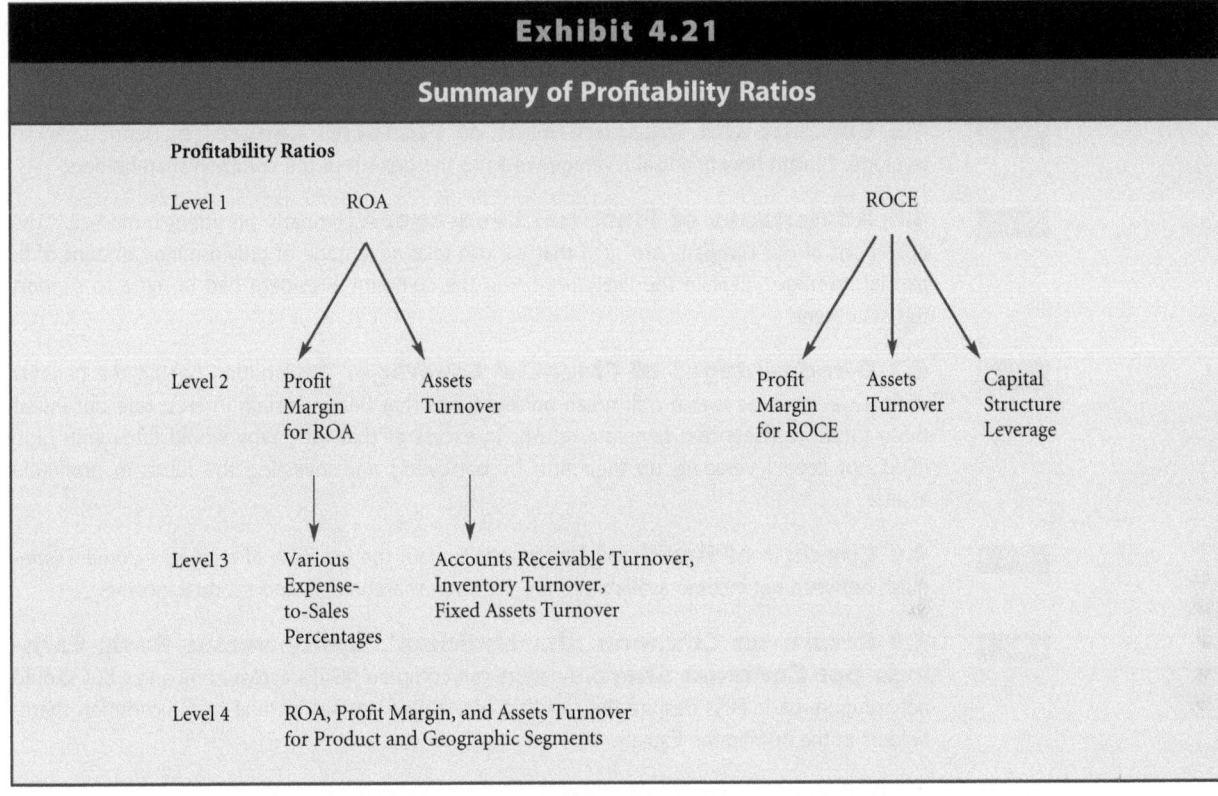

Exhibit 4.21

Summary of Profitability Ratios

- Level 2 disaggregates ROA and ROCE into important components. ROA disaggregates into profit margin for ROA and assets turnover. ROCE disaggregates into profit margin for ROCE, assets turnover, and capital structure leverage components.
- Level 3 disaggregates the profit margin into various expense-to-sales percentages and disaggregates assets turnover into individual asset turnovers.
- Level 4 uses product and geographic segment data to study ROA, profit margin, and assets turnover more fully.

Questions, Exercises, Problems, and Cases

Questions and Exercises

4.1 Common-Size Analysis. Common-size analysis is a simple way to make financial statements of different firms comparable. What are possible shortcomings of comparing two different firms using common-size analysis?

LO 4-1

4.2 Earnings per Share. Firm A reports an increase in earnings per share; Firm B reports a decrease in earnings per share. Is this unconditionally informative about each firm's performance? If not, why is earnings per share so commonly discussed in the financial press?

LO 4-1

4.3 Pro Forma Earnings. Firms often provide supplemental disclosures that report and discuss income figures that do not necessarily equal bottom-line net income from the income statement. For example, in Twitter's initial public offering filings with the SEC, the company reported a net loss of $79.4 million, but prominently disclosed "adjusted EBITDA" of (positive) $21.2 million. Discuss the merits and shortcomings of this managerial practice.

LO 4-1

LO 4-2

4.4 Profit Margin for ROA versus ROCE. Describe the difference between the profit margin for ROA and the profit margin for ROCE. Explain why each profit margin is appropriate for measuring the rate of ROA and the rate of ROCE, respectively.

LO 4-3

4.5 Concept and Measurement of Financial Leverage. Define financial leverage. Explain how financial leverage works to the benefit of the common shareholders.

LO 4-3

4.6 Advantages of Financial Leverage. A company president remarked, "The operations of our company are such that we can take advantage of only a minor amount of financial leverage." Explain the likely reasoning the company president had in mind to support this statement.

LO 4-3

4.7 Disadvantages of Financial Leverage. The intuition behind the benefits of financial leverage is that a firm can borrow funds that bear a certain interest rate but invest those funds in assets that generate returns in excess of that rate. Why would firms with high ROAs not keep leveraging up their firm by borrowing and investing the funds in profitable assets?

LO 4-3

4.8 Concept of Residual Income. Explain the intuition of residual income. Distinguish between net income available to the common shareholders and residual income.

LO 4-3

4.9 Return on Common Shareholders' Equity versus Basic Earnings per Common Share. Analysts can compare ROCEs across companies but should not compare basic EPSs despite the fact that both ratios use net income to the common shareholders in the numerator. Explain.

LO 4-2

4.10 Calculating ROA and Its Components. Nucor, a steel manufacturer, reported net income for 2008 of $1,831 million on sales of $23,663 million. Interest expense for 2008 was $135 million, and noncontrolling interest was $314 million for 2008. The income tax rate is 35%. Total assets were $9,826 million at the beginning of 2008 and $13,874 million at the end of 2008. Compute the rate of ROA for 2008 and disaggregate ROA into profit margin for ROA and assets turnover components.

LO 4-3

4.11 Calculating ROCE and Its Components. Phillips-Van Heusen, an apparel manufacturer, reported net income (amounts in thousands) for Year 4 of $58,615 on sales of $1,460,235. It declared preferred dividends of $21,122. Preferred shareholders' equity totaled $264,746 at both the beginning and end of Year 4. Common shareholders' equity totaled $296,157 at the beginning of Year 4 and $364,026 at the end of Year 4. Phillips-Van Heusen had no noncontrolling interest in its equity. Total assets were $1,439,283 at the beginning of Year 4 and $1,549,582 at the end of Year 4. Compute the rate of ROCE for Year 4 and disaggregate it into profit margin for ROCE, assets turnover, and capital structure leverage ratio components.

LO 4-1

4.12 Calculating Basic and Diluted EPS. TJX, Inc., an apparel retailer, reported net income (amounts in thousands) of $609,699 for Year 4. The weighted average of common shares outstanding during Year 4 was 488,809 shares. TJX, Inc., subtracted interest expense net of tax saving on convertible debt of $4,482. If the convertible debt had been converted into common stock, it would have increased the weighted-average common shares outstanding by 16,905 shares. TJX, Inc., has outstanding stock options that, if exercised, would increase the weighted average of common shares outstanding by 6,935 shares. Compute basic and diluted earnings per share for Year 4, showing supporting computations.

4.13 Relating ROA and ROCE. **Boston Scientific**, a medical device manufacturer, reported net income (amounts in millions) of $1,062 on sales of $5,624 during Year 4. Interest expense totaled $64. The income tax rate was 35%. Average total assets were $6,934.5, and average common shareholders' equity was $3,443.5. The firm did not have preferred stock outstanding or noncontrolling interest in its equity.

    a. Compute the rate of ROA. Disaggregate ROA into profit margin for ROA and assets turnover components.

    b. Compute the rate of ROCE. Disaggregate ROCE into profit margin for ROCE, assets turnover, and capital structure leverage ratio components.

    c. Calculate the amount of net income to common shareholders derived from the excess return on creditors' capital and the amount from the return on common shareholders' capital.

4.14 Relating ROA and ROCE. **Valero Energy**, a petroleum company, reported net income (amounts in millions) of $1,803.8 on revenues of $54,618.6 for Year 4. Interest expense totaled $359.7, and preferred dividends totaled $12.5. Average total assets for Year 4 were $17,527.9. The income tax rate is 35%. Average preferred shareholders' equity totaled $204.3, and average common shareholders' equity totaled $6,562.3.

    a. Compute the rate of ROA. Disaggregate ROA into profit margin for ROA and assets turnover components.

    b. Compute the rate of ROCE. Disaggregate ROCE into profit margin for ROCE, assets turnover, and capital leverage ratio components.

    c. Calculate the amount of net income to common shareholders derived from the excess return on creditors' capital, the excess return on preferred shareholders' capital, and the return on common shareholders' capital.

Problems and Cases

4.15 Analyzing Operating Profitability. Exhibit 4.22 presents selected operating data for three retailers for a recent year. **Macy's** operates several department store chains selling consumer products such as brand-name clothing, china, cosmetics, and bedding and has a large presence in the bridal and formalwear markets (under store names Macy's and **Bloomingdale's**). **Home Depot** sells a wide range of building materials and home improvement products, which includes lumber and tools, riding lawn mowers, lighting fixtures, and

Exhibit 4.22

Selected Data for Three Retailers
(amounts in millions)
(Problem 4.15)

	Macy's	Home Depot	Supervalu
Sales	$24,892	$71,288	$44,564
Cost of goods sold	15,009	47,298	34,451
Interest expense	588	624	633
Net income	(4,803)	2,260	(2,855)
Average inventory	4,915	11,202	2,743
Average fixed assets	10,717	26,855	7,531
Average total assets	24,967	42,744	19,333

kitchen cabinets and appliances. **Supervalu** operates grocery stores under numerous brands (including **Albertsons, Cub Foods, Jewel-Osco, Shaw's,** and **Star Market**).

REQUIRED

 a. Compute the rate of ROA for each firm. Disaggregate the rate of ROA into profit margin for ROA and assets turnover components. Assume that the income tax rate is 35% for all companies.
 b. Based on your knowledge of the three retail stores and their respective industry concentrations, describe the likely reasons for the differences in the profit margins for ROA and assets turnovers.

LO 4-4   **4.16 Calculating and Interpreting Accounts Receivable Turnover Ratios.** Microsoft Corporation (Microsoft) and **Oracle Corporation** (Oracle) engage in the design, manufacture, and sale of computer software. Microsoft sells and licenses a wide range of systems and application software to businesses, computer hardware manufacturers, and consumer retailers. Oracle sells software for information management almost exclusively to businesses. Exhibit 4.23 presents selected data for the two firms for three recent years.

Exhibit 4.23			
Selected Data for Microsoft and Oracle (amounts in millions) (Problem 4.16)			
	Year 3	Year 2	Year 1
Microsoft			
Sales	$58,437	$60,420	$51,122
Average accounts receivable	12,391	12,464	10,327
Change in sales from previous year	(3.3)%	+18.2%	+15.5%
Oracle			
Sales	$23,252	$22,430	$17,996
Average accounts receivable	4,430	5,799	4,589
Change in sales from previous year	+3.7%	+24.6%	+25.2%

REQUIRED

 a. Calculate the accounts receivable turnover ratio for Microsoft and Oracle for Year 1, Year 2, and Year 3.
 b. Suggest possible reasons for the differences in the accounts receivable turnovers of Microsoft and Oracle during the three-year period.
 c. Suggest possible reasons for the trends in the accounts receivable turnover for the two firms over the three-year period.

LO 4-4   **4.17 Calculating and Interpreting Inventory Turnover Ratios.** Dell produces computers and related equipment on a made-to-order basis for consumers and businesses. **Sun Microsystems** designs and manufactures higher-end computers that function as servers and for use in computer-aided design. Sun Microsystems sells primarily to businesses. It also provides services to business customers in addition to product sales of computers. Selected data for each firm for three recent years appear in Exhibit 4.24. (Dell's fiscal year-end is in January; Sun's fiscal year-end is in June. Subsequently, in 2010, Oracle acquired Sun.)

Exhibit 4.24			
Selected Data for Dell and Sun Microsystems (amounts in millions) (Problem 4.17)			
	Year 3	Year 2	Year 1
Dell			
Cost of goods sold	$49,375	$48,855	$47,433
Average inventories	1,024	920	618
Change in sales from previous year	+1.1%	+3.0%	+4.1%
Sun Microsystems			
Cost of goods sold	$ 5,948	$ 6,639	$ 6,778
Average inventories	623	602	532
Change in sales from previous year	(10.4)%	(2.1)%	+3.7%

REQUIRED

a. Calculate the inventory turnover ratio for each firm for the three years.
b. Suggest reasons for the differences in the inventory turnover ratios of these two firms.
c. Suggest reasons for the trends in the inventory turnover ratios during the three-year period.

4.18 Calculating and Interpreting Accounts Receivable and Inventory Turnover Ratios. Nucor and AK Steel are steel manufacturers. Nucor produces steel in mini-mills. Mini-mills transform scrap ferrous metals into standard sizes of rolled steel, which Nucor then sells to steel service centers and distributors. Its steel falls on the lower end in terms of quality (strength and durability). AK Steel is an integrated steel producer, transforming ferrous metals into rolled steel and then into various steel products for the automobile, appliance, construction, and other industries. Its steel falls on the higher end in terms of quality. Exhibit 4.25 sets forth various data for these two companies for two recent years.

LO 4-4

REQUIRED

a. Calculate the accounts receivable turnovers for Nucor and AK Steel for Year 1 and Year 2.
b. Describe the likely reasons for the differences in the accounts receivable turnovers for these two firms.
c. Describe the likely reasons for the trend in the accounts receivable turnovers of these two firms during the two-year period.
d. Calculate the inventory turnovers for Nucor and AK Steel for Year 1 and Year 2.
e. Describe the likely reasons for the differences in the inventory turnovers of these two firms.
f. Describe the likely reasons for the changes in the inventory turnovers of these two firms during the two-year period.

4.19 Calculating and Interpreting Fixed Assets Turnover Ratios. Texas Instruments (TI) designs and manufactures semiconductor products for use in computers, telecommunications equipment, automobiles, and other electronics-based products. The manufacturing of semiconductors is highly capital-intensive. **Hewlett-Packard Corporation** (HP) manufactures computer hardware and various imaging products, such as printers and fax machines. Exhibit 4.26 presents selected data for TI and HP for three recent years.

LO 4-4

Exhibit 4.25

Selected Data for Nucor and AK Steel
(amounts in millions)
(Problem 4.18)

	Year 2	Year 1
Nucor		
Sales	$23,663	$16,593
Cost of goods sold	19,612	13,035
Average accounts receivable	1,420	1,340
Average inventories	2,005	1,371
Change in sales from previous year	+42.6%	+12.5%
AK Steel		
Sales	$ 7,644	$ 7,003
Cost of goods sold	6,479	5,904
Average accounts receivable	572	686
Average inventories	607	752
Change in sales from previous year	+9.2%	+15.3%

Exhibit 4.26

Selected Data for Texas Instruments and Hewlett-Packard
(amounts in millions)
(Problem 4.19)

	Year 3	Year 2	Year 1
Texas Instruments			
Sales	$ 12,501	$ 13,835	$ 14,255
Cost of goods sold	6,256	5,432	5,775
Capital expenditures	763	686	1,272
Average fixed assets	3,457	3,780	3,925
Percentage fixed assets depreciated	54.9%	52.3%	49.0%
Percentage change in sales	(9.6)%	(3.0)%	+6.4%
Hewlett-Packard			
Sales	$114,552	$118,364	$104,286
Cost of goods sold	86,351	87,065	76,965
Capital expenditures	3,695	2,990	3,040
Average fixed assets	11,050	9,318	7,331
Percentage fixed assets depreciated	74.7%	72.4%	87.0%
Percentage change in sales	(3.2)%	+13.5%	+13.8%

REQUIRED

a. Compute the fixed assets turnover for each firm for Years 1, 2, and 3.
b. Suggest reasons for the differences in the fixed assets turnovers of TI and HP.
c. Suggest reasons for the changes in the fixed assets turnovers of TI and HP during the three-year period.

4.20 Calculating and Interpreting the Return on Common Share-holders' Equity and Its Components. JCPenney operates a chain of retail

LO 4-1, LO 4-2,
LO 4-3, LO 4-4

department stores, selling apparel, shoes, jewelry, and home furnishings. It also offers most of its products through catalog distribution. During fiscal Year 5, it sold **Eckerd Drugs**, a chain of retail drugstores, and used the cash proceeds, in part, to repurchase shares of its common stock. Exhibit 4.27 presents selected data for JCPenney for fiscal Year 3, Year 4, and Year 5.

REQUIRED

a. Calculate the rate of ROA for fiscal Year 3, Year 4, and Year 5. Disaggregate ROA into the profit margin for ROA and total assets turnover components. The income tax rate is 35%.
b. Calculate the rate of ROCE for fiscal Year 3, Year 4, and Year 5. Disaggregate ROCE into the profit margin for ROCE, assets turnover, and capital structure leverage components.
c. Suggest reasons for the changes in ROCE over the three years.
d. Compute the ratio of ROCE to ROA for each year.
e. Calculate the amount of net income available to common stockholders derived from the use of financial leverage with respect to creditors' capital, the amount derived from the use of preferred shareholders' capital, and the amount derived from common sharehold-ers' capital for each year.
f. Did financial leverage work to the advantage of the common shareholders in each of the three years? Explain.

Exhibit 4.27

Selected Data for JCPenney
(amounts in millions)
(Problem 4.20)

	Year Ended January 31,			
	Year 5	Year 4	Year 3	
Sales	$18,424	$17,786	$17,633	
Net income (loss)	524	(928)	405	
Interest expense	279	271	245	
Preferred stock dividend	12	25	27	
Income tax rate	35%	35%	35%	
January 31:	**Year 5**	**Year 4**	**Year 3**	**Year 2**
Total assets	$14,127	$18,300	$17,787	$18,048
Preferred stock	0	304	333	363
Total common shareholders' equity	4,856	5,121	6,037	5,766

LO 4-3, LO 4-4   **4.21 Interpreting the Return on Common Shareholders' Equity and Its Components.** Selected financial data for **Georgia-Pacific Corporation**, a forest products and paper firm, appear in Exhibit 4.28.

Exhibit 4.28

Selected Data for Georgia-Pacific Corporation (Problem 4.21)

	Year 4	Year 3	Year 2	Year 1	Year 0
ROCE	10.8%	6.5%	(4.2%)	(9.1%)	7.4%
ROA	4.8%	3.7%	1.5%	0.8%	3.3%
Profit margin for ROA	5.8%	4.6%	1.7%	0.9%	3.3%
Profit margin for ROCE	3.2%	1.6%	(0.9%)	(1.9%)	1.6%
Assets turnover	0.8	0.8	0.9	0.9	1.0
Capital structure leverage	4.1	4.9	5.4	5.3	4.8
Growth rate in sales	0.0%	(13.5%)	(9.2%)	13.4%	24.1%

REQUIRED

a. In which years did financial leverage work to the advantage of the common shareholders? In which years did it work to their disadvantage? Explain.

b. Identify possible reasons for the changes in the capital structure leverage ratio during the five-year period.

LO 4-1, LO 4-3, LO 4-4   **4.22 Calculating and Interpreting the Return on Common Shareholders' Equity and Earnings per Common Share.** Selected data for **General Mills** for 2007, 2008, and 2009 appear below (amounts in millions).

	2009	2008	2007
Net income	$1,304.4	$1,294.7	$1,144.0
Weighted-average number of common shares outstanding	331.9	333.0	346.5
Average common shareholders' equity	$5,695.3	$5,767.4	$5,545.5

REQUIRED

a. Compute the rate of ROCE for 2007, 2008, and 2009.

b. Compute basic EPS for 2007, 2008, and 2009.

c. Interpret the changes in ROCE versus EPS over the three-year period.

LO 4-1, LO 4-2, LO 4-3, LO 4-4   **4.23 Interpreting Several Measures of Profitability.** Selected data for **The Hershey Company** for Year 1 through Year 3 appear in Exhibit 4.29.

REQUIRED

a. Compute ROA and its decomposition for Year 2 and Year 3. Assume a tax rate of 35%.

b. Compute ROCE and its decomposition for Year 2 and Year 3.

c. Interpret the trends in reported net income, EPS, ROA, and ROCE over the three-year period.

Exhibit 4.29			
Selected Data for The Hershey Company **(amounts in millions except per-share data)** **(Problem 4.23)**			
	Year 3	**Year 2**	**Year 1**
Sales	$6,644,252	$6,080,788	$5,671,009
Interest expense	95,569	92,183	96,434
Net income	628,962	509,799	435,994
Diluted EPS	2.89	2.74	2.21
Minority interest in net income	12,950	5,817	8,183
Total assets	4,754,839	4,407,094	4,272,732
Total shareholders' equity	1,048,373	880,943	937,601
Noncontrolling interests in subsidiaries	11,624	23,626	35,285

4.24 Calculating and Interpreting Profitability Ratios. Hasbro is a leading firm in the toy, game, and amusement industry. Its promoted brands group includes products from Playskool, Tonka, Milton Bradley, Parker Brothers, Tiger, and Wizards of the Coast. Sales of toys and games are highly variable from year to year depending on whether the latest products meet consumer interests. Hasbro also faces increasing competition from electronic and online games. Hasbro develops and promotes its core brands and manufactures and distributes products created by others under license arrangements. Hasbro pays a royalty to the creator of such products. In recent years, Hasbro has attempted to reduce its reliance on license arrangements, placing more emphasis on its core brands. Hasbro also has embarked on a strategy of reducing fixed selling and administrative costs in an effort to offset the negative effects on earnings of highly variable sales. Exhibit 4.30 presents the balance sheets for Hasbro for the

LO 4-1, LO 4-2, LO 4-3, LO 4-4

Exhibit 4.30				
Hasbro **Balance Sheets** **(amounts in millions)** **(Problem 4.24)**				
	Year 4	**Year 3**	**Year 2**	**Year 1**
ASSETS				
Cash	$ 725	$ 521	$ 496	$ 233
Accounts receivable	579	607	555	572
Inventories	195	169	190	217
Prepayments	219	212	191	346
Total Current Assets	$1,718	$1,509	$1,432	$1,368

(Continued)

years ended December 31, Years 1 through 4. Exhibit 4.31 presents the income statements and Exhibit 4.32 presents the statements of cash flows for Years 2 through 4.

Exhibit 4.30 (Continued)

Property, plant, and equipment, net	207	200	213	236
Other assets	1,316	1,454	1,498	1,765
Total Assets	**$3,241**	**$3,163**	**$3,143**	**$3,369**
LIABILITIES AND SHAREHOLDERS' EQUITY				
Accounts payable	$ 168	$ 159	$ 166	$ 123
Short-term borrowing	342	24	223	36
Other current liabilities	639	747	578	599
Total Current Liabilities	**$1,149**	**$ 930**	**$ 967**	**$ 758**
Long-term debt	303	687	857	1,166
Other noncurrent liabilities	149	141	128	92
Total Liabilities	**$1,601**	**$1,758**	**$1,952**	**$2,016**
Common stock	$ 105	$ 105	$ 105	$ 105
Additional paid-in capital	381	398	458	455
Retained earnings	1,721	1,567	1,430	1,622
Accumulated other comprehensive income (loss)	82	30	(47)	(68)
Treasury stock	(649)	(695)	(755)	(761)
Total Shareholders' Equity	**$1,640**	**$1,405**	**$1,191**	**$1,353**
Total Liabilities and Shareholders' Equity	**$3,241**	**$3,163**	**$3,143**	**$3,369**

Exhibit 4.31

Hasbro
Income Statements
(amounts in millions)
(Problem 4.24)

	Year 4	Year 3	Year 2
Sales	$ 2,998	$ 3,139	$ 2,816
Cost of goods sold	(1,252)	(1,288)	(1,099)
Selling and administrative expenses:			
Advertising	(387)	(364)	(297)
Research and development	(157)	(143)	(154)
Royalty expense	(223)	(248)	(296)
Other selling and administrative	(687)	(799)	(788)

(Continued)

Exhibit 4.31 (Continued)

Interest expense	(32)	(53)	(78)
Income tax expense	(64)	(69)	(29)
Net Income	$ 196	$ 175	$ 75

Exhibit 4.32

Hasbro
Statements of Cash Flows
(amounts in millions)
(Problem 4.24)

	Year 4	Year 3	Year 2
OPERATIONS			
Net income	$196	$ 175	$ 75
Depreciation and amortization	146	164	184
Addbacks and subtractions, net	17	68	(67)
(Increase) Decrease in accounts receivable	76	(13)	34
(Increase) Decrease in inventories	(16)	35	39
(Increase) Decrease in prepayments	29	8	185
Increase (Decrease) in accounts payable and other current liabilities	(90)	17	23
Cash Flow from Operations	$358	$ 454	$ 473
INVESTING			
Property, plant, and equipment acquired	$ (79)	$ (63)	$ (59)
Other investing transactions	(6)	(2)	(3)
Cash Flow from Investing	$ (85)	$ (65)	$ (62)
FINANCING			
Increase in common stock	$ 3	$ 40	$ 3
Decrease in short-term borrowing	(7)	—	(15)
Decrease in long-term borrowing	(58)	(389)	(127)
Acquisition of common stock	—	(3)	—
Dividends	(37)	(21)	(21)
Other financing transactions	7	9	12
Cash Flow from Financing	$ (69)	$(364)	$(148)
Change in Cash	$204	$ 25	$ 263
Cash—Beginning of year	521	496	233
Cash—End of Year	$725	$ 521	$ 496

REQUIRED

a. Exhibit 4.33 presents profitability ratios for Hasbro for Year 2 and Year 3. Calculate each of these financial ratios for Year 4. The income tax rate is 35%.

b. Analyze the changes in ROA and its components for Hasbro over the three-year period, suggesting reasons for the changes observed.

c. Analyze the changes in ROCE and its components for Hasbro over the three-year period, suggesting reasons for the changes observed.

Exhibit 4.33

Hasbro
Financial Statement Ratio Analysis
(Problem 4.24)

	Year 4	Year 3	Year 2
Profit margin for ROA		6.7%	4.5%
Assets turnover		1.0	0.9
ROA		6.6%	3.9%
Profit margin for ROCE		5.6%	2.7%
Capital structure leverage		2.4	2.6
ROCE		13.5%	5.9%
Cost of goods sold/Sales		41.0%	39.0%
Advertising expense/Sales		11.6%	10.5%
Research and development expense/Sales		4.6%	5.5%
Royalty expense/Sales		7.9%	10.5%
Other selling and administrative expense/Sales		25.4%	28.0%
Income tax expense (excluding tax effects of interest expense)/Sales		2.8%	2.0%
Accounts receivable turnover		5.4	5.0
Inventory turnover		7.2	5.4
Fixed assets turnover		15.2	12.5

LO 4-1, LO 4-2,
LO 4-3, LO 4-4

4.25 Calculating and Interpreting Profitability Ratios. **Abercrombie & Fitch** sells casual apparel and personal care products for men, women, and children through retail stores located primarily in shopping malls. Its fiscal year ends January 31 of each year. Financial statements for Abercrombie & Fitch for fiscal years ending January 31, Year 3, Year 4, and Year 5 appear in Exhibit 4.34 (balance sheets), Exhibit 4.35 (income statements), and Exhibit 4.36 (statements of cash flows). These financial statements reflect the capitalization of operating leases in property, plant, and equipment and long-term debt, a topic discussed in Chapter 6. Exhibit 4.37 (page 257) presents financial statement ratios for Abercrombie & Fitch for Years 3 and 4. Selected data for Abercrombie & Fitch appear here.

Exhibit 4.34

Abercrombie & Fitch
Balance Sheets
(amounts in millions)
(Problem 4.25)

	January 31,			
	Year 5	Year 4	Year 3	Year 2
ASSETS				
Cash	$ 350	$ 56	$ 43	$ 188
Marketable securities	—	465	387	51
Accounts receivable	26	7	10	21
Inventories	248	201	169	130
Prepayments	28	24	20	15
Total Current Assets	$ 652	$ 753	$ 629	$ 405
Property, plant, and equipment, net	1,560	1,342	1,172	947
Other assets	8	1	1	—
Total Assets	$2,220	$2,096	$1,802	$1,352
LIABILITIES AND SHAREHOLDERS' EQUITY				
Accounts payable	$ 84	$ 58	$ 79	$ 32
Short-term borrowing	54	33	—	—
Other current liabilities	276	220	193	132
Total Current Liabilities	$ 414	$ 311	$ 272	$ 164
Long-term debt	872	713	629	581
Other noncurrent liabilities	265	214	165	12
Total Liabilities	$1,551	$1,238	$1,066	$ 757
Common stock	$ 1	$ 1	$ 1	$ 1
Additional paid-in capital	140	139	143	141
Retained earnings	1,076	906	701	520
Treasury stock	(548)	(188)	(109)	(67)
Total Shareholders' Equity	$ 669	$ 858	$ 736	$ 595
Total Liabilities and Shareholders' Equity	$2,220	$2,096	$1,802	$1,352

REQUIRED

a. Calculate the ratios in Exhibit 4.37 for Year 5. The income tax rate is 35%.
b. Analyze the changes in ROA for Abercrombie & Fitch during the three-year period, suggesting possible reasons for the changes observed.
c. Analyze the changes in ROCE for Abercrombie & Fitch during the three-year period, suggesting possible reasons for the changes observed.

Exhibit 4.35

Abercrombie & Fitch
Income Statements
(amounts in millions except retail space and employees)
(Problem 4.25)

	For the Year Ended January 31,		
	Year 5	Year 4	Year 3
Sales	$ 2,021	$1,708	$1,596
Cost of goods sold	(1,048)	(936)	(893)
Selling and administrative expenses	(562)	(386)	(343)
Interest expense	(63)	(54)	(48)
Interest income	5	4	4
Income tax expense	(137)	(131)	(121)
Net Income	$ 216	$ 205	$ 195
	Year 5	Year 4	Year 3
Square feet of retail space (in thousands)	5,590	5,016	4,358
Number of employees	48,500	30,200	22,000
Growth rate in sales	18.3%	7.0%	16.9%
Comparable store sales increase	2.0%	(9.0%)	5.0%

Source: Abercrombie & Fitch Co., Form 10-K for the Fiscal Years Ended 2003–2005.

Exhibit 4.36

Abercrombie & Fitch
Statements of Cash Flows
(amounts in millions)
(Problem 4.25)

	For the Year Ended January 31,		
	Year 5	Year 4	Year 3
OPERATIONS			
Net income	$ 216	$ 205	$ 195
Depreciation and amortization	106	90	76
Addbacks and subtractions, net	13	56	49
(Increase) Decrease in inventories	(34)	(27)	(34)
Increase (Decrease) in current liabilities	125	19	60
Cash Flow from Operations	$ 426	$ 343	$ 346

(Continued)

Exhibit 4.36 (Continued)

INVESTING			
Property, plant, and equipment acquired	$ (185)	$ (160)	$ (146)
Marketable securities sold	4,779	3,771	2,419
Marketable securities purchased	(4,314)	(3,849)	(2,729)
Other investing transactions	—	—	5
Cash Flow from Investing	$ (280)	$ (238)	$ (451)
FINANCING			
Increase in short-term borrowing	$ 20	$ 4	$ 4
Increase in common stock	49	20	—
Acquisition of common stock	(435)	(116)	(43)
Dividends	(46)	—	—
Cash Flow from Financing	$ (412)	$ (92)	$ (39)
Change in Cash	$ 294	$ 13	$ (144)
Cash—Beginning of year	56	43	188
Cash—End of Year	$ 350	$ 56	$ 43

Source: Abercrombie & Fitch Co., Form 10-K for the Fiscal Years Ended 2003–2005.

Exhibit 4.37

Abercrombie & Fitch Financial Statement Ratio Analysis (Problem 4.25)

	Year 5	Year 4	Year 3
Profit margin for ROA		14.1%	14.2%
Assets turnover		0.9	1.0
ROA		12.3%	14.3%
Profit margin for ROCE		12.0%	12.2%
Capital structure leverage		2.4	2.4
ROCE		25.7%	29.3%
Cost of goods sold/Sales		54.8%	56.0%
Selling and administrative expense/Sales		22.6%	21.5%
Interest revenue/Sales		0.2%	0.3%
Income tax expense (excluding tax effects of interest expense)/Sales		8.8%	8.6%
Accounts receivable turnover		200.9	103.0
Inventory turnover		5.1	6.0
Fixed assets turnover		1.4	1.5
Sales per store		$2,440,000	$2,673,367
Sales per square foot		$ 340.51	$ 366.22
Sales per employee		$ 56,556	$ 72,545

LO 4-1, LO 4-2,
LO 4-3, LO 4-4

4.26 Analyzing the Profitability of a Service Firm. Kelly Services (Kelly) places employees at clients' businesses on a temporary basis. It segments its services into (1) commercial, (2) professional and technical, and (3) international. Kelly recognizes revenues for the amount billed to clients. Kelly includes the amount it pays to temporary employees in cost of services sold. It includes the compensation paid to permanent employees that administer its offices in selling and administrative expenses. The latter expense also includes data processing costs relating to payroll records for all employees, rent, taxes, and insurance on office space. Amounts receivable from clients appear in accounts receivable, and amounts payable to permanent and temporary employees appear in current liabilities.

The temporary personnel business offers clients flexibility in adjusting the number of workers to meet changing capacity needs. Temporary employees are typically less costly than permanent workers because they have fewer fringe benefits. However, temporary workers generally are not as well trained as permanent workers and have less loyalty to clients.

Barriers to entry in the personnel supply business are low. This business does not require capital for physical facilities (most space is rented), does not need specialized assets (most temporary employees do not possess unique skills; needed data processing technology is readily available), and operates with little government regulation. Thus, competition is intense and margins tend to be thin.

Exhibit 4.38 presents selected profitability ratios and other data for Kelly Services, the largest temporary personnel supply firm in the United States. Note that the data in Exhibit 4.38 reflect the capitalization of operating leases in property, plant, and equipment and long-term debt, a topic discussed in Chapter 6.

Exhibit 4.38

Profitability Ratios and Other Data for Kelly Services (Problem 4.26)

	Year 4	Year 3	Year 2
Profit margin for ROA	0.6%	0.3%	0.6%
Assets turnover	3.8	3.5	3.5
ROA	2.2%	0.9%	2.1%
Profit margin for ROCE	0.4%	0.1%	0.4%
Capital structure leverage	2.1	2.0	1.9
ROCE	3.3%	0.8%	2.9%
Revenues	100.0%	100.0%	100.0%
Compensation of temporary employees/Revenues	84.0%	83.9%	82.9%
Selling and administrative expense/Revenues	15.1%	15.7%	16.1%
Income tax expense/Revenues	0.3%	0.2%	0.4%
Accounts receivable turnover	7.2	7.1	7.3
Fixed assets turnover	16.0	14.0	12.9
Sales mix data:			
Commercial	46.7%	49.3%	51.9%
Professional and technical	20.7	20.7	21.4
International	32.6	30.0	26.7
Total	100.0%	100.0%	100.0%

(Continued)

Exhibit 4.38 (Continued)			
Segment profit margin:			
Commercial	5.1%	4.4%	5.6%
Professional and technical	6.0%	5.9%	5.8%
International	0.8%	0.0%	0.5%
Number of offices	2,600	2,500	2,400
Number of permanent employees	8,400	7,900	8,200
Number of temporary employees, approximate	700,000	700,000	700,000
Growth rate in revenues	15.2%	6.9%	(4.7%)
Per-office data:			
Revenues	$1,916,923	$1,730,000	$1,690,417
Net income	$ 8,077	$ 2,000	$ 7,500
Permanent employees	3.2	3.2	3.4
Temporary employees	269	280	292
Per-permanent-employee data:			
Revenues	$ 593,333	$ 547,468	$ 494,756
Net income	$ 2,500	$ 633	$ 2,195
Temporary employees	83.3	88.6	85.4
Per-temporary-employee data:			
Revenues	$ 7,120	$ 6,177	$ 5,796
Net income	$ 30	$ 7	$ 26

REQUIRED

Analyze the changes in the profitability of Kelly Services during the three-year period in as much depth as permitted by the data provided.

4.27 Analyzing the Profitability of Two Hotels. Starwood Hotels (Starwood) owns and operates many hotel properties under well-known brand names, including Sheraton, W, Westin, and St. Regis. Starwood focuses on the upper end of the lodging industry. **Choice Hotels** (Choice) is primarily a franchisor of several hotel chains, including Comfort Inn, Sleep Inn, Clarion, EconoLodge, and Rodeway Inn. Choice properties represent primarily the midscale and economy segments of the lodging industry. Exhibit 4.39 presents selected profitability ratios and other data for Starwood, and Exhibit 4.40 presents data for Choice. (Note that ROCE is not meaningful for Choice because of negative common shareholders' equity due to open-market share repurchases, not accumulated deficits. As of the end of 2008, Choice had repurchased over one-third of all common shares issued: 34,640,510 out of 95,345,362 shares.) One of the closely followed metrics in the lodging industry is occupancy rate, which gives an indication of the capacity utilization of available hotel rooms. A second measure is the ADR (average daily rate), which measures the amount actually collected for an average room per night. Finally, REVPAR (revenue per available room) also is an important measure, which measures period-to-period growth in revenues per room for comparable properties (adjusted for properties sold or closed or otherwise not comparable across years). The interaction of occupancy rate and ADR is REVPAR.

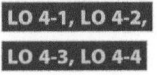

LO 4-1, LO 4-2,
LO 4-3, LO 4-4

Exhibit 4.39

Profitablity Ratios and Other Data for Starwood Hotels
(Problem 4.27)

	2008	2007	2006
Sales growth	(4.0%)	2.9%	0.0%
Profit margin for ROA	7.8%	10.4%	19.8%
Assets turnover	0.61	0.65	0.55
ROA	4.8%	6.8%	10.9%
Profit margin for ROCE	5.6%	8.8%	17.4%
Capital structure leverage	5.23	3.72	2.65
ROCE	17.8%	21.3%	25.4%
Number of hotels	942	925	871
Number of rooms	285,000	282,000	266,000
Rooms per hotel	303	305	305
Occupancy rate	71.1%	72.7%	71.2%
Revenue per available room night	$ 168.93	$ 171.01	$ 136.33
Average daily rate	$ 237.45	$ 235.18	$ 191.56

Exhibit 4.40

Profitability Ratios and Other Data for Choice Hotels
(Problem 4.27)

	2008	2007	2006
Sales growth	4.2%	14.0%	13.1%
Profit margin for ROA	16.7%	19.6%	22.6%
Assets turnover	1.95	1.95	1.90
ROA	32.6%	38.2%	42.9%
Profit margin for ROCE	15.6%	18.1%	20.9%
Capital structure leverage	(2.23)	(2.88)	(2.48)
ROCE	N/M*	N/M*	N/M*
Number of hotels	4,716	4,445	4,211
Number of rooms	373,884	354,139	339,441
Rooms per hotel	79	80	81
Occupancy rate	55.3%	57.9%	58.4%
Revenue per available room night	$ 40.98	$ 41.75	$ 40.13
Average daily rate	$ 74.11	$ 72.07	$ 68.71

*N/M: Not meaningful due to negative common shareholders' equity

Source: Choice Hotels International, Form 10-K for the Fiscal Years Ended 2006–2008.

REQUIRED

Analyze the changes and the differences in the profitability of these two hotel chains to the deepest levels available given the data provided. Compare and contrast the ROAs and ROCEs of both companies. Do the results match your prior expectations given the type of lodging for which each company specializes?

4.28 Analyzing the Profitability of Two Rental Car Companies. Select data for **Avis** and **Hertz** for 2012 follow. Based only on this information and ratios that you construct, speculate on similarities and differences in the operations and financing decisions of the two companies based on similarities and differences in the ratios. Amounts are in millions.

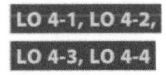

	Avis Budget Group	Hertz Global Holdings
Sales	$ 7,357	$ 9,021
Interest expense	268	650
Net income	290	243
Average total assets	14,078	20,480
Average shareholders' equity	585	2,371

4.29 Analyzing the Profitability of Two Restaurant Chains. Analyzing the profitability of restaurants requires consideration of their strategies with respect to ownership of restaurants versus franchising. Firms that own and operate their restaurants report the assets and financing of those restaurants on their balance sheets and the revenues and operating expenses of the restaurants on their income statements. Firms that franchise their restaurants to others (that is, franchisees) often own the land and buildings of franchised restaurants and lease them to the franchisees. The income statement includes fees received from franchisees in the form of license fees for using the franchiser's name; rent for facilities and equipment; and various fees for advertising, menu planning, and food and paper products used by the franchisee. The revenues and operating expenses of the franchised restaurants appear on the financial statements of the franchisees.

LO 4-4

Exhibit 4.41 presents profitability ratios and other data for **Brinker International**, and Exhibit 4.42 presents similar data for **McDonald's**. Brinker operates chains of specialty sit-down restaurants in the United States under the names of Chili's, Romano's Macaroni Grill, On the Border, Maggiano's Little Italy, and Corner Bakery Cafe. Its restaurants average approximately 7,000 square feet. Brinker owns and operates approximately 81% of its restaurants. McDonald's operates chains of fast-food restaurants in the United States and other countries under the names of McDonald's, Boston Market, Chipotle Mexican Grill, and Donatos Pizza. Its restaurants average approximately 2,800 square feet. McDonald's owns and operates approximately 29% of its restaurants. It also owns approximately 25% of the restaurant land and buildings of franchisees. The financial ratios and other data in Exhibits 4.41 and 4.42 reflect the capitalization of operating leases in property, plant, and equipment and long-term debt, a topic discussed in Chapter 6.

REQUIRED

a. Suggest reasons for the changes in the profitability of Brinker during the three-year period.
b. Suggest reasons for the changes in the profitability of McDonald's during the three-year period.
c. Suggest reasons for differences in the profitability of Brinker and McDonald's during the three-year period.

Exhibit 4.41

Profitability Ratios and Other Data for
Brinker International (dollar amounts in thousands)
(Problem 4.29)

	Year 4	Year 3	Year 2
Profit margin for ROA	5.1%	6.2%	6.5%
Assets turnover	1.4	1.3	1.3
ROA	7.1%	8.4%	8.8%
Profit margin for ROCE	4.1%	5.1%	5.2%
Capital structure leverage	2.5	2.3	2.3
ROCE	14.1%	15.8%	16.1%
Cost of goods sold/Revenues	81.2%	80.9%	81.0%
Selling and administrative expenses/Revenues	10.9%	9.8%	9.1%
Income tax expense (excluding tax effects of interest expense)/Revenues	2.8%	3.1%	3.4%
Accounts receivable turnover	100.2	106.0	101.3
Inventory turnover	97.1	115.5	95.5
Fixed assets turnover	1.7	1.6	1.6
Revenues per restaurant	$2,516	$2,343	$2,277
Operating income per restaurant	$ 129	$ 145	$ 148
Fixed assets per restaurant	$1,476	$1,493	$1,506
Percentage of restaurants owned and operated	80.1%	81.7%	81.9%
Growth in revenues	12.8%	13.8%	16.7%
Growth in number of restaurants	5.3%	10.6%	10.9%

Exhibit 4.42

Profitability Ratios and Other Data for
McDonald's (dollar amounts in thousands)
(Problem 4.29)

	Year 4	Year 3	Year 2
Profit margin for ROA	15.1%	12.2%	10.0%
Assets turnover	0.6	0.5	0.5
ROA	8.5%	6.7%	5.3%
Profit margin for ROCE	12.0%	8.8%	6.4%
Capital structure leverage	2.6	2.8	2.9
ROCE	17.4%	13.5%	9.8%
Cost of goods sold/Revenues	65.8%	66.7%	66.7%
Selling and administrative expenses/Revenues	12.6%	14.4%	17.0%
Income tax expense (excluding tax effects of interest expense)/Revenues	6.5%	6.7%	6.3%

(Continued)

Exhibit 4.42 (Continued)			
Accounts receivable turnover	25.7	21.6	17.7
Inventory turnover	90.9	94.8	94.2
Fixed assets turnover	0.7	0.6	0.6
Revenues per restaurant	$ 605	$ 551	$ 495
Operating income per restaurant	$ 91	$ 67	$ 50
Fixed assets per restaurant	$ 881	$ 856	$ 795
Percentage of restaurants owned and operated	29.2%	28.8%	28.9%
Growth in revenues	11.2%	11.3%	3.6%
Growth in number of restaurants	1.4%	0.1%	3.4%

INTEGRATIVE CASE 4.1

Profitability and Risk Analysis of Walmart Stores

Part A

Walmart Stores (Walmart) is the world's largest retailer. It employs an "everyday low price" strategy and operates stores as three business segments: Walmart Stores U.S., International, and Sam's Club.

1. **Walmart Stores U.S.:** This segment represented 62.3% of all 2015 sales and operates stores in three different formats: Discount stores (104,000 average square feet), Supercenters (178,000 average square feet), and Neighborhood Markets (42,000 average square feet). Each format carries a variety of clothing, housewares, electronic equipment, pharmaceuticals, health and beauty products, sporting goods, and similar items, and Supercenters include a full-line supermarket.[28] Walmart U.S. stores are in all 50 states; Washington, D.C.; and Puerto Rico. Discount stores are in 41 states, Supercenters are in 49 states, and Neighborhood Markets are in 31 states. Customers also can purchase many items through the company's website at www.walmart.com.

2. **International:** The International segment includes wholly owned subsidiaries in Argentina, Brazil, Canada, Chile, China, India, Japan, and the United Kingdom; majority-owned subsidiaries are in Africa, Central America, and Mexico. The merchandising strategy for the International segment is similar to that of the Walmart U.S. segment.

3. **Sam's Clubs:** Sam's Clubs are membership club warehouses that operate in 48 states. The average Sam's Club is approximately 134,000 square feet, and customers can purchase many items through the company's website at www.samsclub.com. These warehouses offer bulk displays of brand name merchandise, including hard goods, some soft goods, institutional-size grocery items, and certain private-label items. Gross margins for Sam's Clubs stores are lower than those of the U.S. and International segments.

---

[28]Walmart's fiscal year ends at the end of January of each year. Despite Walmart's convention of referring to its year ending January 31, 2016, as its fiscal 2016, we follow the common practice of referring to it as 2015 because 11 of the 12 months fall within 2015. This same convention holds true for Carrefour and Target in Part B of this case.

Walmart uses centralized purchasing through its home office for substantially all of its merchandise. It distributes products to its stores through regional distribution centers. During fiscal 2015, the proportion of merchandise channeled through its regional distribution centers was as follows:

Walmart Discount Stores, Supercenters, and Neighborhood Markets	79%
Sam's Club (nonfuel)	69%
International	77%

Exhibit 4.43 sets out various operating data for Walmart for 2013 through 2015. Exhibit 4.44 presents segment data. Exhibit 4.45 presents comparative balance sheets for Walmart for 2012 through 2015 (an extra year to enable average balance computations when necessary), Exhibit 4.46 presents comparative income statements for 2013 through 2015, and Exhibit 4.47 presents comparative statements of cash flows for 2013 through 2015. Exhibit 4.48 presents selected financial statement ratios for Walmart for 2013 through 2015. The statutory income tax rate is 35%.

REQUIRED

a. What are the likely reasons for the changes in Walmart's rate of ROA during the three-year period? Analyze the financial ratios to the maximum depth possible.
b. What are the likely reasons for the changes in Walmart's rate of ROCE during the three-year period?
   Note: Requirements c and d require coverage of material from Chapter 5.
c. How has the short-term liquidity risk of Walmart changed during the three-year period?
d. How has the long-term solvency risk of Walmart changed during the three-year period?

Exhibit 4.43

Walmart Stores
Operating Data
(Integrative Case 4.1, Part A)

	2015	2014	2013
Walmart Discount Stores, Supercenters, and Neighborhood Markets (U.S.)			
Number	4,574	4,516	4,203
Square footage (millions)	689.6	680.1	659.1
Sales per square foot	$432.68	$423.54	$423.92
Operating income per square foot	$ 27.68	$ 31.37	$ 33.06
International			
Number	6,299	6,290	6,107
Square footage (millions)	372.2	367.6	358.2
Sales per square foot	$331.56	$370.40	$381.11
Operating income per square foot	$ 14.36	$ 16.79	$ 14.39
Sam's Club (Domestic)			
Number	655	647	632
Square footage (millions)	87.6	86.5	84.4
Sales per square foot	$597.37	$596.88	$599.22
Operating income per square foot	$ 19.93	$ 21.43	$ 21.53

Exhibit 4.44

Walmart Stores
Segment Profitability Analysis
(Integrative Case 4.1, Part A)

	2015	2014	2013
Sales Mix			
Walmart Discount Stores, Supercenters, and Neighborhood Markets	62.9%	60.5%	59.9%
International	26.0	28.6	29.3
Sam's Club	11.10	10.9	10.8
	100.00%	100.00%	100.00%
Walmart Discount Stores, Supercenters, and Neighborhood Markets			
Operating profit margin	6.40%	7.41%	7.80%
Total assets turnover	2.89	2.84	2.83
ROA	18.51%	21.05%	22.06%
International			
Operating profit margin	4.33%	4.53%	3.77%
Total assets turnover	1.67	1.69	1.60
ROA	7.25%	7.67%	6.04%
Sam's Club			
Operating profit margin	3.34%	3.59%	3.59%
Total assets turnover	3.74	3.69	3.60
ROA	12.47%	13.25%	12.93%

Exhibit 4.45

Walmart Stores
Balance Sheets (amounts in millions)
(Integrative Case 4.1, Part A)

	2015	2014	2013	2012
ASSETS				
Current assets:				
Cash and cash equivalents	$ 8,705	$ 9,135	$ 7,281	$ 7,781
Receivables, net	5,624	6,778	6,677	6,768
Inventories	44,469	45,141	44,858	43,803
Prepaid expenses and other	1,441	2,224	1,909	1,588
Total current assets	60,239	63,278	61,185	59,940
Property and equipment	176,958	177,395	173,089	165,825
Less accumulated depreciation	(66,787)	(63,115)	(57,725)	(51,896)
Property and equipment, net	110,171	114,280	115,364	113,929

(Continued)

Exhibit 4.45 (Continued)

Property under capital lease and financing obligations:				
Property under capital lease and financing obligations	11,096	5,239	5,589	5,899
Less accumulated amortization	(4,751)	(2,864)	(3,046)	(3,147)
Property under capital lease and financing obligations, net	6,345	2,375	2,543	2,752
Goodwill	16,695	18,102	19,510	20,497
Other assets and deferred charges	6,131	5,455	6,149	5,987
Total assets	$199,581	$203,490	$204,751	$203,105
LIABILITIES AND EQUITY				
Current liabilities:				
Short-term borrowings	$ 2,708	$ 1,592	$ 7,670	$ 6,805
Accounts payable	38,487	38,410	37,415	38,080
Accrued liabilities	19,607	19,152	18,793	18,808
Accrued income taxes	521	1,021	966	2,211
Long-term debt due within one year	2,745	4,791	4,103	5,587
Capital lease and financing obligations due within one year	551	287	309	327
Total current liabilities	64,619	65,253	69,345	71,818
Long-term debt	38,214	40,889	41,771	38,394
Long-term capital lease and financing obligations	5,816	2,606	2,788	3,023
Deferred income taxes and other	7,321	8,805	8,017	7,613
Commitments and contingencies	—	—	1,491	519
Equity:				
Common stock	317	323	323	332
Capital in excess of par value	1,805	2,462	2,362	3,620
Retained earnings	90,021	85,777	76,566	72,978
Accumulated other comprehensive income (loss)	(11,597)	(7,168)	(2,996)	(587)
Total Walmart shareholders' equity	80,546	81,394	76,255	76,343
Nonredeemable noncontrolling interest	3,065	4,543	5,084	5,395
Total equity	83,611	85,937	81,339	81,738
Total liabilities and equity	$199,581	$203,490	$204,751	$203,105

Exhibit 4.46

Walmart Stores
Income Statements (amounts in millions)
(Integrative Case 4.1, Part A)

	2015	2014	2013
Net sales	$478,614	$482,229	$473,076
Membership and other income	3,516	3,422	3,218
Total revenues	482,130	485,651	476,294

(Continued)

Exhibit 4.46 (Continued)

Cost of sales	360,984	365,086	358,069
Operating, selling, general, and administrative expenses	97,041	93,418	91,353
Operating income	24,105	27,147	26,872
Interest:			
Debt	2,027	2,161	2,072
Capital lease and financing obligations	521	300	263
Interest income	(81)	(113)	(119)
Income from continuing operations before income taxes	21,638	24,799	24,656
Total provision for income taxes	6,558	7,985	8,105
Income from continuing operations	15,080	16,814	16,551
Income from discontinued operations, net of income taxes	—	285	144
Consolidated net income	15,080	17,099	16,695
Less consolidated net income attributable to nonredeemable noncontrolling interest	(386)	(736)	(606)
Consolidated net income attributable to Walmart	14,694	16,363	16,022

Exhibit 4.47

Walmart Stores
Statements of Cash Flows (amounts in millions)
(Integrative Case 4.1, Part A)

	2015	2014	2013
Consolidated net income	$ 15,080	$ 17,099	$ 16,695
Income from discontinued operations, net of income taxes	—	(285)	(144)
Income from continuing operations	15,080	16,814	16,551
Adjustments to reconcile income from continuing operations to net cash provided by operating activities:			
Depreciation and amortization	9,454	9,173	8,870
Deferred income taxes	(672)	(503)	(279)
Other operating activities	1,410	785	938
Changes in certain assets and liabilities, net of effects of acquisitions:			
Receivables, net	(19)	(569)	(566)
Inventories	(703)	(1,229)	(1,667)
Accounts payable	2,008	2,678	531
Accrued liabilities	1,303	1,249	103
Accrued income taxes	(472)	166	(1,224)
Net cash provided by operating activities	27,389	28,564	23,257
Payments for property and equipment	(11,477)	(12,174)	(13,115)
Proceeds from disposal of property and equipment	635	570	727

(Continued)

Exhibit 4.47 (Continued)

Proceeds from disposal of certain operations	246	671	—
Other investing activities	(79)	(192)	(138)
Net cash used in investing activities	(10,675)	(11,125)	(12,526)
Net change in short-term borrowings	1,235	(6,288)	911
Proceeds from issuance of long-term debt	39	5,174	7,072
Payments of long-term debt	(4,432)	(3,904)	(4,968)
Dividends paid	(6,294)	(6,185)	(6,139)
Purchase of Company stock	(4,112)	(1,015)	(6,683)
Dividends paid to noncontrolling interest	(719)	(600)	(426)
Purchase of noncontrolling interest	(1,326)	(1,844)	(296)
Other financing activities	(513)	(409)	(260)
Net cash used in financing activities	(16,122)	(15,071)	(10,789)
Effect of exchange rates on cash and cash equivalents	(1,022)	(514)	(442)
Net increase (decrease) in cash and cash equivalents	(430)	1,854	(500)
Cash and cash equivalents at beginning of year	9,135	7,281	7,781
Cash and cash equivalents at end of period	$ 8,705	$ 9,135	$ 7,281

Exhibit 4.48

Walmart Stores
Financial Ratio Analysis
(Integrative Case 4.1, Part A)

	2015	2014	2013
Profitability Ratios			
ROA	8.30%	9.16%	8.93%
Profit margin for ROA	3.47%	3.85%	3.82%
Total assets turnover	2.39	2.38	2.34
Cost of goods sold/Sales	74.87%	75.17%	75.18%
Operating, selling, general, and administrative expenses/Sales	20.13%	19.24%	19.18%
Interest expense (net of taxes)/Sales	0.34%	0.33%	0.32%
Income tax expense (excluding tax effects of interest expense)/Sales	1.55%	1.82%	1.87%
Accounts receivable turnover	77.8	72.2	70.9
Inventory turnover	8.1	8.1	8.1
Fixed assets turnover	4.1	4.1	4.1
ROCE	18.15%	20.76%	21.00%
Profit margin for ROCE	3.05%	3.37%	3.36%
Capital structure leverage	2.49	2.59	2.67

(Continued)

Exhibit 4.48 (Continued)			
Risk Ratios			
Current ratio	0.93	0.97	0.88
Quick ratio	0.22	0.24	0.20
Accounts payable turnover	9.37	9.64	9.51
Cash flow from operations to current liabilities ratio	42.18%	42.44%	32.95%
Long-term debt to Long-term capital	34.50%	33.60%	35.39%
Total liabilities/Total assets ratio	58.11%	57.77%	60.27%
Cash flow from operations to total liabilities ratio	23.46%	23.71%	19.00%
Interest coverage ratio	9.2	10.6	11.1

Part B

Part A of Integrative Case 4.1 analyzed the profitability and risk of **Walmart Stores** for its fiscal years 2013, 2014, and 2015. Part B of this case compares the profitability and risk ratios of Walmart and two other leading discount retailers, **Carrefour** and **Target**, for their 2013 through 2015 fiscal years.

Carrefour

Carrefour, headquartered in France, is Europe's largest retailer and the second largest retailer in the world. Carrefour is organized by geographic region (France, Europe excluding France, Asia, and Latin America). Each segment is organized according to store formats, which include the following (2015 number of stores in parentheses):

- **Hypermarkets (1,481):** Offer a wide variety of household and food products at competitively low prices under the Carrefour store brand.
- **Supermarkets (3,462):** Sell traditional grocery products under the Market, Bairro, and Supeco store brands.
- **Convenience Stores (7,181):** Offer a limited variety of food products in smaller stores than those of hypermarkets and supermarkets at aggressively low prices under Express, City, Contact, Bio, Montagne, and other store brands.
- **Cash & Carry (172):** Provides professional restaurant and shop owners food and non-food products at wholesale prices, under the Promocash and other store brands.

Carrefour derived approximately 47% of its 2015 sales in France, 25% in Europe excluding France, 19% in Latin America, and 9% in Asia.

Target

Target Corporation, headquartered in the United States, is a retailer that includes large-format general merchandise and food discount stores as well as an online business at www.target.com. Target stores offer a wide variety of clothing, household, electronics, sports, toy, and entertainment products at discount prices. Target stores attempt to differentiate themselves from Walmart's discount stores by pushing trendy merchandising with more brand-name products. Target emphasizes customer service, referring to its customers as "guests" and focusing on the theme of "Expect More, Pay Less." Target Corporation attempts to differentiate itself from competitors by providing wider aisles and a less cluttered store appearance. Target discontinued its Canadian operations in 2014, which led to a significant nonrecurring loss in that year.

Exhibits 4.49 and 4.50 present profitability ratios for Carrefour, Target, and Walmart for their 2013 through 2015 fiscal years. Exhibit 4.51 presents risk ratios for the three firms. Exhibit 4.52 presents selected other data for these firms. The financial statements include the present value of commitments under all leases in property, plant, and equipment and in long-term debt.

Exhibit 4.49

Carrefour, Target, and Walmart
Cross-Section ROA Profitability Analysis
(Integrative Case 4.1, Part B)

ROA

	2015	2014	2013
Carrefour	3.0%	3.6%	3.7%
Target	9.2%	(2.5%)	6.3%
Walmart	8.3%	9.2%	8.9%

	Profit Margin for ROA			Assets Turnover		
	2015	2014	2013	2015	2014	2013
Carrefour	1.7%	2.1%	2.1%	1.7	1.7	1.7
Target	5.1%	(1.5%)	3.7%	1.8	1.7	1.7
Walmart	3.5%	3.9%	3.8%	2.4	2.4	2.3

	Carrefour			Target			Walmart		
	2015	2014	2013	2015	2014	2013	2015	2014	2013
Sales	100.0%	100.0%	100.0%	100.0%	100.0%	100.0%	100.0%	100.0%	100.0%
Other revenues	3.2%	3.0%	3.2%	0.0%	0.0%	0.0%	0.7%	0.7%	0.7%
Cost of goods sold	79.6%	80.0%	80.5%	70.5%	70.6%	70.2%	75.4%	75.7%	75.7%
Selling and administrative	20.4%	19.8%	19.7%	22.0%	28.8%	23.6%	20.3%	19.4%	19.3%
Interest expense	0.5%	0.5%	0.6%	0.8%	1.2%	1.5%	0.5%	0.5%	0.5%
Income taxes	0.8%	1.0%	0.8%	2.2%	1.7%	2.0%	1.4%	1.7%	1.7%
Profit margin for ROA*	1.71%	2.13%	2.14%	9.23%	−2.48%	5.72%	3.47%	3.85%	3.82%
Receivables turnover	13.6	13.7	14.1	n.a.	n.a.	n.a.	77.8	72.2	70.9
Inventory turnover	9.7	9.9	10.5	6.2	6.2	6.2	8.1	8.1	8.1
Fixed assets turnover	6.5	6.5	6.8	2.9	2.8	2.5	4.1	4.1	4.1

*Amounts do not sum because profit margin for ROA is reduced by taxes on operating profits, which do not equal total taxes reported on the income statement.

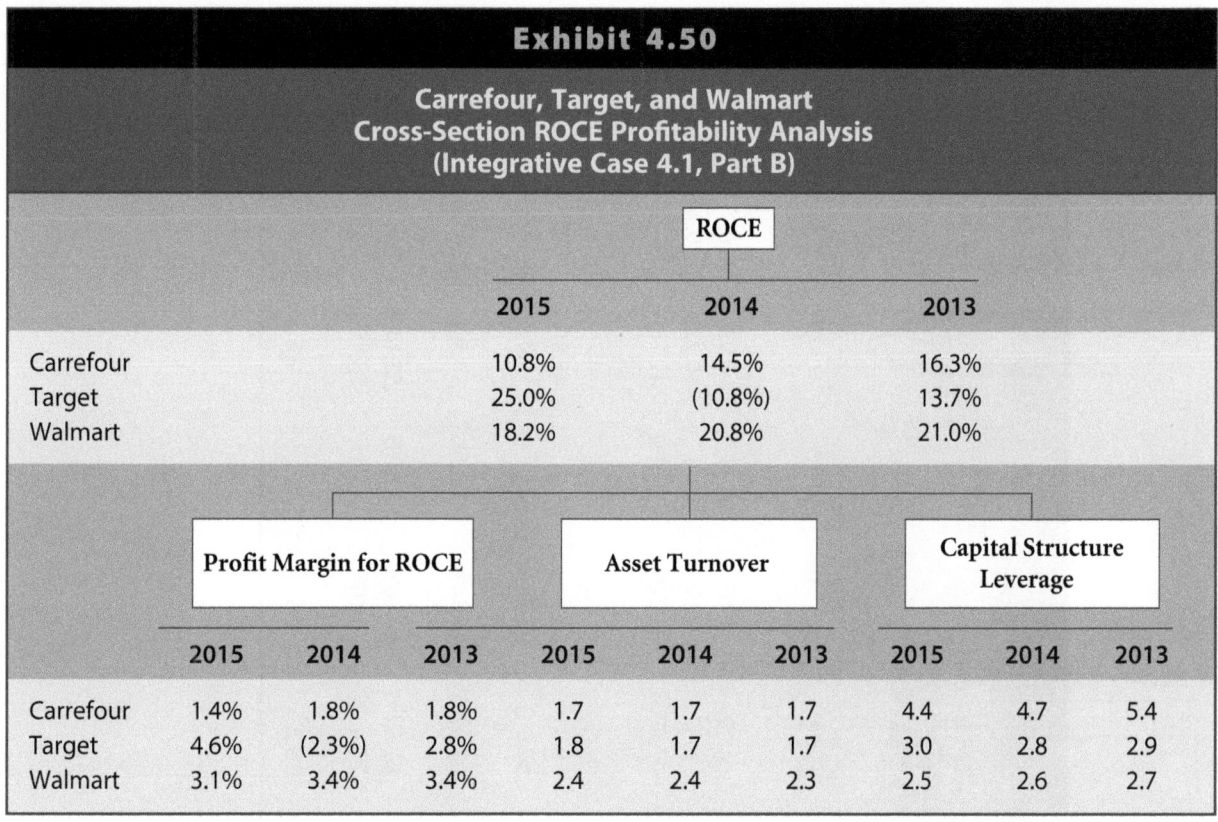

	ROCE		
	2015	2014	2013
Carrefour	10.8%	14.5%	16.3%
Target	25.0%	(10.8%)	13.7%
Walmart	18.2%	20.8%	21.0%

	Profit Margin for ROCE			Asset Turnover			Capital Structure Leverage		
	2015	2014	2013	2015	2014	2013	2015	2014	2013
Carrefour	1.4%	1.8%	1.8%	1.7	1.7	1.7	4.4	4.7	5.4
Target	4.6%	(2.3%)	2.8%	1.8	1.7	1.7	3.0	2.8	2.9
Walmart	3.1%	3.4%	3.4%	2.4	2.4	2.3	2.5	2.6	2.7

Exhibit 4.50

**Carrefour, Target, and Walmart
Cross-Section ROCE Profitability Analysis
(Integrative Case 4.1, Part B)**

Exhibit 4.51

Carrefour, Target, and Walmart Cross-Section Risk Analysis for (Integrative Case 4.1, Part B)

	Carrefour			Target			Walmart		
	2015	2014	2013	2015	2014	2013	2015	2014	2013
Short-Term Liquidity									
Current ratio	0.78	0.76	0.85	1.12	1.16	0.91	0.93	0.97	0.88
Quick ratio	0.12	0.14	0.22	0.32	0.19	0.05	0.22	0.24	0.20
Cash flow from operations/ Average current liabilities	12.42%	11.74%	8.98%	47.98%	36.22%	48.64%	42.18%	42.44%	32.95%
Days receivables	26.9	26.6	25.9	n.a.	n.a.	n.a.	4.7	5.1	5.2
Days inventory	37.7	36.8	40.7	59.3	58.9	59.0	45.3	45.0	45.2
Days payable	80.9	80.1	70.9	52.9	53.7	52.1	38.9	37.9	38.4
Long-Term Solvency									
Long-term debt to Long-term capital	38.43%	39.99%	46.52%	47.97%	47.44%	41.32%	34.50%	33.60%	35.39%
Total liabilities/Total assets ratio	76.33%	77.66%	80.06%	67.82%	66.00%	63.57%	58.11%	57.77%	60.27%
Cash flow from operations/ Average total liabilities	8.05%	7.41%	5.39%	21.45%	16.00%	21.76%	23.46%	23.71%	19.00%
Interest coverage ratio	6.0	6.2	5.7	9.2	0.5	4.2	9.2	10.6	11.1

Exhibit 4.52						
Carrefour, Target, and Walmart **Selected Other Financial Data** **(Integrative Case 4.1, Part B)**						
	2015		**2014**		**2013**	
Growth Rate in Sales						
Carrefour	3.1%		(0.3%)		(1.0%)	
Target	1.6%		1.9%		(2.8%)	
Walmart	(0.7)%		1.9%		1.6%	
Number of Stores						
Carrefour	12,296		10,860		10,100	
Target	1,792		1,790		1,793	
Walmart	11,528		11,453		10,942	
Square Footage (000s)						
Carrefour	188,648		179,036		173,826	
Target	239,539		239,963		240,054	
Walmart	1,149,000		1,134,000		1,102,000	
Sales per Square Foot						
Carrefour	€	418	€	426	€	441
Target	$	308	$	303	$	297
Walmart	$	412	$	420	$	423
Sales per Store						
Carrefour	€ 6,413,000		€ 7,027,000		€ 7,592,000	
Target	$ 41,175,000		$ 40,569,000		$ 39,754,000	
Walmart	$ 41,127,000		$ 41,547,000		$ 42,633,000	
Square Feet per Store						
Carrefour	15,342		16,486		17,211	
Target	133,671		134,058		133,884	
Walmart	99,705		99,031		100,685	
Fixed Assets per Square Foot						
Carrefour	€	64	€	69	€	64
Target	$	105	$	108	$	110
Walmart	$	96	$	101	$	105
Sales per Employee						
Carrefour	€	207,017	€	200,190	€	210,580
Target	$	216,378	$	209,274	$	194,751
Walmart	$	206,137	$	216,290	$	212,042
Exchange Rate						
U.S. dollars per euro (€)	$	1.11	$	1.33	$	1.33

REQUIRED

a. Walmart and Target follow somewhat different strategies. Using information in Exhibits 4.49 and 4.52, suggest reasons for these differences in operating profitability.

b. Walmart and Carrefour follow similar strategies, but Walmart consistently outperforms Carrefour on ROA. Using information in Exhibits 4.49 and 4.52, suggest reasons for these differences in operating profitability.

c. Refer to Exhibit 4.50. Which firm appears to have used financial leverage most effectively in enhancing the rate of ROCE? Explain your reasoning.

Note: Requirements d and e require coverage of material from Chapter 5.

d. Refer to Exhibit 4.51. Rank-order these firms in terms of their short-term liquidity risk. Do any of these firms appear unduly risky as of the end of fiscal 2015? Explain.

e. Refer to Exhibit 4.51. Rank-order these firms in terms of their long-term liquidity risk. Do any of these firms appear unduly risky as of the end of fiscal 2015? Explain.

Risk Analysis

LO 5-1 Understand required disclosures about a firm's *risk exposures* and risk management activities.

LO 5-2 Define *financial flexibility* and decompose the return on common equity to assess financial flexibility.

LO 5-3 Apply analytical tools to assess working capital management and *short-term liquidity risk*.

LO 5-4 Explain the benefits and risks of financial leverage and apply analytical tools to assess *long-term solvency risk*.

LO 5-5 Use risk analysis tools to assess *credit risk*.

LO 5-6 Apply predictive statistical models to assess *bankruptcy risk*.

LO 5-7 Recognize the distinction between *firm-specific risks*, indicated by various financial statement ratios, and *systematic risk*, estimated with market equity beta.

Chapter Overview

The concept of *risk* means different things to different people because the potential consequences of risk differ across different contexts and stakeholders. As a result, there are numerous definitions of risk. A general definition is that risk involves exposure to a specified type of loss. The more *specific* definition of risk depends on the loss of interest. For example, equity investors make investment decisions based on the *expected return* from equity investments relative to the *risks* that such investments will fail to generate the expected level of returns, or, worse, lose money. Similarly, lenders make lending decisions based on the expected return in the form of interest revenue relative to the risks of the borrower defaulting on repayments. The analysis of risk is central to any decision to commit economic resources to a project or an investment.

This chapter describes disclosures required by U.S. GAAP and IFRS to inform financial statement users about *specific* risks that can affect a firm and how the firm manages those risks. We consider the following specific risks in this chapter:

1. Financial flexibility
2. Short-term liquidity risk
3. Long-term solvency risk
4. Credit risk
5. Bankruptcy risk
6. Systematic risk

These are all measures of risk that are related due to their relation to external investors and creditors. This chapter also demonstrates financial statement ratios that are useful in analyzing various types of risk, and we supplement these with statistical risk prediction models and other analytical tools. In Chapter 6, where we introduce the idea of analyzing the quality of firms' accounting information, we also introduce *accounting fraud risk*, and we provide a methodology to estimate it.

Information about risk appears in numerous places in a firm's annual report, such as the notes to the financial statements, the MD&A, the balance sheet, the income statement, and the statement of cash flows. In this chapter, we discuss how to use this collective information to examine risks faced by a firm.

As discussed in Chapter 4, firms use financial leverage to increase returns to equity shareholders. When firms obtain funds from borrowing and invest those funds in assets that generate a higher return than the after-tax cost of the borrowing, the common shareholders benefit. While capital structure leverage enhances the return to the common shareholders, it involves risk. Therefore, the analysis of profitability discussed in that chapter is linked to the analysis of *financial flexibility* in this chapter. Financial flexibility is the ability of a firm to obtain debt financing conditional on its current leverage and profitability of its operating assets.

The risk associated with leverage arises because satisfying future debt retirements requires cash payments. Exhibit 5.1 relates the factors affecting a firm's ability to generate cash with its need to use cash. Many financial statement analysis techniques designed to assess risk focus on a comparison of the supply of cash and the demand for cash. For example, risk analysis using financial statement information can examine *short-term liquidity risk*, which is the near-term ability to generate cash to meet working capital needs and debt service requirements, as well as *long-term solvency risk*, which is the longer-term ability to generate cash internally or externally to satisfy plant capacity and debt repayment needs.

Financial statement information also enables assessment of two closely related types of firm-specific risk: credit risk and bankruptcy risk. *Credit risk* concerns a firm's ability to make ongoing interest and principal payments on borrowings as they come due. *Bankruptcy risk*, on the other hand, relates to the likelihood that a firm will ultimately be forced to file for bankruptcy and perhaps subsequently liquidate due to a combination of insufficient profitability and cash flows and high debt service requirements. Analysts view these two types of risk as states of financial distress that fall along a continuum of increasing severity, as shown in Exhibit 5.2.

Exhibit 5.1

Framework for Financial Statement Analysis of Risk

Activity	Ability to Generate Cash	Need to Use Cash	Financial Statement Analysis Performed
Operating	Profitability of goods and services sold	Working capital requirements	Short-term liquidity risk
Investing	Sales of existing plant assets or investments	Plant capacity requirements	Long-term solvency risk
Financing	Borrowing capacity	Debt service requirements	

Exhibit 5.2

Severity of Various Credit-Related Events to a Firm's Investors

Firm			
←——→			
Not Severe	**Less Severe**	**More Severe**	**Very Severe**
Stretching out trade payables	Failing to make a required interest payment on time	Restructuring debt	Defaulting on a principal payment on debt	Filing for bankruptcy	Liquidating the firm

Analysts concerned with the economic loss of amounts lent to or invested in a firm would examine a firm's position on this financial distress continuum. We demonstrate how analysts can use tools of short-term liquidity and long-term solvency risk in assessing credit risk and bankruptcy risk.

Less than 5% of publicly traded firms experience financial distress as defined by one of the five states in Exhibit 5.2 spanning Less Severe to Very Severe. The other 95% of firms that are reasonably financially healthy utilize borrowings to finance future expansion or investment opportunities, which is captured by the notion of financial flexibility described earlier. Thus, while it is important to monitor liquidity, solvency, credit, and bankruptcy risk, we are more often interested in the financial flexibility of a firm to strategically utilize leverage through borrowing to enhance the returns to the firm's common equity investors.

The preceding types of risk do not encompass the full range of risks that equity investors must consider as the residual risk bearers of firms. Therefore, to value firms, investors should also assess elements of risk inherent in investing in common shares of a firm relative to the risks that are common to all firms. For example, investors consider *systematic* risk (also known as nondiversifiable or undiversifiable risk) and use it to explain differences in expected rates of return on common stocks. Economic theory demonstrates that differences in risk of an investment relate to differences in expected returns from that investment.

Studies of this risk/return relation use market equity beta as one measure of *systematic risk*. Market equity beta measures the covariability of a firm's returns with an index of returns of all securities in the equity capital market. Research and practice show that market equity betas increase with financial leverage. We briefly discuss the research relating financial statement data and market equity beta later in this chapter but elaborate on it more fully in Chapters 11 and 14. Our primary interest in this chapter is in contrasting market risk with the other risks discussed.

As will become clear, all six of these elements of risk are interrelated. Firms use financial flexibility and leverage to achieve higher returns for equity investors, but doing so involves financial risk. Analysts evaluate short-term liquidity and long-term solvency risk and assess both credit risk and bankruptcy risk. Some of the factors affecting long-term solvency risk and financial flexibility also affect systematic risk.

LO 5-1

Understand required disclosures about a firm's *risk exposures* and risk management activities.

Disclosures Regarding Risk and Risk Management

In the United States, the SEC requires firms to prominently identify specific risks they face as "Item 1A. Risk Factors" in their Form 10-K. In paragraph 229.503(c) of Regulation S-K, the SEC states the following:

> Where appropriate, provide under the caption "Risk Factors" a discussion of the most significant factors that make the offering speculative or risky. This discussion must be concise and organized logically. Do not present risks that could apply to any issuer or any offering. Explain how the risk affects the issuer or the securities being offered.

Examples of such risks include the following:

Source	Type or Nature
Firm-specific	• Ability to attract, retain, and motivate employees • Dependence on one or few customers • Dependence on one or few suppliers • Environmental or political scrutiny • Litigation
Industry	• Availability and price of raw materials or other production inputs • Competition • Technology • Regulation • Labor wages and supply
Domestic	• Political environment • Recessions • Inflation or deflation • Interest rate volatility • Demographic shifts
International	• Exchange rate volatility • Host government regulations and posturing • Political unrest or asset expropriation

Most of these risks are unavoidable, and firms must continually monitor each one to ensure they are taking appropriate actions to mitigate the impacts of detrimental events or changes in circumstances. The focus in this chapter, however, is on how to assess the financial consequences of these types of risk using disclosures and data from financial reports. Various financial reporting standards and financial market regulations require firms to discuss in notes to the financial statements or in regulatory filings how important elements of risk affect a particular firm and how the firm manages these risks. For non-U.S. companies that list securities in the United States, a required Form 20-F includes "Item 3D. Risk Factors." Capital market regulators around the world generally require companies to file similar reports. For example, in France, companies file a Registration Document annually with the Autorité des Marchés Financiers (AMF), and in Singapore, companies file an Annual Return and Audited Accounts with the Accounting and Corporate Regulatory Authority (ACRA).

We refer to the disclosures available in **Starbucks'** Form 10-K under "Item 1A. Risk Factors," as well as disclosures in Note 3, "Derivative Financial Instruments" (Appendix A), and the discussion under the heading "Financial Risk Management" in **Starbucks'** MD&A (Appendix B) to illustrate information that firms provide about risk. The above items list risks across an increasingly broad level, from firm-specific to international. The following section discusses the most common risks that firms face and for which specific disclosures exist, which include both specific and general firm-specific operational risks and structural financial risks, such as commodity prices, foreign exchange rates, and interest rates.

Firm-Specific Risks

Like all companies, **Starbucks** is subject to numerous firm-specific risks that are driven by the nature of the business, competition, supplier relationships, customers, and overall firm strategy. Within Item 1A of Form 10-K, **Starbucks** identifies 15 different risks related to its business, and the following are several excerpts:

- *Our success depends substantially on the value of our brands and failure to preserve their value, either through our actions or those of our business partners, could have a negative impact on our financial results.*
- *We rely heavily on information technology in our operations, and any material failure, inadequacy, interruption or security failure of that technology could harm our ability to effectively operate our business and could adversely affect our financial results.*
- *We are increasingly dependent on the success of our CAP and EMEA operating segments in order to achieve our growth targets.*
- *Increases in the cost of high-quality arabica coffee beans or other commodities or decreases in the availability of high-quality arabica coffee beans or other commodities could have an adverse impact on our business and financial results.*
- *Failure to meet market expectations for our financial performance will likely adversely affect the market price and volatility of our stock.*

Although many of the disclosures **Starbucks** provides seem general and applicable to any company, each is discussed in more detail in later sections of the company's Form 10-K. For example, in discussing the effects of meeting market expectations, **Starbucks** gives the following detail, which is true for many companies:

Failure to meet market expectations going forward, particularly with respect to operating margins, earnings per share, comparable store sales, operating cash flows, and net revenues, will likely result in a decline and/or increased volatility in the market price of our stock. In addition, price and volume fluctuations in the stock market as a whole may affect the market price of our stock in ways that may be unrelated to our financial performance.

On the other hand, the following discussion provides more detail about coffee bean and other input commodities:

The supply and price of coffee we purchase can also be affected by multiple factors in the producing countries, including weather, natural disasters, crop disease, general increase in farm inputs and costs of production, inventory levels and political and economic conditions, as well as the actions of certain organizations and associations that have historically attempted to influence prices of green coffee through agreements establishing export quotas or by restricting coffee supplies.

The identification and discussion of firm-specific risks provides a useful bridge between understanding a company's industry, business strategy, and profitability and identifying specific risks that may have an impact on the company's ability to grow, be profitable, and ultimately create value for debt and equity stakeholders. Of the firm-specific risks identified above, some are quantifiable and subject to required disclosures in the footnotes to financial statements. The remaining discussion in this section focuses on examples of such disclosures.

Commodity Prices

Changes in the prices of raw materials used to manufacture products affect future profitability (favorably or unfavorably) unless the firm can pass along price increases to customers, engage in fixed-price contractual arrangements with suppliers, or hedge with commodity futures contracts. For example, some firms attempt to manage this risk by engaging in a purchase commitment with suppliers to purchase certain quantities at a specified price over a particular period of time. Alternatively, a firm might acquire a futures contract or another hedging instrument to neutralize the risk of changes in prices. **Starbucks** discloses the following with respect to commodity price risk in Note 3, "Derivative Financial Instruments":

Depending on market conditions, we enter into coffee futures contracts and collars (the combination of a purchased call option and a sold put option) to hedge a portion of anticipated cash flows under our price-to-be-fixed green coffee contracts, which are described further in Note 5, Inventories. The effective portion of the derivative's gain or loss is recorded in AOCI and is subsequently reclassified to cost of sales including occupancy costs when the hedged exposure affects net earnings.

To mitigate the price uncertainty of a portion of our future purchases of dairy products and diesel fuel, we enter into swaps, futures and collars that are not designated as hedging instruments. Gains and losses from these derivatives are recorded in net interest income and other and help offset price fluctuations on our dairy purchases and the financial impact of diesel fuel fluctuations on our shipping costs, which are included in cost of sales including occupancy costs on our consolidated statements of earnings.

Note 5, "Inventories," indicates that **Starbucks** has purchase commitments for green coffee that total $819 million under fixed-price contracts and $266 million under price-to-be-fixed contracts. Chapter 9 discusses the accounting for commodity derivative contracts in detail, including what types of contracts qualify for hedge accounting treatment. However, at this point, it is important to understand that Footnote 4, "Fair Value Measurements," indicates **Starbucks** had $54.7 million as the fair value of derivative contracts classified as assets at the end of 2015, and only $33.7 million of contracts classified as liabilities. Thus, overall it appears that **Starbucks'** derivative contracts are in a net favorable position at the end of 2015 (because the fair value of derivative contract assets exceed liabilities).

Under "Commodity Price Risk" in the MD&A (Appendix B, which can be found online at the book's companion website at www.cengagebrain.com), **Starbucks** states that, if commodity prices declined 10% at the end of 2015, **Starbucks'** unrealized net losses on commodity derivative instruments (that qualify for hedge accounting) would only increase by $4 million, and realized losses (for derivatives that do not qualify for hedge accounting) would only increase by $6 million. Although accounting for derivatives is complex, disclosures like these are helpful as you assess the relative exposure faced by **Starbucks** for a specific risk like commodity prices. For example, the combined $10 million exposure—assuming a 10% decrease in commodity prices—is only 0.3% of income before income taxes of $3,903.0 million, indicating minimum risk from changes in commodity prices.

Foreign Exchange

Changes in foreign exchange rates can affect a firm in multiple ways, including

- amounts paid to acquire raw materials from suppliers abroad.
- amounts received for products sold to customers abroad.
- amounts collected from an account receivable, a loan receivable, or another receivable denominated in a foreign currency.
- amounts paid to settle an account payable, a loan payable, or another payable denominated in a foreign currency.
- amounts collected from remittances from a foreign branch or dividends from a foreign subsidiary.
- cash-equivalent value of assets invested abroad and liabilities borrowed abroad in the event the firm liquidates a foreign subsidiary.

Firms often use forward foreign exchange contracts to hedge some or all of these risks. Chapter 8 discusses the effect of exchange rate changes on reporting the operations of foreign units, and Chapter 9 discusses forward contracts used to hedge such risks.

Starbucks states the following in Note 3, "Derivative Financial Instruments":

> To reduce cash flow volatility from foreign currency fluctuations, we enter into forward and swap contracts to hedge portions of cash flows of anticipated revenue streams and inventory purchases in currencies other than the entity's functional currency. The effective portion of the derivative's gain or loss is recorded in AOCI and is subsequently reclassified to revenue or cost of sales including occupancy costs when the hedged exposure affects net earnings.

> We also enter into forward contracts to hedge the foreign currency exposure of our net investment in certain foreign operations. The effective portion of the derivative's gain or loss is recorded in AOCI and will be subsequently reclassified to net earnings when the hedged net investment is either sold or substantially liquidated.

Starbucks also entered into specific hedge cross-currency swap contracts in connection with the acquisition of **Starbucks Japan** discussed in Chapter 4. Under "Foreign Exchange Risk," the MD&A indicates that for foreign currency derivatives that qualify for hedge accounting, a 10% unfavorable change in exchange rates would have increased unrealized losses by $120 million for 2015, and realized losses by $10 million. The combined amount of potential loss exposure represents approximately 3.3% of income before income taxes. Thus, unlike commodity risk that is minimal for **Starbucks**, foreign exchange risk is more significant, consistent with **Starbucks'** growing international presence.

Interest Rates

Changes in interest rates can affect

- the fair values of investments in bonds, investment securities, loans, and receivables with fixed interest rates, as well as liabilities with fixed interest rates.
- returns a firm generates from pension fund investments.

Firms often use interest rate swaps to hedge, or neutralize, the risk of interest rate changes. As Chapter 7 discusses, locking in a *fixed* rate insulates the cash flows received or paid for interest payments but exposes the fair value of the principal. Locking in a *variable* rate protects the fair value of the principal but induces volatility in the cash flows for interest payments. Firms, especially financial institutions, also hedge some interest rate risk by matching investments in fixed-interest-rate assets with fixed-rate liabilities of equivalent amounts and duration.

Starbucks discloses the following in Note 3, "Derivative Financial Instruments":

> *Depending on market conditions, we enter into interest rate swap agreements to hedge the variability in cash flows due to changes in the benchmark interest rate related to anticipated debt issuances. These agreements are cash settled at the time of the pricing of the related debt. The effective portion of the derivative's gain or loss is recorded in accumulated other comprehensive income ("AOCI") and is subsequently reclassified to interest expense over the life of the related debt.*

The note explains that **Starbucks** often enters into interest rate swap agreements for specific debt issues, and did so for several during 2015. The agreements are settled when the interest rate on the debt issue is locked in. The notional amount of outstanding interest rate swap agreements at the end of 2015 is $125 million, slightly higher than that for commodities ($95 million), but significantly less than those for foreign exchange ($1,294 million).

Other Risk-Related Disclosures

The particular elements of risk that firms include in their risk management disclosures depend on the types of risks to which a firm is exposed, and many of the financial statement footnotes include qualitative discussions or quantitative indicators of such risks. For example, **Starbucks** discloses in Note 1, "Summary of Significant Accounting Policies," how the company assesses possible impairments of fixed and intangible assets. The required disclosures in Note 12, "Employee Stock and Benefit Plans," enable financial statement users to assess the impact of different assumptions underlying the valuation of stock options and gauge the dilutive effects of those plans and employee stock purchase plans. Similarly, information in Note 13, "Income Taxes," includes discussion of uncertain tax positions and the risk of losing certain tax benefits due to expiration. Finally, Note 15, "Commitments and Contingencies," indicates that although **Starbucks** is party to various legal proceedings, it is "not currently a party to any legal proceeding that management believes could have a material adverse effect on our consolidated financial position, results of operations or cash flows."

Firms now disclose considerably more information for you to use in assessing the effect of various risks. Increasingly, standard setters and regulators require firms to disclose the sensitivity of reported amounts to changes in various variables and assumptions, like those mentioned above. The disclosed information increases in value as analysts and other users of financial statements become familiar with the new reporting.

Analyzing Financial Flexibility by Disaggregating ROCE

LO 5-2

Define *financial flexibility* and decompose the return on common equity to assess financial flexibility.

Financial flexibility is the ability of a firm to strategically use debt financing to increase returns to investments by common shareholders. Firms that borrow funds and invest those funds in assets that generate a higher return than the after-tax cost of the borrowing create value for the common shareholders, as described for ROCE in Chapter 4. Common shareholders benefit from increasing proportions of debt in the capital structure *as long as the firm maintains a rate of return on assets above the after-tax cost of the debt.* Therefore, financial leverage can enhance the return to common shareholders. In this section, we present a method for decomposing ROCE that enables you to gauge the firm's financial flexibility, and thus the extent to which a firm can (or cannot) strategically use debt to generate greater returns for shareholders. The analysis of financial flexibility provides a linkage between the analysis of profitability in the prior chapter and the analysis of risk in the remainder of this chapter.

From Chapter 4, the disaggregation of ROCE into components of profit margin for ROCE, assets turnover, and capital structure leverage is as follows:

ROCE	=	**Profit Margin for ROCE**	×	**Assets Turnover**	×	**Capital Structure Leverage**
$\dfrac{\text{Net Income Attributable to Common Shareholders}}{\text{Average Common Shareholders' Equity}}$	=	$\dfrac{\text{Net Income Attributable to Common Shareholders}}{\text{Sales}}$	×	$\dfrac{\text{Sales}}{\text{Average Total Assets}}$	×	$\dfrac{\text{Average Total Assets}}{\text{Average Common Shareholders' Equity}}$

The disaggregation of ROCE suggests that common equity shareholders benefit from increasing leverage (that is, the third term in the ROCE disaggregation). However, there are two offsetting effects of increasing leverage:

- First, increasing leverage assumes the firm can deploy the financing proceeds into assets that maintain the current levels of profitability and turnover (that is, the first and second terms). This deployment is surely not instantaneous and further depends on the firm's ability to scale up operations without experiencing diminishing returns on investments, market saturation, and other strategic roadblocks.
- Second, increasing leverage increases interest expense because of higher debt levels, but also because of higher interest rates on incremental debt. These effects reduce profit margins (that is, the first term in the disaggregation) and increase demands for future cash.

Thus, increasing leverage has potential benefits and risks. A shortcoming of this standard disaggregation of ROCE is the inability to directly gauge the extent to which a firm can strategically increase leverage to increase returns to common shareholders without offsetting profitability. We refer to this as *financial flexibility*. To gauge a firm's financial flexibility, we can disaggregate ROCE to separate the *operating* and *financing* impacts on ROCE.

The alternative disaggregation discussed next requires that we first reformulate the balance sheet and income statement into operating and financing groupings.[1] Exhibit 5.3 presents the standard balance sheet equation in which assets are equal to liabilities plus equity. Each of these amounts is decomposed into primary components.

- Assets = Operating Assets + Financial Assets
- Liabilities = Operating Liabilities + Financial Liabilities (including Preferred Equity)
- Equity = Common Equity

The important task is to designate assets and liabilities as either *operating* or *financing*. Operating assets and liabilities are those that are necessary for the actual operations of the company, whereas financial assets and liabilities represent sources of capital that provide the funding for net operating assets.

Exhibit 5.3

Reformulation of Standard Balance Sheet into Net Operating Assets, Financing Obligations, and Common Equity Components

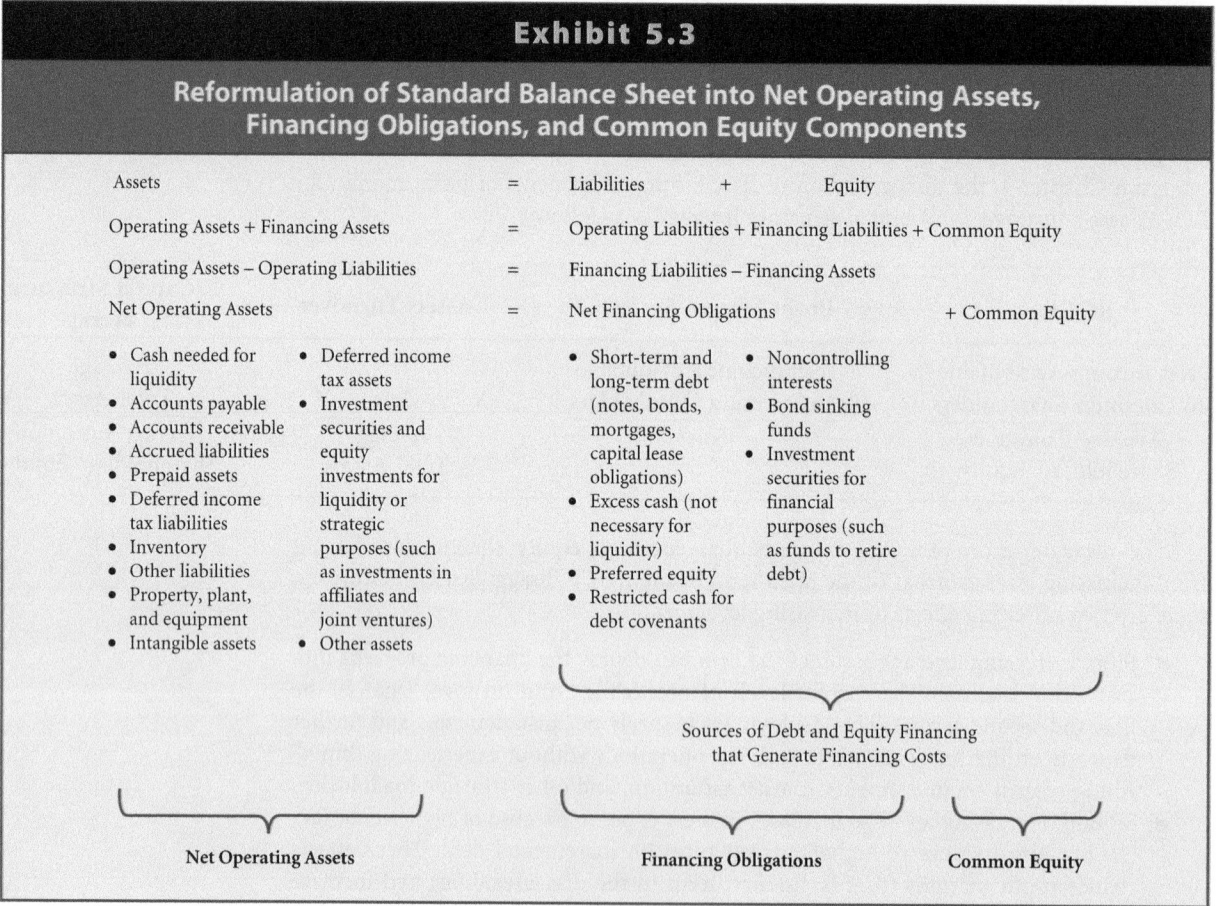

---

[1]This alternative disaggregation of ROCE is sometimes referred to as the "Penman decomposition," following pioneering work by Stephen H. Penman in articulating the operating and financing activities of firms. For a more detailed discussion, see Chapter 11 of Stephen H. Penman, *Financial Statement Analysis and Security Valuation* (New York: McGraw-Hill Irwin, 2004).

We treat noncontrolling interests similar to how we treat preferred equity (that is, a financing obligation) because our focus is from an equity holder's point of view. However, some analysts make the argument that noncontrolling interests should be netted against operating assets. Either approach can be justified so long as consistent treatment is used for noncontrolling interests on the income statement (discussed below).

The reformulated balance sheet equation is as follows:

$$\text{Net Operating Assets} = \text{Net Financing Obligations} + \text{Common Equity}$$

The primary change of this financial statement reformulation is that operating liabilities—both current and noncurrent—are netted against operating assets, leaving net financing obligations as the net of financing liabilities and financing assets and common equity on the right side of the equation. Note that we include noncontrolling interests and preferred equity in financing obligations to be distinct from common equity. The equation still balances, but the totals differ from the standard balance sheet equation.

All firms maintain some financial assets, which include cash, marketable equity securities, and short-term investments. These financial assets must be allocated to operating versus financing categories, depending on their purpose. This allocation requires that you make a judgment call. Some financial assets are necessary elements of the firm's day-to-day operating liquidity (such as the cash and marketable securities necessary to conduct business each day and for liquidity over different seasons and business cycles). In addition, some financial assets may be held for strategic purposes (such as investments in affiliate firms). These types of financial assets are directly related to the operations of the firm, and for most firms they comprise all or the vast majority of financial assets. However, by contrast, some firms will also hold some amounts of financial assets that are specifically intended to be part of the financial structure of the firm, as savings to be used to retire debt. These financial assets might include bond sinking funds, restricted cash (for debt covenants), and/or excess cash and marketable securities (above the amounts needed for liquidity) that the firm intends to use to retire debt. Such *financial* assets should be netted against financing obligations, which yield *net* financing obligations (similar to how operating liabilities are netted against operating assets to yield net operating assets).

A challenging judgment is how to treat cash. All firms need some amount of cash as part of working capital; this amount should be treated as an operating asset. However, some firms hold *excess cash*. There is no magic formula for computing excess cash, and any estimation of excess cash must consider possible reasons a firm holds what appears to be excess cash. For example, in 2004, investors criticized **Microsoft** for holding excess cash. At the end of 2004, cash and short-term investments amounted to over $60 billion, representing almost two-thirds of the firm's $94 billion of total assets. Microsoft subsequently paid a $3-per-share special dividend, totaling $33 billion, and announced a plan to buy back up to $30 billion of outstanding common stock. It was difficult to quantify how much excess cash Microsoft held, but any approximation would have resulted in *negative* net financing obligations for Microsoft (which had no short- or long-term debt). Negative net financing obligations are not a problem as long as the partition of the income statement, discussed below, is done consistently with the allocation of assets and liabilities to operating and financing components.

To be consistent, we also reformulate the income statement. We designate each line item as either an operating or financing component of reported profitability. Once the reformulation of the balance sheet is done, the allocation of line items on the income statement to either operating or financing activities is straightforward. Any item designated as a financing asset or liability should have a corresponding "flow" amount on the income statement, most commonly interest income (for financing assets) or interest expense (for financing liabilities). Also, note that because we designate preferred equity as a financing liability, we treat preferred dividends as a financing cost. Similarly, because we designate noncontrolling interests as a financing liability, we treat income attributable to noncontrolling interests as a financing cost.

The reformulated balance sheets for **Starbucks** for 2012 through 2015 are shown in Exhibit 5.4. Assuming that **Starbucks** holds no financial assets intended for financing

Exhibit 5.4

Reformulated Balance Sheets for Starbucks
(amounts in millions)

	2015	2014	2013	2012
OPERATING ASSETS				
Cash and cash equivalents	$ 1,530.1	$ 1,708.4	$ 2,575.7	$ 1,188.6
Short-term investments	81.3	135.4	658.1	848.4
Accounts receivable, net	719.0	631.0	561.4	485.9
Inventories	1,306.4	1,090.9	1,111.2	1,241.5
Prepaid expenses and other current assets	334.2	285.6	287.7	196.5
Current deferred income taxes, net	381.7	317.4	277.3	238.7
Long-term investments	312.5	318.4	58.3	116.0
Equity and cost investments	352.0	514.9	496.5	459.9
Property, plant, and equipment, net	4,088.3	3,519.0	3,200.5	2,658.9
Noncurrent deferred income taxes, net	828.9	903.3	967.0	97.3
Other long-term assets	415.9	198.9	185.3	144.7
Other intangible assets	520.4	273.5	274.8	143.7
Goodwill	1,575.4	856.2	862.9	399.1
LESS: OPERATING LIABILITIES				
Accounts payable	(684.2)	(533.7)	(491.7)	(398.1)
Accrued liabilities	(1,760.7)	(1,514.4)	(4,053.4)	(1,133.8)
Insurance reserves	(224.8)	(196.1)	(178.5)	(167.7)
Stored value card liability	(983.8)	(794.5)	(653.7)	(510.2)
Other long-term liabilities	(625.3)	(392.2)	(357.7)	(345.3)
Net Operating Assets	$ 8,167.3	$ 7,322.0	$ 5,781.7	$ 5,664.1
FINANCING OBLIGATIONS				
Long-term debt	$ 2,347.5	$ 2,048.3	$ 1,299.4	$ 549.6
Noncontrolling interest	1.8	1.7	2.1	5.5
Financing Obligations	$ 2,349.3	$ 2,050.0	$ 1,301.5	$ 555.1
COMMON EQUITY				
Common stock	$ 1.5	$ 0.7	$ 0.8	$ 0.7
Additional paid-in capital	41.1	39.4	282.1	39.4
Retained earnings	5,974.8	5,206.6	4,130.3	5,046.2
Accumulated other comprehensive income/(loss)	(199.4)	25.3	67.0	22.7
Common Equity	$ 5,818.0	$ 5,272.0	$ 4,480.2	$ 5,109.0
Total Financing Obligations and Common Equity	$8,167.30	$7,322.00	$5,781.70	$5,664.10

purposes (such as a bond sinking fund), we classify all of **Starbucks'** cash, cash equivalents, and short-term investments as operating assets. As a result of this choice, all of **Starbucks'** assets are classified as operating. Current liabilities and other long-term liabilities (not long-term debt) are netted against operating assets, resulting in net operating assets of $8,167.3 million for 2015, compared to $12,446.1 million in total assets reported on the balance sheet.

Exhibit 5.5 presents the reformulated income statements for **Starbucks** for 2012 through 2015. They demonstrate the straightforward identification of costs associated with financing for **Starbucks,** which includes only interest expense and earnings attributable to noncontrolling interests. If **Starbucks** had preferred stock outstanding, we would classify any preferred dividends as financing expense. All other income

Exhibit 5.5

Reformulated Income Statements for Starbucks
(amounts in millions)

	2015	2014	2013
Total net revenues	$19,162.7	$16,447.8	$14,866.8
Cost of sales including occupancy costs	(7,787.5)	(6,858.8)	(6,382.3)
Store operating expenses	(5,411.1)	(4,638.2)	(4,286.1)
Other operating expenses	(522.4)	(457.3)	(431.8)
Depreciation and amortization expenses	(893.9)	(709.6)	(621.4)
General and administrative expenses	(1,196.7)	(991.3)	(937.9)
Litigation charge/(credit)	0.0	20.2	(2,784.1)
Income from equity investees	249.9	268.3	251.4
Gain resulting from acquisition of joint venture	390.6	0.0	0.0
Loss on extinguishment of debt	(61.1)	0.0	0.0
Interest income and other, net	43.0	142.7	123.6
Operating Profit/(Loss) before Taxes	$ 3,973.5	$ 3,223.8	(201.8)
Provision for income taxes at effective tax rate*	(1,164.4)	(1,114.2)	228.9
Net Operating Profit after Taxes (NOPAT)	$ 2,809.1	$ 2,109.6	$ 27.1
FINANCING EXPENSE			
Interest expense × (1 − Effective tax rate)*	(49.8)	(41.9)	(18.3)
Net earnings/(loss) attributable to noncontrolling interests	(1.9)	0.4	(0.5)
Net Financing Expense (After Taxes)	$ (51.7)	$ (41.5)	$ (18.8)
Net Income to Common Shareholders	$ 2,757.4	$ 2,068.1	$ 8.3
Effective Tax Rate	29.3%	34.6%	103.8%

*Because of the unusual 2013 effective tax rate due to the large litigation charge, we use the statutory tax rate of 35% to compute after-tax interest expense and allocate the as-reported income tax expense, less the assumed 35% tax effect for interest expense, to NOPAT.

statement line items are elements of operating profit.[2] Operating profits are reduced by a provision for income taxes, generating the revised measure of profitability—NOPAT (net operating profit after taxes). Finance texts sometimes refer to this construct as EBIAT (earnings before interest after tax), which is the same as NOPAT with consistent treatment of operating and financing activities and proper treatment of taxes (discussed next).[3]

Note how the reformulated income statement allocates part of **Starbucks'** provision for income taxes to NOPAT and part to Net Financing Expense. For 2015, **Starbucks'** total reported tax provision is $1,143.7 million, but Exhibit 5.5 indicates a provision on Operating Profit before Taxes of $1,164.4 million (0.293 × $3,973.5, where the 29.3% effective tax rate is income tax expense of $1,143.7 ÷ earnings before taxes of $3,903.0). The higher provision in Exhibit 5.5 is due to the removal of interest expense from income before income taxes. The tax benefit from interest expense reduces *effective* interest expense from $70.5 million to $49.8 million, as shown in Exhibit 5.5. The difference of $20.7 ($70.5 − $49.8) is the difference between the reported tax provision of $1,143.7 million and the adjusted provision in Exhibit 5.5 of $1,164.4, and reflects the benefits accruing to common shareholders from using debt and tax-deductible interest. Also note the following:

$$\text{NOPAT} - \text{Net Financing Expense (after taxes)} = \text{Net Income Available to Common Shareholders}$$

If we had decided to categorize **Starbucks'** long-term investments as a financial asset, we would have netted it against **Starbucks'** financing obligations in Exhibit 5.4. Accordingly, to be consistent with the treatment on the balance sheet, we would have netted interest revenues (after tax) pertaining to the short-term investments against interest expense (after tax) to compute net financing expense (after tax) in Exhibit 5.5. The reformulated balance sheets would still balance, with different totals, and the reformulated income statements would still reflect the same net income available to common shareholders, but the allocation to operating and financing components would differ. The same argument holds true for the treatment of noncontrolling interests. We treat noncontrolling interests as part of financing obligations (Exhibit 5.3); therefore, we also include the share of net income attributable to noncontrolling interests in net financing expense.

With these new financial statement classifications, Exhibit 5.6 demonstrates the algebraic disaggregation of ROCE into operating and financing components. The result is an alternative disaggregation of ROCE:

$$\text{ROCE} = \text{Operating ROA} + (\text{Leverage} \times \text{Spread})$$

Operating ROA is the rate of return the firm generates on its *net* operating assets (NOPAT/Net Operating Assets). Operating ROA is the rate of return available to *all* sources of financing, including debt, preferred equity, and common equity. It is different

---

[2]Chapter 4 emphasized that judgment could be exercised in the preparation of profitability ratios. The exposition there used adjusted net income based on a subjective assessment of nonrecurring components of reported profitability. For purposes here, we revert to the amounts reported in the 2012 financial statements *without* adjustment for nonrecurring components; doing so would complicate the exposition here. Further, we deliberately use net income available to common shareholders, which requires that preferred dividends and the component of net income attributable to noncontrolling interests be deducted from net income as shown on the income statement in Appendix A.

[3]NOPAT is more common than EBIAT. A simple online search of each term indicates approximately 20 times as many results for NOPAT.

from the definition of ROA discussed in Chapter 4, primarily because the denominator is net operating assets (as opposed to total assets).[4]

In addition to operating ROA, the right side of the new ROCE equation consists of two other factors: leverage and spread. As noted in Exhibit 5.6, leverage is captured by the total financial obligations divided by common equity, similar to the standard debt-to-equity ratio, except that preferred equity and noncontrolling interests are included as financial obligations. Spread is the difference between operating ROA and the net borrowing rate, which is the combined effective rate of interest and preferred dividends. Put simply, the greater the spread between the firm's operating ROA and the net borrowing rate, the more beneficial incremental borrowing will be for the firm's common equity shareholders.

The intuition of the new ROCE equation is that returns to common equity shareholders increase with

- increases in the rate of return on the firm's net operating assets.
- increases in leverage.
- decreases in the after-tax cost of debt and preferred equity.

Note that, like ROA, Operating ROA can be disaggregated into profit margin and net operating assets turnover. Operating ROA is thus the product of profit margin for operating ROA and net operating assets turnover in the same way that ROA is the product of profit margin for ROA and total assets turnover.

Financial flexibility is the ability of a company to use debt financing to strategically take advantage of investment opportunities that arise or to respond to unforeseen expenditures that surface in the normal course of business. For example, a company with extremely high levels of debt, high borrowing rates, low profitability, or insufficient cash flows to satisfy operating or financing obligations has low financial flexibility. In contrast, a company with unused lines of credit, low borrowing rates, high profitability, and high cash flows relative to operating and financing obligations has high financial flexibility.

In addition to ready access to capital, the concept of "spread" is important to fully understanding financial flexibility. Spread reflects the difference between the rate of return on the operating assets (for example, 15%) and the borrowing rate on financial obligations (for example, 8%). Larger spread means the company can obtain capital at a lower borrowing rate and deploy that capital into operating assets that generate a higher rate of return that covers the borrowing costs; any excess is retained by the common equity investors.

Incremental increases in leverage are likely associated with increased borrowing costs, in terms of both nominal borrowing costs and marginally higher borrowing rates. As an applied example, second mortgages on homes generally carry higher interest rates

---

[4]An easy way to understand how the classification of financial statement amounts can vary while still resulting in components that combine mathematically to ROCE is to consider reformulated financial statements where all assets and all liabilities are categorized as operating. Thus, short- and long-term debt, preferred stock (if any), and minority interest are netted against assets to compute net operating assets. By definition, this equals common equity. Then, to be consistent with this treatment in reformulating the income statement, any interest expense, preferred dividends, and noncontrolling interests would be categorized as operating items. The result would be net income available to common shareholders. The alternative disaggregation of ROCE into Operating ROA + (Leverage × Spread) would reduce to ROCE = Operating ROA, where Operating ROA = Net Income Available to Common/Common Equity. This would not accomplish much, but the point of this exercise is to emphasize the mathematical equivalence of this ROCE decomposition regardless of how assets or liabilities are reformulated.

Exhibit 5.6

Algebra Demonstrating the Disaggregation of Return on Common Equity (ROCE)

$$\text{ROCE} = \frac{\text{Net Income Available to Common Shareholders}}{\text{Common Equity}}$$

$$= \frac{\text{NOPAT} - \text{Net Financing Expense (after tax)}}{\text{Common Equity}}$$

$$= \left(\frac{\text{NOPAT}}{\text{Net Operating Assets}} \times \frac{\text{Net Operating Assets}}{\text{Common Equity}}\right) - \left(\frac{\text{Net Financing Expense (after tax)}}{\text{Financing Obligations}} \times \frac{\text{Financing Obligations}}{\text{Common Equity}}\right)$$

$$= \left(\frac{\text{NOPAT}}{\text{Net Operating Assets}} \times \frac{\text{Common Equity} + \text{Financing Obligations}}{\text{Common Equity}}\right) - \left(\frac{\text{Net Financing Expense (after tax)}}{\text{Financing Obligations}} \times \frac{\text{Financing Obligations}}{\text{Common Equity}}\right)$$

$$= \frac{\text{NOPAT}}{\text{Net Operating Assets}} \times \left(1 + \frac{\text{Financing Obligations}}{\text{Common Equity}}\right) - \left(\frac{\text{Net Financing Expense (after tax)}}{\text{Financing Obligations}} \times \frac{\text{Financing Obligations}}{\text{Common Equity}}\right)$$

$$= \text{Operating ROA} \times \left(1 + \frac{\text{Financing Obligations}}{\text{Common Equity}}\right) - \left(\frac{\text{Net Financing Expense (after tax)}}{\text{Financing Obligations}} \times \frac{\text{Financing Obligations}}{\text{Common Equity}}\right)$$

$$= \text{Operating ROA} + \left(\text{Operating ROA} \times \frac{\text{Financing Obligations}}{\text{Common Equity}}\right) - \left(\frac{\text{Net Financing Expense (after tax)}}{\text{Financing Obligations}} \times \frac{\text{Financing Obligations}}{\text{Common Equity}}\right)$$

$$= \text{Operating ROA} + \frac{\text{Financing Obligations}}{\text{Common Equity}} \times \left(\text{Operating ROA} - \frac{\text{Net Financing Expense (after tax)}}{\text{Financing Obligations}}\right)$$

$$= \text{Operating ROA} + [\text{Leverage} \times (\text{Operating ROA} - \text{Net Borrowing Rate})]$$

$$= \text{Operating ROA} + \text{Leverage} \times \text{Spread}$$

than first mortgages. Similarly, increases in debt or preferred equity incrementally increase the net borrowing rate, which decreases spread, lowering the incremental benefits of increasing leverage.

Nevertheless, even though a firm might have a large spread, there may be strategic issues that prevent the firm from simply deploying more capital and achieving historical returns on investment. For example, a firm might have saturated a market, and opening additional facilities or locations might only cannibalize profits from existing locations. However, firms that generate very high operating ROA relative to the cost of borrowing can likely increase the level of borrowings—with either debt or preferred equity—and thus are characterized as having greater financial flexibility. Financial flexibility also is associated with lower short-term and long-term solvency risk, discussed in the next two sections.

To illustrate the disaggregation of ROCE into operating ROA, leverage, and spread, Exhibit 5.7 uses the amounts from the reformulated financial statements in Exhibits 5.4 and 5.5 to compute ROCE. For comparison, Exhibit 5.7 presents the standard and alternative decompositions of ROCE from Chapter 4. Of course, both computations produce the same ROCE.

The alternative ROCE decomposition reveals that **Starbucks** generates a significant spread between operating ROA and the net borrowing rate. For 2015 and 2014, Operating ROA is 36.3% and 32.2%, respectively; operating ROA for 2013 is noncomparable because it includes the $2,784.1 million litigation charge. Nevertheless, based on the more recent data from 2015 and 2014, **Starbucks** clearly utilizes operating assets very profitably. The net borrowing rates were 2.4% in 2015, 2.5% in 2014, and 2.0% in 2013.

Therefore, **Starbucks**' spread between operating ROA and the net borrowing rate was a remarkable 33.9% in 2015 (36.3% operating ROA − 2.4% net borrowing rate), 12.6% in 2014, and 15.4% in 2013. An interpretation of **Starbucks**' spread in 2015 is that for every dollar **Starbucks** currently borrows and deploys in operating assets, it generates 36.3¢ in operating profit after tax, whereas the borrowing triggers only 2.4¢ in net borrowing costs (after tax), resulting in 33.9¢ accruing directly to common equity shareholders. ***This is the essence of the strategic use of leverage by equity investors: borrowing capital at a low cost to generate returns that more than offset the cost of borrowing***.

The extremely large spread generated by **Starbucks** indicates that the company enjoys a high level of financial flexibility. Creditors are comfortable lending money to companies that generate rates of returns on assets that far exceed debt service costs. The trends shown in Exhibit 5.7 suggest that **Starbucks** is gradually increasing its leverage. **Starbucks**' leverage was only 0.19 in 2013, but has climbed to 0.40 in 2015.

The alternative ROCE decomposition reveals that **Starbucks**' ROCE in 2015 of 49.7% is the result of an operating ROA of 36.3% plus leverage of 0.40 times the spread of 33.9% [49.7% = 36.3% + (0.40 × 33.9%)]. In comparison to 2014, this decomposition reveals that **Starbucks**' 2015 operating ROA has increased, and combined with the moderate increase in leverage and stable borrowing rate, ROCE has risen.

Both approaches to the decomposition of ROCE indicate similar increases in margins. However, the traditional decomposition indicates fluctuating turnover and leverage, whereas the alternative decomposition indicates declining turnover and increasing leverage from 2013 to 2015. The alternative ROCE decomposition provides additional insights about the nature of the change in leverage that are masked in the traditional ROCE decomposition at the top of Exhibit 5.7. For the alternative ROCE decomposition in the bottom part of Exhibit 5.7, the increase in leverage is more dramatic, especially between 2013 and 2014 when it rose 79% (0.34/0.19); under the standard ROE

Exhibit 5.7

Computations of ROCE Decomposition Using Standard and Alternative Approaches for Starbucks 2013–2015 (reported amounts, dollar amounts in millions)

Standard ROCE Decomposition		Calculation for 2015	2015	2014	2013
Profit Margin for ROCE	Net Income to Common Equity/Sales	$2,757.4/$19,162.7	14.4%	12.6%	0.06%
× Assets Turnover	Sales/Average Total Assets	$19,162.7/[0.5($12,446.1 + $10,752.9)]	1.65	1.48	1.51
× Capital Structure Leverage	Average Total Assets/(Average Common Equity–Noncontrolling Interests)	[0.5($12,446.1 + $10,752.9)]/[0.5($5,818.0 + $5,272.0)]	2.09	2.28	2.06
= ROCE	Net Income to Common/Average Common Equity	$2,757.4/[0.5($5,818.0 + $5,272.0)]	49.7%	42.4%	0.2%

Alternative ROCE Decomposition			2015	2014	2013
Net Margin for Operating ROA	NOPAT/Sales	$2,809.1/$19,162.7	14.7%	12.8%	0.2%
× Net Operating Assets Turnover	Sales/Average Net Operating Assets	$19,162.7/[0.5($8,167.3 + $7,322.0)]	2.47	2.51	2.60
= Operating ROA	NOPAT/Average Net Operating Assets	$2,809.1/[0.5($8,167.3 + $7,322.0)]	36.3%	32.2%	0.5%
+ Leverage	Average Financing Obligations/Average Common Equity	[0.5($2,349.3 + $2,050.0)]/[0.5($5,818.0 + $5,272.0)]	0.40	0.34	0.19
× Spread	Operating ROA – Net Borrowing Rate [Net Financing Expense (after tax)/Average Financing Obligations]	36.3% – 2.4%	33.9%	29.7%	(1.5%)
= ROCE	Operating ROA + (Leverage × Spread)	36.3% + (0.40 × 33.9%)	49.7%	42.4%	0.2%
Net Borrowing Rate	Net Financing Expense (after tax)/Average Financing Obligations	$51.7/[0.5($2,349.3 + $2,050.0)]	2.4%	2.5%	2.0%

decomposition, capital structure leverage only increased 11% between 2013 and 2014 $(2.28/2.06)$.[5] The difference is that in our alternative ROCE decomposition, we obtain additional information by focusing specifically on interest-bearing liabilities as leverage, rather than including non-interest-bearing liabilities, and quantifying spread as a gauge of financial flexibility.

■ Financial flexibility is the ability of a firm to strategically use debt financing to increase returns to investments by common shareholders.

■ An alternative decomposition of ROCE requires the reformulation of financial statements into operating and financing components, which highlight the benefits available to common shareholders through strategic use of leverage.

■ Firms with large spreads—return on net operating assets minus the net after-tax borrowing rate—stand to benefit from leverage. Starbucks, for example, generates large returns on net operating assets and has limited debt, so it has a large degree of financial flexibility.

■ The analysis of financial flexibility provides a natural link between profitability analysis discussed in the previous chapter and the analysis of numerous risks, discussed next.

Quick Check

Analyzing Short-Term Liquidity Risk

LO 5-3

Apply analytical tools to assess working capital management and *short-term liquidity risk.*

Short-term liquidity is the firm's ability to satisfy near-term payment obligations to suppliers, employees, and creditors for short-term borrowings, the current portion of long-term debt, and other short-term liabilities. Thus, the analysis of short-term liquidity risk requires an understanding of the *operating cycle* of a firm. Consider a typical manufacturing firm that acquires raw materials on account, promising to pay suppliers within 30 to 60 days. The firm then combines these raw materials with labor and other inputs to produce a product. It pays for some of these costs at the time of incurrence and delays payment of other costs. At some point, the firm sells the product to a customer, probably on account. It subsequently collects the customer's account and pays suppliers and others for purchases on its own account.

If a firm (1) can delay all cash outflows to suppliers, employees, and others until it receives cash from customers and (2) receives more cash than it must disburse, the firm will not likely encounter short-term liquidity problems. Most firms, however, cannot time their cash inflows and outflows precisely, especially firms in the start-up or growth phase. Employees may require weekly or semimonthly payments, whereas customers may delay payments for 30 days or more.

Firms may experience rapid growth and need to produce more units of product than they sell during a period. Even if perfectly timed, the cash outflows to support the higher level of production in this period can exceed inflows of cash from customers due to the lower level of sales during prior periods. Firms that operate at a net loss for a period often find that the completion of the operating cycle results in a net cash outflow instead of a net cash inflow. As an extreme example, consider a single malt Scotch whisky distillery that incurs significant cash outflows for grains and other ingredients,

---

[5]Note 1, "Summary of Significant Accounting Policies," indicates **Starbucks** occasionally engages in lease financing arrangements, where financing obligations are included within accrued liabilities and other long-term liabilities. Because these amounts are likely immaterial, we do not attempt to separately add them as financing obligations or the amortization of interest components.

distills the whisky, and then ages it in wooden barrels for 10 to 18 years before finally generating cash inflows from sales to customers.

To satisfy short-term financial needs, firms often use long-term leverage. However, long-term leverage can trigger short-term liquidity problems. For example, a firm may assume a relatively high percentage of long-term debt in its capital structure that typically requires periodic interest payments and may also require repayments of principal. For some firms, especially financial, real estate, and energy firms, interest expense is among the largest single costs. The operating cycle must generate sufficient cash not only to supply operating working capital needs, but also to service debt.

Financially healthy firms frequently bridge temporary cash flow gaps in their operating cycles with short-term borrowing. Such firms issue *commercial paper* or obtain three- to six-month *bank loans*. Most firms maintain lines of credit with their banks to obtain cash quickly for working capital needs. Notes to financial statement usually disclose parameters for any lines of credit and the level of borrowing used on that line during the year, as well as any financial covenant restrictions imposed by the line of credit agreements. **Starbucks**, for example, discloses the following in Note 9, "Debt":

> *Our $750 million unsecured, revolving credit facility with various banks, of which $150 million may be used for issuances of letters of credit, is available for working capital, capital expenditures and other corporate purposes, including acquisitions and share repurchases. During the second quarter of fiscal 2015, we extended the duration of our credit facility, which is now set to mature on January 21, 2020, and amended certain facility fees and borrowing rates. Starbucks has the option, subject to negotiation and agreement with the related banks, to increase the maximum commitment amount by an additional $750 million.*

> *Under our commercial paper program, we may issue unsecured commercial paper notes up to a maximum aggregate amount outstanding at any time of $1 billion, with individual maturities that may vary, but not exceed 397 days from the date of issue. Amounts outstanding under the commercial paper program are required to be backstopped by available commitments under our credit facility discussed above. As of September 27, 2015, availability under our commercial paper program was approximately $750 million (which represents the full committed credit facility amount, as the amount of outstanding letters of credit was not material as of September 27, 2015).*

It is important to note available but untapped borrowing capacity when assessing the overall financial risk profile of a firm. These amounts represent potential increases in leverage and increased financial risk, but at the same time, they provide the firm with beneficial financial flexibility (as discussed in the previous section).

A simple way to quickly grasp short-term liquidity issues is to examine common-size balance sheets, as discussed in Chapter 1. Common-size balance sheets provide a basic quantification of the relative amounts invested in various types of assets versus liabilities. For example, Exhibit 1.15 shows that in 2015 **Starbucks'** current assets represent 31.9% of total assets, but total assets are only financed 29.4% with current liabilities. This imbalance suggests lower short-term liquidity risk. We discuss six financial statement ratios for assessing short-term liquidity risk:

1. Current ratio
2. Quick ratio

3. Operating cash flow to current liabilities ratio
4. Accounts receivable turnover
5. Inventory turnover
6. Accounts payable turnover

Current Ratio

The current ratio equals current assets divided by current liabilities. It indicates the amount of cash available at the balance sheet date plus the amount of other current assets the firm expects to convert into cash within one year of the balance sheet date (from collection of receivables, sale of inventory, and sale or maturity of short-term investment securities) relative to obligations coming due during the period. Large current ratios indicate substantial amounts of current assets are available to repay obligations coming due within the next year. Small ratios, on the other hand, indicate that current assets may not be sufficient to repay short-term obligations.

The current ratio for **Starbucks** at the end of 2015 is as follows:

$$\text{Current Ratio} = \frac{\text{Current Assets}}{\text{Current Liabilities}}$$

$$1.19 = \frac{\$4,352.7}{\$3,653.5}$$

The current ratio for **Starbucks** was 1.37 at the end of 2014. Thus, **Starbucks** experienced a decreasing current ratio during 2015, consistent with an increase in current liabilities relative to its current assets. We can gain further understanding of this ratio by examining individual current assets and liabilities. Note that **Starbucks'** second largest current liability is "stored value card liability" ($983.8 million). This liability represents deferred revenue from customer prepayments on loyalty cards. Although these represent liabilities to provide customers with future coffee or other products, **Starbucks** will settle such liabilities with coffee (or other products), rather than with cash. Excluding this liability from current liabilities yields a current ratio of 1.63 in 2015 and 1.86 in 2014.

Banks, suppliers, and others that extend short-term credit to a firm generally prefer a current ratio in excess of 1.0, but current ratios should not be evaluated in isolation and should be assessed in the context of other factors affecting a firm's liquidity. Banks typically evaluate the appropriate level of a firm's current ratio based on the length of the firm's operating cycle, the expected cash flows from operations, the extent to which the firm has noncurrent assets that could be used for liquidity if necessary, the extent to which the firm's current liabilities do not require cash outflows (such as liabilities for deferred revenues), and similar factors.

Prior to the 1980s, the average current ratios for most industries exceeded 2.0. As interest rates increased in the early 1980s, firms attempted to stretch accounts payable, effectively using suppliers to finance a greater portion of their working capital needs (that is, receivables and inventories). Also, firms increasingly instituted just-in-time inventory systems that reduced the amount of raw materials and finished goods inventories. As a consequence, current ratios hovering around 1.0, or even just below 1.0, are now common. Although this decline suggests an increase in short-term liquidity risk, most investors view this level of risk as tolerable.

Wide variation exists in current ratios across firms and industries, as evident in the descriptive statistics on current ratios in Appendix D. Therefore, you should consider several additional interpretive issues when evaluating the current ratio:

- Be aware that an increase of equal amounts in current assets and current liabilities (for example, purchasing inventory on account) results in a decrease in the current ratio when the ratio is greater than 1.0 before the transaction but an increase in the current ratio when it is less than 1.0 before the transaction. The opposite effects occur when current assets and current liabilities decrease by equal amounts.
- For certain firms, a high or increasing current ratio is not desirable and may accompany poor business conditions, whereas a low or decreasing ratio may be a sign of financial health, and may accompany profitable operations. For example, during a recession, firms may encounter difficulties in selling inventories and collecting receivables, causing the current ratio to increase to higher levels due to the growth in receivables and inventory. In a boom period, the reverse can occur.
- A firm with a very strong ability to generate large and stable amounts of cash flows from operations may function very effectively with a low current ratio, whereas a firm with slow or volatile cash flows from operations may need to maintain a higher current ratio.
- The current ratio is susceptible to window dressing; that is, management can take deliberate steps prior to the balance sheet date to produce a better current ratio than is the normal or average ratio for the period. For example, toward the end of the period, a firm may accelerate purchases of inventory on account (if the current ratio is less than 1.0) or delay such purchases (if the current ratio is greater than 1.0) in an effort to improve the current ratio. Alternatively, a firm may sell off fixed assets, and the cash inflow increases current assets relative to current liabilities.

Despite these interpretive issues with the current ratio, you will find widespread use of the current ratio as a measure of short-term liquidity risk. Empirical studies (discussed later in this chapter) of bond default, bankruptcy, and other conditions of financial distress have found that the current ratio has strong predictive power for costly financial outcomes.

Quick Ratio

A variation of the current ratio is the quick ratio, also called the acid-test ratio, computed by including in the numerator only those current assets the firm could convert *quickly* into cash, often interpreted as within 90 days. The numerator customarily includes cash, marketable securities, other short-term investments, and receivables. However, you should study the facts in each case before deciding whether to include receivables and exclude inventories. Some businesses can convert their inventory into cash more quickly (for example, a firm that carries a large amount of readily salable commodities in inventory) relative to other businesses (for example, an equipment manufacturer such as **John Deere**).

Assuming we include accounts receivable but exclude inventories, **Starbucks'** quick ratio at the end of 2015 is as follows:

$$\text{Quick Ratio} = \frac{\text{Cash and Cash Equivalents} + \text{Short-Term Investments} + \text{Accounts Receivable}}{\text{Current Liabilities}}$$

$$0.64 = \frac{\$1,530.1 + \$81.3 + \$719.0}{\$3,653.5}$$

The quick ratio for **Starbucks** was 0.81 at the end of 2014. The trends in the quick ratio and the current ratio correlate highly. However, the decrease in the quick ratio is more pronounced. In 2015, current assets increased 4.4%, whereas current liabilities increased 20.2%. By contrast, the sum of cash, short-term investments, and accounts receivable decreased 5.8% in 2015, leading to the more pronounced decrease in the quick ratio. As we did for the current ratio, if we exclude amounts for stored value card liability from current liabilities, **Starbucks'** quick ratio is 0.87 for 2015 and 1.10 for 2014.

The quick ratio requires a similar contextual interpretation as the current ratio. That is, you should interpret quick ratios in the context of the many other factors that affect the firm's liquidity, including the firm's ability to generate cash flows from operations. Appendix D again reveals significant variation in quick ratios across firms and industries.

Operating Cash Flow to Current Liabilities Ratio

In addition to balance sheet-based metrics like the current or quick ratio, you also can analyze indicators of a firm's ability to generate cash in the near term, such as ratios based on cash flow from operations. An intuitive measure is the ratio of cash flow from operations to current liabilities, which captures cash generated over a period relative to the level of liabilities due within one year. Because the numerator of this ratio uses amounts for a period of time, the denominator typically uses an average of current liabilities for the same period. This ratio for **Starbucks** for 2015 is as follows:

$$\text{Operating Cash Flow to Current Liabilities Ratio} = \frac{\text{Cash Flow from Operations}}{\text{Average Current Liabilities}}$$

$$1.12 = \frac{\$3,749.1}{0.5(\$3,653.5 + \$3,038.7)}$$

The ratio was 0.14 for 2014 and 0.77 for 2013. A ratio of 0.40 or more is common for a typical healthy manufacturing or retailing firm. The low ratio in 2014 reflects the significant negative cash outflow for a litigation charge. Nevertheless, the 2015 ratio indicates **Starbucks** generates very high cash flows relative to current liabilities, well above 0.40. Thus, this measure suggests **Starbucks** has very low short-term liquidity risk in terms of operating cash flows relative to current liabilities.

Working Capital Turnover Ratios

Our final three measures capture the rate of activity in working capital accounts to calibrate the cash-generating ability of operations and the short-term liquidity risk of a firm:

$$\text{Accounts Receivable Turnover} = \frac{\text{Sales}}{\text{Average Accounts Receivable}}$$

$$\text{Inventory Turnover} = \frac{\text{Cost of Goods Sold}}{\text{Average Inventories}}$$

$$\text{Accounts Payable Turnover} = \frac{\text{Purchases}}{\text{Average Accounts Payable}}$$

Chapter 4 discussed the accounts receivable and inventory turnovers, which are components of *total* assets turnover, as measures of profitability. These same ratios are used here as measures of the speed with which firms sell inventories and turn accounts receivable into cash. The accounts payable turnover indicates the speed at which a manufacturing or retailing firm pays for purchases of raw materials and inventories on account. Firms typically do not disclose the amount of inventory purchases, but this amount can be easily computed. Recall that the inventory account primarily reflects the following:

$$\text{Ending Inventory} = \text{Beginning Inventory} + \text{Purchases} - \text{Cost of Goods Sold}$$

Thus, you can approximate purchases as follows:[6]

$$\text{Purchases} = \text{Cost of Goods Sold} + \text{Ending Inventory} - \text{Beginning Inventory}$$

Note that Purchases is used to generically capture retailing firms' purchase of inventory or manufacturing firms' purchase of raw materials and production costs.

These turnover ratios are often stated in terms of the average number of days each balance sheet item (that is, receivables, inventories, and accounts payable) is outstanding. To do so, divide 365 days by each turnover metric.[7] Mathematically equivalent, but more intuitive, you can divide the balance sheet amount by the appropriate flow variable converted to a daily average. For example, the days accounts receivable outstanding can be calculated equivalently as 365/Accounts Receivable Turnover or, more intuitively, as Average Accounts Receivable/Daily Sales, where Daily Sales = Sales/365.

Exhibit 5.8 presents the calculation of these three turnover ratios and the related number of days for **Starbucks** for 2015. Recall a finer point demonstrated in Chapter 4 that we should only use credit sales and exclude cash sales for the accounts receivable turnover. However, it is often not possible to partition sales into credit and cash sales. For firms like **Starbucks** with significant cash retail sales, the A/R turnover ratio will be higher than average without adjusting for the mix of sales.

Exhibit 5.8

Working Capital Activity Ratios for Starbucks for 2015
(dollar amounts in millions)

Accounts Receivable Turnover

$$\frac{\$19,162.7}{0.5(\$719.0 + \$631.0)} = 28.4 \text{ times per year}$$

Days Accounts Receivable Outstanding

$$\frac{365}{28.4} = 12.9 \text{ days}$$

Inventory Turnover

$$\frac{\$7,787.5}{0.5(\$1,306.4 + \$1,090.9)} = 6.5 \text{ times per year}$$

Days Inventory Held

$$\frac{365}{6.5} = 56.2 \text{ days}$$

Accounts Payable Turnover

$$\frac{\$8,003.0}{0.5(\$684.2 + \$533.7)} = 13.1 \text{ times per year}$$

Days Accounts Payable Outstanding

$$\frac{365}{13.1} = 27.8 \text{ days}$$

---

[6]The accounts payable turnover ratio will be skewed upward if cost of goods sold includes a high proportion of costs (such as depreciation and labor) that do not flow through accounts payable. This bias is more of a concern for (i) manufacturing firms relative to retailing firms and (ii) cross-sectional comparisons relative to time-series analyses.

[7]To be technically correct, you should use 366 days in leap years and 371 days in a 53-week year for firms that use 52/53-week years.

The number of days firms hold inventory until sale plus the number of days firms hold accounts receivable until collection indicates the total number of days from the production or purchase of inventory until collection of cash from the sale of inventory to customers. This combined number of days indicates the length of time for which the firm must obtain financing for its primary working capital assets. The number of days accounts payable are outstanding indicates the working capital financing the firm obtained from suppliers.

The difference between the total number of days for which the firm requires financing for its working capital and the number of days for which it obtains financing from suppliers indicates the additional days for which it must obtain financing. This difference is known as the *cash-to-cash cycle* (also known as the cash operating cycle), and it quantifies the length of time between cash outlays that ultimately result in cash collections. We depict these relations here.

Days of Working Capital Financing Required:

Days Inventory Held	Days Accounts Receivable Outstanding

Days of Working Capital Financing Provided:

Days Account Payable Outstanding	Days of Working Capital Financing Needed from Other Sources

In general, the shorter the number of days of needed financing, the larger the cash flow from operations to average current liabilities ratio. A small number of net days indicates relatively little need to finance accounts receivable and inventories (that is, the firm sells inventory quickly and receives cash from customers soon after sale) or aggressive use of credit from suppliers to finance these current assets (that is, the firm delays paying cash to suppliers). Both scenarios enhance cash flow from operations in the numerator of this ratio. Furthermore, firms with a shorter number of days of financing required from other sources are less dependent on short-term borrowing from banks and other financial institutions. Such borrowing increases current liabilities in the denominator of the operating cash flow to current liabilities ratio, thereby lowering this ratio.

Exhibit 5.9 shows the net number of days of financing needed from other sources for **Starbucks** for 2013, 2014, and 2015. **Starbucks'** days inventory is largest of the

Exhibit 5.9

Net Number of Days of Working Capital Financing Needed from Other Sources for Starbucks

Year	Days Accounts Receivable Outstanding	+	Days Inventory Held	−	Days Accounts Payable Outstanding	=	Days Other Financing Required
2013	12.9		67.3		(26.0)		54.2
2014	13.2		58.6		(27.4)		44.5
2015	12.9		56.2		(27.8)		41.3

Exhibit 5.10

Net Number of Days of Working Capital Financing Needed from Other Sources for Amazon.com, Inc., 2013–2014 (amounts in millions)

	2015	2014	2013
Sales	$107,006	$88,988	$74,452
Cost of goods sold	$ 71,651	$62,752	$54,181
Purchases	$ 73,595	$63,640	$55,561
Accounts receivable	$ 6,423	$ 5,612	$ 4,767
Inventory	$ 10,243	$ 8,299	$ 7,411
Accounts payable	$ 20,397	$16,459	$15,133
Days receivables outstanding	21	21	21
Days inventory held	47	46	45
Days accounts payable outstanding	(101)	(94)	(99)
Days other financing required	(33)	(27)	(33)

three, indicating that **Starbucks** requires significant capital to stock inventory. The days accounts payable exceeds that for accounts receivable, consistent with **Starbucks** obtaining financing from suppliers more than sufficient to cover days in accounts receivable but not sufficient for days in inventory. Overall, **Starbucks'** days needed from other sources of financing has declined steadily from 54.2 in 2013 to 41.3 in 2015, largely due to declining days sales held in inventory and slight increases in the use of suppliers for accounts payable financing.

As an example of a company with extremely favorable working capital requirements, Exhibit 5.10 shows the working capital financing investments for **Amazon.com, Inc.**, a well-known large online retailer of books, electronic media, and numerous other products. Due to low levels of accounts receivable and inventory and extended accounts payable, Amazon has a *negative* value for days of other financing required. Not surprisingly, Amazon does not require any short-term debt financing. The only other liabilities Amazon has at the end of 2012 are (1) accrued expenses of $5,684 million, (2) long-term debt of $3,084 million, and (3) other long-term liabilities of $2,277 million (relative to total assets of $32,555 million). At the other extreme, a jeweler like **Tiffany & Co.** has a very long cash operating cycle with over 500 days of inventory.

Quick Check

- Short-term liquidity risk ratios are helpful in assessing a firm's near-term ability to meet cash flow requirements.
- Analysis of profitability and cash flow levels is an integral part of understanding short-term liquidity risk.

- Profitable firms that generate significant cash flows are characterized as having financial flexibility, and such firms often have credit agreements with banks that further enhance financial flexibility.

Analyzing Long-Term Solvency Risk

Financial leverage enhances ROCE when firms borrow funds and invest those funds in assets that generate a higher return than the after-tax cost of borrowing. We saw this in our discussion of financial flexibility. Common shareholders benefit from increasing proportions of debt in the capital structure as long as the firm maintains ROA in excess of the after-tax cost of the debt. However, increasing the proportion of debt in the capital structure increases the risk that the firm cannot pay interest and repay the principal on the amount borrowed. As credit and bankruptcy risks increase, the incremental cost of borrowing is also likely to increase. The analysis of long-term solvency risk highlights a firm's ability to make interest and principal payments on long-term debt and similar obligations as they come due.

A firm's ability to generate earnings over a period of years is the best indicator for assessing long-term solvency risk. Profitable firms generate sufficient cash from operations, but also are able to obtain needed cash from creditors or equity investors. Therefore, the measures of profitability discussed in Chapter 4 in the context of analyzing ROA and ROCE are also useful in assessing long-term solvency risk. Additionally, analysis of long-term solvency risk must begin with an assessment of the level of and trends in financial flexibility and with an analysis of short-term liquidity risk, already discussed. However, our most direct analysis in examining long-term solvency risk arises from the following measures:

1. Debt ratios
2. Interest coverage ratios
3. Operating cash flow to total liabilities ratio

Debt Ratios

Debt ratios measure the relative amount of liabilities, particularly long-term debt, in a firm's capital structure. The higher a debt ratio, the greater is long-term solvency risk. The capital structure leverage ratio discussed in Chapter 4, one of the disaggregated components of ROCE, is one example of a debt ratio. Similarly, the assessment of financial flexibility discussed earlier in the chapter provides another computation of leverage. Several additional variations of debt ratios exist, including the following four common measures:

$$\text{Liabilities to Assets Ratio} = \frac{\text{Total Liabilities}}{\text{Total Assets}}$$

$$\text{Liabilities to Shareholders' Equity Ratio} = \frac{\text{Total Liabilities}}{\text{Total Shareholders' Equity}}$$

$$\text{Long-Term Debt to Long-Term Capital Ratio} = \frac{\text{Long-Term Debt}}{\text{Long-Term Debt} + \text{Total Shareholders' Equity}}$$

$$\text{Long-Term Debt to Shareholders' Equity Ratio} = \frac{\text{Long-Term Debt}}{\text{Total Shareholders' Equity}}$$

The debt ratios for **Starbucks** at the end of 2015 are as follows:

$$\text{Liabilities to Assets Ratio} = \frac{\$6,626.3}{\$12,446.1} = 0.53$$

$$\text{Liabilities to Shareholders' Equity Ratio} = \frac{\$6,626.3}{\$5,818.0} = 1.14$$

$$\text{Long-Term Debt to Long-Term Capital Ratio} = \frac{\$2,347.5}{\$2,347.5 + \$5,818.0} = 0.29$$

$$\text{Long-Term Debt to Shareholders' Equity Ratio} = \frac{\$2,347.5}{\$5,818.0} = 0.40$$

Exhibit 5.11 shows the debt ratios for **Starbucks** at the end of 2013, 2014, and 2015. In general, the median firm typically has a liabilities to equity ratio of approximately 1, and hence a liabilities to assets ratio of approximately 0.5. **Starbucks'** debt ratios are somewhat higher than these, which is to be expected given **Starbucks'** size, profitability, and strong capacity for strategic debt financing. The debt ratios involving total liabilities exhibit a slight decrease from 2013 to the end of 2015.

However, long-term debt ratios indicate a slightly increasing trend. This is consistent with the insights generated in the previous discussion of **Starbucks'** increasing cash flows relative to short-term working capital requirements. Increasing cash flows permit an increasing use of low-cost debt to generate high returns on assets deployed.

Note the high correlations between changes in the two debt ratios involving total liabilities over time and in the two long-term debt ratios over time. Generally, you can select one of these ratios without losing much information based on an armada of similar ratios. Because different debt ratios exist, you should use caution when reading financial periodicals and discussing debt ratios with others because variations in definitions are pervasive. For example, a liabilities to shareholders' equity ratio greater than 1.0 (that is, more liabilities than shareholders' equity) is not unusual, but a liabilities to assets ratio or a long-term debt to long-term capital ratio greater than 1.0 is highly unusual (because it requires a negative shareholders' equity).

In addition to computing debt ratios, you may gather information from the financial statement note on long-term debt. The note includes information on the types of debt a firm has issued, as well as their interest rates and maturity dates. In some situations, it may be necessary to access public filings of debt contracts to monitor the firm's

Exhibit 5.11

Debt Ratios for Starbucks at the End of 2013–2015

	2015	2014	2013
Liabilities to assets ratio	0.53	0.51	0.61
Liabilities to shareholders' equity ratio	1.14	1.04	1.57
Long-term debt to long-term capital ratio	0.29	0.28	0.22
Long-term debt to shareholders' equity ratio	0.40	0.39	0.29

closeness to debt covenants. **Starbucks'** Note 9, "Debt," provides information about the schedule of long-term debt obligations as well as significant issuances. During 2015, **Starbucks** issued $850 million of senior notes payable (with interest rates of 2.7% and 4.3%) and redeemed $550 million of higher cost senior notes payable (with an interest rate of 6.25%; this debt redemption triggered the $61.1 million loss on early extinguishment of debt). **Starbucks** does not say so, but the company is clearly taking advantage of a lower interest rate environment by refinancing and increasing long-term borrowings at favorable interest rates.

To appear less risky and to lower their cost of financing or perhaps to avoid violating debt covenants in existing borrowing arrangements, some firms attempt to structure financing in a manner that keeps debt off the balance sheet. You should recognize the possibility of such actions when interpreting debt ratios and perhaps adjust the reported amounts, as illustrated for leases in Chapter 7 and several other arrangements in Chapter 6.

Interest Coverage Ratios

Interest coverage ratios indicate the number of times a firm's income or cash flows could cover interest charges. For example, one common approach to the interest coverage ratio divides net income before interest expense and income taxes by interest expense. This income-based interest coverage ratio for **Starbucks**, using the amounts reported for net income and income tax expense for 2015, is as follows:

$$\text{Interest Coverage Ratio (Net Income Basis)} = \frac{\begin{array}{c}\text{Net Income} + \text{Interest Expense} + \text{Income Tax Expense} \\ + \text{Net Income Attributable to Noncontrolling Interests}\end{array}}{\text{Interest Expense}}$$

$$56.4 = \frac{\$2,757.4 + \$70.5 + \$1,143.7 + \$1.9}{\$70.5}$$

The interest coverage ratio for **Starbucks** was 50.3 in 2014. Both are extremely high relative to average firms. Analysts typically view coverage ratios of less than 2.0 as indicators of solvency risk. Clearly, **Starbucks** exhibits very low long-term solvency risk, even with the increase in leverage over the period 2013 through 2015.

Sometimes firms are able to capitalize interest as part of the cost basis of tangible assets. You should be aware of significant interest capitalization when examining net borrowing costs. Similarly, if a firm must make other required periodic payments (such as pensions or leases), you could include these amounts in the calculation as well. If so, the ratio is referred to as the *fixed charges coverage ratio*.

One criticism of the interest and the fixed charges coverage ratios as measures of long-term solvency risk is that they use earnings rather than cash flows in the numerator. Firms pay interest and other fixed charges with cash, not earnings. Notwithstanding the merits of earnings relative to cash flows as a summary performance measure (discussed in Chapters 2 and 3), you can create cash-flow-based variations of these coverage ratios by using cash flow from operations (before interest and income taxes) in the numerator. When the value of the ratios based on earnings is relatively low (that is, less than approximately 2.0), you might also want to examine the cash-flow-based alternatives.

To illustrate, cash flow from operations for **Starbucks** for 2015 was $3,749.1 million. The statement of cash flows provides supplementary information (at the bottom), indicating that **Starbucks** paid $69.5 million for interest and $1,072.2 million for income taxes during 2015. The calculation of the interest coverage ratio using cash flows is as follows:

$$\text{Interest Coverage Ratio (Cash Flow Basis)} = \frac{\text{Cash Flow from Operations} + \text{Payments for Interest and Income Taxes}}{\text{Cash Payments for Interest}}$$

$$3.3 = \frac{\$3{,}749.1 + \$69.5 + \$1{,}072.2}{\$69.5}$$

Interest coverage ratios on a cash flow basis also must be interpreted with caution.[8] Firms incur interest expense on zero-coupon or otherwise deeply discounted bonds and notes but do not pay periodic cash interest. Also, some firms with financial difficulties negotiate deferral of cash interest payment arrangements with lenders to stave off bankruptcy. Interest expense is incurred on these arrangements as well.

Operating Cash Flow to Total Liabilities Ratio

Balance-sheet-based debt ratios such as the liabilities to assets ratio ignore the firm's ability to generate cash flow from operations to service debt. The ratio of cash flow from operations to average total liabilities overcomes this deficiency. This cash flow ratio is similar to the one we use in assessing short-term liquidity, but the denominator includes all liabilities (current and noncurrent).

The operating cash flow to total liabilities ratio for 2015 for **Starbucks** is as follows:

$$\text{Operating Cash Flow to Total Liabilities Ratio} = \frac{\text{Cash Flow from Operations}}{\text{Average Total Liabilities}}$$

$$0.62 = \frac{\$3{,}749.1}{0.5(\$6{,}626.3 + \$5{,}479.2)}$$

The ratio for **Starbucks** was 0.10 in 2014 and 0.57 in 2013. A ratio of 0.20 or more is common for a financially healthy company. The low ratio in 2014 reflects the negative cash flows for the litigation payment of $2,763.9 million. Thus, **Starbucks** appears to be well above the range of financially healthy companies, consistent with our findings with the other long-term solvency ratios.

Quick Check

- Debt, interest coverage, and cash flow ratios measure long-term solvency risk.
- Profitability and cash flows are indicators of the ability of a firm to service its debt.

- In addition to levels, trends are important for monitoring solvency risk.
- A sharp drop in financial flexibility could be an early indicator of potential liquidity and solvency problems.

---

[8]Increased precision suggests that the denominator should include total interest cost for the year, not just the amount recognized as interest expense. If a firm self-constructs fixed assets, it must capitalize a portion of its interest cost each year and add it to the cost of the self-constructed assets. The cost benefit of doing this probably justifies this refinement for industries like electric utilities, which engage in heavy borrowing to construct capital-intensive plants.

Analyzing Credit Risk

LO 5-5

Use risk analysis tools to assess *credit risk*.

Credit risk is the likelihood that a firm will be unable to repay periodic interest and all principal borrowed. Credit risk analysis is a holistic assessment of the creditworthiness of a borrower. To assess credit risk, lenders will start with the short-term liquidity and long-term solvency ratios already discussed in the chapter. However, in addition, lenders also consider other factors, such as the following:

- Circumstances leading to the need for the loan
- Credit history
- Cash flows
- Assets that may be used as collateral
- Capacity for debt
- Contingencies
- Character of management
- Communication
- Conditions or covenants

This list is neither an exhaustive catalog of such factors nor a mandatory list of factors that must be examined, but provides a context within which you can consider various firms.

Circumstances Leading to Need for the Loan

The reason a firm needs to borrow affects the riskiness of the loan and the likelihood of repayment. Consider the following examples.

Example 1: **W. T. Grant Company**, a discount retail chain, filed for bankruptcy in 1975. Its bankruptcy has become a classic example of how poorly designed and implemented controls can lead a firm into financial distress. Between 1968 and 1975, Grant experienced increasing difficulty collecting accounts receivable from credit card customers. To finance the buildup of its accounts receivable, Grant borrowed short-term funds from commercial banks. However, Grant failed to fix the credit extension and cash collection problems with its receivables. As a result, the bank loans simply kept Grant in business in an ever-worsening credit situation. Lending to satisfy cash-flow needs related to an unsolved problem or difficulty can be highly risky.

Example 2: **Toys"R"Us** purchases toys, games, and other entertainment products in September and October in anticipation of heavy demand during the holiday season. It typically pays its suppliers within 30 days for these purchases but does not collect cash from customers until December, January, or later. To finance its inventory, Toys "R"Us borrows short term from its banks. It repays these loans with cash collected from customers. Lending to satisfy cash-flow needs related to ongoing seasonal business operations is generally relatively low risk. Toys"R"Us has an established brand name and predictable demand. Although some risk exists that the products offered will not meet customer preferences in a particular year, Toys"R"Us offers a sufficiently diverse product line that the likelihood of failure to collect sufficient cash is low.

Example 3: **Texas Instruments** designs and manufactures semiconductors for use in computers and other electronic products. Assume that Texas Instruments wants to develop new semiconductors and needs to borrow funds to finance the design and development effort. Such a loan would likely be relatively high risk. Technological change occurs rapidly in semiconductors, which could make semiconductors developed by Texas Instruments obsolete.

Credit History

Lenders like to see that a firm has borrowed in the past and successfully repaid the loans. Young firms sometimes shy away from borrowing to avoid constraints that such borrowing may impose. However, such firms often find that an inadequate credit history precludes them from borrowing later when they need to do so. On the other hand, developing a poor credit history early on can doom a firm to failure because of the difficulty of overcoming initial impressions.

Cash Flows

Lenders prefer that firms generate sufficient cash flows to pay interest and repay principal (collectively referred to as *debt service*) on a loan rather than having to rely on selling the collateral, consistent with the ratios we examined earlier in the chapter. Tools for studying the cash-generating ability of a firm include examining the statement of cash flows for recent years, computing various cash flow financial ratios, and studying cash flows in projected financial statements.

Statement of Cash Flows

We examine a firm's statement of cash flows for recent years to assess whether a firm is experiencing potential cash flow problems. We discussed cash flows in detail in Chapter 3. Some of the indicators of potential cash flow problems, if observed for several years in a row, include

- growth rate in accounts receivable or inventories that exceeds the growth rate in sales.
- increases in accounts payable that exceed the increase in inventories.
- persistent negative cash flows from operations because of net losses or substantial increases in net working capital (current assets minus current liabilities).
- capital expenditures that substantially exceed cash flows from operations. Although you should expect such an excess for a rapidly growing, capital-intensive firm, for a nongrowth firm it indicates a firm's continuing need for external financing to maintain productive capacity.
- reductions in capital expenditures that occur over time. Although such reductions conserve cash in the near term, they might signal that a firm expects declines in future sales, earnings, and operating cash flows.
- net sales of marketable securities that provide cash immediately but might signal the inability of a firm's operations to provide adequate cash flow to finance working capital and long-term investments.
- a reduction or elimination of dividend payments or stock repurchases. Although such actions conserve cash in the near term, dividend reductions or omissions and cessation of share repurchase plans can provide a negative signal about a firm's future prospects.
- available revolving lines of credit that are fully utilized.

Although none of these indicators by themselves represents conclusive evidence of cash flow problems, they do signal the need to obtain explanations from management to see whether a cash flow problem exists. Just as analysts must understand a firm's industry and strategy to effectively analyze profitability, lenders must follow the same analysis steps.

Cash Flows in Projected Financial Statements

In addition to cash flow ratios discussed earlier in the chapter, projected financial statements represent forecasted income statements, balance sheets, and statements of cash flows for some number of years in the future. Lenders may require potential borrowers to prepare such statements (which are rarely made publicly available) to demonstrate the borrower's ability to repay the loan with interest as it comes due. A credit analyst privy to such forecasts should question each of the important assumptions (such as sales growth, cost structure, or capital expenditures plans) underlying these projected financial statements. Chapter 10 illustrates the preparation of financial statement forecasts.

Collateral

The availability and value of collateral for a loan are important determinants of a firm's ability to borrow. Then, if a company's cash flows prove insufficient to pay interest and repay the principal when due, the lender has the right to take possession of any collateral pledged in support of the loan. Commonly collateralized assets include marketable securities; accounts receivable; inventories; and property, plant, and equipment. By contrast, intangible assets such as goodwill, brand names, and customer lists generally do not serve well as collateral for a loan because lenders cannot easily repossess the intangible asset or generate cash from it in the event of a loan default. Firms are increasingly disclosing fair value estimates for various assets, which makes it easier to assess whether the value of collateral serves as an adequate safeguard for a firm's ability to satisfy collateralized obligations.

Capacity for Debt

Closely related to a firm's cash-generating ability and available collateral is a firm's capacity to assume additional debt, discussed earlier as financial flexibility. The cash flows and the collateral represent the means to repay the debt. Most firms do not borrow up to the limit of their debt capacity, and lenders like to see a "margin of safety." In addition to the factors discussed as part of financial flexibility, footnote disclosures highlight the amount of unused credit lines, which provide additional, direct evidence of capacity for debt.

Earlier, we described several ratios that relate the amount of long-term debt or total liabilities to shareholders' equity or total assets as measures of the proportion of liabilities in the capital structure. When measuring debt ratios, you must be careful to consider possible off-balance-sheet obligations (such as operating lease commitments or underfunded pension or health care benefit obligations).

As discussed earlier, the number of times interest payments are covered by operating income before interest and income taxes serves as a gauge of the margin of safety provided by operations to service debt. When the interest coverage ratio falls below approximately 2, the credit risk is generally considered high.

Contingencies

The credit standing of a firm can change abruptly if current uncertainties turn out negatively for the firm. Thus, you should assess the likelihood that contingent outcomes occur. Firms often describe general risks they face in Form 10-K under Item 1A, "Risk Factors." Firms facing specific significant contingent liabilities or risks typically describe them in a footnote to the financial statements. As an example, **Starbucks'** Note 15, "Commitments and Contingencies," describes the outcome of its legal arbitration with Kraft. The following are examples of potential contingencies:

- Is the firm a defendant in a major lawsuit involving its principal products, its technological advantages, its income tax returns, or other core endeavors that could change its profitability and cash flows in the future? Most large firms are continually engaged in lawsuits as a normal part of their business. Sometimes losses are insured, but often they are not, such as the litigation settlement **Starbucks** experienced in 2013.
- Has the firm sold receivables with recourse or served as guarantor on a loan by a subsidiary, joint venture, special-purpose entity, or corporate officer that, if payment is required, will consume cash flows otherwise available to service other debt obligations?
- Is the firm exposed to making payments related to derivative financial instruments that could adversely affect future cash flows if interest rates, exchange rates, or other prices change significantly in an unexpected direction? (See the discussions of derivatives in Chapters 7 and 9.)
- Is the firm dependent on one or a few key employees, contracts or license agreements, or technologies, the loss of which could substantially affect the viability of the business?

Obtaining answers to such questions requires you to read the notes to the financial statement carefully and to ask astute questions of management, attorneys, and others.

Character of Management

The character of the firm's management is an intangible element that can offset to some extent otherwise weak signals about the creditworthiness of a firm. Has the management team successively weathered previous operating problems and challenges that could have bankrupted most firms? Has the management team delivered in the past on projections regarding sales levels, cost reductions, new product development, and similar operating targets? Lenders also are more comfortable lending to firms in which management has a substantial portion of its personal wealth invested in the firm's common equity. The importance of this factor is why analysts sometimes receive training from organizations like the Federal Bureau of Investigation (FBI) on how to recognize deception through voice or visual cues.

Communication

Developing relationships with lenders requires effective communication at the outset and on an ongoing basis. If lenders are unfamiliar with the business or its managers, they must diligently understand the nature of a firm's products and services and the strategies the firm pursues to gain competitive advantage. Lenders do not like surprises, so they monitor the firm's profitability and financial position, much like we have done earlier in this chapter.

Conditions or Covenants

Lenders often place restrictions, or constraints, on a firm to protect their interests. The banking industry refers to these as *covenants*. Such restrictions might include minimum or maximum levels of certain financial ratios. For example, the current ratio cannot fall below 1.2 and the long-term debt to shareholders' equity ratio cannot exceed 75%. Covenants also may preclude firms from paying dividends, repurchasing common stock, or taking on new financing with rights senior to existing lenders in the event of bankruptcy. Violation of such covenants can trigger immediate repayment of loans, higher interest rates, or other burdensome restrictions.

Analyzing Bankruptcy Risk

LO 5-6

Apply predictive statistical models to assess *bankruptcy risk.*

This section discusses the analysis of bankruptcy risk by using information in the financial statements.

The Bankruptcy Process

During the recession of 2008 to 2009, a staggering number of large, well-known firms filed for bankruptcy, including **IndyMac Bancorp** (July 2008), **Lehman Brothers** (September 2008), **Washington Mutual** (September 2008), **Circuit City** (November 2008), **Tribune Group** (December 2008), **Saab Automobile** (February 2009), **Chrysler** (April 2009), **General Motors** (June 2009), **Eddie Bauer** (June 2009), **The Jolt Company** (September 2009), and **Simmons Bedding** (November 2009). Subsequently, many more typically healthy firms filed for bankruptcy, including the publisher of this book.

Most firms that file for bankruptcy in the United States file under Chapter 11 of the National Bankruptcy Code. Under Chapter 11, firms have six months in which to present a plan of reorganization to the court. After that period elapses, creditors, employees, and others can file their plans of reorganization. One such plan might include immediately selling the assets of the business and paying creditors the amounts due. The court decides which plan provides the fairest treatment for all parties concerned. While the firm is in bankruptcy, creditors cannot demand payment of their claims. The court oversees the execution of the reorganization. When the court determines that the firm has executed the plan of reorganization successfully and appears to be a viable entity, the firm is released from bankruptcy. In contrast to Chapter 11, a Chapter 7 filing entails an immediate sale, or liquidation, of the firm's assets and a distribution of the proceeds to various claimants in the order of priority.

Firms typically file for bankruptcy when they have insufficient cash to pay creditors' claims coming due. If such firms did not file for bankruptcy, creditors could exercise their right to take possession of any collateral pledged to secure their lending and effectively begin liquidation of the firm. To keep assets intact and operating activities functioning and to allow time for the firm to reorganize, the firm files for bankruptcy.

Models of Bankruptcy Prediction

Empirical studies of bankruptcy attempt to distinguish the financial characteristics of firms that file for bankruptcy from those that do not. The objective is to develop a model that predicts which firms will likely file for bankruptcy within the near-term. These models use financial statement ratios.

Multivariate Bankruptcy Prediction Models

Early research on bankruptcy prediction in the mid-1960s used univariate analysis to predict the likelihood of bankruptcy. For example, William Beaver studied 29 financial statement ratios for the five years preceding bankruptcy using a sample of 79 bankrupt and 79 nonbankrupt firms.[9] The objective was to identify the ratios that best differentiated between these two groups of firms and to determine how many years prior to bankruptcy the differences in the ratios emerged. The six ratios with the best discriminating power (and the nature of the risk that each ratio measures) were as follows:

1. Net Income plus Depreciation, Depletion, and Amortization/Total Liabilities (long-term solvency risk)[10]
2. Net Income/Total Assets (profitability)
3. Total Debt/Total Assets (long-term solvency risk)
4. Net Working Capital/Total Assets (short-term liquidity risk)
5. Current Assets/Current Liabilities (short-term liquidity risk)
6. Cash, Marketable Securities, Accounts Receivable/Operating Expenses Excluding Depreciation, Depletion, and Amortization (short-term liquidity risk)[11]

Note that this list includes profitability, short-term liquidity risk, and long-term solvency risk ratios, consistent with our analysis in this chapter.

During the late 1960s and throughout the 1970s, deficiencies of univariate analysis led researchers to use multiple discriminant analysis (MDA), a multivariate statistical technique, to develop bankruptcy prediction models. Researchers typically selected a sample of bankrupt firms and matched them with healthy firms of approximately the same size in the same industry. This matching procedure attempts to control factors for size and industry so you can examine the impact of other factors that might explain bankruptcy.

---

[9]William Beaver, "Financial Ratios as Predictors of Failure," *Empirical Research in Accounting: Selected Studies, 1966*, supplement to *Journal of Accounting Research* (1966), pp. 71–102.

[10]This ratio is similar to the operating cash flow to total liabilities ratio discussed earlier in this chapter except that the numerator of Beaver's ratio does not include changes in working capital accounts. Published "funds flow" statements at the time of Beaver's study defined funds as working capital (instead of cash).

[11]This ratio, referred to as the *defensive interval*, indicates the proportion of a year that a firm could continue to operate by paying cash operating expenses with cash and near-cash assets.

You can then calculate a large number of financial statement ratios expected a priori to explain bankruptcy. Using these financial ratios as inputs, an MDA model selects the subset (usually four to six ratios) that best discriminates between bankrupt and non-bankrupt firms. The resulting MDA model includes a set of coefficients that, when multiplied by the particular financial statement ratios and then summed, yields a multivariate score that is the basis of predicting the likelihood of a firm going bankrupt.

Perhaps the best-known MDA bankruptcy prediction model is Altman's Z-score.[12] Altman used data for manufacturing firms to develop the model. Following is the calculation of the Z-score:

$$\text{Z-score} = 1.2\left(\frac{\text{Net Working Capital}}{\text{Total Assets}}\right) + 1.4\left(\frac{\text{Retained Earnings}}{\text{Total Assets}}\right)$$
$$+ 3.3\left(\frac{\text{Earnings before Interest and Taxes}}{\text{Total Assets}}\right) + 0.6\left(\frac{\text{Market Value of Equity}}{\text{Book Value of Liabilities}}\right)$$
$$+ 1.0\left(\frac{\text{Sales}}{\text{Total Assets}}\right)$$

Each ratio captures a different dimension of profitability or risk, as follows:

1. Net Working Capital/Total Assets: The proportion of total assets comprising relatively liquid net current assets (current assets minus current liabilities). This ratio serves as a measure of short-term liquidity risk.
2. Retained Earnings/Total Assets: Accumulated profitability and relative age of a firm.
3. Earnings before Interest and Taxes/Total Assets: A variant of ROA. This ratio measures current profitability.
4. Market Value of Equity/Book Value of Liabilities: A form of the debt-to-equity ratio, but it incorporates the market's assessment of the value of the firm's shareholders' equity. Therefore, this ratio measures long-term solvency risk and the market's overall assessment of the profitability and risk of the firm.
5. Sales/Total Assets: This is the total assets turnover ratio discussed in Chapter 4 and indicates the ability of a firm to use assets to generate sales.

In applying this model, Altman found that Z-scores of less than 1.81 indicated a high probability of bankruptcy, while Z-scores higher than 3.00 indicated a low probability of bankruptcy. Scores between 1.81 and 3.00 were in the gray area.

We can convert the Z-score into a more intuitive probability of bankruptcy using the normal density function in Excel.[13] A Z-score of 3.00 translates into a probability of bankruptcy of 2.75%. A Z-score of 1.81 translates into a probability of bankruptcy of 20.90%. Thus, Z-scores that correspond to probabilities of less than 2.75% indicate low probability of bankruptcy, probabilities between 2.75% and 20.90% are in the gray area, and probabilities above 20.90% are in the high probability area. Altman obtained a 95%

[12]Edward Altman, "Financial Ratios, Discriminant Analysis, and the Prediction of Corporate Bankruptcy," *The Journal of Finance* (September 1968), pp. 589–609.

[13]The formula in Excel is =NORMSDIST(1–Z score). Altman developed his model so that higher positive Z-scores mean lower probability of bankruptcy; thus, computing the probability of bankruptcy requires that the normal density function be applied to 1 minus the Z-score. The website for this book (www.cengagebrain.com) contains an Excel spreadsheet for computing Altman's Z-score and the probability of bankruptcy. FSAP also computes these values.

correct prediction accuracy rate one year prior to bankruptcy. The correct prediction rate two years before bankruptcy was 83%.

Exhibit 5.12 shows the calculation of Altman's Z-score for **Starbucks** for 2015. We use the originally reported amounts for **Starbucks** instead of the adjusted amounts that eliminate nonrecurring items because Altman developed his model using originally reported amounts. Not surprisingly, **Starbucks'** Z-score of 10.98 clearly indicates a very low probability of bankruptcy (0.0%). FSAP computes Altman's Z-scores and the corresponding probabilities of bankruptcy (Appendix C).

The principal strengths of MDA are as follows:

- It incorporates multiple financial ratios simultaneously.
- It provides the appropriate coefficients for combining the independent variables.
- It is easy to apply once the initial model has been developed.

The principal criticisms of MDA are as follows:

- The researcher cannot be sure that the MDA model includes all relevant discriminating financial ratios. MDA selects the best ratios from those provided, but that set does not necessarily provide the best explanatory power.
- The researcher must subjectively judge the value of the cutoff score that best distinguishes bankrupt from nonbankrupt firms.
- The development and application of the MDA model requires firms to disclose the information needed to compute each financial ratio. Firms excluded because they do not provide the necessary data may bias the MDA model.
- MDA assumes that each of the financial ratios for bankrupt and nonbankrupt firms is normally distributed. Firms experiencing financial distress often display unusually large or small ratios that can skew the distribution away from normal.

Exhibit 5.12

Altman's Z-Score for Starbucks, 2015
(dollar amounts in millions)

Ratio	Weight	Score
Net Working Capital/Total Assets ($4,352.7 − $3,653.5)/$12,446.1	1.2	0.0674
Retained Earnings/Total Assets $5,974.8/$12,446.1	1.4	0.6721
Earnings before Interest and Taxes/Total Assets ($2,759.3 + $70.5 + $1,143.7)/$12,446.1	3.3	1.0535
Market Value of Equity/Book Value of Liabilities ($56.84 × 1,485.1)/$6,626.3	0.6	7.6435
Sales/Total Assets $19,162.7/$12,446.1	1.0	1.5397
Z-Score		10.9762

In addition, the researcher cannot include dummy variables (for example, 0 if financial statements are audited and 1 if they are not audited). Dummy variables are not normally distributed.

■ MDA requires that the variance-covariance matrix of the explanatory variables be the same for bankrupt and nonbankrupt firms.[14]

Bankruptcy Prediction Models Using Logit Analysis

A third stage in the methodological development of bankruptcy prediction research was the move during the 1980s and early 1990s to using logit analysis instead of MDA. Logit does not require that the data display the underlying statistical properties described previously for MDA.

The use of logit analysis to develop a bankruptcy prediction model follows a procedure that is similar to that of MDA: (1) initial calculation of a large set of financial ratios, (2) reduction of the set of financial ratios to a subset that best predicts bankrupt and nonbankrupt firms, and (3) estimation of coefficients for each included variable.

The logit model defines the probability of bankruptcy as follows:

$$\text{Probability of Bankruptcy for a Firm} = \frac{1}{1 + e^{-y}}$$

where e equals approximately 2.718282. The exponent y is a multivariate function that includes a constant and coefficients for a set of explanatory variables (that is, financial statement ratios that discriminate bankrupt and nonbankrupt firms).

Ohlson[15] and Zavgren[16] used logit analysis to develop bankruptcy prediction models. Their models use different financial statement ratios than Altman's model, and they are somewhat more complex to apply. We do not discuss their models in depth here, but interested readers can consult the research cited. Despite the shortcomings of discriminant models, Altman's Z-score model is still the most widely referenced and the one emphasized in this chapter.

Application of Altman's Bankruptcy Prediction Model to W. T. Grant Company

W. T. Grant Company (Grant), one of the largest retailers in the United States at the time, filed for bankruptcy in October 1975. Exhibit 5.13 shows the calculation of Altman's Z-score for years leading up to the actual bankruptcy.

Altman's model shows a low probability of bankruptcy prior to the 1973 fiscal year, a move into the gray area in 1973 and 1974, and a high probability of bankruptcy in 1975. The absolute levels of these Z-scores are inflated because Grant was a retailer, whereas Altman developed the model using manufacturing firms. Retailing firms typically have a faster assets turnover than do manufacturing firms. In this case, the trend of the Z-score is more meaningful than its absolute level. Note that the Z-score declined

---

[14]For an elaboration of these criticisms, see James A. Ohlson, "Financial Ratios and the Probabilistic Prediction of Bankruptcy," *Journal of Accounting Research* (Spring 1980), pp. 109–131; and Mark E. Zmijewski, "Methodological Issues Related to the Estimation of Financial Distress Prediction Models," *Journal of Accounting Research*, Supplement (1984), pp. 59–82.

[15]Ohlson, *op. cit.*

[16]Christine V. Zavgren, "Assessing the Vulnerability to Failure of American Industrial Firms: A Logistic Analysis," *Journal of Business Finance and Accounting* (Spring 1985), pp. 19–45.

Exhibit 5.13

Application of Altman's Bankruptcy Prediction Models to W. T. Grant

Fiscal Year	1968	1969	1970	1971	1972	1973	1974	1975
Altman's Z-Score Model								
Net Working Capital/Assets	0.54353	0.51341	0.44430	0.37791	0.44814	0.36508	0.38524	0.19390
Retained Earnings/Assets	0.43738	0.42669	0.41929	0.38511	0.34513	0.31023	0.25712	0.04873
EBIT/Assets	0.41358	0.44611	0.44228	0.38848	0.27820	0.26029	0.25470	(0.63644)
Market Value Equity/Book Value Liabilities	0.86643	1.01740	0.95543	0.89539	0.69788	0.50578	0.10211	0.01730
Sales/Assets	1.77564	1.76199	1.71325	1.67974	1.57005	1.58678	1.54797	1.62802
Z-score	4.03656	4.16560	3.97455	3.72663	3.33940	3.02816	2.54714	1.25151
Probability of Bankruptcy Range	Low	Low	Low	Low	Low	Gray	Gray	High
Probability of Bankruptcy	0.12%	0.07%	0.15%	0.32%	0.97%	2.13%	6.09%	40.07%

steadily beginning in the 1970 fiscal year. With a few exceptions in individual years, each of the five components also declined steadily.[17]

Synthesis of Bankruptcy Prediction Research

The preceding sections of this chapter discussed bankruptcy prediction models. Similar streams of research relate to commercial bank lending, bond ratings, corporate restructurings, and corporate liquidations. Although statistical models and relevant financial statement ratios vary across studies, certain commonalities do appear. This section summarizes the factors that explain bankruptcy most consistently across various studies.

Investment Factors. The probability of financial distress decreases as the relative liquidity of a firm's assets increases. Greater asset liquidity means that the firm has or will soon generate the necessary cash to meet creditors' claims. Firms with relatively large proportions of current assets tend to experience less financial distress than firms with fixed assets or intangible assets as the dominant assets.

Positive returns from any asset investment are ultimately realized in cash. Firms acquire fixed assets or create intangibles to produce a salable product (inventory) or to create a desired service, which they sell to customers and then collect cash. The faster assets turn over, the more quickly a firm generates cash. We discussed turnover ratios earlier in the chapter.

Financing Factors. Firms experience bankruptcy because they are unable to pay liabilities as they come due. The higher the proportion of short-term debt and total liabilities in the capital structure, the higher the probability that firms will experience bankruptcy. Commonly used ratios include total liabilities/total assets, total liabilities/shareholders' equity, and current liabilities/total assets, discussed earlier in the chapter.

Operating Factors. Profitable firms ultimately generate positive cash flows and are usually able to borrow funds more easily and at lower borrowing rates. Research has demonstrated that most bankruptcies initiate with one or several consecutive years of poor operating performance. Firms with unused debt capacity can often borrow for a year or two until they solve operating difficulties. Commonly used financial ratios for profitability are net income/assets, income before interest and taxes/assets, net income/sales, and cash flow from operations/assets.

Additionally, firms that experience variability in operations (for example, from cyclical sales patterns) exhibit a greater likelihood of bankruptcy. During down times in economic cycles, such firms often struggle to obtain financing to meet financial commitments and maintain operating levels.

Other Possible Explanatory Variables. Several other factors examined in bankruptcy research warrant discussion.

1. *Cash flows.* Casey and Bartczak, among others, found that adding cash flow from operations/current liabilities and cash flow from operations/total liabilities did not significantly add explanatory power to models based on accrual-basis

---

[17]The solution to the Grant case indicates that prior to its 1975 fiscal year, Grant failed to provide adequately for uncollectible accounts. The effect of this action was to overstate the net working capital/assets, retained earnings/assets, and EBIT/assets components of the Z-score; understate the sales/assets component; and probably overstate the overall Z-score.

amounts. However, other researchers have found contrary results, suggesting that the use of cash flow variables may enhance bankruptcy prediction.[18] The standard predictive results of earnings and mixed results for cash flows are consistent with our focus in this book that earnings are more predictive of future cash flows than are current cash flows.

2. *Size.* Larger firms generally have access to a wider range of financing sources and more flexibility to redeploy assets than do smaller firms. Most studies measure size using total assets.

3. *Growth.* Rapidly growing firms often need external financing to cover cash shortfalls from operations and to permit acquisitions of fixed assets. These firms often display financial ratios typical of a firm in financial difficulty (that is, high debt ratios and weak profitability). However, their perceived growth potential provides access to capital that allows them to survive. On the other hand, firms in the late maturity or early decline phase of their life cycle may experience slow (or even negative) growth but display healthy financial ratios. For such firms, future profitability can be low and, as a result, the probability of future financial difficulty will be high.

4. *Qualified Audit Opinion.* Auditors with doubts about a firm's ability to continue as a going concern may issue a qualified audit opinion. Such opinions are predictors of financial difficulties. This result is not surprising because auditors can use bankruptcy prediction models as one of their inputs into such decisions.

Some Final Thoughts

Bankruptcy prediction research represents an effort to integrate traditional financial statement analysis with statistical modeling. The models developed by Altman, Ohlson, and others rely on data that are decades old and are based on business activities and bankruptcy laws that differ from those currently encountered. Nevertheless, security analysts and academic researchers continue to use these models and they appear relatively robust despite the numerous limitations discussed previously. More recently, Begley, Ming, and Watts applied Altman's MDA model and Ohlson's logit model to a sample of bankrupt and nonbankrupt firms in the 1980s, a later period than that used by Altman and Ohlson. Begley, Ming, and Watts found that predictive ability of the Altman model deteriorated somewhat, but the Ohlson model performed well.[19]

Measuring Systematic Risk

Firms face additional risks besides credit and bankruptcy risk. Recessions, inflation, changes in interest rates, foreign currency fluctuations, rising unemployment, and similar economic factors affect all firms, but to varying degrees depending on the nature of their operations. An investor in a firm's common stock must consider these dimensions of risk when making investment decisions. In this section, we briefly discuss how equity

---

[18]Cornelius Casey and Norman Bartczak, "Cash Flow—It's Not the Bottom Line," *Harvard Business Review* (July–August 1984), pp. 61–66. For a summary of this research, see Michael J. Gombola, Mark E. Haskins, J. Edward Ketz, and David D. Williams, "Cash Flow in Bankruptcy Prediction," *Financial Management* (Winter 1987), pp. 55–65.

[19]See Joy Begley, Jin Ming, and Susan Watts, "Bankruptcy Classification Errors in the 1980s: An Empirical Analysis of Altman's and Ohlson's Models," *Review of Accounting Studies* 1, no. 4 (1996), pp. 267–284.

markets are used to obtain a broader measure of risk. Then we briefly relate this market measure of risk to financial statement information.

Studies of market rates of return have traditionally used the CAPM (capital asset pricing model) as the basis for an individual firm's risk-based required rate of return. The research typically regresses the rate of returns on a particular firm's common shares [dividends plus (minus) capital gains (losses)/beginning-of-period share price] over some period of time on the excess of the returns of all common stocks over the risk-free rate. The regression takes the following form:

$$
\begin{array}{c} \text{Returns on} \\ \text{Common Stock of} \\ \text{a Particular Firm} \end{array} = \begin{array}{c} \text{Risk-Free} \\ \text{Interest} \\ \text{Rate} \end{array} + \begin{array}{c} \text{Market} \\ \text{Beta} \end{array} \times \left(\begin{array}{c} \text{Market} \\ \text{Return} \end{array} - \begin{array}{c} \text{Risk-Free} \\ \text{Interest} \\ \text{Rate} \end{array} \right) + \text{Error}
$$

The beta coefficient measures the covariability of a firm's returns with the returns of a diversified portfolio of all shares traded on the market (in excess of the risk-free interest rate).

- Firms with a market beta close to 1.0 experience covariability of returns *equal* to the average covariability of the stock market as a whole.
- Firms with a beta greater than 1.0 experience *greater* covariability than the average.
- Firms with a beta less than 1.0 experience *less* covariability than the average firm.

Beta is a measure of the *systematic* (or *undiversifiable*) *risk* of the firm. The market, through the pricing of a firm's shares, rewards shareholders for bearing systematic risk. We refer to elements of risk that are not systematic as *unsystematic* (or *diversifiable*) *risk*. Unsystematic risk factors include diversifiable firm-specific risks such as specific product obsolescence; labor strikes; loss of a lawsuit; and damages from fire, weather, or natural disaster. By constructing a diversified portfolio of securities, the investor can eliminate the effects of unsystematic risk on the returns to the portfolio as a whole. Thus, market pricing should provide no returns for the assumption of nonsystematic risk.

Several firm-specific factors are intuitively related to a firm's market beta, including

- operating leverage.
- financial leverage.
- variability of sales.

Each of these factors causes the earnings of a particular firm to vary over time, and due to the association between earnings and stock prices, these factors are associated with a firm's market beta.

Operating leverage refers to the extent of fixed operating costs in the cost structure. Costs such as depreciation and amortization do *not* vary with the level of sales. Other costs, such as insurance and executive and administrative salaries and benefits, may vary somewhat with the level of sales, but they remain relatively fixed for any particular period. The presence of fixed operating costs leads to variation in operating earnings that is greater than contemporaneous variation in sales. Likewise, financial leverage (discussed earlier in the chapter) adds a fixed cost for interest and creates the potential for earnings to vary more than sales vary. Thus, both operating and financial leverage create variations in earnings when sales vary but firms cannot simultaneously alter the level of fixed costs.

Research demonstrates a strong link between changes in earnings and changes in stock prices.[20] Thus, operating leverage, financial leverage, and variability of sales should result in fluctuations in the market returns for a particular firm's common shares.

---

[20]Ray Ball and Philip Brown, "An Empirical Evaluation of Accounting Income Numbers," *Journal of Accounting Research* (Autumn 1968), pp. 159–178; Ball and Brown, *op. cit.*

The average returns for all firms in the market should reflect the average level of operating leverage, financial leverage, and sales variability of these firms. Therefore, the market beta for a particular firm reflects its degree of variability relative to the average firm. Chapters 11 and 14 discuss more fully the relation between financial statement information and market beta and the use of market beta in the valuation of firms.

Summary

Risk analysis requires you to consider a wide range of factors (for example, government regulations and posturing, industry competition, technological change, quality of management, competitors' actions, profitability, and financial reporting risk). This chapter examines dimensions of risk that have financial consequences and impact the financial statements.

We began with a discussion of financial flexibility, which is an extension of profitability analysis, but with an emphasis on partitioning the firm's financial statements into operating and financing components. With an understanding of how leverage can be strategically used to increase returns available to shareholders, we then examined the analysis of financial risk associated with the use of leverage along the following three dimensions:

1. *With respect to time frame:* We examined the analysis of a firm's ability to pay liabilities coming due the next year (short-term liquidity risk analysis) and its ability to pay liabilities coming due over a longer term (long-term solvency risk analysis).

2. *With respect to the degree of and likelihood of financial distress:* We emphasized the need to consider risk as falling along a continuum from low risk to high risk of financial distress. Firms with a great deal of financial flexibility fall on the low side of this continuum. Firms at risk for missing credit payment deadlines or bankruptcy fall on the low- to medium-risk side of this continuum. We also described a multivariate model to predict the likelihood a firm will become financially distressed.

3. *With respect to covariability of returns with other securities in the market:* We briefly highlighted the use of market equity beta as an indicator of systematic risk with the market, which is affected by the types of risk analyzed in this chapter.

Common factors come into play in all three settings of risk analysis. Fixed costs related to operations or to financing constrain the flexibility of a firm to adapt to changing economic, business, and firm-specific conditions. The profitability and cash-generating ability of a firm allow it to operate within its constraints or to change the constraints in some desirable direction. If the constraints are too high or the capabilities to adapt are too low, a firm faces the risk of financial distress.[21]

Questions, Exercises, Problems, and Cases

Questions and Exercises

LO 5-1

5.1 Interpreting Risk Disclosures. Obtain the latest Form 10-K for **Facebook, Inc.** (www.investor.fb.com). Locate and describe the significant risks the company identifies. Are any of these unexpected based on your previous familiarity with the company?

---

[21]Firms facing potential financial distress are more likely to manipulate earnings and accounting information, as we discuss in Chapter 6.

5.2 Interpreting the Alternative Decomposition of ROCE with Negative Net Financial Obligations. Suppose an analyst reformulates financial statements to prepare the alternative decomposition of ROCE for a firm with no debt. The analyst determines that the company holds excess cash as large marketable equity securities. The result will be net financial obligations that are negative. Assume that operating ROA is positive and large. How will this affect the decomposition of ROCE = Operating ROA + (Leverage × Spread)? How do you interpret the net borrowing rate for this firm? `LO 5-2`

5.3 Relation between Current Ratio and Operating Cash Flow to Current Liabilities Ratio. A firm has experienced an increasing current ratio but a decreasing operating cash flow to current liabilities ratio during the last three years. What is the likely explanation for these results? `LO 5-3`

5.4 Relation between Current Ratio and Quick Ratio. A firm has experienced a decrease in its current ratio but an increase in its quick ratio during the last three years. What is the likely explanation for these results? `LO 5-3`

5.5 Relation between Working Capital Turnover Ratios and Cash Flow from Operations. While a firm's sales and net income have been steady during the last three years, the firm has experienced a decrease in its accounts receivable and inventory turnovers and an increase in its accounts payable turnover. What is the likely direction of change in cash flow from operations? How would your answer be different if sales and net income were increasing? `LO 5-3`

5.6 Effect of Transactions on Debt Ratios. A firm had the following values for the four debt ratios discussed in the chapter: `LO 5-4`

Liabilities to Assets Ratio: less than 1.0
Liabilities to Shareholders' Equity Ratio: equal to 1.0
Long-Term Debt to Long-Term Capital Ratio: less than 1.0
Long-Term Debt to Shareholders' Equity Ratio: less than 1.0

a. Indicate whether each of the following independent transactions increases, decreases, or has no effect on each of the four debt ratios.
   (1) The firm issued long-term debt for cash.
   (2) The firm issued short-term debt and used the cash proceeds to redeem long-term debt (treat as a unified transaction).
   (3) The firm redeemed short-term debt with cash.
   (4) The firm issued long-term debt and used the cash proceeds to repurchase shares of its common stock (treat as a unified transaction).
b. The text states that analysts need not compute all four debt ratios each year because the debt ratios are highly correlated. Does your analysis in Part a support this statement? Explain.

5.7 Interest Coverage Ratio as a Measure of Long-Term Solvency Risk. Identify the assumptions underlying the interest coverage ratio needed to make it an appropriate measure for analyzing long-term solvency risk. `LO 5-4`

5.8 Interest Coverage Ratio as a Measure of Short-Term Liquidity Risk. In what sense is the interest coverage ratio more a measure for assessing short-term liquidity risk than it is a measure for assessing long-term solvency risk? `LO 5-3`

LO 5-3, LO 5-4

5.9 Interpreting Operating Cash Flow to Current and Total Liabilities Ratios.
Empirical research cited in the text indicates that firms with an operating cash flow to current liabilities ratio exceeding 0.40 portray low short-term liquidity risk. Similarly, firms with an operating cash flow to total liabilities ratio exceeding 20% portray low long-term solvency risk. What do these empirical results suggest about the mix of current and noncurrent liabilities for a financially healthy firm? What do they suggest about the mix of liabilities versus shareholders' equity financing?

LO 5-6

5.10 Interpreting Altman's Z-score Bankruptcy Prediction Model.
Altman's bankruptcy prediction model places a coefficient of 3.3 on the earnings before interest and taxes divided by total assets variable but a coefficient of only 1.0 on the sales to total assets variable. Does this mean that the earnings variable is 3.3 times as important in predicting bankruptcy as the assets turnover variable? Explain.

LO 5-7

5.11 Market Equity Beta in Relation to Systematic and Nonsystematic Risk.
Market equity beta measures the covariability of a firm's returns with all shares traded on the market (in excess of the risk-free interest rate). We refer to the degree of covariability as systematic risk. The market prices securities so that the expected returns should compensate the investor for the systematic risk of a particular stock. Stocks carrying a market equity beta of 1.20 should generate a higher return than stocks carrying a market equity beta of 0.90. Nonsystematic risk is any source of risk that does not affect the covariability of a firm's returns with the market. Some writers refer to nonsystematic risk as firm-specific risk. Why is the characterization of nonsystematic risk as firm-specific risk a misnomer?

LO 5-6

5.12 Levels versus Changes in Altman's Bankruptcy Prediction Model.
Altman's bankruptcy risk model utilizes the values of the variables at a particular point in time (balance sheet variables) or for a period of time (income statement values). An alternative would be to use changes in balance sheet or income statement amounts. Why might the levels of values in Altman's model be more appropriate than changes for predicting bankruptcy?

Problems and Cases

LO 5-3, LO 5-4

5.13 Calculating and Interpreting Risk Ratios.
Refer to the financial statement data for **Hasbro** in Problem 4.24 in Chapter 4. Exhibit 5.14 presents risk ratios for Hasbro for Year 2 and Year 3.

REQUIRED
a. Calculate these ratios for Year 4.
b. Assess the changes in the short-term liquidity risk of Hasbro between Year 2 and Year 4 and the level of that risk at the end of Year 4.
c. Assess the changes in the long-term solvency risk of Hasbro between Year 2 and Year 4 and the level of that risk at the end of Year 4.

LO 5-3, LO 5-4

5.14 Calculating and Interpreting Risk Ratios.
Refer to the financial statement data for **Abercrombie & Fitch** in Problem 4.25 in Chapter 4. Exhibit 5.15 presents risk ratios for Abercrombie & Fitch for fiscal Year 3 and Year 4.

REQUIRED
a. Compute these ratios for fiscal Year 5.
b. Assess the changes in the short-term liquidity risk of Abercrombie & Fitch between fiscal Year 3 and fiscal Year 5 and the level of that risk at the end of fiscal Year 5.

c. Assess the changes in the long-term solvency risk of Abercrombie & Fitch between fiscal Year 3 and fiscal Year 5 and the level of that risk at the end of fiscal Year 5.

Exhibit 5.14

Risk Ratios for Hasbro (Problem 5.13)

	Year 4	Year 3	Year 2
Current ratio		1.6	1.5
Quick ratio		1.2	1.1
Operating cash flow to current liabilities ratio		0.479	0.548
Days accounts receivable outstanding		68	73
Days inventory held		51	68
Days accounts payable outstanding		47	49
Net days of working capital financing needed		72	91
Liabilities to assets ratio		0.556	0.621
Liabilities to shareholders' equity ratio		1.251	1.639
Long-term debt to long-term capital ratio		0.328	0.418
Long-term debt to shareholders' equity ratio		0.489	0.720
Operating cash flow to total liabilities ratio		0.245	0.238
Interest coverage ratio		5.6	2.3

Exhibit 5.15

Risk Ratios for Abercrombie & Fitch (Problem 5.14)

	Year 5	Year 4	Year 3
Current ratio		2.4	2.3
Quick ratio		1.7	1.6
Operating cash flow to current liabilities ratio		1.177	1.587
Days accounts receivable outstanding		2	4
Days inventory held		72	61
Days accounts payable outstanding		26	22
Net days of working capital financing needed		48	43
Liabilities to assets ratio		0.591	0.592
Liabilities to shareholders' equity ratio		1.443	1.448
Long-term debt to long-term capital ratio		0.454	0.461
Long-term debt to shareholders' equity ratio		0.831	0.855
Operating cash flow to total liabilities ratio		0.298	0.380
Interest coverage ratio		7.2	7.6

 **5.15 Interpreting Risk Ratios.** Exhibit 5.16 presents risk ratios for Coca-Cola for Year 1 through Year 3.

REQUIRED

a. Assess the changes in the short-term liquidity risk of Coca-Cola between Year 1 and Year 3.
b. Assess the changes in the long-term solvency risk of Coca-Cola between Year 1 and Year 3.

Exhibit 5.16			
Risk Ratios for Coca-Cola (Problem 5.15)			
	Year 3	**Year 2**	**Year 1**
Current ratio	0.9	0.9	0.9
Quick ratio	0.6	0.6	0.6
Operating cash flow to current liabilities ratio	0.578	0.647	0.636
Days accounts receivable outstanding	37	37	37
Days inventory held	71	68	68
Days accounts payable outstanding	44	38	40
Net days of working capital financing needed	64	67	65
Liabilities to assets ratio	0.495	0.497	0.435
Liabilities to shareholders' equity ratio	0.979	0.990	0.771
Long-term debt to long-term capital ratio	0.120	0.131	0.072
Long-term debt to shareholders' equity ratio	0.136	0.151	0.078
Operating cash flow to average total liabilities ratio	0.364	0.414	0.456
Interest coverage ratio	17.0	17.3	29.9

 5.16 Computing and Interpreting Risk and Bankruptcy Prediction Ratios for a Firm That Declared Bankruptcy. Delta Air Lines, Inc., is one of the largest airlines in the United States. It has operated on the verge of bankruptcy for several years. Exhibit 5.17 presents selected financial data for Delta Air Lines for each of the five years ending December 31, 2000, to December 31, 2004. Delta Air Lines filed for bankruptcy on September 14, 2005. We recommend that you create an Excel spreadsheet to compute the values of the ratios and the Altman's Z-score in Requirements a and b, respectively.

REQUIRED

a. Compute the value of each the following risk ratios.
 (1) Current ratio (at the end of 2000–2004)
 (2) Operating cash flow to current liabilities ratio (for 2001–2004)
 (3) Liabilities to assets ratio (at the end of 2000–2004)
 (4) Long-term debt to long-term capital ratio (at the end of 2000–2004)
 (5) Operating cash flow to total liabilities ratio (for 2001–2004)
 (6) Interest coverage ratio (for 2000–2004)
b. Compute the value of Altman's Z-score for Delta Air Lines for each year from 2000 to 2004.
c. Using the analyses in Requirements a and b, discuss the most important factors that signaled the likelihood of bankruptcy of Delta Air Lines in 2005.

Exhibit 5.17

Financial Data for Delta Air Lines, Inc.
(amounts in millions, except per-share amounts)
(Problem 5.16)

	For Year Ended December 31,				
	2004	**2003**	**2002**	**2001**	**2000**
Sales	$15,002	$14,087	$13,866	$13,879	$15,657
Net income (loss) before interest and taxes	$(3,168)	$(432)	$(1,337)	$(1,365)	$1,829
Interest expense	$824	$757	$665	$499	$380
Net income (loss)	$(5,198)	$(773)	$(1,272)	$(1,216)	$828
Current assets	$3,606	$4,550	$3,902	$3,567	$3,205
Total assets	$21,801	$25,939	$24,720	$23,605	$21,931
Current liabilities	$5,941	$6,157	$6,455	$6,403	$5,245
Long-term debt	$12,507	$11,040	$9,576	$7,781	$5,797
Total liabilities	$27,320	$26,323	$23,563	$19,581	$16,354
Retained earnings (deficit)	$(4,373)	$844	$1,639	$2,930	$4,176
Shareholders' equity	$(5,519)	$(384)	$1,157	$4,024	$5,577
Cash flow provided by operations	$(1,123)	$142	$225	$236	$2,898
Common shares outstanding	139.8	123.5	123.4	123.2	123.0
Market price per share	$7.48	$11.81	$12.10	$29.26	$50.18

Source: Delta Airlines, Inc., Forms 10-K for the Fiscal Years Ended June 2000–June 2004.

5.17 Alternative ROCE Decomposition. VF Corporation is an apparel company that owns recognizable brands like Timberland, Vans, Reef, and 7 For All Mankind. Exhibit 5.18 and 5.19 present balance sheets and income statements, respectively, for Year 1 and Year 2. (VF Corporation previously had noncontrolling interests, which were acquired during Year 1. Nevertheless, there is a negative balance at the end of Year 1, presumably pertaining to losses absorbed or currency adjustments. The noncontrolling interests will only affect your calculations through the use of average balances of financing obligations where noncontrolling interests should be allocated.)   `LO 5-2`

REQUIRED

a. Compute ROCE for Year 2 under the traditional calculation discussed in Chapter 4.
b. Compute ROCE for Year 2 using the alternative decomposition, highlighting each component (NOPAT, leverage, spread). HINT: First, allocate individual line items on the balance sheet and income statement to operating and financing activities. Then compute each of the following for Year 2:
   (1) Net operating assets
   (2) Net financing obligations
   (3) Common equity
   (4) NOPAT
   (5) Net financing expense (after tax)
   (6) Operating ROA
   (7) Leverage
   (8) Net borrowing rate
   (9) Spread

Exhibit 5.18

VF Corporation
Consolidated Balance Sheets
(amounts in thousands)
(Problem 5.17)

	December	
	Year 2	Year 1
ASSETS		
Current assets		
Cash and equivalents	$ 597,461	$ 341,228
Accounts receivable, net	1,222,345	1,120,246
Inventories	1,354,158	1,453,645
Deferred income taxes	140,515	106,717
Other current assets	135,104	166,108
Total current assets	3,449,583	3,187,944
Property, plant and equipment	828,218	737,451
Intangible assets	2,917,058	2,958,463
Goodwill	2,009,757	2,023,460
Other assets	428,405	405,808
Total assets	$9,633,021	$9,313,126
LIABILITIES AND STOCKHOLDERS' EQUITY		
Current liabilities		
Short-term borrowings	$ 12,559	$ 281,686
Current portion of long-term debt	402,873	2,744
Accounts payable	562,638	637,116
Accrued liabilities	754,142	744,486
Total current liabilities	1,732,212	1,666,032
Long-term debt	1,429,166	1,831,781
Other liabilities	1,346,018	1,290,138
Commitments and contingencies		
Stockholders' equity		
Preferred stock, par value $1, shares authorized, 25,000,000; no shares outstanding in Year 2 and Year 1	—	—
Common stock, stated value $1; shares authorized, 300,000,000; 110,204,734 shares outstanding in Year 2 and 110,556,981 in Year 1	110,205	110,557
Additional paid-in capital	2,527,868	2,316,107
Accumulated other comprehensive income (loss)	(453,895)	(421,477)
Retained earnings	2,941,447	2,520,804
Total equity attributable to VF corporation	5,125,625	4,525,991
Noncontrolling interests	—	(816)
Total stockholders' equity	5,125,625	4,525,175
Total liabilities and stockholders' equity	$9,633,021	$9,313,126

Source: VF Corporation, Form 10-K for the Fiscal Year Ended December 2012.

Exhibit 5.19

VF Corporation
Consolidated Statements of Income
(amounts in thousands)
(Problem 5.17)

| | Year Ended December | | |
	Year 2	Year 1	Year 0
Net sales	$10,766,020	$9,365,477	$7,624,599
Royalty income	113,835	93,755	77,990
Total revenues	10,879,855	9,459,232	7,702,589
Costs and operating expenses			
Cost of goods sold	5,817,880	5,128,602	4,105,201
Marketing, administrative, and general expenses	3,596,708	3,085,839	2,574,790
Impairment of goodwill and intangible assets	—	—	201,738
	9,414,588	8,214,441	6,881,729
Operating income	1,465,267	1,244,791	820,860
Interest income	3,353	4,778	2,336
Interest expense	(93,605)	(77,578)	(77,738)
Other income (expense), net	46,860	(7,248)	4,754
Income before income taxes	1,421,875	1,164,743	750,212
Income taxes	335,737	274,350	176,700
Net income	1,086,138	890,393	573,512
Net (income) loss attributable to noncontrolling interests	(139)	(2,304)	(2,150)
Net income attributable to VF Corporation	$ 1,085,999	$ 888,089	$ 571,362

Source: VF Corporation, Form 10-K for the Fiscal Year Ended December 2012.

5.18 Computing and Interpreting Risk and Bankruptcy Prediction Ratios for a Firm That Was Acquired. Sun Microsystems, Inc., develops, manufactures, and sells computers for network systems. Exhibit 5.20 presents selected financial data for Sun Microsystems for each of the five years ending June 30, Year 1, to June 30, Year 5. The company did not go bankrupt, but instead was acquired in Year 6 by **Oracle**. We recommend that you create an Excel spreadsheet to compute the values of the ratios and the Altman's Z-score in Requirements a and b, respectively.

`LO 5-3, LO 5-4, LO 5-6`

REQUIRED

a. Compute the value of each of the following risk ratios.
 (1) Current ratio (at the end of Year 1–Year 5)
 (2) Operating cash flow to current liabilities ratio (for Year 2–Year 5)
 (3) Liabilities to assets ratio (at the end of Year 1–Year 5)
 (4) Long-term debt to long-term capital ratio (at the end of Year 1–Year 5)
 (5) Operating cash flow to total liabilities ratio (for Year 2–Year 5)
 (6) Interest coverage ratio (for Year 1–Year 5)

	For Year Ended June 30,				
Exhibit 5.20					
Select Financial Data for Sun Microsystems, Inc. **(amounts in millions, except per-share amounts)** **(Problem 5.18)**					
	Year 5	**Year 4**	**Year 3**	**Year 2**	**Year 1**
Sales	$11,449	$13,880	$13,873	$13,086	$11,070
Net income (loss) before interest and taxes	$(2,166)	$640	$622	$(620)	$(150)
Interest expense	$17	$30	$39	$55	$34
Net income (loss)	$(2,234)	$403	$473	$(864)	$(107)
Current assets	$6,864	$7,834	$9,328	$8,460	$7,191
Total assets	$11,232	$14,340	$15,838	$15,082	$14,190
Current liabilities	$5,621	$5,668	$5,451	$6,165	$4,766
Long-term debt	$695	$1,265	$1,264	$575	$1,123
Total liabilities	$7,927	$8,752	$8,659	$8,738	$7,516
Retained earnings	$(2,055)	$430	$189	$(257)	$1,387
Shareholders' equity	$3,305	$5,588	$7,179	$6,344	$6,674
Cash flow provided by operations	$457	$1,329	$958	$567	$279
Common shares outstanding	752	752	884	876	852
Market price per share	$9.22	$10.88	$20.76	$16.60	$14.92

Source: Sun Microsystems, Inc., Forms 10-K for the Fiscal Years Ended June 2005–2009.

b. Compute the value of Altman's Z-score for Sun Microsystems for each year from Year 1 to Year 5.

c. Using the analyses in Requirements a and b, discuss the most important factors that signal the likelihood of bankruptcy of Sun Microsystems in Year 6.

LO 5-6

5.19 Computing and Interpreting Bankruptcy Prediction Ratios.
Exhibit 5.21 presents selected financial data for **Best Buy Co., Inc.**, and **Circuit City Stores, Inc.**, for fiscal 2008 and 2007. Best Buy and Circuit City operate as specialty retailers offering a wide range of consumer electronics, service contracts, product repairs, and home installation. Competition from **Walmart**, **Costco**, and Internet retailers put downward pressure on prices and margins. In November 2008, Circuit City filed Chapter 7 bankruptcy. In the media, Circuit City's bankruptcy was largely blamed on its poor treatment of employees. In early 2007, Circuit City laid off 3,400 high-paid salespersons, or approximately 8% of its workforce, which left inexperienced, low-paid workers in charge of customer service. Customer service quality plummeted, which was especially harmful for a retail business providing expensive electronic items, warranty products, and installation services.

REQUIRED
a. Compute Altman's Z-score for Best Buy and Circuit City for 2007 and 2008.
b. How did the bankruptcy risk of Best Buy change between 2007 and 2008? Explain.
c. How did the bankruptcy risk of Circuit City change between 2007 and 2008? Explain.

Exhibit 5.21

Select Financial Data for Best Buy and Circuit City
(amounts in thousands, except per-share amounts)
(Problem 5.19)

	Best Buy		Circuit City	
	Year Ended March 1,		Year Ended Feb. 28,	
	2008	2007	2008	2007
Sales	$40,023	$35,934	$11,744	$12,430
Net income (loss) before interest and taxes	$2,290	$2,161	$(352)	$22
Net income (loss)	$1,407	$1,377	$(321)	$(10)
Current assets	$7,342	$9,081	$2,440	$2,884
Total assets	$12,758	$13,570	$3,746	$4,007
Current liabilities	$6,769	$6,301	$1,606	$1,714
Total liabilities	$8,274	$7,369	$2,243	$2,216
Retained earnings	$3,933	$5,507	$981	$1,336
Common shares outstanding	411	481	169	171
Market price per share	$42.00	$44.97	$4.38	$18.47

Source: Best Buy Co., Inc., Form 10-K for the Fiscal Year Ended March 1, 2008, and Circuit City Stores, Inc., Form 10-K for the Fiscal Year Ended February 28, 2008.

d. As noted, Circuit City filed Chapter 7 bankruptcy in November 2008. Using the analysis from Requirements b and c, would you have predicted Circuit City or Best Buy to file bankruptcy in 2008? Explain.

5.20 Applying and Interpreting Bankruptcy Prediction Models. LO 5-6

Exhibit 5.22 presents selected financial data for ABC Auto and XYZ Comics for fiscal Year 5 and Year 6. ABC Auto manufactures automobile components that it sells to automobile manufacturers. Competitive conditions in the automobile industry in recent years have led automobile manufacturers to put pressure on suppliers such as ABC Auto to reduce costs and selling prices. XYZ Comics creates and sells comic books, trading cards, and other youth entertainment products and licenses others to use fictional characters created by XYZ Comics in their products. Youth readership of comic books and interest in trading cards have been declining steadily in recent years. XYZ Comics recognized a significant asset impairment charge in fiscal Year 6.

REQUIRED

a. Compute Altman's Z-score for ABC Auto and XYZ Comics for fiscal Year 5 and Year 6.
b. How did the bankruptcy risk of ABC Auto change between fiscal Year 5 and Year 6? Explain.

	Exhibit 5.22			

**Select Financial Data for ABC Auto and XYZ Comics
(amounts in thousands, except per-share amounts)
(Problem 5.20)**

	ABC Auto		XYZ Comics	
	Year 6	Year 5	Year 6	Year 5
Sales	$824,835	$631,832	$745,400	$828,900
Net income (loss) before interest and taxes	$(11,012)	$40,258	$(370,200)	$25,100
Net income (loss)	$(68,712)	$6,921	$(464,400)	$(48,400)
Current assets	$156,226	$195,417	$399,500	$490,600
Total assets	$617,705	$662,262	$844,000	$1,226,310
Current liabilities	$163,384	$176,000	$345,800	$318,100
Total liabilities	$648,934	$624,817	$999,700	$948,100
Retained earnings	$(184,308)	$(115,596)	$(350,300)	$114,100
Common shares outstanding	7,014	6,995	101,810	101,703
Market price per share	$85.00	$100.50	$1.625	$10.625

  c. How did the bankruptcy risk of XYZ Comics change between Year 5 and Year 6? Explain.
  d. Which firm is more likely to file for bankruptcy during fiscal Year 7? Explain using the analyses from Requirement b.

 5.21 Applying and Interpreting Bankruptcy Prediction Models.
Exhibit 5.23 presents selected financial data for **The Tribune Company** and **The Washington Post Company** for fiscal 2006 and 2007. The Washington Post Company is an education and media company. It owns, among others, Kaplan, Inc.; Cable ONE Inc.; *Newsweek* magazine; and Washington Post Media. The Tribune Company is a media and entertainment company, which also is diversified, owning the *Chicago Tribune*, the *Los Angeles Times*, television and radio affiliates such as The CW Network and WGN, and the Chicago Cubs. The Tribune Company filed for bankruptcy in December 2008.

REQUIRED

  a. Compute Altman's Z-score for The Tribune Company and The Washington Post Company for fiscal 2006 and 2007.
  b. How did the bankruptcy risk of The Tribune Company change between fiscal 2006 and 2007? Explain.
  c. How did the bankruptcy risk of The Washington Post Company change between fiscal 2006 and 2007? Explain.
  d. The Tribune Company filed Chapter 7 bankruptcy in December 2008. Using the analysis from Requirements b and c, would you have predicted The Tribune Company or The Washington Post Company to file bankruptcy? Explain.

Exhibit 5.23

Select Financial Data for The Tribune Company and The Washington Post Company (amounts in millions, except per-share amounts) (Problem 5.21)

	Tribune		Washington Post	
	2007	2006	2007	2006
Sales	$5,063	$5,444	$4,180	$3,905
Net income (loss) before interest and taxes	$619	$1,085	$505	$544
Net income (loss)	$87	$594	$289	$324
Current assets	$1,385	$1,346	$995	$935
Total assets	$13,150	$13,401	$6,005	$5,381
Current liabilities	$2,190	$2,549	$1,013	$812
Total liabilities	$16,664	$9,081	$2,543	$2,222
Retained earnings (deficit)	$(3,474)	$3,138	$4,330	$4,120
Common shares outstanding	239	307	10	10
Market price per share	$45.04	$58.69	$759.25	$711.53

Source: The Tribune Company, Form 10-K for the Fiscal Year Ended December 31, 2007, and The Washington Post Company, Form 10-K for the Fiscal Year Ended December 31, 2007.

5.22 Reformulating Financial Statements, Preparing an Alternative Decomposition of ROCE, and Assessing Financial Flexibility. LO 5-2

Exhibit 5.24 presents balance sheets for Year 2 and Year 3 for **Whole Foods Market, Inc.;** Exhibit 5.25 presents income statements for Year 1 through Year 3.

REQUIRED

a. For Year 3, prepare the standard decomposition of ROCE into margin, turnover, and leverage. Use average balances for balance sheet amounts.

b. Assume that all cash is operating cash (that is, no excess cash). Also assume that deferred lease liabilities are operating. Prepare the alternative decomposition of ROCE by computing NOPAT, net financing expense (after tax), operating profit margin, net operating assets turnover, operating ROA, leverage, and spread for Year 3. Use average balances for balance sheet amounts.

c. Use the same assumptions as in Requirement b, except that all cash is a financing asset (that is, all cash is excess cash) and deferred lease liabilities are a financing obligation. Prepare the alternative decomposition of ROCE by computing NOPAT, net financing expense (after tax), operating profit margin, net operating assets turnover, operating ROA, leverage, and spread for Year 3. Use average balances for balance sheet amounts.

d. Does the different treatment of financial assets and liabilities affect inferences you draw from the decomposition of ROCE? Explain.

Exhibit 5.24

Whole Foods Market, Inc., Balance Sheets
(amounts in thousands)
(Problem 5.22)

	Year 3	Year 2
ASSETS		
Cash and cash equivalents	$ 31,151	$ 2,310
Accounts receivable and other receivables	115,424	270,263
Merchandise inventories	327,452	288,112
Prepaid expenses and other current assets	68,150	40,402
Deferred income taxes	80,429	66,899
Total Current Assets	$ 622,606	$ 667,986
Property and equipment, net of accumulated depreciation and amortization	1,900,117	1,666,559
Goodwill	659,559	668,850
Intangible assets, net of accumulated amortization	78,499	97,683
Deferred income taxes	109,002	104,877
Other assets	10,953	7,173
Total Assets	$3,380,736	$3,213,128
LIABILITIES AND SHAREHOLDERS' EQUITY		
Current installments of long-term debt and capital lease obligations	$ 380	$ 24,781
Accounts payable	183,134	225,728
Accrued payroll, bonus, and other benefits due team members	196,233	181,290
Other current liabilities	286,430	340,551
Total Current Liabilities	$ 666,177	$ 772,350
Long-term debt and capital lease obligations, less current installments	928,790	736,087
Deferred lease liabilities	199,635	152,552
Other long-term liabilities	80,110	93,335
Total Liabilities	$1,874,712	$1,754,324
Common stock, no par value, 300,000 shares authorized; 140,286 and 143,787 shares issued, 140,286 and 139,240 shares outstanding in Year 3 and Year 2, respectively	$1,066,180	$1,232,845
Common stock in treasury, at cost	—	(199,961)
Accumulated other comprehensive income	422	15,722
Retained earnings	439,422	410,198
Total Shareholders' Equity	$1,506,024	$1,458,804
Total Liabilities and Shareholders' Equity	$3,380,736	$3,213,128

Source: Whole Foods Market, Inc., Form 10-K for the Fiscal Year Ended September 28, 2008.

Exhibit 5.25

Whole Foods Market, Inc., Income Statements (amounts in thousands) (Problem 5.22)

	Year 3	Year 2	Year 1
Sales	$7,953,912	$6,591,773	$5,607,376
Cost of goods sold and occupancy costs	5,247,207	4,295,170	3,647,734
Gross Profit	$2,706,705	$2,296,603	$1,959,642
Direct store expenses	2,107,940	1,711,229	1,421,968
General and administrative expenses	270,428	217,743	181,244
Pre-opening expenses	55,554	59,319	32,058
Relocation, store closure, and lease termination	36,545	10,861	5,363
Operating Income	$ 236,238	$ 297,451	$ 319,009
Interest expense	(36,416)	(4,208)	(32)
Investment and other income	6,697	11,324	20,736
Income before income taxes	$ 206,519	$ 304,567	$ 339,713
Provision for income taxes	91,995	121,827	135,885
Net Income	$ 114,524	$ 182,740	$ 203,828

Source: Whole Foods Market, Inc., Form 10-K for the Fiscal Year Ended September 28, 2008.

INTEGRATIVE CASE 5.1

LO 5-2, LO 5-3, LO 5-4, LO 5-6

Walmart

Exhibit 5.26 presents risk ratios for **Walmart** for 2014 and 2013. Exhibits 1.19, 1.20, and 1.21 in Chapter 1 present the financial statements for Walmart.

REQUIRED

a. Compute the values of each of the ratios in Exhibit 5.26 for Walmart for 2015. Walmart had 3,162 million common shares outstanding at the end of fiscal 2015, and the market price per share was $66.36. For 2014, the comparable shares and price per share were 3,228 million and $84.98, and for 2013, they were 3,233 million and $74.68, respectively. For days accounts receivable outstanding, use total revenues in your calculations.

b. Interpret the changes in Walmart's risk ratios during the three-year period, indicating any areas of concern.

Exhibit 5.26

Walmart
Risk Ratios
(Integrative Case 5.1)

	2015	2014	2013
Current ratio		0.97	0.88
Quick ratio		0.24	0.20
Operating cash flow to current liabilities ratio		0.42	0.33
Days accounts receivable outstanding		5.06	5.15
Days inventory held		44.99	45.19
Days accounts payable outstanding		37.87	38.37
Net days of working capital financing needed		12.17	11.98
Liabilities to assets ratio		0.58	0.60
Liabilities to shareholders' equity ratio		1.44	1.62
Long-term debt to long-term capital ratio		0.33	0.35
Long-term debt to shareholders' equity ratio		0.50	0.55
Interest coverage ratio		11.68	12.19
Operating cash flow to total liabilities ratio		0.24	0.19
Altman's Z-score		4.81	4.41
Probability of bankruptcy		0.00%	0.00%

LO 5-5

CASE 5.2

Massachusetts Stove Company—Bank Lending Decision

Massachusetts Stove Company manufactures wood-burning stoves for the heating of homes and businesses. The company has approached you, as chief lending officer for the Massachusetts Regional Bank, seeking to increase its loan from the current level of $93,091 as of January 15, Year 12, to $143,091. Jane O'Neil, chief executive officer and majority stockholder of the company, indicates that the company needs the loan to finance the working capital required for an expected 25% annual increase in sales during the next two years, including to pay suppliers and provide funds for expected nonrecurring legal and retooling costs.

The company's woodstoves have two distinguishing characteristics: (1) the metal frame of the stoves includes inlaid soapstone, which increases the intensity and duration of the heat provided by the stoves and enhances their appearance as an attractive piece of furniture, and (2) a catalytic combustor, which adds heating potential to the stoves and reduces air pollution.

The company manufactures wood-burning stoves in a single plant in Greenfield, Massachusetts. It purchases metal castings for the stoves from foundries in Germany and Belgium. The soapstone comes from a supplier in Canada. These purchases are denominated in U.S. dollars. The catalytic combustor is purchased from a supplier in the United States. The manufacturing process is essentially an assembly operation. The plant employs an average of eight workers. The two keys to quality control are structural airtightness and effective operation of the catalytic combustor.

The company rents approximately 60% of the 25,000-square-foot building it uses for manufacturing and administrative activities. This building also houses the company's factory showroom. The remaining 40% of the building is not currently rented.

The company's marketing of woodstoves follows three channels:

1. Wholesaling of stoves to retail hardware stores. This channel represents approximately 20% of the company's sales in units.
2. Retail direct marketing to individuals in all 50 states. This channel utilizes (a) national advertising in construction and design magazines and (b) the sending of brochures to potential customers identified from personal inquiries. This channel represents approximately 70% of the company's sales in units. The company is the only firm in the industry with a strategic emphasis on retail direct marketing.
3. Retailing from the company's showroom. This channel represents approximately 10% of the company's sales in units.

The company offers three payment options to retail purchasers of its stoves:

1. Full payment: Check, money order, or charge to a third-party credit card is used to pay in full.
2. Layaway plan: Monthly payments are made over a period not exceeding one year. The company ships the stove after receiving the final payment.
3. Installment financing plan: The company has a financing arrangement with a local bank to finance the purchase of stoves by credit-approved customers. The company is liable if customers fail to repay their installment bank loans.

The imposition of strict air emission standards by the Environmental Protection Agency (EPA) has resulted in a major change in the woodstove industry. By December 31, Year 9, firms were required by EPA regulations to demonstrate that their woodstoves met or surpassed specified air emission standards. These standards were stricter than industry practices accommodated at the time, and firms had to engage in numerous company-sponsored and independent testing of their stoves to satisfy EPA regulators. As a consequence, the number of firms in the woodstove industry decreased from more than 200 in the years prior to Year 10 to approximately 35 by December 31, Year 11.

The company received approval for its Soapstone Stove I in Year 11, after incurring retooling and testing costs of $63,001. It capitalized these costs in the Property, Plant, and Equipment account. It depreciates these costs over the five-year EPA approval period. A second stove, Soapstone Stove II, is currently undergoing retooling and testing. For this stove, the company incurred costs of $19,311 in Year 10 and $8,548 in Year 11 and has received preliminary EPA approval. It anticipates additional design, tooling, and testing costs of approximately $55,000 in Year 12 and $33,000 in Year 13 to obtain final EPA approval.

The company holds an option to purchase the building in which it is located for $608,400. The option also permits the company to assume the unpaid balance on a low-interest-rate loan on the building from the New England Regional Industrial Development Authority. The interest rate on this loan is adjusted annually and equals 80% of the bank prime interest rate. The unpaid balance on the loan exceeds the option price and will result in a cash transfer to the company from the owner of the building at the time of transfer. The company exercised its option in Year 9, but the owner of the building refused to comply with the option provisions. The company sued the owner. The case has gone through the lower court system in Massachusetts and is currently under review by the Massachusetts Supreme Court. The company incurred legal costs totaling $68,465 through Year 11 and anticipates additional costs of approximately $45,000 in Year 12. The lower courts have ruled in favor of the company's position on all of the major issues in the case. The company expects the Massachusetts Supreme Court to concur with the decisions of the lower courts when it renders its final decision in the spring of Year 12. The company has held discussions with two prospective tenants for the building's 10,000 square feet that Massachusetts Stove Company does not use in its operations.

Jane O'Neil owns 51% of the company's common stock. The remaining stockholders include John O'Neil (chief financial officer and father of Jane O'Neil), Mark Forest (vice president of manufacturing), and four independent local investors.

To assist in the loan decision, the company provides you with financial statements (see the first three columns of Exhibits 5.27–5.29) and notes for the three years ending December 31, Year 9, Year 10, and Year 11. These financial statements were prepared by John O'Neil, chief financial officer, and are not audited. The company also provides you with projected financial statements for Year 12 and Year 13 (see the last two columns of Exhibits 5.27–5.29) to demonstrate its need for the loan and its ability to repay. The loan requested involves an increase in the current loan amount from $93,091 to $143,091. The company will pay monthly interest and repay the $50,000 additional amount borrowed by December 31, Year 13. Exhibit 5.30 presents financial statement ratios for the company.

The assumptions underlying the projected financial statements are as follows:

- *Sales:* Sales are projected to increase 25% annually during the next two years, after increasing 17.7% in Year 10 and 21.9% in Year 11. The increase reflects continuing market opportunities related to the company's strategic emphasis on retail direct marketing and to the expected continuing contraction in the number of competitors in the industry.

- *Cost of Goods Sold:* Most manufacturing costs vary with sales. The company projects cost of goods sold to equal 51% of sales in Year 12 and 49% of sales in Year 13, having declined from 69.2% of sales in Year 9 to 53.9% of sales in Year 11. The reductions resulted from a higher proportion of retail sales in the sales mix (which have a higher gross margin than wholesale sales), a more favorable pricing environment in the industry (fewer competitors), a switch to lower-cost suppliers, and more efficient production.

- *Selling and Administrative Expenses:* The company projects these costs to equal 41% of sales, having increased from 26.7% of sales in Year 9 to 40.9% of sales in Year 11. The increases resulted from a heavier emphasis on retail sales, which require more aggressive marketing than wholesale sales.

- *Legal Expenses:* The additional $45,000 of legal costs represents the best estimate by the company's attorneys.

- *Interest Expense:* Interest expense has averaged approximately 6% of short- and long-term borrowing during the last three years. The projected income statement assumes a continuation of the 6% average rate.

- *Income Tax Expense:* The company has elected to be taxed as a Subchapter S corporation, which means that the net income of the firm is taxed at the level of the individual shareholders, not at the corporate level. Thus, the pro forma financial statements include no income tax expense. The firm operated at a net loss for several years prior to Year 11, primarily because of losses of a lawn products business that it acquired 10 years ago. The company discontinued the lawn products business in Year 10.

- *Cash:* The projected amounts for cash represent a plug to equate projected assets with projected liabilities and shareholders' equity. Projected liabilities include the requested loan during Year 12 and its repayment at the end of Year 13.

- *Accounts Receivable:* Days accounts receivable outstanding, calculated on the average accounts receivable balances, will be 11 days in Year 12 and Year 13.

- *Inventories:* Days inventory held, calculated on the average inventory balances, will be 155 days in Year 12 and Year 13.
- *Property, Plant, and Equipment:* Capital expenditures for Year 12 include a $55,000 cost for retooling the Soapstone Stove II and $7,500 for other equipment; for Year 13, they include $33,000 for retooling the Soapstone Stove II and $14,500 for other equipment. The projected balance excludes the cost of acquiring the building, its related debt, the cash received at the time of transfer, and rental revenues from leasing the unused 40% of the building to other businesses.
- *Accumulated Depreciation:* This is a continuation of the historical relation between depreciation expense and the cost of property, plant, and equipment.
- *Other Assets:* A new financial reporting standard no longer requires amortization of intangibles after Year 11.
- *Accounts Payable:* Days accounts payable outstanding, based on the average accounts payable balances, will be 97 days in Year 12 and 89 days in Year 13. The decrease in days payable reflects the ability to pay suppliers more quickly with the proceeds of the increased bank loan.
- *Notes Payable:* Notes payable is projected to increase by the amount of the bank loan in Year 12 and to decrease by the loan repayment at the end of Year 13.
- *Other Current Liabilities:* The large increase at the end of Year 11 resulted from a major promotional offer in the fall of Year 11, which increased the amount of deposits by customers. The projected amounts for Year 12 and Year 13 represent more normal expected levels of deposits.
- *Long-Term Debt:* Long-term borrowing represents loans from shareholders to the company. The company does not plan to repay any of these loans in the near future.
- *Retained Earnings:* The change each year represents net income or net loss from operations. The company does not pay dividends.
- *Statement of Cash Flows:* Amounts are taken from the changes in various accounts on the actual and projected balance sheets.

Exhibit 5.27

Massachusetts Stove Company
Income Statements
(Case 5.2)

	Actual			Projected	
	Year 9	Year 10	Year 11	Year 12	Year 13
Sales	$ 665,771	$ 783,754	$ 955,629	$1,194,535	$1,493,170
Cost of goods sold	(460,797)	(474,156)	(514,907)	(609,213)	(731,653)
Selling and administrative	(177,631)	(290,719)	(390,503)	(489,760)	(612,200)
Legal (Note 1)	(28,577)	(30,092)	(9,796)	(45,000)	—
Interest	(25,948)	(24,122)	(23,974)	(26,510)	(26,510)
Income tax (Note 2)	—	—	—	—	—
Net Income (Loss)	$ (27,182)	$ (35,335)	$ 16,449	$ 24,052	$ 122,807

Exhibit 5.28

Massachusetts Stove Company
Balance Sheets
(Case 5.2)

December 31	Actual				Projected	
	Year 8	Year 9	Year 10	Year 11	Year 12	Year 13
ASSETS						
Cash	$ 3,925	$ 11,707	$ 8,344	$ 37,726	$ 11,289	$ 6,512
Accounts receivable	94,606	54,772	44,397	31,964	40,035	49,964
Inventories	239,458	208,260	209,004	225,490	291,924	329,480
Total Current Assets	$ 337,989	$ 274,739	$ 261,745	$ 295,180	$ 343,248	$ 385,956
Property, plant, and equipment, at cost	$ 258,870	$ 316,854	$ 362,399	$ 377,784	$ 440,284	$ 487,784
Accumulated depreciation	(205,338)	(228,985)	(250,189)	(274,347)	(302,502)	(333,694)
Property, plant, and equipment, net	$ 53,532	$ 87,869	$ 112,210	$ 103,437	$ 137,782	$ 154,090
Other assets	$ 17,888	$ 17,888	$ 17,594	$ 17,006	$ 17,006	$ 17,006
Total Assets	$ 409,409	$ 380,496	$ 391,549	$ 415,623	$ 498,036	$ 557,052
LIABILITIES AND SHAREHOLDERS' EQUITY						
Accounts payable	$ 148,579	$ 139,879	$ 189,889	$ 160,905	$ 198,206	$ 176,915
Notes payable—banks (Note 3)	152,985	140,854	125,256	93,091	143,091	93,091
Other current liabilities (Note 4)	13,340	11,440	23,466	62,440	33,500	41,000
Total Current Liabilities	$ 314,904	$ 292,173	$ 338,611	$ 316,436	$ 374,797	$ 311,006
Long-term debt (Note 3)	248,000	269,000	268,950	298,750	298,750	298,750
Total Liabilities	$ 562,904	$ 561,173	$ 607,561	$ 615,186	$ 673,547	$ 609,756
Common stock	$ 2,000	$ 2,000	$ 2,000	$ 2,000	$ 2,000	$ 2,000
Additional paid-in capital	435,630	435,630	435,630	435,630	435,630	435,630
Accumulated deficit	(591,125)	(618,307)	(653,642)	(637,193)	(613,141)	(490,334)
Total Shareholders' Equity	$(153,495)	$(180,677)	$(216,012)	$(199,563)	$(175,511)	$ (52,704)
Total Liabilities and Shareholders' Equity	$ 409,409	$ 380,496	$ 391,549	$ 415,623	$ 498,036	$ 557,052

Exhibit 5.29

Massachusetts Stove Company
Statements of Cash Flows
(Case 5.2)

	Actual			Projected	
	Year 9	Year 10	Year 11	Year 12	Year 13
OPERATIONS					
Net income (loss)	$(27,182)	$(35,335)	$ 16,449	$ 24,052	$122,807
Depreciation and amortization	23,647	21,204	24,158	28,155	31,192
(Increase) Decrease in accounts receivable	39,834	10,375	12,433	(8,071)	(9,929)
(Increase) Decrease in inventories	31,198	(744)	(16,486)	(66,434)	(37,556)
Increase (Decrease) in accounts payable	(8,700)	50,010	(28,984)	37,301	(21,291)
Increase (Decrease) in other current liabilities	(1,900)	12,026	38,974	(28,940)	7,500
Cash Flow from Operations	$ 56,897	$ 57,536	$ 46,544	$(13,937)	$ 92,723
INVESTING					
Fixed assets acquired	$(57,984)	$(45,545)	$(15,385)	$(62,500)	$ (47,500)
Other investing	—	294	588	—	—
Cash Flow from Investing	$(57,984)	$(45,251)	$(14,797)	$(62,500)	$ (47,500)
FINANCING					
Increase (Decrease) in short-term borrowing	$(12,131)	$(15,598)	$(32,165)	$ 50,000	$ (50,000)
Increase (Decrease) in long-term borrowing	21,000	(50)	29,800	—	—
Cash Flow from Financing	$ 8,869	$(15,648)	$ (2,365)	$ 50,000	$ (50,000)
Change in Cash	$ 7,782	$ (3,363)	$ 29,382	$(26,437)	$ (4,777)
Cash—beginning of year	3,925	11,707	8,344	37,726	11,289
Cash—End of Year	$ 11,707	$ 8,344	$ 37,726	$ 11,289	$ 6,512

Notes to Financial Statements

Note 1: The company has incurred legal costs to enforce its option to purchase the building used in its manufacturing and administrative activities. The case is under review by the Massachusetts Supreme Court, with a decision expected in the spring of Year 12.

Note 2: The company is not subject to income tax because it has elected Subchapter S tax status.

Note 3: The notes payable to banks are secured by machinery and equipment, shares of common stock of companies traded on the New York Stock Exchange owned by two shareholders, and personal guarantees of three shareholders. The long-term debt consists of unsecured loans from three shareholders.

Exhibit 5.30

Massachusetts Stove Company
Profitability and Risk Ratios
(Case 5.2)

	Actual			Projected	
	Year 9	Year 10	Year 11	Year 12	Year 13
Profit margin for ROA	(0.2%)	(1.4%)	4.2%	4.2%	10.0%
Assets turnover	1.7	2.0	2.4	2.6	2.8
Return on assets	(0.3%)	(2.9%)	10.0%	11.1%	28.3%
Cost of goods sold/Sales	69.2%	60.5%	53.9%	51.0%	49.0%
Selling and administrative expenses/Sales	26.7%	37.1%	40.9%	41.0%	41.0%
Legal expense/Sales	4.3%	3.8%	1.0%	3.8%	—
Interest expense/Sales	3.9%	3.1%	2.5%	2.2%	1.8%
Days accounts receivable outstanding	41	23	15	11	11
Days inventory held	177	161	154	155	155
Days accounts payable outstanding	122	127	122	96	89
Fixed assets turnover	9.4	7.8	8.9	9.9	10.2
Current ratio	0.9	0.8	0.9	0.9	1.2
Quick ratio	0.2	0.2	0.2	0.1	0.2
Operating cash flow to current liabilities ratio	0.187	0.182	0.142	(0.040)	0.270
Liabilities to assets ratio	1.475	1.552	1.480	1.352	1.095
Long-term debt to shareholders' equity ratio	0.707	0.687	0.719	0.600	0.536
Operating cash flow to total liabilities ratio	0.101	0.098	0.076	(0.022)	0.145
Interest coverage ratio	0.0	(0.5)	1.7	1.9	5.6

Note 4: Other current liabilities include the following:

	Year 8	Year 9	Year 10	Year 11
Customer deposits	$11,278	$ 9,132	$20,236	$59,072
Employee taxes withheld	2,062	2,308	3,230	3,368
	$13,340	$11,440	$23,466	$62,440

REQUIRED

Would you make the loan to the company in accordance with the stated terms? Explain. In responding, consider the reasonableness of the company's projections, positive and negative factors affecting the industry and the company, and the likely ability of the company to repay the loan. (Excel spreadsheet for this case is available at www.cengagebrain.com.)

CASE 5.3

Fly-by-Night International Group: Can This Company Be Saved?

Douglas C. Mather, founder, chair, and chief executive of Fly-by-Night International Group (FBN), lived the fast-paced, risk-seeking life that he tried to inject into his company. Flying the company's Learjets, he logged 28 world speed records. Once he throttled a company plane to the top of Mount Everest in three and a half minutes.

These activities seemed perfectly appropriate at the time. Mather was a Navy fighter pilot in Vietnam and then flew commercial airlines. In the mid-1970s, he started FBN as a pilot training school. With the defense buildup beginning in the early 1980s, Mather branched out into government contracting. He equipped the company's Learjets with radar jammers and other sophisticated electronic devices to mimic enemy aircraft. He then contracted his "rent-an-enemy" fleet to the Navy and Air Force for use in fighter pilot training. The Pentagon liked the idea, and FBN's revenues grew to $55 million in the fiscal year ending April 30, Year 14. Its common stock, issued to the public in Year 9 at $8.50 a share, reached a high of $16.50 in mid-Year 13. Mather and FBN received glowing write-ups in *Business Week* and *Fortune*.

In mid-Year 14, however, FBN began a rapid descent. Although still growing rapidly, its cash flow was inadequate to service its debt. According to Mather, he was "just dumbfounded. There was never an inkling of a problem with cash."

In the fall of Year 14, the board of directors withdrew the company's financial statements for the year ending April 30, Year 14, stating that there appeared to be material misstatements that needed investigation. In December of Year 14, Mather was asked to step aside as manager and director of the company pending completion of an investigation of certain transactions between Mather and the company. On December 29, Year 14, NASDAQ (over-the-counter stock market) discontinued quoting the company's common shares. In February, Year 15, following its investigation, the board of directors terminated Mather's employment and membership on the board.

Exhibits 5.31–5.33 present the financial statements and related notes of FBN for the five years ending April, Year 10, through April, Year 14. The financial statements for Year 10 to Year 12 use the amounts originally reported for each year. The amounts reported on the statement of cash flows for Year 10 (for example, the change in accounts receivable) do not precisely reconcile to the amounts on the balance sheet at the beginning and end of the year because certain items classified as relating to continuing operations on the balance sheet at the end of Year 9 were reclassified as relating to discontinued operations on the balance sheet at the end of Year 10. The financial statements for Year 13 and Year 14 represent the restated financial statements for those years after the board of directors completed its investigation of suspected material misstatements that caused it to withdraw the originally issued financial statements for fiscal Year 14. Exhibit 5.34 lists the members of the board of directors. Exhibit 5.35 presents profitability and risk ratios for FBN.

REQUIRED

Study these financial statements and notes and respond to the following questions:

a. What evidence do you observe from analyzing the financial statements that might signal the cash flow problems experienced in mid-Year 14?

b. Can FBN avoid bankruptcy during Year 15? What changes in the design or implementation of FBN's strategy would you recommend? To compute Altman's Z-score, use the low-bid market price for the year to determine the market value of common shareholders' equity.

Exhibit 5.31

Fly-by-Night International Group
Comparative Balance Sheets
(amounts in thousands)
(Case 5.3)

April 30,

	Year 14	Year 13	Year 12	Year 11	Year 10	Year 9
ASSETS						
Cash	$ 159	$ 583	$ 313	$ 142	$ 753	$ 192
Notes receivable				1,000		
Accounts receivable	6,545	4,874	2,675	1,490	1,083	2,036
Inventories	5,106	2,514	1,552	602	642	686
Prepayments	665	829	469	57	303	387
Net assets of discontinued businesses	—	—	—	—	1,926	—
Total Current Assets	$ 12,475	$ 8,800	$ 5,009	$ 3,291	$ 4,707	$ 3,301
Property, plant, and equipment	$106,529	$76,975	$24,039	$17,809	$37,250	$17,471
Less accumulated depreciation	(17,231)	(8,843)	(5,713)	(4,288)	(4,462)	(2,593)
Net	$ 89,298	$68,132	$18,326	$13,521	$32,788	$14,878
Other assets	$ 470	$ 665	$ 641	$ 1,112	$ 1,566	$ 1,278
Total Assets	$102,243	$77,597	$23,976	$17,924	$39,061	$19,457
LIABILITIES AND SHAREHOLDERS' EQUITY						
Accounts payable	$ 12,428	$ 6,279	$ 993	$ 939	$ 2,285	$ 1,436
Notes payable	—	945	140	1,021	4,766	—
Current portion of long-term debt	60,590	7,018	1,789	1,104	2,774	1,239
Other current liabilities	12,903	12,124	2,423	1,310	1,845	435
Total Current Liabilities	$ 85,921	$26,366	$ 5,345	$ 4,374	$11,670	$ 3,110
Long-term debt	—	41,021	9,804	6,738	20,041	9,060
Deferred income taxes	—	900	803	—	1,322	1,412
Other noncurrent liabilities	—	—	226	—	248	—
Total Liabilities	$ 85,921	$68,287	$16,178	$11,112	$33,281	$13,582
Common stock	$ 34	$ 22	$ 21	$ 20	$ 20	$ 20
Additional paid-in capital	16,516	5,685	4,569	4,323	3,611	3,611
Retained earnings	(29)	3,802	3,208	2,469	2,149	2,244
Treasury stock	(199)	(199)	—	—	—	—
Total Shareholders' Equity	$ 16,322	$ 9,310	$ 7,798	$ 6,812	$ 5,780	$ 5,875
Total Liabilities and Shareholders' Equity	$102,243	$77,597	$23,976	$17,924	$39,061	$19,457

Exhibit 5.32

Fly-by-Night International Group
Comparative Income Statements
(amounts in thousands)
(Case 5.3)

	Year Ended April 30,				
	Year 14	Year 13	Year 12	Year 11	Year 10
CONTINUING OPERATIONS					
Sales	$54,988	$36,597	$20,758	$19,266	$31,992
EXPENSES					
Cost of services	$38,187	$26,444	$12,544	$ 9,087	$22,003
Selling and administrative	5,880	3,020	3,467	2,989	4,236
Depreciation	9,810	3,150	1,703	2,798	3,003
Interest	5,841	3,058	1,101	2,743	2,600
Income taxes	(900)	379	803	671	74
Total Expenses	$58,818	$36,051	$19,618	$18,288	$31,916
Income—continuing operations	$ (3,830)	$ 546	$ 1,140	$ 978	$ 76
Income—discontinued operations	—	47	(400)	(659)	(171)
Net Income	$ (3,830)	$ 593	$ 740	$ 319	$ (95)

Notes to Financial Statements

1. Summary of Significant Accounting Policies

Consolidation. The consolidated financial statements include the accounts of the company and its wholly owned subsidiaries. The company uses the equity method for subsidiaries that are not majority owned (50% or less) and eliminates significant intercompany transactions and balances.

    Inventories. Inventories, which consist of aircraft fuel, spare parts, and supplies, appear at lower of FIFO cost or market.

    Property and Equipment. Property and equipment appear at acquisition cost. The company capitalizes major inspections, renewals, and improvements, while it expenses replacements, maintenance, and repairs that do not improve or extend the life of the respective assets. The company computes depreciation of property and equipment using the straight-line method.

    Contract Income Recognition. Contractual specifications (such as revenue rates, reimbursement terms, and functional considerations) vary among contracts; accordingly, the company recognizes guaranteed contract income (guaranteed revenue minus related direct costs) as it logs flight hours or on a straight-line monthly basis over the contract year, whichever method better reflects the economics of the contract. The company recognizes income from discretionary hours flown in excess of the minimum guaranteed amount each month as it logs such discretionary hours.

    Income Taxes. The company recognizes deferred income taxes for temporary differences between financial and tax reporting amounts.

Exhibit 5.33

**Fly-by-Night International Group
Comparative Statements of Cash Flows
(amounts in thousands)
(Case 5.3)**

	Year 14	Year 13	Year 12	Year 11	Year 10
			Year Ended April 30,		
OPERATIONS					
Income—continuing operations	$ (3,830)	$ 546	$ 1,140	$ 978	$ 76
Depreciation	9,810	3,150	1,703	2,798	3,003
Other adjustments	1,074	1,817	1,119	671	74
Changes in working capital:					
(Increase) Decrease in receivables	(1,671)	(2,199)	(1,185)	(407)	403
(Increase) Decrease in inventories	(2,592)	(962)	(950)	40	19
(Increase) Decrease in prepayment	164	(360)	(412)	246	36
Increase (Decrease) in accounts payable	6,149	5,286	54	(1,346)	359
Increase (Decrease) in other current liabilities	779	9,701	1,113	(535)	596
Cash Flow from Continuing Operations	$ 9,883	$ 16,979	$ 2,582	$ 2,445	$ 4,566
Cash flow from discontinued operations	—	(77)	(472)	(752)	(335)
Net Cash Flow from Operations	$ 9,883	$ 16,902	$ 2,110	$ 1,693	$ 4,231
INVESTING					
Sale of property, plant, and equipment	$ 259	$ 3	$ 119	$ 18,387	$ 12
Acquisition of property, plant, and equipment	(33,035)	(52,960)	(6,573)	(2,424)	(20,953)
Other	(1,484)	78	1,017	(679)	30
Net Cash Flow from Investing	$(34,260)	$(52,879)	$(5,437)	$ 15,284	$(20,911)
FINANCING					
Increase in short-term borrowing	$ —	$ 805	$ —	$ —	$ 4,766
Increase in long-term borrowing	43,279	42,152	5,397	5,869	14,739
Issue of common stock	12,266	191	428	—	—
Decrease in short-term borrowing	(945)	—	(881)	(3,745)	—
Decrease in long-term borrowing	(30,522)	(7,024)	(1,647)	(19,712)	(2,264)
Acquisition of common stock	—	(198)	—	—	—
Other	(125)	321	201	—	—
Net Cash Flow from Financing	$ 23,953	$ 36,247	$ 3,498	$(17,588)	$ 17,241
Change in Cash	$ (424)	$ 270	$ 171	$ (611)	$ 561
Cash—beginning of year	583	313	142	753	192
Cash—End of Year	$ 159	$ 583	$ 313	$ 142	$ 753

Exhibit 5.34

Fly-by-Night International Group
Members of the Board of Directors
(Case 5.3)

Charles A. Barry, USAF (Ret.), Executive Vice President of Wicks and Associates, Inc., a management consulting firm
Thomas P. Gilkey, Vice President, Marketing
Lawrence G. Hicks, Secretary and General Counsel
Michael S. Holt, Vice President, Finance, and Chief Financial Officer
Gordon K. John, Executive Vice President and Chief Operating Officer
Douglas C. Mather, Chair of the Board, President, and Chief Executive Officer
Edward F. O'Hara, President of the O'Hara Companies, which manufactures aircraft products
E. William Shapiro, Professor of Law, Emory University

Exhibit 5.35

Profitability and Risk Ratios for FBN
(Case 5.3)

	Year 14	Year 13	Year 12	Year 11	Year 10
Profit margin for ROA	(0.1%)	6.9%	9.0%	14.5	5.6%
Assets turnover	0.6	0.7	1.0	0.7	1.1
ROA	0.0%	5.0%	8.9%	9.8%	6.1%
Cost of goods and services/Sales	69.4%	72.3%	60.4%	47.2%	68.8%
Selling and administrative/Sales	10.7%	8.3%	16.7%	15.5%	13.2%
Depreciation expense/Sales	17.8%	8.6%	8.2%	14.5%	9.4%
Income tax expense (excluding tax effects of interest)/Sales	2.1%	4.0%	5.7%	8.3%	3.0%
Interest expense/Sales	10.6%	8.4%	5.3%	14.2%	8.1%
Days accounts receivable outstanding	38	38	37	24	18
Days accounts payable outstanding	84	48	26	65	31
Fixed assets turnover	0.7	0.8	1.3	0.8	1.3
Profit margin for ROCE	(7.0%)	1.5%	5.5%	5.1%	0.2%
Capital structure leverage	7.0	5.9	2.9	4.5	5.0
ROCE	(29.9%)	6.4%	15.6%	15.5%	1.3%
Current ratio	0.2	0.3	0.9	0.8	0.4
Quick ratio	0.1	0.2	0.6	0.6	0.2
Operating cash flow to current liabilities ratio	0.176	1.071	0.531	0.305	0.618
Liabilities to assets ratio	0.840	0.880	0.675	0.620	0.852
Long-term debt to long-term capital ratio	0.000	0.815	0.557	0.497	0.776
Operating cash flow to total liabilities ratio	0.128	0.402	0.189	0.112	0.195
Interest coverage ratio	0.2	1.3	2.8	1.6	1.1

2. Transactions with Major Customers

The company provides contract flight services to three major customers: the U.S. Air Force, the U.S. Navy, and the Federal Reserve Bank System. These contracts have termination dates in Year 16 or Year 17. Revenues from all government contracts as a percentage of total revenues were as follows: Year 14, 62%; Year 13, 72%; Year 12, 73%; Year 11, 68%; and Year 10, 31%.

3. Segment Data

During Year 10, the company operated in the following five business segments:

Flight Operations—Business. Provides combat readiness training to the military and nightly transfer of negotiable instruments for the Federal Reserve Bank System, both under multiyear contracts.

Flight Operations—Transport. Provides charter transport services to a variety of customers.

Fixed-Base Operations. Provides ground support operations (fuel and maintenance) to commercial airlines at several major airports.

Education and Training. Provides training for nonmilitary pilots.

Aircraft Sales and Leasing. Acquires aircraft that the company then resells or leases to various firms.

The company discontinued the Flight Operations—Transport and Education and Training segments in Year 11. It sold most of the assets of the Aircraft Sales and Leasing segment in Year 11.

Segment revenue, operating profit, and asset data for the various segments are as follows (amounts in thousands):

	Year Ended April 30,				
	Year 14	Year 13	Year 12	Year 11	Year 10
Revenues					
Flight Operations—Business	$ 44,062	$31,297	$16,026	$11,236	$10,803
Flight Operations—Transport	—	—	—	—	13,805
Fixed-Base Operations	9,597	4,832	4,651	3,911	3,647
Education and Training	—	—	—	—	542
Aircraft Sales and Leasing	1,329	468	81	4,119	3,195
Total	$ 54,988	$36,597	$20,758	$19,266	$31,992
Operating Profit					
Flight Operations—Business	$ 5,707	$ 4,863	$ 3,455	$ 2,463	$ 849
Flight Operations—Transport	—	—	—	—	(994)
Fixed-Base Operations	(2,041)	1,362	1,038	174	332
Education and Training	—	—	—	—	12
Aircraft Sales and Leasing	1,175	378	(15)	1,217[b]	2,726[a]
Total	$ 4,841	$ 6,603	$ 4,478	$ 3,854	$ 2,925
Assets					
Flight Operations—Business	$ 85,263	$64,162	$17,738	$11,130	$13,684
Flight Operations—Transport	—	—	—	—	1,771
Fixed-Base Operations	16,544	13,209	5,754	5,011	4,784
Education and Training	—	—	—	—	1,789
Aircraft Sales and Leasing	436	226	438	1,262	18,524
Total	$102,243	$77,597	$23,930	$17,403	$40,552

[a]Includes a gain of $1.2 million on the sale of aircraft.
[b]Includes a gain of $2.6 million on the sale of aircraft.

4. Discontinued Operations

Income from discontinued operations consists of the following (amounts in thousands):

Year 13

Income from operations of Flight Operations—Transport ($78), net of income taxes of $31	$ 47
Year 12	
Loss from write-off of airline operations certificates in Flight Operations— Transport business	$(400)
Year 11	
Loss from operations of Flight Operations—Transport ($1,261) and Education and Training ($172) segments, net of income tax benefits of $685	$(748)
Gain on disposal of Education and Training business, net of income taxes of $85	89
Total	$(659)
Year 10	
Loss from operations of Charter Tour business, net of income tax benefits of $164	$(171)

5. Related-Party Transactions

On April 30, Year 11, the company sold most of the net assets of the Aircraft Sales and Leasing segment to Interlease, Inc., a Georgia corporation wholly owned by the company's majority stockholder, whose personal holdings at that time represented approximately 75% of the company.

Under the terms of the sale, the sales price was $1,368,000, of which the buyer paid $368,000 in cash and gave a promissory note for the remaining $1,000,000. The company treated the proceeds received in excess of the book value of the net assets sold of $712,367 as a capital contribution due to the related-party nature of the transaction. FBN originally acquired the assets of the Aircraft Sales and Leasing segment during Year 10.

On September 29, Year 14, FBN's board of directors established a Transaction Committee to examine certain transactions between the company and Douglas Mather, FBN's chair, president, and majority stockholder. These transactions appear here.

Certain Loans to Mather. In early September, Year 13, the board of directors authorized a $1 million loan to Mather at the company's cost of borrowing plus $1/8$%. On September 19, Year 13, Mather tendered a $1 million check to the company in repayment of the loan. On September 22, Year 13, at Mather's direction, the company made an additional $1 million loan to him, the proceeds of which Mather apparently used to cover his check in repayment of the first $1 million loan. The Transaction Committee concluded that the board of directors did not authorize the September 22, Year 13, loan to Mather, nor was any director other than Mather aware of the loan at the time. The company's Year 13 Proxy Statement, dated September 27, Year 13, incorrectly stated that "as of September 19, Year 13, Mather had repaid the principal amount of his indebtedness to the company." Mather's $1 million loan remained outstanding until it was canceled in connection with the ESOP (employee stock ownership plan) transaction discussed next.

ESOP Transaction. On February 28, Year 14, the company's ESOP acquired 100,000 shares of the company's common stock from Mather at $14.25 per share. FBN financed the purchase. The ESOP gave the company a $1,425,000 unsecured demand note. To complete the transaction, the company canceled a $1,000,000 promissory note from Mather and paid the remaining $425,000 in cash. The Transaction Committee determined that the board of directors did not authorize the $1,425,000 loan to the ESOP, the cancellation of Mather's $1,000,000 note, or the payment of $425,000 in cash.

Eastwind Transaction. On April 27, Year 14, the company acquired four Eastwind aircraft from a German company. FBN subsequently sold these aircraft to Transreco, a corporation owned by Douglas Mather, for a profit of $1,600,000. In late September and early October, Transreco sold these four aircraft at a profit of $780,000 to unaffiliated third parties. The Transactions Committee determined that none of the officers or directors of the company were aware of the Eastwind transaction until late September, Year 14.

On December 12, Year 14, the company announced that Mather had agreed to step aside as chair and director and take no part in management of the company pending resolution of the matters presented to the board by the Transactions Committee. On February 13, Year 15, the company announced that it had entered into a settlement agreement with Mather and Transreco resolving certain of the issues addressed by the Transactions Committee. Pursuant to the agreement, the company will receive $211,000, the bonus paid to Mather for fiscal Year 14, and $780,000, the gain recognized by Transreco on the sale of the Eastwind aircraft. Also pursuant to the settlement, Mather will resign all positions with the company and waive his rights under his employment agreement to any future compensation or benefits to which he might otherwise have a claim.

6. Long-Term Debt

Long-term debt consists of the following (amounts in thousands):

	April 30,				
	Year 14	Year 13	Year 12	Year 11	Year 10
Notes payable to banks:					
Variable rate	$ 44,702	$30,495	$ 2,086	$ 2,504	$ 3,497
Fixed rate	13,555	14,679	6,292	3,562	1,228
Notes payable to finance companies:					
Variable rate	—	—	1,320	1,737	10,808
Fixed rate	—	—	—	—	325
Capitalized lease obligations	2,333	2,865	1,295	—	5,297
Other	—	—	600	39	1,660
Total	$ 60,590	$48,039	$11,593	$ 7,842	$22,815
Less current portion	(60,590)	(7,018)	(1,789)	(1,104)	(2,774)
Net long-term debt	$ —	$41,021	$ 9,804	$ 6,738	$20,041

Substantially all of the company's property, plant, and equipment serve as collateral for this debt. The borrowings from bank and finance companies contain restrictive covenants, the most restrictive of which appear in the following table:

	Year 14	Year 13	Year 12	Year 11	Year 10
Liabilities/Tangible net worth	<2.5	<3.0	<4.2	<5.5	<6.7
Tangible net worth	>$20,000	>$5,800	>$5,400	>$5.300	>$5,100
Working capital	>$5,000	—	—	—	—
Interest coverage ratio	>1.15	—	—	—	—

As of April 30, Year 14, the company is in default of its debt covenants. It is also in default with respect to covenants underlying its capitalized lease obligations. As a result, lenders have the right to accelerate repayment of their loans. Accordingly, the company has classified all of its long-term debt as a current liability.

The company has entered into operating leases for aircraft and other equipment. The estimated present value of the minimum lease payments under these operating leases as of April 30 of each year is as follows:

Year 14	$2,706
Year 13	3,142
Year 12	3,594
Year 11	3,971
Year 10	4,083

7. Income Taxes

Income tax expense consists of the following:

	Year Ended April 30,				
	Year 14	Year 13	Year 12	Year 11	Year 10
Current					
Federal	$ —	$ —	$ —	$—	$ —
State	—	—	—	—	—
Deferred					
Federal	$(845)	$380	$685	$67	$(85)
State	(55)	30	118	4	(5)
Total	$(900)	$410	$803	$71	$(90)

The cumulative tax loss and tax credit carryovers as of April 30 of each year are as follows:

April 30,	Tax Loss	Tax Credit
Year 14	$10,300	$250
Year 13	5,200	280
Year 12	1,400	300
Year 11	2,100	450
Year 10	4,500	750

The deferred tax provision results from temporary differences in the recognition of revenues and expenses for income tax and financial reporting. The sources and amounts of these differences for each year are as follows:

	Year 14	Year 13	Year 12	Year 11	Year 10
Depreciation	$ —	$ 503	$ 336	$(770)	$ 778
Aircraft modification costs	—	1,218	382	982	703
Net operating losses	(900)	(1,384)	290	—	(1,729)
Other	—	73	(205)	(141)	158
Total	$(900)	$ 410	$ 803	$ 71	$ (90)

A reconciliation of the effective tax rate with the statutory tax rate is as follows:

	Year 14	Year 13	Year 12	Year 11	Year 10
Federal taxes at statutory rate	(35.0%)	35.0%	34.0%	34.0%	(34.0%)
State income taxes	(2.5)	3.0	3.0	3.0	(3.0)
Effect of net operating loss and investment credits	16.5	—	(7.2)	(29.9)	—
Other	2.0	2.9	22.2	11.1	(12.0)
Effect tax rate	(19.0%)	40.9%	52.0%	18.2%	(49.0%)

8. Market Price Information

The company's common stock trades on the NASDAQ National Market System under the symbol FBN. Trading in the company common stock commenced on January 10, Year 10. High- and low-bid prices during each fiscal year are as follows:

Fiscal Year	High Bid	Low Bid
Year 14	$16.50	$9.50
Year 13	14.63	6.25
Year 12	11.25	3.25
Year 11	4.63	3.00
Year 10	5.25	3.25

On December 29, Year 14, the company announced that NASDAQ had decided to discontinue quoting the company's common stock because of the company's failure to comply with NASDAQ's filing requirements.

Ownership of the company's stock at various dates appears as follows:

	April 30,				
	Year 14	Year 13	Year 12	Year 11	Year 10
Douglas Mather	42%	68%	72%	75%	75%
Public	48	23	24	25	25
Company ESOP	10	9	4	—	—
	100%	100%	100%	100%	100%
Common shares outstanding (000's)	3,357.5	2,222.8	2,095.0	2,000.0	2,000.0

Accounting Quality

LEARNING OBJECTIVES

LO 6-1 Describe the concept of quality of accounting information, including the attributes of economic content and earnings persistence.

LO 6-2 Describe the characteristics of balance sheet quality and earnings quality.

LO 6-3 Define earnings management and describe the conditions under which managers might be likely to engage in it.

LO 6-4 Identify the different types of liabilities, how judgment can affect liability recognition and measurement, and how off-balance-sheet financing can affect accounting quality.

LO 6-5 Identify how asset recognition and measurement rules and judgments can affect accounting quality.

LO 6-6 Evaluate the effects on profitability assessment and earnings persistence of various items that occur infrequently but can have a large impact on reported financial statements.

LO 6-7 Assess accounting quality by partitioning earnings into its accrual and cash flow components.

LO 6-8 Compute the Beneish Manipulation Index to assess the likelihood of earnings manipulation.

LO 6-9 Explain the effect of two sets of accounting rules (IFRS and U.S. GAAP) on worldwide financial comparability.

Chapter Overview

C hapters 4 and 5 provide tools for analyzing the profitability and risk of a firm using financial statement information. We presume that reported financial statement information accurately portrays the economic effects of a firm's decisions and actions during the current period, appropriately characterizes the firm's financial position at the end of the period, and is informative about the firm's likely future profitability and risk.

If the presumption is incorrect, the financial statement information is low quality and should be adjusted to obtain better insights. This chapter discusses the critical role of accounting quality as it relates to analyzing a firm's profitability and risk and forecasting its future financial statements. To accomplish this objective, we

- describe earnings management both within and outside the limits of U.S. GAAP or IFRS and managers' incentives to engage in it.
- discuss the effects of a number of accounting issues on balance sheet and earnings quality, including judgment in the recognition and measurement of liabilities and assets and the impact of various types of nonrecurring events on reported earnings.

- demonstrate two useful tools for assessing earnings management and manipulation.
- consider how two sets of accounting standards, U.S. GAAP and IFRS, impact financial statement analysis.

LO 6-1

Describe the concept of quality of accounting information, including the attributes of economic content and earnings persistence.

Accounting Quality

Financial reporting abuses by companies such as **HealthSouth**, **AIG**, **Adelphia**, **Enron**, **WorldCom**, **Parmalat**, **Ahold**, **Satayam**, and **Global Crossing** are rare but dramatic examples of why it is so important to assess the quality of accounting information. These firms reported accounting information that misrepresented their underlying economics and earnings potential. In addition, it is important to realize that even correctly applied accounting rules may, on occasion, fail to indicate future earnings potential and limit the balance sheet's usefulness in assessing financial position and risk.

We frame our discussion by focusing on the following accounting quality issues that are central to analysis and valuation:

- Accounting information should be a fair and complete representation of the firm's economic performance, financial position, and risk.
- Accounting information should provide relevant information to forecast the firm's expected future earnings and cash flows.

Our notion of *accounting quality* encompasses the economic information contained in the income statement, the balance sheet, the statement of cash flows, notes to the financial statements, and MD&A (management's discussion and analysis). Each of these financial statements and supplemental disclosures integrates and articulates with the others, and each aids financial statement users to assess profitability, risk, and value.

Our view of accounting quality is broader than accounting *conservatism*, which is sometimes construed as an attribute of reporting quality. Because conservative accounting numbers are biased, they are not, in their own right, high quality for purposes of financial statement analysis and valuation. Conservatism is simply a prudent response by accountants and managers when faced with uncertainty in measuring the economic effects of transactions, events, and commercial arrangements.

Our approach to accounting quality is also broader and more demanding than merely asking whether the firm used U.S. GAAP or IFRS and received an unqualified opinion from the independent auditor. We instead apply a rigorous test to reported financial statements to determine whether they provide users with useful information that is relevant and reliable for understanding the firm's financial position, performance, and risk, and that aids the projection of the firm's future earnings and cash flows.

High Quality Reflects Economic Reality

Conceptually, accounting amounts may reflect three elements:

- Economics
- Measurement error (or noise)
- Bias

High-quality accounting information portrays fairly and completely the economic effects of a firm's decisions and actions and paints an accurate economic portrait of the firm's financial position, performance, and risk. That is, high-quality accounting information maximizes economic content and minimizes measurement error and bias.

Measurement error occurs when managers, in good faith, make estimates that turn out to be wrong. Accounting standards require managers to make many (often difficult) estimates each period, such as the collectability of receivables, the fair values of financial assets, pension liabilities, and many others. Given the high degree of uncertainty in some of these estimates, some measurement errors are inevitable. Good faith, well-informed estimates yield small measurement errors in directions that are not predictable. The errors tend to cancel out over time and across the many estimates that managers must make in a given year, yielding high-quality accounting numbers. *Bias* occurs when managers apply accounting standards that are inherently biased (for example, standards that require asset write-downs and do not permit asset write-ups) and when managers take advantage of the estimation process to report intentionally optimistic or pessimistic accounting numbers. Neutral application of accounting standards reduces bias and yields high-quality accounting numbers.[1]

Quality in Financial Statements and Disclosures

The following paragraphs decompose the accounting-related portion of a 10-K SEC filing into its major parts and define how each part can achieve high accounting quality.

Balance Sheet. A high-quality balance sheet portrays

- the economic resources that can be reasonably expected to generate future economic benefits (assets) and
- the claims on those resources (liabilities and owners' equity)

at a point in time. Balance sheet quality is low if assets or liabilities are misrepresented.

Income Statement. A high-quality income statement includes

- all revenues the firm earned during the period and can reasonably expect to collect.
- the costs of all resources consumed, including resources consumed in the production process to generate revenues.
- resources consumed during the period that indirectly relate to revenues (such as fixed administrative costs and interest expenses).
- the effects of any gains or losses during the period.

Accounting quality is low if net income

- includes revenues the firm did not earn during the period or may not be able to collect.
- understates or fails to include expenses or losses of the period.
- includes expenses or losses that are attributable to other periods.
- misclassifies or disguises key income items.

The Statement of Cash Flows. A high-quality statement of cash flows

- summarizes all of the cash flow implications of the firm's performance and changes in the firm's financial position over a period of time.
- reports significant noncash investing and financing activities in an accompanying note.
- appropriately classifies cash flows into operating, investing, and financing activities in sufficient detail.

---

[1]Some level of bias (for example, conservative accounting standards) may be preferred by creditors.

Notes to the Financial Statements. High-quality notes to the financial statements

- provide additional information that enhances the users' understanding of the accounting methods used and the judgments and estimates the firm's managers made.
- provide useful disaggregation of summarized disclosures on the face of the financial statements and key contractual terms that underlie financial statement measurements.

Management's Discussion and Analysis. A high-quality MD&A section in the Form 10-K and the annual report

- enhances these disclosures with qualitative discussions of operations and risks.
- provides an in-depth qualitative analysis of the quantitative data reported in the financial statements.

Management's Role in Achieving Quality

Achieving high accounting quality begins with management. Managers' choices and estimates within U.S. GAAP or IFRS should be determined by firms' underlying economic circumstances, including conditions in their industry, competitive strategy, and technology. For example, U.S. GAAP and IFRS allow alternative depreciation methods such as straight-line and accelerated depreciation. Thus, to obtain quality accounting information, management should select the accounting principles that best portray the economic reality from the set permitted.

Even when managers select the most appropriate accounting methods, they still must make numerous estimates in applying those methods. Almost all accounting measurement requires some degree of estimation. In the prior example, the manager must also estimate useful lives of individual assets. Given that managers have discretion in choosing accounting methods and estimating amounts, managers should disclose sufficient information in the financial statements and notes to permit users to assess the economic appropriateness of those choices.

Standard Setters' Role in Achieving Quality

Accounting standard setters establish principles to provide firms with guidance and rules for measuring and reporting the economic effects of firms' activities, performance, and financial position in order to achieve high-quality accounting. Standard setters also establish principles to enhance comparability for users and to provide auditors with a common basis for auditing the fairness of firms' reporting. Standard setters recognize, however, that measuring economic effects requires judgment. As the degree of subjectivity increases, so does the potential for firms to report accounting information that includes unintentional measurement error or opportunistic bias.

In some cases, standard setters have removed choice altogether, resulting in accounting principles that do not faithfully portray underlying circumstances. For example, **Starbucks** cannot recognize its valuable brand name as an asset because U.S. GAAP views internally developed intangible assets as very difficult to value. Similarly, **Apple**, **Google**, and **Eli Lilly** rely heavily on investments made in R&D and have proven technologies, patents, and intellectual property that can be traced to R&D expenditures. Nevertheless, because of a lack of reliable measurements for such assets, U.S. GAAP does not permit companies like these to capitalize these resources. In other words, companies can faithfully apply U.S. GAAP or IFRS and still produce lower-quality financial statements.

Analysts' Role in Achieving Quality

An analyst may conclude that the reported financial statements for a particular firm exhibit poor accounting quality. In these cases, the analyst might adjust reported amounts to enhance the accounting quality before using them to assess operating performance, financial position, or risk. For example, the analyst might judge that an accelerated depreciation rather than a straight-line method more accurately reflects the use of a building or machine, or that a higher bad debts provision is necessary to measure uncollectible accounts. In this chapter, we discuss, at a general level, such choices and the types of adjustments that you might make to reported amounts to enhance accounting quality.[2]

Users of financial statements should consider the following when evaluating the quality of accounting information:

- Whether accounting recognition, measurements, and classifications fit a firm's economic activities.
- Reliability of the measurements.

- Reasonableness of the estimates made.
- Adequacy of disclosures and credibility of qualitative discussions.

Quick Check

High Quality Leads to the Ability to Assess Earnings Persistence over Time

In the preceding section, we described the first key quality of accounting information, to faithfully measure and report current-period financial performance and financial position. The second key quality of financial accounting information is the extent to which it measures and reports current earnings that are likely to persist into the future versus earnings that are transitory. Clearly, the best-case scenario is when current period earnings are high quality, and provide high-quality information about future earnings persistence. In this scenario, high accounting quality helps the analyst assess current period performance, forecast future earnings and cash flows, and value the firm's shares.

Prior to the publication of the 10-K report and the accompanying income statement, firms issue press releases that disclose current quarterly or annual earnings (and semi-annual earnings in some countries outside of the United States). Prior to the earnings press release, analysts and investors hold expectations (i.e., prior predictions) about what the soon-to-be-released earnings will be. A high-quality earnings release will reveal their forecast errors and allow them to make new predictions about future earnings. Thus, the changes in stock prices when the release is made public capture investors' reassessment of firms' equity values. If earnings are not informative about either current or future performance (i.e., they are of low quality), then investors will not use the earnings number to revalue the firm. Further, the lack of information in low-quality earnings will cause investors to pay a lower price to acquire the firm's stock to protect themselves from others who might privately possess higher-quality information about the firm's performance.

---

[2]Chapters 7–9 go into greater detail.

For these reasons, managers have a strong incentive to produce high-quality earnings. Managers also have an incentive to supplement the press release with statements about whether current earnings will persist into the future. Managers also use the MD&A and notes to the financial statements for this purpose. When necessary, managers will highlight certain transitory components of earnings such as a one-time gain or loss to assist investors in forecasting future earnings, or, alternatively, managers might forecast future earnings directly in the press release or in a conference call that is scheduled shortly after the earnings release. These types of voluntary management disclosures are high quality if managers are unbiased and as accurate as possible with respect to identifying the one-time items and in making the direct forecasts.

Your diligence in reading the financial statements, notes to the financial statements, MD&A, and press releases that convey actual earnings and management earnings forecasts will help you reduce errors and bias in your forecasts of future earnings and cash flows.

Quick Check

- Accounting quality is a broad concept encompassing all of the financial statements, notes, and supplemental disclosures and discussion.
- High-quality accounting accurately reflects economic reality and earnings persistence.

- High-quality past earnings and current earnings allow the analyst to develop informed expectations of future earnings and assess firm value.

LO 6-2

Describe the characteristics of balance sheet quality and earnings quality.

Earnings Quality versus Balance Sheet Quality

Given that accounting quality is a property of all financial statements, it is useful to distinguish between the concept of earnings quality (an income statement concept) and the concept of balance sheet quality. While earnings quality permits an accurate assessment of current performance and a foundation for predicting future performance, balance sheet quality permits an accurate assessment of key descriptions of risk: liquidity, financial flexibility, and solvency. See Chapter 5 for a detailed discussion of these ratios. Insightful analyses of each element of risk depend on appropriate, high-quality measures of assets and liabilities.

Earnings and Balance Sheet Quality Are Linked by Financial Statement Articulation

As discussed in Chapters 2 and 3, financial statements articulate. In accounting, income statement amounts reflect changes in the measurement and recognition of assets and liabilities. Thus, high-quality accounting for assets and liabilities usually creates high-quality income measurement. Alternately, low-quality accounting for revenues or expenses usually gives rise to low-quality measures of assets and liabilities on the balance sheet. Thus, an unrealistic estimate, bad judgment, or unjustifiable choice can affect both balance sheet quality and earnings quality.

Occasionally, due to the different objectives of the balance sheet and income statement, an accounting choice intended to create a high-quality income statement can reduce the quality of the balance sheet to some extent. For example, managers choose whether to use the last-in, first-out (LIFO) or first-in, first-out (FIFO) inventory method. If inventory acquisition prices have been rising over time, measuring the balance sheet inventory amount using LIFO yields out-of-date costs on the balance sheet. LIFO assumes that recently purchased inventory (at higher acquisition prices) are sold first and that inventory purchased in previous periods (at lower acquisition prices) remain in inventory. Thus, balance sheet inventory is reported at older costs that understate the future cash flow potential from selling the inventory. Balance sheet quality is impaired because the balance sheet does not capture liquidity adequately. However, gross margins on the income statement are equal to a recent selling price minus a recent acquisition cost, and thus capture economic content and yield a more persistent earnings number. These are characteristics of a high-quality income statement. If management chose to use the FIFO method under these circumstances, then liquidity measurement would be improved on the balance sheet, but income statement quality might suffer.[3]

Earnings Management

High-quality accounting occurs when managers measure and report firm performance and financial position with very little measurement error or bias. However, management's influence over accounting practices can result in *earnings management*, low accounting quality, and the need to adjust financial data to better reflect their economic information content. Earnings management connotes different things to different users of the term. Healy and Wahlen provide the following definition of earnings management:

> Earnings management occurs when managers use judgment in financial reporting and in structuring transactions to alter financial reports to either mislead some stakeholders about the underlying economic performance of the company or to influence contractual outcomes that depend on reporting accounting numbers.[4]

Note that the definition includes managers' choices, judgments, and estimates that are necessary but that mask the underlying economic performance of a firm.

In addition, structuring transactions may also be used as an earnings management tool. For example, managers might delay maintenance to increase reported income. This is often referred to as *real earnings management* because, although no estimates or judgments were involved, a real decision to delay maintenance was undertaken to influence a decision maker's understanding of the earnings signal for future profitability.

Detecting earnings management is difficult because managers can exercise judgment in financial reporting in many ways. Moreover, earnings management is often intended to create the appearance of fundamental economic growth (for example, increasing sales and earnings).

LO 6-3

Define earnings management and describe the conditions under which managers might be likely to engage in it.

---

[3]In Chapter 9, we describe the disclosure of the LIFO reserve in financial statement notes and show how an analyst can use this information to achieve high quality in both financial statements.

[4]Paul M. Healy and James M. Wahlen, "A Review of the Earnings Management Literature and Its Implications for Standard Setting," *Accounting Horizons* (December 1999), pp. 365–383. Another useful definition is provided in Katherine Schipper, "Commentary: Earnings Management," *Accounting Horizons* (December 1989), pp. 91–102: "a purposeful intervention in the external financial reporting process, with the intent of obtaining some private gain (as opposed to, say, merely facilitating the neutral operation of the process)...."

Incentives to Practice Earnings Management

Managers may engage in earnings management if choices and estimates allowed in U.S. GAAP or IFRS benefit them personally or if doing so leads to benefits for the firm and its stakeholders. Examples of reasons for earnings management are:

- Managing earnings upward might increase the manager's compensation under compensation contracts based on earnings or stock prices.
- Managing earnings upward might enhance job security for senior management by influencing the outcomes of transactions that affect corporate control, such as proxy fights and takeovers.
- Managing earnings upward might allow the firm to obtain debt financing at a lower cost by appearing more profitable or less risky, avoid violation of debt covenants, or influence the effects of other binding constraints from accounting-based contracts.
- Managing earnings upward might influence short-term share price performance and increase the economic benefits to the firm from engaging in initial public and seasoned equity offerings and using firm shares in acquisitions.
- Managing earnings upward prior to managers' sale of their personal ownership interests (insider selling) might increase share prices and maximize manager gains from the sale.
- Managing earnings upward might influence stock prices positively (or delay stock price declines) by meeting or beating the market's expectations for earnings, managers' own earnings forecasts, and prior period's earnings, and might also maintain a smooth earnings time-series to cause the firm to appear less risky.
- Managing earnings downward might discourage entry into the industry by potential competitors.
- Managing earnings downward might reduce the probability of antitrust actions against the firm or other regulatory interventions or political interference related to tax issues, capital requirements (e.g., for banks), and import relief.
- Managing earnings downward might suppress stock prices and thus yield favorable terms when taking a company private.
- Managing earnings downward prior to managers' insider share purchases might decrease share prices and maximize manager gains from future share sales.
- Managing earnings downward might create opportunities to report higher earnings in future periods.

Deterrents to Earnings Management

Managers may be deterred from engaging in earnings management for the following reasons:

- Capital markets and regulators such as the SEC penalize firms identified as flagrant earnings managers.
- Firms and managers who are perceived as practicing aggressive earnings management will lose their reputation for being honest and trustworthy among capital market participants and stakeholders. When it is revealed that a firm has managed earnings, its stock price usually falls dramatically and firm managers are often punished or fired.
- Strong corporate governance can deter earnings management. The board of directors monitors management actions and enforces corporate accounting and

disclosure policies. A well-functioning board is enhanced by the presence of informed outside directors. Strong internal controls and effective internal auditors who report directly to the board are also deterrents.

- Legal consequences can result from aggressive earnings management and fraud.
- Securities regulations and stock exchanges require annual audits by independent accountants. External auditors assess and opine on the fairness of measurements and disclosures within U.S. GAAP and IFRS and can monitor particularly aggressive actions taken by management to influence earnings (although an auditor's power to thwart actions taken within the bounds of U.S. GAAP or IFRS is limited).
- The ongoing scrutiny of financial analysts also serves as a check on earnings management.

Although deterrents exist, the existence of incentives to practice earnings management indicates that you are best served by increasing your analysis of accounting quality when these incentives are present. And, as a general rule, you should carefully monitor the frequency, timeliness, and quality of management's communications, which signal the forthrightness of managers and the likelihood of earnings being managed.

Recognizing and Measuring Liabilities

LO 6-4

Identify the different types of liabilities, how judgment can affect liability recognition and measurement, and how off-balance-sheet financing can affect accounting quality.

A high-quality balance sheet is extremely important in assessing financial flexibility (i.e., the debt capacity of the firm for funding new projects) and financial risk, which depend on proper recognition, measurement, and classification of liabilities. So, we begin by discussing what balance sheet liabilities should capture. Financial reporting recognizes a liability if it satisfies the following criteria:

- The obligation involves a probable future sacrifice of economic benefits, e.g., a future transfer of cash, goods, or services; the forgoing of a future cash receipt; or the transfer of equity shares. The firm can measure with reasonable precision the cash-equivalent value of the resources needed to satisfy the obligation.
- The firm has a present obligation (not a possible future obligation) and little or no discretion to avoid the transfer.
- The transaction or event that gave rise to the obligation has already occurred.[5]

While the criteria for liability recognition may appear straightforward and unambiguous, this is often not the case. Various obligations of an enterprise fall along a continuum with respect to how well they satisfy these criteria. Exhibit 6.1 classifies obligations into six groups.

Obligations with Fixed Payment Dates and Amounts

The obligations that most clearly satisfy the liability recognition criteria are those with fixed payment dates and amounts (typically set by contract). Most obligations arising from borrowing arrangements (classified as financing activities) fall into this category. The borrowing agreement specifies the timing and amount of interest and principal payments.

---

[5]Financial Accounting Standards Board, *Statement of Financial Accounting Concepts No. 6*, "Elements of Financial Statements" (1985). Financial Accounting Standards Board, *Statement of Financial Accounting Standards No. 150*, "Accounting for Certain Financial Instruments with Characteristics of Both Liabilities and Equity," (2008) requires certain obligations settled in equity shares to be classified as liabilities; *FASB Codification Topic 480*.

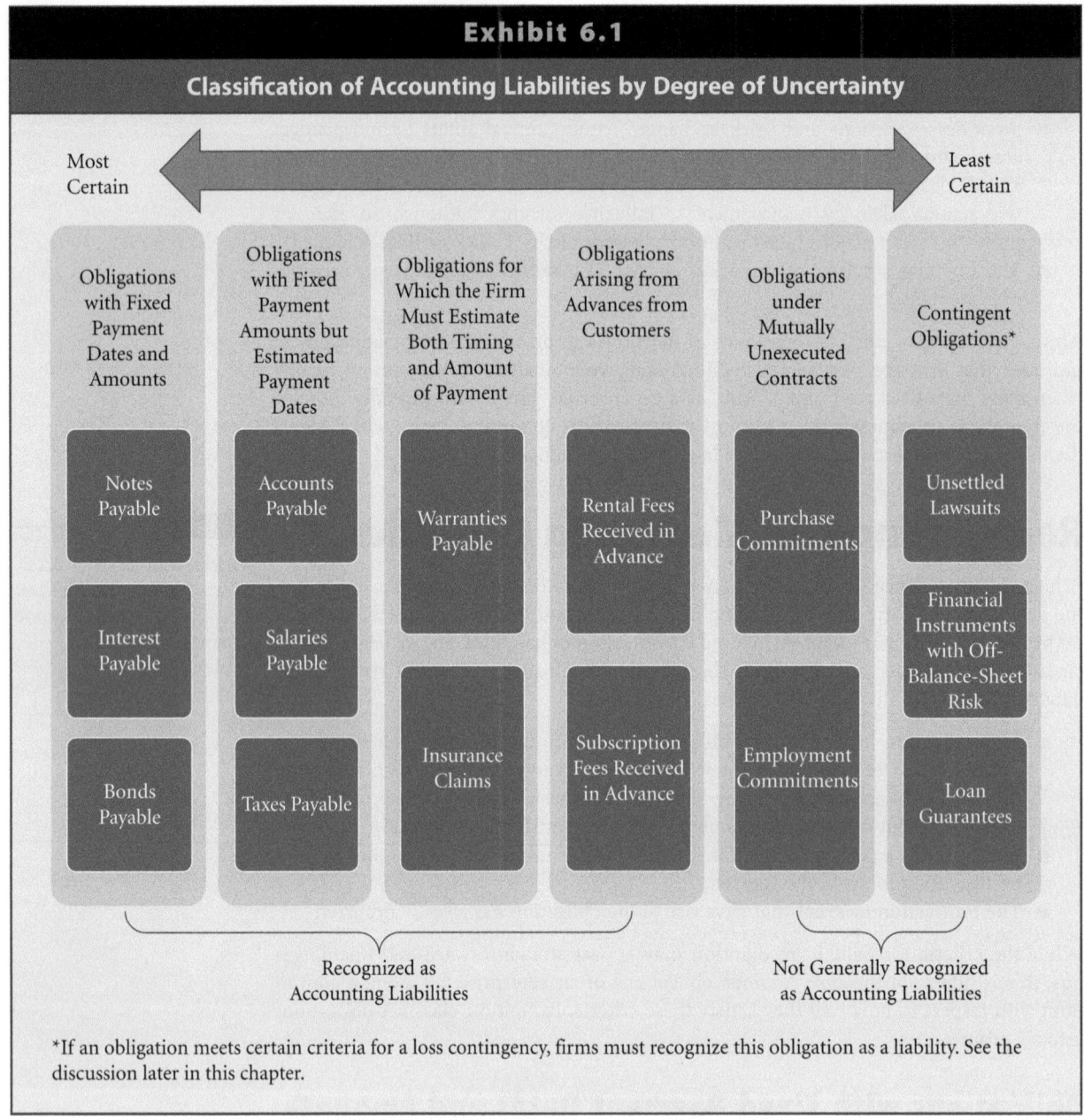

Exhibit 6.1

Classification of Accounting Liabilities by Degree of Uncertainty

Most Certain ⟵——————————————————————⟶ Least Certain

Obligations with Fixed Payment Dates and Amounts	Obligations with Fixed Payment Amounts but Estimated Payment Dates	Obligations for Which the Firm Must Estimate Both Timing and Amount of Payment	Obligations Arising from Advances from Customers	Obligations under Mutually Unexecuted Contracts	Contingent Obligations*
Notes Payable	Accounts Payable	Warranties Payable	Rental Fees Received in Advance	Purchase Commitments	Unsettled Lawsuits
Interest Payable	Salaries Payable				Financial Instruments with Off-Balance-Sheet Risk
Bonds Payable	Taxes Payable	Insurance Claims	Subscription Fees Received in Advance	Employment Commitments	Loan Guarantees

Recognized as Accounting Liabilities   Not Generally Recognized as Accounting Liabilities

*If an obligation meets certain criteria for a loss contingency, firms must recognize this obligation as a liability. See the discussion later in this chapter.

However, even with payment dates and amounts set by contract, long-term liabilities require the choice of an interest rate. At the date of the original transaction, the appropriate interest rate is the effective interest rate implied by the cash transfer from the lender. However, revaluations of long-term liabilities (i.e., fair value measurements) are required for the notes to the financial statements, and managers may choose to use fair value as a basis for reporting in the balance sheet (with changes in fair value affecting the income statement).[6]

---

[6]*FASB Codification Topic 825*; International Accounting Standards Board, *International Accounting Standard 39*, "Financial Instruments: Recognition and Measurement."

To the extent possible, you should ascertain how those fair value measurements were determined by thoroughly reading the long-term debt note and the note describing accounting policy. If fair value is determined by reference to market prices or based on market prices of similar instruments (which implies a market-determined interest rate), then management discretion is minimized, and accounting quality is likely higher. If interest rates are firm-estimated, then material changes in long-term liability fair values require greater scrutiny because using too high of an assumed discount rate reduces liability fair values.[7]

Starbucks reported one note issue due in 2017 at a book value of $550 million on the face of its September 28, 2014, Consolidated Balance Sheet as part of its total long-term notes payable of $2,048.3 million at that date. In Note 9, it reported an estimated fair value for that note of $625 million, which implies a $75 million unrealized (and unrecognized) loss. **Starbucks** retired the note early by paying $610.1 million in 2015 (see **Starbucks'** September 27, 2015, Consolidated Statement of Cash Flows), recognizing a $61.1 million loss on extinguishment of debt in its September 27, 2015, income statement. The difference between the estimated fair value of the note and the price paid later to extinguish it might be due to management error in estimating fair values (a signal of the low quality of the initial fair value estimate), or, alternatively, a slight reversal of the recent decline in interest rates between the estimation date and extinguishment date. Even a management dedicated to high-quality accounting would not be expected to accurately forecast interest rate changes. It is high-quality disclosure to explain the transaction and to segregate the material nonrecurring gain in the income statement.

Obligations with Fixed Payment Amounts but Estimated Payment Dates

Most current operating liabilities fall into this category. Oral agreements, written agreements, or legal statutes fix the amounts payable to suppliers, employees, and government agencies. Firms normally settle these obligations within a few months after incurring them. The firm can estimate the settlement date with sufficient accuracy to warrant recognizing a liability.

Aside from concerns over outright fraudulent attempts to hide liabilities, the lack of an interest rate assumption in measuring these liabilities, their short-run nature, and the tendency for amounts to be fixed by contract causes few quality concerns.

Obligations with Estimated Payment Dates and Amounts

Obligations in this group require estimation because the firm cannot precisely compute what amount of resources it will transfer in the future or when the transfers will occur. For example, when a firm sells products under a warranty agreement, it promises to replace defective parts or perform certain repair services for a specified period of time. At the time of sale, the firm can neither identify the specific customers who will receive warranty benefits nor ascertain the timing or amounts of

---

[7]Because most companies report liability fair values only in the notes to financial statements, this issue primarily affects note quality as it relates to balance sheet quality. Interestingly, increases in a firm's own risk increase discount rates and decrease liability fair values, making the firm look less risky if fair values are used in ratio analysis. Barclays reported a £2.7 billion gain from downward revaluation of its own debt in its 2011 IFRS-based financial statements.

customers' claims. Past experience, however, often provides the necessary information for estimating the likely proportion of customers who will make claims and the probable average amount of their claims. As long as the firm can reasonably estimate the probable amount of the obligation, it satisfies the first criterion for liability recognition. Both balance sheet and earnings quality are similarly affected by this category of liability. Managers must judge if and when future resource outflows will occur. They also must estimate the cost of satisfying the obligations.

High-quality note disclosure assists your quality assessment task. Quite often, firms report estimates, realizations, and estimate changes in their notes. For example, **Harley Davidson** reports estimated motorcycle repair expenses under its warranties, how much repair expense actually was incurred to fix motorcycles, and changes in the balance of the warranty obligation going forward due to historical repair experience and any new warranty issues discovered. Insurance companies also provide detailed note disclosures of estimated obligations under insurance contracts and their loss experiences.

You should study these notes carefully, with a particular eye on unexpected changes in this type of liability. Managers can manipulate earnings by under-reserving to meet or beat street earnings expectations or over-reserving when earnings are high to permit under-reserving in future periods. Current period over-reserving followed by future period opportunistic under-reserving is an example of establishing and using "cookie jar reserves."

Obligations Arising from Advances from Customers

A firm sometimes receives cash from customers in advance for goods or services it will provide at a future time. Many types of revenues involve prepayments from customers, such as airfares, subscriptions, insurance premiums, membership dues, and license fees, among others, which create service obligations for firms. Revenue recognition usually requires that the firm deliver the goods or provide the services before recognizing revenue.[8] The important balance sheet and earnings quality issue is whether revenue has been recognized too early, in which case balance sheet quality is impaired by an understatement of liabilities and earnings quality is impaired by an overstatement of revenue. Therefore, you should study the accounting policy on revenue recognition and decide whether the policy makes sense in light of the economics of the industry and corporate operating strategy.

Starbucks describes its accounting policy relating to stored value cards in Note 1 to its September 27, 2015, Consolidated Financial Statements. You will note from looking at its balance sheet that **Starbucks** has a very large balance in the stored value card liability at that date ($983.8 million), an amount larger than the deposit liability of some banks. This liability is increased each time a card holder puts a deposit on the card and also each time a customer makes a purchase and earns stars under the customer loyalty program. A key accounting quality issue for **Starbucks** is how it accounts for the "breakage" on the stored value card. Note 1 states:

> While we will continue to honor all stored value cards presented for payment, management may determine the likelihood of redemption, based on historical experience, is deemed to be remote for certain cards due to long periods of inactivity. In these circumstances, if management also determines there is no requirement for remitting balances to government agencies under unclaimed

---

[8]We analyze revenue recognition in great detail in Chapter 9.

property laws, unredeemed card balances may then be recognized as breakage income, which is included in net interest income and other on our consolidated statements of earnings. In fiscal 2015, 2014, and 2013, we recognized breakage income of $39.3 million, $38.3 million, and $33.0 million, respectively.

You should probably treat this item as persistent given the history of this income source. In fiscal 2012, 2011, and 2010, **Starbucks** recognized breakage income of $65.8 million, $46.9 million, and $31.2 million, respectively, with the blip in 2012 caused by a one-time court ruling on who has a right to the income.

Obligations under Mutually Unexecuted Contracts

Mutually unexecuted contracts arise when two entities agree to transfer resources but *neither* entity has yet made a transfer. **Starbucks**, for example, reports in Note 5 to its September 27, 2015, Consolidated Financial Statements that it has agreed to purchase green coffee beans from its suppliers over the next two years in the amount of $1,085 million. A baseball organization may agree to pay its "franchise" player a certain sum as compensation for services the player will render over the next five years. A bank may agree to provide lines of credit to its business customers in the event these firms need funds in the future. Both parties have exchanged promises, but neither party has transferred resources. Thus, no accounting liability arises at the time of the exchange of promises. A liability arises only when one party or the other transfers resources. This category of obligation, called *executory contracts*, differs from the preceding two categories in Exhibit 6.1, in which the contracts or agreements are partially executed. With warranty agreements, a firm receives cash but has not fulfilled its warranty obligation. With advances from customers, a firm receives cash but has not provided the required goods or services.

U.S. GAAP and IFRS generally do not require firms to recognize as accounting liabilities obligations under mutually unexecuted contracts. If the amounts involved are material, the firm must disclose the nature of the obligation and its amount in notes to the financial statements. You might conclude, however, that these obligations create sufficient risk for the firm to justify adjusting the reported financial statements to include such obligations.

Purchase commitments are one kind of mutually unexecuted contract bearing such risk. In a purchase commitment, a firm promises to make a future fixed-price payment for a future delivery of inventory. Because payment has not been made and inventory has not been delivered, the contract is not recorded as a liability. The firm, however, bears the risk of changes in the fair value of the inventory reflected in the market price it would pay to acquire the inventory if it did not have the contract in place. You can read the required financial statement note on commitments that will show the expected cash flows under purchase commitments. Further, under U.S. GAAP, the firm must report a loss on purchase commitments if the price to acquire inventory on the open market as of the balance sheet date falls below the fixed price in the contract.

Purchase commitments can be extremely large, especially when the commitment is to purchase capacity. For example, airlines enter into commitments to purchase or lease aircraft in the future. In Note 10 to its December 31, 2015, Consolidated Financial Statements, **Delta Airlines** reports future aircraft purchase commitments of $13.6 billion. In addition, Delta enters into contract carrier agreements with regional airlines to obtain future capacity on their planes. These executory contracts are a similarly large $12.3 billion.

Contingent Obligations

An event whose future outcome is unknown may create an obligation for the future transfer of resources. For example, a firm may be a defendant in a lawsuit, the outcome of which depends on the results of legal proceedings. Or a firm may guarantee loans of a subsidiary, the outcome of which depends on the future solvency of the subsidiary. Or an insurer may promise to pay certain amounts or reimburse certain expenses if particular future events occur. Obligations such as these are *contingent* on future events.

Contingent obligations may or may not trigger recognition of accounting liabilities. Financial reporting requires firms to recognize an estimated loss from a contingency (called a *loss contingency*) and a related liability only if both of the following conditions are met:

- Information available prior to the issuance of the financial statements indicates that it is probable that an asset has been impaired or that a liability has been incurred.
- The firm can estimate the amount of the loss with reasonable precision.[9]

For the first criterion, clear guidance as to what probability cutoff defines *likely* or *probable* does not exist. The FASB has stated that "probable is used with its usual general meaning, rather than in a specific accounting or technical sense, and refers to that which can be expected or believed on the basis of available evidence or logic but is neither certain or proved."[10]

For the second criterion, the concept of *reasonably estimable* is not defined in precise terms. If the firm can narrow the amount of the loss to a reasonable range, however large, the firm has achieved sufficient precision to justify recognition of a liability. The amount to be reported is the most likely estimate within the range. If no amount within the range is more likely than another, the firm should use the amount at the lower end of the range. As might be suspected, the contingent liability estimates are fraught with measurement error, and possibly managerial bias, rendering lower balance sheet and earnings quality.

Closely related to the concept of a loss contingency is a *guarantee*. For example, one firm may guarantee the repayment of another entity's borrowing in the event the other entity cannot repay the loan at maturity. As another example, a firm may sell a portion of its accounts receivable to another entity, promising to reimburse the other entity if uncollectible accounts exceed a specified amount. The need to make future cash payments is contingent on future events. U.S. GAAP requires firms to recognize the fair value of the guarantee as a liability.[11] Measuring this fair value involves estimating the likelihood, timing, and amount that might be payable. However, a guarantee can have a fair value even when the likelihood of making a future payment is low. A guarantee by a financially strong firm of a financially weaker firm's debt will reduce the weaker firm's cost of borrowing. The guarantor recognizes a receivable and a liability for the fair value of the benefit it granted to the borrower. The obligation to reimburse a purchaser of accounts receivable for excess uncollectibles likely increases the amount the buyer pays

---

[9]*FASB Codification Topic 450.*

[10]*Statement of Financial Accounting Concepts No. 6* (1985). Although the FASB has not defined *probable*, practice demands that firms and auditors define it. Currently, most firms and auditors appear to use *probable* to mean at least 80%–85% likelihood.

[11]*FASB Codification Topic 460.*

the seller for the receivables. Recognizing the fair value of this guarantee as a liability affects the amount of gain or loss the seller recognizes on the sale of the receivables. In addition to recognizing the fair value of guarantees as liabilities, firms must disclose the maximum amount that could become payable and any available collateral that the guarantor could recover in the event it must execute the guarantee.

Guarantees are contractual. Their disclosure provides you with a clear indication of potential liabilities of the guarantor if default occurs. In addition to these explicit guarantees, you should use the knowledge gained in the strategy analysis step to consider whether a firm will assist a strategic partner with financing even if it is not legally liable for the strategic partner's debt. For example, prior to consolidating their bottling affiliates, both **PepsiCo** and **Coca-Cola** held large, but not controlling, stakes in their affiliates. It is likely that both firms would consider extending financing to a strategically important bottler that was experiencing financial difficulties.

Off-Balance-Sheet Financing Arrangements

Investors and lenders often use the proportion of debt in a firm's capital structure as a measure of risk and therefore as a factor in establishing the cost of funds.[12] Other things being equal, firms prefer to obtain funds without showing a liability on the balance sheet in the hope that future lenders or investors will ignore the risks associated with such financing. Firms sometimes structure innovative financing arrangements in ways that may not satisfy the criteria for the recognition of a liability, often transacting on situations where financial reporting treats the obligation (if any) as an executory contract or a contingency. The principal aim of such arrangements is to reduce the amount shown as liabilities on the balance sheet. Firms accomplish off-balance-sheet financing using a variety of approaches, including leases, the sale of receivables, product financing arrangements, use of another entity, use of joint ventures, and take-or-pay contracts.

Leases

The most common and potentially largest source of off-balance-sheet financing is the use of operating leases. Lease accounting is complex and will be discussed in detail in Chapter 7. The balance sheet quality issues are that operating leases substantially understate reported long-term, interest-bearing liabilities and property, plant, and equipment, which lead you to understate long-term solvency risk ratios and overstate return on assets. Retailers such as **Macy's** and **Finish Line**, restaurants such as **Starbucks**, and airlines such as **Delta** and **AirFrance/KLM** are heavy users of operating leases.[13]

New lease standards exist that will mitigate the operating lease problem and the need to effectively capitalize leases. However, these standards are delayed to be in effect for financial statements covering years beginning after December 15, 2018. We discuss these new standards in Chapter 7 as well.

Sale of Receivables

Firms sometimes sell their receivables as a means of obtaining financing or use a special-purpose entity (an SPE) to issue securities backed by the receivables (for example, mortgage-backed securities issued by financial institutions or their SPEs). Exhibit 6.2

[12]Chapter 5 discusses various ratios for measuring risk, and Chapter 11 describes techniques for using a firm's capital structure to compute the weighted average cost of capital.

[13]In Chapter 7, we illustrate a method to adjust operating to capital leases.

Exhibit 6.2

Obtaining Financing by Transferring Receivables to an SPE

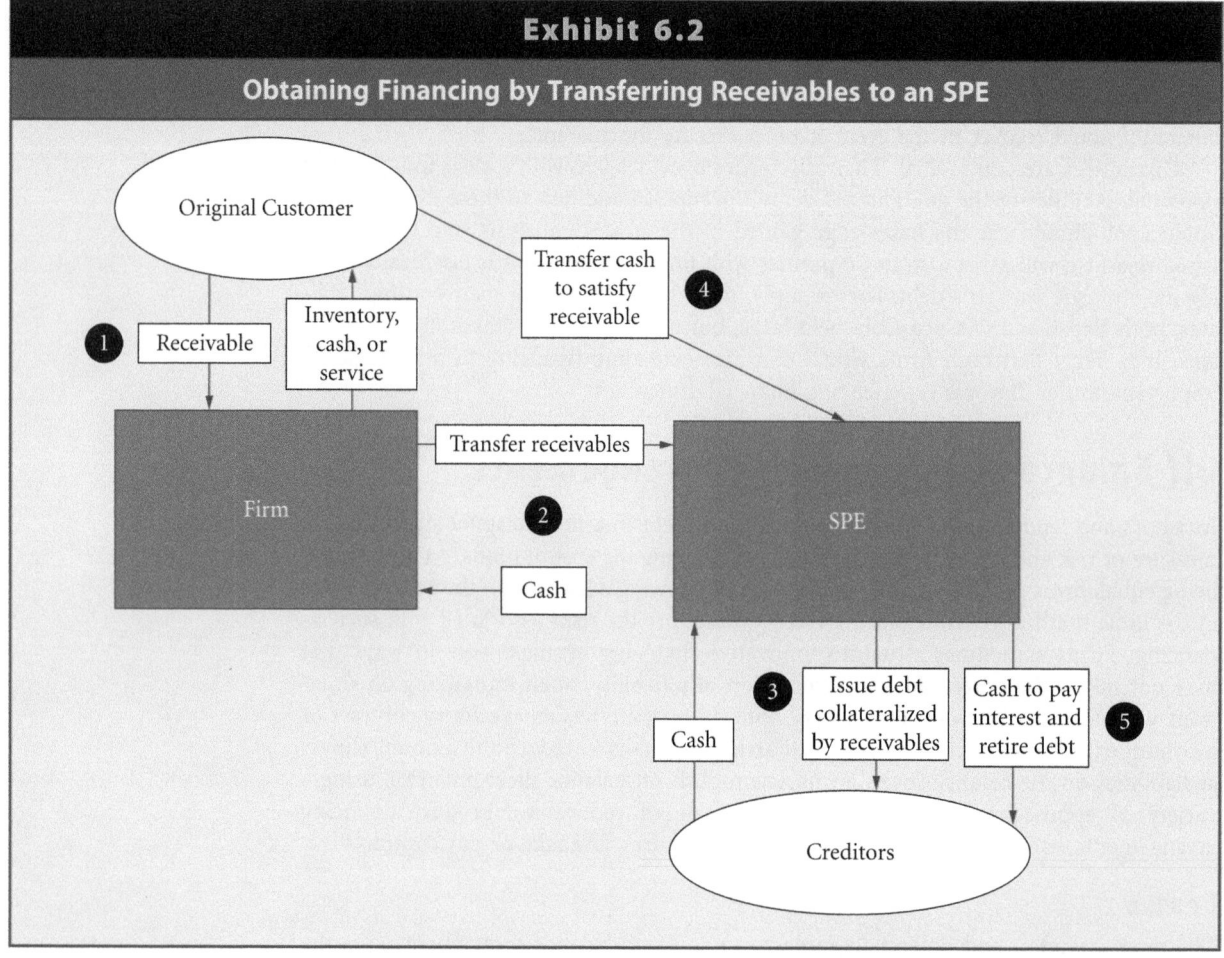

illustrates the use of an SPE to accomplish the sale of receivables. In transaction 1, the firm sells inventory, lends cash, or provides services to an original customer in exchange for a receivable. Rather than wait for customer payment, the firm transfers the receivables to the SPE in exchange for cash (transaction 2). The SPE obtains the cash it transfers to the firm from creditors by issuing debt (transaction 3). The debt is collateralized by the receivables. In transaction 4, the original customer pays off the receivables to the SPE, and in transaction 5, the SPE uses the cash to pay interest and principal to creditors. If collections from customers are not sufficient to repay the amount borrowed plus interest, the transferring firm may have to pay the difference; that is, the lender has recourse against the borrowing firm.[14]

The question arises as to whether the recourse provision creates an accounting liability. Some argue that the arrangement is similar to a collateralized loan. The firm should leave the receivables on its books and recognize a liability in the amount of the cash received in transaction 2. Others argue that the firm has sold an asset; it should recognize a liability only if it is probable that collections from customers will be insufficient and the firm will be required to repay some portion of the amount received.

---

[14]To understand the same transaction without using an SPE, replace the SPE with the creditors and eliminate transactions 3 and 5.

The FASB and IASB provide accounting rules to guide the decision of whether to classify a transfer of receivables as a sale or a loan.[15] For example, U.S. GAAP requires that firms recognize transfers of receivables as sales only if the transferor surrenders control of the receivables. Firms surrender control only if all of the following conditions are met:

- The assets transferred (that is, receivables) have been isolated from the selling ("transferor") firm; that is, neither the transferor nor a creditor of the selling firm could access the receivables in the event of the seller's bankruptcy.
- The buying ("transferee") firm obtains the right to pledge or exchange the transferred assets, and no condition both constrains the transferee from taking advantage of its right and provides more than a trivial benefit to the transferor.
- The selling firm does not maintain effective control over the assets transferred through (a) an agreement that both entitles and obligates it to repurchase the assets or (b) the ability to unilaterally cause the transferee to return specific assets.

The principal refinement to the concept of an accounting liability is in identification of which party enjoys the economic benefits and sustains the economic risk of the assets (receivables in this case). If the selling (borrowing) firm controls the economic benefits/risks, the transaction is a collateralized loan. If the arrangement transfers these benefits/risks to the buying (lending) firm, the transaction is a sale.

Other Examples of Off-Balance-Sheet Financing Arrangements

Several other off-balance-sheet arrangements exist, such as product financing arrangements, the use of another entity to obtain financing, research and development financing arrangements, take-or-pay contracts, and throughput contracts. We illustrate each of these other arrangements in the Chapter 6 Online Appendix found at this text's website.

Quick Check

- Financial reporting typically recognizes events when an exchange takes place.
- Financial reporting recognizes liabilities when a firm incurs an obligation to sacrifice resources in the future for benefits already received.
- Financial reporting has typically not recognized mutually unexecuted contracts as liabilities because the parties have merely exchanged promises to perform in the future.
- Financial reporting does not generally require the recognition of contingent obligations as liabilities because some future obligating event must occur to establish the existence of a liability.
- Exchanges of promises can have economic substance even though a legal obligation to pay does not immediately arise. When a firm controls the determination of which party enjoys the economic benefits and/or incurs the economic risks from an asset, the firm should recognize the asset and its related financial obligations.
- The FASB and IASB closely monitor reporting issues related to off-balance-sheet commitments of firms, but continue to be challenged because of the ever-changing nature of business financing arrangements and the flexible and fluid organizational arrangements that firms create.[16]

---

[15]*FASB Codification Topic 860*; Financial Accounting Standards Board, *Statement of Financial Accounting Standards No. 156*, "Accounting for Servicing of Financial Assets" (2006); International Accounting Standards Board, *International Accounting Standard No. 39*, "Financial Instruments: Recognition and Measurement" (revised 2003).

[16]Specific IFRS rules relating to off-balance-sheet financing are rare. However, guidelines may be found in IASB, *SIC Interpretation 12*, "Consolidating Special Purpose Entities" (1998).

LO 6-5

Identify how asset
recognition and
measurement rules and
judgments can affect
accounting quality.

Asset Recognition and Measurement

A high-quality balance sheet reflects asset values in a way that promotes a proper assessment of liquidity risk and, when considered relative to properly recognized liabilities, helps gauge financial risk.[17] Further, as we learned in Chapter 4, profitability analysis (i.e., ROA) and the efficiency element of profitability analysis (i.e., various asset turnover ratios) critically depend on proper asset recognition and measurement. Chapters 8 and 9 discuss different kinds of assets and their varying characteristics in detail. Here, we focus on a more general understanding of how application of asset measurement rules and management discretion can affect balance sheet quality and earnings quality.

Current Assets

Ratios that measure short-term liquidity risk depend on the proper measurement and reporting of cash, short-term investments, accounts receivable, and inventories.

Cash and Short-Term Investments

Cash usually does not have significant measurement problems. Even cash amounts in foreign currencies can be readily estimated and measured in their U.S. dollar (or corporate home country currency) amounts. However, inclusion of cash as a current asset requires that it be available to satisfy current obligations, and you should carefully read the notes to the financial statements to ascertain whether there are any restrictions on the company's use of cash for that purpose. Cash restricted for longer-term disbursements (e.g., bond sinking funds, plant expansions, etc.) should be reported as noncurrent. Short-term investments are usually measured with readily available market prices and thus are fairly reliable.

Accounts Receivable

Accounts receivable are initially measured at the fair value of the exchange in a credit sale or service arrangement. At the balance sheet date, accounts receivable are reduced by management's estimate of uncollectible amounts arising from customer defaults or customer returns. Accounting quality for receivables is thus determined by the company's revenue recognition policy and the quality of management's uncollectible account estimation. If revenue is recognized too early or if it is recognized fraudulently, then accounts receivable will be overstated on the balance sheet. Further, accounts receivable are overstated if management underestimates uncollectible accounts.

Because balance sheets and income statements articulate, low-quality accounts receivable measurement also affects earnings quality. Aggressive recognition of receivables from sales and services will lead to overstated revenues and overstated net income. Underestimating uncollectible accounts receivable will give rise to understated bad debt expense and overstated income.

Inventory

Inventory is initially recorded at the original cost incurred to obtain the inventory. There are two primary asset measurement issues for inventory that affect accounting quality. The first is the choice of inventory method. LIFO is a popular method for

---

[17]See Chapter 5 for the various risk-related ratios.

inventory valuation under U.S. GAAP (but not allowed under IFRS).[18] LIFO assumes that goods purchased more recently (generally at a higher cost) are sold first. LIFO generally yields higher earnings quality because most-recent costs are matched with most-recent revenues, earnings better capture the economist's definition of income (based on replacement costs of goods sold), and earnings tend to be more persistent. However, LIFO results in far more conservative estimates of inventory value on the balance sheet relative to other methods such as FIFO or average cost because only older costs are reflected in the inventory valuation. Thus, LIFO results in a more conservative assessment of a firm's liquidity.

The second inventory measurement issue that affects accounting quality arises from the lower-of-cost-or-market rule, under which companies annually assess whether inventory costs exceed their market value due to obsolescence, unfavorable supply and demand conditions, or some other economic factor that causes the inventory to decline in value. If so, then the inventory must be written down to market value, triggering an associated loss on the income statement. Management judgments play a large role in the amount and timing of these write-downs and, thus, accounting quality can be compromised.[19]

Noncurrent Assets

Recognition and measurement rules for noncurrent assets have major implications for accounting quality. The following general process describes the accounting for most noncurrent assets:

- A noncurrent asset is initially recognized when a past transaction or event enables a firm to control probable benefits of the asset.
- A noncurrent asset is initially measured at the fair value sacrificed to obtain the asset or the fair value of the asset obtained if more clearly determinable.
- Changes in noncurrent assets must be evaluated to ensure that periodic income captures any value declines.

The accounting rules for noncurrent assets are complex and vary greatly across asset classes. We discuss noncurrent assets in detail in Chapters 8 and 9, where we reconsider the effects of management judgments, estimates, and incentives on accounting quality. At this point, we consider how the aforementioned parts of the measurement process can yield accounting quality problems in more general terms.

Control

The initial recognition of a noncurrent asset emphasizes acquiring control of an asset and its future economic benefits. The issue here concerns the difference between control and ownership. This distinction is critical for SPEs and leases.[20] Historically, the assets of SPEs had not been reported as part of the sponsoring entity's balance sheet because the sponsoring entity's ownership of voting common equity shares was minimal. However, recent rules require SPEs to be consolidated as part of a firm's balance sheet if the

---

[18]Chapter 9 discusses LIFO in greater detail.

[19]Another complicated inventory issue affecting accounting quality discussed in Chapter 9 is a LIFO layer liquidation. Such liquidations are transitory and can seriously affect estimates of future earnings unless adjusted by the analyst.

[20]We discuss SPEs further in Chapter 9.

firm exerts control in some way over the SPE or the firm is the substantial beneficiary of asset benefits held by the SPE. These new rules improve balance sheet quality. Similarly, leased assets under operating leases are not recognized as assets on the balance sheet under the lease accounting rules as of the writing of this text. However, new lease rules that become effective in 2018 improve balance sheet quality by recognizing as assets the right of use and control of benefits obtained by the lessee.

Probability

Initial recognition of a noncurrent asset also requires that the future economic benefits are probable. Management judgment of what is probable is a potential source of low accounting quality. You should read the accounting policy note to understand what costs are capitalized as part of property, plant, and equipment and intangible assets. Often, standard setters don't give companies a choice, prohibiting capitalization of costs from internal R&D and marketing activities as noncurrent assets. On one hand, this improves balance sheet quality by limiting management judgment in some cases. On the other hand, balance sheet quality can be reduced by keeping valuable assets such as brands and intellectual property from research off the balance sheet.

Fair Value

In an arm's-length exchange of regularly traded assets, the initial fair value measurement is generally easy to determine. However, unique transactions can be difficult to measure and value and thus can lead to low accounting quality. Consider, for example, a company that provides unique consulting or design services in exchange for a long-term note receivable. The note receivable should be reported initially as a noncurrent asset at its fair value. However, if the services are unique and have no established market value, accountants must estimate the fair value of the note and use it as a basis to record the transaction. The fair value is determined by contractual cash inflows (i.e., periodic interest and final maturity value) and an interest rate that is appropriate for the risk level of the note. Considerable management judgment might be necessary in this situation, and errors in judgment, whether intentional or not, could yield a low-quality fair value estimate. Because financial statements articulate, revenue is also valued too high or too low if the note is valued too high or too low, and earnings quality is compromised. Companies have controls in place and auditors have incentives to make sure that these transactions are recorded in a reasonable, unbiased way. However, you should also identify if substantial amounts of revenues or asset acquisitions are a result of unique transactions and how the company accounts for these transactions.

Changes in Value

On an ongoing basis, long-lived productive assets such as buildings and equipment must be depreciated over estimated useful lives to an estimated salvage value using a depreciation method. Changing useful life estimates changes depreciation expense, possibly in a way that could help a company achieve an earnings target. Biased or opportunistic management estimates of depreciation can lead to low earnings quality.[21]

When a firm acquires assets such as property, plant, and equipment and intangible assets, it expects that those assets will generate future benefits. However, various events or other factors may reduce the future benefits originally anticipated from the assets. In an attempt to improve balance sheet quality in the accounting for real noncurrent assets

---

[21]Chapter 8 presents methods of detecting whether depreciation estimates are opportunistic.

(as opposed to financial assets), standard setters have created a set of tests for asset impairment. The general process is to estimate whether the fair value of a noncurrent asset has declined below its recorded book value. If so, balance sheet quality is improved by writing down the value of the asset and representing the asset at its lower probable future economic benefits. Earnings quality, especially as it relates to earnings persistence, often suffers when noncurrent asset impairment losses are included in current period income from continuing operations, and if those losses should have been recorded in prior periods, the quality of those earnings will have turned out to be low as well. Again, high-quality disclosure can increase earnings quality. If the notes to the income statement clearly designate the nature of the write-down so that you can assess when the asset decline occurred and its likely persistence, earnings quality remains high.

The FASB cites the following events or circumstances as examples that may signal impairment problems for a long-lived asset or group of assets:

- A significant decrease in the market price of a long-lived asset.
- A significant adverse change in the extent or manner in which a long-lived asset is being used or in its physical condition.
- A significant adverse change in legal factors or in the business climate that affects the value of a long-lived asset.
- A current-period operating or cash flow loss combined with a projection or forecast that demonstrates continuing losses associated with the use of a long-lived asset.
- A current expectation that, more likely than not, a long-lived asset will be sold or otherwise disposed of significantly before the end of its previously estimated useful life.[22]

What is particularly noteworthy about this list is that a firm, in effect, must recognize impairment when it anticipates that assets previously acquired will no longer provide the future benefits initially anticipated. This is a valuable disclosure to consider when you attempt to assess a firm's past strategic decisions.

Firms must include impairment losses in income before taxes from continuing operations. Asset impairments do not warrant presentation in a separate section of the income statement, such as that given for discontinued operations (discussed later). However, alternative methods for reporting the losses include a separate line item on the income statement or a detailed note that describes what line items on the income statement include the impairment losses.

- Choices, estimates, judgments, and accounting standards play an important role in asset and liability measurement and hence the ability of the balance sheet to accurately reflect liquidity risk, solvency risk, and financial flexibility.

- Given the articulation between the balance sheet and income statement, balance sheet quality almost always affects earnings quality.

Quick Check

---

[22]The term *more likely than not* refers to a level of likelihood that is more than 50%. *FASB Codification Topic 360 (-10-35-21)*. Also, see Hugo Nurnberg and Nelson Dittmar, "Reporting Impairments of Long-Lived Assets: New Rules and Disclosures," *Journal of Financial Statement Analysis* (Winter 1997), pp. 37–50. The article includes examples of how these impairment indicators are applied by firms in the oil and gas, restaurant, retail food, and service-related industries.

Specific Events and Conditions That Affect Earnings Persistence

In this section, we turn our attention to a set of specific conditions and transactions that affect earnings quality, primarily with respect to earnings persistence. To provide a framework for our discussion, Exhibit 6.3 presents a hypothetical statement of comprehensive income that shows the reporting of special items (in capital letters) if they receive separate line-item treatment.

Gains and Losses from Peripheral Activities

Firms often enter into transactions that are peripheral to their core operations but generate gains and losses that must be reported on the income statement. For example, firms may sell buildings and equipment, which often results in a gain or loss. Or a firm might extinguish a long-term liability as **Starbucks** did in 2015, which generated a $61.1 million loss. Gains and losses from activities peripheral to the primary activities of a firm are included in income from continuing operations. You should search for such items and decide whether to exclude them when assessing current profitability and forecasting future earnings. Because gains and losses tend to be generated from sales of long-term assets or extinguishment of long-term liabilities, it is not clear that the change in asset or liability value is related to the current period. For example, a gain on a sale of a building might have been the result of an economic gain from appreciation in a prior period. Or depreciation in prior years might have been too high because of an unrealistically low useful-life estimate. In either case, including the gain to assess current period profitability is not warranted.

Exhibit 6.3	
XYZ Company **Statement of Comprehensive Income**	
Sales revenue	X
Cost of goods sold	(X)
Selling and administrative expenses	(X)
Operating Income	X
GAINS (LOSSES) FROM PERIPHERAL ACTIVITIES	(X)
RESTRUCTURING CHARGES AND IMPAIRMENT LOSSES	(X)
Interest income	X
Interest expense	(X)
Income before Income Taxes	X
Income tax expense	(X)
Income from Continuing Operations	X
INCOME FROM DISCONTINUED OPERATIONS, NET OF TAXES	X
Net Income	X
OTHER COMPREHENSIVE INCOME, NET OF TAXES	X
Comprehensive Income	X

	Exhibit 6.4		
Summary of Singapore Airlines Aircraft Disposal Gains **(Singapore dollar amounts in millions)**			
Fiscal Year	**Surplus on Disposal**	**Pretax Income**	**Percentage of Pretax Income**
2010–2011	$103.3	$1,419.0	7.3%
2011–2012	(1.4)	448.2	0.0
2012–2013	56.0	482.0	11.6
2013–2014	51.2	367.9	13.9
2014–2015	51.9	442.9	11.7

Firms report peripheral gains and losses on a *pretax* basis. Income tax expense includes any tax effects of the gain or loss. If you decide to eliminate the gain or loss from income from continuing operations, you also must eliminate the related tax effect from income tax expense using specific information disclosed about the tax effects or using the statutory rate if the firm does not disclose specific information about the tax effects.

Gains and losses can be recurring, material, and a part of corporate strategy. For example, Exhibit 6.4 shows how **Singapore Airlines** reported surplus (gains) on disposal of aircraft, spare parts, and spare engines over the years 2010 to 2015. Singapore Airlines maintains a reputation for flying newer, technologically advanced aircraft, which results in the use of aircraft for fewer years than other airlines. Thus, the sale of aircraft and spare parts is a significant portion of Singapore Airlines' profitability and should be treated as recurring when forecasting future earnings.

Restructuring Charges and Impairment Losses

Firms may decide to remain in a segment of their business but elect to make major changes in the strategic direction or level of operations of that business.[23] In many of these cases, firms record a restructuring charge against earnings for the cost of implementing the decision, which might include terminating or transferring employees, closing down certain types of operations, or substantially changing production and sales processes. Employee-related costs from downsizing or employee retraining and reassignment typically make up a substantial portion of restructuring costs. Restructuring plans also tend to trigger the asset impairments discussed in the earlier section on accounting quality related to noncurrent assets.

The treatment of restructuring charges in analyzing profitability and assessing earnings persistence is important because recessionary conditions often induce firms to include restructuring charges in their reported earnings for the current period. Whether the recessionary conditions are expected to persist will have a bearing on forecasting earnings in the future. Further, restructurings are expected to yield operating efficiencies or strategic benefits, and, thus, may be associated with lower future expenses and higher

---

[23]If the firm decides to abandon a business segment or component altogether, the reporting policies discussed later for discontinued operations apply. In many cases, however, firms are not abandoning current areas of business, but are "restructuring" them to improve profitability.

future revenues. Consistent with this value-added characteristic of restructurings, announcements of restructurings are typically associated with stock price increases.

Interpreting a particular firm's restructuring charge is difficult because firms vary in their treatment of these items, as follows:

- Firms that apply accounting principles conservatively (for example, use relatively short lives for depreciable assets, immediately expense expenditures for repairs of equipment, or use shorter amortization lives for intangible assets) have smaller amounts to write off as restructuring charges than firms that are less conservative.
- Firms that sidestep proper financial reporting treatment by spreading out restructuring charges to minimize the impact of the restructuring charge on current period earnings often must take restructuring charges for several years to provide adequately for restructuring costs.
- Firms that maximize the amount of the restructuring charge in a particular year communicate the "bad news" all at once (referred to as the "big bath" approach) and reduce or eliminate the need for additional restructuring charges in the future. If the restructuring charge later turns out to have been too large, income from continuing operations in a later period includes a restructuring credit that increases reported earnings.

The prevalence of restructuring charges in recent years has prompted standard setters to address these measurement and reporting issues. Although differences between U.S. GAAP and IFRS often caused differences in the timing of the charges in past years, recent revisions to *IAS 19*, effective January 1, 2013, substantially align the two sets of rules related to restructurings.[24] The basic rules are that firms record a *restructuring liability* on the balance sheet and the associated *restructuring charge* (an expense) on the income statement when these two conditions are present:

- Management has committed to the restructuring plan and has informed employees of termination benefits.
- Restructuring costs meet the definition of a liability.

PepsiCo's December 26, 2015, Consolidated Financial Statements provide a good example of restructuring and impairment charges that have different levels of persistence. PepsiCo's income statement reports an enormous impairment charge of $1.359 billion (15.4% of its pretax income before the charge) on its Venezuelan wholly owned subsidiary and joint venture. PepsiCo explained that the markets used to exchange bolivars for U.S. dollars had become illiquid, causing difficulty in the subsidiary's and joint venture's abilities to pay invoices in U.S. dollars, which, in turn, disrupted the supply chain. Venezuelan government actions also disrupted PepsiCo's ability to make certain operating decisions and financial decisions such as the ability to pay dividends. For these reasons, PepsiCo no longer believed that it had the control or significant influence necessary to justify consolidation or the equity method (discussed further in Chapter 8). PepsiCo converted the accounting to the cost method, which required a downward revaluation of the investment to its fair value, resulting in the impairment charge. This is an example of a transitory impairment charge (although it is within the realm of possibility to have future charges with respect to the investment).

---

[24]*FASB Codification Topic 420*; International Accounting Standards Board, *International Accounting Standard 37*, "Provisions, Contingent Assets and Contingent Liabilities" (1998); International Accounting Standards Board, *International Accounting Standard 19* (Revised), "Employee Benefits" (2011).

Exhibit 6.5

Excerpt from PepsiCo's Note 3
(amounts in millions)

Note 3 — Restructuring and Impairment Charges
A summary of our restructuring and impairment charges and other productivity initiatives is as follows:

	2015	2014	2013
2014 Productivity Plan	$169	$357	$ 53
2012 Productivity Plan	61	61	110
Total restructuring and impairment charges	230	418	163
Other productivity initiatives	90	67	—
Total restructuring and impairment charges and other productivity initiatives	$320	$485	$163

Source: PepsiCo's 2015 10-K.

The magnitude of the charge warrants line-item reporting in the income statement. However, other, likely more persistent, restructuring and impairment charges are also buried in PepsiCo's "Selling, general, and administrative expenses" line item. Exhibit 6.5 from Note 3 details charges from two separate productivity improvement and other initiatives.

Discontinued Operations

When a firm decides to exit a particular component of its business, it classifies that business as a discontinued operation. This classification provides analysts and other financial statements users with information to distinguish the effects of continuing versus discontinuing operations on current period performance and provides a basis for forecasting future income from the continuing operations of the firm. Recent pronouncements have substantially aligned U.S. GAAP and IFRS on the issue of identifying a discontinued operation. Under U.S. GAAP, discontinued operations are strategic shifts of the company that have or will have a major effect on operations and financial results. Consistent with the IFRS definition of a discontinued operation, examples provided by recent U.S. GAAP standards are disposals of a major geographical area, line of business, and major equity method investments.

Firms with discontinued items are required to report the net income or loss from the discontinued business (including the results of operating the segment and any disposal gains and losses) as a separate item in the discontinued operations section of the income statement (net of tax effects). Most U.S. firms include three years of income statement information in their income statements. A firm that decides to divest a business during the current year includes the net income or loss of this business as discontinued operations for the current year and in comparative income statements for the preceding two years. (Previously, the firm reported the latter income in continuing operations in the income statements originally prepared for those two years.) If the final sale has not occurred as of the end of the period, the remaining assets held for sale are assessed for impairment and an impairment loss (net of tax) is included as part of the discontinued operations disclosure. The assets and liabilities of the discontinued operations are isolated and receive separate disclosure on the balance sheet or in notes that support the balance sheet. Further, recent pronouncements have emphasized the requirement for disaggregated disclosure in the notes to the financial statements that emphasize major revenue and expense line items included in the results of the discontinued operations, as well as operating and investing cash flows related to the discontinued operations. Examination of these disaggregated disclosures and the separation of discontinued items from continuing operations in the primary financial statements will allow you to better identify the persistence of earnings and cash flows.

For most firms, income from discontinued operations represents a source of earnings that does not persist. Thus, in most cases, you should exclude income from discontinued operations from forecasts of future earnings, focusing instead on income from continuing operations.[25]

Other Comprehensive Income Items

U.S. GAAP and IFRS require firms to revalue certain assets and liabilities each period even though firms have not yet realized the value change in a market transaction. As discussed in Chapter 2, the recognition and valuation of these assets and liabilities do not immediately affect net income and retained earnings. Instead, these unrealized gains and losses are reported as other comprehensive income for the period and are included within accumulated other comprehensive income or loss in the shareholders' equity section of the balance sheet.

Under current U.S. GAAP, four balance sheet items receive this accounting treatment:[26]

- Fair value gains and losses on investment securities deemed available-for-sale.
- Fair value gains and losses on derivatives held as cash flow hedges.
- Certain adjustments to pensions and other postemployment benefits obligations.
- Foreign currency adjustments for assets and liabilities in certain foreign operations.

IFRS also permits upward revaluations of tangible fixed assets used in operations.

You must decide whether to include the unrealized gains and losses when assessing earnings persistence and predicting future profitability:

- These gains and losses are more likely to be part of future earnings when
  - they closely relate to ongoing operating activities.
  - measuring the amount of the gain or loss is relatively objective (i.e., when active markets exist to indicate the amount of the value changes).
- These gains and losses are less likely to be part of future earnings when
  - they are not directly related to the firm's ongoing operating activities.
  - the amount of gain or loss that firms ultimately realize when they sell the assets or settle the liabilities will likely differ from the amount reported each period and might reverse in future years prior to disposal or settlement.
  - measuring the amount of the gain or loss on certain types of assets can be subjective because they are not traded in active markets.

[25]For some firms that regularly pursue a strategy to acquire firms and subsequently sell them, income from discontinued operations is an ongoing source of profitability, and you might decide to include this income in forecasts of future earnings. Expectations about whether discontinued operations will continue to occur are best developed in the industry and strategy analysis stages of the analysis process.

[26]Chapters 7–9 discuss the accounting for each of these items in great detail. New rules go into effect for fiscal years beginning after December 15, 2017 that eliminate the available-for-sale classification. The changes in fair value of securities previously classified as available-for-sale will be reflected in current year income in the same manner as trading securities, eliminating the other comprehensive income treatment of gains and losses.

Comprehensive income items are generally treated as transitory and thus excluded from future earnings predictions.

Changes in Accounting Principles

Firms occasionally change the accounting principles used to generate financial statements. Sometimes standard setters mandate the changes. Regardless of the source of the change, for consistency, firms following U.S. GAAP and IFRS must report amounts for the current and prior years as if the new accounting principle had been applied all along (termed *retrospective treatment*). This reporting results in net income amounts for the current and prior periods measured using the same accounting principles the firm intends to use in future periods, thereby enhancing the information content of reported earnings in forecasting future earnings.[27]

Firms need not restate prior-year earnings retrospectively if it is impracticable to determine the period-specific effects of the change. In this case, firms must apply the new accounting policy to the balances of assets and liabilities as of the earliest period for which retrospective application is practicable and to make a corresponding adjustment to retained earnings for that period. When it is impracticable to determine the cumulative effect of applying a change in accounting principle to *all* prior periods to which it relates, firms must apply the new accounting principle as if it were made prospectively from the start of the year of the change.

For example, if a firm switches from the FIFO cost-flow assumption to the LIFO cost-flow assumption for inventories and cost of goods sold, typically it is impracticable to reconstruct the effects of the accounting change on prior years. In this case, the change to the LIFO cost-flow assumption will be applied prospectively (that is, in current and future years) at the start of the year in which the accounting change takes place.

Firms may choose retrospective treatment on a voluntary basis as well. For example, Exhibit 6.6 presents **Apple Inc.**'s Form 10-K/A to amend its 2009 Form 10-K. In the amendment, Apple explains the financial statement effects when it applied new required accounting methods to account for the iPhone and Apple TV. Prior accounting methods required Apple to defer all revenues and expenses related to sales of iPhone and Apple TV and recognize these revenues and expenses on a straight-line basis over the expected product life because Apple had promised the possibility of free future upgrades and features. The justification for deferral is typically that revenue has not been earned. New standards require Apple to recognize revenue and expenses relating to existing delivered hardware and software at the time of sale and to defer the estimated fair value of the right to receive free future upgrades and features. Apple had a choice of applying the new standards prospectively (in current and future periods) or retrospectively (adjust prior years' results and then use the new standard in current and future periods). Apple chose retrospective application to enhance comparability. Note the huge amounts involved. Adoption of the new standards increased Apple's sales by $6.4 billion in 2009, $5.0 billion in 2008, and $572 million in 2007.

---

[27]*FASB Codification Topic 250*; International Accounting Standards Board, *International Accounting Standard 8*, "Accounting Policies, Change in Accounting Estimates, and Errors" (revised 2003).

Exhibit 6.6

Excerpt from Apple's Explanation of Change in Revenue Recognition Method

Under the historical accounting principles, the Company was required to account for sales of both iPhone and Apple TV using subscription accounting because the Company indicated it might from time-to-time provide future unspecified software upgrades and features for those products free of charge. Under subscription accounting, revenue and associated product cost of sales for iPhone and Apple TV were deferred at the time of sale and recognized on a straight-line basis over each product's estimated economic life. This resulted in the deferral of significant amounts of revenue and cost of sales related to iPhone and Apple TV. Costs incurred by the Company for engineering, sales, marketing and warranty were expensed as incurred. As of September 26, 2009, based on the historical accounting principles, total accumulated deferred revenue and deferred costs associated with past iPhone and Apple TV sales were $12.1 billion and $5.2 billion, respectively.

The new accounting principles generally require the Company to account for the sale of both iPhone and Apple TV as two deliverables. The first deliverable is the hardware and software delivered at the time of sale, and the second deliverable is the right included with the purchase of iPhone and Apple TV to receive on a when-and-if-available basis future unspecified software upgrades and features relating to the product's software. The new accounting principles result in the recognition of substantially all of the revenue and product costs from sales of iPhone and Apple TV at the time of sale. Additionally, the Company is required to estimate a standalone selling price for the unspecified software upgrade right included with the sale of iPhone and Apple TV and recognizes that amount ratably over the 24-month estimated life of the related hardware device. For all periods presented, the Company's estimated selling price for the software upgrade right included with each iPhone and Apple TV sold is $25 and $10, respectively. The adoption of the new accounting principles increased the Company's net sales by $6.4 billion, $5.0 billion and $572 million for 2009, 2008 and 2007, respectively. As of September 26, 2009, the revised total accumulated deferred revenue associated with iPhone and Apple TV sales to date was $483 million; revised accumulated deferred costs for such sales were zero.

The Company had the option of adopting the new accounting principles on a prospective or retrospective basis. Prospective adoption would have required the Company to apply the new accounting principles to sales beginning in fiscal year 2010 without reflecting the impact of the new accounting principles on iPhone and Apple TV sales made prior to September 2009. Accordingly, the Company's financial results for the two years following adoption would have included the impact of amortizing the significant amounts of deferred revenue and cost of sales related to historical iPhone and Apple TV sales. The Company believes prospective adoption would have resulted in financial information that was not comparable between financial periods because of the significant amount of past iPhone sales; therefore, the Company elected retrospective adoption. Retrospective adoption required the Company to revise its previously issued financial statements as if the new accounting principles had always been applied. The Company believes retrospective adoption provides the most comparable and useful financial information for financial statement users, is more consistent with the information the Company's management uses to evaluate its business, and better reflects the underlying economic performance of the Company. Accordingly, the Company has revised its financial statements for 2009, 2008 and 2007 in this Form 10-K/A to reflect the retrospective adoption of the new accounting principles. There was no impact from the retrospective adoption of the new accounting principles for 2006 and 2005. Those years predated the Company's introduction of iPhone and Apple TV.

Source: Apple Corporation, Form 10-K/A for the Fiscal Year Ended September 26, 2009.

Changes in Accounting Estimates

As discussed earlier in this chapter, application of accounting standards requires firms to make many estimates. Examples include the amount of uncollectible accounts receivable; the useful lives for fixed assets and intangible assets; the percentage-of-completion rate for a long-term project; the return rate for warranties; and interest, compensation, and inflation rates for pensions, health care, and other retirement benefits. Firms periodically change these estimates. Current accounting standards require firms to account for changes in estimates by using the new estimates in the current year and in future years.

You should attempt to determine whether estimate changes exist and are significant. We will provide specific examples of how to do this in Chapters 7 to 9. Managers sometimes explain the impact of estimate changes in the MD&A or notes. However, often you must infer their existence and impact.

Some estimate changes are opportunistic; managers make them to achieve their earnings goals and thus to mislead investors. However, you must remember that estimates change over time for legitimate reasons. One of the main determinants of the value of accrual-based financial statements is that the amounts of reported assets and liabilities can reflect management's informed beliefs. Again, knowledge of a company's industry economics and strategy allows for a more informed judgment of whether an estimate change is opportunistic or supportable by a change in economic conditions.

You also must decide whether to use the financial statement data as originally reported for each year or as restated to reflect the new conditions. Because the objective of most financial statement analysis is to evaluate the past as a guide for projecting the future, the logical response is to use the restated data. When a firm provides sufficient information so that you can restate prior years' financial statements using reasonable assumptions, you should use retroactively restated financial statement data. When the firm does not provide sufficient information to do the restatements (as is often the case), you should use the amounts as originally reported for each year. To interpret the resulting ratios, attempt to assess how much of the change in the ratios results from the new reporting condition and how much relates to economic profitability and risk.

Accounting Classification Differences

While accounting quality is primarily a firm-specific concept, a related concern arises when you wish to compare two firms that use different accounting classifications for the same economic item. For example, consider two luxury goods retailers, **Coach** and **Tiffany & Co**. Coach includes shipping and handling expense (for shipping products to retail locations and to customers) in selling, general, and administrative (SG&A) expenses, while Tiffany includes it in cost of goods sold. This creates a source of difference in their gross margins. If the amounts of shipping and handling expense are disclosed, then you can adjust SG&A and cost of goods sold. If the amounts are not disclosed, then you must take the difference into account when making profitability comparisons.

The account classification issue is exacerbated when comparing firms in different countries. Exhibit 6.7 presents the December 31, 2015, consolidated income statement of the Finnish company **Stora Enso**, prepared in accordance with IFRS. Stora Enso is a global paper, packaging, and wood products company that produces newsprint and book paper, magazine paper, fine paper, consumer board, industrial packaging, and wood products.

Exhibit 6.7

Stora Enso Consolidated Income Statement (amounts in EUR millions)

	Year Ended 31 December	
	2015	2014
Sales	10 040	10 213
Other operating income	128	168
Changes in inventories of finished goods and work in progress	18	3
Change in net value of biological assets	(89)	(114)
Materials and services	(6 008)	(6 244)
Freight and sales commissions	(970)	(939)
Personnel expenses	(1 313)	(1 383)
Other operating expenses	(503)	(625)
Share of results of equity accounted investments	519	87
Depreciation, amortisation and impairment charges	(763)	(766)
Operating Profit	1 059	400
Financial income	25	79
Financial expense	(270)	(359)
Profit before Tax	814	120
Income tax	(31)	(30)
Net Profit for the Year	783	90
Attributable to:		
Owners of the parent	807	99
Non-controlling interests	(24)	(9)
Net Profit for the Year	783	90
Earnings per Share		
Basic and diluted earnings per share, EUR	1.02	0.13

Source: Stora Enso, Annual Report for the Fiscal Year Ended December 31, 2015.

Typical of the financial statements for a non-U.S. company, Stora Enso classifies expenses by source instead of function. For example, a U.S. paper company includes as operating expenses cost of goods sold, SG&A expenses, possibly some other gains and losses, restructuring charges, and impairments. Wages and salary costs and depreciation costs are allocated to cost of goods sold and SG&A expenses. Cost of goods sold includes the costs allocated to inventory sold that period, such as wages and depreciation (that is, manufacturing overhead) costs, as well as materials costs. Wages, salaries, and depreciation not related to production appear in SG&A. In contrast, Stora Enso does not make those allocations. For example, "Personnel expenses" are listed, but one does not know the portion of those expenses that would be included in inventory and therefore included in cost of goods sold in the U.S. company. Likewise, Stora Enso reports "Depreciation, amortisation, and impairment charge," which is different from what is done in the U.S. reporting approach. Instead of cost of goods sold, Stora Enso reports "Materials and services" and "Changes in inventories of finished goods and work in progress." An analyst estimating cost of goods sold would have to include these two accounts, an estimated portion of personnel expenses to be included in inventory, and an estimated portion of depreciation to be included in inventory.

When you can easily and unambiguously reclassify accounts, the reclassified data should serve as the basis for analysis. If the reclassifications require numerous assumptions, you should make them as precisely as possible or avoid making them and note the differences in account classification for further reference when interpreting the financial statement analysis.

- Infrequent and unusual items that can have a large impact on reported financial statements include
  - gains and losses from peripheral activities.
  - restructuring charges and impairment losses.
  - discontinued operations.
  - other comprehensive income items.
  - changes in accounting principles.
  - changes in accounting estimates.
  - accounting classification differences.

- These items may affect the quality of the accounting information as a descriptor of current profitability and as a predictor of future earnings.
- The process of deciding whether to exclude these items from income is more art than science and requires considerable judgment on your part.
- The ability to make good judgment is enhanced by understanding the industry economic characteristics and firm strategy.

Tools in the Assessment of Accounting Quality

In the preceding sections, we identified areas of potential low accounting quality and suggested how you might read the financial statements and notes in order to identify low accounting quality and make necessary adjustments to profitability and risk assessment. In the next two sections, we present two additional tools that can be used to assess accounting quality. The first is a partition of earnings into its cash flow and accrual components to gain a better understanding of the persistence of earnings. The second tool is a model to assess the likelihood of financial statement manipulation.

Partitioning Earnings into Operating Cash Flow and Accrual Components

LO 6-7

Assess accounting quality by partitioning earnings into its accrual and cash flow components.

Operating cash inflows and outflows are easy to identify and measure. However, accrual accounting requires a consideration of changes in noncash assets and liabilities to measure earnings. Noncash assets and liabilities are called accruals. Earnings are the sum of cash flow and accrual changes. For example, suppose a firm performs a service for $1,000, collecting $700 in cash and a $300 account receivable from a customer and promising to pay an employee $200 in wages. Under accrual accounting, the firm's earnings equal $800:

Income statement:	Service revenue	$1,000
	Wages expense	(200)
	Earnings	$ 800

Alternatively, earnings can be expressed as the sum of a cash component and an accrual component:

Balance sheet effects: Increase in cash from sale (cash component)		$700
Increase in accruals (accrual component)		
Increase in accounts receivable	$ 300	
Increase in wages payable	(200)	100
Earnings		$800

Accrual accounting is superior to cash accounting on the dimensions of capturing economic content and predicting future cash flows. The $100 net increase in accruals is a prediction of future cash flows. Next period, the firm will collect the $300 accounts receivable in cash and pay the $200 wages payable in cash, yielding a net inflow of $100 in cash.

Analyzing Patterns in Accruals

If managers attempt to manage reported earnings, they will typically do so through accruals estimates. Even if managers do not introduce bias into the financial statements, the accrual component of net income will exhibit a persistence that differs from the operating cash flow component of net income. To further clarify what is meant by "accruals," Exhibit 6.8 provides a schematic of a statement of cash flows and identifies accruals. Accruals are the adjustments that reconcile cash flows from operations and net income. They are components of earnings because they map underlying economics into reported profitability. Investors who fixate on net income or operating cash flows without understanding the relation between the two may make erroneous inferences regarding the persistence of cash flows or earnings.

Sloan examined the relation between net income and operating cash flows by focusing on the behavior of net income conditional on the magnitude of accruals.[28] He defines the accrual component of current earnings as net income minus operating cash flows, and then scales the amount by dividing by the average of beginning and ending total assets so that firms can be compared regardless of their size. He then ranked firms based on this measure of accruals. He plotted net income (scaled by average total assets) for five years before and after the year in which he measured the accruals.

Exhibit 6.9 provides the plots for the decile of firms with the lowest (most negative) accruals and the decile of firms with the highest (most positive) accruals. The top line on the graph indicates that in the ranking year, firms with the highest current accruals have very high income. Moreover, this high income represents a spike relative to the previous five years. More importantly, it represents a spike that reverses almost entirely in the next year. On the other side, firms with the most negative current accruals report net income that is extremely low relative to prior years, but this decline turns around over the following years. When net income is high relative to operating cash flows, we describe the firm as having recorded *income-increasing* accruals; when net income is

---

[28]Richard G. Sloan, "Do Stock Prices Fully Reflect Information in Accruals and Cash Flows about Future Earnings?," *The Accounting Review* (1996), pp. 289–315.

Exhibit 6.8

Simplified Schematic of the Computation of Accruals from the Operating Section of the Statement of Cash Flows

Statement of Cash Flows

Net income   NI

Accruals
- + Depreciation
- + Amortization
- + Deferred taxes

Adjustments for working capital
- +/– Accounts receivable
- +/– Prepaid expenses
- +/– Inventory
- +/– Other assets
- +/– Accounts payable
- +/– Accrued liabilities
- +/– Other liabilities

$$\frac{NI - OCF}{\text{Avg. Total Assets}}$$

Possibly low earnings quality if this is large and positive (i.e., when income-increasing accruals are big)

Operating cash flows   OCF

Cash flows from investing activities   I

Cash flows from financing activities   F

Net change in cash   CHANGE

Exhibit 6.9

Patterns of Earnings Surrounding High and Low Accruals

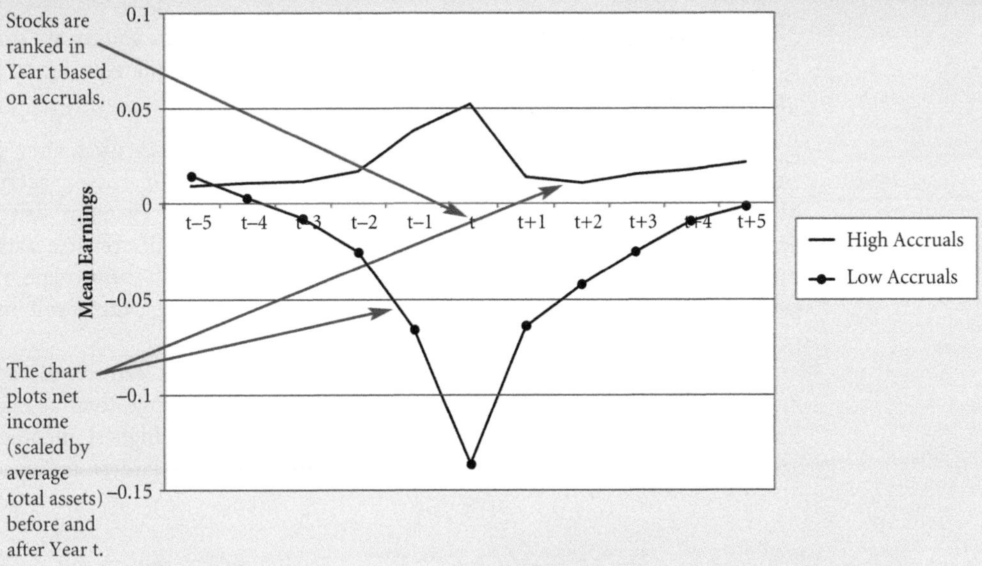

Stocks are ranked in Year t based on accruals.

The chart plots net income (scaled by average total assets) before and after Year t.

— High Accruals
—•— Low Accruals

Source: Sloan (1996), op. cit.

low relative to operating cash flows, we describe the firm as having recorded *income-decreasing* accruals. Non–working capital accruals (e.g., depreciation) tend to be more persistent than working capital accruals (e.g., accounts receivable, accounts payable, inventory), which tend to go up and down and generally fluctuate around zero for mature firms.

The patterns of net income in Exhibit 6.9 indicate that when net income is high because of large income-increasing accruals, the reversal of these accruals generates predictable decreases in the level of earnings in future years. The same is true for income-decreasing accruals; they are followed by increases in the level of earnings in future years. This reversal effect should be intuitive. For example, if a firm generates a spike in sales made on credit, this increases accounts receivable and recognized sales. In the following year, the firm will have to generate incremental sales to maintain the level (or growth) in sales, which is difficult to do if the prior year's high levels were unusual or transitory. The statement of cash flows highlights the evolution of receivables by quantifying period-to-period changes in the balance. If a firm with a high increase in sales made on credit does not replenish these with more sales, the statement of cash flows in the following period will indicate a decrease in receivables. Although the collection of cash will contribute to cash flows from operations, net income will tend to fall because of the relative reduction in sales due to the nonreplenishment of prior-period credit sales. Ultimately, declines in earnings are strongly associated with declines in security prices.

Total accruals divided by average total assets can be thought of as an inverse measure of earnings quality: the higher the measure, the lower the earnings quality in the sense that reported earnings may not be as persistent in the future and will likely decline. The lack of persistence might be due to low earnings quality in the sense that managers introduced bias into accruals, which will have to reverse under double-entry accounting, or it might be due to the tyranny of mean reversion whereby shocks like large increases in credit sales or big decreases in expenses are not sustainable. Increasingly, investors and the financial press are focusing on the link between accruals and earnings quality. For example, in an article profiling **Microsoft**'s 2009 second-quarter earnings announcement, TheStreet.com stated:

> Companies that report lukewarm results on poor earnings quality are prime candidates to miss estimates by a wide margin in future quarters due to the reversal of accruals.[29]

If investors neglect to examine the components of net income, they may fail to appreciate the fact that large earnings driven by large *income-increasing* accruals are less persistent. Similarly, they might fail to appreciate that low earnings driven by large *income-decreasing* accruals also are less persistent and generally reverse with improved earnings in future periods. If enough investors fail to fully appreciate the relation between components of current earnings and future earnings, the result may be mispricing a firm's common stock.

Exhibit 6.10 plots one- and two-year-ahead future stock returns for a ranking of firms by the sign and magnitude of accruals (scaled by average total assets) shown in Exhibit 6.9. Decile 1 consists of the 10% of firms with the highest income-increasing accruals. Decile 10 consists of the 10% of firms with the largest income-decreasing

[29]David MacDougall, "Analyst's Toolkit: Don't Hate on Microsoft," *TheStreet.com* (July 29, 2009).

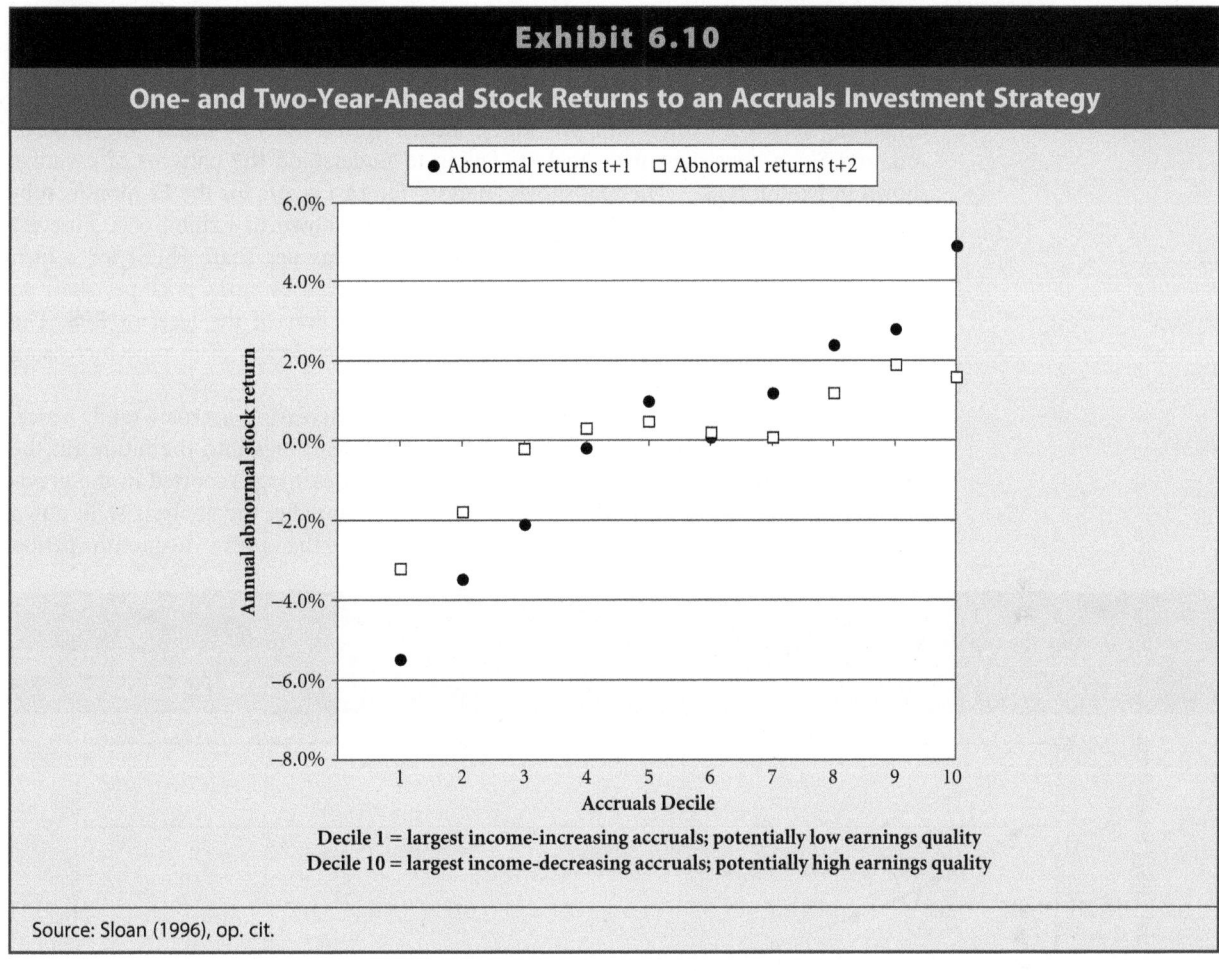

Exhibit 6.10

One- and Two-Year-Ahead Stock Returns to an Accruals Investment Strategy

● Abnormal returns t+1   □ Abnormal returns t+2

Decile 1 = largest income-increasing accruals; potentially low earnings quality
Decile 10 = largest income-decreasing accruals; potentially high earnings quality

Source: Sloan (1996), op. cit.

accruals. The stock returns plotted in Exhibit 6.10 are the average stock return for all firms in the decile, where each firm's return is first adjusted for the return of a portfolio of similarly sized firms. Thus, the returns are referred to as "abnormal" returns. Positive abnormal returns indicate that the firm's stock price performed much better than similar-sized firms, and negative abnormal returns indicate worse performance than similar-sized firms. Exhibit 6.10 indicates that in the first year after firms are ranked based on the magnitude of their accruals, the firms with the highest income-increasing accruals experience the worst stock returns and firms with the highest income-decreasing accruals experience the best stock returns. The plots show a similar ranking of stock returns in the second year after stocks are ranked based on accruals, but the effect diminishes somewhat. Overall, these patterns of returns are consistent with investors, on average, not realizing how important the accrual components of reported earnings are in helping them form expectations of future earnings and, as a consequence, in predicting future stock returns. As firms report quarterly results in years subsequent to large income-increasing or income-decreasing accruals, investors gradually see the turnaround in earnings that is shown in Exhibit 6.9. As this occurs, stock prices gradually adjust to the investors' revised expectations of future earnings.

Do Analysts Recognize These Earnings Patterns?

Analysts ought to be familiar with financial statements and be adept at understanding when earnings are temporarily high or low due to large income-increasing or income-decreasing accruals. Exhibit 6.11 provides evidence from a study by Bradshaw, Richardson, and Sloan consistent with analysts failing to understand the patterns of earnings shown in Exhibit 6.11.[30] The plot shows analysts' forecast errors for the 12 months subsequent to the ranking of firms based on accruals (as shown in Exhibit 6.9). Forecast errors are computed as the analysts' forecast of earnings per share (EPS) for a firm minus the actual reported EPS, and this difference is scaled by stock price per share so that forecast errors can be averaged across firms regardless of the level of EPS. The exhibit displays the average forecast errors for the highest deciles of income-increasing and income-decreasing accrual firms.

It is clear that for firms with the highest income-increasing accruals (and, hence, high earnings), analysts tend to extrapolate those high earnings into the future (in the first several months), but gradually realize that the high earnings reported in the previous year are not repeating in the subsequent year. Eventually, the analysts walk down their forecasts to the amount reported, but it takes the entire 12-month period

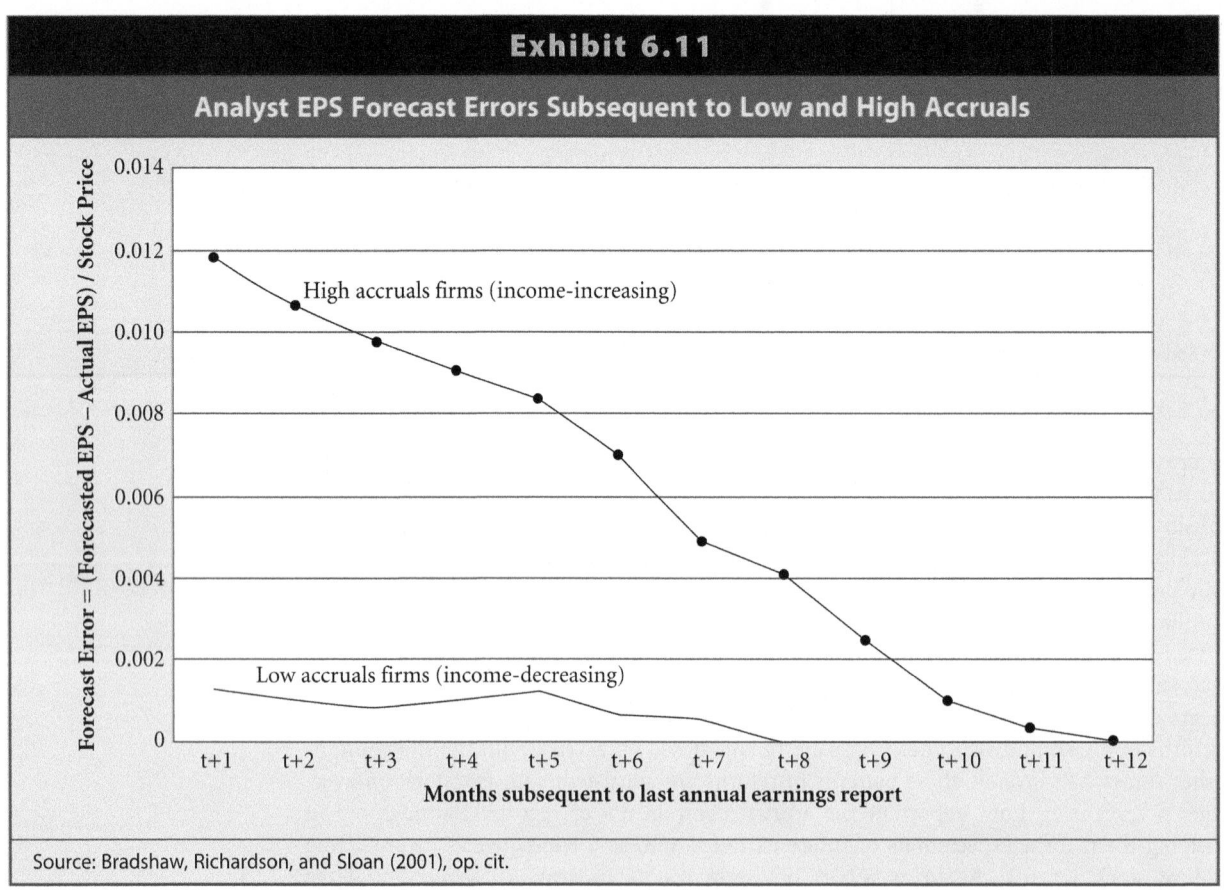

Exhibit 6.11

Analyst EPS Forecast Errors Subsequent to Low and High Accruals

Source: Bradshaw, Richardson, and Sloan (2001), op. cit.

---

[30]Mark T. Bradshaw, Scott A. Richardson, and Richard G. Sloan, "Do Analysts and Auditors Use Information in Accruals?," *Journal of Accounting Research* (June 2001), pp. 45–74.

subsequent to the announcement of the previous year's earnings for them to get it right. As was shown in Exhibit 6.10, during this time, the firms' stock prices are falling as well due to the same phenomenon whereby investors are walking down their expectations and valuations from elevated levels driven by the high earnings composed of income-increasing accruals in the previous year.[31]

The patterns of earnings, stock returns, and analysts' forecasts shown in Exhibits 6.9 to 6.11 suggest that investors who utilize the statement of cash flows to identify circumstances in which earnings are supported by accruals that tend to reverse will have an advantage over other investors, including professional analysts.

A Caveat: The Relative Quality of Cash Flows, EBITDA, and Earnings

Given our previous discussion of earnings management, earnings manipulation, and the tendency for extreme accruals to reverse, one could be left with the feeling that accrual accounting yields earnings numbers that are quite deficient relative to some other measure of performance such as cash flows or a measure to approximate cash flows: *earnings before interest, taxes, depreciation, and amortization* (EBITDA).

Some analysts champion EBITDA as an approximation of a cash-based measure of pretax operating earnings. Prior to the availability of the statement of cash flows, EBITDA was a "quick and dirty" calculation for cash flows, which certainly contributed to the growth of its popularity. However, cash flows from operations or operating income are more complete measures of operating performance that are easier to calculate because they are reported directly in the financial statements.

More importantly, EBITDA excludes four significant expenses. It excludes depreciation and amortization, which, for most firms, are the two largest noncash expenses. The presumption is that EBITDA roughly approximates cash flow from operations. However, EBITDA can differ significantly depending on other activities of the firm. For example, for rapidly growing firms, EBITDA ignores additional investments in working capital required to sustain that growth. The exclusion of depreciation expense, without a similar exclusion for rent expense, can also create inconsistent treatment of expenses for assets that a firm owns and depreciates versus expenses for "assets" that a firm leases. Similarly, comparing firms based on EBITDA can lead to inconsistent comparisons for firms that own depreciable assets relative to firms that lease assets.

The exclusion of interest expense provides a measure of earnings independent of financing costs. The exclusion of interest in computing EBITDA has an element of logic if the analyst is interested in EBITDA as a crude measure of the firm's ability to cover the costs of leverage or if the analyst uses EBITDA for enterprise valuation using a discount rate or earnings multiple that incorporates the cost of both debt and equity capital. However, as emphasized in Chapter 4, analysts must be careful not to confuse measures of profitability at the enterprise level (e.g., ROA) versus those at the common equity level (e.g., ROE). Finally, the rationale for the exclusion of income taxes is not at all clear. Firms that generate positive earnings must pay income taxes just as they must pay suppliers, employees, and other providers of goods and services. It is difficult to

---

[31]Note that analysts are typically optimistic in their forecasts early in a year. This optimistic bias early in a fiscal year results in the forecasts for the firms with the lowest earnings (driven by large income-decreasing accruals) being optimistic, but not nearly to the extent that they are for the income-increasing accrual firms.

construct a cogent argument for why tax expense should be ignored in the assessment of a firm's profitability.

Academic research has examined the correlation between market rates of return on common stock and (1) net income, (2) cash flow from operations, and (3) EBITDA.[32] The results of these studies indicate that stock returns are more highly correlated with net income than with either cash flow from operations or EBITDA. For example, Chapter 2 discussed research by Dechow, who examined the relative ability of cash flows and net income to explain stock returns. Her study confirms that as the measurement window increases (she aggregated firm performance measures over several years), cash flows and net income become similar in their association with stock returns. Dechow showed that over long windows such as five years, both aggregate cash flows and aggregate earnings capture economics well and are closely associated with changes in stock prices. It is over short horizons (such as a quarter or a year) that net income is more closely associated with changes in stock price. Moreover, the primary conclusion supported by many studies, including Dechow's, is that "earnings better reflect firm performance than cash flows, in firms with more volatile operating, investment and financing activities."[33] Also, refer again to Exhibit 1.14 in Chapter 1, which shows that the spread in abnormal returns between increases and decreases in earnings averages 35.6%, whereas the spread between positive and negative changes in cash flows from operations is only 15.0%.

These findings are not surprising given that net income is a bottom-line measure of profitability that does not omit working capital adjustments that have information content for future cash flows. Further, if net income is negative in a given period, it is generally indicative of poor performance and value destruction. On the other hand, if cash flow from operations is negative, it is ambiguous and may reflect very good performance and value creation (for example, start-up and growth firms). In the same manner that operating cash flows omits important elements of performance, EBITDA excludes expenses that are value-relevant for profitable, capital-intensive, or leveraged firms.

Given that operating income, net income, and cash flow from operations are required disclosures, you might wonder why analysts often use EBITDA as an approximation of these measures. As noted, EBITDA not only ignores four important costs of conducting business, but also ignores changes in operating working capital accounts that can fluctuate depending on growth, operating cycles, and managerial discretion, all crucial to the assessment of firm profitability and valuation. A better measure of the cash flows of a firm can be directly obtained from the statement of cash flows.

A Model to Detect the Likelihood of Fraud

LO 6-8

Compute the Beneish Manipulation Index to assess the likelihood of earnings manipulation.

Accounting research has examined potential conditions that could enable (or possibly signal the likelihood of) fraudulent reporting. Dechow, Sloan, and Sweeney[34] examined

[32]Mary E. Barth, Donald P. Cram, and Karen K. Nelson, "Accruals and the Prediction of Future Cash Flows," *Accounting Review* (January 2001), pp. 27–58.

[33]Patricia M. Dechow, "Accounting Earnings and Cash Flows as Measures of Firm Performance: The Role of Accounting Accruals," *Journal of Accounting and Economics* (1994), p. 7.

[34]Patricia M. Dechow, Richard G. Sloan, and Amy P. Sweeney, "Causes and Consequences of Earnings Manipulation: An Analysis of Firms Subject to Enforcement Actions by the SEC," *Contemporary Accounting Research* (Spring 1996), pp. 1–36.

the governance characteristics of firms subject to accounting and auditing enforcement actions by the SEC (i.e., formal charges of manipulation). They found that such firms have weak corporate governance structures, including the absence of an audit committee within their board of directors, the appointment of the founder of the company as the CEO (chief executive officer), the appointment of the CEO as chairperson of the board, and the domination of the board by insiders (employees, consultants, or individuals otherwise closely associated with the firm). The SEC enforcement actions led to declines in stock prices by an average of 9%, increases in the bid-ask spread,[35] increases in the dispersions in analyst earnings forecasts, and increases in short interest,[36] each of which likely increased the firms' cost of capital. Nevertheless, governance is neither a solution nor a well-defined concept. For example, the World Council for Corporate Governance awarded **Satyam** its coveted Golden Peacock Award for Corporate Governance in 2008, shortly before it was uncovered that the company had perpetrated one of the largest financial reporting frauds in corporate history.

Messod D. Beneish developed both a 12- and an 8-factor model to identify the financial characteristics of firms likely to engage in earnings manipulation:[37]

- The 12-factor model relies on a combination of financial statement items and changes in stock prices for a firm's shares.
- The 8-factor model uses only financial statement items.

Beneish developed the models using data for firms subject to SEC enforcement actions related to fraudulent accounting reports.

Developing these models involves identifying characteristics of firms likely to manipulate earnings, selecting financial statement ratios or other measures of these characteristics, and then using probit regressions to select the significant factors and the appropriate coefficient for each factor.[38] The general approach is to estimate a probit regression equation to obtain coefficients on factors associated with earnings manipulation, and then use those coefficients along with a firm's measured factors to calculate a manipulation score, which we will denote y. A probit model converts y into a probability using a standardized normal distribution and a specified prior probability of earnings manipulation. The command NORMSDIST in Excel®, when applied to a particular value of y, converts it to the appropriate probability value. Positive coefficients increase the probability of earnings manipulation.

Beneish's eight factors and the rationale for their inclusion are discussed below. Note that some of these factors attempt to capture the existence of earnings manipulation (e.g., *DSRI*), whereas other factors attempt to capture the existence of heightened incentives managers might face that might lead to earnings manipulation (e.g., *GMI*).

---

[35]Bid-ask spread is the difference between the highest stock price that a buyer is willing to pay and the lowest price for which a seller is willing to sell.

[36]Short interest is the number of shares investors have sold short but not yet covered or closed out. It represents market sentiment about whether a stock's price will fall.

[37]Messod D. Beneish, "Detecting GAAP Violations: Implications for Assessing Earnings Management among Firms with Extreme Financial Performance," *Journal of Accounting and Public Policy* (1997), pp. 271–309. For an instructional case applying this model to an actual company, see Christine I. Wiedman, "Instructional Case: Detecting Earnings Manipulation," *Issues in Accounting Education* (February 1999), pp. 145–176. Also see Messod D. Beneish, "A Note on Wiedman's (1999) Instructional Case: Detecting Earnings Manipulation," *Issues in Accounting Education* (May 1999), pp. 369–370; and Messod D. Beneish, "The Detection of Earnings Manipulation," *Financial Analyst Journal* (September/October 1999), pp. 24–36.

[38]This process is similar to the approaches for identifying predictors of bankruptcy, described in Chapter 5.

1. ***Days' Sales in Receivables Index (DSRI).*** This index relates the ratio of accounts receivable at the end of the current year as a percentage of sales for the current year to the corresponding amounts for the preceding year. A large increase in accounts receivable as a percentage of sales might indicate an overstatement of accounts receivable and sales during the current year to boost earnings. Such an increase also might result from a change in the firm's credit policy (for example, liberalizing credit terms).

2. ***Gross Margin Index (GMI).*** This index relates gross margin (that is, sales minus cost of goods sold) as a percentage of sales last year to the gross margin as a percentage of sales for the current year. A decline in the gross margin percentage will result in an index greater than 1.0. Firms with weaker profitability this year are more likely to engage in earnings manipulation.

3. ***Asset Quality Index (AQI).*** Asset quality refers to the proportion of total assets comprising assets other than (1) current assets; (2) property, plant, and equipment; and (3) investments in securities. The remaining assets include intangibles for which future benefits are less certain than for current assets and property, plant, and equipment. The AQI equals the proportion of these potentially lower-quality assets during the current year relative to the preceding year. An increase in the proportion might suggest an increased effort to capitalize and defer costs the firm should have expensed.

4. ***Sales Growth Index (SGI).*** This index equals sales of the current year relative to sales of the preceding year. Growth does not necessarily imply manipulation. However, growing companies usually rely on external financing more than do mature companies. The need for low-cost external financing might motivate managers to manipulate sales and earnings. Growing companies are often young and tend to have less-developed governance practices to monitor managers' manipulation efforts.

5. ***Depreciation Index (DEPI).*** This index equals depreciation expense as a percentage of net property, plant, and equipment before depreciation for the preceding year relative to the corresponding percentage for the current year. A ratio greater than 1.0 indicates that the firm has slowed the rate of depreciation, perhaps by lengthening depreciable lives, thereby increasing earnings.

6. ***Selling and Administrative Expense Index (SAI).*** This index equals selling and administrative expenses as a percentage of sales for the current year relative to the corresponding percentage for the preceding year. An index greater than 1.0 might suggest increased marketing expenditures that would lead to increased sales in future periods. Firms not able to sustain the sales growth might be induced to engage in earnings manipulation. An alternative interpretation is that an index greater than 1.0 suggests that the firm has not taken advantage of capitalizing various costs; instead, it has expensed them. Firms attempting to manipulate earnings would defer costs, and the index value would be less than 1.0. If this latter explanation is descriptive, the coefficient on this variable will be negative. Thus, the interpretation of this component of Beneish's fraud model is conditional.

7. ***Leverage Index (LVGI).*** This index equals the proportion of total financing comprising current liabilities and long-term debt for the current year relative to the proportion for the preceding year. An increase in the proportion of debt likely subjects a firm to a greater risk of violating debt covenants and the need to manipulate earnings to avoid the violation.

8. ***Total Accruals to Total Assets (TATA).*** Total accruals equals the difference between income from continuing operations and cash flow from operations. Dividing total accruals by total assets at the end of the year scales total accruals across firms and across time. Beneish used this variable as an indicator of the extent to which earnings result from accruals instead of from cash flows. A large excess of income from continuing operations over cash flow from operations indicates that accruals play a large part in measuring income. Accruals can serve as a means of manipulating earnings.

Beneish developed a weighted probit model that takes the proportion of earnings manipulations into account and an unweighted probit model. We illustrate the unweighted model in this section, and FSAP uses the unweighted model to compute Beneish's Manipulation Index and the corresponding probabilities of earnings manipulation. The unweighted model tends to classify more nonmanipulating firms as manipulators (higher Type II error), but lowers the most costly Type I error rate. The value of y is computed as follows:

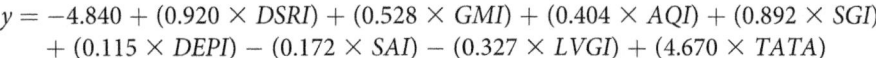

$$y = -4.840 + (0.920 \times DSRI) + (0.528 \times GMI) + (0.404 \times AQI) + (0.892 \times SGI)$$
$$+ (0.115 \times DEPI) - (0.172 \times SAI) - (0.327 \times LVGI) + (4.670 \times TATA)$$

The coefficient on *SAI* is negative, suggesting that a lower selling and administrative expense to sales percentage in the current year relative to the preceding year increases the likelihood that the firm engaged in earnings manipulation to boost earnings. The coefficient on the leverage variable also is negative. A decrease in the proportion of debt in the capital structure may suggest decreased ability to obtain funds from borrowing and the need to engage in earnings manipulation to portray a healthier firm. The coefficients on the *SAI* and *LVGI* variables were not statistically significant. However, one cannot interpret the sign or statistical significance of a coefficient in a multivariate model independent of the other variables in the model, so these factors must be included.

Application of Beneish's Model to Sunbeam Corporation

We illustrate the application of Beneish's probit model to **Sunbeam Corporation**'s financial statements. Sunbeam manufactures countertop kitchen appliances and barbecue grills. Its sales growth and profitability slowed considerably in the mid-1990s, and the firm experienced market price declines for its common stock. The firm hired Al Dunlap in mid-1996 as CEO. Known as "Chainsaw Al," he had developed a reputation for dispassionately cutting costs and strategically redirecting troubled companies. Dunlap laid off half the workforce, closed or consolidated more than half of Sunbeam's factories, and divested several businesses in 1996 and 1997. He also announced major growth initiatives centering on new products and corporate acquisitions.

The reported results for 1997 showed significant improvement over 1996. Sales increased 18.7% while gross margin increased from 8.5% to 28.3%. The stock price more than doubled between the announcement of Dunlap's hiring in mid-1996 and the end of 1997.

The turnaround appeared to proceed according to plan until the firm announced earnings for the first quarter of 1998, seven quarters into the turnaround effort. To the surprise of analysts and the stock market, Sunbeam reported a net loss for the quarter. Close scrutiny by analysts and the media suggested that Sunbeam might have manipulated earnings in 1997. The SEC instituted a formal investigation into this possibility in mid-1997. Sunbeam responded in October 1998 by restating its financial statements from the fourth quarter of 1996 to the first quarter of 1998. The restatements revealed that Sunbeam had engaged in various actions that boosted earnings for 1997. The actions included the following:

- Sunbeam instituted "early buy" and "bill and hold" programs in 1997 to encourage retailers to purchase inventory from Sunbeam during the last few months of 1997. Sunbeam did not adequately provide for returns and canceled transactions, resulting in an overstatement of sales and net income for 1997.
- Sunbeam overstated a restructuring charge in the fourth quarter of 1996 for expenses that should have appeared on the income statement for 1997.
- Sunbeam understated bad debt expense for 1997.

Exhibit 6.12 shows the application of Beneish's earnings manipulation model to the originally reported financial statement amounts and the restated amounts for 1996 and 1997.[39]

Selecting the cutoff probability that signals earnings manipulation involves trade-offs between Type I and Type II errors in a manner similar to that of Beaver's bankruptcy prediction tests discussed in Chapter 5:

- A Type I error involves failing to identify a firm as an income manipulator when it turns out to be one.
- A Type II error involves identifying a firm as an income manipulator when it turns out not to be one.

Exhibit 6.12

Application of Beneish's Earnings Manipulation Model to Sunbeam Corporation

Value of Variable Before Applying Coefficient	Originally Reported 1996	1997	Restated 1996	1997
Days' sales in receivables index	1.020	1.167	1.020	0.982
Gross margin index	2.403	0.300	2.303	0.393
Asset quality index	0.912	0.928	0.912	0.919
Sales growth index	0.968	1.187	0.968	1.090
Depreciation index	0.752	1.284	0.752	1.290
Selling and administrative expense index	1.608	0.516	1.665	0.632
Leverage index	1.457	0.795	1.457	0.917
Total accruals/Total assets	(0.196)	0.117	(0.208)	0.055
Beneish's manipulation y value	(2.983)	(1.827)	(3.101)	(2.388)
Probability of manipulation	0.143%	3.386%	0.096%	0.848%

Note: The amounts in this table are rounded to three decimal places.

[39]The website for this book contains an Excel spreadsheet called Beneish's Manipulation Index for use in calculating the probability of earnings manipulation using Beneish's probit model. This spreadsheet is adapted from one prepared by Professor Christine I. Wiedman (see Wiedman 1999, op. cit.). FSAP also computes Beneish's Manipulation Index and the corresponding probability of earnings manipulation.

The Type I error is more costly to the investor than a Type II error. The cutoff probability depends on the analyst's view of the relative cost of the Type I error compared to a Type II error. That is, how much more costly is it to classify an actual earnings manipulator as a nonmanipulator than to classify an actual nonmanipulator as a manipulator? A Type I error can result in an investor losing *all* of the investment in a firm when the manipulation comes to light. In contrast, misclassifying an actual nonmanipulator results only in a forgone investment opportunity, the amount being the return that could have been earned had an investment been made in the firm. However, the investor presumably invested the funds in another firm. Thus, as with bankruptcy prediction, the Type I error is more costly. If a particular investment makes up a small proportion of an investor's diversified portfolio of investments, a Type I error is less costly than if the investment comprises a more significant proportion of a less diversified portfolio of investments. The cutoff probabilities for various relative mixtures of Type I and Type II error costs follow.

Cost of Type I Error Relative to Type II Error	Cutoff Probability
10:1	6.85%
20:1	3.76
30:1	3.76
40:1 or higher	2.94

Exhibit 6.12 indicates that the probability of manipulation for Sunbeam for 1996 is 0.143% based on its originally reported amounts. This probability level falls well below the cutoff probabilities listed previously for all mixtures of Type I and Type II errors; therefore, it does not suggest earnings manipulation. On the other hand, the probability for 1997 jumps to 3.386%. Under the assumption of a 40:1 Type I to Type II cost relation, you would conclude that Sunbeam is a manipulator. An examination of changes in the individual variables between 1996 and 1997 signals the nature of the manipulation that might have occurred. The total accruals to total assets index increased significantly. Sunbeam reported a significant increase in income from continuing operations from a net loss of $196.7 million in 1996 to a net profit of $123.1 million in 1997, but cash flow from operations turned from $13.3 million in 1996 to a negative $8.2 million in 1997. Buildups of accounts receivable and inventories are major reasons for the negative cash flow from operations in 1997. The days' sales in receivables index increased between these two years, consistent with the buildup of receivables related to the early buy-and-bill and hold programs. The sales growth index also increased, consistent with the aggressive recognition of revenues. The depreciation index increased between the two years, but the firm's financial statements and notes provide no obvious explanation to suggest manipulation. The gross margin index improved significantly between the two years, moderating the increased probability of earnings manipulation. However, this improvement is misleading because of failure to provide adequately for returns and canceled transactions.

Exhibit 6.12 indicates that the probabilities of manipulation based on the restated data are below the cutoff points for 1996 and 1997. The most important difference between the reported and restated probabilities arises for 1997. The downward restatement of income from continuing operations results in fewer accruals, moderating the influence of this variable on the manipulation index. Interestingly, the model would not indicate that Sunbeam was an earnings manipulator if it had reported accurately to begin with (that is, reported the restated data). Initially reporting the restated data, however, would likely have decreased Sunbeam's stock price, which Dunlap presumably wanted to avoid.

The recent revelations of corporate reporting abuses add to the importance of assessing whether firms have intentionally manipulated earnings. Academic research on earnings manipulation is at an early stage of development. The data in the studies discussed previously deal with reporting violations prior to the mid-1990s. The business environment since that time has changed dramatically, particularly for technology-based companies. Additional research in this area might be expected in coming years.

The assessment of earnings manipulation risk is not restricted to the construction of financial ratios. Also relevant are qualitative factors that might change the incentives of managers to incur the potential costs of manipulating earnings, such as an increase in compensation based on stock options, an expectation of growth, or extensive related-party transactions.

LO 6-9

Explain the effect of two sets of accounting rules (IFRS and U.S. GAAP) on worldwide financial comparability.

Financial Reporting Worldwide

Thus far, we have identified many accounting quality and comparability issues. The concerns discussed in the chapter to this point apply equally to firms that follow reporting systems employed outside of the United States, such as IFRS. However, important additional concerns also exist in comparing financial data for firms that operate in different countries.

Cross-national analysis of firms entails a two-step approach:

- Achieve comparability of the reporting methods and accounting principles employed by the firms under scrutiny.
- Understand corporate strategies, institutional structures, and cultural practices unique to the countries in which the firms operate.

Beginning in 2005, the financial statements of firms in the European Community were required to conform to IFRS pronouncements. In addition, the convergence of IFRS and U.S. GAAP will be central to achieving worldwide conformity of financial reporting. The IASB and FASB pledged to use their best efforts to make existing U.S. and IASB standards fully compatible as soon as practicable and to coordinate their future work programs to ensure that, once achieved, compatibility is maintained. For example, the "Projects" section of the FASB website (fasb.org) indicates projects that are being jointly addressed by the IASB and FASB.

Firms headquartered outside of the United States that have debt or equity securities traded in U.S. capital markets are required to file a Form 10-K using U.S. GAAP or a Form 20-F report with the SEC each year. In past years, Form 20-F had to include a reconciliation of shareholders' equity and net income as reported under IFRS (or standards of the firm's local country) with U.S. GAAP. With this information, the analyst could convert the financial statements of a non-U.S. firm to achieve comparable accounting principles with U.S. firms.

Preparation of the reconciliation—essentially requiring a foreign filer in the United States to maintain two sets of financial records—is a costly endeavor and a potential deterrent to companies interested in listing on U.S. exchanges. Thus, the SEC recently relaxed the reporting requirements of non-U.S. filers and now accepts financial reports prepared in accordance with IFRS as legislated by the IASB without reconciliation to U.S. GAAP. SEC Final Rule No. 33-8879 provides U.S. investors with two sets of accounting principles—IFRS and U.S. GAAP. The elimination of the reconciliation is a controversial issue because research suggests that material differences between IFRS and

U.S. GAAP remain and eliminating the reconciliation diminishes the relevant information set available to investors in the United States and around the world.[40]

Achieving comparability in reporting is important to the analysis of multinational firms, but the data must be carefully interpreted. Analysis of multinational firms is complicated by the fact that the environments in which the firms operate may vary extensively across countries. A firm may implement operational strategies in its home country that it cannot implement in other countries. Institutional arrangements, such as significant alliances with banks and extensive intercorporate holdings, may be common in one country but not in another. Cultural characteristics may exist in one country that affect how firms do business in that country—with those same characteristics foreign to other business settings.[41]

Summary

The financial analysis framework discussed in Chapters 1 to 5 and the discussion of forecasting and valuation presented in Chapters 10 to 14 assume that a firm's reported financial statement data accurately reflect the economic effects of a firm's decisions. Another assumption is that the financial data are informative about the firm's likely future profitability and risk. This chapter develops the concept of accounting quality as the basis for assessing the information content of reported financial statement data and for adjusting those data before assessing a firm's profitability and risk or forecasting or valuing the firm.

We discuss earnings management, liability and asset measurement and reporting quality, and the conditions that can trigger low accounting quality. The concepts of accounting quality and earnings management often are linked in discussions of the need to adjust financial data to better reflect its economic information content. In Chapters 7 to 9, we illustrate the financial reporting for financing, investing, and operating activities and we examine accounting quality in greater detail.

Questions, Exercises, Problems, and Cases

Questions and Exercises

6.1 Concept of Earnings Quality. The concept of accounting quality has several dimensions, but two characteristics often dominate: the accounting information should be a fair representation of performance for the reporting period and it should provide relevant information to forecast expected future earnings. Provide a specific example of poor accounting quality that would hinder the forecasting of expected future earnings.

LO 6-1

6.2 Balance Sheet Quality and Earnings Quality. How are balance sheet quality and earnings quality related? Provide a specific example of a management judgment, estimate, or choice that could decrease both balance sheet and earnings quality. Be specific as to how the judgment decreased quality in each of the two financial statements. Give a different

LO 6-2

---

[40]Not all firms domiciled in non-U.S. locations use IFRS. Many are required to file financial statements using home-country standards or IFRS modified for local laws and preferences, and thus would be required to reconcile to U.S. GAAP if listed on U.S. exchanges.

[41]See Don Herrmann, Tatsuo Inoue, and Wayne Thomas, "Are There Benefits to Restating Japanese Financial Statements According to U.S. GAAP?," *Journal of Financial Statement Analysis* (Fall 1996), pp. 61–73, for an example of environmental factors that must be considered in order to effectively interpret foreign financial statements even after adjusting them to be comparable to U.S. GAAP.

example of how a management judgment, estimate, or choice could increase balance sheet quality, but potentially impair earnings quality.

LO 6-3

6.3 Concept of Earnings Management. Define earnings management. Discuss why it is difficult to discern whether a firm does in fact practice earnings management.

LO 6-5, LO 6-6

6.4 Own Debt Profits. Most economists describe three determinants of the interest rates on a borrower's debt: a real interest rate, which is a charge for using capital; an adjustment for expected inflation to insure that debt is repaid in dollars having the same purchasing power; and an adjustment for the borrower's credit risk, which is intended to compensate the lender for the possibility that the borrower will default. Certain companies book gains and losses on their own debt on the income statement due to a revaluation of debt to fair value. For example, if expectations for inflation were to rise, the appropriate interest rate to charge borrowers would rise above the contractual historical interest rate initially used to value and record the debt. If the debt is adjusted to fair value (i.e., rediscounted at the new higher interest rate), the debt book value falls, and because a liability has decreased, a gain is recorded on the income statement. The counterparty to the debt (e.g., the lender) records a loss. These adjustments can be extremely large for banks. For example, **Citi**'s 2011 third quarter net income was $3.7 billion, which included a $1.9 billion gain from revaluing its own debt (before tax) in revenues and income. In Citi's case, the gain was driven from a widening in its credit-default swap spreads, which is an indication of its higher probability of default on its obligations and derivative contracts. How should an analyst view gains on the revaluation of a company's own debt due to changes in its credit risk? Is the gain a persistent component of earnings? How would a debtor realize such gains (i.e., how does such a gain affect cash flows)?

LO 6-4, LO 6-5

6.5 Incentives to Manage the Balance Sheet. Assume that a corporation needs to enter the private debt market to raise funds for plant expansion. The corporation expects debt covenants to place restrictions on the levels of its current ratio and total-liabilities-to-assets ratio. Considering the accounts that comprise these ratios, give examples of accounting estimates, accounting judgments, and structured transactions that the lender should examine closely.

LO 6-3

6.6 Incentives to Manage Earnings Upward. Identify conditions that would lead an analyst to expect that management might attempt to manage earnings upward.

LO 6-3

6.7 Incentives to Manage Earnings Downward. Identify conditions that would lead an analyst to expect that management might attempt to manage earnings downward.

LO 6-6

6.8 Criteria to Identify Nonrecurring Items. The chapter discusses eight items that occur infrequently but that can have a large impact on financial statements. What criteria should an analyst employ to assess whether to include or eliminate items from the financial statements related to these topics?

LO 6-6

6.9 Restating Earnings for Litigation Loss. Rock of Ages, Inc., a large North American integrated granite quarrier, manufacturer, and retailer of finished granite memorials, reported a net loss for 2004 of $3.2 million. In 2004, the firm reported a pretax litigation settlement loss of $6.5 million, and management stated that, in its opinion, the litigation settlement loss did not reflect the current year's operations because it was the first year in five years that the firm reported such a loss. (Rock of Ages' exclusion of an item from the calculation of net income is an example of what the financial press calls "reporting pro forma earnings.") Calculate pro forma earnings for 2004 excluding the settlement costs and speculate on management's reasoning as to why it believes that pro forma earnings is a better measure of performance for Rock of Ages. State any assumptions you make in your calculations. Assume a tax rate of 35%.

6.10 Reporting Impairment and Restructuring Charges. Checkpoint **LO 6-6**
Systems, a leading provider of source tagging, handheld labeling systems, retail merchandising systems, and bar-code labeling systems, stated the following in a press release:

> GAAP reported net loss for the fourth quarter of 2004 was $29.3 million, or $0.78 per diluted share, compared to net earnings of $4.5 million, or $0.13 per diluted share, for the fourth quarter 2003. Excluding impairment and restructuring charges, net of tax, the Company's net income for the fourth quarter 2004 was $0.30 per diluted share, compared to $0.27 per diluted share in the fourth quarter 2003.

Calculate the amount of the impairment and restructuring charges Checkpoint reported in 2004 and 2003. Discuss why the firm reported earnings both including and excluding impairment and restructuring charges.

6.11 Concept of a Peripheral Activity. Firms often enter into transactions that **LO 6-6** are peripheral to their core operations but generate gains and losses that must be reported on the income statement. Provide an example in which a gain generated from the sale of an equity security may be labeled a peripheral activity by one firm but is considered a core activity by another firm.

6.12 Reporting Impairment Charges. Financial accounting rules require firms **LO 6-6** to assess whether they will recover carrying amounts of long-lived assets and, if not, to write down the assets to their fair value and recognize an impairment loss in income from continuing operations. Impairment charges often appear as a separate line item on the income statement of companies that experience reductions in the future benefits originally anticipated from the long-lived assets. Conduct a search to identify a firm (other than those given in this chapter) that has recently reported an impairment charge. Discuss how the firm (a) reported the charge on the income statement, (b) determined the amount of the charge, and (c) used cash related to the charge.

6.13 Effect of Alternative Accounting Standards on Financial **LO 6-9**
Statement Analysis. Nestlé Group, a multinational food products firm based in Switzerland, recently issued its financial statements. The auditor's opinion attached to the financial statements stated the following: "In our opinion, the financial statements for the year ended 31 December 2012 comply with Swiss law and the Company's Articles of Incorporation." In the notes to its financial statements, Nestlé's states that its financial reports are prepared using IFRS standards. One of Nestlé's competitors is **PepsiCo**, which prepares financial reports following U.S. GAAP. Describe the necessary steps an analyst should consider to develop comparable accounting data when conducting a profitability and risk analysis of these two firms.

6.14 Accounting for Loss Contingencies. Loss contingencies may or may not **LO 6-4** give rise to accounting liabilities. Financial reporting requires firms to recognize a loss contingency when two criteria are met. Describe the two criteria and provide an example in which applying the criteria would trigger booking the loss contingency as an accounting liability.

6.15 Securitization of Receivables. Firms such as **Deere & Company** and **LO 6-4**
Macy's, Inc., often sell their receivables as a means of obtaining financing. Should firms selling receivables remove the receivables from the balance sheet, or should the receivables remain on the balance sheet? Should the firms recognize a liability in the amount of the cash received for the receivables? Describe the applicable criteria to determine whether the transfer of receivables can be recorded as a sale.

Problems and Cases

LO 6-4 **6.16 Achieving Off-Balance-Sheet Financing.** *(Adapted from materials by R. Dieter, D. Landsittel, J. Stewart, and A. Wyatt)* Diviney Company wants to raise $50 million cash but for various reasons does not want to do so in a way that results in a newly recorded liability. The firm is sufficiently solvent and profitable, so its bank is willing to lend up to $50 million at the prime interest rate. Diviney's financial executives have devised six different plans, described in the following sections.

TRANSFER OF RECEIVABLES WITH RECOURSE

Diviney will transfer to Condon Company its long-term accounts receivable, which call for payments over the next two years. Condon will pay an amount equal to the present value of the receivables, minus an allowance for uncollectibles, as well as a discount, because it is paying now but will collect cash later. Diviney must repurchase from Condon at face value any receivables that become uncollectible in excess of the allowance. In addition, Diviney may repurchase any of the receivables not yet due at face value minus a discount specified by formula and based on the prime rate at the time of the initial transfer. (This option permits Diviney to benefit if an unexpected drop in interest rates occurs after the transfer.) The accounting issue is whether the transfer is a sale (in which Diviney increases Cash, reduces Accounts Receivable, and recognizes expense or loss on transfer) or merely a loan collateralized by the receivables (in which Diviney increases Cash and increases Notes Payable at the time of transfer).

PRODUCT FINANCING ARRANGEMENT

Diviney will transfer inventory to Condon, which will store the inventory in a public warehouse. Condon may use the inventory as collateral for its own borrowings, the proceeds from which will be used to pay Diviney. Diviney will pay storage costs and will repurchase the entire inventory within the next four years at contractually fixed prices plus interest accrued for the time elapsed between the transfer and later repurchase. The accounting issue is whether the inventory is sold to Condon, with later repurchases treated as new acquisitions for Diviney's inventory, or whether the transaction is merely a loan, with the inventory remaining on Diviney's balance sheet.

THROUGHPUT CONTRACT

Diviney wants a branch line of a railroad built from the main rail line to carry raw material directly to its plant. It could, of course, borrow the funds and build the branch line itself. Instead, it will sign an agreement with the railroad to ship specified amounts of material each month for 10 years. Even if Diviney does not ship the specified amounts of material, it will pay the agreed shipping costs. The railroad will take the contract to its bank and, using it as collateral, borrow the funds to build the branch line. The accounting issue is whether Diviney should increase an asset for future rail services and increase a liability for payments to the railroad. The alternative is to make no accounting entry except when Diviney makes payments to the railroad.

CONSTRUCTION PARTNERSHIP

Diviney and Mission Company will jointly build a plant to manufacture chemicals that both need in their production processes. Each will contribute $5 million to the project, called Chemical. Chemical will borrow another $40 million from a bank, with Diviney being the only guarantor of the debt. Diviney and Mission are each to contribute equally to future operating expenses and debt service payments of Chemical, but in return for its guaranteeing the debt, Diviney will have an option to purchase Mission's interest for $20 million four years hence. The accounting issue is whether Diviney should recognize a liability for the funds borrowed by Chemical. Because of the debt guarantee, debt service payments ultimately will be Diviney's responsibility. Alternatively, the debt guarantee would be treated as a commitment merely to be disclosed in the notes to Diviney's financial statements.

RESEARCH AND DEVELOPMENT PARTNERSHIP

Diviney will contribute a laboratory and preliminary findings about a potentially profitable gene-splicing discovery to a partnership, called Venture. Venture will raise funds by selling the remaining interest in the partnership to outside investors for $2 million and borrowing $48 million from a bank, with Diviney guaranteeing the debt. Although Venture will operate under Diviney's management, it will be free to sell the results of its further discoveries and development efforts to anyone, including Diviney. Diviney is not obligated to purchase any of Venture's output. The accounting issue is whether Diviney would recognize the liability.

HOTEL FINANCING

Diviney owns and operates a profitable hotel. It could use the hotel as collateral for a conventional mortgage loan. Instead, it considers selling the hotel to a partnership for $50 million cash. The partnership will sell ownership interests to outside investors for $5 million and borrow $45 million from a bank on a conventional mortgage loan, using the hotel as collateral. Diviney guarantees the debt. The accounting issue is whether Diviney would record the liability for the guaranteed debt of the partnership.

REQUIRED

Discuss the appropriate treatment of each proposed arrangement from the viewpoint of the auditor, who must apply U.S. GAAP in deciding whether the transaction will result in a liability to be recorded or whether note disclosure will suffice. Does U.S. GAAP reporting result in an accurate portrayal of the economics of the arrangement in each case? Explain.

6.17 Accounting Scandals. Recent years have witnessed some of the most significant accounting scandals in history. For each scandal listed in Exhibit 6.13, identify how balance sheet quality and earnings quality were impaired.

`LO 6-5`

Exhibit 6.13	
Accounting Scandals **(Problem 6.17)**	
Scandal	**Alleged Accounting Wrongdoing**
Waste Management (1988; waste management industry)	Falsely increased the useful lives of long-lived tangible assets
Enron (2001; energy)	Underreported balance sheet long-term debt
WorldCom (2002; telecommunications)	Capitalized rather than expensed expenditures to maintain transmission lines
AIG (2003; health care)	Booked debt as revenue
Lehman Brothers (2008; financial services)	Sold toxic assets (i.e., financial investments) to other banks with a buyback agreement, removing the toxic assets from its books
Saytam (2009; IT and accounting services)	Created fictitious revenue recognition journal entries

LO 6-6 **6.18 Adjusting for Unusual Income Statement and Classification Items.** Henry Company is a marketer of branded foods to retail and foodservice channels. Exhibit 6.14 presents Henry's income statements for Year 10, Year 11, and Year 12.

Exhibit 6.14			
Henry Company **Income Statement** **(amounts in millions)** **(Problem 6.18)**			
	Year 12	**Year 11**	**Year 10**
Sales	$ 9,431	$ 8,821	$ 8,939
Gain on sale of branded product line	—	—	465
Cost of goods sold	(6,094)	(5,884)	(5,789)
Selling and administrative expenses	(1,746)	(1,955)	(1,882)
Interest income	27	23	25
Interest expense	(294)	(333)	(270)
Other income (expense)	(45)	1	(25)
Income before Income Taxes and Cumulative			
Effect of Accounting Changes	$ 1,279	$ 673	$ 1,463
Income tax expense	(445)	(178)	(573)
Income before Extraordinary Item	$ 834	$ 495	$ 890
Extraordinary loss (net of taxes)	—	(17)	—
Net Income	$ 834	$ 478	$ 890

Notes to the financial statements reveal the following information:

1. **Gain on sale of a portion of the branded product line.** In Year 10, Henry completed the sale of a portion of one of its branded product lines for $735 million. The transaction resulted in a pretax gain of $464.5 million. The sale did not qualify as a discontinued operation. Henry did not disclose the tax effect of the gain reported in Exhibit 6.14.

2. **Extraordinary loss.** In Year 11, Henry experienced an extraordinary loss when a subsidiary was expropriated during a military coup in a previously stable country. The loss was $17 million, net of income taxes of $10 million. Note: Recently, U.S. GAAP and IFRS have prohibited the extraordinary item classification, which in the past was used to segregate peripheral gains and losses that were unusual in nature and infrequent in occurrence. Very few items were reported as extraordinary. Treat this item as you would treat any infrequent peripheral gain or loss.

3. **Sale and promotion costs.** In Year 11, Henry changed the classification of certain sale and promotion incentives provided to customers and consumers. In the past, Henry classified these incentives as selling and administrative expenses (see Exhibit 6.14), with the gross amount of the revenue associated with the incentives reported in sales. Beginning in Year 11, Henry changed to reporting the incentives as a reduction of revenues. As a result of this change, the firm reduced reported revenues by $693 million in Year 12, $610 million in Year 11, and $469 million in Year 10. The firm stated that selling and administrative expenses were "correspondingly reduced such that net earnings were not

affected." Exhibit 6.14 already reflects the adjustments to sales revenues and selling and administrative expenses for Years 10 through 12.

4. **Tax rate.** The U.S. federal statutory income tax rate was 35% for each of the years presented in Exhibit 6.14.

REQUIRED

a. Discuss whether you would adjust for each of the following items when using earnings to forecast the future profitability of Henry:

   1. Gain on sale of a portion of the branded product line
   2. Extraordinary loss

b. Indicate the adjustment you would make to Henry's net income for each item in Requirement a.

c. Discuss whether you believe the reclassification adjustments made by Henry for the sale and promotion incentive costs (Item 3) are appropriate.

d. Prepare a common-size income statement for Year 10, Year 11, and Year 12 using the amounts in Exhibit 6.14. Set sales equal to 100%. Round percentages to one decimal point.

e. Repeat Requirement d after making the income statement adjustments in Requirement b.

f. Assess the changes in the profitability of Henry during the three-year period.

LO 6-6

6.19 Unusual Income Statement Items. Vulcan Materials Company, a

member of the S&P 500 Index, is the nation's largest producer of construction aggregates, a major producer of asphalt mix and concrete, and a leading producer of cement in Florida. Exhibit 6.15 presents Vulcan's summarized income statement.

In Note 2 to the consolidated financial statements, "Discontinued Operations," Vulcan describes a June 2005 sale of substantially all assets of its chemicals business, known as Vulcan Chemicals, to **Basic Chemicals**, a subsidiary of **Occidental Chemical Corporation**. Basic Chemicals assumed certain liabilities relating to the chemicals business, including the obligation to monitor and remediate all releases of hazardous materials at or from the Wichita, Geismar, and Port Edwards plant facilities. The decision to sell the chemicals business was based on Vulcan's desire to focus its resources on the construction materials business. The amounts reported as discontinued operations are not revenues and expenses from Vulcan operating the discontinued segment. Instead, the amounts represent a continual updating of the amount payable by the segment buyer. The receivable held by Vulcan from the sale is dependent on the levels of gas and chemical prices through the end of 2012. Vulcan classifies this financial instrument as a derivative contract that must be marked to market. The derivative does not hedge an existing transaction; therefore, its value changes are reflected in income as part of discontinued operations. As of 2008, Vulcan reported that final gains on disposal (if any) would occur after December 31, 2008.

Goodwill impairment relates to Vulcan's cement segment. Vulcan explains the need for the impairment as arising from the need to increase discount rates due to disruptions in credit markets as well as weak levels of construction activity.

REQUIRED

a. Discuss the appropriate treatment of the following when forecasting future earnings of Vulcan Materials: (1) goodwill impairment; (2) discontinued operations; and (3) loss (gain) on sale of property, plant, and equipment and businesses (net).

b. Prepare common-size income statements for Vulcan Materials. Interpret changes in profit margin over the three-year period in light of the special items. Round percentages to one decimal point.

Exhibit 6.15

Vulcan Materials Company
Summarized Income Statement
(amounts in thousands)
(Problem 6.19)

	2008	2007	2006
Total revenues	$3,651,438	$3,327,787	$3,342,475
Cost of revenues	2,901,726	2,376,884	2,410,571
SG&A	342,584	289,604	264,276
Goodwill impairment	252,664	—	—
Loss (gain) on sale of property, plant & equipment and businesses, net	(94,227)	(58,659)	(5,557)
Other operating (income) expense, net	(411)	5,541	(21,904)
Total operating expenses, net	3,402,336	2,613,370	2,647,386
Operating earnings	249,102	714,417	695,089
Other income (expense), net	(4,357)	(5,322)	28,541
Interest income	3,126	6,625	6,171
Interest expense	(172,813)	(48,218)	(26,310)
Earnings from continuing operations before income taxes	75,058	667,502	703,491
Provision for income taxes	(76,724)	(204,416)	(223,313)
Earnings from continuing operations	(1,666)	463,086	480,178
Discontinued operations (Note 2):			
Loss from results of discontinued operations	(4,059)	(19,327)	(16,624)
Income tax benefit	1,610	7,151	6,660
Loss on discontinued operations, net of income taxes	(2,449)	(12,176)	(9,964)
Net earnings (loss)	$ (4,115)	$ 450,910	$ 470,214

Source: Vulcan Materials Company, Form 10-K for the Fiscal Years Ended December 31, 2008, 2007, and 2006.

LO 6-6

6.20 Implications of a Goodwill Impairment Charge for Future Cash Flow and Profitability. Northrop Grumman Corporation is a leading global security company that provides innovative systems products and solutions in aerospace, electronics, information systems, shipbuilding, and technical services to government and commercial customers worldwide. In an early 2009 press release, Northrop reported that it would record a noncash, after-tax charge of between $3.0 billion and $3.4 billion for impairment of goodwill in its 2008 fourth-quarter income statement. As a result of the charge, Northrop reported net losses for the fourth quarter and all of 2008.

Northrop explained how it determined the impairment as follows: "The company performed its required annual testing of goodwill as of Nov. 30, 2008 using a discounted cash flow analysis supported by comparative market multiples to determine the fair value of its businesses versus their book values. Testing as of Nov. 30, 2008 indicated that book values for Shipbuilding and Space Technology exceeded the fair values of these businesses.... This non-cash charge does not impact the company's normal business operations."

REQUIRED

a. Explain how a company computes a goodwill impairment. Describe the usefulness of discounted cash flow and comparative market multiples in the computation of an impairment.

b. Explain the consequences of a goodwill impairment for the assessment of (1) current period profitability as measured by ROA, (2) future earnings projections, and (3) future period profitability as measured by ROA.

6.21 Restructuring Charges at Intel. Intel Corporation's consolidated income statement appears in Exhibit 6.16.

LO 6-6

Note 15, which follows, explains the source of the restructuring charges, the breakdown of the charges into employee-related costs and asset impairments, and the balance of the accrued restructuring liability account.

Exhibit 6.16			
Intel Corporation Consolidated Income Statement (amounts in millions, except per share amounts) (Problem 6.21)			
	2008	2007	2006
Net revenue	$37,586	$38,334	$35,382
Cost of sales	16,742	18,430	17,164
Gross margin	20,844	19,904	18,218
Research and development	5,722	5,755	5,873
Marketing, general and administrative	5,458	5,417	6,138
Restructuring and asset impairment charges	710	516	555
Operating expenses	11,890	11,688	12,566
Operating income	8,954	8,216	5,652
Gains (losses) on equity method investments, net	(1,380)	3	2
Gains (losses) on other equity investments, net	(376)	154	212
Interest and other, net	488	793	1,202
Income before taxes	7,686	9,166	7,068
Provision for taxes	2,394	2,190	2,024
Net income	$ 5,292	$ 6,976	$ 5,044
Basic earnings per common share	$ 0.93	$ 1.20	$ 0.87

Source: Intel Corporation, Form 10-K for the Fiscal Year Ended December 27, 2008.

Note 15: Restructuring and Asset Impairment Charges

The following table summarizes restructuring and asset impairment charges by plan for the three years ended December 27, 2008:

(in millions)	2008	2007	2006
2008 NAND plan	$ 215	—	—
2006 efficiency program	495	$ 516	$ 555
Total restructuring and asset impairment charges	**$710**	**$516**	**$555**

We may incur additional restructuring charges in the future for employee severance and benefit arrangements, and facility-related or other exit activities. Subsequent to the end of 2008, management approved plans to restructure some of our manufacturing and assembly and test operations, and align our manufacturing and assembly and test capacity to current market conditions. These actions, which are expected to take place beginning in 2009, include closing two assembly and test facilities in Malaysia, one facility in the Philippines, and one facility in China; stopping production at a 200mm wafer fabrication facility in Oregon; and ending production at our 200mm wafer fabrication facility in California.

2008 NAND PLAN

In the fourth quarter of 2008, management approved a plan with Micron to discontinue the supply of NAND flash memory from the 200mm facility within the IMFT manufacturing network. The agreement resulted in a $215 million restructuring charge, primarily related to the IMFT 200mm supply agreement. The restructuring charge resulted in a reduction of our investment in IMFT of $184 million, a cash payment to Micron of $24 million, and other cash payments of $7 million.

2006 EFFICIENCY PROGRAM

The following table summarizes charges for the 2006 efficiency program for the three years ended December 27, 2008:

(in millions)	2008	2007	2006
Employee severance and benefit arrangements	$ 151	$ 289	$ 238
Asset impairments	344	227	317
Total	**$495**	**$516**	**$555**

The following table summarizes the restructuring and asset impairment activity for the 2006 efficiency program during 2007 and 2008:

(in millions)	Employee Severance and Benefits	Asset Impairments	Total
Accrued restructuring balance as of December 30, 2006	$ 48	$ —	$ 48
Additional accruals	299	227	526
Adjustments	(10)	—	(10)
Cash payments	(210)	—	(210)
Non-cash settlements	—	(227)	(227)
Accrued restructuring balance as of December 29, 2007	$ 127	$ —	$ 127
Additional accruals	167	344	511
Adjustments	(16)	—	(16)
Cash payments	(221)	—	(221)
Non-cash settlements	—	(344)	(344)
Accrued restructuring balance as of December 27, 2008	$ 57	$ —	$ 57

We recorded the additional accruals, net of adjustments, as restructuring and asset impairment charges. The remaining accrual as of December 27, 2008 was related to severance benefits that we recorded within accrued compensation and benefits.

From the third quarter of 2006 through the fourth quarter of 2008, we incurred a total of $1.6 billion in restructuring and asset impairment charges related to this program. These charges included a total of $678 million related to employee severance and benefit arrangements for approximately 11,900 employees, and $888 million in asset impairment charges.

REQUIRED

a. Based on your reading of the note, how would you treat Intel's restructuring charges in the assessment of current profitability and the prediction of future earnings?

b. Why is the balance of the "accrued restructuring" limited to employee-related costs?

c. Describe the effect on net income of each entry in the "accrued restructuring balance" account reconciliation. (For example, what is the effect of "Additional accruals" on net income?)

d. How do U.S. GAAP and IFRS differ on the rules used to compute the restructuring charge?

6.22 Interpreting the Statement of Cash Flows. Sunbeam Corporation   `LO 6-7`

manufactures and sells a variety of small household appliances, including toasters, food processors, and waffle grills. Exhibit 6.17 presents a statement of cash flows for Sunbeam for Year 5, Year 6, and Year 7. After experiencing decreased sales in Year 5, Sunbeam hired Albert Dunlap in Year 6 to turn the company around. The restructuring effort involved firing employees and cutting costs aggressively. Most of these restructuring efforts took place during Year 6. The market expected significantly improved results in Year 7. Reported sales increased 18.7% between Year 6 and Year 7, and net income improved. However, subsequent revelations showed that almost half of the sales increase resulted from fraudulent early recognition of revenues in the fourth quarter of Year 7 that the firm should have recognized in the first quarter of Year 8. Growth in revenues as originally reported for Years 5, 6, and 7 was −2.6%, −3.2%, and 18.7%, respectively.

Exhibit 6.17

Sunbeam Corporation
Statement of Cash Flows
(amounts in millions)
(Problem 6.22)

	Year 7	Year 6	Year 5
OPERATIONS			
Net income (loss)	$ 109.4	$(228.3)	$ 50.5
Depreciation and amortization	38.6	47.4	44.2
Restructuring and asset impairment charges	—	283.7	—
Deferred income taxes	57.8	(77.8)	25.1
Other additions	13.7	46.2	10.8
Other subtractions	(84.6)	(27.1)	(21.7)
(Increase) Decrease in accounts receivable	(84.6)	(13.8)	(4.5)
(Increase) Decrease in inventories	(100.8)	(11.6)	(4.9)
(Increase) Decrease in prepayments	(9.0)	2.7	(8.8)
Increase (Decrease) in accounts payable	(1.6)	14.7	9.2
Increase (Decrease) in other current liabilities	52.8	(21.9)	(18.4)
Cash Flow from Operations	$ (8.3)	$ 14.2	$ 81.5
INVESTING			
Fixed assets acquired	$ (58.3)	$ (75.3)	$(140.1)
Sale of businesses	91.0	—	65.3
Acquisitions of businesses	—	(.9)	(33.0)
Cash Flow from Investing	$ 32.7	$ (76.2)	$(107.4)
FINANCING			
Increase (Decrease) in short-term borrowing	$ 5.0	$ 30.0	$ 40.0
Increase in long-term debt	—	11.5	—
Issue of common stock	26.6	9.2	9.8
Decrease in long-term debt	(12.2)	(1.8)	(5.4)
Acquisition of common stock	—	—	(13.0)
Dividends	(3.4)	(3.3)	(3.3)
Other financing transactions	.5	(.4)	(.2)
Cash Flow from Financing	$ 16.5	$ 45.2	$ 27.9
Change in Cash	$ 40.9	$ (16.8)	$ 2.0
Cash—Beginning of year	11.5	28.3	26.3
Cash—End of Year	$ 52.4	$ 11.5	$ 28.3

Source: Sunbeam Corporation, Form 10-K for the Fiscal Year Ended December 28, 1997.

REQUIRED

a. Using the information provided and the statement of cash flows for Year 5 in Exhibit 6.17, identify any signals before the turnaround effort that Sunbeam was experiencing operating difficulties and was in need of restructuring.

b. Using information in the statement of cash flows for Year 6, identify indicators of the turnaround efforts and any relations between cash flows that trouble you.

c. Using information in the statement of cash flows for Year 7, indicate any signals that the firm might have engaged in aggressive revenue recognition and had not yet fixed its general operating problems.

6.23 Applying and Interpreting the Earnings Manipulation Model. Exhibit 6.18 presents selected financial statement data for **Enron Corporation** as originally reported for 1997, 1998, 1999, and 2000. In 2001, Enron restated its financial statements for earlier years because it reported several items beyond the limits of U.S. GAAP.

Exhibit 6.18				
Enron Corporation **Financial Statement Data** **(amounts in millions)** **(Problem 6.23)**				
	2000	**1999**	**1998**	**1997**
Accounts receivable	$ 10,396	$ 3,030	$ 2,060	$ 1,697
Current assets	30,381	7,255	5,933	4,669
Property, plant, and equipment, net	11,743	10,681	10,657	9,170
Total assets	65,503	33,381	29,350	23,422
Current liabilities	28,406	6,759	6,107	4,412
Long-term debt	8,550	7,151	7,357	6,254
Sales	$100,789	$40,112	$31,260	$20,273
Cost of goods sold	94,517	34,761	26,381	17,311
Selling and administrative expenses	3,184	3,045	2,473	1,406
Income from continuing operations	979	1,024	703	105
Cash flow from operations	4,779	1,228	1,640	501
Depreciation expense	485	565	563	480

Source: Enron Corporation, Form 10-K for the Fiscal Years Ended December 31, 1997, 1998, 1999, and 2000.

REQUIRED

a. Use Beneish's earnings manipulation model to compute the probability that Enron engaged in earnings manipulation for 1998, 1999, and 2000.

b. Identify the major reasons for the changes in the probability of earnings manipulation during the three-year period.

6.24 Using Originally Reported versus Restated Data. Prior to Year 8, Cooper Corporation engaged in a wide variety of industries, including weapons manufacturing under government contracts, information technologies, commercial aircraft manufacturing, missile systems, coal mining, material service, ship management, and ship financing. During Year 8,

Cooper sold its information technologies business. During Year 9, Cooper sold its commercial aircraft manufacturing business. During Year 9, it also announced its intention to sell its missile systems, coal mining, material service, ship management, and ship financing businesses. These strategic moves left Cooper with only its weapons manufacturing business. Financial statements for Cooper for Year 9 as reported, Year 8 as restated in the Year 9 annual report for discontinued operations, and Year 8 as originally reported appear in Exhibit 6.19 (balance sheet), Exhibit 6.20 (income statement), and Exhibit 6.21 (statement of cash flows).

Exhibit 6.19

Cooper Corporation
Balance Sheet
(amounts in millions)
(Problem 6.24)

	Year 9 as Reported	Year 8 as Restated in Year 9 Annual Report	Year 8 as Originally Reported
ASSETS			
Cash and cash equivalents	$ 513	$ 507	$ 513
Marketable securities	432	307	307
Accounts receivable	64	99	444
Contracts in process	1,550	1,474	2,606
Net assets of discontinued businesses	767	1,468	—
Other current assets	329	145	449
Total Current Assets	$3,655	$4,000	$4,319
Property, plant, and equipment, net	$ 322	$ 372	$1,029
Other assets	245	300	859
Total Assets	$4,222	$4,672	$6,207
LIABILITIES AND SHAREHOLDERS' EQUITY			
Accounts payable and accruals	$ 553	$ 642	$2,593
Current portion of long-term debt	145	450	516
Other current liabilities	1,250	1,174	—
Total Current Liabilities	$1,948	$2,266	$3,109
Long-term debt	38	163	365
Other noncurrent liabilities	362	263	753
Total Liabilities	$2,348	$2,692	$4,227
Common stock	$ 42	$ 55	$ 55
Additional paid-in capital	—	25	25
Retained earnings	2,474	2,651	2,651
Treasury stock	(642)	(751)	(751)
Total Shareholders' Equity	$1,874	$1,980	$1,980
Total Liabilities and Shareholders' Equity	$4,222	$4,672	$6,207

Exhibit 6.20

Cooper Corporation
Income Statement
(amounts in millions)
(Problem 6.24)

	Year 9 as Reported	Year 8 as Restated in Year 9 Annual Report	Year 8 as Originally Reported
Continuing Operations			
Sales	$ 3,472	$ 3,322	$ 8,751
Operating costs and expenses	(3,297)	(3,207)	(8,359)
Interest income (expense), net	25	4	(34)
Other expense, net	27	(27)	(27)
Earnings before Income Taxes	$ 227	$ 92	$ 331
Income tax credit	21	114	43
Income from Continuing Operations	$ 248	$ 206	$ 374
Discontinued Operations			
Earnings from operations	$ 193	$ 299	$ 131
Gain on disposal	374	—	—
Net Income	$ 815	$ 505	$ 505

Exhibit 6.21

Cooper Corporation
Statement of Cash Flows
(amounts in millions)
(Problem 6.24)

	Year 9 as Reported	Year 8 as Restated in Year 9 Annual Report	Year 8 as Originally Reported
OPERATIONS			
Income from continuing operations	$ 248	$ 206	$ 374
Depreciation and amortization	56	140	303
(Increase) Decrease in accounts receivable	35	4	(91)
(Increase) Decrease in contracts in process	(76)	(83)	237
(Increase) Decrease in other current assets	(6)	8	13
Increase (Decrease) in accounts payable and accruals	(66)	51	262
Increase (Decrease) in other current liabilities	11	(41)	(469)
Cash flow from continuing operations	$ 202	$ 285	$ 629
Cash flow from discontinued operations	288	324	44
Cash Flow from Operations	$ 490	$ 609	$ 673

(Continued)

Exhibit 6.21 (Continued)

INVESTING

Proceeds from sale of discontinued operations	$ 1,039	$ 184	$ 184
Capital expenditures	(18)	(29)	(82)
Purchase of marketable securities	(125)	(307)	(307)
Other	32	3	56
Cash Flow from Investing	$ 928	$(149)	$(149)

FINANCING

Issue of common stock	$ 57	$ —	$ —
Repayment of debt	(454)	(11)	(61)
Purchase of common stock	(960)	—	—
Dividends	(55)	(42)	(42)
Other	—	—	(17)
Cash Flow from Financing	$(1,412)	$ (53)	$(120)
Change in Cash	$ 6	$ 407	$ 404
Cash—Beginning of Year	507	100	109
Cash—End of Year	$ 513	$ 507	$ 513

REQUIRED

a. Refer to Exhibit 6.19. Why does the restated amount for total assets for Year 8 of $4,672 million differ from the originally reported amount of $6,207 million?

b. Refer to Exhibit 6.20. Why are the originally reported and restated net income amounts for Year 8 the same (that is, $505 million) when each of the individual revenues and expenses decreased on restatement?

c. Refer to Exhibit 6.21. Why is the restated amount of cash flow from operations for Year 8 of $609 million less than the originally reported amount of $673 million?

d. If the analyst wanted to analyze changes in the structure of assets and equities between Year 8 and Year 9, which columns and amounts in Exhibit 6.19 would he or she use? Explain.

e. If the analyst wanted to analyze changes in the operating profitability between Year 8 and Year 9, which columns and amounts in Exhibit 6.20 would he or she use? Explain.

f. If the analyst wanted to use cash flow ratios to assess short-term liquidity and long-term solvency risk, which columns and amounts in Exhibit 6.21 would he or she use? Explain.

INTEGRATIVE CASE 6.1

Walmart

Exhibits 1.26–1.28 of Integrative Case 1.1 (Chapter 1) present the financial statements for Walmart for 2012 to 2015. In addition, the website for this text contains Walmart's December 31, 2015, Form 10-K. You should read the management discussion and analysis (MD&A), financial statements, and notes to the financial statements, especially Note 2, "Summary of Significant Accounting Policies."

REQUIRED

a. Given your knowledge of Walmart's key success and risk factors, use the note information described above to evaluate Walmart's accounting quality.

b. If you believe that Walmart's accounting policy does not yield measurements of assets and liabilities that reflect economic reality and a measurement of net income that is predictive of future earnings, suggest any changes that you would make to assets, liabilities, and earnings to improve accounting quality. (At this point in your learning process, if you do not have specific numerical adjustments to propose, at least describe potential journal entries you would make to change the financial statements, if any, and what information you might need to make those entries.)

c. Evaluate whether your proposed adjustments are necessary for (1) credit analysis and (2) equity valuation.

CASE 6.2

Citi: A Very Bad Year

Citigroup Inc. (Citi) is a leading global financial services company with over 200 million customer accounts and operations in more than 140 countries. Its operating units Citicorp and Citi Holdings provide a broad range of financial products and services to consumers, governments, institutions, and corporations. Services include investment banking, consumer and corporate banking and credit, securities brokerage, and wealth management.

Citi reported a net loss of $27,684 million, or $5.59 per share, in 2008. Exhibit 6.22 presents Citigroup's consolidated statements of income for 2006 to 2008.

Exhibit 6.22

Citigroup Inc.
Consolidated Statements of Income
(amounts in millions, except per share amounts)
(Case 6.2)

| | Citigroup Inc. and Subsidiaries | | |
| | Year ended December 31 | | |
	2008	2007	2006
Revenues			
Interest revenue	$106,655	$121,429	$ 93,611
Interest expense	52,963	76,051	55,683
Net interest revenue	$ 53,692	$ 45,378	$ 37,928
Commissions and fees	$ 11,227	$ 20,706	$ 18,850
Principal transactions	(22,188)	(12,086)	7,990
Administration and other fiduciary fees	8,560	9,132	6,903
Realised gains (losses) from sales of investments	(2,061)	1,168	1,791
Insurance premiums	3,221	3,062	2,769
Other revenue	342	11,135	10,096
Total non-interest revenues	$ (899)	$ 33,117	$ 48,399
Total revenues, net of interest expense	$ 52,793	$ 78,495	$ 86,327

(Continued)

Exhibit 6.22 (Continued)

Provisions, for credit losses and for benefits and claims			
Provision for loan losses	$ 33,674	$ 16,832	$ 6,320
Policyholder benefits and claims	1,403	935	967
Provision for unfunded lending commitments	(363)	150	250
Total provisions for credit losses and for benefits and claims	$ 34,714	$ 17,917	$ 7,537
Operating expenses			
Compensation and benefits	$ 32,440	$ 33,892	$ 29,752
Net occupancy	7,125	6,648	5,794
Technology/communication	4,897	4,511	3,741
Advertising and marketing	2,292	2,803	2,471
Restructuring	1,766	1,528	—
Other operating	22,614	10,420	8,543
Total operating expenses	$ 71,134	$ 59,802	$ 50,301
Income (loss) from continuing operations before income taxes and minority interest	$ (53,055)	$ 776	$ 28,489
Provision (benefit) for income taxes	(20,612)	(2,498)	7,749
Minority interest, net of taxes	(349)	285	289
Income (loss) from continuing operations	$ (32,094)	$ 2,989	$ 20,451
Discontinued operations			
Income from discontinued operations	$ 1,478	$ 925	$ 1,177
Gain on sale	3,139	—	219
Provision (benefit) for income taxes and minority interest, net of taxes	207	297	309
Income from discontinued operations, net of taxes	$ 4,410	$ 628	$ 1,087
Net income (loss)	$ (27,684)	$ 3,617	$ 21,518
Basic earnings per share[1]			
Income (loss) from continuing operations	$ (6.42)	$ 0.60	$ 4.17
Income from discontinued operations, net of taxes	0.83	0.13	0.22
Net income (loss)	$ (5.59)	$ 0.73	$ 4.39
Weighted average common shares outstanding	5,265.4	4,905.8	4,887.3
Diluted earnings per share[1]			
Income (loss) from continuing operations	$ (6.42)	$ 0.59	$ 4.09
Income from discontinued operations, net of taxes	0.83	0.13	0.22
Net income (loss)	$ (5.59)	$ 0.72	$ 4.31
Adjusted weighted average common shares outstanding	$ 5,795.1	$ 4,995.3	$4,986.1

[1]Diluted shares used in the diluted EPS calculation represent basic shares for 2009 due to the net loss. Using actual diluted shares would result in anti-dilution.

Source: Citigroup Inc., Form 10-K for the Fiscal Years Ended December 31, 2008, 2007, and 2006.

Excerpts from Financial Statement Notes:

The following excerpts were disclosed in the notes to Citigroup's 2008 financial statements:

3. Discontinued Operations

Sale of Citigroup's German Retail Banking Operations

On December 5, 2008, Citigroup sold its German retail banking operations to Credit Mutuel for Euro 5.2 billion, in cash plus the German retail bank's operating net earnings accrued in 2008 through the closing. The sale resulted in an after-tax gain of approximately $3.9 billion including the after-tax gain on the foreign currency hedge of $383 million recognised during the fourth quarter of 2008.

The sale does not include the corporate and investment banking business or the Germany-based European data center.

The German retail banking operations had total assets and total liabilities as of November 30, 2008, of $15.6 billion and $11.8 billion, respectively.

Results for all of the German retail banking businesses sold, as well as the net gain recognized in 2008 from this sale, are reported as *Discontinued Operations* for all periods presented.

Summarized financial information for *Discontinued Operations*, including cash flows, related to the sale of the German retail banking operations is as follows:

in millions of dollars	2008	2007	2006
Total revenues, net of interest expense	$6,592	$2,212	$2,126
Income from discontinued operations	$1,438	$ 652	$ 837
Gain on sale	3,695	—	—
Provision for income taxes and minority interest, net of taxes	426	214	266
Income from discontinued operations, net of taxes	$4,707	$ 438	$ 571

in millions of dollars	2008	2007	2006
Cash flows from operating activities	$ (4,719)	$ 2,227	$ 2,246
Cash flows from investing activities	18,547	(1,906)	(3,316)
Cash flows from financing activities	(14,226)	(213)	1,147
Net cash provided by (used in) discontinued operations	$ (398)	$ 108	$ 77

CitiCapital

On July 31, 2008, Citigroup sold substantially all of CitiCapital, the equipment finance unit in *North America*. The total proceeds from the transaction were approximately $12.5 billion and resulted in an after-tax loss to Citigroup of $305 million. This loss is included in *Income from discontinued operations* on the Company's Consolidated Statement of Income for the second quarter of 2008. The assets and liabilities for CitiCapital totaled approximately $12.9 billion and $0.5 billion, respectively, at June 30, 2008.

This transaction encompassed seven CitiCapital equipment finance business lines, including Healthcare Finance, Private Label Equipment Finance, Material Handling Finance, Franchise Finance, Construction Equipment Finance, Bankers Leasing, and CitiCapital Canada. CitiCapital's Tax Exempt Finance business was not part of the transaction and was retained by Citigroup.

CitiCapital had approximately 1,400 employees and 160,000 customers throughout North America.

Results for all of the CitiCapital businesses sold, as well as the net loss recognized in 2008 from this sale, are reported as *Discontinued operations* for all periods presented.

Summarized financial information for *Discontinued operations*, including cash flows, related to the sale of CitiCapital is as follows:

in millions of dollars	2008	2007	2006
Total revenues, net of interest expense	$ 24	$991	$1,162
Income (loss) from discontinued operations	$ 40	$273	$ 313
Loss on sale	(506)	—	—
Provision (benefit) for income taxes and minority interest, net of taxes	(202)	83	86
Income (loss) from discontinued operations, net of taxes	$(264)	$190	$ 227

in millions of dollars	2008	2007	2006
Cash flows from operating activities	$(287)	$(1,148)	$ 2,596
Cash flows from investing activities	349	1,190	(2,664)
Cash flows from financing activities	(61)	(43)	3
Net cash provided by (used in) discontinued operations	$ 1	$ (1)	$ (65)

Sale of the Asset Management Business

On December 1, 2005, the Company completed the sale of substantially all of its Asset Management business to Legg Mason, Inc. (Legg Mason).

On January 31, 2006, the Company completed the sale of its Asset Management business within Bank Handlowy (an indirect banking subsidiary of Citigroup located in Poland) to Legg Mason. This transaction, which was originally part of the overall Asset Management business sold to Legg Mason on December 1, 2005, was postponed due to delays in obtaining local regulatory approval. A gain from this sale of $18 million after-tax and minority interest ($31 million pretax and minority interest) was recognized in the first quarter of 2006 in *Discontinued operations*.

During March 2006, the Company sold 10.3 million shares of Legg Mason stock through an underwritten public offering. The net sale proceeds of $ 1.258 billion resulted in a pretax gain of $24 million in *ICG*.

In September 2006, the Company received from Legg Mason the final closing adjustment payment related to this sale. This payment resulted in an additional after-tax gain of $51 million ($83 million pretax), recorded in *Discontinued operations*.

Sale of the Life Insurance and Annuities Business

On July 1, 2005, the Company completed the sale of Citigroup's Travelers Life & Annuity and substantially all of Citigroup's international insurance businesses to MetLife, Inc. (MetLife).

During the first quarter of 2006, $15 million of the total $657 million federal tax contingency reserve release was reported in *Discontinued operations* as it related to the Life Insurance and Annuities business sold to MetLife.

In July 2006, Citigroup recognized an $85 million after-tax gain from the sale of MetLife shares. This gain was reported in income from continuing operations in *ICG*.

In July 2006, the Company received the final closing adjustment payment related to this sale, resulting in an after-tax gain of $75 million ($115 million pretax), which was recorded in *Discontinued operations.*

In addition, during the third quarter of 2006, a release of $42 million of deferred tax liabilities was reported in *Discontinued operations* as it related to the Life Insurance & Annuities business sold to MetLife.

In December 2008, the Company fulfilled its previously agreed upon obligations with regard to its remaining 10% economic interest in the long-term care business that it had sold to the predecessor of Genworth Financial in 2000. Under the terms of the 2005 sales agreement of Citi's Life Insurance and Annuities business to MetLife, Citi agreed to reimburse MetLife for certain liabilities related to the sale of the long-term-care business to Genworth's predecessor. The assumption of the final 10% block Genworth at December 31, 2008, resulted in a pretax loss of $50 million ($33 million after-tax), which has been reported in *Discontinued operations.*

Combined Results for Discontinued Operations

The following is summarized financial information for the German retail banking operations, CitiCapital, Life Insurance and Annuities business, Asset Management business, and TPC:

in millions of dollars	2008	2007	2006
Total revenues, net of interest expense	**$6,616**	$3,203	$3,507
Income from discontinued operations	**$1,478**	$ 925	$1,177
Gain on sale	**3,139**	—	219
Provision (benefit) for income taxes, and minority interest, net of taxes	**(207)**	(297)	(309)
Income from discontinued operations, net of taxes	**$4,410**	$ 628	$1,087

Cash Flows from Discontinued Operations			
in millions of dollars	2008	2007	2006
Cash flows from operating activities	**$ (5,006)**	$1,079	$ 4,842
Cash flows from investing activities	**18,896**	(716)	(5,871)
Cash flows from financing activities	**(14,287)**	(256)	1,150
Net cash provided by (used in) discontinued operations	**$ (397)**	$ 107	$ 121

5. Interest Revenue and Expense

For the years ended December 31, 2008, 2007, and 2006, respectively, interest revenue and expense consisted of the following:

in millions of dollars	2008	2007	2006
Interest revenue			
Loan interest, including fees	**$ 62,336**	$ 63,201	$52,086
Deposits with banks	**3,119**	3,113	2,240
Federal funds sold and securities purchased under agreements to resell	**9,175**	18,354	14,199
Investments, including dividends	**10,718**	13,423	10,340
Trading account assets[1]	**17,489**	18,507	11,865
Other interest	**3,818**	4,831	2,881
Total interest revenue	**$106,655**	$121,429	$93,611
Interest expense			
Deposits	**$ 20,271**	$ 28,402	$21,336
Federal funds purchased and securities loaned or sold under agreements to repurchase	**11,330**	23,028	17,448
Trading account liabilities[1]	**1,277**	1,440	1,119
Short-term borrowings	**4,039**	7,071	4,632
Long-term debt	**16,046**	16,110	11,148
Total interest expense	**$ 52,963**	$ 76,051	$55,683
Net interest revenue	**$ 53,692**	$ 45,378	$37,928
Provision for loan losses	**33,674**	16,832	6,320
Net interest revenue after provision for loan losses	**$ 20,018**	$ 28,546	$31,608

[1]Interest expense on Trading account facilities of ICG is reported as a reduction of interest revenue from Trading account assets.

6. Commissions and Fees

Commissions and fees revenue includes charges to customers for credit and bank cards, including transaction-processing fees and annual fees; advisory and equity and debt underwriting services; lending and deposit-related transactions, such as loan commitments, standby letters of credit and other deposit and loan servicing activities; investment management-related fees, including brokerage services and custody and trust services; and insurance fees and commissions.

The following table presents commissions and fees revenue for the years ended December 31:

in millions of dollars	2008	2007	2006
Investment banking	**$ 2,284**	$ 5,228	$ 4,093
Credit cards and bank cards	**4,517**	5,036	5,191
Smith Barney	**2,836**	3,265	2,958
ICG trading-related	**2,322**	2,706	2,464
Checking-related	**1,134**	1,108	911
Transaction Services	**1,423**	1,166	859
Other Consumer	**1,211**	649	279

(Continued)

Nikko Cordial-related[1]	**1,086**	834	—
Loan servicing[2]	**(1,731)**	560	660
Primerica	**415**	455	399
Other *ICG*	**747**	295	243
Other	**(141)**	71	58
Corporate finance[3]	**(4,876)**	(667)	735
Total commissions and fees	**$11,227**	$20,706	$18,850

[1]Commissions and fees for Nikko Cordial have not been detailed due to unavailability of the information.
[2]Includes fair value adjustments on mortgage servicing assets. The mark-to-market on the underlying economic hedges of the MSRs is included in Other revenue.
[3]Includes write-downs of approximately $4.9 billion in 2008 and $1.5 billion in 2007, net of underwriting fees, on funded and unfunded highly leveraged finance commitments, recorded at fair value and reported as loans held for sale in Other assets. Write-downs were recorded on all highly leveraged finance commitments where there was value impairment, regardless of funding date.

7. Principal Transactions

Principal transactions revenue consists of realized and unrealized gains and losses from trading activities. Not included in the table below is the impact of net interest revenue related to trading activities, which is an integral part of trading activities' profitability. The following table presents principal transactions revenue for the years ended December 31:

in millions of dollars	**2008**	**2007**	**2006**[1]
Institutional Clients Group			
Fixed income[2]	**$ (6,455)**	$ 4,053	$5,593
Credit products[3]	**(21,614)**	(21,805)	(744)
Equities[4]	**(394)**	682	866
Foreign exchange[5]	**2,316**	1,222	693
Commodities[6]	**667**	686	487
Total *ICG*	**$(25,480)**	$(15,162)	$6,895
Consumer Banking/Global Cards[7]	**1,616**	1,364	504
Global Wealth Management	**836**	1,315	680
Corporate/Other	**840**	397	(89)
Total principal transactions revenue	**$(22,188)**	$(12,086)	$7,990

[1]Reclassified to conform to the current period's presentation.
[2]Includes revenues from government securities and corporate debt, municipal securities, preferred stock, mortgage securities, and other debt instruments. Also includes spot and forward trading of currencies and exchange-traded and over-the-counter (OTC) currency options, options on fixed income securities, interest rate swaps, currency swaps, swap options, caps and floors, financial futures, OTC options, and forward contracts on fixed income securities. Losses in 2008 reflect the volatility and dislocation in the credit and trading markets.
[3]Includes revenues from structured credit products such as North America and Europe collateralized debt obligations. In 2007 and 2008, losses recorded were related to subprime-related exposures in ICG's lending and structuring business and exposures to super senior CDOs.
[4]Includes revenues from common, preferred and convertible preferred stock, convertible corporate debt, equity-linked notes, and exchange-traded and OTC equity options and warrants.
[5]Includes revenues from foreign exchange spot, forward, option and swap contracts, as well as translation gains and losses.
[6]Primarily includes the results of Phibro LLC, which trades crude oil, refined oil products, natural gas, and other commodities.
[7]Includes revenues from various fixed income, equities and foreign exchange transactions.

10. Restructuring

In the fourth quarter of 2008, Citigroup recorded a pretax restructuring expense of $1.797 billion pre-tax related to the implementation of a Company-wide re-engineering plan. This initiative will generate headcount reductions of approximately 20,600. The charges related to the 2008 Re-engineering Projects Restructuring Initiative are reported in the Restructuring line on the Company's Consolidated Statement of Income and are recorded in each segment.

In 2007, the Company completed a review of its structural expense base in a Company-wide effort to create a more streamlined organization, reduce expense growth, and provide investment funds for future growth initiatives. As a result of this review, a pretax restructuring charge of $1.4 billion was recorded in *Corporate/Other* during the first quarter of 2007. Additional net charges of $151 million were recognized in subsequent quarters throughout 2007 and a net release of $31 million in 2008 due to a change in estimates. The charges related to the 2007 Structural Expense Review Restructuring Initiative are reported in the Restructuring line on the Company's Consolidated Statement of Income.

The primary goals of the 2007 Structural Expense Review and Restructuring, and the 2008 Re-engineering Projects and Restructuring Initiatives were:

- eliminate layers of management/improve workforce management;
- consolidate certain back-office, middle-office and corporate functions;
- increase the use of shared services;
- expand centralized procurement; and
- continue to rationalize operational spending on technology.

The implementation of these restructuring initiatives also caused certain related premises and equipment assets to become redundant. The remaining depreciable lives of these assets were shortened, and accelerated depreciation charges began in the second quarter of 2007 and fourth quarter of 2008 for the 2007 and 2008 initiatives, respectively, in addition to normal scheduled depreciation.

19. Goodwill and Intangible Assets

Goodwill

The changes in goodwill during 2007 and 2008 were as follows:

in millions of dollars	Goodwill
Balance at December 31, 2006	$33,264
Acquisition of GFU	865
Acquisition of Quilter	268
Acquisition of Nikko Cordial[1]	892
Acquisition of Grupo Cuscatlán	921
Acquisition of Egg	1,471
Acquisition of Old Lane	516
Acquisition of BISYS	872
Acquisition of BOOC	712
Acquisition of ATD	569
Sale of Avantel	(118)
Foreign exchange translation, smaller acquisitions and other	821

(Continued)

Balance at December 31, 2007	$41,053
Sale of German retail bank	$ (1,047)
Sale of CitiCapital	(221)
Sale of Citigroup Global Services Limited	(85)
Purchase accounting adjustments—BISYS	(184)
Purchase of the remaining shares of Nikko Cordial—net of purchase accounting adjustments	287
Acquisition of Legg Mason Private Portfolio Group	98
Foreign exchange translation	(3,116)
Impairment of goodwill	(9,568)
Smaller acquisitions, purchase accounting adjustments and other	(85)
Balance at December 31, 2008	$27,132

In the following press release, Citi further describes the source of the goodwill impairment:

Citi Announces Fourth Quarter Goodwill Impairment of $9.6 Billion[42]

Results in Additional Net Loss of $9.0 Billion for 2008

New York — Citi announced today that it recorded a pre-tax goodwill impairment charge of approximately $9.6 billion ($8.7 billion after-tax) in the fourth quarter of 2008. Citi had previously announced in its fourth quarter earnings press release (January 16, 2009) that it was continuing to review its goodwill to determine whether a goodwill impairment had occurred as of December 31, 2008, and this charge is the result of that review and testing. The goodwill impairment charge was recorded in North America Consumer Banking, Latin America Consumer Banking, and EMEA Consumer Banking, and resulted in a write-off of the entire amount of goodwill allocated to those reporting units. The charge does not result in a cash outflow or negatively affect the Tier 1 or Total Regulatory Capital ratios, Tangible Common Equity or Citi's liquidity position as of December 31, 2008.

In addition, Citi recorded a $374 million pre-tax charge ($242 million after-tax) to reflect further impairment evident in the intangible asset related to Nikko Asset Management at December 31, 2008.

The primary cause for both the goodwill and the intangible asset impairments mentioned above was the rapid deterioration in the financial markets, as well as in the global economic outlook generally, particularly during the period beginning mid-November through year-end 2008. This deterioration further weakened the near term prospects for the financial services industry.

Giving effect to these charges, Net Income (Loss) from Continuing Operations for 2008 was $(32.1) billion and Net Income (Loss) was $(27.7) billion, resulting in Diluted Earnings per Share of $(6.42) and $(5.59) respectively.

A complete description of Citi's goodwill impairment testing as of December 31, 2008 and the related charges will be included in Citi's Form 10-K to be filed with the Securities and Exchange Commission on or before March 2, 2009.

---

[42]Press release found at www.citigroup.com/citi/press/2009/090227b.htm. Reprinted by permission.

REQUIRED

Consider the following items reported in Citi's Consolidated Statement of Income:

- Principal transactions
- Realized (gain) losses from sales of investments
- Provision for loan losses
- Restructuring
- Other operating expenses (which presumably includes the goodwill impairment)
- Discontinued operations

Discuss whether you would eliminate all or part of each item when assessing current profitability and forecasting the future earnings of Citi. If so, what adjustments would you make to the financial statements (assuming a tax rate of 35%)?

CASE 6.3

Arbortech: Apocalypse Now

Arbortech, a designer, manufacturer, and marketer of PC cards for computers, printers, telecommunications equipment, and equipment diagnostic systems, was the darling of Wall Street during Year 6. Its common stock price was the leading gainer for the year on the New York Stock Exchange. Its bubble burst during the third quarter of Year 7 when revelations about seriously misstated financial statements for prior years became known. This case seeks to identify signals of the financial shenanigans and to assess the likelihood of the firm's future survival.

Industry and Products

Digital computing and processing have expanded now to include a broad array of mobile applications, including tablets, laptops, cell phones, digital cameras, and medical and automobile diagnostic equipment. A PC card is a rugged, lightweight, credit-card-sized device inserted into a dedicated slot in these products that provides programming, processing, and storage capabilities provided on hard drives in conventional desktop computers. The PC card has a high shock and vibration tolerance, low power consumption, a smaller size (relative to previous technologies), and a high access speed. At the time, the market for PC cards was one of the fastest-growing segments of the electronics industry.

Arbortech designs PC cards for four principal industries: (1) communications (routers, cell phones, and local-area networks), (2) transportation (vehicle diagnostics and navigation), (3) mobile computing (handheld data collection terminals and notebook computers), and (4) medical (blood gas analysis systems and defibrillators). The firm targets its engineering and product development, all of which it conducts in-house, to these four industry groups. It works closely with original equipment manufacturers (OEMs) to design PC cards that meet specific needs of products aimed at these four industries. Arbortech also conducts its manufacturing in-house, which allows it to respond quickly to changing requirements and schedules of these OEMs. The firm markets its products using its own salesforce.

In Year 4, Arbortech was incorporated in Delaware. The firm made its initial public offering of common stock (1 million shares) on April 19, Year 4, at a price of $5.625 per share. Each common share issued included a redeemable common stock purchase warrant that permitted the holder to purchase one share of the firm's common stock for $7.20. Prior to its initial public offering, Arbortech obtained a $550,000 bridge loan during Year 4, which it repaid with proceeds from the initial public offering. Holders of the stock purchase warrants exercised their options during Year 5 and Year 6. The firm obtained equity capital during Year 5 as a result of a private placement of its common stock at $5.83 a share. It issued additional shares to the public during Year 6 at $18 a share. Its stock price was $5.25 on June 30, Year 4; $22.625 on June 30, Year 5; $29.875 on June 30, Year 6; and $52 on December 31, Year 7.

Arbortech maintained a line of credit throughout Year 4 to Year 6 with a major Boston bank to finance its accounts receivables and inventories. The borrowing was at the bank's prime lending rate. Substantially all of the assets of the firm collateralized this borrowing.

The firm's chief executive officer, Daniel James, is also its major shareholder. The firm maintains an employment agreement with James under which it pays his compensation to a Swiss executive search firm, which then pays James.

Beginning in Year 6, Arbortech made minority investments in five corporations engaged in technology development, four of which the firm accounts for using the cost method and one of which it accounts for using the equity method. Products developed by these companies could conceivably use PC cards. Arbortech also advanced amounts to some of these companies using interest-bearing notes.

Exhibits 6.23 to 6.25 present Arbortech's financial statements for the fiscal years ended June 30, Year 4, Year 5, and Year 6, based on the amounts originally reported for each year. Exhibit 6.26 presents selected financial statement ratios based on these reported amounts.

Exhibit 6.23

Arbortech
Balance Sheets as Originally Reported
(amounts in thousands)
(Case 6.3)

	Year 6	Year 5	Year 4	Year 3
ASSETS				
Cash	$ 6,182	$ 970	$ 981	$ —
Marketable securities	4,932	—	—	—
Accounts receivable	12,592	3,932	1,662	730
Inventories	18,229	8,609	3,371	2,257
Other current assets	6,256	1,932	306	234
Total Current Assets	$48,191	$15,443	$6,320	$3,221
Investments in securities	2,472	—	—	—
Property, plant, and equipment, net	4,698	1,323	669	208
Other assets	421	1,433	601	666
Total Assets	$55,782	$18,199	$7,590	$4,095
LIABILITIES AND SHAREHOLDERS' EQUITY				
Accounts payable	$ 3,494	$ 3,571	$ 616	$1,590
Notes payable	4,684	1,153	—	980
Current portion of long-term debt	336	103	—	—
Other current liabilities	614	765	516	457
Total Current Liabilities	$ 9,128	$ 5,592	$1,132	$3,027

(Continued)

Exhibit 6.23 (Continued)

Long-term debt	367	162	—	—
Deferred tax liability	242	—	39	24
Total Liabilities	$ 9,737	$ 5,754	$1,171	$3,051
Common stock	$ 165	$ 110	$ 90	$ 60
Additional paid-in capital	38,802	10,159	5,027	146
Retained earnings	7,078	2,176	1,302	838
Total Shareholders' Equity	$46,045	$12,445	$6,419	$1,044
Total Liabilities and Shareholders' Equity	$55,782	$18,199	$7,590	$4,095

Exhibit 6.24

Arbortech
Income Statements as Originally Reported
(amounts in thousands)
(Case 6.3)

	Year 6	Year 5	Year 4
Sales	$ 37,848	$12,445	$ 8,213
Other revenues	353	10	9
Cost of goods sold	(23,636)	(6,833)	(4,523)
Selling and administrative	(4,591)	(3,366)	(1,889)
Research and development	(1,434)	(752)	(567)
Interest	(370)	(74)	(495)*
Income taxes	(3,268)	(556)	(284)
Net Income	$ 4,902	$ 874	$ 464

*Includes the cost of factoring receivables and interest on bridge financing obtained and repaid during the year.

Exhibit 6.25

Arbortech
Statements of Cash Flows as Originally Reported
(amounts in thousands)
(Case 6.3)

	Year 6	Year 5	Year 4
OPERATIONS			
Net income	$ 4,902	$ 874	$ 464
Depreciation	645	337	193
Other addbacks and subtractions, net	1,159	(5)	219
Working capital provided by operations	$ 6,706	$ 1,206	$ 876

(Continued)

Exhibit 6.25 (Continued)

(Increase) Decrease in accounts receivables	(8,940)	(2,433)	(981)
(Increase) Decrease in inventories	(9,620)	(5,238)	(1,115)
(Increase) Decrease in other current assets	(836)	(2,406)	(71)
Increase (Decrease) in accounts payable	(76)	2,955	(974)
Increase (Decrease) in other current liabilities	(152)	251	87
Cash Flow from Operations	$(12,918)	$(5,665)	$(2,178)
INVESTING			
Sale of investments	$ 3,981	$ —	$ —
Acquisition of fixed assets	(3,899)	(862)	(525)
Acquisitions of investments	(11,186)	—	—
Other investing transactions	(2,800)	—	—
Cash Flow from Investing	$(13,904)	$ (862)	$ (525)
FINANCING			
Increase in short-term borrowing	$ 3,531	$ 1,153	$ 550
Increase in long-term borrowing	691	320	—
Increase in common stock	28,064	5,099	4,663
Decrease in short-term borrowing	—	—	(1,529)
Decrease in long-term borrowing	(252)	(56)	—
Cash Flow from Financing	$ 32,034	$ 6,516	$ 3,684
Net Change in Cash	$ 5,212	$ (11)	$ 981
Cash—Beginning of year	970	981	—
Cash—End of Year	$ 6,182	$ 970	$ 981

Exhibit 6.26

Arbortech
Financial Ratios Based on Originally Reported Amounts
(Case 6.3)

	Year 6	Year 5	Year 4
Profit margin for ROA	13.6%	7.4%	9.6%
Assets turnover	1.0	1.0	1.4
ROA	13.9%	7.2%	13.5%
Profit margin for ROCE	13.0%	7.0%	5.6%
Capital structure leverage	1.3	1.4	1.6
ROCE	16.8%	9.3%	12.4%
Cost of goods sold/Sales	62.4%	54.9%	55.1%
Selling and administrative/Sales	12.1%	27.0%	23.0%
Research and development/Sales	3.8%	6.0%	6.9%
Income tax expense (excluding tax effects of interest expense)/Sales	9.0%	4.7%	5.5%

(Continued)

Exhibit 6.26 (Continued)			
Accounts receivable turnover	4.6	4.4	6.9
Inventory turnover	1.8	1.1	1.6
Fixed assets turnover	12.6	12.5	18.7
Current ratio	5.3	2.8	5.6
Quick ratio	2.6	0.9	2.3
Days accounts payable	39	63	71
Operating cash flow to current liabilities ratio	(1.755)	(1.685)	(1.047)
Long-term debt to long-term capital ratio	0.008	0.013	—
Liabilities to assets ratio	0.175	0.316	0.154
Operating cash flow to total liabilities ratio	(1.668)	(1.636)	(1.032)
Interest coverage ratio	23.1	20.3	2.5

Financial Statement Irregularities

On February 10, Year 7, after receiving information regarding various accounting and reporting irregularities, the board of directors fired James and relieved the chief financial officer of his duties. The board formed a special committee of outside directors to investigate the purported irregularities, obtaining the assistance of legal counsel and the firm's independent accountants. On February 21, Year 7, the New York Stock Exchange announced the suspension of trading in the firm's common stock. The stock was delisted on April 25, Year 7. On February 14, Year 7, the major Boston bank providing working capital financing notified the firm that the firm had defaulted on its line of credit agreement. Although this bank subsequently extended the line of credit through July 31, Year 7, it increased the interest rate significantly above prime. Arbortech decided to seek a new lender.

The investigation by the board's special committee revealed the following accounting and reporting irregularities:

■ Recording of invalid sales transactions: The firm created fictitious purchase orders from regular customers using purchase order forms from legitimate purchase transactions. The firm then purportedly shipped empty PC card housings to these customers at bogus addresses. James apparently paid the accounts receivable underlying these sales with his personal funds.

■ Recording of revenues from bill and hold transactions: The firm kept its books open beyond June 30 each year and recorded as sales of each year products that were shipped in July and should have been recorded as revenues of the next fiscal year.

■ Manipulation of physical counts of inventory balances and inclusion of empty PC card housings in finished goods inventories.

■ Failure to write down inventories adequately for product obsolescence.

■ Inclusion of certain costs in property, plant, and equipment that the firm should have expensed in the period incurred.

■ Inclusion in advances to other technology companies of amounts that represented pre-paid license fees. The firm should have amortized these fees over the license period.

■ Failure to provide adequately for uncollectible amounts related to advances to other technology companies.

■ Failure to write down or write off investments in other technology companies when their market value was less than the cost of the investment.

Exhibits 6.27 to 6.29 present Arbortech's restated financial statements for the fiscal years ending June 30, Year 4, Year 5, and Year 6, after correcting for the irregularities. These exhibits also present the financial statements for the nine months ended March 30, Year 7. The firm decided during February of Year 7 to change its fiscal year to a March year-end. Exhibit 6.30 presents selected financial ratios based on the restated financial statements.

Exhibit 6.27

Arbortech
Balance Sheets Using Restated Data
(amounts in thousands)
(Case 6.3)

	Year 7	Year 6	Year 5	Year 4	Year 3
ASSETS					
Cash	$ 57	$ 6,182	$ 970	$ 981	$ —
Marketable securities	—	4,932	—	—	—
Accounts receivable	5,571	11,260	2,802	1,280	730
Inventories	7,356	8,248	2,181	1,581	2,257
Other current assets	14,229	6,395	2,284	839	669
Total Current Assets	$ 27,213	$ 37,017	$ 8,237	$4,681	$3,656
Investments in securities	20,332	1,783	—	—	—
Property, plant, and equipment, net	3,087	2,033	923	399	243
Other assets	566	299	390	123	172
Total Assets	$ 51,198	$ 41,132	$ 9,550	$5,203	$4,071
LIABILITIES AND SHAREHOLDERS' EQUITY					
Accounts payable	$ 4,766	$ 3,025	$ 3,303	$ 772	$1,590
Notes payable	10,090	4,684	1,153	—	980
Current portion of long-term debt	671	336	103	—	—
Other current liabilities	7,117	811	562	116	457
Total Current Liabilities	$ 22,644	$ 8,856	$ 5,121	$ 888	$3,027
Long-term debt	—	367	162	—	—
Total Liabilities	$ 22,644	$ 9,223	$ 5,283	$ 888	$3,027
Common stock	$ 177	$ 165	$ 110	$ 90	$ 60
Additional paid-in capital	82,240	42,712	10,843	5,059	146
Retained earnings	(53,630)	(10,968)	(6,686)	(834)	838
Foreign currency adjustment	(233)	—	—	—	—
Total Shareholders' Equity	$ 28,554	$ 31,909	$ 4,267	$4,315	$1,044
Total Liabilities and Shareholders' Equity	$ 51,198	$ 41,132	$ 9,550	$5,203	$4,071

Exhibit 6.28

Arbortech
Income Statements Using Restated Data
(amounts in thousands)
(Case 6.3)

	Nine Months Ended March 31:	Year Ended June 30:		
	Year 7	Year 6	Year 5	Year 4
Sales	$ 28,263	$ 33,412	$ 8,982	$ 7,801
Other revenues	67	353	10	9
Cost of goods sold	(24,453)	(29,778)	(11,575)	(6,508)
Selling and administrative	(7,318)	(3,803)	(2,442)	(2,083)
Research and development	(1,061)	(1,434)	(753)	(567)
Loss on investments	(14,096)[a]	(2,662)[a]	—	—
Investigation costs	(3,673)[b]	—	—	—
Provision for settlement of shareholder litigation	(20,000)[c]	—	—	—
Interest	(391)	(370)	(74)	(495)
Income taxes	—[d]	—[d]	—[d]	171
Net Income (Loss)	$(42,662)	$ (4,282)	$ (5,852)	$(1,672)

[a]Write-offs of advances (and write-downs or write-offs of investments) in technology companies.
[b]Legal, accounting, and related costs of investigating misstatements of financial statements.
[c]Estimated cost of class-action lawsuits arising from misstatements of financial statements. Arbortech reached an agreement on June 18, Year 7, to pay the plaintiffs $1,475,000 in cash (included in accounts payable on the March 31, Year 7, balance sheet) and common stock of $18,525,000 (included in additional paid-in capital on the March 31, Year 7, balance sheet). The common stock portion of the settlement represents 37% of the common stock of Arbortech.
[d]Arbortech incurred net losses for income tax purposes and maintains a valuation allowance equal to the balance in deferred tax assets.

REQUIRED

a. Using information in the financial statements as originally reported in Exhibits 6.23 to 6.25, compute the value of Beneish's Manipulation Index for fiscal Year 5 and Year 6.

b. Using information from Requirement a and the financial ratios in Exhibit 6.26, indicate possible signals that Arbortech might have been manipulating its financial statements.

c. Describe the effect of each of the eight accounting irregularities on the balance sheet, income statement, and statement of cash flows.

d. Using information in the restated financial statements in Exhibits 6.27 to 6.29, the financial ratios in Exhibit 6.30, and the information provided in this case, as a commercial banker, would you be willing to offer Arbortech a line of credit as of July 31, Year 7? If so, provide the conditions that would induce you to offer such a line of credit.

e. Exhibit 6.31 presents the values of Altman's Z-score for fiscal Year 4, Year 5, and Year 6 based on the originally reported amounts and the restated amounts. Compute the value of Altman's Z-score for the fiscal year ended March 31, Year 7. Although this is not technically correct, use the income amounts for the nine-month period ending March 31, Year 7. Based on the amounts in the proposed settlement of the class-action lawsuits, the value of the common equity on March 31, Year 7, is $50,068,568.

f. Can Arbortech avoid bankruptcy as of mid-Year 7? Explain. Why doesn't the Altman model signal the financial difficulties earlier?

Exhibit 6.29

Arbortech
Statements of Cash Flows Using Restated Data
(amounts in thousands)
(Case 6.3)

	Nine Months Ended March 31,	Year Ended June 30,		
	Year 7	Year 6	Year 5	Year 4
OPERATIONS				
Net loss	$(42,662)	$ (4,282)	$(5,852)	$(1,672)
Depreciation and amortization	831	471	281	176
Other addbacks and subtractions, net	28,812	2,005	224	352
Working capital provided by operations	$(13,019)	$ (1,806)	$(5,347)	$(1,144)
(Increase) Decrease in accounts receivable	5,289	(8,883)	(1,693)	(599)
Increase (Decrease) in inventories	454	(6,067)	(600)	676
(Increase) Decrease in other current assets	$ (8,092)	$ (5,213)	$(1,932)	$ (176)
Increase (Decrease) in accounts payable	6,572	(9)	3,072	(818)
Increase (Decrease) in other current liabilities	—	(20)	(96)	(340)
Cash Flow from Operations	$ (8,796)	$(21,998)	$(6,596)	$(2,401)
INVESTING				
Sale of investments	$ 32,182	$ 3,981	$ —	$ —
Acquisition of fixed assets	(2,074)	(1,459)	(583)	(332)
Acquisition of investments	(38,892)	(11,186)	—	—
Cash Flow from Investing	$ (8,784)	$ (8,664)	$ (583)	$ (332)
FINANCING				
Increase in short-term borrowing	$ 5,406	$ 3,531	$ 1,153	$ 550
Increase in long-term borrowing	250	691	320	—
Increase in capital stock	4,060	28,813	5,099	4,663
Decrease in short-term borrowing	—	—	—	(1,529)
Decrease in long-term borrowing	(282)	(252)	(56)	—
Proceeds from related-party transaction	2,021	3,091	652	30
Cash Flow from Financing	$ 11,455	$ 35,874	$ 7,168	$ 3,714
Change in Cash	$ (6,125)	$ 5,212	$ (11)	$ 981
Cash—Beginning of year	6,182	970	981	—
Cash—End of Year	$ 57	$ 6,182	$ 970	$ 981

Exhibit 6.30

Arbortech Financial Ratios Based on Restated Data (Case 6.3)

	Year 7*	Year 6	Year 5	Year 4
Profit margin for ROA	(150.0%)	(12.1%)	(64.6%)	(17.2%)
Assets turnover	0.6	1.3	1.2	1.7
ROA	(91.9%)	(15.9%)	(78.7%)	(29.0%)
Profit margin for ROCE	(150.9%)	(12.8%)	(65.2%)	(21.4%)
Capital structure leverage	1.5	1.4	1.7	1.7
ROCE	(141.1%)	(23.7%)	(136.4%)	(62.4%)
Cost of goods sold/Sales	86.5%	89.1%	128.9%	83.4%
Selling and administrative/Sales	25.9%	11.4%	27.2%	26.7%
Research and development/Sales	3.8%	4.3%	8.4%	7.3%
Special provisions/Sales	133.6%	8.0%	—	—
Accounts receivable turnover	3.4	4.8	4.4	7.8
Inventory turnover	3.1	5.7	6.2	3.4
Fixed assets turnover	11.0	22.6	13.6	24.3
Current ratio	1.2	4.2	1.6	5.3
Quick ratio	0.3	2.5	0.7	2.6
Days accounts payable	60	32	61	74
Operating cash flow to current liabilities ratio	(0.558)	(3.148)	(2.195)	(1.227)
Long-term debt to long-term capital ratio	—	0.011	0.037	—
Liabilities to assets ratio	0.442	0.224	0.553	0.171
Operating cash flow to total liabilities ratio	(0.552)	(3.033)	(2.138)	(1.227)
Interest coverage ratio	(108.1)	(10.6)	(78.1)	(2.7)

*Amounts based on a nine-month fiscal year.

Exhibit 6.31

Arbortech Altman's Z-Score (Case 6.3)

	Originally Reported Data			Restated Data		
	Year 6	Year 5	Year 4	Year 6	Year 5	Year 4
Net working capital/Total assets	0.8403	0.6496	0.8203	0.8216	0.3915	0.8748
Retained earnings/Total assets	0.1776	0.1674	0.2402	(0.3733)	(0.9801)	(0.2244)
Income before interest and taxes/ Total assets	0.5052	0.2727	0.5404	(0.3139)	(1.9966)	(0.8550)
Market value of equity/Book value of liabilities	15.3089	13.1911	8.0700	16.1620	14.3672	10.6419
Sales/Total assets	0.6785	0.6838	1.0821	0.8123	0.9405	1.4993
Z-score	17.5105	14.9646	10.7530	17.1088	12.7225	11.9366

Financing Activities

LO 7-1 Describe the financial statement reporting of investments by owners (equity issuances) and distributions to owners (dividends and share repurchases).

LO 7-2 Explain the accounting for share-based compensation (stock options, stock appreciation rights, and restricted stock).

LO 7-3 Identify the components of other comprehensive income.

LO 7-4 Apply financial reporting principles to long-term and short-term debt (bonds, notes payable, leases, and troubled debt).

LO 7-5 Explain the accounting for and financial reporting of hybrid securities.

LO 7-6 Describe how operating and capital leases affect financial statements, and make adjustments required to convert operating leases to capital leases.

LO 7-7 Explain how economic effects of derivatives used to hedge interest rate risk are reported in financial statements.

Chapter Overview

Chapter 6 examined the concept of accounting quality. In this and the next two chapters, we describe certain accounting issues in more depth so that you can understand the accounting procedures used by management to, hopefully, best represent the economics of the business. In this chapter, we examine the accounting issues related to *financing* activities, focusing on the right side of the balance sheet, which conveys the results of raising equity capital from investors and debt capital from creditors. We will also examine the effects of financing activities on income and cash flows. Firms engage in financing activities to raise the capital necessary to engage in investing activities (the acquisition of productive and investment assets), which we cover in Chapter 8. Having deployed external capital into productive assets, firms engage in their primary operating activities, which we discuss in Chapter 9. Throughout Chapters 7 to 9, we identify the choices made by management and the principles established by accounting standard setters that lead to published financial statements. Many of the accounting principles are similar under U.S. GAAP and IFRS, but we note significant differences.

We begin with *equity* financing activities, which include raising capital by issuing common stock and preferred stock, the return of capital to shareholders via dividends and share repurchases, and the use of equity (and equity appreciation) to compensate employees via stock options, stock appreciation rights, and restricted stock plans. Then we discuss the effects on shareholders' equity of net income and other comprehensive income. The second section of the chapter deals with *debt* financing activities. We examine the accounting for and reporting of notes payable and bonds, troubled debt, hybrid securities, and liabilities that are not reflected in financial statements (off-balance-sheet financing), including operating leases and their effective capitalization for cross-sectional comparability and risk-analysis purposes. We also discuss the new lease accounting rules set to take effect in 2019. We conclude with a discussion of the use of derivatives to hedge interest rate risk on long-term debt.

LO 7-1

Describe the financial statement reporting of investments by owners (equity issuances) and distributions to owners (dividends and share repurchases).

Equity Financing

Corporations raise a substantial amount of cash by issuing shares of common stock and by deploying the funds received into profitable operations. The amount of shareholders' equity reported in the balance sheet (the *book value* of shareholders' equity) is the investment base for return-on-equity calculations used in profitability analysis (Chapter 4), the measure of owner financing in risk analysis (Chapter 5), and the measure of the value of net assets in place used in residual income-based equity valuation (Chapters 13 and 14). The three primary events that change the book value of shareholders' equity are

- Investments by shareholders, usually net cash received by the company from equity issuance.
- Distributions to shareholders, usually in the form of periodic cash dividend payments to investors and/or share repurchases.
- Profitable operating and investing activities, primarily consisting of net income but also "other comprehensive income."

The following sections discuss the accounting and financial statement disclosures related to these events.[1]

Investments by Shareholders: Common Equity Issuance

The general principle of accounting for common equity issues is to record the equity claim on the balance sheet at the *fair value* of what the corporation initially receives from the investor. If the issuing firm cannot reliably measure fair value of what it receives, it uses the fair value of the equity issued to record the transaction. As long as the fair value of one side of the exchange is determinable, the fair value of the other side of the transaction is implied under the assumption that unrelated parties exchange equal fair values in arm's-length transactions.

Most commonly, an equity investor pays cash to the corporation to acquire shares of stock. However, the investor could transfer assets (such as property) to or perform services for the corporation in return for an equity interest. Instead of issuing common stock to the investor, the corporation could issue other types of equity interests: preferred stock, options to purchase common stock, or stock rights.[2] In any event, the

---

[1] *FASB Codification Topic 505* describes applicable U.S. GAAP on shareholders' equity accounting.

[2] Common shareholders normally possess a preemptive right that enables them to maintain a proportional ownership when the corporation issues additional stock. When a corporation issues stock rights, it receives nothing from investors in return (no effect on financial statements). The issuance of rights is nothing more than a formal recognition of a right that already existed. When investors exercise their stock rights, the resulting issuance of common stock is reported as an issuance of stock for cash. Another type of stock right sometimes issued by a company as a takeover defense, stock purchase rights, allows current shareholders to purchase an additional number of shares in the event that an outside party acquires or attempts to acquire a substantial equity stake in the company.

fair-value rule applies. For example, the fair value received in a common stock issuance is allocated between two contributed capital accounts: common stock (par value) and additional paid-in capital (amount of fair value received that exceeds par value). Additional paid-in capital is generally referred to as *share premium* in many non-U.S. jurisdictions. The partition of proceeds into the par and additional paid-in capital accounts is not important from an analysis viewpoint because par value is declared by the board of directors and has no economic meaning. In fact, some firms issue "no par" common stock.

Common shareholders' equity is the residual interest in the corporation, which equals the assets remaining after all liabilities are paid and all other non–common equity claims (such as preferred stock) are satisfied. Because common shareholders bear both residual upside and downside risk, they generally have control through the right to vote. However, contractual relationships between the firm and other parties can limit common shareholder control. For example, effective control can be obtained through contracts to acquire all of a firm's output or to use all of a firm's productive capacity or through rights to obtain control of productive capacity through purchase at a later date. These types of contracts are common in the area of SPEs (special-purpose entities), which were discussed in Chapter 6. Also, to protect their claims on assets, debtholders often require firms to enter into debt covenants, which restrict common shareholder control of certain operating and financing decisions such as expansion, dividend payment, and additional borrowings.

Corporations sometimes also issue *preferred stock*. Issuing preferred stock involves a trade-off between maintaining corporate control (preferred stock does not have voting rights) and creating a class of shareholders with preference above common equity shareholders in all asset distributions, including dividends. Accounting for the initial issue of preferred stock is no different than accounting for the issue of common stock. The fair-value rule applies when a firm issues preferred stock. Preferred stock (at par) is normally reported before common stock in the shareholders' equity section because preferred shareholders have priority over common shareholders in corporate liquidations. In addition to the preference in dividends and distribution, preferred stock dividends may accumulate if not declared and paid (the cumulative right). These *dividends in arrears* must be declared and paid before common stock dividends are declared and paid and must be disclosed in the notes to the financial statements. Preferred stock may be convertible into common shares (a positive feature for investors) or callable at scheduled dates or at the firm's discretion (a negative feature for investors). The call options that can exist on preferred stock raise the larger issue (discussed in a later section) of whether certain types of preferred stock should be designated as debt rather than equity.

To illustrate basic shareholders' equity accounting, assume that a company raises capital through the following transactions:

1. Issues 100,000 shares of $1 par value common stock for $5 per share.
2. Receives land in exchange for 28,000 shares of $1 par common stock. The equity investor purchased the land for $85,000. Similar land has recently sold for $150,000.
3. Issues 5,000 shares of $10 par value preferred stock for $75,000.

Exhibit 7.1 summarizes the financial statement effects of the transactions. (Let APIC = additional paid-in capital.) Dollar amounts indicate the effects of each transaction on the financial statement elements (that is, on assets, liabilities, or shareholders' equity: contributed capital = CC, accumulated other comprehensive

Exhibit 7.1: Accounting for Common and Preferred Share Issues

Assets	=	Liabilities	+	Shareholders' Equity		
				CC	AOCI	RE
1. Cash 500,000				Common Stock 100,000 APIC 400,000		

```
Cash                        500,000
    Common Stock                    100,000
    APIC                            400,000
```

Assets	=	Liabilities	+	Shareholders' Equity		
				CC	AOCI	RE
2. Cash 150,000				Common Stock 28,000 APIC 122,000		

```
Land                        150,000
    Common Stock                    28,000
    APIC                            122,000
```

Assets	=	Liabilities	+	Shareholders' Equity		
				CC	AOCI	RE
3. Cash 75,000				Preferred Stock 50,000 APIC 25,000		

```
Cash                        75,000
    Preferred Stock                 50,000
    APIC                            25,000
```

income = AOCI, or retained earnings = RE). The applicable journal entry follows each financial statement effect entry.

Shareholders' equity increases by the fair value of the asset (cash) contributed to the corporation in Transaction 1. In Transaction 2, the fair value of the land contributed to the company is a readily determinable $150,000 (cash price of similar land), and this amount becomes the basis for measurement of the transaction. However, often fair values of noncash assets (for example, land) are harder to obtain and may require the corporation to rely on an estimate of the fair value of common shares issued (for example, share price in an active market if available). Note that the entries divide the amounts of contributed capital into par value and additional paid-in capital amounts.

Cash flow effects of these financing activities are reported in the financing section of the statement of cash flows as sources of cash. The issue of stock for land is reported in a separate schedule of "significant investing and financing activities that do not affect cash" that accompanies the statement of cash flows.

Refer to **Starbucks'** September 27, 2015, consolidated balance sheet. In the shareholders' equity section, **Starbucks** discloses that it has *issued and outstanding* 1,485.1 million shares of common stock (out of 2,400 million shares *authorized* for issue by the board of directors). The shares have a par value of $0.001 per share, approximately $1.5 million in total). The balance in additional paid-in capital implies that issue prices over time for common stock and possibly options and warrants (discussed later) have exceeded par value by $41.1 million.

Distributions to Shareholders: Dividends

Net income is accumulated through time in retained earnings, which is reported as part of shareholders' equity on the balance sheet. Dividend distributions reduce retained earnings. They are simply a transfer to shareholders of a portion of what they already own—the increase over time in the net assets of the firm recognized as net income. The portion of net income retained by the firm represents reinvestments by shareholders.

The declaration of dividends is formalized by three important dates because of the administrative complexity of identifying shareholders of record at any given point in time.

- On the date on which the board of directors declares a dividend, called the *date of declaration*, the firm incurs a legal liability to distribute the dividend.
- The recipients of the dividend will be the owners of the stock as of a specific future date, called the *date of record*.
- On the *date of payment*, the dividend distribution occurs.

Typically, these three dates are several weeks apart.

Corporations generally pay dividends in cash. However, corporations can also pay dividends with interest-bearing promissory notes (scrip dividends), investments in other corporations' stock (property dividends), and corporate assets, such as property (dividends in kind).

At the *date of declaration*, the retained earnings component of shareholders' equity is reduced by the fair value of the item to be distributed and a liability is recorded. Dividends decrease the net assets of a corporation, and this decrease is reported in the statement of shareholders' equity. The *date of record* has no impact on the corporation's accounting. No change in equity occurs on the *date of payment* because both assets (cash or property) and liabilities (dividends payable) decrease (that is, no change in *net* assets). If dividends are declared but not paid by year-end, a (nonoperating) liability for dividends payable appears in the current liabilities section of the balance sheet.[3]

In many jurisdictions (especially outside the U.S.), the balance of retained earnings represents the limit for dividend payments. However, payments to shareholders that exceed the balance in retained earnings, called *liquidating dividends*, can occur. If the dividend is greater than the retained earnings balance, in most jurisdictions, the increment must be used to decrease contributed capital. In the extreme case of firm liquidation, the liquidating dividend equals the amount of equity each shareholder is entitled to upon liquidation of the firm.

Stock Dividends and Stock Splits

On occasion, corporations distribute additional shares of their own stock to current stockholders in the form of *stock dividends*. Unlike other forms of dividends, stock dividends

- do *not* involve a transfer of assets to investors.
- do *not* change total shareholders' equity.
- do *not* change the proportional ownership of shareholders.
- do *not* change investor wealth.

---

[3]IFRS (*IAS 1*) requires disclosure of proposed but not yet approved dividends and post-year-end declared dividends.

The effects of stock dividends and splits on retained earnings and contributed capital are determined by accounting rules and jurisdictional legal requirements. In small stock dividends (distributions of less than 20–25% of common shares), the fair value of shares issued is transferred out of retained earnings and into contributed capital. U.S. GAAP is ambiguous with respect to midrange dividends (20–100%), and laws of the state of incorporation frequently determine the accounting treatment. However, in most cases (and consistent with SEC guidance), midrange stock dividends are treated as a transfer of the par value of shares from retained earnings to contributed capital accounts.

Most large distributions that are greater than or equal to 100% are in the form of a *stock split*. Suppose a company wanted to double the number of shares outstanding (which would mechanically result in the price of its stock dropping by half). This could be accomplished by issuing a 100% stock dividend or a 2-for-1 stock split. Similar to midrange stock dividends, accounting for a large stock dividend depends on applicable state law. Most of the time, the par value of the shares is transferred to common stock from either retained earnings or additional paid-in capital. Firms may also wish to reduce the number of shares outstanding using a *reverse stock split*. For example, in a 1-for-2 reverse stock split, the number of shares outstanding is reduced by 50% and the stock price per share doubles. In the past, firms have engaged in reverse stock splits to meet minimum share price requirements to be listed on organized exchanges and to attract institutional investors that may have policies prohibiting the acquisition of shares traded below a threshold price.

In a stock split, U.S. GAAP does not require an amount to be shifted from retained earnings to contributed capital, but state laws may allow an amount to be shifted from either retained earnings or additional paid-in capital to common stock. Accounting rules require that the par value of individual shares be adjusted so that the total par value after the stock split is the same as the total par value before the split. Therefore, in a 2-for-1 split of 50,000 shares of $10 par value stock, a company issues an additional 50,000 shares and reduces par value to $5 on all 100,000 shares.

From an analysis perspective, it is important to remember that

- the accounting for stock dividends and splits simply reallocates amounts *within* shareholders' equity.
- the total amount of shareholders' equity remains unchanged because assets have not been disbursed from the corporation (that is, cash has not been paid out).
- increasing the number of shares outstanding proportionately decreases per-share amounts for earnings, book value, and cash flow.

To illustrate the accounting for stock dividends and splits, assume that Mystic, Inc., reports the following in its 2017 financial statements:

- Common stock, $3 par, 2,263 million shares outstanding
- Average share price during 2017: approximately $20
- Common dividends paid during 2017: $0.20 per share

Exhibit 7.2 shows the financial statement effects of the following events. (Assume the events are independent.)

1. Mystic declares and pays a dividend of $452.6 million (2,263 million shares × $0.20 per share). Assume that the dividends are declared and then paid at a later date.
2. Mystic distributes a property dividend by giving common shareholders common shares of another company that it carries as a short-term investment in

Exhibit 7.2: Accounting for Stock Dividends and Splits (amounts in millions)

Declaration:

	Assets	=	Liabilities	+	Shareholders' Equity		
					CC	AOCI	RE
1.			Dividends Payable 452.6				Retained Earnings (452.6)

Retained Earnings	452.6	
Dividends Payable		452.6

Date of record: No entry

Payment:

	Assets	=	Liabilities	+	Shareholders' Equity		
					CC	AOCI	RE
1.	Cash (452.6)		Dividends Payable 452.6				

Dividends Payable	452.6	
Cash		452.6

	Assets	=	Liabilities	+	Shareholders' Equity		
					CC	AOCI	RE
2.	Investments (2.0)						Retained Earnings (2.0)

Retained Earnings	2.0	
Investments		2.0

	Assets	=	Liabilities	+	Shareholders' Equity		
					CC	AOCI	RE
3.					Common Stock 678.9 APIC 3,847.1		Retained Earnings (4,526.0)

Retained Earnings	4,526.0	
Common Stock		678.9
APIC		3,847.1

	Assets	=	Liabilities	+	Shareholders' Equity		
					CC	AOCI	RE
4.					Common Stock 6,789.3		Retained Earnings (6,789.3)

Retained Earnings	6,789.3	
Common Stock		6,789.3

5. Memorandum entry only to note that the number of shares outstanding doubles to 4,526.2 million and the par value decreases to $1.50 per share.
6. Memorandum entry only to note that number of shares outstanding falls in half to 1,131.6 million and the par value doubles to $6 per share.

marketable securities. The securities have a fair value of $2.0 million and an original cost of $1.8 million. Mystic uses mark-to-market accounting for these securities and declares the dividend shortly after the securities have been marked to market.

3. Mystic distributes a 10% stock dividend (10% × 2,263 million shares outstanding = 226.3 million shares; 226.3 million shares × $3 = $678.9 million par value; 226.3 million shares × $20 market price = $4,526 million fair value).

4. Mystic distributes a 100% stock dividend (2,263 million additional shares; 2,263 × $3 = $6,789 million par value).

5. Mystic declares a 2-for-1 stock split.

6. Mystic declares a 1-for-2 reverse stock split.

Note that dividends distributed in the form of assets (that is, cash and property; Transactions 1 and 2) decrease shareholders' equity (the sum of the last three columns). Dividends distributed in the form of common stock (Transactions 3 and 4) generate a rearrangement of shareholders' equity but no change in total shareholders' equity. Likewise, stock splits (Transactions 5 and 6) have no effect on total shareholders' equity or the balance of any account in shareholders' equity. Cash outflow for cash dividends is reported in the financing section of the statement of cash flows.[4]

Refer to **Starbucks'** consolidated statement of common shareholders' equity. In the retained earnings column, **Starbucks** reports $1,016.2 million cash dividends declared in fiscal 2015 on common stock (see the bottom third of the statement) and a small reduction due to a stock split ($0.8 million). **Starbucks'** consolidated statement of cash flows reports $928.6 million cash dividends paid in the financing activities section. **Starbucks** reports the excess of dividends declared over dividends paid ($87.6 million) as of the balance sheet date as a nonoperating liability, "Accrued dividends payable."[5]

Distributions to Shareholders: Share Repurchases

For several reasons, corporations may distribute cash to shareholders and reduce shareholders' equity via *share repurchases*. For example, employee compensation plans often grant options to acquire common stock. To service the possible exercise of options, companies may repurchase shares to have a supply of their own stock on hand or, alternatively, to offset the dilution of existing shareholders' proportional ownership from share issuances under the option exercises. Corporations also might repurchase stock simply to shift the mix of debt and equity financing or to signal to investors that corporate management believes the stock is undervalued. Finally, fewer shares outstanding mean less dilution of voting power. This may be particularly important if the firm is facing a takeover attempt.

Share repurchases reduce equity, and the effects on the statement of cash flows are simple. Using cash to reduce equity is a cash outflow reported as a financing activity. Similarly, the effects on the income statement are simple: the reduction of equity is a distribution to owners, a transaction that does *not* affect income. Balance sheet effects of share repurchases depend on whether the shares of stock are retired or held as treasury stock for eventual reissue. If the shares are retired, the amounts originally recorded in the common stock (that is, par value) and the additional paid-in capital accounts are removed. **Microsoft** and **Starbucks** are examples of companies that repeatedly engage in large share repurchases and the retirement of the purchased shares, either by choice or because state law requires the retirement. In fact, **Starbucks'** $1,436.1 million cash outflow to repurchase its shares in fiscal 2015 is its single largest use of cash for the year. The typical case is that the cash paid to retire the shares exceeds the amount at which the shares were originally issued. This excess is treated as a dividend, and like regular cash dividends, it is removed from retained earnings. Less typical is the case in which

---

[4]Transactions 3 and 4 assume that Mystic declares a stock dividend and distributes the dividend in the same period. If a financial statement reporting date intervenes, "stock dividend distributable" will be reported as a contra-equity account instead of a reduction in retained earnings as shown in the template.

[5]**Starbucks** reports the accrued dividends payable account in Note 7. The balance increased only $57.2 million between September 28, 2014, and September 27, 2015 ($297.0 million – $239.8 million). The most likely cause of this discrepancy is that a portion of dividends payable was paid off during an acquisition of shares. In its statement of cash flows, **Starbucks** reports cash outflows of $360.8 million to purchase a noncontrolling interest and $1,436.1 million to repurchase shares.

the amount paid to buy back the shares is less than the original issue price. In this case, additional paid-in capital is increased as if the shareholders left amounts in the firm as a permanent capital contribution.

If firms repurchase stock for reissue at a later date, the stock is referred to as *treasury stock*. There are two acceptable methods to account for treasury stock: the cost method and the par method. Because the par method is rarely used, we focus our discussion on the cost method. The cost method was designed under the assumption that any treasury stock acquired would be reissued.

Using cash to acquire stock to be held in the treasury decreases shareholders' equity. The treasury stock acquired is not an asset of the corporation. A corporation cannot own itself. The payment of cash to owners is a distribution to owners. Under the cost method, this distribution is shown as an increase in a contra-equity account called Treasury Stock. The increase in contra-equity is equivalent to a decrease in equity. Under the cost method, the Treasury Stock account is usually shown at the bottom of the shareholders' equity section. Subsequent treasury share reissues reduce the treasury stock contra-equity account and increase (or decrease) additional paid-in capital if the subsequent reissue price is greater than (less than) the cost of the treasury stock. No gain or loss is recorded because the reissue of treasury stock is, in concept, identical to the original issue of common stock (cash invested, common stock issued).

Equity Issued as Compensation: Stock Options

LO 7-2

Explain the accounting for share-based compensation (stock options, stock appreciation rights, and restricted stock).

Firms develop compensation plans to attract, retain, and motivate employees. Many of these plans include a cash compensation component that is fixed (salary) and a component that varies with levels of employee performance (bonus), which is often defined by an accounting-based income measure (such as return on equity) or stock returns. In a typical compensation arrangement, firms give employees the right, or option, to acquire shares of common stock at a fixed price. If share prices increase over time, employees can exercise their option to purchase shares at a price that is less than the market price of the shares. The use of such *stock options* skyrocketed during the 1990s and early 2000s. Firms in the technology sector have used options as a dominant component of their employee compensation packages.[6]

Stock options permit employees to purchase shares of common stock at a price usually equal to (or just above) the market price of the stock at the time the firm grants the stock option. Employees exercise these stock options at a later time if the stock price increases above the stock option exercise price. Corporations grant stock options because they have characteristics that align the interests of the employees with those of the shareholders. Clearly, an increase in stock price benefits shareholders, which is the same way stock options reward employees. Unlike compensation in the form of salaries, however, stock options do not require firms to use cash during the period in which the stock options are granted. In addition, the ability of a corporation to attract and retain employees is enhanced when firms offer equity incentives such as stock options as part of the compensation package. Employees with unvested stock options have an incentive to continue their employment with the company until they can exercise their options.

---

[6]Due to more recent concerns about excessive executive compensation, the use of stock options has declined to some degree. However, many companies still use stock option plans for incentive compensation.

An understanding of the accounting for stock-based compensation requires understanding several key parameters:

- A firm gives a stock option to an employee on the *grant date*.
- Employees can first exercise their stock options on the *vesting date*.
  - Employees cannot exercise options before the vesting date or after the end of the option's life.
  - To enhance employee retention and increase motivation during the vesting period, firms usually structure stock option plans so that a period of time elapses between the grant date and the vesting date (often two or three years).
  - Firms may preclude employees from exercising the option for one or more years, or they may set an exercise price so high that employees would not want to exercise the option until the stock price increases.
- Employees elect to exchange the options plus cash for shares of common stock on the *exercise date*.
- The *exercise price* is the price specified in the stock option contract for purchasing the common stock.
- The *market price* is the price of the stock as it trades in the market.
- In theory, the value of a stock option has two elements: (1) the benefit realized on the exercise date because the market price of the stock exceeds the exercise price (the *benefit element*) and (2) the length of the period during which the holder can exercise the option (the *time-value element*).

The amount of the benefit element is not known until the exercise date. In general, stock options with exercise prices less than the current market price of the stock (described as *in the money*) have a higher value than stock options with exercise prices exceeding the current market price of the stock (described as *out of the money*).

The time-value element of an option results from the benefit it provides its holder if the market price of the stock increases during the exercise period. The greater the market price of the stock exceeds the exercise price during the exercise period, the greater the benefit to the option holder. This time-value element of an option will have more value the longer the exercise period, the more volatile the market price of the stock, the lower the dividend yield, and the lower the discount rate. Note that a stock option may have an exercise price that exceeds the current market price (zero value for the benefit element) but still have value because of the possibility that the market price will exceed the exercise price on the exercise date (positive value for the time-value element). As the expiration date of the option approaches, the value of the time-value element approaches zero.

Fair value is the basis for stock option accounting.[7] Firms must measure the fair value of stock options on the date of grant. Because the value of employee stock options typically cannot be measured with an observable value established by trading in an active market, most firms will estimate the fair value of the options with the Black-Scholes model or a lattice model (for example, the binomial model). A detailed discussion of option valuation models can be found in the finance literature and is beyond the scope of this text. However, any model employed must incorporate a variety of factors, including the exercise price of the option, the term of the option, the current market

---

[7] *FASB Codification Topic 718*. The promulgation of FASB *Statement No. 123 (Revised 2004)* represents a convergence with international standards. International Accounting Standards Board, *International Financial Reporting Standard 2*, "Share-Based Payment."

price of each share of underlying stock, expected stock price volatility, dividends, and the risk-free interest rate.[8]

Once the firm estimates the fair value of stock options as of the grant date, it must recognize this amount as compensation expense ratably over the period in which an employee provides services (commonly, the vesting period) and disclose the effects of the stock option grants on total compensation expense, the methodology (model) used to value the stock options, and the key assumptions made to estimate the value of the stock options.[9]

Illustration of Accounting for Stock Options

Assume that an Internet-based company decides to conserve cash and align management incentives with shareholders' incentives by compensating managers with 9,000 options to purchase $1 par value common stock for $10 per share. The current stock price is $10 per share. The vesting period is three years, and the options can be exercised during the following seven years. Using an appropriate options pricing model, the company values the options at $2 each.

Exhibit 7.3 illustrates the financial statement effects of these transactions:

1. Grant date.
2. Recognition of compensation expense for each of the three years in the vesting period.
3. Exercise of an option when a share of common stock is trading at $18.
4. Expiration of an option.
5. Forfeiture of an option early in the third year of the vesting period when a manager leaves the firm.

The options' fair value is $18,000 ($2 per option × 9,000 options). No financial statement effects occur at the grant date because the manager has yet to provide service to the firm. The $18,000 fair value is allocated over the three-year vesting period, $6,000 per year, as an increase in compensation expense (a decrease in net income, which is also a decrease in retained earnings). Rather than accepting cash compensation, the manager accepts an option to acquire an equity interest; therefore, APIC from stock options increases shareholders' equity. Note that the net effect of Transaction 2 on total shareholders' equity (the sum of the last three columns) is zero (retained earnings decreases, but APIC increases).

Exercise of an option (Transaction 3) involves a transfer of the stock option plus a $10 exercise price from the manager to the corporation. Through the effects on three

---

[8]For an elaboration on the history of options pricing, see Fischer Black and Myron Scholes, "The Pricing of Options and Corporate Liabilities," *Journal of Political Economy* (May/June 1973), pp. 637–654. A critique of the reliability of various valuation models can be found in American Accounting Association's Financial Accounting Standards Committee, "Response to the FASB's Exposure Draft on Share-Based Payment: An Amendment of FASB *Statements No. 123* and *No. 95*," *Accounting Horizons* (June 2005), pp. 101–114.

[9]Recently, the FASB issued an accounting update (No. 2014-12, June 2014) to Topic 718, *Compensation—Stock Compensation*, which clarified the accounting for situations where a performance condition for management extends beyond the service period. For example, the vesting of an option might be conditional on whether the firm engages in an IPO. In this type of situation, compensation expense should be recognized in the period when the IPO becomes probable. This accounting could create a situation in which no compensation expense is recognized during the period in which managers render service, and all of the compensation expense is recognized in a later period. IFRS has different rules. In a December 2013 amendment to IFRS 2, the IASB decided that performance conditions that could be achieved after the vesting period should be treated as nonvesting conditions and taken into account when determining the grant-date fair value of the award.

Exhibit 7.3: Accounting for Stock Options

1. No entry at grant date. (The contract is executory.) However, the fair value of the options is measured at the grant date. Fair value = 9,000 options ×
$2 per option = $18,000.

Years 1, 2, and 3:

	Assets	=	Liabilities	+	Shareholders' Equity		
					CC	AOCI	RE
2.					APIC—Stock Options 6,000		Compensation Expense (6,000)

Each year		
Compensation Expense	6,000	
APIC—Stock Options		6,000

Exercise:

	Assets	=	Liabilities	+	Shareholders' Equity		
					CC	AOCI	RE
3.	Cash 10				Common Stock 1 APIC 11 APIC—Stock Options (2)		

Cash	10	
APIC—Stock Options	2	
Common Stock		1
APIC		11

Expiration:

	Assets	=	Liabilities	+	Shareholders' Equity		
					CC	AOCI	RE
4.					APIC—Expired Options 2 APIC—Stock Options (2)		

APIC—Stock Options	2	
APIC—Expired Options		2

Revocation:

	Assets	=	Liabilities	+	Shareholders' Equity		
					CC	AOCI	RE
5.					APIC—Stock Options (2)		Compensation Expense 2

APIC—Stock Options	2	
Compensation Expense		2

shareholders' equity accounts, total shareholders' equity increases by $10, the fair value of the cash received. Note that the cash received is not equal to the fair value of the common equity, which is trading at $18. The amount reflected in the equity accounts after this transaction is posted is $1 in common stock and $11 in additional paid-in capital. Thus, common stock issued is recorded at $12, which equals the fair value of the cash surrendered ($10) plus the grant date estimate of the fair value of the option surrendered ($2).[10]

If stock options expire (Transaction 4), the capital contributed to the firm by the manager's employment is reclassified as a permanent contribution to shareholders' equity. If a manager fails to perform the three years of service, the option is revoked (Transaction 5). The amount of the compensation expense related to revoked options is removed from compensation expense of the current period. This treatment is an

---

[10]If previously acquired treasury shares rather than new shares are issued, treasury stock is reduced by the amount of the original acquisition cost and APIC is used to record the remainder of the equity increase.

example of a change in estimate handled prospectively. The firm estimated that compensation expense was $6,000 per year based on the expected three-year service of employees. If an employee leaves the firm and an option is revoked, estimates must be revised *going forward*. Prior period adjustments to expenses are not made.[11]

Option events create two cash flows. The exercise of an option increases cash from equity issues and is reported as a financing activity. Although not shown in the preceding template, the corporation will receive a tax deduction at the date the manager exercises the option, equal to the market price at the exercise date minus the exercise price. (The manager will be taxed on this same amount because it is compensation.) The tax savings is treated as a financing cash inflow.

Options "Overhang"

The existence of unexercised options and the expected future issuance of shares create a potentially dilutive effect on firm value. When options are exercised, firms receive cash equal to the exercise price but must transfer shares to the option holder. The exercise price is often considerably less than the market price of a share, so the firm must use additional cash, which would have been free cash flow to current shareholders, to buy back outstanding shares from the market. Alternatively, the firm could issue new shares, but again, this has a dilutive effect on value per share for existing shareholders.

Options "overhang" is the ratio of outstanding options to outstanding shares, and it can be significant, especially for technology firms that tend to compensate with options. For example, **Cisco**'s options overhang was slightly under 10% as of the end of 2012, but exceeded 20% five years earlier. Cisco's options overhang was reduced by substantial exercises and open market share repurchases to satisfy the exercises.

Firms disclose the potential cash flow consequences of options overhang to existing shareholders, measured by the difference between current market price and the exercise price (i.e., the intrinsic value of the options), in the notes to the financial statements. For example, in Note 12, **Starbucks** discloses that the intrinsic values of exercisable stock options and restricted stock units as of September 27, 2015, are $1,150 million and $620 million, respectively. The cash flow consequences will be mitigated by the tax deduction taken by the firm when the employee exercises. Also, some of these options are not currently exercisable. For example, **Starbucks** also discloses that, of the $1,150 million as of September 27, 2015, the intrinsic values of currently exercisable options and currently vested or expected-to-vest options are $872 million and $1,125 million, respectively. This disclosure suggests that most of the $1,150 million relates to stock that will be exercised.

Alternative Share-Based Compensation: Restricted Stock and RSUs

Exercising stock options can create a cash flow problem for employees. The employee must pay the exercise price and may have to pay taxes on compensation in order to acquire the stock, which he or she may want to hold rather than sell. An alternative

---

[11]We assume that the forfeiture was unexpected. If forfeitures are expected, then the firm has the option to lower the original estimate of compensation expense and use the treatment we show for unexpected additional forfeitures, or not account for expected forfeitures initially and just account for them as they occur using the method we illustrate. This is a recent effort to simplify the accounting in *FASB Topic 718*. Also, we reduced compensation expense by the entire amount of the option (instead of the two-thirds already recognized as compensation expense) assuming that the last year's worth of the compensation expense allocation would be unaffected. An alternative would be to reduce compensation expense by $2 \times 2/3$ and reduce the $6,000 compensation expense for Year 3 by the same amount.

share-based compensation program eliminates a manager's need to pay the exercise price. At the grant date, the manager could be given shares of stock rather than options (far fewer shares than options because the fair value of a share is usually greater than the fair value of an option to purchase the stock), which cannot be traded until after a vesting period (*restricted stock*).[12] Or the manager could receive nontradable rights for a number of shares of stock once the vesting period is completed (called *restricted stock units*, or RSUs).

To illustrate the accounting for restricted stock, assume that an Internet-based company decides to compensate managers by giving them 1,000 shares of $1 par value common stock when the market price is $10 per share. The vesting period is two years, and the stock cannot be traded until after the vesting period. Exhibit 7.4 illustrates the financial statement effects of the following transactions:

1. Grant date.
2. Recognition of compensation expense during the vesting period.

In contrast to an option grant, the firm issues common stock at the grant date, so it makes an entry to recognize the issuance of the common stock (Transaction 1). Note that no change in net assets occurred, so total shareholders' equity does not change. The amount of compensation is more reliably measured (relative to an option) given that the fair value of the stock is more easily measured by reference to market prices. During the vesting period, as managers earn the compensation under the restricted stock plan (Transaction 2), the firm recognizes compensation expenses, which reduces net income and therefore retained earnings, and it reduces deferred compensation expense, a contra-equity account. The net effect of the second transaction is a shift of amounts out of retained earnings into contributed capital. Again, no change in assets or liabilities occurred, so total shareholders' equity does not change.

Exhibit 7.4: Accounting for Restricted Stock

Grant Date:

	Assets	=	Liabilities	+	Shareholders' Equity		
					CC	AOCI	RE
1.					Common Stock 1,000 APIC 9,000 Deferred Compensation (10,000)		

	Deferred Compensation
	   Common Stock
	   APIC
					10,000
					1,000
					9,000		

Years 1 and 2:

	Assets	=	Liabilities	+	Shareholders' Equity		
					CC	AOCI	RE
2.					Deferred Compensation 5,000		Compensation Expenses (5,000)
	Each Year: Compensation Expense Deferred Compensation				5,000 5,000		

---

[12]The descriptor *restricted* simply means that the stock granted is generally restricted from being traded until it vests; the holder of restricted shares is usually entitled to dividends and voting rights.

The decrease in stock option use in recent years has been offset by an increase in the use of restricted stock plans and cash settlement plans. Once the FASB disallowed the use of the previously acceptable intrinsic value method to value stock options (usually at $0), one benefit of using stock options for compensation—no expense on the income statement—disappeared. As a consequence, the use of restricted stock became more common, and although there are some tax ramifications to the employee, a primary benefit to the employee of restricted stock grants relative to option grants is that options can expire worthless but restricted stock almost always has a nonzero value.

Alternative Share-Based Compensation: Cash-Settled Share-Based Plans

The number, complexity, and diversity of share-based compensation plans do not permit a comprehensive treatment in any given textbook. However, the stock option, restricted stock, and RSU plans illustrated in this chapter represent the large majority of share-based compensation plans.

In recent years, a number of firms have created compensation plans that provide cash compensation to employees based on share-price appreciation. These plans, often called *stock appreciation rights* plans, are cash-settled plans and, accordingly, do not result in increases in the contributed capital portion of shareholders' equity pursuant to a distribution of an option or a share of common stock. Conceptually, cash-settled share appreciation plans are similar to compensating employees with cash bonuses for output (for example, exceeding sales quotes or earnings targets). The key difference is that the firm relies on the stock market's assessment of the value of the firm to determine the amount of the cash payment.

The essence of the accounting for cash-settled compensation plans is an increase in an operating liability for the estimated cash payments to the employee and a corresponding increase in compensation expense. For example, **SAP AG**'s IFRS-based financial statements describe the workings of its STAR plan and note the following: "As our STAR plans are settled in cash, rather than by issuing equity instruments, a liability is recorded for such plans based on the current fair value of the STAR awards at the reporting date."

Note 12, "Employee Stock and Benefit Plans," describes **Starbucks'** stock option and RSU plans. **Starbucks** reports four line items in its 2015 consolidated statement of cash flows that relate to share-based compensation arrangements. In the financing activities section, cash proceeds from the issuance of common stock (which includes primarily the exercise of stock options) totaled $191.8 million. The financing activities section also includes the excess tax benefits from the deduction afforded **Starbucks** when employees exercise their options, $132.4 million in 2015. Because stock option–based compensation is an operating expense that reduces net income (and the tax savings increases net income), two line items exist in the operating activities section as well. Under the indirect method of preparing this section, stock-based compensation expense is a noncash expense; thus, **Starbucks** adds back the $209.8 million to net income. Also, although the excess tax benefits are a source of cash, the source is not considered an operating activity by rule; thus, **Starbucks** deducts the $132.4 million tax benefits in the operating activities section.[13]

---

[13]In March 2016, the FASB issued an update intended to simplify accounting and reporting in the stock-based compensation area (*Topic 718*). In future financial statements, the cash flow benefit from the excess tax deduction will be classified as an operating cash flow.

- Although there are many kinds of capital transactions with owners, each involves the exchange of something of value (cash, property, services, labor, etc.) for a right to the item of value (for example, a share of common stock or an option to acquire it).
- Fair value is the basis for recording each of the transactions.

- When the item of value is transferred to the firm, such as cash to purchase shares or labor to acquire stock options, owners' equity increases. When the item of value is transferred to the owner, such as cash to pay dividends or to reacquire shares, owners' equity decreases.

LO 7-3

Identify the components of other comprehensive income.

Net Income, Retained Earnings, Accumulated Other Comprehensive Income, and Reserves

In addition to contributed capital, earned capital is available to finance investing and operating activities. The following sections describe the reporting of earned capital.

Net Income and Retained Earnings

Many of the financing events examined so far—equity issues, share buybacks, and cash dividends—are transactions with shareholders that change shareholders' equity directly. Profitable investing and operating activities also lead to increases in shareholders' equity via net income. Through the accounting closing process, net income increases retained earnings on the statement of shareholders' equity, which supports the balance in retained earnings reported on the balance sheet.

The bottom third of **Starbucks'** 2015 consolidated statement of shareholders' equity reconciles the balance of retained earnings at the beginning of fiscal 2015 ($5,206.6 million) to its balance at the balance sheet date, September 27, 2015 ($5,974.8 million). The first reconciling item is net earnings of $2,757.4 million, which increases retained earnings (and, thus, shareholders' equity). Cash dividends declared ($1,016.2 million) and share repurchases ($972.2 million) decrease retained earnings.

Accumulated Other Comprehensive Income

Another component of shareholders' equity, *AOCI (accumulated other comprehensive income)*, is a consequence of standard setters allowing certain asset and liability revaluations (called *other comprehensive income items*) to bypass the income statement and be reported directly in shareholders' equity (as opposed to the treatment of net income, which first appears on the income statement and then increases shareholders' equity via retained earnings).[14] Chapter 3 introduced the comprehensive income concept. This chapter provides a brief discussion of the items comprising AOCI, with subsequent chapters discussing the detailed accounting and reporting. Under U.S. GAAP, firms recognize four items in AOCI, and IFRS adds a fifth item:

- *Unrealized gains and losses from investments in available-for-sale securities.* Other comprehensive income arises when firms experience unrealized fair value gains

---

[14]*FASB Codification Topic 220*; International Accounting Standards Board, *International Accounting Standard 1, "Presentation of Financial Statements."*

or losses on securities deemed available for sale (described in detail in Chapter 8). Each year, a firm will recognize in the statement of comprehensive income the net change in unrealized fair value gains or losses on available-for-sale securities, which are reported cumulatively in AOCI. When the firm sells the securities, it eliminates the unrealized gain or loss account and recognizes a realized gain or loss in measuring net income.[15]

- *Unrealized gains and losses from translation of foreign financial statements during the consolidation process.* U.S. firms with foreign operations usually translate the financial statements of their foreign entities into U.S. dollars each period using the exchange rate at the end of the period (also discussed in detail in Chapter 8). Changes in the exchange rate cause an unrealized foreign currency gain or loss. Firms do not recognize this gain or loss in measuring net income each period; instead, they recognize foreign currency translation gains and losses in the statement of comprehensive income, and accordingly increase or decrease AOCI in shareholders' equity. Presumably, using AOCI to capture such unrealized gains and losses minimizes the impact of the volatility of foreign currency exchange rates on reported profits while reflecting current values of assets and liabilities. If exchange rates reverse or the firm disposes of the foreign unit, it eliminates the unrealized foreign currency adjustment from AOCI and, in the case of a disposal, recognizes a gain or loss in net income.

- *Unrealized gains and losses from certain hedging activities.* Discussed in a latter part of this chapter and again in Chapter 9, changes in the fair value of cash flow hedges are also reported as other comprehensive income and accumulated in other comprehensive income on the balance sheet. When the hedged cash flows occur and generate an income statement effect, an offsetting portion of the AOCI is reclassified into current net income.

- *Unrealized gains and losses from changes in certain pension assets and liabilities.* Pension accounting (discussed in detail in Chapter 9) is driven by changes in two key economic amounts: the pension liability, which is the present value of all future expected pension payments to retirees, and the pension asset, which is the fair value of cash and securities set aside to make those payments. *Expected* changes in the liability, determined by the discount rate used to compute the liability's present value and the service credits earned during the period by current employees, and *expected* changes in the asset, determined by the expected return on asset investments, are reflected in current period net income through pension expense. *Unexpected* changes in the asset and liability, driven by changes in the discount rate, actual returns on assets, and changes in other actuarial assumptions such as life expectancy, are treated as unrealized gains and losses and reported in AOCI. They are amortized to current period net income over time.

- *Unrealized gains and losses from revaluations of long-lived operating assets (IFRS).* IFRS permits periodic revaluations of fixed assets and intangible assets to their current market value (discussed in Chapter 8). Increased valuation of assets leads

---

[15]On January 5, 2016, the FASB issued *Accounting Standards Update 2016-01*, "Financial Instruments—Overall: Recognitions and Measurement of Financial Assets and Financial Liabilities." Under this new rule, effective for financial statements covering fiscal years beginning after December 15, 2017 (essentially 2018 financial statements), the available-for-sale classification will be removed, causing all gains and losses on revaluation of such investments to pass through net income instead of accumulate in other comprehensive income. Also, that new rule adds a new comprehensive income item to reflect gains and losses on changes in firm-specific credit risk for firms that choose the fair value option to report financial liabilities (discussed later in this chapter).

to an increase in a revaluation reserve account included in the shareholders' equity section of the balance sheet (similar to AOCI). Depreciation or amortization of the revalued assets may appear fully on the income statement each period as an expense or may be split between the income statement (depreciation or amortization based on acquisition cost) and a reduction in the revaluation reserve (depreciation or amortization based on the excess of current market value over acquisition cost).

Given that total shareholders' equity is the same regardless of whether the unrealized gain or loss immediately affects net income or affects another shareholders' equity account (AOCI) and later affects net income, your primary concern with other comprehensive income is the appropriateness of revaluing the associated asset or liability and delaying recognition of its effect in net income. To the extent that the changes in AOCI are transitory (it is, after all, difficult to predict future changes in interest rates, market returns, and exchange rates), the amounts should be excluded from predictions of future earnings. However, you should consider whether management can control the timing of reclassifications of AOCI to current income. We consider this issue in the context of trading securities in Chapter 8.

Fluctuations in comprehensive income and AOCI reflect risks. The fluctuations are quantifications of the effect on value of the firms' exposures to interest rate, market return, exchange rate, and commodity price risk. A look at a firm's comprehensive income through time confirms that comprehensive income is generally far more volatile than net income. A good example of this volatility appears in Exhibit 7.5.

The Statement of Comprehensive Income reports the current period changes in the accumulated comprehensive income items included in shareholders' equity. **Delta** has substantial fluctuation in net income over the three-year period, from a low of $659 million profit in 2014 to a high of $10,540 million profit in 2013. The fluctuation in comprehensive income is greater, from a low of $1,522 million loss in 2014 to a high of $13,987 million profit in 2013. The large fluctuations occurred because the discount rates used to compute Delta's 2014 pension liabilities decreased, causing the liability to

Exhibit 7.5

Fluctuations in Delta Airlines, Inc.'s Net Income and Comprehensive Income

DELTA AIR LINES, INC.

Consolidated Statements of Comprehensive Income (Loss)

(in millions)	Year Ended December 31,		
	2015	2014	2013
Net Income	$4,526	$ 659	$10,540
Other comprehensive income (loss):			
Net (loss) gain on foreign currency and interest rate derivatives	(82)	3	482
Net change in pension and other benefits	163	(2,194)	2,984
Net (loss) gain on investments	(45)	10	(19)
Total Other Comprehensive Income (Loss)	36	(2,181)	3,447
Comprehensive Income (Loss)	$4,562	$(1,522)	$13,987

be much larger (a loss reflected in other comprehensive income). Assumed life expectancy increased as well, causing the liability to become larger (more months of future payouts), which adds to that loss. Discount rates used to compute the 2013 pension liability increased, reducing the pension liability (a gain reflected in other comprehensive income). It is clear that changes in rates used to remeasure certain assets and liabilities can cause large, and generally transitory, fluctuations in comprehensive income.

Refer to the common shareholders' equity section of **Starbucks'** consolidated balance sheet. At September 27, 2015, **Starbucks** reports retained earnings of $5,974.8 million and an accumulated other comprehensive loss of $199.4 million. The retained earnings balance represents accumulated (over the life of **Starbucks**) increases in net assets of the company, *which were reported in net income*, minus dividends declared and share repurchases. The accumulated other comprehensive loss represents decreases in net assets of the company from asset and liability revaluations, *which have not yet been reported in net income*. **Starbucks'** consolidated statement of common shareholders' equity describes how accumulated other comprehensive loss changed during fiscal 2015 from a beginning accumulated income of $25.3 million to the ending accumulated loss of $199.4 million reported in the balance sheet. The change in the balance is explained by other comprehensive income of the period and any change due to acquisitions and divestitures. Aside from a relatively small change in accumulated comprehensive income recognized when it acquired a noncontrolling interest in its subsidiaries (a $31.1 million decrease), the change in balance primarily relates to other comprehensive income of the period (a $193.6 million decrease). **Starbucks** shows the other comprehensive income items in a consolidated statement of comprehensive income. The primary source of other comprehensive income in fiscal 2015 is a $222.7 currency translation loss. One argument for recognizing such gains and losses in other comprehensive income and in the Accumulated Other Comprehensive Income/Loss account is that these types of revaluations of assets and liabilities tend to be transitory; that is, they have the potential to reverse over time. You should examine the behavior of accumulated other comprehensive income through time to see whether including elements of other comprehensive income in current income would aid in the assessment of the risk of the firm and in the prediction of future income.

Summary and Interpretation of Equity

Common shareholders' equity represents the book value of equity investor claims. Dividing common shareholders' equity by the number of common shares outstanding yields *book value per share*. Securities markets determine the *market price per share* of common stock by the interaction of supply and demand for shares. The ratio of book and market value, called the *market-to-book ratio*, is as follows:

Market-to-Book Ratio = Market Price per Share/Book Value per Share

Market-to-book ratios that are exactly equal to one imply the market value and the accounting value of equity are the same. In many cases, market-to-book ratios are greater than one for two primary reasons. First, conservatism in financial reporting (as a result of accounting standards themselves or management's application of accounting standards) can lead to book values of individual assets that are equal to or less than their fair values (but not greater than their fair values). For example, if a company's operations include a great deal of R&D (research and development) that is expensed immediately under U.S. GAAP, the unrecorded economic assets created by such expenditures cause book value per share to be lower than fair value. Second, future growth opportunities increase market price per share but have not been reflected in accounting measurements of book value.

For book value to be recognized in financial statements, U.S. GAAP and IFRS require that transactions have taken place or that unresolved future events can be estimated reliably. Therefore, book value of shareholders' equity tends to lag market value. Chapters 13 and 14 describe a valuation approach that relates book value to market value through the expectations of future accounting earnings not yet embedded in book value.

Quick Check

- Changes in shareholders' equity result from transactions with owners (issuances of stock and distributions such as dividends and share buybacks).
- Changes in shareholders' equity also result from transactions with nonowners, which are reflected in one of the two parts of comprehensive income, either net income or other comprehensive income.

- Financing strategy drives the changes in shareholders' equity from transactions with owners.
- Operating and investing strategies drive profitability and the changes in shareholders' equity from transactions with nonowners.

LO 7-4

Apply financial reporting principles to long-term and short-term debt (bonds, notes payable, leases, and troubled debt).

Debt Financing

As discussed in Chapter 5, the use of debt to finance investments and operations levers up the return on common equity, which can benefit common shareholders. However, the use of debt also has its risks and costs. Debt increases solvency risk, and therefore the required return to common shareholders (that is, the cost of equity capital) is increasing in the amount of debt in a corporation's capital structure. Further, net income is reduced by interest charges on debt. Accordingly, the financial reporting and analysis of debt is critical to understanding the profitability and risk of a firm.

In this section, we address the accounting for traditional debt financing activities that receive balance sheet recognition, including the issue of long-term notes and bonds, debt reduction, accounting for troubled debt, and the issue and conversion of hybrid securities, as well as other financing activities that may or may not result in balance sheet recognition (sales of receivables and operating leases). We give special attention to lease financing, we show how you can adjust financial statements to incorporate off-balance-sheet lease financing in the assessment of financial risk, and we describe recent improvements in lease accounting that mitigate the effects of off-balance-sheet debt on your analysis of leverage.

Financing with Long-Term Debt

As illustrated in Chapters 4 and 5, profitable firms can use leverage to increase the rate of return on common equity. The primary source of leverage for most firms is the issuance of long-term debt in the form of notes payable (primarily to banks and other financial institutions), bonds payable (to bondholders, including open-market debt investors), and leases (entered into with property owners, equipment dealers, or finance companies). Debt issuance is evidenced by a bond indenture, promissory note, or lease agreement. These documents will specify

- promises to pay principal amounts at specified dates.
- promises to pay cash interest (or lease payments) of specified amounts at specified dates.
- call provisions.
- descriptions of property pledged as security.
- whether the debt is convertible to another claim and the conversion rate.
- covenants and restrictions that specify sinking fund requirements, working capital restrictions, dividend payment restrictions, restrictions on new debt issues, and others.

This section illustrates the accounting for long-term debt using notes payable. Accounting for bonds payable is similar except for the possibility that bonds may be traded in active markets, thus having more readily determinable fair values. As discussed in the following sections, the fair value of financial instruments is a required disclosure in the notes to the financial statements and an optional measurement for recognition in the financial statements. Assume that on January 1, 2017, **Starbucks** issues a $100 million promissory note to a bank. The note matures in five years on January 1, 2022, and pays 5% interest once a year on January 1. The bank transfers $95.79 million (rounded) to **Starbucks** (the proceeds of the issue minus issue costs).

Starbucks' cash flows over the life of the note are as follows (in millions):

Cash inflow at issue		$ 95.79
Annual cash outflows (interest payments):		
Face amount of note	$100.00	
Coupon or stated interest rate	×5%	
Annual cash interest payment	$ 5.00	
Years	×5	
Total interest payments		(25.00)
Cash outflow at retirement date		(100.00)
Net cash outflow		$ (29.21)

The $29.21 million net cash outflow represents the total interest cost on the note. Accrual accounting recognizes the interest cost on the note over the five-year period in an economically meaningful way.

By paying less than $100 million for the note, the bank will earn a return that is greater than the 5% stated interest rate. That is, this investment is sufficiently risky such that the yield or effective interest rate should be higher than 5%, and therefore, the bank "discounts" the note. *Effective interest*, also known as the *yield*, *yield-to-maturity*, or *rate of return*, is a function of the risk characteristics of the transaction. It is the economic return on the transaction to creditors and the economic cost to debtors. In contrast, *cash interest* is determined by the *coupon rate* or *stated rate* of interest multiplied by the face value of the debt. The stated rate of interest is negotiated in a note or private bond placement or simply presented to potential buyers in a public bond issuance.[16]

A number of factors determine the effective interest rate. A portion of any effective interest rate contains compensation for the use of the lender's funds. While the funds are on loan, alternative, possibly more profitable opportunities may become available. Also,

---

[16]If the effective rate of interest and the stated rate of interest are equal, computing the present value of the note will yield a present value equal to the face value of the note. When the debt holder pays the face value to acquire a bond or note, the bond or note is said to be "issued at par."

the effective interest rate will reflect expected inflation, which causes future dollars to have less purchasing power. In addition, if the loan is denominated in a foreign currency, relative changes in economic conditions across countries could result in an unfavorable transformation of foreign currency into the dollar. Finally, firm-specific liquidity and solvency risk (as discussed in Chapter 5) explains differences in effective interest rates.

You solve for a loan's effective rate of return (i) using the following formula:

$$\text{Present Value} = \sum_{n=1}^{t} \frac{\text{Cash Interest}}{(1+i)^n} + \frac{\text{Maturity Value}}{(1+i)^t}$$

$$\$95.79 \text{ million} = \sum_{n=1}^{5} \frac{\$5 \text{ million}}{(1+i)^n} + \frac{\$100 \text{ million}}{(1+i)^5}$$

Solving for i results in a yield of 6%.[17]

Starbucks must use the effective interest method to account for the note. Exhibit 7.6 presents the effective interest amortization table. Amounts in the Cash Interest column are obtained by multiplying the face value of the debt by the stated interest rate of 5%, and amounts in the Effective Interest column are obtained by multiplying the beginning-of-the-period book value of the note (previous row) by the 6% effective interest rate charged by the bank. The difference between them is the amortization of the discount.

The beginning book value of $95.79 million represents the amount lent to **Starbucks** on 1/1/17. In 2017, **Starbucks** incurs a 6% interest charge on its $95.79 million initial borrowing, $5.75 million of effective interest expense. Essentially, the debt has grown by $5.75 million. Because **Starbucks** pays only $5 million in cash interest to the bank, the difference between the effective interest expense reported on the income statement and cash interest paid [shown in the Amortization column ($0.75 million)] increases the book value of the debt. Note that the amount of effective interest expense increases each period because the amount owed increases each period as **Starbucks** incurs a constant 6% economic interest charge on the debt. The annual increases in the debt from the amortization of the discount are paid off as part of the $100 million maturity payment. Exhibit 7.7 shows the financial statement effects of these transactions and events for the first three years.

Exhibit 7.6

Effective Interest Amortization Table (amounts in millions)

Date	5% Cash Interest	6% Effective Interest Expense	Amortization	Book Value of Note
1/1/17				$ 95.79
12/31/17	$ 5.00	$ 5.75	$0.75	96.54
12/31/18	5.00	5.79	0.79	97.33
12/31/19	5.00	5.84	0.84	98.17
12/31/20	5.00	5.89	0.89	99.06
12/31/21	5.00	5.94	0.94	100.00
	$25.00	$29.21		

[17]Using a financial calculator to solve for i involves setting n (number of annual interest payments) = 5, payment (annual cash interest payment) = $5 million, present value = $95.79 million, and future value = $100 million.

Exhibit 7.7: Accounting for Notes Payable

1/1/17 Signing:

Assets		=	Liabilities		+	Shareholders' Equity		
						CC	AOCI	RE
Cash	95.79		Note Payable	95.79				

Cash	95.79	
Note Payable		95.79

12/31/17 Year-End Interest Accrual:

Assets		=	Liabilities		+	Shareholders' Equity		
						CC	AOCI	RE
			Note Payable	0.75				Interest Expense (5.75)
			Interest Payable	5.00				

Interest Expense	5.75	
Note Payable		0.75
Interest Payable		5.00

1/1/18 Interest Payment Date:

Assets		=	Liabilities		+	Shareholders' Equity		
						CC	AOCI	RE
Cash	(5.00)		Interest Payable	(5.00)				

Interest Payable	5.00	
Cash		5.00

12/31/18 Year-End Interest Accrual:

Assets		=	Liabilities		+	Shareholders' Equity		
						CC	AOCI	RE
			Note Payable	0.79				Interest Expense (5.79)
			Interest Payable	5.00				

Interest Expense	5.79	
Note Payable		0.79
Interest Payable		5.00

1/1/19 Interest Payment Date:

Assets		=	Liabilities		+	Shareholders' Equity		
						CC	AOCI	RE
Cash	(5.00)		Interest Payable	(5.00)				

Interest Payable	5.00	
Cash		5.00

12/31/19 Year-End Interest Accrual:

Assets		=	Liabilities		+	Shareholders' Equity		
						CC	AOCI	RE
			Note Payable	0.84				Interest Expense (5.84)
			Interest Payable	5.00				

Interest Expense	5.84	
Note Payable		0.84
Interest Payable		5.00

Financial Reporting of Long-Term Debt

On the balance sheet, companies report bonds and notes payable at the present value of future cash flows using the historical effective rate of interest at the issue date. Note that the effective interest amortization table provides the book values of the note at each year end.

At December 31, 2021, the $100 million maturity value must be reclassified as a current liability because funds will be disbursed within one year of the balance sheet date (actually, the next day). A reclassification of a large note payable from long-term to current may have a material adverse impact on working capital (current assets minus current liabilities) and the current ratio (current assets divided by current liabilities). In practice, this potential adverse impact is alleviated two ways. First, a firm may set up a sinking fund in liquid assets (because of debt covenants or as part of the firm's cash management policy) to be used to repay the debt. The sinking fund and debt classifications will have countervailing effects on working capital.[18]

Another means of avoiding the reclassification of long-term debt to a current liability is to enter into a refinancing agreement. If the firm has the intent and ability to refinance the debt on a long-term basis, U.S. GAAP allows the obligation to remain in the long-term classification at the balance sheet date (with appropriate footnote disclosure). Auditors will investigate whether the ability to refinance is present by searching for a refinancing agreement with a lender or for evidence that actual refinancing has taken place before the financial statements are issued.[19]

The statement of cash flows reports the net proceeds of debt issues, interest payments, and maturity payments. Under both U.S. GAAP and IFRS, cash flows relating to principal amounts of debt are reported as financing activities. Under U.S. GAAP, the cash flow portion of interest expense is implicitly included as an operating cash outflow because interest expense reduces net income. Under the indirect method, net income is adjusted for the portions of interest expense that are not cash flows, including accrued amounts of interest payable as well as amortizations of bond discounts and premiums.[20]

Many companies disclose cash interest payments in the notes to the financial statements or in a supplementary schedule provided with the cash flow statement. **Starbucks** discloses cash paid for interest at the bottom of the statement of cash flows. Under IFRS, cash payments for interest can be reported as an operating or financing cash outflow. Under both U.S. GAAP and IFRS, the income statement reports interest expense as a nonoperating charge.

Fair Value Disclosure and the Fair Value Option

Long-term notes and bonds are financial instruments; therefore, firms must disclose the fair values in the notes to the financial statements.[21] In referring back to Exhibit 7.6, the December 31, 2019, book value of the note payable is $98.17 million. This amount is referred to as *amortized cost* because it represents the original "cost" of the debt, $95.79 million, adjusted for the amortization of the bank's discount for 2017–2019.

---

[18]Firms must provide note disclosure of sinking fund and bond retirement payments for each of the next five years after the balance sheet date. *FASB Codification Topic 440.*

[19]*FASB Codification Topics 440* and *470.*

[20]As discussed in Chapter 8, some interest can be capitalized when self-constructing an asset, which also causes a difference between interest expense and interest paid. Capitalized interest is a cash outflow in the investment activities section of the cash flow statement, reported as part of capital expenditures.

[21]*FASB Codification Topic 825*; International Accounting Standards Board, *International Financial Reporting Standard 7*, "Financial Instruments: Disclosures."

The amount also represents the present value of the remaining cash flows (two more $5 million interest payments and one final $100 million principal payment) at the historical 6% effective rate of interest.

$$\$98.17 \text{ million} = \sum_{n=1}^{2} \frac{\$5 \text{ million}}{(1+0.06)^n} + \frac{\$100 \text{ million}}{(1+0.06)^2}$$

If the market's required rate of interest has changed since the original signing date of the note, the fair value of the debt will change as well. Suppose the market requires a 7% return on **Starbucks'** note at December 31, 2019. The fair value of the note would then be

$$\$96.38 \text{ million} = \sum_{n=1}^{2} \frac{\$5 \text{ million}}{(1+0.07)^n} + \frac{\$100 \text{ million}}{(1+0.07)^2}$$

Starbucks would report the amortized cost of $98.17 million on the face of the balance sheet (probably in a group with other long-term debt) and the fair value of $96.38 million in the notes to the financial statements.

Recently, both the FASB and IASB passed a rule allowing firms the option to use fair value as the basis for measuring and reporting financial liabilities (and financial assets) instead of amortized cost.[22] If **Starbucks** were to adopt the *fair value option* for this debt, it would report $96.38 million of notes payable on the face of the balance sheet and an unrealized gain on remeasurement of long-term debt equal to $1.79 million ($98.17 million – $96.38 million) on the income statement (see Exhibit 7.8).[23] The standards are silent on how to recognize interest expense on this new long-term-debt basis. However, using the effective interest method (as described previously) with the new market rate and new book value would be consistent with current practice. Firms must choose whether to elect the fair value option with the inception of each new financing instrument, and be consistent over the life of the instrument. Firms do not

Exhibit 7.8: Accounting for Revaluation of Notes Payable

12/31/19 Year-End Remeasurement at Fair Value:

Assets	=	Liabilities		+	Shareholders' Equity		
					CC	AOCI	RE
		Note Payable	(1.79)				Unrealized Gain 1.79
Note Payable		1.79					
Unrealized Gain					1.79		

---

[22]Financial Accounting Standards Board, *Statement of Financial Accounting Standards No.159*, "The Fair Value Option for Financial Assets and Financial Liabilities" (2008); *FASB Codification Topic 825*; International Accounting Standards Board, *International Financial Reporting Standard 39*, "Financial Instruments: Recognition and Measurement."

[23]Firms that choose the fair value option on debt report a gain on the income statement when the fair value of their debt decreases. The fair value of debt decreases when the interest rate appropriate for discounting increases. However, the appropriate interest rate can increase simply because of increases in firm-specific risk. If this is the cause of the interest rate increase, firms end up reporting gains as they become riskier. On January 5, 2016, the FASB issued *Accounting Standards Update 2016-01*, "Financial Instruments—Overall: Recognitions and Measurement of Financial Assets and Financial Liabilities," effective for financial statements covering fiscal years beginning after December 15, 2017 (essentially 2018 financial statements). This new rule requires firms choosing the fair value option to reflect gains and losses on changes in firm-specific credit risk as other comprehensive income rather than in net income of the period.

have to be consistent from one instrument to the next, so some firms may have some financing instruments reported on the balance sheet at amortized cost and other instruments reported at fair value.

Measuring Fair Value

The challenge that companies face in providing fair value disclosures is obtaining reliable data. Historically, standard setters have eschewed fair value measurement in favor of reliable historical data obtained from arm's-length transactions between the company and outside parties. Recently, however, the potential relevance of fair values in decision making has been judged to outweigh potential measurement reliability issues, especially for financial assets and financial liabilities, and the company can provide information on the level of data reliability. For example, you may wish to use debt fair value estimates in weighted average cost of capital computations if the fair value differs significantly from book value.

Authoritative guidance identifies a hierarchy of inputs for fair value measurements, which were introduced in Chapter 2. Level 1 (observable market prices) inputs provide the most reliable measure and should be used if possible, followed by Level 2 (adjusted market prices) and then Level 3 (estimated models). The level used for each asset or liability measurement must be disclosed. If a firm uses multiple levels for a measurement, then it must disclose the least reliable level having a significant influence on the measurement. Most long-term debt can be measured with Level 1 and Level 2 approaches. In Note 9, **Starbucks** describes the estimated fair values of each of its debt issues. It also describes the early extinguishment of debt (discussed in Chapter 6) that caused the difference between its debt fair value and debt book value ($61.1 million) to be realized as a transitory loss in fiscal 2015.

While few question the relevance of fair value measurement, many worry about the reliability of Level 2 and Level 3 estimates of fair values. While the quoted market prices of Level 1 valuations have intuitive appeal, the reliability of a Level 1 valuation is compromised if the market from which it comes is not "orderly." The market for mortgage-backed securities in 2008–2009 exhibited a volatility that caused some to question its orderliness.

Reducing Debt

Outstanding debt can be reduced by paying off the principal when the debt matures. Alternatively, debt can be retired earlier through open-market purchase of traded debt, exercising call options (if available), or through conversion (if available). The difference between the amounts used to extinguish the debt and the book value of the debt is reported as a realized gain or loss on the income statement. Cash flows used to reduce debt are reported as cash outflows from financing activities in the statement of cash flows. *In-substance defeasance* of debt, transferring or pledging assets to an irrevocable trust to satisfy debt while remaining contingently obligated, used to be another popular way of removing debt from the balance sheet. U.S. GAAP and IFRS (*IAS 39*) now prohibit de-recognition of debt via in-substance defeasance.

Accounting for Troubled Debt

The financial crisis of the late 2000s found many firms struggling to make debt payments. Many firms ended up declaring bankruptcy or renegotiating the terms of outstanding debt obligations. This section examines how the debtor accounts for the restructuring of troubled debt.[24] From the debtor's perspective, two situations exist for handling troubled debt: settlement and modification of terms.

The *settlement* of troubled debt results in an economic gain to the debtor because the creditor settles for less than the book value of the debt. If a noncash asset is transferred to settle the debt (for example, a collateral asset), the noncash asset must be adjusted to fair value prior to its transfer, with the resulting gain or loss reported in income. A gain on debt settlement is recognized as the difference between the book value of the debt (principal plus any accrued interest) and the fair value of the noncash asset or cash transferred to retire the debt. Alternatively, if the debt is settled by issuing capital stock, then the stock issue is recorded at fair value and the gain to the debtor is the excess of the book value of the debt relative to the fair value of the stock issued.

Instead of accepting an asset or common stock to retire the debt, a creditor might *modify the terms* of the debt (for example, reducing the payments or lengthening the amount of time to pay), hoping a debtor will be able to perform under less stringent debt service requirements. Under U.S. GAAP, if terms are modified, the debtor must compare the total (undiscounted) future cash flows of the restructured debt to the current book value of the debt. If the total restructured future cash flows remain greater than the book value of the debt, the debtor will make no adjustment to book value (that is, record no gain). Future recognition of interest expense will follow the effective interest method using a new interest rate that discounts the total restructured future cash flows to the current book value.

If the total undiscounted restructured future cash flows are less than the book value of the debt, the debtor will reduce the book value of the debt to equal the total of the new restructured future cash flows, recording a gain in the process. Future interest expense will not be recognized because all future cash flows represent the repayment of principal; that is, the discount rate is assumed to be zero. This accounting is conservative because future cash flows must fall significantly before the debtor actually recognizes a gain. The result of the conservative accounting is to minimize any gains recognized by debtors who experience difficulty and must restructure debt agreements. These conservative accounting rules for troubled debt are subject to frequent (and deserved) criticism because they ignore the present value of future restructured cash flows for determining book values of troubled debt and gains from debt restructuring, and they often result in subsequent recognition of interest expense based on an unrealistic interest rate assumption.

To see specific examples of accounting for troubled debt restructurings and a contrast of U.S. GAAP with IFRS, please see the Chapter 7 online appendix at the text's website.

Hybrid Securities

Difficulties arise in the measurement and classification of certain debt and preferred stock securities when they have option features with both debt and equity characteristics (for example, convertible bonds). These securities are referred to as *hybrid securities* or

LO 7-5

Explain the accounting for and financial reporting of hybrid securities.

---

[24]U.S. GAAP for the debtor is found in *FASB Codification Topic 470*. We address creditor accounting for troubled debt in Chapter 8. In a troubled-debt restructuring, a creditor makes concessions to a debtor experiencing financial difficulties. Recently, the FASB issued *Accounting Standards Update No. 2011-02*, "A Creditor's Determination of Whether a Restructuring Is a Troubled Debt Restructuring" (2011), which clarifies that a concession involves the creditor receiving restructured cash flows that are lower than original contractual cash flows and that financial difficulties mean that it is probable that the debtor will not pay some or all of the original contractual cash flows. IFRS (*International Accounting Standard No. 39*, "Financial Instruments: Recognition and Measurement," as amended effective January 1, 2011) requires similar identification of a restructuring except that, under IFRS, objective evidence of a loss event leading to the expected impairment is required.

compound financing instruments. For example, firms sometimes issue preferred stock that is subject to certain rights of redemption in either cash or common shares after some period of time.[25] The classification of preferred stock as debt or equity depends on who holds the power to trigger redemption and whether the firm reports under U.S. GAAP or IFRS. If redemption will occur at a specific time or upon a specific event (for example, death of the holder), both U.S. GAAP and IFRS treat the preferred stock as a liability. This situation is typically referred to as *mandatorily redeemable preferred stock.* If the redemption is at the option of the issuing firm (that is, the preferred stock can be called by the firm), U.S. GAAP and IFRS will treat the preferred stock as equity. If redemption is at the holder's discretion (that is, the preferred stock can be put to the firm for payment), U.S. GAAP will require that the stock be disclosed between debt and equity (the so-called "mezzanine" disclosure) and IFRS will require disclosure as a liability.

Convertible preferred stock gives the holder the option to exchange the convertible preferred stock for common stock at a prespecified exchange rate. For example, a holder of 1,000 shares of $100 par, 7% convertible preferred stock may have the right to exchange each share of convertible preferred for five shares of $10 par common stock. Convertible preferred stock is treated as preferred stock at the date of issue. (Equity increases by the fair value of the consideration received at the issue date.) If converted to common stock, the recorded amounts are simply shifted from preferred stock to common stock.

Convertible debt may, at the creditor's option, be converted into common shares at a prespecified exchange rate. The creditor holds (1) debt with a stated interest rate and maturity date and (2) an option to exchange the debt for equity. However, the debt and option features do not trade separately in secondary markets. While holding the convertible debt, the creditor receives interest payments. Under U.S. GAAP, accountants have historically recorded convertible debt as a financial liability and recorded interest expense. The option to exchange the debt for equity is not valued and recorded. IFRS differs in that the debt and equity features are recorded separately to the extent that the separate components can be reliably estimated at fair value.

Under both U.S. GAAP and IFRS, most companies use the *book value method* to record conversion. The book value method is based on the idea that the conversion is a culmination of the original transaction. Whatever amounts are recorded in debt are simply shifted to shareholders' equity when the debt is converted into equity. Both U.S. GAAP and IFRS allow the use of the *market value method*, under which the market value of the common stock determines the basis of the conversion transaction. This approach is rarely used because it generates potentially large losses.

We illustrate the accounting for hybrid securities. The December 31, 2008, Consolidated Balance Sheet of **Digital River, Inc.**, reports 1.25%, 20-year convertible senior notes originally issued in 2004 at a par value of $195 million. Each $1,000 of note principal may be converted into 22.6948 shares of Digital River $0.01 par value common stock, a conversion price of $44.063 per share (= $1,000 ÷ 22.6948 shares). Exhibit 7.9 shows the financial statement effects under both U.S. GAAP and IFRS of the following transactions:

1. Recording of the original issue. For the IFRS treatment, assume that Digital River would have borrowed at 4% if it did not offer a conversion privilege.

---

[25]The following discussion is based on *FASB Codification Topic 480*; Securities and Exchange Commission *Accounting Series Release No. 268*, "Presentation in Financial Statements of Redeemable Preferred Stock"; and International Accounting Standards Board, *International Accounting Standard 32*, "Financial Instruments: Presentation" (as amended effective January 1, 2011).

Exhibit 7.9: Accounting for Hybrid Securities (amounts in millions)

U.S. GAAP:

	Assets		=	Liabilities		+	Shareholders' Equity		
							CC	AOCI	RE
1.	Cash	195.00		Notes Payable	195.00				

Cash	195.00
Note Payable	195.00

IFRS:

	Assets		=	Liabilities		+	Shareholders' Equity		
							CC	AOCI	RE
1.	Cash	195.00		Notes Payable	122.12		APIC—Notes Payable 72.88		

Cash	195.00
Notes Payable	122.12
APIC—Notes Payable	72.88

U.S. GAAP:

	Assets		=	Liabilities		+	Shareholders' Equity		
							CC	AOCI	RE
2.	Cash	(2.4375)							Interest Expense (2.4375)

Interest Expense	2.4375
Cash	2.4375

IFRS:

	Assets		=	Liabilities		+	Shareholders' Equity		
							CC	AOCI	RE
2.	Cash	(2.4375)		Notes Payable	2.4473				Interest Expense (4.8848)

Interest Expense	4.8848
Notes Payable	2.4473
Cash	2.4375

U.S. GAAP:

	Assets		=	Liabilities		+	Shareholders' Equity		
							CC	AOCI	RE
3.				Notes Payable	(195.0000)		Common Stock 0.0443 APIC 194.9557		

Notes Payable	195.0000
Common Stock	0.0443
APIC	194.9557

IFRS:

	Assets		=	Liabilities		+	Shareholders' Equity		
							CC	AOCI	RE
3.				Notes Payable	(124.5273)		APIC—Notes Payable (72.8800) Common Stock 0.0443 APIC 197.3630		

Notes Payable	124.5273
APIC—Notes Payable	72.8800
Common Stock	0.0443
APIC	197.3630

2. Recognition of one year's interest effect.
3. Conversion of the notes using the book value method, assuming a share of Digital River trades at $50.

U.S. GAAP treats the entire convertible note issue proceeds as debt. Under IFRS, the proceeds are allocated between the fair values of the notes (debt) and the conversion options (equity). If Digital would have paid 4% interest on the notes issued without the conversion option, the fair value of the notes could be approximated by discounting the notes' contractual cash flows at 4%. The present value of $195 million received in 20 years and a contractual cash interest payment of $2.4375 million ($195 million × 1.25%) each period for 20 years equals $122.12 million. Thus, the note payable is recorded at $122.12 million and the remainder of the proceeds ($195 million – $122.12 million = $72.88 million) is classified as equity. The account Additional Paid-in Capital—Note Payable would be reported in the shareholders' equity section as part of additional paid-in capital.

U.S. GAAP records the $2.4375 million annual payment as interest expense in Transaction 2. The cash interest and effective interest are equal because Digital River issued the notes payable at par. Under IFRS treatment, the notes were discounted at the effective interest rate of 4%. Therefore, the effective interest of $4.8848 million ($122.12 million beginning note book value times 4% effective interest rate) does not equal the contractual cash interest, and the note payable discount ($2.4473 million) is amortized.[26]

The book value method (Transaction 3) is based on the idea that the conversion is a culmination of a transaction to issue equity. The amounts recorded as debt are simply shifted to shareholders' equity when the debt is converted into equity. Under U.S. GAAP, the original issue was recorded as debt. Therefore, the $195 million is removed from notes payable. The common shares issued at conversion total 4,425,486, which is computed by multiplying the 22.6948 contractual conversion rate per $1,000 of note principal by 195,000 notes ($195 million divided by $1,000 per note). The common stock account is increased by the par value of those shares ($0.01 × 4,425,486 shares), and the rest is treated as additional paid-in capital. Under IFRS, the original issue was treated as part debt (recorded as notes payable) and part equity (recorded as additional paid-in capital—notes payable). Upon conversion, the amounts are shifted into common stock (at par) and additional paid-in capital. The amount shifted out of notes payable is equal to its original issue price from Transaction 1 plus the increase in notes payable from the amortization of the note in Transaction 2.

Bonds issued with detachable warrants provide a good example of where debt and equity features may be more easily separated and are accounted for separately under both U.S. GAAP and IFRS. Typically, after issuance, the bonds and detachable warrants trade separately in secondary markets. When purchasing bonds with detachable warrants, an investor buys a debt instrument (the bond) and the option to acquire equity at a fixed price (the stock warrants). Because the debt and equity features trade separately after issuance, accountants allocate the proceeds from the issue between the bond and the stock warrants on the basis of the two instruments' relative fair market values. As a simple example, assume that bonds with a face value of $1,000,000 plus detachable warrants are issued for $975,000. Assume that immediately after issue, the bonds trade for

---

[26] As is the case with any long-term debt, accrual of interest expense at the effective rate increases the amount owed by Digital River and contractual cash payments decrease the amount owed. Given that the effective interest is greater than the cash payment, Digital River's debt has increased, as evidenced by the increase in notes payable.

$900,000 and the warrants trade for $100,000. Accountants would allocate 90% ($900,000 value of the bonds/$1,000,000 value of bonds plus warrants) of the $975,000 value received to the bonds ($975,000 × 90% = $877,500) and 10% to the warrants ($975,000 × 10% = $97,500).

Transfers of Receivables

Firms sometimes transfer their receivables as a means of obtaining financing or use an SPE to issue securities backed by the receivables (for example, mortgage-backed securities issued by financial institutions or their SPEs). If collections from customers are not sufficient to repay the amount borrowed plus interest, the transferring firm may have to pay the difference; that is, the lender may have recourse against the borrowing firm.[27]

Does the recourse provision create an accounting liability? Some argue that the arrangement is similar to a collateralized loan and that the firm should leave the receivables on its books and recognize a liability for the cash received. Others argue that the firm has sold an asset; it should recognize a liability only if it is probable that collections from customers will be insufficient and the firm will be required to repay some portion of the amount received.

To illustrate the accounting for the transfer of receivables, assume that **Sears** transfers $1,000,000 of installment receivables to a bank in exchange for $950,000. Sears is liable to the bank for uncollectible receivables (a "with recourse" transfer), and the estimated fair value of the recourse obligation is $20,000. Exhibit 7.10 shows the financial statement effects if reported as a borrowing and if reported as a sale.

In the "borrowing" transaction, Sears does not surrender control of the receivables (that is, does not meet the FASB's three conditions to record a sale). Therefore, Sears keeps the accounts receivable on its books and records the receipt of cash and the incurrence of a liability (loan payable). In the "sale" transaction, Sears removes the accounts

Exhibit 7.10: Accounting for a Transfer of Receivables

Borrowing:

Assets		=	Liabilities		+	Shareholders' Equity		
						CC	AOCI	RE
1. Cash	950,000		Loan Payable	950,000				

Cash	950,000	
Loan Payable		950,000

Sale:

Assets		=	Liabilities		+	Shareholders' Equity			
						CC	AOCI	RE	
Cash	950,000		Recourse Liability	20,000				Loss on Sale	(70,000)
Accounts Receivable	(1,000,000)								

Cash	950,000	
Loss on Sale	70,000	
Accounts Receivable		1,000,000
Recourse Liability		20,000

---

[27]The contract of sale will specify whether the purchaser has recourse or whether the sale has taken place on a without-recourse basis, in which case the purchaser assumes all risk of collection.

receivable from the balance sheet because Sears no longer controls the accounts receivable. Sears also records the expected cash outflow to satisfy the recourse provisions of the agreement should customers fail to pay. Because net assets decrease by $50,000 and liabilities increase by $20,000, Sears records a loss on sale of $70,000, which is reported on the income statement and reduces retained earnings.

LO 7-6

Describe how operating and capital leases affect financial statements, and make adjustments required to convert operating leases to capital leases.

Leases

The FASB and the IASB adopted new lease accounting standards in 2016, and they take effect on January 1, 2019 (although firms are permitted to adopt them early). The rules that govern the measurement and reporting of leases will therefore depend on when you are reading this text and the fiscal year of the financial statements that you are analyzing. Because you are likely to have to deal with financial statements under "old" and "new" rules, we will cover both. It is important to closely read the notes to the financial statements to see whether the firm you are analyzing has adopted the new standards or is continuing to use the old standards. We will begin with the old rules.

Many firms acquire rights to use assets through leases. For example, a company might agree to lease computer equipment for three years, an office suite for five years, or an entire building for 40 years, promising to pay a fixed periodic fee for the duration of the lease. Leasing provides benefits to lessees (the users of the leased assets) such as the following:

■ Ability to shift the tax benefits from depreciation and other deductions from a lessee that has little or no taxable income (such as an airline) to a lessor, or owner of the asset, that has substantial taxable income. The lessee negotiates with the lessor to share some of the benefits of these tax deductions through lower lease payments.
■ Flexibility to change capacity as needed without having to purchase or sell assets.
■ Ability to reduce the risk of technological obsolescence, relative to outright ownership, by maintaining the flexibility to shift to more technologically advanced assets.
■ Ability to finance the acquisition of an asset using lessor financing when alternative sources of financing are unavailable or more costly.

These potential benefits of leasing to lessees come with a cost. When the lessor assumes the risks of ownership, it requires the lessee to make larger lease payments than if the lessee faces these risks. Which party bears the risks is a matter of negotiation between lessor and lessee.

An obligation to make a series of lease payments commits the firm just as surely as a bond indenture or a mortgage, and the accounting is similar in many cases.[28] This section describes the "old" lease accounting rules by examining the two methods of accounting for long-term leases: the operating lease method and the capital (sometimes called finance) lease method.[29] The following examples illustrate the accounting by the lessee, the user of the leased asset.

---

[28]Lease disclosures often use the term *noncancelable leases* to capture the contractual lease commitments of the lessee. Under noncancelable leases, the lessee typically can cancel the lease after incurring a severe penalty.

[29]*FASB Codification Topic 840*; International Accounting Standards Board, *International Accounting Standard 17*, "Leases" (revised 2003).

To illustrate these two methods, suppose Myers Company wants to acquire a computer that has a three-year life and that Myers Company can pay 10% per year to borrow money for three years. The computer manufacturer is willing to sell the equipment for $45,000 or to lease it for three years. Myers Company is responsible for property taxes, maintenance, and repairs of the computer whether it leases or purchases the computer.

Assume that Myers Company signs a lease on January 1, Year 1, and must make payments on the lease on December 31, each year. (In practice, lessees usually make lease payments in advance, but the assumption of year-end payments simplifies the computations.) The lessor sets the lease payments to return the $45,000 principal and 10% interest in three equal end-of-year payments. Similar to bond and note calculations, the payment is the amount that solves the following equation:

$$\$45,000 = \sum_{n=1}^{3} \frac{\text{Payment}}{(1 + 0.10)^n}$$

Solving this equation for the payment using a financial calculator ($i = 0.10$, $n = 3$, future value = 0, present value = $45,000) yields an annual payment of $18,095.

Operating Lease Method

In an operating lease, the owner, or lessor, transfers only the rights to use the property to the lessee for a specified period of time. At the end of the lease period, the lessee returns the property to the lessor. For example, car rental companies lease cars by the day or week. If the lessee neither assumes the risks nor enjoys the rewards of ownership, the lessee should treat the lease as an operating lease (under current but soon to be old rules). The lessee reports neither the leased asset nor a lease liability on its balance sheet; the lease is simply a mutually unexecuted contract. Over the life of the lease, the lessee recognizes rent expense in measuring net income each year. The effect of the operating lease on the financial statements of Myers Company each year (ignoring income taxes) appears in Exhibit 7.11.

The total income statement effect over the three years is the sum of the rent expense ($54,285), which also equals the total cash outflow from lease payments.

Capital Lease Method

In leasing arrangements in which the lessee assumes the risks and enjoys the rewards of ownership, the lease contract is considered a capital lease (again, under current but soon to be old rules). In a capital lease, the lessee recognizes the signing of the lease as the simultaneous acquisition of a long-term asset and the incurring of a long-term liability for lease payments. Lessees recognize two expense items each year on capital leases. First, the

Exhibit 7.11: **Operating Lease Treatment**

12/31/Year 1, Year 2, and Year 3:

Assets		=	Liabilities	+	Shareholders' Equity		
					CC	AOCI	RE
Cash	(18,095)						Rent Expense (18,095)
Rent Expense				18,095			
Cash					18,095		

lessee must depreciate the leased asset over the time period it uses the asset (that is, the lease term or the asset's economic useful life if the asset is expected to remain with the lessee after the lease term expires). Assuming that Myers Company uses straight-line depreciation, it recognizes depreciation expense of $15,000 ($45,000/3) each year. Second, as shown in the amortization schedule in Exhibit 7.12, the lease payment made each year is part interest expense and part reduction of the lease obligation.

The effects of (1) the signing of the capital lease on January 1, Year 1, and the recognition of (2) depreciation and (3) interest for each year appear in Exhibit 7.13.

Myers recognizes the leased asset and liability on the balance sheet as of the signing of the lease. Then in each year, Myers uses the effective interest method to account for the lease liability as was illustrated earlier for a note payable, and it depreciates the leased asset. Notice that in the capital lease method, the total expense over the three years is $54,285, comprising $45,000 for depreciation expense and $9,285 for interest expense. This total expense is the same as that recognized under the operating lease method described previously ($18,095 × 3 = $54,285). The capital lease method recognizes expenses sooner than the operating lease method does, but over the life of the lease, total expense equals the cash expenditure under both methods. The capital lease method recognizes both the asset and the liability on the balance sheet.[30]

Choosing the Accounting Method

When a lessee treats a lease as a capital lease, it recognizes an asset and a liability, thereby increasing total liabilities and making the company appear riskier. Given a choice, most lessees prefer not to show the asset and a related liability on the balance sheet. For this reason, lessees prefer an operating lease to an installment purchase or a capital lease. Lessees also prefer to recognize expenses for financial reporting later rather than sooner. These preferences have led a number of lessees to structure asset acquisitions so that the financing takes the form of an operating lease, thereby achieving off-balance-sheet financing.

U.S. GAAP provides detailed rules for accounting for long-term leases. Under the old rules, the lessor and lessee must account for a lease as a capital lease if the lease meets any one of four conditions.[31] These conditions attempt to identify which party,

Exhibit 7.12

Lease Amortization Table

Date	Payment	10% Effective Interest Expense	Amortization	Book Value of Lease Liability
1/1/Year 1				$45,000
12/31/Year 1	$18,095	$4,500	$13,595	31,405
12/31/Year 2	18,095	3,141	14,954	16,451
12/31/Year 3	18,095	1,644	16,451	0
	$54,285	$9,285	$45,000	

[30]The fair value option is not allowed for assets and liabilities reported under capital leases.

[31]FASB Codification Topic 840.

Exhibit 7.13: Capital Lease Treatment

1/1/Year 1 Signing:

Assets		=	Liabilities		+	Shareholders' Equity		
						CC	AOCI	RE
Leased Asset	45,000		Lease Liability	45,000				
Leased Asset				45,000				
Leased Liability						45,000		

12/31/Year 1 Payment:

Assets		=	Liabilities		+	Shareholders' Equity			
						CC	AOCI	RE	
Cash	(18,095)		Lease Liability	(13,595)				Interest Expense	(4,500)
Interest Expense				4,500					
Lease Liability				13,595					
Cash						18,095			

12/31/Year 1 Depreciation:

Assets		=	Liabilities	+	Shareholders' Equity			
					CC	AOCI	RE	
Leased Asset (Net)	(15,000)						Depreciation Expense	(15,000)
Depreciation Expense				15,000				
Leased Asset (Net)					15,000			

12/31/Year 2 Payment:

Assets		=	Liabilities		+	Shareholders' Equity			
						CC	AOCI	RE	
Cash	(18,095)		Leased Liability	(14,954)				Interest Expense	(3,141)
Interest Expense				3,141					
Lease Liability				14,954					
Cash						18,095			

12/31/Year 2 Depreciation:

Assets		=	Liabilities	+	Shareholders' Equity			
					CC	AOCI	RE	
Leased Asset (Net)	(15,000)						Depreciation Expense	(15,000)
Depreciation Expense				15,000				
Leased Asset (Net)					15,000			

12/31/Year 3 Payment:

Assets		=	Liabilities		+	Shareholders' Equity			
						CC	AOCI	RE	
Cash	(18,095)		Lease Liability	(16,451)				Interest Expense	(1,644)
Interest Expense				1,644					
Lease Liability				16,451					
Cash						18,095			

12/31/Year 3 Depreciation:

Assets		=	Liabilities	+	Shareholders' Equity			
					CC	AOCI	RE	
Leased Asset (Net)	(15,000)						Depreciation Expense	(15,000)
Depreciation Expense				15,000				
Leased Asset (Net)					15,000			

the lessor or the lessee, bears most of the risk related to the asset under lease. When the lessor bears most of the risk, the lease is an operating lease. When the lessee bears most of the risk, the lease is a capital lease.

A lease is a capital lease if it meets any one of the following conditions:

- If it extends for at least 75% of the asset's total expected economic life (that is, the lessee uses the asset for most of its life).
- If it transfers ownership to the lessee at the end of the lease term (that is, the lessee bears the risk of changes in the residual value of the asset at the end of the lease term).
- If it seems likely the lessor will transfer ownership to the lessee because of a "bargain purchase" option (that is, the lessee again bears the residual value risk; a bargain purchase option gives the lessee the right to purchase the asset for a price less than the expected fair market value of the asset when the lessee exercises its option).
- The present value of the contractual minimum lease payments equals or exceeds 90% of the fair market value of the asset at the time of signing.[32]

The first three conditions are relatively easy to avoid in lease contracts if lessors and lessees prefer to treat a lease as an operating lease instead of a capital lease. The most difficult of the four conditions to avoid is the fourth. When the present value of the contractual minimum lease payments equals or exceeds 90% of the fair market value of the asset at the time of signing, the lessor has less than or equal to 10% of the asset's value at risk to an uncertain residual value at the end of the lease term. Therefore, the lease transfers the major risks and rewards of ownership from the lessor to the lessee. In economic substance, the lessee has acquired an asset and has agreed to pay for it under a long-term contract, which the lessee recognizes as a liability. When the present value of the minimum lease payments is less than 90% of the fair market value of the asset at the time of signing, the lessor bears the major risks and rewards of ownership and the lease is an operating lease.

Firms often report both operating and capital leases because certain lease agreements meet one or more of these conditions while others do not. As an example of the significance of leasing activities, consider a typical firm in the airline industry that leases many of its aircraft and ground facilities. In Note 7 to its December 31, 2015, consolidated financial statements, **Southwest Airlines** provides schedules of capital and operating lease commitments, as shown in Exhibit 7.14. Southwest Airlines also reports $3,181 million of combined long-term debt and current maturities of long-term debt in its December 31, 2015, consolidated balance sheet. Note that the capitalized lease payments ($346 million) are not a large portion of Southwest's long-term debt. Southwest's commitments under operating leases (gross future cash flows of $3,819 million) are more substantial, representing an important off-balance-sheet cash flow commitment of the firm.

Converting Operating Leases to Capital Leases for Analysis

Lease commitments by lessees accounted for as operating leases do not appear as assets or liabilities on the balance sheet and, if you believe these obligations are essentially financial commitments, can cause you to understate the short-term liquidity or long-term

---

[32]IFRS criteria are similar, although, as is often the case with IFRS, the criteria do not provide "bright-line" percentages such as 75% or 90%. Instead, judgment is relied upon to implement the following: (1) Does ownership transfer from the lessor to the lessee at the end of the lease? (2) Is there a bargain purchase option? (3) Does the lease extend for the major portion of the asset's useful life? (4) Does the present value of the minimum lease payments equal substantially all of the asset's fair value? (5) Is the leased asset specialized for use by the lessee?

Exhibit 7.14

Southwest Airlines Excerpts from December 31, 2015, 10-K (amounts in millions)

Note 7 (partial). Total rental expense for operating leases, both aircraft and other, charged to operations in 2015, 2014, and 2013 was $909 million, $931 million, and $997 million, respectively.... Future minimum lease payments under capital leases and noncancelable operating leases and capital leases with initial or remaining terms in excess of one year at December 31, 2015 were:

	Capital Leases	Operating Leases
2016	$ 46	$ 557
2017	46	545
2018	45	474
2019	45	407
2020	44	307
Thereafter	209	1,529
Total minimum lease payments	$435	$3,819
Less amount representing interest	79	
Present value of minimum lease payments	$356	
Less current portion	32	
Long-term portion	$324	

---

solvency risk of the firm. In cross-sectional comparisons of different firms, you may want to treat all leases as capital leases with the objective of making all firms more comparable in terms of assets and liabilities. Restating the financial statements of lessees in this way provides a more conservative measure of total liabilities.

To illustrate the conversion of operating to capital leases, refer to the **Southwest Airlines** (SWA) operating lease disclosures in Exhibit 7.14. To convert these operating lease cash payments to a capital lease, you must discount the lease commitments to present value. The discount rate you should use is the lessee's incremental borrowing rate for secured debt with similar risk to that of the leasing arrangement. SWA's interest expense as a percentage of average short- and long-term borrowing for 2015 is 4.1%. We assume a 4% rate to compute the present value of operating lease commitments.

Exhibit 7.15 illustrates the computation of the present value of the operating lease payments. To discount payments in 2021 and beyond, you must assume the number of years over which SWA will pay the $1,529 million and the amount of each annual payment. Presuming that payments will continue at the same amount as the $307 million payment in 2020, SWA will pay the remaining $1,529 million in about five periods ($1,529/$307 = 4.98). We assume that the remainder is spread over five periods, yielding a payment of $305.8 million per year ($1,529 million/5 years).

Exhibit 7.15

Southwest Airlines' Capitalization of Operating Leases
(amounts in millions)

Year	Operating Lease Commitments	Present Value Factor at 4%	Present Value
2016	$ 557	0.96153	$ 535.6
2017	545	0.92455	503.9
2018	474	0.88899	421.4
2019	407	0.85480	347.9
2020	307	0.82192	252.3
2021 and beyond	1,529	—	1,118.9
	$2,061		$3,180*

*Present value of an annuity of $305.8 million for five periods at 4%, then that present value discounted back five periods at 4%.

The $1,118.9 million present value is obtained by computing the present value of an annuity of $305.8 million for five periods at 4% to yield a present value at the end of 2020 and then discounting that amount for five additional periods at 4%. The present value of all of SWA's operating lease payments is $3,180 million.

To add the operating lease assets and liabilities to SWA's balance sheet, you add the $3,180 million to property, plant, and equipment; the $535.6 million present value of the 2016 lease payments to short-term debt; and the $2,654.4 ($3,180 − $535.6) million present value of lease payments in 2017 and beyond to long-term debt on the December 31, 2015, balance sheet. Certain ratios could be affected substantially by the operating lease capitalization. For example, SWA's ratio of long-term debt to shareholders' equity based on reported amounts is 34.5% ($2,541/$7,358). Adding the long-term portion of the capital lease liability of $2,654.4 million to the numerator more than doubles the ratio to 70.6% ($2,541 + $2,654.4)/$7,358).

If you convert operating leases to capital leases on the balance sheet for comparison purposes across firms, you also should convert the income statement from the operating to the capital lease method by

- eliminating rent expense.
- including depreciation expense on the capitalized asset.
- including interest expense on the lease obligation.

In general, if the average lease is in the first half of its life, total expenses under the capital lease method tend to exceed total expenses under the operating lease method; so adjusted income will tend to be less than reported income. If the average lease is in the last half of its life, total expenses under the capital lease method tend to be less than under the operating lease method; so adjusted income tends to be greater than reported income. The two expense amounts are approximately equal at the midlife point.

You can calculate the income statement effect of operating lease capitalization for SWA by comparing the operating lease payment in 2016 ($557 million), which would be treated as rent expense for an operating lease, to the following rough approximations for expenses under a capital lease:

$$\text{Depreciation expense} = \$3{,}180 \text{ million asset}/8.67 \text{ years remaining lease life}^{33}$$
$$= \$366.78 \text{ million}$$
$$\text{Interest expense} = \$3{,}180 \text{ million lease liability} \times 4\%$$
$$= \$127.2 \text{ million}$$

The sum of depreciation expense and interest expense (capital lease treatment) is $498.98 million, which is less than the $557.0 million in rent expense (operating lease treatment).

Therefore, constructive capitalization of the operating leases would increase net income by the difference between these two expenses ($58.02 million) times one minus the statutory tax rate, or $37.71 million [$58.02 million $\times$ (1 − 0.35)]. This amount is approximately 1.7% of SWA's 2015 net income of $2,181 million.

The effects on other commonly used performance measures are more pronounced. For example, EBITDA excludes depreciation, interest, and tax expenses (and therefore any adjustments for these items when operating leases are effectively capitalized). Constructive capitalization of operating leases causes EBITDA to increase by the full $557 million excluded rent expense, but is not increased by depreciation and interest expense. The adjustment would increase SWA's 2015 EBITDA of $5,689 million by 9.8% [$557 million ÷ $5,689 million]. As we mentioned in earlier chapters, EBITDA is a somewhat entrenched profitability measure in the financial community and multiples of EBITDA are sometimes used in valuation. The operating lease problem has a particularly strong effect on EBITDA. The strong effect is not limited to airlines. Using a similar capitalization method, **Starbucks'** fiscal 2015 EBITDA increases by more than 6% when its operating leases are capitalized. Often, balance sheet restatements are more significant than income statement restatements. Consequently, you usually can ignore restatements of the income statement, particularly if the emphasis is assessment of a firm's credit risk, as discussed in Chapter 5. However, note that even for firms with leases at the midlife point, where the income statement effect may be immaterial, the effect on the balance sheet can be substantial.[34]

---

[33]Using a weighted average approach, we calculated the 8.67 years as follows: If the rent payments are equal over the 2016 to 2025 period, it would be reasonable to assume that all leased assets are going to be used over the 10-year period. However, the rent payments decline, implying that some assets are used up and, thus, off-lease. Working backwards in the schedule, $305.8 million cash flow appears in each year, $1.2 million additional cash flow ($305.8 + $1.2 = $307) in cash flow appears in the first five years, $100 million additional cash flow appears for the first four years ($307 + $100 = $407), $69 million additional cash flow appears for the first three years ($407 + $69 = $474), $71 million additional cash flow appears for the first two years ($474 + $71 = $545), and $12 million additional cash flow ($545 + $12 = $557) appears in 2016. Therefore, 80% of the cash flows relate to assets in use for 10 years ($305.8 per year × 10 years = $3,058 out of a total of $3,819), 0.15% of the cash flows relates to assets in use for five years ($1.2 per year × 5 years = $6 out of a total of $3,819), 10.47% of the cash flows relates to assets in use for four years ($100 per year × 4 years = $400 out of a total of $3,819), and, by a similar process, 5.42% of the cash flows relates to assets in use for three years, 3.72% of the cash flows relates to assets in use for two years, and 0.31% of the cash flows relates to assets in use for one year. Weighting a 10-year life by 80%, a five-year life by 0.15%, a four-year life by 10.47%, and so on, yields an average useful life of 8.67 years.

[34]For an alternative procedure for converting operating leases into capital leases, see Eugene A. Imhoff Jr., Robert C. Lipe, and David W. Wright, "Operating Leases: Impact of Constructive Capitalization," *Accounting Horizons* (March 1991), pp. 51–63. In this study, the authors found that capitalizing operating leases decreased the rate of return on assets 34% for high-lease firms and 10% for low-lease firms and increased the debt-to-equity ratio 191% for high-lease firms and 47% for low-lease firms.

You can restate the statement of cash flows for the capitalization of operating leases. Under the operating lease method, the lease payment for the year is an operating use of cash. It is implicitly included because it is an expense in computing net income. Under the capital lease method, a portion of the cash payment represents a repayment of the lease liability, a financing use of cash instead of an operating use of cash. You should reclassify this portion of the cash payment from the operating section to the financing section of the statement of cash flows. The net effect of the depreciation expense portion on operating cash flows is zero because it is a noncash expense.

Lease footnote disclosures allow you to capitalize operating leases effectively, but with some error. You will need to make a number of assumptions and estimates (sometimes rough), and these assumptions may not be valid for all firms in all industries. As a result, credit-rating agencies such as Moody's and Fitch have developed standard, simplified methodologies. For example, some analysts estimate the lease liability and leased asset to be capitalized simply using an "8X" rule. That is, a simple method of computing the capitalized liability and asset is to multiply the amount of annual rent expense times eight. Because this "8X" heuristic is based on specific assumptions (e.g., a 9% interest rate and an asset life of 15 years or a 4% interest rate, or an asset life of 4 years, both of which yield a present value factor of approximately 8 for a $1 annuity, etc.), Moody's uses a modified approach that takes into account industry differences in useful lives and the "seasoning" (that is, age) of the leased assets. Thus, for any given firm, a factor of 5X, 6X, 8X, or greater might be applied, with firms with long-lived assets such as airlines, shipping, and public utilities receiving the highest factor. Fitch also uses the 8X heuristic, a present value approach if sufficient data exist, and individual analysis about the validity of the approach for a given firm.[35]

Virtually all firms have some amount of operating leases. The change in debt ratios for some firms is relatively minor. For other firms, particularly airlines and retail stores, the effect can be significant. Even for firms for which the effect is relatively small, adding the effect of capitalizing operating leases to the effect of other off-balance-sheet obligations can result in a combined material effect. Thus, you should examine the effect of leases when assessing the risk and accounting quality of a firm's financial statements. You should also consider the effects of off-balance-sheet leases when determining capital structure weights and debt costs for the weighted average cost of capital calculations used in enterprise valuation.

The New Lease Standard

The FASB's new lease standard is scheduled to take effect on January 1, 2019, with early adoption permitted. You should carefully read the notes to the financial statements to determine if the company you are analyzing has chosen early adoption. Typically, companies will review new standards and state whether they have adopted them in the accounting policy note, usually the first note presented.[36]

Many of the old rules are kept by the new standard, so we will focus on the differences. Most importantly, while the distinction between operating and capital (i.e., financing) lease classifications will remain, the balance sheet reporting of operating leases will change so

---

[35]Moody's Approach to Global Standard Adjustments in the Analysis of Financial Statements for Non-Financial Corporations—Part I, *Standardized Adjustments to Enable Global Consistency for US and Canadian GAAP Issuers* (March 2005); "Capitalization of Operating Leases by Credit Rating Agencies," *ELT* (February 2007).

[36]*FASB Accounting Standards Update 2016-02*, "Leases."

that a leased asset and lease liability will now appear. This new reporting will remove the need to effectively capitalize operating leases using footnote information.

To illustrate, we will continue the Myers Company example. Recall that a lease was classified as a capital lease if one of four conditions was met. These conditions remain in the new rules with one more added—a lease is classified as capital if "the underlying asset is of such a specialized nature that it is expected to have no alternative use to the lessor at the end of the lease term." Also, the "bright lines" included in the four conditions, such as 90% of fair value and 75% of economic useful lives, are replaced with more general terms such as "substantially all" and "a major part of," which essentially makes the conditions much like the more judgment-based conditions under IFRS. The effect of these five newly worded conditions is likely to be that most leases now classified as capital will remain that way, especially because the standard recognizes the bright lines as one reasonable approach to executing the classification judgment. If the lease is classified as a capital lease, the accounting shown in Exhibit 7.13 remains the same under the new rules.

Also, if the lease is classified as an operating lease and the lease is one year or shorter, the accounting shown in Exhibit 7.11 remains the same under the new rules. However, if the lease is classified as an operating lease and the lease is longer than one year, the treatment substantially changes. Instead of making no entry at the date of inception under an operating lease, a right-of-use (i.e., a leased) asset is recorded along with the lease liability, both at present value, like what was done under the old rules for a capital lease. Exhibit 7.16 shows the lease inception date effects.

Each time the $18,095 rent is paid, cash is reduced. Lease expense equals the total of the undiscounted cash payments over the life of the lease ($18,095 × 3 payments = $54,285) amortized over that time period on a straight-line basis ($54,285/3 years = $18,095). Lease expense equals the cash payment in our example, but only because our example has level rent payments each year. If the cash rent payments are not level, lease expense remains level over the lease term under the new accounting rules.

The lease liability is reduced according to the "amortization" column in Exhibit 7.12. The leased asset is reduced by the difference between the lease expense ($18,095) and the effective interest from Exhibit 7.12 ($4,500). Although the leased asset reduction equals the lease liability reduction in our example, it is only because of the level rent payments.

Exhibit 7.16: Accounting for Operating Leases of Longer Than One Year under the New FASB Lease Standard

1/1/Year 1 Signing

Assets	=	Liabilities	+	Shareholders' Equity CC	AOCI	RE
Leased Asset 45,000		Lease Liability 45,000				
Leased Asset			45,000			
Leased Liability				45,000		

12/31/Year 1, Year 2, and Year 3 Payments

Assets	=	Liabilities	+	Shareholders' Equity CC	AOCI	RE
Cash (18,095) Leased Asset (13,595)		Lease Liability (13,595)				Lease Expense (18,095)
Lease Expense			18,095			
Lease Liability			13,595			
Cash				18,095		
Leased Asset				13,595		

For analysis purposes, it will no longer be necessary to adjust balance sheet assets and debt under the new rules. The accounting process will measure and report the lease asset and lease liability appropriately. If, however, your analysis objective requires proper measurement of net income and cash flow from operations, you might consider adjustments to be necessary. The straight-line recognition of lease expense for operating leases longer than one year under the new rules will generally not equal the sum of depreciation and interest expense that would have been recognized had the leases been capitalized. If the average lease for a company is not near the midpoint of the lease term, substantial differences might exist. Also, cash flow from operations will reflect the full lease payment as an operating item for operating leases. Recall that capital lease treatment requires the reporting of the cash flow related to principal reduction as a financing cash flow and the cash flow related to interest as an operating cash flow. In contrast, under the new IFRS standard on leases, the distinction between operating and capital leases has been removed. All leases will be capitalized.[37]

Quick Check

- Proper measurement and reporting of long-term debt are crucial for an accurate assessment of long-term solvency risk.
- Long-term debt is initially reported at fair value, which is, in theory, the present value of future cash outflows discounted at a rate of interest commensurate with the issuer's risk.
- Interest expense is based on the effective interest rate determined by the economics of the transaction while cash interest is determined by the stated rate of interest in the note agreement or bond indenture.

- Some operating-type leases are structured in a way that avoids long-term debt reporting. However, standard setters have adopted a new standard (becoming effective in 2019) that will limit the use of the operating lease treatment and thus will improve long-term debt reporting.
- Long-term debt other than capital leases may be reported at fair value subsequent to the date of issue.
- Long-term debt is a financial instrument for which note reporting of fair value is required.

LO 7-7

Explain how economic effects of derivatives used to hedge changes in long-term debt interest rates are reported in financial statements.

The Use of Derivatives to Hedge Interest Rate Risk

Long-term borrowing subjects firms to the risk of interest rate changes. *Derivative instruments* can help a firm mitigate interest rate (and other types of) risks. This section discusses the nature, use, accounting, and reporting of derivative instruments, with a primary focus on the use of derivatives to hedge interest rate risk.[38] To facilitate this discussion, we use the following two scenarios:

Scenario 1: Firm A gives a note payable to a supplier on January 1, 2017, to acquire manufacturing equipment. The note has a face value of $100,000 and bears a fixed interest rate of 8% per year. Interest is payable annually on December 31, and the note

[37]International Accounting Standards Board, *International Financial Reporting Standard 16*, "Leases" (January 2016).

[38]U.S. GAAP and IFRS have similar derivative accounting rules. *FASB Codification Topics 815* and *825*; International Accounting Standards Board, *International Accounting Standard 39*, "Financial Instruments: Recognition and Measurement" (revised 2003); International Accounting Standards Board, *International Financial Reporting Standard 7*, "Financial Instruments: Disclosures" (2005).

matures on December 31, 2019. Firm A has the option of repaying the note prior to maturity. The prepayment will be based on the fair value of the note on the prepayment date, which is based on prevailing market interest rates on that date. Firm A is concerned that the value of the note will increase if interest rates decrease and that it will have to pay more than $100,000 if it decides to repay the note early.

Firm A wants to neutralize the effect of changes in the market value of the note payable caused by changes in market interest rates. It engages a derivative instrument, an interest rate swap contract, with a notional value of $100,000 with its bank. In effect, the swap allows Firm A to swap its fixed-interest-rate obligation for a variable-interest-rate obligation. That is, in the swap contract, Firm A agrees to pay the bank a variable rate of interest on $100,000, and in exchange the bank will pay Firm A a fixed rate of interest (8%). The market value of the note will remain at $100,000 as long as the variable interest rate in the swap is the same as the variable rate used by the supplier to revalue the note while it is outstanding. The swap causes Firm A's interest payments to vary as the variable interest rate changes, but it locks the value of the note payable at $100,000.

Scenario 2: Firm B gives a note payable to a supplier on January 1, 2017, to acquire manufacturing equipment. The note has a face value of $100,000 and bears interest at the prime lending rate. Assume that the prime lending rate is 8% on January 1, 2017. The supplier will reset the interest rate each December 31 to establish the interest charge for the next calendar year. Interest is payable on December 31 of each year, and the note matures on December 31, 2019. Firm B is concerned that interest rates will increase to more than 8% during the term of the note and negatively affect its cash flows.

Firm B wants to protect its future cash flows against increases in the variable interest rate to more than the initial 8% rate. It also engages in an interest rate swap contract with a notional value of $100,000 with its bank. In effect, the swap allows Firm B to swap its variable-interest-rate obligation for a fixed-interest-rate obligation. That is, in the swap contract, Firm B agrees to pay the bank a fixed rate of 8% interest on $100,000, and in exchange the bank will pay Firm B a variable rate of interest. The swap fixes the firm's annual interest expense and cash expenditure to 8% of the $100,000 note, which eliminates Firm B's risk of interest rate increases. By engaging in the swap, however, Firm B cannot take advantage of decreases in interest rates to less than 8%, which it could have done with its variable-rate note. In this example, the swap locks in Firm B's interest payments on the note, but the value of the note to the supplier will vary as the variable interest rate changes.

Nature and Use of Derivative Instruments

A derivative is a financial instrument that *derives* its value from some other financial instrument or observable market prices, such as stock prices, interest rates, currency exchange rates, commodity prices, and the like. For example, an option to purchase a share of stock (an option contract) derives its value from the market price of the stock. A commitment to purchase a certain amount of foreign currency in the future (a forward contract) derives its value from changes in the exchange rate for that currency. Firms typically use derivative instruments (option, forward, and swap contracts) to hedge the risk of losses from changes in market prices, interest rates, foreign exchange rates, and commodity prices. The general idea is that changes in the value of the derivative instrument offset changes in the value of an asset or a liability or changes in future cash flows, thereby neutralizing the economic loss.

Banks and other financial intermediaries structure derivatives for a fee to suit the needs of their customers. Thus, the nature and complexity of derivatives vary widely. We focus our discussion on the interest rate swap contracts in the two scenarios to illustrate the accounting and reporting of derivatives. Consider the following elements of a derivative:

- A derivative has an *underlying*. An underlying is the specified item to which the derivative applies, such as an interest rate, a commodity price, a foreign exchange rate, or another variable. Interest rates are the underlying in the two scenarios.
- A derivative has a *notional amount*. A notional amount is the number of units (dollar amounts, foreign currency units, bushels, barrels, gallons, shares, or other units) specified in a contract. The $100,000 face value of the note is the notional amount in the two scenarios.
- A derivative may or may not require an initial investment. The firm usually acquires a derivative by exchanging promises with a *counterparty*, such as a commercial or investment bank. The acquisition of a derivative is usually an exchange of promises, a mutually unexecuted contract.
- Derivatives typically require, or permit, *net settlement*. For example, Firm A in Scenario 1 will pay the supplier the 8% interest established in the fixed-rate note. If the variable interest rate used in the swap contract decreases to 6%, the counterparty bank will pay Firm A an amount equal to 2% (8% − 6%) of the notional amount of the note, $100,000. Paying interest of 8% to the supplier and receiving cash of 2% from the counterparty results in net interest cost of 6%. If the variable interest rate increases to 10%, Firm A still pays the supplier interest of 8% as specified in the original note. It would then pay the counterparty bank an additional 2% (10% − 8%), resulting in total interest expense equal to the variable rate of 10%.

Accounting for Derivatives

Firms recognize derivatives as assets or liabilities depending on the rights and obligations under the contract. The swap contracts in Scenarios 1 and 2 may be assets or liabilities depending on the level of interest rates. A later section discusses the initial valuation of these assets and liabilities.

Firms must revalue the derivatives to fair value each period. In addition to increasing or decreasing the derivative asset or liability, the revaluation amount also affects net income immediately, or other comprehensive income immediately and net income later (depending on U.S. GAAP and IFRS requirements discussed shortly). Whether the income effect is reported in net income or other comprehensive income depends on the nature of the hedge for which a firm acquires a derivative. Under U.S. GAAP and IFRS, there are three classifications of derivatives:

- Speculative investments
- Fair value hedges
- Cash flow hedges

Speculative Investment

Firms that acquire derivatives for reasons other than hedging a specific risk classify the derivative as a *speculative investment*. Firms must revalue derivatives held as speculative investments to fair value each period and recognize the resulting gain or loss in net income.

Fair Value Hedges

Derivative instruments acquired to hedge exposure to changes in the fair values of assets or liabilities are *fair value hedges*. Fair value hedges are of two general types: hedges of a *recognized* asset or liability and hedges of an *unrecognized* firm commitment.[39] Firm A in Scenario1 entered into the interest swap agreement to neutralize the effect of changes in interest rates on the market value of its notes payable, a hedge of a recognized liability. Therefore, this derivative instrument is a fair value hedge.

Cash Flow Hedges

Derivative instruments acquired to hedge exposure to variability in expected future cash flows are *cash flow hedges*. Cash flow hedges are of two general types: hedges of cash flows of an *existing* asset or liability and hedges of cash flows of *forecasted* transactions.[40] Firm B in Scenario 2 entered into the interest swap agreement to neutralize changes in cash flows for interest payments on its variable-rate notes payable, a hedge of an existing liability. Therefore, this derivative instrument is a cash flow hedge.

In summary:

Scenario	Type of Hedge	Derivative Instrument Used
1	Fair Value—Liability	Swap Contract—Variable for Fixed Rate
2	Cash Flow—Interest Payments	Swap Contract—Fixed for Variable Rate

Treatment of Derivatives and Hedging Gains and Losses

For a derivative financial instrument classified as a *fair value hedge*, U.S. GAAP and IFRS require firms to recognize the derivative as an asset or liability in the amount of the gain and loss from changes in the fair value of the derivative and to recognize the fair value gain or loss in net income each period while the firm holds the financial instrument. U.S. GAAP and IFRS also require firms to revalue the asset or liability that is hedged to fair value and to recognize a corresponding loss or gain. If the hedge is fully effective, the gain (loss) on the derivative financial instrument will precisely offset the loss (gain) on the asset or liability hedged. The net effect on earnings is zero. If the hedge is not fully effective, the net gain or loss increases or decreases net income.

U.S. GAAP and IFRS require firms to include gains and losses from changes in the fair value of a derivative financial instrument classified as a *cash flow hedge* in other comprehensive income each period to the extent that the financial instrument is "highly effective" in neutralizing the risk. Firms must include the ineffective portion currently in net income. Financial reporting rules give general guidelines but leave the meaning of "highly effective" to professional judgment. The firm removes the accumulated amount in other comprehensive income related to a particular derivative instrument and transfers it to net income periodically during the life of the derivative instrument or at the time of settlement, depending on the type of derivative instrument used.

The logic for the different treatment of gains and losses from changes in fair value of derivative financial instruments is as follows. In a fair value hedge of a recognized asset or liability, the hedged asset (or liability) and its related derivative generally appear on the balance sheet. The firm revalues the hedged asset (or liability) and its related derivative to fair value each period, and reports the gain or loss on the hedged asset (or liability) as well as the loss or gain on the derivative in net income. Net income

---

[39]We discuss the hedge of an unrecognized firm commitment in Chapter 9.

[40]We discuss the hedge of a forecasted transaction in Chapter 9.

therefore includes the net gain or loss based on the effectiveness of the hedge in neutralizing the risk. In a cash flow hedge of an anticipated transaction, the hedged cash flow commitment does not yet appear on the balance sheet but the derivative instrument does. When a gain or loss occurs on the derivative, it is recognized as an asset or liability on the balance sheet, but there is no asset or liability on the balance sheet yet in which to recognize the corresponding change in fair value. Therefore, the change in the fair value is recognized in AOCI. For this reason, the firm classifies the corresponding gain or loss on the derivative instrument in other comprehensive income and later reclassifies the gain or loss to net income when it records the actual transaction.

For further information and numerical example of the accounting for Scenarios 1 and 2, please refer to the Chapter 7 online appendix at the text's website.

Disclosures Related to Derivative Instruments

Firms must disclose the book value and the fair value of financial instruments. Financial instruments impose on one entity a right to receive cash and an obligation on another entity to pay cash. Financial instruments include accounts receivable, notes receivable, notes payable, bonds payable, forward contracts, swap contracts, and most derivatives. Fair value is the current amount at which two willing parties exchange the instrument for cash. In addition, firms must disclose the following with respect to derivatives:

- Firms must describe their risk management strategy and how particular derivatives help accomplish their hedging objectives. The description should distinguish between derivative instruments designated as fair value hedges, cash flow hedges, and all other derivatives.
- For fair value and cash flow hedges, firms must disclose the net gain or loss recognized in earnings resulting from the hedges' ineffectiveness (that is, not offsetting the risk hedged) and the line item on the income statement that includes this net gain or loss.
- For cash flow hedges, firms must describe the transactions or events that will result in reclassifying gains and losses from other comprehensive income to net income and the estimated amount of such reclassifications during the next 12 months.
- Firms must disclose the net amount of gains and losses recognized in earnings because a hedged firm commitment no longer qualifies as a fair value hedge or because a hedged forecasted transaction no longer qualifies as a cash flow hedge.[41]

Starbucks' Derivatives Disclosures

Starbucks uses derivatives to hedge commodity prices, foreign exchange rates, and interest rates. On page 42 of the MD&A section of its 10-K report, its management states: "We utilize short-term and long-term financing and may use interest rate hedges to manage our overall interest expense related to our existing fixed-rate debt, as well as to hedge the variability in cash flows due to changes in the benchmark interest rate related to

[41]U.S. GAAP requires qualitative disclosures about objectives and strategies for using derivatives, quantitative disclosures about fair value amounts of and gains and losses on derivative instruments, and disclosures about credit-risk-related contingent features in derivative agreements. *FASB Codification Topic 815.*

anticipated debt issuances." **Starbucks** then provides a table summarizing the impact of a change in interest rates as of September 27, 2015, on the fair value of **Starbucks'** debt. **Starbucks** has several debt issues outstanding. For example, a 1% (i.e., 100 basis point) increase (decrease) in interest rates would decrease (increase) the fair value of its $400 million 2016 notes by $5 million. The effect on its $355 million 2045 notes would be much larger (a $61 million change in fair value).

Accounting Quality Issues and Derivatives

Firms must mark derivatives to fair value each period. Fair values are usually reliable and easy to obtain when active, established markets exist for derivatives, as is the case for many forward contracts and interest and currency swaps. When firms engage in derivative transactions for which active markets do not exist, questions arise about the reliability of the fair values. **Enron**, for example, purchased and sold derivatives on the price and availability of broadband services. Broadband services were an emerging market at the time, with Enron one of only a few firms engaging in this type of derivative trading. Enron also held billions of dollars of notional value in derivatives for long-forward sales and purchases of various energy commodities, including oil, natural gas, and electricity, with some as far as 25 years in the future. Enron was the largest market maker (and one of the only market makers) for such derivatives, which were not widely traded.

A second accounting quality concern involves the classification of derivatives as fair value hedges versus cash flow hedges. In some cases, firms can classify exchange and commodity contracts as fair value hedges or cash flow hedges. Gains and losses on cash flow hedges affect earnings later than those on fair value hedges. When gains and losses on cash flow hedges substantially exceed the gains and losses on fair value hedges included in earnings, the analyst must at least question the firm's classification of its hedges.

When firms use derivatives to manage risks effectively, the net gain or loss each period should be relatively small. Large and varying amounts of gains or losses usually signal an ineffective use of derivatives.

Summary

This chapter explores various accounting issues related to measuring the financing activities of the firm. Both profitability analysis and risk analysis are affected by management's choice between shareholders' equity and interest-bearing debt to finance the acquisition of operating capacity. The proper measurement and reporting of liabilities enables you to understand the risk of investing in the firm's debt and equity instruments, and the existence of off-balance-sheet arrangements complicates the analysis.

This chapter focuses primarily on the set of liabilities arising from transactions with lending institutions that generate notes and bonds payable. Typically, these liabilities are generated to raise funds for investments in long-term assets used in operations. The next chapter (Chapter 8) examines the accounting issues surrounding these long-term assets. Chapter 9 returns to measuring and reporting liabilities generated from operating activities, such as accounts payable, provisions, deferred tax liabilities, and pension liabilities.

Questions, Exercises, Problems, and Cases

Questions and Exercises

7.1 Common Equity Transactions. Describe the directional effect (increase, decrease, or no effect) of each transaction on the components of the book value of common shareholders' equity shown in the chart below.

   a. Issuance of $1 par value common stock at an amount greater than par value
   b. Donation of land by a governmental unit to a corporation
   c. Cash dividend declared
   d. Previously declared cash dividend paid
   e. Property dividend declared and paid
   f. Large stock dividend declared and issued
   g. Small stock dividend declared and issued
   h. 2-for-1 stock split announced and issued
   i. Stock options granted
   j. Recognition of compensation expense on stock options
   k. Stock options exercised
   l. Stock options expired
   m. Treasury stock acquired (company uses the cost method)
   n. Treasury stock in Transaction m reissued at an amount greater than the original acquisition price
   o. Treasury stock in Transaction m reissued at an amount less than the original acquisition price
   p. Restricted stock issued (grant date)
   q. Recognition of compensation expense related to restricted stock
   r. Granting of stock appreciation rights to be settled with cash
   s. Recognition of compensation expense on stock appreciation rights
   t. Reacquisition and retirement of common stock at an amount greater than original issue price

Item	Common Stock	Additional Paid-in Capital	Deferred Compensation	Retained Earnings (use * to indicate income statement effect)	Treasury Stock at Cost	Total Common Shareholders' Equity
a.						
b.						
c.						
...						

7.2 Common Equity Issue. Assume that a start-up manufacturing company raises capital through a series of equity issues.

   a. Using the financial statement template below, summarize the financial statement effects of the following transactions. Identify the account affected and use plus and minus signs to indicate the increases and decreases in the specific element of the balance sheet (assets, liabilities, components of shareholders' equity).

   (1) Issues 100,000 shares of $1 par value common stock for $10 per share.

(2) Receives land in exchange for 10,000 shares of $1 par common stock when the common stock is trading in the market at $15 per share. The land has no readily determinable market value.

Assets	=	Liabilities	+	Shareholders' Equity		
				CC	AOCI	RE
Journal entry:						

b. In each case, how does the company measure the transaction? What measurement attribute is used?

7.3 Dividends. Following is the shareholders' equity section of All-Wood Doors on a day its common stock is trading at $130 per share.   `LO 7-1`

Common stock ($2 par value, 40,000 shares issued and outstanding)	$80,000
Additional paid-in capital on common stock	1,600,000
Retained earnings	3,000,000

a. Use the financial statement template below to show the financial statement effects of the following dividend events. (Assume that the events are independent.)
  (1) Cash dividend declaration and payment of $1 per share
  (2) Property dividend declaration and payment of shares representing a short-term investment in Screen Products, Ltd., with a fair value of $10,000
  (3) 10% stock dividend
  (4) 100% stock dividend
  (5) 3-for-1 stock split
  (6) 1-for-2 reverse stock split

Assets	=	Liabilities	+	Shareholders' Equity		
				CC	AOCI	RE
Journal entry:						

b. Which events changed the book value of common equity? Under what conditions will these events lead to future increases and decreases in ROCE (see Chapter 4 for the ROCE definition)?

7.4 Cash Flow Effects of Equity and Debt Financing. Identify where the cash flow effect of each of the following transactions is reported in the statement of cash flows: operating, investing, or financing section. State the direction of each change. State *None* if there is no cash flow effect.   `LO 7-1, LO 7-4, LO 7-5`
  a. Issuance of stock for cash
  b. Issuance of stock for land
  c. Acquisition of treasury stock
  d. Reissuance of treasury stock
  e. Declaration of a cash dividend
  f. Payment of a cash dividend previously declared
  g. Declaration and issuance of a large stock dividend
  h. Declaration and issuance of a small stock dividend
  i. Granting of stock options
  j. Exercise of stock options
  k. Granting of RSUs
  l. Issuance of long-term notes payable

    m. Issuance of convertible bonds

    n. Conversion of convertible bonds to common stock

    o. Payment of interest on bonds

    p. Retirement of bonds at book value

    q. Retirement of bonds at a gain

    r. Retirement of bonds at a loss

LO 7-4

7.5 Accounting for a Note Payable. Assume that on December 31, 2017, The Coca-Cola Company borrows money from a consortium of banks by issuing a $900 million promissory note. The note matures in four years on December 31, 2021, and pays 3% interest once a year on December 31. The consortium transfers $867.331 million (rounded) to Coca-Cola, implying that the bank expects a 4% return on the note.

    a. Using the effective interest method, complete the template below to show the financial statement effects of (1) the December 31, 2017, issue; (2) the December 31, 2018, interest payment and interest expense accrual; and (3) the December 31, 2019, interest payment and interest expense accrual.

Assets	=	Liabilities	+	Shareholders' Equity		
				CC	AOCI	RE
Journal entry:						

    b. Assume that events involving foreign operations have increased the risk of The Coca-Cola Company to the point where creditors expect a 5% return on the note as of December 31, 2019. What amounts would Coca-Cola report for long-term debt (1) on the face of its December 31, 2019, balance sheet and (2) in the notes to the financial statements?

    c. In addition to the information in Requirement b, assume that The Coca-Cola Company has chosen the fair value option for the reporting of this note. What amounts would Coca-Cola report for long-term debt (1) on the face of its December 31, 2019, balance sheet and (2) on the income statement with respect to the note's fair value change?

LO 7-4

7.6 Accounting for Troubled Debt: Settlement (Based on material in the online appendix for Chapter 7). Assume that Circuit City owes Synovus Bank $1,000,000 on a four-year, 7% note originally issued at par. After one year of making scheduled payments, Circuit City faces financial difficulty. At the end of the second year, Circuit City owes Synovus $1,000,000 plus $70,000 of accrued but unpaid interest. Circuit City settles the debt by paying $700,000 in cash and transferring investments to Synovus. Circuit City recently purchased the investments for $120,000 and carried them on the books at that amount. The investments are worth $135,000 at the date of the debt settlement. Use the template below to show the financial statement effects of the debt settlement.

Assets	=	Liabilities	+	Shareholders' Equity		
				CC	AOCI	RE
Journal entry:						

LO 7-4

7.7 Accounting for Troubled Debt: Modification of Terms (Based on material in the online appendix for Chapter 7). Assume that Great Beef Co. owes Bank of America $5,000,000 on a three-year, 9% note originally issued at par. After one year of making scheduled payments, the firm faces financial difficulty. At the end of the second year, Great Beef owes Bank of America $5,000,000 plus $450,000 of accrued but unpaid interest. (Assume that the financial difficulty has increased the riskiness of Great Beef Co. to the point where it would have to pay 15% to borrow money.)

a. Assume that Bank of America restructures the note by forgiving the $450,000 interest payable, reducing the note principal to $4,500,000, and reducing the interest rate to 6%. Show the financial statement effects at the date of restructuring using the template below assuming that Great Beef Co. uses
(1) U.S. GAAP.
(2) IFRS.

Assets	=	Liabilities	+	Shareholders' Equity		
				CC	AOCI	RE
Journal entry:						

b. Assume that Bank of America restructures the note by forgiving the $450,000 interest payable, reducing the note principal to $4,800,000, and reducing the interest rate to 7%. Show the financial statement effects at the date of restructuring using the template below assuming that Great Beef Co. uses
(1) U.S. GAAP.
(2) IFRS.

Assets	=	Liabilities	+	Shareholders' Equity		
				CC	AOCI	RE
Journal entry:						

c. Comment on the differences between the two systems. Which reporting system better represents the underlying economics of the debt restructuring? Will U.S. GAAP supplemental disclosures provide similar information? Explain.

7.8 Redeemable Preferred Stock. Determine and compare the financial reporting (debt versus equity classification) of redeemable preferred stock with the following characteristics under U.S. GAAP and IFRS.   `LO 7-1, LO 7-4, LO 7-5`
a. Redemption will occur at a specific time or upon a specific event (for example, death of the holder).
b. Redemption is at the option of the issuing firm; that is, the preferred stock is "callable."
c. Redemption is at the holder's discretion; that is, the preferred stock is "putable."

7.9 Convertible Preferred Stock. Assume that John Deere Co. issues 2,000 shares of $100 par, 6% convertible preferred stock for $105 per share. Shareholders have the right to exchange each share of convertible preferred stock for five shares of $10 par common stock. Use the template below to show the financial statement effects of the following events.   `LO 7-1, LO 7-4, LO 7-5`
a. Issuance of the preferred stock
b. Declaration and payment of the cash dividend on the preferred stock
c. Conversion of the preferred stock to common stock when the market value of the common stock is $29 per share

Assets	=	Liabilities	+	Shareholders' Equity		
				CC	AOCI	RE
Journal entry:						

7.10 Convertible Debt under IFRS and U.S. GAAP. ARTL Company issued 3%, 10-year convertible bonds on January 1 at their par value of $500 million. Each $1,000 bond is convertible into 40 shares of ARTL's $1 par value common stock. Use the template below to show the financial statement effects under U.S. GAAP and IFRS of the following transactions.   `LO 7-5`

a. Original issue (For the IFRS treatment, assume that ARTL would have borrowed at 8% if it did not offer a conversion privilege.)

b. Recognition of one year's interest effect

c. Conversion of the bonds when a share of ARTL common stock trades at $30

Assets	=	Liabilities	+	Shareholders' Equity		
				CC	AOCI	RE
Journal entry:						

LO 7-5

7.11 Bonds Issued with Detachable Warrants. Assume that Motorola, Inc., issues bonds with a face value of $10,000,000 for $9,200,000. The bonds have detachable warrants that may be traded in for shares of common stock. Assume that immediately after issue, bonds with warrants detached trade for $9,000,000; the warrants, for $400,000. Use the template below to show the financial statement effects at the date of issue.

Assets	=	Liabilities	+	Shareholders' Equity		
				CC	AOCI	RE
Journal entry:						

LO 7-6

7.12 Effect of Capital and Operating Leases on the Financial Statements. All leases for financial reporting purposes are treated as either capital (finance) leases or operating leases. The effects of the two reporting techniques on the financial statements differ substantially. From the perspective of the lessee, prepare a chart that lists the line items reported on the (a) income statement, (b) balance sheet, and (c) statement of cash flows under each reporting technique.

LO 7-6

7.13 New Lease Standards. New lease standards become effective January 1, 2019. These standards affect the accounting for operating leases. Assume Swift Company acquires a machine with a fair value of $100,000 on January 1 of Year 1 by signing a five-year lease. Swift must make payments of $16,275 each December 31. The appropriate interest rate on the lease is 10%. Assume that this lease meets the criteria for an operating lease. Compute the following amounts under (a) the lease standards in effect before January 1, 2019, and (b) the new lease standards (an amortization table will be useful in solving this problem):

- The leased asset at December 31 of each of the first three years.
- The lease liability at December 31 of each of the first three years.
- Rent expense for each of the first three years.
- Interest expense for each of the first three years.
- Depreciation expense for each of the first three years.

LO 7-2

7.14 Accounting for Stock-Based Compensation. Historically, technology firms have been the most aggressive users of stock-based compensation in the form of stock options granted to almost all employees of the firms. What is the rationale for offering stock options as compensation? Why has this form of compensation been particularly popular with technology firms in the past?

LO 7-7

7.15 Valuation of Derivatives. Financial reporting classifies derivatives as (a) speculative investments, (b) fair value hedges, or (c) cash flow hedges. However, firms revalue all derivatives to market value each period regardless of the firm's reason for acquiring the derivatives. In addition to increasing or decreasing the derivative asset or liability, the revaluation amount either affects net income immediately or affects other comprehensive income immediately and net income later. For each type of derivative, describe where firms report the revaluation amount on the financial statements in each period. Your answer should include a description of the treatment in the period of settlement, including any transfers among accounts.

Problems and Cases

7.16 Accounting for Securitization of Receivables. Ford Motor Credit
Company discloses the following information with respect to finance receivables (amounts in millions).

December 31:	2004	2003
Finance Receivables	$146,451	$152,276
Securitized Receivables Sold	$ (35,600)	$ (46,900)
Finance Receivables on Balance Sheet	$110,851	$105,376
Retained Interest in Securitized Receivables Sold	$ 9,166	$ 12,569

Notes to Financial Statements

The Company periodically sells finance receivables in securitization transactions to fund operations and to maintain liquidity. The securitization process involves the sale of interest-bearing securities to investors, the payment of which is secured by a pool of receivables. In many securitization transactions, the Company surrenders control over certain of its finance receivables by selling these assets to SPEs. SPEs then securitize the receivables by issuing certificates representing undivided interests in the SPEs' assets to outside investors and to the Company (retained interest). These certificates entitle the holder to a series of scheduled cash flows under present terms and conditions, the receipt of which is dependent upon cash flows generated by the related SPEs' assets. The cash flows on the underlying receivables are used to pay principal and interest on the debt securities as well as transaction expenses.

In each securitization transaction, the Company retains certain subordinated interests in the SPE, which are the first to absorb credit losses on the sold receivables. As a result, the credit quality of certificates held by outside investors is enhanced. However, the investors and the trusts have no recourse against the Company beyond the trust assets. The Company also retains the servicing rights to the sold receivables and receives a servicing fee. While servicing the sold receivables for the SPE, the Company applies the same servicing policies and procedures that it applies to its own receivables and maintains a normal relationship with its financing customers.

Source: Ford Motor Credit Company, Form 10-K for the Fiscal Year Ended December 31, 2004.

REQUIRED

a. Applying the criteria for the sale of receivables, justify Ford Motor Credit's treatment of the securitization of finance receivables on December 31, 2003 and 2004, as a sale instead of a collateralized loan.

b. Assume that the receivables disclosed as securitized on December 31, 2003, had been initially securitized on that day. Give the journal entry that Ford Motor Credit would have made to securitize these receivables, assuming that it securitized the receivables at no gain or loss.

c. Assume that Ford Motor Credit decided to consolidate its receivables securitization structure in 2004 and to start accounting for it as secured borrowings. Give the journal entry that the company would make on December 31, 2004, to account for this change, assuming that it recognized no gain or loss on this event.

d. Most firms prefer to report the securitization of receivables as a sale. The alternative is to view the arrangement as a collateralized loan with the receivables remaining on the firm's balance sheet. Speculate on why firms prefer to report the securitization of receivables as a sale.

7.17 Accounting for Off-Balance-Sheet Financing. On June 24, Year 4, a
major airline entered into a revolving accounts receivable facility (Facility) providing for the sale of $489 million of a defined pool of accounts receivable (Receivables) through a wholly owned

subsidiary to a trust in exchange for a senior certificate in the principal amount of $300 million (Senior Certificate) and a subordinate certificate in the principal amount of $189 million (Subordinate Certificate). The subsidiary retained the Subordinate Certificate, and the company received $300 million in cash from the sale of the Senior Certificate to a third party. The principal amount of the Subordinate Certificate fluctuates daily depending on the volume of Receivables sold and is payable to the subsidiary only to the extent that the collections received on the Receivables exceed amounts due on the Senior Certificate. The full amount of the allowance for doubtful accounts related to the Receivables sold has been retained, as the company has substantially the same credit risk as if the Receivables had not been sold. Under the terms of the Facility, the company is obligated to pay fees that approximate the purchaser's cost of issuing a like amount of commercial paper plus certain administrative costs.

REQUIRED

The airline's management requests your advice on the appropriate accounting for this transaction. How would you respond?

`LO 7-6`

7.18 Effect of Capitalizing Operating Leases on Balance Sheet Ratios. Some retailing companies own their own stores or acquire their premises under capital leases. Other retailing companies acquire the use of store facilities under operating leases, contracting to make future payments. An analyst comparing the capital structure risks of retailing companies may want to adjust reported financial statement data to put all firms on a comparable basis. Certain data from the financial statements of **Gap Inc.** and **Limited Brands** follow (amounts in millions).

Balance Sheet as of January 31, 2009	Gap Inc.	Limited Brands
Current liabilities	$2,158	$1,255
Long-term debt	0	2,897
Other noncurrent liabilities	1,019	946
Shareholders' equity	4,387	1,874
Total	$7,564	$6,972
Minimum Payments under Operating Leases		
2009	$1,069	$ 478
2010	927	455
2011	712	416
2012	520	373
2013	386	341
After 2013	1,080	1,334
Total	$4,694	$3,397

REQUIRED

a. Compute the present value of operating lease obligations using an 8% discount rate for Gap Inc. and Limited Brands as of January 31, 2009. Assume that all cash flows occur at the end of each year. Also assume that the minimum lease payment each year after 2013 equals $360 million per year for three years for Gap Inc. and $333.5 million for four years for Limited Brands. (This payment scheduling assumption can be obtained by assuming that the payment amount for 2013 continues until the aggregate payments after 2013 have been made, rounding the number of years upward, and then assuming level payments for that number of years. For Gap Inc.: $1,080/$386 = 2.8 years. Rounding up to three years creates a three-year annuity of $1,080/3 years = $360 million per year.)

b. Compute each of the following ratios for Gap Inc. and Limited Brands as of January 31, 2009, using the amounts originally reported in their balance sheets for the year.
   (1) Liabilities to Assets Ratio = Total Liabilities/Total Assets
   (2) Long-Term Debt to Long-Term Capital Ratio = Long-Term Debt/(Long-Term Debt + Shareholders' Equity)
c. Repeat Requirement b but assume that these firms capitalize operating leases.
d. Comment on the results from Requirements b and c.

7.19 Stock-Based Compensation. Exhibit 7.17 includes a footnote excerpt from the annual report of **The Coca-Cola Company** for 2004. The beverage company offers stock options to key employees under plans approved by stockholders.

LO 7-2

REQUIRED

Review Exhibit 7.17 and answer the following questions.
   a. Coca-Cola reports both pretax and after-tax stock-based compensation in its notes to the financial statements. What is the tax savings for 2002, 2003, and 2004 that Coca-Cola

Exhibit 7.17

The Coca-Cola Company
Stock Option Disclosures
(Problem 7.19)

Note—Stock-Based Compensation (partial footnote disclosure)

Our Company currently sponsors stock option plans. Effective January 1, 2002, our Company adopted the preferable fair value recognition provisions of Statement of Financial Accounting Standards ("SFAS") No. 123, "Accounting for Stock-Based Compensation." The fair values of the stock awards are determined using a single estimated expected life. The compensation expense is recognized on a straight-line basis over the vesting period. The total stock-based compensation expense, net of related tax effects, was $254 million in 2004, $308 million in 2003, and $267 million in 2002.

	2004	2003	2002
Stock-Based Compensation Expense, pretax[a]	$ 345	$ 422	$ 365
Number of Options Granted[b]	31	24	29
Average Option Price per Share	$ 41.63	$ 49.67	$ 44.69
Average Market Price per Share at Time of Grant	$ 41.63	$ 49.67	$ 44.69
Fair Value of Option Granted per Share	$ 8.84	$ 13.49	$ 13.10
Vesting Period of Options Granted, years	1–4	1–4	1–4
Life of Options, years	10	10	10
Option Valuation Assumptions for Black-Scholes Model[b]			
Risk-Free Interest Rate	3.8%	3.5%	3.4%
Dividend Yield	2.5%	1.9%	1.7%
Stock Volatility	23.0%	28.1%	30.2%
Expected Option Life, years	6.0	6.0	6.0
Number of Options Exercised[a]	5	4	3
Average Option Exercise Price	$ 35.54	$ 26.96	$ 31.09

[a]Amounts in millions.

[b]Weighted averages.

Source: The Coca-Cola Company, Form 10-K for the Fiscal Year Ended December 31, 2004.

generates from the stock-based compensation provided to its employees? Speculate on what income statement line item includes this tax savings as well as what income statement line item includes the stock-based compensation expense. (The income statement is not provided in this problem.)

b. The average option price per share and market price per share at time of grant is equal each year ($44.69 for 2002, $49.67 for 2003, and $41.63 for 2004). Discuss why Coca-Cola structured the stock option grants this way each year.

c. What are the likely reasons that the fair value of options granted per share increased from 2002 to 2003 and then decreased from 2003 to 2004?

d. Coca-Cola does not report the market price of its stock at the time employees exercised options (3 million in 2002, 4 million in 2003, and 5 million in 2004), but in each year the end-of-year market price is substantially higher than the average option exercise price reported in Exhibit 7.17. Discuss why Coca-Cola is willing to sell shares of its stock to employees at a price (option exercise price) much lower than the firm could obtain for shares sold on the market (market price at time of exercise).

e. Coca-Cola employs the Black-Scholes valuation model for valuing stock option grants. Speculate on the directional effects of the key assumptions made in applying the Black-Scholes options pricing model. That is, which assumptions will result in a higher fair value for stock options and which will result in a lower fair value? Why?

LO 7-2 **7.20 Stock-Based Compensation.** **Eli Lilly and Company** produces pharmaceutical products for humans and animals. Exhibit 7.18 includes a footnote excerpt from the annual report of Lilly for the period ending December 31, 2004.

REQUIRED

Review Exhibit 7.18 and answer the following questions.

a. Lilly's statement of cash flows (not provided in this problem) includes an addback for stock-based compensation in calculating cash flows from operations of $108.2 million for 2004 and $25.2 million for 2003. Why does Lilly add stock-based compensation back to net income?

b. Refer to Requirement a. Lilly's statement of cash flows includes a cash inflow in the section on cash flows from financing activities of $12.5 million for 2004 and $46.5 million for 2003. The amounts are labeled "Issuance of common stock under stock plans." Who provided these cash inflows to Lilly? In general terms, how are the amounts determined?

c. Lilly states in the note: "Stock options are granted to employees at exercise prices equal to the fair market value of our stock at the dates of grant." Discuss why Lilly structured the stock option grants this way.

d. The note reports $397.5 million of remaining unrecognized compensation cost related to nonvested stock options. What portion of this amount will be reported as compensation expense in the second quarter ending June 30, 2004? Does this amount represent total stock-based compensation expense for the quarter?

e. In the past, firms were required to report pro forma earnings per share, taking into consideration stock-based compensation. Current financial reporting requires stock-based compensation to be reported in the income statement, and thus included in the calculations of reported earnings per share. Many firms also present non-GAAP earnings numbers before deducting the effects of stock compensation as a supplemental disclosure in their annual reports (which is comparable to the reported earnings number under the older rules). Why do companies do this? Which earnings number is more meaningful, net income or this non-GAAP measure?

LO 7-2 **7.21 Stock-Based Compensation—Vesting and Valuation Models.** Exhibits 7.17 and 7.18 provide footnote excerpts to the financial reports of **The Coca-Cola Company** and **Eli Lilly and Company** that discuss the stock option grants given to the employees of the two firms. Each firm uses options extensively to reward employees for their performance.

Exhibit 7.18

Eli Lilly and Company
Stock Option Disclosures
(Problem 7.20)

Note—Stock-Based Compensation (partial footnote disclosure)

We adopted Statement of Financial Accounting Standards No. 123 (revised 2004), Share-Based Payment (SFAS 123R), effective January 1, 2004. SFAS 123R requires the recognition of the fair value of stock-based compensation in net income. Stock options are granted to employees at exercise prices equal to the fair market value of our stock at the dates of grant. Generally, options fully vest three years from the grant date and have a term of 10 years. We recognize the stock-based compensation expense over the requisite service period of the individual grantees, which generally equals the vesting period.

We recognized compensation cost in the amount of $108.2 million and $25.2 million in the first quarter of 2004 and 2003, respectively, as well as related tax benefits of $32.8 million and $8.8 million, respectively.

Beginning with the 2004 stock option grant, we utilized a lattice-based option valuation model for estimating the fair value of the stock options. The lattice model allows the use of a range of assumptions related to volatility, risk-free interest rate, and employee exercise behavior. Expected volatilities utilized in the lattice model are based on implied volatilities from traded options on our stock, historical volatility of our stock price, and other factors. Similarly, the dividend yield is based on historical experience and our estimate of future dividend yields. The risk-free interest rate is derived from the U.S. Treasury yield curve in effect at the time of grant. The model incorporates exercise and post-vesting forfeiture assumptions based on an analysis of historical data. The expected life of the 2004 grants is derived from the output of the lattice model.

The weighted-average fair values of the options granted in the first quarter of 2004 were $16.06 per option, determined using the following assumptions:

Dividend Yield	2.0%
Weighted-Average Volatility	27.8%
Range of Volatilities	27.6%–30.7%
Risk-Free Interest Rate	2.5%–4.5%
Weighted-Average Expected Life	7.2 years

As of March 31, 2004, the total remaining unrecognized compensation cost related to non-vested stock options amounted to $397.5 million which will be amortized over the weighted-average remaining requisite service period of 2 years.

Source: Elli Lilly and Company, Form 10-K for the Fiscal Year Ended December 31, 2004.

REQUIRED

Review Exhibits 7.17 and 7.18 and answer the following questions.

a. Explain the concept of vesting. Discuss why firms typically include a vesting feature in the stock-based compensation plans that they offer to their employees.

b. What are the vesting characteristics of the two plans discussed in the exhibits? What effect do they have on stock-based compensation expense using the fair value method?

c. For each firm, (1) what is the life of the options granted, (2) how does option life relate to the vesting period, and (3) why might the weighted-average *expected* life of the options be less than the full life of the options?

d. The Coca-Cola Company uses the Black-Scholes valuation model for estimating the fair value of the stock options, whereas Eli Lilly and Company utilizes a lattice-based option valuation model. Both valuation techniques are permitted by U.S. GAAP. Perform an Internet search to determine which valuation model is more commonly used by the largest publicly held firms. Speculate on why this is the case.

Exhibit 7.19

Stock Options (Problem 7.22)

	Year 4	Year 3	Year 2
Number of options granted[a]	27.141	8.261	46.928
Average option price per share	$ 32.26	$ 31.19	$ 27.37
Average market price per share at time of grant	$ 32.26	$ 31.19	$ 27.37
Fair value of option granted per share	$ 8.33	$ 9.44	$ 7.73
Vesting period of options granted, years	1–5	1–5	1–5
Option valuation assumptions:			
Discount rate	4.0%	3.5%	3.5%
Volatility	27.7%	34.7%	33.7%
Dividend yield	2.5%	2.5%	2.7%
Expected option life, years	6.0	6.0	6.0
Number of options exercised (in millions)	43.110	43.829	29.146
Average option exercise price	$ 10.54	$ 9.45	$ 9.45
Average market price at time of exercise	$ 32.68	$ 27.59	$ 31.86

LO 7-2 **7.22 Interpreting Stock Option Disclosures.** Exhibit 7.19 summarizes the information disclosed by a large conglomerate regarding its stock option plans for Years 2–4. Assume an income tax rate of 35%.

REQUIRED

a. The average option price per share and market price per share at time of grant are equal in each year ($27.37 for Year 2, $31.19 for Year 3, and $32.26 for Year 4). Speculate on why the company structured the stock option grants this way in each year.

b. What are the likely reasons that the fair value of options granted per share increased from Year 2 to Year 3?

c. Compute the amount that the company received from the exercise of stock options each year versus the amount it would have received if it had issued the same number of shares on the market.

d. Refer to your answer to Requirement c. Discuss why the company is willing to sell shares of its stock to employees at a price (average option exercise price) much lower than the firm could obtain for shares sold on the market (average market price at time of exercise).

e. Refer again to your answer to Requirement c. Compute the effect of stock-based compensation on net income for each year, assuming that stock option compensation expense equaled the difference between the market price and the exercise price of options exercised.

f. Discuss the strengths and weaknesses of each of the following approaches to recognizing the cost of stock options: (1) no expense as long as the option price equals the market price on the date stock options are granted, (2) expense in the year of the grant equal to value of options granted, and (3) expense in the year of exercise equal to the benefit realized by employees from purchasing shares for less than market value.

LO 7-7 **7.23 Hedging Interest Rate Risk (Based on material in the online appendix for Chapter 7). Part A.** Floral Delivery, Inc. (FD) acquired a fleet of vans on January 1, 2017, by issuing a $500,000, four-year, 4% fixed rate note, with interest payable annually on December 3. FD has the option to repay the note prior to maturity at the note's fair value. FD engages in a contract with the bank to swap its fixed-interest-rate obligation for a variable-interest-rate obligation; the variable rate in the swap is intended to track the variable rate used by the supplier to revalue the note while it is outstanding. The swap causes FD's interest payments to vary as the variable interest rate changes, but it locks the value of the note payable at $100,000, and thus qualifies the swap as a hedge of value changes in an existing liability. Under the terms of the swap, the counterparty (the bank) resets the interest rate each December 31. Assume that the interest rate is reset to 3% at December 31, 2017, and to 5% at December 31, 2018. Interest rates remain steady from that date forward.

REQUIRED

Use the financial template used throughout the chapter to record the financial statement effects and journal entries of these transactions and events through December 31, 2019.

Part B.
REQUIRED

Repeat Part A assuming that the 4% interest rate is variable and that the supplier resets the interest rate each December 31 to establish the interest charge for the next calendar year. In this case, FD wants to protect its future cash flows against increases in the variable interest rate to more than the initial 4% rate, so it contracts with the bank to swap its variable-interest-rate obligation for a fixed-interest-rate obligation. The swap fixes the firm's annual interest expense and cash expenditure to 4% of the $500,000 note. FD designates the swap contract as a cash flow hedge.

INTEGRATIVE CASE 7.1

Walmart

It is common practice for retail outlets to lease their store locations and distribution centers. **Walmart** is no exception. Note 11 to Walmart's consolidated financial statements for the fiscal year ending January 31, 2016 (found online at the text website or available for download in the investor relations section of Walmart's website), provides information on future operating lease commitments.

`LO 7-4, LO 7-6`

REQUIRED

a. Effectively capitalize the operating lease obligations. You must first choose and justify an interest rate. Assume that all cash flows occur at the end of each year.
b. Recompute the long-term debt to long-term capital ratio (see Chapter 5) using your capitalized operating leases. Comment on the results.

CASE 7.2

Oracle Corporation: Share-Based Compensation Effects/Statement of Shareholders' Equity

A sales-based ranking of software companies provided by **Yahoo! Finance** on November 5, 2008, places **Oracle Corporation** third behind sales leaders **Microsoft Corporation** and **IBM Software**. Typical of high-tech companies in the software industry, Oracle Corporation uses share-based compensation plans extensively to motivate its employees. In Note 11 of its May 31, 2008, annual report, Oracle states that it settles employee stock option exercises primarily with newly issued common shares.

`LO 7-1, LO 7-2`

As indicated by the selected data from Oracle's May 31, 2008, consolidated balance sheet in Exhibit 7.20, Oracle finances operations using substantially more common shareholder's equity than it does long-term debt. However, Oracle's long-term debt to shareholders' equity ratio of 44.5% is substantially larger than that of major U.S. competitor Microsoft Corporation and major foreign competitor **SAP AG**, both of which report almost no long-term financial debt. Exhibit 7.21 presents the consolidated statement of shareholders' equity for 2008. Exhibit 7.22 presents portions of financial statement Notes 10 and 11.

REQUIRED

a. Compute Oracle's long-term debt to shareholders' equity ratio for May 31, 2008 and 2007. Identify the increases in shareholders' equity in 2008 from share-based compensation plans. Calculate the long-term debt to shareholders' equity ratio that would have occurred had Oracle not implemented the stock repurchase plan. Comment on the potential effect on future ROE of Oracle's financing strategy.

b. Retained earnings increase because of net income and decrease because of dividends declared. Why, then, did Oracle decrease retained earnings when it repurchased common stock?

c. Of the first five changes listed in the shareholders' equity section, one of them, the common stock repurchase, clearly represents a cash outflow. Identify the cash flow effects of the other four items. Where will each cash flow effect be reported in the statement of cash flows?

d. Oracle engages in many transactions with nonowners (that is, customers, suppliers, and the government) that increase net assets. For example, Oracle's foreign subsidiaries perform services on credit with unrelated third-party customers. The accounts receivable generated by the transactions are denominated in a foreign currency and thus are reported on the foreign subsidiaries' balance sheet in that foreign currency. The consolidation process causes the subsidiary's accounts receivable to be added to the parent company's (Oracle's) accounts receivable and reported on Oracle's Consolidated Balance Sheet. Assuming that the foreign currency strengthens relative to the U.S. dollar, how does Oracle's Consolidated Statement of Shareholders' Equity capture the increases in accounts receivable described in this example transaction?

Exhibit 7.20

Oracle Corporation
May 31, 2008, Consolidated Balance Sheet
(in millions of dollars)
(Case 7.2)

	May 31,	
	2008	2007
Non-current notes payable and other non-current borrowings	$10,235	$ 6,235
Stockholders' equity		
Common stock, $0.01 par value and additional paid-in capital— authorized: 11,000 shares; outstanding: 5,150 shares and 5,107 shares as of May 31, 2008 and 2007	$12,446	$10,293
Retained earnings	9,961	6,223
Accumulated other comprehensive income	618	403
Total stockholders' equity	$23,025	$16,919

Source: Oracle Corporation, Form 10-K for the Fiscal Year Ended May 31, 2008.

Exhibit 7.21

Oracle Corporation
Consolidated Statements of Stockholders' Equity at May 31, 2008
(in millions of dollars)
(Case 7.2)

	Comprehensive Income	Common Stock and Additional Paid-in Capital		Retained Earnings	Accumulated Other Comprehensive Income	Total
		Number of Shares	Amount			
Balances as of May 31, 2007		5,107	$10,293	$ 6,223	$403	$16,919
Common stock issued under stock award plans		137	1,229			1,229
Common stock issued under stock purchase plans		3	59			59
Assumption of stock award in conjunction with acquisitions			240			240
Stock-based compensation			367			367
Repurchase of common stock		(97)	(214)	(1, 786)		(2,000)
Tax benefits from stock plans			472			472
Adjustment to retained earnings upon adoption of FIN 48				3		3
Net unrealized loss on defined benefit plan assets, net of tax	$ (9)				(9)	(9)
Foreign currency translation	300				300	300
Net unrealized losses on derivative financial instruments, net of tax	(77)				(77)	(77)
Net unrealized gain on marketable securities, net of tax	1				1	1
Net income	5,521			5,521		5,521
Comprehensive income	$5,736					
Balances as of May 31, 2008		5,150	$12,446	$ 9,961	$618	$23,025

Source: Oracle Corporation, Form 10-K for the Fiscal Year Ended May 31, 2008.

Exhibit 7.22

Oracle Corporation
Portions of Notes 10 and 11
(Case 7.2)

10. Stockholders' Equity (partial)

Stock Repurchases

Our Board of Directors has approved a program for Oracle to repurchase shares of our common stock to reduce the dilutive effect of our stock option and stock purchase plans. In April 2007, our Board of Directors expanded our repurchase program by $4.0 billion and as of May 31, 2008, $2.2 billion was available for share repurchases pursuant to our stock repurchase program. We repurchased 97.3 million shares for $2.0 billion (including 1.1 million shares for $24 million that were repurchased but not settled), 233.5 million shares for $4.0 billion and 146.9 million shares for $2.1 billion in fiscal 2008, 2007 and 2006, respectively.

Our stock repurchase authorization does not have an expiration date and the pace of our repurchase activity will depend on factors such as our working capital needs, our cash requirements for acquisitions, our debt repayment obligations (as described above), our stock price, and economic and market conditions. Our stock repurchases may be affected from time to time through open market purchases or pursuant to a Rule 10b5-1 plan. Our stock repurchase program may be accelerated, suspended, delayed or discontinued at any time.

11. Employee Benefit Plans (partial)

Stock-based Compensation Plans

Stock Option Plans

… In connection with certain of our acquisitions, including PeopleSoft, BEA, Siebel and Hyperion, we assumed all of the outstanding stock options and other stock awards of each acquiree's respective stock plans. These stock options and other stock awards generally retain all of the rights, terms and conditions of the respective plans under which they were originally granted. As of May 31, 2008, options to purchase 77 million shares of common stock and 1 million shares of restricted stock were outstanding under these plans.

Tax Benefits from Option Exercises

We settle employee stock option exercises primarily with newly issued common shares and may, on occasion, settle employee stock option exercises with our treasury shares. Total cash received as a result of option exercises was approximately $1.2 billion, $873 million and $573 million for fiscal 2008, 2007 and 2006, respectively. The aggregate intrinsic value of options exercised was $2.0 billion, $986 million and $594 million for fiscal 2008, 2007 and 2006, respectively. In connection with these exercises, the tax benefits realized by us were $588 million, $338 million and $169 million for fiscal 2008, 2007 and 2006, respectively. The adoption of Statement 123(R) required us to change our cash flow classification of certain tax benefits received from stock option exercises beginning in fiscal 2007. Of the total tax benefits received, we classified excess tax benefits from stock-based compensation of $454 million and $259 million as cash flows from financing activities rather than cash flows from operating activities for fiscal 2008 and 2007, respectively.

Employee Stock Purchase Plan

We have an Employee Stock Purchase Plan (Purchase Plan). Starting with the April 1, 2005 semi-annual option period, we amended the Purchase Plan such that employees can purchase shares of common stock at a price per share that is 95% of the fair value of Oracle stock as of the end of the semi-annual option period. As of May 31, 2008, 81 million shares were reserved for future issuances under the Purchase Plan. During fiscal 2008, 2007 and 2006, we issued 3 million, 3 million and 6 million shares, respectively, under the Purchase Plan.

Source: Oracle Corporation, Form 10-K for the Fiscal Year Ended May 31, 2008.

e. Using the foreign currency translation gain of $300 million as a context, present an argument for including the gain on Oracle's income statement and an argument for excluding the gain as Oracle does under U.S. GAAP.

f. Under Oracle's Employee Stock Purchase Plan, employees can purchase common shares at 95% of their fair values. Will Oracle report a loss on this transaction? Why or why not?

CASE 7.3

Long-Term Solvency Risk: Southwest and Lufthansa Airlines

The first decade of the 21st century witnessed a flurry of losses, bankruptcies, acquisitions, and strategic partnerships in the airline industry. The heavily levered firms in the industry are particularly susceptible to increases in fuel prices, economic changes that affect travel, and safety concerns. These conditions require you to have a strong understanding of the long-term solvency risk of firms in the airline industry.

LO 7-6

Two of the larger liabilities of airlines relate to promises to provide free flights to customers (frequent-flyer programs) and promises to make cash payments under flight equipment and ground facilities agreements. The former liability is captured in the total liabilities to assets ratio. The latter promise is captured in the total liabilities to assets ratio and in the long-term debt to shareholders' equity ratio, but only if the promises are treated as long-term debt.

Exhibits 7.23 to 7.28 present the income statements, balance sheets, and other key information for U.S. airline **Southwest**, which prepares financial statements under U.S. GAAP, and German airline **Lufthansa**, which prepares financial statements under IFRS.

REQUIRED

a. Using the information in the exhibits, provide a comprehensive and detailed comparison of the long-term solvency risk of Southwest to Lufthansa as of December 31, 2008, and as of December 31, 2007. (Ignore tax effects. Deferred taxes are covered in Chapter 8 on operating activities.)

(1) Consider the following ratios in your analysis:

$$\text{Liabilities to Assets Ratio} = \text{Total Liabilities/Total Assets}$$

$$\text{Long-Term Debt to Shareholders' Equity Ratio} = \text{Long-Term Debt/Total Shareholders' Equity}$$

$$\text{Operating Cash Flow to Average Total Liabilities Ratio} = \text{Operating Cash Flow/AverageTotal Liabilities}$$

$$\text{Interest Coverage Ratio (cash basis)} = \text{(Operating Cash Flow + Interest Paid + Taxes Paid)/Interest Paid}$$

(2) Compute the ratios using financial information (a) as reported and (b) after capitalization of operating leases. (Hint: Adjusting operating cash flow for assumed lease capitalization requires the removal of rent paid from operating cash flows and the inclusion of interest paid in operating cash flows. Use rent expense and interest expense to approximate rent paid and interest paid, respectively.

b. An analyst who compares the debt ratios of firms under U.S. GAAP and IFRS must consider key differences in the two sets of standards related to convertible debt and troubled debt restructurings. In general, which system would most likely yield lower debt and higher equity? Explain.

Exhibit 7.23

Southwest Airlines Co.
Consolidated Balance Sheet
(in millions, except share data)
(Case 7.3)

	December 31	
	2008	2007
ASSETS		
Current assets:		
Cash and cash equivalents	$ 1, 368	$ 2, 213
Short-term investments	435	566
Accounts and other receivables	209	279
Inventories of parts and supplies, at cost	203	259
Fuel derivative contracts	—	1,069
Deferred income taxes	365	—
Prepaid expenses and other current assets	313	57
Total current assets	2,893	4,443
Property and equipment, at cost:		
Flight equipment	13,722	13,019
Ground property and equipment	1,769	1,515
Deposits on flight equipment purchase contracts	380	626
	15,871	15,160
Less allowance for depreciation and amortization	4,831	4,286
	11,040	10,874
Other assets	375	1,455
	$14,308	$16,772
LIABILITIES AND STOCKHOLDERS' EQUITY		
Current liabilities:		
Accounts payable	$ 668	$ 759
Accrued liabilities	1,012	3,107
Air traffic liability	963	931
Current maturities of long-term debt	163	41
Total current liabilities	2,806	4,838
Long-term debt less current maturities	3,498	2,050
Deferred income taxes	1,904	2,535
Deferred gains from sale and leaseback of aircraft	105	106
Other deferred liabilities	1,042	302
Commitments and contingencies		
Stockholders' equity:		
Common stock, $1.00 par value: 2,000,000,000 shares authorized;		
807,611,634 shares issued in 2008 and 2007	808	808
Capital in excess of par value	1,215	1,207
Retained earnings	4,919	4,788
Accumulated other comprehensive income (loss)	(984)	1,241

(Continued)

Exhibit 7.23 (Continued)

Treasury stock, at cost: 67,619,062 and 72,814,104 shares in 2008 and 2007, respectively	(1,005)	(1,103)
Total stockholders' equity	4,953	6,941
See accompanying notes.	$14,308	$16,772

Source: Southwest Airlines Co., Form 10-K for the Fiscal Year Ended December 31, 2008.

Exhibit 7.24

Southwest Airlines Co.
Consolidated Statement of Income
(in millions, except per-share amounts)
(Case 7.3)

	Years Ended December 31,		
	2008	2007	2006
OPERATING REVENUES:			
Passenger	$10,549	$9,457	$8,750
Freight	145	130	134
Other	329	274	202
Total operating revenues	11,023	9,861	9,086
OPERATING EXPENSES:			
Salaries, wages, and benefits	3,340	3,213	3,052
Fuel and oil	3,713	2,690	2,284
Maintenance materials and repairs	721	616	468
Aircraft rentals	154	156	158
Landing fees and other rentals	662	560	495
Depreciation and amortization	599	555	515
Other operating expenses	1,385	1,280	1,180
Total operating expenses	10,574	9,070	8,152
OPERATING INCOME	449	791	934
OTHER EXPENSES (INCOME):			
Interest expense	10	119	128
Capitalized interest	(25)	(50)	(51)
Interest income	(26)	(44)	(84)
Other (gains) losses, net	92	(292)	151
Total other expenses (income)	171	(267)	144
INCOME BEFORE INCOME TAXES	278	1,058	790
PROVISION FOR INCOME TAXES	100	413	291
NET INCOME	$ 178	$ 645	$ 499
NET INCOME PER SHARE, BASIC	$ .24	$ .85	$ .63
NET INCOME PER SHARE, DILUTED	$ .24	$ .84	$ .61

Source: Southwest Airlines Co., Form 10-K for the Fiscal Year Ended December 31, 2008.

Exhibit 7.25

Southwest Airlines Co.
Additional Data from December 31, 2008, 10-K Filing
(Case 7.3)

From Consolidated Statement of Cash Flows (in millions):	2008	2007
Net cash provided by (used in) operating activities	$(1,521)	$2,845
Interest paid	$ 100	$ 63
Income taxes	$ 71	$ 94

From 2008 Note 8 (Leases)

... Total rental expense for operating leases, both aircraft and other, charged to operations in 2008, 2007, and 2006 was $527 million, $469 million, and $433 million, respectively. The majority of the Company's terminal operations space as well as 82 aircraft were under operating leases at December 31, 2008. Future minimum lease payments under capital leases and noncancelable operating leases with initial or remaining terms in excess of one year at December 31, 2008, are provided in the following table.

in millions	Capital Leases	Operating Leases
2009	$16	$ 376
2010	15	324
2011	12	249
2012	—	203
2013	—	152
After 2013	—	728
Total minimum lease payments	43	$2,032
Less amount representing interest	4	
Present value of minimum lease payments	39	
Less current portion	14	
Long-term portion	$25	

From 2007 Note 8 (Leases)

... Total rental expense for operating leases, both aircraft and other, charged to operations in 2007, 2006, and 2005 was $469 million, $433 million, and $409 million, respectively. The majority of the Company's terminal operations space as well as 86 aircraft were under operating leases at December 31, 2007. Future minimum lease payments under capital leases and noncancelable operating leases with initial or remaining terms in excess of one year at December 31, 2007, are provided in the following table.

in millions	Capital Leases	Operating Leases
2008	$16	$ 400
2009	17	335
2010	15	298
2011	12	235
2012	—	195
After 2012	—	876
Total minimum lease payments	60	$2,339

(Continued)

Exhibit 7.25 (Continued)	
Less amount representing interest	8
Present value of minimum lease payments	52
Less current portion	13
Long-term portion	$39

Source: Southwest Airlines Co., Form 10-K for the Fiscal Year Ended December 31, 2008.

Exhibit 7.26

Lufthansa
Consolidated Balance Sheet as of 31 December 2008
(Case 7.3)

Assets

in €m	Notes	31.12.2008	31.12.2007
Intangible assets with indefinite useful life*	17)	821	797
Other intangible assets	18)	261	252
Aircraft and reserve engines	19) 22)	8,764	8,380
Repairable spare parts for aircraft		669	586
Property, plant and other equipment	20) 22)	1,931	1,773
Investment property	21)	3	3
Investments accounted for using the equity method	23)	298	323
Other equity investments	24) 25)	790	777
Non-current securities	24) 25)	509	298
Loans and receivables	24) 26)	475	399
Derivative financial instruments	24) 27)	339	368
Accrued income and advance payments	30)	15	22
Effective income tax receivables	14)	72	79
Deferred claims for income tax rebates	14)	28	19
Non-current assets		**14,975**	**14,076**
Inventories	28)	581	511
Trade receivables and other receivables	24) 29)	3,015	3,448
Derivative financial instruments	24) 27)	213	481
Accrued income and advance payments	30)	119	110
Effective income tax receivables		130	62
Securities	24) 31)	1,834	1,528
Cash and cash equivalents	24) 32)	1,444	2,079
Assets held for sale	33)	97	25
Current assets		**7,433**	**8,244**
Total assets		**22,408**	**22,320**

(Continued)

Exhibit 7.26 (Continued)

Shareholders' equity and liabilities

In €m	Notes	31.12.2008	31.12.2007
Issued capital	34) 35)	1,172	1,172
Capital reserve	36)	1,366	1,366
Retained earnings	36)	3,140	2,063
Other neutral reserves	36)	579	589
Net profit for the period	36)	599	1,655
Equity attributable to shareholders of Deutsche Lufthansa AG		6,856	6,845
Minority interests		63	55
Shareholders' equity		**6,919**	**6,900**
Pension provisions	37)	2,400	2,461
Other provisions	38)	291	349
Borrowings	39) 40)	3,161	3,098
Other financial liabilities	41)	51	55
Advance payments received, accruals and deferrals and other non-financial liabilities	42)	64	66
Derivative financial instruments	27) 39)	118	371
Deferred income tax liabilities	14)	813	749
Non-current provisions and liabilities		**6,898**	**7,149**
Other provisions	38)	1,873	1,686
Borrowings	39) 40)	420	247
Trade payables and other financial liabilities	39) 43)	3,626	3,959
Liabilities from unused flight documents		1,693	1,546
Advance payments received, accruals and deferrals and other non-financial liabilities	44)	388	289
Derivative financial instruments	27) 39)	492	481
Actual income tax liabilities		99	51
Provisions and liabilities included in disposal groups	45)	—	12
Current provisions and liabilities		**8,591**	**8,271**
Total shareholders' equity and liabilities		**22,408**	**22,320**

*Incl. goodwill.

Source: Lufthansa Group, Annual Report for the Fiscal Year Ended December 31, 2008.

Exhibit 7.27

Lufthansa
Consolidated Income Statement for the 2008 Financial Year
(Case 7.3)

in €m	Notes	2008	2007
Traffic revenue	3)	19,998	17,568
Other revenue	4)	4,872	4,852
Total revenue		**24,870**	**22,420**
Changes in inventories and work performed by the enterprise and capitalised	5)	178	119
Other operating income	6)	1,969	1,571
Cost of materials and services	7)	(13,707)	(11,553)
Staff costs	8)	(5,692)	(5,498)
Depreciation, amortisation and impairment	9)	(1,289)	(1,204)
Other operating expenses	10)	(4,946)	(4,269)
Profit from operating activities		**1,383**	**1,586**
Result of equity investments accounted for using the equity method	11)	(22)	223
Result from other equity investments	11)	42	131
Interest income	12)	202	177
Interest expense	12)	(374)	(371)
Other financial items	13)	(427)	(133)
Financial result		**(579)**	**27**
Profit before income taxes		**804**	**1,613**
Income taxes	14)	(195)	(356)
Profit from continuing operations		**609**	**1, 257**
Profit from the discontinued Leisure Travel segment	15)	—	503
Profit after income taxes		**609**	**1, 760**
Minority interests		(10)	(105)
Net profit attributable to shareholders of Lufthansa AG		**599**	**1, 655**
Basic earnings per share in €	16)	1.31	3.61
Diluted earnings per share in €	16)	1.30	3.60

Source: Lufthansa Group, Annual Report for the Fiscal Year Ended December 31, 2008.

Exhibit 7.28

Lufthansa
Additional Data from December 31, 2008, Annual Report
(Case 7.3)

From Consolidated Statement of Cash Flows (In €m):	2008	2007
Net cash provided by (used in) operating activities	2,473	2,862
Net interest paid	172	194
Income taxes	123	274

12) Net interest

Net Interest

In €m	2008	2007
Income from other securities and financial loans	11	13
Other interest and similar income	191	164
Interest income	**202**	**177**
Interest expenses on pensions obligations	(119)	(154)
Interest expense on other provisions	(16)	(9)
Interest and other similar expenses	(239)	(208)
Interest expenses	**(374)**	**(371)**
	(172)	(194)

Operating leases

In addition to the finance leases, a large number of leases have been signed which, on the basis of their economic parameters, are qualified as operating leases, i.e., the leased asset is deemed to belong to the lessor. As well as 106 additional aircraft on operating leases, these are mainly aircraft leased as part of the Lufthansa Regional concept and leases for buildings.

The operating leases for aircraft have a term of between one and nine years. These agreements generally end automatically after the term has expired, but there is sometimes an option for extending the agreement.

The leases for buildings generally run for up to 25 years. The fixtures at the airports in Frankfurt and Munich are leased for 30 years.

The following payments are due in the years ahead (amounts in millions; p.a. denotes per annum):

in €m	2009	2010–2013	from 2014
Aircraft	209	343	—
Various buildings	213	872	215 p.a.
Other leases	70	273	56 p.a.
	492	**1,488**	**271 p.a.**
Payments from sub-leasing	9	13	1 p.a.

In the previous year the following figures were given for operating leases:

in €m	2008	2009–2012	from 2013
Aircraft	196	418	—
Various buildings	236	920	227 p.a.
Other leases	80	306	65 p.a.
	512	**1,644**	**292 p.a.**
Payments from sub-leasing	14	13	2 p.a.

Source: Lufthansa Group, Annual Report for the Fiscal Year Ended December 31, 2008.

Investing Activities

LO 8-1 Describe the accounting and reporting for a firm's investments in tangible and intangible productive assets.

LO 8-2 Discuss the exercise of judgment used in the allocation of costs through the depreciation and amortization process.

LO 8-3 Apply the rules for testing the impairment of different categories of long-lived assets, including goodwill.

LO 8-4 Describe the accounting and reporting for investments in debt and equity securities.

LO 8-5 Describe variable-interest entities, sometimes referred to as special-purpose entities, and explain the need for the primary beneficiary to consolidate them.

LO 8-6 Understand the translation process for subsidiary financial statements denominated in a foreign currency to facilitate consolidation with a U.S. parent.

Chapter Overview

In Chapter 7, we discussed the financial reporting for financing activities, which are the primary sources of capital for investing and operating activities. In this chapter, we discuss the financial reporting for investing activities. Once a firm obtains financing, it must invest the proceeds effectively to generate returns that cover the costs of the financing and generate profit, in order to create value for shareholders.

Investing activities fall into two broad categories:

- Investments in *long-lived operating assets* (which include long-lived tangible assets such as land, buildings, and equipment; intangible assets such as patents, brand names, customer lists, and goodwill; and natural resources such as oil reserves and timberlands).
- Investments in the *securities* of other firms (including stocks and bonds).[1]

Firms also make operating investments in net working capital, such as accounts receivable, inventory, and accounts payable. However, because working capital relates more to day-to-day operations, we discuss these investments separately as part of operating activities in Chapter 9.

To illustrate the scope of this chapter, refer to the Assets section of **Starbucks'** September 27, 2015, consolidated balance sheet (Appendix A). **Starbucks** shows short-term investments (in the current assets section) and many investments in long-lived assets and securities after current assets (that is, long-term investments; equity and cost investments; property, plant, and equipment, net; other long-term assets; other intangible assets;

---

[1]Because a significant subset of stock investments are controlling investments in foreign subsidiaries, we discuss the translation of foreign subsidiary financial statements denominated in a foreign currency in this chapter as well.

and goodwill). Collectively, these assets sum to $7,345.8 million, about 59% of **Starbucks'** total assets.

Because this chapter focuses on a major portion of a company's assets, we should revisit the definition of *assets* we discussed in Chapter 1 prior to consideration of the two major classifications of assets created by investing activities. An asset has four characteristics (the first three form the definition of an asset and the fourth is necessary for measurement):

1. Provides probable future benefits.
2. Is obtained/controlled by the entity.
3. Is a result of past transactions or events.
4. Can be reliably measured (at acquisition cost or fair value).[2]

For many long-lived productive assets, such as machinery, determining whether the item acquired is an asset and measuring its cost are not difficult tasks. However, some transactions present challenges. For example, certain expenditures might fail the probable future benefits test, such as those related to research and development, marketing and brand-building activities, and exploration for natural resources. Also, consideration of the "control" characteristic will determine which assets are recognized in the financial statements of the investor in an intercompany investment. Finally, the availability of reliable fair value information will drive the measurement for many financial assets.

LO 8-1

Describe the accounting and reporting for a firm's investments in tangible and intangible productive assets.

Investments in Long-Lived Operating Assets

Each of the following sections identifies an important issue in financial statement analysis related to investments in long-lived operating assets. The section headings are in the form of analysts' questions. The answers determine accounting quality in the long-lived asset investments area. We also consider how the answers affect your ability to conduct profitability and risk analysis and to forecast future financial statements.

Assets or Expenses?

Firms generally capitalize and recognize investments as assets when the four conditions for asset recognition and measurement are met. However, sometimes measurement of the value of the investment is so difficult as to preclude recognizing an asset, and such investments are required to be expensed immediately. For the more common scenario where investments are capitalized, subsequent cost allocation decreases the long-lived asset over its useful life, through depreciation or amortization expense. Subsequently, the net book value of the asset (its *adjusted acquisition cost*) is reported on the balance sheet.

Because of the very different effects of capitalizing and expensing investments on balance sheets and income statements, your analysis of the quality of accounting for such investments must focus on several related questions: Are capitalized investments justified or should the costs be expensed? Are the firm's capitalization policies clear and in line with competitors and economic reality? Were some economic assets created even though accounting rules require expense treatment? To inform your analysis, we

---

[2]Financial Accounting Standards Board, *Statement of Financial Accounting Concepts No. 5,* "Recognition and Measurement in Financial Statements of a Business Enterprise" (1984); Financial Accounting Standards Board, *Statement of Financial Accounting Concepts No. 6,* "Elements of Financial Statements" (1985).

examine issues related to the financial reporting of activities relating to tangible and intangible assets. We consider

- property, plant, and equipment.
- research and development costs.
- software development costs.
- subsequent expenditures to enhance or maintain property, plant, and equipment.
- costs of self-construction.
- costs of acquiring intangible assets.
- costs of acquiring natural resources.

Accounting for the Acquisition of Property, Plant, and Equipment

In many cases, it is clear that the costs to acquire a piece of property, plant, and equipment will yield future benefits; thus, asset recognition is warranted. The general rule for recognizing the acquisition of an asset is that it should be recorded at the fair value of what has been given up to acquire the asset (whether it be cash, debt, or equity shares) and to prepare the asset for its intended use (including costs to ship, temporarily store, insure, set up, test, and calibrate).

Cash used to acquire property, plant, and equipment is reported as a cash outflow in the investing activities section of the statement of cash flows. If property, plant, and equipment is acquired using debt or equity (both of which are noncash transactions), the investing activity will be reported as a significant noncash investing and financing activity in a separate schedule. **Starbucks** reports capital spending of $1,303.7 million in the investing section of its 2015 Consolidated Statement of Cash Flows (Appendix A). Because operating cash inflows ($3,749.1 million) are greater than capital expenditure cash outflows, **Starbucks** could fund its current investments in property, plant, and equipment without raising additional capital.

Accounting for Research and Development Costs

R&D (research and development) are important activities for many firms. However, because of the inherent uncertainty in determining whether R&D activities will produce sufficient and reliably *measurable* future economic benefits to warrant being capitalized as an asset, U.S. GAAP requires firms to expense immediately all internal R&D costs.[3] For industries with high R&D expenditures, such as the biotechnology industry, significant R&D assets rarely appear on the balance sheet. On the other hand, externally acquired patents or licenses (derived from R&D performed by other firms) can be capitalized because the arm's-length transaction between two market participants provides a reliable measure of acquisition cost and is an indicator of the existence of future economic benefits.

The different accounting treatment of external and internal R&D activities causes an analysis problem when firms use different strategies to carry out similar R&D activities. Some firms develop products *internally* in research laboratories, and thus expense the costs. Some firms make *acquisitions* of other technology companies, in which they acquire established technologies, patent rights, and R&D work that is in process. These firms report intangible assets on their balance sheets for established core technologies and patent rights and the fair value of in-process R&D.[4] Some firms follow a strategy of

---

[3]*FASB Codification Topic 730.* Long-lived assets, such as buildings, computers, and lab equipment, used in multiple R&D projects are initially capitalized; then the depreciation of the assets is assigned to R&D expense.

[4]Capitalization of the fair value of in-process R&D obtained in a merger or acquisition is now required. *FASB Codification Topic 805* reflects the 2007 rule change for U.S. GAAP, and International Accounting Standards Board, *International Financial Reporting Standard 3*, "Business Combinations" (2007), describes the IFRS rule.

external development through a series of joint ventures, licensing relationships, and partnerships. For example, a sponsoring firm might contribute preliminary research findings to obtain its interest in these joint ventures and partnerships. The other participants provide funding to continue development of this preliminary research. In some cases, these firms contract with the joint venture or partnership to perform the continued development in its own laboratories. In this case, the firm receives a fee each period in an amount approximately equal to the R&D costs incurred in conducting the research (resulting in no net R&D cost). In other cases, the joint venture or partnership entity conducts the research, in which case the firm may show no R&D expense on its books. Finally, some firms use several of the aforementioned R&D strategies.

You could address this lack of comparability by choosing a single method to account for all R&D expenditures and modify financial statements by capitalizing and subsequently amortizing all expenditures on R&D that have future service potential and expense all R&D expenditures that are not likely to have future service potential. This approach would also require the consolidation of the firm's share of the assets, liabilities, revenues, and expenses of R&D joint ventures or partnerships. Unfortunately, you would quickly discover that the inherent uncertainty about future benefits that led accounting standard setters to require all internal R&D expenditures to be expensed creates difficulties in judging future service potential from financial statement disclosures alone. Reliance on firm disclosures of scientific and other information outside the financial reporting model is necessary. Also, the consolidation of joint ventures might prove to be difficult because only some R&D joint venture data will be present in notes to the financial statements.

Even when modification of the financial statements is not possible because of lack of data, you should be aware of the effects of R&D expense on profitability analysis. The effects on ROA are countervailing between numerator and denominator. Missing assets understate total assets in the denominator. The numerator of ROA (net income adjusted for interest expense) is affected in two offsetting ways. The numerator is understated because R&D is treated as a current expense, and it is overstated because the amortization of R&D assets from prior successful R&D efforts is excluded. When R&D expenditures are growing, the net effect on the numerator will be understatement because current R&D expenses exceed the amortizations. A mature firm may reach a steady state where current R&D expense approximates total amortization. At that point, the numerator of ROA would be unaffected (assuming current R&D is approximately equal to amortization of previously capitalized R&D), but the denominator would still be understated due to the omission of R&D assets. IFRS rules mitigate the likely overstatement of ROA because *research* costs are expensed and product *development* costs (the costs incurred after the research yields a product or process that is technologically feasible) are capitalized.[5]

In general, capitalization and amortization (relative to immediate expensing) result in a smoother income series and thus produce net income that is easier to predict. Although managers and others view R&D as a necessary investing activity, statement of cash flow reporting treats R&D as an operating activity. Thus, R&D generally reduces both current period net income and cash flows from operating activities.

Accounting for Software Development Costs

U.S. GAAP treats the cost of developing computer software somewhat differently than it treats R&D costs. Firms must expense all internally incurred costs of developing computer software until such development achieves the "technological feasibility" of a

---

[5]International Accounting Standards Board, *International Accounting Standard 38*, "Intangible Assets" (1998).

product. Thereafter, the firm must capitalize and subsequently amortize additional development costs.[6] U.S. GAAP defines technological feasibility as "completion of a detailed program design or, in its absence, completion of a working model." Clearly, determining when a software development project achieves technological feasibility requires significant judgment by managers and other personnel. For example, **IBM**'s R&D expense includes costs for conceptual formulation of software products as well as amortization of software costs previously capitalized for products that had reached the technological feasibility stage. In contrast, **Adobe Systems**, whose Acrobat® and Reader® products are well known, develops new software internally and through aggressive acquisitions of other software companies. Adobe also expenses initial software development costs incurred internally as R&D expense and capitalizes those costs related to developing software deemed technologically feasible. In addition, it capitalizes the cost of software acquired in corporate acquisitions if the software has achieved technological feasibility. **Microsoft** appears to capitalize only a very small portion of the development costs of subsequent generations of Windows® or Office because of the lateness of the point at which it believes that technological feasibility is reached, which is after most development costs have been incurred. Fortunately, because of the very rapid pace of technology development where software products have short life cycles of only a few years, the differences between capitalization and immediate expensing are getting shorter and much less significant.

Subsequent Expenditures for Enhancement or Improvements

After acquiring long-lived operating assets, firms make additional expenditures to enhance or improve them. Proper accounting capitalizes (that is, adds to the asset's book value) expenditures that increase the service life or potential (in either quantity or quality) of an asset beyond that originally anticipated. Firms should expense repairs and maintenance that merely maintain the originally expected service potential. For example, replacing tires on a delivery truck does not qualify as a capital expenditure because the original useful life was determined with the assumption that tires would be replaced regularly. However, if a refrigeration unit was added to the cargo area of the truck to add the capability to transport perishable cargo, the expenditure would be capitalized because the quality of service was improved beyond original expectations.

Maintenance costs can be significant. **American Airlines**, one of the largest airlines in the world, follows a rigorous maintenance program for all of its aircraft. In its 2015 10-K, American Airlines reports nearly $2 billion of maintenance and repairs in operating expenses, relative to pretax income of $4.6 billion.

Management judgment about whether to expense or capitalize such costs creates ample opportunity for earnings management. One way to increase earnings is to (incorrectly) classify routine maintenance and repair costs as capital expenditures. For example, **Waste Management's** founder and several managers were charged with accounting fraud in 2002 for accounting manipulations in the accounting for property, plant, and equipment. Included among the many GAAP violations was their improper capitalization of maintenance expenses. Investors must rely on management integrity and auditor monitoring as protection against self-interested managers manipulating earnings through biased application of the judgment necessary in many settings. Strong corporate governance and auditor reporting of internal control weaknesses assist the assessment of accounting quality.

---

[6]*FASB Codification Topic 985.* These rules on costs of computer software relate to software to be sold, leased, or otherwise marketed, not to software created for internal use that is capitalized and amortized.

Costs of Self-Construction

A company might choose to self-construct plant and equipment because it wants to reduce costs or because no external supplier is available. **Walmart**, for example, might construct its own stores. The cost of a self-constructed asset includes all necessary costs incurred to produce it, including materials, labor, and overhead. For example, self-construction projects frequently use existing equipment and do not create the need for additional expenditures on equipment, plant management supervision, and property taxes. However, these fixed costs are necessary for the construction to occur, and both U.S. GAAP and IFRS require an allocation of part of the fixed overhead cost to self-construction costs. If internal expenditures exceed the cost of acquiring the asset externally, the capitalized costs are limited to the benchmark external acquisition cost; any excess of costs incurred over the external fair value is recorded as a loss of the period. The objective is to prevent an asset from being recorded at an amount greater than its fair value.

As a general rule, interest costs on debt are treated as a period expense, as illustrated in Chapter 7. However, both U.S. GAAP and IFRS have an exception to this rule for interest incurred during the self-construction of a long-lived productive asset intended for the company's own use.[7] Interest on incremental debt used to finance asset construction is a valid and often necessary cost of constructing an asset. By capitalizing interest on self-constructed assets, the firm better captures the true cost to acquire the asset. The capitalized interest cost becomes part of the asset's historical cost (depreciation basis) and, hence, annual depreciation expense in future years.

Costs of Acquiring Natural Resources

Oil fields, timber tracts, and mineral deposits are examples of natural resources. Three types of costs incurred in connection with natural resources are as follows:

- Acquisition costs
- Exploration costs
- Development costs[8]

Acquisition Costs and Restoration Costs. Acquisition costs include the costs of acquiring the natural resources, and restoration costs are the costs associated with returning the resource site to an acceptable condition after the resources have been obtained. Often, the natural resource is attached to land that is salvageable at the end of production. If that is the case, the initial cost is separated into two accounts, with the portion of cost attributable to land reported separately in a "land" or "property" account. All other costs of acquisition are capitalized as part of the "natural resources" account and reported in the property, plant, and equipment section with the other productive, operational assets.

---

[7]Interest costs also may be capitalized on construction of certain types of inventory (discussed in Chapter 9). *FASB Codification Topic 835*; International Accounting Standards Board, *International Accounting Standard 23*, "Borrowing Costs" (revised 2007).

[8]*FASB Codification Topics 930* and *932*; International Accounting Standards Board, *International Financial Reporting Standard 6*, "Exploration for and Evaluation of Mineral Resources" (2004). IFRS cost classifications are slightly different from U.S. GAAP classifications. IFRS requires a clear and consistent accounting policy in the natural resource area involving judgment as to whether costs are capitalized or expensed. Given that the U.S. GAAP rules described in this section yield asset measurements that can be justified by reasonable judgment and permit some choice in the capitalization versus expensing decision, one can conclude that U.S. GAAP and IFRS treatments are not likely to yield variations in natural resource valuations that are greater than the variations in valuations that occur in U.S. GAAP.

Frequently, a natural resource asset is subject to *reclamation costs* or *restoration costs* at the end of the life of a project. For example, at the end of a coal strip mine's productive life, the mine operator incurs substantial costs to fill in the mine and return the land to its original contour. The need to incur costs to reclaim a natural resource is an example of an *ARO (asset retirement obligation)*. The fair value of the obligation (usually determined by discounting expected future reclamation costs) is capitalized and amortized over the life of the related natural resource asset.[9]

Exploration Costs. Exploration costs are incurred to discover the existence and exact location of a natural resource. For example, a petroleum manufacturer acquires an oil field (acquisition cost) and then drills to discover oil. The costs of engaging in the drilling activity, including supplies, labor, and machinery depreciation charges, are exploration costs. The accounting for exploration costs has emerged as one of the most controversial topics in accounting history. At the center of the controversy is the determination of whether the costs of unsuccessful exploration activities are assets or expenses. The following two schools of thought on that issue have emerged:

- *Successful efforts* (exploration costs of successful wells are capitalized as assets, but unsuccessful wells are expensed).
- *Full costing* (exploration costs of successful and unsuccessful wells are assets).

The successful-efforts approach maintains that if six wells are drilled and two produce oil, then the exploration costs of the two successful wells are capitalized in the natural resources account and the costs of the four unsuccessful wells are expensed. This argument is rational because only the successful wells yield probable future economic benefits (that is, the sale of oil) and, hence, should be recognized as assets.

The full-costing approach capitalizes exploration costs for all six wells as part of the natural resources account. The argument is that it was necessary to drill all of the wells in order to discover oil. The cost of exploring all six locations is deemed a necessary investment to generate future economic benefits. Therefore, all costs are capitalizable. This argument also is rational, and it has precedence in other areas of accounting. The costs of producing defective or spoiled inventory, for example, are included as part of the cost of producing good inventory if it is necessary to destroy or spoil some goods in the production of good output. For example, the rapid filling of beverage bottles involves some waste; however, the cost of the wasted beverage is capitalized as part of beverage inventory.

Because reasonable arguments can be made to support both the successful efforts and the full-costing approaches, either method may be used to account for natural resource exploration costs. Managers choose the method they believe is best for their company. Firms in the same industry frequently choose different approaches, and the resulting financial statements can be difficult to compare across firms. Currently, larger producers tend to use the successful-efforts method, while smaller producers tend to use full costing. Accordingly, you should consider the differential treatment of exploration costs when comparing the profitability and risk of small and large firms in the extractive industry. Firms disclose their method choice in the accounting policies note to the financial statements.

Development Costs. Once the natural resource has been acquired and exploration has determined the location of deposits, the natural resource must be developed. Development costs are both tangible (for example, heavy equipment to drill and

---

[9]*FASB Codification Topic 410*; International Accounting Standards Board, *International Accounting Standard 16*, "Property, Plant and Equipment" (1998).

transport the resource) and intangible (for example, the costs of drilling wells and constructing mine shafts). Tangible development costs are capitalized as part of the equipment (or another property, plant, and equipment) account. Intangible development costs are capitalized as part of the natural resources account because the costs are not separable from the natural resource; for example, the costs associated with drilling a specific oil well cannot be moved to another well site.[10]

Summing acquisition costs, exploration costs (of successful efforts or all efforts depending on the method used), and intangible development costs yields the capitalized natural resource asset. Costs are expensed as the natural resource is consumed. Depletion expense represents an estimate of the percentage amount of consumption.

Costs of Acquiring Intangible Assets

Intangible assets include trade and brand names, trademarks, patents, copyrights, franchise rights, customer lists, and goodwill. Under both U.S. GAAP and IFRS, firms expense the cost of *internally* developing intangibles in the period incurred. The rationale for immediate expensing of such costs is the difficulty and uncertainty in ascertaining whether a particular expenditure results in a future benefit (which would trigger asset recognition) or not (in which case the costs are expensed). Thus, although **Starbucks** spends millions of dollars each year promoting its brand, **Starbucks** is not permitted to recognize its brand as an asset. The rationale for not recognizing the value of internally developed intangible assets such as brand names is that the error in estimating such valuations and management incentives to misuse discretion over the capitalization of such costs are so great as to offset the relevance of such estimates in the financial statements.

On the other hand, firms capitalize the costs to acquire intangible assets from others because the existence of an external market transaction provides a reliable measure of its value. In Note 8, "Other Intangible Assets and Goodwill," to its fiscal 2015 financial statements (Appendix A), **Starbucks** shows $217.9 million of indefinite life intangible assets (mainly trade names, trademarks, and patents) and $302.5 million of finite life intangible assets (mainly acquired rights). As already noted, **Starbucks** does not report an asset for the **Starbucks** brand, estimated by Interbrand to be $6,266 million in early 2016.

Because intangible assets, by definition, involve an inherently high degree of uncertainty regarding future economic benefits, most analysts prefer immediate expensing of all costs to internally produce intangible assets.[11] Some analysts also remove from the balance sheet any capitalized R&D costs, software development costs, and goodwill before performing financial analysis. To balance the balance sheet, they reduce retained earnings by the costs of the intangible assets as if intangible acquisition costs had been expensed over time. These analysts argue that the quality of earnings information improves because the ability to manage earnings through expense deferral is reduced. (Often the term *tangible equity* is used to describe the remaining shareholders' equity.) The financial analysis must be interpreted carefully, however, because the analyst may understate a firm's asset base by eliminating these assets.

---

[10]The accounting system captures costs incurred with respect to natural resources, including additional costs incurred to protect the environment. Some costs are incurred to minimize the environmental risk. For example, in the aftermath of the *Exxon Valdez* oil spill, double-hull oil tankers, which are more expensive to produce than single-hull tankers, are now used to transport Alaskan crude oil. The direct cost to **Exxon** to clean up the oil spill and indirect costs associated with tarnishing Exxon's reputation were substantial.

[11]For a stable or moderate-growth firm, the expense each year from immediate expensing is approximately the same as the expense from capitalizing expenditures and subsequently amortizing them.

Goodwill

In corporate acquisitions, acquiring firms allocate the purchase price to the fair values of identifiable, tangible assets (inventories, land, and equipment) and liabilities first. They then allocate any excess purchase price to the fair values of specifically identifiable intangible assets such as patents, customer lists, and trade names, with the remainder allocated to goodwill. *Goodwill* is a residual and effectively represents all intangibles that are not specifically identifiable. **Starbucks'** September 27, 2015, Consolidated Balance Sheet (Appendix A) reports $1.575 billion in goodwill, the second largest asset behind property, plant, and equipment (PP&E).

How should you treat goodwill that appears on a firm's balance sheet? One approach is to follow financial reporting rules and view goodwill like any other productive asset of the firm. The justification is that the initial valuation of goodwill arose from an arm's-length investment in another corporate entity and represents valuable resources that the firm cannot reliably identify and measure separately.

Another approach is to eliminate goodwill from assets and retained earnings. The justification for this approach is that the amount allocated to goodwill from a corporate acquisition may occur simply because the firm overpaid. The corresponding deduction from retained earnings treats the excess purchase price as a loss. Later in this chapter, we discuss corporate acquisitions, and we address goodwill in further detail.

Quick Check

- Firms capitalize costs to acquire and maintain long-lived tangible and intangible assets if future benefits are probable and reasonably estimated; otherwise, the costs are expensed.
- Management conveys information to investors and analysts about whether they believe these costs will result in future economic benefits through the capitalization decision. However, management discretion can also lead to manipulated financial statements by capitalizing costs that are more appropriately expensed.
- In some cases, standard setters do not permit management discretion and require investing activities to be expensed, leading to valuable assets being omitted from the balance sheet.
- It is important to understand a firm's capitalization policy, the unique types of assets it possesses, and why its capitalization policy might differ from industry norms.

How Do Managers Allocate Acquisition Costs over Time?

LO 8-2

Discuss the exercise of judgment used in the allocation of costs through the depreciation and amortization process.

Cost allocation includes the processes of depreciation (for tangible fixed assets), amortization (for limited-life intangible assets), and depletion (for natural resources). When allocating acquisition costs over time, managers must (1) choose an allocation method, (2) estimate useful life, and (3) estimate salvage value. Also, throughout the life of a long-lived asset, the book value must be tested for reasonableness relative to economic values, which may result in revaluing the asset downward for impairment (U.S. GAAP and IFRS) or upward for appreciation (an option under IFRS). Such assessments often require a significant amount of judgment and estimation.

Given the magnitude of long-lived assets on most balance sheets and the importance of understanding accounting judgments available to managers, the following subsections discuss these choices and estimates to help you answer the following questions:

- Are depreciation methods, useful lives, and salvage values reasonable given the economic service and value of the assets?
- Are they in line with competitors?
- Can changes in methods, average useful life estimates, and salvage values be explained by strategy or economic reality, or do they appear to be opportunistic?

Useful Life for Long-Lived Tangible and Limited-Life Intangible Assets

Physical wear and tear and technological obsolescence affect the total useful life and salvage value for long-lived tangible assets and limited-life intangible assets. Managers have an opportunity to convey information to the firm's stakeholders about their expectations of the future usefulness of long-lived assets. However, the estimation process also provides an opportunity to introduce bias into reported earnings. For example, a manager wanting to report higher earnings could bias the estimated useful lives or salvage values of assets upward, or use inflated salvage value estimates, which would result in lower annual depreciation expense.

Unfortunately, firms' disclosures about depreciable lives are usually not very helpful in assessing a firm's aggressiveness in lengthening or shortening depreciable lives or changing estimated salvage values to manage earnings. The problems include the aggregated nature of the disclosures, the fact that firms usually disclose broad ranges of useful lives for asset categories, and the rare disclosure of expected salvage values. For example, **Starbucks** reports the average useful lives of depreciable assets in Note 1 to its 2015 10-K (Appendix A) to be 2 to 15 years for equipment and 30 to 40 years for buildings.

However, there is enough information in financial statements and notes for you to estimate average useful lives over time. Because most U.S. firms use the straight-line depreciation method for financial reporting purposes, you can estimate the average useful life of depreciable assets (PP&E gross minus non-depreciable land and work in progress) by dividing average depreciable cost (gross, assuming zero salvage value) by depreciation expense for the year. The calculations for **Starbucks** for 2012 through 2015 are presented in Exhibit 8.1 and they are included in FSAP.

In 2015, the average useful life estimate is 9.88 years for property, plant, and equipment. Compared to the 2014 estimate (10.48 years), the average total useful life used in depreciation computations has decreased. This decrease is the continuation of a trend over the past few years. If **Starbucks** had used 10.48 years for the depreciation computation in 2015, depreciation expense would have been $833.6 million ($8,735.8 million average depreciable base/10.48 years) instead of $883.4 million reported in 2015. The $49.8 million pretax difference is 1.27% of the $3,903 million pretax income in 2015. The estimate change from 10.48 to 9.88 years in 2015 results in a *lower* reported net income. Generally, estimate changes leading to lower reported earnings are of less concern unless the firm in question regularly disposes of the assets (which **Starbucks** does not, as evidenced by rare disclosure of material gains or losses from asset sales over time). You should, however, be concerned when firms increase depreciation rates over time and also engage in frequent long-lived-asset sales resulting in gains. This is an example of creating "cookie jar" reserves (see Chapter 6) and using them later to manage earnings.

Exhibit 8.1							
Calculation of Starbucks' Average Useful Life for PP&E **(amounts in millions)**							
FYE	**PP&E**	**Land**	**Work in Progress**	**Depreciable Base**	**Average Base**	**Depreciation Expense**	**Avg. Life Estimate**
2011	$6,163.1	$44.8	$127.4	$5,990.9			
2012	$6,903.1	$46.2	$264.1	$6,592.8	$6,291.9	$576.1	10.92
2013	$7,782.1	$47.0	$342.4	$7,392.7	$6,992.8	$647.9	10.79
2014	$8,581.1	$46.7	$415.6	$8,118.8	$7,755.8	$739.7	10.48
2015	$9,641.8	$46.6	$242.5	$9,352.7	$8,735.8	$883.8	9.88

Depreciable base = PP&E – Land – Work in Progress
Average base = Sum of the current and past years' depreciable base divided by 2
Depreciation expense = Depreciation and amortization from statement of cash flows – Amortization disclosed in the notes
Average life estimate = Average depreciable base/Depreciation expense

Even with such aggregated data, you can gain insight by comparing the average useful life of depreciable assets across firms. Firms with similar asset composition (such as direct competitors) should have similar useful lives; if not, you should assess why they differ. A firm's strategy may be associated with different useful lives. For example, an airline choosing a shorter useful life (e.g., **Singapore Airlines**) might do so because its strategy requires it to fly newer planes, and, thus, its aircraft have shorter useful lives. Conversely, a competitor airline might have much longer useful lives for its planes if it utilizes a strategy with more frequent maintenance, extending the lives of the planes. You also need to question firms that report dramatic changes in the useful lives of depreciable assets over time.[12] Is the change because of changes in the assumed useful lives of the assets, has the composition of the firm's assets changed over time, or has the firm made a strategic decision to use assets differently? Firms choosing useful lives that accurately (and consistently) represent the period of time they expect to use the assets report the highest-quality accounting data for depreciable assets.

Both U.S. GAAP and IFRS allow managers to classify certain intangible assets such as goodwill (reported by **Starbucks** in Note 7) as having an indefinite life; therefore, they are not amortized. Rather than having costs allocate across periods through amortization, these nonamortizable intangibles are assessed for impairment (discussed in a later section).

Cost Allocation (Depreciation/Amortization/ Depletion) Method

Firms may allocate the acquisition costs over the useful life of the asset using *any* systematic and rational method. The allocation of cost is charged to depreciation expense

---

[12]When a firm changes a useful life or salvage value estimate, it handles the change prospectively. That is, it simply depreciates the remaining book value over the remaining useful life. *FASB Codification Topic 250*; International Accounting Standards Board, *International Accounting Standard 16*, "Property, Plant and Equipment" (1998).

(for tangible fixed assets), amortization expense (for intangibles), or depletion expense (for natural resources) and is reported on the income statement.[13]

Most firms depreciate tangible long-lived assets evenly over their useful lives (straight-line method). Nearly all firms amortize intangible assets using the straight-line method. Firms generally deplete natural resources using the straight-line method or in proportion to the amount of natural resources consumed (for example, number of board feet of lumber harvested relative to an estimate of the total amount of board feet of lumber in a forest). Regardless of the cost allocation method chosen, the total depreciation over an asset's life generally does not exceed acquisition costs (except in rare cases when firms revalue such assets to current fair values under IFRS). Thus, the various depreciation methods differ only in the *timing* of expense, not in its total amount over time.

Virtually all U.S. firms use accelerated depreciation methods for tax reporting purposes based on depreciable lives specified in the income tax law, which are usually shorter than the depreciable lives that firms use for financial reporting purposes. This is important because too frequently observers make false claims such as, "a manager would choose an accelerated depreciation method for financial reporting to save on taxes." The depreciation method chosen for financial reporting in the U.S. is independent of the depreciation required under tax reporting. In countries where tax laws heavily influence financial reporting (such as Germany, France, and Japan), many firms use accelerated depreciation methods for both financial and tax reporting. Thus, comparisons of U.S. to foreign firms require an assessment of the effects of different depreciation methods and assumptions. To increase comparability, you can restate reported U.S. amounts to an accelerated basis or convert reported amounts for other countries to a straight-line basis by using the tax note. Firms must report in the tax note the portion of the deferred tax liability that is attributable to book versus tax depreciation timing differences at the beginning and end of the year.

To illustrate, in the fourth schedule presented in **Starbucks'** Note 13, "Income Taxes" (Appendix A), **Starbucks** reports a net deferred tax liability attributable to property, plant, and equipment of $96.1 million ($217.5 million deferred tax liability – $121.4 million deferred tax asset) on September 27, 2015, and $69.7 million on September 28, 2014 (computed similarly). An increase in a deferred tax liability relating to differences in depreciation expense for book (i.e., financial statement) and tax purposes indicates that **Starbucks** depreciated fixed assets faster for tax purposes than for book purposes in the current year. If you want to compare **Starbucks'** profitability and risk to another company that uses accelerated methods of depreciation, you must convert key amounts for **Starbucks**, including the asset PP&E (net) and net income, to an accelerated depreciation method basis or convert those amounts for the comparable firm to a straight-line basis. The following computations demonstrate the former approach, converting **Starbucks'** amounts to an accelerated depreciation basis. (**Starbucks** discloses a 35% federal statutory tax rate in Note 13.)

Starbucks measures the net deferred tax liability attributable to property, plant, and equipment of $96.1 million by multiplying the excess tax depreciation over time by 35%. Therefore, we can obtain the excess accumulated tax depreciation over time by dividing the deferred tax liability amount by 35%. Then, to measure PP&E under the tax depreciation method, we can deduct the excess tax depreciation from PP&E reported on the balance sheet under the book depreciation method. We summarize these steps in the following computation:

---

[13]If the long-lived asset is used in production, the depreciation/amortization/depletion is initially added to inventory as a product cost and then expensed as cost of goods sold when the inventory is sold.

Conversion of PP&E (net) to an accelerated basis (amounts in millions):

PP&E (net) as reported at September 27, 2015, using book depreciation method		$4,088.3
Excess accumulated depreciation over time using tax method:		
Net deferred tax liability related to excess depreciation (measured originally by multiplying the excess depreciation by the tax rate)	$ 96.1	
÷ tax rate	÷0.35	(274.6)
PP&E (net) using tax depreciation method		$3,813.7

To restate net income under the tax depreciation method, we rely on the fact that income is affected by the *change* in the deferred tax liability amount, which, when divided by the tax rate, represents the higher tax depreciation expense if an accelerated method is used:

Increase in deferred tax liability during the year ($96.1 − $69.7)	$ 26.4	
÷ tax rate	÷0.35	$ 75.4
Decrease in tax expense ($75.4 × 0.35)		(26.4)
Decrease in 2015 net income if tax depreciation method is used		$ 49.0

If **Starbucks** had used the tax method, it would have had a lower pretax income and, hence, a lower tax expense of $26.4 million. Thus, changing **Starbucks'** book depreciation to a tax-based method would decrease 2015 net income by $49.0 million, approximately 1.8% of 2015 net income.

When Will the Long-Lived Assets Be Replaced?

Forecasting future financial statements requires expectations of future tangible asset acquisitions for replacement of existing production or service capacity and for growing capacity. Although you must rely on knowledge of industry conditions and firm strategy to estimate capacity growth, you can make two computations to gain a better understanding of when existing long-lived assets must be replaced.

Because the amount of accumulated depreciation depends on the number of years for which depreciation has been taken, the *average age of depreciable assets* equals the amount of accumulated depreciation divided by depreciation expense. Based on **Starbucks'** Note 7, "Supplemental Balance Sheet Information" (Appendix A), and the depreciation expense from Exhibit 8.1, the average age equals 6.3 years ($5,553.5/$883.8). Also, the *proportion of depreciable assets consumed* equals total accumulated depreciation divided by acquisition cost. For **Starbucks**, $5,553.5/$9,352.7 = 59.4%. In the same vein, you also can estimate the *remaining useful life* by dividing net depreciable PP&E by annual depreciation expense. For **Starbucks**, ($9,352.7 − $5,553.5)/$883.8 equals 4.3 years average remaining life. You can track average age and proportion consumed through time and compare them to those of competitors to ascertain whether assets are getting older (on average) and whether large capital expenditures may be necessary to replace them. Also, the combination of older, mostly depreciated assets provides an indication that the firm is in a later stage of average product life cycles.

If older assets are taken out of service and scrapped, any remaining book value must be removed and reported as a realized loss on disposal in operating income. In Note 1, **Starbucks** reports some small losses from dispositions ($12.5 million loss in the most recent year). If assets are sold, rather than scrapped, cash inflows from sales are reported in the investing section of the statement of cash flows; gains or losses appear on the income statement, and appear as adjustments in the operating section of the statement of cash flows. Finally, assets may be traded in for newer assets. Both U.S. GAAP and IFRS require firms to record the new asset acquired at fair value with resulting gains and losses on trade-ins reported in net income. An exception to this rule occurs if the transaction lacks commercial substance, in which case the acquired asset is recorded at the book value of the assets surrendered (including the traded-in asset) and liabilities assumed with no recognition of gain or loss.[14]

Quick Check

- Managers must choose depreciation, amortization, and depletion methods to allocate the acquisition costs of limited-life tangible and intangible operational assets to the expected useful life.
- They must also estimate useful lives and salvage values. Managers can use these estimates to convey their beliefs or to manipulate financial statements.
- You should consider the consequences of changes in methods or different methods across firms when performing ratio analysis.

- If long-lived assets are material to the firm's balance sheet, changes in depreciation methods, useful life, or salvage value estimates can have material effects on the income statement through depreciation and amortization expense. You should examine whether any changes in estimates are material and consistent with economic conditions.

LO 8-3

Apply the rules for testing the impairment of different categories of long-lived assets, including goodwill.

What Is the Relation between the Book Values and Market Values of Long-Lived Assets?

Firms report long-lived operational assets at acquisition costs minus the accumulated depreciation to date (adjusted acquisition cost). Remember that depreciation is a cost allocation system, not a valuation system. Fair values are different than reported book values. Difficulties encountered in determining fair values include

- the absence of active markets for many used fixed assets, particularly those specific to a particular firm's needs.
- the need to identify comparable assets currently available in the market to value assets in place.

---

[14]*FASB Codification Topic 845*; International Accounting Standards Board, *International Accounting Standard 16*, "Property, Plant and Equipment" (revised 1998). A lack of commercial substance is evidenced by relatively little change in the cash flows to the firm after it replaces the asset. This provision exists to remove the past abuse of asset trading rules in which two firms trade nearly identical assets with book values below their fair values simply to record the gain on the difference between fair and book value rather than for any commercial reason.

- the need to make assumptions about the effect of technological and other improvements when using the prices of new assets currently available on the market in the valuation process.

Nevertheless, accounting standards require firms to determine whether the net book values of long-lived assets are not overstated relative to the economic reality of fair values. In particular, accounting standards state that long-lived asset values must be tested for impairments and written down if impairment losses have occurred.

To understand how accounting measurement rules affect your analysis of the profitability of a firm and your expectations of future profitability, you should address the following questions:

- Are asset impairment charges consistent with the firm's economic environment?
- Are the charges transitory or do they occur frequently?
- Are asset impairment charges or IFRS upward revaluations based on reliable fair value estimates?

To sharpen your ability to make these judgments, the following sections examine the U.S. GAAP and IFRS standards related to reporting long-lived assets when book values and market values differ. The next three sections deal with three basic types of long-lived operating assets: (1) long-lived assets subject to depreciation and amortization (including land, even though it is not depreciated), (2) intangible assets not subject to amortization because of indefinite lives, and (3) goodwill. A fourth section addresses upward revaluations of long-lived assets under IFRS.

Impairment of Long-Lived Assets Subject to Depreciation and Amortization

The development of new technologies by competitors, changes in government regulations, changes in demographic trends, and other external factors may reduce the future benefits originally anticipated from long-lived assets. Firms are required to assess whether conditions exist implying that the carrying amounts of fixed assets are not recoverable. If they are not, firms must write down the assets to their fair values and recognize impairment losses in income from continuing operations.[15]

U.S. GAAP defines a carrying amount (book value) as not being recoverable if it is greater than the sum of the *undiscounted* cash flows expected from the asset's use and disposal. If the asset's carrying amount is not recoverable, the impairment charge equals the amount by which the carrying value exceeds the asset's fair value. Under U.S. GAAP, although the firm uses undiscounted future cash flows to decide whether an impairment charge is necessary, it must use fair value to determine the actual impairment charge. Fair value is measured using the three-level FASB designation described in Chapter 2. Because of the difficulty of observing prices of the same or similar assets in organized markets, firms often must estimate fair values by computing the present (*discounted*) value of expected cash flows from using the fixed asset (Level 3 inputs used in a valuation approach applying present value techniques, like those presented in Chapter 12).

---

[15]*FASB Codification Topic 360*; International Accounting Standards Board, *International Accounting Standard 36*, "Impairment of Assets."

In requiring firms to use undiscounted cash flows to test for impairment of long-lived tangible assets, U.S. standard setters reasoned that a loss had not occurred if the firm could recover in future cash flows an amount equal to or larger than the current book value. Accounting theorists and practitioners question the logic of using undiscounted, instead of discounted, cash flows in testing for impairment. In some cases, the economic value of the long-lived asset may decline below its carrying value, but the firm would recognize no impairment because the *undiscounted* future cash flows from the asset exceed its carrying value.

IFRS uses rules that are more theoretically defensible. Firms are required to determine whether an impairment has occurred and to measure impairment by comparing the book value of the long-lived asset to the greater of (1) the fair value of the asset minus estimated costs to *sell* the asset or (2) the value of the asset *in use* (which is the present value of estimated future cash flows from using the asset).

Differences in U.S. GAAP and IFRS Impairment of Long-Lived Assets

To illustrate the differences between U.S. GAAP and IFRS, assume that a real estate company owns an apartment building that originally cost $20 million, with a current carrying amount of $15 million. The company originally expected to collect rents of $1.67 million each year for 30 years before selling the apartment complex for $8 million. Deteriorating neighborhood conditions, however, have caused the company to reassess the future rentals, especially given a recent appraisal that set a fair value for the apartment building at $10 million. The company now estimates that it will receive rentals of $1.35 million per year for 15 years and then will sell the building for a net $5 million. The company uses an 8% discount rate to compute the present value for this investment. Costs to sell today are estimated at $300,000.

U.S. GAAP Treatment. Because total undiscounted future cash flows of $25.25 million [($1.35 × 15) + $5] exceed the carrying value of $15 million, the real estate company reports no impairment loss. In essence, the firm has suffered an economic loss but will not report any loss for financial reporting. If the total undiscounted future cash flows in this illustration were estimated to fall below the carrying value of $15 million, the real estate company would compute an impairment loss as the difference between the carrying value and the fair value of the apartment building (in this case, $10 million). The company would report the impairment loss of $5 million in income from continuing operations, and the apartment building would be recorded at the new carrying value of $10 million.

IFRS Treatment. Under IFRS, the greater of the asset's value in use and fair value from sale is identified first. Value in use is $13.1 million, obtained by using the 8% discount rate to compute the present value of a 15-year annuity of $1.35 million cash inflow plus the present value of $5 million received at the end of Year 15. The value from a sale is $9.7 million, the $10 million fair value minus $0.3 million in disposal costs. The larger of the two, $13.1 million, is then compared to the carrying value of $15 million, triggering a $1.9 million impairment. The company would report an impairment loss of $1.9 million in income from continuing operations, and the apartment building would be recorded at the new carrying value of $13.1 million.

Impairment of Intangible Assets Not Subject to Amortization

For intangibles *not requiring* amortization (that is, intangible assets with an indefinite life), firms must test for asset impairment annually—or more frequently if events and circumstances indicate that the asset may be impaired. Unlike the impairment test for depreciable assets and amortizable intangible assets, U.S. GAAP defines impairment of intangible assets not subject to amortization as occurring when the fair value of the intangible asset is below its carrying amount. This approach is more defendable from a theoretical viewpoint because fair value is more closely related to discounted cash flows than to the undiscounted cash flows used in the impairment tests for limited-life assets. IFRS impairment tests for intangible assets not subject to amortization mirror its tests for depreciable and amortizable assets.

Impairment of Goodwill

The U.S. GAAP and IFRS goodwill impairment tests are similar. Both sets of standards view goodwill as not being separable from other assets and therefore require the impairment test to be conducted at the unit level. U.S. GAAP (FASB Codification Topic 350) defines a *reporting unit* as a segment or a component of a segment that is a business with separate financial information that management regularly reviews. IFRS (IAS 36) defines a *cash generating unit* as "the smallest identifiable group of assets that generates cash inflows that are largely independent of the cash inflows from other assets or groups of assets." The impairment test is basically a simulation of a transaction between the firm and an outsider in an organized market to acquire the unit.

Example: Impairment of Goodwill

To illustrate goodwill impairment, assume that Cabrera Co. acquires Golf Tech, Inc., on January 1, 2017, by paying $1,000,000 in cash. At the date of acquisition, the price is allocated as follows:[16]

Price paid	$1,000,000
Fair value of Golf Tech's long-lived tangible assets	(400,000)
Fair value of a brand name with an indefinite useful life	(100,000)
Goodwill	$ 500,000

One year later on December 31, 2017, Cabrera estimates the fair value of the Golf Tech unit to be $800,000. The book and fair values of Golf Tech's long-lived tangible assets are $400,000, and the fair value of the brand name is $70,000.

U.S. GAAP Treatment. Firms following U.S. GAAP would first apply impairment tests to its non-goodwill assets. The fair value of the brand name has declined by $30,000. Therefore, a $30,000 intangible asset impairment charge is reported by

---

[16]In an acquisition, the fair value transferred by the acquirer ($1,000,000 in this example) is assigned to the assets acquired, which are recorded at their fair values. The excess is recorded as goodwill. The acquisition process is discussed in greater detail later in the chapter.

reducing the carrying value of the brand name to $70,000. The second step in the process is to compare the carrying amount of the unit to the unit's fair value, as follows:

Fair value of Golf Tech unit at 12/31/17		$800,000
Carrying values of Golf Tech assets at 12/31/17:		
Long-lived tangible assets	$400,000	
Brand name (after its reduction to fair value)	70,000	
Goodwill	500,000	
Carrying value of Golf Tech unit at 12/31/17		$970,000

If the fair value of the unit exceeds the carrying value, goodwill is not deemed to be impaired. However, in this example, the carrying value exceeds the fair value, so Cabrera must measure the amount of goodwill impairment by simulating a reacquisition. Cabrera compares the fair value of the unit to the fair value of the identifiable assets to yield an implied goodwill, as follows:

Fair value of Golf Tech unit at 12/31/17		$ 800,000
Fair values of Golf Tech's assets other than goodwill		
at 12/31/17:		
Long-lived tangible assets	$400,000	
Brand name	70,000	(470,000)
Implied goodwill at 12/31/17		$ 330,000

Goodwill is written down from $500,000 to $330,000, and a $170,000 impairment loss is reflected in operating income. Exhibit 8.2 shows the brand name and goodwill impairment charges, which total $200,000.[17]

Note that the new carrying amounts for individual assets are as follows:

Long-lived tangible assets	$400,000
Brand name ($100,000 − $30,000 impairment)	70,000
Goodwill ($500,000 − $170,000 impairment)	330,000
Total new carrying value	$800,000

IFRS Treatment. Under IFRS, the recoverable amount of the assets is compared to their original carrying amounts. For long-lived tangible assets and brand names, the recoverable amount is the higher of fair value in use or from sale (less disposal costs). For goodwill, the recoverable amount is the implied goodwill of $330,000 computed in the same way as previously illustrated for the U.S. GAAP treatment.

Exhibit 8.2: Goodwill Impairment under U.S. GAAP

Assets		=	Liabilities	+	Total Shareholders' Equity		
					CC	AOCI	RE
Brand Name	(30,000)						Impairment
Goodwill	(170,000)						Losses (200,000)
Impairment Losses			200,000				
Brand Name					30,000		
Goodwill					170,000		

	Original Carrying Amount	Recoverable Amount
Long-lived tangible assets	$ 400,000	$400,000
Brand name	100,000	70,000
Goodwill	500,000	330,000
Total	$1,000,000	$800,000

The financial statement effects are the same as those shown in Exhibit 8.2. These amounts support the write-down of brand name and goodwill by $30,000 and $170,000, respectively.

It is clear from the example above that managers (and their valuation consultants) make several estimates of future cash flows or fair values to support a goodwill impairment charge. You should consider several issues when assessing current profitability and predicting future earnings. First, the relatively unpredictable and volatile goodwill impairment charge has replaced the inherently certain and constant goodwill amortization charge. You should examine a firm's past goodwill impairment charges as well as the reasonableness of prices paid in recent acquisitions to forecast whether additional impairments are likely. Second, you should attempt to determine whether the goodwill impairment charge is indicative of management paying too much for the acquisition, poor management performance in operating the unit, or uncontrollable external factors. Finally, the substantial estimation involved in goodwill impairments permits earnings management.

Impairment Shortly after Acquisition

The impairment of goodwill can occur shortly after an acquisition. In 2008, **Nike** acquired **Umbro**. Exhibit 8.3 provides an excerpt from Nike's June 2009 10-K.

Note that Nike uses a combination of models (discounted cash flow analysis and market comparables) because it argues that these models are used by market participants. Also note the assumptions to develop the projections used in the discounted cash flow analysis, the use of a weighted-average discount rate, and the sensitivity analysis performed. Return to this example after studying financial statement forecasts and valuations covered in Chapters 10 through 14.

If a company reports an impairment of any kind, net income is reduced. However, impairments are not cash outflows. Accordingly, impairments are added back to net income in the operating section of the statement of cash flows. Impairments that reflect management's beliefs and that are not opportunistically timed are informative to investors and analysts about future cash flows. In its Note 1, **Starbucks** reported small but growing impairment charges on property, plant, and equipment ($12.5, $14.7, and $25.8 million in 2013, 2014, and 2015, respectively). These growing charges appear persistent, but they may not be given our prior analysis indicating that **Starbucks** is decreasing its useful life estimates. A reduction in useful life used in depreciation computations causes book values to decrease more rapidly over time, thus making impairment charges less likely (unless, of course, economic conditions decay further).

Exhibit 8.3

Excerpts from Nike's Reporting of Umbro Impairment

In accordance with FAS 142 "Goodwill and Other Intangible Assets," the Company performs annual impairment tests on goodwill and intangible assets with indefinite lives in the fourth quarter of each fiscal year, or when events occur or circumstances change that would, more likely than not, reduce the fair value of a reporting unit or intangible assets with an indefinite life below its carrying value. As a result of a significant decline in global consumer demand and continued weakness in the macro-economic environment, as well as decisions by Company management to adjust planned investment in the Umbro brand, the Company concluded that sufficient indicators of impairment existed to require the performance of an interim assessment of Umbro's goodwill and indefinite lived intangible assets as of February 1, 2009. Accordingly, the Company performed the first step of the goodwill impairment assessment for Umbro by comparing the estimated fair value of Umbro to its carrying amount, and determined there was a potential impairment of goodwill as the carrying amount exceeded the estimated fair value. Therefore, the Company performed the second step of the assessment which compared the implied fair value of Umbro's goodwill to the book value of goodwill. The implied fair value of goodwill is determined by allocating the estimated fair value of Umbro to all of its assets and liabilities, including both recognized and unrecognized intangibles, in the same manner as goodwill was determined in the original business combination.

The Company measured the fair value of Umbro by using an equal weighting of the fair value implied by a discounted cash flow analysis and by comparisons with the market values of similar publicly traded companies. The Company believes the blended use of both models compensates for the inherent risk associated with either model if used on a stand-alone basis, and this combination is indicative of the factors a market participant would consider when performing a similar valuation .... The assessments of the Company resulted in the recognition of impairment charges of $199.3 million and $181.3 million related to Umbro's goodwill and trademark, respectively, during the third quarter ended February 28, 2009. A deferred tax benefit of $54.5 million was recognized as a result of the trademark impairment charge. In addition to the above impairment analysis, the Company determined an equity investment held by Umbro was impaired, and recognized a charge of $20.7 million related to the impairment of this investment. These charges are included in the Company's "Other" category for segment reporting purposes.

The discounted cash flow analysis calculated the fair value of Umbro using management's business plans and projections as the basis for expected cash flows for the next twelve years and a 3% residual growth rate thereafter. The Company used a weighted average discount rate of 14% in its analysis, which was derived primarily from published sources as well as our adjustment for increased market risk given current market conditions. Other significant estimates used in the discounted cash flow analysis include the rates of projected growth and profitability of Umbro's business and working capital effects. The market valuation approach indicates the fair value of Umbro based on a comparison of Umbro to publicly traded companies in similar lines of business. Significant estimates in the market valuation approach include identifying similar companies with comparable business factors such as size, growth, profitability, mix of revenue generated from licensed and direct distribution and risk of return on investment.

Holding all other assumptions constant at the test date, a 100 basis point increase in the discount rate would reduce the adjusted carrying value of Umbro's net assets by 12%.

Source: From Nike's June 2009 10-K.

IFRS Treatment of Upward Asset Revaluations

U.S. GAAP does not permit upward revaluations of long-lived assets. However, IFRS gives firms the option to revalue upward both intangible and tangible long-lived assets.[18] Firms must choose the classes of asset to which revaluations will apply and then perform the revaluations on a regular basis. The choice is irrevocable, and the fair value of nonfinancial assets in active markets is difficult to obtain. The significant cost associated with obtaining reliable measurements and the potential cost of reporting volatility in profits from frequent revaluations often exceeds the benefits of presenting a relevant asset valuation on the balance sheet. The fact that many firms choose not to exercise the upward revaluation option is a testimony to the time and effort required for its implementation.

When fair value remains above original acquisition cost, upward and downward revaluations are reported as other comprehensive income and are accumulated in the shareholders' equity section of the balance sheet. The account typically used in the other comprehensive income classification is "Revaluation Surplus." If fair value is less than or equal to cost, reversals of previous downward revaluations (that were reported as losses on the income statement) are treated as gains on the income statement.

To illustrate the IFRS treatment, assume that a French company following IFRS has vineyard land originally costing €2,000,000. At the next four year-ends, the land is worth the following:

2017:	€2,500,000
2018:	€2,300,000
2019:	€1,900,000
2020:	€2,000,000

Exhibit 8.4 shows the effects of upward and downward revaluations of the asset.

Fair value increases above original acquisition cost in 2017, causing an upward revaluation of the land and an increase in other comprehensive income (OCI) but not net income. The increase is recognized in accumulated other comprehensive income in the shareholders' equity section. In 2018, the land is revalued downward, causing a partial reversal in the accumulated unrealized gains. Such reversals of previously unrealized gains are reported as losses in other comprehensive income and reduce accumulated other comprehensive income on the balance sheet, as long as fair value is greater than original acquisition cost. In 2019, fair value falls below original acquisition cost, causing a reversal of the remainder of the accumulated unrealized gains in accumulated other comprehensive income via the recognition in other comprehensive income of €300,000 unrealized loss and recognition in net income of €100,000 unrealized loss. The land recovers its value in 2020, and the reversal of the 2019 unrealized loss reported in net income is reported in 2020 net income as an unrealized gain.[19]

---

[18]International Accounting Standards Board, *International Accounting Standard 16*, "Property, Plant and Equipment" (1998).

[19]A final category of long-lived assets exists that is unique to IFRS. Biological assets are living plants and animals that will be transformed into items for sale, agricultural produce, or additional biological assets. For example, in the production of wine, the vintner has vines that produce grapes that ultimately produce wine. The vines are the biological asset. Unless fair value is clearly unreliable, biological assets are reported at fair value less estimated disposal costs at each balance sheet date, with all value changes reflected in current net income. International Accounting Standards Board, *International Accounting Standard 41*, "Agriculture" (2001).

Exhibit 8.4: Upward Asset Revaluations under IFRS

Assets	=	Liabilities	+	Total Shareholders' Equity		
				CC	AOCI	RE
2017: Land 500,000					Unrealized Gains 500,000	
2018: Land (200,000)					Unrealized Gains (200,000)	
2019: Land (400,000)					Unrealized Gains (300,000)	Unrealized Losses (100,000)
2020: Land 100,000						Unrealized Gains 100,000

2017:			
Land	500,000		
Unrealized Gains (OCI)		500,000	
2018:			
Unrealized Gains (OCI)	200,000		
Land		200,000	
2019:			
Unrealized Gains (OCI)	300,000		
Unrealized Losses (NI)	100,000		
Land		400,000	
2020:			
Land	100,000		
Unrealized Gains (NI)		100,000	

Quick Check

- Book and fair values of long-lived tangible and intangible assets diverge over time due to changes in economic conditions and from depreciation methods that focus on cost allocation rather than measuring asset fair value declines.
- Firms must assess whether fair values have declined below book values and recognize impairments. Impairments that reflect changes

  in management's beliefs about an asset's future cash flows and that are not timed opportunistically are informative to investors and analysts.
- You should remember that fair values are often difficult to obtain for real assets.
- IFRS impairment rules differ from U.S. GAAP rules and are more closely related to economic conditions.

Summary

It is important that you understand the firm's accounting policy for long-lived assets when a firm invests heavily in tangible and intangible long-lived assets. The choices that managers make can convey a wealth of information to financial statement users, but this freedom also permits managers to bias or manipulate the financial statements. Pay particular attention to changes in estimates used in the depreciation and amortization process and the reasons for and timing of asset impairment charges and gains and losses on sales of long-lived assets. These sometimes discretionary management decisions shift earnings among periods and bias long-lived asset balance sheet valuations.

Investments in Securities

LO 8-4

Describe the accounting and reporting for investments in debt and equity securities.

Firms also may invest in the securities of other firms, such as common stock and long-term debt, thus acquiring claims to the returns from other firms' operations. In computing ROA, financial assets increase total assets in the denominator, and profits from the investments increase both the denominator (assets) and numerator (net income). This section examines the accounting, reporting, and analysis issues surrounding investments in securities.

Firms invest in the securities of governments, corporations, variable-interest entities, joint ventures, and partnerships for a variety of reasons, including to

- earn interest or dividends.
- speculate on potential price appreciation of the securities.
- provide financial support to, exert significant influence over, or gain control of an important raw materials supplier, customer, technological innovator, or other valued entity.
- achieve other strategic purposes.

The appropriate accounting for investments depends on the level of "controlling financial interest" by the firm making the investment, determined by the degree of influence and control one firm has over another entity—which may be minority, passive; minority, active; or majority, active—and by whether the reporting firm is deemed the primary beneficiary of the investment it has made in a VIE (variable-interest entity).

Minority, Passive Investments

Firms often invest in the debt securities, preferred stock, or common stock of another corporation for the anticipated interest or dividends and capital gains. These investments are deemed minority, passive investments when the percentage that a firm owns of another corporation's voting shares is relatively small (less than 20%) and the investing firm is not deemed the VIE's primary beneficiary (discussed in a later section).

To account for minority, passive investments:[20]

- firms initially record investments at acquisition cost.
- income each period equals interest and dividends earned.
- the accounting at the end of each period and at time of sale depends on the type of security and the firm's ability and intent to hold it, as follows:
  - Firms must account for debt securities they expect to *hold to maturity* at amortized acquisition cost. That is, the firm must amortize any difference between the acquisition cost and maturity value of these debt securities as an adjustment to interest revenue over the life of the debt using the effective interest method as demonstrated in Chapter 7. If the firm sells the security, it reports a realized gain or loss in net income for the difference between the proceeds and the security's amortized cost.

---

[20]U.S. GAAP and IFRS are consistent in the accounting and reporting of minority, passive investments. *FASB Codification Topic 320*; International Accounting Standards Board, *International Accounting Standard 39*, "Financial Instruments: Recognition and Measurement" (revised 2003); International Accounting Standards Board, *International Financial Reporting Standard 7*, "Financial Instruments: Disclosure" (2005). Two key differences exist: (1) Under U.S. GAAP, unless the firm is a broker/dealer, an investment company, an insurance company, or a defined benefit plan, *unlisted* equity securities are generally carried at cost unless impaired or the fair value option is chosen, while IFRS simply requires reliably measurable fair value. (2) U.S. GAAP distinguishes between debt securities (for example, a bond) and a loan (for example, a promissory note) and limits the rules discussed in this section to securities, while IFRS makes no such distinction.

- Firms must account for *trading securities* at fair value. These are securities a firm actively buys and sells to take advantage of short-term changes in market values. They are reported as a current asset on the balance sheet and are marked to market at the end of each period. Broker/dealers, banks, and insurers, for example, often trade securities in different capital markets worldwide to take advantage of temporary differences in market prices. Manufacturers, retailers, and other nonfinancial firms occasionally invest funds for trading purposes, but such situations are unusual. Firms include unrealized holding gains and losses on trading securities in net income each period. When a firm sells a trading security, it recognizes the difference between the selling price and the book value (that is, the market value at the end of the most recent accounting period prior to sale) as a realized gain or loss in net income.

- Under current U.S. GAAP, firms must account for *available-for-sale securities* at fair value, reporting them as either current or noncurrent assets, depending on the expected holding period. These are all other minority, passive investments that do not fit into one of the first two categories. Unrealized holding gains or losses on securities available for sale are not included in net income each period; instead, they appear as a component of other comprehensive income, labeled Unrealized Holding Gain or Loss on Securities Available for Sale. The cumulative unrealized holding gain or loss on securities available for sale appears in the shareholders' equity section of the balance sheet as part of accumulated other comprehensive income. When a firm sells an available-for-sale security, it recognizes the difference between the selling price and the acquisition cost (or amortized cost if it is a bond) as a realized gain or loss on the income statement. At the time of sale, the firm must remove any unrealized gain or loss from accumulated other comprehensive income and the full amount of the realized gain or loss is then recognized in net income and retained earnings. Note that new rules go into effect for fiscal years beginning after December 15, 2017, that eliminate the available-for-sale classification. The changes in fair value of securities previously classified as available-for-sale will be reflected in current year income in the same manner as trading securities, eliminating the other comprehensive income treatment of gains and losses.[21]

An Illustration of Accounting for Minority, Passive Investments in Trading and Available-for-Sale Securities

Assume that James Company had no equity investments prior to the transactions indicated below. During 2017, James Company purchased the following common stocks:

Oden Company	10,000 shares @ $5/sh.	$50,000	
Miller Company	5,000 shares @ $4/sh.	20,000	
Haslem Company	2,000 shares @ $6/sh.	12,000	
Allen Company	3,000 shares @ $20/sh.	60,000	$142,000
Wade Company	10,000 shares @ $3/sh.	$30,000	
Bosh Company	10,000 shares @ $2/sh.	20,000	50,000
Total			$192,000

[21]Financial Accounting Standards Board, *Accounting Standards Update 2016-1*, "Recognition and Measurement of Financial Assets and Liabilities" (January 2016); *FASB Codification Topic 825.*

James intends to hold the Oden, Miller, Haslem, and Allen shares as trading securities while holding the Wade and Bosh shares as available-for-sale securities for an indefinite period. James does not have significant influence with any of the companies. During 2017 and 2018, James received $25,000 and $20,000, respectively, in dividends from the stock investments. James sold the investment in Allen Company in 2018 for $62,000. At the end of 2017 and 2018, market values were as follows:[22]

	2017	2018
Oden	$ 30,000	$55,000
Miller	20,000	23,000
Haslem	10,000	10,000
Allen	63,000	0
Total	$123,000	$88,000
Wade	$ 25,000	$20,000
Bosh	30,000	22,000
Total	$ 55,000	$42,000

Because James has no significant influence with the investee companies, James accounts for these investments using the market method. Exhibit 8.5 analyzes the costs and fair values of the two portfolios of investments in trading and available-for-sale securities at each balance sheet date.

In the current assets section of the balance sheet, investments in trading securities are reported at their December 31, 2017, and December 31, 2018, fair values of $123,000 and $88,000, respectively. In the long-term investments section, the invest- ments in available-for-sale securities also are reported at fair values as of December 31, 2017, and December 31, 2018, at $55,000 and $42,000, respectively. The year-to-year fluctuations in the trading security fair values—a $19,000 unrealized loss in 2017 and a $28,000 unrealized gain in 2018—are reported in the income statement. In contrast, the unrealized gain of $5,000 in 2017 and the unrealized loss of $13,000 in 2018 on revalua- tions of available-for-sale securities are reported as other comprehensive income on the statement of comprehensive income. The cumulative adjustment from cost to fair value is reported in the accumulated other comprehensive income section of the owners' equity section. Dividend income of $25,000 and $20,000 is also reported in 2017 and 2018, respectively.

In Exhibit 8.5, the costs and fair values of the investment in Allen trading securities do not factor into the analysis in 2018 because the securities were sold. A realized loss

---

[22]Note that in this example, James holds three of the trading securities over a two-year period. By definition, a trading security is held for a short period of time (for example, 90 days). A security that is held for two years should not be classified as trading. However, the purpose of this problem is to compare and contrast the accounting for trading and available-for-sale equity security investments. Accordingly, the trading securities are artificially held over two periods so that you can compare and contrast the accounting for trading and available-for-sale equity security investments.

Exhibit 8.5

Application of Market Method to Trading Securities
(amounts in thousands)

Trading Securities:	December 31, 2017		December 31, 2018	
	Cost	Fair Value	New Basis	Fair Value
Oden	$ 50	$ 30	$ 30	$55
Miller	20	20	20	23
Haslem	12	10	10	10
Allen	60	63	—	—
Totals	$142	$123	$ 60	$88
(Loss) Gain reported on income statement as unrealized	$ (19)		$ 28	
Available-for-Sale Securities:				
Wade	$ 30	$ 25	$ 30	$20
Bosh	20	30	20	22
Totals	$ 50	$ 55	$ 50	$42
Unrealized gain (loss) reported on balance sheet in shareholders' equity as accumulated other comprehensive income	$ 5		$ (8)	
Change from prior year reported in other comprehensive income as unrealized gain (loss)	$ 5		$(13)	

occurred on that sale, computed by comparing the new basis (that is, the fair value at the end of 2017) to the selling price, as follows:

Sales price	$ 62,000
December 31, 2017 basis of Allen Company securities	(63,000)
Realized loss on sale	$ (1,000)

The realized loss is recognized in net income in 2018.

The statement of cash flows reports the initial investments in the trading securities as cash outflows in the operating activities section because the majority of firms that invest in trading securities are financial firms that make the investments for operating purposes. The initial investments in available-for-sale securities are reported as cash outflows in the investing activities section. Dividends received are also reported as cash inflows in the operating section under U.S. GAAP. IFRS permits the reporting of dividend receipts in the operating or investing section of the cash flow statement.

Exhibit 8.6 summarizes the financial statement effects and shows the journal entries that would be made to account for the investments in trading and available-for-sale securities.

Exhibit 8.6: Financial Statement Effects of Trading and Available-for-Sale Securities

Assets	=	Liabilities	+	Total Shareholders' Equity		
				CC	AOCI	RE
2017 Purchase of Investments:						
Trading Securities 142,000						
AFS Securities 50,000						
Cash (192,000)						
2017 Dividend Receipts:						
Cash 25,000						Dividend Revenue 25,000
12/31/2017 Adjustments to Fair Value:						
Trading Securities (19,000)					Cumulative Unrealized Loss/Gain on Adjustment of AFS Securities to Fair Value (OCI) 5,000	Unrealized Loss on Adjustment of Trading Securities to Fair Value (19,000)
AFS Securities 5,000						
2018 Dividend Receipts:						
Cash 20,000						Dividend Revenue 20,000
2018 Sale of Allen Company Securities:						
Cash 62,000						Realized Loss on Sale of Trading Securities (1,000)
Trading Securities (63,000)						
12/31/2018 Adjustments to Fair Value:						
Trading Securities 28,000					Cumulative Unrealized Loss/Gain on Adjustment of AFS Securities to Fair Value (OCI) (13,000)	Unrealized Gain on Adjustment of Trading Securities to Fair Value 28,000
AFS Securities (13,000)						

	Debit	Credit
2017 Purchase of Investments:		
Trading Securities	142,000	
AFS Securities	50,000	
Cash		192,000
2017 Dividend Receipts:		
Cash	25,000	
Dividend Revenue		25,000
12/31/2017 Adjustments to Fair Value:		
Unrealized Loss on Adjustment of Trading Securities to Fair Value	19,000	
Trading Securities		19,000
AFS Securities	5,000	
Cumulative Unrealized Loss/Gain on Adjustment of AFS Securities to Fair Value		5,000
2018 Dividend Receipts:		
Cash	20,000	
Dividend Revenue		20,000
2018 Sale of Allen Company Securities:		
Cash	62,000	
Realized Loss on Sale of Trading Securities	1,000	
Trading Securities		63,000
12/31/2018 Adjustments to Fair Value:		
Trading Securities	28,000	
Unrealized Gain on Adjustment of Trading Securities to Fair Value		28,000
Cumulative Unrealized Loss/Gain on Adjustment of AFS Securities to Fair Value	13,000	
AFS Securities		13,000

Security Classification, Potential Earnings Management, and Rule Changes

The reporting of unrealized gains and losses on available-for-sale securities in owners' equity rather than income has the advantage of deferring short-term value fluctuations on longer-term transactions. However, earnings management opportunities are available through available-for-sale securities: "winners" can be sold and "losers" can be held in the portfolio. This allows realized gains to be reported as income, while unrealized losses as a component of owners' equity are deferred. For example, suppose a company made two recent investments in available-for-sale equity securities. Both were purchased for $10,000. Investment A has appreciated to $11,000 during the current period, and Investment B has declined in fair value to $9,500. If the company wanted to report more income during the current period, Investment A could be sold at a gain of $1,000. Otherwise, the $1,000 would be disclosed as an unrealized gain in other comprehensive income. Similar discretion to generate a loss exists with respect to Investment B. Comprehensive income would reflect both the unrealized gain and the unrealized loss, and would not be affected by attempts to manipulate reported net income. Available-for-sale security gains and losses, realized or unrealized, are part of comprehensive income.

The different treatment given to unrealized gains and losses on available-for-sale securities in net income versus other comprehensive income creates the need to *recycle* realized gains and losses through net income when an available-for-sale security is sold. Extending our example, assume that the portfolio of available-for-sale securities is sold during 2019 for $42,000, the portfolio's fair value at December 31, 2018. At that date, the portfolio had a cost of $50,000 and the accumulated comprehensive loss reported in shareholders' equity was $8,000 to reflect the downward valuation of the portfolio. When the portfolio is sold, the loss of $8,000 is realized and reported in (recycled through) net income and then included in retained earnings. The accumulated other comprehensive loss of $8,000 is removed from shareholders' equity by being reversed through OCI in 2019. Therefore, the unrealized fair value gains and losses flow through accumulated other comprehensive income (described in Chapter 2 as a temporary "holding tank") until they are realized in cash, at which time they flow through net income (and ultimately into retained earnings). Because the realized loss is reported in net income and the decrease in the accumulated other comprehensive loss also is reported in other comprehensive income, the two income effects cancel each other, avoiding double-counting in comprehensive income. In other words, comprehensive income reflects fair value gains and losses in the available-for-sale portfolio when they occur during the first two years, not when the securities are sold.

The new rules effective for fiscal years beginning after December 15, 2017 (see footnote 21) eliminate the available-for-sale classification. The changes in fair value of securities classified as available-for-sale will be reflected in current year income in the same manner as trading securities, thus mitigating the potential earnings management in this area, eliminating the other comprehensive income treatment of gains and losses, and eliminating the need to recycle gains and losses through net income.

Held-to-Maturity Investments in Debt Securities

Debt securities do not convey voting rights, so controlling influence is not an issue. Therefore, accounting for debt securities classified as trading and available for sale parallels the rules for investments in equity securities. Interest revenue determined using the effective interest method illustrated in Chapter 7 is reported on the income statement, and debt amortization is added back to net income in the case of a discount in the operating section of the statement of cash flows (amortization of a premium is deducted from net income in the operating section). At each reporting date, the debt securities are reported at fair value on the balance sheet.

In contrast, *held-to-maturity* debt securities are investments for which managers have the intent and ability to hold to maturity. (Note that "maturity" does not necessarily imply a long-term holding period. If a held-to-maturity debt security is due to mature within one year, it is reported as a current asset.) While intent is quite subjective, ability is less subjective. If, for example, a company has a large liability coming due before the debt investment matures, the investment may have to be liquidated to extinguish the liability. Thus, the matching of maturities of assets and liabilities central to financial management is important in documenting the ability to hold to maturity. Held-to-maturity debt investments are reported at amortized cost at each balance sheet date. Standard setters have concluded that short-run fluctuations in market value are less relevant in predicting the level of cash flows because the debt security will not be sold before it matures. Accordingly, held-to-maturity debt securities are *not* marked to market on the balance sheet, but fair values are *disclosed* in the notes.

"Other Than Temporarily Impaired" Securities

As you have learned in the preceding sections, declines in fair values of available-for-sale and held-to-maturity investments are not reflected in net income until they are realized through the sale or maturity of the security. This reflects the assumptions that fair value declines might reverse for available-for-sale securities, and the investor will hold the debt securities to maturity and collect the interest and maturity value.

If managers of the firm determine that the securities are "other than temporarily impaired," the securities must be written down to fair value with the unrealized loss reported in net income of the period. For this reason, in each period, managers must test whether securities that have experienced unrealized losses are "other than temporarily impaired." Firms disclose how long "temporarily" impaired securities have remained impaired and often discuss the reasons for management's belief that interest and maturity values of debt securities will be collected.

When assessing the quality of accounting information, you must decide whether to include any change in the unrealized holding gain or loss on available-for-sale securities in earnings for the period. The principal argument for excluding such amounts is that the unrealized gain or loss may likely reverse or may not be realized for many years, if ever. The principal argument for including the change in earnings is that regardless of whether it is realized, the gain or loss has economic significance and is relevant to an evaluation of the firm's investment performance. The various disclosures of investment gains and losses are particularly important for financial services firms such as banks and insurers because performance and management of their investment portfolios are critically important to the profitability and risk of such firms and because of the sheer magnitude of the numbers. For example, during the financial crisis, **Citigroup, Inc.**'s 2008 annual report disclosed unrealized losses on available-for-sale securities totaling $10,118 million. Although this amount appears in Citigroup's comprehensive income, it is not part of its $27,684 million net loss for 2008. Insurance giant **AIG** also reported a 2008 net unrealized loss on available-for-sale securities of $8,722 million.

- The accounting for minority, passive investments is driven by the lack of a firm's influence generally associated with relatively small equity share holdings or holdings of nonvoting financial instruments such as debt.
- The accounting is also influenced by management's intent to trade the security, hold it as available for sale, or hold it to maturity. Unless held to maturity, minority, passive investments are marked to market at the end of each reporting period.
- Value fluctuations are always a part of comprehensive income, but appear as part of net income only for trading securities.
- You should assess whether sales of available-for-sale securities are timed opportunistically (e.g., to generate a gain to meet or beat street earnings expectations).

Minority, Active Investments

Firms often acquire shares of another corporation to exert significant influence over that company's activities. This significant influence is usually at a strategic management level through representation on the board of directors. Because of wide dispersion of ownership of most publicly held corporations, and the fact that many shareholders do not vote their shares, firms can exert significant influence (but not outright control) over another corporation with ownership of less than a majority of the voting shares. In general, investments of between 20% and 50% of the voting shares of another company are generally deemed minority, active investments unless evidence indicates that the acquiring firm cannot exert significant influence, other circumstances give the investor firm control over the investee, or the investing firm is deemed the VIE's primary beneficiary.

U.S. GAAP and IFRS require firms to account for minority, active investments, generally those for which ownership is between 20% and 50%, using the *equity method*.[23] Under the equity method, the firm owning shares in another firm recognizes as income (loss) each period its proportionate share of the net income (loss) of the other firm.

Illustration of the Equity Method for Minority, Active Investments

On January 1, 2017, Lake Co. bought 40% of Pond Co. common stock at a cost of $500,000. Pond Co.'s net assets have a book value of $1,000,000. Assume that the individual fair values of identifiable net assets are equal to the book values of Pond's assets except for a building that has a fair value that is $150,000 above book value. The building has an estimated remaining useful life of 10 years. During 2017, Pond's net income is $50,000 and it pays $30,000 in dividends.

Lake Co. paid $500,000 to acquire 40% of Pond Co., which implies that $460,000 was paid for identifiable net assets and $40,000 for unidentifiable assets, as follows:

Price paid	$ 500,000
Fair value of identifiable net assets acquired ($1,150,000 × 40%)	(460,000)
Unidentifiable asset acquired (implied goodwill)	$ 40,000

If Lake were to use the market method, the investment in Pond Co. would be marked to market at year-end. Further, $12,000 in dividend revenue ($30,000 × 40%) would be

---

[23]*FASB Codification Topic 323*; International Accounting Standards Board, *International Accounting Standard 28*, "Investments in Associates" (1989).

reported on the income statement. Under the equity method, however, the investee's income, rather than the distribution of dividends, triggers the investor's income recognition. Lake's investment income is determined as follows:

Investee earnings ($50,000 × 40%)	$20,000
Excess building depreciation ($150,000 × 40%/10 years)	(6,000)
Investment revenue	$14,000

The investee (Pond Co.) calculated its $50,000 income by basing depreciation charges on the book values of its assets. Under the equity method, the investor (Lake) records its pro rata share of investee income of $20,000 ($50,000 × 40%). However, from Lake's point of view, the resources committed to generating 40% of Pond's revenues are greater than 40% of Pond's costs because Lake paid $60,000 extra for the appreciated building when it purchased the 40% interest. Allocation of the cost of that extra investment also must be reflected in income measurement (hence, the $6,000 additional depreciation expense).

Lake reports the Investment in Pond Co. account in the long-term investments section of the balance sheet at the original cost plus increases in the investment from the investee's income less decreases in the investment from dividend distribution, as follows:

Investment in Pond (original cost) at January 1, 2017	$500,000
Lake's adjusted share of Pond's earnings	14,000
Lake's share of Pond's dividends ($30,000 × 40%)	(12,000)
Investment in Pond reported at December 31, 2017	$502,000

Exhibit 8.7 summarizes the financial statement effects for Lake Company of its equity method investment in Pond.

Although Lake's net income includes an increment of $14,000 from investment revenue, it received only $12,000 of cash dividends. Therefore, the operating activities section of Lake's statement of cash flows will report a $14,000 subtraction from net income for this noncash component of income, as well as a $12,000 cash inflow from dividends (or, alternately, a net $2,000 deduction for undistributed earnings of affiliates).

Minority, active investments are *related parties*. Sales to and purchases from related parties, including any receivable and payable relationships, must be disclosed in the notes to the financial statements.[24] Related-party transactions with minority, active investments are not eliminated from the investor's financial statements. However, profit lodged in inventory from intercompany sales or purchases must be eliminated by reducing both equity in net income of the affiliate and the Investment in Affiliate account. Assume that Lake sold inventory costing $75 to Pond for $100. Pond holds $10 of the inventory at year-end. Lake must eliminate $1 profit because, based on the gross margin percentage of 25% ($25 profit/$100 selling price), the $10 inventory contains $2.50 in profit and Lake owns 40% of Pond ($2.50 × 40% = $1).[25]

[24]*FASB Codification Topic 850*; International Accounting Standards Board, *International Accounting Standard 24*, "Related Party Disclosures" (revised 2003); International Accounting Standards Board, *International Accounting Standard 1*, "Presentation of Financial Statements" (revised 2007).

[25]Companies also may choose the fair value option to report minority, active investments, recording all gains and losses from revaluation in operating income.

Exhibit 8.7: Financial Statement Effects for Lake Company (Equity Method of Accounting for Minority, Active Investments)

Assets	=	Liabilities	+	Total Shareholders' Equity		
				CC	AOCI	RE
Acquisition of Investment:						
Investment in Pond 500,000						
Cash (500,000)						
Dividends Received:						
Investment in Pond (12,000)						
Cash 12,000						
Recognition of Pond's Earnings:						
Investment in Pond 14,000						Equity in Affiliate Earnings 14,000
Acquisition of Investment:						
Investment in Pond		500,000				
Cash				500,000		
Dividends Received:						
Cash		12,000				
Investment in Pond				12,000		
Recognition of Share of Pond's Earnings:						
Investment in Pond		14,000				
Equity in Affiliate Earnings				14,000		

The Equity Method for Starbucks

Starbucks reports $249.9 million income from equity investees (income statement) for the year ended September 27, 2015, from a $352.0 million equity investment (balance sheet). This very high rate of return of nearly 71% can largely be explained by two main conditions. First, as **Starbucks** discloses in Note 6, it follows the disclosure practice of including the gross profit from sales to equity affiliates in this amount. The gross profit totaled $58.9 million in 2015, which is 24% of total reported equity income for the year. Second, under the equity method, the investment account is not adjusted upward over time to current market value. Current market values would likely be much higher to reflect the substantial earnings that **Starbucks** makes from the investment.

Starbucks' 2015 acquisition of one of those investments, **Starbucks Japan**, provides evidence that the market values of **Starbucks'** equity method investments exceed book value. In a two-stage transaction, **Starbucks** acquired the 60.5% of **Starbucks Japan** that it did not own. In the first stage, it acquired an additional 39.5% interest and therefore converted the investment from an equity affiliate to being a 79% controlled and consolidated subsidiary. In the process, it wrote up the minority share of stock (39.5%) that it had already owned to its fair value, recording a large gain of $390 million. It acquired the remaining 21% interest in the second stage, booking $777 million goodwill in the process. The fair value write-up resulting in the gain is clear evidence that the book value of the original 39.5% interest in **Starbucks Japan** was well below its fair value.

Quick Check

- When a firm can significantly influence the decisions of an investee's management, equity method accounting is required.

- The equity method recognizes the income effects of the investment when the investee earns income, not when the investee remits dividends to the firm.

Majority, Active Investments

When one investor firm owns more than 50% of the voting stock of another company, the investor firm generally has control. This control may occur at both a strategic management level and a day-to-day operational level. The majority investor in this case is the *parent* and the majority-owned company is the *subsidiary*. Financial reporting requires combining, or *consolidating*, the financial statements of majority-owned companies with those of the parent (unless for legal or other reasons the parent cannot exercise control).[26]

Purpose of Consolidated Statements

A consolidation of the financial statements of the parent and each of its subsidiaries presents the results of operations, financial position, and changes in cash flows of an affiliated group of companies under the control of a parent, essentially as if the group of companies were a single entity. The parent and each subsidiary are legally separate entities, but they operate as one centrally controlled economic entity. Consolidated financial statements generally provide more useful information to the shareholders of the parent corporation than do separate financial statements of the parent and each subsidiary.

In general, consolidated financial statements also provide more useful information than does the equity method used to account for minority, active investments. The parent, because of its voting interest, can effectively control the use of the subsidiary's assets, financial leverage, dividend policy, and strategies. Consolidation of the individual assets, liabilities, revenues, and expenses of both the parent and the subsidiary provides a more complete and realistic picture of the operations and financial position of the whole economic entity.

Corporate Acquisitions and Consolidated Financial Statements Illustrated

Corporate acquisitions occur when one corporation acquires a majority ownership interest in another corporation. Current standards are the result of a joint project between the FASB and IASB on business combinations.[27] This section deals with two types of business combinations: (1) *statutory mergers*, which result when one entity acquires all of the assets and liabilities of another entity and places the acquired assets and liabilities on its books, and (2) *acquisitions* of between 51% and 100% of the common stock of an acquired entity, where the acquired entity continues to operate as a separate legal entity with separate financial records.[28] Both types of business combinations use the *acquisition method* and have the same financial statement effects.

---

[26]*FASB Codification Topics 805* and *810*; International Accounting Standards Board, *International Accounting Standard 28*, "Investments in Associates" (1989); International Accounting Standards Board, *International Accounting Standard 27*, "Consolidated and Separate Financial Statements" (revised 2003); International Accounting Standards Board, *International Financial Reporting Standard 3*, "Business Combinations" (revised 2008); International Accounting Standards Board, *Standing Interpretations Committee Interpretation 12*, "Special Purpose Entities" (1998).

[27]The FASB Codification incorporates Financial Accounting Standards Board, *Statement No. 141R* (which requires the acquisition method for business combinations), and which replaces *Statement No. 141* (which required firms to account for all corporate acquisitions using the purchase method). For many years prior to the issuance of *Statement No. 141*, U.S. GAAP required firms to use one of two methods to account for corporate acquisitions: a version of the purchase method or the pooling-of-interests method. Most firms preferred to account for corporate acquisitions as pooling of interests rather than as purchases because of the positive effect on earnings subsequent to the acquisition. Pooling, however, has not been an allowable method for some time.

[28]A parent company may prefer to operate as a group of legally separate corporations rather than as a single legal entity. For example, separate operations isolate subsidiary financial and legal risk from the parent; permit a firm doing business in many states and countries to more efficiently contend with overlapping and inconsistent taxation, regulations, and legal requirements; and might improve incentive alignment between managers and investors when appreciation of stock in a focused firm can be part of the compensation formula.

To illustrate merger and acquisition accounting, assume that, on December 31, 2016, **Parent** Company issues 100,000 shares of its common stock to acquire 100% of the common stock of **Sub** Company. In addition, **Parent** agrees to pay former **Sub** Company shareholders an additional $500,000 in cash if certain earnings projections are achieved over the next two years. Based on probabilities of achieving the earnings projections, **Parent** estimates the fair value of this promise to be $300,000. **Parent** pays $20,000 in legal fees and $25,000 in stock issue costs to effect the acquisition. **Parent** also incurs $10,000 in internal costs related to management's time to complete the transaction. **Parent**'s shares have a fair value of $30 per share at the date of acquisition. Exhibit 8.8 provides the book values of **Parent** Company and the book and fair values of **Sub** Company at the date of acquisition.

Statutory Merger. To record the acquisition assuming that **Sub** Company is dissolved (a statutory merger), the acquisition method is applied to this business combination using the three steps that follow.

Exhibit 8.8

Date of Acquisition Book and Fair Values for Parent Company and Sub Company

	Parent Company Book Values at 12/31/16	Sub Company Book Values at 12/31/16	Sub Company Fair Values at 12/31/16
Cash	$ 900,000	$ 400,000	$ 400,000
Receivables	1,400,000	500,000	450,000
Inventory	1,700,000	1,200,000	1,400,000
PP&E (net)	14,000,000	1,600,000	2,000,000
Customer lists	0	0	100,000
Unpatented technology	0	0	200,000
In-process R&D	0	0	300,000
Total Assets	**$ 18,000,000**	**$ 3,700,000**	**$ 4,850,000**
Accounts payable	$ (600,000)	$ (400,000)	$ (400,000)
Notes payable	(5,100,000)	(2,100,000)	(2,100,000)
Total Liabilities	**$ (5,700,000)**	**$(2,500,000)**	**$(2,500,000)**
Common stock ($1 par)	$ (200,000)	$ (100,000)	
Additional paid-in capital	(4,400,000)	(500,000)	
Retained earnings	(3,700,000)	(300,000)	
Revenues	(9,000,000)	(2,000,000)	
Expenses	5,000,000	1,700,000	
Total Shareholders' Equity	**$(12,300,000)**	**$(1,200,000)**	

Liabilities and shareholders' equity accounts are in parentheses to indicate that they are claims against assets; that is, they are credits for those interpreting the worksheet from the accountant's traditional debit/credit approach. Revenues, gains, and net income are in parentheses to indicate that their signs are opposite those of expenses and losses; again, they are credits in the traditional debit/credit framework.

1. *Measure the fair value of the consideration transferred to acquire Sub.* A key concept underlying the acquisition method is measurement of the transaction at the fair value transferred by **Parent**. **Parent** chose to issue common stock with a fair value of $3,000,000 (10,000 shares × $30 fair value per share) and to incur a liability (the contingent consideration obligation) with a fair value of $300,000. **Parent** also incurred $55,000 in related legal costs, internal costs, and stock issue costs. Because accounting standards define fair value as the price received to sell an asset or the price paid to transfer a liability in an orderly transaction between market participants at the measurement date, standard setters concluded that the fair value of the transaction is the net proceeds from the stock issue, $2,975,000 ($3,000,000 − $25,000 costs to issue), plus the fair value of the stock issue costs, $25,000, plus the fair value of the liability assumed, $300,000, which sum to $3,300,000. (Alternatively, just add the fair value of the stock issued to the fair value of the liability assumed because stock issue costs appear as an addition to and subtraction from fair value.) The legal costs of $20,000 and the internal costs of $10,000 are considered expenses of the period, not part of the acquisition price.
2. *Measure the fair values of the identifiable assets acquired, liabilities assumed, and noncontrolling interests (if any).* In arriving at the $3,300,000 acquisition price, **Parent** estimated the value of the net assets of **Sub** Company whether or not they were recorded on **Sub**'s books. The information provided in Exhibit 8.8 indicates that cash, accounts payable, and notes payable had acquisition date fair values equal to their book values. The equality of book and fair values for short-term monetary assets and liabilities (that is, assets and liabilities with fixed cash flows set by contract) is common. Also, with the advent of the fair value option, the likelihood that book values and fair values will be identical increases. **Parent** estimates the fair value of receivables to be $450,000, which is $50,000 less than book value, an indication that **Parent** believes that **Sub** has under-reserved for potential uncollectible accounts. **Parent** estimates that **Sub**'s nonmonetary assets, inventory, and property, plant, and equipment have fair values that are greater than their book values. The acquirer must recognize separately from goodwill any intangible assets that arise from legal or contractual rights or that can be sold or otherwise separated from the acquired enterprise. The FASB has identified a non-exhaustive list of possible identifiable intangible assets other than goodwill that meet the criteria for recognition as assets. (See Exhibit 8.9.) **Parent** identifies three such intangible assets that are not recorded on **Sub**'s books. **Sub** has customer lists with fair values of $100,000, unpatented technology that has a fair value of $200,000, and in-process R&D that has a fair value of $300,000. These assets have no book value because **Sub** engaged in internal marketing, advertising, and R&D activities to create them, and, by rule, expensed them previously.
3. *Assign any excess consideration to goodwill or record a gain from a bargain purchase.* The difference between the fair value given by the acquirer and the fair values of the individual identifiable assets is goodwill. In this example, **Parent** gave $3,300,000 to acquire net assets of **Sub** that had a fair value of $2,350,000 ($4,850,000 fair value assets − $2,500,000 fair value liabilities). Therefore, goodwill is the difference, $950,000 ($3,300,000 − $2,350,000). The parties, in their negotiation, assign an enterprise value to **Sub** that exceeds the sum of the fair values of identifiable assets. Goodwill represents the superior expected profitability of **Sub**'s operations that exceeds what one would expect from **Sub**'s assets considered individually.

Exhibit 8.9

Examples of Intangible Assets That Meet the Criteria of Recognition Separately from Goodwill

Marketing-Related Intangible Assets
Trademarks, trade names[CL]
Service marks, collective marks, certification marks[CL]
Trade dress (unique color, shape, or package design)[CL]
Newspaper mastheads[CL]
Internet domain names[CL]
Noncompetition agreements[CL]

Customer-Related Intangible Assets
Customer lists[S]
Order or production backlog[S]
Customer contracts and related customer relationships[S]
Noncontractual customer relationships[S]

Artistic-Related Intangible Assets
Plays, operas, and ballets[CL]
Books, magazines, newspapers, and other literary works[CL]
Musical works such as compositions, song lyrics, advertising jingles[CL]
Pictures and photographs[CL]
Video ad audiovisual material, including motion pictures, music videos, television programs[CL]

Contract-Based Intangible Assets
Licensing, royalty, standstill agreements[CL]
Advertising, construction, management, service, or supply contracts[CL]
Lease agreements[CL]
Construction permits[CL]
Franchise agreements[CL]
Operating and broadcast rights[CL]
Use rights such as landing, drilling, water, air, mineral, timber cutting, and route authorities[CL]
Servicing contracts such as mortgage servicing contracts[CL]
Employment contracts[CL]

Technology-Based Intangible Assets
Patented technology
Computer software and mask works[CL]
Unpatented technology[S]
Databases, including title plants[S]
Trade secrets, including secret formulas, processes recipes[CL]

Source: *SFAS 141* and *SFAS 141R*.
[CL]indicates that the assets meet the *Contractual/Legal* criterion. (The asset also might meet the *Separability* criterion, but that is not necessary for recognition.)
[S]indicates that the asset does not meet the contractual/legal criterion but does meet the *Separability* criterion.

If **Parent** acquired **Sub** at a bargain, the fair value given would have been less than the fair values of the individual identifiable assets. Bargain purchases rarely occur given the rational behavior of owners. However, they do exist, often because of some unusual circumstance that requires a quick liquidation of a company, such as the death of an owner or forced liquidation due to bankruptcy or other financial distress. If a bargain purchase occurs, the acquirer has an economic gain equal to the fair value received less the fair value given. The gain is reported on the acquirer's income statement. For example, during the recent financial crisis, a number of healthy banks recognized gains on bargain purchases of distressed banks (and often the acquisitions were assisted by the FDIC). In 2008, for example, **J. P. Morgan Chase & Co.** acquired **Washington Mutual**, recognizing a $1.9 billion gain from the bargain purchase.

Exhibit 8.10 shows the effects of the acquisition and the journal entry to record the acquisition on **Parent**'s books at December 31, 2016. **Parent** records the fair value of assets and liabilities received from **Sub** and the fair values of consideration given to

Exhibit 8.10: Financial Statement Effects of a Merger (Acquisition Date)

Assets		=	Liabilities		+	Total Shareholders' Equity		
						CC	AOCI	RE
Primary Consideration:								
Cash	400,000		Accounts Payable	400,000		Common		
Receivables	450,000		Notes Payable	2,100,000		Stock 100,000		
Inventory	1,400,000		Contingent			APIC 2,900,000		
PP&E	2,000,000		Performance					
Customer Lists	100,000		Obligation	300,000				
Unpatented								
Technology	200,000							
In-Process R&D	300,000							
Goodwill	950,000							
Legal and Management Costs:								
Cash	(30,000)							Operating Expenses (30,000)
Stock Issue Costs:								
Cash	(25,000)						APIC (25,000)	

Primary Consideration:		
Cash	400,000	
Receivables	450,000	
Inventory	1,400,000	
PP&E	2,000,000	
Customer Lists	100,000	
Unpatented Technology	200,000	
In-Process R&D	300,000	
Goodwill	950,000	
Accounts Payable		400,000
Notes Payable		2,100,000
Contingent Performance Obligation		300,000
Common Stock		100,000
APIC		2,900,000
Legal and Management Costs:		
Operating Expenses	30,000	
Cash		30,000
Stock Issue Costs:		
APIC	25,000	
Cash		25,000

Sub's shareholders (the contingent performance obligation and the common stock issued). Note that identifiable intangible assets, in-process R&D, and goodwill are recorded at their fair values, even though their original book values on **Sub**'s books were zero. Given that many firms expensed in-process R&D in the past, the change in U.S. GAAP and IFRS to the current acquisition accounting standards is a significant change for firms acquiring technology-intensive firms. Legal costs and management time related to the combination are expensed as part of operating expenses. Stock issue costs reduce the proceeds of the issue and thus are treated as a reduction of additional paid-in capital.

Because **Sub**'s assets and liabilities now appear on **Parent**'s books and **Sub** no longer exists as a separate legal entity, **Parent** does not have to prepare consolidated financial statements.

Acquisition. If the terms of the business combination cause **Sub** to continue as a separate legal entity (an acquisition), the date of acquisition journal entry differs from the entry used to record a statutory merger. Exhibit 8.11 shows the effects of the acquisition and the journal entry to record the acquisition on **Parent**'s books if **Sub** continues

Exhibit 8.11: Financial Statement Effects of an Acquisition (Acquisition Date)

Assets	=	Liabilities	+	Total Shareholders' Equity		
				CC	AOCI	RE
Primary Consideration:						

Investment in Sub 3,300,000		Contingent
		    Performance
		    Obligation 300,000
				Common
				    Stock 100,000
				APIC 2,900,000		

Legal and Management Costs:						
Cash (30,000)						Operating Expenses (30,000)
Stock Issue Costs:						
Cash (25,000)				APIC (25,000)		
Primary Consideration:						
Investment in Sub		3,300,000				
Contingent Performance Obligation				300,000		
Common Stock				100,000		
APIC				2,900,000		
Legal and Management Costs:						
Operating Expenses		30,000				
Cash				30,000		
Stock Issue Costs:						
APIC		25,000				
Cash				25,000		

as a separate legal entity. In an acquisition, **Parent** records a single account, "Investment in Sub," to represent its interest in the fair values of **Sub**. The remaining entries are identical to the entries for a merger.

Because **Sub**'s assets and liabilities do not appear on **Parent**'s books and **Parent** controls **Sub**, **Parent** must prepare consolidated financial statements to reflect the substance of the entity over its legal form. The following schedule is a review of why **Parent** paid $3,300,000 to acquire **Sub**'s shares. The fair value allocation schedule shows three components present in the $3,300,000 acquisition price. The first two are (1) the book value of **Sub** and (2) the amounts by which individual identifiable assets exceed their book values. The sum of the first two components equals the fair value of the identifiable assets of **Sub**. The third component is goodwill.

Fair value allocation schedule (date of acquisition):

Fair value of consideration transferred by **Parent**		$ 3,300,000
Book value of **Sub** (total shareholders' equity from Exhibit 8.8)		(1,200,000)
Excess		$ 2,100,000
Allocation to differences between fair value and book value at acquisition:		
Receivables ($450,000 − $500,000)	$ (50,000)	
Inventory ($1,400,000 − $1,200,000)	200,000	
PP&E ($2,000,000 − $1,600,000)	400,000	
Customer lists ($100,000 − $0)	100,000	
Unpatented technology ($200,000 − $0)	200,000	
In-process R&D ($300,000 − $0)	300,000	(1,150,000)
Allocated to goodwill		$ 950,000

Preparing Consolidated Statements at the Date of Acquisition

Exhibit 8.12 presents the worksheet necessary to consolidate **Parent** and **Sub** at the date of acquisition. The primary objective of the worksheet is to replace the Investment in **Sub** account with the aforementioned three components in the account.

Exhibit 8.12

Date of Acquisition Consolidation Worksheet (December 31, 2016)

	Parent (adjusted for the acquisition effects)	Sub	Eliminations	Consolidated
INCOME STATEMENT				
Revenues	$ (9,000,000)	—	—	$ (9,000,000)
Expenses	5,030,000	—	—	5,030,000
Net Income	$ (3,970,000)	—	—	$ (3,970,000)
BALANCE SHEET				
Cash	$ 845,000	$ 400,000		$ 1,245,000
Receivables	1,400,000	500,000	$ (50,000)	1,850,000
Inventory	1,700,000	1,200,000	200,000	3,100,000
PP&E (net)	14,000,000	1,600,000	400,000	16,000,000
Investment in Sub	3,300,000	—	(3,300,000)	—
Customer lists	—	—	100,000	100,000
Unpatented technology	—	—	200,000	200,000
In-process R&D	—	—	300,000	300,000
Goodwill	—	—	950,000	950,000
Total Assets	$ 21,245,000	$ 3,700,000	$(1,200,000)	$ 23,745,000
Accounts payable	$ (600,000)	$ (400,000)		$ (1,000,000)
Notes payable	(5,100,000)	(2,100,000)	—	(7,200,000)
Contingent performance obligation	(300,000)	—	—	(300,000)
Common stock	(300,000)	(100,000)	$ 100,000	(300,000)
Additional paid-in capital	(7,275,000)	(500,000)	500,000	(7,275,000)
Retained earnings, Dec. 31, 2016	(7,670,000)	(600,000)	600,000	(7,670,000)
Total Liabilities and Shareholders' Equity	$(21,245,000)	$(3,700,000)	$ 1,200,000	$(23,745,000)

Revenues, gains, and net income are in parentheses to indicate that their signs are opposite those of expenses and losses; that is, they are credits for those interpreting the worksheet from the accountant's traditional debit/credit approach. Liabilities and shareholders' equity accounts are in parentheses to indicate that they are claims against assets; again, they are credits in the traditional debit/credit framework.

1. In the Eliminations column, "Investment in Sub" is removed so that, after the row is summed, the account does not appear in the Consolidated column. From a consolidated viewpoint, the combined **Parent** and **Sub** entity does not have an investment in **Sub** separate from the entity's ownership of all of **Sub**'s assets. Because **Parent** will add the individual assets and liabilities of **Sub** into the consolidated totals, maintaining the Investment in **Sub** account would be double-counting.

2. All of the individual assets and liabilities from **Sub** Company's own financial statements are added to **Parent**'s individual assets and liabilities by summing each row to obtain the consolidated total. **Sub**'s shareholders' equity accounts are eliminated because no outside ownership of **Sub**'s shares exists. These steps accomplish the objective of having the first component of the acquisition price, *book value of Sub*, appear in the consolidated totals.

3. The remainder of the eliminations adds the second (*differences between fair and book values of Sub's identifiable net assets*) and third (*goodwill*) components of the acquisition price into the consolidated totals.

The consolidated assets and liabilities appearing in **Parent**'s consolidated financial statements are equal to the sum of **Parent**'s book values and **Sub**'s fair values as remeasured at the acquisition date. **Sub**'s income statement amounts are not part of the consolidation process because the consolidated entity has not yet engaged in operations. The elimination entries are worksheet entries only, meaning they are not part of the financial records of **Parent** or **Sub**. Therefore, the consolidation worksheet must be prepared each reporting period.

A Note on Acquisition Reserves

Use of the acquisition method often entails establishing specific "acquisition reserves" at the time one company acquires another company because the acquiring company may not know the potential losses inherent in the acquired assets or the potential liabilities of the acquired company.[29] Acquisition reserve accounts increase a liability or reduce an asset. The acquiring company will allocate a portion of the purchase price to various types of acquisition reserves (for example, estimated losses on long-term contracts and estimated liabilities for unsettled lawsuits). An acquiring company has up to one year after the date of acquisition to revalue these acquisition reserves as new information becomes available. After that, the acquisition reserve amounts remain in the accounts and absorb losses as they occur. That is, the acquiring firm charges actual losses against the specific acquisition reserves established, instead of against income, to measure the expected loss.

To illustrate, assume that an acquired company has an unsettled lawsuit for which the acquiring company anticipates a $10 million pretax loss will ultimately result. It allocates $10 million to an acquisition reserve (estimated liability from lawsuit). The acquiring firm would presumably pay less for this company because of the potential liability. Assume that settlement of the lawsuit occurs three years after the date of the acquisition for $8 million (pretax). The accountant offsets the $8 million loss against the $10 million reserve instead of against net income for the year. Furthermore, the accountant reverses the $2 million remaining in the acquisition reserve, increasing net income in the year of the settlement.

---

[29]The term *reserve* is generally unacceptable unless it includes a descriptor as to its purpose. U.S. firms generally use more precise titles for reserve accounts, such as allowance for uncollectible accounts and estimated warranty liability.

Acquisition reserves can affect assessments of the quality of accounting information, and regulators carefully monitor their use (and abuse). When used properly, an acquisition reserve is an accounting mechanism that helps ensure that the assets and liabilities of an acquired company reflect fair values. However, given the estimates required in establishing such reserves, management has some latitude in managing earnings.

Consolidated Financial Statements Subsequent to Date of Acquisition

Subsequent to acquisition, the consolidation process must take into account the operating activities of both firms. Therefore, in addition to a consolidated balance sheet, the other statements must reflect the consolidated entity. To illustrate the consolidation process one year later, refer to the original data in Exhibit 8.8 that listed differences between **Sub**'s fair values and book values at the date of acquisition and assume that PP&E, customer lists, unpatented technology, and in-process R&D have remaining useful lives of 10 years. Exhibit 8.13 presents the consolidated worksheet one year later on December 31, 2017. To focus on eliminations and the meaning of the resulting

Exhibit 8.13

Consolidation Worksheet One Year after Date of Acquisition

	Parent 12/31/17	Sub 12/31/17	Eliminations	Consolidated 12/31/17
INCOME STATEMENT				
Revenues	(P)	(S)		(P) + (S)
Cost of goods sold	P	S	$ 200,000	P + S + $200,000
Bad debts expense	P	S	($50,000)	P + S − $50,000
Depreciation expense	P	S	40,000	P + S + $40,000
Amortization expense	P	S	10,000	
			20,000	P + S + $60,000
			30,000	
Equity in Sub's earnings	(P)		Pª	$0
Net Income	(P)	(S)	S	(P)
BALANCE SHEET				
Cash	P	S		P + S
Receivables	P	S		P + S
Inventory	P	S		P + S
PP&E (net)	P	S	$ 360,000	P + S + $360,000
Investment in Sub	P		(P)ᵇ	$0
Customer lists	P		$ 90,000	P + S + $90,000
Unpatented technology	P		$ 180,000	P + S + $180,000
In-process R&D	P		$ 270,000	P + S + $270,000
Goodwill			$ 950,000	$950,000
Total Assets	P	S	$1,850,000	P + S + $1,850,000

(Continued)

Exhibit 8.13 (Continued)

Accounts payable	(P)	(S)		(P) + (S)
Notes payable	(P)	(S)		(P) + (S)
Contingent performance obligation	(P)	(S)		(P) + (S)
Common stock	(P)	(S)	S[c]	(P)
Additional paid-in capital	(P)	(S)	S	(P)
Retained earnings, 12/31/17	(P)	(S)	S	(P)
Total Liabilities and Shareholders' Equity	(P)	(S)	S	(P) + (S's liabilities)

[a]To eliminate S's net income adjusted for amortizations of the excesses of fair values over book values.
[b]To eliminate equity method balance equal to original investment + S's net income adjusted for amortizations of the excesses of fair values over book values – S's dividends paid.
[c]To eliminate S's shareholders' equity.

Revenues, gains, and net income are in parentheses to indicate that their signs are opposite those of expenses and losses; that is, they are credits for those interpreting the worksheet from the accountant's traditional debit/credit approach. Liabilities and shareholders' equity accounts are in parentheses to indicate that they are claims against assets; again, they are credits in the traditional debit/credit framework.

consolidated numbers, we use P and S for **Parent** and **Sub**'s own financial statement amounts, respectively. In the passages that follow, we also describe the differences between consolidation at acquisition and consolidation subsequent to acquisition.

1. In the Eliminations column, "Investment in Sub" is removed so that, after the row is summed, it does not appear in the Consolidated column. "Investment in Sub" includes the original investment plus **Parent**'s equity in **Sub**'s earnings for the period (all of **Sub**'s earnings because of 100% ownership adjusted for amortizations of the differences between fair and book value) minus **Parent**'s share of **Sub**'s dividends (again, all of **Sub**'s dividends because of 100% ownership).
2. **Parent** adds all of the individual assets and liabilities from **Sub**'s financial statements to **Parent**'s individual assets and liabilities by summing each row to obtain the consolidated total. **Parent** eliminates **Sub**'s shareholders' equity accounts because no outside ownership of **Sub**'s shares exists. These steps accomplish the objective of having the first component of the acquisition price, book value of **Sub**, appear in the consolidated totals. **Sub**'s assets, liabilities, and owners' equity reflect the book value of **Sub** at the date of acquisition plus the changes in assets and liabilities from **Sub**'s activities during the year. The changes in assets and liabilities reflected in **Sub**'s income are based on the book value of **Sub**'s assets and liabilities. For example, **Sub** charges cost of goods sold for the book value of inventory when inventory is sold, not the fair value established at the date of acquisition.
3. A set of adjustments adds the second component (differences between fair and book values of **Sub**'s identifiable net assets) and the third component (goodwill) of the acquisition price into the consolidated totals. Exhibit 8.14 supports the entries in the Eliminations column. At the date of acquisition, we deducted $50,000 from receivables in the consolidated worksheet to reflect the lower fair value of the receivables. Assuming that **Parent** was correct in believing

Exhibit 8.14		
Differences between Fair and Book Values of Identifiable Assets One Year after Acquisition		
Date of Acquisition Differences	**Charged (Credited) to Expense**	**Balance One Year Later**
Receivables: ($50,000)	($50,000) reduction of bad debt expense	$ 0
Inventory: $200,000	$200,000 increase in cost of goods sold	$ 0
PP&E: $400,000	$400,000/10 years = $40,000 increase in depreciation expense	$ 360,000
Customer lists: $100,000	$100,000/10 years = $10,000 increase in amortization expense	$ 90,000
Unpatented technology: $200,000	$200,000/10 years = $20,000 increase in amortization expense	$ 180,000
In-process R&D: $300,000	$300,000/10 years = $30,000 increase in amortization expense	$ 270,000
Allocated to goodwill: $950,000	$0 unless impaired	$ 950,000
Net effects	Decrease income by $250,000	Increase assets by $1,850,000

that the receivables would not be collected (that is, customers defaulted), **Sub** has shown a larger bad debt expense on its own financial statements due to the unexpected (from its viewpoint) customer defaults in the current year. As Exhibit 8.14 shows, the consolidated worksheet in Exhibit 8.13 reduces bad debts expense by $50,000 and makes no adjustment to accounts receivable. The allocation of all of the fair value/book value acquisition date differences to expenses and none to the asset will occur when an item (accounts receivable in this case) is a current asset. Given that inventory also is a current asset (that is, the inventory is sold in less than a year), Exhibit 8.14 allocates all of the acquisition date $200,000 fair value excess to cost of goods sold and none to inventory. As noted in Item 2 above, **Sub** based cost of goods sold on book value when it sold the inventory. **Parent** uses the worksheet to adjust cost of goods sold to the consolidated point of view. The remaining items in Exhibit 8.14 are long term; therefore, if the items are depreciable or amortizable, a portion of the acquisition date excess fair value will be allocated to expense based on the item's estimated remaining useful life, with the remainder allocated to the asset. Goodwill is not amortized, so the full amount is reflected in the Eliminations column as an adjustment to the asset.

4. Equity in Sub's earnings is eliminated. The one-line consolidation of **Sub** has been converted to an item-by-item income statement consolidation through addition of revenues and expenses of **Parent** and **Sub** across columns.

We use the letters *P* and *S* instead of numbers in the financial statements of **Parent** and **Sub**, respectively, one year later to concentrate on what appears in the Consolidated column subsequent to the date of acquisitions. "Investment in Sub" and "Equity in Sub's earnings" do not appear. The consolidated assets and liabilities appearing in **Parent**'s consolidated financial statements are equal to the sum of **Parent**'s book values and **Sub**'s fair values as measured at the acquisition date and are adjusted for **Parent**'s expensing of a portion of the fair value/book value differences to calculate net income on a consolidated basis. Note that in the case of 100% ownership, consolidated net income is simply **P**'s net income under the equity method. Individual revenues and expenses replace the summary of **S**'s income in the Equity in Sub's earnings account, which is already in **Parent**'s net income because of its use of the equity method.

Related-Party Transactions

Several additional transactions must be considered in the preparation of consolidated financial statements. Transactions between the parent and the subsidiary affect their individual financial statements but should *not* affect the consolidated financial statements. Thus, additional eliminations should be made for

- Intercompany loans and receivables and the interest expense and revenues from those arrangements: Parents often provide loans to subsidiaries, and the subsidiary's accounting system will show a payable and accrued interest expense on its own books. Similarly, the parent will show a receivable and accrued interest revenue.
- Intercompany sales and purchases and the profits lodged in ending inventory: An earlier section of this chapter discussed investments in affiliates (minority, active investments). Recall that intercompany sales and purchases are disclosed as related-party transactions but are not eliminated. An example also was provided of how profits lodged in inventory on such sales must be eliminated. In the preparation of consolidated financial statements, the intercompany sales and purchases also must be eliminated because the purchases and sales were not with a party outside the consolidated entity.
- Intercompany payables and receivables as a result of intercompany sales and purchases: For example, if the parent company purchases inventory from the subsidiary company on credit, the subsidiary will recognize receivables that include payables from the parent.

Other extremely complex transactions that occur between parents and subsidiaries are beyond the scope of this text. However, the guiding principle in the preparation of consolidated financial statements is the need to view the substance of transactions from the consolidated entity's point of view.

What Are Noncontrolling Interests?

If an investing firm owns less than 100% of the voting shares of another firm, a *noncontrolling interest* will exist. Many companies use the term *minority interest* to describe the noncontrolling interest in their financial statements. The noncontrolling interest, which may be widely held, is entitled to a pro rata portion of net assets, earnings, and dividends. Recent accounting standards have drastically changed accounting for noncontrolling interests. Under current standards (the acquisition method), the basis for recording the acquisition transaction is the fair value of the acquired firm. For example, in a 70% acquisition, land with a book value of $100 and fair value of $110 would be remeasured to its fair value of $110, with a pro rata share allocated to parent and noncontrolling interests. The measurement of noncontrolling interests also extends to goodwill, which puts both controlling and noncontrolling interests at full fair value. However, under IFRS, firms have an option (on a transaction-by-transaction basis) to assign to noncontrolling interests only their pro rata share of differences between fair value and book value of identifiable assets and liabilities, but not goodwill.

Prior to the issuance of the current accounting standards, noncontrolling interests received disclosure on the balance sheet between liabilities and shareholders' equity ("mezzanine" disclosure). Under current accounting standards, noncontrolling interests are a component of shareholders' equity.

To illustrate an acquisition of less than 100%, Exhibit 8.15 presents the separate financial statements at December 31, 2018, of Power Company and its 80%-owned subsidiary, Small Technologies. Two years earlier, on January 1, 2017, Power acquired 80% of the common shares of Small for $3,900 in cash. Small's 2017 net income was $350, but Small paid no dividends in that year. Small's 2018 income was $450, and it paid $250 in dividends on common stock during 2018.

Shortly after the date of acquisition, Small common stock traded at a share price that was close to the share price Power paid in the acquisition. Because this condition indicated the lack of a control premium, the fair value of Small Technologies was computed as $4,875 ($3,900 acquisition price ÷ 80%). Recording the acquisition at $4,875

Exhibit 8.15

Power Company and Small Technologies Financial Statements at December 31, 2018

	Power Company	Small Technologies
Revenues	$ (4,550)	$(2,150)
Cost of goods sold	1,720	1,000
Depreciation expense	300	100
Amortization expense	500	375
Interest expense	350	225
Equity in subsidiary earnings	(320)	0
Net Income	$ (2,000)	$ (450)
Cash	$ 2,600	$ 2,000
Short-term investments	1,030	225
Land	1,520	1,475
Equipment (net)	1,950	800
Investment in Small Technologies	4,260	0
Patented technologies	4,400	2,700
Total Assets	$ 15,760	$ 7,200
Long-term liabilities	$ (5,410)	$(2,950)
Common stock	(4,350)	(1,150)
Retained earnings	(6,000)	(3,100)
Total Liabilities and Shareholders' Equity	$(15,760)	$(7,200)

Revenues, gains, and net income are in parentheses to indicate that their signs are opposite those of expenses and losses; that is, they are credits for those interpreting the worksheet from the accountant's traditional debit/credit approach. Liabilities and shareholders' equity accounts are in parentheses to indicate that they are claims against assets; again, they are credits in the traditional debit/credit framework.

(the acquisition method based on fair value) rather than $3,900 (the purchase method) causes the noncontrolling interest to reflect fair value as well.[30]

Exhibit 8.16 presents Power's allocation of Small's fair value at the date of acquisition, updated through the current balance sheet date, December 31, 2018. One year of excess fair value amortization must be reflected in consolidated net income each year, and the balance sheet amounts have accumulated two years of amortization as of December 31, 2018. For example, patented technologies had a fair value that exceeded Small's book value by $600. If the estimated life is 20 years, patent amortization expense on a consolidated basis must be increased by $30 in a given year. After two years have passed, the consolidated balance sheet reports the excess fair value at $540.

Exhibit 8.17 traces Power Company's equity method accounting for Small. Power paid $3,900 at the acquisition date (1/1/17), increased the investment account to recognize its equity in Small's earnings (percent ownership times Small's earnings, adjusted for the excess amortizations from Exhibit 8.16), and decreased the investment when it received its share of Small's dividends. The $320 equity in Small's earnings for 2018 appears in Power's own income statement, and the $4,260 investment in Small Technologies appears on Power's own December 31, 2018, balance sheet. The noncontrolling interest computations follow the same process, yielding a noncontrolling interest in 2018 net income of $80 and a noncontrolling interest in the net assets of Small of $1,065 at December 31, 2018.

Exhibit 8.18 presents the consolidation worksheet at December 31, 2018. The eliminations have been coded to facilitate the explanation. The consolidation process for less than 100% ownership follows the same process as illustrated for 100% ownership, with

Exhibit 8.16

Power Company's Fair Value Allocation at the Date of Acquisition of Small Technologies

	Allocation of Fair Values	Estimated Life	Charged (Credited) to Expense Each Year	Balance on December 31, 2018
Small fair value at acquisition date	$ 4,875			
Small book value at acquisition date	(3,700)			
Fair value in excess of book value	$ 1,175			
Land (not depreciated)	300	NA	$ 0	$300
Equipment	(50)	10	(5)	(40)
Patented technologies	600	20	30	540
Long-term liabilities	200	8	25	150
Goodwill	$ 125	Indefinite	0	125
			$50	

---

[30]If Small common stock trades at a lower amount than the per-share price paid by Power, a control premium exists. The fair value of the acquisition (and, hence, the fair value assigned to the noncontrolling interest) would be based on the price paid by Power plus the lower fair value of the remaining noncontrolling shares.

Exhibit 8.17

Investor Interests in Small Technologies
(in millions)

	Power Company Controlling Interest (80%)		Noncontrolling Interest (20%)
Acquisition date fair value (1/1/17) = $4,875		$3,900	$ 975
2017 net income of Small = $350	$280		$ 70
Annual excess amortizations = $50 (Exhibit 8.16)	(40)		(10)
Equity in Small's earnings for 2017		240	60
Investment in Small Technologies (12/31/17)		$4,140	$1,035
2018 net income of Small = $450	$360		$ 90
Annual excess amortizations = $50 (Exhibit 8.18)	(40)		(10)
Equity in Small's earnings for 2018		320	80
Dividends paid by Small in 2018 = $250		(200)	(50)
Investment in Small Technologies (12/31/18)		$4,260	$1,065

Exhibit 8.18

Consolidation Worksheet at December 31, 2018
(in millions)

	Power	Small	Eliminations		Consolidated
Revenues	$ (4,550)	$(2,150)			$ (6,700)
Cost of goods sold	1,720	1,000			2,720
Depreciation expense	300	100	C $	(5)	395
Amortization expense	500	375	C	30	905
Interest expense	350	225	C	25	600
Equity in subsidiary earnings	(320)	0	D	320	0
Net Income	$ (2,000)	$ (450)			
Consolidated net income					$ (2,080)
Noncontrolling interest in net income			E	80	80
Net income to controlling interest					$ (2,000)
Cash	$ 2,600	$ 2,000			$ 4,600
Short-term investments	1,030	225			1,255
Land	1,520	1,475	C	300	3,295
Equipment (net)	1,950	800	C	(40)	2,710
Investment in Small Technologies	4,260	0	A	(4,260)	0
Patented technologies	4,400	2,700	C	540	7,640
Goodwill			C	125	125
Total Assets	$ 15,760	$ 7,200			$ 19,625

(Continued)

Exhibit 8.18 (Continued)

Long-term liabilities	$ (5,410)	$(2,950)		150	$ (8,210)
Common stock	(4,350)	(1,150)	B	1,150	(4,350)
Noncontrolling interests			E	(1,065)	(1,065)
Retained earnings	(6,000)	(3,100)	B	3,100	(6,000)
Total Liabilities and Shareholders' Equity	$(15,760)	$ 7,200		$ 0	$(19,625)

Revenues, gains, and net income are in parentheses to indicate that their signs are opposite those of expenses and losses; that is, they are credits for those interpreting the worksheet from the accountant's traditional debit/credit approach. Liabilities and shareholders' equity accounts are in parentheses to indicate that they are claims against assets; again, they are credits in the traditional debit/credit framework.

the addition of recognizing the noncontrolling interest in net income and net assets computed in Exhibit 8.17. The eliminations are as follows:

A = Elimination of the Investment in Small Technologies account
B = Elimination of Small's shareholders' equity accounts
C = Allocation of excess fair value amounts at the date of acquisition to expenses and to the balance sheet as computed in Exhibit 8.16
D = Elimination of the equity in subsidiary earnings account
E = Recognition of an $80 noncontrolling claim on consolidated net income and of noncontrolling equity of $1,065

The noncontrolling equity interest of $1,065 should be reported as a component of shareholders' equity. As noted in Chapter 4, if the denominator of the ROA computation includes all assets (as it typically does), the numerator should be calculated *before* the allocation of consolidated net income to the noncontrolling interest. A tax effect adjustment is not necessary because the noncontrolling interest is in after-tax net income.

Corporate Acquisitions and Income Taxes

Most corporate acquisitions involve a transaction between the acquiring corporation and the *shareholders* of the acquired corporation. Although the board of directors and management of the acquired company are usually deeply involved in discussions and negotiations, the acquisition usually takes place with the acquiring corporation giving some type of consideration to the shareholders of the acquired corporation in exchange for their stock. The acquired corporation remains a legally separate entity that has simply had a change in the makeup of its shareholder group.

In many acquisitions, the acquired company does not restate its assets and liabilities for tax purposes to reflect the amount that was paid by the acquirer to shareholders for their shares of common stock. Instead, the tax basis of assets and liabilities of the acquired company before the acquisition carries over after the acquisition (termed a *nontaxable reorganization* by the Internal Revenue Code).

The preceding examples ignored the tax effects to focus on the acquisition and consolidation process. However, the following illustrates how deferred taxes would be recognized on a given difference between fair and book values. Assume that inventory had a book value of $70 and a fair value of $80; the tax rate is 35%. In the fair value allocation at the date of acquisition (and in the elimination entries during consolidation), inventory is increased by $10 and a deferred tax liability is increased by $3.50 ($10 × 35%). The deferred tax liability is accrued at the date of acquisition to recognize the increase in tax liability when the inventory is sold in the future. If during the next year the subsidiary sells the inventory at its $80 fair value, the subsidiary will have a pretax profit (for book purposes) and a taxable income (for tax purposes) of $10. However, the consolidated financial statements recognize no profit on the sale because of two counterbalancing effects: the subsidiary shows a $10 pretax profit, but the $10 additional cost of goods sold (the $10 extra paid by the parent to acquire the inventory) is recognized through the elimination process. Accordingly, consolidated pretax profit on the transaction is zero; thus, consolidated income tax expense is zero. However, the tax basis of the inventory has not been "stepped up" to $80 at the date of acquisition. Therefore, the subsidiary must pay taxes of $3.50 when the inventory is sold (the reversal of the deferred tax liability).

Consolidation of Unconsolidated Affiliates and Joint Ventures

In some cases, firms have joint ventures or minority-owned affiliates that comprise strategically important components integral to the operations of the firm but that are not consolidated. To get a more complete picture of the economic position and performance of the firm, you may want to assess the firm after consolidating all important minority-owned affiliates. For example, firms frequently work together in joint ventures to carry out their business activities. These companies do not consolidate the financial statements of the joint ventures with their financial statements, but instead use the equity method to account for the joint ventures because they are not majority-owned by the firm.

The procedure to consolidate unconsolidated affiliates and joint ventures follows the consolidated worksheet illustrated earlier. Basically, you eliminate the investment account, add the assets and liabilities of the affiliate or joint venture to the parent's assets and liabilities, adjust the assets and liabilities for any unamortized differences between the affiliate or joint venture's book and fair values (if that information is available in the notes to the parent's financial statements), and recognize the noncontrolling interest in net assets.

Proportionate consolidation is an alternative to full consolidation. Under proportionate consolidation, the investor's *share* of the affiliate's assets and liabilities appears in separate sections on the asset and liabilities sides of the balance sheet, with the equity investment account eliminated, and no noncontrolling interest is recognized. This alternative is particularly appealing for firms that enter into joint ventures in which ownership of the venture is split equally between two firms. Under U.S. GAAP, firms account for investments in joint ventures using the equity method because these investments fall between minority, active investments and majority, active investments. IFRS permits use of proportionate consolidation for joint ventures, arguing that proportionate consolidation better captures the economics of transactions in which joint control is present.

LO 8-5

Describe variable-interest entities, sometimes referred to as special-purpose entities, and explain the need for the primary beneficiary to consolidate them.

Primary Beneficiary of a Variable-Interest Entity

Control achieved by ownership of more than 50% of voting shares justifies the preparation of consolidated financial statements. However, firms can have less than 50% ownership in an entity but still be the primary beneficiary of the entity's operations and achieve control over the entity's decision-making process by contractual relationships. Special-purpose entities, now more generically termed variable-interest entities (VIEs), were part of the massive fraud infamously perpetrated by **Enron**, and such arrangements now tend to conjure up images of corporate malfeasance. However, companies may establish VIEs for legitimate business purposes. VIEs can take the form of a corporation, partnership, trust, or any other legal structure used for business purposes. Examples include entities that administer real estate leases, R&D agreements, and energy-related foreign exchange contracts. Often VIEs hold financial assets (such as accounts or loans receivable), real estate, or other property. The VIE may be passive and simply carry out a function on behalf of one or more firms (administering a commercial real estate lease, for example), or it may actively engage in some activity on behalf of one or more firms (such as conducting R&D activities). VIEs can be quite large and significant relative to the sponsoring firms. For example, in 2004, **The Walt Disney Company** announced that it would consolidate VIEs Euro Disney and Hong Kong Disneyland. The Walt Disney Company owned slightly more than 40% of each affiliate.

One of the primary benefits of the VIE is low-cost financing of asset purchases. For example, a sponsoring firm can create a VIE by using minimal amounts of equity investment, some debt investment, and probably some guarantee of VIE debt or other loss protection to outside investors. The VIE could acquire an asset and lease it to the sponsoring firm. Isolation of the asset from the sponsor's operations, the collateral presented by the asset, and sponsor debt guarantees motivate lenders to provide a lower interest rate loan to the VIE to acquire the asset.

Because of the low level of equity investment, the sponsoring firm would not consolidate a VIE under the percentage-of-ownership criterion. However, the sponsoring firm might possess the rights of a typical equity investor via contractual control of a VIE's operating, investing, and financing activities and may bear losses and reap profits as if it were an equity investor.

When Is an Entity Classified as a VIE?

A firm's investment in another entity is classified as a VIE investment if either of the following conditions exists:[31]

- The total equity investment at risk is not sufficient to permit the entity to finance its activities without additional subordinated financial support from other parties, including equity holders. The presumption is that an equity investment of less than 10% of the entity's total assets is not sufficient to permit the entity to

---

[31]*FASB Codification Topics 810 and 860.*

finance its activities without additional support. However, entities that are holding high-risk assets, engaging in high-risk activities, or exposed to risks beyond their reported assets and liabilities may be required to have more than a 10% investment.

- The equity-investing firms lack any one of the following three characteristics of a controlling financial interest:
  - The direct or indirect ability to make decisions about the entity's activities through voting rights or similar rights. Contractual arrangements with the subordinated providers of funds usually restrict the ability of the equity-investing firms to make decisions about the entity's activities.
  - The obligation to absorb all of the expected losses of the entity if they occur. The subordinated providers of funds absorb some of the expected losses.
  - The right to receive all of the expected residual returns of the entity if they occur. The subordinated providers of funds have a claim on some of the expected residual returns.

Which Entity Should Consolidate the VIE?

If a firm has a relationship with an entity deemed to be a VIE, it must ascertain whether it is the primary beneficiary of the VIE. If it is, it must consolidate the VIE's assets, liabilities, revenues, expenses, and noncontrolling interests. The firm is the primary beneficiary if it has

- the direct or indirect ability to make decisions about the entity's activities.
- the obligation to absorb the entity's expected losses if they occur.
- the right to receive the entity's expected residual returns if they occur.

These criteria recognize that contractual rights can cause a sponsoring firm to have *variable interests* similar to those possessed by traditional equity owners. Examples of variable interests and links to potential losses and returns are as follows:

- Participation rights (entitling holders to the VIE's residual profits).
- Asset purchase options (entitling holders to benefit from increases in fair values, often versus bargain repurchase rights).
- Guarantees of debt (the maker of the guarantee must stand ready to repay a VIE's liabilities if the VIE cannot).
- Subordinated debt instruments (the subordinated creditor provides the cash flow to pay senior debt when the VIE cannot).
- Lease residual value guarantees (the maker of the guarantee covers losses when a leased asset's value falls below its expected residual value).

The presence of these variable interests leads to control in the absence of equity ownership. Therefore, consolidation of the VIE is appropriate because the primary beneficiary controls the net assets of the VIE. Consolidation of a VIE follows the same process as that illustrated for majority, active investments.

If material to the financial statements, the primary beneficiary must disclose

- the nature, purpose, size, and activities of the VIE.
- the carrying amount and classification of the consolidated assets that represent collateral for the VIE's obligations.
- the status of VIE creditors' recourse (if any) to the assets of the primary beneficiary.

Firms holding significant variable interest in a VIE must disclose

- the nature of its involvement with the VIE and the start of that involvement.
- the nature, purpose, size, and activities of the VIE.
- the investing firm's maximum exposure to loss given its involvement with the VIE.

Ford Motor Company describes its VIEs in Note 15 of its 2015 10-K. As diagrammed in Exhibit 8.19, Ford Motor Company's finance subsidiary, Ford Credit, sponsors (that is, creates) a VIE with a minimal amount of equity investment. The VIE's balance sheet shows relatively small amounts of cash. The VIE must acquire assets of some kind to carry out its operations; therefore, it must attract capital from other parties. When a potential capital provider (for example, bank, insurer, or equity investor) assesses the risk of the VIE, Ford Motor Company's risk is irrelevant. The VIE is a legally separate entity from Ford Motor Company. The term used to describe the VIE status is *bankruptcy remote*. Because of bankruptcy remote status, the VIE should be able to obtain better financing terms. The VIE will determine its capital structure based on the risk of cash flows from the assets it acquires to carry on its stated purpose. In the case of Ford's financial services, the VIEs acquire customer receivables from Ford Credit and securitize the receivables. That is, the VIEs issue rights to investors to the cash flows from receivable collection. The cash it collects from investors upon selling the secured interests is transferred back to Ford Credit as payment for the receivables acquired. Customers pay cash on their receivables to Ford Credit, and Ford Credit delivers scheduled cash payments to the VIEs' investors.

The benefit to Ford Motor Company of this arrangement is clear: Ford quickly converts its receivables to cash, and Ford Credit can offer more financing to stimulate future sales. This benefit comes at a cost because investors in the VIE demand a return on their investment. The bankruptcy remote status of the VIE will help incent VIE investors to accept a lower return, but the investors often require more guarantees that Ford Credit will share in the risk that the securitized receivables will not generate sufficient cash flows. Because Ford Motor Company is the primary beneficiary of the VIE, it appropriately consolidates the VIE.

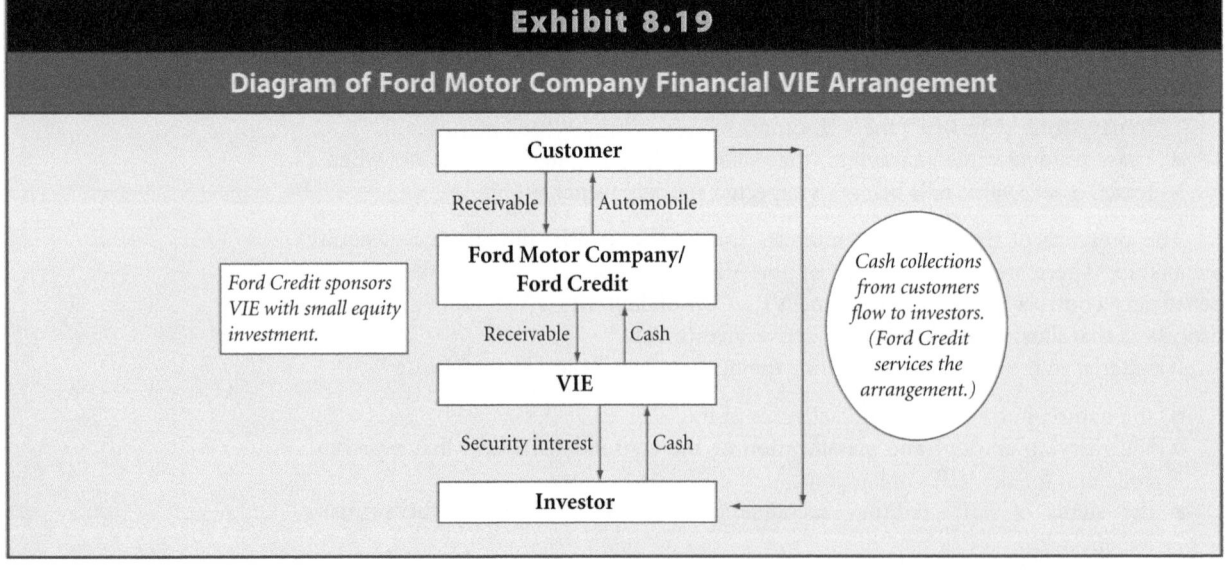

Exhibit 8.19

Diagram of Ford Motor Company Financial VIE Arrangement

Foreign Currency Translation

Firms headquartered in a particular country often have substantial operations outside of that country.[32] For some firms (such as **Coca-Cola**), international sales dominate even though the firm is headquartered in the United States. U.S. parent companies must translate the financial statements of foreign branches and subsidiaries into U.S. dollars before preparing consolidated financial statements for shareholders and creditors. This section describes the translation methodology and discusses the implications of the methodology for interpreting financial statement disclosures.[33]

The following general issues arise in translating the financial statements of a foreign branch or subsidiary:

■ Should the firm translate individual financial statement items using the exchange rate at the time of the transaction (referred to as the *historical exchange rate*) or the exchange rate during or at the end of the current period (referred to as the *current exchange rate*)? Financial statement items that firms translate using the historical exchange rates appear in the financial statements at the same U.S.-dollar-equivalent amount each period regardless of changes in the exchange rate. For example, land acquired in France for €10,000 when the exchange rate was $1.05 per euro appears on the balance sheet at $10,500 each period. Financial statement items that firms translate using the current exchange rate appear in the financial statements at a different U.S. dollar amount each period when exchange rates change. Thus, a change in the exchange rate to $1.40 per euro results in reporting the land at $14,000 in the balance sheet. Financial statement items for which firms use the current exchange rate give rise to a *foreign exchange translation adjustment* each period.

■ Should the firm recognize the foreign exchange adjustment as a gain or loss in measuring net income each period as it arises, or should the firm defer its recognition until a future period? The foreign exchange translation adjustment represents an unrealized gain or loss, much the same as changes in the market value of derivatives, marketable securities, inventories, and other assets.

The sections that follow address these two questions.

---

[32]Financial reporting requires firms to disclose segment data by geographic location (foreign versus domestic) as well as by reportable operating segments and major customers. *FASB Codification Topic 280.*

[33]Other than terminology and other relatively minor implementation differences, IFRS and U.S. GAAP are similar in the foreign currency translation area.

Functional Currency Concept

Central to the translation of foreign currency items under U.S. GAAP is the concept of *functional currency*.[34] Determination of the functional currency drives the accounting for translating the financial statements of foreign entities of U.S. firms into U.S. dollars. Foreign entities (whether branches or subsidiaries) are of two general types:

- A self-contained and integrated unit in a particular foreign country. The functional currency for these operations is the currency of that foreign country. The rationale is that management of the foreign unit likely makes operating, investing, and financing decisions based primarily on economic conditions in that foreign country, with secondary concern for economic conditions, exchange rates, and similar factors in other countries.
- A direct and integral component or extension of the parent company's operations. The functional currency for these operations is the U.S. dollar. The rationale is that management of the foreign unit likely makes decisions from the perspective of a U.S. manager concerned with the impact of decisions on U.S. dollar amounts even though day-to-day transactions of the entity are usually conducted in the foreign currency.

U.S. GAAP identifies characteristics for determining whether the currency of the foreign unit or the U.S. dollar is the functional currency, as shown in Exhibit 8.20. The operating characteristics of a particular foreign operation may provide mixed signals regarding which currency is the functional currency. Managers must exercise judgment in determining which functional currency best captures the economic effects of a foreign entity's operations and financial position. As a later section discusses, managers may structure certain financing or other transactions to influence the identification of the functional currency. Once a firm determines the functional currency of a foreign entity, it must use that currency consistently over time unless changes in economic circumstances clearly indicate that a change in the functional currency be made.

There is one exception to the guidelines in Exhibit 8.20. If the foreign entity operates in a highly inflationary country, U.S. GAAP considers its currency too unstable to serve as the functional currency, and the firm must use the U.S. dollar instead. A highly inflationary country is one that has experienced cumulative inflation of at least 100% over a three-year period. Some developing nations fall within this exception.

Translation Methodology—Foreign Currency Is Functional Currency

When the functional currency is the currency of the foreign unit, U.S. GAAP requires firms to use the *all-current translation method*. The rationale for this method is that the firm's investment in the foreign unit is for the long term; therefore, short-term changes

[34]*FASB Codification Topics 220 and 830.*

Exhibit 8.20		
Factors for Determining Functional Currency of a Foreign Unit of a U.S.-Based Firm		
	Functional Currency Is:	
	Foreign Currency	**U.S. Dollar**
Cash flows of foreign entity	Receivables and payables denominated in foreign currency and not usually remitted to parent currently	Receivables and payables denominated in U.S. dollars and readily available for remittance to parent
Sales prices	Influenced primarily by local competitive conditions and not responsive on a short-term basis to exchange rate changes	Influenced by worldwide competitive conditions and responsive on a short-term basis to exchange rate changes
Cost factors	Foreign unit obtains labor, materials, and other inputs primarily from its own country	Foreign unit obtains labor, materials, and other inputs primarily from the United States
Financing	Financing denominated in currency of foreign unit or generated internally by the foreign unit	Financing denominated in U.S. dollars or ongoing fund transfers by the parent
Relations between parent and foreign unit	Low volume of intercompany transactions and little operational interrelations between parent and foreign unit	High volume of intercompany transactions and extensive operational interrelations between parent and foreign unit

in exchange rates should not affect periodic net income. Under the all-current translation method:

- translate revenues and expenses at the average exchange rate during the period.
- translate balance sheet items at the end-of-the-period exchange rate.
- include the resulting translation adjustment (the amount needed to balance the balance sheet) as a component of other comprehensive income rather than net income.
- recognize the cumulative amount in the translation adjustment account in net income when measuring any gain or loss in the case of a sale or disposal of a foreign unit.

The "translation adjustment" reported by a firm can include a second component in addition to the effect of exchange rate changes on the parent's equity investment in foreign subsidiaries or branches. The second component would reflect a firm's use of forward contracts, currency swaps, or other derivative instruments. As part of the translation adjustment, firms report the change in fair value of a derivative that qualifies as a hedge of the net investment in a foreign entity.[35] In this sense, the foreign currency hedge is treated similar to a cash flow hedge (discussed and illustrated in Chapter 7) in

---

[35]*FASB Codification Topic 815.* However, if the foreign currency hedge does not qualify as a hedge of the net investment, the criteria established in this standard for fair value and cash flow hedges are applied to determine the appropriate accounting. See Chapter 7 for a discussion of the accounting for derivatives used in fair value and cash flow hedging activities.

that the change in the fair value of the hedge appears in other comprehensive income. The difference is that firms do not separately disclose the change in the fair value of the hedge, but rather embed it in the translation adjustment, which also captures the effect of exchange rate changes on the parent's equity investment in the foreign entity.

Translation Methodology—U.S. Dollar Is Functional Currency

When the functional currency is the U.S. dollar, firms must use the *monetary/nonmonetary translation method*. The underlying premise of the monetary/nonmonetary method is that the translated amounts reflect amounts that the firm would have reported if it had originally made all measurements in U.S. dollars. To implement this underlying premise, it is necessary to distinguish between monetary items and nonmonetary items and translate each item at the appropriate exchange rate:

- A monetary item is an item with a fixed nominal maturity amount, which does not change as the exchange rate changes (for example, a €10,000 receivable).
- From a U.S. dollar perspective, monetary items give rise to exchange gains and losses because the number of U.S. dollars required to settle the fixed foreign currency amounts fluctuates over time with exchange rate changes.
- Monetary items include cash, marketable securities, receivables, accounts payable, other accrued liabilities, and short-term and long-term debt.
- Firms translate monetary items using the *end-of-the-period exchange rate* and recognize translation gains and losses.
- These translation gains and losses increase or decrease net income each period. The rationale for the recognition of unrealized translation gains and losses in net income is that the foreign unit will likely make a currency conversion in the near future to settle monetary assets and liabilities or to convert foreign currency into U.S. dollars to remit a dividend to the parent. These activities are consistent with foreign units that operate as extensions of the U.S. parent.
- Nonmonetary items include inventories, fixed assets, common stock, revenues, and expenses.
- Firms translate nonmonetary items using the *historical exchange rate* in effect when the foreign unit initially made the measurements underlying these accounts.
  - Inventories and cost of goods sold translate at the exchange rate when the foreign unit acquired the inventory items.
  - Fixed assets and depreciation expense translate at the exchange rate when the foreign unit acquired the fixed assets.
  - Most revenues and operating expenses other than cost of goods sold and depreciation translate at the average exchange rate during the period.
  - The objective is to state these accounts at their U.S.-dollar-equivalent historical cost amounts. In this way, the translated amounts reflect the U.S. dollar perspective that is appropriate when the U.S. dollar is the functional currency.

The organizational structure and operating policies of a particular foreign unit determine its functional currency. The two acceptable choices and the corresponding translation methods were designed to capture the different economic and operational relationships between a parent and its foreign affiliates. However, firms have some latitude in deciding the functional currency (and therefore the translation method) for each foreign unit. Actions that management might consider to swing the balance of factors toward use of the foreign currency as the functional currency include the following:

- *Decentralize decision making to the foreign unit.* The greater the degree of autonomy of the foreign unit, the more likely its currency will be the functional currency. The U.S. parent company can design effective control systems to monitor the activities of the foreign unit while permitting the foreign unit to operate with considerable freedom.
- *Minimize remittances/dividends.* The greater the degree of earnings retention by the foreign unit, the more likely its currency will be the functional currency. The parent may obtain cash from a foreign unit indirectly rather than directly through remittances or dividends. For example, a foreign unit with mixed signals about its functional currency might, through loans or transfer prices for goods or services, send cash to another foreign unit whose functional currency is clearly its own currency. This second foreign unit can then remit it to the parent. Other possibilities for interunit transactions are acceptable as well to ensure that *some* foreign currency rather than the U.S. dollar is the functional currency.

Most U.S. firms with foreign operations use the foreign currency as the functional currency. When the U.S. dollar is chosen as the functional currency, it is most often because the subsidiary is in a highly inflationary country, where firms must use the U.S. dollar as the functional currency. Thus, it appears that firms prefer the all-current translation method, in large part because they can exclude unrealized foreign currency gains and losses from earnings, shielding earnings from exchange rate volatility.

The question to consider when assessing earnings quality is whether to include the change in the foreign currency translation account in earnings or leave it as a component of other comprehensive income. The principal argument for excluding it is that the unrealized gains or losses may well reverse in the long term and, in any case, may not be realized for many years. The principal arguments for including it in earnings are that (1) management has purposely chosen the foreign currency as the functional currency to avoid including such gains or losses in earnings, not because the firm allows its foreign units to operate as independent units, and (2) the change in the foreign currency translation adjustment represents the current period's portion of the eventual net gain or loss that *will* be realized. When using earnings to value a firm, Chapter 13 suggests that earnings should include all recognized value changes regardless of whether U.S. GAAP includes them in net income or other comprehensive income.

A study examined the valuation relevance of the translation adjustment. The study's results suggest that the market considers the translation adjustment relevant for security valuation but less persistent than earnings excluding gains and losses.[36] Given this finding, the FASB's decision to require firms to report the translation adjustment change as a *separate and distinct* component of comprehensive income appears to be helpful for investors.

The online appendix to this chapter provides detailed computational illustrations of the two methods for foreign currency translation.

---

[36]Billy S. Soo and Lisa Gilbert Soo, "Accounting for the Multinational Firm: Is the Translation Process Valued by the Stock Market?," *The Accounting Review* (October 1995), pp. 617–637.

Interpreting the Effects of Exchange Rate Changes on Operating Results

In addition to understanding the effects of the foreign currency translation method on a firm's financial statements, you should consider how changes in exchange rates affect changes in sales levels, sales mix, and net income. For example, assume that a firm generated sales of $10,000 in the United States and €2,000 in Italy during Year 1. The exchange rate between the U.S. dollar and Italy was $2.0:1€ during Year 1. The €2,000 of sales translates into $4,000 of foreign sales, resulting in a mix of 71.4% domestic sales and 28.6% foreign sales. For illustration, assume that domestic sales for Year 2 are $10,000 and foreign sales are €2,000. Also assume first that the U.S. dollar increases in value relative to the euro during Year 2, with an average exchange rate of $1.8:1€. The €2,000 of foreign sales translates into $3,600, resulting in a mix of 73.5% domestic sales and 26.5% foreign sales. Alternatively, assume that the U.S. dollar decreases in value during Year 2, with an average exchange rate of $2.4:1€. The €2,000 of foreign sales translates into $4,800, resulting in a mix of 67.6% domestic sales and 32.4% foreign sales. Without considering the effects of changes in selling price and volume, changes in exchange rates affect the level and mix of domestic versus foreign sales.

	Exchange Rate	Domestic Sales	Foreign Sales	Total Sales	Sales Domestic	Mix Foreign
Year 1	$2.0:€1	$10,000	$4,000[a]	$14,000	71.4%	28.6%
Year 2	$1.8:€1	$10,000	$3,600[b]	$13,600	73.5%	26.5%
Year 2	$2.4:€1	$10,000	$4,800[c]	$14,800	67.6%	32.4%

[a]€2,000 × $2.0:€1 = $4,000
[b]€2,000 × $1.8:€1 = $3,600
[c]€2,000 × $2.4:€1 = $4,800

Changes in exchange rates also affect profit margins and rates of return. The profit margin for a firm is a weighted average of the profit margins of its domestic and foreign units, for which the weights are the sales mix percentages. Changes in exchange rates affect the sales mix proportions (in addition to any effects on the amount for foreign-source earnings) and thereby the firm's overall profit margin.

Quick Check

- During the consolidation process, firms must translate foreign subsidiary financial statements into U.S. dollars. The translation results in an unrealized gain or loss for the period.
- If the foreign currency is the functional currency, the unrealized gains and losses are reported in other comprehensive income and accumulated in accumulated other comprehensive income in the shareholders' equity section of the balance sheet.
- If the U.S. dollar is the functional currency, the unrealized gains and losses are reported in net income.

Summary

Investing activities create the capacity for operations. Firms invest in assets for their own operations. Their balance sheets report the balances of property, plant, and equipment; intangible assets (including goodwill); and natural resources. Firms also invest in the operations of other firms. Their balance sheets report passive investments in marketable debt and equity securities; active equity method investments in affiliates; and because they are consolidated with the entities they control, the individual assets, liabilities, revenues, and expenses of majority investments in subsidiaries and VIEs for which they are the primary beneficiary.

Firms undertake investing activities on behalf of the claimants to the firm's assets—debtholders, preferred shareholders, controlling interests in shareholders' equity, and noncontrolling interests in shareholders' equity. Management's goal is to generate returns on these investments through operating activities. The next chapter examines the operating process and presents the accounting and reporting for operating activities.

Questions, Exercises, Problems, and Cases

Questions and Exercises

8.1 Capitalization versus Expensing Decision. When a firm incurs costs on an item to be used in operations, management must decide whether to treat the cost as an asset or an expense. Assume that a company used cash to acquire machinery expected to contribute to the generation of revenues over a three-year period and the company erroneously expensed the cost to acquire the machine.   `LO 8-1`

    a. Describe the effects on ROA of the error over the three-year period.
    b. Explain how the error would affect the statement of cash flows.

8.2 Self-Constructed Assets. Assume that a company needs to acquire a large special-purpose materials handling facility. Given that no outside vendor exists for this type of facility and that the company has available engineering, management, and productive capacity, the company borrows funds and builds the facility itself. Identify the costs to construct this facility that should be capitalized as assets.   `LO 8-1`

8.3 Natural Resources. The three types of costs incurred in oil production are acquisition costs (costs to acquire the oil fields, minus the cost of the land, plus the present value of future cash flows necessary to restore the site), exploration costs (costs of drilling), and development costs (pipes, roads, and so on, to extract and transport the oil to refineries). Should each of these costs be capitalized or expensed? Explain.   `LO 8-1`

8.4 Research and Development Costs. U.S. GAAP requires firms to expense immediately all internal expenditures for R&D costs. Alternatively, U.S. GAAP could require firms to capitalize and subsequently amortize all internal expenditures on R&D that have future potential. Why have standard setters chosen not to allow the capitalization alternative? How would analysts be better served if U.S. GAAP required capitalization of R&D costs?   `LO 8-1`

8.5 Capitalization of Software Development Costs. In practice, very few firms capitalize costs of developing computer software. However, U.S. GAAP requires that firms capitalize (and subsequently amortize) development costs once the "technological feasibility"   `LO 8-1` stage of a product is reached. Review the Adobe Systems illustration in the chapter (page 501) and discuss why the firm does not capitalize any software development costs.

LO 8-3 **8.6 Testing for Goodwill Impairment.** Goodwill is an intangible asset that firms report on their balance sheets as a result of acquiring other firms. Goodwill generally has an indefinite life and should not be amortized, but it should be tested for impairment at least annually. Describe the procedures prescribed by U.S. GAAP and IFRS to test for goodwill impairment. How do these procedures differ from the procedure followed for testing the impairment of a patent, which is an intangible asset with a definite life?

LO 8-2 **8.7 Earnings Management and Depreciation Measurement.** Earnings management entails managers using judgment and reporting estimates in such a way as to alter reported earnings to their favor.

   a. Discuss the three factors that must be estimated in measuring depreciation.
   b. Provide an illustration as to how each of these factors can be employed to manage earnings.

LO 8-1 **8.8 Corporate Acquisitions and Goodwill.** Not every acquisition results in goodwill reported in the consolidated balance sheet. Describe the valuation procedures followed by the acquiring firms to determine whether any goodwill should be recorded as a result of an acquisition and the circumstances that could lead to no recognition of goodwill in an acquisition.

LO 8-4 **8.9 Corporate Acquisitions and Acquisition Reserves.** Often the application of the acquisitions method entails establishing one or more acquisition reserves. Define an acquisition reserve, provide two examples of such reserves, and discuss how the quality of accounting information can be diminished as a result of misusing acquisition reserves.

LO 8-4 **8.10 Accounting for Available-for-Sale and Trading Marketable Equity Securities.** Firms invest in marketable securities for a variety of reasons. One of the most common reasons is to temporarily invest excess cash. Securities that qualify for the available-for-sale reporting classification are accounted for differently from those that qualify for the trading reporting classification. Describe the similarity between the reporting for the two classifications. Also describe the differences in reporting between the two classifications.

LO 8-4 **8.11 Equity Method for Minority, Active Investments.** U.S. GAAP requires firms to account for equity investments in which ownership is between 20% and 50% using the equity method. Ace Corporation owns 35% of Spear Corporation during 2017. Spear Corporation reported net income of $100.4 million for 2017 and declared and paid dividends of $25 million during the year.

   a. Calculate the equity income that Ace Corporation reports in 2017 related to its ownership in Spear Corporation.
   b. What does Ace Corporation report in its statement of cash flows for 2017 related to its ownership in Spear Corporation?
   c. Assuming that Ace Corporation's balance sheet account, Investment in Spear Corporation, is $1,100 million at the beginning of 2017, what is the balance in the account at the end of 2017? Support your answers with calculations.

8.12 Consolidation of Variable-Interest Entities. Some accounting theo- `LO 8-5` rists propose that firms should consolidate any entity in which they have a "controlling financial interest." Typically, the percentage of equity ownership that one firm has in another entity determines whether consolidation is appropriate, with greater than 50% ownership requiring consolidation. Why is the percentage of ownership criterion often *not* appropriate for judging whether a VIE should be consolidated? What criterion is used to determine whether a VIE should be consolidated?

8.13 Choice of a Functional Currency. Choosing the functional currency is a `LO 8-6` key decision for translating the financial statements of foreign entities of U.S. firms into U.S. dollars. Qing Corporation, a U.S. firm that sells car batteries, formed a wholly owned subsidiary in Mexico to manufacture components needed in the production of the batteries. Approximately 50% of the subsidiary's sales are to Qing Corporation. The subsidiary also sells the components it manufactures to independent third parties, and these sales are denominated in Mexican pesos. Financing for the manufacturing plants in Mexico is denominated in U.S. dollars, but labor contracts are denominated in both dollars and pesos. All materials contracts are denominated in Mexican pesos. Senior managers of the subsidi- ary are employees of Qing Corporation who have been transferred to the subsidiary for a tour of international service. Is the functional currency of the subsidiary the peso or the U.S. dollar? Explain your reasoning using the five criteria of FASB Statement 52.

8.14 Foreign Currency as Functional Currency. Identify the exchange `LO 8-6` rates used to translate income statement and balance sheet items when the foreign currency is defined as the functional currency. Discuss the logic for the use of the exchange rates you identified.

Problems and Cases

8.15 Analyzing Disclosures Regarding Fixed Assets. Exhibit 8.21 presents `LO 8-2` selected financial statement data for three chemical companies: **Monsanto Company**, **Olin Corporation**, and **NewMarket Corporation**. (NewMarket was formed from a merger of Ethyl Corporation and Afton Chemical Corporation.)

REQUIRED

- a. Compute the average total depreciable life of assets in use for each firm.
- b. Compute the average age to date of depreciable assets in use for each firm at the end of the year.
- c. Compute the amount of depreciation expense recognized for tax purposes for each firm for the year using the amount of the deferred taxes liability related to depreciation tim- ing differences.
- d. Compute the amount of net income for the year for each firm assuming that depreciation expense for financial reporting equals the amount computed in Requirement c for tax reporting.
- e. Compute the amount each company would report for property, plant, and equipment (net) at the end of the year if it had used accelerated (tax reporting) depreciation instead of straight-line depreciation.
- f. What factors might explain the difference in average total life of the assets of NewMarket Corporation and Olin Corporation relative to the assets of Monsanto Company?
- g. What factors might explain the older average age for depreciable assets of NewMarket Corporation and Olin Corporation relative to Monsanto Company?

Exhibit 8.21

Three Chemical Companies' Selected Financial Statement Data on Depreciable Assets (amounts in millions) (Problem 8.15)

	NewMarket Corporation	Monsanto Company	Olin Corporation
Depreciable assets at cost:			
Beginning of year	$752	$4,611	$1,796
End of year	777	4,604	1,826
Accumulated depreciation:			
Beginning of year	584	2,331	1,301
End of year	611	2,517	1,348
Net income	33	267	55
Depreciation expense	27	328	72
Deferred tax liability relating to depreciable assets:			
Beginning of year	13	267	83
End of year	9	256	96
Income tax rate	35%	35%	35%
Depreciation method for financial reporting	Straight-line	Straight-line	Straight-line
Depreciation method for tax reporting	Accelerated	Accelerated	Accelerated

Sources: NewMarket Corporation, Form 10-K for the Fiscal Year ended December 31, 2004; Monsanto Company, Form 10-K for the Fiscal Year ended August 31, 2004; and Olin Corporation, Form 10-K for the Fiscal Year ended December 31, 2004.

LO 8-3   **8.16 Asset Impairments.** Nonrelated scenarios for Hammerhead Paper Company and Sterling Company follow:

Scenario 1: Hammerhead Paper Company owns a press used in the production of fine paper products. The press originally cost $2,000,000, and it has a current carrying amount of $1,200,000. A decrease in the demand for fine paper products has caused the company to reassess the future cash flows from using the machine. The company now estimates that it will receive cash flows of $160,000 per year for 12 years. The company uses a 10% discount rate to compute the present value for this investment. A similar machine recently sold for $1,000,000 in the secondhand market. Hammerhead estimates that it would cost $50,000 to sell the machine.

REQUIRED

   a. Compute the amount of Hammerhead's press impairment, if any, under U.S. GAAP and IFRS.

Scenario 2: Sterling Co. acquires Vineyard Aging, Inc., on January 1, 2017, by paying $2,000,000 in cash. At the date of acquisition, the price is allocated as follows:

Price paid	$ 2,000,000
Fair value of Vineyard's identifiable assets	(1,600,000)
Goodwill	$ 400,000

One year later, on December 31, 2017, Sterling estimates the fair value of the unit to be $1,800,000. The carrying value of Vineyard's identifiable assets is $1,500,000 after impairment tests are applied.

REQUIRED

    b. Compute the amount of Sterling's goodwill impairment, if any.

    c. How is the goodwill impairment reflected in the financial statements?

8.17 Upward Revaluations under IFRS. Bed and Breakfast (B&B), an Italian company operating in the Tuscany region, follows IFRS and has made the choice to remeasure long-lived assets at fair value. B&B purchased land in 2016 for €150,000. At December 31 of the next four years, the land is worth €160,000 in 2016, €155,000 in 2017, €140,000 in 2018, and €145,000 in 2019.

REQUIRED

    a. Describe how B&B will reflect the changes in the land's value in each of its annual financial statements.

    b. Assume that the asset was a building with a 10-year remaining useful life as of the end of 2016. After writing the building upward to €160,000, how much should B&B charge to depreciation expense in 2016?

8.18 Application of Statement No. 115 for Investments in Marketable Equity Securities. SunTrust Banks, Inc., owns a large block of The Coca-Cola Company (Coke) common stock that it has held for many years. SunTrust indicates in a note to its financial statements that all equity securities held by the bank, including its investment in Coke stock, are classified as available for sale. In its 2006 Form 10-K, SunTrust reports the following information for its Coke investment (amounts in thousands):

Coke common stock investment, market value on December 31, 2006	$2,324,826
Coke common stock investment, market value on December 31, 2005	1,945,622
Net income for 2006	2,109,742

REQUIRED

    a. Calculate the effect of the change in the market value of SunTrust's investment in Coke's common stock on SunTrust's 2006 (1) net income and (2) shareholders' equity. Ignore taxes.

    b. How would your answer to Requirement a differ if SunTrust classified its investment in Coke's common stock as a trading security?

    c. Does the value reported on SunTrust's balance sheet for the investment in Coke's stock differ depending on the firm's reason for holding the stock (that is, whether it is classified as available for sale versus trading by management)? Explain.

8.19 Effect of an Acquisition on the Date of Acquisition Balance Sheet. Lexington Corporation acquired all of the outstanding common stock of Chalfont, Inc., on January 1, 2016. Lexington gave shares of its no par common stock with a market value of $504 million in exchange for the Chalfont common stock. Chalfont will remain a legally separate entity after the exchange, but Lexington will prepare consolidated financial statements with Chalfont each period. Exhibit 8.22 presents the balance sheets of Lexington and Chalfont on January 1, 2016, just prior to the acquisition. The market value of Chalfont's fixed assets exceeds

Exhibit 8.22

Lexington Corporation and Chalfont, Inc., Balance Sheets January 1, 2016 (amounts in millions) (Problem 8.19)

	Lexington Corporation	Chalfont, Inc.
Cash	$ 100	$ 30
Accounts receivable	240	90
Fixed assets (net)	1,000	360
Copyright	—	—
Deferred tax asset	40	—
Goodwill	—	—
Total Assets	$1,380	$480
Accounts payable and accruals	$ 240	$ 80
Long-term debt	480	100
Deferred tax liability	160	—
Other noncurrent liabilities	120	—
Common stock	320	100
Retained earnings	60	200
Total Liabilities and Shareholders' Equity	$1,380	$480

their book value by $80 million. Chalfont owns a copyright with a market value of $50 million. Chalfont is a defendant in a lawsuit that it expects to settle during 2016 at a cost of $30 million. The firm carries no insurance against such lawsuits. Lexington plans to establish an acquisition reserve for this lawsuit.

REQUIRED
a. Prepare a schedule that shows the allocation of the consideration given to individual assets and liabilities under the acquisition method. Ignore deferred tax effects.
b. Prepare a consolidated balance sheet for Lexington and Chalfont on January 1, 2016. Show your supporting calculations for any amount that is not simply the sum of the amounts for Lexington and Chalfont from their separate financial records.

LO 8-4

8.20 Effect of an Acquisition on the Postacquisition Balance Sheet and Income Statement. Ormond Co. acquired all of the outstanding common stock of Daytona Co. on January 1, 2017. Ormond Co. gave shares of its common stock with a fair value of $312 million in exchange for 100% of the Daytona Co. common stock. Daytona Co. will remain a legally separate entity after the exchange, but Ormond Co. will prepare consolidated financial statements with Daytona Co. each period. Exhibit 8.23 presents the balance sheets of Ormond Co. and Daytona Co. on January 1, 2017, just after the acquisition. The following information applies to Daytona Co.:

1. The market value of Daytona Co.'s fixed assets exceeds their book value by $50 million.
2. Daytona Co. owns a patent with a market value of $40 million.

Exhibit 8.23

Ormond Co. and Daytona Co.
Balance Sheets on January 1, 2017
(amounts in millions)
(Problem 8.20)

	Ormond Co.	Daytona Co.
Cash	$ 25	$ 15
Accounts receivable	60	40
Investment in Daytona	312	—
Fixed assets (net)	250	170
Patent	—	—
Deferred tax asset	10	—
Goodwill	—	—
Total Assets	$657	$225
Accounts payable and accruals	$ 60	$ 40
Long-term debt	120	60
Deferred tax liability	40	—
Other noncurrent liabilities	30	—
Common stock	392	50
Retained earnings	15	75
Total Liabilities and Shareholders' Equity	$657	$225

3. Daytona Co. is a defendant in a lawsuit that it expects to settle during 2017 at a cost of $25 million. The firm carries no insurance against such lawsuits. If permitted, Ormond Co. wants to establish an acquisition reserve for this lawsuit.
4. Daytona Co. has an unrecognized and unfunded retirement health care benefits obligation totaling $20 million on January 1, 2017.

REQUIRED

a. Prepare a consolidated balance sheet for Ormond Co. and Daytona Co. on January 1, 2017. Ignore deferred tax effects. (A consolidated worksheet is not required, but recommended.)
b. Exhibit 8.24 presents income statements and balance sheets taken from the separate-company books at the end of 2017. The following information applies to these companies:
  - The fixed assets of Daytona Co. had an average remaining life of five years on January 1, 2017. The firms use the straight-line depreciation method.
  - The patent of Daytona Co. had a remaining life of 10 years on January 1, 2017.
  - Daytona Co. settled the lawsuit during 2017 and expects no further liability.
  - Daytona Co. will amortize and fund its retirement health care benefits obligation over 20 years. It included $1 million in operating expenses during 2017 related to amounts unrecognized and unfunded as of January 1, 2017.
  - The test for goodwill impairment indicates that no impairment charge is necessary for 2017.

Exhibit 8.24

Ormond Co. and Daytona Co.
Income Statement and Balance Sheet for 2017
(in millions)
(Problem 8.20)

	Ormond Co.	Daytona Co.
Income Statement for 2017		
Sales	$ 600	$ 450
Equity in earnings of Daytona Co.	30	—
Operating expenses	(550)	(395)
Interest expense	(10)	(5)
Loss on lawsuit	—	(20)
Income tax expense	(28)	(12)
Net Income	$ 42	$ 18
Balance Sheet on December 31, 2017		
Cash	$ 45	$ 25
Accounts receivable	80	50
Investment in Daytona Co.	339	—
Fixed assets	280	195
Patent	—	—
Deferred tax asset	15	—
Goodwill	—	—
Total Assets	$ 759	$ 270
Accounts payable and accruals	$ 90	$ 55
Long-term debt	140	75
Deferred tax liability	50	—
Other noncurrent liabilities	40	—
Common stock	392	50
Retained earnings	47	90
Total Liabilities and Shareholders' Equity	$ 759	$ 270

Prepare a consolidated income statement for 2017 and a consolidated balance sheet on December 31, 2017. (A consolidated worksheet is not required, but it will be illustrated in the solution.)

LO 8-5 **8.21 Variable-Interest Entities.** Molson Coors Brewing Company (Molson Coors) is the fifth-largest brewer in the world. It is one of the leading brewers in the United States and Canada; the company's brands include Coors, Molson Canadian, Carling, and Killian's Irish Red. Molson and Adolph Coors Brewing Company merged in early 2005. In the final annual report of Adolph Coors Brewing Company for the year ended December 26, 2004, sales exceeded 32 million barrels (1 U.S. barrel equals 31 gallons). Coors reported $4.3 billion of net sales for 2004. The firm invests in various entities to carry out its brewing, bottling, and canning activities. The investments take the legal form of partnerships, joint ventures, and limited liability corporations, among other arrangements. The firm states in its 2004 annual report, issued under the Molson Coors name, that each of these arrangements has been tested to determine whether it qualifies as a VIE.

The following excerpt is taken from the firm's note on VIEs in its 2004 annual report:

Note 3. Variable-Interest Entities. Once an entity is determined to be a VIE, the party with the controlling financial interest, the primary beneficiary, is required to consolidate it. We have investments in VIEs, of which we are the primary beneficiary. Accordingly, we have consolidated three joint ventures in 2004, effective December 29, 2003, the first day of 2004. These include Rocky Mountain Metal Container (RMMC), Rocky Mountain Bottle Company (RMBC) and Grolsch (UK) Limited (Grolsch). The impacts to our balance sheet include the addition of net fixed assets of RMMC and RMBC totaling approximately $65 million, RMMC debt of approximately $40 million, and Grolsch net intangibles of approximately $20 million (at current exchange rates). The most significant impact to our cash flow statement for the year ended December 26, 2004, was to increase depreciation expense by approximately $13.2 million and cash recognized on initial consolidation of the entities of $20.8 million. Our partners' share of the operating results of the ventures is eliminated in the minority interests line of the Consolidated Statements of Income.

Molson Coors also provides additional information in its annual report on each of the consolidated joint ventures, as follows:

1. RMBC is a joint venture with Owens-Brockway Glass Container, Inc., in which we hold a 50% interest. RMBC produces glass bottles at a glass-manufacturing facility for use at the Golden, Colorado brewery. Under this agreement, RMBC supplies our bottle requirements and Owens-Brockway has a contract to supply the majority of our bottle requirements not met by RMBC. In 2003 and 2002, the firm's share of pretax joint venture profits for the venture, totaling $7.8 million and $13.2 million, respectively, was included in cost of goods sold on the consolidated income statement.

2. RMMC, a Colorado limited liability company, is a joint venture with Ball Corporation in which we hold a 50% interest. RMMC supplies the firm with substantially all of the cans for our Golden, Colorado brewery. RMMC manufactures the cans at our manufacturing facilities, which RMMC operates under a use and license agreement. In 2003 and 2002, the firm's share of pretax joint venture profits (losses), totaling $0.1 million and ($0.6) million, respectively, was included in cost of goods sold on the consolidated income statement. As stated previously, on consolidation of RMMC, debt of approximately $40 million was added to the balance sheet. As of December 26, 2004, Coors is the guarantor of this debt.

3. Grolsch is a joint venture between CBL and Royal Grolsch N.V. in which we hold a 49% interest. The Grolsch joint venture markets Grolsch branded beer in the United Kingdom and the Republic of Ireland. The majority of the Grolsch branded beer is produced by CBL under a contract brewing arrangement with the joint venture. CBL and Royal Grolsch N.V. sell beer to the joint venture, which sells the beer back to CBL (for onward sale to customers) for a price equal to what it paid plus a marketing and overhead charge and a profit margin. In 2003 and 2002, the firm's share of pretax profits for this venture, totaling $3.6 million and $2.0 million, respectively, was included in cost of goods sold on the consolidated income statement. As stated previously, on consolidation, net fixed assets of approximately $4 million and net intangibles of approximately $20 million were added to our balance sheet.

REQUIRED

a. Describe the operational purpose of the three VIEs consolidated by Molson Coors.

b. Molson Coors is the primary beneficiary for three investments that the firm identified as VIEs. What criteria did Molson Coors apply to determine that the firm is the primary beneficiary for these three investments?

c. For each investment, Molson Coors reports the income statement impact as a reduction of cost of goods sold on the consolidated income statement. What is the rationale for reporting the impact this way on the income statement?

d. The firm states, "Our partners share of the operating results of the ventures is eliminated in the minority interests line of the Consolidated Statements of Income." Define *minority interests* as it appears on the income statement. Discuss why Molson Coors subtracts it to calculate consolidated net income.

e. RMBC, RMMC, and Grolsch are consolidated with the financial statements of Molson Coors because the three investments qualify as VIEs as defined in *Interpretation No. 46* and the firm determined that it is the primary beneficiary for the investments. Explain what reporting technique Molson Coors would use to account for the investments if, in fact, they did not qualify as VIEs. What would be the impact on the balance sheet? What would be the impact on the income statement? What would be the impact on the statement of cash flows?

f. The firm reports that the depreciation expense on the statement of cash flows for 2004 increased by approximately $13.2 million as a result of consolidating the VIEs. Why did consolidating the VIEs increase depreciation expense?

LO 8-4

8.22 Accounting for a Merger under the Acquisition Method. On December 31, 2017, Pace Co. paid $3,000,000 to Sanders Corp. shareholders to acquire 100% of the net assets of Sanders Corp. Pace Co. also agreed to pay former Sanders shareholders $200,000 in cash if certain earnings projections were achieved over the next two years. Based on probabilities of achieving the earnings projections, Pace estimated the fair value of this promise to be $150,000. Pace paid $10,000 in legal fees and incurred $10,000 in internal cash costs related to management's time to complete the transaction. Exhibit 8.25 provides the book and fair values of Sanders Corp. at the date of acquisition.

Exhibit 8.25		
Sanders Corp. Book and Fair Values as of December 31, 2017 (Problem 8.22)		
	Sanders Corp. Book Values at 12/31/17	**Sanders Corp. Fair Values at 12/31/17**
Cash	$ 400,000	$ 400,000
Receivables	500,000	500,000
Inventory	1,200,000	1,600,000
PP&E (net)	1,600,000	2,000,000
Unpatented technology	0	300,000
In-process R&D	0	200,000
Total Assets	$ 3,700,000	$ 5,000,000

(Continued)

Exhibit 8.25 (Continued)

Accounts payable	$ (400,000)	$ (400,000)
Notes payable	(2,100,000)	(2,200,000)
Total Liabilities	$(2,500,000)	$(2,600,000)
Common stock ($1 par)	$ (100,000)	
Additional paid-in capital	(500,000)	
Retained earnings	(300,000)	
Revenues	(2,000,000)	
Expenses	1,700,000	
Total Shareholders' Equity	$(1,200,000)	

Revenues, gains, and net income are in parentheses to indicate that their signs are opposite those of expenses and losses; that is, they are credits for those interpreting the worksheet from the accountant's traditional debit/credit approach. Liabilities and shareholders' equity accounts are in parentheses to indicate that they are claims against assets; again, they are credits in the traditional debit/credit framework.

REQUIRED

a. Record the merger using the financial statement effects template or journal entries.

b. How would the financial effects *change* if the cash paid was $2,000,000?

8.23 Consolidation Subsequent to the Date of Acquisition (Noncontrolling Interests).  Exhibit 8.26 presents the separate financial statements at December 31, 2018, of Prestige Resorts and its 80%-owned subsidiary Booking, Inc. Two years earlier on January 1, 2017, Prestige acquired 80% of the common shares of Booking for $1,170 million in cash. Booking's 2017 net income was $105 million, and Booking paid no dividends in 2017. Booking's 2018 income was $135 million, and it paid $75 million in dividends on common stock during 2018. Booking's pre- and postacquisition stock prices do not support the existence of a control premium. Exhibit 8.27 shows the allocation of fair value at the date of acquisition, January 1, 2017. Exhibit 8.28 traces Prestige Resorts' equity method accounting for Booking, Inc. Ignore deferred tax effects.

Exhibit 8.26

Prestige Resorts and Booking, Inc., Financial Statements at December 31, 2018 (in millions) (Problem 8.23)

	Prestige Resorts	Booking, Inc.
Revenues	$(1,365)	$ (645)
Cost of goods sold	516	300
Depreciation expense	90	30
Amortization expense	150	112.5
Interest expense	105	67.5
Equity in subsidiary earnings	(96)	0
Net Income	$ (600)	$ (135)

(Continued)

Exhibit 8.26 (Continued)

Cash	$ 780	$ 600
Short-term investments	309	67.5
Land	456	442.5
Equipment (net)	585	240
Investment in Small Technologies	1,278	0
Customer lists	1,320	810
Total Assets	**$ 4,728**	**$ 2,160**
Long-term liabilities	$(1,623)	$ (885)
Common stock	(1,305)	(345)
Retained earnings	(1,800)	(930)
Total Liabilities and Shareholders' Equity	**$(4,728)**	**$(2,160)**

Revenues, gains, and net income are in parentheses to indicate that their signs are opposite those of expenses and losses; that is, they are credits for those interpreting the worksheet from the accountant's traditional debit/credit approach. Liabilities and shareholders' equity accounts are in parentheses to indicate that they are claims against assets; again, they are credits in the traditional debit/credit framework.

REQUIRED

a. Complete Exhibit 8.27 to show income effects and balance sheet adjustments to be reflected in the December 31, 2018, Eliminations column of the consolidated worksheet.

b. Complete Exhibit 8.28 to trace the noncontrolling interests in Booking, Inc.'s earnings and net assets.

c. Prepare a worksheet to consolidate Prestige and Booking at December 31, 2018.

Exhibit 8.27

Allocations of Fair Value (in millions)
(Problem 8.23)

	Allocation of Fair Values	Estimated Life	Charged (Credited) to Expense Each Year	Balance on December 31, 2018
Booking fair value at acquisition date	$ 1,462.5			
Booking book value at acquisition date	(1,110.0)			
Fair value in excess of book value	$ 352.5			
Land (not depreciated)	(90)	NA		
Equipment	15	10		
Customer lists	(180)	20		
Long-term liabilities (lower fair value)	(60)	8		
Goodwill	$ 37.5	Indefinite		

Exhibit 8.28

Investor Interests in Booking, Inc. (in millions)
(Problem 8.23)

	Prestige Properties (80% Controlling Interest)	Noncontrolling Interest (20%)
Acquisition date fair value (1/1/17) = $1,462.5	$1,170	
2014 net income of Booking = $105	$ 84	
Annual excess amortizations = $15	(12)	
Equity in Booking's earnings for 2017	72	
Investment in Booking, Inc. (12/31/17)	$1,242	
2018 net income of Booking = $135	$108	
Annual excess amortizations = $15	(12)	
Equity in Booking's earnings for 2018	96	
Dividends paid by Booking in 2018 = $75	(60)	
Investment in Booking, Inc. (12/31/18)	$1,278	

8.24 Calculating the Translation Adjustment under the All-Current Method and the Monetary/Nonmonetary Method (Based on material in the online appendix for Chapter 8). LO 8-6

Foreign Sub is a wholly owned subsidiary of U.S. Domestic Corporation. U.S. Domestic Corporation acquired the subsidiary several years ago. The financial statements for Foreign Sub for 2017 in its own currency appear in Exhibit 8.29.

The exchange rates between the U.S. dollar and the foreign currency of the subsidiary are

December 31, 2016	$10.0:1FC
Average, 2017	$ 8.0:1FC
December 31, 2017	$ 6.0:1FC

Exhibit 8.29

Foreign Sub
Financial Statement Data
(Problem 8.24)

	December 31	
	2016	2017
Cash	FC 100	FC 150
Accounts receivable	300	350
Inventories	350	400
Land	500	700
Total Assets	FC 1,250	FC 1,600

(Continued)

Exhibit 8.29 (Continued)

Accounts payable	FC 150	FC 250
Long-term debt	200	300
Common stock	500	600
Retained earnings	400	450
Total Liabilities and Equities	FC 1,250	FC 1,600

	For 2017
Sales	FC 4,000
Cost of goods sold	(3,200)
Selling and administrative expenses	(400)
Income taxes	(160)
Net Income	FC 240
Dividend declared and paid on December 31	(190)
Increase in Retained Earnings	FC 50

On January 1, 2017, Foreign Sub issued FC100 of long-term debt and FC100 of common stock in the acquisition of land costing FC200. Operating activities occurred evenly over the year.

REQUIRED

a. Assume that the currency of Foreign Sub is the functional currency. Compute the change in the cumulative translation adjustment for 2017. Indicate whether the change increases or decreases shareholders' equity.

b. Assume that the U.S. dollar is the functional currency. Compute the amount of the translation gain or loss for 2017. Indicate whether the amount is a gain or loss.

LO 8-6   **8.25 Translating the Financial Statements of a Foreign Subsidiary; Comparison of Translation Methods (Based on material in the online appendix for Chapter 8).** Stebbins Corporation established a wholly owned Canadian subsidiary on January 1, Year 1, by contributing US$500,000 for all of the subsidiary's common stock. The exchange rate on that date was C$1:US$0.90 (that is, one Canadian dollar equaled 90 U.S. cents). The Canadian subsidiary invested C$500,000 in a building with an expected life of 20 years and rented it to various tenants for the year. The average exchange rate during Year 1 was C$1:US$0.85, and the exchange rate on December 31, Year 1, was C$1:US$0.80. Exhibit 8.30 shows the amounts taken from the books of the Canadian subsidiary at the end of Year 1, measured in Canadian dollars.

REQUIRED

a. Prepare a balance sheet, an income statement, and a retained earnings statement for the Canadian subsidiary for Year 1 in U.S. dollars assuming that the Canadian dollar is the functional currency. Include a separate schedule showing the computation of the translation adjustment account.

b. Repeat Requirement a assuming that the U.S. dollar is the functional currency. Include a separate schedule showing the computation of the translation gain or loss.

Exhibit 8.30
Canadian Subsidiary Financial Statements Year 1 (Problem 8.25)

Balance Sheet as of December 31, Year 1

ASSETS

Cash	C$ 77,555
Rent receivable	25,000
Building (net)	475,000
	C$577,555

LIABILITIES AND EQUITY

Accounts payable	C$ 6,000
Salaries payable	4,000
Common stock	555,555
Retained earnings	12,000
	C$577,555

Income Statement for Year 1

Rent revenue	C$125,000
Operating expenses	(28,000)
Depreciation expense	(25,000)
Translation exchange loss	—
Net Income	C$ 72,000

Retained Earnings Statement for Year 1

Balance, January 1, Year 1	C$ —
Net income	72,000
Dividends	(60,000)
Balance, December 31, Year 1	C$ 12,000

c. Why is the sign of the translation adjustment for Year 1 under the all-current translation method and the translation gain or loss for Year 1 under the monetary/nonmonetary translation method the same? Why do their amounts differ?

d. Assuming that the firm could justify either translation method, which method would the management of Stebbins Corporation likely prefer for Year 1? Why?

8.26 Translating the Financial Statements of a Foreign Subsidiary; Second Year of Operations (Based on the material in the online appendix for Chapter 8). Refer to Problem 8.25 for Stebbins Corporation for Year 1, its first year of operations. Exhibit 8.31 shows the amounts for the Canadian subsidiary for Year 2. The average exchange rate during Year 2 was C$1:US$0.82, and the exchange rate on December 31, Year 2, was C$1:US$0.84. The Canadian subsidiary declared and paid dividends on December 31, Year 2.

LO 8-6

Exhibit 8.31

Canadian Subsidiary
Financial Statements
Year 2
(Problem 8.26)

Balance Sheet

ASSETS

Cash	C$116,555
Rent receivable	30,000
Building (net)	450,000
	C$596,555

LIABILITIES AND EQUITY

Accounts payable	C$ 7,500
Salaries payable	5,500
Common stock	555,555
Retained earnings	28,000
	C$596,555

Income Statement

Rent revenue	C$150,000
Operating expenses	(34,000)
Depreciation expense	(25,000)
Translation exchange gain	—
Net Income	C$ 91,000

Retained Earnings Statement

Balance, January 1, Year 2	C$ 12,000
Net income	91,000
Dividends	(75,000)
Balance, December 31, Year 2	C$ 28,000

REQUIRED

a. Prepare a balance sheet, an income statement, and a retained earnings statement for the Canadian subsidiary for Year 2 in U.S. dollars, assuming that the Canadian dollar is the functional currency. Include a separate schedule showing the computation of the translation adjustment for Year 2 and the change in the translation adjustment account.

b. Repeat Requirement a assuming that the U.S. dollar is the functional currency. Include a separate schedule showing the computation of the translation gain or loss.

c. Why is the sign of the translation adjustment for Year 2 under the all-current translation method and the translation gain or loss under the monetary/nonmonetary translation method the same? Why do their amounts differ?

d. Assuming that the firm could justify either translation method, which method would management of Stebbins Corporation likely prefer for Year 2? Why?

8.27 Identifying the Functional Currency. Alpha Computer Systems (ACS)   `LO 8-6`
designs, manufactures, sells, and services networked computer systems; associated peripheral
equipment; and related network, communications, and software products. Exhibit 8.32 presents
geographic segment data. ACS conducts sales and marketing operations outside the United
States, principally through sales subsidiaries in Canada, Europe, Central and South America, and
the Far East; by direct sales from the parent corporation; and through various representative

Exhibit 8.32

Alpha Computer Systems
Geographic Segment Data
(amounts in thousands)
(Problem 8.27)

	Year 3	Year 4	Year 5
Revenues			
United States Customers	$ 4,472,195	$ 5,016,606	$ 5,810,598
Intercompany	1,354,339	1,921,043	2,017,928
Total	$ 5,826,534	$ 6,937,649	$ 7,828,526
Europe Customers	$ 2,259,743	$ 3,252,482	$ 4,221,631
Intercompany	82,649	114,582	137,669
Total	$ 2,342,392	$ 3,367,064	$ 4,359,300
Canada, Far East, Americas Customers	$ 858,419	$ 1,120,356	$ 1,443,217
Intercompany	577,934	659,204	912,786
Total	$ 1,436,353	$ 1,779,560	$ 2,356,003
Eliminations	$(2,014,922)	$(2,694,829)	$ (3,068,383)
Net Revenue	$ 7,590,357	$ 9,389,444	$11,475,446
Income			
United States	$ 342,657	$ 758,795	$ 512,754
Europe	405,636	634,543	770,135
Canada, Far East, Americas	207,187	278,359	390,787
Eliminations	(126,771)	(59,690)	(38,676)
Operating Income	$ 828,709	$ 1,612,007	$ 1,635,000
Interest Income	116,899	122,149	143,665
Interest Expense	(88,079)	(45,203)	(37,820)
Income before Income Taxes	$ 857,529	$ 1,688,953	$ 1,740,845
Assets			
United States	$ 3,911,491	$ 4,627,838	$ 5,245,439
Europe	1,817,584	2,246,333	3,093,818
Canada, Far East, Americas	815,067	843,067	1,293,906
Corporate Assets (temporary cash investments)	2,035,557	1,979,470	2,057,528
Eliminations	(1,406,373)	(1,289,322)	(1,579,135)
Total Assets	$ 7,173,326	$ 8,407,386	$10,111,556

and distributorship arrangements. The company's international manufacturing operations include plants in Canada, the Far East, and Europe. These manufacturing plants sell their output to the company's sales subsidiaries, the parent corporation, or other manufacturing plants for further processing.

ACS accounts for intercompany transfers between geographic areas at prices representative of unaffiliated-party transactions. Sales to unaffiliated customers outside the United States, including U.S. export sales, were $5,729,879,000 for Year 5, $4,412,527,000 for Year 4, and $3,179,143,000 for Year 3, which represented 50%, 47%, and 42%, respectively, of total operating revenues. The international subsidiaries have reinvested substantially all of their earnings to support operations. These accumulated retained earnings, before elimination of intercompany transactions, aggregated $2,793,239,000 at the end of Year 5, $2,070,337,000 at the end of Year 4, and $1,473,081,000 at the end of Year 3. The company enters into forward exchange contracts to reduce the impact of foreign currency fluctuations on operations and the asset and liability positions of foreign subsidiaries. The gains and losses on these contracts increase or decrease net income in the same period as the related revenues and expenses; for assets and liabilities, in the period in which the exchange rate changes.

REQUIRED

Discuss whether ACS should use the U.S. dollar or the currencies of its foreign subsidiaries as its functional currency. Use the five criteria in FASB Statement 52.

INTEGRATIVE CASE 8.1

Walmart

Walmart makes significant investments in operating capacity, primarily via investments in property, plant, and equipment, but also via investments in wholly and partially owned subsidiaries. Walmart also has significant non-U.S. operations in its Walmart International segment. The Chapter 8 online appendix provides Walmart's January 31, 2016, Consolidated Financial Statements and accompanying notes, which describe these significant investments.

REQUIRED

a. Estimate the average total estimated useful life of depreciable property, plant, and equipment. Does the estimate reconcile with stated accounting policy on useful lives for property, plant, and equipment? Explain.
b. How should an analyst interpret fluctuations in this estimate for a given company over time? How should an analyst interpret differences in this estimate between a company and its competitors?
c. Estimate the average age of depreciable assets, the percentage of PP&E that has been used up, and the remaining useful life. How might an analyst use this information?
d. Has Walmart recognized impairment of property, plant, and equipment or goodwill during the fiscal year ending January 31, 2016? Why is it important for the analyst to know the answer to this question?
e. Under U.S. GAAP, the impairment tests for goodwill and PP&E are different. Describe the main difference.
f. Walmart must consolidate subsidiaries that are partially owned. Evidence of this fact can be found in the income statement, the balance sheet, and the statement of cash flows, where noncontrolling interests in net income, noncontrolling interest in net assets, and

cash flows related to noncontrolling interests are referenced. Explain the meaning of the noncontrolling interest in net income and the noncontrolling interest in net assets.

g. Generally speaking, firms, including firms that are partially owned subsidiaries, pay out only a portion of their net income during a period (i.e., the dividend payout ratio is generally less than one). The January 31, 2016, balance sheet reports a decrease in noncontrolling interest in net assets. Do other statements (and note information) provide evidence as to what might have happened?

h. What was the gain or loss from foreign currency translation for the year ended January 31, 2016? Where is it reported, and what is the rationale for reporting it there?

i. What happened to foreign exchange rates during the year?

CASE 8.2

Disney Acquisition of Marvel Entertainment

In August 2009, **The Walt Disney Company** announced that it would acquire **Marvel Entertainment, Inc.,** in a $4 billion cash and common stock deal. On a per-share basis, the consideration given by Disney to Marvel shareholders represents a 29% premium over Marvel's share price at the date of acquisition. Disney acquires the more than 5,000 characters in Marvel's library, including Iron Man, Spider-Man, X-Men, Captain America, and the Fantastic Four. Exhibit 8.33 presents the condensed consolidated balance sheet of Marvel at the end of its June 30, 2009, second quarter.

Exhibit 8.33

Marvel Entertainment, Inc., Condensed Consolidated Balance Sheets (unaudited) (in thousands, except per-share amounts)

	June 30	December 31
	2009	2008
ASSETS		
Current assets:		
Cash and cash equivalents	$ 81,039	$ 105,335
Restricted cash	38,220	12,272
Short-term investments	—	32,975
Accounts receivable, net	29,471	144,487
Inventories, net	13,473	11,362
Income tax receivable	206	2,029
Deferred income taxes, net	25,497	34,072
Prepaid expenses and other current assets	9,164	5,135
Total current assets	$ 197,070	$ 347,667
Fixed assets, net	$ 4,194	$ 3,432
Film inventory, net	192,068	181,564
Goodwill	346,152	346,152

(Continued)

Exhibit 8.33 (Continued)

Accounts receivable, non-current portion	7,010	1,321
Income tax receivable, non-current portion	5,906	5,906
Deferred income taxes, net—non-current portion	17,046	13,032
Deferred financing costs	3,320	5,810
Restricted cash, non-current portion	42,274	31,375
Other assets	5,489	455
Total assets	$ 820,529	$ 936,714
LIABILITIES AND EQUITY		
Current liabilities:		
Accounts payable	$ 2,860	$ 2,025
Accrued royalties	89,912	76,580
Accrued expenses and other current liabilities	33,826	40,635
Deferred revenue	67,468	81,335
Film facility	—	204,800
Total current liabilities	$ 194,066	$ 405,375
Accrued royalties, non-current portion	806	10,499
Deferred revenue, non-current portion	93,696	48,939
Film facility, non-current portion	—	8,201
Income tax payable	66,522	59,267
Other liabilities	10,680	8,612
Total liabilities	$ 365,770	$ 540,893
Commitments and contingencies	—	—
Marvel Entertainment, Inc. stockholders' equity:		
Preferred stock, $.01 par value, 100,000,000 shares authorized, none issued	—	—
Common stock, $.01 par value, 250,000,000 shares authorized, 134,681,030 issued and 77,997,619 outstanding in 2009 and 134,397,258 issued and 78,408,082 outstanding in 2008	$ 1,347	$ 1,344
Additional paid-in capital	752,438	750,132
Retained earnings	628,628	555,125
Accumulated other comprehensive loss	(4,574)	(4,617)
Total Marvel Entertainment, Inc. stockholders' equity before treasury stock	$1,377,839	$1,301,984
Treasury stock, at cost, 56,683,411 shares in 2009 and 55,989,176 shares in 2008	(921,700)	(905,293)
Total Marvel Entertainment, Inc. stockholders' equity	$ 456,139	$ 396,691
Noncontrolling interest in consolidated Joint Venture	(1,380)	(870)
Total equity	$ 454,759	$ 395,821
Total liabilities and equity	$ 820,529	$ 936,714

Source: Marvel Entertainment, Inc., Quarterly Reports, June 30, 2009, and December 31, 2008.

REQUIRED

a. From a strategic perspective, discuss why you believe Disney would make this acquisition. Note: If you are not familiar with this acquisition, search online for articles relating to the acquisition to help you formulate your answer.

b. Assuming that the assets and liabilities of Marvel approximate their individual fair values at the date of acquisition, compute goodwill.

c. This is a 100% acquisition. What role does the 29% premium play in the computation of goodwill? If this were a less-than-100% acquisition, how would the 29% premium affect the computation of the noncontrolling interest?

d. Disney will record a decrease in its cash and an increase in its shareholders' equity totaling $4 billion at the date of acquisition. Contrast the rest of the financial statement effects on Disney's own records and on its consolidated balance sheet between two scenarios: Marvel is dissolved (a merger) and Marvel continues to exist as a separate legal entity (an acquisition).

e. It is unlikely that the assets and liabilities of Marvel as shown in the condensed quarterly balance sheet approximate their individual fair values at the date of acquisition. Indeed, some of Marvel's most valuable resources might not be recognized on their balance sheet. As a result, the entire excess acquisition price is not likely to be assigned to goodwill. Identify items that are likely to receive a portion of the allocation based on the differences between their book values and fair values.

Operating Activities

LEARNING OBJECTIVES

LO 9-1 Discuss and apply the criteria for the recognition of *revenues* from operating activities, as well as the related assets, liabilities, and cash flows.

LO 9-2 Discuss and apply the criteria for the recognition of *expenses* from operating activities, as well as the related assets, liabilities, and cash flows.

LO 9-3 Use the financial statement and note information for corporate *income taxes* to analyze the firm's tax strategies.

LO 9-4 Identify the effects of *pensions and other postemployment benefits* on the financial statements.

Chapter Overview

The ultimate objective of most financing (Chapter 7) and investing (Chapter 8) activities is to create the capacity for operations. For the majority of firms, operating activities are the source of value creation. The results of a firm's operating activities are reported in the operating income section of the income statement (on an accrual basis) and in the operating cash flows section of the statement of cash flows (on a cash basis). Also, the balance sheet reflects a number of working capital and longer-term assets and liabilities generated for or by operations.

Starbucks' consolidated statement of income (Appendix A) reports pretax operating income for the year ended September 27, 2015, of $3,601.0 million. After including other investment- and financing-related income and expenses and the provision for income taxes, **Starbucks** reports consolidated net income of $2,759.3 million, of which $1.9 million is attributable to the noncontrolling interests. **Starbucks'** consolidated statement of cash flows (Appendix A) shows net cash provided by operating activities of $3,749.1 million for the same year, a measure of current period operating performance on a cash basis. Like most firms, **Starbucks** uses the indirect method to derive cash flow from operations and thus begins the section with consolidated net income of $2,759.3 million. **Starbucks** then adjusts for all of the noncash income items (such as depreciation and amortization expenses) as well as cash flows triggered by changes in operating assets and liabilities (that is, working capital). As described in Chapter 3, the operating activities section prepared using the indirect method reconciles the two measures of operating results: accrual-basis net income and cash flow from operations.

Because of the superiority of accrual accounting in measuring value creation beyond cash flows, we follow the organization of the income statement to explain operating activities. We begin with the important topic of revenue recognition and the related balance sheet items created by delayed receipt of cash (accounts receivable) and accelerated receipt of cash (deferred revenues). Then we examine the accounting and reporting for the major income statement expenses, including cost of sales (along with inventory and accounts payable); selling, general, and administrative (SG&A) expenses (including accounts such as prepaid and accrued expenses); income tax expenses (and current and deferred taxes payable); and compensation expenses (including pensions and other postemployment benefits obligations).

LO 9-1

Discuss and apply the criteria for the recognition of *revenues* from operating activities, as well as the related assets, liabilities, and cash flows.

Revenue Recognition

The income statement begins with revenues from sales and services. Revenues are typically the single largest item on the income statement, and thus a major determinant of a firm's profitability. As we will discuss in Chapter 10, financial statement forecasting begins with a projection of future revenues, and many expense, asset, and liability forecasts are conditional on projected revenues. Therefore, understanding how and when firms recognize revenues is a crucial part of accounting analysis.

The following sections discuss the current criteria for revenue recognition and practical application of the criteria. Recently, the IASB and FASB jointly completed a long-awaited new standard on revenue recognition.[1] The new guidance will apply to financial statements with reporting periods beginning after December 15, 2017. We focus the body of the chapter on the new rules because they supersede all prior revenue-related standards and their implementation is relatively soon (relative to the date of this textbook's creation).[2]

The Revenue Recognition Problem

Revenue recognition is primarily a question of timing. That is, one of the most important financial reporting decisions firms must make is *when* to recognize revenue. For most firms, revenue recognition occurs at the point of product or service delivery. On the balance sheet, cash or accounts receivable increases for the amount of the sale. If returns and rebates are allowed and can be reliably estimated, the sales revenue and associated accounts receivable are reported net of the expected returns and rebates.

The recognition of revenue at the time of sale (delivery) is common, but it is important that you assess whether this timing is appropriate for a particular firm. Firms may attempt to increase reported earnings by accelerating the timing of revenues or estimating the collectible amounts too aggressively. In addition, some firms may alter their definition of a *sale*. Does the receipt of customer orders for goods held in inventory constitute a sale? Or does the sale depend on physical delivery of the product and transfer of legal title to the customer? Is completion of custom-produced goods sufficient to recognize revenue, or is physical delivery necessary? In an effort to achieve sales targets for a period, firms sometimes record sales earlier than physical delivery. In fact, some firms, eager to report higher sales revenues or growth, might be inclined to violate revenue recognition rules by recording sales based merely on an indication of interest in a product by a customer. The pressure that sales personnel face can lead to such a violation. A related violation of the spirit of reporting sustainable revenue growth is to accelerate the shipment of products and the recognition of sales revenues to closely related

---

[1]Financial Accounting Standards Board, *Codification Topic 606*, "Revenue from Contracts with Customers" (May 2014).

[2]It is likely that you will come across accounting under the superseded rules if you analyze financial statements prior to the date of implementation. In the online appendix to the chapter, we provide a short description of revenue recognition concepts prior to the new rules.

customers (such as dealerships, franchisees, and affiliates) at the end of the year and then understate the likely sales returns by those customers (a practice known as channel-stuffing). This practice robs future periods of revenues to report current period revenues, casting great doubt on the persistence of those revenues. Even more aggressively, some firms go so far as to commit fraud, creating artificial sales invoices and shipping and storing the goods in a remote or independently owned warehouse, hoping an independent auditor will not detect them.

Revenue recognition becomes more complex as business models deviate from the typical point-of-sale transaction. For example, customers sometimes pay well in advance of receiving goods or services, and revenue recognition must be delayed until the firm satisfies its obligation to deliver goods or render services. Common examples are sales of gift cards redeemable for products (at **Starbucks** or **Nordstrom**), subscriptions to magazines (from *Time* or *The Economist*), airfares (**Delta** or **United**), and memberships (**Sam's Club**). These firms must link revenue recognition with the future delivery of a product or service or with the passage of time.

In addition, some companies' revenue generation models are quite complex, as the following examples show:

- ■ *Bundled deliverables in leases*. **Xerox Corporation** typically manufactures copiers and either sells them to customers or leases them to customers under multiyear leases. If Xerox sells a copier to a creditworthy customer, it recognizes revenue from the sale of the copier at the time of delivery. When Xerox leases copiers to customers, the length of the leases often approximates the useful life of the copiers. Thus, the arrangement is equivalent to a sale of the copier, with Xerox providing financing to the customer signing the lease. The accounting becomes complex, however, because the lease contract usually entails bundled monthly payments that cover not just use of the copier by the customer over the life of the lease, but also maintenance services, photocopying supplies (paper and toner cartridges) up to certain maximum usage, and financing costs. The revenue recognition question is *when* Xerox should recognize revenue from the four services covered in the lease: (1) copier use, (2) maintenance, (3) supplies, and (4) financing.
- ■ *Uncertain revenue timing*. Founded in 1810, the **Hartford Financial Services Group** is one of the largest investment and insurance companies in the United States. Hartford is a leading provider of (1) life insurance and group and employee benefits, (2) automobile and homeowners' insurance, and (3) business insurance. Hartford's automobile insurance unit receives cash from both premiums and investments each period. It invests in readily marketable securities for the most part, so it can measure objectively the changes in the fair value of its investments. Measuring the amount of revenue each period while the automobile insurance policy is outstanding presents few difficulties because of the (generally) one-year policy coverage period. In contrast, Harford's life insurance revenue recognition timing is more complex. In a term policy (five years, for example), it makes sense to recognize revenue over the five-year period. In a whole life policy, revenue recognition timing depends on the expected life of the policyholder. Further, straight-line revenue recognition over a whole life policy may not make sense because the probability of death increases over time. Another issue is whether firms like Hartford should recognize as revenue the interest and dividend income from investments as well as realized and unrealized gains and losses from changes in the market value of investments.

■ *Bundled service deliverables*. **MicroStrategy, Inc.**, is a software and consulting firm in the information technology sector. The firm specializes in tailoring proprietary software to analyze large databases of clients. Clients often sign two- or three-year contracts with the firm that cover customizing the software to the specific needs of the client and then licensing (as opposed to selling) the use of the software for the length of the contract. The contracts often require MicroStrategy to train the client's personnel to use the software to mine large databases and to assist the client in designing reports and analyses based on this data mining. The contracts establish key deliverables, together with a schedule for the payment of fees over the life of the contract. Assuming reasonable assurance of the collectability of fees from the client, the important revenue recognition issue is *when* MicroStrategy meets the substantial performance criterion for revenue recognition. The situation is complicated because MicroStrategy provides (1) a license to use its proprietary software tailored to the client's needs and (2) a consulting service to ensure that client personnel produce value-added reports and analyses. What proportion of the contract relates to the software, and what proportion relates to the consulting services? How precise are the deliverables requirements, which determine when MicroStrategy has completed the process to earn the revenue?

■ *Gross versus net: Online advertising*. **AOL**, formerly the Internet services division of AOL Time Warner (it was spun off as a separate company in December 2009), generates subscription revenues from subscribers to its online services, as well as advertising revenues for advertisements it places on various websites. In the past, AOL entered into an advertising arrangement with **eBay**. Under the arrangement, AOL located firms that wanted to advertise on the eBay website. AOL sold the advertising space to various companies and remitted a portion of this amount to eBay. AOL bore no credit risk if the firms failed to pay for the advertising space. AOL guaranteed the sale of a minimum amount of advertising space each month. Failure to sell the minimum space required AOL to make payments to eBay. AOL booked the amount to be received from the various companies as revenues and the amount paid to eBay as an expense. In turn, eBay booked the net amount received from AOL as revenue. The accounting issue for this revenue stream is whether AOL is a principal or an agent in purchasing and selling advertising space, and thus whether it should recognize the gross amount of revenue or the next amount. The revenue recognition described above considers AOL a principal because it entails booking the full revenue and expense. However, U.S. GAAP requires a firm to assume substantial product risk if it is to be considered a principal, which would not characterize the AOL–eBay arrangement if AOL is highly likely to sell sufficient advertising space each month to cover the minimum obligation to eBay. AOL bears little risk of unsold advertising space. Thus, it serves as an agent, which requires that only the *net* amount be recognized as revenue. The net amount would be the amount collected from purchasers of advertising minus the amount AOL remits to eBay. The distinction is an important one because, although there is no effect on bottom-line net income, the magnitude of revenues reported as a principal is substantially higher than that reported as an agent. Revenues often are a driver for assessing firms, particularly technology and Internet firms such as AOL.

■ *Gross versus net: Online sales*. **Priceline.com**'s business model, allowing customers to "name their price" when booking hotel rooms, generates similar revenue recognition questions. Should Priceline recognize the price of the hotel room as revenue (a practice known as grossing up) and the cost of the hotel room charged by the hotel to Priceline as cost of goods sold? Or should Priceline record only the difference between the price and the hotel cost as its fee revenue? The latter approach is probably the better measure of Priceline's revenue because recording the full revenue and full cost assumes that Priceline consumed an asset (the right to stay in a hotel room for a night) that caused the expense, cost of goods sold. However, Priceline did not bear the risk of ownership of this asset. In fact, Priceline's only significant risk is its contention that it is "the merchant of record" in the transaction. The SEC does not permit the grossing up of revenue for agents, but controversy continues to surround revenue recognition in business models such as Priceline's.

- **Gross versus net: Efficient inventory management.** Although the revenue-generating models of AOL and Priceline are unique, the grossing up of revenue also can be seen in more traditional situations where efficient inventory management practices exist. For example, if **Dell Inc.** receives an order and has its supplier ship inventory directly to the customer, as it often does, should Dell record the grossed-up revenue and associated cost of goods sold for the cost of the inventory that it has probably not even purchased at the time the customer's order was received? Should the French retailer **Carrefour** gross up revenues when it sells items on its floor that it does not purchase until the point of sale? If you want to compare ratios such as gross margin percentages across firms and forecast sales growth, you must read the notes to the financial statements carefully to understand the revenue recognition practices of firms and industries. Dell Inc. and Carrefour never bore risks of holding inventory because neither had title to the goods before the sale. However, both companies bear the risks of product performance and the risks of resale if the products are returned. They are the merchants of record and should probably not be treated as agents.

The preceding examples illustrate the difficulty of applying general principles for recognizing revenues. You need to increase the usual degree of healthy skepticism when analyzing reported financial data when the activities of the firms or industries under scrutiny involve heightened levels of uncertainty or subjectivity. In recent years, the SEC has emphasized the importance of investors understanding revenue recognition practices and initiated a stepped-up enforcement of firms' providing clear and complete descriptions of their revenue recognition practices.

The IASB and FASB's Revenue Recognition Project

The IASB and FASB responded to the revenue recognition problem by issuing new guidance. The core principle of the new revenue guidance is as follows: "An entity should recognize revenue to depict the transfer of promised goods or services to customers in an amount that reflects the consideration to which the entity expects to be entitled in exchange for those goods or services."[3] Entities will apply the new standard retrospectively and restate prior years' earnings, or use a more simplified cumulative adjustment to the beginning retained earnings balance without restating prior years' earnings.

---

[3]*Codification Topic 606.* In addition to the typical transfer of goods or services, the guidance applies to the sale of nonfinancial assets, such as property, plant, and equipment and intangible assets, but it does not apply to leases, insurance, financial instruments, or certain nonmonetary exchanges.

To apply the core principle, firms must follow five steps:

1. *Identify the contract with a customer.* The contract can be oral, written, or simply implied by an entity's customary business practices as long as it has commercial substance and creates enforceable rights and obligations (e.g., identifies the rights of the parties to the contract and establishes terms for probable payments).

2. *Identify the separate performance obligations in the contract.* This is a significant part of the new guidance. It requires a firm to identify whether a given good or service is "distinct," and thus accounted for separately, or indistinct, and thus combined with other promised goods or services until the firm is able to identify a bundle of goods or services that is distinct. A good or service is distinct if it meets either of the following criteria:
    *   The entity regularly sells the good or service separately.
    *   The customer can benefit from the good or service either on its own or together with other resources that are readily available to the customer.

    A good or service is not considered distinct if it is part of an interrelated bundle that the entity has combined and modified or customized for the customer to fulfill the contract.

3. *Determine the transaction price.* When determining the transaction price, an entity would consider the effects of all of the following:
    *   If the payment from the customer is a fixed amount, then that amount is the transaction price. However, if payment from the customer is variable, then the transaction price is either the expected (i.e., probability-weighted) or most likely (i.e., outcome with the highest probability) variable consideration amount, depending on which one the firm expects to better predict the amount of consideration. This guidance will require a great deal of judgment. In addition, it is likely that firms will have to defend their experience with a particular contingency that determines variable consideration outcomes. For example, if a company has no experience with similar contracts, it will be constrained from recognizing variable consideration until uncertainty about the amount of consideration is substantially resolved. Even if the company has experience with a particular kind of contract, the variable consideration might be a function of something outside of management's control and highly uncertain, such as stock prices, judgments by third parties, weather conditions, exchange rate fluctuations, etc. or might remain unresolved for long periods of time. Again, recognition of the variable consideration would not be allowed until the amount of consideration is substantially resolved.
    *   The time value of money if the contract has a significant financing component (only if contract completion will be beyond one year).
    *   Noncash consideration, either directly measured at fair value or, if not reasonably estimated, indirectly measured by reference to the stand-alone selling price of the goods or services promised to the customer in exchange for the consideration.
    *   Consideration payable to the customer, which should be treated as a reduction of the transaction price unless the payment is in exchange for a distinct good or service.

    Customer credit risk (that is, collectability) is not to be considered when determining the transaction price. Firms are to follow current standards to recognize bad debt expense.

4. *Allocate the transaction price to the separate performance obligations in the contract.* After observing the stand-alone selling price of each separate performance obligation, or estimating it if it is not observable, the firm should allocate the transaction price on a relative stand-alone selling price basis. Estimation approaches, in order of preference, are
   - the adjusted market assessment approach (basically, an estimate of what customers will be willing to pay),
   - the expected cost plus margin approach (cost to produce the good or service plus an appropriate profit margin), and
   - the residual approach (total transaction price minus observable stand-alone prices of the other goods or services in the contract). This latter approach should be used only when the stand-alone selling price of the good or service is highly variable or uncertain.

5. *Recognize revenue when (or as) the entity satisfies a performance obligation.* Satisfaction occurs when (or as) the customer obtains control of the good or service. Firms must estimate whether performance obligations are satisfied by transferring control of a good or service *over time*. If not, then the performance obligation is satisfied *at a point in time*. The standard outlines a number of criteria for determining when performance obligations are satisfied over time, such as when the entity's performance creates or enhances an asset that the customer controls. If the performance is satisfied over time, revenue is measured by the progress toward complete satisfaction of that performance obligation using either output or input methods. For example, revenues recognized from progress on road construction could be measured by considering the miles of pavement installed (an output measure) or cost incurred to date to install the pavement (an input measure). If performance occurs at a point in time, revenue recognition is based on indicators of the transfer of control that include the following:
   - The entity has a present right to payment for the asset.
   - The customer has legal title to the asset.
   - The entity has transferred physical possession of the asset.
   - The customer has the significant risks and rewards of ownership.
   - The customer has accepted the asset.

There are two clear general implications of the new guidance. First and foremost, the standard improves revenue recognition under both U.S. GAAP and IFRS, and it more closely aligns the two sets of standards. U.S. GAAP has many bright line rules for revenue recognition in different business models. The new guidance is a judgment-based unified standard that would replace these bright-line rules. Second, the volume of disclosures will increase significantly. The guidance requires disclosures about the contracts, the basis for judgments about the performance obligations and their satisfaction, and many other related items.

Application of the New Revenue Recognition Method

In the following discussions, we provide examples of applying the new revenue recognition standard to various revenue models.

Retail Sales

The retail sales situation is a good example of how informality and standard business practices enter into the revenue recognition decision. Assume that you order a $4 latte at **Starbucks**. No formal contract is written, but the essential elements of a contract are present. You are agreeing that if **Starbucks** brews and hands you the latte, you will pay. **Starbucks'** performance obligation is clear—deliver one latte. The probable transaction price has been established, and **Starbucks** allocates it to its single performance observation. **Starbucks** hands you the latte, you pay, and **Starbucks** recognizes revenue.

This example also illustrates some other concepts. First, it is quite possible that you paid with a **Starbucks** "stored value card" rather than with cash or a credit card. You obtained the **Starbucks** card by gift or by going online and putting cash on the card. How does **Starbucks** apply the revenue recognition rules when it initially receives the cash? By accepting the cash, **Starbucks** incurs performance obligations to deliver food and/or drinks of a value equivalent to the cash received. It cannot recognize any revenue until satisfying at least one of the performance obligations, and therefore records a liability, deferred revenue, to recognize the performance obligation. For example, if you put $40 cash on the card and then use the card to acquire a $4 latte, then **Starbucks** can recognize $4 of revenue and reduce the performance obligation by $4. But what if **Starbucks'** experience tells it that, say, 2% of the cards will never be redeemed? The amounts that **Starbucks** predicts will go unredeemed are often called "breakage." Note 1 to **Starbucks'** Consolidated Financial Statements recognizes that **Starbucks** will have to adopt the new revenue recognition standard for the first quarter of Fiscal 2019 (October–December 2018) and states that **Starbucks'** management is evaluating the likely effects of the new rules on **Starbucks'** financial statements. One of the biggest changes **Starbucks** anticipates is the way that it accounts for breakage income. Currently, it reports revenue from **Starbucks'** cards that it believes will not be used by the customer as breakage income in the period in which management assesses the likelihood of redemption to be remote. Under the new standards, it will likely measure its performance obligations taking the breakage into account and thus spreading the breakage income over the performance obligations that it expects to perform.

Second, a latte consists of espresso and milk. Does this mean that **Starbucks** has two performance obligations? Although it is conceivable that **Starbucks** could sell the espresso and milk separately, the contract is for a mixture of the two and thus dependent. In contrast, a sale of a cup of coffee and a slice of chocolate chip banana cake would be a sale of independent products, and thus two performance obligations.

Sales of Bundled Products

Assume that Markets Plus develops complex client-specific software systems to mine big data on real estate markets, provides annual reprogramming to take advantage of new databases that are created during the year, and also has a segment of its business that creates new databases on real estate markets. Markets Plus signs a contract with Classic City Properties to create and install custom software and necessary hardware in early January 2017, and to provide the annual reprogramming over a two-year period ending in late December 2018. The reprogramming services are not customized and Markets Plus regularly sells similar reprogramming services to other clients who produce their own software. Assume that Markets Plus priced the transaction at $300,000, payable in two equal installments: $150,000 upon delivery and installation of the software in early January 2017 and $150,000 in September 2017.

Clearly, a contract exists (Step 1), and Markets Plus has two independent performance obligations, creation and installation of custom software and necessary hardware and performance of reprogramming services (Step 2). The consideration is fixed (i.e., no variable consideration), and the cash payments are within one year (i.e., no significant financing component that would require discounting for the time value of money). Therefore, the transaction price is $300,000 (Step 3).

When more than one performance obligation exists, the new standards require the allocation of the transaction price to the various obligations (Step 4). If the installation has a stand-alone selling price of $250,000 and the reprogramming has a stand-alone price of $50,000, the allocation would be obvious. Often, however, bundled pricing is at a discount. So, if the installation has a stand-alone selling price of $275,000 and the reprogramming has a stand-alone price of $75,000, the allocation of the $300,000 transaction price is based on relative fair values as follows:

To the installation: $300,000 \times [\$275,000/(\$275,000 + \$75,000)] = \$235,714$
To the reprogramming: $300,000 \times [\$75,000/(\$275,000 + \$75,000)] = \$64,286$

Another complication often arises: Suppose the stand-alone selling price of the installation is $250,000 and the reprogramming has no stand-alone selling price because Markets Plus does not sell it independently (possibly because it has to be tailored to its system). In this case, Markets Plus would have to estimate what the stand-alone price would be by considering prices of similar programming services in the market place or by taking its expected cost to reprogram plus a normal profit margin. In the event that the stand-alone prices are highly variable or uncertain, Markets Plus could use a residual approach and assign the difference between the transaction price and the stand-alone selling price (i.e., the residual) to the reprogramming services ($300,000 – $275,000 = $25,000).

The final step (Step 5) is recognizing the revenue when a specific performance obligation is removed. Regardless of how the transaction price was allocated, Markets Plus recognizes the amount allocated to the installation when it is installed (i.e., *at a point in time*) and the promise to reprogram as necessary equally over the two-year period (i.e., *over time*).

Starbucks has bundled performance obligations through its licensed stores. **Starbucks** charges an initial fee for providing assistance in store site selection, store design, and employee and management training. This represents one performance obligation because of the necessary dependence of these actions in a typical franchising operation. **Starbucks** recognizes this initial fee revenue at a point in time, when it substantially discharges the performance obligation. **Starbucks** also collects royalties from product sales of the licensees, which is a separate performance obligation. The obligation is to allow the licensee to operate a **Starbucks** store. This is variable consideration (see next section) that is highly uncertain and over which **Starbucks** has little control. **Starbucks** recognizes any revenue from royalties over time as it allows the licensee to operate and the licensee reports the royalty earned to **Starbucks**.

Sales with Variable Consideration

Let's reconsider the Markets Plus example with a slight twist. Assume that Classic City Properties is not willing to risk the possibility that no new databases will be created during the two-year period during which reprogramming will be necessary. Accordingly, the two parties agree that $15,000 will be refunded for each year in which a new database to mine does not become available. This is an example of variable consideration.

When performing the Step 3 calculation of the transaction price to be allocated in Step 4, variable consideration must be taken into account. Because Markets Plus is also a creator of this type of database, it has a reasonable idea of the likelihood that new databases will be created. According to Markets Plus's management, the possible outcomes and likelihoods are as follows:

New databases become available in:

> Both years: Markets Plus receives $300,000 (70% chance)
> Only one of the years: Markets Plus receives $285,000 (20% chance)
> Neither year: Markets Plus receives $270,000 (10% chance)

Market Plus's goal is to measure the transaction price at what it believes it will receive, either the *expected value* or the *most likely amount*. The expected value is $294,000, the sum of each outcome weighted by its likelihood (= $300,000 $\times$ .7 + $285,000 $\times$ .2 + $270,000 $\times$ .1). The most likely amount is $300,000. Market Plus uses the method that is the best predictor of the consideration it will receive. The expected value approach will be used more often when there are several potential outcomes that Market Plus has witnessed over time due to its experience with this kind of contract. The most likely amount approach will be used more often when the outcome is binary.

If Market Plus was not also a creator of the databases, a case could be made (within the new revenue recognition rules) that the contract price should be measured at $270,000, the outcome if no new databases are created during the two-year period. The creation of new databases is out of Market Plus's control, and the uncertainty surrounding their creation would require the additional revenue amounts to be recognized as new databases become available ($15,000 per year).

Sales with Warranties

How should Markets Plus treat a warranty that they provide on the installation? Is it a separate performance obligation? The standard setters identified two kinds of warranties:

- Assurance-type warranty (a warranty that the goods or services meet the contract specifications at the time of sale).
- Service-type warranty (a warranty providing services beyond those provided by the assurance-type warranty).

The assurance-type warranty is not a separate performance obligation. Its expected cost is treated as an expense of the period in which the revenue is reported. The service-type warranty is treated as a separate performance obligation and recognized as revenue over the agreed-upon service period (i.e., over time).

Sales with Delayed Delivery (Bill-and-Hold Arrangements)

In some cases, revenue can be recognized before delivery. In a bill-and-hold arrangement, the selling firm does not deliver goods for the convenience of a buyer. For example, assume that **Starbucks** orders furniture for several stores that it plans to open in the upcoming year. The furniture is ready for delivery, but the stores are not yet open.

Starbucks and the furniture manufacturer agree that the furniture will be held at the seller's warehouse until the stores are ready. To determine whether the furniture manufacturer should recognize revenue, the following conditions must be met:

- The reason for the arrangement must be substantive.
- The product must be identified separately as belonging to **Starbucks**.
- The products must be ready for delivery to **Starbucks**.
- The seller cannot have the ability to use the goods to fill another order.

In this kind of agreement, title passes to **Starbucks** before the delivery takes place, and the selling firm is allowed to recognize revenue because it has satisfied its performance obligation.

Principal–Agent Relationships

Some firms do not acquire and sell inventory or services, but instead facilitate the sales process for a commission by acting as an agent for the seller. **Priceline.com** is a good example of this type of firm. The key question is whether the performance obligation is delivering inventory or a service or facilitating the sales process. Indicators of the agency relationship[4] are

- the principal (not the agent) is primarily responsible for fulfilling the contract.
- the agent does not bear the inventory risk before or after the customer places the order or during shipping.
- the agent's benefit is constrained by the fact that it does not have the latitude in establishing prices for the goods or services.
- the consideration is in the form of a commission.
- the agent does not bear the customer's credit risk from any receivable arising from the facilitated transaction.

In the past, some agents, Priceline.com being an example, recorded the cost of the inventory as an expense and the full sales price as revenue (a *gross method*). Financial accounting rules, however, require agents to record revenue equal to the amount of the commission (a *net approach*). The principle will follow the gross method when it satisfies the performance obligation by delivering the good or service.

Revenue Recognition over Time (Long-Term Contracts)

The operating cycle for a long-term contractor (such as a commercial or industrial building contractor, an aerospace manufacturer, or a ship builder) differs from that of a typical manufacturing firm in three important respects:

- The period of construction (production) may span many accounting periods.
- Contractors identify customers and agree to build customized projects for the customers for a contract price and terms agreed upon in advance of construction (or at least in the early stages).
- Customers often make periodic payments of the contract price as work progresses.

The operating activities of long-term contractors often satisfy the criteria for the recognition of revenue during the period of construction and prior to completion. The existence of a contract indicates that the contractor has identified a buyer and the contractor and

---

[4]*Codification Topic 606.*

buyer have agreed on the scope of the construction project and a price. In agreeing to a contract price, the contractor should have some confidence in the estimates of the total costs it will incur on the contract.

Prior to the new revenue standard, long-term contracts were accounted for under one of two methods, the *percentage-of-completion method* or the *completed contract method*. Most contracts are accounted for under the preferred percentage-of-completion method to recognize the economic fact that many long-term contractors meet the criteria for revenue recognition during the construction process, as they complete certain construction milestones. Under this method, contractors recognize a portion of the total contract price, based on the degree of completion of the work during the period, as revenue for the period. They base this proportion on engineers' or architects' estimates of the degree of completion or on the ratio of costs incurred to date to the total expected costs for the contract. As contractors recognize portions of the contract price as revenues, they recognize corresponding proportions of the total estimated costs of the contract as expenses.

The new revenue standard supersedes prior industry-specific guidance such as the percentage-of-completion method. However, although the terminology of the new standard is different, the new standard still requires firms to recognize revenue and profit over time based on physical or cost-to-cost estimates of the percentage of the performance obligation that has been satisfied to date. In fact, industry publications on the new revenue standard refer to the idea that the percentage-of-completion approach is going away as a "myth."[5] Therefore, we illustrate the percentage-of-completion approach with the following example.

Assume that a firm agrees to construct a bridge for $5,000,000. Estimated costs are as follows: Year 1, $1,500,000; Year 2, $2,000,000; Year 3, $500,000. Thus, the expected gross margin from the contract is $1,000,000 ($5,000,000 − $1,500,000 − $2,000,000 − $500,000). The firm bills the customer (and collects) $2,000,000 in Year 1, $2,000,000 in Year 2, and $1,000,000 in Year 3. Assuming that the contractor bases the degree of completion on the percentage of total costs incurred to date and that it incurs actual costs as anticipated, revenues and expenses from the contract are as follows:

Year	Degree of Completion	Revenues	Expenses	Gross Margin
1	$1,500,000/$4,000,000 = 37.5%	$1,875,000	$1,500,000	$ 375,000
2	$2,000,000/$4,000,000 = 50.0%	2,500,000	2,000,000	500,000
3	$500,000/$4,000,000 = 12.5%	625,000	500,000	125,000
	Totals	$5,000,000	$4,000,000	$1,000,000

Notice that the cash amounts collected are not the amounts used for revenues. Rather, the income statement effect is to recognize pro rata revenues, expenses, and gross margins based on the degree of completion, thus providing a better measure of the operating success of the contractor each period during the contract. Exhibit 9.1

---

[5]Timothy T. Wilson and Michael J. Sobolewski, "It's Finally Here: FASB Issues New Revenue Recognition Standard," *Construction Financial Management Association*, http://www.cfma.org/news/content.cfm!ItemNumber=2982.

Exhibit 9.1: Long-Term Construction Accounting

	Assets	=	Liabilities	+	Total Shareholders' Equity		
					CC	AOCI	RE
1.	*Year 1:* Cash (1,500,000) Contracts in Progress 1,500,000						
	Contracts in Progress 1,500,000 Cash				1,500,000		

2.	Accounts
	  Receivable 2,000,000
	Accounts
	  Receivable (2,000,000)
	Cash 2,000,000
			Progress Billings 2,000,000				

	Accounts Receivable 2,000,000
	  Progress Billings
	Cash 2,000,000
	  Accounts Receivable
					2,000,000
					
					2,000,000		

3.	Contracts
	  in Progress 375,000
							Contract
							  Revenue 1,875,000
							Contract
							  Expense (1,500,000)

	Contracts in Progress 375,000 Contract Expense 1,500,000 Contract Revenue				1,875,000		
4.	*Year 2:* Cash (2,000,000) Contracts in Progress 2,000,000						
	Contracts in Progress 2,000,000 Cash				2,000,000		

5.	Accounts
	  Receivable 2,000,000
	Accounts
	  Receivable (2,000,000)
	Cash 2,000,000
			Progress Billings 2,000,000				

	Accounts Receivable 2,000,000
	  Progress Billings
	Cash 2,000,000
	  Accounts Receivable
					2,000,000
					
					2,000,000		

6.	Contracts
	  in Progress 500,000
							Contract
							  Revenue 2,500,000
							Contract
							  Expense (2,000,000)

	Contracts in Progress 500,000 Contract Expense 2,000,000 Contract Revenue				2,500,000		
7.	*Year 3:* Cash (500,000) Contracts in Progress 500,000						
	Contracts in Progress 500,000 Cash				500,000		

8.	Accounts
	  Receivable 1,000,000
	Accounts
	  Receivable (1,000,000)
	Cash 1,000,000
			Progress Billings 1,000,000				

	Accounts Receivable 1,000,000
	  Progress Billings
	Cash 1,000,000
	  Accounts Receivable
					1,000,000
					
					1,000,000		

(Continued)

Exhibit 9.1 (Continued)

9.	Contracts					Contract	
	in Progress	125,000				Revenue	625,000
						Contract	
						Expense	(500,000)
	Contracts in Progress		125,000				
	Contract Expense		500,000				
	Contract Revenue				625,000		

provides a more detailed look at the financial statement impacts of the following underlying transactions in this example:

Year 1

1. Incur $1,500,000 costs. (Assume that all costs are paid in cash.)
2. Bill customer for $2,000,000. Collect cash in full.
3. Recognize $1,875,000 of revenue and $1,500,000 of expenses using the percentage-of-completion method.

Year 2

4. Incur $2,000,000 costs. (Assume that all costs are paid in cash.)
5. Bill customer for $2,000,000. Collect cash in full.
6. Recognize $2,500,000 of revenue and $2,000,000 of expenses using the percentage-of-completion method.

Year 3

7. Incur $500,000 costs. (Assume that all costs are paid in cash.)
8. Bill customer for $1,000,000. Collect cash in full.
9. Recognize $625,000 of revenue and $500,000 of expenses using the percentage-of-completion method.

The two primary balance sheet accounts that are unique in the long-term contracts area are the liability account *Progress Billings* and the asset account *Contracts in Process*. Contractors report actual contract costs on the balance sheet in a Contracts in Process account (Transactions 1, 4, and 7), which is an asset that represents future economic benefits (the project being constructed). It is measured as the accumulated costs and gross margin on construction to date, which totals over the life of the contract to the contract price (gross margin added in Transactions 3, 6, and 9). When the contractor invoices the customer for progress payments, the contractor increases Accounts Receivable and an account called Progress Billings, which is a liability account (Transactions 2, 5, and 8). Progress billings is a liability because the customer is billed for promised work at the contract price and the contractor is obligated to deliver the asset under construction to the customer upon completion. The net amount of these two accounts (contracts in progress minus progress billings) is disclosed as a net obligation (if more has been billed than work performed) or as a net asset (if more work has been performed than billed). For example, at the end of Year 2, Contracts in Progress totals $4,375,000 ($1,500,000 + $375,000 + $2,000,000 + $500,000) and Progress Billings totals $4,000,000 ($2,000,000 + $2,000,000). Therefore, the Year 2 balance sheet reports contracts in progress in excess of billings of $375,000 as an asset. Upon completing the project at the end of Year 3, Contracts in Progress and Progress Billings will have equal balances and will be closed out.

Actual costs on contracts seldom coincide precisely with expectations. As new information on expected total costs becomes available, contractors must adjust reported revenues and income in current and future periods rather than retroactively restating income of prior periods. Assume that actual costs incurred in Year 2 for the contract were $2,200,000 instead of $2,000,000 and that total expected costs on the contract increase to $4,200,000. Revenue, expense, and gross margin from the contract are as follows:

Year	Cumulative Degree of Completion	Revenue	Expense	Margin
1	$1,500,000/$4,000,000 = 37.5%	$1,875,000	$1,500,000	$375,000
2	$3,700,000/$4,200,000 = 88.1%	2,530,000[a]	2,200,000	330,000
3	$4,200,000/$4,200,000 = 100.0%	595,000[b]	500,000	95,000
		$5,000,000	$4,200,000	$800,000

[a]$(0.881 \times \$5,000,000) - \$1,875,000 = \$2,530,000$
[b]$\$5,000,000 - \$1,875,000 - \$2,530,000 = \$595,000$

The unexpected costs are a *change in estimate*. Therefore, Year 2 revenue is cumulative revenue recognized to date based on the new estimate of costs minus past cumulative revenue recognition based on the old cost estimate.

If it appears that the contractor will ultimately realize a loss on completion of a contract, the contractor must recognize the loss in full as soon as it becomes evident. For example, if at the end of Year 2 the contractor expects to realize a loss of $200,000 on the total contract, it must recognize a loss of $575,000 in Year 2. The $575,000 amount offsets the income of $375,000 recognized in Year 1 plus a loss of $200,000 anticipated on the overall contract.

Under U.S. GAAP prior to the new revenue standard, when the contract price, costs, or degree of completion are not reasonably estimable, long-term contractors postpone the recognition of revenue until they complete the construction project under the completed-contract method. If the firm in our original example had used the completed-contract method, it would have recognized no revenue or expense from the contract during Year 1 or Year 2. It would recognize contract revenue of $5,000,000 and contract expenses of $4,000,000 in Year 3. Note that total gross margin is $1,000,000 under both the percentage-of-completion and completed-contract methods, equal to cash inflows of $5,000,000 minus cash outflows of $4,000,000. However, if the contractor anticipates a loss on a contract, it recognizes the loss as soon as the loss becomes evident, even if the contract is incomplete.

In some cases, contractors use the completed-contract method because the contracts are of such short duration (such as a few months) that earnings reported with the percentage-of-completion and the completed-contract methods are not significantly different. In these cases, the lower costs of implementing the completed-contract method justify its use. Contractors also use the completed-contract method when they have not obtained a specific buyer during the construction phase, as is sometimes the case in the construction of residential housing. These cases require future selling efforts. Substantial uncertainty may exist regarding the ultimate contract price and the amount of cash that the contractor will receive.

The preceding examples illustrate the dramatic level of estimation and uncertainty involved with income recognition for long-term contractors. Sometimes a project can take a number of years to complete. In some cases, contractors work with hundreds of subcontractors. Renegotiating contracts several times during the course of a large contract is commonplace. Analysts estimating persistent earnings using historical data for firms that construct and sell long-term projects must consider these and other firm factors, including the volume of projects currently under way, the success in completing projects on time and within budget, the length of typical projects, the types of projects undertaken, and the nature of the customer (if that information is available).

Investment in Working Capital: Accounts Receivable and Deferred Revenues

Revenues generate cash inflows, but the two are not necessarily equal in a given period. From the examples given previously, it is clear that cash inflows often occur after revenue is recognized, resulting in a working capital asset, accounts receivable, or before revenue is recognized, resulting in a working capital liability, deferred revenues (also called unearned revenues or advances from customers). Relative to when revenues are recognized, cash flows from operations are delayed with accounts receivable but are accelerated with deferred revenues.

Retail coffee and fast-food franchisers typically have both receivables and deferred revenues. **Starbucks**, for example, has point-of-sale revenues (retail sales of coffee and food), receivables (royalties from licensees and product sales to affiliates and food distributors), and deferred revenues (gift cards, **Starbucks'** stored value card, and up-front license payments from licensees). When analyzing liquidity, you should take into account that deferred or unearned revenue liabilities can sometimes be large, but they are not cash-settled obligations; they are settled with the performance of services. For **Starbucks**, for example, the deferred revenue "stored value card liability" at the end of 2015 was $983.8 million, or 23% of the company's total current liabilities. **Starbucks** satisfies this liability by delivering coffee to card-holding customers.

Discuss and apply the criteria for the recognition of *expenses* from operating activities, as well as the related assets, liabilities, and cash flows.

Expense Recognition

When engaging in operating activities, firms consume assets and incur liabilities and, thus, incur operating expenses. The next several sections discuss the general criteria for expense recognition and apply the criteria to explain how firms recognize the various operating expenses reported on the income statement.

Criteria for Expense Recognition

Both U.S. GAAP and IFRS require the recognition of expenses under the accrual basis of accounting as follows:

1. Costs *directly* associated with revenues must be recognized as expenses in the period when a firm recognizes the revenues.
2. Costs *not directly* associated with revenues must be recognized as expenses in the period when a firm consumes the services or benefits of the costs in operations.

Most of the costs of purchasing inventory or manufacturing inventory can be directly linked or reliably allocated to particular products. When the products are sold, the firm recognizes revenue and these directly linked expenses, referred to as *product* costs. Other costs (rent, insurance and property taxes, salaries of corporate officers and staff, and depreciation and amortization on tangible and intangible assets that are not part of the manufacturing process) are related to doing business in a particular period and bear only an indirect relation to revenues generated during the period. Such costs become expenses in the period in which the firm consumes the benefits of these types of services. Accountants refer to such costs as *period* costs.

Because a proportion of the expenses that firms report on the income statement associate directly with revenue recognized and because another proportion of the expenses relate to doing business during the reporting period, income statements provide generally reliable assessments of firms' economic performance each period. However, certain period expenses are more susceptible to management control than others. Expenditures that are somewhat discretionary and reported on the income statement as period costs are prime candidates for managing earnings. You should carefully monitor bad debts expense, advertising, R&D, and maintenance expenditures, as examples, to discern whether substantive reasons exist for changes in the levels of these expenditures (especially relative to sales) or whether the changes are intended to manage earnings. For example, if a firm's earnings in a period just barely meet or beat the consensus analyst forecast and discretionary expenses suddenly decrease for no apparent reason, managers might be cutting these expenses to meet or beat that period's earnings target.

Cost of Sales

For most retail and manufacturing firms, cost of sales represents the single largest expense reported on the income statement. Retailers accumulate the net costs of inventory purchases (invoice cost minus purchase discounts and purchase returns plus freight costs paid by the purchaser) in the inventory account. Manufacturers accumulate the same costs in raw materials inventory. Then as the raw materials are used in production, the raw materials costs are assigned to work-in-process inventory along with production-related labor, supplies, and overhead costs (including depreciation on production-related property, plant, and equipment). As products are finished, the costs are transferred to finished goods inventory. Finally, as products are sold, inventory costs are reported as cost of goods sold.

Firms selling relatively high-dollar-value items such as automobiles, airplanes, and real estate can ascertain from the accounting records the specific cost of each item sold. They recognize revenue when each item is sold and then may choose to recognize the specific cost of each item sold as cost of goods sold.

In most cases, however, firms cannot identify the cost of the specific items sold. Sometimes inventory items are so similar and their unit costs so small that firms cannot justify economically the cost of designing an accounting system to keep track of specific unit costs. To measure cost of goods sold in these cases, firms must make some assumption about the flow of costs. Three cost-flow assumptions exist:

- Average cost
- First-in, first-out (FIFO)
- Last-in, first-out (LIFO)

These assumptions about cost flows do not necessarily reflect the physical flow of units. For example, a grocery store could use any of the methods to account for its milk inventory, even though they would certainly sell the oldest milk first (a physical FIFO flow). Also, many firms use a combination of cost-flow assumptions for different items of inventory in different subsidiaries or business segments or in different countries.

With the introduction of cost-flow assumptions into the reporting system, however, comes the possibility of earnings management and varying degrees of earnings quality.

Analyzing earnings quality in the context of inventory accounting requires understanding the implications of the reporting options available to management.

Average Cost

The average cost-flow assumption simply determines the weighted-average cost of all inventory units available for sale during the period (units in beginning inventory plus units purchased), then it assigns that cost to each unit sold and to each unit in ending inventory. When inventory turns over rapidly, purchases during the current period receive a heavy weight in the weighted-average unit cost.

FIFO

FIFO assigns the cost of the earliest purchases to the units sold and the cost of the most recent purchases to ending inventory. FIFO results in a balance sheet amount for ending inventory that is closest to current replacement cost. The income statement amount for cost of goods sold can be somewhat out of date, however, because FIFO recognizes costs of goods sold based on the costs of beginning inventory and the earliest purchases during the year. When inventory costs are rising, FIFO leads to the highest reported net income (lowest cost of goods sold) and the highest balance sheet value for inventory of the three methods, and when inventory costs fall, FIFO leads to the smallest net income and the lowest balance sheet value of inventory.

LIFO

LIFO assigns the cost of the most recent purchases to the cost of goods sold and the cost of the earliest purchases to inventory. LIFO results in amounts for cost of goods sold on the income statement that closely approximate current replacement costs. Balance sheet amounts, however, can contain the cost of inventory acquisitions made many years previously. During periods of rising inventory costs, LIFO generally results in the highest cost of goods sold and the lowest net income of the three cost-flow assumptions. For this reason, firms usually prefer LIFO for income tax purposes. If a firm chooses a LIFO cost-flow assumption for tax purposes, the income tax law requires the firm to use LIFO for financial reporting to shareholders. IFRS does not permit the use of LIFO.

LIFO Liquidation

One exception to the generalization that LIFO produces the lowest net income during periods of rising prices occurs when a firm sells more units during a period than it purchases (referred to as a *LIFO layer liquidation*). In this case, LIFO assigns the cost of all current period purchases plus the costs assigned to the liquidated LIFO layers to the cost of goods sold. During periods of rising prices, the liquidated layers of LIFO inventory may be at much lower costs than current costs, which can cause costs of goods sold to be relatively low and net income to be relatively high. When firms experience LIFO liquidations, two cash-flow effects likely occur. First, firms have delayed purchasing inventory items, thereby delaying a cash outflow. Second, firms increase taxable income and the required cash outflow for taxes. In Note 7, "Inventory," to its December 31, 2008, consolidated financial statements, **General Motors Corporation** (GM) reported a LIFO reserve of $1,233 million. GM also reported a LIFO layer liquidation as follows:

> In 2008 and 2007, U.S. LIFO eligible inventory quantities were reduced. This reduction resulted in a liquidation of LIFO inventory quantities carried at

lower costs prevailing in prior years as compared with the cost of 2008 and 2007 purchases, the effect of which decreased automotive cost of sales by approximately $355 million and $100 million in 2008 and 2007, respectively.

If GM's LIFO layer liquidation is a transitory event, then GM's current period profits are not indicative of future earnings.

Characteristics of LIFO Adopters

Researchers have examined the characteristics of firms that do and do not adopt LIFO. Although these research studies do not always show consistent results, the following factors appear related to the decision to adopt LIFO.[6]

Firms Following U.S. GAAP. IFRS does not permit the use of LIFO, but U.S. and non-U.S.-domiciled firms that follow U.S. GAAP for consolidated reporting are permitted to use LIFO. Some of these firms have subsidiaries that are domiciled in countries that follow IFRS, so they may be prohibited from using LIFO for the inventory of those subsidiaries even though they use LIFO for inventory in the subsidiaries in U.S. GAAP jurisdictions.

Direction and Rate of Factor Price Changes for Inventory Items. Firms experiencing rapidly increasing factor prices for raw materials, labor, or other product costs obtain greater tax benefits from LIFO than firms that experience smaller factor price increases or that experience price decreases. Although adopting LIFO implies future tax savings (good news), it also implies higher expected future factor prices for inventory (bad news).

Variability in the Rate of Inventory Growth. LIFO adopters show more variable rates of inventory growth before adopting LIFO than do firms that remain on FIFO. The variability of inventory growth declines after LIFO is adopted. Because LIFO tends to match more recent inventory costs with sales than does FIFO or weighted average (these methods sometimes use costs that are 6–15 months old relative to current replacement costs), LIFO tends to result in less variability in the gross margin percentage over the business cycle. Firms with variable rates of inventory growth (perhaps because of cyclicality in their industry) can more easily accomplish an income-smoothing reporting objective using LIFO than if they use FIFO or average cost. Income smoothing is achieved by creating additional LIFO layers to match against sales through additional end-of-period purchases.

Tax Savings Opportunities. LIFO adopters tend to adopt LIFO to provide future tax savings. LIFO adopters also realize larger tax savings in the year of adoption than in the surrounding years, suggesting that the decision is in part motivated by tax rather than financial reporting considerations.

Industry Membership. Firms in certain industries are more likely to adopt LIFO. Because firms in a particular industry face similar factor price changes and

---

[6]For a review of these studies, see Frederick W. Lindahl, "Dynamic Analysis of Inventory Accounting Choice," *Journal of Accounting Research* (Autumn 1989), pp. 201–226; and Nicholas Dopuch and Morton Pincus, "Evidence on the Choice of Inventory Accounting Methods: LIFO versus FIFO," *Journal of Accounting Research* (Spring 1988), pp. 28–59.

variability in their inventory growth rates, those firms are likely to make similar choices of cost-flow assumptions.

Asset Size. Larger firms are more likely to adopt LIFO than are smaller firms. LIFO increases record-keeping costs relative to FIFO, both in the year of adoption and in subsequent years. To absorb the adoption and ongoing record-keeping costs of LIFO, larger firms realize larger amounts of tax savings than do smaller firms.

One hypothesis examined in this research is the relation between LIFO adoption and managerial compensation. Because LIFO usually results in lower earnings, managerial compensation of LIFO adopters would likely be less than compensation of non-LIFO adopters or include a lower component of compensation based on earnings. Studies have found no difference in managerial compensation of LIFO and non-LIFO adopters, although adopters had a smaller earnings component to their compensation.

Conversion from LIFO to FIFO

Costs of goods sold under LIFO more closely reflect replacement cost and, thus, net income under the LIFO method is generally considered to be high quality. However, under LIFO, the balance sheet amount for ending inventory might contain some very old costs (relative to FIFO, which approximates inventory closer to "current cost"). If LIFO inventory valuation results in low out-of-date inventory values, the balance sheet amounts for inventory reflect poor accounting information quality and provide potentially misleading information to users of financial statements.[7] Accordingly, the SEC requires firms using LIFO to disclose in notes to the financial statements the amounts by which LIFO inventories differ from the amounts the firm would recognize for inventories under FIFO. Analysts sometimes refer to the difference in ending inventory valuation between LIFO and FIFO as the *LIFO reserve*. From this disclosure, it is possible to restate a LIFO firm's income and inventory to a FIFO basis. In this way, you can place firms using LIFO on a basis more comparable to firms using FIFO.

The main inventory item for **Starbucks**, coffee, has a relatively short holding period, and as a result, LIFO and FIFO costs are similar. Firms with long inventory holding periods, however, often have significant LIFO reserves. **Nucor Corporation**, a primarily North American steel manufacturer, was incorporated in 1958. Exhibit 9.2 shows selected annual report data from Nucor's December 31, 2015, Form 10-K. Nucor uses the LIFO inventory method for much of its inventory.

To convert Nucor Corporation to FIFO, we use balance sheet amounts based on LIFO for beginning and ending inventory and the income statement amount for cost of sales to infer purchases during the period. Then, to convert the beginning inventory, ending inventory, and cost of sales to the FIFO basis, we use the information from the financial statement note that provides the amount by which beginning and ending inventories would be larger under FIFO. The notes to Nucor's financial statements indicate that the FIFO-basis beginning (December 31, 2014) and ending (December 31, 2015) inventories are $567.4 million and $100.8 million higher,

---

[7]Researchers examining the relation between market returns on equity securities and earnings based on LIFO versus FIFO cost of goods sold found that earnings numbers based on LIFO explain more of the cross-sectional variation in returns than do earnings numbers based on FIFO. Ross Jennings, Paul J. Simko, and Robert B. Thompson II, "Does LIFO Inventory Accounting Improve the Income Statement at the Expense of the Balance Sheet?," *Journal of Accounting Research* (Spring 1996), pp. 85–109.

Exhibit 9.2

Nucor Corporation
Selected Financial Statement Information
(amounts in millions)

Balance Sheet	December 31, 2015	December 31, 2014
Inventories	$2,145.4	$2,745.0
Current assets (including inventory)	5,754.3	6,441.8
Current liabilities	1,385.1	2,097.7

Income Statement	2015	
Sales	$16,439.2	
Cost of sales	14,858.0	
Net income before allocation to noncontrolling interest	496.0	

respectively, than the amounts reported on the balance sheets under LIFO. The conversion to FIFO is as follows:

(amounts in millions)	LIFO Basis (as reported)	Adjustments	FIFO Basis
Sales (a)	$16,439.2		$16,439.2
Beginning inventory	$ 2,745.0	$ 567.4	$ 3,312.4
Purchases	14,258.4		14,258.4
Goods available for sale	$17,003.4		$17,570.8
Ending inventory	(2,145.4)	(100.8)	(2,246.2)
Cost of sales	$14,858.0	$ 466.6	$15,324.6
Gross margin (b)	$ 1,581.2		$ 1,114.6

In periods of *declining* input prices into the manufacturing process, FIFO yields a higher cost of sales and therefore a lower gross margin percentage (b/a):

$$\text{Gross margin percentage as reported under LIFO} = 9.62\%$$
$$\text{Gross margin percentage on a FIFO basis} = 6.78\%$$

Net income for allocation to the controlling and noncontrolling interests (as reported under LIFO) is $496.0 million. To adjust net income to a FIFO basis, deduct the increase in cost of sales times one minus the tax rate to obtain a $303.2 million decrease in net income [$466.8 million $\times$ (1 − 0.35)], which is 61.6% of reported net income. Adjusted net income would therefore have been $192.6 million if Nucor had used FIFO. This, of course, is a substantial difference in net income. In the Management, Discussion, and Analysis that accompanies the financial statements, Nucor discusses the substantial "LIFO credit" that they received in net income from use of the LIFO method and attributed the effect to falling input prices, particularly scrap metal.

As shown in Chapter 4, the inventory turnover ratio (cost of sales/average inventory) is a measure of the efficiency with which a firm manages its inventory, as follows:

As reported under LIFO: $14,858.0/[0.5 \times (\$2,745.0 + \$2,145.4)] = 6.07$
On a FIFO basis: $15,324.8/[0.5 \times (\$3,312.4 + \$2,246.0)] = 5.51$

The difference in the inventory turnover ratio under LIFO and FIFO reflects the fact that FIFO inventory cost is larger than LIFO inventory cost. The inventory turnover ratio based on LIFO amounts gives a poor indication of the actual turnover of inventory items because it divides a cost of goods sold amount reflecting current costs by an average inventory amount reflecting older costs. The inventory turnover ratio under FIFO provides a better indication of the turnover of inventory items because it divides a cost of goods sold reflecting relatively current costs by an average inventory reflecting relatively recent costs. Although the trend in the inventory turnover ratio for most firms is likely to be similar under LIFO and FIFO, cross-sectional comparisons can be misleading if one firm uses LIFO and the other firm uses FIFO during times when inventory input prices are rising or falling. This example illustrates the trade-off that can exist between balance sheet and earnings quality. As we discussed earlier, while LIFO may not be the best method for valuing inventory on the balance sheet, it does produce a high-quality earnings number by reflecting current costs in cost of goods sold.

The inventory cost-flow assumption also affects the current ratio (current assets/current liabilities), a measure commonly used to assess short-term liquidity risk that was introduced in Chapter 5, as follows:

(amounts in millions)	2015	2014
Current assets (as reported)	$5,754.3	$6,441.8
Adjust inventory to FIFO	100.8	567.4
Current assets (FIFO)	$5,855.1	$7,009.2
Current liabilities	$1,385.1	$2,097.7
Current ratio (as reported)	4.15	3.07
Current ratio (FIFO)	4.22	3.34

Nucor's current ratio would be higher in each year if it used FIFO, again due to the fact that FIFO costs remaining in inventory are generally higher than LIFO costs remaining in inventory.

Reporting Changes in the Value of Inventory

FIFO, LIFO, and weighted average are methods for assigning costs to ending inventory and cost of sales. For many firms, market values of inventory will likely differ from acquisition costs at balance sheet reporting dates. Under both U.S. GAAP and IFRS, firms are required to follow the conservative lower-of-cost-or-market method to report inventory at each balance sheet date.[8] Increases in market value are not reflected in the financial statements until the inventory is sold. If market value has increased and firms are able to pass the market value increases on to customers by increasing selling price, sales of inventory will realize higher gross profits and greater amounts of cash or accounts receivable. This effect should occur relatively quickly because inventory is a current asset.

---

[8]*FASB Codification Topic 330*; International Accounting Standards Board, *International Accounting Standard 2*, "Inventories."

Under U.S. GAAP and IFRS, when inventory market values decline below cost, the losses must be reflected in the financial statements as decreases in inventory and increases in cost of goods sold or, if material, as a separate income statement line item for the loss on decline in inventory market value. Subsequent recoveries in market value are not reflected under U.S. GAAP, but they are under IFRS. Write-downs of inventory in the current period due to market decline are intended to appropriately reflect the value of inventory on the balance sheet and to yield a normal gross margin on a subsequent period's sale. That is, sales price in the subsequent period will be lower due to the market decline, and cost of goods sold in the subsequent period will be lower by the same amount because cost of goods sold is determined by the (now lower) cost of the inventory.

Starbucks reports in Note 1 (Appendix A) under the "Inventories" heading that inventory reserves were $33.8 million and $31.2 million as of September 27, 2015, and September 28, 2014, respectively. The change in the reserve (a $2.6 million increase) is the income statement effect (a $2.6 million decrease in pretax income), which is immaterial relative to pretax income of $3,903.0 million (only 0.066% of pretax income). However, it is also useful to gauge the magnitude of the reserve relative to the inventory balance before the reserve. The ratio of the reserve to inventories on the balance sheet before being reduced by reserves is 2.5% [= $33.8 million/($1,306.4 million + $33.8 million] in 2015 and 2.8% [= $31.2 million/($1,090.9 million + $31.2 million)] in 2014. Therefore, Starbucks has reduced the magnitude of the reserve relative to inventory. This might be explainable by lower spoilage rates or lower expected inventory obsolescence. Had Starbucks used 2.8% as the reserve rate in 2015, the reserve would have been $36.6 million instead of $33.8 million. In this case, again the amounts are relatively small, but, for other companies, they might not be.

Investment in Working Capital: Inventory and Accounts Payable

Combining Starbucks' two largest working capital assets (receivables and inventory) yields $2,025.4 million of working capital investments at September 27, 2015, roughly 16% of total assets. To offset the effect of having cash invested in inventory pending sale and collection of receivables, firms delay payments to suppliers, employees, and taxing authorities as long as possible. Starbucks' current liabilities section shows $2,444.9 million for accounts payable and other accrued current liabilities at the same date.

Buying, holding, paying for, and selling inventory involves risk. Some of the risk can be mitigated through hedging activities. In the Chapter 9 online appendix to this chapter found at the text's website, we provide specific examples of the accounting for derivatives used to hedge foreign currency and commodity risks associated with operating activities.

SG&A Costs

While costs like sales commissions vary directly with sales, most of the SG&A costs generally bear a less direct relation with sales. SG&A expenses reported on the income statement as part of operating profit represent the consumption of assets and incurrence of liabilities to carry on corporate functions other than production, such as advertising, marketing, sales, administration, accounting, information systems, and credit functions. The sections that follow describe the accounting and reporting of SG&A expenses.

Advertising and Marketing Costs

Many firms in the consumer products industry have large expenditures for advertising and marketing. Although these expenditures are undertaken with the expectation that they will create value, quantifying the value is difficult. Thus, both U.S. GAAP and IFRS require immediate expensing of these costs. As discussed in detail in Chapter 8, these expenditures fail to meet the definition of an asset. Prepayments for advertising (such as prepayments for commercial time on broadcast media such as television and radio or prepayments for advertising space in publications) create working capital assets (usually titled prepaid expenses). Delays in paying suppliers and service providers for advertising and marketing costs also create working capital liabilities (usually reported as accrued expenses).

Compensation

Wages, salaries, payroll taxes, bonuses, commissions, and fringe benefits are capitalized as part of inventory if incurred in the production process and then expensed as part of cost of goods sold when the inventory is sold. If compensation costs are related to the selling, advertising, marketing, or administrative functions, they are reported as compensation expenses within SG&A.

Depreciation, Depletion, and Amortization

Recall from Chapter 8 that depreciation, amortization, and depletion of long-lived productive assets are allocations of the costs of assets to the periods benefited. If the long-lived assets are used in production, the allocated costs are capitalized as part of inventory. If not, the allocated costs are expensed as part of SG&A. The materiality of these expenses requires that they be disclosed in the notes to the financial statements. Also, depreciation, depletion, and amortization typically represent the largest addbacks to net income in the operating section of the statement of cash flows.

Credit Policy

In an effort to increase sales, most firms allow customers to delay payment. If cash collection is not highly likely, the sale should not be recorded in the first place. However, even if cash collection is generally likely to occur at an individual customer level, at a portfolio level some customers will not pay. Also, customers' ability to pay can change in the period between the initial sale and dates of scheduled cash payments.

Accounts receivable must be reported on the balance sheet at the amount of cash that is expected to be realized (that is, the *net realizable value*). Net realizable value reporting requires an estimate, at each balance sheet date, of the two causes of uncollectible receivables: sales returns and bad debts.

If sales returns are small in dollar amount and infrequent, they are recorded as incurred by simultaneously reducing sales and accounts receivable. If sales returns are material, they should be accounted for using the *allowance method*. Basically, the expected returns are estimated and reported as a subtraction from sales revenue in the income statement ("estimated sales returns") and as a subtraction from accounts receivable on the balance sheet ("allowance for sales returns"). For example, if a company had $1,000 of credit sales of which $200 was collected in the period and the company estimated $50 in sales returns, the company reports $950 in "net sales" and $750 in accounts receivable. Note that sales returns are a direct reduction in sales, not an SG&A expense.

Bad debts also are accounted for using the allowance method. The proper balance in the "allowance for doubtful accounts" is typically determined by a percentage of ending accounts receivable, or an aging of accounts receivable. By determining the allowance using the aging method, the firm uses its historical experience with past bad debts and its expectations going forward to estimate the proportion of accounts receivable that will not be collected based on the length of time receivables have been outstanding. The likelihood an account will not be collected increases with its age. For example, experience may show that bad debts arise from 1% of receivables less than 60 days old, 5% of the receivables that are between 61 and 180 days old, and 40% of receivables that are more than 180 days old. At the end of each period, the firm estimates the necessary balance in the allowance for doubtful accounts. The necessary adjustment to increase the allowance for doubtful accounts is recognized as bad debts expense (often called provision for bad debts), which is reported as a component of SG&A expenses.

Under U.S. GAAP, an analogous treatment is given to receivables with maturity dates beyond one year, such as notes receivable. These receivables are initially reported at their present value. Then at each balance sheet date, an allowance for uncollectible notes (often referred to as an allowance or reserve for loan losses) is established. Actual loan impairments are written off against the allowance for loan losses, much like the procedure for bad debts. In contrast, under IFRS, notes receivable balance sheet reporting follows the fair value reporting rules for investments illustrated in Chapter 8.

Time series and cross-sectional analyses of accounts receivable, bad debt expense, and sales can alert you to possible revenue and expense manipulation. If a firm experiences a substantial increase in the number of days accounts receivable are outstanding, it is possible that the company has intentionally extended credit to additional groups to generate sales or that the company has entered different product markets that have different payment practices. However, it is also possible that customers are taking longer to pay their invoices because they are experiencing financial difficulties (suggesting that more bad debt expense should be accrued or that future additional sales to the same parties are less likely) or, in the extreme, the customers are not paying because they don't exist (i.e., sales are fraudulent). Examining the income statement ratio of bad debt expense to sales and the balance sheet ratio of allowance for doubtful accounts to accounts receivable can detect inadequate recognition of bad debt exposure.

Warranty Expense

Another method of increasing sales is to guarantee the performance of the product sold. Estimated costs under warranties must be accrued in the period in which the guaranteed goods are sold by increasing a warranty obligation and increasing warranty expense (a portion of SG&A expense). Then, as warranty claims arise, the costs of servicing the warranty claims reduce the estimated warranty obligation. As in the case of bad debts expense, accounting quality is compromised if inappropriate or inconsistent amounts represent opportunistic bias.

Operating Profit

Sales revenue minus cost of sales and SG&A expenses yields operating profit before income taxes. From this amount, firms deduct "other" revenues and expenses from financing and investing activities (primarily interest income and interest expense), including equity in the earnings of affiliates. Finally, income tax expense is subtracted to obtain net income.

Income Taxes

Income taxes are a significant operating expense. Chapter 2 provides an introduction to income taxes and illustrates the accounting that leads to income tax expense and deferred tax assets and liabilities. You may wish to review it at this time. In this section, we focus on the income tax note to the financial statements to illustrate how to assess a firm's income tax position.

LO 9-3

Use the financial statement and note information for corporate *income taxes* to analyze the firm's tax strategies.

Required Income Tax Disclosures

The income tax note is a rich source of information. This section describes four required and useful disclosures:

- Components of the provision for income taxes (i.e., income tax expense).
- Reconciliation of income taxes at the statutory rate with the provision for income taxes.
- Components of deferred tax assets and liabilities.
- Information regarding uncertain tax positions and related reserves.

We analyze each disclosure using **Starbucks'** income tax disclosures in Note 13, "Income Taxes," to its financial statements (Appendix A). To facilitate our discussion, we reproduce portions of Note 13 in each section.

Components of Income Tax Expense

Exhibit 9.3 shows **Starbucks'** disclosure of income before taxes and the components of income tax expense. **Starbucks** partitions income before taxes by income source—U.S. and foreign. Foreign income increases as a percentage of total income in every year presented. In fiscal 2013, foreign income is 17.4% of total income. (We compute the percentage in fiscal 2013 using the "all other" column, which excludes the effect of the litigation charge related to the Kraft lawsuit. We will use that column in all of our analyses in this section.) The percentage increases to 18.5% in fiscal 2014, and then to 27.3% in fiscal 2015. The shift in income source has potentially significant tax implications given that foreign tax rates are often lower than U.S. tax rates. The next portion of the disclosure shows the provision for income taxes (i.e., the $1,143.7 million reported on **Starbucks'** 2015 consolidated income statement shown as the sum of the 2015 column) partitioned by taxing jurisdiction—U.S. federal, foreign, and state—and by whether the component of income tax expense is current or deferred. Note that the current provision, the tax currently due, makes up the bulk of the total provision.

 Starbucks' average, or effective, tax rates for the three years are as follows:

	2015	2014	2013
All sources of income:			
Total income tax expense	$1,143.7	$1,092.0	$ 832.3
÷ Total income before taxes	3,903.0	3,159.7	2,554.2
= Effective tax rate on total income	29.3%	34.6%	32.6%
U.S. income:			
Federal, state, and local current and deferred taxes	$1,011.6	$ 962.7	$ 738.6
÷ Total U.S. income before taxes	2,837.2	2,572.4	2,110.1
= Effective tax rate on U.S. income	35.6%	37.4%	35.0%
Foreign income:			
Foreign current and deferred taxes	$ 132.1	$ 129.3	$ 93.7
÷ Total foreign income before taxes	1,065.8	587.3	444.1
= Effective tax rate on foreign income	12.4%	22.0%	20.9%

Exhibit 9.3

Portion of Starbucks' Tax Note 13 from 2015 10-K (Income Before Taxes and Tax Provision)

Components of earnings/(loss) before income taxes *(in millions)*:

			Sep 29, 2013		
Fiscal Year Ended	Sep 27, 2015	Sep 28, 2014	Total	Litigation charge	All Other
United States	$2,837.2	$2,572.4	$(674.0)	$(2,784.1)	$2,110.1
Foreign	1,065.8	587.3	444.1	—	444.1
Total earnings/(loss) before income taxes	$3,903.0	$3,159.7	$(229.9)	$(2,784.1)	$2,554.2

Provision/(benefit) for income taxes *(in millions)*:

			Sep 29, 2013		
Fiscal Year Ended	Sep 27, 2015	Sep 28, 2014	Total	Litigation charge	All Other
Current taxes:					
U.S. federal	$ 801.0	$ 822.7	$ 616.6	$ —	$616.6
U.S. state and local	150.1	132.9	93.8	—	93.8
Foreign	172.2	128.8	95.9	—	95.9
Total current taxes	1,123.3	1,084.4	806.3	—	806.3
Deferred taxes:					
U.S. federal	56.5	12.0	(898.8)	(922.3)	23.5
U.S. state and local	4.0	(4.9)	(144.0)	(148.7)	4.7
Foreign	(40.1)	0.5	(2.2)	—	(2.2)
Total deferred taxes	20.4	7.6	(1,045.0)	(1,071.0)	26.0
Total income tax expense/(benefit)	$1,143.7	$1,092.0	$ (238.7)	$(1,071.0)	$832.3

The effective tax rate on all income decreased over the three-year period, and it varied quite a bit. The effective tax rates are lower than statutory rates because **Starbucks** generates a substantial amount of income in lower-tax jurisdictions. In general U.S. tax rules require U.S. companies to pay taxes on earnings regardless of the jurisdiction in which the earnings were generated. An exception exists, however, for foreign earnings that are reinvested rather than repatriated to the United States in the form of dividends. **Starbucks** reports in Note 13 that it has $2.8 billion of undistributed foreign earnings that it intends to continue to reinvest outside the United States for the foreseeable future. Note the substantially lower effective tax rates on foreign income relative to U.S.-sourced income, and that the substantial decrease in effective tax rates on foreign income from 2014 to 2015 is the driver of **Starbucks'** lower 2015 overall effective tax rate.

Reconciliation of Income Taxes at Statutory Rate with Income Tax Expense

U.S. firms are also required to disclose why the average tax rates shown previously differ from the statutory federal tax rate on income before taxes. Firms can express reconciling items in dollar amounts or in percentage terms. Exhibit 9.4 presents **Starbucks'** tax rate reconciliation.

The initial assumption in this reconciliation is that all income is subject to taxes at a rate equal to the U.S. federal statutory rate of 35%. This is a reasonable assumption given the general tendency for the United States to tax all income regardless of where it is earned. State and local income taxes trigger increases in firms' average tax rates beyond the federal statutory tax rate (net of their U.S. federal tax benefit because they are deductible). In **Starbucks'** case, state taxes increased the average tax rate by between 2.4% and 2.8%, and it is growing over time.

As we learned in the previous section, the lower tax rates on **Starbucks'** income from foreign operations lower the overall effective tax rate. It is noteworthy, however, that the benefit of these lower tax rates appears to be slightly dwindling, from a −3.4% adjustment in 2013 to only a −2.1% adjustment in 2015.

Some of the foreign tax benefit reduction is likely beyond a firm's control, especially if it is simply caused by foreign jurisdictions raising tax rates. But you might assess whether a firm's tax strategy will shift income from higher to lower tax jurisdictions by

---

Exhibit 9.4

Portion of Starbucks' Tax Note 13 from 2015 10-K (Tax Rate Reconciliation)

Reconciliation of the statutory U.S. federal income tax rate with our effective income tax rate:

| | | | Sep 29, 2013 | | |
Fiscal Year Ended	Sep 27, 2015	Sep 28, 2014	Total	Litigation charge	All Other
Statutory rate	35.0%	35.0%	35.0%	35.0%	35.0%
State income taxes, net of federal tax benefit	2.8	2.6	15.8	3.5	2.4
Benefits and taxes related to foreign operations	(2.1)	(1.9)	37.5	—	(3.4)
Domestic production activity deduction	(2.2)	(0.7)	8.1	—	(0.7)
Domestic tax credits	(0.2)	(0.2)	2.8	—	(0.3)
Charitable contributions	(0.3)	(0.4)	3.9	—	(0.3)
Gain resulting from acquisition of joint venture	(3.7)	—	—	—	—
Other, net	—	0.2	0.7	—	(0.1)
Effective tax rate	29.3%	34.6%	103.8%	38.5%	32.6%

- physically shifting operations (for example, manufacturing or marketing).
- adjusting transfer prices or cost allocations to shift income.
- shifting borrowing between jurisdictions or shifting financing between debt and equity in a given jurisdiction to maximize the tax benefits of interest deductions.

While the federal, state, and foreign components are generally persistent, many items in the tax rate reconciliation are transitory. In 2015, **Starbucks'** effective tax rate is lower as a result of two such items, a domestic productivity activity deduction and a gain resulting from acquisition of the remaining shares of a joint venture (generally nontaxable under IRS rules). When you assess profitability, be sure to consider whether a portion of after-tax profitability is driven by a transitory event such as an acquisition or resolution of an audit. When predicting future provisions for income taxes, you should determine the expected future tax rate by analyzing the tax rate reconciliation over time. Generally, the more persistent portion of the rate is obtained by summing federal and state rates minus the foreign tax benefit.

Components of Deferred Tax Assets and Liabilities

Firms also must disclose the components of deferred tax assets and the deferred tax liabilities. The components describe the *cumulative* extent to which accrual accounting differs from the cash-flow-based tax treatments for many items over time. Exhibit 9.5 presents **Starbucks'** disclosure in Note 13 of the components of deferred tax assets and liabilities.

Exhibit 9.5

Components of Deferred Tax Assets and Liabilities from Starbucks' 2015 10-K

Tax effect of temporary differences and carryforwards that comprise significant portions of deferred tax assets and liabilities *(in millions)*:

	Sep 27, 2015	Sep 28, 2014
Deferred tax assets:		
Property, plant and equipment	$ 121.4	$ 78.5
Accrued occupancy costs	98.4	58.8
Accrued compensation and related costs	81.7	75.3
Other accrued liabilities	49.0	27.6
Asset retirement obligation asset	29.0	18.6
Stored value card liability	99.1	63.4
Asset impairments	26.2	49.5
Tax credits	20.8	20.3
Stock-based compensation	135.5	131.5
Net operating losses	93.4	104.4
Litigation charge	931.0	1,002.0
Other	104.5	77.0
Total	$1,790.0	$1,706.9

(Continued)

Exhibit 9.5 (Continued)		
Valuation allowance	(143.7)	(166.8)
Total deferred tax asset, net of valuation allowance	$1,646.3	$1,540.1
Deferred tax liabilities:		
Property, plant and equipment	(217.5)	(148.2)
Intangible assets and goodwill	(177.3)	(92.9)
Other	(114.1)	(89.4)
Total	(508.9)	(330.5)
Net deferred tax asset	$1,137.4	$1,209.6
Reported as:		
Current deferred income tax assets	$ 381.7	$ 317.4
Long-term deferred income tax assets	828.9	903.3
Current deferred income tax liabilities (included in Accrued liabilities)	(5.4)	(4.2)
Long-term deferred income tax liabilities (included in Other long-term liabilities)	(67.8)	(6.9)
Net deferred tax asset	$1,137.4	$1,209.6

Starbucks reports many components of deferred tax assets. One way these components arise is when revenues are taxed before they are recognized in the financial statements. The stored value card liability is a good example because the tax must be paid when cash is received up front but the revenue is recognized later. In latter periods the revenue will be recognized but not taxed. The other way the deferred tax asset component arises is when expenses are recognized before cash outflow occurs, but a tax deduction is not allowed until the cash outflow occurs. Two common examples present in **Starbucks'** disclosure are stock-based compensation and the litigation charge. For financial reporting, **Starbucks** records its stock-based compensation expense by determining option values on the date of the grant of stock options and then recognizing the expense over the vesting period. For tax reporting, the expense is recognized later, when the stock options are exercised by employees. Upon exercise, U.S. tax law permits firms to deduct the difference between market price and exercise price of the shares being issued. **Starbucks** also has accrued a litigation charge for which it did not receive a tax deduction. Like future nontaxed revenues, these future tax deductions will cause future tax payments to be lower, and thus they are assets.

Another common and special kind of deferred tax asset is present in **Starbucks'** disclosure, net operating loss (NOL) carryforwards. Suppose a firm generates a net loss for tax reporting for the year. The firm can carry back this net loss to offset taxable income of the two preceding years and receive a refund for income taxes paid in those years. The firm recognizes the refund as an income tax credit in the year of the net loss. If the firm has no positive taxable income in the two preceding years against which to carry back the net loss or if the net loss exceeds the taxable income of those years, the firm can carry forward the net loss up to 20 years. This carryforward provides future tax benefits in that it can offset positive taxable income and thereby reduce income taxes otherwise payable. The benefits of the NOL carryforward give rise to a deferred tax asset.

Starbucks reports two main components of deferred tax liabilities: property, plant, and equipment of $217.5 million and intangible assets and goodwill of $177.3 million for the year ended September 27, 2015. Firms claim depreciation deductions on their tax returns using accelerated methods over periods shorter than the expected useful lives of depreciable and amortizable assets. Most firms depreciate and amortize assets for financial reporting using the straight-line method over the expected useful lives of such assets. Thus, the book bases of depreciable assets will likely exceed their tax bases. Depreciation and amortization expense for tax reporting in future years will be less than the amounts for financial reporting, giving rise to a liability for future tax payments. The deferred tax liability relating to depreciable and amortizable assets is very large, consistent with good tax planning to defer taxes. The liability increased during the year, which is typical of a growing firm adding more depreciable assets.

Deferred Tax Asset Valuation Allowances. Firms must recognize a valuation allowance for any deferred tax assets they are not likely to realize as tax benefits so that deferred tax assets will be reported at the most likely net realizable value. Often, the valuation allowance is similar in amount to the deferred tax asset for NOL carryforwards each year. This occurs because the company is profitable and paying taxes, so the net loss is most likely related to its subsidiaries. The net loss of the subsidiary can offset only net income of that subsidiary in a later year. NOLs generally are not transferable between subsidiaries because the tax law treats the subsidiaries as different taxable entities. If a company is generally very profitable and paying taxes but the subsidiary is not, both now and in the future, the deferred tax assets associated with NOL carryforwards may go unused and a valuation allowance is appropriate.

The deferred tax valuation allowance is a tax reserve that leads to greater tax expense and thus lower net income (changes in the valuation allowance affect income tax expense directly). Any large change in this reserve will have a substantial effect on net income and should be investigated further.

Starbucks' deferred tax allowance has decreased over the two-year period, which represents an *increase* in earnings. You should be skeptical of such decreases when there is a decrease in the ratio of the valuation allowance to deferred tax assets as well. **Starbucks'** valuation allowance was 9.7% of deferred tax assets in the prior year (= $166.8/$1,709.6) and only 8.0% of deferred tax assets in the current year (= $143.7/$1,790.0). If the percentage had been held constant at 9.7% in the year ended September 27, 2015, **Starbucks** would have reported $30.43 million [= (9.7% − 8.0%) × $1,790.0] less in net income, which represents more than 1% of net income for the year.

Starbucks discloses the following in the note: "The valuation allowance as of September 27, 2015 and September 28, 2014 is primarily related to net operating losses and other deferred tax assets of consolidated foreign subsidiaries. The net change in the total valuation allowance was a decrease of $23.1 million and an increase of $6.3 million for fiscal 2015 and 2014, respectively." The decrease in the valuation allowance is consistent with this explanation. The net operating loss carryforwards decreased by $11 million in fiscal 2015 ($104.4 million − $93.4 million). The remaining $12.1 million decrease

($23.1 million total decrease − $11 million) is likely explained by the other deferred tax assets of consolidated foreign subsidiaries. Note the **Starbucks'** valuation allowance is always substantially larger than its NOL carryforwards, suggesting that it also believes that some of these deferred tax assets will also fail to be realized.

Information Regarding Uncertain Tax Positions and Related Reserves

Financial reporting standards require that firms report reserves for the tax benefits of uncertain tax positions. For example, assume a firm takes a tax deduction or excludes income when filing its corporate return. The firm is uncertain about whether its position will be supported in the event of an audit by the IRS or other taxing authority. If it is more likely than not that the tax position would be upheld in the audit or subsequent litigation and appeal, then the firm is allowed to recognize the benefit as a reduction of tax expense. Otherwise, a reserve must be established. **Starbucks** has established a $150.4 million reserve and Exhibit 9.6 presents the required reconciliation of the beginning and ending balances of the reserve.

As in the case of the deferred tax asset valuation allowance, this tax reserve increase leads to greater tax expense and thus lower net income on a dollar-per-dollar basis. You want to pay close attention to material changes in tax reserves during a period.

Exhibit 9.6

Portion of Starbucks' Tax Note 13 from 2015 10-K (Tax Reserve)

The following table summarizes the activity related to our unrecognized tax benefits *(in millions):*

	Sep 27, 2015	Sep 28, 2014	Sep 29, 2013
Beginning balance	$112.7	$ 88.8	$75.3
Increase related to prior year tax positions	7.9	1.4	8.9
Decrease related to prior year tax positions	(0.9)	(2.2)	(9.3)
Increase related to current year tax positions	32.0	26.7	19.3
Decrease related to current year tax positions	(0.6)	(1.9)	(0.4)
Decreases related to settlements with taxing authorities	(0.7)	(0.1)	—
Decreases related to lapsing of statute of limitations	—	—	(5.0)
Ending balance	$150.4	$112.7	$88.8

- The income statement reports the amount of income tax expense. You can compute the relation between income tax expense and income before taxes, resulting in a firm's *average (or effective) tax rate*. The income tax note explains the major reasons why the average tax rate differs from the statutory federal tax rate. Most differences between average and statutory tax rates are transitory and thus do not affect the prediction of future periods' net income. However, shifts between domestic and foreign operations may create persistent tax rate changes.

- The income tax note indicates the mix of currently payable and deferred taxes and the extent to which a firm has delayed or accelerated the payment of income taxes. It also indicates the components of deferred tax assets and liabilities, which you can tie to the analysis of various other transactions of the firm.

- Accounting quality can be compromised in the process by which tax reserves are estimated. The dollar-for-dollar nature of tax reserves, the estimation required in their measurement, and the magnitude of tax rates combine to cause reserves to be a potentially material part of a company's profitability.

Pensions and Other Postretirement Benefits

LO 9-4

Identify the effects of *pensions and other postemployment benefits* on the financial statements.

In addition to salaries, bonuses, wages, vacation time, and share-based compensation, most employers provide benefits to employees when they retire. This section deals with pension benefits. Later, we provide a brief summary of similar financial reporting for other postretirement benefits such as health care.[9]

To provide for retiree pension benefits, employers sponsor *defined contribution plans* or *defined benefit plans*. In a *defined contribution plan*, employers promise to place a certain percentage of an employee's earnings into an investment vehicle as specified by the employee. During the past decade, more employers have begun to offer defined contribution plans, typically 401(k) plans. The employer makes a cash contribution to an investment account each year based on a percentage of the employee's salary. The employer's obligation under the plan is satisfied once the funds are placed into the investment account. The employer does not guarantee a given benefit payment when the employee retires. Instead, the fund balance at retirement depends on the investing success of the investment company and the employee's allocation of the contribution across different types of investments. The accounting for a defined contribution plan is straightforward. Because of the plan contract, the employee's current service generates the employer's obligation to make periodic payments, and the employer records pension expense for the amount of the defined contribution obligation. **Starbucks** uses such a plan as its primary post-employment benefit. From Note 12: "We maintain voluntary defined contribution plans, both qualified and non-qualified, covering eligible employees as defined in the plan documents. Participating employees may elect to defer and contribute a portion of their eligible compensation to the plans up to limits stated in the plan documents, not to exceed the dollar amounts set by applicable laws. Our matching

---

[9]Standards on pensions and postemployment benefits are *Codification Topics 715* and *958*; International Accounting Standards Board, *International Accounting Standard 19*, "Employee Benefits" (revised 1998).

contributions to all U.S. and non-U.S. plans were $70.9 million, $73.0 million, and $54.7 million in fiscal years 2015, 2014, and 2013, respectively."

In a *defined benefit plan*, employers incur the obligation to provide a pension payment to employees throughout the employee's retirement period. The final obligation is determined by the terms of a pension plan, which are negotiated by employers and employees. Normally, many factors affect the determination of the final obligation, including the length of the employee's service to the company, expected employee longevity, status at retirement, and final pay. The intricacies of determining the obligation and assigning pension cost to particular periods create complex accounting.

Normally, a corporation hires a third-party trustee, usually an insurance company or another financial services company, to administer defined benefit plans. Each year the employer makes an annual contribution to the trustee, which is invested in plan assets (usually a portfolio of cash, debt, and equity securities) managed by the trustee. The trustee keeps records of the plan's obligations to individual employees and makes pension payments to eligible employees. The remaining discussion of pensions relates to understanding the accounting for these more complex defined benefit plans.

The Economics of Pension Accounting in a Defined Benefit Plan

The underlying economic explanation of defined benefit pension plans involves understanding and comparing two key amounts: *pension obligations* and *pension assets*.

Pension Obligation (Liability)

In a typical defined benefit arrangement, employees are promised a lump-sum payment or periodic monthly payments when they retire based on a plan formula. A typical plan formula considers the number of years of employee service, a credit for each year of annual service (usually expressed as a percentage of final salary), and final salary at retirement date. For example, assume that a pension plan is governed by the following formula:

Annual Benefits = Annual Credit × Years of Service × Salary at Retirement Date

If the annual credit is 1%, the interpretation of the formula is that for each year of service, an employee's annual retirement benefit increases by 1% of the salary at retirement date. An employee who worked 30 years under the plan would retire at 30% of final salary. The PBO (*projected benefit obligation*) is the actuarially determined present value of estimated retirement payments calculated according to the benefit formula (using expected future salary levels) to be paid to employees because employees have worked and earned benefits until the current date. The discount (interest) rate used for the present value computation is called the settlement rate, which represents the current market rate at which an outside party would effectively settle the obligation.

Pension Assets

To have the funds available to make pension payments when due, employers accumulate pension assets by setting aside funds for that purpose (self-administration of the plan) or by making cash payments to a plan trustee with the expectation that the trustee will invest the cash and increase the fund by generating returns on the investments.

If the employer self-administers the plan, it is referred to as an unfunded plan. If a plan trustee is used, the plan is considered a funded plan. Unless otherwise noted, we assume that all plans are administered by a third-party trustee. The employer and third-party trustee, in consultation with an actuary, make decisions about payments to the trustee based on an assumption about the expected long-term rate of return on plan assets.

Pension fund assets are measured at their fair value (FV) at the end of each year. Employers use the year-end FV or an average FV over a period of time, usually five years (the average is referred to as the *market-related fair value*), in financial reporting. Determining the fair value of the assets in the fund usually is not a problem because prudent investing of fund assets generally yields funds comprising cash and widely held, often-traded securities.

The Economic Status of the Plan

The economic status of the plan is determined by comparing the two amounts: the PBO and the FV of plan assets:

If PBO > FV of plan assets, the plan is underfunded, resulting in a *net obligation*.
If PBO < FV of plan assets, the plan is overfunded, resulting in a *net asset*.

The economic status of the plan is reflected on the balance sheet. Underfunded plans are net liabilities on the firm's balance sheet, whereas overfunded plans are net assets. If a firm has several different plans (across employee groups, subsidiaries, countries, etc.), then the firm determines the net funded status for each one separately. Plans with net asset status and plans with net obligation status are accumulated and reported separately.

What Changes the Economic Status of the Plan during the Year?

Other than funding (that is, payments by the firm to the trustee), changes in the economic status of the plan are reported in comprehensive income.

What Changes PBO (the Pension Plan Liability)? Five events have the potential of changing the PBO during a given period: service cost, interest on PBO, prior service cost, liability (actuarial) gains and losses, and benefit payments to retirees.

1. Employees earn benefits in the current year (*service cost*).
   By working one additional year, employees earn an increase in future benefits. The actuarially determined present value of the increase in future benefits represents an increase in the employer's pension liability. This liability increase is called service cost.
2. Time passes (*interest on PBO*).
   PBO represents the present value of future benefits payable to retirees. As time passes without the liability being extinguished, the liability accumulates interest at the settlement interest rate. That is, the long-term liability PBO grows at a rate of interest equal to the settlement interest rate. The liability increase due to the passage of time is called interest cost.
3. Plan amendments grant retroactive benefits (*prior service cost*).
   From time to time, employers and employees negotiate and decide to change the pension plan benefit formula. Usually, the negotiation leads to increased retirement benefits, which are applied retroactively. Recall the pension plan formula example described earlier. Now assume that the employer amends the pension

plan agreement to increase the annual credit from 1% to 2%. If the amendment is retroactive, the employee now is entitled to an annual benefit equal to 60% of final salary. This sudden increase in retirement payments translates into a sudden increase in PBO because PBO is the actuarially determined present value of the estimated future retirement payments. The increase in PBO from amending a pension plan and retroactively granting benefits is defined as prior service cost. Employers often justify the sudden increase in the liability with the argument that the current employee group benefiting from the retroactive amendment represents a more loyal workforce with a higher morale. These conditions translate into a future economic benefit for the employer over the remaining service life of the affected group.

4. Actuarial assumptions about future retirement payments change [*liability (actuarial) gains and losses*].

    Each period the actuary estimates PBO using the most current assumptions about items such as interest rates, mortality, pay increases, and job classifications. If experience during the period indicates that assumptions should be changed, the actuary recomputes the PBO based on the new assumptions. The resulting increase or decrease in PBO is referred to as a liability (actuarial) gain or loss. For example, if new information becomes available that employees are estimated to live longer after retirement than previously thought, increased future retirement payments will occur, and, consequently, PBO increases. The unexpected increase in PBO is a liability loss. Other changes in plan assumptions could lead to decreased PBO, which would be classified as a liability gain.

5. Retirement benefits are paid (*benefit payments*).

    Actually paying retirement benefits to retired employees reduces the PBO.

What Changes the FV of Pension Plan Assets?   Three events may change the FV of pension plan assets during a given period: employer cash payments to the pension plan, actual return on plan assets, and retirement benefits payments.

1. Employer cash payments are made to the plan trustee (*employer contributions*).

    Funding the plan by making a cash contribution to the pension plan increases the FV of pension plan assets. Within certain boundaries, company management decides how much cash to contribute to the pension plan each year. The U.S. federal government mandates minimum funding amounts for defined benefit pension plans, which become the minimum company contribution amounts. Internal Revenue Service regulations allow only a certain amount to be tax deductible, which most firms treat as the maximum company contribution amount. Firms normally make a pension plan contribution between these minimum and maximum amounts. Note that this contribution amount reduces the obligation to retired employees, the PBO.

2. There are actual returns on invested plan assets (*return on plan assets*).

    The pension plan trustee invests the cash contributed by the employer in stocks, bonds, and other assets, which earn a return (for example, dividends or interest) and experience changes in market value. The change in the FV of plan assets during the period, adjusted for employer contributions and benefit payments, leads to the computation of an *actual return* on plan assets. If the return is positive, the FV of the assets increased during the period. The return, however, can be negative. The actual return on plan assets can be thought of as comprising two components: expected return and unexpected return.

- The *expected return on plan assets*, which is always positive, is based on long-run expected rates of return on diversified portfolios of assets similar to those of the pension fund.
- The *unexpected return on plan assets* is based on deviations of actual rates of return from expected rates (*asset gains and losses*).

For example, if a company expects a 10% return and the actual return is 9%, the two components of actual return are an expected return of 10% and a plan asset loss of 1%. The PBO increases due to accruing interest at the settlement rate. Similarly, the FV of plan assets increases based on the expected return. The PBO increases or decreases if the settlement rate (or other assumptions) turns out to be different than expected. The FV of plan assets also increases (a gain) or decreases (a loss) if the actual return turns out to be higher or lower than expected.

3. Retirement benefits are paid (*benefit payments*).

Finally, actually paying retirement benefits to retired employees reduces the FV of available plan assets. Note that this amount also reduces the obligation to retired employees, the PBO.

Reporting the Income Effects in Net Income and Other Comprehensive Income

Each noncash change in PBO and the FV of plan assets is given (1) immediate recognition as a part of pension expense of the current period or (2) delayed recognition as part of other comprehensive income.

Type of Change in Pension Plan	Treatment
Changes in PBO:	
Service cost	Increase pension expense
Interest cost on PBO	Increase pension expense
Prior service cost	Decrease other comprehensive income
Liability gains/losses on PBO	Increase/decrease other comprehensive income
Changes in FV of plan assets:	
Actual return on plan assets (two components):	
Expected return on plan assets	Decrease pension expense
Asset gains/losses	Increase/decrease other comprehensive income

Items receiving immediate recognition in net income are service cost, interest cost, and expected return on plan assets. Immediate recognition of service cost and interest on PBO increases pension expense because both represent an increase in the PBO liability. The expected return on plan assets is always positive. Because it represents an increase in the FV of plan assets, it decreases pension expense.[10]

---

[10]We use the terms *pension expense* and *net pension cost* interchangeably. This is not always correct because a cost can be an expense or an asset depending on whether economic benefits are expected to exist beyond the current period. We have abstracted from the idea that pension cost can be part of inventory (for example, if it is the pension of a direct laborer) to make the discussion easier. However, if pension cost is deemed to be part of inventory, it is not reported as pension expense; instead, it is allocated to inventory as a product cost and then becomes part of cost of goods sold when the inventory is sold.

Prior service cost is generally an increase in the PBO liability, and it is recognized as a decrease in other comprehensive income. However, prior service cost is recognized in net income over time through an amortization process. The recognition of prior service cost in net income over time is consistent with the idea that prior service costs generate employee goodwill, with the benefits of such goodwill realized over the remaining service period of the employees to whom the retroactive benefits were granted.

Recognition of gains and losses on pension liabilities and assets is delayed because of a smoothing objective inherent in the accounting for pensions. A primary argument in support of this objective is that most gains and losses are transitory fluctuations for which current recognition should not be given. The rules for the specific delayed recognition of gains and losses are complex, and we discuss them subsequently in the chapter. The basic idea is that only if transitory gains and losses become very large are they amortized and reflected in net income. However, in the period in which they occur, all liability gains and losses are reflected in other comprehensive income.

The sum of the amounts currently recognized in net income is reported as pension expense on the income statement. To strengthen your understanding of pension expense computation and to illustrate the balance sheet and note presentations, we consider the following simplified example.

Pension Expense Calculation with Balance Sheet and Note Disclosures

On January 1, 2016, Moreno Co. adopted a defined benefit pension plan, at which time both its PBO and FV of plan assets equaled zero. In early 2017, Moreno granted retroactive benefits of $100,000 to employees who have an average remaining service period of 10 years from that date. Moreno decided to fund the plan at the end of each year by sending $60,000 to a plan trustee. Service cost is $50,000 each year. Moreno earns 10% on investments and can settle the obligation by purchasing an annuity with a 7% interest rate. To simplify this first example, assume that (1) actual and expected returns on plan assets are equal (that is, no asset gains or losses) and (2) actual and expected PBO are equal (that is, no liability gains or losses). Our goal is to prepare financial statement disclosures for 2016–2018.

To compute many of the pension disclosures, it is necessary to reconcile PBO and FV of plan assets. Exhibit 9.7 shows the reconciliations for Moreno Co.

In 2016, PBO began at $0 and increased $50,000 due to employees' current service. Because there was no beginning PBO, it did not grow due to the passage of time; thus, interest cost on PBO is $0. No other changes in PBO occurred in 2016. (Two possible other changes intentionally not considered in this example are liability gains/losses and payments to retired employees.) The FV of plan assets began at zero, no return was earned on the $0 investment, and $60,000 was contributed to the plan trustee at the end of the year. (Again, by construction of the example, no payments were made to retirees.) Comparing PBO and FV of plan assets at 12/31/16, we see that Moreno contributed $10,000 more than the pension plan obligation to employees. Thus, the plan is overfunded by $10,000. That is, the pension plan is in a $10,000 net asset position, which will be reported on Moreno's balance sheet as of 12/31/16.

In 2017, the situation changes substantially. Again, service cost of $50,000 increases PBO. But now the $50,000 beginning PBO accrues interest at the 7% settlement rate such that PBO goes up by an additional $3,500 (interest cost on PBO). Also, 2017 is the year in which Moreno granted retroactive benefits in a plan amendment causing PBO

Exhibit 9.7

Moreno Co. Reconciliation of Pension Liability and Assets

Changes in PBO		2016		2017		2018
PBO, 1/1		$ 0		$ 50,000		$203,500
Service cost		50,000		50,000		50,000
Interest cost on PBO:						
Beginning PBO balance	$0		$50,000		$203,500	
Settlement rate	×0.07		× 0.07		× 0.07	
Interest cost		0		3,500		14,245
Prior service cost		0		100,000		0
PBO, 12/31		$50,000		$203,500		$267,745

Changes in FV of Plan Assets		2016		2017		2018
FV of plan assets, 1/1		$ 0		$ 60,000		$126,000
Expected return on plan assets:						
Beginning balance	$0		$60,000		$126,000	
Long-term expected return on plan assets	×0.10		× 0.10		× 0.10	
Expected return		0		6,000		12,600
Contributions		60,000		60,000		60,000
FV of plan assets, 12/31		$60,000		$126,000		$198,600

to increase $100,000 for prior service cost. Therefore, at December 31, 2017, PBO is $203,500. Moreno did not choose to immediately fund the prior service cost PBO increase. The FV of plan assets increased only by the 10% return on the beginning plan assets plus the annual end-of-period payment of $60,000 to the trustee. Therefore, at December 31, 2017, Moreno is in a net liability position of $77,500, which can be found by comparing the $203,500 PBO to the $126,000 FV of plan assets. This will be reported as a liability on Moreno's 2017 balance sheet. Under certain laws, severe underfunding of a plan can trigger a legal requirement to purchase insurance on the plan. Even if underfunding does not trigger legal actions, it can trigger employee disenchantment and represents a formidable headwind for the firm's future earnings and cash flows.

The events that change PBO and FV of plan assets in 2018 are similar. However, interest on PBO ($14,245) now exceeds the actual return on plan assets ($12,600). When this occurs, an employer would have to fund at a rate higher than annual service cost to keep the underfunded position (that is, net obligation) from growing.

Income Statement Effects

Service cost, interest on PBO, and expected return on plan assets received immediate recognition as part of pension expense on Moreno's books. Prior service cost and gains and losses receive delayed recognition by initially recognizing the increase in PBO in other comprehensive income and then recycling it through net income by amortizing the beginning balances over the average remaining service period of employees.

Computation of Net Pension Expense	2016	2017	2018
Service cost	$50,000	$50,000	$ 50,000
Interest on PBO	0	3,500	14,245
Expected return on assets	0	(6,000)	(12,600)
Amortization of PSC*	0	0	10,000
Amortization of gain/loss	0	0	0
Net pension expense	$50,000	$47,500	$ 61,645

*Assumes that the December 31, 2017, prior service cost is amortized beginning in 2018. The amount is amortized over average remaining service life of the workforce at December 31, 2017, which is assumed to be 10 years.

Note that amortization of prior service cost is $0 in 2016, $0 in 2017 (because there was no beginning balance to amortize), and $10,000 in 2018 ($100,000 prior service cost/10 years). The amortization of prior service cost will continue for nine more years.

Net pension expense is reflected in the income statement in each of the three years. For merchandising firms, it appears as an operating expense. For manufacturing firms, the portion that pertains to employees involved in manufacturing inventory is capitalized as part of inventory and then expensed as a portion of cost of goods sold when the inventory is sold.

Exhibit 9.8 presents the previous discussion within the financial statement effects template. In 2016, an increase in the pension liability occurs that causes $50,000 in pension expense. Funding increases the pension asset by $60,000. In 2017, the plan amendment increases the pension liability by the $100,000 prior service cost. Prior service cost receives delayed recognition (that is, it is not reflected in current pension expense). Instead, other comprehensive income is reduced. The remainder of the changes in the pension liability (increase of $53,500) and pension asset (increase of $6,000) is from events receiving immediate recognition in pension expense (increase of $47,500). Again, funding increases the pension asset further ($60,000 increase). In 2018, similar events occur to change the pension asset and liability. In addition, the prior service cost is amortized to pension expense by removing $10,000 from other comprehensive income.

Exhibit 9.8: Financial Statement Effects of Pension Accounting

Assets		=	Liabilities		+	Total Shareholders' Equity		
						CC	AOCI	RE
2016								
Record Pension Expense:								
			Pension Liability	50,000				Pension Expense (50,000)
Record Cash Payment:								
Cash	(60,000)							
Pension Asset	60,000							
Pension Expense			50,000					
Pension Liability						50,000		
Pension Asset			60,000					
Cash						60,000		

(*Continued*)

Exhibit 9.8 (Continued)

2017								
Record Plan Amendment:	Pension Liability	100,000			OCI	(100,000)		
Record Pension Expense:								
Pension Asset	6,000	Pension Liability	53,500				Pension Expense	(47,500)
Record Cash Payment:								
Cash	(60,000)							
Pension Asset	60,000							

OCI	100,000	
Pension Liability		100,000
Pension Expense	47,500	
Pension Asset	6,000	
Pension Liability		53,500
Pension Asset	60,000	
Cash		60,000

2018								
Record Pension Expense:								
Pension Asset	12,600	Pension Liability	64,245		OCI	10,000	Pension Expense	(61,645)
Record Cash Payment:								
Cash	(60,000)							
Pension Asset	60,000							

Pension Expense	61,645	
Pension Asset	12,600	
OCI		10,000
Pension Liability		64,245
Pension Asset	60,000	
Cash		60,000

In the notes, Moreno will disclose the components of the net periodic pension expense, as shown in the table illustrating the pension expense computations on page 616. Additional required disclosures reconcile beginning PBO to ending PBO and beginning FV of plan assets to ending FV of plan assets.

Note Disclosures: Reconciliations of PBO and FV of Plan Assets	2016	2017	2018
January 1, PBO	$ 0	$ 50,000	$203,500
Service cost	50,000	50,000	50,000
Interest cost	0	3,500	14,245
Prior service cost	0	100,000	0
Benefit payments	0	0	0
December 31, PBO	$ 50,000	$203,500	$267,745
January 1, FV of plan assets	$ 0	$ 60,000	$126,000
Company contributions	60,000	60,000	60,000
Benefit payments	0	0	0
Actual return on plan assets	0	6,000	12,600
December 31, FV of plan assets	$ 60,000	$126,000	$198,600
Net pension liability (asset)	$(10,000)	$ 77,500	$ 69,145

Gain and Loss Recognition

To this point, we have assumed that all actual and expected amounts are equal. Gains and losses occur when expectations turn out to be different than realizations. That is:

Expected PBO $\neq$ Actual PBO, which results in liability gains or losses
Expected FV $\neq$ Actual FV, which results in asset gains or losses

Pension plan accounting defers both asset and liability gains and losses. The net deferred gain/loss amount is amortized only if it becomes very large. The FASB set an arbitrary amount, called the *corridor* amount, as the threshold for deferred gain or loss amortization. The *corridor* is defined as 10% of the greater of actual PBO or actual FV. The logic behind this treatment is simple. Gains and losses are deviations from expectations. If expectations are unbiased, gains and losses will offset over time and the net gain or loss should fluctuate around zero. If, however, the gains and losses do not offset over time, the accumulated gains or losses will become large, with *large* defined as exceeding the corridor. The FASB prescribes amortization only if the balance becomes larger than the corridor. The decision to amortize net deferred gains or losses is made each year, and that decision is independent of any decision made in prior years. Also, the decision is made based upon *beginning-of-the-year balances* (that is, using prior year-end balances for net deferred gain or loss, PBO, and FV). The financial statement effects of amortizing a net loss are identical to the effects of amortizing prior service cost. Amortizing a net gain decreases other comprehensive income and increases net income via a reduction in pension expense.

Impact of Actuarial Assumptions

Firms must disclose in notes to the financial statements the assumptions made with respect to

- the discount rate used to compute the pension benefit obligation.
- the expected rate of return on pension investments (including the pension plan investment guidelines that form the basis for establishing the expected rate of return).
- the rate of compensation increase, which affects the amount of the PBO.

The amount of the pension benefit obligation is inversely related to the discount rate. U.S. GAAP specifies that firms should use a long-term government bond rate as the discount rate. Thus, the discount rates firms use should not vary significantly. However, even small differences in the discount rate can materially affect the size of the pension benefit obligation.

Firms use different expected rates of return on pension investments, in part because of different mixtures of investments in their pension portfolios. For example, a firm with equal proportions of debt and equity should have a lower expected return (and lower risk) than a firm that invests fully in equities. Firms must report their target allocation for plan assets. For example, a target allocation could be 40% investment in fixed income securities, 33% in U.S. equity, 22% in international equity, and 5% in real estate. Firms also report how they obtained the fair values of each type of plan asset. Calculating the percentage fair values across different asset classes allows you to assess whether target allocations are being achieved.

These transparent disclosures of target and actual investment allocations exist because of concerns that firms may use different expected rates of return in an effort to manage earnings. The assumed long-term rate of return on pension assets impacts the analysis of pensions in several ways. First, if the firm cannot generate returns, on average, equal to this rate, the firm will need to contribute additional assets in the future.

Second, the expected return on pension investments reduces pension expense each period and increases earnings. Firms must amortize any combined difference between expected and actual returns and liability gains and losses if the accumulated gains and losses exceed the corridor, so a deficiency resulting from expecting too high a level of returns shows up slowly in pension expense.

The problem also exists with the assumed rate of compensation increases, which is determined by management and thus not as externally verifiable as the discount rate for the PBO and the expected return on plan assets. The amount of the pension benefit obligation is directly related to the assumed rate of compensation increases. Firms have incentives to use a lower rather than higher assumed rate of compensation increases, both to lower their PBO and to create lower expectations among employees about future compensation increases. You should compare a firm's assumptions over time with other firms to evaluate the firm's level of aggressiveness in making assumptions.

Other Postretirement Benefits

Employers provide postretirement benefits other than pensions to employees as well as to employees' spouses and dependents. These benefits may include medical and hospitalization coverage, college tuition assistance, and life insurance coverage. As in the case of pensions, current employee service triggers these promises, and the expected obligation for these benefits can be computed as the actuarially determined present value of future payments.

A good understanding of postretirement benefits accounting can be obtained by adopting the same framework for expense recognition, balance sheet presentation, and note reconciliation as that discussed for pensions. However, there are two major differences. First, many companies simply pay these benefits when retirees make claims and do not fund a portfolio of plan assets dedicated to pay for other postretirement benefits because government regulations do not specify minimum funding for postretirement benefits other than pensions. As a result, the FV of postretirement plan assets is zero for many companies. Second, there are two additional required disclosures for postretirement benefits other than pensions: (1) the assumed health care cost trend rate(s) used in actuarial computations and (2) the effects of a one-percentage-point increase and decrease in the assumed health care cost trend rate on the accumulated postretirement benefit obligation for health care benefits and on the aggregate of the service and interest cost components of the net periodic postretirement health care benefit cost.

Signals about Earnings Persistence

Firms with large, unfunded pension obligations can face a significant headwind to future profitability because of future pension expenses, and a constraint on future cash flows because of required cash payments to fund the pension obligations. By contrast, firms with large amounts of pension assets will not face as much future pressure on earnings and cash flows. Large swings in the market values of investments can impact pension expense and earnings significantly. Although firms use long-term expected returns on investments to compute the expected return on assets each period, they apply this rate to the market value of assets in the pension portfolio. When market values increase, as they did in the early to late 1990s, many firms found that their pension expenses became pension income. During this period, some firms' pension income was a substantial portion of their increased earnings. In the stock market downturn that followed, companies recognized pension expense rather than pension income, exacerbating the downward pressure on earnings from weakened economic conditions. When using earnings of the current period to forecast earnings in the future, you should recognize the impact of changing stock prices on the measurement of pension expense.

- Pensions and other postemployment benefits have two key economic amounts: the present value of expected payments to retirees and the fair value of assets that have been set aside to make those payments.
- Noncash expected changes in these two economic amounts are accumulated into pension expense.

- Noncash unexpected changes are reported as other comprehensive income and accumulated other comprehensive income. The amounts either reverse or are recycled through pension expense in later periods.
- The difference between the two key economic amounts is reported as either a net asset or a net liability in the balance sheet.

Summary

Operating profitability is the key driver of firm value. This chapter examined the accounting and reporting issues surrounding operating activities. Our discussion of operating profitability followed the generally occurring order of the income statement. We began with a study of revenue recognition and followed with discussions of the major expense categories: cost of sales, SG&A expense, and income tax expense. These operating activities require investments in working capital. Accordingly, we examined issues surrounding inventory and accounts receivable reporting and the reporting of many working capital assets and liabilities that arise when accrual measurement and cash flow timing do not coincide. Finally, we considered the financial statement effects of pensions, an important area that illustrates the reporting of profitability, which is divided between current recognition on the income statement and delayed recognition in other comprehensive income.

Questions, Exercises, Problems, and Cases

Questions and Exercises

LO 9-1

9.1 Delayed Revenue Recognition. Software companies often bundle upgrades and technical support services with their software. Assume that a software company promises to automatically deliver upgrades for two years when a customer purchases software costing $100. Describe how the software company should determine the amount of revenue to recognize at the date of sale and subsequent to the date of sale.

LO 9-1

9.2 Measuring the Transaction Price. Bookman Co. develops digital accounting systems and provides accounting-related consulting services.

a. On January 1, 2017, Bookman signs a contract with Brock Florists to install a system and provide consulting services over a two-year period ending in late December 2018. The contract calls for an upfront payment of $25,000 a second payment of $10,000 in March 2017, and a third payment of $20,000 in December 2017. What is the transaction price?

b. Use the same information in Part a, but assume that the payment schedule is an upfront payment of $15,000, a second payment of $20,000 one year later, and a third payment of $20,000 two years later; Brock Florists typically borrows at an interest rate of 10%. What is the transaction price?

c. Use the same information in Part a, but assume that the third payment in December 2017 is contingent on Brock's need for the accounting consulting, specifically whether Brock Florists successfully completes a planned merger with a small privately owned pottery company. Brock has completed several mergers in the past and the Brock's management believes that the completion of the current merger is probable. The possible outcomes and likelihoods are (1) the merger occurs as planned (80% chance) or (2) the merger fails to occur (20% chance). What is the transaction price?

9.3 Allocating the Transaction Price. HeavyEQ produces large conveyor belt systems for heavy manufacturing. HeavyEQ signs a $2 million fixed-price contract under which it makes three promises:

- Install a conveyor belt system: fair value $1.6 million
- Service the system over a five-year period: fair value $0.6 million
- Provide a warranty assuring that the conveyer belt meets the contract specification at the time of sale: fair value $0.2 million

REQUIRED
- **a.** Allocate the transaction price to the performance obligations.
- **b.** Reallocate the transaction price under the notion that HeavyEQ has no reasonable basis for determining the fair value of the servicing because the conveyor system is of such a unique nature that the servicing activities are highly variable and uncertain.

9.4 Working Capital. Identify the working capital accounts related to (a) revenues recognized and deferred, (b) cost of goods sold, (c) employee salary and wages, and (d) income tax expense. For each account, indicate whether an increase in the working capital asset or liability would be an addition or subtraction when reconciling from net income to cash flows from operations.

9.5 Expense Recognition. Provide three examples of expense recognition justified by (a) a direct relation with revenue (cause and effect) and (b) an indirect relation with revenue (the consumption of an asset or an increase in a liability during a period in which revenue is recognized).

9.6 Accounts Receivable. Using the following key, identify the effects of the following transactions or conditions on the various financial statement elements: I = increases; D = decreases; NE = no effect.

	Assets	Liabilities	Shareholders' Equity	Net Income
a. A credit sale				
b. Collection of a portion of accounts receivable				
c. Estimate of bad debts				
d. Write-off of a specific uncollectible account				

9.7 Inventory Costing and Valuation. The acquisition cost of inventory remaining at the end of a period is measured using LIFO, FIFO, or average cost.

- **a.** Rank cost of goods sold, gross profit, and ending inventory from highest to lowest under the three cost-flow assumptions when input prices are rising.
- **b.** How should differences between acquisition cost and the market value of inventory be reported on the balance sheet under IFRS and U.S. GAAP?

LO 9-1

LO 9-1, LO 9-2

LO 9-2

LO 9-1, LO 9-2

LO 9-2

LO 9-2

9.8 LIFO Layer Liquidation. What is a LIFO layer liquidation? How does it affect the prediction of future earnings?

LO 9-2

9.9 Effect of Weighted-Average Cost-Flow Assumption on Inventory. The weighted-average cost-flow assumption is a common technique used to value inventory and determine cost of goods sold. It falls between LIFO and FIFO as to the differential effect on inventory and cost of goods sold amounts, although normally it is more like FIFO than LIFO in its effect on the balance sheet. Why?

LO 9-4

9.10 Reconcile PBO/FMV of Plan Assets. Given the following information, compute December 31, 2017, projected benefit obligation (PBO) and fair market value (FMV) of plan assets for Lee Company. What amount of asset or liability will be reported on the balance sheet at December 31, 2017?

Prior service cost granted in a 2017 plan amendment	$110,000
Interest on PBO	70,000
Actual return on plan assets	100,000
Service cost	80,000
Contribution sent to plan trustee	60,000
Benefit payments to retirees	20,000
Liability loss (gain)	(30,000)
FMV of plan assets, January 1, 2017	750,000
PBO, January 1, 2017	800,000

LO 9-4

9.11 Financial Statement Effects of Pension Plan Events. Using the following key, identify the effects of the following transactions or conditions on the various financial statement elements: I = increases; D = decreases; NE = no effect.

Note that the questions pertain to the employer's financial statements, not to the pension plan's financial statements. Analyze effects on the current year only.

Pension Plan Events or Conditions	Assets	Liabilities	Shareholders' Equity	Net Income
a. Employees performing current service				
b. Plan amendment grants retroactive benefits				
c. Projected benefit obligation accrues interest at the settlement rate				
d. Unexpected increases in PBO due to changes in actuarial assumptions				
e. Retired employees are paid benefits				
f. Contributions made to plan trustee				
g. Plan assets increase by expected return from investing				
h. Unexpected decrease in FMV of plan assets due to an asset loss				
i. Amortization of prior service cost				
j. Amortization of gain				

9.12 Components of Pension Expense. Pension expense typically consists of five components. Answer the following questions related to each component.

a. Service cost: Is it possible for the service cost component to *reduce* pension expense for the year? Explain your answer.

b. Interest cost: Is it possible for the interest cost component to *reduce* pension expense for the year? Explain your answer.

c. Expected return on plan assets: U.S. GAAP requires firms to reduce pension expense each year by the expected, not the actual, return on investments. What is the logic employed by policy makers in reaching this decision?

d. Amortization of prior service cost: What is a prior service cost? Provide an example of a plan change that would generate an amount labeled prior service cost.

e. Amortization of actuarial gains and losses: What circumstances give rise to actuarial gains and losses?

9.13 Postretirement Benefits Other Than Pensions. The notes to a firm's financial statements reveal that the obligations for postretirement health care benefits at the end of 2017 total $2.1 billion. The fair value of plan assets for these benefits at the end of 2017 is reported at zero, with an unrecognized net actuarial loss of $310 million reported for the same year. Calculate the amount of the postretirement health care benefit obligation reported by the firm at the end of 2017. Discuss what classification category (or categories) on the balance sheet would appropriately include the obligation.

Problems and Cases

9.14 Income Recognition for Various Types of Businesses. Discuss when each of the following types of businesses is likely to recognize revenues and expenses.

a. A bank lends money for home mortgages.

b. A travel agency books hotels, transportation, and similar services for customers and earns a commission from the providers of these services.

c. A major league baseball team sells season tickets before the season begins and signs its players to multiyear contracts. These contracts typically defer the payment of a significant portion of the compensation provided by the contract until the player retires.

d. A producer of fine whiskey ages the whiskey 12 years before sale.

e. A timber-growing firm contracts to sell all timber in a particular tract when it reaches 20 years of age. Each year it harvests another tract. The price per board foot of timber equals the market price when the customer signs the purchase contract plus 10% for each year until harvest.

f. An airline provides transportation services to customers. Each flight grants frequent-flier miles to customers. Customers earn a free flight when they accumulate sufficient frequent-flier miles.

9.15 Measuring Income for a Software Manufacturer. DataTech (DT) is a software manufacturer. It develops, markets, and supports software that helps manufacturers improve the competitiveness of their products. DT provides a detailed description of its revenue streams in its SEC 10-K filing, excerpts of which are as follows:

> We derive revenues from three primary sources: (1) software licenses, (2) maintenance services and (3) other services, which include consulting and education services. We exercise judgment and use estimates in connection with the determination of the amounts of software license and services revenues to be recognized in each accounting period.
>
> For software license arrangements that do not require significant modification or customization of the underlying software, we recognize revenue when (1) persuasive

evidence of an arrangement exists, (2) delivery has occurred (generally, FOB shipping point or electronic distribution), (3) the fee is fixed or determinable, and (4) collection is probable. Substantially all of our license revenues are recognized in this manner. Our software is distributed primarily through our direct sales force. However, our indirect distribution channel continues to expand through alliances with resellers. Revenue arrangements with resellers are recognized on a sell-through basis; that is, when we receive persuasive evidence that the reseller has sold the products to an end-user customer. We do not offer contractual rights of return, stock balancing, or price protection to our resellers, and actual product returns from them have been insignificant to date. As a result, we do not maintain reserves for product returns and related allowances.

At the time of each sale transaction, we must make an assessment of the collectability of the amount due from the customer. Revenue is only recognized at that time if management deems that collection is probable. In making this assessment, we consider customer creditworthiness and historical payment experience. At that same time, we assess whether fees are fixed or determinable and free of contingencies or significant uncertainties. If the fee is not fixed or determinable, revenue is recognized only as payments become due from the customer, provided that all other revenue recognition criteria are met. In assessing whether the fee is fixed or determinable, we consider the payment terms of the transaction and our collection experience in similar transactions without making concessions, among other factors. Our software license arrangements generally do not include customer acceptance provisions. However, if an arrangement includes an acceptance provision, we record revenue only upon the earlier of (1) receipt of written acceptance from the customer or (2) expiration of the acceptance period.

Our software arrangements often include implementation and consulting services that are sold separately under consulting engagement contracts or as part of the software license arrangement. When we determine that such services are not essential to the functionality of the licensed software and qualify as "service transactions," we record revenue separately for the license and service elements of these arrangements.

Maintenance services generally include rights to unspecified upgrades (when and if available), telephone and Internet-based support, updates, and bug fixes. Maintenance revenue is recognized ratably over the term of the maintenance contract on a straight-line basis. It is uncommon for us to offer a specified upgrade to an existing product; however, in such instances, all revenue of the arrangement is deferred until the future upgrade is delivered.

When consulting qualifies for separate accounting, consulting revenues under time and materials billing arrangements are recognized as the services are performed.

Education services include on-site training, classroom training, and computer-based training and assessment. Education revenues are recognized as the related training services are provided.

REQUIRED

a. DT generates revenues from software licenses. Discuss the appropriateness of revenue recognition techniques employed by the firm for software licenses.
b. DT recognizes maintenance service revenue ratably over the term of the maintenance contract unless a specific software upgrade is promised to the customer as part of the maintenance contract. Describe the revenue recognition policy of DT for maintenance contracts that include a specific upgrade. Justify the logic for the policy.
c. DT provides educational services to its clients, such as on-site training and assessment, and recognizes revenue when the services are provided. Speculate on the criteria employed by DT to justify when the services have been provided.

d. DT states that the firm must "exercise judgment and use estimates in connection with the determination of the amounts of software license and services revenues to be recognized in each accounting period." Provide several illustrations of judgments or estimates that DT must employ for determining the amount of software license and service revenues to report each accounting period.

9.16 Measuring Income for a Consultancy Firm. Sanders Company is a LO 9-1, LO 9-2
technology consultancy firm. Sanders' disclosures in a recent Form 10-K filing provided an extensive discussion of its revenue recognition policies, excerpts of which follow:

> We recognize revenue from the provision of professional services under written service contracts with our clients. We derive a significant portion of our revenue from fixed-price, fixed-time contracts. Revenue generated from fixed-price contracts, with the exception of support and maintenance contracts, is recognized based on the ratio of labor hours incurred to estimated total labor hours. This method is used because reasonably dependable estimates of the revenues and costs applicable to various stages of a contract can be made, based on historical experience and milestones set in the contract.
>
> Revenue generated from fixed-price support and maintenance contracts is recognized ratably over the contract term.
>
> Certain contracts provide for revenue to be generated based upon the achievement of certain performance standards. Revenue is recognized when such performance standards are achieved.
>
> For these arrangements, we evaluate all deliverables in the contract to determine whether they represent separate units of accounting. If the deliverables represent separate units of accounting, we then measure and allocate the consideration from the arrangement to the separate units, based on reliable evidence of the fair value of each deliverable. This evaluation is performed at the inception of the arrangement and as each item in the arrangement is delivered, and involves significant judgments regarding the nature of the services and deliverables being provided and whether these services and deliverables can reasonably be divided into the separate units of accounting.

REQUIRED

a. Sanders recognizes revenues based on the provisions of the written service contracts generated for each client. The primary types of contracts are (1) fixed-price, fixed-time contracts; (2) support and maintenance contracts; and (3) performance standards contracts. Discuss the criteria used to recognize revenue for each type of contract and the difficulties in applying the criteria.

b. Discuss the appropriateness of the revenue recognition techniques employed by Sanders.

c. As detailed earlier, some contracts have multiple-element arrangements with separate deliverable components. Discuss the criteria used to distinguish among multiple components of the contract. Also speculate on how the firm recognizes revenue when the contract cannot be separated into distinct deliverable components.

9.17 Measuring Income for a Long-Haul Transport Firm. Canadian LO 9-1, LO 9-2
National Railway Company (CN) spans Canada and mid-America and provides freight transport services from the Atlantic Ocean to the Pacific Ocean and to the Gulf of Mexico. It is currently the largest private rail system in Canada and was privatized by the Canadian government when it was considered one of the worst rail transport companies in North America. CN has been a success story since its privatization and is now considered one of the strongest and most efficient rail freight transport companies. Its success is partly due to a fundamental change in the way it offers freight services to customers. CN runs what the firm refers to as a *scheduled*

railroad. Similar to rail passenger service, as much as possible CN maintains a fixed operating schedule and a fixed freight-car fleet movement across the continent. Thus, customers know what shipment options are available to them and with a high degree of accuracy when shipments will arrive at designated locations.

Typically, a customer contracts a fixed fee with CN to ship its freight from the point of origination (for example, the Port of Halifax) to the point of destination (for example, the Port of Vancouver). CN provides the entire transport (that is, CN does not contract out a portion of the shipment to other rail transport companies), and the length of time taken to deliver the freight depends on the distance and the type of service (fast delivery versus normal delivery, for example) purchased by the customer. In a recent annual report, CN succinctly states its policy on recognizing revenue: "Freight revenues are recognized on services performed by the Company, based on the percentage of complete service method. Costs associated with movements are recognized as the service is performed."

REQUIRED

Discuss the appropriateness of the revenue recognition techniques employed by CN for recognizing freight revenues.

LO 9-1, LO 9-2

9.18 Measuring Income from Long-Term Contracts. On January 1, 2017, assume that Turner Construction Company agreed to construct an observatory for Dartmouth College for $120 million. Dartmouth College must pay $60 million upon signing and $30 million in 2018 and 2019. Expected construction costs are $10 million for 2017, $60 million for 2018, and $30 million for 2019.

REQUIRED

  a. Indicate the amount and nature of income (revenue and expense) that Turner would recognize during 2017, 2018, and 2019 if it uses the completed-contract method. Ignore income taxes.
  b. Repeat Requirement a using the percentage-of-completion method.
  c. Indicate the balance in the Construction in Process account on December 31, 2017, 2018, and 2019 (just prior to completion of the contract), under the completed-contract and the percentage-of-completion methods.

LO 9-1, LO 9-2

9.19 Interpreting Financial Statement Disclosures Relating to Income Recognition. **Deere & Company** manufactures agricultural and industrial equipment and provides financing services for its independent dealers and their retail customers. In Note 2 to its October 31, 2012, Form 10-K, Deere discloses the following revenue recognition policy:

Sales of equipment and service parts are recorded when the sales price is determinable and the risks and rewards of ownership are transferred to independent parties based on the sales agreements in effect. In the U.S. and most international locations, this transfer occurs primarily when goods are shipped. In Canada and some other international locations, certain goods are shipped to dealers on a consignment basis under which the risks and rewards of ownership are not transferred to the dealer. Accordingly, in these locations, sales are not recorded until a retail customer has purchased the goods. In all cases, when a sale is recorded by the company, no significant uncertainty exists surrounding the purchaser's obligation to pay. No right of return exists on sales of equipment.... Financing revenue is recorded over the lives of related receivables using the interest method....

REQUIRED

Justify Deere's timing of revenue recognition for its equipment sales. Consider why recognition of revenue earlier or later than the time of shipment to dealers would not be more appropriate.

9.20 LIFO and FIFO Cost-Flow Assumptions for Inventory. A large manufacturer of truck and car tires recently changed its cost-flow assumption method for inventories at the beginning of 2017. The manufacturer has been in operation for almost 40 years, and for the last decade it has reported moderate growth in revenues. The firm changed from the LIFO method to the FIFO method and reported the following information (amounts in millions):

	December 31	
	2016	**2017**
Inventories at FIFO cost	$ 788.1	$ 861.7
Excess of FIFO cost over LIFO cost	(429.0)	(452.4)
Cost of goods sold (FIFO)	—	4,150.8
Cost of goods sold (LIFO)	—	4,417.1

REQUIRED

Calculate the inventory turnover ratio for 2017 using the LIFO and FIFO cost-flow assumption methods. Explain why the costs assigned to inventory under LIFO at the end of 2016 and 2017 are so much less than they are under FIFO.

9.21 Reconcile PBO/FMV of Plan Assets; Compute Pension Expense. The following information relates to a firm's pension plan.

Prior service cost due to 2017 amendment	$ 60,000
PBO, January 1, 2017	1,000,000
FMV, January 1, 2017	1,200,000
Settlement interest rate	7%
Expected return on plan assets	9%
Actual return on plan assets	8%
Liability loss (gain)	(40,000)
Contribution to plan trustee (made at end of year)	100,000
Service cost	115,000
Payments to retired employees	30,000

REQUIRED

   a. Compute the December 31, 2017, PBO and FMV of pension assets.
   b. Compute 2017 pension expense.
   c. Use the financial statements effects template to show the effects on the 2017 financial statements of the recording of:
      • the plan amendment
      • pension expense
      • the liability gain
      • the asset loss
      • the cash contribution to the trustee
      • payments to retiring employees.

9.22 Accounting for Forward Foreign Exchange Contract as a Fair Value Hedge (Based on Online Appendix).
Lynn Construction enters into a firm purchase commitment for equipment to be delivered on June 30, 2017, for a price of 10,000 GBP. It simultaneously signs a forward foreign exchange contract for 10,000 GBP. The forward rate on June 30, 2017, for settlement on June 30, 2018, is $1.64 per GBP. Lynn designates the forward foreign exchange contract as a fair value hedge of the firm commitment.

REQUIRED

a. U.S. GAAP and IFRS do not require Lynn to record the purchase commitment or the forward foreign exchange contract on the balance sheet as a liability and an asset on June 30, 2017. What is the logic for this accounting?

b. On December 31, 2017, the forward foreign exchange rate for settlement on June 30, 2018, is $1.73 per GBP. Using the financial statement effects template, show the financial statement effects of recording the change in the value of the purchase commitment and the change in the value of the forward contract for 2017. Ignore discounting.

c. On June 30, 2018, the spot foreign exchange rate is $1.75 per GBP. Show the financial statement effects of recording the change in the value of the purchase commitment and the change in the value of the forward contract due to changes in the exchange rate during the first six months of 2018.

d. Show the financial statement effects of the June 30, 2018, purchase of 10,000 GBP with U.S. dollars and acquisition of the equipment.

e. Show the financial statement effects on June 30, 2018, to settle the forward foreign exchange contract.

f. How would the effects in Requirements b–e differ if Lynn had chosen to designate the forward foreign exchange contract as a cash flow hedge instead of a fair value hedge?

g. Suggest a scenario that would justify Lynn treating the forward foreign exchange contract as a fair value hedge and a scenario that would justify the firm treating the contract as a cash flow hedge.

9.23 Accounting for Forward Commodity Price Contract as a Cash Flow Hedge (Based on Online Appendix).
Kentucky Gold (KG) holds 10,000 gallons of whiskey in inventory on October 31, 2017, that costs $225 per gallon. KG contemplates selling the whiskey on March 31, 2018, when it completes the aging process. Uncertainty about the selling price of whiskey on March 31, 2018, leads KG to acquire a forward contract on whiskey. The forward contract does not require an initial investment of funds. KG designates the forward commodity contract as a cash flow hedge of an anticipated transaction. The forward price on October 31, 2017, for delivery on March 31, 2018, is $320 per gallon.

REQUIRED

a. Using the financial statement effects template, show the financial statement effects, if any, that KG would have on October 31, 2017, when it acquires the forward commodity price contract.

b. On December 31, 2017, the end of the accounting period for KG, the forward price of whiskey for March 31, 2018, delivery is $310 per gallon. Show the financial statement effects of recording the change in the value of the forward commodity price contract. Ignore the discounting of cash flows in this part and in the remainder of the problem.

c. Show the financial statement effects of the December 31, 2017, decline in value of the whiskey inventory.

d. On March 31, 2018, the price of whiskey declines to $270 per gallon. Show the financial statement effects of revaluing the forward contract.

e. Show the financial statement effects on March 31, 2018, to reflect the decline in value of the inventory.

f. Show the financial statement effects on March 31, 2018, to settle the forward contract.

g. Assume that KG sells the whiskey on March 31, 2018, for $270 a gallon. Show the financial statement effects of recording the sale and recognizing the cost of goods sold.

h. How would the effects in Requirements b–g differ if KG had chosen to designate the forward commodity price contract as a fair value hedge instead of a cash flow hedge?

i. Suggest a scenario that would justify treating the forward commodity price contract as a fair value hedge and a scenario that would justify treating it as a cash flow hedge.

9.24 Interpreting Derivatives Disclosures (Based on Online Appendix). Excerpts from the disclosures on derivatives made by a large beverage manufacturer in Year 4 appear below:

`Online Appendix`

> Our Company uses derivative financial instruments primarily to reduce our exposure to adverse fluctuations in interest rates and foreign exchange rates, and, to a lesser extent, in commodity prices and other market risks. When entered into, the Company formally designates and documents the financial instrument as a hedge of a specific underlying exposure, as well as the risk management objectives and strategies for undertaking the hedge transaction. The Company formally assesses, both at the inception and at least quarterly thereafter, whether the financial instruments that are used in hedging transactions are effective at offsetting changes in either the fair value or cash flows of the related underlying exposures. Our Company does not enter into derivative financial instruments for trading purposes.
>
> Our Company monitors our mix of fixed-rate and variable-rate debt. This monitoring includes a review of business and other financial risks. We also enter into interest rate swap agreements to manage these risks. These contracts had maturities of less than one year on December 31, Year 4. The fair value of our Company's interest rate swap agreements was approximately $6 million at December 31, Year 4. The Company estimates the fair value of its interest rate management derivatives based on quoted market prices. Interest rate swap agreements are accounted for as fair value hedges. During Year 4, there has been no ineffectiveness related to fair value hedges.
>
> We enter into forward exchange contracts to hedge certain portions of forecasted cash flows denominated in foreign currencies. These contracts had maturities up to one year on December 31, Year 4. The purpose of our foreign currency hedging activities is to reduce the risk that our eventual U.S. dollar net cash inflows resulting from sales outside the United States will be adversely affected by changes in exchange rates. We designate these derivatives as cash flow hedges. During Year 4, we decreased accumulated other comprehensive income by $76 million ($46 million after tax) for changes in the fair value of cash flow hedges. The amount recorded in earnings for the ineffective portion of cash flow hedges during Year 4 was not significant. We also reclassified net losses of $86 million ($52 million after tax) from accumulated other comprehensive income to earnings. The accumulated net loss on cash flow derivatives on December 31, Year 4, is $56 million ($34 million after tax). The carrying and fair value of foreign exchange contracts on December 31, Year 4, is $39 million.
>
> We monitor our exposure to financial market risks using value-at-risk models. Our value-at-risk calculations use a historical simulation model to estimate potential future losses in the fair value of our derivatives and other financial instruments that could occur as a result of adverse movements in foreign currency and interest rates. We examined historical weekly returns over the previous 10 years to calculate our value at risk. The average value at risk represents the simple average of quarterly amounts over the past year.

According to our interest rate value-at-risk calculations, we estimate with 95% confidence that an adverse move in interest rates over a one-week period would not have a material impact on our consolidated financial statements for Year 4. Similar calculations for adverse movements in foreign exchange rates indicate a maximum impact on earnings over a one-week period of $17 million. Net income for Year 4 was $4,847 million.

REQUIRED

a. The company indicates that it "formally specifies the risk management objectives and strategies for undertaking the hedge transactions." Identify the risk management objectives and describe how the particular derivative accomplishes these objectives with respect to interest rate swap agreements.

b. Repeat Requirement a for forward exchange contracts.

c. What is the rationale for the company's designation of the interest rate swaps as fair value hedges and the forward exchange contracts as cash flow hedges?

d. Why does the company assess both initially and at least quarterly the effectiveness of these hedging instruments?

e. Compute the amount that the company initially recorded on its books for foreign exchange contracts outstanding on December 31, Year 4. What events will cause the carrying value of these contracts at any later date to differ from the amounts initially recorded?

f. For Year 4, the company reports a $76 million net loss from changes in the value of cash flow hedges. What does the disclosure that the company recognized a net loss instead of a net gain suggest about the direction of changes in exchange rates between the U.S. dollar and the foreign currencies underlying the foreign exchange contracts? Will the forward exchange contracts likely appear on the company's balance sheet as assets or liabilities? Explain.

g. Justify the company's treatment of the $76 million net loss from changes in the value of cash flow hedges during Year 4 as a decrease in accumulated other comprehensive income instead of an ineffective cash flow hedge that should be included in earnings.

h. The gains and losses from changes in the fair value of foreign exchange contracts are taxed in the period of settlement. Will the tax effects of the $76 million pretax loss for Year 4 affect current taxes payable or deferred taxes? If the answer to the previous question is deferred taxes, will it affect deferred tax assets or deferred tax liabilities? Explain.

i. Describe the likely event that will cause the company to reclassify amounts from accumulated other comprehensive income to earnings.

j. Assess the effectiveness of the company's management of risk changes from interest and foreign exchange rates for Year 4.

 9.25 Interpreting Income Tax Disclosures. Disclosures related to income taxes for **The Coca-Cola Company** (Coca-Cola) for 2006–2008 appear in Exhibit 9.9.

REQUIRED

a. Why are Coca-Cola's average tax rates so low?

b. Is it likely that Coca-Cola has recognized a net asset or a net liability on its balance sheet for pension and other postretirement benefit plans? Explain your reasoning.

c. Coca-Cola discloses that the valuation allowance on deferred tax assets relates primarily to net operating loss carryforwards. Assume for purposes of this question that Coca-Cola had recognized a valuation allowance each year exactly equal to the deferred tax assets recognized for net operating loss carryforwards. Indicate the effect on income tax expense and income tax payable in the year Coca-Cola initially recognizes the net operating loss carryforwards.

d. Refer to Requirement c. Indicate the effect on income tax expense and income tax payable in the year Coca-Cola benefits from the net operating loss carryforwards.

e. Interpret Coca-Cola's recognition of net deferred tax liabilities, instead of deferred tax assets, for equity investments in 2008.

Exhibit 9.9

The Coca-Cola Company
Income Tax Reconciliation and Components of Deferred Taxes
(amounts in millions)
(Problem 9.25)

	2008	2007	2006
Income Tax Reconciliation			
U.S. Statutory Tax Rate	35.0%	35.0%	35.0%
State Taxes, Net of Federal Tax Benefit	0.8	0.6	0.7
Foreign Earnings Taxes at Lower Rates	(14.3)	(10.8)	(11.4)
Equity Income or Loss	0.2	(1.3)	(0.6)
Other Operating Charges	0.7	0.5	0.6
Other	(0.5)	(0.0)	(1.5)
Average Tax Rate	21.9%	24.0%	22.8%

Components of Deferred Taxes on December 31:	2008	2007
Deferred Tax Assets		
Property, Plant and Equipment	$ 33	$ 45
Trademarks and Other Intangible Assets	79	76
Equity Method Investments	339	238
Other Liabilities	447	845
Benefit Plans	1,171	881
Net Operating Loss Carryforwards	494	554
Other	532	266
Total Deferred Tax Assets (Gross)	$ 3,095	$ 2,905
Valuation Allowance	(569)	(611)
Total Deferred Tax Assets (Net)	$ 2,526	$ 2,294
Deferred Tax Liabilities		
Property, Plant and Equipment	$ (667)	$ (670)
Trademarks and Other Intangible Assets	(1,974)	(1,925)
Equity Method Investments	(267)	(841)
Other Liabilities	(101)	(90)
Other	(229)	(383)
Total Deferred Tax Liabilities	$(3,238)	$(3,909)
Net Deferred Tax Assets (Liability)	$ (712)	$(1,615)

Source: The Coca-Cola Company, Form 10-K for the Fiscal Year ended December 31, 2008.

f. Why does Coca-Cola report tax effects of equity income and investments in the income tax reconciliation and in deferred tax liabilities?

g. Interpret Coca-Cola's recognition of deferred tax liabilities, instead of deferred tax assets, for intangible assets.

INTEGRATIVE CASE 9.1

Walmart

Exhibits 1.26–1.28 of Integrative Case 1.1 (Chapter 1) present the financial statements for Walmart for 2012–2015. In addition, the website for this text contains Walmart's December 31, 2015, Form 10-K. You should read the management discussion and analysis (MD&A), financial statements, and notes to the financial statements, especially Note 2, "Summary of Significant Accounting Policies."

REQUIRED

REVENUE RECOGNITION

    a. Does Walmart recognize all of its revenue at a point in time? If not, how is it recognized?

COST OF SALES AND INVENTORY

    b. What costing method does Walmart use to determine cost of sales and inventory?
    c. How does Walmart handle the requirement to report inventory at lower-of-cost-or-market?
    d. Does Walmart have a large LIFO reserve? If not, why?
    e. Walmart receives discounts from suppliers because it purchases large volumes of merchandise. Is this reported as other income or accounted for in another way?

WORKING CAPITAL

    f. Operations create working capital accounts. Which of Walmart's working capital accounts are the most financially significant?
    g. Does Walmart's working capital management yield a positive or negative net investment in working capital? Is this a good situation for Walmart's profitability? Why?

INCOME TAXES

    h. Note 9 to Walmart's consolidated financial statements presents a substantial amount of income tax–related information, including an effective income tax rate reconciliation. Which reconciling items appear to be relatively persistent?
    i. What is the effect of Walmart's generation of income in foreign jurisdictions on the effective tax rate? Is the effect changing over time?
    j. Are Walmart's foreign earnings growing relative to U.S. earnings?
    k. What is the interpretation of the line item "Net impact of repatriated international earnings"? Why is it a positive reconciling item in some years but negative in other years?
    l. What are the two largest deferred tax assets? Explain how they have arisen and why they are assets.
    m. What is the "valuation allowance"? It has decreased during the two-year period. What is the implication of this decrease for earnings?
    n. Why does Walmart report a deferred tax liability for property and equipment? Speculate whether Walmart expanded or contracted based on the information in this section of the tax note.

PENSIONS

    o. What kind of pension plans does Walmart have, and how are earnings affected by each?

CASE 9.2

Coca-Cola Pensions

In its December 31, 2008, Consolidated Financial Statements, **The Cola-Cola Company** (Coca-Cola) reports a substantial shift in its net pension liability ($1,328 million) relative to December 31, 2007 ($85 million).

LO 9-4

REQUIRED

a. Given a portion of Coca-Cola's Note 16 reconciliations provided below, write a memorandum explaining the change in the net pension liability. (Do not assume that the reader knows what items such as *service cost* mean.)

(amounts in millions)	2008
Benefit obligation at the beginning of the year	$3,517
Service cost	114
Interest cost	205
Foreign currency exchange rate changes	(141)
Amendments	(13)
Actuarial loss (gain)	125
Benefits paid*	(199)
Settlements/curtailments	(4)
Special termination benefits	11
Other	3
Benefit obligation at the end of the year	$3,618
Fair value of plan assets at beginning of year	$3,428
Actual return on plan assets	(961)
Employer contributions	96
Foreign currency exchange rate changes	(118)
Benefits paid	(155)
Settlements/curtailments	(3)
Other	3
Fair value of plan assets at the end of the year	$2,290

*Some pension plans are "unfunded," meaning that the company does not hire an independent trustee and send the funds to the trustee for investment, but, instead, pays retirees out of company rather than trustee pension fund assets. Coca-Cola paid $44 million out of company assets to retirees who are covered by unfunded plans.

Source: The Coca-Cola Company, Form 10-K for the Fiscal Year ended December 31, 2008.

b. For each item in the reconciliation, explain whether the effect on the PBO and the fair value of plan assets is reflected in current period pension expense or as a change in other comprehensive income.

c. Provide a general justification for keeping some PBO and fair value of plan asset changes out of current period net income.

d. In the same note, Coca-Cola indicates that it changed a key assumption during the period. The expected rate of increase in compensation levels was decreased by 1%. What effect does this assumption change have on the pension liability (PBO) and current and future pension expense?

Forecasting Financial Statements

LEARNING OBJECTIVES

LO 10-1 List and describe the general forecasting principles and the seven steps of the forecasting framework.

LO 10-2 Build forecasts of future balance sheets, income statements, and statements of cash flows by applying the seven-step forecasting framework to project:
   a. revenues.
   b. operating expenses.
   c. operating assets and liabilities.
   d. financial leverage, capital structure, and financial income items.
   e. provisions for taxes, net income, dividends, share repurchases, and retained earnings.
   f. a balance sheet that balances.
   g. cash flows.

LO 10-3 Understand how and when to use shortcut forecasting techniques.

LO 10-4 Test the validity of your forecast assumptions and results.

LO 10-5 Test the sensitivity of your forecasts to variations in critical assumptions and parameters.

LO 10-6 Develop forecast models that are flexible and comprehensive, enabling you to respond quickly and effectively when a company announces important new information.

Chapter Overview

Thus far, the preceding nine chapters of this text have drawn on the disciplines of accounting, finance, economics, and strategy. These chapters have demonstrated the first four steps of the analysis and valuation framework. They describe how to analyze (1) the economics of a firm's industry, (2) the competitive advantages and risks of the firm's strategy, (3) the information content and quality of the firm's accounting, and (4) the firm's financial performance and risk. The next five chapters cover the two culminating steps of the framework: (5) forecasting the future operating, investing, and financing activities of the firm and then (6) valuing the firm.

In this chapter, we shift our focus to the future because the value of an investment is a function of its *expected future payoffs* conditional on the *risks inherent in those payoffs*. You will use your knowledge about a firm's industry, strategy, accounting quality, past and current profitability, and risk to develop expectations about the firm's future operating, investing, and financing activities. Then you will capture those expectations in forecasts of future financial statements—income statements, balance sheets, and statements of cash flows. The purpose in building financial statement forecasts is to develop unbiased expectations for a firm's future earnings, cash flows, and dividends that you can use to estimate the firm's share value, as well as in a wide array of other decision contexts.

After we develop financial statement forecasts in this chapter, we will then use them in Chapters 11 through 14 to derive and value the future payoffs to the firm's common equity shareholders, including expected future dividends, free cash flows, and earnings.

Introduction to Forecasting

Analysts must develop realistic expectations for the outcomes of a firm's future business activities. To develop these expectations, analysts *forecast* expected future income statements, balance sheets, and statements of cash flows. Financial statement forecasts are integrated projections of a firm's future operating, investing, and financing activities, which will determine the firm's future financial position, profitability, cash flows, and risk. Financial statement forecasts are important tools from which you can derive expected future payoffs to equity shareholders—earnings, cash flows, and dividends— which are the fundamental bases for share value.

Financial statement forecasts also are important tools in many other decision contexts. Credit risk decisions require expectations for future cash flows available to make required interest and principal payments. Managers' decisions about firm strategy, customer or supplier relationships, mergers or acquisitions, divestitures, and even whether a firm presents a good employment opportunity, all depend on expected future payoffs and the risks of those payoffs.

Developing forecasts is in many ways the most difficult step of the six-step framework of this text because it requires you to confront a high degree of uncertainty. And forecast errors can prove very costly. Optimistic forecasts can lead you to overestimate future earnings and cash flows or underestimate risk and therefore overstate the value of the firm. Pessimistic or conservative forecasts can lead you to understate future earnings and cash flows or overstate risk and consequently miss valuable investment opportunities. As an analyst, you need to develop *realistic*—unbiased and objective, not optimistic or conservative—expectations of future earnings and cash flows that enable you to make well-informed investment decisions.

Superior forecasting has the potential to help you pick stocks that will generate superior returns. As Chapter 1 discussed, empirical research results from Nichols and Wahlen (2004) show that firms that generated increases in annual earnings also experienced stock returns that beat the market average by roughly 19% per year, whereas firms that generated decreases in annual earnings experienced stock returns that were roughly 16% below the average market return.[1] You should consider these results encouraging because they suggest that by increasing your ability to forecast future changes in annual earnings, you will have a greater potential to distinguish future winning stocks from losing stocks.

The first four steps of the analytical framework of this text have provided you with the necessary foundation for forecasting. To maximize your ability to develop reliable forecasts of financial statements and to avoid costly forecast errors, your expectations should reflect (1) the economics of the industry, (2) the competitive advantages and

---

[1] D. Craig Nichols and James M. Wahlen, "How Do Earnings Numbers Relate to Stock Returns? A Review of Classic Accounting Research with Updated Evidence," *Accounting Horizons* 18 (December 2004), pp. 263–286. This study uses data from 1988 to 2001 to replicate the seminal findings in Ray Ball and Philip Brown, "An Evaluation of Accounting Income Numbers," *Journal of Accounting Research* (Autumn 1968), pp. 159–178, and several other seminal studies.

risks of the firm's strategy, (3) the quality of the firm's accounting, and (4) the drivers of the firm's profitability and risk. These four steps inform you about the critical risk and success factors of the firm and the key drivers of the firm's profitability and risk. The critical factors that are the focal points of the firm's strategy, accounting quality, profitability, and risk are the most important building blocks for forecasting a firm's future financial statements.

This chapter first outlines general forecasting principles, describes a seven-step process for forecasting financial statements, and offers several practical coaching tips on forecasting. The chapter then applies each step to **Starbucks**, developing forecasts for income statements, balance sheets, and statements of cash flows for the next five years. The chapter then describes techniques to enhance the reliability of forecasts, including sensitivity analysis, iteration, and validity checks. The chapter also describes some shortcut forecasting techniques and the conditions under which such shortcuts are more reliable.

Preparing Financial Statement Forecasts

LO 10-1

In this section, we first describe general principles of building forecasts, and then a seven-step forecasting procedure, along with some practical forecasting tips. We also briefly describe how to use FSAP to build financial statement forecasts.

List and describe the general forecasting principles and the seven steps of the forecasting framework.

General Forecasting Principles

Several key principles of forecasting deserve mention at the outset.

- **Forecasts should project the firm's future operating, investing, and financing activities. Projected future financial statements measure the outcomes from those activities.** You should focus on *projecting the firm's future business activities*. For example, when will a manufacturer invest in a new plant? How much will it cost? How will it be financed? How much will that plant produce? The financial statements measure the projected outcomes of the firm's future business activities.

- **The objective of forecasting is to produce realistic expectations of future earnings, cash flows, and dividends, which determine the future payoffs to investment.** To maximize reliability and avoid costly forecast errors, your financial statement forecasts should provide *unbiased* and *objective* predictions of the firm's future operating, investing, and financing activities. Firm managers tend to be optimistic, and accountants tend to be conservative. Ideally, your forecasts will be neither optimistic nor conservative. Instead, they should be accurate and realistic.

- **Forecasts should avoid wishful thinking.** Do not create forecasts based on strategies you *hope* the firm will pursue or think the firm *should* pursue. Instead, your forecasts should capture the strategies you believe the firm *actually will execute and achieve* in the future.

- **Financial statement forecasts should be comprehensive.** Your forecasts should *include all expected future operating, investing, and financing activities*. For example, suppose you take a quick-and-dirty approach and simply use the prior year's sales growth rate to extrapolate expected future sales and then project expected future earnings by assuming a constant profit margin. This approach fails to consider all of the elements that will determine future profitability, which can cause your earnings forecasts to be incomplete and erroneous. By assuming a constant profit margin, you ignore important considerations, such as whether the cost of goods sold and operating expenses will increase more quickly or more slowly than sales.

- **Financial statement forecasts must be internally consistent.** Your forecasts should rely on the *additivity* within financial statements and the *articulation* across the financial statements to avoid internal inconsistencies and to reduce the possibility of errors from inconsistent assumptions. The income statement should measure profit or loss appropriately by including all revenues, expenses, gains, and losses each period. The balance sheet should capture all of the assets, liabilities, and equities, and should balance. The statement of cash flows should reflect all cash inflows and outflows implied by the income statement and all changes in the firm's balance sheet. Forecasts of each of the financial statements will impact and be impacted by each of the other statements.
- **Financial statement forecast assumptions must have external validity.** Your forecast assumptions should pass the test of *common sense.* You should impose reality checks on your forecast assumptions. For example, do your sales growth forecast assumptions appropriately reflect the firm's strategy and the industry's competitive conditions, including market demand and price elasticity for the firm's products, as well as the firm's productive capacity? You should benchmark the external validity of your forecast assumptions by comparing them to industry averages and to the firm's past performance and strategies.

Seven-Step Forecasting Game Plan

Exhibit 10.1 summarizes the following seven-step process, which provides you with a logical, sequential process for forecasting future financial statements:

1. Project revenues from selling products and delivering services to customers.
2. Project operating expenses (for example, cost of goods sold and selling, general, and administrative expenses) and derive projected operating income.
3. Project the operating assets (for example, cash; receivables; inventory; property, plant, and equipment) that will be necessary to support the level of operations projected in Steps 1 and 2. Also project the operating liabilities that will be triggered by these activities (for example, accounts payable and accrued expenses).
4. Project the financial liabilities, financial assets, and common equity capital that will be necessary to finance the net operating assets projected in Step 3. In addition, determine the interest expense that will be triggered by the financing liabilities, as well as any interest income the financial assets will generate.
5. Project nonrecurring gains or losses (if any) and derive projected income before tax. Subtract the projected provision for income taxes to derive projected net income. Subtract expected dividends from net income to project the change in retained earnings. Also project other comprehensive income items, if any.
6. At this point the projected balance sheet will likely not balance, so you will have to determine how the firm will likely use its financial flexibility to balance the balance sheet. For example, if projected assets exceed projected liabilities and equities, it indicates the firm will need to raise capital by issuing additional short- or long-term debt or common equity. You will need to repeat steps 4, 5, and 6 until the balance sheet is in balance.
7. Derive the projected statement of cash flows from the projected income statement and the changes in the projected balance sheet amounts.

The analysis techniques in Chapters 1 through 5 emphasize how to analyze operating, investing, and financing activities as drivers of the profitability and risk of the firm. Chapters 6 through 9 demonstrate how to assess the accounting quality of the

Exhibit 10.1

The Seven-Step Process for Preparing Financial Statement Forecasts

Balance Sheet

Assets	Liabilities and Shareholders' Equity
Cash Marketable Securities Accounts Receivable Inventories Other Current Assets Property, Plant, and Equipment Intangible Assets	Accounts Payable Accrued Expenses Income Taxes Payable Pension and Retirement Benefit Obligations Deferred Taxes
Short-Term Investments Long-Term Investments	Short-Term and Long-Term Debt Contributed Equity Capital
	Retained Earnings Accumulated Other Comprehensive Income
Total Assets =	**Total Liabilities and Shareholders' Equity**

Investing Activities
Net Capital Expenditures on
  Property, Plant, and
  Equipment
Purchases or Sales of
  Investments
Other Investing Transactions
	Financing Activities
	Changes in Short-Term and
	  Long-Term Debt
	Issues or Repurchases of
	  Common Equity
	Dividend Payments
	Other Financing Transactions

Cash Flow from Investing	**Cash Flow from Financing**

**STEP 1: Project
Operating Revenues**

**STEP 2: Project Operating
Expenses and Derive
Operating Income**

**STEP 3: Project Operating
Assets and Liabilities**

**STEP 4: Project Financial
Leverage, Financial Assets,
Common Equity Capital, and
Financial Income Items**

**STEP 5: Project
Nonrecurring Items, Provisions
for Income Taxes, Net Income,
Dividends, Changes in
Retained Earnings, and Other
Comprehensive Income Items**

**STEP 6: Balance the
Balance Sheet**

**STEP 7: Derive Cash Flows
from Operating, Investing,
and Financing Activities**

Statement of Cash Flows

**Income Statement and the
Change in Retained Earnings**

Sales Revenues
Other Operating Revenues

Operating Expenses:
– Cost of Goods Sold
– Selling, General, and
   Administrative Expense
– Other Operating Expenses
= **Operating Income**

– Interest Expense
+ Interest Income

– Income Taxes
= **Net Income**
– Dividends
= **Change in Retained Earnings**

Operating Activities
Net Income
Depreciation Expense
Other Adjustments
Changes in Receivables
Changes in Inventories
Changes in Other Current
   Assets
Changes in Payables
Changes in Accrued Expenses

Cash Flow from Operations

financing, investing, and operating activities of the firm. We carry this perspective into forecasting and valuation in Chapters 10 through 14. In this chapter, the seven-step forecasting procedure follows the aforementioned general forecasting principles by focusing on the firm's future operating, investing, and financing activities in order to project the firm's future financial statements.

Coaching Tips for Implementing the Seven-Step Forecasting Game Plan

- **Integrated and interdependent steps.** These seven steps are integrated and interdependent tasks, not necessarily sequential or linear. The order in which you implement these steps and the emphasis you place on each step will depend on the integration of the firm's operating, investing, and financing activities. For example, your forecasts of revenues for a retail or restaurant chain may first require forecasts of the number of new stores that will be open. Your sales forecasts for a manufacturer may depend on building a new plant, which may depend on obtaining long-term financing.
- **Forecast amounts must articulate among the three financial statements.** Most business activities affect all three financial statement forecasts. For example, sales forecasts will affect the revenues on the income statement, receivables on the balance sheet, and operating cash flows on the statement of cash flows. As another example, property, plant, and equipment on the balance sheet will be affected by capital expenditures from the statement of cash flows and depreciation expense, which affects both the income statement and the statement of cash flows. Net cash flow on the statement of cash flows must equal the change in cash on the balance sheet.
- **Financial flexibility and circularity.** Your financial statement forecasts must balance, so you will require at least one flexible financial account and an iterative and circular process. Firms rely on financial flexibility—financial assets, financial liabilities, equity capital, and dividends—that can expand or contract with the firm's supply and demand for capital. For example, a growth firm that requires capital may need to raise cash by issuing short-term or long-term debt or equity shares. A mature cash-cow firm may generate substantial amounts of excess cash and use it to pay down debt, pay dividends, or repurchase common shares. Therefore, you must identify what financial flexibility the firm has and how it will use it. Then you must adjust these flexible financial accounts as necessary to match the firm's future financial capital structure with the firm's future operations and investments. Thus, producing a set of financial statement forecasts will require several iterations and a degree of circularity. For example, your first pass through a set of financial statement forecasts may reveal that the firm must increase long-term debt to finance future capital expenditures. Increased long-term debt, however, will increase interest expense, which will cause net income to fall. As a consequence, retained earnings will fall, so the firm may have to increase long-term debt a bit more. You must repeat this process until the balance sheet balances and articulates with the income statement and the statement of cash flows.
- **Garbage in, garbage out.** The quality of your forecasts—and the quality of your investment decisions based on these forecasts—will depend on the quality of your forecast assumptions. You should thoughtfully justify each assumption, especially the most important assumptions that reflect the critical risk and success factors of the firm's strategy. In addition, you should reality check your assumptions by analyzing the forecasted financial statements using ratios and common-size and

rate-of-change financial statements (discussed in Chapters 1, 4, and 5). They may reveal that certain assumptions are unrealistic or inconsistent.

- **Sweat the big stuff, not the little stuff.** You should devote thoughtful time and effort to developing the most important forecast assumptions—those that reflect the critical business activities that will have the biggest impact on the firm's future growth, profitability, and risk. For most firms, forecasts of revenues, key operating expenses, major assets, and the debt-equity structure deserve a good amount of your thoughtful attention. However, some of the accounts in a set of financial statements are less critical to the risk or success of the business. As such, be efficient and make simple reasonable assumptions about these noncritical accounts, and avoid "analysis-paralysis."
- **Conduct sensitivity analysis on the financial statement forecasts.** Some assumptions have more significant consequences than others, and sensitivity analyses will help you assess the extent to which forecast results depend on key assumptions. You should test, for example, variation in earnings and cash flows across most likely, optimistic, and pessimistic sales growth scenarios.

The subsequent sections of this chapter apply the seven-step forecasting procedure to **Starbucks**. In this chapter we use **Starbucks'** financial statement data for 2013 through 2015 to develop forecast assumptions and to project financial statements for **Starbucks** for 2016 through 2020. We label them Year +1 through Year +5 to denote that they are forecasts of activities we expect to occur one through five years ahead.[2]

Using FSAP to Prepare Forecasted Financial Statements

FSAP, the financial statement analysis package introduced in Chapter 1, contains a Forecasts spreadsheet that you can use to prepare financial statement forecasts. The website for this text (www.cengagebrain.com) contains a blank FSAP template and the FSAP **Starbucks** file for easy download and use. If you have not previously designed an Excel spreadsheet to prepare financial statement forecasts, you should do so *before* using the Forecasts spreadsheet in FSAP. The proper design of a spreadsheet and the preparation of forecasted financial statements provide excellent learning experiences to enhance and solidify your understanding of the relations among various financial statement items. Once you become comfortable with using spreadsheets for forecasting financial statements, using the Forecasts spreadsheet in FSAP will save you time.

The Forecasts spreadsheet in FSAP is a general and adaptable template for forecasting financial statements. In addition, FSAP contains a Forecast Development spreadsheet that you can use to compute various detailed forecast assumptions. To demonstrate, we incorporate in FSAP the specific forecast assumptions we make for **Starbucks** in this chapter, including the Forecasts spreadsheet with explicit financial statement forecast assumptions through Year +5, and the Forecast Development spreadsheet with various supporting computations. FSAP also contains instructions and user guides.

All financial statement amounts throughout this chapter appear in millions. The spreadsheets take all computations to multiple decimal places. Because we express all amounts in millions, some minor rounding differences will arise and make it appear as though various totals disagree with the sum of the individual items that make up the total.

---

[2]Previous chapters also have analyzed data from the most recent three years to evaluate **Starbucks'** current profitability, risk, and accounting quality. In forecasting financial statements that extend five years or more into the future, it is often helpful to draw on a longer time series of historical data to evaluate a firm's long-term trends, particularly for mature and stable firms. For firms in the introduction or growth phase of the life cycle, or for firms that have recently experienced significant mergers or divestitures, a long time series of historical data may not be available or may not permit reliable comparisons with current period data.

Step 1: Project Revenues

The principal business activities of most firms involve generating revenues by selling products or delivering services. Analysts frequently use the expected future level of revenues as a basis for deriving many other amounts in the financial statement forecasts.[3] Therefore, analysts typically begin the forecasting process by projecting revenues.

Revenues are determined by sales volumes (quantities) and prices. Some firms report sales volumes (for example, automobile manufacturers report numbers of vehicles sold and beverage makers report gallons or cases sold), enabling you to assess volume and price separately as drivers of past revenues and predictors of future revenues. Some firms report volume-related measures that you can use to forecast revenues, such as the number of stores for retailers and restaurant chains or the number of passenger and revenue seat miles for airlines. When you perform the industry analysis in the first step of the financial statement analysis process, you will discover industrywide conditions that will influence your volume forecasts. For a stable firm in a mature industry, you might conclude that the firm will not significantly gain or lose market share, but that sales volume will grow with the population in the firm's geographic markets. For a firm that has increased its production capacity in an industry with high anticipated growth (for example, biotechnology or tablet computers), you can use the industry growth rate coupled with the expansion in the firm's capacity to project sales volume increases.

When projecting *prices*, which is difficult, you should consider factors specific to the firm and its industry that will affect demand and price elasticity, such as excess or constrained capacity, raw material surpluses or shortages, substitute products, and technological changes in products or production methods. Capital-intensive firms, such as manufacturers of paper products or computer chips, may require several years to add new capacity. If the firm competes in a capital-intensive industry that you expect will operate near capacity for the next few years, price increases will be more likely. By contrast, if the firm competes in a capital-intensive industry with excess capacity, price increases will be less likely. Further, capital-intensive firms in a competitive industry with excess capacity may face high exit barriers and thus may experience future price decreases. A firm with significant technological improvements in its production processes (for example, some portions of the computer industry or cell phone industry) might expect increases in sales volume but decreases in prices. If a firm has established a brand name or unique characteristics for its products, it may have a greater potential to maintain or increase prices than a competitor with generic products.

You also should consider economywide factors such as the expected rate of inflation and changes in foreign currency exchange rates. If the firm generates some of its revenues in a foreign currency that has appreciated relative to the currency used to prepare the firm's financial statements, the translation process will increase reported revenues due to the foreign exchange rate increase, thus leading to a higher revenue growth unrelated to volume or pricing increases. In addition, your revenue forecasts should also capture the effects of corporate transactions such as acquisitions and divestitures. Acquisitions typically increase revenues, whereas divestitures of subsidiaries usually reduce revenues.

---

[3]Revenue forecasts are particularly important because they have crucial impacts on the projected income statements, balance sheets, and cash flows. You should utilize as much relevant information as possible in developing reliable revenue forecast assumptions. You can often find useful information for forecasts in company disclosures, competitors' financial statements and disclosures, industry data, and regional- and country-specific economic data. This chapter seeks to illustrate the techniques of using such information in developing forecasts, while also being concise and efficient for you, the reader.

If revenues have grown at a reasonably steady rate in prior periods and you expect that economic, industry, and firm-specific factors will remain stable, you can project that the historical growth rate will persist into the future. Projecting revenues for a cyclical firm (for example, heavy machinery manufacturers, property-casualty insurers, and investment banks) involves an additional degree of difficulty because revenue growth rates often exhibit wide variations in both direction and amount over the business cycle. For such firms, you can project revenue growth rates that vary with the stages of the cycle, assuming you can correctly identify the firm's current point in the cycle and how quickly it will progress to the next stages.

It is challenging to project future revenues for firms that depend heavily on new products to generate growth (such as pharmaceutical firms conducting research to discover new drugs, technology firms developing new products, or oil and gas firms exploring for new reserves) because of the inherent uncertainty in the discovery and development process. In those cases, analysts often rely heavily on firms' disclosures about the research and development pipeline. In addition, analysts often seek help from scientists, doctors, or technology experts who can provide knowledgeable advice on the likelihood of the future success of the firm's research and product development efforts.

This discussion reinforces how forecasting depends heavily on the first four steps of the analysis process. Projecting a firm's future business activities, particularly revenues, relies on understanding the economic and competitive forces of the industry, the competitive strategy of the firm, the quality of the firm's accounting, and the drivers of the firm's profitability and risk.

Projecting Revenues for Starbucks

Earlier chapters indicated that the coffee shop industry is very mature and competitive. **Starbucks** has established a very strong niche in this industry as the world's largest chain of coffee shops. It has generated impressive revenue growth, with a compounded annual growth rate of 13.5% from 2013 to 2015.

In **Starbucks'** 2015 Annual Report, the MD&A section titled "Results of Operations" discloses information about revenues and operating profits for each of **Starbucks'** five operating segments. The largest revenue-generating segment is the Americas segment, which consists of company-operated and licensed stores in North America, South America, and Central America. The second-largest segment in terms of revenues is the China/Asia Pacific (CAP) segment, which consists of company-operated and licensed stores in Asia, especially China and Japan. The EMEA segment consists mainly of company-operated and licensed stores in Europe, the Middle East, and Africa. The fourth segment is Channel Development, which consists of sales of coffee beans and other products to grocery stores and foodservice distributors. **Starbucks** also groups other small business it controls into the fifth and smallest segment, the All Other segment. It primarily includes company-operated stores under the Teavana brand.

For each segment, **Starbucks** discloses revenues, operating expenses, and operating income. **Starbucks** also discloses overall revenue growth rates, revenue growth attributable to opening new stores, comparable store sales growth rates (arising from changes in transaction volume and prices), as well as effects of changes in foreign exchange rates and acquisitions and divestitures. The data for **Starbucks'** revenue drivers appear in Exhibit 10.2. These data reveal significant differences in the drivers of growth across the five segments. For example, the Americas segment generated 11% sales growth in 2015 primarily from company-operated stores and comparable store sales growth rates. The CAP segment experienced revenue growth of 112% in 2015, in large part due to

Exhibit 10.2			
Starbucks' Revenue Growth Analysis by Segment (dollar amounts in millions)			
Year	**2013**	**2014**	**2015**
Net Revenues (in millions)			
Company-operated stores	**$11,793.2**	**$12,977.9**	**$15,197.3**
Licensed stores	**1,360.5**	**1,588.6**	**1,861.9**
CPG, foodservice and other	**1,713.1**	**1,881.3**	**2,103.5**
Total Net Revenues	**$14,866.8**	**$16,447.8**	**$19,162.7**
Growth rates		10.6%	16.5%
Americas	**2013**	**2014**	**2015**
Net new stores opened during the year			
Company-operated	276	317	276
Licensed	404	381	336
Total	680	698	612
Total stores			
Company-operated	8,078	8,395	8,671
Licensed	5,415	5,796	6,132
Total	13,493	14,191	14,803
Revenues			
Company-operated	$ 10,038.3	$ 10,866.5	$ 11,925.6
Growth rates		8.3%	9.7%
Revenues per store/year	$ 1.264	$ 1.319	$ 1.398
Growth rates		4.4%	5.9%
Licensed	$ 915.4	$ 1,074.9	$ 1,334.4
Growth rates		17.4%	24.1%
Revenues per store/year	$ 0.176	$ 0.192	$ 0.224
Growth rates		9.2%	16.7%
CAP	**2013**	**2014**	**2015**
Net new stores opened during the year			
Company-operated	239	250	1,320
Licensed	349	492	(482)
Total	588	742	838
Total stores			
Company-operated	882	1,132	2,452
Licensed	3,000	3,492	3,010
Total	3,882	4,624	5,462

(Continued)

Exhibit 10.2 (Continued)

CAP	2013	2014	2015
Revenues			
Company-operated	$ 671.7	$ 859.4	$ 2,127.3
Growth rates		27.9%	147.5%
Revenues per store/year	$ 0.881	$ 0.853	$ 0.926
Growth rates		(3.1%)	8.5%
Licensed	$ 245.3	$ 270.2	$ 264.4
Growth rates		10.2%	(2.1%)
Revenues per store/year	$ 0.087	$ 0.083	$ 0.096
Growth rates		(4.1%)	15.6%

EMEA	2013	2014	2015
Net new stores opened during the year			
Company-operated	(29)	(9)	(80)
Licensed	129	180	302
Total	100	171	222
Total stores			
Company-operated	826	817	737
Licensed	1,143	1,323	1,625
Total	1,969	2,140	2,362
Revenues			
Company-operated	$ 932.8	$ 1,013.8	$ 911.2
Growth rates		8.7%	(10.1%)
Revenues per store/year	$ 1.110	$ 1.234	$ 1.173
Growth rates		11.2%	(5.0%)
Licensed	$ 190.3	$ 238.4	$ 257.2
Growth rates		25.3%	7.9%
Revenues per store/year	$ 0.176	$ 0.193	$ 0.174
Growth rates		9.6%	(9.8%)

Other Stores (including Teavana)	2013	2014	2015
Net new stores opened during the year			
Company-operated	343	12	6
Licensed	(10)	(24)	(1)
Total	333	(12)	5

(Continued)

Exhibit 10.2 (Continued)			
Other Stores (including Teavana)	**2013**	**2014**	**2015**
Other segment stores			
Company-operated	357	369	375
Licensed	66	42	41
Total	423	411	416
Other segment store revenues	$ 159.9	$ 243.3	$ 239.1
Growth rates		52.2%	(1.7%)
CPG, Foodservice, and Other	**2013**	**2014**	**2015**
Revenues	$ 1,713.1	$ 1,881.3	$ 2,103.5
Growth rates		9.8%	11.8%
Total Net Revenues	**$14,866.8**	**$16,447.8**	**$19,162.7**

Starbucks gaining ownership and control of 1,009 company-operated stores by acquiring **Starbucks** Japan. By contrast, the EMEA segment experienced a 6% decline in revenues during 2015, in part due to unfavorable foreign currency exchange rates and net closures of some company-operated stores.

In addition, in **Starbucks'** 2015 Annual Report, the MD&A section titled "Fiscal 2016—The View Ahead" discloses information from **Starbucks'** managers about their expectations. **Starbucks'** managers update those expectations with each quarterly earnings release and quarterly report during fiscal 2016. In these disclosures, **Starbucks** reveals it expects to open roughly 1,800 new stores during fiscal 2016. Of these new stores, **Starbucks** expects to open 700 new stores in the Americas, with roughly half of them being company operated and the other half being licensed stores. **Starbucks** also expects to open 900 new stores in the CAP segment, with roughly one-third being company operated and the other two-thirds being licensed stores. In the EMEA segment, **Starbucks** expects to open 200 net new stores, primarily licensed stores. **Starbucks** does not disclose any plans to open any stores in the All Other segment. **Starbucks** also discloses that it expects comparable store sales growth rates to be "somewhat above mid-single digits."

We analyze the drivers of revenue growth at the segment level by store type (company operated versus licensed) in order to develop more accurate forecasts for **Starbucks'** revenue growth in each segment. In addition, we will consider **Starbucks'** disclosures about expected future store openings and growth rates in 2016. These disclosures are worth considering because in the past **Starbucks** has provided reasonably accurate disclosures about its expected future activities. After we develop our forecast assumptions, we will then discuss and apply an adjustment to our forecast amount for fiscal 2016, which will contain 53 weeks rather than the normal 52 weeks.

Americas Revenue Growth

The Americas segment generates revenues from operating company stores and from licensed stores in the Western Hemisphere—North, South, and Central America. The data in Exhibit 10.2 reveal that company-operated store revenues in the Americas grew by 8.3% in 2014 and by 9.7% in 2015. **Starbucks** discloses that it achieved these growth rates through a combination of opening new stores and same-store sales growth. **Starbucks** opened 317 new company stores in the Americas in 2014 and 276 new stores in 2015. The average sales per store grew by 4.4% to $1.319 million in 2014, followed by an additional 5.9% growth, to $1.398 million, in 2015.

The data in Exhibit 10.2 also reveal that licensed-store revenues in the Americas grew by 17.4% in 2014 and by 24.1% in 2015. **Starbucks** discloses that it achieved these impressive growth rates through a combination of opening new stores and same-store sales growth. **Starbucks** opened 381 new licensed stores in the Americas in 2014 and 336 new licensed stores in 2015. The average revenues per licensed store grew by 9.2% to $0.192 million in 2014, followed by an additional 16.7% growth, to $0.224 million, in 2015. [Recall that **Starbucks**' licensed store revenues are much lower per licensed store compared to company-operated stores because they only consist of royalties and license fees, as well as product sales to licensees.]

In **Starbucks**' 2015 Annual Report, the MD&A section titled "Fiscal 2016—The View Ahead" and in subsequent quarterly reports during fiscal 2016, **Starbucks** discloses that it expects to open roughly 350 net new company-operated stores and roughly 350 net new licensed stores. In prior years, similar projections by **Starbucks** have turned out to be reasonably accurate. These projections are in line with **Starbucks**' recent store openings in the Americas, and the firm seems to have the financial capital and management competence to handle this level of growth. In our forecast assumptions, we will use these projections for new store openings in Year +1 (fiscal 2016). We will also assume that **Starbucks** will sustain the same level of new store openings in Year +2 through Year +5.

As noted earlier, in the 2015 Annual Report, **Starbucks** also discloses that it expects comparable store sales growth rates to be "somewhat above mid-single digits." For stores in the Americas segment, we project that average revenues for company-operated and licensed stores will therefore grow by 6% per year.

We compute future revenue amounts as the average number of stores open during the year times the average revenue per store. So for company-operated stores, **Starbucks** began Year +1 with 8,671 stores in the Americas. If it opens 350 stores during that year, the result will be 9,021 company-operated stores by year-end. If the new stores are open for roughly one-half of the year on average, then there will be roughly 8,846 store-years [(8,671 + 9,021)/2] generating revenues during Year +1. Average revenues per store in 2015 were $1.398 million. If store revenues grow by 6%, then the average store will generate revenues of $1.481 million [$1.398 million × 1.06] during Year +1. Therefore, we project that during Year +1 **Starbucks**' company-operated stores in the Americas segment will generate total revenues amounting to $13,104.8 million [8,846 store-years × $1.481 million average revenues per store-year]. We use similar computations to project revenue amounts for Years +2 to +5.

For licensed stores, **Starbucks** began Year +1 with 6,132 stores in the Americas. If it opens 350 stores during that year, the result will be 6,482 licensed stores by year-end. If the new stores are open for roughly one-half of the year on average, then there will be roughly 6,307 store-years [(6,132 + 6,482)/2] generating revenues during Year +1. Average revenues per store in 2015 were $0.224 million. If licensed store revenues grow by 6%, then the average store will generate revenues of $0.237 million [$0.224 million × 1.06] during Year +1. Therefore, total revenues generated during Year +1 among licensed stores in the Americas segment will be $1,495.8 million [6,307 store-years × $0.237 million average revenues per store-year]. We use similar computations to project revenue amounts for Years +2 to +5.

The revenue projections and growth rates for **Starbucks'** Americas segment over the five-year forecast horizon are as follows (allow for rounding):

Americas	Actuals 2015	Year +1	Year +2	Year +3	Year +4	Year +5
Net new stores during the year						
Company-operated	276	350	350	350	350	350
Licensed	336	350	350	350	350	350
Total	612	700	700	700	700	700
Total stores						
Company-operated	8,671	9,021	9,371	9,721	10,071	10,421
Licensed	6,132	6,482	6,832	7,182	7,532	7,882
Total	14,803	15,503	16,203	16,903	17,603	18,303
Revenues						
Company-operated	$11,925.6	$13,104.8	$14,440.7	$15,889.8	$17,460.7	$19,162.9
Revenues per store/year	$ 1.398	$ 1.481	$ 1.570	$ 1.665	$ 1.764	$ 1.870
Projected growth rates		6.0%	6.0%	6.0%	6.0%	6.0%
Licensed	$ 1,334.4	$ 1,495.8	$ 1,673.5	$ 1,867.2	$ 2,078.1	$ 2,307.6
Revenues per store/year	$ 0.224	$ 0.237	$ 0.251	$ 0.266	$ 0.282	$ 0.299
Projected growth rates		6.0%	6.0%	6.0%	6.0%	6.0%

China/Asia Pacific (CAP) Segment Revenue Growth

The CAP segment generates revenues from company-operated stores and from licensed stores in China, Japan, Korea, and other Asia-Pacific countries. The data in Exhibit 10.2 reveal that company-operated store revenues in the CAP segment grew by 27.9% in 2014 and by 147.5% in 2015. **Starbucks** discloses that it achieved these growth rates through a combination of opening new stores, same-store sales growth, and acquisition. In particular, **Starbucks** acquired 1,009 company-operated stores in Japan by acquiring 100% ownership of a former joint venture partner, **Starbucks** Japan. These stores in Japan had been reported as licensed stores before the acquisition and are company-operated stores after the acquisition. In addition, **Starbucks** also discloses that it opened 250 new company stores in the CAP segment in 2014 and 311 new stores in 2015. The average sales per store fell by 3.1% to $0.853 million in 2014, followed by 8.5% growth, to $0.926 million in 2015.[4]

The data in Exhibit 10.2 also reveal that licensed store revenues in the CAP segment grew by 10.2% in 2014 and then fell by 2.1% in 2015. **Starbucks** opened 492 new licensed stores in 2014 and 527 new licensed stores in 2015 (not including the 1,009 stores in Japan that transitioned from licensed to company operated). The average revenues per licensed store fell by 4.1% to $0.083 million in 2014, and then grew by 15.6%, to $0.096 million in 2015.

In **Starbucks'** 2015 Annual Report, the MD&A section titled "Fiscal 2016—The View Ahead," and in subsequent quarterly reports during fiscal 2016, **Starbucks** discloses that it expects to open roughly 300 net new company-operated stores and roughly 600 net new licensed stores in the CAP segment. These projections are in line with **Starbucks'** recent store openings in the CAP region, and the firm seems to have the financial capital and management competence to handle this level of growth. In our forecast

[4]To compute average store sales in 2015, we include all 1,009 stores acquired from **Starbucks** Japan for the entire year because the acquisition occurred in the early part of the year.

assumptions, we will use these projections for new store openings in Year +1 (fiscal 2016). We will also assume that **Starbucks** will sustain the same level of new store openings in Year +2 through Year +5.

As noted earlier, in the 2015 Annual Report, **Starbucks** also discloses that it expects comparable store sales growth rates to be "somewhat above mid-single digits." For stores in the CAP segment, which is **Starbucks'** fastest-growing segment, we project that average revenues for company-operated and licensed stores will grow by 7% per year.

We again compute future revenue amounts as the average number of stores open during the year times the average revenue per store. So for company-operated stores in the CAP segment, **Starbucks** began Year +1 with 2,452 stores. If it opens 300 stores during that year, the result will be 2,752 company-operated stores by year-end. If the new stores are open for roughly one-half of the year on average, then there will be roughly 2,602 store-years [(2,452 + 2,752)/2] generating revenues during Year +1. Average revenues per store in 2015 were $0.926 million. If store revenues grow by 7%, then the average store will generate revenues of $0.991 million [$0.926 million × 1.07] during Year +1. Therefore, total revenues generated during Year +1 among company-operated stores in the CAP segment will be $2,579.0 million [2,602 store-years × $0.991 million average revenues per store-year]. We use similar computations to project revenue amounts for Years +2 to +5.

For licensed stores, **Starbucks** began Year +1 with 3,010 stores in the CAP segment. If it opens 600 stores during that year, the result will be 3,610 licensed stores by year-end. If the new stores are open for roughly one-half of the year on average, then there will be roughly 3,310 store-years [(3,010 + 3,610)/2] generating revenues during Year +1. Average revenues per store in 2015 were $0.096 million. If licensed store revenues grow by 7%, then the average store will generate revenues of $0.103 million [$0.096 million × 1.07] during Year +1. Therefore, total revenues generated during Year +1 among licensed stores in the CAP segment will be $341.0 million [3,310 store-years × $0.103 million average revenues per store-year]. We use similar computations to project revenue amounts for Years +2 to +5.

The revenue projections and growth rates for **Starbucks'** CAP segment over the five-year forecast horizon are as follows (allow for rounding):

	Actuals	Projections				
CAP	2015	Year +1	Year +2	Year +3	Year +4	Year +5
Net new stores during the year						
Company-operated	276	300	300	300	300	300
Licensed	336	600	600	600	600	600
Total	612	900	900	900	900	900
Total stores						
Company-operated	2,452	2,752	3,052	3,352	3,652	3,952
Licensed	3,010	3,610	4,210	4,810	5,410	6,010
Total	5,462	6,362	7,262	8,162	9,062	9,962
Revenues						
Company-operated	$2,127.3	$2,579.0	$3,077.7	$3,633.6	$4,252.2	$4,939.6
Revenues per store/year	$ 0.926	$ 0.991	$ 1.061	$ 1.135	$ 1.214	$ 1.299
Projected growth rates		7.0%	7.0%	7.0%	7.0%	7.0%
Licensed	$ 264.4	$ 341.0	$ 430.9	$ 531.9	$ 644.8	$ 771.0
Revenues per store/year	$ 0.096	$ 0.103	$ 0.110	$ 0.118	$ 0.126	$ 0.135
Projected growth rates		7.0%	7.0%	7.0%	7.0%	7.0%

Europe, Middle East, and Africa (EMEA) Revenue Growth

The EMEA segment generates revenues from company-operated stores and from licensed stores in countries in Europe, the Middle East, and Africa, including the United Kingdom, Turkey, the UAE, Russia, and many others. The data in Exhibit 10.2 reveal that company-operated store revenues in the EMEA segment grew by 8.7% in 2014 but fell by 10.1% in 2015. The average sales per company-operated store in EMEA grew by 11.2% to $1.234 million in 2014, but then fell by 5.0% to $1.173 million in 2015. During 2014, **Starbucks** closed a net 9 stores, and then it closed another net 80 stores in 2015.

The data in Exhibit 10.2 also reveal that licensed-store revenues in the EMEA segment grew by 25.3% in 2014 and then grew by an additional 7.9% in 2015. **Starbucks** opened 180 new licensed stores in 2014 and 302 new licensed stores in 2015. The average revenues per licensed store grew by 9.6% to $0.193 million in 2014, but then fell by 9.8% to $0.174 million in 2015.

In the 2015 Annual Report, **Starbucks** discloses that it expects to open roughly 200 net new licensed stores in the EMEA segment. In our forecast assumptions, we will project no new company-operated store openings but 200 new licensed stores in EMEA during Year +1 (fiscal 2016). We will also assume that **Starbucks** will sustain the same level of new store openings in Year +2 through Year +5.

Comparable store revenue growth rates in the EMEA segment have been lagging **Starbucks'** growth in other segments for several years, so it seems unlikely that the mid-single-digits average growth rate (noted earlier) will apply to EMEA stores. For stores in the EMEA segment, which is **Starbucks'** slowest-growing segment, we project that average revenues will grow by only 2% per year.

We again compute future revenue amounts as the average number of stores open during the year times the average revenue per store. So for company-operated stores in the EMEA segment, with no new store openings, **Starbucks** will begin and end Year +1 with 737 stores. Average revenues per store in 2015 were $1.173 million. If store revenues grow by 2%, then the average store will generate revenues of $1.196 million [$1.173 million × 1.02] during Year +1. Therefore, total revenues generated by company-operated stores in the EMEA segment during Year +1 will be $881.6 million [737 store-years × $1.196 million average revenues per store-year]. We use similar computations to project revenue amounts for Years +2 to +5.[5]

For licensed stores, **Starbucks** began Year +1 with 1,625 stores in the EMEA segment. If it opens 200 stores during that year, the result will be 1,825 licensed stores by year-end. If the new stores are open for roughly one-half of the year on average, then there will be roughly 1,725 store-years [(1,625 + 1,825)/2] generating revenues during Year +1. Average revenues per store in 2015 were $0.174 million. If licensed store revenues grow by 2%, then the average store will generate revenues of $0.178 million [$0.174 million × 1.02] during Year +1. Therefore, total revenues generated by licensed stores in the EMEA segment during Year +1 will be $307.0 million [1,725 store-years × $0.178 million average revenues per store-year]. We use similar computations to project revenue amounts for Years +2 to +5.

[5]Note that the projected revenue in EMEA for company-operated stores in Year +1 is $881.6 million, which is less than the prior year (2015) revenue of $911.2 million, even though we projected a 2% growth in average store revenues. The projected decline in total revenues results from the fact that in 2015, **Starbucks** generated at least partial-year revenues from the 80 stores it closed. During Year +1, we project no revenues from those closed stores.

The revenue projections and growth rates for **Starbucks'** EMEA segment over the five-year forecast horizon are as follows (allow for rounding):

EMEA	Actuals 2015	Projections Year +1	Year +2	Year +3	Year +4	Year +5
Net new stores during the year						
Company-operated	(80)	0	0	0	0	0
Licensed	302	200	200	200	200	200
Total	222	200	200	200	200	200
Total stores						
Company-operated	737	737	737	737	737	737
Licensed	1,625	1,825	2,025	2,225	2,425	2,625
Total	2,362	2,562	2,762	2,962	3,162	3,362
Revenues						
Company-operated	$911.2	$881.6	$899.2	$917.2	$935.5	$954.2
Revenues per store/year	$1.173	$1.196	$1.220	$1.244	$1.269	$1.295
Projected growth rates		2.0%	2.0%	2.0%	2.0%	2.0%
Licensed	$257.2	$307.0	$349.5	$393.5	$439.1	$486.4
Revenues per store/year	$0.174	$0.178	$0.182	$0.185	$0.189	$0.193
Projected growth rates		2.0%	2.0%	2.0%	2.0%	2.0%

Other Stores Segment Revenue Growth

The Other Stores segment primarily includes company-operated stores operating under the Teavana and Seattle's Best Coffee brands, as well as other businesses. The data in Exhibit 10.2 reveal that revenues in the Other Stores segment grew by 52.2% in 2014 but fell by 1.7% in 2015. Total revenues in the Other Stores segment amounted to $239.1 million in fiscal 2015. During 2014, **Starbucks** opened only 12 stores, and then it opened another 6 stores in 2015, to reach a total of 375 company-operated stores. The Other Stores segment also includes 41 licensed stores as of the end of 2015, and it has been closing licensed stores over the past couple of years.

In **Starbucks'** 2015 Annual Report, it does not disclose plans to open new stores in the Other Stores segment. In our forecast assumptions, we will simply project no new store openings in the Other Stores segment during Year +1 through Year +5. We will also simply project revenues in this segment will grow by only 3% per year.

The revenue projections and growth rates for **Starbucks'** Other Stores segment over the five-year forecast horizon are as follows (allow for rounding):

Other Stores (including Teavana)	Actuals 2015	Projections Year +1	Year +2	Year +3	Year +4	Year +5
Total stores						
Company-operated	375	375	375	375	375	375
Licensed	41	41	41	41	41	41
Total	416	416	416	416	416	416
Revenues	$239.1	$246.3	$253.7	$261.3	$269.1	$277.2
Projected growth rates		3.0%	3.0%	3.0%	3.0%	3.0%

CPG, Foodservice, and Other Segment Revenue Growth

Starbucks' CPG, Foodservice, and Other segment produces and sells various products through different channels. The CPG (Consumer Packaged Goods) business generates domestic and international sales of packaged coffee and tea, ready-to-drink beverages, and single-serve coffee and tea products through grocery stores, warehouse clubs, and specialty retailers. If you purchase a bag of Starbucks' coffee beans from your local grocery store, that store may have purchased them from Starbucks' CPG business. The Foodservice business sells coffee beans, tea, and related products to institutional food-service companies. If you had a cup of Starbucks' coffee in a cafeteria, in a restaurant, or on a flight, it is likely that coffee was originally produced and sold by Starbucks' Foodservice business.

The data in Exhibit 10.2 reveal that revenues in the CPG, Foodservice, and Other segment have been growing steadily, by 9.8% in 2014 and by 11.8% in 2015. Total revenues in the CPG, Foodservice, and Other segment amounted to $2,103.5 million in fiscal 2015.[6]

In the 2015 Annual Report, Starbucks does not disclose specific growth expectations for this segment. In our forecast assumptions, we will simply project that it will sustain roughly 10% growth in revenues per year during Year +1 through Year +5, consistent with recent performance. The revenue projections and growth rates for Starbucks' CPG, Foodservice, and Other segment over the five-year forecast horizon are as follows (allow for rounding):

	Actuals	Projections				
CPG, Foodservice, and Other	2015	Year +1	Year +2	Year +3	Year +4	Year +5
Revenues	$2,103.5	$2,313.9	$2,545.2	$2,799.8	$3,079.7	$3,387.7
Projected growth rates		10.0%	10.0%	10.0%	10.0%	10.0%

Starbucks' Combined Revenue Growth Forecasts, Including the 53rd-Week Effect

The following table combines the revenue forecasts for each of Starbucks' five segments into the three revenue line-items Starbucks reports on its income statements: Company-Operated Stores; Licensed Stores; and CPG, Foodservice, and Other.

Starbucks uses an accounting convention in which each quarter normally consists of 13 weeks, and a fiscal year consists of 52 weeks. However, Starbucks also uses an accounting convention in having the last day of the fiscal year fall on the Sunday closest to September 30th. Together, that means that once every six or seven years, Starbucks has to add a 53rd week to its fiscal year, so the year-end falls close to September 30th. Our forecast Year +1 (fiscal 2016) will be the next time when Starbucks' fiscal year will be 53 weeks instead of only 52 weeks.

It is straightforward to incorporate the 53rd-week effect into our forecasts for Year +1. We simply need to multiply our revenue forecast amounts for that year by a factor of 53/52 (= 1.019). The following table presents the projected revenue amounts for each segment, Starbucks' total net revenues, and annual growth rates after including the 53rd-week effect, for each year through Year +5.

---

[6]In this total we include CPG, Foodservice, and Other revenues that Starbucks reports separately within the Americas, CAP, EMEA, and Other Stores segments.

Starbucks' Combined Revenue Forecasts

Company-Operated Stores	Actuals 2015	Projections Year +1	Year +2	Year +3	Year +4	Year +5
Americas	$11,925.6	$13,104.8	$14,440.7	$15,889.8	$17,460.7	$19,162.9
CAP	$ 2,127.3	$ 2,579.0	$ 3,077.7	$ 3,633.6	$ 4,252.2	$ 4,939.6
EMEA	$ 911.2	$ 881.6	$ 899.2	$ 917.2	$ 935.5	$ 954.2
Other Stores	$ 239.1	$ 246.3	$ 253.7	$ 261.3	$ 269.1	$ 277.2
Subtotals	$15,203.2	$16,811.7	$18,671.3	$20,701.8	$22,917.5	$25,334.0
The 53rd-week effect (53/52)		1.019				
Totals	$15,203.2	$17,135.0	$18,671.3	$20,701.8	$22,917.5	$25,334.0

Licensed Stores	2015	Year +1	Year +2	Year +3	Year +4	Year +5
Americas	$1,334.4	$1,495.8	$1,673.5	$1,867.2	$2,078.1	$2,307.6
CAP	$ 264.4	$ 341.0	$ 430.9	$ 531.9	$ 644.8	$ 771.0
EMEA	$ 257.2	$ 307.0	$ 349.5	$ 393.5	$ 439.1	$ 486.4
Subtotals	$1,856.0	$2,143.8	$2,454.0	$2,792.6	$3,162.1	$3,565.0
The 53rd-week effect (53/52)		1.019				
Totals	$1,856.0	$2,185.0	$2,454.0	$2,792.6	$3,162.1	$3,565.0

CPG, Foodservice, and Other	2015	Year +1	Year +2	Year +3	Year +4	Year +5
Revenues	$ 2,103.5	$ 2,313.9	$ 2,545.2	$ 2,799.8	$ 3,079.7	$ 3,387.7
The 53rd-week effect (53/52)		1.019				
Totals	$ 2,103.5	$ 2,358.3	$ 2,545.2	$ 2,799.8	$ 3,079.7	$ 3,387.7
Total Net Revenues	$19,162.7	$21,678.3	$23,670.5	$26,294.2	$29,159.4	$32,286.7

The Forecasts spreadsheet in FSAP gives you the opportunity to input specific forecast parameters (such as revenue growth rates) for Year +1 through Year +5, as well as general forecast parameters for Year +6 and beyond. For Years +1 through +5, we will enter the revenue growth rates and amounts shown above. The forecast parameters for Year +6 and beyond represent general forecast assumptions over the long-run horizon. We assume **Starbucks** will sustain a 3.0% nominal growth rate in revenue in Year +6 and beyond, consistent with the sum of the expected long-run growth rate in the economy plus the expected long-run inflation rate averaging 3.0% per year.[7]

You can use the Forecast Development spreadsheet in FSAP to develop detailed revenues forecasts, capturing the key drivers of the firm's growth. We have done that here by analyzing and forecasting **Starbucks'** revenue growth drivers separately for each segment and for each type of store, and then aggregating those forecasts into total revenue forecasts through Year +5. Appendix C illustrates how we used the forecast development spreadsheet to develop the revenue forecasts for **Starbucks**.

---

[7]It is not uncommon for analysts to expect that nominal long-run growth rates will average 3.0% in years following Year +5. However, the analyst interested in greater forecast accuracy may want to use longer forecast horizons (for example, 10 years) before adopting a single linear long-run growth rate.

LO 10-2b

Build forecasts of future balance sheets, income statements, and statements of cash flows by applying the seven-step forecasting framework to project: b. operating expenses.

Step 2: Project Operating Expenses

The procedure for projecting operating expenses depends on the degree to which they have fixed or variable components. If certain operating expenses vary directly with sales, you can project these future operating expenses by either multiplying projected sales by the appropriate common-size percentage or by projecting those operating expenses to grow at the same rate as sales.

Some operating expenses reflect cost structures that will not change linearly with sales. For example, the firm may experience economies of scale as sales increase or may face expenses that remain relatively fixed even if sales decrease. In cases like those, using the common-size income statement approach will project operating expenses that are too high or too low.

Some operating expenses have both a fixed component and a portion that varies with sales. For example, a firm's selling, general, and administrative expenses often include fixed components for items such as salaries, rent, insurance, and other corporate overhead expenses but variable components that vary directly with sales, such as sales commissions. A possible clue for the existence of fixed costs can be found in the ratio of the percentage change in an expense relative to the percentage change in sales. Changes in this ratio over time may be due to the existence of fixed costs.

When sales grow at faster rates than costs of goods sold or selling, general, and administrative expenses, it often indicates the presence of fixed costs. You can estimate the variable cost component as a percentage of sales by dividing the amount of the change in the expense by the amount of the change in sales for the same period. You can then multiply sales by the variable-cost percentage to estimate the variable cost component. Subtracting the variable cost component from the total expense yields an estimate of the fixed cost for that particular operating expense. For example, suppose sales grow from $10 million to $12 million, while costs of sales grow from $7 million to $8 million. The $1 million increase in costs of sales divided by the $2 million increase in sales implies that variable costs are roughly 50% of sales. If so, it also implies that fixed costs amount to $2 million per year. In the current year, for example, costs of sales are comprised of $6 million in variable costs ($12 million $\times$ 50%) plus $2 million in fixed costs. Using this approach, you can then project a particular future expense with a fixed component and a component that varies with sales.[8]

When projecting operating expenses as a percentage of sales, you should keep in mind that an expense as a percentage of sales can change over time:

- *Expenses can change, even if sales remain constant.* For example, you may expect an expense to decrease relative to sales over time if the firm will drive down costs by creating operating efficiencies or new production technologies. Alternately, you might expect an expense to increase relative to sales if the firm will face increasing input costs that it cannot pass along to customers by raising prices.
- *Sales can change, even if expenses remain constant.* For example, you may expect that the firm will hold expenses (such as cost of goods sold) relatively steady but will face increased competition for market share and therefore may be forced to lower sales prices, causing the expected expense-to-sales ratio to increase. Alternately, you might expect that sales will increase, but because of fixed costs in the production process, expenses will remain fairly steady.

---

[8]Sometimes more advanced approaches may be necessary, such as using regression analysis to estimate fixed versus variable components of expenses. For example, you might use time-series data to estimate the relation, $COGS = \alpha + \beta \times Sales + \varepsilon$. The intercept, α, is an estimate of the fixed costs, and the variable cost proportion would be reflected by the slope coefficient, β.

- *Sales and expenses can change simultaneously and in the same direction.* If you expect both sales and operating expenses to increase (or decrease) simultaneously, the net result on the projected expense-to-sales percentage will depend on which of the two effects is proportionally greater.
- *Sales and expenses can change simultaneously but in opposite directions.* You might expect sales to increase while operating expenses decrease, which can occur for a firm in transition from the start-up phase to the growth phase of its life cycle. Or you might expect sales will decrease while operating expenses increase, as might occur for a firm in distress. The net result on the projected expense-to-sales percentage will depend on the relative magnitudes of the two effects.

In projecting the future relations between revenues and expenses, it is essential to evaluate the firm's strategies with respect to future growth, shifts in product/portfolio mix, the mix of fixed and variable expenses, competitive pressure on pricing, and many other factors that will impact expected future revenues and expenses.

Projecting Cost of Sales Including Occupancy Costs

Cost of sales and occupancy costs are the largest expenses on **Starbucks'** income statement. These expenses represent the costs of coffee beans and other products that **Starbucks** sells, as well as the occupancy costs (primarily rent) on company-operated stores. As such, these expenses represent a good example of expenses that contain fixed and variable components, as discussed in the preceding section. The rent component is largely fixed for a given company-operated store. The total amount of rent expense grows as **Starbucks** opens new company-operated stores. By contrast, the cost of sales component is likely to be more variable, varying with the amount of sales. We will therefore forecast each of the two components separately to capture the effects of these different drivers, and then we will combine them into the projected total amounts of cost of sales and occupancy costs.

The common-size income statement data discussed in Chapters 1 and 4 (and presented in the Analysis spreadsheet of FSAP) indicate that **Starbucks'** cost of goods sold as a percent of sales has steadily decreased from 42.9% in 2013 to 40.6% in 2015. However, the occupancy cost component has not been decreasing because **Starbucks** has been opening new company-operated stores. **Starbucks** discloses the total amount of annual rent expenses in Note 10, "Leases" (Appendix A). In 2015, for example, **Starbucks** incurred $1,137.8 million in rent expense, up considerably from $974.2 million in 2014. **Starbucks** had 11,474 company-operated stores on average during 2015 [(10,713 stores at the beginning of 2015 + 12,235 stores at the end of 2015)/2]. Therefore, **Starbucks** incurred $0.099 million in rent expense per average store during 2015.

We will project that **Starbucks'** average rent expense per store will increase by 3% due to general inflation in Year +1, so the average rent expense will be $0.102 million. In our revenue forecasts, we projected that **Starbucks** will have 12,885 company-operated stores by the end of Year +1. Thus, **Starbucks** will operate an average of 12,560 stores during Year +1 [(12,235 stores at the beginning + 12,885 stores at the end)/2]. Therefore, we project **Starbucks** will incur a total of $1,282.9 million in rent expense during Year +1 [$0.102 million in rent expense per average store × 12,560 store-years]. We use similar computations to project rent expense amounts for Years +2 through +5.

Starbucks' cost of sales (net of the rent expense component) as a percentage of total revenues has been decreasing steadily, from 36.9% in 2013, to 35.8% in 2014, to 34.7%

in 2015. Clearly, **Starbucks** generates cost efficiencies in its production processes. We project that **Starbucks** will continue to improve its performance and reduce the cost of sales in the future. We project that cost of sales (net of rent expense) as a percentage of total revenues will continue to decline to 34.0% in Year +1, and then continue to decline gradually in Years +2 through +5. Therefore, in Year +1, we project **Starbucks'** cost of sales will total $7,370.6 million [$21,678.3 million × 34.0%].

Combining the two components, we project **Starbucks'** Year +1 cost of sales and occupancy costs will total $8,653.5 million [$1,282.9 million in rent expense + $7,370.6 million in cost of sales]. The cost of sales and occupancy cost forecasts through Year +5 are as follows:

	2013	2014	2015	Year +1	Year +2	Year +3	Year +4	Year +5
Cost of sales and occupancy costs	$6,382.3	$6,858.8	$7,787.5	$8,653.5	$9,390.4	$10,336.7	$11,358.7	$12,461.9
As a percent of total revenues	42.9%	41.7%	40.6%	39.9%	39.7%	39.3%	39.0%	38.6%
Rent expense (Note 10: Leases)	$ 894.7	$ 974.2	$1,137.8	$1,282.9	$1,389.7	$ 1,501.8	$ 1,619.4	$ 1,742.8
Number of company-operated stores at fiscal year-end	10,143	10,713	12,235	12,885	13,535	14,185	14,835	15,485
Average number of company-operated stores		10,428	11,474	12,560	13,210	13,860	14,510	15,160
Average annual rent per company-operated store		$ 0.093	$ 0.099	$ 0.102	$ 0.105	$ 0.108	$ 0.112	$ 0.115
Expected inflation in annual rent				3.0%	3.0%	3.0%	3.0%	3.0%
Cost of sales (net of rent expense)	$5,487.6	$5,884.6	$6,649.7	$7,370.6	$8,000.6	$ 8,834.8	$ 9,739.2	$10,719.2
As a percent of total revenues	36.9%	35.8%	34.7%	34.0%	33.8%	33.6%	33.4%	33.2%

Projecting Store Operating Expenses and Other Operating Expenses

Starbucks' second-most-significant operating expense is store operating expenses, which primarily involve payroll and other costs to manage **Starbucks'** company-operated stores. These expenses tend to vary with the number of company-operated stores. In the MD&A section of the 2015 Annual Report, **Starbucks** even discloses these expenses expressed as a percentage of company-operated store revenues. Store operating expenses have been declining steadily as a percentage of company-operated store revenues, from 36.3% in 2013, to 35.7% in 2014, to 35.6% in 2015. We project that these expenses will continue to decline as a percentage of store-operated revenues, from 35.0% in Year +1 to 34.2% in Year +5.

Starbucks' other operating expenses involve payroll, marketing, and various other costs to manage the licensing, CPG, and foodservice businesses. These expenses seem to vary with the total revenues from licensing, CPG, and Foodservice. In 2014 and 2015, these expenses amounted to 13.2% of those revenues. We will project that other operating expenses will decline slightly to 13.0% of total revenues from licensing, CPG, and

Foodservice in Years +1 through +5. The projected store operating expenses and other operating expenses through Year +5 are as follows:

Store Operating Expenses and Other Operating Expenses	2015	Year +1	Year +2	Year +3	Year +4	Year +5
Company-operated store revenues	$15,203.2	$17,135.0	$18,671.3	$20,701.8	$22,917.5	$25,334.0
Store operating expenses	$ 5,411.1	$ 5,997.2	$ 6,497.6	$ 7,162.8	$ 7,883.6	$ 8,664.2
As a percent of company-operated store revenues	35.6%	35.0%	34.8%	34.6%	34.4%	34.2%
Licensing revenues	$ 1,856.0	$ 2,185.0	$ 2,454.0	$ 2,792.6	$ 3,162.1	$ 3,565.0
CPG, Foodservice, and Other revenues	$ 2,103.5	$ 2,358.3	$ 2,545.2	$ 2,799.8	$ 3,079.7	$ 3,387.7
Totals	$ 3,959.5	$ 4,543.4	$ 4,999.2	$ 5,592.4	$ 6,241.8	$ 6,952.7
Other operating expenses	$ 522.4	$ 590.6	$ 649.9	$ 727.0	$ 811.4	$ 903.9
As a percent of associated revenues	13.2%	13.0%	13.0%	13.0%	13.0%	13.0%

Projecting Property, Plant, and Equipment and Depreciation Expense

For a firm like **Starbucks**, with operating activities that are particularly dependent on property, plant, and equipment, you should create a separate schedule to forecast capital expenditures that lead projected future sales, and to forecast depreciation expense amounts that lag capital expenditures on property, plant, and equipment (PP&E).

In **Starbucks'** 2015 Annual Report, the MD&A section titled "Fiscal 2016—The View Ahead" discloses information about its expectations for the future.[9] In these disclosures, **Starbucks** states that it expects capital expenditures to be $1,400 million during fiscal 2016 (Year +1), primarily for new stores, store renovations, and other investments to support growth initiatives. This projected amount of capital expenditures is roughly 7.3% larger than capital expenditures in 2015, which amounted to $1,303.7 million. In prior years, **Starbucks'** management forecasts of capital expenditures have proven to be reliable, so we will use the projected $1,400 million for our Year +1 forecast.

In Years +2 through +5, we will assume **Starbucks'** capital expenditures will increase considerably. In developing our revenue forecasts, we projected that **Starbucks** will continue to open roughly the same number of new company-operated stores, so capital expenditures for new stores will likely remain fairly stable, growing with inflation. However, we believe **Starbucks** will have to increase capital spending for renovations and replacement of PP&E that is approaching the end of its useful life. At the end of fiscal 2015, **Starbucks** has 12,235 company-operated stores, but roughly 75% of those stores are at least five years old (some much older than that). Indeed, nearly 60% of **Starbucks'** existing PP&E has already been depreciated. Therefore, we project that **Starbucks** will incur capital expenditures of $1,500 million in Year +2; $1,800 million in Year +3; $2,100 million in Year +4; and $2,400 million in Year +5. We will add these capital expenditures to the PP&E totals on the projected balance sheets each year, and

---

[9]**Starbucks'** managers also update those expectations with quarterly reports during fiscal 2016.

subtract these amounts of cash outflows in the investing section of the projected statements of cash flows each year.

For the income statement projections, we need to forecast depreciation expense each year. Starbucks' existing PP&E will continue to depreciate as it uses these assets in daily operations. In addition, Starbucks' capital expenditures on new PP&E will trigger a new layer of depreciation expense each year. Starbucks discloses in Note 1, "Summary of Significant Accounting Policies" (Appendix A), that it uses the straight-line depreciation method over the estimated useful lives of the assets. Note 1 does not disclose information related to salvage values, but we can assume that Starbucks depreciates PP&E to zero salvage value. Based on this assumption, we estimate the average useful life that Starbucks uses for depreciation by taking the average amount in PP&E at acquisition cost and dividing it by depreciation expense for that year. Starbucks discloses the gross amounts of PP&E at cost in Note 7, "Supplemental Balance Sheet Information." In fiscal 2015, for depreciation purposes Starbucks used an average useful life of 10.3 years {[($9,641.8 + $8,581.1)/2]/$883.8}. For simplicity, we will assume that Starbucks will use a 10-year average useful life for depreciation.

In computing depreciation expense for Year +1, we need to forecast two components. The first component is depreciation on the $9,641.8 million of existing PP&E as of the beginning of Year +1, which will be $964.2 million ($9,641.8/10.0 years). The second component is depreciation on the Year +1 capital expenditures of $1,400 million, which will be $140 million ($1,400/10.0 years). Together, total depreciation expense in Year +1 will be $1,104.2 million ($964.2 + $140.0), and accumulated depreciation (the PP&E contra account on the balance sheet) will grow by this amount of depreciation. In Year +2, depreciation expense will be $1,254.2 million, which consists of those two components plus a third component to reflect depreciation expense of $150.0 million ($1,500.0/10.0 years) on Year + 2 capital expenditures on PP&E, and so on. The projected amounts for capital expenditures and depreciation expense through Year +5 are as follows:

Capital Expenditures and Depreciation Expense Forecasts

	2015	Year +1	Year +2	Year +3	Year +4	Year +5
Capital expenditures	$1,303.7	$1,400.0	$1,500.0	$1,800.0	$2,100.0	$2,400.0
Depreciation Expense Forecast Development		Depreciation expense forecast on existing PP&E				
Existing PP&E at cost	$9,641.8	$964.2	$964.2	$964.2	$964.2	$231.6
Remaining balance to be depreciated	$4,088.3	$3,124.1	$2,159.9	$1,195.8	$231.6	$0.0
Depreciation on New PP&E		Depreciation expense forecasts on new PP&E				
Capital expenditures Year +1	$1,400.0	$140.0	$140.0	$140.0	$140.0	$140.0
Capital expenditures Year +2	$1,500.0		$150.0	$150.0	$150.0	$150.0
Capital expenditures Year +3	$1,800.0			$180.0	$180.0	$180.0
Capital expenditures Year +4	$2,100.0				$210.0	$210.0
Capital expenditures Year +5	$2,400.0					$240.0
Total depreciation expense		**$1,104.2**	**$1,254.2**	**$1,434.2**	**$1,644.2**	**$1,151.6**
Portion Reported Separately on Income Statement (95% of total)		$1,049.0	$1,191.5	$1,362.5	$1,562.0	$1,094.0
Portion Reported within Cost of Sales on Income Statement (5% of total)		$55.2	$62.7	$71.7	$82.2	$57.6

Starbucks reports depreciation expense as a separate line item on the income statement, but it allocates a portion of depreciation expense to cost of sales, for depreciation on assets used in production and distribution of products. In 2015, for example, Starbucks added $933.8 million in depreciation and amortization expense back to net income on the statement of cash flows, but it reported only $893.9 million of depreciation and amortization expense on the income statement, which is roughly 95% of the total. The remaining 5% of the depreciation expense was included in cost of sales and occupancy costs. Therefore, in our income statement projections, we include 95% of the projected depreciation expense amounts as a separate line item for depreciation and amortization expense, and we implicitly assume the remaining 5% is included in our projections of cost of sales and occupancy. However, we do add the entire amount of depreciation and amortization expense back to net income in our projected statement of cash flows, discussed in a later section of this chapter.

On our projected balance sheets, we add these projected amounts for capital expenditures and depreciation expenses to PP&E, and accumulated depreciation, as follows (allow for rounding):

Property, Plant and Equipment and Accumulated Depreciation Forecasts

PP&E at cost	2015	Year +1	Year +2	Year +3	Year +4	Year +5
Beginning balance at cost		$ 9,641.8	$11,041.8	$12,541.8	$ 14,341.8	$ 16,441.8
Add: CAPEX forecasts		1,400.0	1,500.0	1,800.0	2,100.0	2,400.0
Ending balance at cost	$ 9,641.8	$11,041.8	$12,541.8	$14,341.8	$ 16,441.8	$ 18,841.8
Accumulated depreciation						
Beginning balance		$ (5,553.5)	$ (6,657.7)	$ (7,911.9)	$ (9,346.0)	$(10,990.2)
Less: Depreciation expense forecasts		(1,104.2)	(1,254.2)	(1,434.2)	(1,644.2)	(1,151.6)
Ending balance	$(5,553.5)	$ (6,657.7)	$ (7,911.9)	$ (9,346.0)	$(10,990.2)	$(12,141.8)
PP&E—net	$ 4,088.3	$ 4,384.1	$ 4,629.9	$ 4,995.8	$ 5,451.6	$ 6,700.0

When you forecast fixed assets for capital-intensive firms (such as manufacturing firms or utility companies) or firms for which fixed-asset growth is a critical driver of future sales growth and earnings (for example, new stores for retail chains or restaurant chains), PP&E will typically be a large proportion of total assets and have a material impact on your forecasts. For such firms, you should invest considerable time and effort in developing detailed forecasts of capital expenditures, PP&E, and depreciation expense.[10] In FSAP, the Forecast Development spreadsheet includes a model for forecasting capital expenditures, PP&E, depreciation expense, and accumulated depreciation. The FSAP output (Appendix C) demonstrates the use of this model to compute the preceding forecasts for Starbucks.

Projecting General and Administrative Expenses

The common-size income statement data reveal that Starbucks' general and administrative expenses are a steady percentage of total revenues, varying in a narrow range

---

[10]Similarly, when you forecast firms that invest heavily in finite-lived intangible assets, you should devote time and effort in developing forecasts of intangible asset expenditures and amortization expense. For Starbucks in 2015, finite-lived intangible assets only amount to $302.5 million and trigger only $50.0 million in amortization expense, so for simplicity we will not develop separate forecast schedules for them. If you are interested in greater precision, that might be a worthwhile exercise.

from 6.3% of total revenues in 2013, to 6.0% in 2014, to 6.2% in 2015. Going forward, we project general and administrative expenses to be roughly 6.0% of total revenues in the future. The projected amounts through Year +5 are as follows:

	2015	Year +1	Year +2	Year +3	Year +4	Year +5
Total net revenues	$19,162.7	$21,678.3	$23,670.5	$26,294.2	$29,159.4	$32,286.7
General and administrative expenses	$ 1,196.7	$ 1,300.7	$ 1,420.2	$ 1,577.7	$ 1,749.6	$ 1,937.2
As a percent of total revenues	6.2%	6.0%	6.0%	6.0%	6.0%	6.0%

Projecting Income from Equity Investees

As Chapter 8 describes, some firms make substantial investments in affiliated companies or joint ventures that enable the investor company to exert significant influence but not control over the operating and financing decisions of the investee. In such cases, the investor might own 20% to 50% of the outstanding shares of the affiliate company but does not own enough of the shares to control the firm's activities, and therefore does not report the investment on a consolidated basis. Instead, under U.S. GAAP and IFRS, the investor company reports in income its proportionate share of the net income of the affiliate. On the balance sheet, equity investees (also called investments in noncontrolled affiliates) should increase with the firm's proportionate share of the net income of the affiliate, minus dividends received from the affiliate each period, plus or minus any additional investments or dispositions of investments in such affiliates.

To forecast future equity income from these types of equity investments, you can project a normal rate of return and the level of investment in equity affiliates. Alternately, a more time-consuming but potentially more accurate approach would be to prepare a full set of financial statement forecasts for the equity affiliates and estimate the investor's share of expected future income. This approach is worthwhile for firms that have very large and important investments in joint ventures and affiliated companies.

Starbucks includes income from equity investees in operating income. It likely makes this reporting choice because many of Starbucks' equity investments involve joint ventures or affiliated firms with operating activities that relate closely to Starbucks' operating activities. For example, prior to 2015, one of the joint ventures was Starbucks Japan, in which Starbucks owned a large but noncontrolling proportion (39.5%) of the shares of the firm that licensed and operated 1,009 Starbucks coffee shops in Japan. In fiscal 2015, Starbucks acquired 100% ownership of the firm, so its financial statements are now consolidated with Starbucks' financial statements, and Starbucks now reports the stores as company-operated stores. Starbucks discloses in Note 6, "Equity and Cost Investments," that at the end of fiscal 2015, equity method investments include roughly 50% ownership interests in joint ventures operating licensed stores in China, Korea, Taiwan, India, Spain, and others, as well as 50% ownership in The North American Coffee Partnership with PepsiCo.

Equity investments generate a substantial amount of operating income for Starbucks. In 2015, Starbucks included $249.9 million in income from equity investees in operating income. As it describes in Note 6, this amount includes Starbucks' proportionate share of the income (and losses) from these equity investees. In addition, Starbucks includes its share of gross profits from selling products to these equity investees, as well as license fees and royalties. Dividing the amount of income from equity investees by the average balance of the investments in equity investees reveals that Starbucks has generated returns in excess of 50% on these investments over the past three years. In 2015, for example, **Starbucks** generated a return of 57.7% ($249.9 million in income divided by an average investment balance of $433.5 million [($514.9 million at the beginning of the year + $352.0 million at the end)/2]. Going forward, we will assume **Starbucks** will continue to generate a 50% return on the average amount invested in equity investees each year. We will also assume that these investments will grow by roughly 5% per year over the five-year forecast horizon.[11] The projected investment amounts and income from equity investees are as follows (allow for rounding):

Investments in and Income from Equity Investees

Equity Investees	2015	Year +1	Year +2	Year +3	Year +4	Year +5
Beginning balance	$352.0	$369.6	$388.1	$407.5	$427.9	$449.3
Assume 5% growth		5.0%	5.0%	5.0%	5.0%	5.0%
Income from equity investees						
Average investment balance		$360.8	$378.8	$397.8	$417.7	$438.6
Projected rate of return		50.0%	50.0%	50.0%	50.0%	50.0%
Projected income		$180.4	$189.4	$198.9	$208.8	$219.3

Projecting Nonrecurring Income Items

As discussed in prior chapters, it is not uncommon for firms' reported income statements to include other nonrecurring gains or losses that are part of operations, unusual gains or losses that are peripheral to operations, and income from discontinued segments. For example, in the 2015 income statement, **Starbucks** recognized a $390.6 million gain resulting from an acquisition of a joint venture, as well as a $61.1 million loss on the early extinguishment of long-term debt. In fiscal 2013, **Starbucks** recognized a huge $2,784.1 million litigation charge for a legal settlement with Kraft.

As previous chapters discussed, you must determine whether items such as these are likely to persist in the future; if so, include them in the financial statement forecasts.[12] It is very difficult to predict specific future amounts of nonrecurring items for **Starbucks** because they seem to be infrequent and nonrecurring. Therefore, we will assume that **Starbucks** will not generate any nonrecurring gains or losses in income over our forecast horizon.

Projecting Operating Income

The revenue forecasts—together with the projected costs of sales and occupancy costs, store operating expenses, other operating expenses, depreciation and amortization expenses, general and administrative expenses, and income from equity investees,

---

[11]For the analyst who needs greater forecast precision, the projections of future balances in Equity Investments in Noncontrolled Affiliates should follow the accounting methods for equity method investments. As such, the balances should grow with the firm's proportionate share of the net income of the affiliate minus dividends received from the affiliate each period, and should increase with additional investments and decrease with dispositions of investments in such affiliates.

[12]By contrast, as Chapter 6 illustrates, **Starbucks** reports gift card breakage in roughly similar amounts in every year, which suggests that the portion of "interest and other income" that represents gift card breakage is likely recurring. Because these amounts are small relative to **Starbucks'** income, we simply include them in our forecasts of interest and other income and do not forecast them separately.

SG&A expenses, and amortization of intangible assets—lead to the following projected amounts of operating income for **Starbucks** for Years +1 through +5:

Operating Income Projections	2015	Year +1	Year +2	Year +3	Year +4	Year +5
Total net revenues	$19,162.7	$21,678.3	$23,670.5	$ 26,294.2	$ 29,159.4	$ 32,286.7
Cost of sales and occupancy	(7,787.5)	(8,653.5)	(9,390.4)	(10,336.7)	(11,358.7)	(12,461.9)
Store operating expenses	(5,411.1)	(5,997.2)	(6,497.6)	(7,162.8)	(7,883.6)	(8,664.2)
Other operating expenses	(522.4)	(590.6)	(649.9)	(727.0)	(811.4)	(903.9)
Depreciation expense	(893.9)	(1,049.0)	(1,191.5)	(1,362.5)	(1,562.0)	(1,094.0)
General and administrative expenses	(1,196.7)	(1,300.7)	(1,420.2)	(1,577.7)	(1,749.6)	(1,937.2)
Income from equity investees	249.9	180.4	189.4	198.9	208.8	219.3
Operating income	$ 3,601.0	$ 4,267.7	$ 4,710.4	$ 5,326.4	$ 6,002.9	$ 7,444.8
Operating income margin	18.8%	19.7%	19.9%	20.3%	20.6%	23.1%

Exhibit 10.3 presents the complete forecasts of **Starbucks'** income statements, as well as comprehensive income, for Years +1 through +5. The exhibit also presents forecast amounts for Year +6, assuming **Starbucks** will grow at a constant rate of 3%. The format of this exhibit mirrors the format of the Forecasts spreadsheet in FSAP. In later sections of this chapter, we discuss the projections of interest income, interest expense, income tax expense, net income, comprehensive income, and the change in retained earnings, after projecting **Starbucks'** balance sheet.

LO 10-2c

Build forecasts of future balance sheets, income statements, and statements of cash flows by applying the seven-step forecasting framework to project: c. operating assets and liabilities.

Step 3: Project Operating Assets and Liabilities on the Balance Sheet

In this section, we describe how the operating activities we projected for the income statement will give rise to future operating assets and liabilities on the balance sheet. We demonstrate how to forecast balance sheet amounts using various drivers of growth in different assets and liabilities.

Techniques to Project Operating Assets and Liabilities

To forecast individual operating assets and liabilities, you must first determine the underlying operating activities that drive them. For some types of assets, such as inventory and property, plant, and equipment, asset growth typically *leads* future sales growth. Growth for other types of assets, such as accounts receivable, typically *lags* sales growth. Certain operating liabilities will be determined by operating assets (such as accounts payable arising from inventory purchases), whereas others will be determined by operating expenses (such as accrued expenses).

After determining the business activities that drive future operating assets and liabilities, you can adopt a number of techniques to forecast the future balance sheet amounts. You might project certain types of assets and liabilities using a growth rate, such as the expected growth in sales, for assets and liabilities that vary with sales, such as future accounts receivable. For some types of assets and liabilities, you might project future growth rates based on past growth trends or expected shifts in

Exhibit 10.3

Starbucks
Actual and Forecasted Statements of Net Income and Comprehensive Income
(amounts in millions; allow for rounding)

Actual and forecasted amounts in bold; below the actual amounts (only) we report historical common-size and rate-of-change percentages. Below the forecast amounts (only) we report the forecast assumptions and brief explanations.

	Actuals			Forecasts					
	2013	2014	2015	Year +1	Year +2	Year +3	Year +4	Year +5	Year +6
INCOME STATEMENT									
Revenues	$14,866.8	$16,447.8	$19,162.7	$21,678.3	$23,670.5	$26,294.2	$29,159.4	$32,286.7	$33,255.3
common size	100.0%	100.0%	100.0%	13.1%	9.2%	11.1%	10.9%	10.7%	10.7%
rate of change		10.6%	16.5%	See Forecast Development worksheet for details of revenues forecasts.					
Cost of sales and occupancy									
expense	(6,382.3)	(6,858.8)	(7,787.5)	(8,653.5)	(9,390.4)	(10,336.7)	(11,358.7)	(12,461.9)	(12,835.8)
common size	(42.9%)	(41.7%)	(40.6%)	(39.9%)	(39.7%)	(39.3%)	(39.0%)	(38.6%)	(38.6%)
rate of change		7.5%	13.5%	See Forecast Development worksheet for details.					
Gross profit	$ 8,484.5	$ 9,589.0	$11,375.2	$13,024.9	$14,280.2	$15,957.5	$ 17,800.7	$ 19,824.8	$ 20,419.5
common size	57.1%	58.3%	59.4%	60.1%	60.3%	60.7%	61.0%	61.4%	61.4%
rate of change		13.0%	18.6%	14.5%	9.6%	11.7%	11.6%	11.4%	11.4%
Store operating expenses	(4,286.1)	(4,638.2)	(5,411.1)	(5,997.2)	(6,497.6)	(7,162.8)	(7,883.6)	(8,664.2)	(8,924.2)
common size	(28.8%)	(28.2%)	(28.2%)	(35.0%)	(34.8%)	(34.6%)	(34.4%)	(34.2%)	(34.2%)
rate of change		8.2%	16.7%	Assume store operating expenses decline as a percent of company-operated store revenues.					
Other operating expenses	(431.8)	(457.3)	(522.4)	(590.6)	(649.9)	(727.0)	(811.4)	(903.9)	(931.0)
common size	(2.9%)	(2.8%)	(2.7%)	(13.0%)	(13.0%)	(13.0%)	(13.0%)	(13.0%)	(13.0%)
rate of change		5.9%	14.2%	Assume steady state percentage of licensed, CPG, Foodservice, and other revenues.					
Depreciation and amortization	(621.4)	(709.6)	(893.9)	(1,049.0)	(1,191.5)	(1,362.5)	(1,562.0)	(1,094.0)	(1,126.8)
common size	(4.2%)	(4.3%)	(4.7%)	Amounts from depreciation schedule, Forecast Development worksheet.					
rate of change		14.2%	26.0%						
Gen. and admin. expenses	(937.9)	(991.3)	(1,196.7)	(1,300.7)	(1,420.2)	(1,577.7)	(1,749.6)	(1,937.2)	(1,995.3)
common size	(6.3%)	(6.0%)	(6.2%)	(6.0%)	(6.0%)	(6.0%)	(6.0%)	(6.0%)	(6.0%)
rate of change		5.7%	20.7%	Assume steady state relative to revenues.					
Income from equity investees	251.4	268.3	249.9	180.4	189.4	198.9	208.8	219.3	225.9
common size	1.7%	1.6%	1.3%	50.0%	50.0%	50.0%	50.0%	50.0%	50.0%
rate of change		6.7%	(6.9%)	Assume 50% rate of return from equity investees.					

(Continued)

Exhibit 10.3 (Continued)

	Actuals			Forecasts					
	2013	2014	2015	Year +1	Year +2	Year +3	Year +4	Year +5	Year +6
Nonrecurring operating gains losses	(2,784.1)	20.2	0.0	0.0	0.0	0.0	0.0	0.0	0.0
common size	(18.7%)	0.1%	0.0%	0.0%	0.0%	0.0%	0.0%	0.0%	
rate of change		(100.7%)	(100.0%)	Assume zero nonrecurring items.					
Operating profit	$ (325.4)	$ 3,081.1	$ 3,601.0	$ 4,267.7	$ 4,710.4	$ 5,326.4	$ 6,002.9	$ 7,444.8	$ 7,668.1
common size	(2.2%)	18.7%	18.8%	19.7%	19.9%	20.3%	20.6%	23.1%	23.1%
rate of change		(1,046.9%)	16.9%	18.5%	10.4%	13.1%	12.7%	24.0%	23.1%
Interest income	123.6	142.7	43.0	43.2	47.8	52.0	57.0	62.5	64.4
common size	0.8%	0.9%	0.2%	2.1%	2.1%	2.1%	2.1%	2.1%	2.1%
rate of change		15.5%	(69.9%)	Interest rate earned on average balance in cash and investment securities.					
Interest expense	(28.1)	(64.1)	(70.5)	(77.1)	(90.6)	(90.6)	(90.6)	(90.6)	(93.3)
common size	(0.2%)	(0.4%)	(0.4%)	(2.71%)	(2.71%)	(2.71%)	(2.71%)	(2.71%)	(2.71%)
rate of change		128.1%	10.0%	Weighted-average interest rate on average balances in long-term debt. See Forecast Development.					
Income before Tax	$ (229.9)	$ 3,159.7	$ 3,903.0	$ 4,233.8	$ 4,667.5	$ 5,287.8	$ 5,969.3	$ 7,416.6	$ 7,639.1
common size	(1.5%)	19.2%	20.4%	19.5%	19.7%	20.1%	20.5%	23.0%	23.0%
rate of change		(1474.4%)	23.5%	8.5%	10.2%	13.3%	12.9%	24.2%	23.0%
Income tax expense	238.7	(1,092.0)	(1,143.7)	(1,439.5)	(1,587.0)	(1,797.9)	(2,029.6)	(2,521.7)	(2,597.3)
common size	1.6%	(6.6%)	(6.0%)	(34.0%)	(34.0%)	(34.0%)	(34.0%)	(34.0%)	(34.0%)
rate of change		(557.5%)	4.7%	Effective income tax rate assumptions.					
Net income	$ 8.8	$ 2,067.7	$ 2,759.3	$ 2,794.3	$ 3,080.6	$ 3,490.0	$ 3,939.8	$ 4,895.0	$ 5,041.8
common size	0.1%	12.6%	14.4%	12.9%	13.0%	13.3%	13.5%	15.2%	15.2%
rate of change		23,396.6%	33.4%	1.3%	10.2%	13.3%	12.9%	24.2%	3.0%
Net income attributable to noncontrolling interests	(0.5)	0.4	(1.9)	0.0	0.0	0.0	0.0	0.0	0.0
common size	0.0%	0.0%	0.0%	0.0%	0.0%	0.0%	0.0%	0.0%	0.0%
rate of change		(180.0%)	(575.0%)	Assume noncontrolling interests are acquired.					
Net income attributable to common shareholders	$ 8.3	$ 2,068.1	$ 2,757.4	$ 2,794.3	$ 3,080.6	$ 3,490.0	$ 3,939.8	$ 4,895.0	$ 5,041.8
common size	0.1%	12.6%	14.4%	12.9%	13.0%	13.3%	13.5%	15.2%	15.2%
rate of change		24,816.9%	33.3%	1.3%	10.2%	13.3%	12.9%	24.2%	3.0%
Other comprehensive income items	43.8	(41.3)	(195.5)	0.0	0.0	0.0	0.0	0.0	0.0
common size	0.3%	(0.3%)	(1.0%)	0.0%	0.0%	0.0%	0.0%	0.0%	0.0%
rate of change		(194.3%)	373.4%	Assume random walk, mean zero.					
Comprehensive income	$ 52.6	$ 2,026.4	$ 2,563.8	$ 2,794.3	$ 3,080.6	$ 3,490.0	$ 3,939.8	$ 4,895.0	$ 5,041.8
common size	0.4%	12.3%	13.4%	12.9%	13.0%	13.3%	13.5%	15.2%	15.2%
rate of change		3,752.5%	26.5%	9.0%	10.2%	13.3%	12.9%	24.2%	3.0%

the firm's strategy. For example, perhaps the firm plans to hold larger amounts of cash than it has held in the past in order to increase its liquidity. In other cases, the firm may have a strategy of maintaining certain types of assets and liabilities at relatively steady proportions of total assets, in which case you might project future amounts using the expected future common-size percentages. This approach would work, for example, if the firm maintains a target percentage of total assets in cash. In some instances, asset and liability amounts can be projected based on large future transactions. For instance, if a firm is expected to borrow a large amount of cash in order to construct a new plant, you might project a large increase in cash after the borrowing and a large decrease following the investment.

You might choose to project future amounts for operating assets and liabilities, such as cash; accounts receivable; inventory; property, plant, and equipment; and accounts payable using the turnover rates demonstrated in Chapter 4. Using turnover rates produces reasonable forecasts of average and year-end account balances if the firm generates revenues evenly throughout the year and if the forecasted account varies reliably with revenues. However, you should not use a turnover-based forecast if the firm will experience substantially different future growth rates in revenues and the forecasted account, or if the turnover rate varies unpredictably over time.

A less desirable feature that can result from using a sales-turnover forecasting approach is that if the firm has exhibited volatility in historical amounts, it can trigger volatility in forecast amounts as well. To illustrate, suppose you expect that sales will remain constant at $12,167 per year over the next five years. Suppose also that you expect the firm will hold roughly 30 days of sales in cash and that it currently has a cash balance of $800. Using the cash turnover rate of 30 days' sales, you would project the firm will maintain an average cash balance of $1,000 ($12,167/365 $\times$ 30).

To compute the year-end cash balance from the average cash balance, you multiply the average by two and then subtract the beginning balance [Ending = (Average $\times$ 2) − Beginning]. Applying this approach, the projected year-end cash balances would be as follows:

	Annual Sales Forecasts	Average Sales per Day	Days' Sales in Cash	Average Cash Balance	Beginning Cash Balance	Ending Cash Balance
Year +1	$12,167	$33.33	30	$1,000	$ 800	$1,200
Year +2	$12,167	$33.33	30	$1,000	$1,200	$ 800
Year +3	$12,167	$33.33	30	$1,000	$ 800	$1,200
Year +4	$12,167	$33.33	30	$1,000	$1,200	$ 800
Year +5	$12,167	$33.33	30	$1,000	$ 800	$1,200

Notice that, because the firm held a smaller-than-average cash balance at the start of the forecast period ($800), the forecast of ending cash will have to compensate with a larger-than-average cash balance ($1,200) at the end of Year +1. The forecast model will then have to compensate again in Year +2 and project a smaller-than-average year-end balance ($800). The relatively small balance at the beginning of Year +1 triggers a relatively large balance at the end of Year +1, which in turn triggers a relatively small balance at the end of Year +2, and so on, creating a sawtooth pattern of variability.

For some firms, this type of variability is a realistic outcome of seasonal or cyclical volatility in the firm's operating activities. Forecasts that capture seasonality or cyclicality are preferable when you are concerned about whether a firm might violate certain contractual constraints, such as debt covenants or regulatory capital requirements. In other contexts, you may prefer smooth forecasts that mitigate variability. Smooth forecasts are often preferable in contexts where you expect random fluctuations around a generally smooth average growth trend over time. Smooth growth forecasts also tend to be easier to present and explain to an audience.

A number of techniques exist for you to produce smooth forecasts. One such technique is to project the ending balances to equal the projected average balances. In the example, one would simply assume that the projected ending balance in cash each year will equal the average balance ($1,000). Another forecast smoothing technique involves using turnover rates to project the ending balance in the forecast account at the end of the forecast horizon (say, Year +5). Then forecast the annual amounts in Year +1, +2, and so on, using the steady growth rate necessary to reach the projected ending amount in Year +5. Alternately, if you expect the ending balance will vary with sales, then you can simply project growth using the expected sales growth rates. In choosing among forecasting techniques, you must trade off the objectives of achieving minimizing forecast error while avoiding unnecessary computational complexity.

In the sections that follow, we project individual operating assets and liabilities for **Starbucks** using a combination of forecast drivers, including common-size percentages, growth rates, and asset turnovers. We proceed in roughly the order in which **Starbucks** presents its accounts on the balance sheet. Exhibit 10.4 provides a preview of the projected balance sheets for **Starbucks** for Year +1 through Year +5, which we developed using the Forecasts spreadsheet in FSAP. The exhibit also presents forecast amounts for Year +6, assuming **Starbucks** will grow at a constant rate of 3%.

Projecting Cash and Cash Equivalents

The Analysis spreadsheet in FSAP computes the average turnover of cash through revenues each year, so we use that turnover rate to project **Starbucks'** ending cash balances. Like all firms, **Starbucks** needs a certain amount of cash on hand for day-to-day liquidity.[13] During 2015, **Starbucks** had average cash balances of roughly 30.8 days of sales (computed as 365 days divided by the ratio of revenues to the average balance in cash; in 2015, 30.8 days = 365/{$19,162.7/[($1,530.1 + $1,708.4)/2]}. We assume that **Starbucks** will maintain ending cash balances equivalent to 30 days of sales in the future.

To apply this approach, we use our forecasts of revenues and the projected number of days' sales in cash to compute the ending balance in cash each year. The Year +1 revenue forecast is $21,678.3 million, or an average of $59.4 million per day.[14] We project **Starbucks** will hold 30 days of sales in cash at the end of Year +1, for a cash

---

[13]Our forecasts assume that **Starbucks** uses cash for day-to-day operating liquidity purposes, so we treat cash as an element of working capital. Some firms maintain excess cash balances far beyond what is needed for daily liquidity. For such firms, you should forecast two separate components: cash necessary for liquidity and excess cash. For these firms, you can then use the excess cash as the flexible financial account to balance the balance sheet.

[14]This computation assumes a 365-day year. For the analyst who needs greater precision, use 364 days in a 52-week fiscal year, 371 days in a 53-week fiscal year, and 366 days in a leap year. For simplicity, we use a 365-day year throughout this chapter.

Exhibit 10.4

Starbucks
Actual and Forecasted Balance Sheets
(amounts in millions; allow for rounding)

The actual and forecasted amounts are in bold. Below the actual amounts (only), we report historical common-size and rate-of-change-percentages. Below the forecast amounts (only), we report the forecast assumptions and brief explanations.

	Actuals			Forecasts					
	2013	2014	2015	Year +1	Year +2	Year +3	Year +4	Year +5	Year +6
BALANCE SHEET									
ASSETS									
Cash and cash equivalents	**$ 2,575.7**	**$ 1,708.4**	**$ 1,530.1**	**$ 1,781.8**	**$ 1,945.5**	**$ 2,161.2**	**$ 2,396.7**	**$ 2,653.7**	**$ 2,733.3**
common size	22.4%	15.9%	12.3%	30.0	30.0	30.0	30.0	30.0	
rate of change		(33.7%)	(10.4%)	Assume ending cash balances equal to 30 days sales.					
Short-term investments	**658.1**	**135.4**	**81.3**	**83.7**	**86.3**	**88.8**	**91.5**	**94.2**	**97.1**
common size	5.7%	1.3%	0.7%	3.0%	3.0%	3.0%	3.0%	3.0%	
rate of change		(79.4%)	(40.0%)	Assume 3% growth.					
Accounts and notes receivable—net	**561.4**	**631.0**	**719.0**	**825.0**	**907.8**	**1,015.5**	**1,133.4**	**1,262.5**	**1,300.4**
common size	4.9%	5.9%	5.8%	14.7%	10.0%	11.9%	11.6%	11.4%	
rate of change		12.4%	13.9%	Assume growth with licensing and CPG revenues					
Inventories	**1,111.2**	**1,090.9**	**1,306.4**	**1,327.7**	**1,440.7**	**1,585.9**	**1,742.7**	**1,912.0**	**1,969.3**
common size	9.6%	10.1%	10.5%	56.0	56.0	56.0	56.0	56.0	
rate of change		(1.8%)	19.8%	Assume ending inventory equals 56 days' cost of goods sold.					
Prepaid expenses and other current assets	**287.7**	**285.6**	**334.2**	**352.0**	**369.7**	**387.5**	**405.2**	**423.0**	**435.7**
common size	2.5%	2.7%	2.7%	5.3%	5.0%	4.8%	4.6%	4.4%	
rate of change		(0.7%)	17.0%	Assume growth with company-operated stores.					
Deferred income taxes—current	**277.3**	**317.4**	**381.8**	**0.0**	**0.0**	**0.0**	**0.0**	**0.0**	**0.0**
common size	2.4%	3.0%	3.1%	0.0%	0.0%	0.0%	0.0%	0.0%	
rate of change		14.5%	20.3%	Assume the current portion of deferred tax assets is fully realized in Year +1.					
Current assets	**$ 5,471.4**	**$ 4,168.7**	**$ 4,352.8**	**$ 4,370.2**	**$ 4,750.0**	**$ 5,238.9**	**$ 5,769.5**	**$ 6,345.4**	**$ 6,535.8**
common size	47.5%	38.8%	35.0%	34.1%	35.1%	36.1%	37.0%	36.2%	36.2%
rate of change		(23.8%)	4.4%	0.4%	8.7%	10.3%	10.1%	10.0%	3.0%
Long-term investments	**58.3**	**318.4**	**312.5**	**321.9**	**331.5**	**341.5**	**351.7**	**362.3**	**373.1**
common size	0.5%	3.0%	2.5%	3.0%	3.0%	3.0%	3.0%	3.0%	
rate of change		446.1%	(1.9%)	Assume steady growth at 3%.					

(Continued)

Exhibit 10.4 (Continued)

	Actuals			Forecasts					
	2013	2014	2015	Year +1	Year +2	Year +3	Year +4	Year +5	Year +6
Equity and cost investments	496.5	514.9	352.0	369.6	388.1	407.5	427.9	449.3	462.7
common size	4.3%	4.8%	2.8%						
rate of change		3.7%	(31.6%)	5.0%	5.0%	5.0%	5.0%	5.0%	
				Assume steady growth at 5%.					
Property, plant, and equipment— at cost	7,782.1	8,581.1	9,641.8	11,041.8	12,541.8	14,341.8	16,441.8	18,841.8	19,407.1
common size	67.6%	79.8%	77.5%						
rate of change		10.3%	12.4%	PP&E assumptions—see schedule in forecast development.					
Accumulated depreciation	(4,581.6)	(5,062.1)	(5,553.5)	(6,657.7)	(7,911.9)	(9,346.0)	(10,990.2)	(12,141.8)	(12,506.1)
common size	(39.8%)	(47.1%)	(44.6%)						
rate of change		10.5%	9.7%	See depreciation schedule in forecast development worksheet.					
Deferred income taxes—noncurrent	967.0	903.3	828.9	746.0	671.4	604.3	543.8	489.5	504.1
common size	8.4%	8.4%	6.7%						
rate of change		(6.6%)	(8.2%)	(10.0%)	(10.0%)	(10.0%)	(10.0%)	(10.0%)	
				Assume noncurrent deferred tax assets decrease 10% per year, as tax benefits are realized.					
Other assets	185.3	198.9	415.9	436.7	458.5	481.5	505.5	530.8	546.7
common size	1.6%	1.8%	3.3%						
rate of change		7.3%	109.1%	5.0%	5.0%	5.0%	5.0%	5.0%	
				Assume 5% growth.					
Other intangible assets	274.8	273.5	520.4	546.4	573.7	602.4	632.5	664.2	684.1
common size	2.4%	2.5%	4.2%						
rate of change		(0.5%)	90.3%	5.0%	5.0%	5.0%	5.0%	5.0%	
				Assume 5% growth.					
Goodwill	862.9	856.2	1,575.4	1,654.2	1,736.9	1,823.7	1,914.9	2,010.7	2,071.0
common size	7.5%	8.0%	12.7%						
rate of change		(0.8%)	84.0%	5.0%	5.0%	5.0%	5.0%	5.0%	
				Assume 5% growth.					
Total Assets	$11,516.7	$10,752.9	$12,446.2	$12,829.0	$13,540.1	$14,495.5	$15,597.5	$17,552.1	$18,078.6
common size	100.0%	100.0%	100.0%	100.0%	100.0%	100.0%	100.0%	100.0%	100.0%
rate of change		(6.6%)	15.7%	3.1%	5.5%	7.1%	7.6%	12.5%	3.0%
LIABILITIES									
Accounts payable	$ 491.7	$ 533.7	$ 684.2	$ 665.5	$ 729.0	$ 804.1	$ 883.4	$ 969.0	$ 998.0
common size	4.3%	5.0%	5.5%						
rate of change		8.5%	28.2%	28.0	28.0	28.0	28.0	28.0	
				Assume a 28-day payment period consistent with recent years.					
Accrued liabilities	1,269.3	1,514.4	1,760.7	1,991.8	2,174.9	2,416.0	2,679.2	2,966.6	3,055.6
common size	11.0%	14.1%	14.1%						
rate of change		19.3%	16.3%	13.1%	9.2%	11.1%	10.9%	10.7%	
				Assume growth with total revenues.					

	Actuals			Forecasts					
	2013	2014	2015	Year +1	Year +2	Year +3	Year +4	Year +5	Year +6
Current maturities of long-term debt	0.0	0.0	0.0	400.0	0.0	350.0	0.0	0.0	0.0
common size	0.0%	0.0%	0.0%	0.0	0.0	0.0	0.0	0.0	0.0
rate of change				Current maturities of long-term debt per long-term debt note (Note 9).					
Insurance reserves	178.5	196.1	224.8	231.5	238.5	245.6	253.0	260.6	268.4
common size	1.5%	1.8%	1.8%						
rate of change		9.9%	14.6%	3.0%	3.0%	3.0%	3.0%	3.0%	3.0%
				Assume 3% growth.					
Stored value card liability	653.7	794.5	983.8	1,113.0	1,215.2	1,349.9	1,497.0	1,657.6	1,707.3
common size	5.7%	7.4%	7.9%						
rate of change		21.5%	23.8%	13.1%	9.2%	11.1%	10.9%	10.7%	
				Assume growth with total revenues.					
Accrued litigation charge	2,784.1	0.0	0.0	0.0	0.0	0.0	0.0	0.0	0.0
common size	24.2%	0.0%	0.0%	0.0	0.0	0.0	0.0	0.0	0.0
rate of change		(100.0%)		Assume nonrecurring.					
Current liabilities	$ 5,377.3	$ 3,038.7	$ 3,653.5	$ 4,401.8	$ 4,357.6	$ 5,165.6	$ 5,312.6	$ 5,853.7	$ 6,029.3
common size	46.7%	28.3%	29.4%	34.3%	32.2%	35.6%	34.1%	33.4%	33.4%
rate of change		(43.5%)	20.2%	20.5%	(1.0%)	18.5%	2.8%	10.2%	
Long-term debt	1,299.4	2,048.3	2,347.5	2,947.5	3,347.5	2,997.5	3,347.5	3,347.5	3,447.9
common size	11.3%	19.0%	18.9%						
rate of change		57.6%	14.6%						
				1,000.00	400.00	0.00	350.00	0.00	
				$1,000 new long-term debt issues in 2016; see debt maturities in Note 9.					
Long-term accrued liabilities	357.7	392.2	625.3	707.4	772.4	858.0	951.5	1,053.6	1,085.2
common size	3.1%	3.6%	5.0%						
rate of change		9.6%	59.4%	13.1%	9.2%	11.1%	10.9%	10.7%	
				Assume growth with G&A expenses, which grow with revenues.					
Total liabilities	$ 7,034.4	$ 5,479.2	$ 6,626.3	$ 8,056.7	$ 8,477.5	$ 9,021.1	$ 9,611.6	$ 10,254.8	$ 10,562.4
common size	61.1%	51.0%	53.2%	62.8%	62.6%	62.2%	61.6%	58.4%	58.4%
rate of change		(22.1%)	20.9%	21.6%	5.2%	6.4%	6.5%	6.7%	
SHAREHOLDERS' EQUITY									
Common stock + additional paid-in capital	282.9	40.1	42.6	43.9	46.3	49.6	53.4	60.1	61.9
common size	2.5%	0.4%	0.342%	0.342%	0.342%	0.342%	0.342%	0.342%	0.342%
rate of change		(85.8%)	6.2%	Assume steady percent of total assets.					
Retained earnings	4,130.3	5,206.6	5,974.8	4,927.8	5,215.6	5,624.1	6,131.9	7,436.6	7,653.7
common size	35.9%	48.4%	48.0%						
rate of change		26.1%	14.8%	Add net income and subtract dividends and share repurchases.					

(Continued)

Exhibit 10.4 (Continued)

	Actuals			Forecasts						
	2013	2014	2015	Year +1	Year +2	Year +3	Year +4	Year +5	Year +6
Accum. other comprehensive income <loss>	67.0	25.3	(199.4)	(199.4)	(199.4)	(199.4)	(199.4)	(199.4)	(199.4)
common size	0.6%	0.2%	(1.6%)	0.0	0.0	0.0	0.0	0.0	
rate of change		(62.2%)	(888.1%)	Add accumulated other comprehensive income items from income statement					
Total common shareholders' equity	$ 4,480.2	$ 5,272.0	$ 5,818.0	$ 4,772.4	$ 5,062.6	$ 5,474.4	$ 5,985.9	$ 7,297.3	$ 7,516.2
common size	38.9%	49.0%	46.7%	37.2%	37.4%	37.8%	38.4%	41.6%	
rate of change		17.7%	10.4%	(18.0%)	6.1%	8.1%	9.3%	21.9%	3.0%
Noncontrolling interests	2.1	1.7	1.8	0.0	0.0	0.0	0.0	0.0	0.0
common size	0.0%	0.0%	0.0%	0.0	0.0	0.0	0.0	0.0	
rate of change		(19.0%)	5.9%	Assume noncontrolling interests are acquired in Year +1.					
Total equity	$ 4,482.3	$ 5,273.7	$ 5,819.8	$ 4,772.4	$ 5,062.6	$ 5,474.4	$ 5,985.9	$ 7,297.3	$ 7,516.2
common size	38.9%	49.0%	46.8%	37.2%	37.4%	37.8%	38.4%	41.6%	
rate of change		17.7%	10.4%	(18.0%)	6.1%	8.1%	9.3%	21.9%	3.0%
Total liabilities and equities	$11,516.7	$10,752.9	$12,446.1	$12,829.0	$13,540.1	$14,495.5	$15,597.5	$17,552.1	$ 18,078.6
common size	100.0%	100.0%	100.0%	100.0%	100.0%	100.0%	100.0%	100.0%	100.0%
rate of change		(6.6%)	15.7%	3.1%	5.5%	7.1%	7.6%	12.5%	3.0%

balance of $1,781.8 million. The projected balances in cash and cash equivalents on the projected **Starbucks** balance sheets follow (allow for rounding):

Cash and Cash Equivalents	2015	Year +1	Year +2	Year +3	Year +4	Year +5
Projected revenues	$19,162.7	$21,678.3	$23,670.5	$26,294.2	$29,159.4	$32,286.7
Revenues per day	$ 52.5	$ 59.4	$ 64.9	$ 72.0	$ 79.9	$ 88.5
Projected cash turnover (in days)	30.8	30.0	30.0	30.0	30.0	30.0
Projected cash balances	$ 1,530.1	$ 1,781.8	$ 1,945.5	$ 2,161.2	$ 2,396.7	$ 2,653.7

For the three primary financial statement forecasts to articulate with each other, the change in the cash balance on the projected balance sheet each year must agree with the change in cash on the projected statement of cash flows. Later in the chapter, we demonstrate how to forecast the implied statement of cash flows.

Projecting Short-Term Investments

From 2013 to 2015, **Starbucks'** short-term investments balances (also known as marketable securities) dropped dramatically, from $658.1 million to $81.3 million. **Starbucks** sold some of the short-term investments in part to pay the large legal settlement with Kraft in 2014. It appears **Starbucks** primarily manages its liquidity through its fairly large cash balances rather than through its very small amount of short-term investments. Going forward, we will simply assume that **Starbucks'** short-term investments balances will grow by 3% per year. Later in this chapter, we will include on the forecasted income statements the future interest income that we expect the cash, short-term, and long-term investments to generate. The projected balances follow:

Short-Term Investments	2015	Year +1	Year +2	Year +3	Year +4	Year +5
Projected balances	$81.3	$83.7	$86.3	$88.8	$91.5	$94.2
Projected growth rate		3.0%	3.0%	3.0%	3.0%	3.0%

Projecting Accounts Receivable

Starbucks' accounts receivable are driven by licensing, CPG, foodservice, and other revenues. **Starbucks'** makes sales to licensees, grocery store chains, and foodservice distributors on credit, which create accounts receivable. By contrast, **Starbucks** makes sales in company-operated stores either for cash, through the redemption of **Starbucks'** stored-value cards (gift cards, which are prepaid), or through third-party credit cards (e.g., Visa or Mastercard), which are reported as "cash equivalents" within the cash account. Company-operated store revenues do not create accounts receivable. We will therefore use the projected rate of growth in licensing, CPG, foodservice, and other revenues to project growth in accounts receivable. The projected amounts are as follows (allow for rounding):

Accounts Receivable	2015	Year +1	Year +2	Year +3	Year +4	Year +5
Licensed store revenues	$1,856.0	$2,185.0	$2,454.0	$2,792.6	$3,162.1	$3,565.0
CPG, foodservice, and other revenues	$2,103.5	$2,358.3	$2,545.2	$2,799.8	$3,079.7	$3,387.7
Total	$3,959.5	$4,543.4	$4,999.2	$5,592.4	$6,241.8	$6,952.7
Growth rate		14.7%	10.0%	11.9%	11.6%	11.4%
Accounts receivable	$ 719.0	$ 825.0	$ 907.8	$1,015.5	$1,133.4	$1,262.5

Projecting Inventories

Chapter 4's analysis of **Starbucks'** inventory turnover ratios revealed that **Starbucks** has generated faster inventory turnover rates of 56 days in 2015, compared to 59 days in 2014 and 67 days in 2013. **Starbucks'** inventory turnover rates slowed considerably in 2012 and 2013, after it took over from Kraft all of the distribution of its products to grocery stores, warehouse clubs, and foodservice distributors. Since then, **Starbucks'** has significantly improved the efficiency of its inventory management. We project **Starbucks'** inventory turnover days will remain steady at 56 days. The projected year-end inventory amounts follow:

Inventory	2015	Year +1	Year +2	Year +3	Year +4	Year +5
Costs of sales and occupancy costs	$7,787.5	$8,653.5	$9,390.4	$10,336.7	$11,358.7	$12,461.9
Costs of sales per day	$ 21.3	$ 23.7	$ 25.7	$ 28.3	$ 31.1	$ 34.1
Projected inventory turnover (in days)	56.0	56.0	56.0	56.0	56.0	56.0
Projected inventory balances	$1,306.4	$1,327.7	$1,440.7	$ 1,585.9	$ 1,742.7	$ 1,912.0

For some firms, such as retail chains, inventory is a large proportion of total assets. For such firms, you should link inventory forecasts to projections of the number of stores that will be operating in future years (or even, more specifically, to the number of square feet of retail space). For retail firms that operate large big-box stores (**Walmart** or **Costco**, for example), inventory projections may grow stepwise because each new store will require millions of dollars of additional inventory. Retail chains with seasonal sales will strive to have new stores (and thus new inventory) in place before heavy selling seasons (such as the back-to-school season for casual clothing and the Christmas season for toys); thus, analysts link inventory forecasts to projections of new stores in advance of these heavy selling seasons.

Projecting Prepaid Expenses and Other Current Assets

Prepaid expenses and other current assets represent items such as prepaid rent, advertising, and insurance. These items often vary in relation to the level of operating activity, such as sales, advertising, production, new stores or restaurants, and total assets. For **Starbucks**, many of these expenses vary with new company-operated stores. We will therefore project prepaid expenses and other current assets will grow in the future at the rate of growth in company-operated stores. The projected amounts are as follows:

Prepaid Expenses and Other Current Assets	2015	Year +1	Year +2	Year +3	Year +4	Year +5
Company-operated stores	12,235	12,885	13,535	14,185	14,835	15,485
Growth rate		5.3%	5.0%	4.8%	4.6%	4.4%
Prepaid expenses and other current assets	$ 334.2	$ 352.0	$ 369.7	$ 387.5	$ 405.2	$ 423.0

Projecting Current and Noncurrent Deferred Income Tax Assets

Current and noncurrent deferred tax assets (and liabilities) are driven by temporary differences between accrued income tax expenses and income taxes paid to the governmental taxing authorities. These are complex, as discussed earlier in Chapter 6. For our purposes here, we will avoid getting too deep into the details of these accounts. However, for firms for which deferred tax assets and liabilities are very important, forecasts of these accounts may warrant more careful treatment.

At the end of fiscal 2015, **Starbucks** reports (net) deferred tax assets, with $381.7 million as current assets and $828.9 million as noncurrent assets. **Starbucks'** net deferred tax assets jumped considerably in 2013, when it recognized over $1.0 billion in new deferred tax assets arising from the litigation settlement with Kraft. In the Annual Report, Note 13, "Income Taxes," **Starbucks** does not disclose any information about when these deferred tax assets will be realized in future tax savings. It is therefore very difficult to predict changes in **Starbucks'** tax-paying status and realizations of tax savings from these deferred tax asset accounts. For simplicity, we will make the (somewhat arbitrary) assumptions that the current deferred tax assets will be fully realized in Year +1 and that the noncurrent deferred tax assets will decline by 10.0% per year during the forecast horizon. Going forward, we would monitor these accounts carefully, and be prepared to adjust these assumptions if **Starbucks'** tax status changes. The projected amounts are:

Current and Noncurrent Deferred Tax Assets	2015	Year +1	Year +2	Year +3	Year +4	Year +5
Current	$381.7	$ 0.0	$ 0.0	$ 0.0	$ 0.0	$ 0.0
		Assume current tax benefits fully realized in Year +1.				
Noncurrent	$828.9	$746.0	$671.4	$604.3	$543.8	$489.5
Growth rate		(10.0%)	(10.0%)	(10.0%)	(10.0%)	(10.0%)

Projecting Long-Term Investments

In 2014 and 2015, **Starbucks'** long-term investments have been fairly steady, at $318.4 million and $312.5 million, respectively. Going forward, we will simply assume that **Starbucks'** long-term investments balances will grow by 3% per year. Later in this chapter we will include on the forecasted income statements the future interest income that we expect the cash, short-term, and long-term investments to generate. The projected balances follow:

Long-Term Investments	2015	Year +1	Year +2	Year +3	Year +4	Year +5
Projected balances	$312.5	$321.9	$331.5	$341.5	$351.7	$362.3
Projected growth rate		3.0%	3.0%	3.0%	3.0%	3.0%

Projecting Equity and Cost Investments

Recall that we developed our forecast projections for equity investments when we projected expected income from equity investees on the income statement. Those projections are on page 661.

Projecting Property, Plant, and Equipment and Accumulated Depreciation

Recall that we developed our forecast projections for PP&E and accumulated depreciation when we projected depreciation expense on the income statement. Those projections are on page 659.

Projecting Other Long-Term Assets, Other Intangible Assets, and Goodwill

At the end of fiscal 2015, the majority of Starbucks' intangible assets involved goodwill ($1,575.4 million). Under U.S. GAAP and IFRS, a firm can only recognize goodwill as an asset when it acquires another company. Goodwill represents the portion of the acquisition price that the firm cannot allocate to other tangible or intangible assets. As Starbucks discloses in Note 8, "Other Intangible Assets and Goodwill," goodwill jumped by over $800 million in 2015 as a consequence of Starbucks acquiring and consolidating Starbucks Japan. U.S. GAAP and IFRS do not require firms to amortize goodwill because it has an indefinite useful life, but firms must test goodwill values annually for impairment and write the carrying values down to fair value if deemed impaired. Thus far, Starbucks has deemed it necessary to recognize only very minor impairment losses on its goodwill (a total of only $9.9 million in accumulated impairment charges).

On the 2015 balance sheet, Starbucks recognizes other intangible assets, including $302.5 million in finite-lived intangibles (primarily acquired rights) and $217.9 million in indefinite-lived intangibles (primarily trade names, trademarks, and patents). Starbucks also recognizes $415.9 million in miscellaneous other long-term assets.

Because of their nature, these various types of assets, especially goodwill and intangibles, tend to grow with company acquisitions, as was the case in 2015. Absent announcements or disclosures about pending acquisitions, these types of transactions are inherently hard to forecast accurately. Therefore, for simplicity, we project that goodwill, other intangible assets, and other long-term assets will grow by 5% per year. We will also assume that no future impairment charges will be necessary for these assets. The projected amounts are as follows (allow for rounding):

Other Long-Term Assets, Other Intangible Assets, and Goodwill	2015	Year +1	Year +2	Year +3	Year +4	Year +5
Other long-term assets	$ 415.9	$ 436.7	$ 458.5	$ 481.5	$ 505.5	$ 530.8
Expected growth rates		5.0%	5.0%	5.0%	5.0%	5.0%
Other intangible assets	$ 520.4	$ 546.4	$ 573.7	$ 602.4	$ 632.5	$ 664.2
Expected growth rates		5.0%	5.0%	5.0%	5.0%	5.0%
Goodwill	$1,575.4	$1,654.2	$1,736.9	$1,823.7	$1,914.9	$2,010.7
Expected growth rates		5.0%	5.0%	5.0%	5.0%	5.0%

Projecting Assets as a Percentage of Total Assets

In some circumstances, you may need to project individual asset amounts that will vary as a percentage of total assets, particularly for firms that maintain a steady proportion of total assets invested in specific types of assets. For example, suppose a firm's strategy is to maintain 7.0% of total assets in cash for liquidity purposes. Also suppose our projected amounts for Year +1 for all of the individual assets *other than cash* amount to $100.0 million. The $100 million subtotal represents 93.0% (1.00 – 0.07) of total assets. Therefore, projected total assets should equal $107.527 million ($100.0 million/0.93).

Thus, in this hypothetical example, the ending cash balance would equal $7.527 million (0.07 × $107.527 million).

Note that this approach to forecasting introduces some circularity into the projected financial statements; the cash balance is a function of total assets, which is a function of the cash balance. This forecast approach is not unrealistic, nor does it create a problem for the computations. A later subsection of this chapter discusses how to solve for such codetermined variables in financial statement forecasts.

Projected Total Assets

We have now projected amounts for each of the assets reported on **Starbucks'** balance sheets. Our projected asset totals are as follows:

	2015	**Year +1**	**Year +2**	**Year +3**	**Year +4**	**Year +5**
Projected total assets	$12,446.1	$12,829.0	$13,540.1	$14,495.5	$15,597.5	$17,552.1

Next, we will turn to forecasting operating liabilities, as well as debt and equity financing.

Projecting Accounts Payable

Starbucks reports $684.2 million in accounts payable on its 2015 balance sheet. Future credit purchases of inventory and **Starbucks'** payment policy to its suppliers will drive future accounts payable. The ratios discussed in Chapter 4 and reported in the Analysis spreadsheet of FSAP show that **Starbucks** maintains a very stable payables policy. Days payable have varied within a narrow range from 26 to 28 days over the past five years. We assume that **Starbucks** will continue to maintain an accounts payable period of 28 days in the future. To forecast future accounts payable balances, we begin by forecasting inventory purchases, which drive payables. We rely on our prior forecasts of **Starbucks'** cost of sales (net of the occupancy costs) and add the changes in the inventory balances to compute inventory purchases, which will flow through accounts payable. We then project ending balances in accounts payable, assuming 28-day payable periods.

As discussed earlier, in Year +1 the projected cost of sales and occupancy costs is $8,653.5 million (page 656).[15] This is the cost of the inventory **Starbucks** will have to purchase simply to replenish the inventory we project it will sell in Year +1. However, in our inventory forecasts (page 672), we projected that **Starbucks'** inventory balance will grow to $1,327.7 million by the end of Year +1, an increase of $21.3 million. This represents additional inventory purchases. The total projected inventory purchases in Year +1 will be $8,674.8 million ($8,653.5 million + $21.3 million), all of which will be on credit terms, driving accounts payable. On an average day during Year +1, **Starbucks** will purchase $23.8 million in inventory, and incur $23.8 million in accounts payable. If **Starbucks** maintains a 28-day payables policy, then the accounts payable

---

[15]For greater precision in your accounts payable forecasts, instead of using total cost of sales and occupancy expense, you could use just the cost of sales portion (computed as $7,370.6 million in Year +1, as shown on page 656.)

balance will be $665.5 million ($23.8 million × 28.0 days). The accounts payable projections for Year +1 to +5 are as follows (allow for rounding):

Accounts Payable	2015	Year +1	Year +2	Year +3	Year +4	Year +5
Costs of sales and occupancy costs	$7,787.5	$8,653.5	$9,390.4	$10,336.7	$11,358.7	$12,461.9
Projected inventory balances	$1,306.4	$1,327.7	$1,440.7	$ 1,585.9	$ 1,742.7	$ 1,912.0
Projected changes in inventory		$ 21.3	$ 113.1	$ 145.2	$ 156.8	$ 169.3
Projected inventory purchases		$8,674.8	$9,503.4	$10,481.9	$11,515.5	$12,631.2
Average inventory purchases per day		$ 23.8	$ 26.0	$ 28.7	$ 31.5	$ 34.6
Projected turnover (in days)	28.0	28.0	28.0	28.0	28.0	28.0
Accounts payable	$ 684.2	$ 665.5	$ 729.0	$ 804.1	$ 883.4	$ 969.0

Projecting Accrued Liabilities

In **Starbucks'** 2015 Annual Report, Note 8, "Supplemental Balance Sheet Information" (Appendix A), discloses that at the end of 2015 accrued liabilities consisted of amounts payable for various activities, including compensation and benefits, occupancy costs, taxes, dividends, and other expenses. In recent years, accrued liabilities have been growing at roughly the same rate of growth as revenues (and, in some years, faster). In 2015, for example, revenues grew by 16.5% and accrued liabilities grew by 16.3%. We therefore forecast that accrued liabilities will grow with revenues (allow for rounding).

Accrued Liabilities	2015	Year +1	Year +2	Year +3	Year +4	Year +5
Accrued liabilities	$1,760.7	$1,991.8	$2,174.9	$2,416.0	$2,679.2	$2,966.6
Growth with revenue growth rates		13.1%	9.2%	11.1%	10.9%	10.7%

Projecting Insurance Reserves

In **Starbucks'** 2015 Annual Report, Note 1, "Summary of Significant Accounting Policies" (Appendix A), explains that the firm uses a combination of insurance and self-insurance mechanisms to provide for potential liabilities for certain risks, such as workers' compensation, heath care benefits, general liability, and others. We will simply forecast that insurance reserves will grow 3% per year (allow for rounding).

Insurance Reserves	2015	Year +1	Year +2	Year +3	Year +4	Year +5
Insurance reserves	$224.8	$231.5	$238.5	$245.6	$253.0	$260.6
Growth rates		3.0%	3.0%	3.0%	3.0%	3.0%

Projecting Stored-Value Card Liabilities

Starbucks' stored-value cards can be loaded at company-operated stores, most licensed stores, and online. When a customer loads a card, the customer pays **Starbucks** cash, and the stored-value card can then be redeemed at **Starbucks'** locations for products and services. The stored-value card liability is therefore a service obligation to customers for prepaid revenues. At the end of fiscal 2015, the stored-value card liability amounted to $983.8 million. We forecast that stored-value card liabilities will grow with revenues (allow for rounding).

Stored-Value Card Liabilities	2015	Year +1	Year +2	Year +3	Year +4	Year +5
Stored-value card liabilities	$983.8	$1,113.0	$1,215.2	$1,349.9	$1,497.0	$1,657.6
Growth with revenues		13.1%	9.2%	11.1%	10.9%	10.7%

Projecting Other Long-Term Liabilities

Other long-term liabilities are accrued liabilities for expenses that relate to pension obligations, health care obligations, long-term compensation, and other operating and administrative expenses. We therefore project other noncurrent liabilities will grow with general and administrative expenses, which we assume grow with revenues (allow for rounding):

Other Long-Term Liabilities	2015	Year +1	Year +2	Year +3	Year +4	Year +5
Other long-term liabilities	$625.3	$707.4	$772.4	$858.0	$951.5	$1,053.6
Growth with revenues		13.1%	9.2%	11.1%	10.9%	10.7%

Step 4: Project Financial Leverage, Financial Assets, Common Equity Capital, and Financial Income and Expense Items

LO 10-2d

Build forecasts of future balance sheets, income statements, and statements of cash flows by applying the seven-step forecasting framework to project: d. financial leverage, capital structure, and financial income items.

After completing forecasts of the operating assets and liabilities of the balance sheet, we must now project any financial assets the firm will hold, and the financial debt and shareholders' equity amounts that will be necessary to finance the firm's operating and investing activities. In addition, we project the effects of investing and financing on net income by projecting future interest income, interest expense, and other elements of financial income.

For firms that regularly maintain a particular capital structure over time, you can use the common-size balance sheet percentages to project amounts of debt and equity capital. If the firm has a target capital structure that consists of stable proportions of liabilities and equity (for instance, 60% liabilities and 40% equity), you can use these common-size percentages and the projected amounts of total assets to project future totals of liabilities and equity.

Alternatively, you can project debt capital and shareholders' equity accounts by projecting potential future changes in the financial leverage strategy of the firm. For instance, in recent years, interest rates on corporate debt have been at historically low levels, so many firms have been taking on more financial leverage with greater amounts of short- and long-term debt and using this debt financing to reduce shareholders' equity through repurchases of common shares and increased dividends. In other cases, you may need to project how a firm will alter its capital structure as a result of a merger, acquisition, or divestiture transaction.

In this section, we forecast debt and equity by projecting the financial leverage strategy of **Starbucks** over our forecast horizon. We discuss each account in turn.

Projecting Financial Assets

You must assess the firm's business activities and financial strategy to determine the extent to which the firm uses financial assets for operating liquidity purposes versus financial purposes. Most firms use financial assets, such as cash and short-term and long-term investment securities, to accomplish one or all of the following:

- manage seasonal swings in operating liquidity.
- provide a financial cushion for future uncertainties.
- have financial flexibility to take advantage of profitable opportunities when they arise.

As such, for these firms it makes sense to forecast financial assets as part of the liquidity and operating activities of the firm. For example, **Starbucks'** 2015 balance sheet recognizes cash, short-term investments, long-term investments, and equity investments. As discussed previously, **Starbucks** uses cash and short-term and long-term investments to provide liquidity for operating activities. The equity investments represent investments in joint ventures closely related to **Starbucks'** operating activities. Therefore, we included these types of financial assets in our projections of **Starbucks'** operating activities.

By contrast, some firms hold excess cash and/or investment securities that are not needed for operating liquidity, and are instead intended for future financial purposes, such as debt retirement, corporate acquisitions, repurchase of shares, or payment of dividends. When forecasting the future financial capital structure for firms like these, you must project the future financial assets that represent financial savings that can be used for debt retirement or other financial purposes. Suppose, for example, a firm had issued bonds to finance plant and equipment and the bond indenture agreement required the firm to maintain a bond sinking fund (a reserve of cash and securities to be used for future bond retirement). The cash and securities in the sinking fund would represent financial assets intended for debt retirement and should be projected with the firm's financial structure rather than as part of the firm's operating activities. As of the 2015 balance sheet, **Starbucks** does not report any short-term or long-term investment securities for debt retirement purposes, and because of its ability to generate cash flows from operations, **Starbucks** is not likely to need future reserves for debt retirement.

Projecting Short-Term and Long-Term Debt

As of the end of 2015, **Starbucks** had issued a total of $2,347.5 million in long-term debt. The common-size balance sheet for **Starbucks** (Chapter 1) shows that long-term debt has become an increasingly larger proportion of total assets. From 2013 to 2015, the proportion of long-term debt in **Starbucks'** capital structure jumped considerably, from roughly 11% of total assets to 19%.

Starbucks' statement of cash flows for 2015 (Appendix A) indicates the firm generated $3,749.1 million of net cash flow from operating activities and used $1,520.3 million for investing activities. In terms of financing activities in 2015, **Starbucks** used $928.6 million in cash to pay dividends and $1,436.1 million to repurchase common stock, after issuing $848.5 million in long-term debt and paying down roughly $610.1 million in long-term debt. Clearly, **Starbucks** generates a lot of cash from its operating activities and is choosing to increase its debt obligations in order to return more cash to shareholders through dividends and share repurchases. **Starbucks** appears to be shifting its financial leverage strategy to recapitalize by issuing greater amounts of long-term debt while paying larger dividends and repurchasing more common equity shares.

In fact, during the first half of fiscal 2016 (while this chapter was being written), **Starbucks** issued a total of nearly $1.0 billion of new long-term debt obligations. We include this new additional level of long-term debt in our forecasts for Year +1.

Starbucks' outstanding long-term debt matures at varying dates extending from 2016 to 2045. Note 9, "Debt" (Appendix A), discloses information on the maturities and reveals that $400 million of long-term debt will mature in December 2016 (fiscal

2017; Year +2), and another $350 million will mature in December 2018 (fiscal 2019; Year +4). In our forecasts, we therefore reduce long-term debt by these amounts the year before they mature, and include them in the current liability account "Current Maturities of Long-Term Debt." In the years in which they mature, we forecast that they will be repaid.[16] To keep long-term debt levels stable, we will also project that in the years in which long-term debts mature, **Starbucks** will replace them with new long-term debt issues.

The projected amounts for current maturities and long-term debt are as follows:

Long-Term Debt and Current Maturities of Long-Term Debt	Year +1	Year +2	Year +3	Year +4	Year +5
Long-term debt					
Beginning balance	$2,347.5	$2,947.5	$3,347.5	$2,997.5	$3,347.5
Add: New issues	$1,000.0	$ 400.00	$ 0.0	$ 350.0	$ 0.0
Less: Maturities	$ (400.0)	$ 0.0	$ (350.0)	$ 0.0	$ 0.0
Ending balance	$2,947.5	$3,347.5	$2,997.5	$3,347.5	$3,347.5
Current maturities of long-term debt					
Beginning balance	$ 0.0	$ 400.0	$ 0.0	$ 350.0	$ 0.0
Add: Maturing issues	$ 400.0	$ 0.0	$ 350.0	$ 0.0	$ 0.0
Less: Repayments	$ 0.0	$ (400.0)	$ 0.0	$ (350.0)	$ 0.0
Ending balance	$ 400.0	$ 0.0	$ 350.0	$ 0.0	$ 0.0

We will use these projected amounts for interest-bearing debt to project **Starbucks'** future interest expense.

Projected Total Liabilities

We have now made projections of all of **Starbucks'** liabilities. Combining them, our projected liabilities for **Starbucks** over the forecast horizon are as follows:

Total Liabilities	2015	Year +1	Year +2	Year +3	Year +4	Year +5
Accounts payable	$ 684.2	$ 665.5	$ 729.0	$ 804.1	$ 883.4	$ 969.0
Accrued liabilities	1,760.7	1,991.8	2,174.9	2,416.0	2,679.2	2,966.6
Insurance reserves	224.8	231.5	238.5	245.6	253.0	260.6
Stored-value card liabilities	983.8	1,113.0	1,215.2	1,349.9	1,497.0	1,657.6
Current maturities of long-term debt	0.0	400.0	0.0	350.0	0.0	0.0
Current liabilities	$3,653.5	$4,401.8	$4,357.6	$5,165.6	$5,312.6	$ 5,853.7
Long-term debt	2,347.5	2,947.5	3,347.5	2,997.5	3,347.5	3,347.5
Other long-term liabilities	625.3	707.4	772.4	858.0	951.5	1,053.6
Total liabilities	$6,626.3	$8,056.7	$8,477.5	$9,021.1	$9,611.6	$10,254.8
Total liabilities as a percent of total assets	53.2%	62.8%	62.9%	63.7%	65.0%	63.7%

---

[16]If you are building forecasts for firms that are deleveraging and retiring debt or for firms that are highly leveraged and facing a high probability of distress or bankruptcy, the schedule of future long-term debt maturities is very helpful in projecting when the firm will have to retire or refinance mature debt.

Projecting Interest Expense

We can now project **Starbucks'** interest expense, based on our projected balances in interest-bearing debt. Note 9, "Debt" (Appendix A), discloses the amounts, maturities, and interest rates on the debt issues outstanding. It indicates that at the end of 2015, the interest rates ranged from 0.875% on notes maturing in 2016 to 4.3% on notes maturing in 2045. In addition, the two most recent debt issues are $500 million in 2.1% notes maturing in 2021 and $500 million in 2.45% notes maturing in 2026. We can use all of these disclosures to estimate the weighted-average interest rate on total debt outstanding, as follows:

Long-Term Debt and Weighted-Average Interest Rates

Debt Issues and Maturities	Face Value Amounts	Proportion of Total	Stated Interest Rates	Weighted Average Interest Rates
2016 Notes	$ 400.0	0.119	0.875%	0.1045%
2018 Notes	$ 350.0	0.104	2.000%	0.2090%
2021 Notes	$ 500.0	0.149	2.100%	0.3134%
2022 Notes	$ 500.0	0.149	2.700%	0.4030%
2023 Notes	$ 750.0	0.224	3.850%	0.8619%
2026 Notes	$ 500.0	0.149	2.450%	0.3657%
2045 Notes	$ 350.0	0.104	4.300%	0.4493%
Totals	**$3,350.0**	1.000		**2.7067%**

We therefore project interest expense using the weighted-average interest rate of 2.7067% on the average amount of interest-bearing debt in Year +1 through Year +5 to match the weighted-average interest rate on the outstanding debt. Using the projected amounts of total interest-bearing debt in the prior section, the projected interest expense amounts follow (allow for rounding):

Interest-Bearing Debt and Interest Expense	2015	Year +1	Year +2	Year +3	Year +4	Year +5
Long-term debt	$2,347.5	$2,947.5	$3,347.5	$2,997.5	$3,347.5	$3,347.5
Current maturities of long-term debt	$ 0.0	$ 400.0	$ 0.0	$ 350.0	$ 0.0	$ 0.0
Total interest-bearing debt	$2,347.5	$3,347.5	$3,347.5	$3,347.5	$3,347.5	$3,347.5
Average interest-bearing debt		$2,847.5	$3,347.5	$3,347.5	$3,347.5	$3,347.5
Weighted average interest rate		2.7067%	2.7067%	2.7067%	2.7067%	2.7067%
Projected interest expense	$ 70.5	$ 77.1	$ 90.6	$ 90.6	$ 90.6	$ 90.6

The interest expense projections are higher than recent past interest expense amounts for **Starbucks**, reflecting **Starbucks'** shift in financial strategy in 2015 to greater reliance on long-term debt. We can now enter these interest expense amounts in the projected income statements. If the projected balance sheets imply that **Starbucks** will need larger or smaller amounts of long-term debt to finance future asset growth, then we will need to recompute the interest expense projections to reflect different amounts of debt.

Projecting Interest Income

We can also project our first-pass estimates of **Starbucks'** interest income on financial assets, such as cash and short-term and long-term investments. In 2015, **Starbucks** recognized $43.0 million in interest and other income.[17] The average amount of interest-earning assets (cash and short-term and long-term investments) during 2015 was $2,043.0 million [($1,530.1 + $1,708.4 + $81.3 + $135.4 + $312.5 + $318.4)/2], for an average return of 2.1% ($43.0/$2,043.0). This low average rate of return reflects the very low interest rate environment present during 2015. In addition, it is likely that **Starbucks'** cash and investment securities are low-risk but liquid instruments, and therefore yield low rates of return. At the beginning of Year +1, yields on low-risk, highly liquid short-term and medium-term U.S. Treasury bonds were in the 1.0% to 2.0% range. Assuming interest rates and yields remain stable over the forecast horizon, we project **Starbucks** will earn a 2.1% return on the average balances in cash and short-term and long-term investments each year. The projected amounts for interest income are as follows (allow for rounding):

Interest-Earning Assets and Interest Income	2015	Year +1	Year +2	Year +3	Year +4	Year +5
Cash	$1,530.1	$ 1,781.8	$ 1,945.5	$ 2,161.2	$ 2,396.7	$ 2,653.7
Short-term investments	$ 81.3	$ 83.7	$ 86.3	$ 88.8	$ 91.5	$ 94.2
Long-term investments	$ 312.5	$ 321.9	$ 331.5	$ 341.5	$ 351.7	$ 362.3
Total interest-earning assets	$1,923.9	$ 2,187.4	$ 2,363.3	$ 2,591.5	$ 2,839.9	$ 3,110.2
Average interest-earning assets		$2,055.65	$2,275.35	$2,477.39	$2,715.68	$2,975.06
Weighted-average interest rate		2.1%	2.1%	2.1%	2.1%	2.1%
Projected interest income	$ 43.0	$ 43.2	$ 47.8	$ 52.0	$ 57.0	$ 62.5

If the projected balance sheets imply that **Starbucks** will generate and retain larger amounts of cash and investment securities, then we will recompute the interest income projections to reflect additional interest-earning assets.

Projecting Noncontrolling Interests

Noncontrolling interests in equity are similar to the equity method investments (investments in noncontrolled affiliates) described earlier, but in this case the firm is the controlling shareholder and consolidates the subsidiaries. Noncontrolling interests therefore account for the equity ownership of minority investors that own less than 50% of the shares of the subsidiary company (this is the mirror image of accounting for investments in equity affiliates).

At the end of 2015, **Starbucks** has only $1.8 million of equity capital from noncontrolling interest shareholders. These investors own significant but not controlling proportions of the equity in certain subsidiaries that **Starbucks** controls and consolidates.

---

[17]As discussed in Chapter 6, **Starbucks** includes in "interest and other income" income from breakage of stored-value cards, which does not vary with the average investment in interest-earnings assets. However, in most years, interest income is the largest portion of this account. Therefore, we demonstrate this general forecast approach, and project interest and other income as a function of the average amount invested in interest-earning assets. For the analyst interested in greater forecast precision, you can forecast the interest income portion and the breakage income portion separately.

We should project the future amounts of noncontrolling equity by projecting additional investments by or retirements of these noncontrolling equity investors as well as the proportionate share of income and dividends from these subsidiaries to these investors. In addition, we should reduce net income in our projected income statements by the amount of net income attributable to noncontrolling interests each year, with the remainder of net income attributable to **Starbucks'** shareholders.

Because the amount of noncontrolling interests in equity are so minor (0.03% of total shareholders' equity), for simplicity we will assume that **Starbucks** will retire all of the noncontrolling interests in Year +1, and that **Starbucks'** subsidiaries will not raise any additional noncontrolling equity capital during the forecast horizon.

Projecting Common Stock, Preferred Stock, and Additional Paid-in Capital

As Chapter 7 explains, common stock, preferred stock, and paid-in capital accounts increase as the firm raises capital by selling common and/or preferred shares to investors or by issuing shares in a merger or acquisition. These accounts decrease when the firm retires shares. The paid-in capital accounts also increase when firms award share-based compensation and bonuses, such as stock options or restricted share units, to employees, executives, and board members. Paid-in capital accounts increase (but retained earnings decrease) by the fair value of the share-based compensation expense. Subsequently, if individuals exercise stock options or convert restricted shares into unrestricted shares, then paid-in capital accounts increase by the net amount of any cash received from the individuals (such as the exercise price of the options).

Starbucks' consolidated statement of equity (Appendix A) shows that, in 2015, **Starbucks'** has no preferred stock outstanding. We will assume that **Starbucks** will not issue any preferred shares during the forecast horizon.

The statement of equity also shows that **Starbucks** has 1,485.1 million common shares outstanding with a par value of $0.001 per share, so the common stock at par account is only $1.5 million at the end of fiscal 2015. [Note: **Starbucks** had a 2-for-1 stock split during fiscal 2015, doubling the number of outstanding shares.] The additional paid-in capital account amounts to only $41.1 million at the end of fiscal 2015. The common-sized balance sheet data (Chapter 1) show that **Starbucks'** paid-in capital accounts (par value plus additional paid-in capital) in 2015 amount to only 0.342% of total assets. Given that **Starbucks** has shifted its capital strategy to increase the proportion of long-term debt, we do not expect significant future issues of common equity. We therefore simply project common stock and additional paid-in capital will grow with total assets, remaining at 0.342% of total assets. The projected amounts for common stock and additional paid-in capital are as follows:

Common Stock and Additional Paid-in Capital	2015	Year +1	Year +2	Year +3	Year +4	Year +5
Total assets	$12,446.1	$12,829.0	$13,540.1	$14,495.5	$15,597.5	$17,552.1
Paid-in capital as a percent of total assets	0.342%	0.342%	0.342%	0.342%	0.342%	0.342%
Projected common stock and additional paid-in capital	$ 42.6	$ 43.9	$ 46.3	$ 49.6	$ 53.4	$ 60.1

Projecting Accumulated Other Comprehensive Income or Loss

As described in Chapters 8 and 9, under U.S. GAAP, other comprehensive income items result from four specific types of asset and liability revaluations: fair value gains and losses on available-for-sale securities, foreign currency translation adjustments, adjustments to certain pension and retiree benefit obligations, and fair value gains and losses on cash flow hedges. Because economywide changes in interest rates and foreign exchange rates tend to be transitory and because many firms tend to hedge or mitigate exposure to such risks, it is often very difficult to predict with confidence whether a particular firm will generate persistent gains or losses from such changes over long periods of time. As such, analysts commonly forecast gains or losses from other comprehensive income items to be zero, on average.

On the consolidated statement of comprehensive income (Appendix A), **Starbucks** reported net income of $2,759.3 million for 2015 but comprehensive income of $2,534.6 million—**Starbucks'** other comprehensive income items amounted to a loss of $224.7 million after tax. As that statement shows, these income items were attributable primarily to foreign currency translation adjustments. In 2015, the U.S. dollar's value strengthened against many other currencies in which **Starbucks** holds net assets, which triggered the −$222.7 million translation adjustment. Also in 2015, **Starbucks** recognized various small amounts for fair value gains and losses on available-for-sale securities, and cash flow and net investment hedges. In 2015, **Starbucks** also reclassified net (after-tax) losses of $43.6 million in earnings. According to **Starbucks'** consolidated statement of equity (Appendix A), accumulated other comprehensive income/loss was $25.3 million at the beginning of 2015, and, consequently, by the end of 2015 it had become −$199.4 million.

In prior years, **Starbucks'** other comprehensive income items were much smaller. **Starbucks** recognized other comprehensive losses of only −$41.7 million in fiscal 2014, and other comprehensive income of $44.3 million in fiscal 2013. For simplicity, we project that **Starbucks** will experience neither persistent income nor losses from other comprehensive income items in the future. We are essentially assuming that **Starbucks'** future foreign currency translation adjustments are equally likely to be positive or negative in any given year and that, on average, they will be zero over time. In addition, we assume that available-for-sale investment securities and cash flow hedges are equally likely to generate fair value gains or losses in any given year and that, on average, they will be zero over the forecast horizon. Therefore, we project that accumulated other comprehensive loss will remain at its current level. Accordingly, other comprehensive income items will also be zero in future years.

Step 5: Project Provisions for Taxes, Net Income, Dividends, Share Repurchases, and Retained Earnings

Thus far we have developed forecasts of **Starbucks'** operating activities, including operating income as well as the operating assets and liabilities. We have projected **Starbucks'** future financial liabilities, common equity capital, and financial income items including interest income, interest expense, and income from noncontrolled affiliates. In Step 5, we complete the forecasting of **Starbucks'** net income, dividends, share repurchases, and retained earnings. This will lead us into Step 6, in which we make our balance sheet forecasts balance.

LO 10-2e

Build forecasts of future balance sheets, income statements, and statements of cash flows by applying the seven-step forecasting framework to project: e. provisions for taxes, net income, dividends, share repurchases, and retained earnings.

Projecting Provisions for Income Taxes

As Chapter 9 discusses, **Starbucks'** Note 13, "Income Taxes" (Appendix A), shows the reconciliation between the statutory tax rate and **Starbucks'** average, or effective, tax rate. The statutory U.S. federal income tax rate was 35.0% during 2013–2015. During 2015, **Starbucks** experienced an effective income tax rate of only 29.3%. This relatively low effective tax rate in 2015 includes an additional 2.8% tax that **Starbucks** paid for state income taxes. However, **Starbucks'** effective income tax rate was offset by various tax benefits, including a decrease of 2.1% from lower tax rates in international tax jurisdictions, a benefit of 2.2% from the domestic production activity deduction, a benefit of 3.7% from the tax-deferred gain on the acquisition of the joint venture in Japan, and various other factors. In 2014, **Starbucks** experienced a more normal effective tax rate of 34.6%.

As we noted earlier, **Starbucks'** 2015 Annual Report, the MD&A section titled "Fiscal 2016—The View Ahead," and subsequent quarterly disclosures early in 2016 provide information from **Starbucks'** managers about their expectations. In these disclosures, **Starbucks** reveals it expects an effective tax rate of roughly 34.0% in Year +1. We therefore assume that **Starbucks'** average combined federal, state, and foreign income tax rate for Year +1 through Year +5 will be 34.0%. The projected amounts for income tax expense are reported in the table in the next section.

Also discussed earlier, Note 13 discloses that **Starbucks** has net deferred tax assets of $1,137.4 million at the end of fiscal 2015, a large portion of which stems from deferred tax savings from the litigation settlement with Kraft. When these deferred tax assets are realized, they will enable **Starbucks** to generate future tax savings. Although these deferred tax assets will not reduce **Starbucks'** expected future effective tax rate, they will allow **Starbucks** to pay lower amounts of cash taxes. As we reduce our projections of these deferred tax assets on our projected balance sheets, we will also capture the cash tax savings on our projected statements of cash flows over our forecast horizon.

Net Income Attributable to Starbucks' Common Shareholders

All of the elements of the income statement, including first-iteration estimates of interest expense, interest income, and income taxes, are now complete. Recall that Exhibit 10.3 presents these income statement projections. The projected amounts of net earnings, net profit margins, and the implied earnings growth rates are as follows:

Net Income Projections	2015	Year +1	Year +2	Year +3	Year +4	Year +5
Projected total net revenues	$19,162.7	$21,678.3	$23,670.5	$26,294.2	$29,159.4	$32,286.7
Projected operating income	$ 3,601.0	$ 4,267.7	$ 4,710.4	$ 5,326.4	$ 6,002.9	$ 7,444.8
Projected interest income	43.0	43.2	47.8	52.0	57.0	62.5
Projected interest expense	(70.5)	(77.1)	(90.6)	(90.6)	(90.6)	(90.6)
Gain from acquisition of joint venture	390.6	0.0	0.0	0.0	0.0	0.0
Loss on extinguishment of debt	(61.1)	0.0	0.0	0.0	0.0	0.0
Income before taxes	$ 3,903.0	$ 4,233.8	$ 4,667.5	$ 5,287.8	$ 5,969.3	$ 7,416.6
Effective tax rates	(29.3%)	(34.0%)	(34.0%)	(34.0%)	(34.0%)	(34.0%)
Income tax expense	(1,143.7)	(1,439.5)	(1,587.0)	(1,797.9)	(2,029.6)	(2,521.7)
Projected net earnings	$ 2,759.3	$ 2,794.3	$ 3,080.6	$ 3,490.0	$ 3,939.8	$ 4,895.0
Net profit margin	14.4%	12.9%	13.0%	13.3%	13.5%	15.2%
Net income growth rates	33.4%	1.3%	10.2%	13.3%	12.9%	24.2%

The forecasts of net earnings for **Starbucks** imply a slightly lower profit margin than in 2013–2015 and only modest growth in net income in Year +1, in part because of the increase in the expected tax rate. Profit margins and earnings growth rates return to higher, more normal levels for **Starbucks** in Years +2 through +5.

Projecting Dividends and Share Repurchases

Profitable, mature companies like **Starbucks** can distribute excess cash to shareholders through dividend payments as well as by repurchasing common shares. In recent years, given its profitability and strong cash flows, **Starbucks** has been increasing these cash flows to its shareholders. Dividend payout rates have increased from $0.445 per share in 2013, to $0.550 per share in fiscal 2014, to $0.680 per share in fiscal 2015. For Year +1, **Starbucks'** board of directors approved a further increase to dividend payments of $0.800 per share. Relying on that announcement, and with roughly 1,485 million shares outstanding, it suggests **Starbucks** will pay roughly $1,188.0 million in dividends in Year +1.[18] Given that we forecast **Starbucks** will generate $2,794.3 million in net earnings in Year +1, it implies **Starbucks** will pay out 42.5% of earnings in dividends. We will project that **Starbucks'** dividend payout policy will average 42.5% of projected net earnings in Years +1 through + 5. Therefore, forecasts of dividends to common shareholders will vary over time with net earnings.

In addition to paying dividends, **Starbucks** also distributes large amounts of cash to shareholders through repurchases of common shares. For some firms, repurchases of common shares are accounted for in a treasury stock account, which is a negative (contra) account in shareholders' equity on the balance sheet. The treasury stock account becomes *more* negative when the firm repurchases some of its outstanding common equity shares. The treasury stock account becomes *less* negative when the firm reissues treasury shares on the open market, uses them to meet stock option exercises, issues them in merger or acquisition transactions, or retires them. (See Chapter 7 for more discussion of accounting for treasury stock transactions.)

Starbucks, however, is incorporated in the state of Washington, and state laws require that it subtract amounts paid for common share repurchases from retained earnings.[19] In 2013 through 2015, **Starbucks'** statement of common shareholders' equity (Appendix A) reveals that it has been using increasing amounts of cash to repurchase common shares: $544.1 million in 2013, $769.8 million in 2014, and $1,431.8 million in 2015.[20]

---

[18]The capital markets generally react positively when firms announce plans to increase dividend payouts because market participants infer that this is a signal of managers' favorable private information about expectations for future sustainable earnings and cash flows. Moreover, managers are reluctant to cut or omit dividends because the market usually reacts negatively to such announcements. Thus, managers typically do not increase dividends unless they believe the increase can be sustained.

[19]Note, however, that this accounting differs if a firm repurchases common shares in order to transfer them to employees or officers in stock-based compensation plans. In the case of share transactions with employees, the amounts for stock-based compensation expense, vesting of restricted share units, and any cash received from employees exercising stock options are all added to additional paid-in capital, and the amounts paid by the firm to repurchase common shares is subtracted from additional paid-in capital.

[20]The stock market often interprets share repurchase announcements as "good news," inferring that management, with its in-depth knowledge of the firm, believes that the capital market is underpricing the firm's stock (although, ironically, most stock repurchase plans are not completed at the announced levels). The stock market typically reacts to this positive signal by bidding up the price of the firm's shares. Stock repurchases also may be perceived favorably by capital market participants because they represent a form of implicit dividend to individual shareholders that may be taxed at capital gains rates, which may be lower than the ordinary income tax rates on dividends (depending on the shareholders' holding period and tax status).

In **Starbucks'** 2015 Annual Report, the MD&A section titled "Financial Condition, Liquidity, and Capital Resources" (Appendix B, which can be found online at the book's companion website at www.cengagebrain.com) discloses that in July 2015, **Starbucks** announced the board of directors had approved an increase of 50 million shares to the ongoing share repurchase program. **Starbucks** will likely continue to make substantial repurchases of common shares. We project that **Starbucks** will use $1,500 million in cash each year in Years +1 through +5 to repurchase common shares.

We may need to reduce the projected amount of share repurchases in particular years if we determine later in our analysis that **Starbucks** will not have sufficient cash flow for these repurchases, or if our equity valuation estimates indicate that the capital market has overpriced **Starbucks'** shares. Alternately, we may increase these projected amounts if our analysis reveals that **Starbucks** will have excess future cash flow or if our valuation estimates indicate **Starbucks'** shares are underpriced.

In projecting stock repurchases net of stock reissues, we assume that employees will continue to exercise stock options and other stock-based compensation awards in future years. We may need to revise this assumption later in the analysis if our equity valuation estimates indicate that **Starbucks'** stock options are not likely to be "in the money." We implicitly include an expense for the fair value of stock-based compensation in the projections of general and administrative expense.

The projected amounts for dividends and common share repurchases are as follows:

Dividends and Common Share Repurchases	2015	Year +1	Year +2	Year +3	Year +4	Year +5
Projected net earnings	$2,759.3	$2,794.3	$3,080.6	$3,490.0	$3,939.8	$4,895.0
Dividend payout policy	36.8%	42.5%	42.5%	42.5%	42.5%	42.5%
Projected dividend payments	$1,016.2	$1,187.6	$1,309.2	$1,483.2	$1,674.4	$2,080.4
Repurchases of common shares	$1,431.8	$1,500.0	$1,500.0	$1,500.0	$1,500.0	$1,500.0

Retained Earnings

In general, retained earnings typically increase by the amount of net income and decrease for dividends declared and net losses. For **Starbucks**, amounts paid to repurchase common shares are subtracted from retained earnings, too. The implied changes in retained earnings are as follows (allow for rounding):

Retained Earnings	Year +1	Year +2	Year +3	Year +4	Year +5
Beginning balance	$ 5,974.8	$ 6,081.5	$ 6,352.9	$ 6,859.6	$ 7,625.0
Projected net earnings	2,794.3	3,080.6	3,490.0	3,939.8	4,895.0
Projected dividend payments	(1,187.6)	(1,309.2)	(1,483.2)	(1,674.4)	(2,080.4)
Projected common share Repurchases	(1,500.0)	(1,500.0)	(1,500.0)	(1,500.0)	(1,500.0)
Ending balance	$ 6,081.5	$ 6,352.9	$ 6,859.6	$ 7,625.0	$ 8,939.6

Step 6: Balance the Balance Sheet

LO 10-2f

Build forecasts of future balance sheets, income statements, and statements of cash flows by applying the seven-step forecasting framework to project: f. a balance sheet that balances.

Even though the first-pass forecasts of all amounts on the income statement and balance sheet are complete, the balance sheet does not balance because we have projected individual asset and liability accounts to capture their underlying business activities, which are not perfectly correlated. The difference between the initial projected total assets and the projected total liabilities and shareholders' equity each year represents the amount by which we must adjust a "flexible" financial account to balance the balance sheet. If the difference is a positive amount, projected assets exceed projected liability and equity claims, so the firm must raise additional debt or equity capital or reduce projected assets. If the difference is a negative amount, projected assets are less than projected liability and equity financing, in which case the firm can pay down debt, issue larger dividends, repurchase more shares, or increase investments in financial assets. The change in the difference represents the increment by which we must adjust the flexible financial account each year.

The analyst must evaluate the firm's financial flexibility and adjust the balance sheet accordingly. For some firms (for example, start-ups), financial flexibility may be in cash or marketable securities, which represent financial liquidity "safety valves." These firms often keep relatively large amounts of cash or marketable securities on the balance sheet for financial slack and use the funds when necessary to meet periodic cash requirements. For these firms, large inflows of cash (such as from a new issue of debt or equity shares) build up the cash and marketable securities accounts, and large outflows (such as for the purchase of an asset or R&D expenditures) deplete the accounts. For these firms, analysts can use cash or marketable securities as the financial flexibility account needed to balance the balance sheet after all other balance sheet amounts have been determined.

For profitable growth firms that do not have large reserves of excess cash or marketable securities, financial flexibility may be exercised through short-term or long-term debt or equity. As the firm grows and invests in increasing productive capacity, it must raise the necessary capital through borrowing or issuing equity. As the firm matures and becomes a cash cow, it will shift how it uses its financial flexibility to pay down debt and perhaps initiate or increase dividends and share repurchases. You should consider carefully what financial flexibility the firm has and is likely to use.

Balancing Starbucks' Balance Sheets

Currently, our projections of **Starbucks'** total assets minus total liabilities and shareholders' equity indicate the amounts by which our balance sheets do not balance. These amounts are shown below (allow for rounding):

Projected Balance Sheet Amounts	Year +1	Year +2	Year +3	Year +4	Year +5
Total assets (A)	$12,829.0	$13,540.1	$14,495.5	$15,597.5	$17,552.1
Total liabilities	$ 8,056.7	$ 8,477.5	$ 9,021.1	$ 9,611.6	$10,254.8
Common stock and additional paid-in capital	43.9	46.3	49.6	53.4	60.1
Accumulated other comprehensive loss	(199.4)	(199.4)	(199.4)	(199.4)	(199.4)
Retained earnings	6,081.5	6,352.9	6,859.6	7,625.0	8,939.6
Total liabilities and equity (L + E)	$13,982.7	$14,677.3	$15,730.9	$17,090.6	$19,055.0
Difference: A − (L + E)	$(1,153.7)	$(1,137.2)	$(1,235.4)	$(1,493.0)	$(1,503.0)
Change in the difference	$(1,153.7)	$ 16.5	$ (98.2)	$ (257.6)	$ (9.9)

In Year +1, the first-iteration forecasts project that liabilities and equities exceed assets by $1,153.7 million, so we will need an adjustment for this amount. In Year +2, the first-iteration projections indicate that assets will exceed liabilities and equities by a total of $1,137.2 million, so we need an incremental adjustment of $16.5 million in Year +2, and so on. We could use a number of flexible financial accounts for this adjustment each year, depending on **Starbucks'** strategy for investments and capital structure. Consider the following options:

- Increase short-term and/or long-term investment securities, assuming **Starbucks** will retain excess capital in marketable securities for financial flexibility.
- Reduce short-term or long-term debt, assuming **Starbucks** will use its financial flexibility to reduce leverage.
- Reduce retained earnings by increasing projected dividends.
- Reduce retained earnings by increasing common share repurchases.

Given the fact that **Starbucks** has clearly demonstrated its willingness and ability to pay out increasing amounts of capital to shareholders through dividends and share repurchases, we adjust share repurchases as the flexible financial account. Equivalently, we could assume that **Starbucks** will distribute the excess capital to shareholders through additional dividends rather than treasury stock repurchases. Either assumption, that **Starbucks** will return the excess capital to shareholders through increased dividends and/or common share repurchases, will have the same effect on total assets, total liabilities, total shareholders' equity, and net income. Therefore, in Year +1, we will increase the share repurchase forecast by $1,153.7 million, the amount necessary to balance the balance sheet. This simply means that if **Starbucks'** financial performance and position during Year +1 exactly match our forecasts, then **Starbucks** can use a total of $2,653.7 million (the original forecast of $1,500.0 plus the adjustment of $1,153.7 million) for share repurchases, keeping total assets in balance with total liabilities and equity. In Years +2 through +5, we will also adjust our share repurchase forecasts of $1,500.0 million up or down each year by the incremental amount of the necessary adjustment to balance the balance sheet (that is, –$16.5 million in Year +2, $98.2 million in Year +3, and so on). The projected total amounts of share repurchases are as follows:

Common Share Repurchases	Year +1	Year +2	Year +3	Year +4	Year +5
Original projections of share repurchases	$1,500.0	$1,500.0	$1,500.0	$1,500.0	$1,500.0
Financial flexible adjustments	1,153.7	(16.5)	98.2	257.6	9.9
Adjusted total share repurchases	$2,653.7	$1,483.5	$1,598.2	$1,757.6	$1,509.9

After adjusting our projected share repurchases as necessary to balance the balance sheet, the Retained Earnings projections are as follows (allow for rounding):

Retained Earnings	Year +1	Year +2	Year +3	Year +4	Year +5
Beginning balance	$ 5,974.8	$ 4,927.8	$ 5,215.6	$ 5,624.1	$ 6,131.9
Projected net earnings	2,794.3	3,080.6	3,490.0	3,939.8	4,895.0
Projected dividend payments	(1,187.6)	(1,309.2)	(1,483.2)	(1,674.4)	(2,080.4)
Projected common share repurchases	(2,653.7)	(1,483.5)	(1,598.2)	(1,757.6)	(1,509.9)
Ending balance	$ 4,927.8	$ 5,215.6	$ 5,624.1	$ 6,131.9	$ 7,436.6

The final projections of the balance sheet total amounts, which you should verify by referring back to the projected balance sheets presented in Exhibit 10.4, are as follows (allow for rounding):

Projected Balance Sheet Amounts	Year +1	Year +2	Year +3	Year +4	Year +5
Total assets (A)	$12,829.0	$13,540.1	$14,495.5	$15,597.5	$17,552.1
Total liabilities	$ 8,056.7	$ 8,477.5	$ 9,021.1	$ 9,611.6	$10,254.8
Common stock and additional paid-in capital	43.9	46.3	49.6	53.4	60.1
Accumulated other comprehensive loss	(199.4)	(199.4)	(199.4)	(199.4)	(199.4)
Retained earnings	4,927.8	5,215.6	5,624.1	6,131.9	7,436.6
Total liabilities and equity (L + E)	$12,829.0	$13,540.1	$14,495.5	$15,597.5	$17,552.1
Difference: A − (L + E)	$ 0.0	$ 0.0	$ 0.0	$ 0.0	$ 0.0

Closing the Loop: Solving for Codetermined Variables

If we had added the excess capital to interest-earning asset accounts (for example, investment securities or cash) or subtracted it from interest-bearing short-term or long-term debt, the projected amounts for interest income or interest expense would have to be adjusted on the income statement. This would have created an additional set of codetermined variables in the financial statement forecasts.

For example, suppose we use long-term debt as the flexible financial account and adjust it to balance assets with liabilities and shareholders' equity. To determine the necessary adjustment to long-term debt, we must first forecast all of the other asset, liability, and shareholders' equity amounts, including retained earnings. To forecast retained earnings, we must forecast net income, which depends on interest expense on long-term debt. To determine retained earnings, we must also forecast dividends, which depend on net income. Thus, it is necessary to solve simultaneously for at least five variables.

This problem might seem intractable, but it is not because of the computational capabilities of computer spreadsheet programs such as Excel. To solve for multiple variables simultaneously, check the box in Excel to "Enable iterative calculation" and allow for up to 1,000 iterations. (This box appears in different places in different versions of Excel. In recent versions, it appears within the Formulas menu under the Options tab under the File tab.) Excel will then solve and resolve circular references up to 1,000 times until all calculations fall within the specified tolerance for precision. Then you can program each cell to calculate the variables needed, even if they are simultaneously determined with other variables. The default settings in FSAP allow for iterative simultaneous computations, but some versions of Excel automatically reset the default settings. Follow these steps to double-check that the FSAP spreadsheet will compute codetermined variables simultaneously.

Step 7: Project the Statement of Cash Flows

LO 10-2g

Build forecasts of future balance sheets, income statements, and statements of cash flows by applying the seven-step forecasting framework to project: g. cash flows.

The final step of the seven-step forecasting process involves projecting the statement of cash flows, which we described in Chapter 3. This is a relatively straightforward task because the statement of cash flows simply characterizes all of the changes in the balance sheet in terms of the implications for cash. Thus, we derive the implied cash flows directly from the projected changes in all of the balance sheet accounts (other than the cash account, of course), as follows:

- Increases in assets imply uses of cash.
- Decreases in assets imply sources of cash.
- Increases in liabilities and shareholders' equity imply sources of cash.
- Decreases in liabilities and shareholders' equity imply uses of cash.

Tips for Forecasting Statements of Cash Flows

Here are a few coaching tips for preparing forecasts of statements of cash flows:

- The statement of cash flows will only reconcile with the projected income statement and balance sheets when the balance sheets balance and the income statement articulates with the balance sheets. (That is, net income is included in retained earnings.)
- You should *not* attempt to project future statements of cash flows from historical statements of cash flows. Unfortunately, unlike historical balance sheets and income statements, historical statements of cash flows *do not* provide good bases for projecting future cash flows because many of the line items on the statement of cash flows are difficult to reconcile with historical changes in balance sheet amounts. The reason is that in preparing the statement of cash flows, the accountant can aggregate or disaggregate numerous cash flows on each line item of the statement and you may not be able to determine what amounts have been aggregated or disaggregated. For example, the accountant must report separately the net cash flow implications of a business acquisition on one line of the statement, but the business acquisition causes changes in many asset and liability accounts. In addition, the accountant may choose to disclose details of cash flows that you cannot verify. For example, the accountant might disclose separately in the statement of cash flows the amounts of marketable securities purchased and sold, but you cannot verify those amounts because you can only observe the net change in the marketable securities from the beginning to the end of the year.
- We strongly recommend simply following the steps below to compute the *implied statement of cash flows* from the projected balance sheets and income statements, which you can observe and verify. We have programmed the Forecasts spreadsheet in FSAP (Appendix C) to automatically calculate implied statements of cash flows from the projected income statements and balance sheets.

Specific Steps for Forecasting Implied Statements of Cash Flows

Exhibit 10.5 presents the projected implied statement of cash flows for **Starbucks** for 2015 and for Years +1 through +6. Line item numbers are in the right-most column of the exhibit, and we describe the derivation of the amounts on each line item next. You should verify how the projected implied statements of cash flows in Exhibit 10.5 capture the cash inflows and outflows described in each of the following line items.

(1) **Net Income:** Use the amounts in the forecasted income statements (Exhibit 10.3).
(2) **Depreciation Expense:** Add back the projected amount of depreciation expense included in net income. The depreciation expense forecast should reconcile with the change in accumulated depreciation on property, plant, and equipment on the projected balance sheet (minus the decrease in accumulated depreciation from assets that were sold or retired, if any).

Exhibit 10.5

Starbucks
Actual and Forecasted Statements of Cash Flows
(Actual and forecasted amounts in bold. Amounts in millions; allow for rounding.)

IMPLIED STATEMENTS OF CASH FLOWS	Actuals 2015	Year +1	Year +2	Year +3	Year +4	Year +5	Year +6	line
Net Income	$ 2,759.3	$ 2,794.3	$ 3,080.6	$ 3,490.0	$ 3,939.8	$ 4,895.0	$ 5,041.8	(1)
Add back depreciation expense (net)	491.4	1,104.2	1,254.2	1,434.2	1,644.2	1,151.6	364.3	(2)
Add back amortization expense (net)	0.0	0.0	0.0	0.0	0.0	0.0	0.0	(3)
<Increase> Decrease in receivables—net	(88.0)	(106.0)	(82.8)	(107.7)	(117.9)	(129.1)	(37.9)	(4)
<Increase> Decrease in inventories	(215.5)	(21.3)	(113.1)	(145.2)	(156.8)	(169.3)	(57.4)	(5)
<Increase> Decrease in prepaid expenses	(48.6)	(17.8)	(17.8)	(17.8)	(17.8)	(17.8)	(12.7)	(6)
Increase <Decrease> in accounts payable—trade	150.5	(18.7)	63.6	75.1	79.3	85.6	29.1	(7)
Increase <Decrease> in current accrued liabilities	246.3	231.1	183.0	241.1	263.3	287.3	89.0	(8)
Increase <Decrease> in insurance reserves	28.7	6.7	6.9	7.2	7.4	7.6	7.8	(9)
Increase <Decrease> in stored value card liabilities	189.3	129.2	102.3	134.7	147.1	160.6	49.7	(10)
Net change in deferred tax assets and liabilities	10.0	464.7	74.6	67.1	60.4	54.4	(14.7)	(11)
Increase <Decrease> in long-term accrued liabilities	233.1	82.1	65.0	85.6	93.5	102.0	31.6	(12)
Net Cash Flows from Operations	$ 3,756.5	$ 4,648.5	$ 4,616.6	$ 5,264.2	$ 5,942.4	$ 6,428.0	$ 5,490.7	(13)
<Increase> Decrease in property, plant, & equip. at cost	(1,060.7)	(1,400.0)	(1,500.0)	(1,800.0)	(2,100.0)	(2,400.0)	(565.3)	(14)
<Increase> Decrease in short-term investments	54.1	(2.4)	(2.5)	(2.6)	(2.7)	(2.7)	(2.8)	(15)
<Increase> Decrease in long-term investments	168.8	(27.0)	(28.1)	(29.3)	(30.6)	(31.9)	(24.3)	(16)
<Increase> Decrease in amortizable intangible assets (net)	(246.9)	(26.0)	(27.3)	(28.7)	(30.1)	(31.6)	(19.9)	(17)
<Increase> Decrease in goodwill and nonamort. intangibles	(719.2)	(78.8)	(82.7)	(86.8)	(91.2)	(95.7)	(60.3)	(18)
<Increase> Decrease in other assets	(217.0)	(20.8)	(21.8)	(22.9)	(24.1)	(25.3)	(15.9)	(19)
Net Cash Flows from Investing Activities	$(2,020.9)	$(1,555.0)	$(1,662.5)	$(1,970.4)	$(2,278.7)	$(2,587.3)	$ (688.6)	(20)

Exhibit 10.5 (Continued)

IMPLIED STATEMENTS OF CASH FLOWS	Actuals	Forecasts						line
	2015	Year +1	Year +2	Year +3	Year +4	Year +5	Year +6	
Increase <Decrease> in short-term debt	0.0	400.0	(400.0)	350.0	(350.0)	0.0	0.0	(21)
Increase <Decrease> in long-term debt	299.2	600.0	400.0	(350.0)	350.0	0.0	100.4	(22)
Increase <Decrease> in common stock + paid-in capital	2.5	1.3	2.4	3.3	3.8	6.7	1.8	(23)
Increase <Decrease> in accum. OCI	(224.7)	0.0	0.0	0.0	0.0	0.0	0.0	(24)
Dividends and share repurchases	(1,989.2)	(3,841.3)	(2,792.8)	(3,081.5)	(3,432.0)	(3,590.3)	(4,824.7)	(25)
Increase <Decrease> in noncontrolling interests	(1.8)	(1.8)	0.0	0.0	0.0	0.0	0.0	(26)
Net Cash Flows from Financing Activities	$(1,914.0)	$(2,841.7)	$(2,790.4)	$(3,078.2)	$(3,428.2)	$(3,583.6)	$(4,722.5)	(27)
Net Change in Cash	$ (178.4)	$ 251.8	$ 163.7	$ 215.6	$ 235.5	$ 257.0	$ 79.6	(28)
Beginning Cash Balance	$ 1,708.4	$ 1,530.0	$ 1,781.8	$ 1,945.5	$ 2,161.2	$ 2,396.7	$ 2,653.7	(29)
Ending Cash Balance	$ 1,530.0	$ 1,781.8	$ 1,945.5	$ 2,161.2	$ 2,396.7	$ 2,653.7	$ 2,733.3	(30)
Check figure								
Net change in cash − Change in cash balance	0	0	0	0	0	0	0	

Note: We label the statement of cash flows and amounts for 2015 as "Actual" even though we derive it from the actual balance sheet and income statement amounts in Starbucks' financial statements rather than from the financial statement forecasts. Appendix A presents the actual statements of cash flows for 2013, 2014, and 2015 as reported by Starbucks according to U.S. GAAP.

(3) **Amortization Expense:** Add back amortization expense on amortizable intangible assets.[21] The amount of amortization expense to add back to net income should reconcile with the change in amortizable intangible assets balance, adjusted for any new investments in those assets (which should be included as cash outflows in the investing section of this statement). For some firms, if the amount of amortization expense is not large, you can ignore adding it back to net income to compute cash flow from operating activities and simply include the net change in amortizable intangible assets in the investing section. This will slightly understate cash inflows from operations and slightly understate cash outflows for investing activities, but the two effects will offset so that net cash flow is not affected.

(4)–(10) **Working Capital Accounts:** Adjust net income for changes in all of the various operating current asset and current liability accounts other than cash (such as accounts receivable, inventory, accounts payable, accrued expenses, and others) appearing on the projected balance sheets.

(11), (12) **Deferred Taxes and Long-Term Accrued Expenses:** Adjust net income for changes in deferred taxes, noncurrent liabilities for accrued expenses, and changes in other noncurrent liabilities. These items include changes in long-term accruals for expenses that are part of operations, including deferred taxes, pension and retiree benefit obligations, warranties, and other noncurrent liabilities that appear on the projected balance sheets.

(13) **Net Cash Flows from Operations:** The sum of lines (1) through (12) is the implied amount of net cash flows from operating activities.

(14) **Property, Plant, and Equipment:** The amount on this line captures cash outflows for the projected capital expenditures included in the change in property, plant, and equipment (at cost) on the projected balance sheet in Exhibit 10.4, minus any cash proceeds from sales of property, plant, and equipment. As a check, make sure the statement of cash flows captures all of the net cash flow implications of property, plant, and equipment. To verify this, the amount of depreciation expense added back to net income *minus* cash outflows for capital expenditures *plus* cash inflows for any asset sales or retirements should equal the change in net property, plant, and equipment on the projected balance sheet.

(15), (16) **Investment Securities (net):** The statement of cash flows classifies net purchases and sales of short-term and long-term investment securities as investing transactions. The net changes in these accounts on the projected balance sheets determine the cash flow amounts for these items on the statement of cash flows. Some error in the implied cash flow amount from investment securities can occur. This change should be increased (become less negative) for the excess (if any) of equity earnings over dividends received from noncontrolled affiliates (which is a noncash increase in this asset amount). Similarly, the excess of equity earnings over dividends received also should be subtracted from net income in the operating section of the statement of cash flows. Rather than making assumptions about this relatively immaterial item (the effects of which completely offset each other), we simply treat the entire change in investments as an investing transaction. This choice means that cash flows

---

[21]Note that you should not need to add back any amortization expense for nonamortizable intangible assets such as goodwill and brands with indefinite lives because, under U.S. GAAP and IFRS, goodwill and other intangibles with indefinite lives are not amortized. Thus, no amortization expense for these assets was included in the projected income statements.

from operating activities may be slightly overstated and cash flows from investing activities may be slightly understated by an equivalent amount but that the net change in cash each year is not affected.

(17) **Amortizable Intangible Assets:** Enter the implied net cash flows from any changes in amortizable intangible assets on this line, which should include any projected cash outflows to acquire amortizable intangible assets, net of any cash inflows from sales or retirements of such assets. As discussed in Item (3), we add back amortization expense to net income in the operating section of the statement of cash flows. Thus, our adjustment for cash outflows or inflows for amortizable intangible assets in the investing section of the statement should not include the effects of amortization expense. Given that amortizable intangibles are commonly shown on balance sheets net of accumulated amortization, the change in the net amortizable intangible assets account balance will reflect both effects: cash flows from investing activities and amortization expense. To isolate the cash flows from investing, you should add amortization expense back to the net change in this account balance.

(18) **Goodwill and Indefinite-Lived (Nonamortizable) Intangible Assets:** Enter the implied cash flows from changes in goodwill and indefinite-lived intangible assets on this line. These assets are not amortized, so the net change on the projected balance sheets should reflect cash outflows to acquire new goodwill and nonamortizable intangible assets, net of any cash inflows from selling or retiring such assets. If the account balance for goodwill or nonamortizable intangible assets has declined because of an impairment charge, you should add this noncash charge back to net income in the operating section of the statement of cash flows and adjust accordingly the cash flow implications from net changes in goodwill or nonamortizable intangibles in the investing section (similar to adding back amortization expense).

(19) **Other Noncurrent Assets:** Enter the changes in other noncurrent assets on this line. The changes in the other noncurrent asset accounts on the projected balance sheets measure the cash outflows to acquire such assets net of any cash inflows from sales or retirements of such assets.

(20) **Net Cash Flows from Investing Activities:** The sum of lines (14) through (19) on **Starbucks'** projected implied statement of cash flows measures the implied amount of net cash flows from investing activities.

(21), (22) **Short-Term and Long-Term Debt:** Changes in interest-bearing debt (short-term notes payable, current maturities of long-term debt, and long-term debt) on the projected balance sheets are financing activities.

(23) **Changes in Common Stock and Additional Paid-in Capital:** These amounts represent the financing cash flows from changes in the common stock and paid-in capital accounts on the projected balance sheets.

(24) **Changes in Accumulated Other Comprehensive Income:** These amounts represent the changes in the accumulated other comprehensive income account that is a component of shareholders' equity on the projected balance sheets.

(25) **Dividends and Common Share Repurchases:** The amounts represent the net cash flow implications of dividend payments as well as common share repurchases that are captured in the net change in retained earnings (or in the treasury stock account) on the projected balance sheets.

(26) **Noncontrolling Interests:** Enter the projected amounts of dividends to noncontrolling interests as cash outflows, net of any cash inflows (if any) from additional investments by noncontrolling investors.

(27) **Net Cash Flows from Financing Activities:** The sum of lines (21) through (26) measures the implied amount of net cash flows from financing activities.

(28) **Net Change in Cash:** The aggregate of the amounts of cash flows from operating activities (line 13), investing activities (line 20), and financing activities (line 27). This total should equal the change in cash on the projected balance sheets.

(29), (30) **Beginning and Ending Balance in Cash:** The net change in cash on the statement of cash flows (line 28) should equal the change in cash on the projected balance sheets.

Shortcut Approaches to Forecasting

LO 10-3

Understand how and when to use shortcut forecasting techniques.

This chapter emphasizes and demonstrates a methodical, detailed approach to forecasting drivers of expected future operating, investing, and financing activities that will determine future amounts for individual accounts on the income statement, balance sheet, and statement of cash flows. In some circumstances, however, you may find it necessary to forecast income statement and balance sheet totals directly without carefully considering each account. This shortcut approach has the potential to introduce forecasting error if the shortcut assumptions do not fit each account very well. On the other hand, if the firm is stable and mature in an industry in steady-state equilibrium, shortcut forecasting techniques are efficient approaches to project current steady-state conditions to the future. This section briefly illustrates shortcut approaches for forecasting **Starbucks'** income statements and balance sheets.

Projected Revenues and Income Approach

Shortcut projections for total revenues and net income can be developed using **Starbucks'** recent revenue growth rates and net profit margins. The common-size and rate-of-change income statement data discussed in Chapter 1 reveal that, from 2011 through 2015, **Starbucks** generated a compound annual growth rate in revenues of 12.3% and an average net profit margin of 9.6%. If we simply use these ratios to forecast revenues and net income over Years +1 to +5, the projected amounts are as follows:

Shortcut Projections	2015	Year +1	Year +2	Year +3	Year +4	Year +5
Total net revenues	$19,162.7	$21,519.7	$24,166.6	$27,139.1	$30,477.2	$34,225.9
Compounded annual growth	12.3%	12.3%	12.3%	12.3%	12.3%	12.3%
Net earnings	$ 2,759.3	$ 2,065.9	$ 2,320.0	$ 2,605.4	$ 2,925.8	$ 3,285.7
Historical average profit margin	9.6%	9.6%	9.6%	9.6%	9.6%	9.6%

These shortcut projections for revenues are much higher and the projections for net income are much lower than the detailed revenue and income projections developed for **Starbucks** throughout this chapter. The more detailed projections capture specific factors driving growth in revenues, as well expected changes in individual expenses relative to revenues. The shortcut approach simply assumes that existing relations between revenues and expenses will persist linearly into the future.

Projected Total Assets Approach

For the balance sheet, total assets can be projected using the recent historical growth rate in total assets. Between fiscal 2011 and 2015, **Starbucks'** total assets grew at a compound annual rate of 14.3%. Over that same period, total liabilities averaged 48.7% of total assets, and shareholders' equity averaged 51.3%. If a shortcut approach assumes this historical growth rate and capital structure will continue through Year +5, then projected total assets, liabilities, and equities will be as follows (allow for rounding):

Shortcut Projections	2015	Year +1	Year +2	Year +3	Year +4	Year +5
Total assets	$12,446.1	$14,225.9	$16,260.2	$18,585.4	$21,243.1	$24,280.9
Compounded annual growth	14.3%	14.3%	14.3%	14.3%	14.3%	14.3%
Total liabilities	$ 6,626.3	$ 6,928.0	$ 7,918.7	$ 9,051.1	$10,345.4	$11,824.8
Average as a percent of assets	48.7%	48.7%	48.7%	48.7%	48.7%	48.7%
Total shareholders' equity	$ 5,819.8	$ 7,297.9	$ 8,341.5	$ 9,534.3	$10,897.7	$12,456.1
Average as a percent of assets	51.3%	51.3%	51.3%	51.3%	51.3%	51.3%

Using common-size balance sheet percentages to project individual assets, liabilities, and shareholders' equity encounters (at least) three potential shortcomings. First, in using common-size percentages for forecasting, you assume the firm maintains a constant mix of assets, liabilities, and equities, and that each asset, liability, and equity account grows at the same rate as total assets. This strong assumption may not be valid for a majority of firms, which tend to experience dynamic, nonlinear changes over time. Second, using the common-size percentages does not permit you to change the assumptions about the future behavior of an individual asset or liability. For **Starbucks**, for example, we forecast continued, substantial increases in dividend payments and share repurchases. Third, the common-sized shortcut approaches do not allow you an effective mechanism to forecast major transactions that reflect disproportionate shifts in assets relative to liabilities and equities.

In general, shortcut approaches to forecasting have the benefit of greater efficiency but greater potential for error as compared to more thoughtful and deliberate forecasts of income statement and balance sheet accounts. Given that forecast errors can be very costly if they lead to bad investment decisions, we strongly advocate the careful, detailed approach to projecting financial statements by forecasting the firm's future operating, investing, and financing activities using individual income statement and balance sheet accounts.

LO 10-4

Test the validity of your forecast assumptions and results.

Test Forecast Validity by Analyzing Projected Financial Statements

You should test the validity of your forecast assumptions by analyzing the projected financial statements using the ratios and analytical tools discussed in Chapters 1, 4, and 5. Exhibit 10.6 presents a ratios analysis for **Starbucks** based on the financial statement forecasts for Year +1 to Year +6. The FSAP Forecasts spreadsheet provides these computations (Appendix C).

These data show that our forecast growth rates for revenues are relatively smooth, which is consistent with **Starbucks'** past sales growth performance. The forecasts of net income exhibit growth rates that are less volatile than those **Starbucks** experienced in its recent past. The projected rate of ROA (return on assets) increases steadily from

Exhibit 10.6

Financial Ratio Analysis of Starbucks Based on Actual and Forecasted Financial Statements

	Actuals			Forecasts					
	2013	2014	2015	Year +1	Year +2	Year +3	Year +4	Year +5	Year +6
FORECAST VALIDITY CHECK DATA									
GROWTH									
Revenue Growth Rates	11.8%	10.6%	16.5%	13.1%	9.2%	11.1%	10.9%	10.7%	3.0%
Net Income Growth Rates	99.4%	23,396.6%	33.4%	1.3%	10.2%	13.3%	12.9%	24.2%	3.0%
Total Asset Growth Rates	40.1%	(6.6%)	15.7%	3.1%	5.5%	7.1%	7.6%	12.5%	3.0%
RETURN ON ASSETS (excluding the effects of nonrecurring items)									
Profit Margin for ROA	12.4%	12.7%	13.5%	13.1%	13.3%	13.5%	13.7%	15.3%	15.3%
× Asset Turnover	1.5	1.5	1.7	1.7	1.8	1.9	1.9	1.9	1.9
= Return on Assets	18.6%	18.8%	22.3%	22.5%	23.8%	25.3%	26.6%	29.9%	28.6%
RETURN ON COMMON EQUITY (excluding the effects of nonrecurring items)									
Profit Margin for ROCE	12.2%	12.5%	13.3%	12.9%	13.0%	13.3%	13.5%	15.2%	15.2%
× Asset Turnover	1.5	1.5	1.7	1.7	1.8	1.9	1.9	1.9	1.9
× Capital Structure Leverage	2.1	2.3	2.1	2.4	2.7	2.7	2.6	2.5	2.4
= Return on Common Equity	37.9%	42.1%	45.9%	52.8%	62.6%	66.2%	68.8%	73.7%	68.1%

(Continued)

Exhibit 10.6 (Continued)

	Actuals			Forecasts					
	2013	2014	2015	Year +1	Year +2	Year +3	Year +4	Year +5	Year +6
OPERATING PERFORMANCE									
Gross Profit/Revenues	57.1%	58.3%	59.4%	60.1%	60.3%	60.7%	61.0%	61.4%	61.4%
Operating Profit before Taxes/Revenues	(2.2%)	18.7%	18.8%	19.7%	19.9%	20.3%	20.6%	23.1%	23.1%
ASSET TURNOVER									
Revenues/Avg. Accounts Receivable	28.4	27.6	28.4	28.1	27.3	27.3	27.1	27.0	26.0
Cost of Goods Sold/Avg. Inventory	5.4	6.2	6.5	6.6	6.8	6.8	6.8	6.8	6.6
Revenues/Avg. Fixed Assets	5.1	4.9	5.0	2.0	1.9	1.9	1.8	1.8	1.7
LIQUIDITY									
Current Ratio	1.0	1.4	1.2	1.0	1.1	1.0	1.1	1.1	1.1
Quick Ratio	0.7	0.8	0.6	0.6	0.7	0.6	0.7	0.7	0.7
SOLVENCY									
Total Liabilities/Total Assets	61.1%	51.0%	53.2%	62.8%	62.6%	62.2%	61.6%	58.4%	58.4%
Total Liabilities/Total Equity	156.9%	103.9%	113.9%	168.8%	167.5%	164.8%	160.6%	140.5%	140.5%
Interest Coverage Ratio	(7.2)	50.3	56.4	55.9	52.5	59.4	66.9	82.9	82.9

Year +1 to Year +5, consistent with our projections of increasing profitability and asset efficiency. For the same reasons, and because of the projected increase in capital structure leverage, the projected ROCE (return on common equity) increases considerably from Year +1 to +5.

The projected increase in capital structure leverage over the forecast horizon is the result of **Starbucks'** strategy to increase outstanding long-term debt. In addition, **Starbucks** is distributing increasing amounts of cash to shareholders through dividends and share repurchases. These financial strategy shifts have been ongoing over the past few years, and we project they will continue over the forecast horizon. Together, the net effects of increasing the ratio of long-term debt to assets, while at the same time repurchasing shares and paying dividends, suggests that **Starbucks'** capital structure leverage will increase. Given that we expect **Starbucks** will continue to generate healthy profit margins and high levels of asset efficiency, we expect it will also generate increasingly higher returns to common equity shareholders.

The operating performance ratios, liquidity ratios, assets turnover ratios, and solvency ratios confirm that our forecast assumptions are reasonable given **Starbucks'** expected future financial performance and position. Unfortunately, these ratios cannot confirm whether our forecast assumptions will turn out to be correct. These ratios do not tell us whether we have accurately and realistically captured **Starbucks'** future sales growth, profitability, cash flows, and financial position. For this confirmation, only time will tell.

Sensitivity Analysis

LO 10-5

Test the sensitivity of your forecasts to variations in critical assumptions and parameters.

These financial statement forecasts can serve as a "base case" from which you can assess the impacts of variations in critical forecast assumptions for the firm. For example, with these financial statement forecasts, you can assess the sensitivity of projected net income and cash flows to key assumptions about revenue growth rates, gross profit margins, operating expenses, and others. Using the projected financial statements (Exhibits 10.3, 10.4, and 10.6) as a base case, you can easily assess the impact on **Starbucks's** profitability from an increase or decrease in revenue growth or from an increase or decrease in the gross profit margin.

You also can use the projected financial statements to assess the sensitivity of the firm's liquidity and leverage to changes in key assumptions. For example, you can assess the impact on **Starbucks'** liquidity and solvency ratios by varying the long-term debt to assets assumptions and the interest expense assumptions. Lenders and credit analysts can use the projected financial statements to assess the conditions under which the firm's debt covenants may become binding. For example, suppose **Starbucks'** long-term debt agreements contain covenants that require **Starbucks** to maintain liquidity and interest coverage ratios that exceed certain minimum levels. The financial statement forecasts provide these analysts with a structured approach to assess how far net income and cash flows would need to decrease (and how much long-term debt and interest expense would need to increase) before **Starbucks** would violate these debt covenants.

LO 10-6

Develop forecast models that are flexible and comprehensive, enabling you to respond quickly and effectively when a company announces important new information.

Reactions to Announcements

The projected financial statements also enable you to react quickly and efficiently to new announcements by the firm. Using a dynamic, flexible financial statement forecast model (like the one in FSAP), you can react relatively efficiently and incorporate new

information quickly into your expectations for the firm's future earnings, balance sheets, and cash flows. For example, in early 2016, **Starbucks** announced two major new debt issues, each roughly $500 million. We responded quickly to these announcements by including those new debt issues in our long-term debt forecasts on the projected balance sheets and increasing our projected amounts of interest expense.

As an alternative example, suppose **Starbucks** suddenly announces that it is reversing its recapitalization strategy, such that it will discontinue purchases of common shares in Year +1, and that it intends to use this cash to reduce long-term debt. Our projections included $2,653.7 million in cash used for common share repurchases in Year +1, which must now become zero. Our projections must also change to reflect that **Starbucks** will use this capital to reduce (rather than increase) long-term debt. We can efficiently incorporate the effects of this announcement into the projected financial statements by changing a couple of forecast assumptions. **Starbucks'** original and revised projected ratios for Year +1 are as follows:

	Year +1 Original Projections	Year +1 Revised Projections
Net profit margin for ROA	13.1%	13.1%
ROA	22.5%	22.5%
ROCE	52.8%	42.5%
Capital structure leverage	2.4	1.9
Total liabilities/Total assets	62.8%	42.1%
Interest coverage ratio	55.9	104.7

Thus, the assumptions about common share repurchases and long-term debt have significant effects on projected financial statements and ratios for **Starbucks**, as well as **Starbucks'** ability to generate returns for shareholders. Various other changes in assumptions are possible. By designing a flexible spreadsheet model for projecting financial statements, you can quickly and efficiently change any one or a combination of assumptions and observe the effect on the financial statements and ratios. FSAP provides a flexible spreadsheet for forecasting.

Summary

This chapter demonstrates a seven-step procedure for developing financial statement forecasts. The preparation of financial statement forecasts requires numerous assumptions about the future operating, investing, and financing activities of the firm, including future growth rates in sales, cost behavior of various expenses, levels of investments in working capital and fixed assets, the financial capital structure of the firm, and dividend payouts. You should carefully develop realistic expectations for these activities and capture those expectations in financial statement forecasts that provide an objective and realistic projection of the firm in the future. You should then study the sensitivity of the financial statements to the assumptions made and to the impacts of variations in the assumptions.

After developing careful and realistic expectations for future earnings, cash flows, and dividends using financial statement projections, you can use the information to make a wide array of decisions about the firm, including evaluating the firm as a potential equity investment. The next four chapters demonstrate how to incorporate expectations for future dividends, cash flows, and earnings into estimates of firm value.

Questions, Exercises, Problems, and Cases

Questions and Exercises

10.1 Relying on Accounting to Avoid Forecast Errors. The chapter `LO 10-1` states that forecasts of financial statements should rely on the *additivity* within financial statements and the *articulation* across financial statements to avoid internal inconsistencies in forecasts. Explain how the concepts of additivity and articulation apply to financial statement forecasts. Also explain how these concepts can help you avoid potential forecast errors.

10.2 Objective and Realistic Forecasts. The chapter encourages analysts to de- `LO 10-1` velop forecasts that are realistic, objective, and unbiased. Some firms' managers tend to be optimistic. Some accounting principles tend to be conservative. Describe the different risks and incentives that managers, accountants, and analysts face. Explain how these different risks and incentives lead managers, accountants, and analysts to different biases when predicting uncertain outcomes.

10.3 Projecting Revenues: The Effects of Volume versus Price. Sup- `LO 10-2a` pose a firm has generated 10.25% revenue growth in the past two years, consisting of 5.0% growth in sales volume compounded with 5.0% growth in prices. Describe one firm-specific strategic factor, one industry-specific factor, and one economywide factor that could help this firm sustain 5.0% growth in sales volume next year. Describe one firm-specific strategic factor, one industry-specific factor, and one economywide factor that could help this firm sustain 5.0% growth in prices next year.

10.4 Projecting Gross Profit: The Effects of Volume versus Price. `LO 10-2` Suppose you are analyzing a firm that is successfully executing a strategy that differentiates its products from those of its competitors. Because of this strategy, you project that next year the firm will generate 6.0% revenue growth from price increases and 3.0% revenue growth from sales volume increases. Assume that the firm's production cost structure involves strictly variable costs. (That is, the cost to produce each unit of product remains the same.) Should you project that the firm's gross profit will increase next year? If you project that the gross profit will increase, is the increase a result of volume growth, price growth, or both? Should you project that the firm's gross profit margin (gross profit divided by sales) will increase next year? If you project that the gross profit margin will increase, is the increase a result of volume growth, price growth, or both?

10.5 Projecting Revenues, Cost of Goods Sold, and Inventory. Use `LO 10-2` the following hypothetical data for **Walgreens** in 2014 and 2015 to project revenues, cost of goods sold, and inventory for Year +1. Assume that Walgreens's Year +1 revenue growth rate, gross profit margin growth rate, and inventory turnover will be identical to 2015. Project the average inventory balance in Year +1 and use it to compute the implied ending inventory balance.

Walgreens (data in millions)	2014	2015
Sales revenues	$76,392	$103,444
Cost of goods sold	$54,823	$ 76,520
Ending inventory	$ 6,076	$ 8,678

10.6 The Flexible Financial Account. The chapter describes how firms must use `LO 10-2f` flexible financial accounts to maintain equality between assets and claims on assets from liabilities and equities. Chapter 1 describes how some firms progress through different life-cycle stages—from introduction to growth to maturity to decline—and how firms experience very different cash flows during different stages of the life cycle. For each life-cycle stage, identify the different types of flexible accounts that firms will be more likely to use to balance the balance sheet.

LO 10-2f **10.7 Dividends as a Flexible Financial Account.** The following data for Schwartz Company represent a summary of your first-iteration forecast amounts for Year +1. Schwartz uses dividends as a flexible financial account. Compute the amount of dividends you can assume that Schwartz will pay in order to balance your projected balance sheet. Present the projected balance sheet.

	Year +1
Operating income	$ 58
Interest expense	(8)
Income before tax	$ 50
Tax provision (20.0% effective tax rate)	(10)
Net income	$ 40
Total assets	$200
Accrued liabilities	43
Long-term debt	80
Common stock, at par	20
Retained earnings (at the beginning of Year +1)	34

LO 10-2f **10.8 Long-Term Debt as a Flexible Financial Account.** For this exercise, use the preceding data for Schwartz Company. Now assume that Schwartz pays common shareholders a dividend of $25 in Year +1. Also assume that Schwartz uses long-term debt as a flexible financial account, increasing borrowing when it needs capital and paying down debt when it generates excess capital. For simplicity, assume that Schwartz pays 10.0% interest expense on the ending balance in long-term debt for the year and that interest expense is tax deductible at Schwartz's average tax rate of 20.0%. Present the projected income statement and balance sheet for Year +1. (Hint: Because of the circularity among interest expense, net income, and debt, you may need several iterations to balance the projected balance sheet and to have the projected balance sheet articulate with net income. You may find it helpful to program a spreadsheet to work the iterative computations.)

Problems and Cases

LO 10-2 **10.9 Store-Driven Forecasts.** The Home Depot is a leading specialty retailer of hardware and home improvement products and is the second-largest retail store chain in the United States. It operates large warehouse-style stores. In 2014 and 2015, The Home Depot invested in five new stores. The following table provides summary hypothetical data for The Home Depot.

The Home Depot (amounts in millions except number of stores)	2014	2015
Number of stores	2,269	2,274
Sales revenues	$83,176	$88,519
Inventory	$11,079	$11,809
Capital Expenditures, net	$ 1,442	$ 1,503

REQUIRED

    a. Use the preceding data for The Home Depot to compute average revenues per store, capital spending per new store, and ending inventory per store in 2015.

    b. Assume that The Home Depot will add 10 new stores by the end of Year +1. Use the data from 2015 to project Year +1 sales revenues, capital spending, and ending inventory. Assume that each new store will be open for business for an average of one-half year in Year +1. For simplicity, assume that in Year +1, Home Depot's sales revenues will grow, but only because it will open new stores.

10.10 Projecting Property, Plant, and Equipment. Intel is a global leader in manufacturing microprocessors, which is very capital-intensive. The production processes in microprocessor manufacturing require sophisticated technology, and the technology changes rapidly, particularly with each new generation of microprocessor. As a consequence, production and manufacturing assets in the microprocessor industry tend to have relatively short useful lives. Assume the following selected information relates to Intel's property, plant, and equipment for 2014 and 2015:

Intel (amounts in millions)	2014	2015
Property, plant, and equipment, at cost	$ 79,709	$ 83,396
Accumulated depreciation	$(46,471)	$(51,538)
Property, plant, and equipment, net	$ 33,238	$ 31,858
Depreciation expense		$ 7,821
Capital expenditures, net		$ 7,326

REQUIRED

Assume that Intel depreciates all property, plant, and equipment using the straight-line depreciation method and zero salvage value. Assume that Intel spends $6,000 million on new depreciable assets in Year +1 and does not sell or retire any property, plant, and equipment during Year +1.

    a. Compute the average useful life (in years, rounded to two decimals) that Intel used for depreciation in 2015.

    b. Project total depreciation expense for Year +1 using the following steps:

        1. Project depreciation expense for Year +1 on existing property, plant, and equipment at the end of 2015.

        2. Project depreciation expense on capital expenditures in Year +1 assuming that Intel takes a full year of depreciation in the first year of service.

        3. Sum the results of (1) and (2) to obtain total depreciation expense for Year +1.

    c. Project the Year +1 ending balance in property, plant, and equipment, both at cost and net of accumulated depreciation.

10.11 Identifying the Cost Structure and Projecting Gross Margins for Capital-Intensive, Cyclical Businesses. AK Steel is an integrated manufacturer of high-quality steel and steel products in capital-intensive steel mills. AK Steel produces flat-rolled carbon, stainless and electrical steel products, and carbon and stainless tubular steel products for automotive, appliance, construction, and manufacturing markets. **Nucor** manufactures more commodity-level steel and steel products at the lower end of the market in less capital-intensive mini-mills. The following selected hypothetical data describe sales and cost of products sold for both firms for Years 3 and 4.

LO 10-2

LO 10-2

($ amounts in millions)	Year 3	Year 4
AK Steel		
Sales	$4,042	$ 5,217
Cost of products sold	$3,887	$ 4,554
Gross profit	$ 155	$ 663
Gross margin	3.8%	12.7%
Nucor		
Sales	$6,266	$11,377
Cost of products sold	$5,997	$ 9,129
Gross profit	$ 269	$ 2,248
Gross margin	4.3%	19.8%

Industry analysts anticipate the following annual changes in sales for the next five years: Year +1, 5% increase; Year +2, 10% increase; Year +3, 20% increase; Year +4, 10% decrease; Year +5, 20% decrease.

REQUIRED

a. Estimate the variable cost as a percentage of sales for the cost of products sold by dividing the amount of the change in the cost of products sold by the amount of the change in sales. Then multiply the variable-cost percentage times sales to estimate the total variable cost. Subtract the variable cost from the total cost to estimate the fixed cost for cost of products sold. Follow this procedure to estimate the manufacturing cost structure (variable cost as a percentage of sales, total variable costs, and total fixed costs) for cost of products sold for both AK Steel and Nucor in Year 4.

b. Discuss the structure of manufacturing cost (that is, fixed versus variable) for each firm in light of the manufacturing process and type of steel produced.

c. Using the analysts' forecasts of sales growth rates, compute the projected sales, cost of products sold, gross profit, and gross margin (gross profit as a percentage of sales) of each firm for Year +1 through Year +5.

d. Why do the levels and variability of the gross margin percentages differ for these two firms for Year +1 through Year +5?

LO 10-2   **10.12 Identifying the Cost Structure.** **Sony Corporation** manufactures and markets consumer electronics products. Assume the following are selected income statement data for 2014 and 2015 (amounts in billions of yen):

	2014	2015
Sales	¥ 6,682	¥ 7,036
Cost of goods sold	(5,140)	(5,275)
Selling and administrative expenses	(1,729)	(1,811)
Operating income before income Taxes	¥ (187)	¥ (50)

REQUIRED

a. Estimate the variable cost as a percentage of sales for the cost of goods sold by dividing the amount of the change in the cost of goods sold by the amount of the change in sales. Then multiply the variable-cost percentage times sales to estimate the total variable cost. Subtract the variable cost from the total cost to estimate the fixed cost for cost of goods sold. Follow this procedure to determine the cost structure (fixed cost plus variable cost as a percentage of sales) for cost of goods sold for Sony.

b. Repeat Requirement a for selling and administrative expenses.

c. Suppose that Sony Corporation discloses that it expects sales to grow at the following rates in future years: Year +1, 12%; Year +2, 10%; Year +3, 8%; Year +4, 6%. Project sales, cost of goods sold, selling and administrative expenses, and operating income before income taxes for Sony for Year +1 to Year +4 using the cost structure amounts derived in Requirements a and b.

d. Compute the ratio of operating income before income taxes to sales for Year +1 through Year +4.

e. Interpret the changes in the ratio computed in Requirement d in light of the expected changes in sales.

10.13 Smoothing Changes in Accounts Receivable. Hasbro designs, manufactures, and markets toys and games for children and adults in the United States and in international markets. Hasbro's portfolio of brands and products contains some of the most well-known toys and games under famous brands such as Playskool, Tonka Trucks, Milton Bradley, and Parker Brothers and includes such classic games as Scrabble®, Monopoly®, and Clue®. Assume that sales during 2015 totaled $4,448 million. Also assume that accounts receivable totaled $1,095 million at the beginning of 2014 and $1,218 million at the end of 2015.

LO 10-2, LO 10-3
LO 10-4

REQUIRED

a. Use the average balance to compute the accounts receivable turnover ratio for Hasbro for 2015.

b. Assume that Hasbro's sales will grow at a 13.0% rate each year for Year +1 through Year +5 and that the accounts receivable turnover ratio each year will equal the ratio computed in Requirement a for 2015. Project the amount of accounts receivable at year-end through Year +5 based on the accounts receivable turnover computed in Requirement a. Also compute the percentage change in accounts receivable between each of the year-ends through Year +5.

c. Does the pattern of growth in your projections of Hasbro's accounts receivable seem reasonable considering the assumptions of smooth growth in sales and steady turnover? Explain.

d. The changes in accounts receivable computed in Requirement b display the sawtooth pattern depicted in Exhibit 10.4. Smooth the changes in accounts receivable by computing the year-end accounts receivable balances for Year +1 through Year +5 using the compound annual growth rate in accounts receivable between the end of 2015 and the end of Year +1 from Requirement b.

e. Smooth the changes in accounts receivable using the compound annual growth rate in accounts receivable between the end of 2015 and the end of Year +4 from Requirement b. Apply this growth rate to compute accounts receivable at the end of Year +1 through Year +5. Why do the amounts for ending accounts receivable using the growth rate from Requirement d differ from those using the growth rate from this requirement?

f. Compute the accounts receivable turnover for 2015 by dividing sales by the balance in accounts receivable at the end of 2015 (instead of using average accounts receivable as in Requirement a). Use this accounts receivable turnover ratio to compute the projected balance in accounts receivable at the end of Year +1 through Year +5. Also compute the percentage change in accounts receivable between the year-ends for Year +1 through Year +5.

LO 10-2, LO 10-3
LO 10-4

10.14 Smoothing Changes in Inventories. Barnes & Noble sells books, magazines, music, and videos through retail stores and online. For a retailer like Barnes & Noble, inventory is a critical element of the business, and it is necessary to carry a wide array of titles. Inventories constitute the largest asset on Barnes & Noble's balance sheet, totaling $1,293 million at the end of 2015 and $1,235 million at the end of 2014. Assume that in 2015, sales totaled $6,070 million and cost of sales totaled $4,197 million.

REQUIRED

a. Compute the inventory turnover ratio for Barnes & Noble for 2015.

b. Over the last two years, suppose the number of Barnes & Noble retail stores has remained constant and sales have grown at a compounded annual rate of 11.6%. Assume that the number of stores will remain constant and that sales will continue to grow at an annual rate of 11.6% each year between Year +1 and Year +5. Also assume that the future cost of goods sold to sales percentage will equal that realized in 2015 (which is very similar to the cost of goods sold percentage over the past three years). Project the amount of inventory at the end of Year +1 through Year +5 using the inventory turnover ratio computed in Requirement a. Also compute the percentage change in inventories between each of the year-ends between 2015 and Year +5. Does the pattern of growth in your projections of Barnes & Noble inventory seem reasonable to you considering the assumptions of smooth growth in sales and steady cost of goods sold percentages? Explain.

c. The changes in inventories in Requirement b display the sawtooth pattern depicted in Exhibit 10.4. Smooth the changes in the inventory forecasts between 2015 and Year +5 using the compound annual growth rate in inventories between the end of 2015 and the end of Year +5 implied by the projections in Requirement b. Does this pattern of growth seem more reasonable? Explain.

d. Now suppose that instead of following the smoothing approach in Requirement c, you used the rate of growth in inventory during 2015 to project future inventory balances at the end of Year +1 through Year +5. Use these projections to compute the implied inventory turnover rates. Does this pattern of growth and efficiency in inventory for Barnes & Noble seem reasonable? Explain.

LO 10-2

10.15 Identifying Financial Statement Relations. Partial forecasts of financial statements for Watson Corporation appear in Exhibit 10.7 (income statement), Exhibit 10.8 (balance sheet), and Exhibit 10.9 (statement of cash flows). Selected amounts have been omitted, as have all totals (indicated by XXXX).

REQUIRED

Determine the amount of each of the following items.

a. Dividends declared and paid during Year 1.

b. Depreciation expense for Year 1 assuming that Watson Corporation neither sold nor retired depreciable assets during Year 1.

c. Inventories at the end of Year 2.

d. Interest expense on borrowing during Year 2, with an interest rate of 7%.

e. Other current liabilities at the end of Year 2.

f. Property, plant, and equipment at the end of Year 3 assuming that Watson Corporation neither sold nor retired depreciable assets during Year 3.

g. Retained earnings at the end of Year 3.

h. Long-term debt at the end of Year 3.

i. The income tax rate for Year 4.

j. Purchases of inventories during Year 4.

presented (unless indicated otherwise) beginning with the income statement, then the balance sheet, and then the statement of cash flows. For this portion of the case, assume that Walmart will exercise its financial flexibility with the cash and cash equivalents account to balance the balance sheet.

Exhibit 10.10

Walmart Stores, Inc.
Balance Sheets
(amounts in millions; allow for rounding)
(Integrative Case 10.1)

	2014	2015	2016
Assets			
Cash and cash equivalents	$ 7,281	$ 9,135	$ 8,705
Accounts and notes receivable—net	6,677	6,778	5,624
Inventories	44,858	45,141	44,469
Prepaid expenses and other current assets	1,909	2,224	1,441
Current assets of discontinued segments	460		
Current Assets	**$ 61,185**	**$ 63,278**	**$ 60,239**
Property, plant, and equipment—at cost	178,678	182,634	188,054
Accumulated depreciation	(60,771)	(65,979)	(71,538)
Goodwill	19,510	18,102	16,695
Other assets	6,149	5,455	6,131
Total Assets	**$204,751**	**$203,490**	**$199,581**
Liabilities and Equities			
Accounts payable	$ 37,415	$ 38,410	$ 38,487
Current accrued expenses	18,793	19,152	19,607
Notes payable and short-term debt	7,670	1,592	2,708
Current maturities of long-term debt	4,412	5,078	3,296
Income taxes payable	966	1,021	521
Current liabilities of discontinued operations	89		
Current Liabilities	**$ 69,345**	**$ 65,253**	**$ 64,619**
Long-term debt obligations	44,559	43,495	44,030
Deferred tax liabilities—noncurrent	8,017	8,805	7,321
Redeemable noncontrolling interest	1,491		
Total Liabilities	**$123,412**	**$117,553**	**$115,970**
Common stock + Additional paid-in capital	2,685	2,785	2,122
Retained earnings	76,566	85,777	90,021
Accum. other comprehensive income (loss)	(2,996)	(7,168)	(11,597)
Total Common Shareholders' Equity	**$ 76,255**	**$ 81,394**	**$ 80,546**
Noncontrolling interests	5,084	4,543	3,065
Total Equity	**$ 81,339**	**$ 85,937**	**$ 83,611**
Total Liabilities and Equities	**$204,751**	**$203,490**	**$199,581**

Exhibit 10.11

Walmart Stores, Inc.
Income Statements
(amounts in millions; allow for rounding)
(Integrative Case 10.1)

	2014	2015	2016
Revenues	$ 476,294	$ 485,651	$ 482,130
Cost of goods sold	(358,069)	(365,086)	(360,984)
Gross Profit	**$ 118,225**	**$ 120,565**	**$ 121,146**
Selling, general, and administrative expenses	(91,353)	(93,418)	(97,041)
Operating Profit	**$ 26,872**	**$ 27,147**	**$ 24,105**
Interest income	119	113	81
Interest expense	(2,335)	(2,461)	(2,548)
Income before Tax	**$ 24,656**	**$ 24,799**	**$ 21,638**
Income tax expense	(8,105)	(7,985)	(6,558)
Income (Loss) from discontinued operations	144	285	
Net Income	**$ 16,695**	**$ 17,099**	**$ 15,080**
Net income attributable to noncontrolling interests	(673)	(736)	(386)
Net Income Attributable to Common Shareholders	**$ 16,022**	**$ 16,363**	**$ 14,694**
Other comprehensive income items	(2,409)	(4,172)	(4,429)
Comprehensive Income	**$ 13,613**	**$ 12,191**	**$ 10,265**

Exhibit 10.12

Walmart Stores, Inc.
Statements of Cash Flows
(amounts in millions, allow for rounding)
(Integrative Case 10.1)

	2014	2015	2016
Net Income	**$ 16,695**	**$ 17,099**	**$ 15,080**
Add back depreciation and amortization expenses	8,870	9,173	9,454
Deferred income taxes	(279)	(503)	(672)
(Increase) Decrease in accounts receivable	(566)	(569)	(19)
(Increase) Decrease in inventories	(1,667)	(1,229)	(703)
Increase (Decrease) in accounts payable	531	2,678	2,008
Increase (Decrease) in income taxes payable	(1,224)	166	(472)
Increase (Decrease) in other current liabilities	103	1,249	1,303
(Income) Loss from discontinued segments	(144)	(285)	—
Other operating cash flows	938	785	1,410
Net Cash Flow from Operating Activities	**$ 23,257**	**$ 28,564**	**$ 27,389**

(Continued)

Exhibit 10.12 (Continued)			
	2014	2015	2016
Proceeds from sales of property, plant, and equipment	727	570	635
Property, plant, and equipment acquired	(13,115)	(12,174)	(11,477)
Investments acquired	—	—	—
Other investment transactions	(138)	479	167
Net Cash Flow from Investing Activities	$(12,526)	$(11,125)	$(10,675)
Increase (Decrease) in short-term borrowing	911	(6,288)	1,235
Increase (Decrease) in long-term borrowing	2,104	1,270	(4,393)
Share repurchases—treasury stock	(6,683)	(1,015)	(4,112)
Dividend payments	(6,139)	(6,185)	(6,294)
Other financing activities	(982)	(2,853)	(2,558)
Net Cash Flow from Financing Activities	$(10,789)	$(15,071)	$(16,122)
Effects of exchange rate changes on cash	(442)	(514)	(1,022)
Net Change in Cash	$ (500)	$ 1,854	$ (430)
Cash and cash equivalents, beginning of year	$ 7,781	$ 7,281	$ 9,135
Cash and cash equivalents, end of year	$ 7,281	$ 9,135	$ 8,705

Income Statement Forecast Assumptions

Sales Sales grew by 1.6% in 2014 and 2.0% in 2015, but fell by 0.7% in 2016. The compound annual sales growth rate during the last three years was only 0.6%. Walmart generates sales growth primarily through increasing same-store sales, opening new stores, and acquiring other retailers. In the future, Walmart will likely continue to grow in international markets by opening stores and acquiring other firms and in domestic U.S. markets by converting discount stores to Supercenters. In addition, despite vigorous competition, Walmart will likely continue to generate steady increases in same-store sales, consistent with its experience through 2016. Assume that sales will grow 2.0% each year from Year +1 through Year +5.

Cost of Goods Sold The percentage of costs of goods sold relative to sales decreased slightly from 75.2% of sales in 2014 and 2015 to 74.9% in 2016. Walmart's everyday low-price strategy, its movement into grocery products, and competition will likely prevent Walmart from achieving significant reductions in this expense percentage. Assume that the cost of goods sold to sales percentage will be 75.0% for Year +1 to Year +5.

Selling and Administrative Expenses The selling and administrative expense percentage has increased slightly from 19.2% of sales in 2014 and 2015 to 20.1% in 2016. Walmart has exhibited strong cost control over the years, and is likely to continue to exhibit such control. Assume that the selling and administrative expenses average 20.0% of sales for Year +1 to Year +5.

Interest Income Walmart earns interest income on its cash and cash equivalents accounts. The average interest rate earned on average cash balances was approximately 0.9% during 2016, a bit lower than the rates earned in 2014 and 2015 (1.6% and 1.4%, respectively). Assume that Walmart will earn interest income based on a 1.5% interest rate on average cash balances (that is, the sum of beginning and end-of-year cash balances divided by 2) for Year +1 through Year +5. (Note: Projecting the amount of interest income must await projection of cash on the balance sheet.)

Interest Expense Walmart uses long-term mortgages and capital leases to finance new stores and warehouses and short- and long-term debt to finance corporate acquisitions. The average interest rate on all interest-bearing debt and capital leases was approximately 4.6% and 5.1% during 2015 and 2016, respectively. Assume a 5.0% interest rate for all outstanding borrowing (short-term and long-term debt, including capital leases, and the current portion of long-term debt) for Walmart for Year +1 through Year +5. Compute interest expense on the average amount of interest-bearing debt outstanding each year. (Note: Projecting the amount of interest expense must await projection of the interest-bearing debt accounts on the balance sheet.)

Income Tax Expense Walmart's average income tax rate as a percentage of income before taxes has been roughly 31.8% during the last three years. Assume that Walmart's effective income tax rate will be 32.0% of income before taxes for Year +1 through Year +5. (Note: Projecting the amount of income tax expense must await computation of income before taxes.)

Net Income Attributable to Noncontrolling Interests Noncontrolling interest shareholders in Walmart subsidiaries were entitled to a $386 million share in Walmart's 2016 net income, which amounted to roughly a 12.6% rate of return on investment. Assume that the portion of net income attributable to noncontrolling interests in the future will continue to amount to a 12.6% rate of return in Year +1 through Year +5.

Balance Sheet Forecast Assumptions

Cash We will adjust cash as the flexible financial account to equate total assets with total liabilities plus shareholders' equity. Projecting the amount of cash must await projections of all other balance sheet amounts.

Accounts Receivable As a retailer, a large portion of Walmart's sales are in cash or for third-party credit card charges, which Walmart can convert into cash within a day or two. Walmart has its own credit card that customers can use for purchases at its Sam's Club warehouse stores, but the total amount of receivables outstanding on these credit cards is relatively minor compared to Walmart's total sales. As a consequence, Walmart's receivables turnover is very steady and fast, averaging roughly five days during each of the past two years. Assume that accounts receivable will continue to turn over at the same rate and increase at the growth rate in sales.

Inventories Walmart's overall inventory efficiency has remained steady over the past three years. Inventory turnover has averaged 45 days in 2014, 2015, and 2016. Assume that ending inventory will continue to be equal to 45 days of cost of goods sold, in Year +1 to Year +5.

Prepaid Expenses Current assets include prepayments for ongoing operating costs such as rent and insurance. Assume that prepayments will grow at the growth rate in sales.

Current Assets and Liabilities of Discontinued Segments Walmart's 2014 balance sheet recognized amounts as current assets and current liabilities that are associated with discontinued segments (subsidiaries that Walmart is divesting). Walmart divested these operations in fiscal 2015, so assume that these amounts will be zero in Year +1 through Year +5.

Property, Plant, and Equipment—At Cost With regard to property, plant, and equipment (including assets held under capital leases), Walmart's net capital expenditures (capital expenditures net of proceeds from selling property, plant, and equipment) have declined from roughly

$12.4 billion in 2014, to $11.6 billion in 2015, to $10.8 billion in 2016. Assume that capital spending on new property, plant, and equipment will be $10.0 billion each year from Year +1 through Year +5.

Accumulated Depreciation In 2015 and 2016, Walmart depreciated property, plant, and equipment using an average useful life of approximately 19.7 years. For Year +1 through Year +5, assume that accumulated depreciation will increase each year by depreciation expense. For simplicity, compute straight-line depreciation expense based on an average 20-year useful life and zero salvage value. In computing depreciation expense each year, make sure you depreciate the beginning balance in the existing property, plant, and equipment—at cost. Also add a new layer of depreciation expense for the new property, plant, and equipment acquired through capital expenditures. Assume that Walmart recognizes a full year of depreciation on new property, plant, and equipment in the first year of service.

Goodwill and Other Assets Goodwill and other assets include primarily goodwill arising from corporate acquisitions outside the United States. Such acquisitions increase Walmart sales. Assume that goodwill and other assets will grow at the same rate as revenues. Also assume that goodwill and other assets are not amortizable, and that no impairment charges will be needed.

Accounts Payable Walmart has maintained a steady accounts payable turnover, with payment periods averaging 9.5 times per year (an average turnover of roughly 38 days) during the last three years. Assume that ending accounts payable will continue to approximate 38 days of inventory purchases in Years +1 to +5. To compute the ending accounts payable balance using a 38-day turnover period, remember to add the change in inventory to the cost of goods sold to obtain the total amount of credit purchases of inventory during the year.

Accrued Liabilities Accrued liabilities relate to accrued expenses for ongoing operating activities and are expected to grow at the growth rate in selling and administrative expenses, which are expected to grow with sales.

Income Taxes Payable and Deferred Tax Liabilities—Noncurrent For simplicity, assume that income taxes payable and deferred tax liabilities—noncurrent grow at 2.0% per year in Year +1 through Year +5.

Short-Term Debt, Current Maturities of Long-Term Debt, and Long-Term Debt Walmart uses short-term debt, current maturities of long-term debt, and long-term debt to augment cash from operations to finance capital expenditures on property, plant, and equipment and acquisitions of existing retail chains outside the United States. Over the past two years, individual amounts of debt financing (short-term debt, current maturities of long-term debt, and long-term debt) have fluctuated from year to year, whereas the aggregate amount of debt financing has remained steady, averaging roughly 25.0% of total assets. For simplicity, assume that the total amount of debt financing will continue to remain a steady percentage of total assets for Year +1 through Year +5. Assume that Walmart's short-term debt, current maturities of long-term debt, and long-term debt will grow at 3.0% per year in Year +1 through Year +5, roughly consistent with the projected growth in total assets.

Common Stock and Additional Paid-in Capital Over the past three years, Walmart's common stock and additional paid-in capital have averaged approximately 1.2% of total assets. (Walmart repurchases company shares on the open market and then reissues these shares to employees and executives to satisfy stock option exercises.) Assume that equity financing will continue to be 1.2% of total assets for Year +1 through Year +5. Assume that Walmart's common stock and additional paid-in capital will grow at 3.0% per year in Year +1 through Year +5, roughly consistent with the projected growth in total assets.

Retained Earnings   The increase in retained earnings equals net income minus dividends and share repurchases. In 2016, Walmart paid total dividends of $6,294 million to common shareholders, which amounted to roughly 42% of net income attributable to Walmart shareholders. Assume that Walmart will maintain a policy to pay dividends equivalent to 42% of net income attributable to Walmart shareholders in Year +1 through Year +5. In addition, Walmart has used varying amounts of cash to repurchase common shares: $6,683 million in 2014, $1,015 million in 2015, and $4,112 million in 2016. Assume that Walmart will use $4,000 million per year to repurchase common shares in Year +1 through Year +5.

Accumulated Other Comprehensive Income   Assume that accumulated other comprehensive income will not change. Equivalently, assume that future other comprehensive income items will be zero, on average, in Year +1 through Year +5.

Noncontrolling Interests   Noncontrolling interests amount to equity investments made by third-party investors in subsidiaries that Walmart controls and consolidates. Noncontrolling interests grow each year by their proportionate share of the subsidiary's income, and these interests decrease by any dividends paid to them. We assumed, for purposes of projecting the income statement, that net income attributable to noncontrolling interests would generate a 12.6% rate of return for those investors. For simplicity, assume that the dividends Walmart will pay to the noncontrolling interest shareholders will equal the amount of net income attributable to these noncontrolling interests in Year +1 to Year +5. Therefore, the amount of noncontrolling interests in equity will remain constant.

Cash   At this point, you can project the amount of cash on Walmart's balance sheet at each year-end from Year +1 to Year +5. Assume that Walmart uses cash as the flexible financial account to balance the balance sheet. The resulting cash balance each year should be the total amount of liabilities and shareholders' equity minus the projected ending balances in all non-cash asset accounts.

Statement of Cash Flows Forecast Assumptions

Depreciation Addback   Include depreciation expense, which should equal the change in accumulated depreciation.

Other Addbacks   Assume that changes in other noncurrent liabilities on the balance sheet are operating activities.

Other Investing Transactions   Assume that changes in other noncurrent assets on the balance sheet are investing activities.

REQUIRED (continued from page 708)

    b. If you have programmed your spreadsheet correctly, the projected amount of cash grows steadily from $13,675 million at the end of Year +1 to a whopping $44,459 million at the end of Year +5 (allow for rounding), which is 18.6% of total assets. Identify one problem that so much cash could create for the financial management of Walmart.

c. Suppose that Walmart announces that it will augment its dividend policy by paying out 42% of net income plus the amount of excess cash each year (if any). Assume that during Year +1 to Year +5, Walmart will maintain a constant cash balance of $8,705 million (the ending cash balance in 2016). Revise your forecast model spreadsheets to change the financial flexibility account from cash to dividends. Determine the total amount of dividends that Walmart could pay each year under this scenario. Identify one potential benefit that increased dividends could create for the financial management of Walmart.

d. Calculate and compare the return on common equity for Walmart using the forecast amounts determined in Requirements a and c for Year +1 to Year +5. Why are the two sets of returns different? Which results will Walmart's common shareholders prefer? Why?

CASE 10.2

Massachusetts Stove Company: Analyzing Strategic Options[22]

LO 10-3, LO 10-4
LO 10-5, LO 10-6

The Woodstove Market

Since the early 1990s, woodstove sales have declined from 1,200,000 units per year to approximately 100,000 units per year. The decline has occurred because of (1) stringent new federal EPA regulations, which set maximum limits on stove emissions beginning in 1992; (2) stable energy prices, which reduced the incentive to switch to woodstoves to save on heating costs; and (3) changes in consumers' lifestyles, particularly the growth of two-income families.

During this period of decline in industry sales, the market was flooded with woodstoves at distressed prices as companies closed their doors or liquidated inventories made obsolete by the new EPA regulations. Downward pricing pressure forced surviving companies to cut prices, output, or both. Years of contraction and pricing pressure left many of the surviving manufacturers in a precarious position financially, with excessive inventory, high debt, little cash, uncollectible receivables, and low margins.

The shakeout and consolidation among woodstove manufacturers and, to a lesser extent, woodstove specialty retailers have been dramatic. The number of manufacturers selling more than 2,000 units a year (characterized in the industry as "large manufacturers") has declined from approximately 90 to 35 in the prior 10 years. The number of manufacturers selling less than 2,000 units per year (characterized as "small manufacturers") has declined from approximately 130 to 6. Because the current woodstove market is not large enough to support all of the surviving producers, manufacturers have attempted to diversify in order to stay in business. Seeking relief, nearly all of the survivors have turned to the manufacture of gas appliances.

The Gas Appliance Market

The gas appliance market includes three segments: (1) gas log sets, (2) gas fireplaces, and (3) gas stoves. Gas log sets are "faux fires" that can be installed in an existing fireplace. They are primarily decorative and have little heating value. Gas fireplaces are fully assembled

---

[22]The authors acknowledge the assistance of Tom P. Morrissey in the preparation of this case.

fireboxes that a builder or contractor can install in new construction or in renovated buildings and houses. They are mainly decorative and are less expensive and easier to maintain than a masonry/brick fireplace. Gas stoves are freestanding appliances with a decorative appearance and efficient heating characteristics.

The first two segments of the gas appliance market (log sets and fireplaces) are large, established, stable markets. Established manufacturers control these markets, and distribution is primarily through mass merchandisers. The third segment (gas stoves) is less than five years old. Although it is growing steadily, it has an annual volume of only about 100,000 units (almost identical to the annual volume of the woodstove market). This is the market to which woodstove manufacturers have turned for relief.

The gas stove market is not as heavily regulated as the woodstove market, and there are currently no EPA regulations governing the emissions of gas heating appliances. Gas stoves are perceived as being more appropriate for an aging population because they provide heat and ambiance but require no effort. They can be operated with a wall switch or thermostat or by remote control. Because actual fuel cost (or cost savings) is not an issue for many buyers, a big advantage of heating with wood is no longer a consideration for many consumers. Gas stoves are sold and distributed through mass merchandisers and through natural gas or propane dealers. The gas industry has the financial, promotional, organizational, and lobbying clout to support the development of the gas stove market, attributes that the tiny woodstove industry lacks.

Unfortunately, life has not been rosy for all of the woodstove companies entering this new market. Development costs and selling costs for new products using a different fuel and different distribution system have been substantial. Improvements in gas logs and gas burners have required rapid changes in product design. In contrast, woodstove designs are fairly stable and slow to change. Competition for market share has renewed pricing pressure on gas stove producers. Companies trying to maintain their woodstove sales while introducing gas products must carry large inventories to service both product lines. Failure to forecast demand accurately has left many companies with inventory shortages during the selling season or with large inventories of unsold product at the end of the season.

Many surviving manufacturers who looked to gas stoves for salvation are now quietly looking for suitors to acquire them. A combination of excessive debt and inventory levels, together with high development and distribution costs, has made financial success highly uncertain. Continued consolidation will take place in this difficult market during the next five years.

Massachusetts Stove Company

Massachusetts Stove Company (MSC) is one of the six "small manufacturers" to survive the EPA regulation and industry meltdown. The company has just completed its sixth consecutive year of slow but steady growth in revenue and profit since complying with the EPA regulations. Exhibits 10.13–10.15 present the financial statements of MSC for Year 3–Year 7. Exhibit 10.16 (see page 719) presents selected financial statement ratios.

The success of MSC in recent years is a classic case of a company staying small, marketing in a specific niche, and vigorously applying a "stick-to-your-knitting" policy. MSC is the only woodstove producer that has not developed gas products; 100% of its sales currently come from woodstove sales. MSC is the only woodstove producer that sells by mail order directly to consumers. The mail-order market has sheltered MSC from some of the pricing pressure that other manufacturers have had to bear. The combination of high entry costs and high risks make it unlikely that another competitor will enter the mail-order niche.

Exhibit 10.13

Massachusetts Stove Company
Income Statements
(Case 10.2)

	Year Ended December 31				
	Year 3	Year 4	Year 5	Year 6	Year 7
Sales	$1,480,499	$1,637,128	$ 2,225,745	$ 2,376,673	$ 2,734,986
Cost of goods sold	(727,259)	(759,156)	(1,063,135)	(1,159,466)	(1,380,820)
Depreciation	(56,557)	(73,416)	(64,320)	(66,829)	(72,321)
Facilities costs	(59,329)	(47,122)	(66,226)	(48,090)	(45,309)
Facilities rental income	25,856	37,727	38,702	42,142	41,004
Selling expenses	(452,032)	(563,661)	(776,940)	(874,000)	(926,175)
Administrative expenses	(36,967)	(39,057)	(46,444)	(48,046)	(111,199)
Operating Income	$ 174,211	$ 192,443	$ 247,382	$ 222,384	$ 240,166
Interest income	712	2,242	9,541	9,209	16,665
Interest expense	(48,437)	(44,551)	(47,535)	(52,633)	(42,108)
Income Before Income Taxes	$ 126,486	$ 150,134	$ 209,388	$ 178,960	$ 214,723
Income taxes	(35,416)	(42,259)	(64,142)	(45,794)	(60,122)
Net Income	$ 91,070	$ 107,875	$ 145,246	$ 133,166	$ 154,601

Exhibit 10.14

Massachusetts Stove Company
Balance Sheets
(Case 10.2)

	December 31					
	Year 2	Year 3	Year 4	Year 5	Year 6	Year 7
ASSETS						
Cash	$ 50,794	$ 19,687	$ 145,930	$ 104,383	$ 258,148	$ 351,588
Accounts receivable	12,571	56,706	30,934	41,748	30,989	5,997
Inventories	251,112	327,627	347,883	375,258	409,673	452,709
Other current assets	1,368	—	—	—	—	—
Total Current Assets	$ 315,845	$ 404,020	$ 524,747	$ 521,389	$ 698,810	$ 810,294
PP&E, at cost	1,056,157	1,148,806	1,164,884	1,184,132	1,234,752	1,257,673
Accumulated depreciation	(296,683)	(353,240)	(426,656)	(490,975)	(557,804)	(630,125)
Other assets	121,483	94,000	61,500	12,200	—	—
Total Assets	$1,196,802	$1,293,586	$1,324,475	$1,226,746	$1,375,758	$1,437,842

(Continued)

Exhibit 10.14 (Continued)

| | December 31 | | | | | |
	Year 2	Year 3	Year 4	Year 5	Year 6	Year 7
LIABILITIES AND SHAREHOLDERS' EQUITY						
Accounts payable	$ 137,104	$ 112,815	$ 43,229	$ 60,036	$ 39,170	$ 47,809
Notes payable	25,000	12,000	—	—	—	—
Current portion of long-term debt	27,600	29,000	21,570	113,257	115,076	27,036
Other current liabilities	39,530	100,088	184,194	189,732	244,241	257,252
Total Current Liabilities	$ 229,234	$ 253,903	$ 248,993	$ 363,025	$ 398,487	$ 332,097
Long-term debt	972,446	953,491	881,415	599,408	574,332	547,296
Deferred income taxes	—	—	—	—	5,460	6,369
Total Liabilities	$1,201,680	$1,207,394	$1,130,408	$ 962,433	$ 978,279	$ 885,762
Common stock	2,000	2,000	2,000	2,000	2,000	2,000
Additional paid-in capital	435,630	435,630	435,630	435,630	435,630	435,630
Retained earnings (deficit)	(442,508)	(351,438)	(243,563)	(98,317)	34,849	189,450
Treasury stock	—	—	—	(75,000)	(75,000)	(75,000)
Total Shareholders' Equity	$ (4,878)	$ 86,192	$ 194,067	$ 264,313	$ 397,479	$ 552,080
Total Liabilities and Shareholders' Equity	$1,196,802	$1,293,586	$1,324,475	$1,226,746	$1,375,758	$1,437,842

Exhibit 10.15

Massachusetts Stove Company
Statements of Cash Flows
(Case 10.2)

| | Year Ended December 31 | | | | |
	Year 3	Year 4	Year 5	Year 6	Year 7
OPERATIONS					
Net income	$ 91,070	$107,875	$ 145,246	$133,166	$ 154,601
Depreciation and amortization	56,557	73,416	64,320	66,829	72,321
Other addbacks	27,483	32,500	49,300	17,660	909
(Increase) Decrease in receivables	(44,135)	25,772	(10,814)	10,759	24,992
(Increase) Decrease in inventories	(76,515)	(20,256)	(27,375)	(34,415)	(43,036)
Decrease in other current assets	1,368	—	—	—	—
Increase (Decrease) in payables	(24,289)	(69,586)	16,807	(20,866)	8,639
Increase in other current liabilities	60,558	84,106	5,538	54,509	13,011
Cash Flow from Operations	$ 92,097	$233,827	$ 243,022	$227,642	$ 231,437

(Continued)

Exhibit 10.15 (Continued)

| | Year Ended December 31 | | | | |
	Year 3	Year 4	Year 5	Year 6	Year 7
INVESTING					
Capital expenditures	$(92,649)	$ (16,078)	$ (19,249)	$ (50,620)	$ (22,921)
Cash Flow from Investing	$(92,649)	$ (16,078)	$ (19,249)	$ (50,620)	$ (22,921)
FINANCING					
Increase in long-term debt	$ 10,000	$ —	$ —	$ —	$ —
Decrease in short-term debt	(13,000)	(12,000)	—	—	—
Decrease in long-term debt	(27,555)	(79,506)	(190,320)	(23,257)	(115,076)
Acquisition of common stock	—	—	(75,000)	—	—
Cash Flow from Financing	$(30,555)	$ (91,506)	$(265,320)	$ (23,257)	$(115,076)
Change in Cash	$(31,107)	$126,243	$ (41,547)	$153,765	$ 93,440
Cash—Beginning of year	50,794	19,687	145,930	104,383	258,148
Cash—End of Year	$ 19,687	$145,930	$ 104,383	$258,148	$ 351,588

Exhibit 10.16

Massachusetts Stove Company
Financial Statement Ratios
(Case 10.2)

	Year 3	Year 4	Year 5	Year 6	Year 7
Profit Margin for ROA	8.5%	8.5%	8.1%	7.2%	6.8%
Total Assets Turnover	1.2	1.3	1.7	1.8	1.9
ROA	10.1%	10.7%	14.1%	13.1%	13.1%
Profit Margin for ROCE	6.2%	6.6%	6.5%	5.6%	5.7%
Capital Structure Leverage	30.6	9.3	5.6	3.9	3.0
ROCE	224.0%	77.0%	63.4%	40.2%	32.6%
Cost of Goods Sold/Sales	49.1%	46.4%	47.8%	48.8%	50.5%
Depreciation Expense/Sales	3.8%	4.5%	2.9%	2.8%	2.6%
Facilities Costs Net of Rental Income/Sales	2.3%	0.6%	1.2%	0.3%	0.2%
Selling Expense/Sales	30.5%	34.4%	34.9%	36.8%	33.9%
Administrative Expenses/Sales	2.5%	2.4%	2.1%	2.0%	4.0%
Interest Income/Sales	—	0.1%	0.4%	0.4%	0.6%
Interest Expense/Sales	3.3%	2.7%	2.1%	2.2%	1.5%
Income Tax Expense/Income before Taxes	28.0%	28.1%	30.6%	25.6%	28.0%
Accounts Receivable Turnover	42.7	37.4	61.2	65.3	147.9
Inventory Turnover	2.5	2.2	2.9	3.0	3.2
Fixed Assets Turnover	1.9	2.1	3.1	3.5	4.2
Current Ratio	1.59	2.11	1.44	1.75	2.44

(Continued)

Exhibit 10.16 (Continued)

	Year 3	Year 4	Year 5	Year 6	Year 7
Quick Ratio	0.30	0.71	0.40	0.73	1.08
Days Accounts Receivable	9	10	6	6	3
Days Inventory Held	146	166	126	122	114
Days Accounts Payable	51	33	16	14	11
Cash Flow from Operations/Average Current Liabilities	38.1%	93.0%	79.4%	59.8%	63.4%
Long-Term Debt/Shareholders' Equity	1,106.2%	454.2%	226.8%	144.5%	99.1%
Cash Flow from Operations/Average Total Liabilities	7.6%	20.0%	23.2%	23.5%	24.8%
Interest Coverage Ratio	3.6	4.4	5.4	4.4	6.1

MSC's other competitive advantages are the high efficiency and unique features of its woodstoves. MSC equips its woodstoves with a catalytic combuster, which reburns gases emitted from burning wood. This reburning not only increases the heat generated by the stoves, but also reduces pollutants in the air. MSC offers a woodstove with inlaid soapstone. This soapstone heats up and provides warmth even after the fire in the stove has dwindled. The soapstone also adds to the attractiveness of the stove as a piece of furniture. MSC's customer base includes many middle- and upper-income individuals.

MSC believes that profitable growth of woodstove sales beyond gross revenues of $3 million a year in the mail-order niche is unlikely. However, no one is selling gas appliances by mail order. Many of MSC's customers and prospects have asked whether MSC plans to produce a gas stove.

Management of MSC is contemplating the development of several gas appliances to sell by mail order. There are compelling reasons for MSC to do this, as well as some good reasons to be cautious.

Availability of Space MSC owns a 25,000-square-foot building but occupies only 15,000 square feet. MSC leases the remaining 10,000 square feet to two tenants. The tenants pay rent plus their share of insurance, property taxes, and maintenance costs. The addition of gas appliances to its product line would require MSC to use 5,000 square feet of the space currently rented to one of its tenants. MSC would have to give the tenant six months' notice to cancel its lease.

Availability of Capital MSC has its own internal funds for product development and inventory, as well as an unused line of credit. But it will lose interest income (or incur interest expense) if it invests these funds in development and increased inventory.

Existing Demand MSC receives approximately 50,000 requests for catalogs each year and has a mailing list of approximately 220,000 active prospects and 15,000 recent owners of woodstoves. There is anecdotal evidence of sufficient demand so that MSC could introduce its gas stoves with little or no additional marketing expense, other than the cost of printing some additional catalog pages each year. MSC's management worries about the risk of the gas stove sales cannibalizing its existing woodstove sales. Also, if the current base of woodstove sales is eroded through mismanagement, inattention, or cannibalization, attempts to grow the business through expansion into gas appliances will be self-defeating.

Vacant Market Niche No other manufacturer is selling gas stoves by mail order. Because the entry costs are high and the unit volume is small, it is unlikely that another producer will enter the niche. MSC has had the mail-order market for woodstoves to itself for approximately seven years. MSC believes that this lack of existing competition will give it additional time to develop new products. However, management also believes that a timely entry will help solidify its position in this niche.

Suppliers MSC has existing relationships with many of the suppliers necessary to manufacture new gas products. The foundry that produces MSC's woodstove castings is one of the largest suppliers of gas heating appliances in central Europe. On the other hand, MSC would be a small, new customer for the vendors that provide the ceramic logs and gas burners. This could lead to problems with price, delivery, or service for these parts.

Synergies in Marketing and Manufacturing MSC would sell gas appliances through its existing direct-mail marketing efforts. It would incur additional marketing expenses for photography, printing, and customer service. MSC's existing plant is capable of manufacturing the shell of the gas units. It would require additional expertise to assemble fireboxes for the gas units (valves, burners, and log sets). MSC would have to increase its space and the number of employees to process and paint the metal parts of the new gas stoves. The gross margin for the gas products should be similar to that of the woodstoves.

Lack of Management Experience Managing new product development, larger production levels and inventories, and a more complex business would require MSC to hire more management expertise. MSC also would have to institute a new organizational structure for its more complex business and define responsibilities and accountability more carefully. Up to now, MSC has operated with a fairly loose organizational philosophy.

REQUIRED (additional requirements follow on page 723)

(additional requirements follow on page 723)

a. Identify clues from the financial statements and financial statement ratios for Year 3–Year 7 that might suggest that Massachusetts Stove Company is a mature business.
b. Design a spreadsheet for the preparation of projected income statements, balance sheets, and statements of cash flows for MSC for Year 8–Year 12. Also forecast the financial statements for each of these years under three scenarios: (1) best case, (2) most likely, and (3) worst case. The following sections describe the assumptions you can make.

Development Costs MSC plans to develop two gas stove models, but not concurrently. It will develop the first gas model during Year 8 and begin selling it during Year 9. It will develop the second gas model during Year 9 and begin selling it during Year 10. MSC will capitalize the development costs in the year incurred (Year 8 and Year 9) and amortize them straight-line over five years, beginning with the year the particular stove is initially sold (Year 9 and Year 10). Estimated development cost for each stove are as follows:

Best Case: $100,000
Most Likely Case: $120,000
Worst Case: $160,000

Capital Expenditures Capital expenditures, other than development costs, will be as follows: Year 8, $20,000; Year 9, $30,000; Year 10, $30,000; Year 11, $25,000; Year 12, $25,000. Assume a six-year depreciable life, straight-line depreciation, and a full year of depreciation in the year of acquisition.

Sales Growth Changes in wood and gas stove sales relative to total sales of the preceding year are as follows:

Year	Best Case			Most Likely Case			Worst Case		
	Wood	Gas	Total	Wood	Gas	Total	Wood	Gas	Total
8	+2%	—	+2%	−2%	—	−2%	−4%	—	−4%
9	+2%	+6%	+8%	−2%	+4%	+2%	−4%	+2%	−2%
10	+2%	+12%	+14%	−2%	+8%	+6%	−4%	+4%	+0%
11	+2%	+12%	+14%	−2%	+8%	+6%	−4%	+4%	+0%
12	+2%	+12%	+14%	−2%	+8%	+6%	−4%	+4%	+0%

Because sales of gas stoves will start at zero, the projections of sales should *use the preceding growth rates in total sales*. The growth rates shown for woodstove sales and gas stove sales simply indicate the components of the total sales increase.

Cost of Goods Sold Manufacturing costs of the gas stoves will equal 50% of sales, the same as for woodstoves.

Depreciation Depreciation will increase for the amortization of the product development costs on the gas stoves and depreciation of additional capital expenditures.

Facilities Rental Income and Facilities Costs Facilities rental income will decrease by 50% beginning in Year 9 when MSC takes over 5,000 square feet of its building now rented to another company and will remain at that reduced level for Year 10–Year 12. Facilities costs will increase by $30,000 beginning in Year 9 for facilities costs now paid by a tenant and for additional facilities costs required by gas stove manufacturing. These costs will remain at that increased level for Year 10–Year 12.

Selling Expenses Selling expenses as a percentage of sales are as follows:

Year	Best Case	Most Likely Case	Worst Case
8	34%	34.0%	34%
9	33%	33.5%	35%
10	32%	33.0%	36%
11	31%	32.5%	37%
12	30%	32.0%	38%

Administrative Expenses Administrative expenses will increase by $30,000 in Year 8, $30,000 in Year 9, and $20,000 in Year 10, and then will remain at the Year 10 level in Years 11 and 12.

Interest Income MSC will earn 5% interest on the average balance in cash each year.

Interest Expense The interest rate on interest-bearing debt will be 6.8% on the average amount of debt outstanding each year.

Income Tax Expense MSC is subject to an income tax rate of 28%.

Accounts Receivable and Inventories Accounts receivable and inventories will increase at the growth rate in sales.

Property, Plant, and Equipment Property, plant, and equipment at cost will increase each year by the amounts of capital expenditures and expenditures on development costs. Accumulated depreciation will increase each year by the amount of depreciation and amortization expense.

Accounts Payable and Other Current Liabilities Accounts payable will increase with the growth rate in inventories. Other current liabilities include primarily advances by customers for stoves manufactured soon after the year-end. Other current liabilities will increase with the growth rate in sales.

Current Portion of Long-Term Debt Scheduled repayments of long-term debt are as follows: Year 8, $27,036; Year 9, $29,200; Year 10, $31,400; Year 11, $33,900; Year 12, $36,600; Year 13, $39,500.

Deferred Income Taxes Deferred income taxes relate to the use of accelerated depreciation for tax purposes and the straight-line method for financial reporting. Assume that deferred income taxes will not change.

Shareholders' Equity Assume that there will be no changes in the contributed capital of MSC. Retained earnings will change each year in the amount of net income.

REQUIRED (continued from page 721)

c. Calculate the financial statement ratios listed in Exhibit 10.16 for MSC under each of the three scenarios for Year 8–Year 12.
Note: You should create a fourth spreadsheet as part of your preparation of the projected financial statements that will compute the financial ratios.

d. What advice would you give the management of MSC regarding its decision to enter the gas stove market? Your recommendation should consider the profitability and risks of this action as well as other factors you deem relevant.

Risk-Adjusted Expected Rates of Return and the Dividends Valuation Approach

LEARNING OBJECTIVES

LO 11-1 Describe the general valuation model and its culminating role in the six-step analysis and valuation process that is the focus of this book.

LO 11-2 Explain the fundamental equivalence of valuation based on expected future dividends, free cash flows, and earnings.

LO 11-3 Estimate expected rates of return on equity capital as well as weighted-average costs of capital, which we will use to discount future payoffs to present value.

LO 11-4 Explain the dividends-based valuation approach, including the relation between cash flows to the investor versus cash flows reinvested in the firm.

LO 11-5 Measure dividends, establish a forecast horizon, and value continuing dividends.

LO 11-6 Bring all of the elements together in the dividends-based valuation model, and estimate firm value.

LO 11-7 Assess the sensitivity of firm value estimates to key valuation parameters, such as discount rates and expected long-term growth rates, and make investment decisions.

Chapter Overview

The first portion of this chapter describes the equivalence among valuation approaches that are based on dividends, free cash flows, and earnings. The second portion explains expected rates of return on equity capital and weighted-average costs of capital, which we use as discount rates in the valuation process. The latter portion of this chapter describes and applies the dividends-based valuation model using **Starbucks**.

Looking further ahead, Chapter 12 presents and applies cash-flow-based valuation approaches. Chapter 13 describes and applies earnings-based valuation approaches. Chapters 11 to 13 discuss and illustrate the important issues that determine the conceptual and practical strengths and weaknesses of each approach. All three chapters illustrate the equivalence of these valuation approaches using the theoretical development of the models and applying these approaches to the projected dividends, cash flows, and earnings derived from the financial statements forecasts developed for **Starbucks** in Chapter 10. Chapter 14 describes and applies market multiples such as price-earnings ratios and market-to-book ratios that analysts use in some circumstances to value firms.

The General Valuation Model

Economic theory teaches that the value of an investment equals the present value of the projected future payoffs from the investment discounted at a rate that reflects the time value of money and the risk inherent in those expected payoffs. A general model for the present value of a security at time $t=0$ (denoted as V_0) with an expected life of n future periods is as follows:[1]

$$V_0 = \sum_{t=1}^{n} \frac{\text{Projected Future Payoffs}_t}{(1 + \text{Discount Rate})^t}$$

In securities markets that are less than perfectly efficient, *price* does not necessarily equal *value* for every security at all times. Therefore, it can be very fruitful to search for and analyze securities that may have prices that have deviated temporarily from fundamental values. When buying a security, you pay the security's price and receive the security's value. When selling a security, you receive the selling price and give up the security's value. ***Price is observable, but value is not; value must be estimated.*** Therefore, we must estimate the value of a security to make intelligent investment decisions. Investors, analysts, fund managers, investment bankers, corporate managers, and others engage in financial statement analysis and valuation to determine a reliable appraisal of the value of shares of common equity or the value of whole firms. The questions they typically address include the following:

- What is the value of a particular company's common stock?
- Comparing my estimate of value to the current price in the market, should I buy, sell, or hold a particular firm's common shares?
- What is a reasonable price to accept (or ask) as a seller or pay (or bid) as a buyer for the shares of a firm in an initial public offering or a corporate merger or acquisition?

Equity valuation based on dividends, cash flows, and earnings has been examined in many theoretical and empirical research studies. These studies provide many insights into valuation, but two very compelling general conclusions emerge and motivate the application of valuation models in this text: (a) share prices in the capital markets *generally* relate closely with share values, but *do not always* equal share values; (b) temporary deviations of price from value occur.

First, many empirical studies demonstrate that dividends, cash flows, and earnings-based valuation models generally provide significant explanatory power for share prices observed in the capital markets.[2] Share value estimates determined from these models

---

[1] Throughout this chapter, t refers to accounting periods. The valuation process determines an estimate of firm value, denoted V_0, when $t=0$. The period $t=1$ refers to the first accounting period being discounted to present value. Period $t=n$ is the period of the expected final, or liquidating, payoff.

[2] For examples, see Craig Nichols, James Wahlen, and Matthew Wieland, "Pricing and Mispricing of Accounting Fundamentals in the Time-Series and in the Cross-Section," forthcoming, *Contemporary Accounting Research*; Stephen Penman and Theodore Sougiannis, "A Comparison of Dividend, Cash Flow, and Earnings Approaches to Equity Valuation," *Contemporary Accounting Research* 15, no. 3 (Fall 1998), pp. 343–383; and Jennifer Francis, Per Olsson, and Dennis Oswald, "Comparing the Accuracy and Explainability of Dividend, Free Cash Flow, and Abnormal Earnings Equity Value Estimates," *Journal of Accounting Research* 38 (Spring 2000), pp. 45–70.

correlate closely with the stock prices observed in the capital markets. These correlations hold across different types of firms, during different periods of time, and across different countries. In addition, many empirical research studies also have shown that unexpected *changes* in earnings, dividends, and cash flows correlate closely with *changes* in stock prices.

Second, a number of empirical research studies show that dividends, cash flows, and earnings-based valuation models help identify when share prices are temporarily overpriced or underpriced, representing potentially profitable investment opportunities. For example, Exhibit 11.1 is a graphic depiction of results from a study by Frankel and Lee (1998). They sorted firms each year into five portfolios based on quintiles of their estimate of value (V) to share price (P).[3] Their findings show striking differences in the average 36-month stock returns earned by their portfolios. The highest value-to-price quintile portfolio generated significantly greater average returns than the lowest value-to-price portfolio. These results are very encouraging for those interested in developing fundamental forecasting and valuation skills for investment purposes.

The six-step analysis and valuation framework that forms the structure of this book (Exhibit 1.2 in Chapter 1) is a logical sequence of steps for understanding the fundamentals of a business and for determining intelligent estimates of its value. In the final step, we derive from projected financial statements our forecasts of future earnings, cash flows, and dividends as measures of projected future payoffs for the firm. We use these projected future payoffs as inputs to valuation models to determine the value of the firm. Reliable projections of future payoffs to the firm (the numerator in the general valuation model) depend on unbiased and thoughtful forecasts of future income statements, balance

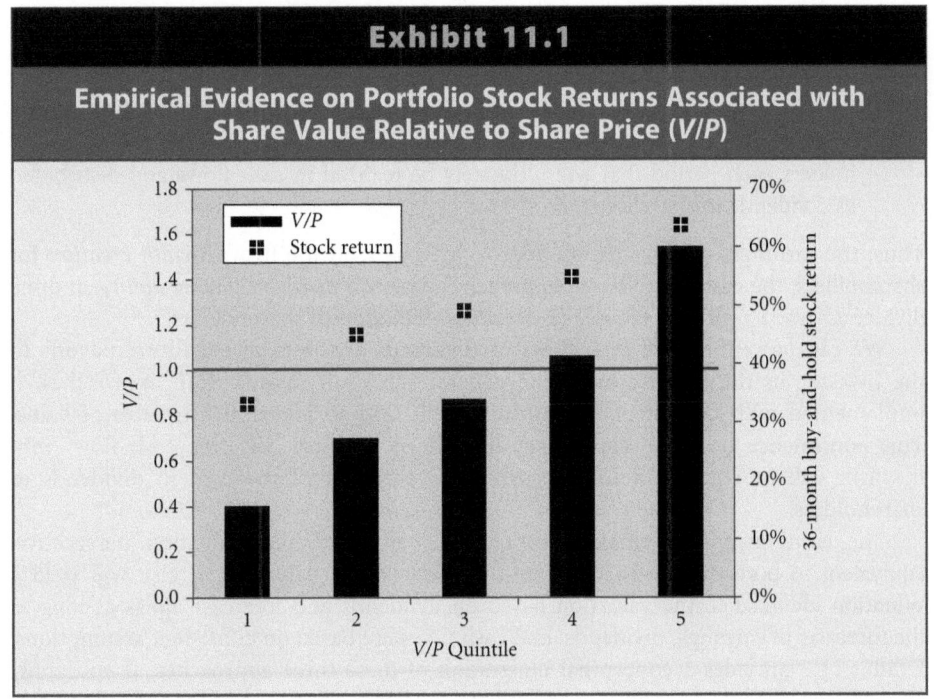

Exhibit 11.1

Empirical Evidence on Portfolio Stock Returns Associated with Share Value Relative to Share Price (*V/P*)

[3]Richard Frankel and Charles Lee, "Accounting Valuation, Market Expectation, and Cross-Sectional Stock Returns," *Journal of Accounting and Economics* 25, no. 3 (1998), pp. 283–319.

sheets, and statements of cash flows, all of which depend on reliable projections of the firm's future operating, investing, and financing activities. Assessing an appropriate risk-adjusted discount rate (the denominator in the general valuation model) requires an assessment of the inherent risk in the set of expected future payoffs. Therefore, reliable estimates of firm value depend on unbiased estimates of expected future payoffs and an appropriate risk-adjusted discount rate, all of which depend on the collective information from the six steps of the framework.

LO 11-2

Explain the fundamental equivalence of valuation based on expected future dividends, free cash flows, and earnings.

Equivalence among Dividends, Cash Flows, and Earnings Valuation

When you derive internally consistent expectations of future earnings, cash flows, and dividends from a set of financial statement forecasts and use the same discount rate to compute the present values of those expected future payoffs, the valuation models yield identical estimates of firm value. That is, dividends-, free-cash-flows-, and earnings-based valuation models are complementary approaches that produce equivalent value estimates.

The dividends-, free-cash-flows-, and earnings-based valuation approaches primarily differ in perspective:

- The dividends-based valuation approach focuses on *wealth distribution* to shareholders. This approach determines share value as the present value of cash flows the shareholder will receive.
- Cash-flow-based valuation focuses on *free cash flow generation*. This approach determines share value as the present value of the *free cash flows* that are available for distribution to shareholders, after necessary investments in operating assets and required payments to debtholders.
- Earnings-based valuation focuses on *wealth creation*. It takes the perspective that earnings measure the capital that firms create (or destroy) for common shareholders each period that will ultimately be realized in cash flows and distributed as dividends to shareholders.

Thus, the earnings-based valuation approach focuses on the firm's *wealth creation* for shareholders, the cash-flows-based approach focuses on *dividend-paying ability*, and the dividends-based approach focuses on *wealth distribution* to shareholders.

We can use either free cash flows or dividends as the expected future payoffs to the investor in the numerator of the general valuation model. Both approaches, if implemented with consistent assumptions, will lead to identical estimates of value. This equivalence occurs because over the life of the firm, the free cash flows into the firm will be equivalent to the cash flows paid out of the firm in dividends to shareholders.

The earnings-based valuation approach is an alternative valuation perspective, equivalent to both dividends- and free-cash-flows-based valuation. It also will yield a valuation identical to the valuation based on dividends and free cash flows as long as the forecasts of earnings, dividends, and cash flows are based on consistent assumptions. Exhibit 11.2 provides a conceptual illustration of these three approaches. If you apply all three approaches, you will gain much better insights about firm value than if you rely on only one approach. You will understand valuation more thoroughly across a wider array of situations when you can triangulate valuation across the dividends-, cash-flows-, and earnings-based approaches.

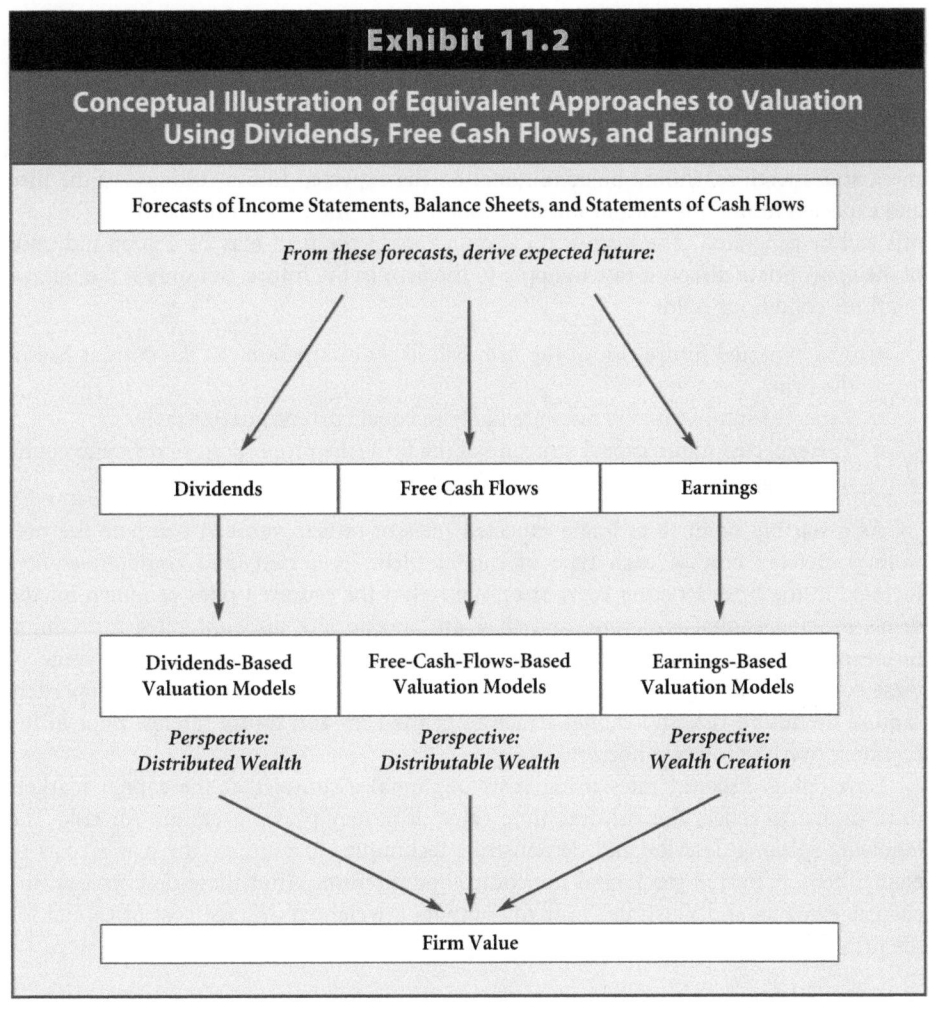

Exhibit 11.2

Conceptual Illustration of Equivalent Approaches to Valuation Using Dividends, Free Cash Flows, and Earnings

Forecasts of Income Statements, Balance Sheets, and Statements of Cash Flows

From these forecasts, derive expected future:

Dividends	Free Cash Flows	Earnings

Dividends-Based Valuation Models	Free-Cash-Flows-Based Valuation Models	Earnings-Based Valuation Models
Perspective: Distributed Wealth	*Perspective: Distributable Wealth*	*Perspective: Wealth Creation*

Firm Value

All four valuation chapters (Chapters 11–14) emphasize that the objective of the valuation process is not a single point estimate of value per se; instead, the objective is to determine a reliable distribution of value estimates across the relevant ranges of critical forecast assumptions and valuation parameters. By estimating share value using cash flows, earnings, and dividends, and by assessing the sensitivity of these value estimates across a distribution of relevant forecast assumptions and parameters, you can determine the most likely range of values for a share, which you can then compare to the share's price in the capital market for an intelligent investment decision.

Expected Rates of Return

All of the valuation approaches we describe and demonstrate in Chapters 11 to 14 use the general valuation model set forth at the beginning of this chapter, in which we determine firm value by discounting projected future payoffs to present value. Therefore, for all of the valuation approaches, we need a discount rate to compute the present value of all projected future payoffs. To compensate for the time value of money and risk, the discount rate should be the required rate of return that investors expect from the firm. When you compute the present value of future payoffs (dividends, free cash flows, or earnings) to *common equity shareholders*, you should use a discount rate that reflects the risk-adjusted required rate of return on *common equity* capital.

The discount rate should be a forecast of the required rate of return on the investment and, therefore, should be conditional on the expected future riskiness of the firm and expected future interest rates in the economy over the period during which the payoffs will be generated. The historical discount rate of the firm may be a good indicator of the appropriate discount rate to apply to the firm in the future, but only if the following three conditions hold:

- The expected future risk of the firm will likely be the same as the current risk of the firm.
- Expected future interest rates are likely to equal current interest rates.
- The expected future capital structure of the firm (the proportions of debt and equity financing) will likely be the same as the existing capital structure of the firm.

As a starting point to estimate expected rates of return, you can compute the prevailing after-tax cost of each type of capital (debt, preferred, and common equity) invested in the firm. Existing costs of capital reflect the required rates of return for the firm's existing capital structure, and they are appropriate discount rates for valuing future payoffs for the firm if the three preceding conditions hold. If one or more of these conditions do not hold, you will need to project discount rates that appropriately capture the future risk and capital structure of the firm and future interest rates in the economy over the forecast horizon.

Developing discount rates using costs of capital assumes that the capital markets price capital to reflect the risk-free time value of money plus a premium for risk. The following sections describe and demonstrate techniques to estimate the firm's costs of equity, debt, preferred stock, and noncontrolling interests. After these descriptions, the chapter explains and illustrates how to compute a weighted-average cost of capital for the firm.

Cost of Common Equity Capital

Analysts commonly estimate the cost of equity capital using the *capital asset pricing model (CAPM)*. The CAPM assumes that for a given level of expected return, risk-averse investors will seek to bear as little risk as possible and will diversify risk across the types of assets they hold in a portfolio. Therefore, the CAPM hypothesizes that in equilibrium, investors should expect to earn a rate of return on a firm's common equity capital that equals the rate of return the market requires to hold that firm's stock in a diversified portfolio of assets. In theory, the market comprises risk-averse investors who demand a rate of return that compensates them for (1) delaying consumption (the time value of money) and (2) bearing *systematic, marketwide risk* that cannot be diversified. Systematic risk arises from economywide factors (such as economic growth or recession, unemployment, unexpected inflation, unexpected changes in prices for natural resources such as oil and gas, unexpected changes in exchange rates, and population growth) that affect all firms to varying degrees and cannot be fully diversified. Therefore, the market's required rate of return on equity capital is a function of prevailing risk-free rates of interest in the economy plus a risk premium for bearing risk, conditional on the level of systematic risk inherent in the firm's common stock.

Note that the CAPM assumes nonsystematic risk factors are diversifiable across a broad portfolio of stocks. Nonsystematic risk factors are industry- and firm-specific, such as the level of competition in an industry, the product portfolio of a particular firm, the sustainability of the firm's strategy, and the firm's ability to generate revenue growth and control expenses. A competitive equilibrium capital market, according to CAPM, does not expect a return for a firm's nonsystematic risk because such risk can be diversified away in a portfolio of stocks.

Analysts estimate systematic risk as the degree of covariation between a firm's stock returns and a marketwide index of stock returns. Analysts commonly estimate systematic risk using the firm's *market beta*, which is the slope coefficient from regressing the firm's stock returns on an index of returns on a marketwide portfolio of stocks over a relevant period of time.[4] If a firm's market beta from such a regression is equal to 1, it indicates that, on average, the firm's stock returns covary identically with returns to a marketwide portfolio, indicating that the firm has the same degree of systematic risk as the market as a whole. If market beta is greater than 1, the firm has a greater degree of systematic risk than the market as a whole. If market beta is less than 1, the firm has less systematic risk than the market as a whole.

Exhibit 11.3 reports industry median, 25th percentile, and 75th percentile market betas for a sample of 48 industries over the years 2006–2015.[5] These data depict wide variation in systematic risk across industries during this 10-year period, with industry median market betas ranging from lows of 0.61 (Tobacco Products) and 0.68 (Beer & Liquor) to highs of 1.73 and 1.75 (Steel Works and Shipbuilding & Railroad Equipment, respectively). Various financial data sources and websites regularly publish market betas for common equity in publicly traded firms. It is not uncommon to find considerable variation in market betas among the various sources. This occurs in part because of differences in the period and methodology used to estimate betas.[6]

The CAPM projects the expected return on common equity capital for Firm j as follows:

$$E[R_{Ej}] = E[R_F] + \beta_j \times \{E[R_M] - E[R_F]\}$$

where E denotes that the related variable is an expectation; R_{Ej} denotes required return on common equity in Firm j; R_F denotes the risk-free rate of return; β_j denotes the market beta for Firm j; and R_M denotes the required return on a diversified, marketwide portfolio of stocks (such as the S&P 500). According to the CAPM, a security with no systematic risk (that is, $\beta_j = 0$) should be expected to earn a return equal to the expected rate of return on risk-free securities. Of course, most equity securities are not risk-free. The subtraction term in brackets in the CAPM represents the average market

---

[4]Researchers and analysts have developed a variety of approaches to estimate market betas. One common approach estimates a firm's market beta by regressing the firm's monthly stock returns on a marketwide index of returns (such as the S&P 500 index) over the last 60 months.

[5]Our sincere thanks to Professor Matt Wieland for help in collecting these data.

[6]Eugene Fama and Kenneth French developed an empirical model that explains realized stock returns using three factors they found to be correlated with returns during their study period. Their model and results indicate that during their sample period (1963–1990), firms' stock returns were related to firms' market betas, market capitalizations (size), and market-to-book ratios [see Eugene F. Fama and Kenneth R. French, "The Cross Section of Expected Stock Returns," *Journal of Finance* 47, no. 2 (June 1992), pp. 427–465]. Data to implement their model can be obtained from French's website (http://mba.tuck.dartmouth.edu/pages/faculty/ken.french/data_library.html).

Exhibit 11.3

Relation between Industry and Systematic Risk over 2006–2015

Industry	25th Percentile	Median	75th Percentile
Tobacco Products	0.52	0.61	0.78
Beer & Liquor	0.46	0.68	0.90
Utilities	0.54	0.75	0.97
Food Products	0.48	0.78	1.12
Candy & Soda	0.51	0.81	1.01
Health Care	0.52	0.87	1.19
Banking	0.24	0.88	1.36
Other	0.39	0.89	1.35
Medical Equipment	0.59	0.92	1.23
Recreation	0.53	0.95	1.41
Real Estate	0.48	0.95	1.52
Insurance	0.74	1.00	1.35
Restaurants, Hotels, Motels	0.70	1.03	1.35
Entertainment	0.63	1.03	1.49
Agriculture	0.72	1.03	1.39
Personal Services	0.65	1.04	1.38
Pharmaceutical Products	0.66	1.05	1.52
Defense	0.72	1.05	1.38
Shipping Containers	0.89	1.05	1.35
Wholesale	0.65	1.05	1.45
Consumer Goods	0.55	1.05	1.43
Communication	0.75	1.07	1.42
Printing & Publishing	0.74	1.08	1.52
Rubber & Plastic Products	0.72	1.08	1.39
Business Services	0.72	1.09	1.46
Textiles	0.48	1.10	1.59
Measuring & Control Equipment	0.69	1.12	1.49
Computers	0.77	1.13	1.50
Trading	0.72	1.13	1.55
Retail	0.81	1.15	1.48
Apparel	0.78	1.17	1.48
Transportation	0.88	1.20	1.55
Precious Metals	0.78	1.21	1.67
Aircraft	0.96	1.22	1.46
Electrical Equipment	0.77	1.24	1.63
Electronic Equipment	0.86	1.27	1.69
Chemicals	1.00	1.31	1.67
Business Supplies	0.91	1.31	1.65
Construction Materials	0.85	1.33	1.70
Machinery	1.09	1.43	1.77

(Continued)

Exhibit 11.3 (Continued)			
Fabricated Products	0.69	1.43	1.83
Petroleum & Natural Gas	1.04	1.45	1.87
Automobiles & Trucks	1.06	1.46	1.86
Nonmetallic & Industrial Metal Mining	1.07	1.56	1.96
Construction	1.30	1.65	1.99
Coal	1.08	1.70	2.12
Steel Works	1.36	1.73	2.09
Shipbuilding & Railroad Equipment	1.23	1.75	1.99
Overall	**0.68**	**1.11**	**1.52**

risk premium, which is equal to the amount of return above the risk-free rate that equity investors in the capital markets require for bearing the average amount of systematic risk in the market as a whole. Therefore,

- An equity security with systematic risk equal to the average amount of systematic risk of all equity securities in the market has a market beta equal to 1, so the cost of common equity capital for such a firm should be equal to the required return on the market portfolio.
- A firm with a market beta greater than 1 has higher-than-average systematic risk and faces a higher cost of equity capital because the capital markets expect the firm to yield a commensurately higher return to compensate investors for bearing greater risk.
- A firm with a market beta less than 1 faces a lower cost of equity capital because the capital markets expect the firm to yield a commensurately lower return to investors for bearing less risk.

Exhibit 11.4 depicts the CAPM graphically.

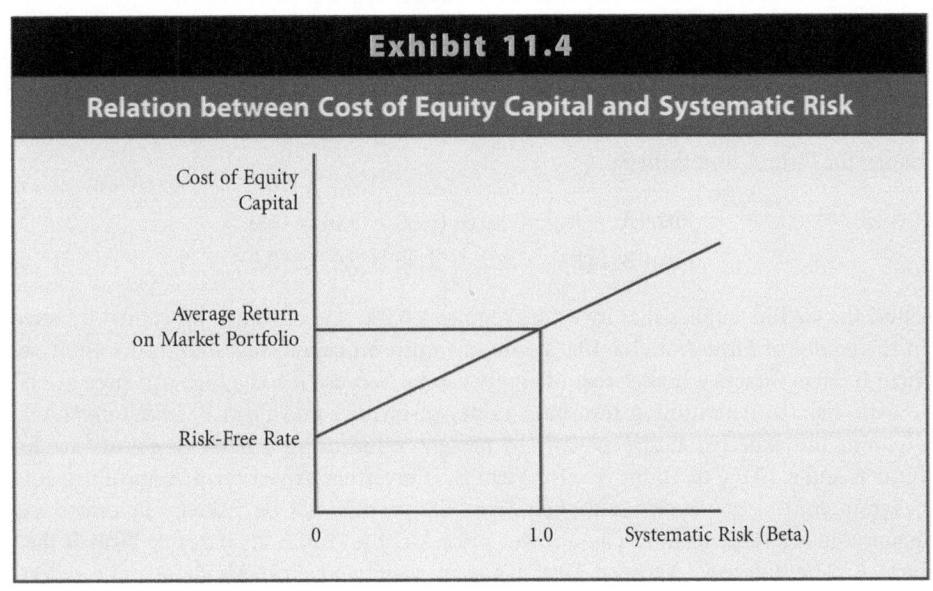

Exhibit 11.4

Relation between Cost of Equity Capital and Systematic Risk

You should use the market return on securities with zero systematic risk as the risk-free interest rate in the CAPM. Returns on such systematic risk-free securities (for example, U.S. Treasury securities) should exhibit no correlation with returns on a diversified marketwide portfolio of stocks. Given that equity securities have indefinitely long lives, it might seem appropriate to use the yield on long-term U.S. Treasury securities as a proxy for a risk-free rate. However, yields on long-term U.S. government securities tend to exhibit greater sensitivity to changes in inflation and interest rates; therefore, they have a greater degree of systematic risk (although the systematic risk is still quite low) compared to short-term U.S. government securities. Common practice uses the yield on intermediate-term U.S. government securities (for example, yields on 10-year U.S. Treasury securities) as the risk-free rate. Historically, these yields have averaged around 6% over the long run, although in recent years, they have been quite low, ranging from roughly 1% to 4%.

The average realized rate of return on the market portfolio depends on the period studied. Historically, the market portfolio return has varied between 9% and 13%. Thus, the risk premium on the market portfolio over the risk-free rate has varied between 3% and 7%. Some financial economists argue that the market risk premium varies over time with investors' demand for consumption. These economists argue that, on the margin, when the economy is healthy and growing (with low unemployment and high consumer confidence), investors' demand for additional consumption is relatively low; therefore, investors demand relatively low rates of return for postponing consumption and bearing risk. Thus, risk premia tend to be lower (perhaps 3%–4%) when economic conditions are strong. Conversely, when the economy is weak and investors face a higher degree of uncertainty, investors' demand for additional consumption is relatively high; therefore, they demand relatively high rates of return for postponing consumption and bearing risk. Thus, risk premia tend to be higher (perhaps 6%–7%) when economic conditions are weak. The theories asserting that risk premia are time-varying (and vary inversely with investors' marginal demand for consumption) seem intuitive and appear to explain risk premia observed in the capital markets quite well, but they are somewhat difficult to integrate into valuations and require more empirical research.

Using the CAPM to Compute Expected Rates of Return

Suppose Firm A has a market beta of 0.60 and Firm B has a market beta of 1.40. Assume that the prevailing yields on 10-year U.S. Treasury bonds are roughly 3.0% and that the capital markets require a 5.0% risk premium for bearing an average amount of systematic risk. Applying the CAPM, we would compute the following expected rates of return for Firm A and Firm B:

$$\text{Firm A: } E[R_A] = 3.0 + (0.60 \times 5.0) = 6.0$$
$$\text{Firm B: } E[R_B] = 3.0 + (1.40 \times 5.0) = 10.0$$

Thus, the CAPM implies that investors require a 6.0% rate of return on capital invested in the equity of Firm A and a 10.0% rate of return on capital invested in the equity of Firm B. Firm B faces a higher cost of equity capital because it has a higher degree of systematic risk. In determining the share values of Firm A and Firm B, investors should discount the expected future payoffs to present value using a 6.0% discount rate for Firm A and a 10.0% discount rate for Firm B. If investors expect Firm A and Firm B to generate equivalent payoffs (although Firm B's payoffs will be riskier), investors will assign a lower value to (and pay a lower price for) the common shares of Firm B than Firm A. The difference between Firm B's share value and Firm A's share value reflects the additional compensation that shareholders demand for holding the riskier Firm B shares relative to shares of Firm A. Shareholders will realize this compensation in the form of the equivalent payoffs, for which shareholders in Firm B paid a lower price than did shareholders in Firm A.

Computing the Required Rate of Return on Equity Capital for Starbucks

At the end of fiscal 2015, different sources provided different estimates of market beta for **Starbucks** common stock, ranging from 0.50 to roughly 1.00. Historically, **Starbucks'** market beta has varied around 0.75 over time, so we will assume that **Starbucks** common stock has a market beta of roughly 0.75 as of the end of fiscal 2015. At that time, U.S. Treasury bills with 10 years to maturity traded with a yield of roughly 2.7%, which we use as the risk-free rate. Additionally, economic conditions were strong, stock market indexes had experienced strong gains, and investors were less risk-averse than normal; so we will assume investors demanded a 6.0% market risk premium. Therefore, the CAPM indicates that **Starbucks** has a cost of common equity capital of 7.20% [2.7 + (0.75 × 6.0)].

Adjusting Market Equity Beta to Reflect a New Capital Structure

Recall from the discussion in Chapter 5 that market beta reflects operating leverage, financial leverage, variability of sales and earnings, and other firm characteristics. The market beta computed using historical market price data reflects the firm's existing capital structure. In some settings, such as a leveraged buyout, firms make significant changes in the financial capital structure. In such cases, you need to project what the market beta is likely to be after the firm changes the capital structure. You can "unlever" the current market beta to remove the effects of leverage and then "relever" it to reflect the new capital structure. The following formula estimates an unlevered market beta (sometimes referred to as an *asset beta*):

$$\text{Current Levered Market Beta} = \text{Unlevered Market Beta} \times$$
$$\left[1 + (1 - \text{Income Tax Rate}) \times \left(\frac{\text{Current Market Value of Debt}}{\text{Current Market Value of Equity}}\right)\right]$$

The intuition is that current market beta reflects two components: (1) the systematic risk of the operations and assets of the firm (the unlevered beta), compounded by (2) the financial leverage of the firm (the debt-to-equity ratio), net of the tax benefit from using leverage (that is, tax savings from interest expense deductions). Estimating the new levered beta requires two steps:

1. Solve for the unlevered beta by rearranging the preceding equation to divide the current levered market beta by the term in square brackets on the right side of the equation, as follows:

   Unlevered Market Beta = Current Levered Market Beta/[1 + (1 − Income Tax Rate) × (Current Market Value of Debt/Current Market Value of Equity)]

2. Project the new levered market beta by multiplying the unlevered beta by the term in square brackets on the right side of the equation after substituting the projected new ratio of the market value of debt to the market value of equity in place of the current ratio of the market value of debt to the market value of equity, as follows:

   New Levered Market Beta = Unlevered Market Beta × [1 + (1 − Income Tax Rate) × (New Market Value of Debt/New Market Value of Equity)]

To illustrate the effects of leverage on beta and expected rates of return, suppose a firm has a market beta of 0.9, is subject to an income tax rate of 35%, and has a market-value-of-debt-to-market-value-of-equity ratio of 60%. If the risk-free rate is 3% and the market risk premium is 6%, then according to the CAPM, the market expects this firm to generate equity returns of 8.4% [3.0% + (0.9 × 6.0%)]. The firm intends to adopt a new capital structure that will increase the debt-to-equity ratio to 140%. To project the firm's levered beta under the new capital structure, the first step is to solve for the unlevered beta, denoted X, as follows:

$$0.9 = X \times [1 + (1 - 0.35) \times (0.60/1.00)]$$
$$X = 0.9/[1 + (1 - 0.35) \times (0.60/1.00)]$$
$$X = 0.65$$

Because financial leverage is positively related to market beta, removing the effect of financial leverage reduces market beta. The unlevered beta should reflect the effects of the firm's operating risk, sales volatility, and other operating factors, but not risk related to financial leverage. The new market beta is projected to reflect the new debt-to-equity ratio as follows:

$$Y = 0.65 \times [1 + (1 - 0.35) \times (1.40/1.00)] = 1.24$$

The new capital structure will increase the leverage and therefore the systematic risk of the firm. According to the CAPM, this firm will face an equity cost of capital of 10.44% [3.0% + (1.24 × 6.0%)] under the new capital structure.

Evaluating the Use of the CAPM to Measure the Cost of Equity Capital

The use of the CAPM to calculate the cost of equity capital is subject to various criticisms:

- Market betas for a firm should vary over time as the systematic risk of the firm changes; however, market beta estimates are quite sensitive to the time period and methodology used in their computation.
- In theory, the CAPM estimates required returns based on the stock's risk relative to a diversified portfolio of assets across the economy, but a return index for a diversified portfolio of assets that spans the entire economy does not exist. Measuring a stock's systematic risk relative to a stock market return index such as the S&P 500 Index fails to consider covariation between the stock's returns and returns on assets outside the stock market, including other financial investments (for example, U.S. government and corporate debt securities and privately held equity), real estate, and human capital.
- The market risk premium is sensitive to the time period used in its calculation. Considerable uncertainty surrounds the appropriate market risk premium. It is not clear whether the appropriate premium should be 3%, 7%, or somewhere in between.[7] As noted earlier, some financial economists now argue that the risk

---

[7]See, for example, James Claus and Jacob Thomas, "Equity Premia as Low as Three Percent? Empirical Evidence from Analysts' Earnings Forecasts for Domestic and International Stock Markets," *Journal of Finance* 56 (October 2001), pp. 1629–1666. Also see Peter Easton, Gary Taylor, Pervin Shroff, and Theodore Sougiannis, "Using Forecasts of Earnings to Simultaneously Estimate Growth and the Rate of Return on Equity Investment," *Journal of Accounting Research* 40 (June 2000), pp. 657–676.

premium is lower in periods of economic health and growth and higher in periods of economic weakness and uncertainty, which seems plausible and consistent with observable variation in marketwide stock returns over time. However, this approach requires more research to develop practical models for measuring firm-specific time-varying risk premia.

In light of these criticisms of the CAPM and considering the crucial role of the risk-adjusted discount rate for common equity valuation, it is important to analyze the sensitivity of share value estimates across different discount rates. For example, you should estimate values for a share of common equity in a particular firm across a relevant range of discount rates for common equity by varying the market risk premium from 3% to 7%.

Chapter 14 describes techniques to reverse-engineer the implicit expected rate of return on common equity securities. This technique does not require the assumption of an asset pricing model such as the CAPM.

Cost of Debt Capital

You should compute the after-tax cost of each component of debt capital, including short-term and long-term notes payable, mortgages, bonds, and capital lease obligations, as the yield to maturity on each type of debt times one minus the statutory tax rate applicable to income tax deductions for interest expense. The yield to maturity is the rate that discounts the contractual cash flows on the debt to the debt's current fair value. If the fair value of the debt is equal to face value (for example, a $1,000 debenture trades on an exchange for $1,000), the yield to maturity equals the stated interest rate on the debt. If the fair value of the debt exceeds the face value of the debt, yield to maturity is lower than the stated rate. This can occur after interest rates fall; previously issued fixed-rate debt will have a stated rate that exceeds current market yields for debt with comparable credit quality and terms. On the other hand, after interest rates rise, existing fixed-rate debt may have a stated rate that is lower than prevailing market rates for comparable debt, in which case the debt will have a fair value that is less than face value and the yield to maturity will be greater than the stated rate.

Firms disclose in notes to their financial statements the stated interest rates on their existing interest-bearing debt capital. Firms also disclose in notes the estimated fair values of their interest-bearing debt, which should reflect the present value of the debt using prevailing market yields to maturity on the debt. Together, these disclosures allow us to estimate prevailing market yields to maturity on the firm's outstanding debt.

In computing costs of debt capital, we typically exclude operating liability accounts (such as accounts payable, accrued expenses, deferred income tax liabilities, and retirement benefit obligations). We typically treat these items as part of the firm's operating activities rather than as part of the firm's financial capital structure.

A capitalized lease obligation will generally have an implicit after-tax cost of capital equal to the after-tax yield to maturity on collateralized borrowing with equivalent risk and maturity. Firms recognize capital lease obligations on the balance sheet as financial liabilities; however, as described in Chapter 7, firms also may have significant off-balance-sheet commitments to make future payments under operating leases. If the firm has significant commitments under operating leases, it may be necessary to include them in the computation of the cost of debt capital. If you elect to adjust the firm's balance sheet to capitalize operating lease commitments as debt (as illustrated in Chapter 7), you should make three sets of adjustments to include the effects of operating leases on the total cost of debt capital:

1. Include the present value of operating lease commitments in calculating the fair value of various components of outstanding debt.
2. Include the discount rate used to compute the present value of the operating lease commitments as the after-tax interest rate on operating leases in the computation of the cost of debt capital. The lessor bears more risk in an operating lease than in a capital lease, so the cost of capital represented by operating leases is likely to be higher than for capital leases.
3. The cash outflows for rent payments under operating leases should be reclassified as interest and principal payments of debt when computing free cash flows. Chapter 7 discusses techniques to convert operating leases to capital leases.

The income tax rate we use to compute the tax effects of interest should be the firm's tax rate applicable to interest expense deductions. For most firms, the tax rate applicable to interest expense deductions is the statutory federal tax rate, which is 35% in the United States in 2016. However, state and foreign taxes or other special tax factors may increase or decrease the combined statutory tax rate depending on where the firm raises its debt capital. Firms generally do not separately disclose statutory state or foreign tax rates, but do summarize the effect of these taxes in the income tax reconciliation found in the income tax note. To achieve greater precision, you could approximate the combined statutory tax rate applicable to interest expense deductions using the effective tax rate disclosed in the income tax footnote.

Cost of Preferred Equity Capital

The cost of preferred stock capital depends on the preference conditions. Preferred stock that has preference over common shares with respect to dividends and priority in liquidation generally sells near its par value. Therefore, its cost of capital is the dividend rate on the preferred stock. Depending on the attributes of the preferred stock, dividends on preferred stock may give rise to a tax deduction, in which case the after-tax cost of capital will be lower than the pretax cost. Preferred stock that is convertible into common stock has both preferred and common equity attributes. Its cost is a blending of the cost of nonconvertible preferred stock and common equity.

Cost of Equity Capital Attributable to Noncontrolling Interests

As described in Chapter 7, noncontrolling interests represent the equity ownership of minority investors who own less than 50% of the shares of a subsidiary company. When a firm reports equity capital attributable to noncontrolling interests in shareholders' equity on the balance sheet, it indicates that the firm is the controlling shareholder and consolidates the subsidiary. The noncontrolling interests account measures and reports the amount of equity capital that has been invested by the noncontrolling investors. The relevant cost of capital depends on the risk of this component of equity capital. In some cases, the subsidiary company may be a publicly traded firm for which you can obtain an estimate of systematic risk (e.g., beta). In those cases, you can use the CAPM to estimate the cost of capital for noncontrolling interests. For subsidiary companies that are not publicly traded, you must estimate the appropriate cost of capital using other methods. For example, if the subsidiary company has very similar risk as the consolidated firm, then it is appropriate to use the parent company's cost of equity capital.

Computing the Weighted-Average Cost of Capital

In some circumstances, you may need to determine the present value of payoffs from all of the assets of a firm, not just the equity capital of the firm. Such circumstances might arise, for example, if you are considering acquiring all of the assets of a firm or considering acquiring controlling interest in a firm. If you need to determine the present value of the payoffs from investing in the total assets of the firm, or, equivalently, acquiring all of the financing claims on the firm, you should use a discount rate that reflects the weighted-average required rate of return that encompasses the debt, preferred, and common equity capital used to finance the net operating assets of the firm.

A formula for the weighted-average cost of capital (denoted as R_A) is given here:

$$R_A = [w_D \times R_D \times (1 - Income\ Tax\ Rate)] + [w_P \times R_P] + [w_E \times R_E] + [w_{NCI} \times R_{NCI}]$$

where: w denotes the weight on each type of capital
D denotes debt capital
P denotes preferred stock capital
E denotes common equity capital
NCI denotes equity capital attributable to noncontrolling interests
R denotes the cost of each type of capital
Income Tax Rate denotes the tax rate applicable to debt capital costs

The weights used to compute the weighted-average cost of capital should be the market values of each type of capital in proportion to the total market value of the financial capital structure of the firm (that is, $w_D + w_P + w_E + w_{NCI} = 1.0$). On the right side of the equation, the first term in brackets measures the weighted after-tax cost of debt capital, the second term measures the weighted cost of preferred stock capital, the third term measures the weighted cost of common equity capital, and the fourth term measures the weighted cost of capital for noncontrolling interests.

To determine the appropriate weights to use in the weighted-average cost of capital, you must first determine the market values of each type of capital (debt, preferred, common, and noncontrolling interests). Market values for debt will be observable only for firms that have issued publicly traded debt; however, U.S. GAAP and IFRS require firms to disclose the fair value of their outstanding debt capital in notes to the financial statements each year. Fair value disclosures may not be available, however, if the firm is privately owned, if it is not required to follow U.S. GAAP or IFRS, or if it is a division and does not publish its own financial statements. If market values are not observable and fair values are not disclosed, you can (1) estimate the fair value of the firm's debt if sufficient data are available about the firm's credit quality and the maturity and terms of the debt or (2) rely on the book value of debt. The book value of debt can be a reliable estimate of fair value if the debt

- is recently issued.
- bears a variable rate of interest.
- bears a fixed rate of interest, but interest rates and the firm's credit quality have been stable since the debt was issued.

Because the yield to maturity on debt is inversely related to its market value, analysts sometimes approximate the cost of debt by simply using the coupon rate and the book value of debt, particularly when interest rates are stable and the market value of debt is likely to be close to book value.

If available, market prices for equity securities provide the amounts for determining the market value of equity. Market prices for equity may not be available, however, if the firm is privately owned or if it is a subsidiary of a parent firm. You can then use the book value of equity as a starting point to compute the weight of equity in the capital structure.

Over time, the weights you assign to debt, preferred, common equity, and noncontrolling interests capital may change if you expect the firm's capital structure to change over the forecast horizon. In addition, you may expect yields to maturity on debt capital and required rates of return on equity capital to change as interest rates in the economy change, the risk of the firm changes, or the firm's tax status changes. To capture these changes, you may need to project the weighted-average cost of capital *for each period* over the forecast horizon.

Computing the Weighted-Average Cost of Capital

To demonstrate how to compute the weighted-average cost of capital, suppose a firm has the following capital structure on its balance sheet:

	Book Value	Fair Value
Long-term bonds, 10% annual coupon, issued at par	$20,000,000	$22,000,000
Preferred stock, 4% dividend, issued at par	5,000,000	5,000,000
Common equity	25,000,000	33,000,000
Total	$50,000,000	$60,000,000

The market has priced the bonds to yield 8.0%. (That is, 8.0% is the interest rate that discounts the annuity of contractual $2,000,000 interest payments and the $20,000,000 maturity value to the bonds' $22,000,000 fair value.) Note that this rate is less than the coupon rate of 10% and that the market value of the debt is greater than its par value. The firm's income tax rate is 35%, so the after-tax cost of debt is 5.2% [(1 − 0.35) × 8.0%]. Use of coupon rates and book values in this case would result in a higher cost of debt capital (6.5% = 0.65 × 10.0%) but a smaller weight for debt in the weighted average. Assuming that the dividend on the preferred stock is not tax deductible, its cost is the dividend rate of 4.0% because it is selling for par value. The equity capital has a market beta of 0.9. Assuming a risk-free interest rate of 6.0% and a market premium of 7.0%, the cost of equity capital is 12.3% [6.0% + (0.9 × 7.0%)]. The calculation of the weighted-average cost of capital is as follows:

Security	Market Value	Weight	After-Tax Cost	Weighted Average
Long-term debt	$22,000,000	37%	5.2%	1.92%
Preferred equity	5,000,000	8	4.0%	0.32
Common equity	33,000,000	55	12.3%	6.77
Total	$60,000,000	100%		9.01%

Computing the Weighted-Average Cost of Capital Iteratively

The preceding discussion reveals circular reasoning in computing weighted-average costs of capital for valuation purposes. We use the market values of debt and equity to compute the weighted-average cost of capital, which we use in turn to compute the value of the debt and equity in the firm. This is circular reasoning because we need to know the market values to determine the weights, but we need to know the weights to determine the weighted-average cost of capital to estimate firm value. In practice, we use two approaches to deal with this circularity. One approach assumes that the firm will maintain a target debt-to-equity structure in the future based on the firm's past debt-to-equity ratios or the firm's stated strategy with respect to financial leverage. The other approach computes iteratively the weighted-average cost of capital and the values of debt and equity capital until the weights and the values converge.

Suppose that you need to compute the weighted-average cost of capital and the market value of equity for a firm for which no market or fair value data are available. Also suppose that the firm has outstanding debt with a book value of $40 million. The firm recently issued this debt, and it carries a stated rate of 8.0%, so you can assume that this is a reliable measure of the cost of debt capital. The firm faces a 35% tax rate. The book value of equity is $60 million. Similar firms in the same industry with comparable risks have a market beta of 1.2. Using the same risk-free rate and market risk premium as in the prior example, the cost of equity capital is 14.4% [6.0% + (1.2 × 7.0%)]. The first estimate of the weighted-average cost of capital is as follows:

Security	Amount	Weight	After-Tax Cost	Weighted Average
Debt	$ 40,000,000	40%	5.2%	2.08%
Common equity	60,000,000	60%	14.4%	8.64%
Total	$100,000,000	100%		10.72%

After using the 10.72% weighted-average cost of capital to discount the free cash flows to present value, you determine that the firm's equity value is roughly $120 million (calculations not shown). Therefore, the values and weights you used to compute the weighted-average cost of capital are inconsistent with your value estimates for equity. Your first-iteration estimates placed too much weight on debt and too little weight on equity. You should use the revised estimate of the value of equity to recompute the weighted-average cost of capital and then recompute the value of the firm. Using the revised estimates produces a weighted-average cost of capital estimate as follows:

Security	Amount	Weight	After-Tax Cost	Weighted Average
Debt	$ 40,000,000	25%	5.2%	1.30%
Common equity	120,000,000	75%	14.4%	10.80%
Total	$160,000,000	100%		12.10%

You should then use the revised estimate of the weighted-average cost of capital of 12.10% to recompute the value of equity once again and then repeat this process until your values of debt and equity converge with your weights of debt and equity.

Computing the Weighted-Average Cost of Capital for Starbucks

Starbucks' balance sheet (Appendix A) at the end of fiscal 2015 shows interest-bearing long-term debt obligations of $2,348 million. Recall that Chapter 10 used information disclosed in Note 9, "Debt" (Appendix A), to assess stated interest rates on Starbucks' interest-bearing debt. In 2015, Starbucks' outstanding debt carries a weighted-average interest rate of approximately 2.71%. In Note 9, Starbucks discloses that the fair value of outstanding debt obligations at the end of fiscal 2015 is $2,402 million. Thus, Starbucks has experienced a small unrealized (and unrecognized) loss of $54 million ($2,348 million − $2,402 million) on its debt capital. This unrealized loss is a bit surprising because the financing activities section of Starbucks' statement of cash flows (Appendix A) reveals that Starbucks issued this outstanding long-term debt over 2013 to 2015 at prevailing market rates. The unrealized loss implies that the firm's prior issues of outstanding long-term fixed-rate debt must carry stated rates of interest that are slightly higher than prevailing market yields, which at the end of 2015 are at relatively low levels. Based on the fact that Starbucks' outstanding debt obligations were recently issued, Chapter 10 projected that Starbucks' cost of debt capital will continue to approximate 2.71% in Year +1 and beyond. We use the current fair value (as a proxy for market value) of Starbucks' debt for weighting purposes. In Chapter 10 we also projected that Starbucks will face average tax rates of roughly 34% in Year +1 and beyond. Therefore, these projections imply that Starbucks faces an after-tax cost of debt capital of 1.79% [2.71 × (1 − 0.34)].

Starbucks has no preferred stock on the 2015 balance sheet. In Chapter 10 we projected that Starbucks would not issue any preferred stock in future years. Therefore, we include no preferred stock in the computation of Starbucks' weighted-average cost of capital.

Starbucks' 2015 balance sheet reports $1.8 million in equity capital attributable to noncontrolling interests. In Chapter 10 we projected that Starbucks would retire this very small amount in Year +1, so we include no capital for noncontrolling interests.

Recall that earlier in this chapter we used the CAPM to determine that Starbucks faces a 7.20% cost of equity capital. At the end of fiscal 2015, Starbucks had 1,485.1 million shares outstanding and a share price of $56.84, for a total market capital of common equity of $84,413 million.

Bringing these costs of debt and equity capital together, we compute Starbucks' weighted-average cost of capital to be 7.05% as follows (allow for rounding):

Capital	Value Basis	Amount	Weight	After-Tax Cost of Capital	Weighted-Average Component
Debt	Fair	$ 2,402	2.77%	1.79%	0.05%
Common Equity	Market	84,413	97.23%	7.20%	7.00%
Total		$86,815	100.00%		7.05%

This is just an initial estimate of Starbucks' weighted-average cost of capital. As described earlier, the weighted-average cost of capital must be computed iteratively until the weights are consistent with the present values of debt and equity capital.

In this chapter, we only use our estimate of Starbucks' equity cost of capital to compute the dividends-based valuation model. However, in Chapter 12 we use Starbucks' weighted-average cost of capital to compute the free-cash-flows-based valuation model. We turn next to the rationale and basic concepts of the dividends-based valuation approach.

Dividends-Based Valuation: Rationale and Basic Concepts

LO 11-4

Explain the dividends-based valuation approach, including the relation between cash flows to the investor versus cash flows reinvested in the firm.

Dividends are the most fundamental expected future payoffs to use to value shares because they represent the distribution of wealth from the firm to the shareholders. The shareholder invests cash to purchase the share and then receives cash as a result of holding the share. In dividends-based valuation, we define *dividends* broadly to include *all* cash flows between the firm and the common equity shareholders. The shareholder can receive cash as a result of holding the share in various ways:

- quarterly or annual dividend payments.
- payment when either the firm repurchases shares or the firm liquidates all of its assets and distributes the capital to shareholders, or when another firm acquires all of the outstanding shares in a merger or acquisition transaction.
- the final "liquidating" dividend when the investor sells the share in the open market.

Therefore, in dividends-based valuation, "dividends" encompass all cash flows from the firm to shareholders through periodic dividend payments, stock repurchases, and/or the liquidating dividend when the investor sells the share.

As a practical matter, however, quarterly or annual dividend payment amounts are established by a dividend policy set by the firm's managers and board of directors. Periodic dividend payments typically do not vary closely with firm performance each period. Some firms do not pay any regular periodic dividends, particularly young, high-growth firms. For most firms, the final liquidating dividend usually represents a large proportion of firm value in a dividends-based valuation. Therefore, to value a firm's shares using dividends, we must forecast dividends over the life of the firm (or the expected length of time the share will be held), including the final liquidating dividend (that is, the future price at which shares will be retired, acquired, or sold). Thus, we face the challenge of needing to forecast the value of shares in the future at the time of the liquidating dividend in order to value the shares today.

Dividends-Based Valuation Concepts

This section describes and illustrates key concepts in dividends-based valuation, first presenting simple examples and then confronting conceptual measurement issues regarding dividends to the investor versus cash flows to the firm, and nominal versus real dividends. Later, we apply this approach to value the shares of **Starbucks**.

Dividends Valuation for a Firm

For the following examples, assume the following:

- You can acquire all of the common equity shares of a firm for $4.0 million.
- You expect the firm will generate pretax net cash flows of $2 million per year.
- The income tax rate is 40%.
- After making any debt service payments and paying taxes, the firm will pay dividends to distribute any remaining cash flows to you each year.
- You plan to own the firm for three years. At the end of the third year, you expect to liquidate the assets of the firm for $3.0 million. The liquidation will not trigger any income tax payments, so the firm will pay out the entire proceeds in a final, liquidating dividend.
- Your cost of equity capital is 10%.

Example: Value of Common Equity in an All-Equity Firm

What is the value of this firm to you, the investor? Should you be willing to pay $4.0 million to buy this firm? You can determine the value of the firm using the present value of the expected future dividends, as follows:

	Year 1	Year 2	Year 3	Liquidation
Pretax cash flows	$2,000,000	$2,000,000	$2,000,000	$3,000,000
Interest payments on debt	0	0	0	0
Income taxes (40%)	($800,000)	($800,000)	($800,000)	0
Dividends	$1,200,000	$1,200,000	$1,200,000	$3,000,000
Present value factor (10%)	0.9091	0.8264	0.7513	0.7513
Present value of dividends	$1,090,909	$ 991,736	$ 901,578	$2,253,944
Value of equity	$5,238,167			

Each year the firm will pay you a dividend of $1,200,000. Also, at the end of the third and final year, the firm will pay you a liquidating dividend of $3,000,000. The present value of this stream of cash flows to you is worth $5,238,167. So it would be a wise investment to purchase the firm for only $4.0 million because the firm is worth $1,238,167 more than your investment ($5,238,167 – $4,000,000).

Example: Value of Common Equity in a Firm with Debt Financing

Assume the same original facts, but now make the following additional assumptions:

- You can purchase all of the equity shares for $4.0 million, and you plan to finance the investment with $3.0 million of equity capital and $1.0 million of debt capital.
- The debt is less risky than equity, so the lenders demand interest of only 6%, payable at the end of each year. Interest expense is deductible for income tax purposes. You will repay the debt with the liquidation proceeds at the end of Year 3.
- This amount of debt in the firm's capital structure does not alter substantially the risk of the firm to you, so you continue to require a 10% rate of return.

Now what is the value of this firm to you, the investor? Should you be willing to pay $3.0 million and borrow $1.0 million to buy this firm? As in the prior example, you can determine the value of the firm using the present value of the expected future dividends, as follows:

	Year 1	Year 2	Year 3	Liquidation
Pretax cash flows	$2,000,000	$2,000,000	$2,000,000	$3,000,000
Interest/Principal payments on debt (6%)	(60,000)	(60,000)	(60,000)	(1,000,000)
Income taxes [40% × ($2,000,000 – $60,000)]	($776,000)	($776,000)	($776,000)	0
Dividends	$1,164,000	$1,164,000	$1,164,000	$2,000,000
Present value factor (10%)	0.9091	0.8264	0.7513	0.7513
Present value of dividends	$1,058,182	$ 961,983	$ 874,530	$1,502,630
Value of equity	$4,397,325			

Each year the firm will pay you a dividend of $1,164,000. Also, at the end of the third and final year, the firm will pay you a liquidating dividend of $2,000,000, after repaying the $1,000,000 debt. The present value of this stream of cash flows to you is worth $4,397,325. It would be a wise investment to purchase the firm for only $3.0 million of equity because it would be worth $1,397,325 more than your original investment ($4,397,325 − $3,000,000).

Note that in this example, the value of the firm to you in excess of your original investment ($1,397,325) is larger than in the previous example ($1,238,167) by $159,159 because

- The debt capital is less expensive than the equity capital (6% rather than 10% on $1,000,000 of financing), creating $99,474 of value from capital structure leverage [the present value of $1,000,000 × (0.10 − 0.06) for three years].
- The net tax savings from interest expense each year is $24,000 ($60,000 interest deduction × 0.40 tax rate). In present value terms, the tax savings creates $59,684 of value [the present value of $24,000 tax savings per year for three years, discounted at 10%].

Note that we assumed that the amount of debt in the capital structure did not alter the risk of the firm or your expected return of 10%. If the increased leverage in the firm did make it riskier, then you would require a higher rate of return on this investment. Given the same payoffs, you would then estimate a lower value for this firm.[8]

Dividends to the Investor versus Cash Flows to the Firm

The beginning of this chapter asserted that you can use dividends expected to be paid to the investor or the free cash flows expected to be generated by the firm (that will ultimately be paid to the investor) as equivalent approaches to measure value-relevant expected payoffs to shareholders. Will using *net cash flows into the firm* result in the same estimate of value as using *dividends paid out of the firm*? Cash flows paid to the investor via dividends and free cash flows to the firm that are available for common equity shareholders will differ each period to the extent that the firm reinvests a portion (or all) of the cash flows generated. However, if the firm generates a rate of return on reinvested free cash flow equal to the discount rate used by the investor (that is, the cost of equity capital), either set of payoffs (dividends or free cash flows) will yield the same valuation. The following scenarios demonstrate this equivalence.

Example: Dividend Policy Irrelevance with 100% Payout versus Zero Payout

In the first example, we computed firm value assuming 100% dividend payout. We assumed the firm would pay out all of the after-tax cash flows to you as a dividend each year. We determined the firm value to be $5,238,167. Now suppose that the firm will pay zero dividends each year, and will instead reinvest all of the cash flows. Also assume that the firm will generate a 10% rate of return on the reinvested capital, equal to your required rate of return. Also assume that all of the reinvested capital will be paid to you

[8]As an exercise, repeat the calculations in this example and use a 15% cost of equity capital rather than 10%, to reflect the higher risk and higher expected return. You should find a value of $3,972,707. The lower value is the net result of two effects. First, the increased risk of the firm causes the equity investors to increase the discount rate from 10% to 15%, which reduces (if considered in isolation) the value of the firm. Second, the debt capital is significantly less expensive than the equity capital, creating greater value from capital structure leverage. The net result is a lower value of the firm because of the incremental effects of risk.

as a final liquidating dividend at the end of Year 3, along with the $3.0 million proceeds from liquidating the assets of the firm.

Under these assumptions of zero dividend payout and a 10% return on invested capital, the Year 1 after-tax cash flows should grow to be $1,452,000 by the end of Year 3 ($1,200,000 × (1.10)^2). The Year 2 after-tax cash flows should grow to be $1,320,000 by the end of Year 3 ($1,200,000 × (1.10)^3). The Year 3 after-tax cash flows occur at the end of Year 3, so they will be $1,200,000. The final liquidating dividend payment at the end of Year 3 should then be $6,972,000, computed as follows:

	After-Tax Cash Flows	Value at the End of Year 3	Present Value Factor	Present Value
Year 1	$1,200,000	$1,452,000	0.7513	$1,090,909
Year 2	$1,200,000	$1,320,000	0.7513	$ 991,736
Year 3	$1,200,000	$1,200,000	0.7513	$ 901,578
Liquidation	$3,000,000	$3,000,000	0.7513	$2,253,944
Final Liquidating Dividend		$6,972,000		
Value of equity				$5,238,167

Note that the present value of the final liquidating dividend will be $5,238,167, which is identical to the value determined under the original scenario with 100% dividend payout.

Alternatively, we could assume a partial dividend payout policy, say 25% of cash flows paid out each year in dividends and the remaining 75% of cash flows reinvested to earn the 10% required rate of return. Under those assumptions, we would again obtain a $5,238,167 value for the firm. These examples illustrate the *relevance* of dividends for valuation, but also the *irrelevance* of the firm's dividend policy in valuation, assuming the firm reinvests cash flows to earn the investors' required rate of return.[9]

Nominal versus Real Dividends

Changes in general price levels (that is, inflation or deflation) cause the purchasing power of the monetary unit to change over time. Should you use projected nominal dividends, which include the effects of inflation or deflation, or real dividends, which filter out the effects of changes in general purchasing power?[10] You should obtain the same valuation of an investment using nominal or real dividend amounts as long as you use a discount rate that is a nominal or real rate of return, respectively, consistent with the dividend measure. That is, if you project nominal dividends that include the effects of inflation, you should use a discount rate that is nominal and includes an inflation component. If you project real dividends (net of the effects of inflation), you should use a discount rate that is a real rate of return, excluding the inflation component. As a

[9]Merton Miller and Franco Modigliani, "Dividend Policy, Growth and the Valuation of Shares," *Journal of Business* 34, no. 4 (October 1961), pp. 411–433. Penman and Sougiannis test empirically the replacement property of dividends for future earnings and find support for the irrelevance of dividend policy in valuation. See Stephen H. Penman and Theodore Sougiannis, "The Dividend Displacement Property and the Substitution of Anticipated Earnings for Dividends in Equity Valuation," *The Accounting Review* 72, no. 1 (January 1997), pp. 1–21.

[10]Note that the issue here is not with specific price changes of a firm's particular assets, liabilities, revenues, and expenses. These specific price changes affect projections of the firm's dividends, cash flows, and earnings and should enter into the valuation of the firm. The issue is whether some portion, all, or more than all of the specific price changes represent economywide changes in the purchasing power of the monetary unit, which should not affect the value of a firm.

practical matter, costs of capital and expected returns are typically quoted in nominal terms, so it is usually more straightforward to discount nominal dividends using nominal discount rates.

Dividends-Based Valuation: Advanced Concepts

LO 11-5

Measure dividends, establish a forecast horizon, and value continuing dividends.

In this section, we explain and demonstrate three advanced concepts that are essential in dividends valuation:

1. Measuring dividends
2. Determining the forecast horizon
3. Projecting and valuing continuing dividends

In the sections that follow, we bring all of these concepts together in the dividends-based valuation model, and then apply it to value **Starbucks**.

Measuring Dividends

The dividends-based approach values the common equity in a firm by measuring the present value of all net cash flows from the firm to the equity shareholders. Therefore, dividends valuation measures the present value of *total net dividends* for common equity shareholders, including *all* of the cash flows the shareholders will receive from holding the shares.

Total net dividends encompass cash flows from the firm to common equity shareholders through periodic (quarterly or annual) dividend payments, based on the firm's dividend payout policy. Total net dividends also include cash flows to common equity shareholders through stock buybacks, merger or acquisition of the firm, or cash distributed to shareholders upon liquidation of the firm. Further, when the firm issues shares to shareholders, the cash flows from the shareholders to the firm are *negative* dividends. Thus, to measure total value-relevant net dividends that encompass all of the cash flows from the firm to common equity shareholders each period, you should include the following three components:

+ Quarterly or annual ordinary dividend payments to common equity shareholders
+ Net cash flows to shareholders from share repurchases (or acquisition or liquidation)
− Net cash flows from shareholders through common equity issues

= Total dividends to common equity shareholders

An alternative and equivalent way of computing total net dividends relies on how we account for shareholders' equity under the assumption of *clean surplus accounting*. Under clean surplus accounting, income must include *all* revenues, expenses, gains, and losses generated by the firm for common equity shareholders. Under U.S. GAAP and IFRS, clean surplus income is measured by comprehensive income (that is, net income plus all of the unrealized gains and losses included in other comprehensive income). Under clean surplus accounting, income does *not* include increases or decreases in the book value of equity as a result of direct capital transactions between the firm and the common equity shareholders, such as periodic dividend payments, share issues, and share repurchases.[11]

---

[11]Also assume that direct capital transactions between the firm and common equity shareholders are arm's-length exchanges of fair value. That is, the firm does not generate gains or losses from trading in its own shares because the shares are issued or repurchased for fair value.

The general principles of clean surplus accounting represent common equity as follows:

$$BV_t = BV_{t-1} + CI_t - D_t$$

where: BV_t denotes the book value of equity at the end of year t

CI_t denotes comprehensive income for year t

D_t denotes net direct capital transactions between the firm and common shareholders (dividend payments, stock issues, stock repurchases) during year t.

To isolate all of the net cash flows between the firm and the shareholders during year t, simply rearrange the equation as follows:

$$D_t = CI_t + BV_{t-1} - BV_t$$

Therefore, total dividends used in valuation should equal comprehensive income each year, adjusted for the change in the book value of common equity as a result of direct capital transactions.

Measuring Dividends for Starbucks

This section illustrates measuring dividends for the valuation of **Starbucks**. We derive our dividends expectations from our projected financial statements for **Starbucks** in Chapter 10. In that chapter, we projected that (amounts in millions, allow for rounding):

- **Starbucks** would pay Year +1 common equity dividends equal to 42.5% of net income attributable to common shareholders, amounting to $1,187.6 million [0.425 × ($2,794.3 million net income attributable to common shareholders)].
- **Starbucks'** common stock and additional paid-in capital would remain roughly 0.342% of total assets. Our projections expect common stock and additional paid-in capital will grow from $42.6 million to $43.9 million by the end of Year +1, implying new stock issues of $1.3 million (in effect, negative dividends of −$1.3 million).
- **Starbucks** would engage in net repurchases of common shares totaling $2,653.7 million ($1,500.0 + $1,153.7) in Year +1:
  - **Starbucks** would pay $1,500.0 million to repurchase common shares, net of any shares reissued for stock options exercises.
  - **Starbucks** would use treasury share repurchases as the flexible financial account to balance the balance sheet, so it would distribute an additional $1,153.7 million in cash to shareholders through additional share repurchases.

Combining them, we project that total value-relevant dividends to common equity shareholders in Year +1 will be as follows (in millions; allow for rounding):

Periodic dividend payments	$1,187.6
Common stock issues	(1.3)
Net purchases of treasury stock	2,653.7
Total dividends to common equity shareholders	$3,839.9

This computation reconciles with the clean surplus accounting approach. The Year +1 forecast of comprehensive income attributable to common shareholders is $2,794.3 million. Total book value of common shareholders' equity (before noncontrolling interests) is \$5,818.0 million at the beginning of Year +1 and \$4,772.4 million at the end of Year +1. Therefore, using the clean surplus accounting approach, total dividends in Year +1 are as follows (in millions; allow for rounding):

$$D_t = CI_t + BV_{t-1} - BV_t = \$2,794.3 + \$5,818.0 - \$4,772.4 = \$3,839.9$$

The projected net amount of dividends to common shareholders using the clean surplus approach is identical to the amount computed above. Exhibit 11.5 demonstrates these computations for Years +1 through +5.

Selecting a Forecast Horizon

For how many future years should you project future payoffs from an investment? The correct answer is the expected life of the investment being valued. This life is a finite number of years for an investment in a machine, a building, or any resource with limits to its physical existence or a financial instrument with a finite stated maturity (such as a bond, mortgage, or lease). In equity valuation, however, the resource to be valued is an ownership claim on the firm, which has an indefinite expected life. Therefore, in the case of an equity security, you must project future dividends that, in theory, extend indefinitely.

Of course, as a practical matter, you cannot precisely predict a firm's dividends very many years into the future. Therefore, analysts commonly develop specific forecasts of dividends over a finite horizon (perhaps 5 or 10 years) depending on the industry, the maturity of the firm, and the expected growth and predictability of the firm's business

Exhibit 11.5

Computation of Starbucks' Total Dividends for the Dividends-Based Valuation Approach (amounts in millions, allow for rounding)

	Computing Total Dividends Using Components				
	Year +1	Year +2	Year +3	Year +4	Year +5
Dividends paid to common shareholders	\$1,187.6	\$1,309.2	\$1,483.2	\$1,674.4	\$2,080.4
Less: Common stock issues	(1.3)	(2.4)	(3.3)	(3.8)	(6.7)
Plus: Common stock repurchases	2,653.7	1,483.5	1,598.2	1,757.6	1,509.9
Total dividends to common equity	\$3,839.9	\$2,790.4	\$3,078.2	\$3,428.2	\$3,583.6

	Computing Total Dividends Using Clean Surplus Accounting				
	Year +1	Year +2	Year +3	Year +4	Year +5
Comprehensive income attributable to common equity	\$ 2,794.3	\$ 3,080.6	\$ 3,490.0	\$ 3,939.8	\$ 4,895.0
Plus: Beginning book value of common equity	5,818.0	4,772.4	5,062.6	5,474.4	5,985.9
Less: Ending book value of common equity	(4,772.4)	(5,062.6)	(5,474.4)	(5,985.9)	(7,297.3)
Total dividends to common equity	\$ 3,839.9	\$ 2,790.4	\$ 3,078.2	\$ 3,428.2	\$ 3,583.6

activities. After the finite forecast horizon, analysts then typically use general steady-state growth assumptions to project the future dividends that will persist indefinitely. Therefore, you will find it desirable to develop specific forecasts of income statements, balance sheets, and cash flows over a forecast horizon that extends until the point when you expect a firm's growth pattern will reach steady state, during which time you can expect dividends will grow (on average) at a stable rate indefinitely.

Selecting a forecast horizon involves trade-offs. You can make reasonably reliable projections over longer forecast horizons for stable and mature firms. Projections for such firms, like **Starbucks** (demonstrated in Chapter 10), or **Walmart** or **Coca-Cola**, capture relatively steady-state operations. On the other hand, it is more difficult to develop reliable projections over long forecast horizons for young high-growth firms, like **Tesla Motors**, because their future operating performance is more uncertain. This difficulty is exacerbated by the fact that a much higher proportion of the value of young growth firms will be achieved in distant future years, after they reach their potential steady-state profitability. Thus, we face the dilemma of depending most heavily on long-run forecasts for young growth firms for which long-run projections are most uncertain. The forecasting and valuation process is particularly difficult for growth firms when we project the near-term dividends will be zero or negative, as is common for rapidly growing firms that finance growth by issuing common stock. In this case, the firm's value depends entirely on dividends to be generated in years far into the future.

Unfortunately, there is no way to avoid this dilemma. The predictive accuracy of our dividend forecasts many years into the future is likely to be limited for even the most stable and predictable firms. Of course, we recognize that forecasts and value estimates for all firms, but especially growth firms, have a high degree of uncertainty and estimation risk. To mitigate this uncertainty and estimation risk, we offer the following coaching tips:

- Diligently follow all six steps of the analysis framework. By thoroughly analyzing the firm's industry, strategy, accounting quality, financial performance and risk, you will have more information to use to develop more reliable long-term forecasts.
- To the extent possible, directly confront the problem of long-term uncertainty by developing specific projections of dividends derived from projected income statements and balance sheets that extend 5 or 10 years into the future, at which point the firm may reasonably be projected to reach steady-state growth.
- Assess the sensitivity of the forecast projections and value estimates across the reasonable range of growth assumptions.

Projecting and Valuing Continuing Dividends

This section describes techniques to project continuing dividends using a steady-state growth rate beyond the explicit forecast horizon and to measure the present value of continuing dividends. We refer to them as *continuing dividends* because they reflect the cash flows from the firm to the common equity shareholders continuing into the long-run future.

In some circumstances, however, you may not find it necessary to forecast dividends continuing beyond the explicit forecast horizon if you can reliably predict that the share will receive a future liquidating dividend. In such circumstances, the liquidating dividend is the final cash flow to the shareholder. The liquidating dividend might arise when the firm liquidates its assets at the end of its business life and distributes the proceeds to shareholders to retire their shares. Alternatively, the liquidating dividend might arise when a firm's shares are acquired by another firm in a merger or acquisition transaction—or when the shareholder sells the share, creating a liquidating dividend from the selling price.

Projecting Continuing Dividends

If you cannot reliably predict whether or when your shares will receive a liquidating dividend, then you need to forecast dividends over a finite forecast horizon until the point when you expect the firm to mature into steady-state growth, and you can assume dividends will grow at a constant steady-state rate. You can project the long-run sustainable growth rate (denoted as g) in future continuing dividends to be positive, negative, or zero. Sustainable growth in dividends will be driven by long-run expectations for inflation, demand for the industry's output, the economy in general, and the firm's strategy. You should select a growth rate that captures realistic long-run expectations for Year T+1 and beyond.

Example: Projecting Continuing Dividends Correctly

To project continuing dividends in Year T+1, you should derive the continuing dividends from the projected Year T+1 income statement and balance sheet. To do so correctly, you should use the expected long-run growth rate (g) to project all of the items of the Year T+1 income statement and balance sheet. Simply multiply each item on the Year T income statement and balance sheet by $(1 + g)$. You can then derive Year T+1 dividends using clean surplus accounting as follows:

$$D_{T+1} = CI_{T+1} + BV_T - BV_{T+1}$$

Comprehensive income and book value in Year T+1 are therefore $CI_{T+1} = CI_T \times (1 + g)$ and $BV_{T+1} = BV_T \times (1 + g)$. Substitute these terms into the D_{T+1} equation, as follows:

$$D_{T+1} = [CI_T \times (1 + g)] + BV_T - [BV_T \times (1 + g)]$$

You must impose the long-run growth rate assumption $(1 + g)$ uniformly on the Year T+1 income statement and balance sheet projections to derive the dividends for Year T+1 correctly. In the long run, assuming that the firm itself will grow at a steady-state rate, all of the elements of the firm—revenues, expenses, income, assets, liabilities, shareholders' equity, cash flows, and, therefore, dividends—will grow on average at the same rate. By applying a uniform growth rate across all of the items of the income statement and balance sheet, you will achieve internally consistent steady-state growth across all of your projections, keeping the balance sheet in balance throughout the continuing forecast horizon and keeping growth in dividends, cash flows, and earnings internally consistent with each other.

As an example, suppose we develop the following forecasts for Year T–1 and Year T:

	Assets	=	Liabilities	+	Shareholders' Equity
Year T–1 forecast amounts	$100	=	$60	+	$40
Net income	+ 20				+ 20
New borrowing	+ 6		+ 6		
Dividends paid	(10)				(10)
Year T forecast amounts	$116	=	$66	+	$50

Suppose we project that the firm will grow at a steady-state rate of 10% in Year T+1 and thereafter. To forecast continuing dividends in Year T+1 correctly, we should project Year T+1 net income, assets, liabilities, and shareholders' equity to grow by 10% each and then compute Year T+1 continuing dividends as follows:

	Assets	=	Liabilities	+	Shareholders' Equity
Year T forecast amounts	$ 116	=	$ 66	+	$ 50
Growth	×1.10		×1.10		×1.10
Year T+1 forecast amounts	$127.6	=	$ 72.6	+	$ 55

The projected net income would be $22 ($20 × 1.10). The Year T+1 dividends projection would therefore be $17 ($22 net income + $50 beginning shareholders' equity − $55 ending shareholders' equity). Also note that the $17 Year T+1 dividend is substantially larger than the $10 dividend amount for Year T. The reason the firm can begin to pay larger dividends in Year T+1 and beyond is that the firm's long-run growth rate of 10% is lower than the Year T growth rate in assets (16%) and shareholders' equity (25%). Thus, this firm will not need to reinvest as much of its earnings to fund growth and will be able to pay larger dividends in Year T+1 and beyond.

In projecting continuing dividends in Year T+1 and beyond, analysts assume that the firm will settle into a long-run sustainable growth rate. Often analysts assume that the firm's long-run sustainable growth rate will be consistent with long-run growth in the economy, on the order of 3% to 5%. For firms that have been growing faster than that in the years leading up to Year T+1, the long-run sustainable growth rate implies that the firm will maintain a lower growth rate in assets and equity and thus will be able to pay out substantially larger dividends. By projecting Year T+1 net income, assets, and equity using the long-run sustainable growth rate, it is possible to solve for the long-run sustainable dividends the firm can pay. The continuing dividend amount derived for Year T+1 may be significantly larger than the amounts the firm actually paid during its higher-growth-rate years. The Year T+1 dividend amount reflects the firm's transition from a high rate of reinvestment to finance high growth in assets to lower reinvestment for lower growth.

Example: Projecting Continuing Dividends Incorrectly

Unfortunately, analysts sometimes take an erroneous shortcut in computing the continuing dividends for Year T+1. The mistake is to multiply the dividends for Year T by one plus the growth rate $(1 + g)$ rather than correctly deriving the Year T+1 dividends from the projected Year T+1 income statement and balance sheet. If you want to avoid this error and compute internally consistent and identical estimates of firm value using dividends, free cash flows, and earnings, you should *not* project dividends for Year T+1 by simply multiplying dividends for Year T by $(1 + g)$. Doing so ignores the necessary growth in all of the elements of the balance sheet and the income statement, which can introduce inconsistent forecast assumptions for dividends, cash flows, and earnings. Even if you simply project that Year T+1 dividends, cash flows, and earnings will grow at an identical rate $(1 + g)$, you may obtain inconsistent value estimates if Year T dividends, cash flows, and earnings are not internally consistent.

To illustrate, suppose we made the same forecasts for the firm in Year T−1 and Year T, as shown in the preceding example. As before, suppose we project that the firm will grow at a steady-state rate of 10% in Year T+1 and thereafter. If we simply (and erroneously) project Year T dividends to grow by 10%, we would project the Year T+1 will be only $11 ($10 Year T dividends × 1.10). Then, if we project that future earnings will grow at the same 10% steady-state rate, we would project Year T+1 earnings will be $22 ($20 Year T net income × 1.10). Even though we have used the same growth rate, we have used inconsistent assumptions. As we show in the next section, if assets, liabilities, and shareholders' equity all increase by 10% in Year T+1, then dividends and net income cannot simultaneously increase by 10%; the clean surplus relationship will not hold. This error will force the estimated value of the firm based on dividends to be lower than the value estimates based on earnings. Note that the correct projected Year T+1 dividend amount of $17 in the preceding example is substantially larger than the erroneous $11 dividend projection in this example.

Computing Continuing Value

Once you have computed continuing dividends for Year T+1, you can compute continuing value (also called terminal value) of dividends in Year T+1 and beyond using the perpetuity-with-growth valuation model. At the end of Year T, assume that the continuing value of the common equity of the firm (denoted as V_T) will equal the present value of all expected future continuing dividends in Year T+1 and beyond, which we can express as follows:

$$V_T = \sum_{t=1}^{\infty} \frac{D_{T+t}}{(1 + R_E)^t}$$

As described in a prior section, we correctly project the Year T+1 dividend by assuming that each line item on the Year T income statement and balance sheet will grow at the long-run steady state growth rate $(1 + g)$ and then by deriving the Year T+1 dividend. As shown above, we assume that accounting for the book value of the shareholders' equity (BV) follows clean surplus accounting, by adding comprehensive income (CI) and subtracting dividends to common shareholders each period (that is, $BV_t = BV_{t-1} + CI_t - D_t$). Comprehensive income and book value in Year T+1 therefore equal $CI_{T+1} = CI_T \times (1 + g)$ and $BV_{T+1} = BV_T \times (1 + g)$. We can then rearrange the D_{T+1} equation as follows:

$$D_{T+1} = CI_{T+1} + BV_T - BV_{T+1} = [CI_T \times (1 + g)] + BV_T - [BV_T \times (1 + g)]$$

Assuming that D_{T+1} will grow in perpetuity at rate g, the firm can be valued at the end of Year T using the perpetuity-with-growth model, as follows:[12]

$$V_T = \sum_{t=1}^{\infty} \frac{D_{T+t}}{(1 + R_E)^t} = \frac{D_{T+t}}{(R_E - g)} = \frac{[CI_T \times (1 + g) + BV_T - BV_T \times (1 + g)]}{(R_E - g)}$$

Example: Valuing Continuing Dividends

Suppose you forecast that the dividends of a firm in Year +5 will be $30 million and that Year +5 earnings and cash flows also will be $30 million. For simplicity in this example, assume you expect that the firm's income statements and balance sheets will grow uniformly over the long run and, therefore, so will cash flows, earnings, and dividends. However, you are uncertain about the steady-state long-run growth rate in Years +6 and beyond. You believe that the growth rate will most likely be zero but could

---

[12]This formula is simply the algebraic simplification for the present value of a growing perpetuity.

reasonably fall in the range between +6% and −6% per year; so you derived the range of Year +6 dividends shown in the following table. Assuming a 15% cost of capital, the table shows the range of possible continuing values (in millions) for the firm in present value at the beginning of the continuing value period (that is, the beginning of Year +6) and in present value as of today; that is, the continuing value is discounted to today using a factor of $1/(1.15)^5$:

Dividends Year +5 (T)	Long-Run Growth Rate	Dividends Year +6 (T+1)	Perpetuity with Growth Factor	Present Value of Continuing Value as of: Beginning of Year +6 (T+1)	Today
$30.00	0%	$30.00	1/(0.15 − 0.0) = 6.67	$200.00	$ 99.44
$30.00	+6%	$31.80	1/(0.15 − 0.06) = 11.11	$353.30	$175.65
$30.00	−6%	$28.20	1/(0.15 + 0.06) = 4.76	$134.23	$ 66.74

Analysts also can estimate continuing value using a multiple of dividends in the first year of the continuing value period. The following table shows the continuing value multiples using $1/(R − g)$ for various costs of equity capital and growth rates. The multiples increase with growth for a given cost of capital, and they decrease as the cost of capital increases for a given level of growth.

Continuing Value Multiples (i.e., Perpetuity with Growth Factors)						
	Long-Run Growth Rates					
Cost of Equity Capital	0%	2%	3%	4%	5%	6%
6%	16.67	25.00	33.33	50.00	100.00	N/A
8%	12.50	16.67	20.00	25.00	33.33	50.00
10%	10.00	12.50	14.29	16.67	20.00	25.00
12%	8.33	10.00	11.11	12.50	14.29	16.67
15%	6.67	7.69	8.33	9.09	10.00	11.11
18%	5.56	6.25	6.67	7.14	7.69	8.33
20%	5.00	5.56	5.88	6.25	6.67	7.14

The continuing value computation using the perpetuity-with-growth model does not work when the growth rate equals or exceeds the discount rate (that is, when $g \geq R$) because the denominator in the computation is zero or negative and the resulting continuing value estimate is meaningless. In this case, you cannot use the perpetuity computation illustrated here. Instead, you must forecast dividend amounts for each year beyond the forecast horizon using the long-run growth rate and then discount each year's dividends to present value using the discount rate. You also should reconsider whether it is realistic to expect the firm's dividend growth rate to exceed the discount rate (the expected rate of return) in perpetuity. This scenario can exist for some years, but is not likely to be sustainable indefinitely. Competition, technological change, new entrants into an industry, and similar dynamic factors eventually reduce growth rates.

An alternative approach for estimating the continuing value is to use the dividend multiples for comparable firms that currently trade in the market. You can identify comparable companies by studying characteristics such as industry, firm size and age, past growth rates in dividends, profitability, risk, and similar factors. Chapter 14 discusses valuation multiples in more depth.

Because of the uncertainty inherent in long-run growth rate forecasts and because continuing value amounts are commonly large proportions of value estimates, you should conduct sensitivity analysis to assess how sensitive the firm value estimate is to variations in the long-run growth assumption. For example, suppose you are valuing a young high-growth company and can reliably forecast dividends five years into the future. After that horizon, you expect the firm to grow at 6% per year, although this is highly uncertain, and long-run growth could range from −3% per year to as much as 9% per year. You should conduct sensitivity analysis on the projections and valuation, varying long-run growth across the range from −3% to 9% per year.

The Dividends-Based Valuation Model

LO 11-6

Bring all of the elements together in the dividends-based valuation model, and estimate firm value.

This section presents the dividends-based valuation model that determines the value of common shareholders' equity in the firm. The sections following demonstrate how to use the model to value **Starbucks**.

The dividends-based valuation model determines the value of common shareholders' equity in the firm (denoted as V_0) as the sum of the present value of all future dividends to shareholders over the remaining life of the firm. The dividends-based valuation model includes dividends (denoted as D) that encompass all of the net cash flows from the firm to shareholders through periodic dividend payments and stock buybacks and subtracts cash flows from the shareholders to the firm when the firm issues shares. We discount the stream of future dividends to present value using the required return on common equity capital in the firm (denoted as R_E). The following general model expresses the dividends valuation approach:

$$V_0 = \sum_{t=1}^{\infty} \frac{D_t}{(1+R_E)^t} = \frac{D_1}{(1+R_E)^1} + \frac{D_2}{(1+R_E)^2} + \frac{D_3}{(1+R_E)^3} + \cdots$$

Suppose we can reliably forecast dividend amounts through Year T. At the end of Year T, we assume that the continuing value of the common equity of the firm (denoted as V_T) will equal the present value of all expected future continuing dividends in Year T+1 and beyond (a perpetuity of D_{T+1} in every year), which can be expressed as follows:

$$V_T = \sum_{t=1}^{\infty} \frac{D_{T+t}}{(1+R_E)^t}$$

Thus, the value of the firm today can be expressed using periodic dividends over a finite horizon to Year T plus continuing value based on dividends in Year T+1 and beyond as follows:

$$V_0 = \sum_{t=1}^{\infty} \frac{D_t}{(1+R_E)^t} = \frac{D_1}{(1+R_E)^1} + \frac{D_2}{(1+R_E)^2} + \frac{D_3}{(1+R_E)^3} + \cdots \frac{D_T}{(1+R_E)^T} + \frac{V_T}{(1+R_E)^T}$$

This equation reveals that the estimate of value today (V_0) depends on the estimate of value in the future (V_T).

As described in a preceding section, we project the Year T+1 dividend by assuming that each line item on the Year T income statement and balance sheet will grow at the expected long-run steady-state growth rate of the firm and then deriving the Year T+1 dividend as follows:

$$D_{T+1} = CI_{T+1} + BV_T - BV_{T+1} = [CI_T \times (1+g)] + BV_T - [BV_T \times (1+g)]$$

Assuming that D_{T+1} will grow in perpetuity at rate g, the firm can be valued at the end of Year T using the perpetuity-with-growth model as follows:

$$V_T = \sum_{t=1}^{\infty} \frac{D_{T+t}}{(1+R_E)^t} = \frac{D_{T+1}}{(R_E - g)} = \frac{[CI_T \times (1+g)] + BV_T - [BV_T \times (1+g)]}{(R_E - g)}$$

Therefore, the dividends-based valuation model estimates the present value of common equity as follows:

$$
\begin{aligned}
V_0 &= \sum_{t=1}^{\infty} \frac{D_t}{(1+R_E)^t} \\
&= \frac{D_1}{(1+R_E)^1} + \frac{D_2}{(1+R_E)^2} + \frac{D_3}{(1+R_E)^3} + \ldots + \frac{D_T}{(1+R_E)^T} + \frac{V_T}{(1+R_E)^T} \\
&= \frac{D_1}{(1+R_E)^1} + \frac{D_2}{(1+R_E)^2} + \frac{D_3}{(1+R_E)^3} + \ldots + \frac{D_T}{(1+R_E)^T} + \frac{[CI_T \times (1+g)] + BV_T - [BV_T \times (1+g)]}{(R_E - g) \times (1+R_E)^T}
\end{aligned}
$$

Applying the Dividends-Based Valuation Model to Value Starbucks

Applying the dividends-based valuation model to determine the value of the common shareholders' equity in a firm involves measuring the following three elements:

1. The discount rate (denoted as R_E in the valuation model) used to compute the present value of the future dividends.
2. The expected future dividends over the forecast horizon (denoted as D_t in periods $t = 1$ through T in the valuation model).
3. The continuing dividend in the final period of the forecast horizon, which we denote as D_{T+1} in the valuation model, and a forecast of the long-run growth rate (denoted as g) in the continuing dividend beyond the forecast horizon.

Prior sections of this chapter have discussed each of these elements. We now bring them all together to estimate the value for **Starbucks** shares at the end of fiscal 2015.

Using the Dividends-Based Valuation Model to Value Starbucks

At the end of fiscal 2015, trading in **Starbucks** shares on the NASDAQ Exchange closed at a *price* of $56.84 per share. But what is our estimate of the *value* of a **Starbucks** share? We will estimate the value of **Starbucks** shares using the techniques described in this chapter and the forecasts we developed in Chapter 10. We develop the forecasts and valuation estimates using the Forecasts and Valuation spreadsheets in FSAP (Appendix B).

Starbucks' Discount Rate and Dividends, Year +1 through Year +5

We estimate the present value of a share of common equity in **Starbucks** at the end of fiscal 2015 (equivalently, the start of Year +1) using the expected rate of return on **Starbucks'** equity capital as the appropriate discount rate. In this chapter, we computed **Starbucks'** cost of equity capital using the CAPM to be 7.2%. Exhibit 11.5 (page 749) summarized the computations of **Starbucks'** projected dividends in Years +1 to +5. Discounting these future dividends using a discount rate of 7.2% yields a present value estimate of $13,636.1 million. The top portion of Exhibit 11.6 illustrates these computations.

Starbucks' Continuing Dividends beyond Year +5

To compute the present value of **Starbucks'** dividends continuing in Year +6 and beyond, we project that continuing dividends will grow at a 3% rate in perpetuity, consistent with long-run average growth in the economy. We forecast Year +6 dividends as follows:

$$D_6 = [CI_5 \times (1 + g)] + BV_5 - [BV_5 \times (1 + g)]$$
$$= [\$4,895.0 \text{ million} \times 1.03] + \$7,297.3 \text{ million} - [\$7,297.3 \text{ million} \times 1.03]$$
$$= \$5,041.8 \text{ million} + \$7,297.3 \text{ million} - \$7,516.2 \text{ million}$$
$$= \$4,822.9 \text{ million}$$

We use the perpetuity-with-growth model to discount dividends in the continuing value period to present value as of the beginning of Year +6 (the beginning of the continuing value period) using **Starbucks'** 7.2% cost of equity capital, as follows (allow for rounding):

$$\text{Continuing Value}_6 = D_6 \times [1/(R_E - g)]$$
$$= \$4,822.9 \text{ million} \times [1/(0.072 - 0.030)]$$
$$= \$4,822.9 \text{ million} \times 23.81$$
$$= \$114,831.3 \text{ million}$$

We then discount the continuing value as of the beginning of Year +6 to present value, as follows (allow for rounding):

$$\text{Present Value of Continuing Value}_0 = \$114,831.3 \text{ million} \times [1/(1 + R_E)^5]$$
$$= \$114,831.3 \text{ million} \times [1/(1 + 0.072)^5]$$
$$= \$114,831.3 \text{ million} \times 0.706$$
$$= \$81,112.2 \text{ million}$$

Starbucks' Total Dividends

The total present value of **Starbucks'** dividends to common equity shareholders is the sum of these two parts:

Present value of dividends through Year +5	$13,636.1 million
Present value of continuing value	81,112.2 million
Present value of common equity	$94,748.3 million

Exhibit 11.6

Valuation of Starbucks
Present Value of Dividends to Common Equity

	Valuation of Dividends in Year +1 through Year +5 (amounts in millions)				
	Year +1	Year +2	Year +3	Year +4	Year +5
Total Dividends to Common Equity (from Exhibit 11.5)	$ 3,839.9	$2,790.4	$3,078.2	$3,428.2	$3,583.6
Present Value Factors ($R_E = 7.20\%$)	0.933	0.870	0.812	0.757	0.706
Present Value of Dividends	$ 3,582.0	$2,428.1	$2,498.7	$2,595.9	$2,531.3
Sum of Present Value Dividends, Years +1 through +5	$13,636.1				

Continuing Value Based on Dividends in Year + 6 and Beyond

Project Year +6 Dividends (allow for rounding):

$D_6 = [CI_5 \times (1 + g)] + BV_5 - [BV_5 \times (1 + g)]$

$\quad = [\$4,895.0 \text{ million} \times 1.03] + \$7,297.3 \text{ million} - [\$7,297.3 \text{ million} \times 1.03]$

$\quad = \$5,041.8 \text{ million} + \$7,297.3 \text{ million} - \$7,516.2 \text{ million}$

$\quad = \$4,822.9 \text{ million}$

$\text{Continuing Value}_0 = D_6 \times [1/(R_E - g)]$

$\qquad = \$4,822.9 \text{ million} \times [1/(0.072 - 0.030)]$

$\qquad = \$4,822.9 \text{ million} \times 23.81$

$\qquad = \$114,831.3 \text{ million}$

$\text{Present Value of Continuing Value}_0 = \$114,831.3 \text{ million} \times [1/(1 + R_E)^5]$

$\qquad = \$114,831.3 \text{ million} \times [1/(1 + 0.072)^5]$

$\qquad = \$114,831.3 \text{ million} \times 0.706$

$\qquad = \$81,112.2 \text{ million}$

Total Value of Starbucks's Dividends

Present value of dividends through Year + 5		$13,636.1	million
+ Present value of continuing value	+	81,112.2	million
Present value of common equity	=	$94,748.3	million
Adjust for midyear discounting (multiply by 1 + [R_E/2])	×	1.0360	
Total present value of common equity	=	$98,159.2	million
Divide by number of shares outstanding	÷	1,485.1	million
Value per share of Starbucks common equity	=	$ 66.10	

Midyear Discounting

Present value calculations like those used here discount amounts for full periods. Thus, the valuation computations discount Year +1 dividends for one full year, Year +2 dividends for two full years, and so on, which is appropriate if the dividends being discounted occur at the end of each year. Dividends often occur throughout the period. If this is the case, present value computations with full-year discounting will over-discount these flows. To avoid over-discounting, you can compute the present value discount factors as of the midpoint of each year, thereby effectively discounting the dividends as if they occur, on average, in the middle of each year. Suppose you use a discount rate of 10% ($R = 0.10$). You would discount the Year +1 dividends from the middle of Year +1 using a factor of $1/(1 + R)^{0.5} = 1/(1.10)^{0.5} = 0.9535$; the Year +2 dividends from the middle of Year +2 using a factor of $1/(1 + R)^{1.5} = 1/(1.10)^{1.5} = 0.8668$; and so on.

You also can use a shortcut approach to this correction by adjusting the total present value to a midyear approximation by adding back one-half year of discounting. To make this midyear adjustment, multiply the total present value of the discounted dividends by a factor of $1 + (R/2)$. For example, if $R = 0.10$, the midyear adjustment is 1.05 [$1 + (0.10/2)$]. The Valuation spreadsheet computations in FSAP use this shortcut adjustment.[13]

Applying the midyear discounting adjustment to the computation of the present value of **Starbucks'** dividends results in the following:

Present value of common equity	$ 94,748.3 million
Midyear adjustment factor [$1 + (0.072/2)$]	× 1.0360
Total present value of common equity	$ 98,159.2 million

Computing Common Equity Value per Share

Dividing the total present value of common equity of $98,159.2 million by 1,485.1 million shares outstanding indicates that **Starbucks'** common equity shares have a value of $66.10 per share. This value estimate is roughly 16% higher than the market price of $56.84 at the end of fiscal 2015. We will obtain identical value estimates for **Starbucks** when we apply the free-cash-flows-based valuation model in Chapter 12 and the earnings-based valuation model in Chapter 13. Exhibit 11.7 presents the dividends-based valuation model from FSAP (Appendix B, which can be found online at the book's companion website at www.cengagebrain.com).

---

[13]The valuation models described in this chapter estimate the present value of the firm as of the first day of the first year of the forecast horizon; for example, January 1 of Year +1 for a firm with an accounting period that matches the calendar year. However, analysts estimate valuations every day of the year. Suppose the analyst values a firm as of June 17 and compares the value estimate to that day's market price. A present value calculation that determines the value of the firm as of January 1 will ignore the value accumulation between January 1 and June 17 of that year. To refine the calculation, the analyst can adjust the present value as of January 1 to a present value as of June 17 by multiplying V_0 by a future value factor that reflects value accumulation for the appropriate number of days (in this case, 168 days). For example, if the valuation date is June 17 and if $R = 0.10$, the analyst can update the January 1 value estimate by multiplying V_0 by $(1 + R)^{(168/365)} = (1 + 0.10)^{(168/365)} = 1.0448$.

Exhibit 11.7

Dividends-Based Valuation of Starbucks in FSAP

Dividends-Based Valuation	1 Year +1	2 Year +2	3 Year +3	4 Year +4	5 Year +5	Continuing Value Year +6
Dividends Paid to Common Shareholders	$ 1,187.6	$1,309.2	$1,483.2	$1,674.4	$2,080.4	
Less: Common Stock Issues	(1.3)	(2.4)	(3.3)	(3.8)	(6.7)	
Plus: Common Stock Repurchases	2,653.7	1,483.5	1,598.2	1,757.6	1,509.9	
Dividends to Common Equity	$ 3,839.9	$2,790.4	$3,078.2	$3,428.2	$3,583.6	$4,822.9
Present Value Factors	0.933	0.870	0.812	0.757	0.706	
Present Value of Dividends	$ 3,582.0	$2,428.1	$2,498.7	$2,595.9	$2,531.3	
Sum of Present Value of Dividends	$ 13,636.1					
Present Value of Continuing Value	$ 81,112.2					
Total	$ 94,748.3					
Adjust to midyear discounting	1.0360					
Total Present Value of Dividends	$98,159.19					
Shares Outstanding	1,485.1					
Estimated Value per Share	$ 66.10					
Current share price	$ 56.84					
Percent difference	16%					

LO 11-7

Assess the sensitivity of firm value estimates to key valuation parameters, such as discount rates and expected long-term growth rates, and make investment decisions.

Sensitivity Analysis and Investment Decision Making

We should not place too much confidence in the *precision* of firm value estimates using these (or any) forecasts over the remaining life of any firm, even a mature firm such as **Starbucks**. Although we have constructed these forecasts and value estimates with care, the forecasting and valuation process has an inherently high degree of uncertainty and estimation error. Therefore, we should not rely too heavily on any single point estimate of the value of a firm's shares and instead should describe a reasonable range of share values.

Two critical forecasting and valuation parameters in most valuations are the long-run growth rate assumption and the cost of equity capital assumption. We conduct sensitivity analyses to test the effects of these and other key valuation parameters and forecast assumptions on the share value estimate. Sensitivity analyses allow us to vary valuation parameters individually and jointly for additional insights into the correlations between share values, growth rates, and discount rates.

For **Starbucks**, the base case assumptions indicate **Starbucks'** share value to be roughly $66.10. The base case valuation assumes a long-run growth rate of 3.0% and a cost of equity capital of 7.2%. We can assess the sensitivity of the estimates of **Starbucks'** share value by varying these two parameters (or any other key parameters in the valuation) across reasonable ranges. Exhibit 11.8 contains the results of sensitivity analysis varying the long-run growth rate from 0% to 5% and the cost of equity capital from 6% to 12%. The data in Exhibit 11.8 (from FSAP) show that as the discount rate increases, holding growth constant, share value estimates fall. Likewise, value estimates fall as growth rates decrease, holding discount rates constant. Note that we should omit value estimates from this analysis when the assumed growth rate equals or exceeds the assumed discount rate because the continuing value computation is meaningless.

Considering the downside possibilities first, consider how sensitive the share value estimate for **Starbucks** is to adverse changes in long-run growth and discount rates. For example, by reducing the long-run growth assumption from 3.0% to 2.5% while holding the discount rate constant at 7.2%, **Starbucks'** share value falls to $60.20, which is above current market price of $56.48. Similarly, while holding constant the long-run growth assumption at 3.0%, increasing the discount rate from 7.2% to 8.0% produces a share value estimate of $55.32, which is just slightly below market price. Increasing the discount rate further to 8.5% produces a value estimate of $50.19, well below market price. If we revise both assumptions at once, reducing the long-run growth assumption to 2.5% and increasing the discount rate assumption to 7.5%, **Starbucks'** share value falls to $56.51, nearly equivalent to current market price of $56.48.

On the upside, reducing the discount rate to 7.0% while holding growth constant at 3.0% suggests **Starbucks** shares could have a value of $69.47. Increasing the long-run

Exhibit 11.8

Valuation of Starbucks:
Sensitivity Analysis of Value to Growth and Equity Cost of Capital

Dividends Valuation Sensitivity Analysis:

		Long-Run Growth Assumptions							
	$66.10	0.0%	1.0%	2.0%	2.5%	3.0%	3.5%	4.0%	5.0%
Discount Rates:	6.00%	52.05	60.26	72.57	81.36	93.09	109.50	134.12	257.23
	6.50%	47.87	54.60	64.32	71.00	79.58	91.04	107.07	171.19
	6.70%	46.38	52.62	61.51	67.54	75.21	85.27	99.05	150.95
	7.00%	44.30	49.89	57.72	62.94	69.47	77.85	89.04	128.18
	7.20%	43.01	48.23	55.44	60.20	66.10	73.58	83.41	116.46
	7.50%	41.21	45.92	52.33	56.51	61.60	67.98	76.17	102.39
	7.70%	40.09	44.49	50.45	54.28	58.93	64.69	72.00	94.75
	8.00%	38.51	42.51	47.85	51.25	55.32	60.30	66.53	85.21
	8.50%	36.13	39.57	44.06	46.87	50.19	54.17	59.03	72.94
	9.00%	34.03	37.00	40.82	43.17	45.91	49.15	53.05	63.74
	9.50%	32.14	34.73	38.01	40.00	42.30	44.98	48.15	56.60
	10.00%	30.45	32.72	35.56	37.26	39.21	41.45	44.07	50.89
	11.00%	27.54	29.32	31.48	32.76	34.20	35.82	37.68	42.33
	12.00%	25.13	26.54	28.24	29.22	30.31	31.53	32.90	36.23

growth assumption from 3.0% to 4.0% while holding the discount rate constant at 7.2%, the value estimates jump to $83.41. If we reduce the discount rate further, or increase the long-run growth rate further, the share value estimates for **Starbucks** jump dramatically higher. For example, increasing the growth rate assumption to 4.0% and decreasing the discount rate assumption to 7.0% moves the share value estimate to $89.

These data suggest that the value estimate is sensitive to slight variations in the baseline assumptions of 3.0% long-run growth and a 7.2% discount rate, which yield a share value estimate of roughly $66. Adverse variations in valuation parameters could reduce **Starbucks**' share value estimates to $55 or lower, whereas favorable variations could increase **Starbucks**' share value to over $80.

If the forecast and valuation assumptions are realistic, the baseline value estimate for **Starbucks** is $66.10 per share at the end of fiscal 2015. At that time, the market price of $56.48 per share indicates that **Starbucks**' shares were underpriced by about 16%. Under our forecast assumptions, **Starbucks**' share value could vary within a range of a low of $55 per share to a high of over $80 per share with only minor perturbations in the growth rate and discount rate assumptions. Given **Starbucks**' $56.48 share price, these value estimates would have supported a buy recommendation at the end of fiscal 2015 because the sensitivity analysis reveals limited downside potential but substantial upside potential for the value of **Starbucks**' shares.

Summary

This chapter illustrated the computation of expected rates of return on equity and the weighted-average cost of capital, which we use as discount rates in valuation models. In valuation, we use these discount rates to compute the present value of future dividends, cash flows, and earnings. This chapter also described the dividends-based valuation model and applied it to value **Starbucks**' shares at the end of fiscal 2015.

The principal *advantages* of the dividends-based valuation method include:

- This valuation method focuses on dividends. Economists argue that dividends provide the classical approach to valuing shares. Dividends reflect cash flows that shareholders can consume.
- Projected amounts of dividends result from projecting expected amounts of revenues, expenses, assets, liabilities, and shareholders' equity. Therefore, they reflect the implications of the analyst's expectations for all of the future operating, investing, and financing decisions of a firm.

The principal *disadvantages* of the dividends-based valuation method include:

- The continuing value (terminal value) tends to dominate the total value in many cases. For firms that do not pay periodic dividends or repurchase shares, the continuing value can comprise the total value of the firm, which requires that we forecast the future value of the firm in order to compute the present value of the firm. Continuing value estimates are sensitive to assumptions made about growth rates after the forecast horizon and discount rates.
- The projection of dividends can be time-consuming, making it costly when we follow many companies and must regularly identify under- and overvalued firms.

As with the preparation of projected financial statements in Chapter 10, the reasonableness of the valuations depends on the reliability of the forecast assumptions and the valuation parameters. We should assess the sensitivity of the valuation to alternative long-run growth and discount rate parameters and to other key value drivers. To validate value estimates using the dividends-based valuation approach, we also will compute the value of the firm using the free-cash-flows-based approach discussed in Chapter 12, the earnings-based approach discussed in Chapter 13, and the valuation-multiples described in Chapter 14.

Questions, Exercises, Problems, and Cases

Questions and Exercises

11.1 The Dividends-Based Valuation Approach. Explain the theory behind the dividends-based valuation approach. Why are dividends value-relevant to common equity shareholders?

`LO 11-4`

11.2 Valuation Approach Equivalence. Conceptually, why should an analyst expect the dividends-based approach to yield equivalent value estimates to the valuation approach that is based on free cash flows available to be distributed to common equity shareholders?

`LO 11-2`

11.3 The Risk-Return Trade-Off. Explain why analysts and investors use risk-adjusted expected rates of return as discount rates in valuation. Why do investors expect rates of return to *increase* with risk?

`LO 11-3`

11.4 The Components of the CAPM. The CAPM computes expected rates of return using the following model (described in the chapter):

$$E[R_{Ej}] = E[R_F] + \beta_j \times \{E[R_M] - E[R_F]\}$$

Explain the role of each of the three components of this model.

`LO 11-3`

11.5 Nondiversifiable and Diversifiable Risk Factors. Identify the types of firm-specific factors that increase a firm's nondiversifiable risk (systematic risk). Identify the types of firm-specific factors that increase a firm's diversifiable risk (nonsystematic risk). Why do expected returns models include no expected return premia for diversifiable risk?

`LO 11-3`

11.6 Debt and the Weighted-Average Cost of Capital. Why do investors typically accept a lower risk-adjusted rate of return on debt capital than equity capital? Suppose a stable, financially healthy, profitable, tax-paying firm that has been financed with all equity now decides to add a reasonable amount of debt to its capital structure. What effect will the change in capital structure likely have on the firm's weighted-average cost of capital?

`LO 11-3`

11.7 Firms That Do Not Pay Periodic Dividends. Why is the dividends-based valuation approach applicable to firms that do not pay periodic (quarterly or annual) dividends?

`LO 11-4`

11.8 Dividend Policy Irrelevance. The chapter asserts that dividends are value-relevant even though the firm's dividend policy is irrelevant. How can that be true? What is the key assumption in the theory of dividend policy irrelevance?

`LO 11-4`

11.9 Measuring Value-Relevant Dividends. The chapter describes how the dividends-based valuation approach measures dividends to encompass various transactions

`LO 11-5`

between the firm and the common shareholders. What transactions should you include in measuring dividends for the purposes of implementing the dividends-based valuation model? Why?

Problems and Cases

LO 11-3

11.10 Calculating Required Rates of Return on Equity Capital across Different Industries. The data in Exhibit 11.3 on industry median betas suggest that firms in the following three sets of related industries have different degrees of systematic risk.

	Median Beta during 2006–2015
Utilities versus Petroleum and Natural Gas	0.75 versus 1.45
Food Products (Grocery Stores) versus Apparel (Retailers)	0.78 versus 1.17
Banking (Depository Institutions) versus Trading (Financial Security and Commodity Brokers)	0.88 versus 1.13

REQUIRED

a. For each matched pair of industries, describe factors that characterize a typical firm's business model in each industry. Describe how such factors would contribute to differences in systematic risk.

b. For each matched pair of industries, use the CAPM to compute the required rate of return on equity capital for the median firm in each industry. Assume that the risk-free rate of return is 4.0% and the market risk premium is 5.0%.

c. For each matched pair of industries, compute the present value of a stream of $1 dividends for the median firm in each industry. Use the perpetuity-with-growth model and assume 3.0% long-run growth for each industry. What effect does the difference in systematic risk across industries have on the per-dollar dividend valuation of the median firm in each industry?

LO 11-3

11.11 Calculating the Cost of Capital. **Whirlpool** manufactures and sells home appliances under various brand names. **IBM** develops and manufactures computer hardware and offers related technology services. **Target** operates a chain of general merchandise discount retail stores. The data in the following table apply to these companies (dollar amounts in millions). For each firm, assume that the market value of the debt equals its book value.

	Whirlpool	IBM	Target
Total assets	$13,532	$109,524	$44,106
Interest-bearing debt	$ 2,597	$ 33,925	$18,752
Average pretax borrowing cost	6.1%	4.3%	4.9%
Common equity:			
Book value	$ 3,006	$ 13,465	$13,712
Market value	$ 2,959	$110,984	$22,521
Income tax rate	35.0%	35.0%	35.0%
Market equity beta	2.27	0.78	1.20

REQUIRED

a. Assume that the intermediate-term yields on U.S. government Treasury securities are 3.5%. Assume that the market risk premium is 5.0%. Compute the cost of equity capital for each of the three companies.

b. Compute the weighted-average cost of capital for each of the three companies.

c. Compute the unlevered market (asset) beta for each of the three companies.

d. Assume that each company is a candidate for a potential leveraged buyout. The buyers intend to implement a capital structure that has 75% debt (with a pretax borrowing cost of 8.0%) and 25% common equity. Project the weighted-average cost of capital for each company based on the new capital structure. To what extent do these revised weighted-average costs of capital differ from those computed in Requirement b?

11.12 Calculation of Dividends-Based Value. Royal Dutch Shell (Shell) is   `LOs 11-3–11-7`

a petroleum and petrochemicals company. It engages primarily in the exploration, production, and sale of crude oil and natural gas and the manufacture, transportation, and sale of petroleum and petrochemical products. The company operates in approximately 200 countries in North America, Europe, Asia-Pacific, Africa, South America, and the Middle East. Assume that during the past three years (Year -2, -1, and 0), Shell generated the following total dividends to common equity shareholders (in USD millions):

	Year -2	Year -1	Year 0
Common dividend payments	$ 8,142	$ 9,001	$ 9,516
Stock repurchases	8,047	4,387	3,573
Total dividends	$16,189	$13,388	$13,089

Analysts project 5% growth in earnings over the next five years. Assuming concurrent 5% growth in dividends, the following table provides the amounts that analysts project for Shell's total dividends for each of the next five years. In Year $+6$, total dividends are projected for Shell assuming that its income statement and balance sheet will grow at a long-term growth rate of 3%.

	Year $+1$	Year $+2$	Year $+3$	Year $+4$	Year $+5$	Year $+6$
Projected growth	5%	5%	5%	5%	5%	3%
Projected total dividends to common equity	$13,743	$14,431	$15,152	$15,910	$16,705	$17,206

At the end of Year 0, Shell had a market beta of 0.71. At that time, yields on intermediate-term U.S. Treasuries were 3.5%. Assume that the market required a 5.0% risk premium. Suppose Shell had 6,241 million shares outstanding at the beginning of Year $+1$ that traded at a share price of $24.87.

REQUIRED

a. Calculate the required rate of return on equity for Shell as of the beginning of Year $+1$.

b. Calculate the sum of the present value of total dividends for Years $+1$ through $+5$.

c. Calculate the continuing value of Shell at the start of Year $+6$ using the perpetuity-with-growth model with Year $+6$ total dividends. Also compute the present value of continuing value as of the beginning of Year $+1$.

d. Compute the total present value of dividends for Shell as of the beginning of Year $+1$. Remember to adjust the present value for midyear discounting.

e. Compute the value per share of Shell as of the beginning of Year $+1$.

f. Given the share price at the start of Year $+1$, do Shell shares appear underpriced, overpriced, or correctly priced?

11.13 Valuing the Equity of a Privately Held Firm. Refer to the financial   `LOs 11-5–11-7`

statement forecasts for Massachusetts Stove Company (MSC) prepared for Case 10.2. The management of MSC wants to know the equity valuation implications of adding gas stoves under the best, most likely, and worst-case scenarios. Under the three scenarios from Case 10.2, the actual amounts of net income and common shareholders' equity for Year 7 and the projected amounts for Years 8 through 12 are as follows:

	Actual	Projected				
	Year 7	Year 8	Year 9	Year 10	Year 11	Year 12
Best-case scenario:						
Net income	$154,601	$148,422	$123,226	$173,336	$ 271,725	$ 390,639
Common equity	$552,080	$700,502	$823,728	$997,064	$1,268,789	$1,659,429
Most likely scenario:						
Net income	$154,601	$135,343	$ 74,437	$ 72,899	$ 109,357	$ 149,977
Common equity	$552,080	$687,423	$761,860	$834,759	$ 944,116	$1,094,093
Worst-case scenario:						
Net income	$154,601	$128,263	$ 18,796	$ (39,902)	$ (58,316)	$ (77,156)
Common equity	$552,080	$680,343	$699,139	$659,238	$ 600,921	$ 523,766

MSC is not publicly traded and therefore does not have a market equity beta. Using the market equity beta of the only publicly traded woodstove and gas stove manufacturing firm and adjusting it for differences in the debt-to-equity ratio, income tax rate, and privately owned status of MSC yields a cost of equity capital for MSC of 13.55%.

REQUIRED

a. Use the clean surplus accounting approach to derive the projected total amount of MSC's dividends to common equity shareholders in Years 8 through 12.
b. Given that MSC is a privately held company, assume that ending book value of common equity at the end of Year 12 is a reasonable estimate of the value at which the common shareholders' equity could be liquidated. Calculate the value of the equity of MSC as of the end of Year 7 under each of the three scenarios. Ignore the midyear discounting adjustment.
c. How do these valuations affect your advice to the management of MSC about adding gas stoves to its woodstove line?

LOs 11-3–11-7

11.14 Dividends-Based Valuation of Common Equity. The Coca-Cola Company is a global soft drink beverage company (ticker: KO) that is a primary and direct competitor with Starbucks. The following data for Coca-Cola include the actual amounts for 2015 and the projected amounts for Years +1 through +5 for comprehensive income and common shareholders' equity (amounts in millions).

	Actual	Projected				
	2015	Year +1	Year +2	Year +3	Year +4	Year +5
Comprehensive income	$ 2,954	$ 7,342	$ 7,575	$ 7,803	$ 8,039	$ 8,283
Common shareholders' equity:						
Paid-in Capital	$ 15,776	$ 15,723	$ 16,279	$ 16,839	$ 17,392	$ 17,939
Retained Earnings	65,018	66,854	68,747	70,698	72,708	74,779
Treasury Stock	(45,066)	(45,952)	(47,818)	(49,797)	(51,892)	(54,107)
Accumulated Other Comprehensive Income	(10,174)	(10,174)	(10,174)	(10,174)	(10,174)	(10,174)
Total Common Equity	$ 25,554	$ 26,451	$ 27,035	$ 27,566	$ 28,033	$ 28,437

The market equity beta for Coca-Cola at the end of 2015 is 0.75. Assume that the risk-free interest rate is 3.0% and the market risk premium is 6.0%. Coca-Cola had 4,324 million shares outstanding at the end of 2015, when the share price was $42.96.

REQUIRED

a. Use the CAPM to compute the required rate of return on common equity capital for Coca-Cola.

b. Compute the weighted-average cost of capital for Coca-Cola as of the start of Year $+1$. At the end of 2015, Coca-Cola had $44,213 million in outstanding interest-bearing debt on the balance sheet and no preferred stock. Assume that the balance sheet value of Coca-Cola's debt is approximately equal to the market value of the debt. Assume that at the start of Year $+1$, it will incur interest expense of 2.0% on debt capital and that its average tax rate will be 24.0%. Coca-Cola also had $210 million in equity capital from noncontrolling interests. Assume that this equity capital carries a 15.0% required rate of return. (For our forecasts, we assume noncontrolling interests receive dividends equal to the required rate of return each year.)

c. Use the clean surplus accounting approach to derive the projected dividends for common shareholders for Years $+1$ through $+5$ based on the projected comprehensive income and shareholders' equity amounts. (Throughout this problem, you can ignore dividends to noncontrolling interests.)

d. Use the clean surplus accounting approach to project the continuing dividend to common shareholders in Year $+6$. Assume that the steady-state long-run growth rate will be 3% in Years $+6$ and beyond.

e. Using the required rate of return on common equity from Requirement a as a discount rate, compute the sum of the present value of dividends to common shareholders for Coca-Cola for Years $+1$ through $+5$.

f. Using the required rate of return on common equity from Requirement a as a discount rate and the long-run growth rate from Requirement d, compute the continuing value of Coca-Cola as of the beginning of Year $+6$ based on its continuing dividends in Years $+6$ and beyond. After computing continuing value, bring continuing value back to present value at the start of Year $+1$.

g. Compute the value of a share of Coca-Cola common stock, as follows:

(1) Compute the sum of the present value of dividends including the present value of continuing value.

(2) Adjust the sum of the present value using the midyear discounting adjustment factor.

(3) Compute the per-share value.

h. Using the same set of forecast assumptions as before, recompute the value of Coca-Cola shares under two alternative scenarios. To quantify the sensitivity of your share value estimate for Coca-Cola to these variations in growth and discount rates, compare (in percentage terms) your value estimates under these two scenarios with your value estimate from Requirement g.

 ● Scenario 1: Assume that Coca-Cola's long-run growth will be 2%, not 3% as before, and assume that its required rate of return on equity is 1 percentage point higher than the rate you computed using the CAPM in Requirement a.

 ● Scenario 2: Assume that Coca-Cola's long-run growth will be 4%, not 3% as before, and assume that its required rate of return on equity is 1 percentage point lower than the rate you computed using the CAPM in Requirement a.

i. What reasonable range of share values would you expect for Coca-Cola common stock? Where is the current price for Coca-Cola shares relative to this range? What do you recommend?

INTEGRATIVE CASE 11.1

Walmart

LOs 11-3–11-7

Dividends-Based Valuation of Walmart's Common Equity

Integrative Case 10.1 involves projecting financial statements for **Walmart** for Years +1 through +5. The following data for Walmart include the actual amounts for 2015 and the projected amounts for Years +1 through +5 for comprehensive income and common shareholders' equity, assuming it will use implied dividends as the financial flexible account to balance the balance sheet (amounts in millions).

	Actual	Projected				
	2015	**Year +1**	**Year +2**	**Year +3**	**Year +4**	**Year +5**
Comprehensive income	$ 10,651	$ 14,696	$ 14,979	$ 15,267	$15,560	$ 15,858
Common shareholders' equity:						
Paid-in Capital	$ 2,122	$ 2,186	$ 2,251	$ 2,319	$ 2,388	$ 2,460
Retained Earnings	90,021	89,589	87,776	85,407	82,491	79,029
Accumulated Other Comprehensive Income	(11,597)	(11,597)	(11,597)	(11,597)	(11,597)	(11,597)
Total Common Equity	$ 80,546	$ 80,178	$ 78,430	$ 76,129	$73,283	$ 69,892

Assume that the market equity beta for Walmart at the end of 2015 was 1.00. Assume that the risk-free interest rate was 3.0% and the market risk premium was 6.0%. Also assume that Walmart had 3,162 million shares outstanding at the end of 2015, and share price was $67.50.

REQUIRED

a. Use the CAPM to compute the required rate of return on common equity capital for Walmart.

b. Compute the weighted-average cost of capital for Walmart as of the start of Year +1. At the end of 2015, Walmart had $50,034 million in outstanding interest-bearing debt on the balance sheet and no preferred stock. Assume that the balance sheet value of Walmart's debt is approximately equal to the market value of the debt. Assume that at the start of Year +1, it will incur interest expense of 5.0% on debt capital and that its average tax rate will be 32.0%. Walmart also had $3,065 million in equity capital from noncontrolling interests. Assume that this equity capital carries a 12.6% required rate of return. (For our forecasts, we assume noncontrolling interests receive dividends equal to the required rate of return each year.)

c. Use the clean surplus accounting approach to derive the projected dividends for common shareholders for Years +1 through +5 based on the projected comprehensive income and shareholders' equity amounts. (Throughout this case, you can ignore dividends to noncontrolling interests.)

d. Use the clean surplus accounting approach to project the continuing dividend to common shareholders in Year +6. Assume that the steady-state long-run growth rate will be 3% in Years +6 and beyond.

e. Using the required rate of return on common equity from Requirement a as a discount rate, compute the sum of the present value of dividends to common shareholders for Walmart for Years +1 through +5.

f. Using the required rate of return on common equity from Requirement a as a discount rate and the long-run growth rate from Requirement d, compute the continuing value of Walmart as of the beginning of Year +6 based on its continuing dividends in Years +6 and beyond. After computing continuing value, bring continuing value back to present value at the start of Year +1.

g. Compute the value of a share of Walmart common stock, as follows:

   (1) Compute the sum of the present value of dividends including the present value of continuing value.

   (2) Adjust the sum of the present value using the midyear discounting adjustment factor.

   (3) Compute the per-share value.

h. Using the same set of forecast assumptions as before, recompute the value of Walmart shares under two alternative scenarios. To quantify the sensitivity of your share value estimate for Walmart to these variations in growth and discount rates, compare (in percentage terms) your value estimates under these two scenarios with your value estimate from Requirement g.

   ● Scenario 1: Assume that Walmart's long-run growth will be 2%, not 3% as before, and assume that its required rate of return on equity is 1 percentage point higher than the rate you computed using the CAPM in Requirement a.

   ● Scenario 2: Assume that Walmart's long-run growth will be 4%, not 3% as before, and assume that its required rate of return on equity is 1 percentage point lower than the rate you computed using the CAPM in Requirement a.

i. What reasonable range of share values would you expect for Walmart common stock? Where is the current price for Walmart shares relative to this range? What do you recommend?

Valuation: Cash-Flow-Based Approaches

Chapter Overview

This chapter develops *free-cash-flows-based* valuation approaches and applies them to **Starbucks**. If you are not familiar with the forecasting techniques we introduced in Chapter 10 and the valuation concepts and techniques we introduced in Chapter 11, we strongly encourage you to read those chapters carefully before proceeding with this chapter. In this chapter, we apply many of the concepts that we explained and demonstrated in those chapters.

Recall that economic theory teaches that the value of an investment equals the present value of the expected future payoffs from the investment, discounted at a rate that reflects the time value of money and the risk inherent in those expected payoffs. The general model for estimating the present value of a security (denoted as V_0, present value at time $t = 0$) with an expected life of n future periods is as follows:[1]

$$V_0 = \sum_{t=1}^{n} \frac{\text{Expected Future Payoffs}_t}{(1 + \textit{Discount Rate})^t}$$

The dividends-based valuation approach in Chapter 11, the free-cash-flows-based approaches demonstrated in this chapter, and the earnings-based approaches

---

[1]As in the previous chapter, t refers to accounting periods. The valuation process determines an estimate of firm value, denoted as V_0, in present value as of today, when $t = 0$. The period $t = 1$ refers to the first accounting period being discounted to present value. Period $t = n$ is the period of the expected final payoff.

demonstrated in the next two chapters are all designed to produce reliable estimates of the value of the firm's equity shares that provide the basis for intelligent investment decisions. Even in relatively efficient securities markets, price does not necessarily equal value for every security at all times. Price is observable, but value is not; value must be estimated. The financial statement analysis and valuation process enables investors, analysts, portfolio managers, investment bankers, and corporate managers to determine a reliable appraisal of the value of shares of common equity. Comparing value to price then yields a reliable basis to assess whether a firm's equity shares are underpriced, overpriced, or fairly priced in the capital markets.

Whether you will produce reliable estimates of share value as a result of the financial statement analysis and valuation process depends entirely on whether you carefully and thoughtfully apply each step of the six-step analysis framework that forms the structure of this book (Exhibit 1.2 in Chapter 1). Following the first three steps, you should first understand the economics of the industry, then assess the particular firm's strategy, and then carefully evaluate the quality of the firm's accounting, making adjustments if necessary. In the fourth step, you should evaluate the firm's profitability and risk. All of these analyses provide you with useful information for the fifth step, projecting the firm's future financial statements. You can then use those financial statement forecasts to derive expectations of future earnings, cash flows, and dividends, which are the fundamental payoff measures used in valuation. In the sixth and final step, you apply valuation models to these expected future payoffs to estimate the value of the firm. Your expectations for future payoffs (the numerator in the valuation model) depend on your forecasts of future earnings, cash flows, and dividends. Assessing an appropriate risk-adjusted discount rate (the denominator in the valuation model) requires an unbiased assessment of the inherent riskiness in the set of expected future payoffs. Therefore, reliable estimates of firm value depend on unbiased expectations of future payoffs and an appropriate risk-adjusted discount rate, all of which depend on all six steps of the framework.

As explained in the previous chapter, when you derive forecasts of future earnings, cash flows, and dividends from a set of internally consistent financial statement forecasts for a firm and use the same discount rate in correctly specified models to compute present values, the earnings-, cash-flows-, and dividends-based valuation models will yield *identical* estimates of value for a firm. In Chapter 11, we applied the dividends-based valuation approach to **Starbucks** and estimated that, given our forecast assumptions and valuation parameters, **Starbucks'** share value should be within a fairly narrow range around $66.10 at the time of our analysis. This chapter demonstrates the practical equivalence of the dividends- and free-cash-flows-based valuation approaches with the valuation of **Starbucks**. The next chapter will describe and apply the earnings-based valuation approach and demonstrate its theoretical and practical equivalence with both the dividends and free-cash-flows approaches.[2]

It is important that you understand the similarities and differences in these valuation approaches, and their theoretical and practical equivalence. Our experience suggests that applying several different valuation approaches yields better insights about the value of a firm than relying on only one approach in all cases. In addition, you will be better equipped to work successfully with different clients, managers, colleagues, and

---

[2]For examples of research on the complementarity of these approaches, see Stephen Penman and Theodore Sougiannis, "A Comparison of Dividend, Cash Flow, and Earnings Approaches to Equity Valuation," *Contemporary Accounting Research* 15, no. 3 (Fall 1998), pp. 343–383; and Jennifer Francis, Per Olsson, and Dennis Oswald, "Comparing the Accuracy and Explainability of Dividend, Free Cash Flow, and Abnormal Earnings Equity Value Estimates," *Journal of Accounting Research* 38, no. 1 (Spring 2000), pp. 45–70.

subordinates in the analysis and valuation process if you thoroughly understand all three valuation approaches.

All four valuation chapters—Chapters 11 to 14—emphasize that the objective is to determine the distribution of value estimates across the relevant ranges of critical forecast assumptions and valuation parameters. By assessing the sensitivity of value estimates across a distribution of relevant forecast assumptions and valuation parameters, we determine the most likely range of values for a share, which we then compare to the share's current price for an intelligent investment decision.

Rationale for Cash-Flow-Based Valuation

LO 12-1

Describe cash-flow-based valuation models and their conceptual and practical strengths and weaknesses.

As we demonstrated in the previous chapter, the value of a share of common equity is the present value of the expected future dividends. You invest cash when you purchase the share, and then you receive cash through dividends as the payoffs from holding the share, including the final liquidating dividend when you sell the share.

You should consider cash-flow-based valuation and dividends-based valuation to be two sides of the same coin: you can value the firm based on the cash flows *into* the firm that will be used to pay dividends or, equivalently, value the firm based on the cash flows *out of* the firm in dividends to common shareholders. We apply the same fundamental valuation concepts to value expected future dividends in Chapter 11 and free cash flows here in Chapter 12. These fundamental concepts are listed in Exhibit 12.1. Instead of focusing on wealth distribution through dividends, the free-cash-flow-based approach focuses on cash flows generated by the firm that create dividend-paying capacity. In any given period, the amount of cash flow into the firm and the amount of dividends paid out of the firm will likely differ; the equivalence of these two valuation approaches arises because, over the lifetime of the firm, the cash flows into and out of the firm will be equivalent.

The cash-flow-based valuation approach measures and values the cash flows that are "*free*" to be distributed to shareholders. *Free cash flows* are the cash flows each period that are available for distribution to shareholders, unencumbered by necessary reinvestments in operating assets or required payments to debtholders, preferred stockholders, or other claimants. We can use free cash flows instead of dividends as the expected future payoffs in the

---

Exhibit 12.1

Fundamental Valuation Concepts

- Risk, expected rates of return, and the weighted-average cost of capital
- Cash flows to the investor versus cash flows to the firm
- Nominal versus real cash flows
- The forecast horizon
- Computing continuing value

Note to Readers: These concepts apply to all the valuation models demonstrated in this text. All of these concepts are explained and demonstrated in Chapter 11 (pages 729–755). To minimize redundancy, we do not repeat them here. If you need a thorough discussion and explanation of these topics, we strongly encourage you to read Chapter 11 carefully.

numerator of the general value model set forth at the outset of this chapter. Both approaches, if implemented with consistent assumptions, lead to identical estimates of value.

The principal advantages of using the free-cash-flows-based valuation methods include the following:

- Free-cash-flows valuation is widely used in practice because it focuses directly on net cash inflows to the entity that are available to be distributed to capital providers, as opposed to focusing on dividends to common equity shareholders. This cash flow perspective is especially pertinent for acquisition decisions.
- Cash is the medium of exchange and therefore a fundamental source of value. An economic resource has value because of its ability to provide future cash flows that will enable investors to consume goods and services in the future. The free-cash-flows approach measures value based on the projected cash flows that the firm will generate that will be distributed to investors.
- Cash is a common measure of payoffs for comparing the future benefits of alternative investment opportunities. One can use the present value of future cash flows to compare very different investment opportunities involving a bond, a stock, or real estate.
- Projected amounts of free cash flows result from projected amounts of revenues, expenses, assets, liabilities, and shareholders' equity, which result from projected future operating, investing, and financing decisions of a firm.

The principal disadvantages of using the free-cash-flows-based valuation methods include the following:

- The projection of free cash flows can be time-consuming, making it costly when you follow many companies and must regularly identify under- and overvalued firms.
- The continuing value (terminal value) tends to dominate the total value in many cases. This continuing value is sensitive to assumptions made about growth rates after the forecast horizon and discount rates.
- You must be very careful that free cash flow computations are internally consistent with long-run assumptions regarding growth and payout. Failure to do so can result in estimation errors that produce poor valuations that are inconsistent with those derived from expected future dividends and earnings.

LO 12-2

Measure free cash flows for all debt and equity stakeholders, as well as free cash flows for common equity shareholders, and explain when each measure is appropriate.

Measuring Free Cash Flows

This section first presents a conceptual framework for measuring free cash flows. Then it describes practical steps to measure free cash flows from two different perspectives—free cash flows to all debt and equity stakeholders and free cash flows to common equity shareholders—and when to use each.

A Conceptual Framework for Free Cash Flows

A conceptual framework for free cash flows emanates from the balance sheet equation:

$$A = L + SE$$

Recall from Chapter 5 the demonstration of an alternative ROCE decomposition into operating and financial leverage components. Using the same approach, separate all of the assets and liabilities into two categories: operating or financing:

$$OA + FA = OL + FL + SE$$

Operating assets (denoted as *OA*) and operating liabilities (denoted as *OL*) relate to the firm's day-to-day operations in the normal course of business. For most firms, operating assets include cash and short-term investment securities necessary for operating liquidity purposes; accounts receivable; inventory; property, plant, and equipment; intangible assets (for example, licenses, patents, trademarks, and goodwill); and investments in affiliated companies. Operating liabilities typically include accrued liabilities, such as accounts payable, accrued expenses, accrued taxes, deferred taxes, pension obligations, and other retirement benefits obligations.

Financial liabilities (denoted as *FL*) include short-term and long-term interest-bearing liabilities that are part of the financial capital structure of the firm. Financial liabilities are those that trigger a cost of financing and include short-term notes payable; current maturities of long-term debt; and long-term debt in the forms of mortgages, bonds, notes, and lease obligations. If outstanding preferred stock contains features that make it economically similar to debt (features such as limited life, mandatory redemption, and guaranteed dividends), you should include preferred stock with financial liabilities.

In some circumstances, firms may hold financial assets (denoted as *FA*) such as excess cash and short- or long-term investment securities to provide the firm with liquidity to repay debt, pay dividends, and repurchase common stock. Distinguishing financial assets that the firm will use for its financial capital structure from cash and marketable securities the firm will use for liquidity for operating purposes requires that you make a judgment call. We typically consider financial assets to be part of the financial structure of the firm if the firm intends to use the financial assets to retire debt or if the financial assets exceed the firm's needs for operating liquidity purposes and therefore could be used to retire debt, pay dividends, or repurchase common equity shares. For example, such financial assets may exist if a firm is accumulating cash or investment securities for the purpose of retiring debt, holding certain amounts of restricted cash under a loan covenant, or accumulating a sinking fund for bond retirement under the terms of a bond debenture. We typically consider cash and cash equivalents and marketable securities to be part of the operating liquidity (and not part of the financial capital structure) of a firm when these assets are necessary to manage the liquidity needs of the firm's operating activities across different seasons or business cycles. We also typically consider investment securities to be part of the operating activities (and not part of the financial capital structure) of a firm when the investments are part of the long-term strategy of the firm, such as investments in affiliated subsidiaries with related operating activities or investments in potential acquisition targets. Capital held in these types of accounts for the purposes of operating liquidity or strategic investments should be considered operating assets, not financial assets.

Once you have separated the assets and liabilities into operating and financing categories, rearrange the equation to put operating accounts on one side and financing accounts and shareholders' equity on the other, as follows:

$$OA - OL = FL - FA + SE,$$

which is equivalent to

$$NetOA = NetFL + SE$$

where $NetOA = OA - OL$ and $NetFL = FL - FA$. For most firms, operating assets exceed operating liabilities and financial liabilities exceed financial assets. (Financial borrowing usually exceeds financial assets because the firm uses the funds obtained from borrowing to purchase operating assets.)

This balance sheet arrangement provides a useful basis to conceptualize free cash flows to the firm. If we substitute for each term the present values of the expected future net cash flows associated with operating activities (*NetOA*), financing activities (*NetFL*), and shareholders' equity (*SE*), we can express the balance sheet as follows:

Present Value of Expected Future Net Cash Flows from Operations
= Present Value of Expected Future Net Cash Flows Available for Debt Financing
+ Present Value of Expected Future Net Cash Flows Available for Shareholders' Equity

This expression indicates that the present value of the expected net cash flows from operations of the firm determines the sum of the values of the debt and equity claims on the firm. Therefore, one can value the debt and equity capital of the firm by valuing the net cash flows from operations that are "free" to service debt and equity claims. We refer to this measure of free cash flows as *the free cash flows for all debt and equity stakeholders* because they reflect the cash flows that are available to all of the debt and equity stakeholders in the firm.

We can rearrange the balance sheet equation slightly further:

$$NetOA - NetFL = SE$$

Using the same present value cash flow terms as before, we can express this form of the balance sheet equation as follows:

Present Value of Expected Future Net Cash Flows from Operations
−Present Value of Expected Future Net Cash Flows Available for Debt Financing
= Present Value of Expected Future Net Cash Flows Available for Shareholders' Equity

With this expression, we can conceptualize free cash flows specifically attributable to the equity shareholders of the firm. The present value of free cash flows produced by the operations of the firm minus the present value of cash flows necessary to service claims of the net debtholders yields *free cash flows available for common equity shareholders*. This measure captures the present value of the net free cash flows available to equity shareholders after debt claims are satisfied.

How Do We Measure Free Cash Flows?

The following sections describe how you should measure *free cash flows for all debt and equity stakeholders* and *free cash flows for common equity shareholders*, and when you should use each measure. In practice, different analysts compute free cash flows from various starting points: the statement of cash flows, net income, EBITDA (earnings before interest, tax, depreciation, and amortization), or NOPAT (net operating profit adjusted for tax). For completeness, we describe how to measure free cash flows from each starting point.

Measuring Free Cash Flows: The Statement of Cash Flows as the Starting Point

Under U.S. GAAP and IFRS, firms report the statement of cash flows by reporting the net cash flows from operating, investing, and financing activities. These three categories do not exactly match the operating and financing classifications we need for computing free cash flows. Thus, we need to reclassify some of the components of the statement of cash flows to compute free cash flows for valuation purposes. Exhibit 12.2 describes the computations.

Exhibit 12.2

Measurement of Free Cash Flows

Free Cash Flows for All Debt and Equity Stakeholders:	Free Cash Flows for Common Equity Shareholders:
Operating Activities:	**Operating Activities:**
Cash Flow from Operations	**Cash Flow from Operations**
Begin with cash flow from operations on the projected statement of cash flows.	Begin with cash flow from operations on the projected statement of cash flows.
+/− **Net Interest after Tax**	
Add back interest expense (net of tax) Also subtract interest income (net of tax) from financial assets (if any) that you deem to be part of the financial capital structure of the firm and not part of the operating activities of the firm.	
+/− **Changes in Cash Required for Liquidity**	+/− **Changes in Cash Required for Liquidity**
Subtract an increase or add a decrease in cash required for purposes of liquidity for operations.	Subtract an increase or add a decrease in cash required for purposes of liquidity for operations.
= *Free Cash Flows from Operations for All Debt and Equity*	= *Free Cash Flows from Operations for Equity*
Investing Activities:	**Investing Activities:**
+/− **Net Capital Expenditures**	+/− **Net Capital Expenditures**
Subtract cash outflows for capital expenditures and add cash inflows from sales of assets that comprise the productive capacity of the operations of the firm (including property, plant, and equipment; affiliated companies; and intangible assets).	Subtract cash outflows for capital expenditures and add cash inflows from sales of assets that comprise the productive capacity of the operations of the firm (including property, plant, and equipment; affiliated companies; and intangible assets).
= *Free Cash Flows for All Debt and Equity Stakeholders*	
	Financing Activities:
	+/− **Debt Cash Flows**
	Add cash inflows from new borrowings and subtract cash outflows for repayments of short- and long-term interest-bearing debt.
	+/− **Financial Asset Cash Flows**
	Subtract cash outflows invested in cash, short-term, and long-term investment securities (or add cash inflows from these accounts) if you deem these financial assets to be part of the financial capital structure of the firm and not part of the operating activities of the firm.

(Continued)

Exhibit 12.2 (Continued)	
Free Cash Flows for All Debt and Equity Stakeholders:	**Free Cash Flows for Common Equity Shareholders:**
	$+/-$ **Preferred Stock Cash Flows**
	Add cash inflows from new issues of preferred stock and subtract cash outflows for preferred stock retirements and dividend payments.
	$+/-$ **Noncontrolling Interest Cash Flows**
	Add cash inflows from new investments by noncontrolling interests and subtract cash outflows for noncontrolling interest retirements and dividend payments.
	$=$ *Free Cash Flows for Common Equity Stakeholders*

Cash flow from operations from the projected statement of cash flows is the most direct starting point for computing both measures of free cash flows because it requires the fewest adjustments. Recall from Chapter 3 that the statement of cash flows measures cash flow from operations by beginning with net income, adding back any noncash expenses or losses (such as depreciation and amortization expenses), subtracting any noncash income or gains (such as income from equity-method affiliates), and then adjusting for changes in receivables, inventory, accounts payable, and accrued expenses.

Free Cash Flows for All Debt and Equity Capital Stakeholders

Free cash flows for all debt and equity capital stakeholders are the cash flows available to make interest and principal payments to debtholders, redeem preferred shares or pay dividends to preferred shareholders, retire or pay dividends to noncontrolling interests, and pay dividends and buy back shares from common equity shareholders. To measure these free cash flows, we begin with cash flows from operations from the projected statement of cash flows, as shown in the left side of Exhibit 12.2. To measure cash flows from operations before the effects of the firm's financial capital structure, you must add back the interest expense on financial liabilities, net of any income tax savings from interest expense. If you make the judgment call that some of the firm's financial assets (such as excess cash holdings or marketable securities) are intended to retire debt and pay dividends and are part of the financial capital structure of the firm (rather than part of the operating liquidity management of the firm), you should subtract the interest income on those financial assets, net of the income taxes paid on that interest income. To adjust interest expense and interest income for tax effects, multiply them by one minus the firm's marginal tax rate.[3]

You should also add or subtract any change in the cash balance that the firm will require for operating liquidity. Cash that the firm must maintain for operating liquidity purposes is not available for distribution to debt or equity stakeholders and therefore is

---

[3]Technically, analysts should make these adjustments using the cash amounts of interest paid and interest received rather than the accrual amounts of interest expense and interest income. However, as a practical matter, it is reasonable to assume that forecasted amounts of interest expense will equal interest paid and forecasted amounts of interest income will equal interest received.

not part of free cash flow. If the firm improves its cash management efficiency and reduces the amount of cash required for operating liquidity, the firm has additional cash that can be distributed to debt or equity stakeholders. If the firm expands its operations into new markets or countries, it will require additional amounts of cash for operating liquidity, reducing free cash flow available for debt and equity stakeholders.[4] Procedurally, you should project the required amounts of cash for working capital purposes each period and add or subtract the change in required cash balances to determine free cash flow from operations for debt and equity stakeholders.

Next, adjust for cash flows related to capital expenditures on long-lived assets that are a part of the firm's productive capacity (for example, property, plant, and equipment; affiliated companies; intangible assets; and other investing activities). You should subtract cash outflows for capital expenditures and investments, and add cash inflows from sales of these types of assets, from the investing activities section of the projected statement of cash flows.

As noted earlier, you must make a judgment call about the amounts of the firm's financial assets (for example, in cash and cash equivalents, short-term securities, or long-term investment securities) that are (1) necessary for the liquidity and operating capacity of the firm or (2) part of the financial capital structure of the firm and therefore distributable to debt or equity stakeholders. For example, if you project that the firm will retain financial assets by saving some portion of its cash flows in a securities account each period and that this cash will ultimately be used to repay debt, pay dividends, or buy back shares, then you should deem these cash flows as free cash flows for debt and equity capital. For instance, the firm may be required by a bond indenture agreement to maintain a sinking fund of cash or liquid securities that will be available to repay the bond when it matures. In this case, you should include the amount of cash added to the bond sinking fund as free cash flows for debt and equity capital.

This adjustment requires a judgment call because in some circumstances, firms retain seemingly excess amounts of cash, marketable securities, or investment securities accounts when these assets are in fact not free for potential distribution to capital stakeholders. For example, in some cases, firms with seasonal business need to maintain large balances in cash or securities accounts in order to provide needed liquidity during particular seasons. In other cases, firms build up large balances in investment securities accounts that represent investments in key affiliates. In scenarios such as these, you should not assess these cash flows as "free" for potential distribution to capital stakeholders, but instead should consider these cash flows necessary investments in the liquidity and productive capacity of the firm.

Together, these computations result in free cash flows available to service debt; pay dividends to preferred, common, and noncontrolling interest shareholders; and buy back shares. A later section describes the approach to estimate the present value of the debt and equity claims on the firm by discounting free cash flows for debt and equity stakeholders using the weighted-average cost of capital of the firm.

Free Cash Flows for Common Equity Shareholders

Free cash flows for common equity shareholders are the cash flows specifically available to the common shareholders after all debt service payments to lenders and dividends to

---

[4]For example, suppose you are valuing a retail store chain and the chain must maintain the equivalent of seven days of sales in cash on hand at each store for purposes of conducting retail sales transactions. When the chain opens new stores, it must hold additional cash as part of operations (as it must also hold additional inventory). These additional cash requirements are not available for debt and equity capital providers if the firm intends to maintain its operations.

preferred and noncontrolling interest shareholders. To measure free cash flows for common equity shareholders, you can again begin with cash flow from operations from the projected statement of cash flows, as presented in the right side of Exhibit 12.2. As in the previous section, you should subtract any increase in the cash balance required for operating liquidity because this cash is not free for distribution to equity shareholders (or add any decrease in the required cash balance because it means more cash is free for equity shareholders).

Note that unlike the computation of free cash flows for all debt and equity stakeholders, we do not adjust for interest expense or interest income after tax when we compute free cash flows for equity. Our measure of free cash flow for equity already reflects net cash flows for interest payments for interest-bearing debt because the statement of cash flows starts with net income to compute cash flow from operations and because net income already reflects interest expense after tax.

Also, as in the previous section, you should adjust for cash flows for capital expenditures on long-lived assets that are a part of the firm's productive capacity. You should subtract cash outflows for purchases and add cash inflows from sales of assets related to the firm's long-term productive activities.

You should also include cash flows related to debt claims by adding cash inflows from new borrowing in short- and long-term debt and subtracting cash outflows for repayments of short- and long-term debt. If you make the judgment call that the firm saves financial capital beyond its liquidity needs in financial asset accounts (such as cash or investment securities), these cash flows reflect financing activities. Therefore, you must (1) subtract the amount of cash outflow to purchase the securities because this cash obviously is not paid out to equity shareholders or (2) add the amount of cash inflow received from selling such securities because this cash inflow is available for distribution to equity shareholders. For example, if the firm maintains a bond sinking fund for the retirement of bonds when they mature, the cash invested in the sinking fund is not available for common equity shareholders. You also should add cash inflows from new issues of preferred stock and subtract cash outflows from preferred-stock retirements and dividend payments. Finally, you should also add cash inflows from new investments of capital by noncontrolling interests, and subtract cash outflows from retirements and dividend payments to noncontrolling interests. These computations result in the free cash flows available to common equity shareholders for dividends, stock buybacks, or reinvestment. As described in a later section of this chapter, we will discount free cash flows for common equity at the cost of equity capital to determine the value of the common equity of the firm.[5]

Measuring Free Cash Flows: Alternative Starting Points

In practice, different analysts use different starting points to compute free cash flows. The approaches described above began with cash flows from operations from the projected statement of cash flows because it is the most direct starting point, requiring the fewest adjustments. However, some analysts compute free cash flows by beginning with projected net income, or EBITDA, or NOPAT, each of which is more complicated and

---

[5]It might seem inappropriate to include changes in debt and preferred stock financing, which appear in the financing section of the statement of cash flows, in the valuation of the equity of a firm. Changes in debt and preferred stock, however, affect the amount of cash available to the common shareholders. You should include cash flows related to debt and preferred stock financing in free cash flows for common equity shareholders but adjust the cost of equity capital to reflect the amounts of such senior financing in the capital structure.

prone to error than starting with cash flows from operations. Exhibit 12.3 describes the steps you must take to adjust each of these starting points to determine free cash flows to all debt and equity stakeholders. Exhibit 12.4 (page 783) describes the steps you must take to adjust each of these starting points to determine free cash flows to common equity shareholders.

If you start with net income and want to determine free cash flows for all debt and equity stakeholders, Exhibit 12.3 indicates that you must add back all noncash expenses (such as depreciation and amortization expenses), subtract all noncash income items (such as accrued income from equity method affiliates), and adjust for changes in working capital accounts (receivables, inventory, payables). These adjustments bring you to our previous starting point, cash flows from operations. You should then incorporate the remaining steps by adjusting for net interest expense after tax, changes in cash required for liquidity, and capital expenditures.

Other analysts compute free cash flows for all debt and equity by starting with EBITDA, which already adds back noncash income items for depreciation and amortization, interest expense (but usually not interest income), and *all* of the provision for income taxes. From this starting point, you must adjust further by adding back any other noncash expenses (other than depreciation and amortization), adjust for noncash income items, and adjust for changes in working capital accounts. In addition, because EBITDA adds back all of the provision for income taxes, you must subtract cash taxes paid, net of tax savings on interest expense. These adjustments bring you to our previous starting point, cash flows from operations. You then incorporate the remaining steps by adjusting for changes in cash required for operating liquidity and capital expenditures.

Finally, other analysts begin the computation of free cash flows for all debt and equity stakeholders using NOPAT, which is net income with net interest expense (adjusted for tax savings) added back. From this starting point, you should add back all noncash expenses (such as depreciation and amortization expenses), subtract all noncash income items (such as accrued income from equity method affiliates), and adjust for cash flows for changes in working capital accounts. You then incorporate the remaining steps by adjusting for changes in cash required for liquidity and capital expenditures.

In practice, some analysts also use net income, or EBITDA, and NOPAT as starting points to compute free cash flows for equity shareholders. Exhibit 12.4 shows the steps necessary to adjust each of these starting point amounts to complete measures of free cash flows for common equity. Note that many, but not all, of the additional adjustments are similar to those in Exhibit 12.3. Also note that although it occurs in practice, starting with EBITDA or NOPAT is inefficient because it is then necessary to subtract interest expense after tax.

The starting point of the computation of free cash flows is less important than the ending point. You can begin the computation with cash flow from operating activities on the statement of cash flows, net income, EBITDA, or NOPAT, so long as you properly make all of the necessary adjustments to compute a complete measure of free cash flows as described in Exhibits 12.2 to 12.4.

Which Free Cash Flow Measure Should We Use?

The appropriate free cash flow measure to use—free cash flows to all debt and equity stakeholders or free cash flows to equity shareholders—depends on your valuation objective.

Exhibit 12.3

Measurement of Free Cash Flows for All Debt and Equity Stakeholders from Alternative Starting Points

Starting Point:

EBITDA:[a]	NOPAT:[b]
Operating Activities:	*Operating Activities:*
EBITDA	NOPAT
+ Add back all noncash expenses other than depreciation and amortization	+ Add back all noncash expenses
− Subtract all noncash income items	− Subtract all noncash income items
+/− Working capital cash flows	+/− Working capital cash flows
− Subtract cash taxes paid, net of tax savings on interest expense	
+/− Changes in cash required for liquidity	+/− Changes in cash required for liquidity
= *Free Cash Flows from Operations for All Debt and Equity Stakeholders*	= *Free Cash Flows from Operations for All Debt and Equity Stakeholders*
Investing Activities:	*Investing Activities:*
+/− Net capital expenditures	+/− Net capital expenditures
= *Free Cash Flows for All Debt and Equity Stakeholders*	= *Free Cash Flows for All Debt and Equity Stakeholders*

Net Income:

Operating Activities:

Net income

+ Add back all noncash expenses

− Subtract all noncash income items

+/− Working capital cash flows

+/− Net interest after tax

+/− Changes in cash required for liquidity

= *Free Cash Flows from Operations for All Debt and Equity Stakeholders*

Investing Activities:

+/− Net capital expenditures

= *Free Cash Flows for All Debt and Equity Stakeholders*

[a]EBITDA denotes earnings before interest, tax, depreciation, and amortization.

[b]NOPAT denotes net operating profit after tax, which equals net income adjusted for net interest expense after tax.

Exhibit 12.4

Measurement of Free Cash Flows for Common Equity Shareholders from Alternative Starting Points

Starting Point:

Net Income:	EBITDA:[a]	NOPAT:[b]
Operating Activities:	*Operating Activities:*	*Operating Activities:*
Net income	EBITDA	NOPAT
+ Add back all noncash expenses	+ Add back all noncash expenses other than depreciation and amortization	+ Add back all noncash expenses
− Subtract all noncash income items	− Subtract all noncash income items	− Subtract all noncash income items
+/− Working capital cash flows	+/− Working capital cash flows	+/− Working capital cash flows
	− Subtract net interest expense	− Subtract net interest expense after tax
	− Subtract taxes	
+/− Changes in cash required for liquidity	+/− Changes in cash required for liquidity	+/− Changes in cash required for liquidity
= *Free Cash Flows from Operations for Equity*	= *Free Cash Flows from Operations for Equity*	= *Free Cash Flows from Operations for Equity*
Investing Activities:	*Investing Activities:*	*Investing Activities:*
+/− Net capital expenditures	+/− Net capital expenditures	+/− Net capital expenditures
Financing Activities:	*Financing Activities:*	*Financing Activities:*
+/− **Debt cash flows**	+/− **Debt cash flows**	+/− **Debt cash flows**
+/− Financial asset cash flows	+/− Financial asset cash flows	+/− Financial asset cash flows
+/− Preferred stock cash flows	+/− Preferred stock cash flows	+/− Preferred stock cash flows
+/− Noncontrolling interest cash flows	+/− Noncontrolling interest cash flows	+/− Noncontrolling interest cash flows
= *Free Cash Flows for Common Equity Stakeholders*	= *Free Cash Flows for Common Equity Stakeholders*	= *Free Cash Flows for Common Equity Stakeholders*

[a]EBITDA denotes earnings before interest, tax, depreciation, and amortization.
[b]NOPAT denotes net operating profit after tax, which equals net income adjusted for net interest expense after tax.

- If your objective is to value net operating assets or, equivalently, the sum of the debt and equity capital of a firm, you should use the free cash flow for all debt and equity stakeholders, discounted using the weighted-average cost of capital.
- If your objective is to value the common shareholders' equity of a firm, or to value a share of common stock, you should use the free cash flow for common equity shareholders, discounted at the cost of equity capital.

The difference between these two valuations is the value of total debt financing, preferred stock, and noncontrolling interests. To reconcile the two valuations, one could value the debt financing instruments by discounting all future debt service cash flows (including repayments of principal) at the after-tax cost of debt capital, all preferred-stock dividends at the cost of preferred equity, and all noncontrolling interest dividends at the appropriate cost of equity capital for the subsidiary firm. Subtracting these present values of debt financing, preferred stock, and noncontrolling interests from the present value of the sum of debt and equity capital yields the present value of common equity.

Example 1: Valuing an Asset Acquisition. One firm wants to acquire the net operating assets of another firm. The acquiring firm will replace the financing structure of the target with a financing structure that matches its own. The relevant free cash flows for valuing the target's net operating assets are the operating cash flows the assets will generate minus the expected capital expenditures in operating assets or, equivalently, the free cash flows for all debt and equity capital. The acquiring firm will discount these projected free cash flows for all debt and equity capital at the expected future weighted-average cost of capital of the acquiring firm because it will use a similar financing structure for the target.

Example 2: Valuing Equity Shares. An investor wants to value 1,000 shares of common stock in a firm. The relevant cash flows are the free cash flows available for common equity shareholders. These free cash flows measure the cash flows generated from using the assets of the firm minus the cash required to service the debt. Thus, free cash flows for common equity shareholders should capture the cash generated by operating the assets of the firm plus any beneficial effects of financial leverage on the value of the common equity minus the cash flows required to service debt capital. The investor should discount these projected free cash flows at the required return on equity capital.

Example 3: Valuing a Leveraged Buyout. The managers of a firm intend to acquire a target firm through a leveraged buyout (LBO). The managers offer to purchase the outstanding shares of the target firm by investing their own equity (usually 20–25% of the total) and borrowing the remainder from various lenders. The tendered shares serve as collateral for the loan (often called a *bridge loan*) during the transaction. After gaining voting control of the firm, the managers will have the firm engage in sufficient new borrowing to repay the bridge loan. After an LBO, the firm will have much more debt in the capital structure from the use of leverage to execute the takeover.

Determining the value of the common shares acquired follows the usual procedure for an equity investment (see prior example). This value should equal the present value of free cash flows for common equity discounted at the cost of common equity capital. The valuation of the equity must reflect the new capital structure and the related increase in debt service costs. Also, the cost of equity capital will likely increase as a result of the higher level of debt in the capital structure; the common shareholders bear more risk as residual claimants on the assets of the firm. Therefore, the valuation must be based on the expected new cost of equity capital.

As an alternative approach that will produce the same value for the common equity, you can treat an LBO as a purchase of assets (similar to Example 1). That is, compute the present value of the free cash flows for all debt and equity capital stakeholders using the expected future weighted-average cost of debt and equity capital, using weights that reflect the newly leveraged capital structure of the acquired firm. This amount represents the value of net operating assets. Subtract from the present value of net operating assets the present value of debt raised to execute the LBO.[6] The result is the present value of the common equity.

Cash-Flow-Based Valuation Models

Thus far, this chapter has focused on measuring free cash flows. We next present the free-cash-flow-based valuation models. In each of these equations, all of the variables used to compute firm value are *expectations* of future free cash flows, future discount rates, and future growth rates.

Estimate firm value using the:
a. present value of future free cash flows for common equity shareholders, discounted at the required rate of return on equity capital.
b. present value of future free cash flows for all debt and equity stakeholders, discounted at the weighted-average cost of capital.

Valuation Models for Free Cash Flows for Common Equity Shareholders

The following equation values the common equity of a firm as of time $t=0$ (denoted as V_0) using the present value of free cash flows for common equity shareholders discounted at the required rate of return on equity capital (R_E):

$$V_0 = \sum_{t=1}^{\infty} \left[Free\ Cash\ Flow\ Equity_t / (1 + R_E)^t \right]$$

This approach expresses the value of the common equity of the firm as a function of the present value of the free cash flows the firm will generate for the common equity shareholders. Given that common equity shareholders are the residual risk-bearers of the firm, this valuation approach estimates common equity value using the residual free cash flows available to them. Therefore, free cash flows available to equity shareholders are the cash flows available after the firm has met all other cash requirements for working capital, capital expenditures, principal and interest payments on debt financing, preferred stock dividends, and noncontrolling interests dividends. It is appropriate to discount these payoffs to present value using a discount rate that reflects the risk-adjusted required rate of return on common equity capital of the firm.

The following equation also computes the present value of common equity, but in this equation, we compute the present value of the expected future free cash flows for common equity shareholders over a finite forecast horizon through Year T plus the present value of free cash flows continuing in Year T+1 and beyond.[7] We compute continuing value based on the forecast assumption that the firm will grow indefinitely at rate g beginning in Year T+1 and continuing thereafter. We derive free cash flows for common equity shareholders in Year T+1 from the projected income statement and

---

[6]It is irrelevant whether any debt on the books of the target firm remains outstanding after the LBO or whether the firm engages in additional borrowing to repay existing debt, as long as the weighted-average cost of capital properly includes the costs of each financing arrangement.

[7]Note that this valuation model is essentially identical to the dividends valuation model described in Chapter 11 (page 755). The only difference between the two models is the payoff being valued—dividends versus free cash flows for equity shareholders.

balance sheet for Year T+1, in which we project all of the elements of the Year T income statement and balance sheet to grow at rate g beginning in Year T+1. The equation is as follows:

$$V_0 = \sum_{t=1}^{T} \left[Free\ Cash\ Flow\ Equity_t / (1 + R_E)^t \right]$$
$$+ Free\ Cash\ Flow\ Equity_{T+1} \times \left[1/(R_E - g) \right] \times \left[1/(1 + R_E)^T \right]$$

Both of these equations represent the value of the common equity of the firm. The Valuations spreadsheet in FSAP provides a template that calculates V_0 using the present value of free cash flows for common equity shareholders, including the continuing value computation.

Valuation Models for Free Cash Flows for All Debt and Equity Stakeholders

The following equation determines the present value of the net operating assets of a firm as of time $t=0$ (denoted as $VNOA_0$) by computing the present value of all future free cash flows for all debt and equity capital stakeholders (denoted as *Free Cash Flow All*):

$$VNOA_0 = \sum_{t=1}^{\infty} \left[Free\ Cash\ Flow\ All_t / (1 + R_A)^t \right]$$

This equation differs from the models in the previous section in three important ways. First, this valuation approach does not compute the value of common shareholders' equity (V_0). Instead, it computes the *value of the net operating assets* ($VNOA_0$) of the firm or, equivalently, the value of all of the debt, preferred, noncontrolling interests, and common equity claims on the net assets of the firm. Second, this model includes expected future free cash flows to all debt and equity stakeholders. The prior equation focused specifically on the expected future free cash flows to common equity shareholders. Third, this equation discounts the free cash flows to present value using R_A, which denotes the expected future weighted-average cost of capital, which should reflect the weighted-average required rate of return on the net operating assets of the firm. [Recall that we explained and demonstrated the computation of the weighted-average cost of capital in Chapter 11.] In the prior model to estimate V_0, we relied on a discount rate using the required rate of return to equity (R_E).

This valuation approach expresses the value of the financial claims on the firm (debt, preferred, noncontrolling interests, and common equity) as a function of the present value of the free cash flows the firm's net operating assets will generate and that can ultimately be distributed to debtholders, preferred stockholders, noncontrolling investors, and common shareholders. Thus, the value-relevant payoffs in this approach are the cash flows the firm's operations generate that will be available to satisfy all financing claims. Given that these free cash flows will be distributed to debt, preferred, noncontrolling, and common equity stakeholders, it is appropriate to discount these payoffs to present value using a discount rate that reflects the weighted-average cost of capital across these different capital claims.

The next equation summarizes the same computation but uses the present value of free cash flows for all debt and equity stakeholders over a finite forecast horizon through Year T (for example, T may be 5 or 10 years in the future) plus the present value of continuing value. We compute continuing value based on the forecast assumption that the firm will grow indefinitely at rate g beginning in Year $T+1$ and continuing thereafter. We derive free cash flows for all debt and equity capital stakeholders in Year $T+1$ from the projected income statement and balance sheet for Year $T+1$, in which we project all elements of the Year T income statement and balance sheet to grow at rate g beginning in Year $T+1$. The equation is as follows:

$$VNOA_0 = \sum_{t=1}^{T} \left[Free\ Cash\ Flow\ All_t / (1 + R_A)^t \right]$$
$$+ Free\ Cash\ Flow\ All_{T+1} \times \left[1/(R_A - g) \right] \times \left[1/(1 + R_A)^T \right]$$

Both of the prior equations estimate the value of the net operating assets of the firm, which is equivalent to the sum of the values of debt, preferred, noncontrolling, and common equity capital. To isolate the value of common equity capital, we must subtract the present value of all interest-bearing debt, preferred stock, and noncontrolling interests. The equation to compute the value of equity (denoted as V_0) is as follows:

$$V_0 = VNOA_0 - VDebt_0 - VPreferred_0 - VNCI_0$$

The Valuations spreadsheet in FSAP provides a template that calculates $VNOA_0$ and V_0 using the present value of free cash flows for all debt and equity capital stakeholders, including the continuing value computation.

In theory, the value of common equity using this valuation approach should be identical to the value of common equity using the free-cash-flows-to-equity approach, the dividends-based valuation approach discussed in the previous chapter, and the earnings-based approaches discussed in the following chapters. As a practical matter, however, it is sometimes difficult to get the equity value estimate from the free cash flows to all debt and equity stakeholders to match the other value estimates. The main reason is the added degrees of circularity in this valuation approach. For these different approaches to agree, the market-value-based weights for debt, preferred stock, noncontrolling interests, and common equity capital used in computing the weighted-average cost of capital must be consistent with the value estimates for debt, preferred stock, noncontrolling interests, and common equity. Thus, additional degrees of circularity arise because the value estimates depend on the weighted-average cost of capital, and the weighted-average cost of capital depends on the value estimates. Obtaining an internally consistent set of value estimates for each type of capital and an internally consistent weighted-average cost of capital may require a number of iterations until all of the weights and value estimates agree.

Free Cash Flows Valuation of Starbucks

LO 12-4

Understand how to implement the free-cash-flows-based valuation approaches by applying them to estimate share value for Starbucks.

At the end of fiscal 2015, trading in **Starbucks** shares on the NASDAQ Exchange closed at $56.84 per share. Therefore, we know the *price* at which we could buy or sell **Starbucks** shares at that time. The free-cash-flows valuation methods enable us to estimate the *value* of these shares. This section illustrates the valuation of **Starbucks** shares using the free-cash-flows valuation techniques described in this chapter and the forecasts developed in Chapter 10. We develop these forecasts and value estimates using the Forecast and Valuation spreadsheets in FSAP (see Appendix C).

In this section, we estimate the value of **Starbucks'** shares at the end of fiscal 2015 (equivalently, the start of forecast Year $+1$) two ways, by estimating (a) the present value of free cash flows to *common equity* shareholders, discounted at the *equity* cost of capital; and (b) the present value of free cash flows to *all debt and equity* stakeholders, discounted using **Starbucks'** *weighted-average* cost of capital; we then subtract the present value of debt claims.

To proceed with each valuation, we follow four steps:

1. Estimate the appropriate discount rates for **Starbucks**.
2. Derive the free cash flows from the projected financial statements for **Starbucks** described in Chapter 10 and make an assumption about free cash flows growth in the continuing periods beyond the forecast horizon.
3. Discount the free cash flows to present value, including continuing value.
4. Make the necessary adjustments to convert the present value computation to an estimate of share value for **Starbucks**.

Once we have our benchmark estimate of **Starbucks'** share value, we conduct sensitivity analysis to determine the reasonable range of values for **Starbucks** shares. Finally, we compare this range of reasonable values to **Starbucks'** share price in the market and suggest an appropriate investment decision indicated by our analysis. As we saw in the previous chapter using the dividends-based valuation approach, our value estimate was $66.10. Because of the equivalence of models, we should obtain the same value estimates here.

Starbucks Discount Rates

To discount free cash flows to common equity shareholders, we need to compute **Starbucks'** required rate of return on equity capital. To discount free cash flows to all debt and equity capital, we need to compute **Starbucks'** weighted-average cost of capital. Recall from Chapter 11 our computations of **Starbucks'** required rate of return on equity capital and weighted-average cost of capital. This section will only briefly review those computations.

Computing the Required Rate of Return on Equity Capital for Starbucks

At the end of fiscal 2015, different sources provided different estimates of market beta for **Starbucks** common stock, ranging from 0.50 to 1.00. Historically, **Starbucks'** market beta has varied around 0.75 over time, so we assume that **Starbucks** common stock has a market beta of 0.75 as of the end of fiscal 2015. At that time, U.S. Treasury bills with 10 years to maturity traded with a yield of approximately 2.7%, which we use as the risk-free rate. Assuming a 6.0% market risk premium, the CAPM indicates that **Starbucks** has a cost of common equity capital of 7.2% [7.2% = 2.7% + (0.75 × 6.0%)]. At the end of fiscal 2015, **Starbucks** had 1,485.1 million shares outstanding and a share price of $56.84, for a total market capital of common equity of $84,413 million.

Computing the Weighted-Average Cost of Capital for Starbucks

The following subsections demonstrate how to compute the costs of capital for the debt and other components of **Starbucks'** capital structure, and then how to compute **Starbucks'** weighted-average cost of capital.

Debt Capital. **Starbucks'** balance sheet (Appendix A) at the end of fiscal 2015 shows interest-bearing long-term debt obligations of $2,348 million. Recall that Chapter 10 used information disclosed in Note 9, "Debt" (Appendix A), to assess stated interest rates on **Starbucks'** interest-bearing debt. In 2015, **Starbucks'** outstanding debt carries a weighted-average interest rate of approximately 2.71%. In Note 9, **Starbucks** discloses that the fair value of outstanding debt obligations at the end of fiscal 2015 is $2,402 million.

Thus, Starbucks has experienced a small unrealized (and unrecognized) loss of $54 million ($2,348 million − $2,402 million) on its debt capital. This unrealized loss is a bit surprising because the financing activities section of **Starbucks'** statement of cash flows (Appendix A) reveals that **Starbucks** issued this outstanding long-term debt over 2013 to 2015 at prevailing market rates. The unrealized loss implies that the firm's prior issues of outstanding long-term fixed-rate debt must carry stated rates of interest that are slightly higher than prevailing market yields, which at the end of 2015 are at relatively low levels. Based on the fact that **Starbucks'** outstanding debt obligations were recently issued, Chapter 10 projected that **Starbucks'** cost of debt capital will continue to approximate 2.71% in Year +1 and beyond. We use the current fair value (as a proxy for market value) of **Starbucks'** debt for weighting purposes. In Chapter 10 we also projected that **Starbucks** will face average tax rates of roughly 34% in Year +1 and beyond. Therefore, these projections imply that Starbucks faces an after-tax cost of debt capital of 1.79% [2.71 × (1 − 0.34)].

Preferred Stock and Noncontrolling Interests. Starbucks has no preferred stock on the 2015 balance sheet. In Chapter 10 we projected that **Starbucks** would not issue any preferred stock in future years. Therefore, we include no preferred stock in the computation of **Starbucks'** weighted-average cost of capital. **Starbucks'** 2015 balance sheet reports $1.8 million in equity capital attributable to noncontrolling interests. In Chapter 10 we projected that **Starbucks** would retire this very small amount in Year +1, so we include no capital for noncontrolling interests.

Starbucks' Weighted-Average Cost of Capital. Combining these costs of debt and equity capital, we compute **Starbucks'** weighted-average cost of capital to be 7.05% as follows (allow for rounding):

Capital	Value Basis	Amount	Weight	After-Tax Cost of Capital	Weighted-Average Component
Debt	Fair	$ 2,402	2.77%	1.79%	0.05%
Common Equity	Market	84,413	97.23%	7.20%	7.00%
Total		$86,815	100.00%		7.05%

This is just an initial estimate of **Starbucks'** weighted-average cost of capital. As described earlier, the weighted-average cost of capital must be computed iteratively until the weights used are consistent with the present values of debt and equity capital.

Valuing Starbucks Using Free Cash Flows

This section first describes valuing **Starbucks** using free cash flows for common equity shareholders, then describes valuing **Starbucks** using free cash flows for all debt and equity stakeholders. Recall that Exhibits 12.2 to 12.4 presented the steps to compute free cash flows, beginning with the statement of cash flows. Chapter 10 described detailed projections of **Starbucks'** future statements of cash flows by making specific assumptions regarding each item on the income statement and balance sheet and then deriving the related cash flow effects over a five-year forecast horizon (see Exhibit 10.6). We use these projections to compute projected free cash flows. We present the projections and present value computations of free cash flows for common equity shareholders in Exhibit 12.5 (page 790).

Exhibit 12.5
Projected Free Cash Flows to Common Equity Shareholders for Starbucks Year +1 through Year +6 (dollar amounts in millions; allow for rounding)

Free Cash Flows for Common Equity Shareholders	Year +1	Year +2	Year +3	Year +4	Year +5	Year +6
Net cash flow from operations	$ 4,648.5	$ 4,616.6	$ 5,264.2	$ 5,942.4	$ 6,428.0	$5,490.7
Decrease (increase) in cash required for operations	(251.8)	(163.7)	(215.6)	(235.5)	(257.0)	(79.6)
Free cash flow from operations for common equity shareholders	$ 4,396.7	$ 4,452.9	$ 5,048.6	$ 5,706.9	$ 6,170.9	$5,411.1
Net cash flows for investing activities	(1,555.0)	(1,662.5)	(1,970.4)	(2,278.7)	(2,587.3)	(688.6)
Net cash flows from debt financing	1,000.0	0.0	0.0	0.0	0.0	100.4
Net cash flows into financial assets	0.0	0.0	0.0	0.0	0.0	0.0
Net cash flows—preferred stock and noncontrolling interests	(1.8)	0.0	0.0	0.0	0.0	0.0
Free cash flow for common equity shareholders	$ 3,839.9	$ 2,790.4	$ 3,078.2	$ 3,428.2	$ 3,583.6	$4,822.9
Present value factors ($R_E = 7.2\%$)	0.933	0.870	0.812	0.757	0.706	
Present value of free cash flows	$ 3,582.0	$ 2,428.1	$ 2,498.7	$ 2,595.9	$ 2,531.3	
Sum of present value free cash flows for common equity shareholders, Year +1 through Year +5	$13,636.1					

Valuing Starbucks Using Free Cash Flows to Common Equity

Exhibit 12.5 presents estimates of **Starbucks'** free cash flows for common equity shareholders through Year +6. The computations begin with the Year +1 projection of $4,648.5 million of cash flows from operations, from the projected statement of cash flows for Year +1 in Chapter 10. We adjust cash flows from operations in Year +1 by subtracting the increment of $251.8 million of additional cash required for liquidity. Recall that in Chapter 10, we projected that **Starbucks** would maintain roughly 30 days of sales in cash for liquidity purposes; therefore, **Starbucks'** required cash balance varies with sales. For example, at the end of Year +1, we project that **Starbucks'** cash balance will be $1,781.8 million, equivalent to 30 days of sales. Given that this balance is higher than **Starbucks'** fiscal 2015 year-end cash balance of $1,530.1 million, it implies that **Starbucks** will increase its cash balance by $251.8 million. This increment of cash is not available in Year +1 to satisfy debt and equity claims, so we subtract it from free cash flows. In Year +2, we project that the cash balance will grow by $163.7 million to $1,945.5 million. This additional increment of cash is required for liquidity in Year +2 and therefore is not a free cash flow, so we again subtract it. As a result of these adjustments, we project that **Starbucks'** free cash flows from operations for equity will be $4,396.7 million in Year +1 and $4,452.9 million in Year +2, and so on.[8]

Next, we subtract cash flows for capital expenditures using the amount of net cash flow for investing from **Starbucks'** projected statements of cash flows. For example, in Year +1, we projected that net cash flows for investing activities will be $1,555.0 million. These investing cash flows include cash outflows for purchases of property, plant, and equipment; acquisitions of goodwill and other intangible assets; and purchases of marketable securities and investment securities. We consider purchases of marketable securities and investment securities to be investing activities (rather than financing activities) because these securities are for the purposes of operating liquidity, so we make no adjustment for cash flows into financial assets. Therefore, we subtract the full amount of net cash flow for investing activities from the free cash flow from operations. We subtract $1,555.0 million of projected cash outflows for capital expenditures and other investing activities in Year +1, $1,662.5 million in Year +2, and so on.

To further refine these cash flows to free cash flows available to common equity, we need to adjust them for cash flows related to debt, preferred stock, and noncontrolling interest financing. We first add any cash inflows from new borrowing and subtract any cash outflows for debt repayments. For example, in Year +1, we add $1,000.0 million in cash flows for our projections of **Starbucks'** additional long-term borrowing. We also subtract any cash outflows and add any cash inflows related to financial asset accounts that are part of **Starbucks'** capital structure (which we have deemed to be zero). Next, we add inflows and subtract outflows related to transactions with preferred stock and noncontrolling interest shareholders (if any). In Year +1, we project **Starbucks** will not have any preferred stock, so no adjustment is needed. However, we subtract $1.8 million for free cash flows for noncontrolling interests because in Chapter 10, we projected that **Starbucks** would retire the very small amount of noncontrolling interests in Year +1. Taken together, these computations project $3,839.9 million in free cash flows for **Starbucks'** common equity shareholders in Year +1. We repeat these steps each year through Year +5.

We estimate the present value of these free cash flows in Year +1 through Year +5 by discounting them using **Starbucks'** 7.2% required rate of return on equity capital. Exhibit 12.5 shows that **Starbucks'** free cash flows for common equity through Year + 5 have a present value of $13,636.1 million.

To project **Starbucks'** free cash flows for common equity continuing in Year +6 and beyond, we again forecast that **Starbucks** will sustain long-run growth of 3.0%. We project the Year +5 income statement and balance sheet amounts to grow at a rate of 3.0% in Year +6 and derive free cash flows to common equity from the projected Year +6 statements. Our computations indicate that free cash flows to common equity in Year +6 will be $4,822.9 million.

We compute **Starbucks'** continuing value as the present value of a growing perpetuity of free cash flows beginning in Year +6. We project these free cash flows ($4,822.9 million in Year +6) to grow at 3.0% and discount them to present value using the 7.2% discount rate. The present value of these cash flows is $81,112.2 million. As shown in

---

[8]Note that we make no adjustment for net interest expense after tax because we need to measure the free cash flows available to equity shareholders net of all debt-related cash flows. Because our starting point, cash flows from operations, is derived from net income (after interest expense), our cash flows amount is net of interest expense.

Exhibit 12.5, the present value of **Starbucks'** free cash flows to common equity share-holders is the sum of these two parts:

Present value free cash flows through Year +5	$13,636.1 million
Present value of continuing value in Year +6 and beyond	81,112.2 million
Present value of common equity	$94,748.3 million

As described in the previous chapter, we need to correct our present value calculations for over-discounting. To make the correction, we multiply the present value sum by the midyear adjustment factor of 1.0360 $[1 + (R_E/2) = 1 + (0.0720/2)]$. The total present value of free cash flows to common equity shareholders should be $98,159.2 million ($94,748.3 million $\times$ 1.0360). Dividing the total value of common equity of **Starbucks** by 1,485.1 million shares outstanding indicates that **Starbucks'** common equity shares have a value of $66.10 per share. This share value estimate is identical to the share value estimate we computed using dividends in the previous chapter. Exhibit 12.6 presents these computations. Exhibit 12.7 presents the same computations from the Valuations spreadsheet in FSAP.

Exhibit 12.6

Valuation of Starbucks Using Free Cash Flows to Common Equity Shareholders (allow for rounding)

Present Value of Free Cash Flows to Common Equity Shareholders in Year +1 through Year +5:

From Exhibit 12.5:	$13,636.1 million

Present Value of Continuing Value of Free Cash Flows to Common Equity in Year +6 and Beyond:

Projected Year +6 Free Cash Flows to Common Equity (Exhibit 12.5): $4,822.9 million

Continuing Value in Present Value ($R_E = 7.2\%$ and $g = 3.0\%$):

Continuing Value
$$= \text{Free Cash Flow Year+6} \times [1/(R_E - g)]$$
$$= \$4,822.9 \text{ million} \times [1/(0.072 - 0.030)]$$
$$= \$4,822.9 \text{ million} \times 23.8095$$
$$= \$114,831.3 \text{ million}$$

Present Value of Continuing Value $= \text{Continuing Value} \times [1/(1 + R_E)^5]$
$$= \$114,831.3 \text{ million} \times [1/(1 + 0.0720)^5]$$
$$= \$114,831.3 \text{ million} \times 0.706 \qquad = \$81,112.2 \text{ million}$$

Total Value of Free Cash Flows to Common Equity Shareholders:

Present value of free cash flows through Year +5	$13,636.1	million
Present value of continuing value	+ 81,112.2	million
Present value of common equity	$94,748.3	million
Adjust for midyear discounting (multiply by 1 + [R_E/2])	× 1.0360	
Total present value of common equity	$98,159.2	million
Divide by number of shares outstanding	÷ 1,485.1	million
Value per share of Starbucks common equity	$ 66.10	

Exhibit 12.7

FSAP Valuation of Starbucks Using Free Cash Flows to Common Equity Shareholders through Year +5 and Beyond (in millions, except per-share amounts; allow for rounding)

Free Cash Flows for Common Equity	1 Year +1	2 Year +2	3 Year +3	4 Year +4	5 Year +5	Continuing Value Year +6
Net cash flow from operations	$ 4,648.5	$ 4,616.6	$ 5,264.2	$ 5,942.4	$ 6,428.0	$5,490.7
Decrease (Increase) in cash required for operations	(251.8)	(163.7)	(215.6)	(235.5)	(257.0)	(79.6)
Net cash flow from investing	(1,555.0)	(1,662.5)	(1,970.4)	(2,278.7)	(2,587.3)	(688.6)
Net CFs from debt financing	1,000.0	0.0	0.0	0.0	0.0	100.4
Net CFs into financial assets	0.0	0.0	0.0	0.0	0.0	0.0
Net CFs—preferred stock and noncontrolling interests	(1.8)	0.0	0.0	0.0	0.0	0.0
Free cash flow for common equity	$ 3,839.9	$ 2,790.4	$ 3,078.2	$ 3,428.2	$ 3,583.6	$4,822.9
Present value factors	0.933	0.870	0.812	0.757	0.706	
Present value free cash flows	$ 3,582.0	$ 2,428.1	$ 2,498.7	$ 2,595.9	$ 2,531.3	
Sum of present value free cash flows	$13,636.1					
Present value of continuing value	$81,112.2					
Total	$94,748.3					
Adjust to midyear discounting	1.036					
Total present value free cash flows to equity	$98,159.2					
Shares outstanding	1,485.1					
Estimated value per share	$ 66.10					
Current share price	$ 56.84					
Percent difference	16%					

Valuing Starbucks Using Free Cash Flows to All Debt and Equity Capital Stakeholders

In Exhibit 12.8, we again begin our computation of free cash flows with cash flows from operations from the projected statements of cash flows developed in Chapter 10 for **Starbucks** for Year +1 through Year +5. In Year +1, for example, we project that **Starbucks'** cash flows from operations will be $4,648.5 million. We then adjust for net interest, adding back interest expense after tax. Specifically, in Year +1, we add back $50.9 million in interest expense after tax [$77.1 million × (1 – 0.34)]. We do not subtract interest income after tax because we assume that all of **Starbucks'** interest income relates to cash, short-term and long-term investments that are used for liquidity in operating activities, and strategic investments that are not part of the capital structure.

As in the prior section, we also adjust cash flow from operations for required investments in operating cash. We project **Starbucks** will require an additional $251.8 million in cash in Year +1, $163.7 million in Year +2, and so on. These additional increments of cash are required for liquidity and are therefore not free cash flows, so we subtract them. As a result of these adjustments, we project that **Starbucks'** free cash flows from

Exhibit 12.8

Projected Free Cash Flows to All Debt and Equity Stakeholders for Starbucks Year +1 through Year +6 (dollar amounts in millions; allow for rounding)

Free Cash Flows for All Debt and Equity	Year +1	Year +2	Year +3	Year +4	Year +5	Year +6
Net cash flow from operations	$ 4,648.5	$ 4,616.6	$ 5,264.2	$ 5,942.4	$ 6,428.0	$5,490.7
Add back: Interest expense after tax	50.9	59.8	59.8	59.8	59.8	61.6
Subtract: Interest income after tax	(0.0)	(0.0)	(0.0)	(0.0)	(0.0)	(0.0)
Decrease (Increase) in cash required for operations	(251.8)	(163.7)	(215.6)	(235.5)	(257.0)	(79.6)
Free cash flow from operations for all debt and equity stakeholders	$ 4,447.6	$ 4,512.7	$ 5,108.4	$ 5,766.7	$ 6,230.7	$5,472.7
Net cash flows for investing activities	(1,555.0)	(1,662.5)	(1,970.4)	(2,278.7)	(2,587.3)	(688.6)
Add back: Net cash flows into financial assets	0.0	0.0	0.0	0.0	0.0	0.0
Free cash flows—all debt and equity stakeholders	$ 2,892.6	$ 2,850.2	$ 3,138.0	$ 3,488.0	$ 3,643.4	$4,784.1
Present value factors (R_A = 7.05%)	0.934	0.873	0.815	0.761	0.711	
Present value free cash flows	$ 2,702.1	$ 2,487.1	$ 2,557.9	$ 2,656.0	$ 2,591.6	
Sum of present value of free cash flows for all debt and equity stakeholders, Year +1 through Year +5	$12,994.7					

operations for all debt and equity stakeholders will be $4,447.6 million in Year +1, $4,512.7 million in Year +2, and so on.

Also as in the prior section, we subtract cash flows for capital expenditures using the amount of net cash flow for investing from **Starbucks'** projected statements of cash flows. In Year +1, we projected that net cash flows for investing activities will be $1,555.0 million. We repeat these steps each year through Year +5.

We estimate the present value of these free cash flows in Year +1 through Year +5 by discounting them using **Starbucks'** weighted-average cost of capital, which we estimated to be 7.05%. Exhibit 12.8 shows that **Starbucks'** free cash flows for all debt and equity stakeholders through Year +5 have a present value of $12,994.7 million.

To project **Starbucks'** free cash flows continuing in Year +6, we project each line item on **Starbucks'** Year +5 income statement and balance sheet to grow at 3.0% per year in Year +6, consistent with expected long-term growth in the economy. We use these Year +6 projected income statement and balance sheet amounts to derive the Year +6 free cash flows for all debt and equity, which we project will be $4,784.1 million. We assume that this free cash flow amount is the beginning of a perpetuity of continuing free cash flows that **Starbucks** will generate beginning in Year +6, growing at 3% each year thereafter. To compute the present value of **Starbucks'** continuing value, we compute the continuing value in Year +6 and beyond using the perpetuity-with-growth model and using a 7.05% weighted-average cost of capital.

Exhibit 12.9 (page 796) demonstrates that in present value, **Starbucks'** continuing value has a present value of $84,020.0 million. The present value of **Starbucks'** free cash flows to all debt and equity capital stakeholders is the sum of these two parts:

Present value free cash flows through Year +5	$12,994.7 million
Present value of continuing value Year +6 and beyond	84,020.0 million
Present value of free cash flows for all debt and equity	$97,014.7 million

Necessary Adjustments to Compute Common Equity Share Value

To narrow this computation to the present value of common equity, we need to subtract the market value of interest-bearing debt, preferred stock, and noncontrolling interests, and add the present value of interest-earning financial assets that are part of the firm's financial capital structure. Exhibit 12.9 summarizes all of these computations, and Exhibit 12.10 (page 797) presents the computations to arrive at **Starbucks'** common equity share value using the Valuations spreadsheet in FSAP.

Relying on **Starbucks'** disclosure, we subtract $2,402.0 million for the fair value of outstanding debt. In our Year +1 cash flow forecasts, we also assumed that **Starbucks** would retire the very minor amount of equity capital attributable to noncontrolling interests. We assume that **Starbucks'** financial assets are not part of the financial capital structure, so we do not adjust for them. After these adjustments, the present value of **Starbucks'** common equity capital is $94,612.7 million ($97,014.7 million − $2,402.0 million).

As described earlier, our present value calculations have over-discounted these cash flows because we have discounted each year's cash flows for a full period when, in fact, **Starbucks** generates cash flows throughout each period and we should discount them from the midpoint of each year to the present. Therefore, to make the correction, we multiply

Exhibit 12.9

Valuation of Starbucks Using Free Cash Flows to All Debt and Equity Stakeholders (allow for rounding)

Present Value of Free Cash Flows to All Debt and Equity Stakeholders in Year +1 through Year +5:

From Exhibit 12.8:	$12,994.7 million

Present Value of Continuing Value of Free Cash Flows to All Debt and Equity Stakeholders in Year +6 and Beyond:

Projected Year +6 Free Cash Flows to All Debt and Equity Stakeholders
(Exhibit 12.8): $4,784.1 million

Continuing Value in Present Value ($R_A = 7.05\%$ and $g = 3.0\%$):

Continuing Value	$= \text{Free Cash Flow} \times [1/(R_A - g)]$	
	$= \$4,784.1 \text{ million} \times [1/(0.0705 - 0.030)]$	
	$= \$4,784.1 \text{ million} \times 24.6914$	
	$= \$118,125.5 \text{ million}$	
Present Value of Continuing Value	$= \text{Continuing Value} \times [1/(1 + R_A)^5]$	
	$= \$118,125.5 \text{ million} \times [1/(1 + 0.0705)^5]$	
	$= \$118,125.5 \text{ million} \times 0.711$	$=\$84,020.0$ million

Total Value of Starbucks's Free Cash Flows to All Debt and Equity Stakeholders:

Present value of free cash flows through Year +5	$12,994.7 million
+ Present value of continuing value	+ 84,020.0 million
Present value of all debt and equity	$97,014.7 million
Subtract fair value of debt	− 2,402.0 million
Subtract fair value to retire preferred stock	− 0.0 million
Subtract book value of noncontrolling interests	− 0.0 million
Add fair value of financial assets in the capital structure	+ 0.0 million
Present value of common equity	$94,612.7 million
Adjust for midyear discounting [multiply by $1 + (R_A/2) = 1 + (0.0705/2)$]	× 1.03525
Total present value of common equity	$97,947.9 million
Divide by number of shares outstanding	÷ 1,485.1 million
Value per share of Starbucks common equity	$ 65.95

the present value sum by the midyear adjustment factor of 1.03525 [$1 + (R_A/2) = 1 + (0.0705/2)$]. Therefore, the total present value of free cash flows to common equity shareholders is $97,947.9 million ($94,612.7 million × 1.03525). Dividing by 1,485.1 million shares outstanding indicates that **Starbucks'** common equity shares have a value of $65.95 per share.

Note that our calculation of a $65.95 value for **Starbucks'** common equity shares is slightly different from the value of $66.10 per share obtained from the free-cash-flows-to-common-equity approach described previously and the dividends-based approach in the previous chapter. This is because we used the current market price per share of **Starbucks**

Exhibit 12.10

FSAP Valuation of Starbucks Using Free Cash Flows to All Debt and Equity Stakeholders through Year +5 and Beyond (in millions, except per-share amounts; allow for rounding)

Free Cash Flows for All Debt and Equity	1 Year +1	2 Year +2	3 Year +3	4 Year +4	5 Year +5	Continuing Value Year +6
Net cash flow from operations	$ 4,648.5	$ 4,616.6	$ 5,264.2	$ 5,942.4	$ 6,428.0	$5,490.7
Add back: Interest expense after tax	50.9	59.8	59.8	59.8	59.8	61.6
Subtract: Interest income after tax	0.0	0.0	0.0	0.0	0.0	0.0
Decrease (Increase) in cash required for operations	(251.8)	(163.7)	(215.6)	(235.5)	(257.0)	(79.6)
Free cash flow from operations	$ 4,447.6	$ 4,512.7	$ 5,108.4	$ 5,766.7	$ 6,230.7	$5,472.7
Net cash flow from investing	(1,555.0)	(1,662.5)	(1,970.4)	(2,278.7)	(2,587.3)	(688.6)
Add back: Net CFs into financial assets	0.0	0.0	0.0	0.0	0.0	0.0
Free cash flows—all debt and equity	$ 2,892.6	$ 2,850.2	$ 3,138.0	$ 3,488.0	$ 3,643.4	$4,784.1
Present value factors	0.934	0.873	0.815	0.761	0.711	
Present value free cash flows	$ 2,702.1	$ 2,487.1	$ 2,557.9	$ 2,656.0	$ 2,591.6	
Sum of present value free cash flows	$12,994.7					
Present value of continuing value	$84,020.0					
Total present value free cash flows to equity and debt	$97,014.7					
Less: Value of outstanding debt	(2,402.0)					
Less: Value of preferred stock	0.0					
Plus: Value of financial assets	0.0					
Present value of equity	$94,612.7					
Adjust to midyear discounting	1.0353					
Total present value of equity	$97,947.9					
Shares outstanding	1,485.1					
Estimated value per share	$ 65.95					
Current share price	$ 56.84					
Percent difference	16%					

common stock ($56.84) in the initial weighted-average cost of capital computation, rather than our previous value estimate of the intrinsic value ($66.10). As a consequence, we did not place enough weight on the market value of equity in the initial cost of capital computation. To iterate the valuation approach, we can use the share value estimate of $66.10 to determine that the total value of **Starbucks** common equity in the weighted-average cost of capital computation. To further iterate the valuation approach, we can recompute the weighted-average cost of equity capital each forecast year because our projections indicate that **Starbucks'** common equity in the capital structure will gradually fall in proportion to the debt financing in the capital structure in future years. After a number of iterations, the valuation computations and the weights we use to compute the weighted-average cost of capital converge. (This exercise highlights the circularity of this approach, namely that we require an estimate of share value to compute share value.) The equity value estimate of $98,159.2 million, or $66.10 per share, is the internally consistent value.

LO 12-5

Assess the sensitivity of firm value estimates to key valuation parameters such as discount rates and expected long-term growth rates.

Sensitivity Analysis and Investment Decision Making

As we emphasized in the previous chapter, forecasts of cash flows over the remaining life of any firm, even a mature firm such as **Starbucks**, contain a high degree of uncertainty; so we should not place too much confidence in the *precision* of value estimates using these forecasts. Although we have constructed these forecasts and value estimates with care, the forecasting and valuation process has an inherently high degree of uncertainty and estimation error. Therefore, do not rely too heavily on any single point estimate of the value of a firm's shares; instead, you should describe a reasonable range of values for a firm's shares.

Two critical forecasting and valuation parameters in most valuations are the long-run growth rate assumption and the cost of equity capital assumption. You should conduct sensitivity analyses to test the effects of these and other key forecast assumptions and valuation parameters on the share value estimate. Sensitivity analyses allow you to vary these assumptions and parameters individually and jointly for additional insights into the correlation between share value, growth rates, and discount rate assumptions.

For **Starbucks**, our base case assumptions indicate share value to be roughly $66.10. Our base case valuation assumptions include a long-run growth rate of 3% and a cost of equity capital of 7.2%. We can assess the sensitivity of our estimates of **Starbucks'** share value by varying these two parameters (or any other key parameters in the valuation) across reasonable ranges. Exhibit 12.11 contains the results of sensitivity analysis varying the long-run growth rate from 0% to 5% and the cost of equity capital from 6% to 12%. The data in Exhibit 12.11 show that as the discount rate increases, holding growth constant, share value estimates fall. Likewise, value estimates fall as growth rates decrease, holding discount rates constant.

Considering the downside possibilities first, consider how sensitive the share value estimate is to adverse changes in long-run growth and discount rates. For example, by reducing the long-run growth assumption from 3.0% to 2.5% while holding the discount rate constant at 7.2%, **Starbucks'** share value falls to $60.20, which is above the current market price of $56.48. Similarly, while holding constant the long-run growth assumption at 3.0%, increasing the discount rate from 7.2% to 8.0% produces a share value estimate of $55.32, which is just slightly below the market price. Increasing the discount rate further to 8.5% produces a value estimate of $50.19, below the market price. If we

Exhibit 12.11								
Valuation of Starbucks: Sensitivity Analysis of Value to Growth and Equity Cost of Capital								

Free Cash Flows Valuation Sensitivity Analysis:

		Long-Run Growth Assumptions							
	66.10	**0.0%**	**1.0%**	**2.0%**	**2.5%**	**3.0%**	**3.5%**	**4.0%**	**5.0%**
Discount Rates:	6.00%	52.05	60.26	72.57	81.36	93.09	109.50	134.12	257.23
	6.50%	47.87	54.60	64.32	71.00	79.58	91.04	107.07	171.19
	6.70%	46.38	52.62	61.51	67.54	75.21	85.27	99.05	150.95
	7.00%	44.30	49.89	57.72	62.94	69.47	77.85	89.04	128.18
	7.20%	43.01	48.23	55.44	60.20	66.10	73.58	83.41	116.46
	7.50%	41.21	45.92	52.33	56.51	61.60	67.98	76.17	102.39
	7.70%	40.09	44.49	50.45	54.28	58.93	64.69	72.00	94.75
	8.00%	38.51	42.51	47.85	51.25	55.32	60.30	66.53	85.21
	8.50%	36.13	39.57	44.06	46.87	50.19	54.17	59.03	72.94
	9.00%	34.03	37.00	40.82	43.17	45.91	49.15	53.05	63.74
	9.50%	32.14	34.73	38.01	40.00	42.30	44.98	48.15	56.60
	10.00%	30.45	32.72	35.56	37.26	39.21	41.45	44.07	50.89
	11.00%	27.54	29.32	31.48	32.76	34.20	35.82	37.68	42.33
	12.00%	25.13	26.54	28.24	29.22	30.31	31.53	32.90	36.23

revise both assumptions at once, and reduce the long-run growth assumption to 2.5% and increase the discount rate assumption to 7.5%, **Starbucks'** share value falls to $56.51, nearly equivalent to the current market price of $56.48.

On the upside, reducing the discount rate to 7.0% while holding growth constant at 3.0% suggests **Starbucks** shares could have a value of $69.47. Increasing the long-run growth assumption from 3.0% to 4.0% while holding the discount rate constant at 7.2%, the value estimates jump to $83.41. If we reduce the discount rate, or increase the long-run growth rate further, the share value estimates for **Starbucks** jump dramatically higher. For example, increasing the growth rate assumption to 4.0% and decreasing the discount rate assumption to 7.0% moves the share value estimate to $89.

These data suggest that the value estimate is sensitive to slight variations in the baseline assumptions of 3.0% long-run growth and a 7.2% discount rate, which yield a share value estimate of roughly $66. Adverse variations in valuation parameters could reduce **Starbucks'** share value estimates to $55 or lower, whereas favorable variations could increase **Starbucks'** share value to over $80.

If the forecast and valuation assumptions are realistic, the baseline value estimate for **Starbucks** is $66.10 per share at the end of fiscal 2015. At that time, the market price of $56.48 per share indicates that **Starbucks** shares were underpriced by about 16%. Under our forecast assumptions, **Starbucks'** share value could vary within a range of a low of $55 per share to a high of over $80 per share with only minor perturbations in the growth rate and discount rate assumptions. Given **Starbucks'** $56.48 share price, these value estimates would have supported a buy recommendation at the end of fiscal 2015 because the sensitivity analysis reveals limited downside potential but substantial upside potential for the value of **Starbucks'** shares.

Summary

This chapter illustrates valuation using the present value of future free cash flows. As with the preparation of financial statement forecasts in Chapter 10, the reasonableness of the valuations depends on the reasonableness of the assumptions. You should assess the sensitivity of the valuation to alternative assumptions regarding growth and discount rates. To validate value estimates using a free-cash-flows-based approach, you also should compute the value of the common equity of the firm using the dividends-based approach in Chapter 11, the earnings-based approach in Chapter 13, and the market-based approaches in Chapter 14.

Questions, Exercises, Problems, and Cases

Questions and Exercises

LO 12-1

12.1 Free Cash Flows. Explain "free" cash flows. Describe which types of cash flows are *free* and which are not. How do free cash flows available for debt and equity stakeholders differ from free cash flows available for common equity shareholders?

LO 12-1

12.2 Free-Cash-Flows-Based Valuation Approaches. Explain the theory behind the free-cash-flows valuation approaches. Why are free cash flows value-relevant to common equity shareholders when they are not cash flows to those shareholders but rather are cash flows into the firm?

LO 12-1

12.3 Valuation Approach Equivalence. Conceptually, why should you expect valuation based on dividends and valuation based on the free cash flows for common equity shareholders to yield identical value estimates?

LO 12-2

12.4 Measuring Value-Relevant Free Cash Flows. The chapter describes free cash flows for common equity shareholders. If the firm borrows cash by issuing debt, how does that transaction affect free cash flows for common equity shareholders in that period? If the firm uses cash to repay debt, how does that transaction affect free cash flows for common equity shareholders in that period?

LO 12-2

12.5 Measuring Value-Relevant Free Cash Flows. The chapter describes free cash flows for common equity shareholders. Suppose a firm has no debt and uses marketable securities to manage operating liquidity. If the firm uses cash to purchase marketable securities, how does that transaction affect free cash flows for common equity shareholders in that period? If the firm sells marketable securities for cash, how does that transaction affect free cash flows for common equity shareholders in that period?

LO 12-3

12.6 Valuation When Free Cash Flows Are Negative. Suppose you are valuing a healthy, growing, profitable firm and you project that the firm will generate negative free cash flows for equity shareholders in each of the next five years. Can you use a free-cash-flows-based valuation approach when cash flows are negative? If so, explain how a free-cash-flows approach can produce positive valuations of firms when they are expected to generate negative free cash flows over the next five years.

LO 12-2, LO 12-3
LO 12-4

12.7 Using Different Free-Cash-Flows-Based Approaches. The chapter describes valuation using free cash flows for all debt and equity stakeholders as well as free cash flows for equity shareholders. For each approach, give one example of valuation settings in which that approach is appropriate.

12.8 Appropriate Discount Rates. Describe valuation settings in which the appropriate discount rate to use is the required rate of return on equity capital versus settings in which it is appropriate to use a weighted-average cost of capital. `LO 12-2, LO 12-3` `LO 12-4`

12.9 Free Cash Flows and Discount Rates. Describe circumstances and give an example of when free cash flows to equity shareholders and free cash flows to all debt and equity stakeholders will be identical. Under those circumstances, will the required rate of return on equity and the weighted-average cost of capital be identical too? Explain. `LO 12-2, LO 12-3` `LO 12-4`

Problems and Cases

12.10 Calculating Free Cash Flows. The **3M Company** is a global diversified technology company active in the following product markets: consumer and office; display and graphics; electronics and communications; health care; industrial; safety, security, and protection services; and transportation. At the consumer level, 3M is probably most widely known for products such as Scotch® Brand transparent tape and Post-it® notes. Exhibit 12.12 presents information from the statement of cash flows and income statement for the 3M Company for 2013 to 2015. From 2013 through 2015, 3M decreased cash and cash equivalents. The interest income reported by 3M pertains to interest earned on cash and marketable securities. 3M holds only small amounts of investments in marketable securities. 3M's income tax rate is 35%. `LO 12-2`

Exhibit 12.12			
3M Company Selected Information from the Statement of Cash Flows (amounts in millions) (Problem 12.10)			
	2015	**2014**	**2013**
Operating Activities:			
Cash Flow from Operating Activities	$ 6,420	$ 6,626	$ 5,817
Investing Activities:			
Fixed assets acquired, net	(1,428)	(1,358)	(1,537)
(Acquisition) Sale of businesses, net	(2,791)	(94)	8
(Purchase) Sale of investments, net	1,300	754	627
Other investing	102	102	46
Cash Flow from Investing Activities	$(2,817)	$ (596)	$ (856)
Financing Activities:			
Increase (Decrease) in short-term borrowing	860	27	(2)
Increase (Decrease) in long-term debt	2,448	853	(20)
Increase (Decrease) in common stock	(4,449)	(5,378)	(3,511)
Dividends paid	(2,561)	(2,216)	(1,730)
Cash Flow from Financing Activities	$(3,702)	$(6,714)	$(5,263)
Net increase (decrease) in cash & equivalents	$ (99)	$ (684)	$ (302)
Cash at beginning of year	$ 1,897	$ 2,581	$ 2,883
Cash at end of year	$ 1,798	$ 1,897	$ 2,581
Interest income	$ 26	$ 33	$ 41
Interest expense	$ 149	$ 142	$ 145

Source: 3M Company, Form 10-K for Fiscal Year Ended December 31, 2015.

REQUIRED

a. Beginning with cash flows from operating activities, calculate the amount of free cash flows to all debt and equity capital stakeholders for 3M for 2013, 2014, and 2015.

b. Beginning with cash flows from operating activities, calculate the amount of free cash flows 3M generated for common equity shareholders in 2013, 2014, and 2015.

c. Reconcile the amounts of free cash flows 3M generated for common equity shareholders in 2013, 2014, and 2015 from Requirement b with 3M's uses of cash flows for equity shareholders, including share repurchases and dividend payments.

LO 12-2

12.11 Calculating Free Cash Flows. Dick's Sporting Goods is a chain of full-line sporting goods retail stores offering a broad assortment of brand name sporting goods equipment, apparel, and footwear. Dick's Sporting Goods had its initial public offering of shares in fiscal 2003. Since then, Dick's Sporting Goods has grown its chain of retail stores rapidly and has acquired several other chains of retail sporting goods stores, including Golf Galaxy and Chick's Sporting Goods. As of the end of the fiscal year ending in 2016, Dick's Sporting Goods operated 736 stores in 47 states of the United States. Exhibit 12.13 presents information from the statement of cash flows and income statement for Dick's Sporting Goods for the fiscal years ending in 2014 through 2016. Dick's Sporting Goods requires all of its cash and cash equivalents for operating liquidity and reports no interest income on the income statement. The effective income tax rate for Dick's Sporting Goods during these years is 35%.

Exhibit 12.13

Dick's Sporting Goods Selected Information from the Statement of Cash Flows (amounts in thousands) (Problem 12.11)

	Fiscal year ended		
	January 30, 2016	January 31, 2015	February 1, 2014
Operating Activities:			
Net cash provided by operating activities	$ 643,514	$ 605,978	$ 403,870
Cash Flows Used in Investing Activities:			
Capital expenditures	(370,028)	(349,007)	(285,668)
Proceeds from sale of other assets	—	74,534	11,000
Deposits & purchases of other assets	(2,406)	(30,547)	(64,507)
Net cash used in investing activities	$(372,434)	$(305,020)	$(339,175)
Cash Flows From Financing Activities:			
Increase (decrease) in bank overdraft	29,121	(29,258)	43,508
Payments on long-term debt and capital leases	(537)	(925)	(8,984)
Proceeds from share issues	19,690	30,532	57,420
Cash paid for treasury stock	(357,276)	(200,000)	(255,602)
Cash dividends paid to stockholders	(64,715)	(61,262)	(64,432)
Net cash provided by financing activities	$(373,823)	$(261,010)	$(228,178)
Net Increase (Decrease) in Cash	$(102,743)	$ 39,948	$(163,483)
Cash, beginning of period	221,679	181,731	345,214
Cash, end of period	$ 118,936	$ 221,679	$ 181,731
Cash paid during the year for interest	$ 3,308	$ 2,631	$ 2,255

Source: Dick's Sporting Goods, Form 10-K for the Fiscal Year Ended January 31, 2016.

REQUIRED

a. Beginning with cash flows from operating activities, calculate free cash flows to all debt and equity capital stakeholders for Dick's Sporting Goods for fiscal years ending in 2014, 2015, and 2016.

b. Beginning with cash flows from operating activities, calculate free cash flows for common equity shareholders for Dick's Sporting Goods for fiscal years ending in 2014, 2015, and 2016.

c. Reconcile the amounts of free cash flows for common equity shareholders for Dick's Sporting Goods for fiscal years ending in 2014, 2015, and 2016 with Dick's Sporting Goods' sources of cash flows from equity shareholders.

d. In each of these three years, why do the free cash flows to all debt and equity capital stakeholders differ from the free cash flows to common equity shareholders?

12.12 Valuing a Leveraged Buyout Candidate. May Department Stores

Company (May) operates retail department store chains throughout the United States. Assume that at the end of Year 2, May's balance sheet reports debt of $4,658 million and common shareholders' equity at book value of $3,923 million. The market value of its common stock is $6,705, and its market equity beta is 0.88.

   Suppose an equity buyout group is considering an LBO of May as of the beginning of Year 3. The group intends to finance the buyout with 25% common equity and 75% debt carrying an interest rate of 10%. Assume the group projects that the free cash flows to all debt and equity capital stakeholders of May will be as follows: Year 3, $798 million; Year 4, $861 million; Year 5, $904 million; Year 6, $850 million; Year 7, $834 million; Year 8, $884 million; Year 9, $919 million; Year 10, $947 million; Year 11, $985 million; and Year 12, $1,034 million. The group projects free cash flows to grow 3% annually after Year 12.

   This problem sets forth the steps you might follow in deciding whether to acquire May and the value to place on the firm.

REQUIRED

a. Compute the unlevered market equity (asset) beta of May before consideration of the LBO. Assume that the book value of the debt equals its market value. The income tax rate is 35%. (See Chapter 11.)

b. Compute the cost of equity capital with the new capital structure that results from the LBO. Assume a risk-free rate of 4.2% and a market risk premium of 5.0%.

c. Compute the weighted-average cost of capital of the new capital structure.

d. Compute the present value of the projected free cash flows to all debt and equity capital stakeholders at the weighted-average cost of capital. Ignore the midyear adjustment related to the assumption that cash flows occur, on average, over the year. In computing the continuing value, apply the projected growth rate in free cash flows after Year 12 of 3% directly to the free cash flows of Year 12.

e. Assume that the buyout group acquires May for the value determined in Requirement d. Assuming that the realized free cash flows coincide with projections, will May generate sufficient cash flow each year to service the interest on the debt? Explain.

12.13 Valuing a Leveraged Buyout Candidate. At the end of Year 5,

Experian Information Solutions, Inc. (Experian), has total assets of $555,443, long-term debt of $1,839, and common equity at book value of $402,759 (amounts in thousands). Suppose an equity buyout group is planning to acquire Experian in an LBO as of the beginning of Year 6. The group plans to finance the buyout with 60% debt that has an interest cost of 10% per year and 40% common equity. Analysts for the buyout group project free cash flows to all debt and

LO 12-4

LO 12-4

equity capital stakeholders as follows (in thousands): Year 6, $52,300; Year 7, $54,915; Year 8, $57,112; Year 9, $59,396; and Year 10, $62,366. Because Experian is not a publicly traded firm, it does not have a market equity beta. The company most comparable to Experian is Equifax. Equifax has an equity beta of 0.86. The market value of Equifax's debt is $366.5 thousand, and its common equity is $4,436.8 thousand. Assume an income tax rate of 35% throughout this problem. This problem sets forth the steps you might follow in valuing an LBO candidate.

REQUIRED

a. Compute the unlevered market equity (asset) beta of Equifax. (See Chapter 11.)

b. Assuming that the unlevered market equity beta of Equifax is appropriate for Experian, compute the equity beta of Experian after the buyout with its new capital structure.

c. Compute the weighted-average cost of capital of Experian after the buyout. Assume a risk-free interest rate of 4.2% and a market risk premium of 5.0%.

d. The analysts at the buyout firm project that free cash flows for all debt and equity capital stakeholders of Experian will increase 5.0% each year after Year 10. Compute the present value of the free cash flows at the weighted-average cost of capital. Ignore the midyear adjustment related to the assumption that cash flows occur, on average, over the year. In computing the continuing value, apply the 5.0% projected growth rate directly to the free cash flows of Year 10.

e. Assume that the buyout group acquires Experian for the value determined in Requirement d. Assuming that actual free cash flows to all debt and equity capital stakeholders coincide with projections, will Experian generate sufficient cash flow each year to service the debt? Explain.

12.14 Applying Various Present Value Approaches to Valuation.

An equity buyout group intends to acquire Wedgewood as of the beginning of Year 8. The buyout group intends to finance 40% of the acquisition price with debt bearing a 10% interest rate and 60% with common equity. The income tax rate is 40%. The cost of equity capital is 14%. Analysts at the buyout firm project the following free cash flows for all debt and equity capital stakeholders for Wedgewood (in millions): Year 8, $2,100; Year 9, $2,268; Year 10, $2,449; Year 11, $2,645; and Year 12, $2,857. The analysts project that free cash flows for all debt and equity capital stakeholders will increase 8% each year after Year 12.

REQUIRED

a. Compute the weighted-average cost of capital for Wedgewood based on the proposed capital structure.

b. Compute the total purchase price of Wedgewood (debt plus common equity). To do this, discount the free cash flows for all debt and equity capital stakeholders at the weighted-average cost of capital. Ignore the midyear adjustment related to the assumption that cash flows occur, on average, over the year. In computing the continuing value, apply the 8% projected growth rate in free cash flows after Year 12 directly to the free cash flows of Year 12.

c. Given the purchase price determined in Requirement b, compute the total amount of debt, the annual interest cost, and the free cash flows to common equity shareholders for Year 8 to Year 12.

d. The present value of the free cash flows for common equity shareholders when discounted at the 14% cost of equity capital should equal the common equity portion of the total purchase price computed in Requirement b. Determine the growth rate in free cash flows for common equity shareholders after Year 12 that will result in a present value of free cash flows for common equity shareholders equal to 60% of the purchase price computed in Requirement b.

e. Why does the implied growth rate in free cash flows to common equity shareholders determined in Requirement d differ from the 8% assumed growth rate in free cash flows for all debt and equity capital stakeholders?

f. The adjusted present value valuation approach separates the total value of the firm into the value of an all-equity firm and the value of the tax savings from interest deductions. Assume that the cost of unlevered equity is 11.33%. Compute the present value of the free cash flows to all debt and equity capital stakeholders at this unlevered equity cost. Compute the present value of the tax savings from interest expense deductions using the pretax cost of debt as the discount rate. Compare the total of these two present values to the purchase price determined in Requirement b.

12.15 Valuing the Equity of a Privately Held Firm.

LO 12-3

Refer to the projected financial statements for Massachusetts Stove Company (MSC) prepared for Case 10.2. The management of MSC wants to know the equity valuation implications of not adding gas stoves versus adding gas stoves under the best, most likely, and worst scenarios. Under the three scenarios from Case 10.2 and a fourth scenario involving not adding gas stoves, the projected free cash flows to common equity shareholders for Year 8 to Year 12, and assumed growth rates thereafter, are as follows:

Year	Best	Most Likely	Worst	No Gas
8	$73,967	$47,034	$3,027	$162,455
9	$52,143	$(3,120)	$(84,800)	$132,708
10	$213,895	$135,939	$48,353	$106,021
11	$315,633	$178,510	$36,605	$81,840
12	$432,232	$220,010	$10,232	$60,007
13–17	20% Growth	10% Growth	Zero Growth	Zero Growth
After Year 17	10% Growth	5% Growth	Zero Growth	Zero Growth

MSC is not publicly traded and therefore does not have a market equity beta. Using the market equity beta of the only publicly traded woodstove and gas stove manufacturing firm and adjusting it for differences in the debt-to-equity ratio, income tax rate, and privately owned status of MSC yields a cost of equity capital for MSC of 13.55%.

REQUIRED

a. Calculate the value of the equity of MSC as of the beginning of Year 8 under each of the four scenarios. Ignore the midyear adjustment related to the assumption that cash flows occur, on average, over the year. Apply the growth rates in free cash flows to common equity shareholders after Year 12 directly to the free cash flow of the preceding year. (That is, Year 13 free cash flow equals the Year 12 free cash flow times the given growth rate; Year 18 free cash flow equals the Year 17 free cash flow times the given growth rate.)

b. How do these valuations affect your advice to the management of MSC regarding the addition of gas stoves to its woodstove line?

12.16 Free-Cash-Flows-Based Valuation.

LO 12-2, LO 12-3
LO 12-4, LO 12-5

The **Coca-Cola Company** is a global soft drink beverage company (ticker symbol = KO) that is a primary and direct competitor with **Starbucks**. The data in Exhibits 12.14 to 12.16 (pages 806–809) include the actual amounts for fiscal 2015 and projected amounts for Year +1 to Year +6 for the income statements, balance sheets, and statements of cash flows for Coca-Cola (in millions). The market

Exhibit 12.14

The Coca-Cola Company
Income Statements for 2015 (Actual) and Year +1 through Year +6 (Projected) (amounts in millions; allow for rounding) (Problem 12.16)

	Actual	Forecasts					
	2015	Year +1	Year +2	Year +3	Year +4	Year +5	Year +6
INCOME STATEMENT							
Revenues	$ 44,294	$ 45,623	$ 46,992	$ 48,401	$ 49,853	$ 51,349	$ 52,889
Cost of goods sold	(17,482)	(18,021)	(18,562)	(19,118)	(19,692)	(20,283)	(20,891)
Gross Profit	$ 26,812	$ 27,602	$ 28,430	$ 29,283	$ 30,161	$ 31,066	$ 31,998
Selling, general, and administrative expenses	(16,427)	(16,880)	(17,387)	(17,908)	(18,446)	(18,999)	(19,569)
Other operating expenses	(1,657)	(1,369)	(1,410)	(1,452)	(1,496)	(1,540)	(1,587)
Operating Profit	$ 8,728	$ 9,353	$ 9,633	$ 9,922	$ 10,220	$ 10,527	$ 10,842
Interest income	613	606	623	642	661	681	701
Interest expense	(856)	(887)	(910)	(951)	(993)	(1,034)	(1,065)
Income from equity affiliates	489	631	663	696	731	767	790
Other gains (losses)	631	0	0	0	0	0	0
Income before Tax	$ 9,605	$ 9,702	$ 10,009	$ 10,309	$ 10,619	$ 10,940	$ 11,269
Income tax expense	(2,239)	(2,329)	(2,402)	(2,474)	(2,549)	(2,626)	(2,704)
Net Income	$ 7,366	$ 7,374	$ 7,607	$ 7,835	$ 8,071	$ 8,315	$ 8,564
Net income attributable to noncontrolling interests	(15)	(32)	(32)	(32)	(32)	(32)	(32)
Net Income attributable to common shareholders	$ 7,351	$ 7,342	$ 7,575	$ 7,803	$ 8,039	$ 8,283	$ 8,532
Other comprehensive income items	(4,412)	0	0	0	0	0	0
Comprehensive Income	$ 2,954	$ 7,342	$ 7,575	$ 7,803	$ 8,039	$ 8,283	$ 8,532

Source for Actuals: The Coca-Cola Company, Form 10-K for the Fiscal Year Ended December 31, 2015.

Exhibit 12.15

The Coca-Cola Company
Balance Sheets for 2015 (Actual) and Year +1 through Year +6 (Projected)
(amounts in millions; allow for rounding) (Problem 12.16)

	Actual			Forecasts			
	2015	Year +1	Year +2	Year +3	Year +4	Year +5	Year +6
ASSETS							
Cash and cash equivalents	$ 7,309	$ 7,500	$ 7,725	$ 7,956	$ 8,195	$ 8,441	$ 8,694
Marketable securities	12,591	12,969	13,358	13,759	14,171	14,596	15,034
Accounts and notes receivable—net	3,941	4,375	4,506	4,641	4,780	4,924	5,072
Inventories	2,902	3,110	3,204	3,300	3,399	3,501	3,606
Prepaid expenses and other current assets	2,752	2,835	2,920	3,007	3,097	3,190	3,286
Assets held for sale	3,900	0	0	0	0	0	0
Current Assets	**$ 33,395**	**$ 30,788**	**$ 31,712**	**$ 32,663**	**$ 33,643**	**$ 34,652**	**$ 35,692**
Investments in noncontrolled affiliates	12,318	12,934	13,581	14,260	14,973	15,721	16,193
Property, plant, and equipment—at cost	22,354	25,091	27,887	30,767	33,734	36,789	37,893
Accumulated depreciation	(9,783)	(11,612)	(13,644)	(15,887)	(18,345)	(21,026)	(21,657)
Amortizable intangible assets (net)	854	705	592	532	475	423	436
Goodwill	11,289	11,628	11,977	12,336	12,706	13,087	13,480
Other nonamortizable intangible assets	11,989	12,349	12,719	13,101	13,494	13,899	14,315
Other assets	7,677	7,907	8,145	8,389	8,641	8,900	9,167
Total Assets	**$ 90,093**	**$ 89,790**	**$ 92,968**	**$ 96,161**	**$ 99,320**	**$102,445**	**$105,518**
LIABILITIES							
Accounts payable	$ 2,795	$ 1,998	$ 2,044	$ 2,106	$ 2,169	$ 2,234	$ 2,301
Current accrued expenses	6,865	7,071	7,283	7,502	7,727	7,958	8,197
Notes payable and short-term debt	13,129	13,216	13,816	14,429	15,047	15,671	16,141
Current maturities of long-term debt	2,677	2,695	2,817	2,942	3,068	3,195	3,291
Income taxes payable	331	449	465	481	497	512	528
Liabilities held for sale	1,133	0	0	0	0	0	0
Current Liabilities	**$ 26,930**	**$ 25,429**	**$ 26,425**	**$ 27,459**	**$ 28,507**	**$ 29,571**	**$ 30,458**

(Continued)

Exhibit 12.15 (Continued)

	Actual	Forecasts					
	2015	Year +1	Year +2	Year +3	Year +4	Year +5	Year +6
Long-term debt obligations	28,407	28,596	29,894	31,219	32,557	33,907	34,924
Long-term accrued liabilities	4,301	4,430	4,563	4,700	4,841	4,986	5,136
Deferred tax liabilities—noncurrent	4,691	4,675	4,841	5,007	5,171	5,334	5,494
Total Liabilities	**$ 64,329**	**$ 63,130**	**$ 65,723**	**$ 68,385**	**$ 71,076**	**$ 73,798**	**$ 76,012**
SHAREHOLDERS' EQUITY							
Common stock + Additional paid-in capital	15,776	15,723	16,279	16,839	17,392	17,939	18,477
Retained earnings	65,018	66,854	68,747	70,698	72,708	74,779	77,022
Accum. other comprehensive income (loss)	(10,174)	(10,174)	(10,174)	(10,174)	(10,174)	(10,174)	(10,174)
Treasury stock	(45,066)	(45,952)	(47,818)	(49,797)	(51,892)	(54,107)	(56,035)
Total Common Shareholders' Equity	**$ 25,554**	**$ 26,451**	**$ 27,035**	**$ 27,566**	**$ 28,033**	**$ 28,437**	**$ 29,290**
Noncontrolling interests	210	210	210	210	210	210	216
Total Equity	**$ 25,764**	**$ 26,661**	**$ 27,245**	**$ 27,776**	**$ 28,243**	**$ 28,647**	**$ 29,506**
Total Liabilities and Equities	**$ 90,093**	**$ 89,790**	**$ 92,968**	**$ 96,161**	**$ 99,320**	**$102,445**	**$105,518**

Source for Actuals: The Coca-Cola Company, Form 10-K for the Fiscal Year Ended December 31, 2015.

Exhibit 12.16

The Coca-Cola Company

Projected Implied Statements of Cash Flows for Year +1 through Year +6
(amounts in millions; allow for rounding) (Problem 12.16)

	Forecasts					
	Year +1	Year +2	Year +3	Year +4	Year +5	Year +6
Net Income	$ 7,374	$ 7,607	$ 7,835	$ 8,071	$ 8,315	$ 8,564
Add back depreciation expense (net)	1,829	2,032	2,242	2,459	2,681	631
<Increase> Decrease in receivables—net	(434)	(131)	(135)	(139)	(143)	(148)
<Increase> Decrease in inventories	(208)	(93)	(96)	(99)	(102)	(105)
<Increase> Decrease in prepaid expenses	(83)	(85)	(88)	(90)	(93)	(96)
<Increase> Decrease in other current assets	3,900	0	0	0	0	0
Increase <Decrease> in accounts payable—trade	(797)	47	61	63	65	67
Increase <Decrease> in current accrued liabilities	206	212	218	225	232	239
Increase <Decrease> in income taxes payable	118	16	16	16	16	15
Increase <Decrease> in other current liabilities	(1,133)	0	0	0	0	0
Net change in deferred tax assets and liabilities	(16)	165	166	164	163	160
Increase <Decrease> in long-term accrued liabilities	129	133	137	141	145	150
Net Cash Flows from Operations	$10,885	$ 9,903	$10,357	$10,810	$11,278	$ 9,477
<Increase> Decrease in property, plant, & equip. at cost	(2,737)	(2,796)	(2,880)	(2,966)	(3,055)	(1,104)
<Increase> Decrease in marketable securities	(378)	(389)	(401)	(413)	(425)	(438)
<Increase> Decrease in investment securities	(616)	(647)	(679)	(713)	(749)	(472)
<Increase> Decrease in amortizable intangible assets (net)	149	113	60	57	52	(13)
<Increase> Decrease in goodwill and nonamort. intangibles	(698)	(719)	(741)	(763)	(786)	(810)
<Increase> Decrease in other noncurrent assets	(230)	(237)	(244)	(252)	(259)	(267)
Net Cash Flows from Investing Activities	$ (4,511)	$(4,675)	$ (4,885)	$ (5,050)	$ (5,222)	$(3,102)
Increase <Decrease> in short-term debt	105	722	738	744	751	566
Increase <Decrease> in long-term debt	189	1,298	1,326	1,338	1,350	1,017
Increase <Decrease> in common stock + paid-in capital	(53)	556	559	553	547	538
Increase <Decrease> in accumulated OCI	0	0	0	0	0	0
Increase <Decrease> in treasury stock	(886)	(1,866)	(1,979)	(2,096)	(2,214)	(1,928)
Dividends	(5,507)	(5,682)	(5,853)	(6,029)	(6,212)	(6,288)
Increase <Decrease> in noncontrolling interests	(32)	(32)	(32)	(32)	(32)	(26)
Net Cash Flows from Financing Activities	$ (6,183)	$(5,002)	$ (5,241)	$ (5,522)	$ (5,810)	$(6,122)
Net Change in Cash	$ 191	$ 225	$ 232	$ 239	$ 246	$ 253

equity beta for Coca-Cola at the end of 2015 is 0.75. Assume that the risk-free interest rate is 3.0% and the market risk premium is 6.0%. Coca-Cola has 4,324 million shares outstanding at the end of 2015, when the share price was $42.96.

REQUIRED

Part I—Computing Coca-Cola's Share Value Using Free Cash Flows to Common Equity Shareholders

   a. Use the CAPM to compute the required rate of return on common equity capital for Coca-Cola.

   b. Derive the projected free cash flows for common equity shareholders for Coca-Cola for Years +1 through +6 based on the projected financial statements. Assume that Coca-Cola's changes in cash each year are necessary for operating liquidity purposes. The financial statement forecasts for Year +6 assume that Coca-Cola will experience a steady-state long-run growth rate of 3% in Year +6 and beyond.

   c. Using the required rate of return on common equity from Requirement a as a discount rate, compute the sum of the present value of free cash flows for common equity shareholders for Coca-Cola for Years +1 through +5.

   d. Using the required rate of return on common equity from Requirement a as a discount rate and the long-run growth rate from Requirement b, compute the continuing value of Coca-Cola as of the start of Year +6 based on Coca-Cola's continuing free cash flows for common equity shareholders in Year +6 and beyond. After computing continuing value as of the start of Year +6, discount it to present value at the start of Year +1.

   e. Compute the value of a share of Coca-Cola common stock.

      (1) Compute the total sum of the present value of all future free cash flows for equity shareholders (from Requirements c and d).

      (2) Adjust the total sum of the present value using the midyear discounting adjustment factor.

      (3) Compute the per-share value estimate.

Part II—Computing Coca-Cola's Share Value Using Free Cash Flows to All Debt and Equity Stakeholders

   f. Compute the weighted-average cost of capital for Coca-Cola as of the start of Year +1. At the end of fiscal 2015, Coca-Cola had $44,213 million in outstanding interest-bearing debt on the balance sheet and no preferred stock. Assume that the balance sheet value of Coca-Cola's debt is approximately equal to the market value of the debt. The forecasts assume that Coca-Cola will face an interest rate of 2.0% on debt capital and that Coca-Cola's average tax rate will be 24% (based on the past five-year average effective tax rate). Coca-Cola also had noncontrolling interests of $210 million at that time. The forecasts assume a 15.0% cost of capital for noncontrolling interests. (For our forecasts, we assume noncontrolling interests receive dividends equal to the required rate of return each year.)

   g. Beginning with projected net cash flows from operations, derive the projected free cash flows for all debt and equity stakeholders for Coca-Cola for Years +1 through +6 based on the projected financial statements. Assume that the change in cash each year is related to operating liquidity needs.

   h. Using the weighted-average cost of capital from Requirement f as a discount rate, compute the sum of the present value of free cash flows for all debt and equity stakeholders for Coca-Cola for Years +1 through +5.

i. Using the weighted-average cost of capital from Requirement f as a discount rate and the long-run growth rate from Requirement b, compute the continuing value of Coca-Cola as of the start of Year +6 based on Coca-Cola's continuing free cash flows for all debt and equity stakeholders in Year +6 and beyond. After computing continuing value as of the start of Year +6, discount it to present value as of the start of Year +1.

j. Compute the value of a share of Coca-Cola common stock.
    (1) Compute the total value of Coca-Cola's net operating assets using the total sum of the present value of free cash flows for all debt and equity stakeholders (from Requirements h and i).
    (2) Subtract the value of outstanding debt to obtain the value of equity.
    (3) Adjust the present value of equity using the midyear discounting adjustment factor.
    (4) Compute the per-share value estimate of Coca-Cola's common equity shares.

Note: Do not be alarmed if your share value estimate from Requirement e is slightly different from your share value estimate from Requirement j. The weighted-average cost of capital computation in Requirement f used the weight of equity based on the market price of Coca-Cola's stock at the end of fiscal 2015. The share value estimates from Requirements e and j likely differ from the market price, so the weights used to compute the weighted-average cost of capital are not internally consistent with the estimated share values.

Part III—Sensitivity Analysis and Recommendation

k. Using the free cash flows to common equity shareholders, recompute the value of Coca-Cola shares under two alternative scenarios.
    Scenario 1: Assume that Coca-Cola's long-run growth will be 2%, not 3% as before, and assume that Coca-Cola's required rate of return on equity is 1% higher than the rate you computed for Requirement a.
    Scenario 2: Assume that Coca-Cola's long-run growth will be 4%, not 3% as before, and assume that Coca-Cola's required rate of return on equity is 1% lower than the rate you computed in Requirement a. To quantify the sensitivity of your share value estimate for Coca-Cola to these variations in growth and discount rates, compare (in percentage terms) your value estimates under these two scenarios with your value estimate from Requirement e.

l. Using these data at the end of 2015, what reasonable range of share values would you have expected for Coca-Cola common stock? At that time, what was the market price for Coca-Cola shares relative to this range? What investment strategy (buy, hold, or sell) would you have recommended?

INTEGRATIVE CASE 12.1

LO 12-2, LO 12-3
LO 12-4, LO 12-5

Walmart: Free-Cash-Flows Valuation of Walmart's Common Equity

In Integrative Case 10.1, we projected financial statements for **Walmart Stores, Inc.** (Walmart), for Years +1 through +5. In this portion of the Walmart Integrative Case, we use the projected financial statements from Integrative Case 10.1 and apply the techniques learned in this chapter to compute Walmart's required rate of return on equity and share value based on the free-cash-flows valuation models. We also compare our value estimate to Walmart's share price at the time of the case development to provide an investment recommendation.

The data in Exhibits 12.17 to 12.19 (pages 812–814) include the actual amounts for fiscal 2015 and the projected amounts for Year +1 to Year +5 for the income statements, balance sheets, and statements of cash flows for Walmart (in millions). These forecast amounts assume Walmart will use implied dividends as the financial flexible account to balance the balance sheet. The market equity beta for Walmart at the end of 2015 was 1.00. Assume that the risk-free interest rate was 3.0% and the market risk premium was 6.0%. Walmart had 3,162 million shares outstanding at the end of fiscal 2015, and a share price of $67.50.

REQUIRED

Part I—Computing Walmart's Share Value Using Free Cash Flows to Common Equity Shareholders

a. Use the CAPM to compute the required rate of return on common equity capital for Walmart.

b. Beginning with projected net cash flows from operations, derive the projected free cash flows for common equity shareholders for Walmart for Years +1 through +5 based on the projected financial statements. Assume that Walmart uses cash for operating liquidity purposes.

Exhibit 12.17

Walmart Stores, Inc.
Income Statements for 2015 (Actual) and Year +1 through Year +5 (Projected)
(amounts in millions; allow for rounding)

	Actual	Forecasts				
	2015	Year +1	Year +2	Year +3	Year +4	Year +5
Revenues	$ 482,130	$ 491,773	$ 501,608	$ 511,640	$ 521,873	$ 532,310
Cost of goods sold	(360,984)	(368,829)	(376,206)	(383,730)	(391,405)	(399,233)
Gross Profit	$ 121,146	$ 122,943	$ 125,402	$ 127,910	$ 130,468	$ 133,078
Selling, general, and administrative expenses	(97,041)	(98,355)	(100,322)	(102,328)	(104,375)	(106,462)
Interest income	81	131	131	131	131	131
Interest expense	(2,548)	(2,539)	(2,615)	(2,694)	(2,775)	(2,858)
Income before Tax	$ 21,638	$ 22,180	$ 22,596	$ 23,019	$ 23,450	$ 23,888
Income tax expense	(6,558)	(7,098)	(7,231)	(7,366)	(7,504)	(7,644)
Net Income	$ 15,080	$ 15,082	$ 15,365	$ 15,653	$ 15,946	$ 16,244
Net income attributable to noncontrolling interests	(386)	(386)	(386)	(386)	(386)	(386)
Net Income attributable to common shareholders	$ 14,694	$ 14,696	$ 14,979	$ 15,267	$ 15,560	$ 15,858
Other comprehensive income items	(4,429)	0	0	0	0	0
Comprehensive Income	$ 10,651	$ 14,696	$ 14,979	$ 15,267	$ 15,560	$ 15,858

Source for Actual 2015: Walmart Stores, Inc., Form 10-K for the Fiscal Year Ended January 31, 2015.

Exhibit 12.18

Walmart Stores, Inc.
Balance Sheets for 2015 (Actual) and Year +1 through Year +5 (Projected)
(amounts in millions; allow for rounding)

	Actual	Forecasts				
	2015	Year +1	Year +2	Year +3	Year +4	Year +5
ASSETS						
Cash and cash equivalents	$ 8,705	$ 8,705	$ 8,705	$ 8,705	$ 8,705	$ 8,705
Accounts and notes receivable—net	5,624	5,736	5,851	5,968	6,088	6,209
Inventories	44,469	45,472	46,382	47,309	48,255	49,220
Prepaid expenses and other current assets	1,441	1,470	1,499	1,529	1,560	1,591
Current Assets	**$ 60,239**	**$ 61,383**	**$ 62,437**	**$ 63,512**	**$ 64,608**	**$ 65,726**
Property, plant, and equipment— at cost	188,054	198,054	208,054	218,054	228,054	238,054
Accumulated depreciation	(71,538)	(81,441)	(91,843)	(102,746)	(114,149)	(126,052)
Goodwill	16,695	17,029	17,369	17,717	18,071	18,433
Other assets	6,131	6,254	6,379	6,506	6,636	6,769
Total Assets	**$199,581**	**$201,279**	**$202,396**	**$203,043**	**$203,221**	**$202,930**
LIABILITIES						
Accounts payable	$ 38,487	$ 38,503	$ 39,261	$ 40,047	$ 40,847	$ 41,664
Current accrued expenses	19,607	19,999	20,399	20,807	21,223	21,648
Notes payable and short-term debt	2,708	2,789	2,873	2,959	3,048	3,139
Current maturities of long-term debt	3,296	3,395	3,497	3,602	3,710	3,821
Income taxes payable	521	531	542	553	564	575
Current Liabilities	**$ 64,619**	**$ 65,218**	**$ 66,572**	**$ 67,967**	**$ 69,392**	**$ 70,848**
Long-term debt obligations	44,030	45,351	46,711	48,113	49,556	51,043
Deferred tax liabilities—noncurrent	7,321	7,467	7,617	7,769	7,924	8,083
Total Liabilities	**$115,970**	**$118,036**	**$120,900**	**$123,849**	**$126,873**	**$129,973**
SHAREHOLDERS' EQUITY						
Common stock + Additional paid-in capital	$ 2,122	$ 2,186	$ 2,251	$ 2,319	$ 2,388	$ 2,460
Retained earnings	90,021	89,589	87,776	85,407	82,491	79,029
Accum. other comprehensive income (loss)	(11,597)	(11,597)	(11,597)	(11,597)	(11,597)	(11,597)
Total Common Shareholders' Equity	**$ 80,546**	**$ 80,178**	**$ 78,430**	**$ 76,129**	**$ 73,283**	**$ 69,892**
Noncontrolling interests	3,065	3,065	3,065	3,065	3,065	3,065
Total Equity	**$ 83,611**	**$ 83,243**	**$ 81,495**	**$ 79,194**	**$ 76,348**	**$ 72,957**
Total Liabilities and Equities	**$199,581**	**$201,279**	**$202,396**	**$203,043**	**$203,221**	**$202,930**

Source for Actual 2015: Walmart Stores, Inc., Form 10-K for the Fiscal Year Ended January 31, 2015.

Exhibit 12.19

Walmart Stores, Inc.
Projected Implied Statements of Cash Flows for Year +1 through Year +5
(amounts in millions; allow for rounding)

			Forecasts		
	Year +1	Year +2	Year +3	Year +4	Year +5
Net Income	$ 15,082	$ 15,365	$ 15,653	$ 15,946	$ 16,244
Add back depreciation expense (net)	9,903	10,403	10,903	11,403	11,903
<Increase> Decrease in receivables—net	(112)	(115)	(117)	(119)	(122)
<Increase> Decrease in inventories	(1,003)	(909)	(928)	(946)	(965)
<Increase> Decrease in prepaid expenses	(29)	(29)	(30)	(31)	(31)
Increase <Decrease> in accounts payable—trade	16	758	785	801	817
Increase <Decrease> in current accrued liabilities	392	400	408	416	424
Increase <Decrease> in income taxes payable	10	11	11	11	11
Net change in deferred tax assets and liabilities	146	149	152	155	158
Net Cash Flows from Operations	**$ 24,406**	**$ 26,032**	**$ 26,837**	**$ 27,636**	**$ 28,440**
<Increase> Decrease in property, plant, & equip. at cost	(10,000)	(10,000)	(10,000)	(10,000)	(10,000)
<Increase> Decrease in goodwill and nonamort. intangibles	(334)	(341)	(347)	(354)	(361)
<Increase> Decrease in other noncurrent assets	(123)	(125)	(128)	(130)	(133)
Net Cash Flows from Investing Activities	**$(10,457)**	**$(10,466)**	**$(10,475)**	**$(10,484)**	**$(10,494)**
Increase <Decrease> in short-term debt	180	186	191	197	203
Increase <Decrease> in long-term debt	1,321	1,361	1,401	1,443	1,487
Increase <Decrease> in common stock + paid-in capital	64	66	68	70	72
Increase <Decrease> in accumulated OCI	0	0	0	0	0
Dividends	(15,128)	(16,792)	(17,636)	(18,475)	(19,321)
Increase <Decrease> in noncontrolling interests	(386)	(386)	(386)	(386)	(386)
Net Cash Flows from Financing Activities	**$(13,949)**	**$(15,567)**	**$(16,362)**	**$(17,151)**	**$(17,946)**
Net Change in Cash	**$ —**	**$ —**	**$ —**	**$ —**	**$ —**

c. Project the continuing free cash flow for common equity shareholders in Year +6. Assume that the steady-state, long-run growth rate will be 3% in Year +6 and beyond. Project that the Year +5 income statement and balance sheet amounts will grow by 3% in Year +6; then derive the projected statement of cash flows for Year +6. Derive the projected free cash flow for common equity shareholders in Year +6 from the projected statement of cash flows for Year +6.

d. Using the required rate of return on common equity from Requirement a as the discount rate, compute the sum of the present value of free cash flows for common equity shareholders for Walmart for Years +1 through +5.

e. Using the required rate of return on common equity from Requirement a as a discount rate and the long-run growth rate from Requirement c, compute the continuing value of Walmart as of the start of Year +6 based on Walmart's continuing free cash flows for common equity shareholders in Year +6 and beyond. After computing continuing value as of the start of Year +6, discount it to present value at the start of Year +1.

f. Compute the value of a share of Walmart common stock.
   (1) Compute the total sum of the present value of all future free cash flows for equity shareholders (from Requirements d and e).
   (2) Adjust the total sum of the present value using the midyear discounting adjustment factor.
   (3) Compute the per-share value estimate.

Note: If you worked Integrative Case 11.1 in Chapter 11 and computed Walmart's share value using the dividends valuation approach, compare your value estimate from that problem with the value estimate you obtain here. They should be the same.

Part II—Computing Walmart's Share Value Using Free Cash Flows to All Debt and Equity Stakeholders

g. Compute the weighted-average cost of capital for Walmart as of the start of Year +1. At the end of fiscal 2015, Walmart had $50,034 million in outstanding interest-bearing debt on the balance sheet and no preferred stock. Assume that the balance sheet value of Walmart's debt is approximately equal to the market value of the debt. Assume that at the start of Year +1, Walmart will incur interest expense of 5.0% on debt capital and that Walmart's average tax rate will be 32.0%. In addition, at the end of fiscal 2015, Walmart had noncontrolling interests of $3,065 million, with an expected return of 12.6%. (For our forecasts, we assume noncontrolling interests receive dividends equal to the required rate of return each year.)

h. Beginning with projected net cash flows from operations, derive the projected free cash flows for all debt and equity stakeholders for Walmart for Years +1 through +5 based on the projected financial statements.

i. Project the continuing free cash flows for all debt and equity stakeholders in Year +6. Use the projected financial statements for Year +6 from Requirement c to derive the projected free cash flow for all debt and equity stakeholders in Year +6.

j. Using the weighted-average cost of capital from Requirement g as a discount rate, compute the sum of the present value of free cash flows for all debt and equity stakeholders for Walmart for Years +1 through +5.

k. Using the weighted-average cost of capital from Requirement g as a discount rate and the long-run growth rate from Requirement c, compute the continuing value of Walmart as of the start of Year +6 based on Walmart's continuing free cash flows for all debt and equity stakeholders in Year +6 and beyond. After computing continuing value as of the start of Year +6, discount it to present value as of the start of Year +1.

l. Compute the value of a share of Walmart common stock.
(1) Compute the total value of Walmart's net operating assets using the total sum of the present value of free cash flows for all debt and equity stakeholders (from Requirements j and k).
(2) Subtract the value of outstanding debt to obtain the value of equity.
(3) Adjust the present value of equity using the midyear discounting adjustment factor.
(4) Compute the per-share value estimate of Walmart's common equity shares.

Note: Do not be alarmed if your share value estimate from Requirement f is slightly different from your share value estimate from Requirement l. The weighted-average cost of capital computation in Requirement g used the weight of equity based on the market price of Walmart's stock at the end of fiscal 2015. The share value estimates from Requirements f and l likely differ from the market price, so the weights used to compute the weighted-average cost of capital are not internally consistent with the estimated share values.

Part III—Sensitivity Analysis and Recommendation

m. Using the free cash flows to common equity shareholders, recompute the value of Walmart shares under two alternative scenarios.
Scenario 1: Assume that Walmart's long-run growth will be 2%, not 3% as before, and assume that Walmart's required rate of return on equity is one percentage point higher than the rate you computed using the CAPM in Requirement a.
Scenario 2: Assume that Walmart's long-run growth will be 4%, not 3% as before, and assume that Walmart's required rate of return on equity is one percentage point lower than the rate you computed using the CAPM in Requirement a. To quantify the sensitivity of your share value estimate for Walmart to these variations in growth and discount rates, compare (in percentage terms) your value estimates under these two scenarios with your value estimate from Requirement f.

n. Using these data at the end of fiscal 2015, what reasonable range of share values would you have expected for Walmart common stock? At that time, what was the market price for Walmart shares relative to this range? What would you have recommended?

CASE 12.2

Holmes Corporation

LBO Valuation

Holmes Corporation is a leading designer and manufacturer of material handling and processing equipment for heavy industry in the United States and abroad. Its sales have more than doubled, and its earnings have increased more than sixfold in the past five years. In material handling, Holmes is a major producer of electric overhead and gantry cranes, ranging from 5 tons in capacity to 600-ton giants, the latter used primarily in nuclear and conventional power-generating plants. It also builds underhung cranes and monorail systems for general industrial use carrying loads up to 40 tons, railcar movers, railroad and mass transit shop maintenance equipment, and a broad line of advanced package conveyors. Holmes is a world leader in evaporation and crystallization systems and furnishes dryers, heat exchangers, and filters to complete its line of chemical-processing equipment sold internationally to the chemical, fertilizer, food, drug, and paper industries. For the metallurgical industry, it designs and manufactures electric arc and induction furnaces, cupolas, ladles, and hot metal distribution equipment.

The information below and on the following pages appears in the Year 15 annual report of Holmes Corporation.

Highlights

	Year 15	Year 14
Net sales	$102,698,836	$109,372,718
Net earnings	$6,601,908	$6,583,360
Net earnings per share	$3.62*	$3.61*
Cash dividends paid	$2,241,892	$1,426,502
Cash dividends per share	$1.22*	$0.78*
Shareholders' equity	$29,333,803	$24,659,214
Shareholders' equity per share	$16.07*	$13.51*
Working capital	$23,100,863	$19,029,626
Orders received	95,436,103	80,707,576
Unfilled orders at end of period	77,455,900	84,718,633
Average number of common shares outstanding during period	1,824,853	1,824,754

*All per-share amounts throughout the case have already been adjusted for June, Year 15, and June, Year 14, 5-for-4 stock distributions.

Net Sales, Net Earnings, and Net Earnings per Share by Quarter

	Year 15			Year 14		
	Net Sales	Net Earnings	Per Share	Net Sales	Net Earnings	Per Share
First quarter	$ 25,931,457	$1,602,837	$0.88	$ 21,768,077	$1,126,470	$0.62
Second quarter	24,390,079	1,727,112	0.95	28,514,298	1,716,910	0.94
Third quarter	25,327,226	1,505,118	0.82	28,798,564	1,510,958	0.82
Fourth quarter	27,050,074	1,766,841	0.97	30,291,779	2,229,022	1.23
	$102,698,836	$6,601,908	$3.62	$109,372,718	$6,583,360	$3.61

Common Stock Prices and Cash Dividends Paid per Common Share by Quarter

	Year 15			Year 14		
	Stock Prices		Cash Dividends per Share	Stock Prices		Cash Dividends per Share
	High	Low		High	Low	
First quarter	$22½	$18½	$0.26	$11¼	$ 9½	$0.16
Second quarter	25¼	19½	0.26	12⅜	8⅞	0.16
Third quarter	26¼	19¾	0.325	15⅞	11⅝	0.20
Fourth quarter	28⅛	23¼	0.375	20⅞	15⅞	0.26
			$1.22			$0.78

Management's Report to Shareholders

Year 15 was a pleasant surprise for all of us at Holmes Corporation. When the year started, it looked as though Year 15 would be a good year but not up to the record performance of Year 14. However, due to the excellent performance of our employees and the benefit of a favorable acquisition, Year 15 produced both record earnings and the largest cash dividend outlay in the company's 93-year history.

There is no doubt that some of the attractive orders received in late Year 12 and early Year 13 contributed to Year 15 profit. But of major significance was our organization's favorable response to several new management policies instituted to emphasize higher corporate profitability. Year 15 showed a net profit on net sales of 6.4%, which not only exceeded the 6.0% of last year but represents the highest net margin in several decades.

Net sales for the year were $102,698,836, down 6% from the $109,372,718 of a year ago but still the second largest volume in our history. Net earnings, however, set a new record at $6,601,908, or $3.62 per common share, which slightly exceeded the $6,583,360, or $3.61 per common share, earned last year.

Cash dividends of $2,241,892 paid in Year 15 were 57% above the $1,426,502 paid a year ago. The record total resulted from your Board's approval of two increases during the year. When we implemented the 5-for-4 stock distribution in June, Year 15, we maintained the quarterly dividend rate of $0.325 on the increased number of shares for the January payment. Then, in December, Year 15, we increased the quarterly rate to $0.375 per share.

Year 15 certainly was not the most exuberant year in the capital equipment markets. Fortunately, our heavy involvement in ecology improvement, power generation, and international markets continued to serve us well, with the result that new orders of $95,436,103 were 18% over the $80,707,576 of Year 14.

Economists have predicted a substantial capital spending upturn for well over a year, but, so far, our customers have displayed stubborn reluctance to place new orders amid the uncertainty concerning the economy. Confidence is the answer. As soon as potential buyers can see clearly the future direction of the economy, we expect the unleashing of a large latent demand for capital goods, producing a much-expanded market for Holmes' products.

Fortunately, the accelerating pace of international markets continues to yield new business. Year 15 was an excellent year on the international front as our foreign customers continue to recognize our technological leadership in several product lines. Net sales of Holmes products shipped overseas and fees from foreign licensees amounted to $30,495,041, which represents a 31% increase over the $23,351,980 of a year ago.

Management fully recognizes and intends to take maximum advantage of our technological leadership in foreign lands. The latest manifestation of this policy was the acquisition of a controlling interest in Société Française Holmes Fermont, our Swenson process equipment licensee located in Paris. Holmes and a partner started this firm 14 years ago as a sales and engineering organization to function in the Common Market. The company currently operates in the same mode. It owns no physical manufacturing assets, subcontracting all production. Its markets have expanded to include Spain and the East European countries.

Holmes Fermont is experiencing strong demand in Europe. For example, in early May, a $5.5 million order for a large potash crystallization system was received from a French engineering company representing a Russian client. Management estimates that Holmes Fermont will contribute approximately $6 to $8 million of net sales in Year 16.

Holmes' other wholly owned subsidiaries—Holmes Equipment Limited in Canada; Ermanco Incorporated in Michigan; and Holmes International, Inc., our FSC (Foreign Sales Corporation)—again contributed substantially to the success of Year 15. Holmes Equipment Limited registered its second-best year. However, capital equipment markets in Canada have virtually come to a standstill in the past two quarters. Ermanco achieved the best year in its history, while Holmes International, Inc., had a truly exceptional year because of the very high level of activity in our international markets.

The financial condition of the company showed further improvement and is now unusually strong as a result of very stringent financial controls. Working capital increased to $23,100,863 from $19,029,626, a 21% improvement. Inventories decreased 6% from $18,559,231 to $17,491,741. The company currently has no long-term or short-term debt, and has considerable cash in short-term instruments. Much of our cash position, however, results from customers' advance payments, which we will absorb as we make shipments on the contracts. Shareholders' equity increased 19% to $29,393,803 from $24,690,214 a year ago.

Plant equipment expenditures for the year were $1,172,057, down 18% from $1,426,347 of Year 14. Several appropriations approved during the year did not require expenditures because of delayed deliveries beyond Year 15. The major emphasis again was on our continuing program of improving capacity and efficiency through the purchase of numerically controlled machine tools. We expanded the Ermanco plant by 50%, but since this is a leasehold arrangement, we made only minor direct investments. We also improved the Canadian operation by adding more manufacturing space and installing energy-saving insulation.

Labor relations were excellent throughout the year. The Harvey plant continues to be nonunion. We negotiated a new labor contract at the Canadian plant, which extends to March 1, Year 17. The Pioneer Division in Alabama has a labor contract that does not expire until April, Year 16. While the union contract at Ermanco expired June 1, Year 15, work continues while negotiation proceeds on a new contract. We anticipate no difficulty in reaching a new agreement.

We exerted considerable effort during the year to improve Holmes' image in the investment community. Management held several informative meetings with security analyst groups to enhance the awareness of our activities and corporate performance.

The outlook for Year 16, while generally favorable, depends in part on the course of capital spending over the next several months. If the spending rate accelerates, the quickening pace of new orders, coupled with present backlogs, will provide the conditions for another fine year. On the other hand, if general industry continues the reluctant spending pattern of the last two years, Year 16 could be a year of maintaining market positions while awaiting better market conditions. Management takes an optimistic view and thus looks for a successful Year 16.

The achievement of record earnings and the highest profit margin in decades demonstrates the capability and the dedication of our employees. Management is most grateful for their efforts throughout the excellent year.

T. R. Varnum
President
March 15, Year 16

T. L. Fuller
Chairman

Review of Operations

Year 15 was a very active year although the pace was not at the hectic tempo of Year 14. It was a year that showed continued strong demand in some product areas but a dampened rate in others. The product areas that had some special economic circumstances enhancing demand fared well. For example, the continuing effort toward ecological improvement fostered excellent activity in Swenson processing equipment. Likewise, the energy concern and the need for more electrical power generation capacity boded well for large overhead cranes. On the other hand, Holmes' products that relate to general industry and depend on the overall capital spending rate for new equipment experienced lesser demand, resulting in lower new orders and reduced backlogs. The affected products were small cranes, underhung cranes, railcar movers, and metallurgical equipment.

Year 15 was the first full year of operations under some major policy changes instituted to improve Holmes' profitability. The two primary revisions were the restructuring of our marketing effort along product division lines and the conversion of the product division incentive plans to a profit-based formula. The corporate organization adapted extremely well to the new policies. The improved profit margin in Year 15, in substantial part, was a result of the changes.

International activity increased markedly during the year. Surging foreign business and the expressed objective to capitalize on Holmes' technological leadership overseas resulted in the elevation of Mr. R. E. Foster to officer status as Vice President–International. The year involved heavy commitments of the product division staffs, engineering groups, and manufacturing organization to such important contracts as the $14 million Swenson order for Poland, the $8 million Swenson project for Mexico, the $2 million crane order for Venezuela, and several millions of dollars of railcar movers for all areas of the world.

The acquisition of control and commencement of operating responsibility of Société Française Holmes Fermont, the Swenson licensee in Paris, was a major milestone in our international strategy. This organization has the potential of becoming a very substantial contributor in the years immediately ahead. Its long-range market opportunities in Europe and Asia are excellent.

Material Handling Products

Material handling equipment activities portrayed conflicting trends. During the year, when total backlog decreased, the crane division backlog increased. This was a result of several multimillion-dollar contracts for power plant cranes. The small crane market, on the other hand, experienced depressed conditions during most of the year as general industry withheld appropriations for new plant and equipment. The underhung crane market experienced similar conditions. However, as congressional attitudes and policies on investment unfold, we expect capital spending to show a substantial upturn.

The Transportation Equipment Division secured the second order for orbital service bridges, a new product for the containment vessels of nuclear power plants. This design is unique and allows considerable cost savings in erecting and maintaining containment shells.

The Ermanco Conveyor Division completed its best year with the growing acceptance of the unique XenoROL design. We expanded the Grand Haven plant by 50% to effect further cost reduction and new concepts of marketing.

The railcar moving line continued to produce more business from international markets. We installed the new 11TM unit in six domestic locations, a product showing signs of exceptional performance. We shipped the first foreign 11TM machine to Sweden.

Processing Equipment Products

Processing equipment again accounted for slightly more than half of the year's business.

Swenson activity reached an all-time high level with much of the division's effort going into international projects. The large foreign orders required considerable additional work to cover the necessary documentation, metrification when required, and general liaison.

We engaged in considerably more subcontracting during the year to accommodate one-piece shipment of the huge vessels pioneered by Swenson to effect greater equipment economies. The division continued to expand the use of computerization for design work and contract administration. We developed more capability during the year to handle the many additional tasks associated with turnkey projects. Swenson's research and development efforts accelerated in search of better technology and new products. We conducted pilot plant test work at our facilities and in the field to convert several sales prospects into new contracts.

The metallurgical business proceeded at a slower pace in Year 15. However, with construction activity showing early signs of improvement and automotive and farm machinery manufacturers increasing their operating rates, we see intensified interest in metallurgical equipment.

Financial Statements

The financial statements of Holmes Corporation and related notes appear in Exhibits 12.20 to 12.22 (pages 821–823). Exhibit 12.23 (page 824) presents five-year summary operating information for Holmes.

Exhibit 12.20

**Holmes Corporation
Balance Sheet
(amounts in thousands)
(Case 12.2)**

	Year 10	Year 11	Year 12	Year 13	Year 14	Year 15
Cash	$ 955	$ 962	$ 865	$ 1,247	$ 1,540	$ 3,857
Marketable securities	0	0	0	0	0	2,990
Accounts/Notes receivable	6,545	7,295	9,718	13,307	18,759	14,303
Inventories	7,298	8,685	12,797	20,426	18,559	17,492
Current Assets	$14,798	$16,942	$23,380	$34,980	$38,858	$38,642
Investments	0	0	0	0	0	422
Property, plant, and equipment	12,216	12,445	13,126	13,792	14,903	15,876
Less: Accumulated depreciation	(7,846)	(8,236)	(8,558)	(8,988)	(9,258)	(9,703)
Other assets	470	420	400	299	343	276
Total Assets	$19,638	$21,571	$28,348	$40,083	$44,846	$45,513
Accounts payable—trade	$ 2,894	$ 4,122	$ 6,496	$ 7,889	$ 6,779	$ 4,400
Notes payable—nontrade	0	0	700	3,500	0	0
Current portion long-term debt	170	170	170	170	170	0
Other current liabilities	550	1,022	3,888	8,624	12,879	11,142
Current Liabilities	$ 3,614	$ 5,314	$11,254	$20,183	$19,828	$15,542
Long-term debt	680	510	340	170	0	0
Deferred tax	0	0	0	216	328	577
Other noncurrent liabilities	0	0	0	0	0	0
Total Liabilities	$ 4,294	$ 5,824	$11,594	$20,569	$20,156	$16,119
Common stock	$ 2,927	$ 2,927	$ 2,927	$ 5,855	$ 7,303	$ 9,214
Additional paid-in capital	5,075	5,075	5,075	5,075	5,061	5,286
Retained earnings	7,342	7,772	8,774	8,599	12,297	14,834
Accumulated other comprehensive income	0	0	5	12	29	60
Treasury stock	0	(27)	(27)	(27)	0	0
Total Shareholders' Equity	$15,344	$15,747	$16,754	$19,514	$24,690	$29,394
Total Liabilities and Shareholders' Equity	$19,638	$21,571	$28,348	$40,083	$44,846	$45,513

Exhibit 12.21

Holmes Corporation
Income Statement
(amounts in thousands)
(Case 12.2)

	Year 11	Year 12	Year 13	Year 14	Year 15
Sales	$ 41,428	$ 53,541	$ 76,328	$109,373	$102,699
Other revenues and gains	0	41	0	0	211
Cost of goods sold	(33,269)	(43,142)	(60,000)	(85,364)	(80,260)
Selling and administrative expense	(6,175)	(7,215)	(9,325)	(13,416)	(12,090)
Other expenses and losses	(2)	0	(11)	(31)	(1)
Operating Income	$ 1,982	$ 3,225	$ 6,992	$ 10,562	$ 10,559
Interest expense	(43)	(21)	(284)	(276)	(13)
Income tax expense	(894)	(1,471)	(2,992)	(3,703)	(3,944)
Net Income	$ 1,045	$ 1,733	$ 3,716	$ 6,583	$ 6,602

Exhibit 12.22

Holmes Corporation
Statement of Cash Flows
(amounts in thousands)
(Case 12.2)

	Year 11	Year 12	Year 13	Year 14	Year 15
OPERATIONS					
Net income	$ 1,045	$ 1,733	$ 3,716	$ 6,583	$ 6,602
Depreciation and amortization	491	490	513	586	643
Other addbacks	20	25	243	151	299
Other subtractions	0	0	0	0	(97)
(Increase) Decrease in receivables	(750)	(2,424)	(3,589)	(5,452)	4,456
(Increase) Decrease in inventories	(1,387)	(4,111)	(7,629)	1,867	1,068
Increase (Decrease) in accounts payable—trade	1,228	2,374	1,393	1,496	(2,608)
Increase (Decrease) in other current liabilities	473	2,865	4,737	1,649	(1,509)
Cash Flow from Operations	$ 1,120	$ 952	$ (616)	$ 6,880	$ 8,854
INVESTING					
Fixed assets acquired, net	$ (347)	$ (849)	$ (749)	$(1,426)	$(1,172)
Investments acquired	0	0	0	0	(3,306)
Other investing transactions	45	0	81	(64)	39
Cash Flow from Investing	$ (302)	$ (849)	$ (668)	$(1,490)	$(4,439)

(Continued)

Exhibit 12.22 (Continued)					
FINANCING					
Increase in short-term borrowing	$ 0	$ 700	$ 2,800	$ 0	$ 0
Decrease in short-term borrowing	0	0	0	(3,500)	0
Increase in long-term borrowing	0	0	0	0	0
Decrease in long-term borrowing	(170)	(170)	(170)	(170)	(170)
Issue of capital stock	0	0	0	0	315
Acquisition of capital stock	(27)	0	0	0	0
Dividends	(614)	(730)	(964)	(1,427)	(2,243)
Other financing transactions	0	0	0	0	0
Cash Flow from Financing	$ (811)	$ (200)	$ 1,666	$(5,097)	$(2,098)
Net Change in Cash	$ 7	$ (97)	$ 382	$ 293	$ 2,317
Cash, beginning of year	955	962	865	1,247	1,540
Cash, End of Year	$ 962	$ 865	$ 1,247	$ 1,540	$ 3,857

Notes to Consolidated Financial Statements Year 15 and Year 14

Note A—Summary of Significant Accounting Policies. Significant accounting policies consistently applied appear below to assist the reader in reviewing the company's consolidated financial statements contained in this report.

Consolidation—The consolidated financial statements include the accounts of the company and its subsidiaries after eliminating all intercompany transactions and balances.

Inventories—Inventories generally appear at the lower of cost or market, with cost determined principally on a first-in, first-out method.

Property, plant, and equipment—Property, plant, and equipment appear at acquisition cost minus accumulated depreciation. When the company retires or disposes of properties, it removes the related costs and accumulated depreciation from the respective accounts and credits, or charges any gain or loss to earnings. The company expenses maintenance and repairs as incurred. It capitalizes major betterments and renewals. Depreciation results from applying the straight-line method over the estimated useful lives of the assets as follows:

Buildings	30 to 45 years
Machinery and equipment	4 to 20 years
Furniture and fixtures	10 years

Intangible assets—The company has amortized the unallocated excess of cost of a subsidiary over net assets acquired (that is, goodwill) over a 17-year period. Beginning in Year 16, U.S. GAAP no longer requires amortization of goodwill.

Research and development costs—The company charges research and development costs to operations as incurred ($479,410 in Year 15 and $467,733 in Year 14).

Pension plans—The company and its subsidiaries have noncontributory pension plans covering substantially all of their employees. The company's policy is to fund accrued pension costs as determined by independent actuaries. Pension costs amounted to $471,826 in Year 15 and $366,802 in Year 14.

Exhibit 12.23

Holmes Corporation
Five-Year Summary of Operations
(Case 12.2)

	Year 11	Year 12	Year 13	Year 14	Year 15
Orders received	$55,454,188	$89,466,793	$121,445,731	$ 80,707,576	$ 95,436,103
Net sales	41,427,702	53,540,699	76,327,664	109,372,718	102,698,836
Backlog of unfilled orders	32,339,614	68,265,708	113,383,775	84,718,633	77,455,900
Earnings before taxes on income	$ 1,939,414	$ 3,203,835	$ 6,708,072	$ 10,285,943	$ 10,546,213
Taxes on income	894,257	1,470,489	2,991,947	3,702,583	3,944,305
Net earnings	1,045,157	1,733,346	3,716,125	6,583,360	6,601,908
Net property, plant, and equipment	$ 4,209,396	$ 4,568,372	$ 4,803,978	$ 5,644,590	$ 6,173,416
Net additions to property	346,549	848,685	748,791	1,426,347	1,172,057
Depreciation and amortization	491,217	490,133	513,402	585,735	643,231
Cash dividends paid	$ 614,378	$ 730,254	$ 963,935	$ 1,426,502	$ 2,242,892
Working capital	11,627,875	12,126,491	14,796,931	19,029,626	23,100,463
Shareholders' equity	15,747,116	15,754,166	19,514,358	24,690,214	29,393,803
Earnings per common share (1)	$ 0.57	$ 0.96	$ 2.03	$ 3.61	$ 3.62
Dividends per common share (1)	0.34	0.40	0.53	0.78	1.22
Book value per common share (1)	8.62	9.18	10.68	13.51	16.07
Number of shareholders, December 31	1,787	1,792	1,834	2,024	2,157
Number of employees, December 31	1,303	1,425	1,551	1,550	1,549
Shares of common outstanding, December 31 (1)	1,827,515	1,824,941	1,824,754	1,824,754	1,824,853
Percent of net sales by product line:					
Material Handling Equipment	63.0%	54.4%	51.3%	43.6%	46.1%
Processing Equipment	37.0%	45.6%	48.7%	56.4%	53.9%

Revenue recognition—The company generally recognizes income on a percentage-of-completion basis. It records advance payments as received and reports them as a deduction from billings when earned. The company recognizes royalties, included in net sales, as income when received. Royalties totaled $656,043 in Year 15 and $723,930 in Year 14.

Income taxes—The company provides no income taxes on unremitted earnings of foreign subsidiaries because it anticipates no significant tax liabilities should foreign units remit such earnings. The company makes provision for deferred income taxes applicable to timing differences between financial statement and income tax accounting, principally on the earnings of a foreign sales subsidiary, which existing statutes defer in part from current taxation.

Note B—Foreign Operations. The consolidated financial statements in Year 15 include net assets of $2,120,648 ($1,847,534 in Year 14), undistributed earnings of $2,061,441 ($1,808,752 in Year 14), sales of $7,287,566 ($8,603,225 in Year 14), and net income of $454,999 ($641,454 in Year 14) applicable to the Canadian subsidiary. The company translates balance sheet accounts of the Canadian subsidiary into U.S. dollars at the exchange rates at the end of the year and translates operating results at the average of exchange rates for the year.

Note C—Inventories. Inventories used in determining cost of sales appear below.

	Year 15	Year 14	Year 13
Raw materials and supplies	$ 8,889,147	$ 9,720,581	$ 8,900,911
Work in process	8,602,594	8,838,650	11,524,805
Total inventories	$17,491,741	$18,559,231	$20,425,716

Note D—Short-Term Borrowing. The company has short-term credit agreements that principally provide for loans of 90-day periods at varying interest rates. There were no borrowings in Year 15. In Year 14, the maximum borrowing at the end of any calendar month was $4,500,000 and the approximate average loan balance and weighted-average interest rate, computed by using the days outstanding method, were $3,435,000 and 7.6%. There were no restrictions upon the company during the period of the loans and no compensating bank balance arrangements required by the lending institutions.

Note E—Income Taxes. Provision for income taxes consists of:

	Year 15	Year 14
Current		
Federal	$2,931,152	$2,633,663
State	466,113	483,240
Canadian	260,306	472,450
Total current provision	$3,657,571	$3,589,353
Deferred		
Federal	$ 263,797	$ 91,524
Canadian	22,937	21,706
Total deferred	$ 286,734	$ 113,230
Total provision for income taxes	$3,944,305	$3,702,583

Reconciliation of the total provision for income taxes to the current federal statutory rate of 35% is as follows:

	Year 15		Year 14	
	Amount	%	Amount	%
Tax at statutory rate	$3,691,000	35.0%	$3,600,100	35.0%
State taxes, net of U.S. tax credit	302,973	2.9	314,106	3.1
All other items	(49,668)	(0.5)	(211,623)	(2.1)
Total provision for income taxes	$3,944,305	37.4%	$3,702,583	36.0%

Note F—Pensions. The components of pension expense appear below.

	Year 15	Year 14
Service cost	$ 476,490	$ 429,700
Interest cost	567,159	446,605
Expected return on pension investments	(558,373)	(494,083)
Amortization of actuarial gains and losses	(13,450)	(15,420)
Pension expense	$ 471,826	$ 366,802

The funded status of the pension plan appears below.

	December 31:	
	Year 15	Year 14
Accumulated benefit obligation	$5,763,450	$5,325,291
Effect of salary increases	1,031,970	976,480
Projected benefit obligation	$6,795,420	$6,301,771
Pension fund assets	6,247,940	5,583,730
Excess pension obligation	$ 547,480	$ 718,041

Assumptions used in accounting for pensions appear below.

	Year 15	Year 14
Expected return on pension assets	10%	10%
Discount rate for projected benefit obligation	9%	8%
Salary increases	5%	5%

Note G—Common Stock. As of March 20, Year 15, the company increased the authorized number of shares of common stock from 1,800,000 shares to 5,000,000 shares. On December 29, Year 15, the company increased its equity interest (from 45% to 85%) in Société Française Holmes Fermont, a French affiliate, in exchange for 18,040 of its common shares in a transaction accounted for as a purchase. The company credited the excess of the fair value ($224,373) of the company's shares issued over their par value ($90,200) to additional contributed capital. The excess of the purchase cost over the underlying value of the assets acquired was insignificant.

The company made a 25% common stock distribution on June 15, Year 14, and on June 19, Year 15, resulting in increases of 291,915 shares in Year 14 and 364,433 shares in Year 15, respectively. We capitalized the par value of these additional shares by a transfer of $1,457,575 in Year 14 and $1,822,165 in Year 15 from retained earnings to the common stock account. In Year 14 and Year 15, we paid cash of $2,611 and $15,340, respectively, in lieu of fractional share interests.

In addition, the company retired 2,570 shares of treasury stock in June, Year 14. The earnings and dividends per share for Year 14 and Year 15 in the accompanying consolidated financial statements reflect the 25% stock distributions.

Note H—Contingent Liabilities. The company has certain contingent liabilities with respect to litigation and claims arising in the ordinary course of business. The company cannot determine the ultimate disposition of these contingent liabilities but, in the opinion of management, they will not result in any material effect upon the company's consolidated financial position or results of operations.

Note I—Quarterly Data (unaudited). Quarterly sales, gross profit, net earnings, and earnings per share for Year 15 appear below (first quarter results restated for 25% stock distribution):

	Net Sales	Gross Profit	Net Earnings	Earnings per Share
First	$ 25,931,457	$ 5,606,013	$1,602,837	$0.88
Second	24,390,079	6,148,725	1,727,112	0.95
Third	25,327,226	5,706,407	1,505,118	0.82
Fourth	27,050,074	4,977,774	1,766,841	0.97
Year	$102,698,836	$22,438,919	$6,601,908	$3.62

Auditors' Report

Board of Directors and Stockholders

Holmes Corporation

We have examined the consolidated balance sheets of Holmes Corporation and Subsidiaries as of December 31, Year 15 and Year 14, and the related consolidated statements of earnings and cash flows for the years then ended. Our examination was made in accordance with generally accepted auditing standards and accordingly included such tests of the accounting records and such other auditing procedures as we considered necessary in the circumstances. In our opinion, the financial statements referred to above present fairly the consolidated financial position of Holmes Corporation and Subsidiaries at December 31, Year 15 and Year 14, and the consolidated results of their operations and changes in cash flows for the years then ended, in conformity with generally accepted accounting principles applied on a consistent basis.

SBW, LLP
Chicago, Illinois
March 15, Year 16

REQUIRED

A group of Holmes' top management is interested in acquiring Holmes in an LBO.
  a. Briefly describe the factors that make Holmes an attractive and, conversely, an unattractive LBO candidate.
  b. (This question requires coverage of Chapter 10.) Prepare projected financial statements for Holmes Corporation for Year 16 through Year 20 excluding all financing. That is, project the amount of operating income after taxes, assets, and cash flows from operating and investing activities. State the underlying assumptions made.

c. Ascertain the value of Holmes' common shareholders' equity using the present value of its future cash flows valuation approach. Assume a risk-free interest rate of 4.2% and a market premium of 5.0%. Note that information in Requirement e may be helpful in this valuation. Assume the following financing structure for the LBO:

Type	Proportion	Interest Rate	Term
Term debt	50%	8%	7-year amortization[a]
Subordinated debt	25	12%	10-year amortization
Shareholders' equity	25		
	100%		

[a]Holmes must repay principal and interest in equal annual payments.

d. (This question requires coverage of Chapter 13.) Ascertain the value of Holmes' common shareholders' equity using the residual income approach.

e. (This question requires coverage of Chapter 14.) Ascertain the value of Holmes' common shareholders' equity using the residual ROCE model and the price-to-earnings ratio and the market value to book value of comparable companies' approaches. Selected data for similar companies for Year 15 appear in the following table (amounts in millions):

Industry:	Agee Robotics Conveyor Systems	GI Handling Systems Conveyor Systems	LJG Industries Cranes	Gelas Corp. Industrial Furnaces
Sales	$4,214	$28,998	$123,034	$75,830
Net income	$ 309	$ 2,020	$ 9,872	$ 5,117
Assets	$2,634	$15,197	$ 72,518	$41,665
Long-term debt	$ 736	$ 5,098	$ 23,745	$ 8,869
Common shareholders' equity	$1,551	$ 7,473	$ 38,939	$26,884
Market value of common equity	$6,915	$20,000	$102,667	$41,962
Market beta	1.12	0.88	0.99	0.93

f. Would you attempt to acquire Holmes Corporation after completing the analyses in Requirements a–e? If not, how would you change the analyses to make this an attractive LBO?

Valuation: Earnings-Based Approach

LEARNING OBJECTIVES

LO 13-1 Describe earnings-based valuation and explain the different valuation implications of earnings, dividends, and free cash flows.

LO 13-2 Explain the conceptual and practical strengths and weaknesses of earnings-based valuation.

LO 13-3 Demonstrate a conceptual understanding of residual income valuation by
   a. utilizing book value of common shareholders' equity, comprehensive income, dividends, and clean surplus accounting.
   b. measuring required income.
   c. measuring residual income.
   d. determining the value of common equity.

LO 13-4 Demonstrate a conceptual understanding of residual income valuation with finite forecast horizons and continuing value computations.

LO 13-5 Demonstrate a practical understanding of residual income valuation by applying the approach to value the common shares of Starbucks.

LO 13-6 Assess the sensitivity of share value estimates to key parameters, such as discount rates and expected long-term growth rates.

LO 13-7 Describe four important implementation issues for the residual income valuation approach.

LO 13-8 Identify potential causes of errors if the residual income, free cash flows, and dividend valuations do not produce identical value estimates.

Chapter Overview

Reported earnings numbers are the single most widely followed measures of firms' financial performance. Accounting standard setters (most notably the FASB and IASB), along with the accounting profession and the community of financial statement users, have designed the accrual accounting process to measure earnings as the bottom line of the firm's profitability each period. As a result, firms' reported earnings numbers are the primary value-relevant measures of performance used in the capital markets for share pricing and capital allocation.

Because of the demand in the capital markets for earnings information, firms usually release quarterly and annual earnings to the public as soon as accountants have prepared and verified the numbers, often weeks *before* the firms actually release their detailed quarterly and annual income statements, balance sheets, statements of cash flows, and notes. Firms commonly announce earnings during conference calls and press conferences attended by investors, analysts, managers, board members, and the financial press. Analysts spend a lot of effort building forecasts of firms' upcoming quarterly and annual earnings, and then revising those earnings forecasts when new information arrives. Sell-side analysts disseminate their earnings forecasts to interested investors, brokers, and fund managers. Commercial firms such as **Thomson Reuters** and **Zacks Investment Research** have built businesses on compiling and distributing data on analysts' earnings forecasts. Recently, **Estimize** has developed crowd-sourced earnings forecasts using a platform for collecting earnings forecasts from thousands of professional and amateur analysts and investors. The financial media (broadcast, print, and online) provide daily coverage of firms' earnings announcements. For example, *The Wall Street Journal* provides daily reports of firms' earnings announcements as well as daily data on each firm's stock price and price-earnings ratio.

Firms' share prices usually react quickly to earnings announcements. The direction and magnitude of the market's reaction depends on the direction and magnitude of the earnings news relative to investors' expectations. Firms that announce earnings beating the market's expectations ("good news") often experience significant jumps in share price during the day of and the days immediately following the announcement. Likewise, firms that announce earnings falling short of the market's expectations ("bad news") often experience immediate sharp declines in share price. As noted in several prior chapters, the seminal Ball and Brown (1968) study and many other research studies, including the Nichols and Wahlen (2004) study described in Chapter 1, have shown that firms' stock returns are highly positively correlated with changes in firms' earnings.[1]

Because earnings provide such important information to investors and other external stakeholders, earnings also play key roles in decisions that firms make with regard to internal capital allocation. New project proposals within firms are often evaluated based on the effects they will have on reported earnings. In addition, corporate boards commonly reward or punish managers with compensation and bonus plans that depend on whether firm performance meets (or fails to meet) certain earnings targets. The following observations highlight the important roles of earnings:

- Earnings is the primary measure of firm performance produced by the accrual accounting system.
- Earnings have a strong impact on the pricing of shares in the capital markets.
- Corporate managers and boards of directors use earnings for internal capital allocation and for aligning the incentives of managers with shareholders.
- Because of the tremendous demand for earnings information among stakeholders, the financial press and the analyst community devote a lot of time and attention to reporting, analyzing, and forecasting earnings.

Therefore, it is logical that accounting earnings also provide a basis for valuation. This chapter describes the conceptual and practical strengths and weaknesses of the *residual income valuation model*. This model bases valuation on expected future earnings and the book value of common shareholders' equity.

This chapter takes three important steps and addresses some key questions:

1. ***Theoretical and Conceptual Foundations:*** What theories and concepts support residual income valuation? How do we measure residual income? What economic construct does it represent?

---

[1]Ray Ball and Philip Brown, "An Evaluation of Accounting Income Numbers," *Journal of Accounting Research* (Autumn 1968), pp. 159–178; D. Craig Nichols and James Wahlen, "How Do Earnings Numbers Relate to Stock Returns? A Review of Classic Accounting Research with Updated Evidence," *Accounting Horizons* (December 2004), pp. 263–286.

2. ***Practical Applications:*** How do we estimate share value using residual income valuation methods? What implementation issues do we need to understand?
3. ***Linking Residual Income Valuation to Dividends Valuation and Free Cash Flow Valuation:*** Conceptually and practically, why is the residual income valuation approach equivalent to the valuation approaches that rely on dividends and free cash flows?

In addition to explaining the rationale and the conceptual and theoretical foundations, we demonstrate the residual income model by applying it to value the common shareholders' equity of **Starbucks**. As we apply the model, we describe the key measurement and implementation issues. Finally, we demonstrate the internal consistency among dividends-based, free-cash-flows-based, and earnings-based valuation models, and how to identify and correct errors if the three models seem to disagree.

The residual income valuation model provides a powerful approach that is equivalent to the classical dividends-based valuation approach presented in Chapter 11 and to the free-cash-flows-based valuation approach presented in Chapter 12. The residual income valuation model also forms the basis for the market-based valuation multiples described in Chapter 14, including the market-to-book ratio and the price-earnings ratio.

Rationale for Earnings-Based Valuation

LO 13-1

Describe earnings-based valuation and explain the different valuation implications of earnings, dividends, and free cash flows.

Economic theory indicates that the value of any resource equals the present value of the expected future payoffs from the resource discounted at a rate that reflects the risk inherent in those expected future payoffs. Like Chapters 11 and 12, we start with the same general model for the present value of a security (denoted as V_0, with present value denoted as of time $t=0$) with an expected life of n future periods, as follows:[2]

$$V_0 = \sum_{t=1}^{n} \frac{\text{Expected Future Payoffs}_t}{(1 + \text{Discount Rate})^t}$$

Chapter 11 demonstrates that the value of a share of common equity should equal the present value of the *expected future dividends* the shareholder will receive. Dividends are the fundamental value-relevant payoffs because they represent the distribution of wealth from the firm to the shareholders. Thus, to value a firm's shares using dividends, you discount to present value the expected future dividends over the life of the firm (or the expected length of time the share will be held), including the final liquidating dividend. This is a *wealth distribution* approach to valuation.

Chapter 12 demonstrates that the value of a share of common equity also should equal the present value of the *expected future free cash flows* that the firm will generate, which it will ultimately distribute in dividends to the common equity shareholders. The free-cash-flows-based valuation approach focuses on the amounts and timing of the cash flows the firm will generate. Thus, to value a firm's shares using free cash flows, you discount to present value the expected future free cash flows for common equity shareholders over the life of the firm (or the expected length of time the share will be held), including the final liquidating cash flows. This is a *distributable wealth* approach to valuation.

The residual income valuation approach presented in this chapter parallels the dividends-based and the free-cash-flows-based valuation approaches, except that it uses

[2]This chapter uses the same notation as in prior chapters, where t refers to accounting periods. The valuation process determines an estimate of firm value, denoted as V_0, in present value as of today, when $t=0$. The period $t=1$ refers to the first accounting period being discounted to present value. Period $t=n$ is the period of the expected final, or liquidating, payoff.

a different measure of payoffs. The residual income valuation approach uses book value of common shareholders' equity and *expected future earnings* to determine the value-relevant expected future payoffs to the investor (the numerator of the general valuation model above) in place of future dividends or future free cash flows.

The rationale for the role of book value of shareholders' equity is straightforward: it is the starting point for valuation because it is the balance sheet measure of the common equity shareholders' claim on the net assets of the firm. The rationale for using expected future earnings as a basis for valuation is also straightforward: future earnings measure the net profits or losses the firm will generate for the shareholders. Over the remaining life of the firm, earnings measure the total wealth to be created by the firm for the shareholders. Rather than focusing on wealth distribution through dividend payments or focusing on distributable wealth through free cash flow realizations, residual income valuation focuses on earnings as a periodic measure of shareholder *wealth creation.* In Chapter 11, Exhibit 11.2 showed the differences in valuation approach perspectives: dividends are measures of *wealth distribution*; free cash flows are measures of *distributable wealth*; and earnings are measures of *wealth creation.*

Using professionally established principles, accrual accounting measures income for the equity shareholders based on the net amount of economic resources generated and consumed by the firm each period. Accrual accounting also produces periodic statements of financial position—balance sheets—that measure and report the economic resources (assets) that the firm controls and uses to produce expected future economic benefits and the claims on those resources by creditors and investors (liabilities and equities). Cash inflows and outflows do not necessarily reflect economic value generated or consumed each period. Thus, to measure a firm's economic performance and position in a given period, it makes sense to measure the following:

- *Revenues earned* during that period, not just the amounts of cash collected from customers that period.
- Expenses for *resources consumed* in that period, not just the amounts of cash paid out of the firm that period.
- Allocated portions of *long-lived resources* used during that period, such as periodic depreciation of a building each year of its useful life (rather than recognize the full cost of the building in the year the firm pays for it and ignore the consumption of the building in all other years the firm uses it).
- *Obligations incurred* in the course of doing business this period that will require payments in future periods, such as pension and other retirement benefits, warranties, taxes, and others (rather than ignore those commitments and measure their effects only when the firm pays cash).

Earnings under accrual accounting are far from perfect performance measures. However, recall the discussion in Chapter 2 that described how accounting standards are intended to optimize the relevance and reliability of asset and liability valuation and income recognition for investors and other stakeholders. By virtue of accounting standards, accounting earnings will more closely match the firm's underlying economic performance—the wealth created or destroyed for equity shareholders—in a given period than will the net cash inflows or outflows of that period.

Over the life of a firm, the cash flows invested in the firm by the shareholders plus the wealth created by the firm for the shareholders will determine the cash flows that will be distributable to shareholders. Thus, valuation of shareholders' equity in a firm using the capital invested in the firm plus earnings over the life of the firm (residual income valuation) is equivalent to valuation using free cash flows over the life of the firm. And both are equivalent to valuation using dividends over the life of the firm.[3]

Earnings-Based Valuation: Practical Advantages and Concerns

LO 13-2

Explain the conceptual and practical strengths and weaknesses of earnings-based valuation.

Although earnings, cash flows, and dividends are equally valid bases for valuation, several practical advantages and concerns arise with earnings-based valuation. The first advantage is that the emphasis placed on earnings by firms and the capital markets makes earnings a logical starting point for valuation. Analysts, investors, the capital markets, managers, boards, and the financial press focus on earnings forecasts and earnings reports rather than free cash flows. It is rare to find a firm holding press conferences to announce free cash flows. Analysts publish earnings forecasts far more frequently than they publish free cash flow forecasts. Boards of directors and compensation committees typically do not base managers' bonus plans on achieving free cash flow targets; instead, those compensation plans most often rely on earnings-based measures of performance. This is because earnings align more closely than dividends or free cash flows with the focus of the capital markets and corporate managers and boards of directors on firm performance.[4]

Another practical advantage arises because it is more direct and efficient for you to go straight from forecasting earnings to valuation rather than take a detour to free cash flows. As Exhibit 13.1 depicts, estimating firm value using free cash flows adds an intermediary step to the valuation process. As demonstrated in Chapter 12, free cash flows valuation requires that we initially forecast future income statements and balance sheets. Then we derive the implied forecasts of cash flows from those projected income statements and balance sheets by making adjustments for the accruals in earnings, for the cash flows invested in working capital, and for capital expenditures. We use these cash flows to determine free cash flows, which we then use to compute value. Under the residual income approach, we begin valuation immediately after we forecast future income statements and balance sheets. The two valuations should ultimately be the same, but the free-cash-flows-based approach requires more computations, which requires more time and effort, and increases the potential for error.[5]

---

[3]Over sufficiently long time periods, net income equals free cash flows to common equity. The effect of year-end accruals to convert cash flows to net income lessens as the measurement period lengthens. The correlation between firms' earnings and stock returns increases as the earnings measurement interval increases. See Peter D. Easton, Trevor S. Harris, and James A. Ohlson, "Aggregate Accounting Earnings Can Explain Most of Security Returns," *Journal of Accounting and Economics* (1992), pp. 119–142.

[4]Numerous research studies show that earnings and cash flows cumulated over long periods of time are highly positively correlated with stock returns over long periods (for example, five-year periods), but that for shorter periods (say, one year), earnings show a stronger association with stock returns than cash flows. See Patricia M. Dechow, "Accounting Earnings and Cash Flows as Measures of Firm Performance: The Role of Accounting Accruals," *Journal of Accounting and Economics* (1994), pp. 3–42; C. S. Cheng, Chao-Shin Liu, and Thomas F. Schaefer, "Earnings Permanence and the Incremental Information Content of Cash Flow from Operations," *Journal of Accounting Research* (Spring 1996), pp. 173–181; Richard G. Sloan, "Do Stock Prices Fully Reflect Information in Accruals and Cash Flows about Future Earnings," *The Accounting Review* (July 1996), pp. 289–315.

[5]Of course, another way to save steps would be simply to forecast future cash flows from the past time series of statements of cash flows, skipping accrual accounting altogether. However, compelling evidence reveals that forecasting models using earnings and accruals are much more accurate than forecasting models using only cash flows. See Kenneth S. Lorek and G. Lee Willinger, "A Multivariate Time-Series Prediction Model for Cash Flow Data," *The Accounting Review* 71 (January 1996), pp. 81–102.

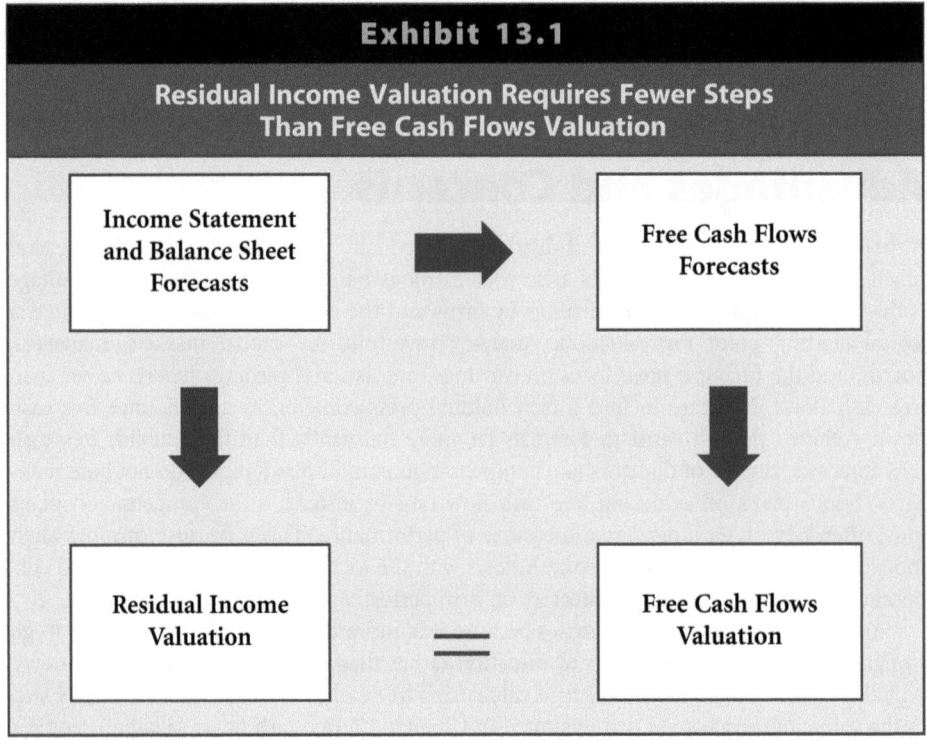

Exhibit 13.1

Residual Income Valuation Requires Fewer Steps Than Free Cash Flows Valuation

Economists sometimes express concern that earnings are not useful for valuation because earnings are not as reliable or as meaningful as cash or dividends for valuing investments. When considering earnings, economists sometimes point out that firms pay dividends in cash, not earnings; investors can spend cash but cannot spend earnings for future consumption. This concern is alleviated in valuation, however, by the fact that the differences between earnings, cash flows, and dividends are merely timing differences: earnings measure when the firm creates wealth, whereas free cash flows measure when the firm realizes wealth in cash, and dividends measure when the firm distributes wealth to shareholders. Over the life of the firm, the present values of future earnings, cash flows, and dividends will be equal.

Some economists worry that accrual accounting earnings reflect accounting methods that no longer capture changes in underlying economic values (for example, depreciation or amortization expenses based on outdated acquisition costs of assets, expenses for research and development that have turned out to be successful, or advertising expenses that have created economically valuable brand equity). Value measurement based on expected earnings over the remaining life of the firm alleviates this concern. Over time, the accrual accounting process will ultimately self-correct measurement errors in accounting numbers. For example, if fixed asset book values are "too high" or "too low" for a company, over time (and it usually does not take long), accrual accounting will naturally correct these measurement errors because the subsequent depreciation expenses will be "too high" or "too low" accordingly. If the current balance sheet does not recognize intellectual capital value created by successful research and development or brand value created by successful marketing, accrual accounting will correct itself over time as the firm generates higher earnings from this intangible capital.[6]

Some economists voice concerns that earnings can be subject to manipulation by a firm. To be sure, we must always be alert to the possibility that earnings management (or worse, fraudulent reporting) may occur in some periods by some firms. But this is more of a concern about whether past and current earnings are useful measures to assess profitability and risk, and therefore lead to reliable forecasts of any of the payoffs, whether they be earnings, dividends, or free cash flows. As long as we perform accounting analysis carefully to ensure that we do not naively forecast future earnings based on past managed earnings, residual earnings valuation will be unaffected. The same can be said for dividends-based and free-cash-flows-based valuations. Earlier chapters devoted considerable attention to helping you understand how to assess firms' accounting quality and how to build reliable forecasts.

Ironically, firms can easily manage cash flows in a given period, but economists rarely voice this concern. Free cash flows each period depend on cash inflows and outflows, which the firm can manipulate by accelerating or delaying certain cash payments or cash collections in that particular period. Over the remaining life of the firm, which is the focus of your forecasting and valuation, the firm's earnings and cash flows will be determined ultimately by the success of the firm's operating, investing, and financing activities, not by the manipulation of earnings or cash flows.

Theoretical and Conceptual Foundations for Residual Income Valuation

LO 13-3

Demonstrate a conceptual understanding of residual income valuation by
a. utilizing book value of common shareholders' equity, comprehensive income, dividends, and clean surplus accounting.
b. measuring required income.
c. measuring residual income.
d. determining the value of common equity.

The foundation for residual income valuation is the classical dividends-based valuation model from Chapter 11, in which the value of common shareholders' equity is the present value of all future dividends to shareholders over the remaining life of the firm. As described in Chapter 11, we define *dividends* to be all-inclusive measures of the cash flows between the firm and the common equity shareholders, encompassing cash flows from the firm to shareholders through periodic dividend payments, stock buybacks, and the firm's liquidating dividend, as well as cash flows from the shareholders to the firm when the firm issues shares (negative dividends).

Chapter 11 demonstrates how to estimate an appropriate discount rate (using the CAPM) based on the rate of return (denoted as R_E) that the capital markets expect for the risk associated with common equity capital in a firm. That chapter also demonstrates the dividends-based valuation approach, which measures the value of common shareholders' equity (denoted as V_0) as the present value of all expected future dividends (denoted as D_t) with the following general model:

$$V_0 = \sum_{t=1}^{\infty} \frac{D_t}{(1 + R_E)^t} = \frac{D_1}{(1 + R_E)^1} + \frac{D_2}{(1 + R_E)^2} + \frac{D_3}{(1 + R_E)^3} + \cdots$$

[6]Indeed, when an analyst asserts that a firm's current balance sheet accounting numbers do not reflect underlying economic values, how does the analyst know that? When an analyst asserts that a firm's balance sheet omits a valuable intangible asset in the form of intellectual property or brand equity, how has the analyst assessed the amount of the omission? Usually, analysts base assertions like these on their assessments that the firm will generate future profits from operations that utilize these economic assets. Earnings-based valuation captures exactly the same idea. Firm value depends on expected future earnings over the remaining life of the firm. In fact, if the balance sheet fully reflected economic values, there would be little need for debt and equity analysts. The value of the firm would be given by total assets on the balance sheet, the value of debt would be given by total debt on the balance sheet, and the value of equity would be given by total shareholders' equity on the balance sheet.

Analysts and investors commonly find it desirable to identify and forecast economic variables that determine the firm's future dividends and can therefore substitute for dividends to yield an equivalent valuation. Accounting numbers provide a solution. Accounting for the book value of common shareholders' equity (denoted as BV) in a firm can be expressed as follows:

$$BV_t = BV_{t-1} + CI_t - D_t$$

In this expression, book value of common shareholders' equity at the end of Year t (BV_t) is equal to book value at the end of Year $t-1$ (BV_{t-1}) plus comprehensive income for Year t (CI_t) minus the all-inclusive dividends during Year t (D_t). As in the dividends valuation approach described in Chapter 11, we assume that accounting for net income and book value of shareholders' equity follows *clean surplus accounting*. Clean surplus accounting simply means that comprehensive income includes all of the recognized elements of income of the firm for common equity shareholders (that is, net income plus all of the other comprehensive income items) and dividends include all direct capital transactions between the firm and the common equity shareholders (that is, periodic dividend payments, share repurchases, and share issues).

We can rearrange the accounting equation for the book value of common equity to isolate dividends as follows:

$$D_t = CI_t + BV_{t-1} - BV_t$$

In this expression, dividends equal comprehensive income plus the change in book value from direct capital transactions with common shareholders.

Example: Clean Surplus

To illustrate clean surplus accounting, suppose a firm had shareholders' equity on the balance sheet at a book value of $5,000 at the end of Year $t-1$. Suppose during Year t, the firm earns comprehensive income of $600, pays dividends to shareholders of $360, issues new stock to raise $250 of capital, and uses $50 to repurchase common shares. The book value of shareholders' equity at the end of Year t is as follows:

$$
\begin{aligned}
BV_t &= BV_{t-1} + CI_t - D_t \\
&= \$5{,}000 + \$600 - (\$360 - \$250 + \$50) \\
&= \$5{,}000 + \$600 - \$160 \\
&= \$5{,}440
\end{aligned}
$$

In this example, all-inclusive dividends (D_t) in Year t amount to $160. Using the expression for dividends shows that

$$D_t = CI_t + BV_{t-1} - BV_t = \$600 + \$5{,}000 - \$5{,}440 = \$160$$

We can therefore substitute comprehensive income plus the change in the book value of common shareholders' equity into the classical dividends valuation model, as follows:

$$V_0 = \sum_{t=1}^{\infty} \frac{D_t}{(1+R_E)^t} = \sum_{t=1}^{\infty} \frac{CI_t + BV_{t-1} - BV_t}{(1-R_E)^t}$$

$$= \frac{CI_1 + BV_0 - BV_1}{(1+R_E)^1} + \frac{CI_2 + BV_1 - BV_2}{(1+R_E)^2} + \frac{CI_3 + BV_2 - BV_3}{(1+R_E)^3} + \cdots$$

Algebraically, the present value of BV_{t-1} can be rewritten as follows:

$$\frac{BV_{t-1}}{(1+R_E)^t} = \frac{BV_{t-1}}{(1+R_E)^{t-1}} - \frac{R_E \times BV_{t-1}}{(1+R_E)^t}$$

We substitute the right side expression for the present value of BV_{t-1} into the equation, rearrange terms, and simplify to obtain the following expression for the *residual income valuation model*:

$$V_0 = BV_0 + \sum_{t=1}^{\infty} \frac{CI_t - (R_E \times BV_{t-1})}{(1+R_E)^t}$$

$$= BV_0 + \frac{CI_1 - (R_E \times BV_0)}{(1+R_E)^1} + \frac{CI_2 - (R_E \times BV_1)}{(1+R_E)^2} + \frac{CI_3 - (R_E \times BV_2)}{(1+R_E)^3} + \cdots$$

The *residual income valuation model* above is therefore a valuation model for common shareholders' equity that is algebraically equivalent to dividends-based valuation, yet relies on earnings and book values.[7]

Intuition for Residual Income Measurement and Valuation

The intuition for the residual income valuation model is straightforward. The value of common shareholders' equity is composed of two parts: the book value of common equity plus the present value of all expected future residual income. The first component, book value of common shareholders' equity (BV_0), captures the value of shareholders' equity already invested in the firm. The second component is the present value of all expected future *residual income*, which is the amount by which expected future earnings exceed the required income each period. The *required income* (also known as *normal earnings*) of the firm equals the product of the required rate of return on common equity capital times the book value of common equity capital at the beginning of each period. We compute required income for period t as $R_E \times BV_{t-1}$. Required income reflects the earnings the firm must generate in period t simply to provide a return to common equity that is equal to the cost of common equity capital. Required income is analogous to a charge for the cost of equity capital, similar to interest expense as a charge for the cost of debt capital.

To summarize, we measure *residual income* (also called *abnormal earnings*) as follows:

$$Residual\ Income_t = CI_t - (R_E \times BV_{t-1})$$

Residual income is the difference between the comprehensive income you expect the firm to generate and the required income of the firm in a given period. Positive residual income indicates an increase in shareholder wealth because the firm generates comprehensive income greater than the income required to cover the cost of equity capital. If residual income is

---

[7]Credit for the rigorous development of the residual income valuation model goes to James A. Ohlson, "A Synthesis of Security Valuation Theory and the Role of Dividends, Cash Flows, and Earnings," *Contemporary Accounting Research* (Spring 1990), pp. 648–676; James A. Ohlson, "Earnings, Book Values, and Dividends in Equity Valuation," *Contemporary Accounting Research* (Spring 1995), pp. 661–687; Gerald A. Feltham and James A. Ohlson, "Valuation and Clean Surplus Accounting for Operating and Financial Activities," *Contemporary Accounting Research* (Spring 1995), pp. 216–230. The ideas underlying the earnings-based valuation approach trace to early work by G. A. D. Preinreich, "Annual Survey of Economic Theory: The Theory of Depreciation," *Econometrica* (1938), pp. 219–241, and Edgar O. Edwards and Philip W. Bell, *The Theory and Measurement of Business Income* (Berkeley, CA: University of California Press, 1961).

negative, the firm destroys shareholder wealth that period because it generates earnings that are below the income required to cover the cost of equity capital. If the firm generates comprehensive income exactly equal to required income in a given period [that is, $CI_t - (R_E \times BV_{t-1}) = 0$], then the firm's earnings exactly cover the cost of equity capital. In that case, the firm generates a normal rate of return to shareholders that period, exactly equal to the equity cost of capital, neither creating nor destroying shareholder wealth.

If you expect the firm will create wealth for the shareholders by earning positive amounts of residual income in future periods, the value of the firm is equal to book value of common shareholders' equity plus the present value of all expected future residual income. However, if you expect the firm will destroy shareholder wealth by generating negative amounts of residual income, the value of the firm is equal to book value of common shareholders' equity *minus* the present value of all expected future residual income. If the firm will generate comprehensive income each period in the future that is exactly equal to required income [that is, $CI_t - (R_E \times BV_{t-1}) = 0$ residual income for all future periods], the value of the firm is exactly equal to the book value of common shareholders' equity.[8]

Illustrations of Residual Income Measurement and Valuation

The following examples illustrate residual income measurement and the residual income valuation model under various assumptions.

Example 1: Zero Residual Income, 100% Dividend Payout

Suppose investors have invested $10,000 in common equity in a company. Given the risk of the company, the investors expect to earn a 12% return, and they expect the company to pay out 100% of income in dividends each year. The required income of the company each period is as follows:

$$R_E \times BV_{t-1} = 0.12 \times \$10,000 = \$1,200$$

Suppose the investors forecast that the company will generate exactly $1,200 in comprehensive income each year. The investors should compute the residual income of the firm as follows:

$$CI_t - (R_E \times BV_{t-1}) = \$1,200 - (0.12 \times \$10,000) = \$0$$

Using the residual income approach, investors would value this firm based on book value plus expected future residual income as follows:

$$V_0 = BV_0 + \sum_{t=1}^{\infty} \frac{CI_t - (R_E \times BV_{t-1})}{(1 + R_E)^t}$$

$$= \$10,000 + \sum_{t=1}^{\infty} \frac{\$1,200 - (0.12 \times \$10,000)}{(1 + 0.12)^t}$$

$$= \$10,000 + \sum_{t=1}^{\infty} \frac{\$0}{(1 + 0.12)^t} = \$10,000$$

---

[8]The concept of residual income in the economics literature and the accounting literature predates the commercialization of "Economic Value Added" by decades. Applications of the concept of residual income in valuation and corporate governance practices can be found in G. Bennett Stewart, *The Quest for Value* (New York: Harper Collins, 1991), and in the expanding literature on economic value added.

In this case, the firm's expected future income exactly equals the required income necessary to cover the cost of equity capital. So residual income is zero and the value of the firm is equal to the book value of common equity invested in the firm. The value of the firm under the residual income model is identical to the value determined using the dividends valuation model, which would value the company as a stream of dividends in perpetuity with no growth as follows:

$$V_0 = \frac{\$1,200}{0.12} = \$10,000$$

Example 2: Zero Residual Income, Zero Dividend Payout

Now assume the same facts as in Example 1, but suppose investors expect the company to pay out no dividends each year and all the earnings will be reinvested in projects that will generate the investors' required 12% rate of return.[9] The required income of the firm in Year $+1$ will be

$$R_E \times BV_0 = 0.12 \times \$10,000 = \$1,200$$

After retained earnings of $1,200 are added to book value of equity at the end of Year $+1$, the required income of the company in Year $+2$ will be

$$R_E \times BV_1 = 0.12 \times [\$10,000 + \$1,200] = \$1,344$$

After retained earnings of $1,344 are added to book value of equity at the end of Year $+2$, the required income of the company in Year $+3$ will be

$$R_E \times BV_2 = 0.12 \times [\$11,200 + \$1,344] = \$1,505$$

These computations show that the firm's required income will grow as it retains and reinvests earnings, on which the investors expect the firm to earn the required rate of return.

Suppose the investors expect the firm to generate future comprehensive income each year that will exactly match required income each year, so it will generate zero residual income each year. Assuming the firm will continue to reinvest all of its earnings and generate the required 12% return each year over its remaining life (that is, continuing in Year $+4$ and beyond), then we can determine the value of equity capital in the firm using the residual income model as follows:

$$V_0 = BV_0 + \sum_{t=1}^{\infty} \frac{CI_t - (R_E \times BV_{t-1})}{(1 + R_E)^t}$$

$$= \$10,000 + \frac{\$1,200 - (0.12 \times \$10,000)}{(1.12)^1} + \frac{\$1,344 - (0.12 \times \$11,200)}{(1.12)^2}$$

$$+ \frac{\$1,505 - (0.12 \times \$12,544)}{(1.12)^3} + \sum_{t=4}^{\infty} \frac{CI_t - (0.12 \times BV_{t-1})}{(1 + 0.12)^t}$$

$$= \$10,000 + \frac{\$0}{(1.12)^1} + \frac{\$0}{(1.12)^2} + \frac{\$0}{(1.12)^3} + \sum_{t=4}^{\infty} \frac{\$0}{(1 + 0.12)^t}$$

$$= \$10,000$$

---

[9] Although this is simply an illustration, note that this is an important assumption because it presumes that the firm can scale up operations without diminishing future returns.

Example 3: Declining Residual Income, Zero Dividend Payout

Now assume the same facts as in Example 2, but suppose investors expect the firm simply to reinvest the earnings in cash or other types of assets that will earn no additional return for each of the next three periods. The investors expect the firm to continue to earn $1,200 each year on the original investment of $10,000, but they expect the reinvestment of earnings in the first three years to produce no incremental return. Also assume for simplicity that in Year +4 and beyond, the firm will invest in projects that will earn a total of 12% return for equity shareholders.

The required income of the firm in Year +1 will be

$$R_E \times BV_0 = 0.12 \times \$10,000 = \$1,200$$

After retained earnings of $1,200 are added to book value of equity at the end of Year +1, the required income in Year +2 will be

$$R_E \times BV_1 = 0.12 \times (\$10,000 + \$1,200) = \$1,344$$

After retained earnings of $1,200 are added to book value of equity at the end of Year +2, the required income in Year +3 will be

$$R_E \times BV_2 = 0.12 \times (\$11,200 + \$1,200) = \$1,488$$

In Year +4 and beyond, we assume the firm will generate a steady 12% return for equity shareholders, equal to the cost of equity capital, so residual income will be zero. We can determine the value of equity capital in the firm using the residual income model as follows:

$$
\begin{aligned}
V_0 &= BV_0 + \sum_{t=1}^{\infty} \frac{CI_t - (R_E \times BV_{t-1})}{(1+R_E)^t} \\
&= \$10,000 + \frac{\$1,200 - (0.12 \times \$10,000)}{(1.12)^1} + \frac{\$1,200 - (0.12 \times \$11,200)}{(1.12)^2} \\
&\quad + \frac{\$1,200 - (0.12 \times \$12,400)}{(1.12)^3} + \sum_{t=4}^{\infty} \frac{CI_t - (0.12 \times BV_{t-1})}{(1+0.12)^t} \\
&= \$10,000 + \frac{\$0}{(1.12)^1} + \frac{\$1,200 - \$1,344}{(1.12)^2} + \frac{\$1,200 - \$1,488}{(1.12)^3} + \sum_{t=4}^{\infty} \frac{\$0}{(1+0.12)^t} \\
&= \$10,000 + \$0 - \$115 - \$205 + \$0 \\
&= \$9,680
\end{aligned}
$$

This example shows that by reinvesting earnings to earn zero incremental return rather than the required 12% return, the firm's reinvested earnings will be $144 less than required income in Year +2 and $288 less than required income in Year +3. In present value terms, the firm will destroy $115 of shareholder value in Year +2 and $205 of shareholder value in Year +3. Therefore, investors would value the firm at only $9,680 in this example, as compared to $10,000 in the preceding two examples.

Example 4: Positive Residual Income

Now assume investors have invested $10,000 in common equity in a firm, they expect to earn a 12% return, and they expect the company to pay out 100% of income in dividends each year. Now suppose these investors expect the firm to earn net income of $1,000 in Year +1, $2,000 in Year +2, $1,500 in Year +3, and $1,200 each year thereafter. Investors should compute the residual income valuation as follows:

$$V_0 = BV_0 + \sum_{t=1}^{\infty} \frac{CI_t - (R_E \times BV_{t-1})}{(1 + R_E)^t}$$

$$= \$10,000 + \frac{\$1,000 - (0.12 \times \$10,000)}{(1.12)^1} + \frac{\$2,000 - (0.12 \times \$10,000)}{(1.12)^2}$$

$$+ \frac{\$1,500 - (0.12 \times \$10,000)}{(1.12)^3} + \sum_{t=4}^{\infty} \frac{\$1,200 - (0.12 \times \$10,000)}{(1 + 0.12)^t}$$

$$= \$10,000 + \frac{-\$200}{(1.12)^1} + \frac{\$800}{(1.12)^2} + \frac{\$300}{(1.12)^3} + \sum_{t=4}^{\infty} \frac{\$0}{(1 + 0.12)^t}$$

$$= \$10,000 - \$179 + \$638 + \$214 + \$0$$

$$= \$10,673$$

In this example, the firm will generate residual income amounts of –$200 in Year +1, $800 in Year +2, $300 in Year +3, and $0 each year thereafter. The firm destroys shareholder wealth in Year +1 by failing to earn sufficient income to cover the cost of equity capital, but the firm generates increasing shareholder wealth in Years +2 and +3 and exactly covers the cost of equity capital each year thereafter. Given these assumptions, the present value of the firm under the residual income model is $10,673.

Example 5: Residual Income Valuation under Different Accounting Treatments

As mentioned earlier, like accrual accounting, the residual income valuation model will naturally correct for differences in accounting methods over the life of a firm. To illustrate, suppose we are valuing a very simple firm under the following assumptions. The firm has only one asset (cash) of $200 and a beginning book value of common equity equal to $200. Investors expect to earn a 10% rate of return. In Year 1, the firm invests $100 cash in an R&D project. In Year 1, the firm realizes no revenues, but in Year 2 it realizes $200 in revenues from the R&D project. These are the only activities of this (admittedly simple) firm.

Suppose the firm immediately expenses the entire R&D in Year 1. Earnings for the firm would equal −$100 in Year 1 ($0 revenues − $100 R&D expense) and +$200 in Year 2 ($200 in revenues − $0 expenses). Using the residual income valuation model, we would value the firm as follows:

$$V_0 = BV_0 + \sum_{t=1}^{\infty} \frac{CI_t - (R_E \times BV_{t-1})}{(1 + R_E)^t}$$

$$= \$200 + \frac{-\$100 - (0.10 \times \$200)}{(1.10)^1} + \frac{\$200 - (0.10 \times \$100)}{(1.10)^2}$$

$$= \$200 + \frac{-\$120}{(1.10)^1} + \frac{\$190}{(1.10)^2}$$

$$= \$200 - \$109 + \$157 = \$248$$

Now suppose the firm capitalizes the entire R&D expenditure as an asset in Year 1 and expenses the R&D in Year 2, the period in which the R&D generates revenues. Earnings for the firm would equal $0 in Year 1 ($0 revenues − $0 R&D expense) and

+$100 in Year 2 ($200 in revenues − $100 R&D expense). Using the residual income valuation model, we would value the firm as follows:

$$V_0 = BV_0 + \sum_{t=1}^{\infty} \frac{CI_t - (R_E \times BV_{t-1})}{(1 + R_E)^t}$$

$$= \$200 + \frac{\$0 - (0.10 \times \$200)}{(1.10)^1} + \frac{\$100 - (0.10 \times \$200)}{(1.1)^2}$$

$$= \$200 + \frac{-\$20}{(1.10)^1} + \frac{\$80}{(1.10)^2}$$

$$= \$200 - \$18 + \$66 = \$248$$

Notice that we arrive at exactly the same value, whether the firm capitalizes or expenses R&D in Year 1.

Now imagine that we value the firm using free-cash-flows-based or dividends-based valuation. At the end of Year 2, the firm has $300 in free cash flows, so it can pay a $300 liquidating dividend, based on the initial $200 cash investment minus $100 in cash spent on R&D in Year 1 plus $200 in cash collected in revenues in Year 2. The present value of a $300 dividend at the end of Year 2, discounted at 10%, is $248, exactly the same value as we determined by the residual income model.

LO 13-4

Demonstrate a conceptual understanding of residual income valuation with finite forecast horizons and continuing value computations.

Residual Income Valuation with Finite Horizon Earnings Forecasts and Continuing Value Computations

No one can precisely forecast firms' income statements and balance sheets for many years into the future. Therefore, we commonly forecast income statements and balance sheets over a foreseeable finite horizon and then make simplifying growth rate assumptions for the years continuing after the forecast horizon. We can modify the residual income valuation model to include explicit forecasts of net income and book value of common equity through Year T (where T is a finite horizon, often 5 or 10 years in the future) and then apply a constant growth rate assumption (denoted as g) to project residual income for Year $T+1$ and all years thereafter. We used similar approaches to forecast dividends in Chapter 11 and free cash flows in Chapter 12.

To deal with the uncertainty in long-run forecasts, you must forecast net income, book value of shareholders' equity, and residual income over an explicit forecast horizon until the point when you expect the firm to settle into steady-state growth, during which time earnings, dividends, and cash flows will grow (on average) at a steady, predictable rate (like we did in the examples above). We refer to residual income in this long-run, steady-state growth period as *continuing residual income* because it reflects residual income earned by the firm continuing into the long-run future. The long-run, steady-state growth rate in future continuing residual income may be positive, negative, or zero. Steady-state growth in residual income may be driven by long-run expectations for inflation, the industry's sales, the economy in general, or the population. In some industries, competitive dynamics eventually drive the future returns earned by the firm (for example, the future ROCE) to an equilibrium level equal to the long-run expected cost of equity capital in the firm. Once a firm reaches that equilibrium, the firm can be expected to earn zero residual income in the future. You should select a continuing growth rate in residual income that captures realistic long-run expectations for the firm.

To compute residual income in Year $T+1$, you should project Year $T+1$ comprehensive income by multiplying Year T comprehensive income by the growth factor $(1+g)$. Year $T+1$ residual income (denoted as RI_{T+1}) can then be computed as follows:

$$RI_{T+1} = [CI_T \times (1+g)] - [R_E \times BV_T]$$

By estimating RI_{T+1} this way, you also will apply the same uniform long-run growth factor $(1+g)$ to estimate Year $T+1$ income statement and balance sheet amounts and to compute internally consistent projections for Year $T+1$ free cash flows and dividends. You can then use them in free-cash-flows-based and dividends-based valuation models to determine internally consistent value estimates. Chapters 11 and 12 demonstrate these approaches.

Next, you can treat RI_{T+1} as a growing perpetuity of residual income beginning in Year $T+1$. You can discount the perpetuity of residual income to present value using the perpetuity-with-growth value model described in Chapters 11 and 12. We include the continuing value computation into the finite horizon residual income model as follows:

$$V_0 = BV_0 + \sum_{t=1}^{\infty} \frac{CI_t - (R_E \times BV_{t-1})}{(1+R_E)^t}$$

$$= BV_0 + \sum_{t=1}^{T} \frac{CI_t - (R_E \times BV_{t-1})}{(1+R_E)^t}$$

$$\underset{(1)}{} \qquad \underset{(2)}{}$$

$$+ \left(\{[CI_T \times (1+g)] - (R_E \times BV_T)\} \times \frac{1}{(R_E - g)} \times \frac{1}{(1+R_E)^T} \right)$$

$$\underset{(3)}{}$$

This model computes the value of common equity based on three parts, identified as (1), (2), and (3) in the preceding equation:

1. Book value of shareholders' equity at time $t=0$ (the BV_0 term).
2. Present value of residual income over the explicit forecast horizon through Year T (the summation term).
3. Present value of continuing value based on residual income as a perpetuity with growth beginning in Year $T+1$ (the term in brackets).

To compute continuing value, we compute residual income in Year $T+1$ {the term $[CI_T \times (1+g)] - (R_E \times BV_T)$}. We assume that residual income in Year $T+1$ will grow at constant rate g in perpetuity beginning in Year $T+1$, so we compute continuing value as of the start of Year $T+1$ using the perpetuity-with-growth valuation factor [the term $1/(R_E - g)$]. Finally, we discount continuing value to present value at time $t = 0$ using the present value factor [the $1/(1+R_E)^T$ term].

Coaching Tip: Avoid This Common Mistake

The preceding section describes how to compute residual income in Year $T+1$, as follows:

$$RI_{T+1} = [CI_T \times (1+g)] - (R_E \times BV_T)$$

By estimating RI_{T+1} this way, you will effectively apply a uniform long-run growth factor $(1+g)$ to comprehensive income to compute residual income. Recall that

Chapters 11 and 12 also demonstrated how to correctly compute free cash flows and dividends in Year $T+1$ by applying the same long-run growth factor $(1 + g)$ to project all of the Year $T+1$ income statement and balance sheet amounts and then deriving internally consistent projections for Year $T+1$ free cash flows and dividends. With this simple but important step, you can determine internally consistent value estimates across all three valuation models (and therefore avoid the all-too-common mistake of deriving *different* values for the *same* firm using *different* valuation models).

The common mistake that analysts make, and that you should avoid with this tip, is simply projecting $RI_{T+1} = RI_T \times (1 + g)$. This shortcut projection implicitly assumes that $RI_T \times (1 + g) = [CI_T - (R_E \times BV_{T-1})] \times (1 + g) = CI_T \times (1 + g) - [R_E \times BV_{T-1} \times (1 + g)]$. This assumption requires BV_T to equal $BV_{T-1} \times (1 + g)$, which is not necessarily true. Residual income in Year $T+1$ depends on book value at the end of Year T. We assume constant growth at rate $(1 + g)$ in residual income beginning in Year $T+1$. Thus, the only way residual income in Year $T+1$ will equal residual income in Year T times $(1 + g)$ is if book value in Year T happened to grow (by coincidence) at the same rate $(1 + g)$. Such a coincidence is rare. You can easily avoid this forecasting and valuation error for RI_{T+1} by correctly computing $RI_{T+1} = [CI_T \times (1 + g)] - (R_E \times BV_T)$.

LO 13-5

Demonstrate a practical understanding of residual income valuation by applying the approach to value the common shares of Starbucks.

Valuation of Starbucks Using the Residual Income Model

This is the practical application step in which we apply the residual income valuation approach to value the common shareholders' equity in **Starbucks**. **Starbucks'** shares closed trading at $56.84 on NASDAQ at the end of fiscal 2015. In Chapter 11, applying the dividends-based valuation approach, we determined our central estimate of the value of **Starbucks'** shares at the end of fiscal 2015 to be roughly $66.10. We obtained the same $66.10 value estimate for **Starbucks'** shares in Chapter 12 using the free-cash-flows-based valuation approaches. Next, we illustrate the valuation of **Starbucks'** shares using the residual income valuation approach described in this chapter and the forecasts developed in Chapter 10. The Forecasts and Valuation spreadsheets of FSAP (Appendix C) also demonstrate the forecasts and valuation estimates.

We value **Starbucks'** common equity shares with the residual income approach following these six steps:

1. Estimate the appropriate discount rate using the risk-adjusted required rate of return on equity capital.
2. Determine the book value of common shareholders' equity on **Starbucks'** fiscal 2015 balance sheet.
3. Project expected future residual income from the financial statement forecasts for **Starbucks** described in Chapter 10.
4. Project long-run growth in residual income in the continuing periods beyond the forecast horizon.
5. Discount the expected future residual income to present value, including continuing value.
6. Add the book value of equity and the present value of expected future residual income to determine the total value of common shareholders' equity, correct for midyear discounting, and divide by the number of shares outstanding to convert this total to an estimate of share value for **Starbucks**.

After illustrating this six-step valuation process, we will run sensitivity analyses to determine the range of reasonable values for **Starbucks'** shares in the market and suggest an appropriate investment decision indicated by the analysis.

Discount Rates for Residual Income

To compute the appropriate discount rate for residual income, we again use the CAPM to estimate the market's required rate of return on **Starbucks'** common shares, as demonstrated in Chapters 11 and 12. At the end of fiscal 2015, **Starbucks'** common stock had a market beta of roughly 0.75. At the same time, U.S. Treasury bills with 10 years to maturity traded with a yield of approximately 2.7%, which we use as the risk-free rate. Assuming a 6.0% market risk premium, the CAPM indicates that **Starbucks** had a cost of common equity capital of 7.2% [$R_E = 7.2\% = 2.7\% + (0.75 \times 6.0\%)$] at the end of fiscal 2015, the beginning of the valuation period. We used this same cost of common equity capital to value **Starbucks'** shares in Chapter 11 using the present value of future dividends and in Chapter 12 using the present value of free cash flows to common equity shareholders.

Using the residual income valuation model, we do not need to compute the weighted-average cost of capital. This does not mean that we ignore debt capital or the costs related to debt capital. Instead, we rely on accounting to capture the effects of debt. We project book value of shareholders' equity after subtracting debt from total assets, and we project net income after subtracting interest expense net of tax savings.

Starbucks' Book Value of Equity and the Projection of Residual Income

According to **Starbucks'** balance sheet (Appendix A), book value of common shareholders' equity is $5,818.0 million at the end of fiscal 2015. This amount is the starting point for the residual income valuation model, the term denoted BV_0 in the valuation equation.

To project residual income in Year +1 through Year +5 in the finite forecast horizon, we begin with our forecasts of expected future comprehensive income and future book value of common shareholders' equity from Chapter 10. (Recall that in Chapter 10 we projected **Starbucks'** future comprehensive income by making specific assumptions regarding each line item on the income statement. We also projected future common shareholders' equity on the balance sheet by projecting **Starbucks'** assets, liabilities, and common equity, including specific forecasts of dividends, stock issues, and stock buybacks.)

We then measure future residual income each period with two computations:

1. Compute expected future *required income*, which is the product of the cost of equity capital times the beginning book value of common shareholders' equity each period ($R_E \times BV_{t-1}$).
2. Determine expected future *residual income* by subtracting expected future required income from expected future comprehensive income [$CI_t - (R_E \times BV_{t-1})$].

Exhibit 13.2 presents projections of **Starbucks'** comprehensive income, book value of shareholders' equity, required income, and residual income through Year +5 using the forecasts discussed in Chapter 10 and a 7.2% cost of equity capital.

In Chapter 10, for example, we projected net income attributable to **Starbucks'** common shareholders will be $2,794.3 million in Year +1. We forecasted other comprehensive income items will be zero, so projected comprehensive income and net income will be equal. (Recall from the earlier discussion that the residual income model requires that we measure income for common equity shareholders comprehensively by using

Exhibit 13.2

Valuation of Starbucks:
Present Value of Residual Income Year +1 through Year +5
(dollar amounts in millions; allow for rounding)

	Year +1	Year +2	Year +3	Year +4	Year +5
Common shareholders' equity at beginning of year (denoted BV_{t-1})	$ 5,818.0	$4,772.4	$5,062.6	$5,474.4	$5,985.9
Comprehensive income available for common shareholders (denoted CI_t)	$ 2,794.3	$3,080.6	$3,490.0	$3,939.8	$4,895.0
Required income ($R_E \times BV_{t-1}$; $R_E = 7.2\%$)	(418.9)	(343.6)	(364.5)	(394.2)	(431.0)
Residual income [$CI_t - (R_E \times BV_{t-1})$]	$ 2,375.4	$2,737.0	$3,125.5	$3,545.6	$4,464.0
Present value factors ($R_E = 7.2\%$)	0.933	0.870	0.812	0.757	0.706
Present value of residual income	$ 2,215.9	$2,381.7	$2,537.1	$2,684.8	$3,153.2
Sum of present value of residual income Year +1 through Year +5	**$12,972.6**				

clean surplus accounting.) Given that **Starbucks'** book value of common shareholders' equity at the beginning of Year +1 is $5,818.0 million and **Starbucks'** cost of equity capital is 7.2%, we project Year +1 required income to be $418.9 million (0.072 × $5,818.0 million). Therefore, we project Year +1 residual income will be $2,375.4 million ($2,794.3 million – $418.9 million).

To project **Starbucks'** residual income continuing in Year +6 and beyond, we forecast that **Starbucks** can sustain long-run growth of 3.0% per year, consistent with long-run average growth in the economy. We made the same assumption in forecasting long-run growth for dividends in Chapter 11 and for free cash flows in Chapter 12. We project Year +6 residual income will be $4,516.4 million, computed by projecting Year +5 comprehensive income to grow by 3.0% and subtracting required income, measured as the equity cost of capital times book value at the end of Year +5, as follows:

$$RI_6 = [CI_5 \times (1 + g)] - (R_E \times BV_5)$$
$$= [\$4,895.0 \text{ million} \times 1.03] - (0.072 \times \$5,985.9 \text{ million})$$
$$= \$5,041.8 \text{ million} - \$525.4 \text{ million}$$
$$= \$4,516.4 \text{ million}$$

Discounting Starbucks' Residual Income to Present Value

We discount residual income to present value using **Starbucks'** 7.2% cost of equity capital. Exhibit 13.2 shows that the sum of the present value of **Starbucks'** residual income from Year +1 through Year +5 is $12,972.6 million.

We compute the present value of **Starbucks'** continuing value of residual income as a perpetuity beginning in Year +6 with growth at a 3.0% rate. To compute the continuing value estimate, we use the perpetuity-with-growth valuation model, which determines the present value of the growing perpetuity at the start of the perpetuity period. We then discount that value back to present value at time $t=0$. We compute the present value of the continuing value of **Starbucks'** residual income as follows (allowing for rounding):

$Present\ Value\ of\ Continuing\ Value_0$

$$= \{[CI_5 \times (1+g)] - (R_E \times BV_5)\} \times [1/(R_E - g)] \times [1/(1+R_E)^5]$$
$$= [\$4{,}895.0\ \text{million} \times 1.03] - (0.072 \times \$5{,}985.9\ \text{million})$$
$$\times [1/(0.072 - 0.03)] \times [1/(1+0.072)^5]$$
$$= (\$5{,}041.8\ \text{million} - \$525.4\ \text{million}) \times 23.8095 \times 0.706$$
$$= \$4{,}516.4\ \text{million} \times 23.8095 \times 0.706$$
$$= \$75{,}957.7\ \text{million}$$

The total present value of **Starbucks'** residual income is the sum of these two parts:

Present value of residual income Year +1 through Year +5 (Exhibit 13.2)	$12,972.6 million
Present value of continuing value in Year +6 and beyond	75,957.7 million
Present value of residual income	$88,930.3 million

Computing Starbucks' Common Equity Share Value

To compute the total value of common equity, we add **Starbucks'** book value of common equity to the present value of residual income. The total value of common equity as of the beginning of Year +1 is the sum of these two amounts:

Present value of residual income	$88,930.3 million
Book value of common shareholders' equity	5,818.0 million
Present value of common shareholders' equity before midyear discounting	$94,748.3 million

As Chapters 11 and 12 describe, our present value calculations over-discount because they discount each year's residual income for full periods when, in fact, residual income is generated throughout each period and should be discounted from the midpoint of each year to the present. Therefore, to make the correction, we multiply the total by the midyear adjustment factor of 1.0360 $[1 + (R_E/2) = 1 + (0.072/2)]$. Therefore, the total present value of common shareholders' equity should be computed as follows:

Present value of common shareholders' equity before midyear discounting	$94,748.3 million
Midyear discounting adjustment factor	× 1.0360
Total present value of common shareholders' equity	$ 98,159.2 million

Dividing the total present value of common shareholders' equity of $98,159.2 million by 1,485.1 million shares outstanding indicates that **Starbucks'** common equity shares have a value of $66.10 per share. This value estimate is identical to the value estimate based on dividends in Chapter 11 and free cash flows to common equity shareholders in Chapter 12. Exhibit 13.3 summarizes the computations to arrive at **Starbucks'** common equity share value. Exhibit 13.4 presents the residual income model application for **Starbucks** from FSAP.

Exhibit 13.3

Valuation of Starbucks Using the Residual Income Valuation Model
(dollar amounts in millions except per-share amounts)

Valuation Steps	Computations	Amounts
Sum of present value of residual income, Year +1 through Year +5	See Exhibit 13.2.	$ 12,972.6
Add present value of continuing value	Year +6 residual income assumed to grow at 3.0%; discounted at 7.2%	+ 75,957.7
Total present value of residual income		$ 88,930.3
Add: Beginning book value of equity	Beginning book value of equity from fiscal 2015 balance sheet	+ 5,818.0
Total		$ 94,748.3
Adjust to midyear discounting	Multiply by $1 + (R_E/2)$	× 1.0360
Total present value of common equity		$ 98,159.2
Divide by shares outstanding	1,485.1 million shares outstanding	÷ 1,485.1
Estimated value per share		$ 66.10
Current price per share		$ 56.84
Percent difference	Positive number indicates underpricing	16%

LO 13-6

Assess the sensitivity of share value estimates to key parameters, such as discount rates and expected long-term growth rates.

Sensitivity Analysis and Investment Decision Making

We cautioned in Chapters 11 and 12 and we reiterate here that you should not place too much confidence in the precision of a single point estimate of firm value using these (or any) forecasts for residual income over the remaining life of any firm, even a mature firm such as **Starbucks**. Although we have constructed these forecasts and value estimates with care, the forecasting and valuation process has an inherently high degree of uncertainty and estimation error. Therefore, rather than relying too heavily on a point estimate of the value of a firm's shares, you should describe a reasonable range of values for a firm's shares.

Two critical forecasting and valuation parameters are the long-run growth assumption (3.0%) and the cost of equity capital (7.2%). With these assumptions, our base case estimate is that **Starbucks** common shares should be valued at roughly $66.10 per share. As in Chapters 11 and 12, we assess the sensitivity of our estimate of **Starbucks'** share value by varying these two parameters across reasonable ranges. Exhibit 13.5 contains the results of sensitivity analysis in FSAP varying the long-run growth assumption from 0% to 5% and the cost of equity capital from 6% to 12%. The data in Exhibit 13.5 show that our share value estimates decline as discount rates increase, holding growth constant. In contrast, our share value estimates increase with growth, holding discount rates constant.[10]

As we observed in our sensitivity analyses in Chapters 11 and 12, these data suggest that our value estimate is sensitive to slight variations of our baseline assumptions of 3.0% long-run growth and a 7.2% discount rate. Slight adverse variations in valuation parameters (such as 2.5%

---

[10]We omit value estimates from sensitivity analysis when the growth rate equals or exceeds the discount rate because the continuing value computation is meaningless.

Exhibit 13.4

Valuation of Starbucks:
Residual Income Valuation Approach in FSAP
(dollar amounts in millions, except per-share amounts)

RESIDUAL INCOME VALUATION	1 Year +1	2 Year +2	3 Year +3	4 Year +4	5 Year +5	Continuing Value Year +6
Comprehensive income available for common shareholders	$ 2,794.3	$3,080.6	$3,490.0	$3,939.8	$4,895.0	$5,041.8
Lagged book value of common shareholders' equity (at t−1)	$ 5,818.0	$4,772.4	$5,062.6	$5,474.4	$5,985.9	$7,297.3
Required income	$ 418.9	$ 343.6	$ 364.5	$ 394.2	$ 431.0	$ 525.4
Residual income	$ 2,375.4	$2,737.0	$3,125.5	$3,545.6	$4,464.0	$4,516.4
Present value factors	0.933	0.870	0.812	0.757	0.706	
Present value residual income	$ 2,215.9	$2,381.7	$2,537.1	$2,684.8	$3,153.2	
Sum of present value residual income	$12,972.6					
Present value of continuing value	$75,957.7					
Total	$88,930.3					
Add: Beginning book value of equity	$ 5,818.0					
Present value of equity	$94,748.3					
Adjust to midyear discounting	1.0360					
Total present value of equity	$98,159.2					
Shares outstanding	1,485.1					
Estimated value per share	$ 66.10					
Current share price	$ 56.84					
Percent difference	16%					

Exhibit 13.5

Valuation of Starbucks: Sensitivity Analysis of Share Value Estimates to Growth and Equity Cost of Capital

	Long-Run Growth Assumptions								
	66.10	**0.0%**	**1.0%**	**2.0%**	**2.5%**	**3.0%**	**3.5%**	**4.0%**	**5.0%**
Discount Rates:	6.00%	52.05	60.26	72.57	81.36	93.09	109.50	134.12	257.23
	6.50%	47.87	54.60	64.32	71.00	79.58	91.04	107.07	171.19
	6.70%	46.38	52.62	61.51	67.54	75.21	85.27	99.05	150.95
	7.00%	44.30	49.89	57.72	62.94	69.47	77.85	89.04	128.18
	7.20%	43.01	48.23	55.44	60.20	66.10	73.58	83.41	116.46
	7.50%	41.21	45.92	52.33	56.51	61.60	67.98	76.17	102.39
	7.70%	40.09	44.49	50.45	54.28	58.93	64.69	72.00	94.75
	8.00%	38.51	42.51	47.85	51.25	55.32	60.30	66.53	85.21
	8.50%	36.13	39.57	44.06	46.87	50.19	54.17	59.03	72.94
	9.00%	34.03	37.00	40.82	43.17	45.91	49.15	53.05	63.74
	9.50%	32.14	34.73	38.01	40.00	42.30	44.98	48.15	56.60
	10.00%	30.45	32.72	35.56	37.26	39.21	41.45	44.07	50.89
	11.00%	27.54	29.32	31.48	32.76	34.20	35.82	37.68	42.33
	12.00%	25.13	26.54	28.24	29.22	30.31	31.53	32.90	36.23

long-run growth and an 8.0% discount rate) reduce Starbucks' share value to roughly $51, whereas slightly more favorable variations (such as 3.5% long-run growth and a 7.0% discount rate) increase Starbucks' share value to roughly $78. If our forecast and valuation assumptions are realistic, our baseline value estimate for Starbucks is $66.10 per share at the end of fiscal 2015. At that time, the market price of $56.84 per share indicates that Starbucks shares were underpriced by about 16%. Under our forecast assumptions, Starbucks' share value could vary within a range of a low of $51 per share to a high of $78 per share with only minor perturbations in our growth rate and discount rate assumptions. Given that Starbucks' $56.84 share price is in the lower end of that range of values, and 16% below our baseline estimate of a $66.10 share value, we would have supported a buy recommendation at the end of fiscal 2015.

LO 13-7

Describe four important implementation issues for the residual income valuation approach.

Residual Income Model Implementation Issues

The residual income valuation model is a rigorous and straightforward valuation approach, but you should be aware of four important implementation issues:

1. "Dirty surplus" accounting items.
2. Common stock transactions.
3. Portions of net income attributable to equity claimants other than common shareholders.
4. Negative book value of equity.

The next four sections describe these issues and how to deal with them.

Dirty Surplus Accounting

The residual income model requires that you follow clean surplus accounting in developing expectations for future comprehensive income, dividends, and book values. This means that the expected future income amounts should include all of the income recognized by the firm for the common equity shareholders and that all-inclusive dividends should include all capital transactions with common equity shareholders. Currently, U.S. GAAP and IFRS do *not* measure net income using clean surplus accounting. U.S. GAAP admits four *dirty surplus* items. These items are the other comprehensive income amounts that firms recognize directly in shareholders' equity. The four dirty surplus items are

1. unrealized fair value gains and losses on available-for-sale investment securities.[11]
2. foreign currency translation gains and losses.
3. changes in assets and liabilities related to pensions and postemployment benefits that arise from plan amendments and actuarial experience.
4. fair value gains and losses from cash flow hedges.

U.S. GAAP requires that firms recognize these items within *comprehensive income* but does not allow firms to recognize them in net income until they are realized (for example, when the firm realizes gains or losses by selling an available-for-sale investment security). Under U.S. GAAP and IFRS, firms usually report comprehensive income in a separate statement of performance to accompany the income statement. In residual income valuation, be sure to use projected comprehensive income (rather than net income) to be consistent with clean surplus accounting.

For example, **Starbucks** reported in its 2015 consolidated statement of comprehensive income (Appendix A) that other comprehensive income items totaled $(224.7) million. As a result of these items, **Starbucks'** comprehensive income was $2,534.6 million (net income of $2,759.3 million minus other comprehensive income items of $224.7 million). By the end of 2015, total accumulated other comprehensive loss (which measures total accumulated other comprehensive income adjustments over the life of **Starbucks** and is included as a component of shareholders' equity) was $(199.4) million. As Chapters 8 and 10 describe, the main culprit driving other comprehensive losses for **Starbucks** has been foreign currency translation adjustments, amounting to $(222.7) million in 2015.

The four dirty surplus items in U.S. GAAP typically arise because of unrealized gains and losses attributable to changes in market prices, such as changes in investment security fair values, foreign currency exchange rates, or interest rates. Thus, in expectation, you may determine that such gains and losses are certain to occur but that it is impossible to predict with precision either the direction or amount of the future unrealized gains and losses. In that case, you would likely forecast the expected future other comprehensive income items to be zero, on average, and therefore forecast net income and comprehensive income to be equal. We used this assumption in building forecasts for **Starbucks** in Chapter 10. On the other hand, if you can reliably project the amounts and timing of any of these items, you should incorporate them in your comprehensive income forecasts.

---

[11]Note that the FASB adopted a new accounting standard in 2016 that will require firms to recognize fair value gains and losses on available-for-sale investment securities in net income rather than in other comprehensive income. The standard will become effective in 2018. At that time, these fair value gains and losses will no longer be "dirty surplus" items.

Common Stock Transactions

Common stock transactions that change the intrinsic value of existing common share-holders' equity also can cause violations of the clean surplus accounting relation and hinder the ability of the residual income model to measure firm value correctly. To illustrate, consider the firm that sells common shares or repurchases common shares at transaction prices that exactly reflect the intrinsic value of the shares. That is, share sales or repurchases have a neutral effect on share value for existing shareholders (neither dilutive nor accretive). Such transactions leave the existing shareholders' value unchanged, and clean surplus accounting holds for these transactions. On the other hand, suppose the firm issues common shares at a price that is lower than their intrinsic value. This transaction has a dilutive effect on (that is, reduces the value of) all of the existing common shares. Comprehensive income and the all-inclusive dividend do not reflect this loss in value to existing shareholders, so it violates clean surplus accounting.

It is reasonable to expect that clean surplus accounting holds for most common stock transactions because most issues and repurchases of common shares are accounted for at market value. As such, they will likely have neutral effects on share value for existing shareholders and will conform to clean surplus accounting. The most prominent exception, however, is the issuance of common equity shares when employees exercise stock options. As Chapter 7 discusses, the exercise of stock options by employees at strike prices below the prevailing market price dilutes the existing share-holders' equity value. If the firm estimates the fair value of the employee stock options at the time it grants them and recognizes the estimated value of the grants as an expense in measuring net income, it mitigates the violation of clean surplus accounting. In this case, you should forecast the fair value of expected future options grants and subtract these estimated expenses when forecasting expected future net income. We implicitly follow this approach in Chapter 10 in building our forecasts of net income for **Starbucks** because **Starbucks** expenses the fair value of stock options at the date of grant. Under Statement No. 123 (Revised 2004) and IAS 2, firms are required to expense the fair value of stock options by amortizing them over the vesting period, beginning at the date of grant.[12]

It is not uncommon for firms to repurchase common equity shares in the open market and then use these shares to fulfill stock option exercises. In that case, the accounting for the stock repurchase at market value and the issue of the treasury shares at the option strike price captures the dilutive effect of the option exercise on shareholders' equity. For example, if the firm repurchases a share in the market for $60 and issues it to an employee exercising an option with a strike price of $40, the net effect of the accounting will capture the $20 decrease in shareholders' equity. On the other hand, if the firm fulfills stock option exercises by issuing new shares (or treasury shares repurchased in prior periods at prices that do not reflect the current period market value), the accounting will reflect the issue of the shares at the option's strike price and the dilutive effect on existing shareholders will violate clean surplus accounting.

For example, **Starbucks** reports in its 2015 consolidated statement of common share-holders' equity (Appendix A) that it repurchased a total of 29 million shares for $1,431.8 million, implying an average cost of $49.37 per share. **Starbucks** also discloses in that statement that it reissued 14.6 million shares for options exercises and vesting of restricted share units, thereby increasing equity capital by $224.4 million, for an average book value of

---

[12]The FASB *Statement No. 123* (Revised 2004), "Accounting for Share-Based Payment," and the IASB *International Financial Reporting Standard 2*, "Share-Based Payment," were issued in 2004.

$15.37 per share issued. The difference between the average cost of $49.37 per share and the average book value of $15.37 per share indicates an average dilution of $34.00 per share issued. Given that **Starbucks** issued 14.6 million shares, the total dilution is $175.0 million. With 1,485.1 million shares outstanding, that amounts to $0.12 dilution per outstanding share, which is roughly 0.2% of the year-end share price of $56.84.

You should devote particular time and attention to stock-based compensation when valuing a firm that has substantial amounts of options outstanding and/or that will likely grant large numbers of options in the future, if you expect that these options will likely be exercised (options that you expect will ultimately expire or be forfeited pose no problems for valuation). In these cases, you should explicitly forecast future stock-based compensation expenses that include the fair values of future options grants. In addition, you should forecast the future dilutive effects of options exercises on the book value of common equity. You should capture both effects in your valuation.[13]

Portions of Net Income Attributable to Equity Claimants Other Than Common Shareholders

Residual income valuation should be based on the comprehensive income available for common equity shareholders. In some circumstances, a portion of comprehensive income is attributable to equity claimants other than common shareholders. For example, preferred stockholders may be entitled to preference in dividends over common shareholders. Also, noncontrolling interest shareholders have a claim on the portion of comprehensive income that is attributable to their share of the equity in the subsidiary they own. For purposes of residual income measurement and valuation, these portions of comprehensive income are not available to the common equity shareholders and should be excluded from residual income (just as we excluded the noncontrolling interest on the balance sheet from our beginning book value of equity in the residual income valuation model). We assumed that **Starbucks** would retire in Year +1 the very small amount ($1.8 million) of noncontrolling interests. So our forecasts of comprehensive income and common shareholders' equity are entirely attributable to **Starbucks'** common shareholders. Thus, our residual income valuation is based correctly on comprehensive income available to common shareholders.

Negative Book Value of Common Shareholders' Equity

Some firms report negative amounts for total common shareholders' equity (liabilities exceed assets). This is not common, but it can arise among firms that are in the start-up phase of the life cycle, when the firm's operations may be generating significant losses. Negative book value of common equity also can arise following a significant releveraging, when a firm uses a significant amount of debt capital to repurchase shares or pay dividends, driving total shareholders' equity below zero. Negative book value of equity also can arise for firms that are in severe distress and at high risk of bankruptcy (essentially, liabilities exceed total assets).

In these uncommon cases, you should not use the residual income valuation approach because the computation of required income ($R_E \times BV_{t-1}$) will be negative.

---

[13]For an illustration of stock options and valuation, see Leonard Soffer, "SFAS No. 123 Disclosures and Discounted Cash Flow Valuation," *Accounting Horizons* 14, no. 2 (June 2000), pp. 169–189.

The computation of residual income $[CI_t - (R_E \times BV_{t-1})]$ will then effectively result in *adding* (subtracting a negative amount) required income to net income, which is not correct. In this situation, you should use only the dividends-based and free-cash-flows-based valuation approaches.[14]

Identify potential causes of errors if the residual income, free cash flows, and dividend valuations do not produce identical value estimates.

Consistency in Residual Income, Dividends, and Free Cash Flows Valuation Estimates

The dividends-based, free-cash-flows-based, and earnings-based valuation approaches should be internally consistent. Throughout Chapters 11 through 13, we have conceptually and theoretically linked each valuation approach to the general valuation model (presented in the introduction to each of these chapters). Along the way, we have demonstrated the internal consistency of these approaches through our analysis and valuation of **Starbucks** and have demonstrated the equivalence of value estimates based on residual income, free cash flows, and dividends.

The former baseball player and coach Yogi Berra is reported to have said, "In theory, practice and theory are the same. In practice, they're not." In theory, all three valuation models, *when correctly implemented with internally consistent assumptions*, will produce the same estimates of value. In practice, you may discover that the three models yield different value estimates. If so, check your analysis for one or more of the following three common errors:[15]

1. *Incomplete or inconsistent earnings and cash flow forecasts.* You should make sure that projected earnings, cash flows, and dividends are complete and based on assumptions that are consistent with one another. As Chapter 10 emphasized, you can reduce the chance of incomplete or inconsistent forecasts by projecting complete financial statements in which the balance sheets balance, the income statements measure comprehensive income for common shareholders, and the statements of cash flows articulate with the income statements and the changes in the balance sheets. You also should make sure that projected shareholders' equity reflects clean surplus accounting.

2. *Inconsistent estimates of weighted-average costs of capital.* Suppose you compute the present value of free cash flows to all debt and equity capital using the weighted-average cost of capital as a discount rate and then subtract the present value of debt and preferred stock to determine the present value of common equity (as shown in Chapter 12). The only way the value estimates from this approach will be identical with value estimates from the residual income approach or the dividends approach is if the weighted-average cost of capital uses weights that are perfectly internally consistent with the present values of debt, preferred stock, and common equity. Thus, you may have to iterate the computation of the weighted-average

---

[14]Note that this implementation issue arises only when total book value of common shareholders' equity is negative. It does not arise when retained earnings is a negative amount (termed *retained deficit*) but total book value of common shareholders' equity is positive. This situation occurs among firms that have generated significant operating losses, particularly during the start-up phase.

[15]For a more complete description of diagnosing errors that can cause differences in the three valuation model estimates, see Russell Lundholm and Terry O'Keefe, "Reconciling Value Estimates from the Discounted Cash Flow Model and the Residual Income Model," *Contemporary Accounting Research* (Summer 2001), pp. 1–26.

cost of capital a number of times until all of the weights and present values are internally consistent.

3. *Incorrect continuing value computations.* Chapters 11 through 13 emphasize that you must carefully estimate continuing value, particularly the Year $T+1$ amount for residual income, free cash flows, and dividends. If you use inconsistent assumptions to project the beginning amounts to compute continuing value, your resulting value estimates will not agree. To avoid this problem, you should first project the Year $T+1$ income statement and balance sheet amounts assuming a uniform rate of growth $(1 + g)$, and then use these projections to derive the Year $T+1$ amounts for residual income, free cash flows, and dividends. The derived amounts for Year $T+1$ can then be used as the starting values of the perpetuity to calculate continuing value. A common error that analysts make is simply to assume that all residual income, free cash flows, and dividends in Year T will grow at the same rate g. This shortcut will likely cause inconsistent assumptions and valuations.

Summary

Chapters 11 through 13 have described and applied three different but equivalent approaches to valuation using the present value of projected dividends, the present value of projected free cash flows, and the present value of projected residual income. Together, these approaches are theoretically sound and practical techniques for estimating a firm's value. Our experience with valuation suggests that using several valuation approaches yields more useful insights than using just one approach in all circumstances. Chapter 14 demonstrates a variety of additional valuation techniques, including the use of market-based valuation multiples, such as market-to-book ratios and price-earnings ratios.

Questions, Exercises, Problems, and Cases

Questions and Exercises

13.1 Valuation Approach Equivalence. Conceptually, why should you expect a valuation based on dividends, a valuation based on the free cash flows for common equity shareholders, and a valuation based on residual income to yield equivalent value estimates for a given firm? `LO 13-1, LO 13-2`

13.2 Required Income. Explain required income. What does required income represent? How is required income conceptually analogous to interest expense? `LO 13-3`

13.3 Residual Income. Explain residual income. How is it measured? What does residual income represent? `LO 13-3`

13.4 Residual Income Valuation Theory. Explain the theory behind the residual income valuation approach. Why is residual income value relevant to common equity shareholders? `LO 13-3`

13.5 Residual Income Valuation Approach. Explain the two roles of book value of common shareholders' equity in the residual income valuation approach. `LO 13-3`

LO 13-3   **13.6 Interpreting Residual Income.** If a firm's residual income for a particular year is positive, does that mean the firm was profitable? Explain. If a firm's residual income for a particular year is negative, does that mean the firm necessarily reported a loss on the income statement? Explain. What does it mean when a firm's residual income is zero?

LO 13-3   **13.7 Effects of Investments on Residual Income.** Assume that the firm's cost of equity capital is 10% and that the firm's existing assets and operations generate a 10% return on common equity. If the firm raises additional equity capital and invests in assets that will generate a return less than 10%, what effect will that investment have on the firm's residual income? If the firm raises additional equity capital and invests in assets that will generate a return that exceeds 10%, what effect will that investment have on the firm's residual income?

LO 13-3   **13.8 Effects of Borrowing on Residual Income.** If the firm borrows capital from a bank and invests it in assets that earn a return greater than the interest rate charged by the bank, what effect will that have on residual income for the firm? How does that effect compare with the effects of capital structure leverage described in Chapters 4 and 5?

LO 13-3   **13.9 Effects of Competition on Residual Income.** If the firm is in a very competitive, mature industry, what effect will the competitive conditions have on residual income for the firm and others in the industry? Now suppose the firm holds a competitive advantage in its industry, but the advantage is not likely to be sustainable for more than a few years. As the firm's competitive advantage diminishes, what effect will that have on that firm's residual income?

LO 13-2   **13.10 Effects of Conservative Accounting on Residual Income Valuation.** Suppose you are applying the residual income valuation model to value a firm with extremely conservative accounting. Suppose, for example, the firm is following U.S. GAAP or IFRS, but the firm does not recognize a substantial intangible asset on the balance sheet. (Perhaps the firm has expensed substantial amounts of R&D expenditures that have led to valuable intellectual property or substantial amounts of advertising expenses that have created a valuable brand name.) As a consequence of this conservative accounting, the firm reports assets and equity at book values that are much lower than their respective economic values. Explain why the residual income value estimates will not be distorted by conservative accounting. How does the residual income valuation model correct for the effects of conservative accounting and understated book values of equity?

LO 13-2   **13.11 Effects of Aggressive Accounting on Residual Income Valuation.** Suppose you are applying the residual income valuation model to value a firm with extremely aggressive accounting. Suppose, for example, the firm has a substantially overvalued asset on the balance sheet. (Perhaps the firm has a large amount of goodwill on the balance sheet from a prior acquisition and has delayed recording a necessary impairment charge that would write off the value of the goodwill.) As a consequence of this aggressive accounting, the firm reports assets and equity at book values that are much higher than their respective economic values. Explain why the residual income value estimates will not be distorted by aggressive accounting. How does the residual income valuation model correct for the effects of aggressive accounting and overstated book values of equity?

LO 13-3, 13-4   **13.12 Appropriate Discount Rates.** Why is it appropriate to use the required rate of return on equity capital (rather than the weighted-average cost of capital) as the discount rate when using the residual income valuation approach?

Problems and Cases

13.13 Computing Residual Income. Suppose the following hypothetical data represent total assets, book value, and market value of common shareholders' equity (dollar amounts in millions) for **Abbott Labs**, **IBM**, and **Target Stores**. Abbott Labs manufactures and sells healthcare products. IBM develops and manufactures computer hardware and offers related technology services. Target Stores operates a chain of general merchandise retail stores. In addition, these data include hypothetical market betas for the three firms and analysts' consensus forecasts of net income for Year +1. Assume that for each firm, analysts expect other comprehensive income items for Year +1 to be zero, so Year +1 net income and comprehensive income will be identical. Assume that the risk-free rate of return in the economy is 4.0% and the market risk premium is 5.0%.

(amounts in millions)	Abbott Labs	IBM	Target Stores
Total assets	$42,419	$109,524	$44,106
Common equity:			
Book value	$17,480	$ 13,466	$13,712
Market value	$83,050	$166,420	$34,600
Market equity beta	0.27	0.73	1.09
Analysts' consensus forecasts			
of net income for Year +1	$ 5,750	$ 12,956	$ 2,384

REQUIRED

  a. Using the CAPM, compute the required rate of return on equity capital for each firm.
  b. Project required income for Year +1 for each firm.
  c. Project residual income for Year +1 for each firm.
  d. What do the different amounts of residual income imply about each firm? Do the projected residual income amounts help explain the differences in market value of equity across these three firms? Explain.

13.14 Computing Residual Income. Suppose the following hypothetical data represent total assets, book value, and market value of common shareholders' equity (dollar amounts in millions) for **Microsoft**, **Intel**, and **Dell**, three firms involved in different aspects of the computer technology industry. Microsoft engages primarily in the development, manufacture, license, and support of software products. Intel develops and manufactures semiconductor chips and microprocessors for the computing and communications industries. Dell designs and manufactures a range of computer hardware systems, such as laptops, desktops, and servers. These data also include hypothetical market betas for these three firms and analysts' consensus forecasts of net income for Year +1. For each firm, analysts expect other comprehensive income items for Year +1 to be zero, so Year +1 net income and comprehensive income will be identical. Assume that the risk-free rate of return in the economy is 4.0% and the market risk premium is 5.0%.

(amounts in millions)	Microsoft	Intel	Dell
Total assets	$ 77,888	$ 50,715	$26,500
Common equity:			
Book value	$ 39,558	$ 39,088	$ 4,271
Market value	$264,510	$112,480	$26,000
Market equity beta	0.96	1.12	1.28
Analysts' consensus forecasts			
of net income for Year +1	$ 16,250	$ 8,060	$ 1,882

REQUIRED

a. Using the CAPM, compute the required rate of return on equity capital for each firm.
b. Project required income for Year +1 for each firm.
c. Project residual income for Year +1 for each firm.
d. Rank the three firms using expected residual income for Year +1 relative to book value of common equity.
e. What do the different amounts of residual income imply about each firm? Do the projected residual income amounts help explain the differences in market value of equity across these three firms? Explain.

LO 13-3

13.15 Computing Residual Income. Suppose the following hypothetical data represent total assets, book value, and market value of common shareholders' equity (dollar amounts in millions) for three firms. Each of these firms, **Southwest Airlines**, **Kroger**, and **Yum! Brands**, operates in a different industry, but all of them operate in very competitive industries. Southwest Airlines is a U.S. domestic airline that provides low-cost point-to-point air transportation services. Kroger operates retail supermarkets across the United States. Yum! Brands operates and franchises quick-service restaurants, including KFC, Pizza Hut, Taco Bell, Long John Silver's, and A&W All American Food restaurants. These data also include hypothetical market betas for the three firms and analysts' consensus forecasts of net income for Year +1. For each firm, analysts expect other comprehensive income items for Year +1 to be zero, so Year +1 net income and comprehensive income will be identical. Assume that the risk-free rate of return in the economy is 4.0% and the market risk premium is 5.0%.

(amounts in millions)	Southwest Airlines	Kroger	Yum! Brands
Total assets	$14,308	$23,211	$ 7,242
Common equity:			
Book value	$ 4,953	$ 5,176	$ 1,139
Market value	$ 7,490	$14,870	$15,950
Market equity beta	1.10	0.35	1.04
Analysts' consensus forecasts			
of net income for Year +1	$ 252	$ 1,263	$ 1,010

REQUIRED

a. Using the CAPM, compute the required rate of return on equity capital for each firm.
b. Project required income for Year +1 for each firm.
c. Project residual income for Year +1 for each firm.

d. Rank the three firms using expected residual income for Year +1 relative to book value of common equity.

e. What do the different amounts of residual income imply about each firm? Do the projected residual income amounts help explain the differences in market value of equity across these three firms? Explain.

13.16 Equity Valuation Using the Residual Income Model. Morrissey

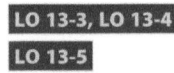

Tool Company manufactures machine tools for other manufacturing firms. The firm is wholly owned by Kelsey Morrissey. The firm's accountant developed the following long-term forecasts of comprehensive income:

Year +1:	$213,948
Year +2:	$192,008
Year +3:	$187,444
Year +4:	$196,442
Year +5:	$206,667

The accountant expects comprehensive income to grow 5% annually after Year +5. Kelsey withdraws 30% of comprehensive income each year as a dividend. Total common shareholders' equity on January 1, Year +1, is $1,111,141. Kelsey expects to earn a rate of return on her invested equity capital of 12% each year.

REQUIRED

a. Using the residual income valuation model, compute the value of Morrissey Tool Company as of January 1, Year +1.

b. What advice would you give Kelsey regarding her ownership of the firm?

13.17 Equity Valuation Using the Residual Income and Dividend

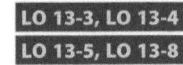

Discount Models. Priority Contractors provides maintenance and cleaning services to various corporate clients in New York City. The firm has provided the following forecasts of comprehensive income for Year +1 to Year +5:

Year +1:	$478,246
Year +2:	$491,882
Year +3:	$485,568
Year +4:	$515,533
Year +5:	$554,198

Total common shareholders' equity was $2,224,401 on January 1, Year +1. The firm does not expect to pay a dividend during the period of Year +1 to Year +5. The cost of equity capital is 12%.

REQUIRED

a. Compute the value of Priority Contractors on January 1, Year +1, using the residual income valuation model. The firm expects comprehensive income to grow 5% annually after Year +5.

b. Compute the value of Priority Contractors on January 1, Year +1, using the dividend discount model. The firm will pay its first dividend in Year +6. (Hint: Solve for the dividend amount using clean surplus accounting and 5% growth in comprehensive income and shareholders' equity in Year +6.)

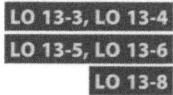

13.18 Equity Valuation Using the Residual Income, Free Cash Flow, and Dividend Discount Models.

Exhibit 13.6 presents selected hypothetical data from projected financial statements for **Steak 'n Shake** for Year +1 to Year +11. The amounts for Year +11 reflect a long-term growth assumption of 3%. The cost of equity capital is 9.34%. Assume net income and comprehensive income will be identical.

REQUIRED

a. Compute the value of Steak 'n Shake as of January 1, Year +1, using the residual income model.

b. Repeat Requirement a using the present value of expected free cash flows to the common equity shareholders.

c. Repeat Requirement a using the dividend discount model.

d. Identify the reasons for any differences in the valuations in Requirements a, b, and c.

e. Suppose the market value of Steak 'n Shake on January 1, Year +1, is $309.98 million. Based on your valuations in Requirements a, b, and c, what is your assessment of the market value of this firm?

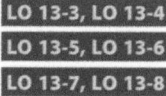

13.19 Residual Income Valuation.

The **Coca-Cola Company** is a global soft drink beverage company (ticker: KO) that is a primary and direct competitor with **Starbucks**. The data in Chapter 12's Exhibits 12.14, 12.15, and 12.16 (pages 806–809) include the actual amounts for 2013, 2014, and 2015 and projected amounts for Year +1 to Year +6 for the income statements, balance sheets, and statements of cash flows, respectively, for Coca-Cola. The market equity beta for Coca-Cola at the end of 2015 is 0.75. Assume that the risk-free interest rate is 3.0% and the market risk premium is 6.0%. Coca-Cola had 4,324 million shares outstanding at the end of 2015, when Coca-Cola's share price was $42.96.

REQUIRED

Part I—Computing Coca-Cola's Share Value Using the Residual Income Valuation Approach

a. Use the CAPM to compute the required rate of return on common equity capital for Coca-Cola.

b. Derive the projected residual income for Coca-Cola for Years +1 through +6 based on the projected financial statements. The financial statement forecasts for Year +6 assume that Coca-Cola will experience a steady-state, long-run growth rate of 3% in Year +6 and beyond.

c. Using the required rate of return on common equity from Requirement a as a discount rate, compute the sum of the present value of residual income for Coca-Cola for Years +1 through +5.

d. Using the required rate of return on common equity from Requirement a as a discount rate and the long-run growth rate from Requirement b, compute the continuing value of Coca-Cola as of the start of Year +6 based on Coca-Cola's continuing residual income in Year +6 and beyond. After computing continuing value as of the start of Year +6, discount it to present value at the start of Year +1.

e. Compute the value of a share of Coca-Cola common stock.

   (1) Compute the total sum of the present value of all residual income (from Requirements c and d).

   (2) Add the book value of equity as of the beginning of the valuation (that is, as of the end of 2015, or the start of Year +1).

   (3) Adjust the total sum of the present value of residual income plus book value of common equity using the midyear discounting adjustment factor.

   (4) Compute the per-share value estimate.

Exhibit 13.6

Steak 'n Shake
Selected Financial Information
(amounts in millions; allow for rounding)
(Problem 13.18)

	Year +1	Year +2	Year +3	Year +4	Year +5	Year +6	Year +7	Year +8	Year +9	Year +10	Year +11[a]
Common equity, beginning of year	$165.8	$177.6	$192.0	$206.0	$216.6	$227.7	$234.2	$238.1	$239.4	$255.8	$269.5
Net income	24.5	25.8	27.6	29.6	31.8	34.2	36.8	39.5	53.9	57.0	58.7
Dividends	(12.7)	(11.4)	(13.6)	(19.0)	(20.8)	(27.7)	(32.9)	(38.2)	(37.4)	(43.3)	(50.6)
Common equity, end of year[b]	$177.6	$192.0	$206.0	$216.6	$227.7	$234.2	$238.1	$239.4	$255.8	$269.5	$277.6
Cash flow from operations	$ 45.4	$ 51.2	$ 56.3	$ 61.5	$ 67.1	$ 72.9	$ 78.9	$ 85.2	$ 85.6	$ 92.4	$ 73.2
Cash flow for investing	(35.2)	(41.1)	(41.9)	(42.7)	(43.5)	(44.4)	(45.2)	(46.0)	(47.3)	(48.1)	(22.1)
Cash flow for long-term debt	(0.5)	2.0	—	1.0	(2.0)	—	—	—	—	—	—
Cash flow for dividends	(12.7)	(11.4)	(13.6)	(19.0)	(20.8)	(27.7)	(32.9)	(38.2)	(37.4)	(43.3)	(50.6)
Net change in cash	$ (3.0)	$ 0.7	$ 0.8	$ 0.8	$ 0.8	$ 0.8	$ 0.8	$ 1.0	$ 0.9	$ 1.0	$ 0.5

[a]The amounts for Year +11 result from increasing each income statement and balance sheet amount by the expected long-term growth rate of 3% and then deriving the amounts for the statement of cash flows.

[b]Amounts on this line may reflect the effects of rounding of intermediate computations.

Part II—Sensitivity Analysis and Recommendation

f. Using the residual income valuation approach, compute the value of Coca-Cola shares under two alternative scenarios.

Scenario 1: Assume that Coca-Cola's long-run growth will be 2%, not 3% as above, and that Coca-Cola's required rate of return on equity is 1% higher than that calculated in Requirement a.

Scenario 2: Assume that Coca-Cola's long-run growth will be 4%, not 3% as above, and that Coca-Cola's required rate of return on equity is 1% lower than that calculated in Requirement a.

To quantify the sensitivity of your share value estimate for Coca-Cola to these variations in growth and discount rates, compare (in percentage terms) your value estimates under these two scenarios with your value estimate from Requirement e.

g. Using these data at the end of 2015, what reasonable range of share values would you have expected for Coca-Cola common stock? At that time, what was the market price for Coca-Cola shares relative to this range? What would you have recommended?

h. If you completed Problem 12.16 in Chapter 12, compare the value estimate you obtained in Requirement e of that problem (using the free cash flows to common equity shareholders valuation approach) with the value estimate you obtained here using the residual income valuation approach. The value estimates should be the same. If you have not completed Problem 12.16, you would benefit from doing so now.

INTEGRATIVE CASE 13.1

Walmart

LO 13-3, LO 13-4
LO 13-5, LO 13-6
LO 13-7, LO 13-8

Residual Income Valuation of Walmart's Common Equity

In Integrative Case 10.1, we projected financial statements for **Walmart Stores, Inc.** (Walmart), for Years +1 through +5. The data in Chapter 12's Exhibits 12.17, 12.18, and 12.19 (pages 812–814) include the actual amounts for 2015 and the projected amounts for Year +1 to Year +5 for the income statements, balance sheets, and statements of cash flows, respectively, for Walmart. The market equity beta for Walmart at the end of 2015 was 1.00. Assume that the risk-free interest rate was 3.0% and the market risk premium was 6.0%. Walmart had 3,162 million shares outstanding at the end of 2015 and a share price of $67.50.

REQUIRED

Part I—Computing Walmart's Share Value Using the Residual Income Valuation Approach

a. Use the CAPM to compute the required rate of return on common equity capital for Walmart.

b. Derive the projected residual income for Walmart for Years +1 through +5 based on the projected financial statements.

c. Project the continuing residual income in Year +6. Assume that the steady-state, long-run growth rate will be 3% in Year +6 and beyond. Project that the Year +5 income statement and balance sheet amounts will grow by 3% in Year +6; then derive the projected amount of residual income for Year +6.

d. Using the required rate of return on common equity from Requirement a as a discount rate, compute the sum of the present value of residual income for Walmart for Years $+1$ through $+5$.

e. Using the required rate of return on common equity from Requirement a as a discount rate and the long-run growth rate from Requirement c, compute the continuing value of Walmart as of the start of Year $+6$ based on Walmart's continuing residual income in Year $+6$ and beyond. After computing continuing value as of the start of Year $+6$, discount it to present value at the start of Year $+1$.

f. Compute the value of a share of Walmart common stock.

    (1) Compute the total sum of the present value of all future residual income (from Requirements d and e).

    (2) Add the book value of equity as of the beginning of the valuation (that is, as of the end of 2015, or the start of Year $+1$).

    (3) Adjust the total sum of the present value of residual income plus book value of common equity using the midyear discounting adjustment factor.

    (4) Compute the per-share value estimate.

Part II—Sensitivity Analysis and Recommendation

g. Using the residual income valuation method, compute the value of Walmart shares under two alternative scenarios.

    Scenario 1: Assume that Walmart's long-run growth will be 2%, not 3% as above, and that Walmart's required rate of return on equity is 1 percentage point higher than the rate you computed using the CAPM in Requirement a.

    Scenario 2: Assume that Walmart's long-run growth will be 4%, not 3% as above, and that Walmart's required rate of return on equity is 1 percentage point lower than the rate you computed using the CAPM in Requirement a.

    To quantify the sensitivity of your share value estimate for Walmart to these variations in growth and discount rates, compare (in percentage terms) your value estimates under these two scenarios with your value estimate from Requirement f.

h. Using these data at the end of 2015, what reasonable range of share values would you have expected for Walmart common stock? At that time, what was the market price for Walmart shares relative to this range? What would you have recommended?

i. If you worked Case 11.1 from Chapter 11 and computed Walmart's share value using the dividends valuation approach, compare your value estimate from Requirement g of that problem with the value estimate you obtained here. Similarly, if you worked Case 12.1 from Chapter 12 and computed Walmart's share value using the free cash flows to common equity shareholders, compare your value estimate from Requirement f of that problem with the value estimate you obtained here. You should obtain the same value estimates for Walmart shares under all three approaches. If you have not worked both of those problems, you would benefit from doing so now.

Valuation: Market-Based Approaches

LO 14-1 Explain the practical advantages and disadvantages of using market-based valuation multiples such as market-to-book (MB) and price-earnings (PE) ratios to assess the capital market's relative valuation of a particular stock.

LO 14-2 For market-to-book (MB) ratios:

   a. Apply a version of the residual income valuation model to compute the value-to-book (VB) ratio.

   b. Make investment decisions by comparing the VB ratio to the MB ratio.

   c. Explain why VB and MB ratios differ across firms and the impact of the following factors on VB and MB ratios: (1) risk and the cost of equity capital, (2) growth, (3) differences between current and expected future earnings, and (4) alternative accounting methods.

LO 14-3 For price-earnings (PE) ratios:

   a. Understand the theory and the practical approach to compute and use the firm's value-earnings (VE) ratio, and compare it to the PE ratio.

   b. Incorporate growth into the PE ratio to compute the price-earnings-growth (PEG) ratio.

   c. Use PE and PEG ratios to analyze share prices over time and across firms, and to make investment decisions.

   d. Explain why VE and PE ratios differ across firms and the impact of (1) risk and the cost of equity capital, (2) growth, (3) differences between current and expected future earnings, and (4) alternative accounting methods.

LO 14-4 Reverse engineer a firm's stock price to determine the implied expected return or the implied expected long-run growth rate.

LO 14-5 Explain the notion of capital market efficiency in valuation and the empirical evidence on the degree to which the capital markets efficiently impound earnings information into share prices.

Chapter Overview

Chapters 1 through 13 establish a disciplined and effective six-step framework that uses firm fundamentals to attack a very difficult but fascinating problem: how to analyze and value a firm. In using this framework, we must first understand the firm's industry and business strategy and then use that understanding to assess the quality of the firm's accounting, making adjustments as necessary. We then evaluate the firm's profitability, risk, growth, efficiency, liquidity, and leverage, using a set of financial ratios. We then forecast the firm's future business activities, measuring the expected outcomes of these activities with projected future balance sheets, income statements, and statements of cash flows. We derive from our financial statement forecasts the firm's expected future dividends, free cash flows, and residual income, which we then use to value the firm. We also assess the sensitivity of our share value estimates to key parameters such as the cost of capital and the expected long-run growth rate. To culminate this process, we compute a range of share value estimates and compare this range to the firm's share price in order to make an intelligent investment decision.

Exhibit 14.1 provides a summary representation of this fundamentals-driven valuation process. The top of the exhibit depicts the firm's value drivers, such as expected future earnings, cash flows, dividends, growth, and risk, which comprise the economic foundations of valuation. We capture these value determinants in forecasts of future financial statements, and then use these forecasts to estimate firm value using the residual income model, the free cash flows model, and the dividends model.

In this chapter, we continue our focus on fundamental characteristics of profitability, risk, growth, and value, but we augment that approach by exploiting the information in *share price*. We apply a variety of techniques that compare the firm's share price to the firm's fundamentals. The techniques described in this chapter include commonly used market multiples—market-to-book (MB) ratios, price-earnings (PE) ratios, and price-earnings-growth (PEG) ratios—which provide efficient shortcuts in the valuation process. As Exhibit 14.2 depicts, market multiples require an understanding of the same set of value drivers—expected earnings, cash flows, dividends, growth, and risk. But market multiples collapse the valuation process. Rather than developing financial statement forecasts and computing present values of expected future payoffs, users of market multiples rely on simple ratios of share price relative to just one summary accounting number, such as earnings per share or book value of common equity per share.

Exhibit 14.1

Fundamentals of Valuation

Analyze Fundamental Determinants of Firm Value:
Earnings, Cash Flows, Dividends, Growth, Risk

Forecast Future Financial Statements and Derive Fundamental Value Drivers over the Remaining Life of the Firm:
Expected Future Earnings, Cash Flows, Dividends, Risk

Compute:
Firm Value
= Book Value of Common Equity + Present Value of Expected Future Residual Income
= Present Value of Expected Future Free Cash Flows to Common Equity Shareholders
= Present Value of Expected Future Dividends

Share Value

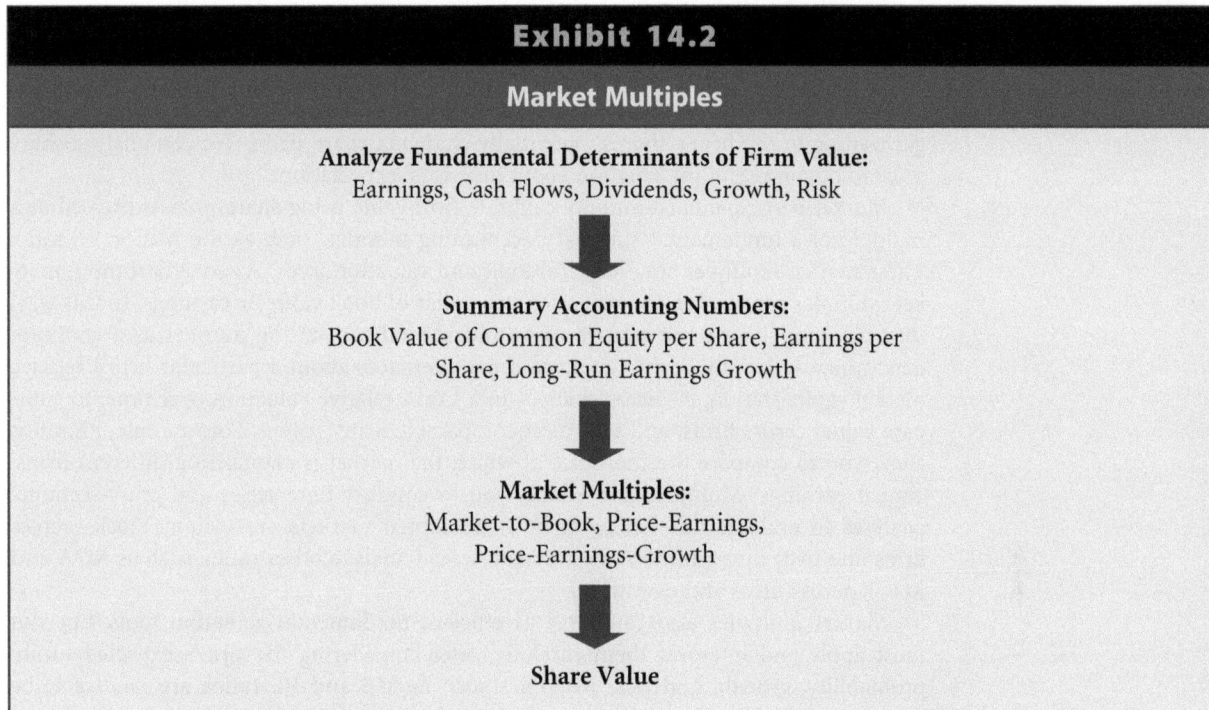

Exhibit 14.2

Market Multiples

Analyze Fundamental Determinants of Firm Value:
Earnings, Cash Flows, Dividends, Growth, Risk

Summary Accounting Numbers:
Book Value of Common Equity per Share, Earnings per Share, Long-Run Earnings Growth

Market Multiples:
Market-to-Book, Price-Earnings, Price-Earnings-Growth

Share Value

In this chapter, we also demonstrate *reverse engineering* share prices, a technique that enables you to infer the assumptions the capital market appears to be making in pricing a particular share. In the last section of the chapter, we summarize a few key insights from the last 50 years of accounting and finance research suggesting that the capital markets are highly but not perfectly efficient in using accounting earnings information to price stocks. These research findings are encouraging for those interested in using earnings and accounting information for fundamental analysis and valuation of stocks and for developing trading strategies to exploit accounting information.

Market Multiples of Accounting Numbers

LO 14-1

Explain the practical advantages and disadvantages of using market-based valuation multiples such as market-to-book (MB) and price-earnings (PE) ratios to assess the capital market's relative valuation of a particular stock.

Throughout this text, we have described how to analyze the wide array of information available in financial statements: earnings, balance sheet amounts, cash flows, footnotes, supplemental management disclosures, financial ratios, growth rates, and others. However, we have not analyzed and exploited the information in one very important number: *share price*. The market price for a share of common equity is a special and informative number; it is the result of the market's trading activity in that stock, so it aggregates the expectations of all market participants (investors, potential investors, market makers, analysts, and others) following that particular stock. It summarizes the information the market participants have about the firm and their aggregate expectations for the firm's future profitability, growth, risk, and value.

The market price of a share does not mean that all market participants agree that that price is the correct value for the share. In fact, the prices at which potential buyers or sellers may be willing to trade may differ widely across market participants and over time. Indeed, the market price simply indicates that momentary point of equilibrium in which the forces of supply (investors willing to sell the stock—the "ask" side of trading) and the forces of demand (market participants willing to buy the stock—the "bid" side of trading) are in balance. Stock prices are dynamic. Discovery of new information can quickly change investors' expectations about share value and trigger trading in the firm's shares, potentially changing share price. We can analyze share price to obtain useful information about investors' expectations.

Market participants commonly calibrate firm value using share price expressed as a multiple of a fundamental summary accounting number, such as the MB or PE ratio. These market multiples are analytical tools and valuation tools. As analytical tools, market multiples capture *relative* valuation per dollar of book value or earnings. In this way, they measure share price relative to a fundamental accounting number as a common denominator, thereby enabling you to draw inferences about a particular firm's relative market capitalization, to assess changes in a firm's relative valuation over time, to compare values across firms, and to project comparable firms' values. For example, PE ratios allow you to compare the multiples at which the market is capitalizing different firms' annual earnings. Multiples also enable you to conduct time-series and cross-sectional analyses to evaluate differences in how the capital markets are valuing stocks across firms and over time (in the same way you would analyze other ratios such as ROA and ROCE across firms and over time).

Market multiples also can serve as efficient fundamental valuation tools, but you must apply and interpret them carefully, after considering the firm's expected future profitability, growth, and risk. Multiples such as MB and PE ratios are *relative* value metrics, in which market value is denominated relative to a summary accounting measure; therefore, they are not meaningful as stand-alone valuation measures. For example, you cannot determine whether a particular firm's PE ratio should be 10, 20, 50, or some other number unless you know the firm's fundamental characteristics: expected future profitability, growth, and risk. Similarly, you cannot determine whether a particular firm's PE ratio should be higher or lower than some other firm's PE ratio or the industry average PE ratio unless you know how the firm's expected future profitability, growth, and risk characteristics compare to those characteristics of the other firm or the industry as a whole.

For example, a firm may have a very high PE ratio at a particular point in time for very different reasons: perhaps the share price is too high; perhaps the market expects and prices very high future earnings growth; or perhaps the firm experienced temporarily low earnings last period (because of a restructuring charge, for example). If you use market multiples to draw simple or naive inferences about the firm's market price without carefully researching the firm's fundamentals, you risk badly misinterpreting market multiples.

Market multiples can be useful shortcut valuation tools. Unfortunately, analysts sometimes apply market multiples to estimate value in ad hoc and simplistic ways, and this "quick-and-dirty" approach may be misleading. A naive analyst might be tempted to value a firm simply by using its historical average or the industry average market multiple. The firm's historical average MB ratio, for example, may be an appropriate fit for the valuation of the firm today, but only if the firm's current fundamental characteristics match those of the past. Similarly, an industry average PE multiple may be an appropriate multiple for valuing a particular firm, but only if that firm's fundamental characteristics match the industry averages. If the firm's fundamentals have changed or do not match the industry averages, then you must adjust market multiples to reflect the firm's fundamental characteristics.

This chapter continues to emphasize the distinction between *value* and *price*. The chapter focuses on how you should compute *value*-based multiples that properly reflect the firm's fundamentals and that you can reliably compare to market *price*-based multiples. This focus also directs your attention to the factors that drive multiples so that you can adjust historical or industry average multiples correctly to reflect the firm's expected future profitability, growth, and risk.

Market-to-Book and Value-to-Book Ratios

LO 14-2

For market-to-book (MB) ratios:
a. Apply a version of the residual income valuation model to compute the value-to-book (VB) ratio.
b. Make investment decisions by comparing the VB ratio to the MB ratio.
c. Explain why VB and MB ratios differ across firms and the impact of the following factors on VB and MB ratios: (1) risk and the cost of equity capital, (2) growth, (3) differences between current and expected future earnings, and (4) alternative accounting methods.

We can compute the MB ratio easily by dividing the firm's market value of common equity at a point in time by the book value of common equity from the firm's most recent balance sheet. For example, on September 27, 2015, **Starbucks'** market value was $84,413 million ($56.84 per share × 1,485.1 million shares) and **Starbucks'** 2015 book value of common shareholders' equity was $5,818.0 million (Appendix A). Thus, **Starbucks** was trading at an MB ratio equal to 14.5 ($84,413 million/$5,818 million). The MB ratio measures market value as a multiple of accounting book value at a point in time. The MB ratio reflects what the market value *is*, but it does not tell us what the ratio *should be* given our estimate of intrinsic value. By computing the VB ratio (share value), we can determine whether the MB ratio (market price) is too high, too low, or about right.

A Model of the Value-to-Book Ratio

We can compute the value-to-book (VB) ratio (the firm's intrinsic value of common shareholders' equity divided by the book value of common shareholders' equity) using a version of the residual income model developed in Chapter 13. In fact, the VB ratio model is simply the residual income model scaled by book value of common shareholders' equity. The numerator of the VB ratio is the estimated intrinsic value of common equity, as shown in Chapter 13. The denominator of the VB ratio (denoted BV_0) is the total book value of common shareholders' equity (excluding equity of noncontrolling interests). You can compare the VB ratio to the MB ratio to make an investment decision the same way previous chapters compared share value to share price. You also can use the VB ratio of one firm to estimate the value of a comparable firm, provided you make whatever adjustments to the VB ratio are necessary so that it reflects the comparable firm's fundamental profitability, risk, and growth characteristics.

Using the same notation from prior chapters, we compute the VB ratio using the following model:

$$\frac{V_0}{BV_0} = 1 + \sum_{t=1}^{\infty} \frac{(ROCE_t - R_E) \times \frac{BV_{t-1}}{BV_0}}{(1 + R_E)^t}$$

In short, the VB ratio should be equal to 1 plus the present value of the expected future residual return on common equity [the $(ROCE_t - R_E)$ term above] times cumulative growth in book value (the BV_{t-1}/BV_0 term above). The growth in book value indicates the increase in net assets on which firms can earn residual income. The growth in book value depends on ROCE, dividend payout, and changes in common stock

assign the firm a VB ratio equal to 1 plus the present value of future residual ROCE times growth, determined as follows:

Year	Expected ROCE	Residual ROCE (ROCE − R_E)	Cumulative Book Value Growth Factor to Year $t-1$	Residual ROCE × Cumulative Growth	PV Factor	PV of Residual ROCE × Cumulative Growth
+1	0.15	0.05	$1.00 = (1.15)^0$	0.05000	0.9091	0.04546
+2	0.15	0.05	$1.15 = (1.15)^1$	0.05750	0.8264	0.04752
+3	0.15	0.05	$1.3225 = (1.15)^2$	0.06613	0.7513	0.04968
+4	0.10	0.00	$1.5209 = (1.15)^3$	0.00000	0.6830	0.00000
					Total	0.14266

The sum of the present values of residual ROCE times cumulative growth through Year +3 equals 0.14266, and the sum in all years after Year +3 is zero. Adding this present value amount to 1 (to reflect the book value of equity already in place), the VB ratio of this firm is 1.14266. Note that we have determined this VB ratio with all of the inputs expressed in rates. We can multiply the VB ratio of 1.14266 by book value of equity ($1,000) to determine that firm value is $1,142.66. We can confirm this value using dollar amounts and the residual income approach from Chapter 13 as follows:

Year	Expected ROCE	Expected Earnings	Cumulative Book Value at the End of Year $t-1$ (BV_{t-1})	Required Income ($BV_{t-1} \times R_E$)	Residual Income	PV Factor	PV of Residual Income
+1	0.15	$150.00 = 0.15 × $1,000	$1,000	$100 = $1,000 × 0.10	$50.00 = $150 − $100	0.9091	$ 45.46
+2	0.15	$172.50 = 0.15 × $1,150	$1,150 = $1,000 + $150	$115 = $1,150 × 0.10	$57.50 = $172.50 − $115	0.8264	47.52
+3	0.15	$198.38 = 0.15 × $1,322.5	$1,322.5 = $1,150 + $172.5	$132.25 = $1,322.5 × 0.10	$66.13 = $198.38 − $132.25	0.7513	49.68
+4	0.10	$152.09 = 0.10 × $1,520.9	$1,520.9 = $1,322.5 + $198.4	$152.09 = $1,520.9 × 0.10	$0.00 = $152.09 − $152.09	0.6830	0.00
						Total	$142.66

The sum of the present values of residual income through Year +3 equals $142.66, the sum in all years after Year +3 is zero, and book value of equity is $1,000; so the residual income model confirms that firm value is $1,142.66.

The Value-to-Book Model with Finite Horizon Earnings Forecasts and Continuing Value

As we discussed in Chapters 11 through 13, analysts commonly forecast income statements, balance sheets, and cash flows over a foreseeable, finite horizon and then make simplifying growth rate assumptions for the years continuing after the forecast horizon.

We can modify the VB model to include specific forecasts of comprehensive income, book value of common equity, and ROCE through Year T (where T is a finite horizon, for example, 5 or 10 years in the future) and then apply a constant growth rate assumption (denoted as g) to project ROCE for Year T+1 and all years thereafter. We used similar approaches to forecast and value dividends in Chapter 11, free cash flows in Chapter 12, and residual income in Chapter 13.

To develop the VB model with finite horizon earnings forecasts and continuing value computations, we use the same approach as in Chapter 13, with only slight modifications. Recall from Chapter 13 that we used specific forecasts of financial statements for a finite horizon through Year T and then projected Year T+1 comprehensive income by multiplying Year T comprehensive income by the long-run growth factor $(1 + g)$. We then computed Year T+1 residual income (denoted as RI_{T+1}) as follows:

$$RI_{T+1} = [CI_T \times (1 + g)] - (R_E \times BV_T)$$

By estimating RI_{T+1} this way, we apply the same uniform long-run growth factor $(1 + g)$ to estimate Year T+1 income statement and balance sheet amounts and compute internally consistent projections for Year T+1 free cash flows, dividends, and residual income.

As we discussed in Chapter 13, you can treat RI_{T+1} as a growing perpetuity of residual income beginning in Year T+1. You can then compute the present value using the perpetuity-with-growth value model as follows:

Present Value of
Continuing Value$_0$ $= \{[CI_T \times (1 + g)] - (R_E \times BV_T)\} \times [1/(R_E - g)] \times [1/(1 + R_E)^T]$

We can modify this computation to adapt it to the value-to-book model with two steps:

1. Divide the term $[CI_T \times (1 + g)]$ by BV_T to convert it to an ROCE measure for Year T+1.
2. Divide the BV_T term by BV_0 to measure the cumulative growth in book value.

The result of these two steps is a continuing value computation based on projected future residual ROCE and book value growth as follows:

Present Value of Continuing Value$_0$

$$= \{[CI_T \times (1 + g)/BV_T] - R_E\} \times (BV_T/BV_0) \times [1/(R_E - g)] \times [1/(1 + R_E)^T]$$
$$= [ROCE_{T+1} - R_E] \times [BV_T/BV_0] \times [1/(R_E - g)] \times [1/(1 + R_E)^T]$$
$$\quad (1) \qquad\qquad (2) \qquad\qquad (3) \qquad\qquad (4)$$

The first term in the computation is projected residual ROCE in Year T+1. The second term is the cumulative growth in book value from present (BV_0) to the beginning of the continuing value period (BV_T). The third term is the perpetuity-with-growth factor, computing the present value of the perpetuity as of the start of the continuing value period. The fourth term is the present value factor that discounts continuing value to present value today.

We include the continuing value computation into the finite horizon VB model as follows:

$$\frac{V_0}{BV_0} = 1 + \sum_{t=1}^{T} \frac{(ROCE_t - R_E) \times \frac{BV_{t-1}}{BV_0}}{(1 + R_E)^t} + \underbrace{(ROCE_{T+1} - R_E) \times (BV_T/BV_0) \times [1/(R_E - g)] \times [1/(1 + R_E)^T]}$$
$$\quad (1) \qquad\qquad (2) \qquad\qquad (3)$$

This model computes the value-to-book ratio of common equity based on three parts: (1) book value scaled by book value (BV_0/BV_0, which is, of course, equal to 1), (2) the present value of residual ROCE over the explicit forecast horizon through Year T (the summation term), and (3) the present value of continuing value based on residual ROCE as a perpetuity with growth beginning in Year T+1.

Why Might VB Ratios and MB Ratios Differ from 1?

The expression for the VB ratio provides some deep insights into valuation. First, let's focus on a number of *economic* reasons why VB and MB ratios may differ from 1:

- *In long-run equilibrium, firms should expect to earn a return equal to the cost of capital (that is, ROCE = R_E).* The VB model indicates that a firm in steady-state equilibrium earning ROCE = R_E will maintain (not create or destroy) shareholder wealth and will be valued at book value. That is, for firms in equilibrium, we expect abnormal earnings will likely be zero, so we would expect VB = 1.
- *The firm may have competitive advantages that enable it to earn an ROCE that is greater than R_E.* To the extent that the firm can sustain these competitive advantages, the firm will increase the magnitude and persistence over time of the degree to which ROCE exceeds R_E, thereby increasing firm value and the VB and MB ratios. A firm's value should be greater than its book value of common equity if the firm is expected to generate wealth for common equity shareholders by earning a return (ROCE) that exceeds the cost of capital (R_E). That is, VB > 1 if ROCE > R_E. By contrast, firms that are expected to earn a return that is less than the cost of equity capital (that is, ROCE < R_E) will destroy shareholder wealth and will be valued below book value (that is, VB < 1).
- *By itself, growth in book value does not create firm value.* Growth creates value for shareholders only if the growth generates additional residual income for common equity shareholders. If expected ROCE equals R_E on new projects (that is, zero NPV projects), these new projects will not create or destroy common shareholders' equity value. New projects will create new wealth for equity shareholders (that is, will be positive NPV projects) only when expected ROCE exceeds R_E.
- *The risk of the firm increases the equity cost of capital, R_E.* Increasing the equity cost of capital reduces firm value in two ways: (1) by increasing the required ROCE the firm must earn to cover the increased R_E (that is, the "hurdle rate" goes up in the numerator) and (2) by increasing the discount rate used to compute the present value of residual income (which increases the denominator).
- A firm's VB ratio will differ from the industry average VB ratio if the firm's expected future ROCE, R_E, and/or book value growth differ from the industry averages.
- A firm's VB ratio will change over time, when current expectations for the firm's future ROCE, R_E, and/or book value growth differ from past expectations for the firm's future ROCE, R_E, and/or book value growth, respectively.

In addition to those economic reasons, a firm's VB and MB ratio may differ from 1 for *accounting* reasons.[4] The firm may have investments in projects for which

---

[4]Stephen Ryan (1995) found that book value changes lag market value changes in part because U.S. GAAP uses historical cost valuations for assets. The lag varies in part based on the degree of capital intensity of firms. See Stephen Ryan, "A Model of Accrual Measurement and Implications for the Evolution of the Book-to-Market Ratio," *Journal of Accounting Research* (Spring 1995), pp. 95–112.

accounting methods and principles cause ROCE to differ from R_E. For example, firms may make substantial investments in successful R&D projects, brand equity, human capital, or other intangible resources. If these investments are internally generated through R&D activities, marketing and advertising activities, or human capital recruiting and training activities, firms are typically required to expense them according to U.S. GAAP and IFRS. If these investments subsequently develop into profitable resources, they will generate substantial net income. However, the firm also will have substantial off-balance-sheet assets and off-balance-sheet common shareholders' equity. Together, these effects will cause common shareholders' equity to be understated, so ROCE will be relatively high. These effects can be observed among certain firms in many industries, such as pharmaceuticals, biotechnology, software, and consumer goods.

Starbucks has created substantial off-balance-sheet brand equity over many years of successful product development, advertising, and brand-building activities (similar to other successful brand name firms like **Apple, Google**, and **Coca-Cola**). Following U.S. GAAP, these firms have expensed their expenditures on these activities. Thus, for these firms, the book value of common shareholders' equity does not recognize the off-balance-sheet value of brand equity. Relative to R_E, ROCE for **Starbucks** is very high and likely will continue to be very high for many years in the future.

Over a sufficiently long period of time, however, the impact of accounting principles on the VB and MB ratio will diminish because economics teaches us to expect that competitive equilibrium forces will drive ROCE to R_E in the long run. Also, the self-correcting nature of accounting will eventually eliminate conservative biases in ROCE and book value of equity. For example, consider a biotechnology company that for several years invests in R&D to develop a particular drug. During the initial years of research, the firm incurs research costs that the firm is required to expense under U.S. GAAP. Its ROCE and book value of equity will be "low" during these years. After successfully developing and marketing the drug, ROCE will be "high" because the firm generates revenues without matching expenses for research costs. The "high" ROCE will increase retained earnings, and, over time, the initial conservative biases in ROCE and book value will eventually be corrected.

Application of the Value-to-Book Model to Starbucks

In Chapter 13, we determined that **Starbucks'** share value at the end of fiscal 2015 should be within a reasonable range centered on $66.10. We determined this amount using the financial statement forecasts developed in Chapter 10 and the residual income valuation model. Given that we already have an estimate of share value, we can simply divide by book value of equity per share to determine the VB ratio. **Starbucks'** book value per share at the end of fiscal 2015 was $3.9176 ($5,818.0 million/1,485.1 million shares). Thus, **Starbucks'** VB ratio at the end of fiscal 2015 should be 16.872 ($66.10 value per share/$3.9176 book value equity per share).

We illustrate the valuation of **Starbucks** shares using the VB model to illustrate the rigor of the VB model and its consistency with the residual income valuation approach in Chapter 13. To apply the VB model to **Starbucks**, we rely on the same financial statement forecasts developed in Chapter 10, the same equity cost of capital (7.2%), the same expected long-run growth rate (3.0%), and the same residual income computations and valuation steps developed in Chapter 13. We summarize the computations to arrive at **Starbucks'** common equity share value using the VB approach in Exhibit 14.3, where

we present the VB model for **Starbucks** from FSAP. We present all of the forecasts and valuation models in the FSAP Forecasts and Valuation spreadsheets in Appendix C.

In applying the VB model to **Starbucks**, note that the first two rows of information in Exhibit 14.3 are identical to the amounts used in Exhibit 13.4 on page 849 to apply the residual income valuation model: the projected amounts of comprehensive income available to common shareholders and projected book values of common shareholders' equity. Using these amounts, the Year +1 projected ROCE is 48.0% ($2,794.3 million/$5,818.0 million). The residual ROCE is 40.8% after subtracting 7.2% for the cost of equity capital. The cumulative growth factor in book value (BV_{t-1}/BV_0) in Year +1 is 1.0 because Year +1 is the first year of the valuation horizon.[5] Therefore, the product of Year +1 residual ROCE times the cumulative growth factor is 40.8%, which we discount to present value using the 7.2% cost of equity capital. Exhibit 14.3 presents these computations for **Starbucks** for Year +1 through Year +5. The sum of the present value of residual ROCE times growth in Year +1 through Year +5 is 2.23.[6]

For purposes of computing continuing value, as described in the previous chapter, we project comprehensive income in Year +6 to grow by the 3.0% long-run growth rate. Using projected book value as of the start of Year +6 (the end of Year +5), we compute implied residual ROCE and multiply by the cumulative growth factor in book value up to the beginning of Year +6. The projected ROCE in Year +6 is 69.1% $\{[CI_5 \times (1 + g)]/BV_5 = ($4,895.0 \text{ million} \times 1.03)/$7,297.3 \text{ million} = $5,041.8 \text{ million}/$7,297.3 \text{ million}\}$. After subtracting the 7.2% cost of equity capital, the projected residual ROCE in Year +6 is 61.9%. Cumulative growth in book value from Year 0 to the beginning of Year +6 (the end of Year +5) is 125.4% $(BV_5/BV_0 = $7,297.3 \text{ million}/$5,818.0 \text{ million})$. Therefore, we project that in Year +6, the product of residual ROCE times cumulative growth is 77.6% (61.9% × 125.4%). The present value of continuing value is computed as follows (allow for rounding):

Present Value of Continuing Value$_0$

$$= [\{NI_5 \times (1+g)/BV_5\} - R_E] \times [BV_5/BV_0] \times [1/(R_E - g)] \times [1/(1 + R_E)^5]$$
$$= [($4,895.0 \times 1.03)/$7,297.3 - 0.072] \times [$7,297.3/$5,818.0]$$
$$\times [1/(0.072 - 0.030)] \times [1/(1 + 0.072)^5]$$
$$= 0.619 \times 1.254 \times 23.8095 \times 0.706 = 13.06$$

To compute the VB ratio, we need to add the present value of future residual income and **Starbucks'** beginning book value of common equity expressed as a ratio of beginning book value of equity, which is, of course, equal to 1. Also, as described in prior chapters, our present value calculations over-discount because they discount each year's residual ROCE for full periods. Therefore, we multiply the present value sum by

[5]We project that **Starbucks'** book value of common equity will decrease to $4,772.4 million by the end of Year +1. Therefore, the cumulative growth factor in book value of common equity as of the start of Year +2 will be 0.820 ($4,772.4 million/$5,818.0 million).

[6]This amount should be interpreted as a component of the VB ratio because all of the computations in the model are scaled by BV_0. Thus, the amount 2.23 is an estimate of the amount of residual income **Starbucks** will create in Years +1 through +5 that, in present value, is equal to 2.23 times the book value of common equity. To reconcile this computation with the residual income model computations in Chapter 13, recognize that 2.23 times book value of $5,818.0 million equals $12,972.6 (allow for rounding), which is the sum of the present value of residual income in Year +1 through Year +5 computed in Exhibit 13.2.

Exhibit 14.3

Valuation of Starbucks
Using the Value-to-Book Approach
(dollar amounts in millions, except per-share amounts; allow for rounding)

RESIDUAL INCOME VALUATION						Continuing Value
	1	2	3	4	5	
Market-to-Book Approach	Year +1	Year +2	Year +3	Year +4	Year +5	Year +6
Comprehensive income available for common shareholders	$ 2,794.3	$3,080.6	$3,490.0	$3,939.8	$4,895.0	$ 5,041.8
Book value of common shareholders' equity (at $t-1$)	$ 5,818.0	$4,772.4	$5,062.6	$5,474.4	$5,985.9	$ 7,297.3
Implied ROCE	48.0%	64.6%	68.9%	72.0%	81.8%	69.1%
Residual ROCE	40.8%	57.4%	61.7%	64.8%	74.6%	61.9%
Cumulative growth factor in common equity as of $t-1$	100.0%	82.0%	87.0%	94.1%	102.9%	125.4%
Residual ROCE times cumulative growth	40.8%	47.0%	53.7%	60.9%	76.7%	77.6%
Present value factors	0.933	0.870	0.812	0.757	0.706	
Present value residual ROCE times growth	0.381	0.409	0.436	0.461	0.542	
Sum of present value residual ROCE times growth	2.23					
Present value of continuing value	13.06					
Total present value residual ROCE	15.29					
Add one for book value of equity at $t-1$	1.00					
Sum	16.29					
Adjust to midyear discounting	1.036					
Implied market-to-book ratio	16.872					
Times beginning book value of equity	$ 5,818.0					
Total present value of equity	$98,159.2					
Shares outstanding	1,485.1					
Estimated value per share	$ 66.10					
Current share price	$ 56.84					
Percent difference	16%					

the midyear discounting adjustment factor of 1.036 $[1 + (R_E/2) = 1 + (0.072/2)]$. The implied VB ratio is computed as follows:

Present value of residual ROCE in Year +1 through Year +5	2.23
Present value of continuing value of residual ROCE in Year +6 and beyond	13.06
Present value of all future residual ROCE	15.29
Add: Beginning book value	+1.00
Total	16.29
Multiply by the midyear discounting factor	×1.036
Implied VB ratio	16.872

These computations confirm that **Starbucks'** common equity should be valued at 16.872 times the book value of equity at the end of fiscal 2015. At that time, **Starbucks'** market value was $84,413 million ($56.84 per share × 1,485.1 million shares) and **Starbucks'** book value of common shareholders' equity was $5,818.0 million. Thus, **Starbucks** was trading at an MB ratio equal to 14.509 ($84,413.0 million/$5,818.0 million). The VB ratio of 16.872 is 16% greater than the MB ratio of 14.509, implying that **Starbucks'** shares were underpriced by 16% at that time.

Equivalently, we can convert the VB ratio into a share value estimate for purposes of comparing to market price per share. If we multiply book value equity by the VB ratio, we obtain the value estimate of **Starbucks'** common equity of $98,159.2 million ($5,818.0 million × 16.872 VB ratio). Dividing by 1,485.1 million shares outstanding indicates that **Starbucks'** common equity shares have a value of $66.10 per share, which is identical to the value estimates we obtained from the residual income model in Chapter 13, the free cash flows to common equity shareholders model in Chapter 12, and the dividend models in Chapter 11. Comparing the share value estimate of $66.10 to market price per share of $56.84 also indicates that **Starbucks'** shares were underpriced by 16% at the end of fiscal 2015.

We can conduct a sensitivity analysis for the estimate of **Starbucks'** VB ratio to assess a reasonable range of VB ratios for **Starbucks**. We will find that the sensitivity of the VB ratio estimate is identical to the sensitivity of the residual income model value estimates demonstrated in Chapter 13. This is to be expected because both models use the same forecasts and valuation assumptions and the VB model is a scaled version of the residual income model.

Empirical Data on MB Ratios

Exhibit 14.4 presents descriptive statistics for MB ratios across 48 industries during the decade from 2006 to 2015 (the same industries and years for which Exhibit 11.3 provided data on market betas).[7] The median MB ratio for the 45,103 firm-years in this sample is 1.77.[8] These data reveal substantial variation in MB ratios across industries and within industries during this period. The descriptive statistics on MB and other ratios across industries and years in Appendix D (which can be found online at the

---

[7]Our sincere thanks to Professor Matt Wieland for providing these data and the data in Exhibits 11.3 and 14.6.

[8]To compute these descriptive statistics on market-to-book value ratios, we deleted firm-years with negative book value of equity. We also deleted firm-year observations in the top 1% of the distribution to reduce the influence of potential outliers.

Exhibit 14.4

Descriptive Statistics on Market-to-Book Ratios, 2006–2015
Forty-Eight Industries Sorted by Median Market-to-Book Ratios

Industry:	25th Percentile	Median	75th Percentile
Full sample (45,103 firm-years)	**1.09**	**1.77**	**3.12**
Banking	0.75	1.08	1.53
Insurance	0.81	1.09	1.59
Other	0.91	1.31	2.52
Fabricated Products	0.98	1.39	2.08
Real Estate	0.82	1.43	2.64
Textiles	0.92	1.48	2.43
Construction	1.09	1.52	2.08
Trading	1.00	1.53	2.63
Agriculture	0.93	1.54	2.59
Steel Works, etc.	1.02	1.57	2.25
Transportation	0.95	1.60	2.73
Utilities	1.30	1.63	2.14
Recreation	1.00	1.63	2.52
Electronic Equipment	1.07	1.65	2.76
Printing and Publishing	1.12	1.67	2.60
Wholesale	1.07	1.68	2.70
Petroleum and Natural Gas	1.08	1.70	2.69
Construction Materials	1.11	1.77	2.66
Business Supplies	1.13	1.78	2.77
Shipbuilding, Railroad Equipment	1.31	1.81	3.05
Entertainment	1.10	1.81	3.13
Precious Metals	1.10	1.87	3.24
Consumer Goods	1.02	1.87	3.32
Apparel	1.12	1.89	3.11
Automobiles and Trucks	1.16	1.90	3.30
Rubber and Plastic Products	1.24	1.94	3.24
Electrical Equipment	1.26	1.96	3.07
Measuring and Control Equipment	1.33	1.97	3.27
Retail	1.22	2.00	3.34
Communication	1.17	2.03	3.68
Food Products	1.29	2.07	3.56
Machinery	1.32	2.07	3.26
Healthcare	1.20	2.09	3.22
Personal Services	1.34	2.17	3.77
Aircraft	1.39	2.17	3.39
Non-Metallic and Industrial Metal Mining	1.36	2.19	3.82
Computers	1.42	2.28	3.74

(Continued)

Exhibit 14.4 (Continued)			
Chemicals	1.53	2.36	3.78
Business Services	1.40	2.40	4.32
Coal	1.33	2.43	4.51
Defense	1.67	2.52	5.21
Shipping Containers	1.86	2.57	3.89
Restaurants, Hotels, Motels	1.37	2.67	4.67
Medical Equipment	1.61	2.68	4.33
Beer & Liquor	1.50	2.76	5.09
Candy & Soda	1.90	3.20	4.48
Pharmaceutical Products	2.11	3.65	6.37
Tobacco Products	5.21	8.59	13.51

book's companion website at www.cengagebrain.com) also reveal substantial variation in MB ratios.

The differences across industries in median MB ratios in Exhibit 14.4 likely relate, in part, to differences in competitive conditions driving differences in growth and ROCE relative to R_E as well as differences in applicable accounting principles across firms and time. Economically, in a mature and competitive industry, the median firm will likely generate ROCE that is close to R_E and will not likely generate unusually high rates of growth. Such firms tend to have median MB ratios closer to 1. For example, firms in mature competitive industries such as banking, insurance, fabrication, real estate, textiles, construction, securities trading, agriculture, steel works, transportation, and utilities tend to have MB ratios that are lower than the sample average.

The assets of firms in some of these industries—particularly banks and insurers—are primarily investments in financial assets, some of which appear on the balance sheet at fair value; thus, MB ratios are closer to 1. In contrast, some of the industries with relatively high MB ratios are more likely to have off-balance-sheet assets and shareholders' equity. For example, the tobacco industry contains firms with significant off-balance-sheet brand equity and the pharmaceutical industry includes firms with substantial value in off-balance-sheet R&D assets. The balance sheet understates the economic value of key resources in these industries. These industries have MB ratios considerably greater than 1.

Empirical Research Results on the Predictive Power of MB Ratios

Several empirical studies have found that MB ratios are fairly stable and mean reverting slowly over time, and that MB ratios are reliable predictors of future growth in book value and expected future ROCE (implying that ROCE also mean reverts slowly).[9] For

[9]Victor L. Bernard, "Accounting-Based Valuation Methods, Determinants of Market-to-Book Ratios and Implications for Financial Statement Analysis," *Working Paper*, University of Michigan (1993); Jane A. Ou and Stephen H. Penman, "Financial Statement Analysis and the Evaluation of Market-to-Book Ratios," *Working Paper*, Columbia University (1995); Stephen H. Penman, "The Articulation of Price-Earnings Ratios and Market-to-Book Ratios and the Evaluation of Growth," *Journal of Accounting Research* 34, no. 2 (Autumn 1996), pp. 235–259; William H. Beaver and Stephen G. Ryan, "Biases and Lags in Book Value and Their Effects on the Ability of the Book-to-Market Ratio to Predict Book Return on Equity," *Journal of Accounting Research* 38, no. 1 (Spring 2000), pp. 127–149.

Exhibit 14.5

Relations among MB Ratios, Future ROCE, and Future Book Value Growth

MB Portfolio	Mean MB Ratio	Median ROCE for Year:			
		0	+1	+5	+10
Low	0.67	0.11	0.09	0.12	0.12
Medium	1.15	0.11	0.13	0.14	0.14
High	2.65	0.10	0.17	0.16	0.20

MB Portfolio	Mean MB Ratio	Cumulative Percentage Increase in Book Value through Year:			
		0	+1	+5	+10
Low	0.67	0%	15%	54%	190%
Medium	1.15	0%	15%	69%	204%
High	2.65	0%	21%	139%	394%

example, Victor Bernard grouped roughly 1,900 firms into 10 portfolios each year between 1972 and 1981 based on their MB ratios. He then computed the mean ROCE for each portfolio in the formation year and for each of the 10 subsequent years. Exhibit 14.5 summarizes a portion of Bernard's results, grouping firms in the lowest three MB portfolios, middle four MB portfolios, and highest three MB portfolios.[10]

The data in Exhibit 14.5 indicate that firms with the highest MB ratios tend to have the highest ROCEs through Year +10 and firms with the lowest MB ratios tend to have the lowest ROCEs through Year +10. The results from the Bernard study also indicate that firms with the highest MB ratios have the highest growth rates in book value of equity through Year +10 and firms with the lowest MB ratios have the lowest growth rates through Year +10. In addition, the results in the Bernard study indicate (although it is not apparent from the summary of results in Exhibit 14.5) that the predictive power of MB ratios for future ROCEs tends to diminish as the horizon lengthens. In Year +10, for example, there is relatively little difference in ROCEs across firms in the third through ninth MB portfolios, as these firms experience ROCEs that tended to converge to 14% during Bernard's sample period. These results are consistent with the mean reversion in ROCEs over time, consistent with movement toward competitive equilibrium.

Price-Earnings and Value-Earnings Ratios

The capital markets devote enormous amounts of time and energy to forecasting and analyzing firms' earnings. So it is no surprise that the PE ratio is the market multiple receiving the most frequent use and attention. Analysts' reports and the financial press frequently refer to PE ratios. *The Wall Street Journal* reports PE ratios as part of the

LO 14-3

For price-earnings (PE) ratios:
a. Understand the theory and the practical approach to compute and use the firm's value-earnings (VE) ratio, and compare it to the PE ratio.
b. Incorporate growth into the PE ratio to compute the price-earnings-growth (PEG) ratio.
c. Use PE and PEG ratios to analyze share prices over time and across firms, and to make investment decisions.
d. Explain why VE and PE ratios differ across firms and the impact of (1) risk and the cost of equity capital, (2) growth, (3) differences between current and expected future earnings, and (4) alternative accounting methods.

---

[10]To reduce the effects of survivorship bias, Bernard included firms that did not survive the entire 10-year future horizon and included any final gain or loss (from bankruptcy, takeover, or liquidation) in the final-year ROCE.

daily coverage of stock prices and trading activity. The capital markets increasingly integrate the PE ratio with expected future earnings growth to capture explicitly the links between price, profitability, and growth using the PEG ratio.

This section begins by computing the value-earnings (VE) ratio for **Starbucks**, followed by a theoretical model for VE ratios. The section then describes computing and using PE ratios from a practical perspective. It discusses the strict assumptions implied by PE ratios, the conditions in which PE ratios may not capture appropriately the theoretical relation between value and earnings, and the difficulties encountered in reconciling actual PE ratios with those indicated by the VE model. This section also incorporates earnings growth and examines PEG ratios. The section concludes by describing empirical data on PE ratios, the predictive power of PE ratios, and the empirical evidence on the articulation between PE ratios and MB ratios.

A Model for the Value-Earnings Ratio with Application to Starbucks

Beginning from a theoretically correct standpoint, we should compute the VE ratio as the value of common shareholders' equity divided by earnings for a single period. The previous chapter described how to determine common equity value as a function of the present value of expected *future* earnings using the residual income model. In the residual income model, we use clean surplus accounting and expected future comprehensive income available to common shareholders. Thus, in theory, you should measure the VE ratio as the value of common equity divided by the next period's expected comprehensive income. This way, the VE ratio achieves consistent alignment of the numerator and denominator in *perspective* (both forward-looking) and *measurement* (both based on comprehensive income).

If we have already computed share value using the forecasting and valuation models developed in the last four chapters, computing the theoretically correct VE ratio is a simple matter of division. For example, in the preceding section and in prior chapters, we estimated **Starbucks'** common shareholders' equity value to be $98,159.2 million at the end of fiscal 2015. We also projected that Year $+1$ comprehensive income will equal net income available for common shareholders, which will equal $2,794.3 million. Thus, we can compute the VE ratio for **Starbucks** at the end of fiscal 2015 as follows:

$$V_0/E_1 = \$98,159.2 \text{ million}/\$2,794.3 \text{ million} = 35.13$$

Or, equivalently, the VE ratio can be computed on a per-share basis, as follows:

$$V_0/E_1 = (\$98,159.2 \text{ million}/1,485.1 \text{ million shares})/(\$2,794.3 \text{ million}/1,485.1 \text{ million shares})$$
$$= \$66.10/\$1.88 = 35.13$$

We also can derive the VE ratio from the VB ratio determined in the previous section. For this derivation, we employ a simple algebraic step, as follows:

$$V_0/E_1 = V_0/BV_0 \times BV_0/E_1 = V_0/BV_0 \times (1/ROCE_1)$$

This equation shows that the same factors that drive the VB ratio (V_0/BV_0) also drive the VE ratio. In fact, the model shows that the VE ratio should be a multiple of the VB ratio, where the multiple is the inverse of ROCE. However, the VE ratio also makes an important simplifying and restrictive assumption: that value can be summarized by one-period-ahead ROCE. A consequence of this assumption is that VE ratios vary *inversely* with expected future ROCE. Holding the VB ratio constant, a firm with a temporarily high level of expected ROCE next period will have a temporarily low VE ratio, and vice versa.

Using this approach, we can derive **Starbucks'** VE ratio from the VB ratio we computed in the previous section, as follows:

$$V_0/E_1 = V_0/BV_0 \times BV_0/E_1 = V_0/BV_0 \times (1/ROCE_1)$$
$$= (\$98{,}159.2 \text{ million}/\$5{,}818.0 \text{ million}) \times (\$5{,}818.0 \text{ million}/\$2{,}794.3 \text{ million})$$
$$= 16.872 \times 2.082 = 16.872 \times (1/0.480) = 35.13$$

Thus, **Starbucks'** VE ratio should equal 35.13. We convert **Starbucks'** VB ratio of 16.872 into the VE ratio by multiplying by $1/ROCE_1$, which we project will be the inverse of 48.0%.

Notice that we derived the VE ratio simply from the computation that **Starbucks'** value is equal to $98,159.2 million, which is based on specific forecasts of **Starbucks'** future earnings. Obviously, using value to compute a VE ratio will not provide any new information about **Starbucks'** value. So what is the point of computing a VE ratio?

The VE ratio provides you with a theoretically correct benchmark to evaluate the firm's PE ratio. We can compare **Starbucks'** VE ratio of 35.13 to **Starbucks'** PE ratio to assess the market value of **Starbucks'** shares. This comparison is equivalent to comparing V to P (that is, value to price). We compute the PE ratio for **Starbucks** as of the end of fiscal 2015 using our forecast that Year +1 earnings (comprehensive income available to common shareholders) will be $2,794.1 million as follows:

$$P_0/E_1 = Price\ per\ share_0/Earnings\ per\ share_1$$
$$= \$56.84/(\$2{,}794.3 \text{ million}/1{,}485.1 \text{ million shares})$$
$$= \$56.84/\$1.88 = 30.21$$

Thus, at the end of fiscal 2015, **Starbucks'** shares traded at a multiple of 30.21 times the Year +1 earnings forecast. **Starbucks'** VE ratio of 35.13 is 16% greater than **Starbucks'** PE ratio of 30.21 at the end of 2015, consistent with our prior estimates of **Starbucks'** value.

With the theoretically correct VE ratio, we also can project VE ratios for other firms after we have made any necessary adjustments to capture the other firms' fundamental characteristics of profitability, growth, and risk. In addition, with the theoretically correct VE ratio, we have a benchmark to gauge other firms' PE ratios to assess whether the market is under- or overpricing their shares.

In the next section, we describe how to use PE ratios as shortcut valuation metrics, highlighting the necessary assumptions in the process and evaluating their theoretical soundness. We also discuss the practical advantages and disadvantages in using PE ratios as shortcut valuation metrics.

PE Ratios from a Theoretical Perspective: Projecting Firm Value from Permanent Earnings

PE ratios are practical tools used by analysts interested in valuation shortcuts. In some circumstances, you may need to react with timely ballpark share value estimates, and PE ratios can provide a quick way to estimate firm value as a multiple of earnings. You can assess benchmark PE ratios that you might expect a firm to have based on past PE ratios for that firm, on industry averages, or on comparable firms' PE ratios. You use these benchmarks to project a firm's PE ratio, using one-period earnings as a common denominator for relative valuations rather than engaging in the extensive computations necessary to value the firm's shares appropriately. But what *should* a firm's PE ratio be? If you have not computed firm value to determine the VE ratio and need to use a short-cut PE ratio instead, what is the correct PE ratio to use?

In projecting firm value using a simple PE ratio (that is, one that uses only one period of earnings and ignores earnings growth), you impose a *very strong assumption*: you treat these earnings as the beginning amount of a *permanent* stream of earnings, valued as a perpetuity. In essence, the PE assumes that one year of earnings is sufficient information to value a firm and to determine share price. Conceptually, suppose you assume that the market is highly efficient and the firm's share value equals its market price (value = price), the firm's earnings will be constant in the future, and the firm's investors expect a constant rate of return R_E. Under these restrictive conditions, we can value the firm's common equity using one-year-ahead earnings (denoted as E_1) as a perpetuity, as follows:

$$V_0 = P_0 = E_1/R_E$$

Rearranged slightly, under these assumptions, the firm's VE and PE ratios are

$$V_0/E_1 = P_0/E_1 = 1/R_E$$

Thus, strictly speaking, the PE multiple assumes that firm value is the present value of a constant stream of expected future earnings, which is discounted at a constant expected future discount rate. Under these conditions, you can value the firm using a simple multiple of one-period-ahead earnings, and the PE ratio of the firm is simply the inverse of the discount rate.

To illustrate this model, assume that the market expects the firm to generate earnings of $700 next period and requires a 14% return on equity capital. The market value of the firm at the beginning of the next period should be $5,000 ($700/0.14). Note that the inverse of the 14% discount rate translates into a PE ratio of 7.14 (1/0.14). Thus, $700 times 7.14 equals $5,000.

The simple PE ratio assumes that future earnings will be permanent, which is not realistic for most firms. Most firms' earnings are expected to grow, not remain constant. We have already seen that such strict assumptions do not fit **Starbucks**. Under the assumptions that **Starbucks'** earnings will be constant in the future and that **Starbucks'** constant future ROCE will equal the 7.2% cost of equity capital, **Starbucks'** PE ratio should be 13.89 (1/0.072). This PE ratio is far below the theoretically derived VE ratio of 35.13 for **Starbucks**.

Price-Earnings Ratios from a Practical Perspective

As a practical matter, analysts, the financial press, and financial databases commonly measure PE ratios as current share price divided by reported (historical) earnings per share for the most recent prior fiscal year or the most recent four quarters (sometimes referred to as the *lagged* or *trailing-12-months earnings per share*).[11] *The Wall Street Journal* and financial data websites such as Yahoo! Finance commonly compute PE

---

[11] In theory, to be consistent with clean surplus accounting and residual income valuation, the denominator should be based on comprehensive income per share. However, analysts, the financial press, and financial databases rarely compute PE ratios based on comprehensive income per share, in part because (1) U.S. GAAP does not yet require reporting comprehensive income on a per-share basis and (2) the other comprehensive income items are usually unrealized gains and losses that are not likely to be a permanent component of income each period. We follow common practice in this chapter and compute PE ratios using reported earnings figures.

ratios this way. With this approach, the PE ratio for **Starbucks** as of the end of fiscal 2015 is equal to $56.84/$1.84 = 30.89. Thus, with a share price of $56.84 at the end of fiscal 2015 and basic earnings per share of $1.84 for fiscal 2015, **Starbucks** shares traded at a PE multiple of 30.89.

The common approach to compute the PE ratio by dividing share price by basic earnings per share for the most recent year is practical because you can readily observe price and earnings per share for most firms. This approach is efficient because it does not require you to produce a computation of value or a forecast of earnings. However, this common approach creates a logical misalignment for valuation purposes because it divides *historical* earnings into share price, which reflects the present value of *future* earnings. If historical earnings contain unusual or nonrecurring gains or losses that are not expected to persist in future earnings, you should normalize the reported historical earnings by removing these effects to compute a PE ratio that reflects earnings that are likely to persist in the future. Chapters 3 and 6 describe techniques to identify elements of income that are unusual and nonrecurring; adjust reported earnings to eliminate their effects and thereby measure recurring, persistent earnings.

As an alternative approach to create a more logical alignment of price and earnings, you can compute the *forward PE ratio* by dividing share price by a forecast of future earnings per share (for example, analysts' consensus forecast of expected earnings per share one year ahead). A PE ratio based on expected future earnings, however, requires you to forecast future earnings (or have access to an analyst's forecast). Thus, the reliability of a forward PE ratio depends on the reliability of the earnings forecast. Earnings forecast errors will distort forward PE ratios. In addition, as discussed previously for VE ratios, PE ratios will vary inversely with transitory earnings components. If you use trailing or forward earnings that are temporarily increased by transitory gains or temporarily decreased by transitory losses, the PE ratio will be temporarily biased down or up, respectively.

Recall that, in the preceding subsection, we computed the forward PE ratio for **Starbucks** as of the end of fiscal 2015 using our forecast for Year +1 earnings (comprehensive income available to common shareholders) as follows: price per share$_0$/earnings per share$_1$ = $56.84 per share/($2,794.3 million/1,485.1 million shares) = $56.84/$1.88 = 30.21. Thus, at the end of fiscal 2015, **Starbucks'** shares traded at a forward PE multiple of 30.21 times the Year +1 earnings forecast. **Starbucks'** VE ratio of 35.13 is 16% greater than **Starbucks'** forward PE ratio of 30.21, consistent with our prior estimates of **Starbucks'** value.[12]

Notice that we derived the PE ratios in this section simply by dividing **Starbucks'** market share price by earnings per share of the past year or by our forecasts of **Starbucks'** future earnings per share. Obviously, using price to compute a PE ratio will not provide any new information about **Starbucks'** share *value*.

PE Ratio Measurement Issues

Thus far, we have discussed a variety of different measurement issues for PE ratios. Forward-looking PE ratios divide share price by one-year-ahead earnings forecasts, which is theoretically more correct. However, at least two problems arise in using forward PE ratios. First, one-year-ahead earnings forecasts are not readily available for all firms. Second, the reliability of forward PE ratios depends on the accuracy of the earnings forecasts, which can differ widely. Therefore, as noted earlier, in practice analysts

---

[12]In this case, our forecasts of net income and comprehensive income for **Starbucks** in Year +1 are the same, so the PE ratio using earnings per share is equal to that using comprehensive income per share.

commonly compute PE ratios as share price divided by earnings per share for the most recent prior fiscal year or for the most recent four quarters. This is sensible because historical earnings are observable and unique; however, computation of PE ratios using historical earnings introduces the potential for bias. To recap, you should be aware of (at least) the following types of potential measurement errors in PE ratios:

1. *Growth.* Simple PE ratios do not explicitly consider firm-specific differences in long-term earnings growth. The price-earnings-growth ratio described in a later section provides a mechanism that addresses this potential bias by incorporating growth into price-earnings multiples.

2. *Transitory earnings.* Past earnings are historical and may not be indicative of expected future "permanent" earnings levels. Insofar as historic earnings contain transitory gains or losses (or other elements that are not expected to recur), temporarily high or low earnings can cause the PE ratio to vary widely. You should normalize the earnings amount by removing the effects of nonrecurring or unusual gains or losses.

3. *Dividends.* A potential bias in PE ratios can arise because of differences in firms' dividend payouts. Dividends displace future earnings. A dividend paid in Year t reduces market price by the amount of the dividend, but the dividend is not subtracted from earnings. The dividend paid will cause future earnings to decline, all else equal, because the firm has paid out a portion of its resources to shareholders. Therefore, price should decline by the present value of the firm's forgone amount of expected future income distributed as dividends. Thus, for dividend-paying firms, dividends cause a mismatch between current period price and lagged earnings. To eliminate this mismatch, you can compute a PE ratio for a dividend-paying firm as follows: $(P_t + D_t)/E_t$.[13]

Benchmarking Relative Valuation: Using Market Multiples of Comparable Firms

In addition to using PE ratios as shortcut valuation metrics, you also can use PE ratios as potentially informative benchmarks to compare valuations across companies or to project the valuations of other companies. For example, you could compare **Starbucks'** PE ratio to the PE ratios of competitors like **McDonald's** or the **Panera Bread Company**. You also might use **Starbucks'** PE ratio to project valuations for these companies. You also can value privately held firms (whose common shares are not publicly traded) or divisions of companies by using PE ratios (and MB ratios) of comparable firms that are publicly traded. Investment bankers use comparable companies' PE ratios to benchmark reasonable ranges of share prices for IPOs (initial public offerings) and merger and acquisition transactions.

PE ratios have the advantage of speed and efficiency, but they are not precise value estimates. Therefore, when using PE ratios, you must be careful to adjust them to match the fundamental characteristics of different companies. For example, **Starbucks'** PE ratio should differ from that of McDonald's insofar as the fundamental characteristics of profitability, growth, and risk differ across the two firms. Such differences might arise, for example, because **Starbucks** derives a major portion of earnings from the coffee beverage sales, whereas McDonald's derives most of its earnings from food sales.

---

[13]While this adjustment to PE ratios for differences in dividend policies is technically correct, it is not commonly implemented in practice.

These and other factors cause the profitability, growth, and risk of **Starbucks** and McDonald's to differ and therefore cause their PE ratios to differ. In later sections, we describe PE ratio differences in more detail and provide descriptive data.

Selecting appropriate firms to use as comparable or peer firms in relative valuation analysis using PE ratios (or MB ratios) can be a challenging task. The theoretical models assist in this task by identifying the variables you should use in selecting comparable firms. Bhojraj and Lee (2002) demonstrate a technique for selecting comparable firms in multiples-based valuation by computing "warranted multiples" based on factors that drive cross-sectional differences in multiples, such as expected profitability, growth, and cost of capital.[14] Alford (1992) examined the accuracy of the PE valuation models using industry, risk, ROCE, and earnings growth in selecting comparable firms.[15] The results indicate that industry membership, particularly at a three-digit SIC code level, provides a useful basis for comparisons if firms in the same industry experience similar profitability, risks, and growth rates. Thus, in some circumstances, industry membership serves as an effective proxy for the variables in the PE valuation model. However, data described in the next section reveal substantial differences in PE across firms in the same industry. The warranted-multiples approach of Bhojraj and Lee provides a mechanism to determine comparable companies within similar industries and across different industries.

Descriptive Data on PE Ratios

Exhibit 14.6 includes descriptive statistics on forward PE ratios (market value divided by one-year-ahead earnings before extraordinary items: P_t/E_{t+1}) for the same 48 industries described in Exhibit 14.4 (MB ratios) and Exhibit 11.3 (market betas) during 2006 through 2015. These data represent a broad cross-sectional sample of 26,162 firm-years drawn from the Compustat database.[16] Exhibit 14.6 lists the industries in ascending order of the median PE ratios. Descriptive statistics on PE and other ratios across industries also appear in Appendix D.

These descriptive data indicate substantial differences in median PE ratios across industries during 2006 through 2015. The firms in the insurance, defense, autos and trucks, coal, petroleum and natural gas, and banking industries experienced the lowest median PE ratios during the period, whereas firms in the precious metals, entertainment, medical equipment, trading, computers, and business services industries experienced the highest median PE ratios. These data also depict wide variation in PE ratios across firms in each industry. For example, most of these 48 industries experienced wide differences between the 25th percentile and the 75th percentile PE ratio during 2006 through 2015. With only a few exceptions, the 75th percentile PE ratio in most industries was more than double the 25th percentile PE ratio.[17]

---

[14]Sanjeev Bhojraj and Charles M.C. Lee, "Who Is My Peer? A Valuation-Based Approach to the Selection of Comparable Firms," *Journal of Accounting Research* 40, no. 2 (May 2002), pp. 407–439.

[15]Andrew W. Alford, "The Effect of the Set of Comparable Firms on the Accuracy of the Price-Earnings Valuation Method," *Journal of Accounting Research* (Spring 1992), pp. 94–108.

[16]To compute these descriptive statistics on price-earnings ratios, we divided firm value (computed as year-end closing price times number of shares outstanding) by one-year-ahead net income before extraordinary items. We deleted firm-years with negative one-year-ahead net income. It does not make sense to compute PE ratios using negative earnings because PE ratios assume earnings are permanent. Negative earnings cannot be permanent.

[17]You must be careful with PE ratios because they are sensitive to earnings that are near zero. Firms with earnings that are positive but temporarily very low will experience PE ratios that are temporarily very high.

Exhibit 14.6

Descriptive Statistics on Forward Price-Earnings Ratios (P_t/E_{t+1}), 2006–2015
Forty-Eight Industries Sorted by Median Forward PE Ratio

Industry	25th Percentile	Median	75th Percentile
Full Sample	**11.15**	**16.38**	**25.65**
Insurance	7.52	10.81	17.03
Defense	8.50	13.10	20.52
Automobiles and Trucks	8.61	13.39	20.04
Coal	8.18	13.46	22.15
Petroleum and Natural Gas	9.40	13.96	22.65
Banking	10.31	14.27	20.73
Shipping Containers	12.67	14.43	16.72
Printing and Publishing	9.98	14.55	21.74
Chemicals	9.93	14.56	20.31
Tobacco Products	13.23	14.81	18.48
Business Supplies	10.19	14.85	20.19
Wholesale	10.43	14.90	20.46
Shipbuilding, Railroad Equipment	10.18	14.92	27.92
Electrical Equipment	10.95	15.01	20.03
Recreation	9.09	15.08	26.36
Aircraft	12.36	15.10	19.94
Utilities	12.86	15.35	19.39
Steel Works, etc.	10.41	15.52	25.62
Healthcare	11.73	15.56	22.20
Apparel	11.46	15.68	22.69
Communication	10.67	15.72	24.45
Transportation	10.24	15.73	22.70
Retail	11.65	15.78	23.58
Candy & Soda	12.44	15.78	23.40
Construction	11.44	15.85	24.59
Machinery	11.95	16.36	22.50
Textiles	9.18	16.76	24.78
Consumer Goods	11.31	16.96	23.33
Food Products	11.94	17.24	25.13
Rubber and Plastic Products	12.26	17.28	26.19
Other	10.90	17.34	31.22
Electronic Equipment	11.22	17.41	28.96
Pharmaceutical Products	11.13	17.60	27.56
Beer & Liquor	13.72	17.75	22.43
Fabricated Products	9.39	18.06	23.25
Non-Metallic and Industrial Metal Mining	11.45	18.10	30.69
Agriculture	10.45	18.73	34.34

(Continued)

Exhibit 14.6 (Continued)			
Real Estate	9.83	19.26	44.57
Measuring and Control Equipment	13.51	19.30	31.06
Personal Services	13.57	19.45	29.93
Restaurants, Hotels, Motels	14.14	19.48	31.72
Construction Materials	13.08	19.69	31.05
Business Services	13.30	20.14	33.80
Computers	13.56	20.65	35.87
Trading	12.64	20.79	36.96
Medical Equipment	15.35	21.36	33.05
Entertainment	15.19	22.21	37.04
Precious Metals	16.10	25.47	44.46

What Factors Cause PE Ratios to Differ across Firms?

The same set of economic factors that can cause firms' MB ratios to differ also can cause firms' PE ratios to differ. The primary drivers of variation in PE ratios across firms are the fundamental drivers of value: risk, profitability, and growth. In addition to economic factors, differences across firms in accounting methods and accounting principles and differences in earnings across time also can drive differences in PE ratios.

Risk and the Cost of Capital. Firms with equivalent amounts of earnings but different levels of risk and therefore different costs of equity capital will experience different PE and VE ratios. All else equal, a riskier firm will experience a lower VE and PE ratio.

Profitability. A firm with competitive advantages will be able to earn ROCE that exceeds R_E. Firms with sustainable competitive advantages will be able to generate ROCE that exceeds R_E for longer, thereby increasing the PE ratio relative to similar firms that do not have sustainable competitive advantages. Thus, both the magnitude and persistence of the amount by which ROCE exceeds R_E will increase PE ratios across firms.

Accounting Differences. In addition to economic factors, firms' PE ratios may differ for a variety of accounting reasons, including the periodic nature of earnings measurement and differences in accounting methods. Some firms select accounting methods that are conservative with respect to income recognition and asset measurement (for example, LIFO for inventories during periods of rising input prices and accelerated depreciation of fixed assets). Some firms invest in projects for which accounting principles are conservative. For example, firms may make substantial expenditures on intangible activities that must be expensed under conservative accounting principles, leading to economic assets that are off-balance-sheet, such as intellectual property, brand equity, and/or human capital. The effects of accounting methods and principles on reported earnings and PE ratios will likely change over the life of the firm. All else equal, conservative accounting will reduce reported earnings early in the life of the firm (for example, when accelerated depreciation charges are high or R&D is being expensed), thereby increasing the PE ratio. Ironically, later in the life of the firm, after the investments have been completely expensed, reported earnings will be higher and PE ratios will be lower.

Accounting Measures Earnings in Annual Periods. Firms' PE ratios will be significantly different when one-period earnings are unusually high or low and therefore not representative of persistent earnings. In particular, if you use PE ratios based on trailing-12-months earnings that include nonrecurring gains or losses that will not persist, the PE ratios will be artificially volatile. The impact of unusual and nonrecurring items on net income will have an inverse impact on PE ratios. That is, nonrecurring gains will temporarily drive net income up and PE ratios down, whereas nonrecurring losses will temporarily drive net income down but PE ratios up.

Continuing the simple example introduced earlier, assume that you expect the firm to generate earnings of $600 next period instead of $700 because the firm will recognize a nonrecurring $100 restructuring charge. Because this charge is nonrecurring (not a permanent change in earnings), the market price should fall to roughly $4,900 ($5,000 − $100) in the no-growth scenario and the PE ratio for that period will be 8.17 ($4,900/$600) instead of 7.14 ($5,000/$700). Conversely, if the current period's earnings exceed their expected permanent level, the PE ratio will be lower than normal.

You must assess whether the lower or higher level of earnings for the period (and therefore higher or lower PE ratio) represents a transitory event or a change to a new level of permanent earnings. If you expect that the decrease in earnings from $700 to $600 will be permanent, the market price (assuming no change in risk or growth) should decrease to $4,286 ($600/0.14). Thus, the PE ratio remains the same at 7.14 (1/0.14).

To illustrate the effects of accounting differences on PE ratios across firms, consider the historical data in the following table, which includes PE ratios (computed as year-end share price over trailing earnings per share) for **Starbucks** for 2012 through 2015.

	Starbucks's PE Ratios:		
Year	PE Ratio	Price per Share	Earnings per Share
2012	27.16	$25.08	$0.92
2013	3,802.50	$38.03	$0.01
2014	27.54	$37.73	$1.37
2015	30.89	$56.84	$1.84

Considered at face value, the PE ratio in 2013 implies the market valued **Starbucks'** earnings at a multiple of 3,802.50, more than 100 times **Starbucks'** earnings multiples in 2012, 2014, or 2015. Did the market suddenly assess an enormous jump in the value in **Starbucks'** shares? No. In 2013, **Starbucks** recognized a large litigation charge in income, driving EPS down to only $0.01, thereby temporarily wildly inflating the PE ratio. Thus, the big jump in **Starbucks's** PE ratio occurred because earnings temporarily declined that year and did not reflect the market's expectations for **Starbucks'** long-term earnings. In 2014 and 2015, **Starbucks** reported earnings at more normal levels and PE ratios returned to normal levels.

Incorporating Earnings Growth into PE Ratios

All else equal, VE and PE ratios will be greater for firms that the market expects will generate greater earnings growth with future investments in abnormally profitable projects. Analysts commonly modify the PE ratio to incorporate earnings growth. In this section, we demonstrate two ways to include expected future earnings growth in the PE ratio computation: (1) the perpetuity-with-growth approach and (2) the price-earnings-growth approach.

The Perpetuity-with-Growth Approach

The perpetuity-with-growth approach assumes that the firm's current period earnings will grow at a constant rate g. Therefore, the firm can be valued as the present value of a permanent stream of future earnings that will grow at constant rate g. In this case, we can express forward VE and forward PE ratios as perpetuity-with-growth models as follows:

$$V_0 = P_0 = \frac{E_0 \times (1+g)}{(R_E - g)} = \frac{E_1}{(R_E - g)}, \quad \text{so} \quad \frac{V_0}{E_1} = \frac{P_0}{E_1} = \frac{1}{(R_E - g)}$$

To continue the illustration, assume that the firm generated \$666.67 in earnings in the current period. The market expects the firm's earnings to grow 5% next year and each year thereafter, so that Year +1 earnings will be \$700. The model suggests that the forward PE ratio incorporating growth should be 11.11 [1.0/(0.14 − 0.05)] and market value should be \$7,778 (\$700 × 11.11). The present value of the expected future growth in earnings adds \$2,778 (\$7,778 − \$5,000) to the value of the firm.

Note that the above expression describes forward VE and forward PE ratios because they use E_1 (one-year-ahead earnings). However, if current period (historical) earnings are expected to grow at the constant rate g in Year +1, then the VE and PE ratios can be expressed as multiples of current period (historical) earnings (E_0):

$$V_0 = P_0 = \frac{E_1}{(R_E - g)} = \frac{E_0 \times (1+g)}{(R_E - g)}, \quad \text{so} \quad \frac{V_0}{E_0} = \frac{P_0}{E_0} = \frac{(1+g)}{(R_E - g)}$$

Continuing with the illustration, the VE and PE ratios based on current period earnings would then be 11.667 [(1 + g)/(R_E − g) = 1.05/(0.14 − 0.05)]. Note that using this VE and PE ratio will lead to market value for the firm of \$7,778 (\$666.67 × 11.667). This is the same market value as we determined using the forward VE and PE ratios.

PE ratios are particularly sensitive to the growth rate. If the growth rate in our illustration becomes 6% instead of 5%, the forward PE ratio becomes 12.50 [1.0/(0.14 − 0.06)] and the market value becomes \$8,750 (\$700 × 12.50). The sensitivity occurs because the model assumes that the firm will grow at the specified growth rate in perpetuity. Competition, new discoveries or technologies, or other factors eventually erode rapid growth rates in an industry. In using the constant growth version of the PE ratio, you should select a long-run equilibrium growth rate in earnings.

This expression for the VE and PE ratio underscores the joint importance of risk and growth in valuation. Given the relation between expected return (R_E) and risk, the VE and PE ratios should be inversely related to risk. Holding earnings and growth constant, higher risk should translate into lower PE and VE ratios. Risk-averse investors will not pay as much for a higher-risk security as for a lower-risk security with identical expected earnings and growth. In contrast, VE and PE should relate positively to growth. Holding earnings and R_E constant, firms with higher expected long-run growth rates in earnings should experience higher VE and PE ratios.

With respect to our valuation of **Starbucks** at the end of fiscal 2015, we assumed that **Starbucks** would experience a long-run growth rate of 3.0% beginning in Year +6 and beyond. If we were instead to assume that **Starbucks** will experience a 3.0% constant growth rate in earnings beginning in Year +1, using the perpetuity-with-growth approach, we would calculate the forward PE ratio for **Starbucks** as follows:

$$\frac{P_0}{E_1} = \frac{1}{(R_E - g)} = \frac{1}{(0.072 - 0.030)} = 23.81$$

Clearly, incorporating growth makes a big difference in **Starbucks'** forward PE ratio [as compared to the PE ratio of 13.89 (1/0.072) that ignores growth]. Assuming that **Starbucks'** earnings will grow at 3.0% per year beginning in Year +1, this forward PE-with-growth ratio would value **Starbucks** shares at a multiple of 23.81 times the Year +1 earnings forecast. This PE ratio is substantially lower than the theoretically correct VE ratio of 35.13, which takes into account much higher growth rates in earnings for **Starbucks** through Year +5.

The Price-Earnings-Growth Approach

An alternative ad hoc approach to incorporate growth into PE ratios has emerged from practice in recent years. Using this approach, we divide the PE ratio by the expected medium-term earnings growth rate (expressed as a percent). Some analysts use the expected earnings growth rate over a three- to five-year horizon. This approach produces the so-called PEG ratio seen with increasing frequency in practice. You can compute the PEG ratio as follows:

$$PEG = (Price\ per\ Share_0/Expected\ Earnings\ per\ Share_1)/(g \times 100)$$

Analysts and the financial press use the PEG ratio as a rule of thumb to assess share price relative to earnings and expected future earnings growth. Although there is little theoretical foundation for this rule of thumb (which tends to vary among analysts), proponents of PEG ratios generally assert that firms should have PEG ratios roughly equal to 1.0, indicating that market price fairly reflects expected earnings and growth.

This rule of thumb for the PEG ratio makes the following assumptions:

- The firm's earnings behave as a perpetuity with growth.
- The firm's earnings generate an ROCE equivalent to R_E.
- All of the firm's growth arises from reinvesting all of its earnings.
- All of the reinvested earnings generate an ROCE equivalent to R_E, so the firm's earnings growth rate is equivalent to R_E.

Using the rule of thumb that PEG ratios should equal 1, proponents assert that market prices for firms with PEG ratios below 1 are underpriced given earnings and expected earnings growth and that market prices for firms with PEG ratios above 1 are overpriced relative to earnings and expected earnings growth. Proponents of PEG ratios argue that this heuristic provides a convenient means to rank stocks, taking into account one-year-ahead earnings and expected earnings growth.[18]

In Chapter 10, we assumed that **Starbucks** would experience earnings growth of roughly 12.2% per year through Year +5. Using this growth rate assumption and our projected earnings per share of $1.88 for Year +1, we compute **Starbucks'** PEG ratio at the end of fiscal 2015 as follows:

$$
\begin{aligned}
PEG_{2015} &= (Price\ per\ share_{2015}/Expected\ Earnings\ per\ share_1)/(g \times 100) \\
&= (\$56.84/\$1.88)/(0.122 \times 100) \\
&= 30.21/12.2 = 2.48
\end{aligned}
$$

Thus, **Starbucks'** shares traded at the end of fiscal 2015 at a PEG ratio of 2.48. Based on the PEG heuristic, **Starbucks'** PEG ratio suggests that the market price for **Starbucks**

---

[18]Mark Bradshaw (2002) demonstrates that sell-side analysts' target price estimates are highly correlated with valuation estimates based on the PEG model in "The Use of Target Prices to Justify Sell-Side Analysts' Stock Recommendations," *Accounting Horizons* 16, no. 1 (March 2002), pp. 27–41.

shares reflect substantial *overpricing* of **Starbucks'** earnings and expected earnings growth. However, the PEG ratio heuristic does not take into account differences in risk and costs of equity capital across firms. For example, **Starbucks'** PEG ratio seems high because it does not account for the fact that **Starbucks'** expected future ROCE is significantly greater than **Starbucks'** R_E because of **Starbucks'** substantial off-balance-sheet brand equity. In addition, this heuristic does not take into account the fact that **Starbucks** is likely to achieve this future earnings growth with relatively low risk. (**Starbucks'** beta is 0.75.) The PEG ratio deserves considerable attention from researchers and practitioners so that its uses and limitations can be tested and understood.

Empirical Properties of PE Ratios

The theoretical models indicate that the PE ratio is related to R_E, the cost of equity capital, and g, the growth rate in future earnings. Several empirical studies have examined the relations among PE ratios, risk (measured using market beta), and growth (measured using realized prior earnings growth rates or analysts' forecasts of future growth). These studies have found that approximately 50–70% of the variability in PE ratios across firms relates to risk and growth.[19]

PE Ratios as Predictors of Future Earnings Growth

Stephen Penman, a leading scholar in the relations among earnings, book values, and market values, studied the relation between PE ratios and changes in earnings per share. Penman collected data from the CRSP and Compustat databases on roughly 2,574 firms during 1968 through 1985.[20] For each year, Penman grouped firms into 20 portfolios based on the level of their PE ratios, computed using lagged earnings per share. He then computed the percentage change in earnings per share for the portfolio formation year and for each of the nine subsequent years. Penman then aggregated the results across years. The table below presents a subset of the aggregate results.

PE Portfolio	Median Percentage Change in Earnings per Share in:				
	Year 0	Year +1	Year +2	Year +3	Year +4
High	3.9%	52.2%	17.5%	17.8%	15.0%
Medium	14.0%	11.8%	11.6%	13.7%	15.8%
Low	18.4%	4.8%	10.2%	12.3%	13.1%

The results for the portfolio formation year are consistent with PE ratios being inversely related to changes in earnings in Year 0. Firms with high PE ratios experienced, on average, low percentage changes in earnings (and many experienced earnings declines) during Year 0 relative to the preceding year. Firms with low PE ratios experienced high percentage changes in earnings during Year 0. The results for Year +1 suggest a counterbalancing change in earnings in the next year. A low percentage increase in earnings in Year 0 is followed by a high percentage increase in earnings in Year +1 for the high PE portfolios, and vice versa for the low PE portfolios.

---

[19]See William Beaver and Dale Morse, "What Determines Price-Earnings Ratios?," *Financial Analysts Journal* (July–August 1978), pp. 65–76; Paul Zarowin, "What Determines Earnings-Price Ratios: Revisited," *Journal of Accounting, Auditing and Finance* (Summer 1990), pp. 439–454.

[20]Stephen H. Penman, "The Articulation of Price-Earnings Ratios and Market-to-Book Ratios and the Evaluation of Growth," *Journal of Accounting Research* 34, no. 2 (Autumn 1996), pp. 235–259.

The results for subsequent years reflect the tendency toward mean reversion in percentage earnings changes to a level in the mid-teens. This result is consistent with the data presented in Exhibit 14.5 for ROCE, where Victor Bernard observed a mean reversion in ROCE toward the mid-teens during his sample period. The mean reversion suggests systematic directional changes in earnings growth over time (that is, serial autocorrelation), but the reversion takes several years to occur.

Articulation of MB and PE Ratios. In the same study, Penman also ranked and grouped the firms into three MB ratio portfolios, classifying MB ratios below 0.90 as low, MB ratios above 1.10 as high, and MB ratios between 0.90 and 1.10 as normal. He then utilized the residual income valuation model and empirical data to examine the articulation between firms' PE and MB ratios.[21] Exhibit 14.7 presents a matrix summarizing some of the results from Penman's study. The matrix presents residual income scaled by book value of equity (essentially, residual ROCE) figures after assuming a 10.0% cost of capital for all firm-years. We denote current period residual income as CRI and future residual income one year ahead and six years ahead as FRI1 and FRI6, respectively.

Penman's research results generally support his predictions and shed light on the residual income conditions that cause MB ratios and PE ratios to covary. His results show that future residual income is substantially *higher* for high MB firms than for low MB firms. Examining future residual income across columns of the matrix, Penman's results

Exhibit 14.7

The Articulation of Market-to-Book (MB) and Price-Earnings (PE) Ratios

PE Ratio Portfolios	MB Ratio Portfolios		
	High	Normal	Low
High (Portfolios 15–20)	CRI < FRI > 0 CRI: −0.50 to 0.07 FRI1: −0.07 to 0.08 FRI6: 0.01 to 0.11	CRI < FRI = 0 CRI: −0.36 to −0.04 FRI1: −0.13 to −0.03 FRI6: −0.06 to 0.07	CRI < FRI < 0 CRI: −0.24 to −0.06 FRI1: −0.13 to −0.06 FRI6: −0.01 to 0.02
Normal (Portfolios 7–14)	CRI = FRI > 0 CRI: 0.07 to 0.10 FRI1: 0.08 to 0.10 FRI6: 0.11 to 0.14	CRI = FRI = 0 CRI: −0.02 to 0.04 FRI1: −0.02 to 0.04 FRI6: 0.01 to 0.06	CRI = FRI < 0 CRI: −0.05 to 0.00 FRI1: −0.04 to 0.00 FRI6: −0.02 to 0.03
Low (Portfolios 1–6)	CRI > FRI > 0 CRI: 0.12 to 0.41 FRI1: 0.12 to 0.25 FRI6: 0.11 to 0.24	CRI > FRI = 0 CRI: 0.05 to 0.22 FRI1: 0.05 to 0.15 FRI6: 0.07 to 0.12	CRI > FRI < 0 CRI: 0.00 to 0.06 FRI1: −0.01 to 0.04 FRI6: 0.03 to 0.05

Source: We obtained these data from Table 4 in Stephen H. Penman, "The Articulation of Price-Earnings Ratios and Market-to-Book Ratios and the Evaluation of Growth," *Journal of Accounting Research*, Vol. 34, No. 2 (Autumn 1996), pp. 235–259.
Note: CRI denotes current period residual income and FRI denotes future residual income.

[21]*Ibid.*

show that MB ratios are positive predictors of future residual income, consistent with the results from Bernard in Exhibit 14.5. Examining the results across rows, high PE ratio firms tend to have current period residual income that is much *lower than* future residual income, suggesting that PE ratios for these firms are temporarily high because residual income is temporarily low. In contrast, firms with low PE ratios tend to have current residual income amounts that are *greater than* the future residual income amounts, suggesting that these firms are experiencing low PE ratios because residual income is temporarily high. Penman's results provide intuition about when MB ratios should be high, low, or normal and, concurrently, when PE ratios should be high, low, or normal.

Reverse Engineering

LO 14-4

Reverse engineer a firm's stock price to determine the implied expected return or the implied expected long-run growth rate.

Reverse engineering is an analytical approach through which you can deduce and evaluate the assumptions implicit in a stock price. Throughout this text, we have emphasized the process of using a firm's fundamental characteristics to estimate firm value independent of the prevailing market value. The valuation process can be characterized essentially as a puzzle with four pieces, or as an equation with four variables:

1. Expected future profitability
2. Expected long-run future growth
3. Expected risk-adjusted discount rates
4. Firm value

Thus far, we have developed forecasts and expectations about three of the variables—expected future profitability, long-run growth, and risk-adjusted discount rates—and have used them to solve for the fourth variable: firm value. In fact, if we can make assumptions about any three of the four variables, we can then solve for the fourth variable.

For example, we can treat the market value of common equity as one of the "known" variables by assuming that V_0 equals market price. (That is, we can assume that the market price equals value.) We can then forecast any two other variables and solve for the missing fourth variable. We refer to this process as *reverse engineering* stock prices because it takes the valuation process and reverses it. It is a process in which you assume that share value equals market price, and then solve for the assumptions the market appears to be making to price the firm's shares. For example, if we assume that a firm's share value equals the market's share price and use the consensus analysts' forecasts for future earnings and long-run growth as reasonable proxies for the market's expectations, we can solve for the implied expected risk-adjusted rate of return on common equity that is consistent with the observed market price. This is essentially equivalent to solving for the internal rate of return on the stock.[22]

As another example, suppose we assume that share value equals market price, that the market's risk-adjusted expected return on a stock can be determined by an expected returns model such as the CAPM, and that analysts' consensus earnings forecasts through Year +5 are reasonable proxies for the market's earnings expectations. We can then solve for the long-run growth rate implicit in the firm's stock price, conditional on the other assumptions.

Reverse engineering allows you to infer a set of assumptions that the market appears to have impounded into a share price. You can then assess whether the assumptions the market appears to be making are realistic, optimistic, or pessimistic. If you determine that the market's assumptions are optimistic, it suggests that the market has overpriced the stock. Alternatively, if you determine that the market's assumptions are pessimistic, it suggests that the market has underpriced the stock.

Reverse Engineering Starbucks's Stock Price

To illustrate the process of reverse engineering, we apply the approach to **Starbucks** using the September 30, 2015 (shortly after the close of the 2015 fiscal year) market price of $56.84 per share. To reverse engineer **Starbucks'** share price, we again rely on the residual income model in Chapter 13 and the forecasts developed in Chapter 10.

Assume that we want to solve for the expected rate of return (that is, the risk-adjusted discount rate) implied by **Starbucks'** share price of $56.84. Also assume that our forecasts of earnings and book value of common equity for **Starbucks** through Year +5 and our forecast of 3.0% long-run growth are realistic proxies for the market's expectations. Armed with share price, earnings and growth forecasts through Year +5, and a constant long-run growth assumption beyond Year +5, we can use the residual

---

[22]A related technique computes the "price differential," which is a straightforward approach to compute the amount by which a share price has been discounted by the market for risk. This technique involves using the risk-free rate as the expected return in the residual income valuation model and computing "risk-neutral share value." You can then subtract the market's share price from the risk-neutral share value in order to compute the price differential, which is the amount by which the market has discounted the share price for risk. For more guidance on how to implement this approach, and empirical evidence on its efficacy, see Stephen Baginski and James Wahlen, "Residual Income Risk, Intrinsic Values, and Share Prices," *The Accounting Review* 78, no. 1 (January 2003), pp. 327–351.

income value model to solve for the discount rate that reduces future earnings and book value to a present value equal to the $56.84 market price per share.

Procedurally, one way to solve for the implied expected return on **Starbucks'** stock, conditional on the price, earnings, and growth assumptions, is to first estimate the value of common equity using the risk-free rate as the discount rate. This will compute the "risk-neutral share value." The risk-neutral share value will likely far exceed the market price because the future residual income has not been discounted for risk. To reverse engineer the share price, steadily increase the discount rate until the residual income model value exactly agrees with the market price of $56.84 per share. Following this approach, the implied expected rate of return on **Starbucks'** shares is 7.869%. At this discount rate, conditional on our residual income and growth assumptions, the present value of **Starbucks'** shares is $56.84 per share, exactly equal to market price. Recall that we assumed that **Starbucks'** common equity had a required rate of return of 7.2% based on the CAPM. However, this reverse engineering approach indicates that if we buy a share of **Starbucks'** stock at the market price of $56.84, *it will yield a 7.869% rate of return*, conditional on our other assumptions. The Valuation spreadsheet in FSAP allows you to make these iterative computations easily by varying the discount rate for equity capital.

To demonstrate another example, we can reverse engineer **Starbucks'** stock price to solve for the implicit long-run growth assumption. To illustrate, we again take the market price of $56.84 per share as given and our earnings and book value forecasts through Year +5 as reasonable proxies for the market's expectations. We return to our original assumption that the CAPM risk-adjusted discount rate for **Starbucks'** stock is 7.2%. With this, we have established three assumptions—value, earnings through Year +5, and the risk-adjusted discount rate—and can solve for the missing piece of the puzzle: long-run implied growth. We begin with the long-run growth assumption set at zero. We compute our first estimate of firm value using a zero growth assumption and compare that estimate to market price. The first estimate is normally substantially lower than market price because market price includes the present value of the market's expectations for long-run growth. This turns out to be the case for **Starbucks**, as the initial value estimate assuming zero long-run growth is only $43.01 per share—well below current share price. To determine the implied long-run growth rate impounded in price, we steadily increase the long-run growth parameter assumption until the present value from the residual income model equals market price.[23] In the case of **Starbucks**, at the end of fiscal 2015, market price of $56.84 reflects *long-run growth of 2.157%*, which is significantly lower than our expectation of 3.0% long-run growth. That is, conditional on our assumptions for residual income through Year +5, on **Starbucks'** cost of equity capital at 7.2%, and on the market's expectations for long-run growth at 2.157% per year, the present value of **Starbucks** shares exactly agrees with the market price of $56.84. Given that **Starbucks** will likely experience higher long-run growth, it further confirms our assessment that **Starbucks'** shares are underpriced at the end of fiscal 2015. Again, note that the Valuation spreadsheet in FSAP is a useful tool that allows you to establish assumptions for earnings and cost of capital and then vary the long-run growth assumption for reverse engineering.

---

[23]Note that you must vary the long-run growth parameter assumption in two places: (1) projecting the terminal year financial statement amounts and (2) calculating the valuation equations.

The Relevance of Academic Research for the Work of the Security Analyst

As demonstrated in Exhibit 1.14 in Chapter 1, the Nichols and Wahlen (2004) replication of the Ball and Brown (1968)[24] results indicate that during their sample period 1988 through 2002, merely the difference in the sign of the change in annual earnings (whether positive or negative) was associated with nearly a 35% difference in annual market-adjusted stock returns. The average sample firm that reported an earnings increase in a given year experienced stock returns that, on average, "beat" the market average returns by 19%, while the average sample firm that reported an earnings decrease in a given year experienced stock returns that, on average, fell 16% short of the market average returns. The results suggest earnings numbers are very informative for the capital markets.

The results of academic research in accounting have provided many insights into multifaceted dimensions of the relations between accounting numbers and a variety of capital market variables such as stock prices, stock price reactions around earnings announcements, stock returns cumulated over long periods of time, trading volume, analysts' and managements' earnings forecasts, equity costs of capital, implied market risk premia, market betas and other risk factors, bankruptcy, earnings management, and fraud. This concluding section summarizes the role of market efficiency and describes some striking empirical evidence on the relative degree of market efficiency with respect to accounting information. We consider the results to date to be very encouraging for analysts and investors.

What Does "Capital Market Efficiency" Really Mean?

Academics generally examine market efficiency from the perspective of the big picture, testing for predictable market returns in large portfolios of shares. In contrast, analysts and investors view their task as the constant pursuit of market inefficiencies—temporarily mispriced securities. Investors see market efficiency from the front lines, experiencing daily swings in market prices that are sometimes hard to explain in the context of an efficient market. Thus, it is not surprising that the perspective on the degree of market efficiency differs substantially between academics and professional investors. This section seeks to reach a common understanding.

Capital markets may be described as "efficient" with regard to accounting information based on the degree to which market prices react *completely* and *quickly* to available accounting information. Notice that efficiency should be described as a matter of *degree*, not as an absolute. The issue is not whether the capital markets are or are not efficient. Rather, the issue is the degree to which the capital markets impound in prices all the available value-relevant information.

The term *completely* in this description implies the degree to which share prices reflect the value-relevant implications of all available accounting information without systematic bias. A capital market that is relatively efficient will price all value-relevant financial statement information, even including accounting items that may be disclosed in the notes.

[24]D. Craig Nichols and James Wahlen, "How Do Earnings Numbers Relate to Stock Returns? A Review of Classic Accounting Research with Updated Evidence," *Accounting Horizons* (December 2004), pp. 263–286; Ray Ball and Philip Brown, "An Empirical Evaluation of Accounting Income Numbers," *Journal of Accounting Research* (Autumn 1968), pp. 159–178.

The term *quickly* in this description suggests that market participants cannot consistently earn abnormal returns using accounting information for a long period of time after the information has been made public. If capital markets exhibit a high degree of efficiency, market prices should react quickly (within a matter of days) to capture any value-relevant signals in the accounting information or other information about the firm.

The degree of efficiency, or the completeness and speed of price reactions, in an information-efficient capital market depends on analysts and financial statement analysis. Analysts and investors study accounting information to assess appropriate values for stocks and to take positions in under- or overpriced securities, thereby driving stock market prices to efficient levels. Share prices move to new efficient levels based on the speed with which investors and analysts can forecast and anticipate accounting information before it is released and on the speed with which they can analyze and react to surprises in accounting information when it is released.

What does a high degree of market efficiency *not* imply? A capital market with a high degree of information efficiency does not necessarily price all stocks correctly every day. As a practical matter, relatively efficient markets experience temporary deviations of share price from fundamental value at the level of the individual firm, but these random inefficiencies should cancel out at an aggregated market level and should not persist for long periods of time.[25] Analysts and investors are driving forces involved in identifying and correcting security mispricing. A capital market with a high degree of information efficiency does not necessarily have perfect foresight—surprises happen. Firms frequently surprise the market by announcing earnings that are higher or lower than the market's expectations. Again, analysts and investors drive market prices to higher levels of efficiency by reacting quickly and completely to new information.

Striking Evidence on the Degree of Market Efficiency and Inefficiency with Respect to Earnings

Two studies by Victor Bernard and Jacob Thomas (1989 and 1990) provide the most striking evidence to date on the degree of market efficiency and inefficiency with respect to accounting earnings.[26] The Bernard and Thomas results during the post-earnings-announcement period suggest that the market's reaction to quarterly earnings news is highly, but not completely, efficient. Nichols and Wahlen (2004) used data from 1988 through 2002 to replicate the seminal results in Bernard and Thomas (which were based on data from 1974 to 1986). Nichols and Wahlen collected a sample of 90,470 quarterly earnings announcements for firms on the CRSP and Compustat databases. They ranked all sample firms each quarter into 10 portfolios on the basis of each firm's unexpected earnings. [Unexpected earnings (denoted as UE) equal actual earnings per share minus analysts' consensus forecast of earnings per share, scaled by price per share as of 60 trading days prior to the earnings announcement for cross-sectional comparability.] They studied the average abnormal (market-adjusted) stock returns to each portfolio over the 60 trading days leading up to the quarterly earnings announcement and over

---

[25]For a discussion of these issues, see Ray Ball, "The Earnings-Price Anomaly," *Journal of Accounting and Economics* (1992), pp. 319–345.

[26]Victor Bernard and Jacob Thomas, "Post-Earnings Announcement Drift: Delayed Price Response or Risk Premium?," *Journal of Accounting Research* 27, Supplement (1989), pp. 1–36; and "Evidence That Stock Prices Do Not Fully Reflect the Implications of Current Earnings for Future Earnings," *Journal of Accounting and Economics* 13, no. 4 (1990), pp. 305–340.

the 60 trading days following the announcement. Exhibit 14.8 depicts a portion of the Nichols and Wahlen results, which mirror the Bernard and Thomas results.

The results in the left side of Exhibit 14.8 indicate that the market is highly efficient in anticipating and reacting to quarterly earnings surprises. Firms with quarterly earnings surprises in the "good news" portfolios—UE portfolios 7 through 10—experience positive cumulative abnormal returns during the 60 days prior to and including the release of earnings. Firms with quarterly earnings surprises in the "bad news" portfolios—UE portfolios 1 through 3—experience negative cumulative abnormal returns during the 60 days prior to and including the release of earnings. The average difference in cumulative abnormal returns between UE portfolio 10 (roughly +6.7%) and UE portfolio 1 (roughly −6.8%) was 13.5% *per quarter*. These results suggest that the market anticipates and reacts quickly to quarterly earnings information.

Exhibit 14.8

Evidence from Nichols and Wahlen (2004) Replication of Bernard and Thomas (1989) on Market Efficiency with Respect to Quarterly Earnings

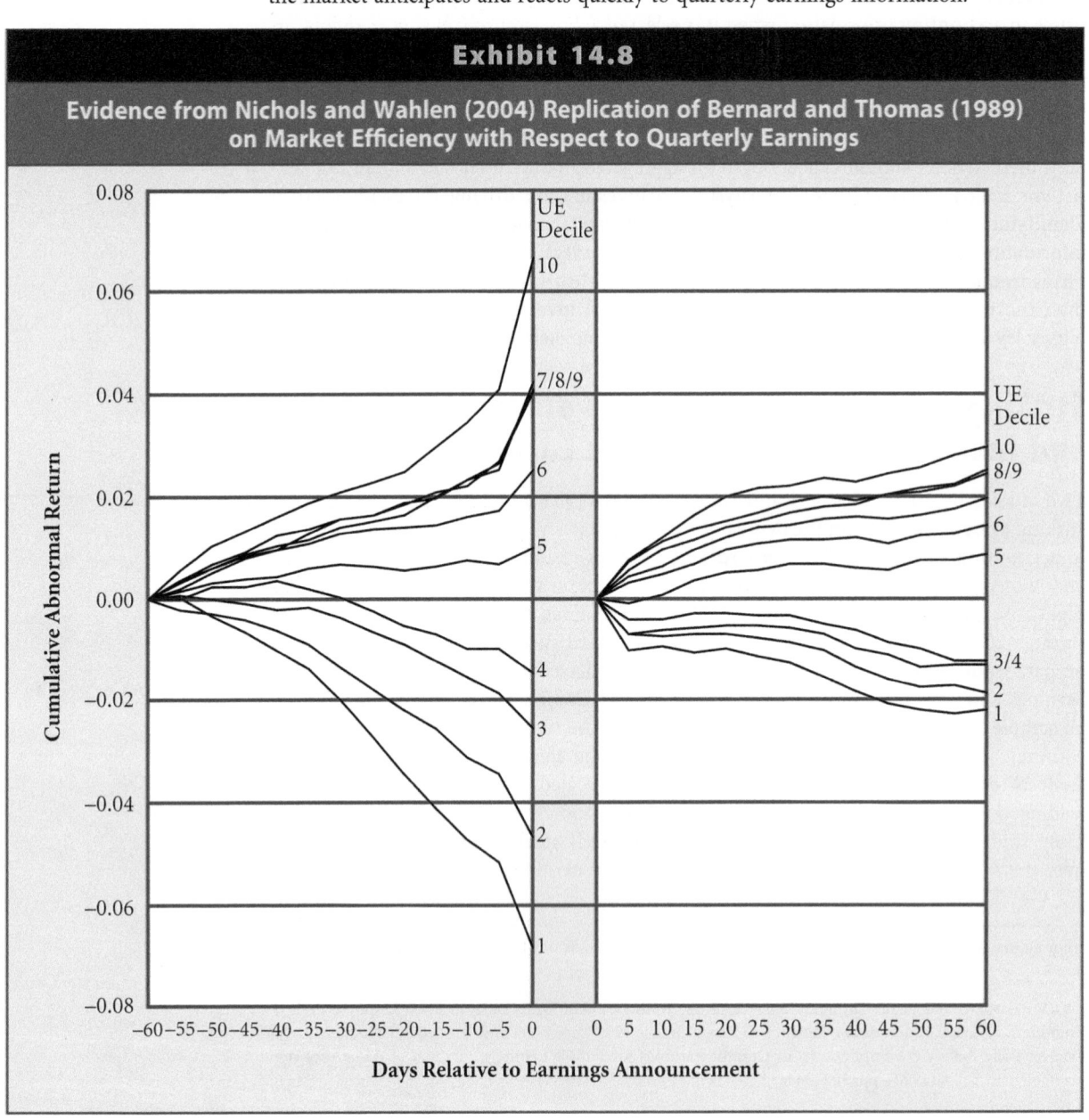

The results in the left side of Exhibit 14.8 report the cumulative abnormal returns to the exact same portfolios over the 60 trading days *after* the earnings announcements. These results suggest that the market's reaction to quarterly earnings news is highly, but not completely, efficient. If the market's reactions to quarterly earnings announcements were, on average, quick and complete, these portfolios should exhibit no systematic abnormal returns in the post-announcement period. Market prices should adjust efficiently within a few days of the earnings announcement. Post-announcement abnormal returns should arise only from new information that arrives during those 60 days, and the post-announcement abnormal returns should not be associated with the prior quarter's earnings news.

The results for the post-announcement period clearly indicate significant cumulative abnormal returns for the firms in UE portfolio 10 (best news) and UE portfolio 1 (worst news). Mean cumulative abnormal returns amount to roughly +3.0% and −2.2% for the best and worst unexpected earnings news portfolios, respectively. In a follow-up study, Bernard and Thomas (1990) show that, in part, the market seems to underreact to the persistence in current period earnings for future period earnings, failing to fully anticipate the momentum in quarterly earnings changes.

Taken together, the Bernard and Thomas studies reveal that the market is highly, but not completely, efficient with respect to quarterly earnings. The results from the Nichols and Wahlen study using more recent data suggest that the Bernard and Thomas findings still hold. We interpret these results to be very encouraging. Analysts who can forecast future earnings and take long positions in (buy) shares of firms likely to experience earnings increases and short positions in (sell) shares of firms likely to experience earnings decreases during the 60-day pre-announcement period have the potential to earn some portion of the pre-announcement abnormal returns. Similarly, analysts who react appropriately once earnings are announced have some potential to earn a portion of the post-announcement abnormal returns. These findings suggest that there are returns to be earned by being good at forecasting and reacting to earnings.

We believe that the state of the art of market efficiency is exactly where we would like it to be. The market is very efficient with respect to accounting information, but not perfectly efficient. Some stocks are temporarily mispriced, but the market tends to correct mispricing in a relatively short time. Financial statement analysis, particularly focusing on earnings, can help us identify stocks whose prices may be temporarily out of equilibrium. Insightful financial statement analysis can lead to intelligent investment decisions and better-than-average returns.

Striking Evidence on the Use of Valuation Models to Form Portfolios

An empirical study by Richard Frankel and Charles Lee (1998) provides compelling evidence on the use of the residual income valuation models (this chapter and Chapter 13) to pick stocks and form portfolios.[27] Frankel and Lee implemented the residual income model to compute fundamental share value for 18,162 firm-year observations from 1976 through 1993.

Frankel and Lee implemented the residual income valuation model for each firm-year in this large sample. For earnings forecasts, Frankel and Lee collected from I/B/E/S the consensus analysts' forecasts of one-year-ahead and two-years-ahead earnings per share as well as consensus earnings growth rate forecasts for Year +3. They collected

---

[27]Richard Frankel and Charles M. C. Lee, "Accounting Valuation, Market Expectation, and Cross-Sectional Stock Returns," *Journal of Accounting and Economics* 25 (1998), pp. 283–319.

book-value-per-share data from Compustat and projected that future book value per share would grow with the consensus earnings-per-share forecast minus future dividends, assuming that each firm would maintain the current dividend payout policy. Finally, to determine the cost of equity capital, Frankel and Lee used an industry-average, three-factor (beta, size, and market-to-book) expected returns model. They also assumed a constant cost of capital (11%, 12%, or 13%) across time and firms. Their results were not very sensitive to the R_E estimate.

Applying the three-year-horizon residual income model enabled Frankel and Lee to compute value per share (denoted as V) for each sample observation. They then scaled each firm's V by market share price (P) to compute a V/P ratio. If a firm's V/P ratio is exactly 1, it suggests that the market price per share is exactly equal to value per share. A V/P ratio that is greater than 1 suggests that the share is underpriced, whereas a V/P ratio less than 1 suggests that the share is overpriced. During each year of the study, Frankel and Lee ranked all of the sample firms from highest to lowest V/P. They then formed five portfolios, from the top 20% of firms with the highest V/P ratios each year down to the bottom 20% of firms with the lowest V/P ratios. They cumulated average returns over a 36-month holding period for these portfolios.

Exhibit 14.9 presents the Frankel and Lee results averaged across all of the years of their study. Judging by the bars in the graph and the axis on the left side of the exhibit,

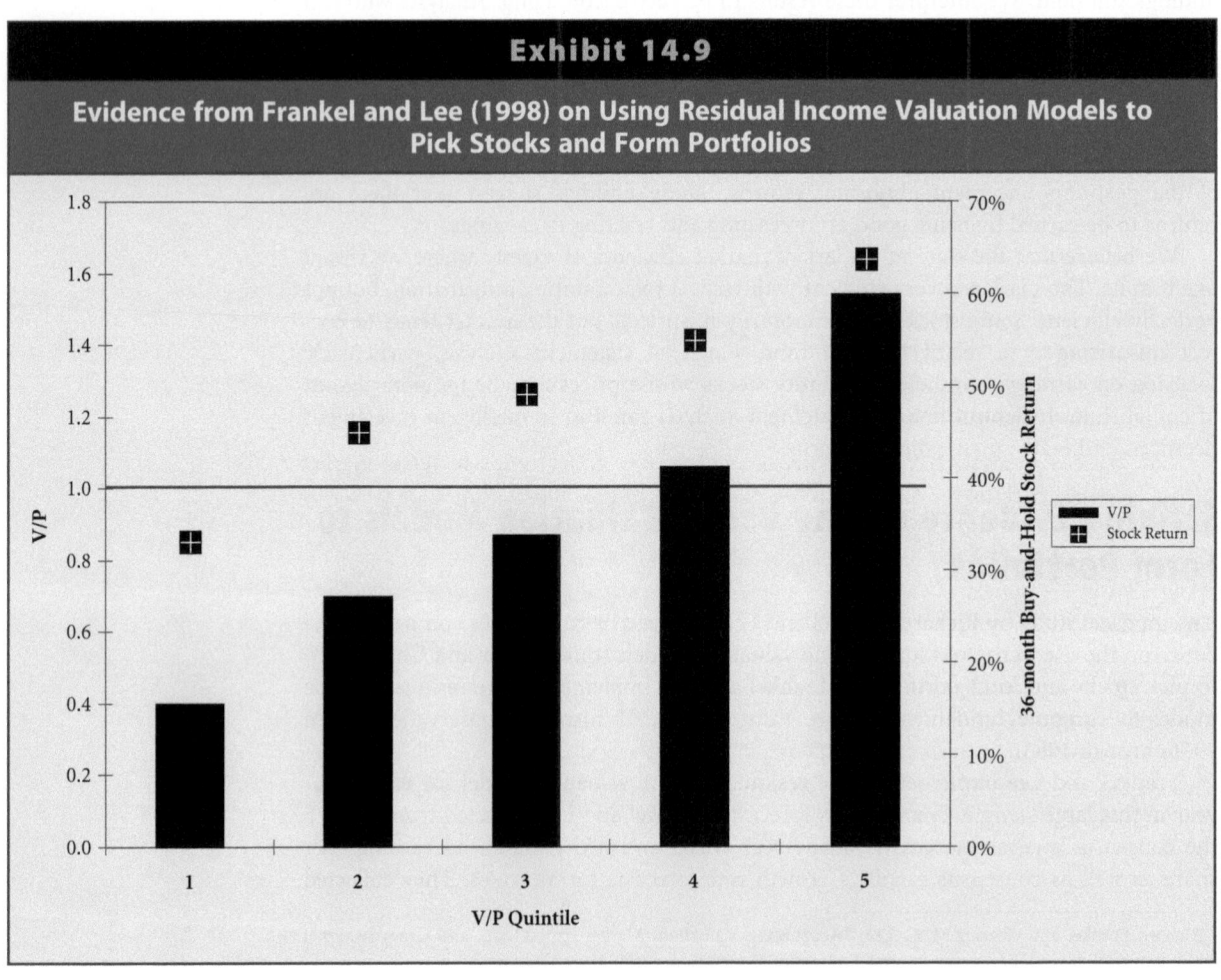

Exhibit 14.9

Evidence from Frankel and Lee (1998) on Using Residual Income Valuation Models to Pick Stocks and Form Portfolios

the bottom quintile portfolio had an average V/P ratio of only 0.40 (potentially overpriced). The top quintile portfolio had an average V/P ratio of roughly 1.5 (potentially underpriced). The square dots and the right axis of the graph indicate the average buy-and-hold returns cumulated by each portfolio over the 36 months after portfolio formation. Notice that the lowest quintile V/P firms generated, on average, cumulative three-year returns of only 35%, whereas the highest quintile V/P firms generated average cumulative three-year returns of nearly 65%. Frankel and Lee's study also included various sensitivity analyses and control tests indicating that their results were robust. The V/P ratio seemingly distinguished under- and overpriced stocks.

These results suggest that the valuation models we have discussed and demonstrated are useful in estimating share values and identifying which stocks are more likely to be under- or overpriced. Although these results are very encouraging, the results do not imply that the valuation process is easy or error-proof. Indeed, we strongly encourage you to carefully apply all six steps of the analysis framework demonstrated throughout this book to conduct thorough financial statement analysis, develop accurate forecasts, and determine reliable estimates of value to increase the likelihood of making good investment decisions.

Summary

This chapter examines the use of market multiples in valuation by relying on the residual income model to develop the theoretical rationale relating market prices to economic drivers of value and to accounting fundamentals. This chapter describes the conceptual bases and practical applications of the market-to-book ratio, the price-earnings ratio, and the price-earnings-growth ratio. The chapter focuses on four factors that affect these market multiples:

1. Risk and the cost of equity capital.
2. Expected future growth in earnings.
3. The presence of permanent and transitory components in the earnings of a particular year.
4. The effects of accounting methods and principles on reported earnings and the book value of common shareholders' equity.

For decades, analysts have relied heavily on price-earnings ratios to relate market prices to earnings. However, in recent years, analysts and academics alike increasingly have recognized that transitory elements in earnings and earnings growth can cloud the interpretation of the price-earnings ratio as an indicator of value. Analysts and academics are shifting emphasis to the market-to-book ratio and to the price-earnings-growth ratio. Transitory earnings elements of a particular period have less effect on the market-to-book ratio. This chapter also demonstrates techniques to exploit the information in market price by reverse engineering stock prices to infer the assumptions the market appears to be making. The chapter concludes by describing the relevance of academic research for the professional analyst, including highlighting key research results that appear to be very encouraging for those interested in using earnings and financial statement data to analyze and value firms.

Questions, Exercises, Problems, and Cases

Questions and Exercises

LO 14-1   **14.1 Value Determinants.** What are the fundamental determinants of share value, and how do they affect market-based valuation multiples, such as market-to-book and price-earnings ratios?

LO 14-2   **14.2 Residual ROCE.** Explain *residual* ROCE (return on common shareholders' equity). What does residual ROCE represent? What does residual ROCE measure?

LO 14-2   **14.3 Value-to-Book Valuation Approach.** In conceptual terms, explain the value-to-book valuation approach. Explain how the value-to-book approach described and demonstrated in this chapter relates to the residual income valuation approach described and demonstrated in Chapter 13.

LO 14-2   **14.4 Interpreting Value-to-Book Ratios.** Explain the implications of a value-to-book ratio that is exactly equal to 1. Compare the implications of a value-to-book ratio that is greater than 1 to those of a value-to-book ratio that is less than 1.

LO 14-2   **14.5 Interpreting Value-to-Book Ratios.** Explain the implications of a value-to-book ratio that is greater than the market-to-book ratio. Explain the implications of a value-to-book ratio that is less than the market-to-book ratio.

LO 14-2   **14.6 Value-to-Book Ratio Drivers.** Identify three economic factors that will drive a firm's value-to-book ratio to be higher than that of other firms in the same industry. Identify three accounting factors that will drive a firm's value-to-book ratio to be higher than that of other firms in the same industry.

LO 14-2   **14.7 Value-to-Book Ratio Drivers.** Identify three economic factors that will drive a firm's value-to-book ratio to decrease over time. Identify three accounting factors that will drive a firm's value-to-book ratio to decrease over time.

LO 14-3   **14.8 The Value-Earnings Ratio.** In conceptual terms, explain the value-earnings ratio. Explain the difference between the value-earnings ratio and the price-earnings ratio. What is the critical assumption about future earnings in both the value-earnings and price-earnings ratio?

LO 14-3   **14.9 The Price-Earnings Ratio.** In practice, it is common to observe price-earnings ratios measured as current period price divided by trailing-12-months (or most recent annual) earnings per share. Identify and explain three potential flaws inherent in this measurement of the price-earnings ratio as a valuation multiple.

LO 14-3   **14.10 Price-Earnings Ratio Drivers.** Identify three economic factors that will drive a firm's price-earnings ratio to be higher than that of other firms in the same industry. Identify three accounting factors that will drive a firm's price-earnings ratio in a given period to be higher than that of other firms in the same industry.

LO 14-3   **14.11 Price-Earnings Ratio Drivers.** Identify three economic factors that will drive a firm's price-earnings ratio to decrease over time. Identify three accounting factors that will drive a firm's price-earnings ratio down in a given period.

14.12 Market-to-Book versus Price-Earnings Ratios. Explain why market-to-book valuation multiples demonstrate less variance over time and across firms than do price-earnings valuation multiples.

LO 14-2, LO 14-3

14.13 Reverse Engineering Share Prices. Explain reverse engineering of share prices in conceptual terms. How does reverse engineering of share prices enable an analyst to infer (or deduce) the assumptions that the capital markets appear to impound in share price?

LO 14-4

14.14 Market Efficiency. What does market efficiency mean? What does market efficiency not mean? Explain how market efficiency relates to the *amount* of information that affects share prices and the *speed* with which information affects share prices.

LO 14-5

14.15 Analysts' Role in Market Efficiency. Explain the role of analysts in increasing capital market efficiency.

LO 14-5

14.16 Market Efficiency with Respect to Quarterly Earnings Surprises. Using the evidence presented in Exhibit 14.8, describe the extent to which the market is efficient with respect to quarterly earnings surprises during the 60 trading days *prior to* quarterly earnings announcements. Using the evidence presented in Exhibit 14.8, describe the extent to which the market is efficient with respect to quarterly earnings surprises during the 60 trading days *following* quarterly earnings announcements.

LO 14-5

Problems and Cases

14.17 Using Market Multiples to Assess Values and Market Prices. Problem 13.18 and Exhibit 13.6 in Chapter 13 present selected hypothetical data from projected financial statements for Steak 'n Shake for Year +1 to Year +11. The amounts for Year +11 reflect a long-term growth assumption of 3%. The cost of equity capital is 9.34%. The market value of common shareholders' equity in **Steak 'n Shake** on January 1, Year +1, is $309.98 million.

LO 14-2, LO 14-3, LO 14-4, LO 14-5

REQUIRED

a. Compute the value-to-book ratio as of January 1, Year +1, using the residual ROCE valuation method.

b. Using the analyses developed in Requirement a, prepare an exhibit summarizing the following ratios for Steak 'n Shake as of January 1, Year +1:
1. Value-to-book ratio (using the amounts from Requirement a)
2. Market-to-book ratio
3. Value-earnings ratio, using reported earnings for Year 0 of $21.8 million
4. Price-earnings ratio, using reported earnings for Year 0 of $21.8 million
5. Value-earnings ratio, using projected earnings for Year +1 of $24.5 million
6. Price-earnings ratio, using projected earnings for Year +1 of $24.5 million

c. Use reverse engineering to solve for the long-run growth rate in continuing residual income in Year +11 and beyond that is implicitly impounded in the market value of Steak 'n Shake on January 1, Year +1. Use the 9.34% cost of equity capital and the projected earnings amounts for Year +1 to Year +10 in Exhibit 13.6 before solving for the long-run growth rate in continuing residual income.

d. Using the analyses in Requirements a–c, evaluate the extent of the market's mispricing (if any) of Steak 'n Shake.

Exhibit 14.10

Selected Data for Pharmaceutical Companies
(Problem 14.18)

Company	MB	ROCE	Cost of Equity Capital	Dividend Payout Ratio	PE	Growth in Earnings	Excess Earnings Years
Bristol-Myers Squibb	13.9	0.489	0.134	0.77	32.4	0.068	58.3
Warner-Lambert	13.0	0.350	0.133	0.48	42.7	0.051	32.2
Eli Lilly	12.4	0.281	0.155	0.42	49.3	0.110	89.8
Pfizer	11.2	0.350	0.143	0.43	40.4	0.152	27.8
Abbott Laboratories	10.4	0.428	0.113	0.39	26.9	0.116	13.5
Merck	10.3	0.331	0.154	0.46	31.8	0.130	41.9
Wyeth	6.9	0.340	0.138	0.51	25.0	0.065	24.6

LO 14-2

14.18 Interpreting Market-to-Book Ratios. Exhibit 14.10 presents data on market-to-book (MB) ratios, ROCE, the cost of equity capital, and price-earnings (PE) ratios for seven pharmaceutical companies. (Note that PE ratios for these firms typically fall in the 30–35 range.) Exhibit 14.10 also provides historical data on the five-year average rate of growth in earnings and dividend payout ratios for each firm. The data on excess earnings years represent the number of years that each firm would need to earn a rate of return on common shareholders' equity (ROCE) equal to that in Exhibit 14.10 in order to produce value-to-book ratios that equal the market-to-book ratios shown. For example, **Bristol-Myers Squibb** would need to earn an ROCE of 48.9% for 58.3 years in order for the present value of the excess earnings over the cost of equity capital to produce a value-to-book ratio that matches the market-to-book ratio of 13.9.

REQUIRED

Assume that market share prices for each firm are reasonably efficient. That is, do not simply assume that the market has over- or undervalued these firms. Considering the theoretical determinants of the market-to-book ratio, discuss the likely reasons for the relative ordering of these seven companies on their market-to-book ratios.

LO 14-2, LO 14-3

14.19 Sensitivity of Value-Earnings and Value-to-Book to Changes in Assumptions. This problem explores the sensitivity of the value-earnings and value-to-book models to changes in underlying assumptions. We recommend that you design a computer spreadsheet to perform the calculations, particularly for the value-to-book ratio.

REQUIRED

a. Assume that current period earnings per share were $1.00 for each of the following nine scenarios (A through I). Compute the value-earnings ratio based on projected one-year-ahead earnings under each of the following sets of assumptions:

Scenario	Cost of Equity Capital	Growth Rate in Earnings
A	0.15	0.06
B	0.15	0.08
C	0.15	0.10
D	0.13	0.06
E	0.13	0.08
F	0.13	0.10
G	0.11	0.06
H	0.11	0.08
I	0.11	0.10

b. Assess the sensitivity of the value-earnings ratio to changes in the cost of equity capital and changes in the growth rate.

c. Compute the value-to-book ratio under each of the following nine sets of assumptions (A through I). Assume zero abnormal ROCE in the periods following the number of years of excess earnings.

Scenario	ROCE	Cost of Equity Capital	Dividend Payout Percentage	Years of Excess Earnings
A	0.20	0.13	0.30	10
B	0.18	0.13	0.30	10
C	0.14	0.13	0.30	10
D	0.18	0.15	0.30	10
E	0.18	0.11	0.30	10
F	0.18	0.13	0.40	10
G	0.18	0.13	0.20	10
H	0.18	0.13	0.30	15
I	0.18	0.13	0.30	20

d. Assess the sensitivity of the value-to-book ratio to changes in the assumptions made about the various underlying variables.

14.20 Market Multiples and Reverse Engineering Share Prices. In

LO 14-4

2000, **Enron** enjoyed remarkable success in the capital markets. During that year, Enron's shares increased in value by 89%, while the S&P 500 index fell by 9%. At the end of 2000, Enron's shares were trading at roughly $83 per share, and all of the sell-side analysts following Enron recommended the shares as a "buy" or a "strong buy." With 752.2 million shares outstanding, Enron had a market capitalization of $62,530 million and was one of the largest firms (in terms of market capital) in the United States. At year-end 2000, Enron's book value of common shareholders' equity was $11,470 million. At year-end 2000, Enron posted earnings per share of $1.19. Among sell-side analysts following Enron, the consensus forecast for earnings per share was $1.31 per share for 2001 and $1.44 per share for 2002, with 10% earnings growth expected from 2003 to 2005. At the time, Enron was paying dividends equivalent to roughly 40% of earnings and was expected to maintain that payout policy. At year-end 2000, Enron had a market beta of 1.7. The risk-free rate of return was 4.3%, and the market risk premium was

5.0%. (Note: The data provided in this problem, and the inferences you draw from them, do not depend on foresight of Enron's declaring bankruptcy by the end of 2001.)

REQUIRED

a. Use the CAPM to compute the required rate of return on common equity capital for Enron.

b. Use year-end 2000 data to compute the following ratios for Enron:
   (1) Market-to-book
   (2) Price-earnings (using 2000 earnings per share)
   (3) Forward price-earnings (using consensus forecast earnings per share for 2001)

c. Reverse engineer Enron's $83 share price to solve for the implied expected return on Enron shares at year-end 2000. Do the reverse engineering under the following assumptions:
   (1) Enron's market price equals value.
   (2) The consensus analysts' earnings-per-share forecasts through 2005 are reliable proxies for market expectations.
   (3) Enron will maintain a 40% dividend payout rate.
   (4) Beyond 2005, Enron's long-run earnings growth rate will be 3.0%.

d. What do these analyses suggest about investing in Enron's shares at a price of $83?

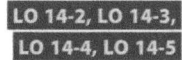

14.21 Valuation of Coca-Cola Using Market Multiples. The Coca-Cola **Company** is a global soft-drink beverage company that is a direct competitor with **Starbucks**. The data in Chapter 12, Exhibits 12.14 through 12.16 (pages 806–809), include the actual amounts for 2015 and projected amounts for Year +1 to Year +6 for the income statements, balance sheets, and statements of cash flows for Coca-Cola.

The market equity beta for Coca-Cola at the end of 2015 is 0.75. Assume that the risk-free interest rate is 3.0% and the market risk premium is 6.0%. Coca-Cola has 4,324 million shares outstanding at the end of 2015, when Coca-Cola's share price was $42.96.

REQUIRED

Part I—Computing Coca-Cola's Value-to-Book Ratio Using the Value-to-Book Valuation Approach

a. Use the CAPM to compute the required rate of return on common equity capital for Coca-Cola.

b. Using the projected financial statements in Exhibits 12.14 through 12.16, derive the projected residual ROCE (return on common shareholders' equity) for Coca-Cola for Years +1 through +5.

c. The projected income statements and balance sheets for Year +6 assume Coca-Cola will grow at a steady-state growth rate of 3.0%. Derive the projected residual ROCE for Year +6 for Coca-Cola.

d. Using the required rate of return on common equity from Requirement a as a discount rate, compute the sum of the present value of residual ROCE for Coca-Cola for Years +1 through +5.

e. Using the required rate of return on common equity from Requirement a as a discount rate and the long-run growth rate from Requirement c, compute the continuing value of Coca-Cola as of the start of Year +6 based on Coca-Cola's continuing residual ROCE in Year +6 and beyond. After computing continuing value as of the start of Year +6, discount it to present value at the start of Year +1.

f. Compute Coca-Cola's value-to-book ratio as of the end of 2015 with the following three steps:

(1) Compute the total sum of the present value of all future residual ROCE (from Requirements d and e).

(2) To the total from Requirement f(1), add 1 (representing the book value of equity as of the beginning of the valuation as of the end of 2015).

(3) Adjust the total sum from Requirement f(2) using the midyear discounting adjustment factor.

g. Compute Coca-Cola's market-to-book ratio as of the end of 2015. Compare the value-to-book ratio to the market-to-book ratio. What investment decision does the comparison suggest? What does the comparison suggest regarding the pricing of Coca-Cola shares in the market: underpriced, overpriced, or fairly priced?

h. Use the value-to-book ratio to project the value of a share of common equity in Coca-Cola.

i. If you computed Coca-Cola's common equity share value using the free cash flows to common equity valuation approach in Problem 12.16 in Chapter 12 and/or the residual income valuation approach in Problem 13.19 in Chapter 13, compare the value estimate you obtained in those problems with the estimate you obtained in this case. You should obtain the same value estimates under all three approaches. If you have not yet worked those problems, you would benefit from doing so now.

Part II—Analyzing Coca-Cola's Share Price Using the Value-Earnings Ratio, Price-Earnings Ratio, and Reverse Engineering

j. Use the forecast data for Year +1 to project Year +1 earnings per share. To do so, divide the projection of Coca-Cola's comprehensive income available for common shareholders in Year +1 by the number of common shares outstanding at the end of 2015. Using this Year +1 earnings-per-share forecast and the share value computed in Requirement h, compute Coca-Cola's value-earnings ratio.

k. Using the Year +1 earnings-per-share forecast from Requirement j and using the share price at the end of 2015, compute Coca-Cola's price-earnings ratio. Compare Coca-Cola's value-earnings ratio with its price-earnings ratio. What investment decision does the comparison suggest? What does the comparison suggest regarding the pricing of Coca-Cola shares in the market: underpriced, overpriced, or fairly priced? Does this comparison lead to the same conclusions you reached when comparing value-to-book ratios with market-to-book ratios in Requirement g?

l. Reverse engineer Coca-Cola's share price at the end of 2015 to solve for the implied expected rate of return. First, assume that value equals price and that the earnings and 3% long-run growth forecasts through Year +6 and beyond are reliable proxies for the market's expectations for Coca-Cola. Then solve for the implied expected rate of return (the discount rate) the market has impounded in Coca-Cola's share price. (Hint: Begin with the forecast and valuation spreadsheet you developed to value Coca-Cola shares. Vary the discount rate until you solve for the discount rate that makes your value estimate exactly equal the end-of-2015 market price of $42.96 per share.)

m. Reverse engineer Coca-Cola's share price at the end of 2015 to solve for the implied expected long-run growth. First, assume that value equals price and that the earnings forecasts through Year +5 are reliable proxies for the market's expectations for Coca-Cola. Also assume that the discount rate implied by the CAPM (computed in Requirement a) is a reliable proxy for the market's expected rate of return. Then solve for the implied expected long-run growth rate the market has impounded in Coca-Cola's share price. [Hint: Begin with the forecast and valuation spreadsheet you developed to value Coca-Cola shares and use the CAPM discount rate. Set the long-run growth parameter initially to zero. Increase the long-run growth rate until you solve for the growth rate that makes your value estimate exactly equal the end-of-2015 market price of $42.96 per share.]

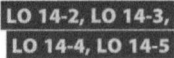

14.22 Analysis of Comparable Companies Using Market Multiples.

In this chapter, we evaluated shares of common equity in **Starbucks** using the value-to-book approach, market multiples, and reverse engineering. **The Coca-Cola Company** competes directly with **Starbucks**. The data in Chapter 12, Exhibits 12.14 through 12.16, include the actual amounts for 2015 and projected amounts for Year +1 to Year +6 for the income statements, balance sheets, and statements of cash flows for Coca-Cola. In Problem 14.21, you evaluated shares of common equity in Coca-Cola using the value-to-book approach, market multiples, and reverse engineering.

REQUIRED

a. Prepare an exhibit using the data and analyses for **Starbucks** from this chapter and the data and analyses for Coca-Cola from the previous problem that will allow you to compare these two competitors on the following dimensions:
   1. Cost of equity capital (R_E)
   2. ROCE for 2015
   3. Projected ROCE for Year +1
   4. Book value of common shareholders' equity
   5. Market value of common shareholders' equity
   6. Intrinsic value of common shareholders' equity
   7. Value-to-book ratio
   8. Market-to-book ratio
   9. Value-earnings ratio (using Year +1 projected comprehensive income)
   10. Price-earnings ratio (using Year +1 projected comprehensive income)
   11. Value-earnings ratio (using 2015 reported earnings per share)
   12. Price-earnings ratio (using 2015 reported earnings per share)
   13. Reverse engineer share price to solve for implied expected rate of return (assuming 3% long-run growth)
   14. Reverse engineer share price to solve for implied long-run growth (assuming the cost of equity capital as the discount rate)

b. What inferences can you draw from these comparisons about the valuation of **Starbucks** versus Coca-Cola? In the chapter, we concluded that **Starbucks** shares were underpriced by roughly 16% in the market at the end of 2015. In the previous problem, you determined whether Coca-Cola was under- or overpriced. Are the comparisons here consistent with your previous conclusions regarding both **Starbucks** and Coca-Cola shares at the end of 2015? Explain.

INTEGRATIVE CASE 14.1

Walmart

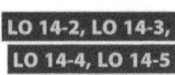

Valuation of Walmart's Common Equity Using Market Multiples

In Integrative Case 10.1, we projected financial statements for **Walmart Stores** for Years +1 through +5. The data in Chapter 12, Exhibits 12.17 through 12.19 (pages 812–814), include the actual amounts for 2015 and the projected amounts for Year +1 to Year +5 for the income statements, balance sheets, and statements of cash flows for Walmart (in millions). In this portion of the Walmart Integrative Case, we use the projected financial statements from Chapter 12 and apply the techniques in Chapter 14 to compute Walmart's required rate of return on equity and share value based on the value-to-book valuation model. We also compare our value-to-book ratio estimate to Walmart's market-to-book ratio at the time of the case to determine an investment recommendation. In addition, we compute the value-earnings and price-earnings ratios, and we reverse engineer Walmart's share price as of the end of 2015. The market equity beta for Walmart at the end of 2015 was 1.00. Assume that the risk-free interest rate was 3.0% and the market risk premium was 6.0%. Walmart had 3,162 million shares outstanding at the end of 2015, and the share price was $67.50.

REQUIRED

Part I—Computing Walmart's Value-to-Book Ratio Using the Value-to-Book Valuation Approach

a. Use the CAPM to compute the required rate of return on common equity capital for Walmart.

b. Using the projected financial statements in Chapter 12, Exhibits 12.17 through 12.19, derive the projected residual ROCE (return on common shareholders' equity) for Walmart for Years +1 through +5.

c. Assume that the steady-state, long-run growth rate will be 3% in Year +6 and beyond. Project that the Year +5 income statement and balance sheet amounts will grow by 3% in Year +6; then derive the projected residual ROCE for Year +6 for Walmart.

d. Using the required rate of return on common equity from Requirement a as a discount rate, compute the sum of the present value of residual ROCE for Walmart for Years +1 through +5.

e. Using the required rate of return on common equity from Requirement a as a discount rate and the long-run growth rate from Requirement c, compute the continuing value of Walmart as of the start of Year +6 based on Walmart's continuing residual ROCE in Year +6 and beyond. After computing continuing value as of the start of Year +6, discount it to present value at the start of Year +1.

f. Compute Walmart's value-to-book ratio as of the end of 2015 with the following three steps:

   (1) Compute the total sum of the present value of all future residual ROCE (from Requirements d and e).

   (2) To the total from Requirement f(1), add 1 (representing the book value of equity as of the beginning of the valuation as of the end of 2015).

   (3) Adjust the total sum from Requirement f(2) using the midyear discounting adjustment factor.

g. Compute Walmart's market-to-book ratio as of the end of 2015. Compare the value-to-book ratio to the market-to-book ratio. What investment decision does the comparison suggest? What does the comparison suggest regarding the pricing of Walmart shares in the market: underpriced, overpriced, or fairly priced?

h. Use the value-to-book ratio to project Walmart's share value.

i. If you computed Walmart's common equity share value using the dividends valuation approach in Integrative Case 11.1, and/or the free cash flows to common equity valuation approach in Integrative Case 12.1, and/or the residual income valuation approach in Integrative Case 13.1, compare the value estimate you obtained in those problems with the estimate you obtained in this case. You should obtain the same value estimates under all four approaches. If you have not yet worked those cases, you would benefit from doing so now.

Part II—Analyzing Walmart's Share Price Using the Value-Earnings Ratio, Price-Earnings Ratio, and Reverse Engineering

j. Use the forecast data for Year +1 to project Year +1 earnings per share. To do so, divide Walmart's projected comprehensive income available for common shareholders in Year +1 by the number of common shares outstanding at the end of 2015. Using this Year +1 earnings-per-share forecast and the share value computed in Requirement h, compute Walmart's value-earnings ratio.

k. Using the Year +1 earnings-per-share forecast from Requirement j and using the share price of $67.50 at the end of 2015, compute Walmart's price-earnings ratio. Compare Walmart's value-earnings ratio with its price-earnings ratio. What does the comparison suggest regarding the pricing of Walmart shares in the market: underpriced, overpriced, or fairly priced? What investment decision does the comparison suggest? Does this comparison lead to the same conclusions you reached when comparing value-to-book ratios with market-to-book ratios in Requirement g?

l. Reverse engineer Walmart's share price at the end of 2015 to solve for the implied expected rate of return. First, assume that value equals price and that the earnings and 3% long-run growth forecasts in Year +6 and beyond are reliable proxies for the market's expectations for Walmart. Then solve for the implied expected rate of return (the discount rate) the market has impounded in Walmart's share price. (Hint: Begin with the forecast and valuation spreadsheet you developed to value Walmart shares. Vary the discount rate until you solve for the discount rate that makes your value estimate exactly equal the end-of-2015 market price of $67.50 per share.)

m. Reverse engineer Walmart's share price at the end of 2015 to solve for the implied expected long-run growth. First, assume that value equals price and that the earnings forecasts through Year +5 are reliable proxies for the market's expectations for Walmart. Also assume that the discount rate implied by the CAPM (computed in Requirement a) is a reliable proxy for the market's expected rate of return. Then solve for the implied expected long-run growth rate the market has impounded in Walmart's share price. (Hint: Begin with the forecast and valuation spreadsheet you developed to value Walmart shares and use the CAPM discount rate. Set the long-run growth parameter initially to zero. Increase the long-run growth rate until you solve for the growth rate that makes your value estimate exactly equal the end-of-2015 market price of $67.50 per share.)

Financial Statements and Notes for Starbucks Corporation

UNITED STATES SECURITIES AND EXCHANGE COMMISSION
Washington, DC 20549
Form 10-K

☒ ANNUAL REPORT PURSUANT TO SECTION 13 OR 15(d) OF THE SECURITIES EXCHANGE ACT OF 1934
For the Fiscal Year Ended September 27, 2015

or

☐ TRANSITION REPORT PURSUANT TO SECTION 13 OR 15(d) OF THE SECURITIES EXCHANGE ACT OF 1934
For the transition period from   to   .
Commission File Number: 0-20322

Starbucks Corporation
(Exact Name of Registrant as Specified in its Charter)

Washington	91-1325671
(State of Incorporation)	*(IRS Employer ID)*

2401 Utah Avenue South, Seattle, Washington 98134
(206) 447-1575
(Address of principal executive offices, zip code, telephone number)
Securities Registered Pursuant to Section 12(b) of the Act:

Title of Each Class	Name of Each Exchange on Which Registered
Common Stock, $0.001 par value per share	Nasdaq Global Select Market

Securities Registered Pursuant to Section 12(g) of the Act: None

Indicate by check mark if the registrant is a well-known seasoned issuer, as defined in Rule 405 of the Securities Act. Yes ☒ No ☐
Indicate by check mark if the registrant is not required to file reports pursuant to Section 13 or Section 15(d) of the Act. Yes ☐ No ☒
Indicate by check mark whether the registrant: (1) has filed all reports required to be filed by Section 13 or 15(d) of the Securities Exchange Act of 1934 during the preceding 12 months (or for such shorter period that the registrant was required to file such reports), and (2) has been subject to such filing requirements for the past 90 days. Yes ☒ No ☐

Indicate by check mark whether the registrant has submitted electronically and posted on its corporate Web site, if any, every Interactive Data File required to be submitted and posted pursuant to Rule 405 of Regulation S-T (§ 232.405 of this chapter) during the preceding 12 months (or for such shorter period that the registrant was required to submit and post such files). Yes ☒ No ☐
Indicate by check mark if disclosure of delinquent filers pursuant to Item 405 of Regulation of S-K (§ 229.405 of this chapter) is not contained herein, and will not be contained, to the best of the registrant's knowledge, in definitive proxy or information statements incorporated by reference in Part III of this Form 10-K or any amendment to this Form 10-K.   ☐
Indicate by check mark whether the registrant is a large accelerated filer, an accelerated filer, a non-accelerated filer, or a smaller reporting company. See the definitions of "large accelerated filer," "accelerated filer" and "smaller reporting company" in Rule 12b-2 of the Exchange Act. (Check one):

Large accelerated filer   ☒   Accelerated filer   ☐

Non-accelerated filer   ☐ (Do not check if a smaller reporting company)   Smaller reporting company   ☐

Indicate by check mark whether the registrant is a shell company (as defined in Rule 12b-2 of the Act).   Yes ☐   No ☒
The aggregate market value of the voting stock held by non-affiliates of the registrant as of the last business day of the registrant's most recently completed second fiscal quarter, based upon the closing sale price of the registrant's common stock on March 29, 2015 as reported on the NASDAQ Global Select Market was $69 billion. As of November 6, 2015, there were 1,484.8 million shares of the registrant's Common Stock outstanding.

DOCUMENTS INCORPORATED BY REFERENCE

Portions of the definitive Proxy Statement for the registrant's Annual Meeting of Shareholders to be held on March 23, 2016 have been incorporated by reference into Part III of this Annual Report on Form 10-K.

Item 8.   *Financial Statements and Supplementary Data*

STARBUCKS CORPORATION
CONSOLIDATED STATEMENTS OF EARNINGS
(in millions, except per share data)

Fiscal Year Ended	Sep 27, 2015	Sep 28, 2014	Sep 29, 2013
Net revenues:			
Company-operated stores	$ 15,197.3	$ 12,977.9	$ 11,793.2
Licensed stores	1,861.9	1,588.6	1,360.5
CPG, foodservice and other	2,103.5	1,881.3	1,713.1
Total net revenues	19,162.7	16,447.8	14,866.8
Cost of sales including occupancy costs	7,787.5	6,858.8	6,382.3
Store operating expenses	5,411.1	4,638.2	4,286.1
Other operating expenses	522.4	457.3	431.8
Depreciation and amortization expenses	893.9	709.6	621.4
General and administrative expenses	1,196.7	991.3	937.9
Litigation charge/(credit)	—	(20.2)	2,784.1
Total operating expenses	15,811.6	13,635.0	15,443.6
Income from equity investees	249.9	268.3	251.4
Operating income/(loss)	3,601.0	3,081.1	(325.4)
Gain resulting from acquisition of joint venture	390.6	—	—
Loss on extinguishment of debt	(61.1)	—	—
Interest income and other, net	43.0	142.7	123.6
Interest expense	(70.5)	(64.1)	(28.1)
Earnings/(loss) before income taxes	3,903.0	3,159.7	(229.9)
Income tax expense/(benefit)	1,143.7	1,092.0	(238.7)
Net earnings including noncontrolling interests	2,759.3	2,067.7	8.8
Net earnings/(loss) attributable to noncontrolling interests	1.9	(0.4)	0.5
Net earnings attributable to Starbucks	$ 2,757.4	$ 2,068.1	$ 8.3
Earnings per share — basic	$ 1.84	$ 1.37	$ 0.01
Earnings per share — diluted	$ 1.82	$ 1.35	$ 0.01
Weighted average shares outstanding:			
Basic	1,495.9	1,506.3	1,498.5
Diluted	1,513.4	1,526.3	1,524.5

See Notes to Consolidated Financial Statements.

46

STARBUCKS CORPORATION
CONSOLIDATED STATEMENTS OF COMPREHENSIVE INCOME
(in millions)

	Sep 27, 2015	Sep 28, 2014	Sep 29, 2013
Net earnings including noncontrolling interests	$ 2,759.3	$ 2,067.7	$ 8.8
Other comprehensive income/(loss), net of tax:			
Unrealized holding gains/(losses) on available-for-sale securities	1.4	1.6	(0.6)
Tax (expense)/benefit	(0.5)	(0.6)	0.2
Unrealized gains/(losses) on cash flow hedging instruments	47.6	24.1	47.1
Tax (expense)/benefit	(16.8)	(7.8)	(24.6)
Unrealized gains/(losses) on net investment hedging instruments	4.3	25.5	32.8
Tax (expense)/benefit	(1.6)	(9.4)	(12.1)
Translation adjustment	(222.7)	(75.8)	(41.6)
Tax (expense)/benefit	6.0	(1.6)	0.3
Reclassification adjustment for net (gains)/losses realized in net earnings for available-for-sale securities, hedging instruments, and translation adjustment	(65.9)	(1.5)	46.3
Tax expense/(benefit)	23.5	3.8	(3.5)
Other comprehensive income/(loss)	(224.7)	(41.7)	44.3
Comprehensive income including noncontrolling interests	2,534.6	2,026.0	53.1
Comprehensive income/(loss) attributable to noncontrolling interests	(29.2)	(0.4)	0.5
Comprehensive income attributable to Starbucks	$ 2,563.8	$ 2,026.4	$ 52.6

See Notes to Consolidated Financial Statements.

47

STARBUCKS CORPORATION
CONSOLIDATED BALANCE SHEETS
(in millions, except per share data)

	Sep 27, 2015		Sep 28, 2014
ASSETS			
Current assets:			
Cash and cash equivalents	$ 1,530.1	$	1,708.4
Short-term investments	81.3		135.4
Accounts receivable, net	719.0		631.0
Inventories	1,306.4		1,090.9
Prepaid expenses and other current assets	334.2		285.6
Deferred income taxes, net	381.7		317.4
Total current assets	4,352.7		4,168.7
Long-term investments	312.5		318.4
Equity and cost investments	352.0		514.9
Property, plant and equipment, net	4,088.3		3,519.0
Deferred income taxes, net	828.9		903.3
Other long-term assets	415.9		198.9
Other intangible assets	520.4		273.5
Goodwill	1,575.4		856.2
TOTAL ASSETS	$ 12,446.1	$	10,752.9
LIABILITIES AND EQUITY			
Current liabilities:			
Accounts payable	$ 684.2	$	533.7
Accrued liabilities	1,760.7		1,514.4
Insurance reserves	224.8		196.1
Stored value card liability	983.8		794.5
Total current liabilities	3,653.5		3,038.7
Long-term debt	2,347.5		2,048.3
Other long-term liabilities	625.3		392.2
Total liabilities	6,626.3		5,479.2
Shareholders' equity:			
Common stock ($0.001 par value) — authorized, 2,400.0 shares; issued and outstanding, 1,485.1 and 1,499.1 shares, respectively	1.5		0.7
Additional paid-in capital	41.1		39.4
Retained earnings	5,974.8		5,206.6
Accumulated other comprehensive income/(loss)	(199.4)		25.3
Total shareholders' equity	5,818.0		5,272.0
Noncontrolling interest	1.8		1.7
Total equity	5,819.8		5,273.7
TOTAL LIABILITIES AND EQUITY	$ 12,446.1	$	10,752.9

See Notes to Consolidated Financial Statements.

STARBUCKS CORPORATION
CONSOLIDATED STATEMENTS OF CASH FLOWS
(in millions)

Fiscal Year Ended	Sep 27, 2015	Sep 28, 2014	Sep 29, 2013
OPERATING ACTIVITIES:			
Net earnings including noncontrolling interests	$ 2,759.3	$ 2,067.7	$ 8.8
Adjustments to reconcile net earnings to net cash provided by operating activities:			
Depreciation and amortization	933.8	748.4	655.6
Litigation charge	—	—	2,784.1
Deferred income taxes, net	21.2	10.2	(1,045.9)
Income earned from equity method investees	(190.2)	(182.7)	(171.8)
Distributions received from equity method investees	148.2	139.2	115.6
Gain resulting from acquisition/sale of equity in joint ventures and certain retail operations	(394.3)	(70.2)	(80.1)
Loss on extinguishment of debt	61.1	—	—
Stock-based compensation	209.8	183.2	142.3
Excess tax benefit on share-based awards	(132.4)	(114.4)	(258.1)
Other	53.8	36.2	23.0
Cash provided/(used) by changes in operating assets and liabilities:			
Accounts receivable	(82.8)	(79.7)	(68.3)
Inventories	(207.9)	14.3	152.5
Accounts payable	137.7	60.4	88.7
Accrued litigation charge	—	(2,763.9)	—
Income taxes payable, net	87.6	309.8	298.4
Accrued liabilities and insurance reserves	124.4	103.9	47.3
Stored value card liability	170.3	140.8	139.9
Prepaid expenses, other current assets and other long-term assets	49.5	4.6	76.3
Net cash provided by operating activities	3,749.1	607.8	2,908.3
INVESTING ACTIVITIES:			
Purchases of investments	(567.4)	(1,652.5)	(785.9)
Sales of investments	600.6	1,454.8	60.2
Maturities and calls of investments	18.8	456.1	980.0
Acquisitions, net of cash acquired	(284.3)	—	(610.4)
Additions to property, plant and equipment	(1,303.7)	(1,160.9)	(1,151.2)
Proceeds from sale of equity in joint ventures and certain retail operations	8.9	103.9	108.0
Other	6.8	(19.1)	(11.9)
Net cash used by investing activities	(1,520.3)	(817.7)	(1,411.2)
FINANCING ACTIVITIES:			
Proceeds from issuance of long-term debt	848.5	748.5	749.7
Repayments of long-term debt	(610.1)	—	(35.2)
Cash used for purchase of non-controlling interest	(360.8)	—	—
Proceeds from issuance of common stock	191.8	139.7	247.2
Excess tax benefit on share-based awards	132.4	114.4	258.1
Cash dividends paid	(928.6)	(783.1)	(628.9)
Repurchase of common stock	(1,436.1)	(758.6)	(588.1)
Minimum tax withholdings on share-based awards	(75.5)	(77.3)	(121.4)
Other	(18.1)	(6.9)	10.4
Net cash used by financing activities	(2,256.5)	(623.3)	(108.2)
Effect of exchange rate changes on cash and cash equivalents	(150.6)	(34.1)	(1.8)
Net (decrease)/increase in cash and cash equivalents	(178.3)	(867.3)	1,387.1
CASH AND CASH EQUIVALENTS:			
Beginning of period	1,708.4	2,575.7	1,188.6
End of period	$ 1,530.1	$ 1,708.4	$ 2,575.7
SUPPLEMENTAL DISCLOSURE OF CASH FLOW INFORMATION:			
Cash paid during the period for:			
Interest, net of capitalized interest	$ 69.5	$ 56.2	$ 34.4
Income taxes, net of refunds	$ 1,072.2	$ 766.3	$ 539.1

See Notes to Consolidated Financial Statements.

STARBUCKS CORPORATION
CONSOLIDATED STATEMENTS OF EQUITY
(in millions, except per share data)

	Common Stock		Additional Paid-in Capital	Retained Earnings	Accumulated Other Comprehensive Income/(Loss)	Shareholders' Equity	Noncontrolling Interest	Total
	Shares	Amount						
Balance, September 30, 2012	749.3	$0.7	$39.4	$5,046.2	$22.7	$5,109.0	$5.5	$5,114.5
Net earnings				8.3		8.3	0.5	8.8
Other comprehensive income/(loss)					44.3	44.3	—	44.3
Stock-based compensation expense			144.1			144.1		144.1
Exercise of stock options/vesting of RSUs, including tax benefit of $259.9	14.4	0.1	366.7	—		366.8	—	366.8
Sale of common stock, including tax benefit of $0.2	0.3		20.4	—		20.4	—	20.4
Repurchase of common stock	(10.8)		(288.5)	(255.6)		(544.1)	—	(544.1)
Cash dividends declared, $0.445 per share				(668.6)		(668.6)	—	(668.6)
Noncontrolling interest resulting from divestiture							(3.9)	(3.9)
Balance, September 29, 2013	753.2	$0.8	$282.1	$4,130.3	$67.0	$4,480.2	$2.1	$4,482.3
Net earnings				2,068.1		2,068.1	(0.4)	2,067.7
Other comprehensive income/(loss)					(41.7)	(41.7)	—	(41.7)
Stock-based compensation expense			185.1			185.1		185.1
Exercise of stock options/vesting of RSUs, including tax benefit of $114.8	6.5		154.8			154.8	—	154.8
Sale of common stock, including tax benefit of $0.2	0.3		22.3			22.3	—	22.3
Repurchase of common stock	(10.5)	(0.1)	(604.9)	(164.8)		(769.8)	—	(769.8)
Cash dividends declared, $0.550 per share				(827.0)		(827.0)	—	(827.0)
Balance, September 28, 2014	749.5	$0.7	$39.4	$5,206.6	$25.3	$5,272.0	$1.7	$5,273.7
Net earnings				2,757.4		2,757.4	1.9	2,759.3
Other comprehensive income/(loss)					(193.6)	(193.6)	(31.1)	(224.7)
Stock-based compensation expense			211.7			211.7	—	211.7
Exercise of stock options/vesting of RSUs, including tax benefit of $131.3	14.6		224.4	—		224.4	—	224.4
Sale of common stock, including tax benefit of $0.2	0.6		23.5	—		23.5	—	23.5
Repurchase of common stock	(29.0)		(459.6)	(972.2)		(1,431.8)	—	(1,431.8)
Cash dividends declared, $0.680 per share				(1,016.2)		(1,016.2)	—	(1,016.2)
Two-for-one stock split	749.4	0.8		(0.8)		—	—	
Noncontrolling interest resulting from acquisition							411.1	411.1
Purchase of noncontrolling interest			1.7		(31.1)	(29.4)	(381.7)	(411.1)
Balance, September 27, 2015	1,485.1	$1.5	$41.1	$5,974.8	$(199.4)	$5,818.0	$1.8	$5,819.8

See Notes to Consolidated Financial Statements.

STARBUCKS CORPORATION
INDEX FOR NOTES TO CONSOLIDATED FINANCIAL STATEMENTS

STARBUCKS CORPORATION
NOTES TO CONSOLIDATED FINANCIAL STATEMENTS
Fiscal Years ended September 27, 2015, September 28, 2014 and September 29, 2013

Note 1: Summary of Significant Accounting Policies

Description of Business

We purchase and roast high-quality coffees that we sell, along with handcrafted coffee and tea beverages and a variety of fresh food items, through our company-operated stores. We also sell a variety of coffee and tea products and license our trademarks through other channels such as licensed stores, grocery and national foodservice accounts.

In this 10-K, Starbucks Corporation (together with its subsidiaries) is referred to as "Starbucks," the "Company," "we," "us" or "our."

We have four reportable operating segments: 1) Americas, which is inclusive of the U.S., Canada, and Latin America; 2) China/Asia Pacific ("CAP"); 3) Europe, Middle East, and Africa ("EMEA") and 4) Channel Development. We also have several non-reportable operating segments, including Teavana, Seattle's Best Coffee, Evolution Fresh, and our Digital Ventures business, as well as certain developing businesses such as the Starbucks Reserve® Roastery & Tasting Room, which are combined and referred to as All Other Segments. Unallocated corporate operating expenses, which pertain primarily to corporate administrative functions that support the operating segments but are not specifically attributable to or managed by any segment, are presented as a reconciling item between total segment operating results and consolidated financial results.

Additional details on the nature of our business and our reportable operating segments are included in Note 16, Segment Reporting, of these Consolidated Financial Statements.

Principles of Consolidation

Our consolidated financial statements reflect the financial position and operating results of Starbucks, including wholly-owned subsidiaries and investees that we control. Investments in entities that we do not control, but have the ability to exercise significant influence over operating and financial policies, are accounted for under the equity method. Investments in entities in which we do not have the ability to exercise significant influence are accounted for under the cost method. Intercompany transactions and balances have been eliminated.

Fiscal Year End

Our fiscal year ends on the Sunday closest to September 30. Fiscal years 2015, 2014 and 2013 included 52 weeks.

Estimates and Assumptions

Preparing financial statements in conformity with accounting principles generally accepted in the United States of America ("GAAP") requires management to make estimates and assumptions that affect the reported amounts of assets, liabilities, revenues and expenses. Examples include, but are not limited to, estimates for inventory reserves, asset and goodwill impairments, assumptions underlying self-insurance reserves, income from unredeemed stored value cards, stock-based compensation forfeiture rates, future asset retirement obligations, and the potential outcome of future tax consequences of events that have been recognized in the financial statements. Actual results and outcomes may differ from these estimates and assumptions.

Cash and Cash Equivalents

We consider all highly liquid instruments with maturities of three months or less at the time of purchase, as well as credit card receivables for sales to customers in our company-operated stores that generally settle within two to five days, to be cash equivalents. We maintain cash and cash equivalent balances with financial institutions that exceed federally-insured limits. We have not experienced any losses related to these balances and we believe credit risk to be minimal.

Our cash management system provides for the funding of all major bank disbursement accounts on a daily basis as checks are presented for payment. Under this system, outstanding checks are in excess of the cash balances at certain banks, which creates book overdrafts. Book overdrafts are presented as a current liability in accrued liabilities on our consolidated balance sheets.

52

Investments

Available-for-sale Securities

Our short-term and long-term investments consist primarily of investment-grade debt securities, all of which are classified as available-for-sale. Available-for-sale securities are recorded at fair value, and unrealized holding gains and losses are recorded, net of tax, as a component of accumulated other comprehensive income. Available-for-sale securities with remaining maturities of less than one year and those identified by management at the time of purchase to be used to fund operations within one year are classified as short-term. All other available-for-sale securities are classified as long-term. We evaluate our available-for-sale securities for other than temporary impairment on a quarterly basis. Unrealized losses are charged against net earnings when a decline in fair value is determined to be other than temporary. We review several factors to determine whether a loss is other than temporary, such as the length and extent of the fair value decline, the financial condition and near-term prospects of the issuer, and whether we have the intent to sell or will more likely than not be required to sell before the securities' anticipated recovery, which may be at maturity. Realized gains and losses are accounted for using the specific identification method. Purchases and sales are recorded on a trade date basis.

Trading Securities

We also have a trading securities portfolio, which is comprised of marketable equity mutual funds and equity exchange-traded funds. Trading securities are recorded at fair value with unrealized holding gains and losses recorded in net interest income and other on our consolidated statements of earnings. Our trading securities portfolio approximates a portion of our liability under our Management Deferred Compensation Plan ("MDCP"), which is included in accrued compensation and related costs, within accrued liabilities on our consolidated balance sheets. Changes in our MDCP liability are recorded in general and administrative expenses on our consolidated statements of earnings.

Equity and Cost Method Investments

We evaluate our equity and cost method investments for impairment annually and when facts and circumstances indicate that the carrying value of such investments may not be recoverable. We review several factors to determine whether the loss is other than temporary, such as the length and extent of the fair value decline, the financial condition and near-term prospects of the investee, and whether we have the intent to sell or will more likely than not be required to sell before the investment's anticipated recovery. If a decline in fair value is determined to be other than temporary, an impairment charge is recorded in net earnings.

Fair Value

Fair value is the price we would receive to sell an asset or pay to transfer a liability (exit price) in an orderly transaction between market participants. For assets and liabilities recorded or disclosed at fair value on a recurring basis, we determine fair value based on the following:

Level 1: The carrying value of cash and cash equivalents approximates fair value because of the short-term nature of these instruments. For trading and U.S. government treasury securities and commodity futures contracts, we use quoted prices in active markets for identical assets to determine fair value.

Level 2: When quoted prices in active markets for identical assets are not available, we determine the fair value of our available-for-sale securities and our over-the-counter forward contracts, collars, and swaps based upon factors such as the quoted market price of similar assets or a discounted cash flow model using readily observable market data, which may include interest rate curves and forward and spot prices for currencies and commodities, depending on the nature of the investment. The fair value of our long-term debt is estimated based on the quoted market prices for the same or similar issues or on the current rates offered to us for debt of the same remaining maturities.

Level 3: We determine the fair value of our auction rate securities using an internally-developed valuation model, using inputs that include interest rate curves, credit and liquidity spreads, and effective maturity.

Assets and liabilities recognized or disclosed at fair value on a nonrecurring basis include items such as property, plant and equipment, goodwill and other intangible assets, equity and cost method investments, and other assets. We determine the fair value of these items using Level 3 inputs, as described in the related sections below.

Derivative Instruments

We manage our exposure to various risks within our consolidated financial statements according to a market price risk management policy. Under this policy, we may engage in transactions involving various derivative instruments to hedge interest rates, commodity prices and foreign currency denominated revenue streams, inventory purchases, assets and liabilities, and investments in certain foreign operations. We record all derivatives on our consolidated balance sheets at fair value. We generally do not offset derivative assets and liabilities in our consolidated balance sheets or enter into derivative instruments

53

with maturities longer than three years. Refer to Note 3, Derivative Financial Instruments, for further discussion of our derivative instruments. We do not enter into derivative instruments for trading purposes.

We use various types of derivative instruments including forward contracts, commodity futures contracts, collars and swaps. Forward contracts and commodity futures contracts are agreements to buy or sell a quantity of a currency or commodity at a predetermined future date, and at a predetermined rate or price. A collar is a strategy that uses a combination of a purchased call option and a sold put option with equal premiums to hedge a portion of anticipated cash flows, or to limit the range of possible gains or losses on an underlying asset or liability to a specific range. A swap agreement is a contract between two parties to exchange cash flows based on specified underlying notional amounts, assets and/or indices.

Cash Flow Hedges

For derivative instruments that are designated and qualify as a cash flow hedge, the effective portion of the derivative's gain or loss is reported as a component of other comprehensive income ("OCI") and recorded in accumulated other comprehensive income ("AOCI") on our consolidated balance sheets. The gain or loss is subsequently reclassified into net earnings when the hedged exposure affects net earnings.

To the extent that the change in the fair value of the contract corresponds to the change in the value of the anticipated transaction using forward rates on a monthly basis, the hedge is considered effective and is recognized as described above. The remaining change in fair value of the contract represents the ineffective portion, which is immediately recorded in net interest income and other on our consolidated statements of earnings.

Cash flow hedges related to anticipated transactions are designated and documented at the inception of each hedge by matching the terms of the contract to the underlying transaction. Cash flows from hedging transactions are classified in the same categories as the cash flows from the respective hedged items, which is discussed further at Note 3, Derivative Financial Instruments. Once established, cash flow hedges generally remain designated as such until the hedge item impacts net earnings, or the anticipated transaction is no longer likely to occur. For dedesignated cash flow hedges or for transactions that are no longer likely to occur, the related accumulated derivative gains or losses are recognized in net interest income and other or interest expense on our consolidated statements of earnings based on the nature of the underlying transaction.

Net Investment Hedges

For derivative instruments that are designated and qualify as a net investment hedge, the effective portion of the derivative's gain or loss is reported as a component of OCI and recorded in AOCI. The gain or loss will be subsequently reclassified into net earnings when the hedged net investment is either sold or substantially liquidated.

To the extent that the change in the fair value of the forward contract corresponds to the change in value of the anticipated transactions using spot rates on a monthly basis, the hedge is considered effective and is recognized as described above. The remaining change in fair value of the forward contract represents the ineffective portion, which is immediately recognized in net interest income and other on our consolidated statements of earnings.

Derivatives Not Designated As Hedging Instruments

We also enter into certain foreign currency forward contracts, commodity futures contracts, collars and swaps that are not designated as hedging instruments for accounting purposes. The change in the fair value of these contracts is immediately recognized in net interest income and other on our consolidated statements of earnings.

Normal Purchase Normal Sale

We enter into fixed-price and price-to-be-fixed green coffee purchase commitments, which are described further at Note 5, Inventories. For both fixed-price and price-to-be-fixed purchase commitments, we expect to take delivery of and to utilize the coffee in a reasonable period of time and in the conduct of normal business. Accordingly, these purchase commitments qualify as normal purchases and are not recorded at fair value on our balance sheets.

Receivables, net of Allowance for Doubtful Accounts

Our receivables are mainly comprised of receivables for product and equipment sales to and royalties from our licensees, as well as receivables from our CPG and foodservice business customers. Our allowance for doubtful accounts is calculated based on historical experience, customer credit risk and application of the specific identification method. As of September 27, 2015 and September 28, 2014, the allowance for doubtful accounts was $10.8 million and $6.7 million, respectively.

Inventories

Inventories are stated at the lower of cost (primarily moving average cost) or market. We record inventory reserves for obsolete and slow-moving inventory and for estimated shrinkage between physical inventory counts. Inventory reserves are based on inventory obsolescence trends, historical experience and application of the specific identification method. As of September 27, 2015 and September 28, 2014, inventory reserves were $33.8 million and $31.2 million, respectively.

Property, Plant and Equipment

Property, plant and equipment, which includes assets under capital leases, are carried at cost less accumulated depreciation. Cost includes all direct costs necessary to acquire and prepare assets for use, including internal labor and overhead in some cases. Depreciation is computed using the straight-line method over estimated useful lives of the assets, generally ranging from 2 to 15 years for equipment and 30 to 40 years for buildings. Leasehold improvements are amortized over the shorter of their estimated useful lives or the related lease life, generally 10 years. For leases with renewal periods at our option, we generally use the original lease term, excluding renewal option periods, to determine estimated useful lives. If failure to exercise a renewal option imposes an economic penalty to us, we may determine at the inception of the lease that renewal is reasonably assured and include the renewal option period in the determination of the appropriate estimated useful lives.

The portion of depreciation expense related to production and distribution facilities is included in cost of sales including occupancy costs on our consolidated statements of earnings. The costs of repairs and maintenance are expensed when incurred, while expenditures for refurbishments and improvements that significantly add to the productive capacity or extend the useful life of an asset are capitalized. When assets are disposed of, whether through retirement or sale, the net gain or loss is recognized in net earnings. Long-lived assets to be disposed of are reported at the lower of their carrying amount or fair value less estimated costs to sell.

We evaluate property, plant and equipment for impairment when facts and circumstances indicate that the carrying values of such assets may not be recoverable. When evaluating for impairment, we first compare the carrying value of the asset to the asset's estimated future undiscounted cash flows. If the estimated undiscounted future cash flows are less than the carrying value of the asset, we determine if we have an impairment loss by comparing the carrying value of the asset to the asset's estimated fair value and recognize an impairment charge when the asset's carrying value exceeds its estimated fair value. The fair value of the asset is estimated using a discounted cash flow model based on forecasted future revenues and operating costs, using internal projections. Property, plant and equipment assets are grouped at the lowest level for which identifiable cash flows are largely independent of the cash flows of other assets and liabilities. For company-operated store assets, the impairment test is performed at the individual store asset group level.

We recognized net disposition charges of $12.5 million, $14.7 million, and $17.4 million and net impairment charges of $25.8 million, $19.0 million, and $12.7 million in fiscal 2015, 2014, and 2013, respectively. The nature of the underlying asset that is impaired or disposed of will determine the operating expense line on which the related impact is recorded on our consolidated statements of earnings. For assets within our retail operations, net impairment and disposition charges are recorded in store operating expenses. For all other assets, these charges are recorded in cost of sales including occupancy costs, other operating expenses, or general and administrative expenses.

Goodwill

We evaluate goodwill for impairment annually during our third fiscal quarter, or more frequently if an event occurs or circumstances change, such as material deterioration in performance or a significant number of store closures, that would indicate that impairment may exist. When evaluating goodwill for impairment, we may first perform a qualitative assessment to determine whether it is more likely than not that a reporting unit is impaired. If we do not perform a qualitative assessment, or if we determine that it is not more likely than not that the fair value of the reporting unit exceeds its carrying amount, we calculate the estimated fair value of the reporting unit. Fair value is the price a willing buyer would pay for the reporting unit and is typically calculated using a discounted cash flow model. For certain reporting units, where deemed appropriate, we may also utilize a market approach for estimating fair value. If the carrying amount of the reporting unit exceeds the estimated fair value, an impairment charge is recorded to reduce the carrying value to the estimated fair value.

As part of our ongoing operations, we may close certain stores within a reporting unit containing goodwill due to underperformance of the store or inability to renew our lease, among other reasons. We may abandon certain assets associated with a closed store, including leasehold improvements and other non-transferable assets. When a portion of a reporting unit that constitutes a business is to be disposed of, goodwill associated with the business is included in the carrying amount of the business in determining any loss on disposal. Our evaluation of whether the portion of a reporting unit being disposed of constitutes a business occurs on the date of abandonment. Although an operating store meets the accounting definition of a business prior to abandonment, it does not constitute a business on the closure date because the remaining assets on that date do not constitute an integrated set of assets that are capable of being managed for the purpose of providing a return to investors. As a result, when closing individual stores, we do not include goodwill in the calculation of any loss on disposal of the related assets. As noted above, if store closures are indicative of potential impairment of goodwill at the reporting unit level, we perform an evaluation of our reporting unit goodwill when such closures occur. There were no material goodwill impairment charges recorded during fiscal 2015, 2014, and 2013.

Other Intangible Assets

Other intangible assets consist primarily of finite-lived intangible assets, which mainly consist of acquired and reacquired rights, trade secrets, licensing agreements, contract-based patents and copyrights, are amortized over their estimated useful lives, and are tested for impairment using a similar methodology to our property, plant and equipment, as described above.

Indefinite-lived intangibles, which consist primarily of trade names and trademarks, are tested for impairment annually during the third fiscal quarter, or more frequently if an event occurs or circumstances change that would indicate that impairment may exist. When evaluating other intangible assets for impairment, we may first perform a qualitative assessment to determine whether it is more likely than not that an intangible asset group is impaired. If we do not perform the qualitative assessment, or if we determine that it is not more likely than not that the fair value of the intangible asset group exceeds its carrying amount, we calculate the estimated fair value of the intangible asset group. Fair value is the price a willing buyer would pay for the reporting unit and is typically calculated using an income approach, such as a relief-from-royalty model. If the carrying amount of the intangible asset group exceeds the estimated fair value, an impairment charge is recorded to reduce the carrying value to the estimated fair value. In addition, we continuously monitor and may revise our intangible asset useful lives if and when facts and circumstances change.

There were no other intangible asset impairment charges recorded during fiscal 2015, 2014, and 2013.

Insurance Reserves

We use a combination of insurance and self-insurance mechanisms, including a wholly-owned captive insurance entity and participation in a reinsurance treaty, to provide for the potential liabilities for certain risks, including workers' compensation, healthcare benefits, general liability, property insurance, and director and officers' liability insurance. Liabilities associated with the risks that are retained by us are not discounted and are estimated, in part, by considering historical claims experience, demographics, exposure and severity factors, and other actuarial assumptions.

Revenue Recognition

Consolidated revenues are presented net of intercompany eliminations for wholly-owned subsidiaries and investees controlled by us and for product sales to and royalty and other fees from licensees accounted for under the equity method. Additionally, consolidated revenues are recognized net of any discounts, returns, allowances and sales incentives, including coupon redemptions and rebates.

Company-operated Store Revenues

Company-operated store revenues are recognized when payment is tendered at the point of sale. Company-operated store revenues are reported net of sales, use or other transaction taxes that are collected from customers and remitted to taxing authorities.

Licensed Store Revenues

Licensed store revenues consist of product and equipment sales to licensees, as well as royalties and other fees paid by licensees to use the Starbucks brand. Sales of coffee, tea, food and related products are generally recognized upon shipment to licensees, depending on contract terms. Shipping charges billed to licensees are also recognized as revenue, and the related shipping costs are included in cost of sales including occupancy costs on our consolidated statements of earnings.

Initial nonrefundable development fees for licensed stores are recognized upon substantial performance of services for new market business development activities, such as initial business, real estate and store development planning, as well as providing operational materials and functional training courses for opening new licensed retail markets. Additional store licensing fees are recognized when new licensed stores are opened. Royalty revenues based upon a percentage of reported sales, and other continuing fees, such as marketing and service fees, are recognized on a monthly basis when earned.

CPG, Foodservice and Other Revenues

CPG, foodservice and other revenues primarily include sales of packaged coffee and tea as well as a variety of ready-to-drink beverages and single-serve coffee and tea products to grocery, warehouse clubs and specialty retail stores, sales to our national foodservice accounts, and revenues from sales of products to and license fee revenues from manufacturers that produce and market Starbucks-, Seattle's Best Coffee- and Tazo-branded products through licensing agreements. Sales of coffee, tea, ready-to-drink beverages and related products to grocery and warehouse club stores are generally recognized when received by the customer or distributor, depending on contract terms. Revenues are recorded net of sales discounts given to customers for trade promotions and other incentives and for sales return allowances, which are determined based on historical patterns.

Revenues from sales of products to manufacturers that produce and market Starbucks-, Seattle's Best Coffee- and Tazo-branded products through licensing agreements are generally recognized when the product is received by the manufacturer or

56

distributor. License fee revenues from manufacturers are based on a percentage of sales and are recognized on a monthly basis when earned. National foodservice account revenues are recognized, when the product is received by the customer or distributor.

Sales to customers through CPG channels and national foodservice accounts, including sales to national distributors, are recognized net of certain fees paid to the customer. We characterize these fees as a reduction of revenue unless we are able to identify a sufficiently separable benefit from the customer's purchase of our products such that we could have entered into an exchange transaction with a party other than the customer in order to receive such benefit, and we can reasonably estimate the fair value of such benefit.

Stored Value Cards

Stored value cards, primarily Starbucks Cards, can be loaded at our company-operated and most licensed store locations, online at StarbucksStore.com or via mobile devices held by our customers, and at certain other third party locations, such as grocery stores. When an amount is loaded onto a stored value card at any of these locations, we recognize a corresponding liability for the full amount loaded onto the card, which is recorded within stored value card liability on our consolidated balance sheets.

Stored value cards can be redeemed at company-operated and most licensed stores, as well as online. When a stored value card is redeemed at a company-operated store or online, we recognize revenue by reducing the stored value card liability. When a stored value card is redeemed at a licensed store location, we reduce the corresponding stored value card liability and cash, which is reimbursed to the licensee.

There are no expiration dates on our stored value cards, and we do not charge service fees that cause a decrement to customer balances. While we will continue to honor all stored value cards presented for payment, management may determine the likelihood of redemption, based on historical experience, is deemed to be remote for certain cards due to long periods of inactivity. In these circumstances, if management also determines there is no requirement for remitting balances to government agencies under unclaimed property laws, unredeemed card balances may then be recognized as breakage income, which is included in net interest income and other on our consolidated statements of earnings. In fiscal 2015, 2014, and 2013, we recognized breakage income of $39.3 million, $38.3 million, and $33.0 million, respectively.

Loyalty Program

Starbucks has a loyalty program called My Starbucks Rewards® ("MSR"). Customers in the U.S., Canada, and certain other countries who register their Starbucks Card are automatically enrolled in that program. They earn loyalty points ("Stars") with each purchase at participating Starbucks®, Teavana®, and Evolution Fresh™ stores, as well as on certain packaged coffee products purchased in select Starbucks® stores, online, and through CPG channels. After accumulating a certain number of Stars, the customer earns a reward that can be redeemed for free product that, regardless of where the related Stars were earned within that country, will be honored at company-operated stores and certain participating licensed store locations in that same country.

We defer revenue associated with the estimated selling price of Stars earned by our program members towards free product as each Star is earned, and a corresponding liability is established within stored value card liability on our consolidated balance sheets. The estimated selling price of each Star earned is based on the estimated value of the product for which the reward is expected to be redeemed, net of Stars we do not expect to be redeemed, based on historical redemption patterns. Fully earned rewards generally expire if unredeemed after approximately 30 days. Stars generally expire if inactive for a period of one year.

When a customer redeems an earned reward, we recognize revenue for the redeemed product and reduce the related loyalty program liability.

Marketing & Advertising

Our annual marketing expenses include many components, one of which is advertising costs. We expense most advertising costs as they are incurred, except for certain production costs that are expensed the first time the advertising takes place.

Marketing expenses totaled $351.5 million, $315.5 million and $306.8 million in fiscal 2015, 2014, and 2013, respectively. Included in these costs were advertising expenses, which totaled $227.9 million, $198.9 million and $205.8 million in fiscal 2015, 2014, and 2013, respectively.

Store Preopening Expenses

Costs incurred in connection with the start-up and promotion of new store openings are expensed as incurred.

Leases

Operating Leases

We lease retail stores, roasting, distribution and warehouse facilities, and office space for corporate administrative purposes under operating leases. Most lease agreements contain tenant improvement allowances, rent holidays, lease premiums, rent escalation clauses and/or contingent rent provisions. We recognize amortization of lease incentives, premiums and minimum rent expenses on a straight-line basis beginning on the date of initial possession, which is generally when we enter the space and begin to make improvements in preparation for intended use.

For tenant improvement allowances and rent holidays, we record a deferred rent liability within accrued liabilities, or other long-term liabilities, on our consolidated balance sheets and amortize the deferred rent over the terms of the leases as reductions to rent expense in cost of sales including occupancy costs on our consolidated statements of earnings.

For premiums paid upfront to enter a lease agreement, we record a prepaid rent asset in prepaid expenses and other current assets on our consolidated balance sheets and amortize the deferred rent over the terms of the leases as additional rent expense in cost of sales including occupancy costs on our consolidated statements of earnings.

For scheduled rent escalation clauses during the lease terms or for rental payments commencing at a date other than the date of initial possession, we record minimum rent expense on a straight-line basis over the terms of the leases in cost of sales including occupancy costs on our consolidated statements of earnings.

Certain leases provide for contingent rent, which is determined as a percentage of gross sales in excess of specified levels. We record a contingent rent liability in accrued occupancy costs within accrued liabilities on our consolidated balance sheets and the corresponding rent expense when specified levels have been achieved or when we determine that achieving the specified levels during the fiscal year is probable.

When ceasing operations of company-operated stores under operating leases, in cases where the lease contract specifies a termination fee due to the landlord, we record such expense at the time written notice is given to the landlord. In cases where terms, including termination fees, are yet to be negotiated with the landlord, we will record the expense upon signing of an agreement with the landlord. In cases where the landlord does not allow us to prematurely exit the lease, but allows for subleasing, we estimate the fair value of any sublease income that can be generated from the location and recognize an expense equal to the present value of the remaining lease payments to the landlord less any projected sublease income at the cease-use date.

Lease Financing Arrangements

We are sometimes involved in the construction of leased buildings, primarily stores. When we qualify as the deemed owner of these buildings due to significant involvement during the construction period under build-to-suit lease accounting requirements and do not qualify for sales recognition under sales-leaseback accounting guidance, we record the cost of the related buildings in property, plant and equipment. The offsetting lease financing obligations are recorded in other long-term liabilities, with the current portion recorded in in accrued occupancy costs within accrued liabilities on our consolidated balance sheets. These assets and obligations are amortized in depreciation and amortization and interest expense, respectively, on our consolidated statements of earnings based on the terms of the related lease agreements.

Asset Retirement Obligations

We recognize a liability for the fair value of required asset retirement obligations ("ARO") when such obligations are incurred. Our AROs are primarily associated with leasehold improvements, which, at the end of a lease, we are contractually obligated to remove in order to comply with the lease agreement. At the inception of a lease with such conditions, we record an ARO liability and a corresponding capital asset in an amount equal to the estimated fair value of the obligation. We estimate the liability using a number of assumptions, including store closing costs, cost inflation rates and discount rates, and accrete to its projected future value over time. The capitalized asset is depreciated using the same depreciation convention as leasehold improvement assets. Upon satisfaction of the ARO conditions, any difference between the recorded ARO liability and the actual retirement costs incurred is recognized as a gain or loss in cost of sales including occupancy costs on our consolidated statements of earnings. As of September 27, 2015 and September 28, 2014, our net ARO assets included in property, plant and equipment were $5.8 million and $4.1 million, respectively, and our net ARO liabilities included in other long-term liabilities were $60.1 million and $28.4 million, respectively. The increases in our net ARO assets and net ARO liabilities in fiscal 2015 were primarily due to the acquisition of Starbucks Japan, which is discussed in Note 2, Acquisitions and Divestitures.

Stock-based Compensation

We maintain several equity incentive plans under which we may grant non-qualified stock options, incentive stock options, restricted stock, restricted stock units ("RSUs") or stock appreciation rights to employees, non-employee directors and consultants. We also have an employee stock purchase plan ("ESPP"). RSUs issued by us are equivalent to nonvested shares under the applicable accounting guidance. We record stock-based compensation expense based on the fair value of stock awards at the grant date and recognize the expense over the related service period following a graded vesting expense schedule. Expense for performance-based RSUs is recognized when it is probable the performance goal will be achieved. Performance goals are determined by the Board of Directors and may include measures such as earnings per share, operating income and return on invested capital. The fair value of each stock option granted is estimated on the grant date using the Black-Scholes-Merton option valuation model. The assumptions used to calculate the fair value of options granted are evaluated and revised, as necessary, to reflect market conditions and our historical experience. The fair value of RSUs is based on the closing price of Starbucks common stock on the award date, less the present value of expected dividends not received during the vesting period. Compensation expense is recognized over the requisite service period for each separately vesting portion of the award, and only for those options expected to vest, with forfeitures estimated at the date of grant based on our historical experience and future expectations.

Foreign Currency Translation

Our international operations generally use their local currency as their functional currency. Assets and liabilities are translated at exchange rates in effect at the balance sheet date. Income and expense accounts are translated at the average monthly exchange rates during the year. Resulting translation adjustments are reported as a component of OCI and recorded in AOCI on our consolidated balance sheets.

Income Taxes

We compute income taxes using the asset and liability method, under which deferred income taxes are recognized based on the differences between the financial statement carrying amounts and the respective tax basis of our assets and liabilities. Deferred tax assets and liabilities are measured using current enacted tax rates expected to apply to taxable income in the years in which we expect the temporary differences to reverse. The effect of a change in tax rates on deferred taxes is recognized in income in the period that includes the enactment date.

We routinely evaluate the likelihood of realizing the benefit of our deferred tax assets and may record a valuation allowance if, based on all available evidence, we determine that some portion of the tax benefit will not be realized. In evaluating our ability to recover our deferred tax assets within the jurisdiction from which they arise, we consider all available positive and negative evidence, including scheduled reversals of deferred tax liabilities, projected future taxable income, tax-planning strategies, and results of recent operations. If we determine that we would be able to realize our deferred tax assets in the future in excess of their net recorded amount, we would make an adjustment to the deferred tax asset valuation allowance, which would reduce the provision for income taxes.

In addition, our income tax returns are periodically audited by domestic and foreign tax authorities. These audits include review of our tax filing positions, including the timing and amount of deductions taken and the allocation of income between tax jurisdictions. We evaluate our exposures associated with our various tax filing positions and recognize a tax benefit from an uncertain tax position only if it is more likely than not that the tax position will be sustained upon examination by the relevant taxing authorities, including resolutions of any related appeals or litigation processes, based on the technical merits of our position. The tax benefits recognized in the financial statements from such a position are measured based on the largest benefit that has a greater than 50% likelihood of being realized upon ultimate settlement. For uncertain tax positions that do not meet this threshold, we record a related liability. We adjust our unrecognized tax benefit liability and income tax expense in the period in which the uncertain tax position is effectively settled, the statute of limitations expires for the relevant taxing authority to examine the tax position, or when new information becomes available.

Starbucks recognizes interest and penalties related to income tax matters in income tax expense on our consolidated statements of earnings. Accrued interest and penalties are included within the related tax liability on our consolidated balance sheets.

Stock Split

On April 9, 2015, we effected a two-for-one stock split of our $0.001 par value common stock for shareholders of record as of March 30, 2015. All share and per-share data in our consolidated financial statements and notes has been retroactively adjusted to reflect this stock split. We adjusted shareholders' equity to reflect the stock split by reclassifying an amount equal to the par value of the additional shares arising from the split from retained earnings to common stock during the second quarter of fiscal 2015, resulting in no net impact to shareholders' equity on our consolidated balance sheets.

Earnings per Share

Basic earnings per share is computed based on the weighted average number of shares of common stock outstanding during the period. Diluted earnings per share is computed based on the weighted average number of shares of common stock and the effect of dilutive potential common shares outstanding during the period, calculated using the treasury stock method. Dilutive potential common shares include outstanding stock options and RSUs. Performance-based RSUs are considered dilutive when the related performance criterion has been met.

Common Stock Share Repurchases

We may repurchase shares of Starbucks common stock under a program authorized by our Board of Directors, including pursuant to a contract, instruction or written plan meeting the requirements of Rule 10b5-1(c)(1) of the Securities Exchange Act of 1934. Under applicable Washington State law, shares repurchased are retired and not displayed separately as treasury stock on the financial statements. Instead, the par value of repurchased shares is deducted from common stock and the excess repurchase price over par value is deducted from additional paid-in capital and from retained earnings, once additional paid-in capital is depleted.

Recent Accounting Pronouncements

In September 2015, the Financial Accounting Standards Board ("FASB") issued guidance on the recognition of adjustments to preliminary amounts recognized in a business combination, which removes the requirement to retrospectively account for these adjustments. The guidance will become effective for us at the beginning of our first quarter of fiscal 2017. We will apply the guidance prospectively and do not expect the adoption will have a material impact on our consolidated financial statements.

In July 2015, the FASB issued guidance on the subsequent measurement of inventory, which changes the measurement from lower of cost or market to lower of cost and net realizable value. The guidance will require prospective application at the beginning of our first quarter of fiscal 2018, but permits adoption in an earlier period. We are currently evaluating the impact this guidance will have on our consolidated financial statements and the timing of adoption.

In April 2015, the FASB issued guidance on the financial statement presentation of debt issuance costs. This guidance requires debt issuance costs to be presented in the balance sheet as a reduction of the related debt liability rather than an asset. The guidance will become effective for us at the beginning of our first quarter of fiscal 2017 and will only result in an immaterial change in presentation of these costs on our consolidated balance sheets.

In February 2015, the FASB issued guidance that changes the evaluation criteria for consolidation and related disclosure requirements. This guidance introduces evaluation criteria specific to limited partnerships and other similar entities, as well as amends the criteria for evaluating variable interest entities with which the reporting entity is involved and certain investment funds. The guidance will become effective for us at the beginning of our first quarter of fiscal 2017. We do not expect the adoption of this guidance will have a material impact on our consolidated financial statements.

In May 2014, the FASB issued guidance outlining a single comprehensive model for entities to use in accounting for revenue arising from contracts with customers that supersedes most current revenue recognition guidance. This guidance requires an entity to recognize revenue when it transfers promised goods or services to customers in an amount that reflects the consideration to which the entity expects to be entitled in exchange for those goods or services. The original effective date of the guidance would have required us to adopt at the beginning of our first quarter of fiscal 2018. In July 2015, the FASB approved an optional one-year deferral of the effective date. The new guidance may be applied retrospectively to each prior period presented or retrospectively with the cumulative effect recognized as of the date of adoption. We are currently evaluating the overall impact this guidance will have on our consolidated financial statements, as well as the expected timing and method of adoption. Based on our preliminary assessment, we determined the adoption will change the timing of recognition and classification of our stored value card breakage income, which is currently recognized using the remote method and recorded in net interest income and other. The new guidance will require application of the proportional method and classification within total net revenues on our consolidated statements of earnings. Additionally, the new guidance requires enhanced disclosures, including revenue recognition policies to identify performance obligations to customers and significant judgments in measurement and recognition. We are continuing our assessment, which may identify other impacts.

In April 2014, the FASB issued guidance that changes the criteria for reporting discontinued operations. To qualify as a discontinued operation under the amended guidance, a component or group of components of an entity that has been disposed of or is classified as held for sale must represent a strategic shift that has or will have a major effect on the entity's operations and financial results. This guidance also expands related disclosure requirements. The guidance will become effective for us at the beginning of our first quarter of fiscal 2016. We do not expect the adoption of this guidance will have a material impact on our financial statements.

In July 2013, the FASB issued guidance on the financial statement presentation of an unrecognized tax benefit when a net operating loss carryforward, a similar tax loss, or a tax credit carryforward exists. This guidance requires the unrecognized tax benefit to be presented in the financial statements as a reduction to a deferred tax asset. When a deferred tax asset is not available, or the asset is not intended to be used for this purpose, the unrecognized tax benefit should be presented in the financial statements as a liability and not netted with a deferred tax asset. The guidance became effective for us at the beginning of our first quarter of fiscal 2015 and did not have a material impact on our consolidated financial statements.

In March 2013, the FASB issued guidance on a parent's accounting for the cumulative translation adjustment upon derecognition of certain subsidiaries or groups of assets within a foreign entity or of an investment in a foreign entity. This guidance requires a parent to release any related cumulative translation adjustment into net income only if the sale or transfer results in the complete or substantially complete liquidation of the foreign entity in which the subsidiary or group of assets had resided. The guidance became effective for us at the beginning of our first quarter of fiscal 2015 and did not have a material impact on our consolidated financial statements.

Note 2: Acquisitions and Divestitures

Fiscal 2015

During the fourth quarter of fiscal 2015, we sold our company-operated retail store assets and operations in Puerto Rico to Baristas Del Caribe, LLC, converting these operations to a fully licensed market, for a total of $8.9 million. This transaction resulted in a pre-tax gain of $3.7 million, which was included in net interest income and other on the consolidated statements of earnings.

On September 23, 2014, we entered into a tender offer bid agreement with Starbucks Coffee Japan, Ltd. ("Starbucks Japan"), at the time a 39.5% owned equity method investment, and our former joint venture partner, Sazaby League, Ltd. ("Sazaby"), to acquire the remaining 60.5% ownership interest in Starbucks Japan. Acquiring Starbucks Japan further leverages our existing infrastructure to continue disciplined retail store growth and expand our presence into other channels in the Japan market, such as consumer packaged goods ("CPG"), licensing and foodservice. This acquisition was structured as a two-step tender offer.

On October 31, 2014, we acquired Sazaby's 39.5% ownership interest in Starbucks Japan through the first tender offer step for ¥55 billion in cash, or $509 million with Japanese yen converted into U.S. dollars at a reference conversion rate of 108.13 JPY to USD, based on a spot rate that approximates the rate as of the acquisition date, bringing our total ownership in Starbucks Japan to a controlling 79% interest.

The following table summarizes the allocation of the total consideration to the fair values of the assets acquired and liabilities assumed as of October 31, 2014 *(in millions)*:

Consideration:		
Cash paid for Sazaby's 39.5% equity interest	$	508.7
Fair value of our preexisting 39.5% equity interest		577.0
Total consideration	$	1,085.7
Fair value of assets acquired and liabilities assumed:		
Cash and cash equivalents	$	224.4
Accounts receivable, net		37.4
Inventories		26.4
Prepaid expenses and other current assets		35.7
Deferred income taxes, net (current)		23.4
Property, plant and equipment		282.9
Other long-term assets		141.4
Other intangible assets		323.0
Goodwill		815.6
Total assets acquired		1,910.2
Accounts payable		(54.5)
Accrued liabilities		(115.9)
Stored value card liability		(36.5)
Deferred income taxes (noncurrent)		(90.7)
Other long-term liabilities		(115.8)
Total liabilities assumed		(413.4)
Noncontrolling interest		(411.1)
Total consideration	$	1,085.7

During fiscal 2015, the acquisition date fair value of goodwill increased due to revisions that decreased the acquisition date fair value of accrued liabilities and deferred income taxes (noncurrent) and increased the acquisition date fair value of other-long-term liabilities. None of the adjustments had a material effect on our current or interim period consolidated financial statements.

The assets acquired and liabilities assumed are reported within our China/Asia Pacific segment. Other current and long-term assets acquired primarily include various deposits, specifically lease and key money deposits. Accrued liabilities and other long-term liabilities assumed primarily include the financing obligations associated with the build-to-suit leases discussed below, as well as asset retirement obligations.

The intangible assets are finite-lived and include reacquired rights, licensing agreements with Starbucks Japan's current licensees and Starbucks Japan's customer loyalty program. The reacquired rights of $305.0 million represent the fair value, calculated over the remaining original contractual period, to exclusively operate licensed Starbucks® retail stores in Japan. These rights will be amortized on a straight-line basis through March 2021, or over a period of approximately 6.4 years. The licensing agreements were valued at $15.0 million and will be amortized on a straight-line basis over a period of approximately 10.9 years, which is based on the remaining terms of the respective licensing agreements. The customer loyalty program was valued at $3.0 million and will be amortized on a straight-line basis over a period of 4.0 years, which represents the period during which we expect to benefit from these customer relationships.

Below is a tabular summary of the acquired intangible assets as of September 27, 2015, for which the gross balances in total are $33.7 million lower than as of the October 31, 2014 acquisition date due to foreign currency translation *(in millions)*:

	Sep 27, 2015				
	Gross Carrying Amount		Accumulated Amortization		Net Carrying Amount
Reacquired rights	$	273.2	$	(39.0)	$	234.2
Licensing agreements		13.4		(1.1)		12.3
Customer loyalty program		2.7		(0.6)		2.1
Total acquired finite-lived intangible assets	$	289.3	$	(40.7)	$	248.6

Amortization expense for these finite-lived intangible assets for the year ended September 27, 2015 was $41.0 million and is estimated to be approximately $44 million each year for the next five years and approximately $29 million thereafter.

The $815.6 million of goodwill represents the intangible assets that do not qualify for separate recognition and primarily includes the acquired customer base, the acquired workforce including store partners in the region that have strong relationships with these customers, the existing geographic retail and online presence, and the expected geographic presence in new channels. The goodwill was allocated to the China/Asia Pacific segment and is not deductible for income tax purposes. Due to foreign currency translation, the balance of goodwill related to the acquisition declined $85.1 million to $730.5 million as of September 27, 2015.

As a part of this acquisition, we acquired a significant number of operating leases, including $7.5 million of favorable lease assets, which are included in prepaid expenses and other current assets and other long-term assets, and $15.5 million of unfavorable lease liabilities, which are included in accrued liabilities and other long-term liabilities on the consolidated balance sheets. The fair values of these assets and liabilities were determined based on market terms for similar leases as of the date of the acquisition, and will be amortized on a straight-line basis as rent expense, or a reduction of rent expense, respectively, in cost of sales including occupancy costs on the consolidated statements of earnings over the remaining terms of the leases, for which the weighted-average period was 9.4 years as of the October 31, 2014 acquisition date. We recorded a net reduction of rent expense of $0.8 million for the year ended September 27, 2015, in connection with the leases acquired.

Additionally, we acquired a number of build-to-suit lease arrangements that are accounted for as financing leases. Starbucks Japan is the deemed owner of buildings under build-to-suit lease accounting requirements since Starbucks Japan has significant involvement with the respective lessors and does not qualify for sales recognition under sale-leaseback accounting guidance. Accordingly, we have recorded the acquired buildings in property, plant and equipment, and the assumed lease financing obligations, representing the related future minimum lease payments, in other long-term liabilities, with the current portion recorded in accrued occupancy costs within accrued liabilities on the consolidated balance sheets. These financing obligations will be amortized based on the terms of the related lease agreements.

The table below summarizes our estimated minimum future rental payments under the acquired non-cancelable operating leases and lease financing arrangements as of September 27, 2015 *(in millions)*:

	Operating Leases		Lease Financing Arrangements
Year 1	$	83.7	$	2.8
Year 2		66.5		2.8
Year 3		49.0		2.8
Year 4		37.5		2.8
Year 5		30.3		2.7
Thereafter		129.4		24.8
Total minimum lease payments	$	396.4	$	38.7

The fair value of the noncontrolling interest in Starbucks Japan was estimated by applying the market approach. Specifically, the fair value was determined based on the purchase price we expected to pay for the remaining 21% noncontrolling interest, which was comprised of a set market price and a premium above the market price. The market price premium is a customary business practice for public tender offer transactions in Japan, so we believe this is what a market participant would pay and should be included in the fair value determination.

As a result of this acquisition, we remeasured the carrying value of our preexisting 39.5% equity method investment to fair value, which resulted in a pre-tax gain of $390.6 million that was presented separately as gain resulting from acquisition of joint venture within other income and expenses on the consolidated statements of earnings. The fair value of $577.0 million was calculated using an average of the income and market approach. The income approach fair value measurement was based on significant inputs that are not observable in the market and thus represents a fair value measurement categorized within Level 3 of the fair value hierarchy. Key assumptions used in estimating future cash flows included projected revenue growth and operating expenses, as well as the selection of an appropriate discount rate. Estimates of revenue growth and operating expenses were based on internal projections and considered the historical performance of stores, local market economics and the business environment impacting the stores' performance. The discount rate applied was based on Starbucks Japan's weighted-average cost of capital and included a company-specific risk premium. The market approach fair value measurement was based on the implied fair value of Starbucks Japan using the purchase price of Sazaby's 39.5% ownership interest and the expected purchase price of the 21% remaining noncontrolling interest.

We began consolidating Starbucks Japan's results of operations and cash flows into our consolidated financial statements beginning after October 31, 2014. For the year ended September 27, 2015, Starbucks Japan's net revenues and net earnings included in our consolidated statements of earnings were $1.1 billion and $108.5 million, respectively.

The following table provides the supplemental pro forma revenue and net earnings of the combined entity had the acquisition date of Starbucks Japan been the first day of our first quarter of fiscal 2014 rather than during our first quarter of fiscal 2015 *(in millions)*:

	Pro Forma (unaudited)			
	Year Ended			
	Sep 27, 2015		Sep 28, 2014	
Revenue	$	19,254.5	$	17,646.4
Net earnings attributable to Starbucks[1]		2,380.9		2,449.9

[1] The pro forma net earnings attributable to Starbucks for fiscal 2014 includes the acquisition-related gain of $390.6 million, and transaction and integration costs of $13.6 million for the year ended September 28, 2014.

The amounts in the supplemental pro forma earnings for the periods presented above fully eliminate intercompany transactions, apply our accounting policies and reflect adjustments for additional occupancy costs, depreciation and amortization that would have been charged assuming the same fair value adjustments to leases, property, plant and equipment and acquired intangibles had been applied on September 30, 2013. These pro forma results are unaudited and are not necessarily indicative of results of operations that would have occurred had the acquisition actually occurred in the prior year period or indicative of the results of operations for any future period.

We initiated the second tender offer step on November 10, 2014 to acquire the remaining 21% ownership interest held by the public shareholders and option holders of Starbucks Japan's common stock, with the objective of acquiring all of the remaining outstanding shares including outstanding stock options. At the close of the second tender offer period on December 22, 2014, we funded the second tender offer step to acquire an additional 14.7% ownership interest for ¥31 billion in cash, or $258 million with Japanese yen converted into U.S. dollars at a reference conversion rate of 120.39 JPY to USD. However, we did not complete the second tender offer nor obtain control of these shares until the settlement date of December 29, 2014, which was the first day of our second quarter of fiscal 2015.

Subsequent to the completion of the second tender offer step, we commenced a cash-out procedure under Japanese law (the "Cash-out") to acquire all remaining shares of Starbucks Japan (an approximate 6.3% interest). On March 26, 2015, we obtained control of these shares resulting in 100% ownership of Starbucks Japan. The purchase price for the Cash-out was ¥13.5 billion, or $109 million. During the third quarter of fiscal 2015, we settled ¥9.6 billion, or $78 million, of the purchase price in cash, with Japanese yen converted into U.S. dollars at a reference conversion rate of 123.87 JPY to USD. During the fourth quarter of fiscal 2015, we settled ¥3.2 billion, or $26 million, of the purchase price in cash, with Japanese yen converted into U.S. dollars at a reference conversion rate of 120.72 JPY to USD. The remaining ¥674 million ($6 million) was recorded in accrued liabilities on our consolidated balance sheets and represents cash that was unclaimed by minority shareholders as of September 27, 2015. There are no legal restrictions on the remaining unclaimed balance.

For the first quarter of fiscal 2015, net earnings attributable to noncontrolling interests in our consolidated statement of earnings related to Starbucks Japan reflects the 21% of minority shareholders' interests that we did not own as of the end of the first quarter of fiscal 2015. For the second quarter of fiscal 2015, net earnings attributable to noncontrolling interests in our consolidated statement of earnings related to Starbucks Japan reflects the approximate 6.3% of minority shareholders' interests that we did not obtain control of until March 26, 2015.

The following table shows the effects of the change in Starbucks ownership interest in Starbucks Japan on Starbucks equity:

	Year Ended	
	Sep 27, 2015	Sep 28, 2014
Net earnings attributable to Starbucks	$ 2,757.4	$ 2,068.1
Transfers (to)/from the noncontrolling interest:		
Increase/(decrease) in additional paid-in capital for purchase of interest in subsidiary	1.7	—
Change from net earnings attributable to Starbucks and transfers (to)/from noncontrolling interest	$ 2,759.1	$ 2,068.1

During the year ended September 27, 2015, we incurred approximately $11.9 million of acquisition-related costs, such as regulatory, legal, and advisory fees, which we have recorded within unallocated corporate general and administrative expenses.

Fiscal 2014

During the fourth quarter of fiscal 2014, we sold our Australian company-operated retail store assets and operations to the Withers Group, converting these operations to a fully licensed market, for a total of $15.9 million. This transaction resulted in a pre-tax gain of $2.4 million, which was included in net interest income and other on our consolidated statements of earnings. On an after-tax basis, this transaction resulted in a loss that was not material to our financial statements.

Fiscal 2013

During the fourth quarter of fiscal 2013, we sold our 82% interest in Starbucks Coffee Chile S.A. to our joint venture partner Alsea, S.A.B. de C.V., converting this market to a 100% licensed market, for a total purchase price of $68.6 million, which includes final working capital adjustments. This transaction resulted in a gain of $45.9 million, which was included in net interest income and other on our consolidated statements of earnings.

In the third quarter of fiscal 2013, we acquired 100% ownership of a coffee farm in Costa Rica for $8.1 million in cash. The fair value of the net assets acquired on the acquisition date primarily comprised property, plant and equipment.

On December 31, 2012, we acquired 100% of the outstanding shares of Teavana Holdings, Inc. ("Teavana"), a specialty retailer of premium loose-leaf teas, authentic artisanal teawares and other tea-related merchandise, to elevate our tea offerings as well as expand our domestic and global tea footprint. We acquired Teavana for $615.8 million in cash. Of the total cash paid, $12.2 million was excluded from the purchase price allocation below as it represented contingent consideration receivable, all of which has been settled. At closing, we also repaid $35.2 million for long-term debt outstanding on Teavana's balance sheet, which was recognized separately from the business combination. The following table summarizes the allocation of the purchase price to the fair values of the assets acquired and liabilities assumed on the closing date *(in millions)*:

	Fair Value at Dec 31, 2012
Cash and cash equivalents	$ 47.0
Inventories	21.3
Property, plant and equipment	59.7
Other intangible assets	120.8
Goodwill	467.5
Other current and noncurrent assets	19.8
Current liabilities	(36.0)
Deferred income taxes (noncurrent)	(54.3)
Long-term debt	(35.2)
Other long-term liabilities	(7.0)
Total consideration	$ 603.6

The assets acquired and liabilities assumed are reported within All Other Segments. Other current and noncurrent assets acquired primarily include prepaid expenses, trade receivables, and deferred tax assets. In addition, we assumed various current liabilities primarily consisting of accounts payable, accrued payroll-related liabilities and other accrued operating expenses. The intangible assets acquired as part of the transaction include the Teavana trade name, tea blends and non-compete agreements. The Teavana trade name was valued at $105.5 million and determined to have an indefinite life, based on our expectation that the brand will be used indefinitely and has no contractual limitations. The intangible asset related to the tea blends was valued at $13.0 million and will be amortized on a straight-line basis over a period of 10 years, and the intangible asset related to the non-compete agreements was valued at $2.3 million and will be amortized on a straight-line basis over a period of 3 years. The $467.5 million of goodwill represents the intangible assets that do not qualify for separate recognition, primarily including Teavana's established global store presence in high traffic mall locations and other high-sales-volume retail venues, Teavana's global customer base, and Teavana's "Heaven of tea" retail experience in which store employees engage and educate customers about the ritual and enjoyment of tea. The goodwill was allocated to All Other Segments and is not deductible for income tax purposes.

Note 3: Derivative Financial Instruments

Interest Rates

Depending on market conditions, we enter into interest rate swap agreements to hedge the variability in cash flows due to changes in the benchmark interest rate related to anticipated debt issuances. These agreements are cash settled at the time of the pricing of the related debt. The effective portion of the derivative's gain or loss is recorded in accumulated other comprehensive income ("AOCI") and is subsequently reclassified to interest expense over the life of the related debt.

During the first quarter of fiscal 2015, we entered into forward-starting interest rate swap agreements with an aggregate notional amount of $250.0 million related to the $500 million of 7-year 2.700% Senior Notes (the "2022 notes") due in June 2022 issued in the third quarter of fiscal 2015. During the third quarter of fiscal 2015, we entered into forward-starting interest rate swap agreements with an aggregate notional amount of $250.0 million related to the $350 million of 30-year 4.300% Senior Notes (the "2045 notes") due in June 2045 issued in the third quarter of fiscal 2015. We cash settled these swap agreements at the time of the pricing of the 2022 and the 2045 notes, effectively locking in the benchmark interest rate in effect at the time the swap agreements were initiated. In July 2015, we redeemed our $550 million of 6.250% Senior Notes (the "2017 notes") originally scheduled to mature in August 2017. In connection with the redemption in the fourth quarter of fiscal 2015, we reclassified $2.0 million from accumulated other comprehensive income to interest expense on our consolidated statements of earnings related to remaining unrecognized losses from interest rate contracts entered into in conjunction with the 2017 notes and designated as cash flow hedges. In the fourth quarter of fiscal 2015, we entered into forward-starting interest rate swap agreements with an aggregate notional amount of $125 million related to an anticipated debt issuance in fiscal 2016. Refer to Note 9, Debt, for details of the components of our long-term debt.

Foreign Currency

To reduce cash flow volatility from foreign currency fluctuations, we enter into forward and swap contracts to hedge portions of cash flows of anticipated revenue streams and inventory purchases in currencies other than the entity's functional currency. The effective portion of the derivative's gain or loss is recorded in AOCI and is subsequently reclassified to revenue or cost of sales including occupancy costs when the hedged exposure affects net earnings.

In connection with the acquisition of Starbucks Japan that is discussed in Note 2, Acquisitions and Divestitures, we entered into cross-currency swap contracts during the first and third quarters of fiscal 2015 to hedge the foreign currency transaction risk of certain yen-denominated intercompany loans with a total notional value of ¥86.5 billion, or approximately $717 million as of September 27, 2015. Gains and losses from these swaps offset the changes in value of interest and principal payments as a result of changes in foreign exchange rates, which are also recorded in net interest income and other on the consolidated statements of earnings. We recognize the difference between the U.S. dollar interest payments received from the swap counterparty and the U.S. dollar equivalent of the Japanese yen interest payments made to the swap counterparty in interest income and other, net or interest expense on our consolidated statements of earnings. This difference varies over time and is driven by a number of market factors, including relevant interest rate differentials and foreign exchange rates. These swaps have been designated as cash flow hedges and mature in September 2016 and November 2024 at the same time as the related loans. There are no credit-risk-related contingent features associated with these swaps, although we may hold or post collateral depending upon the gain or loss position of the swap agreements.

We also enter into forward contracts to hedge the foreign currency exposure of our net investment in certain foreign operations. The effective portion of the derivative's gain or loss is recorded in AOCI and will be subsequently reclassified to net earnings when the hedged net investment is either sold or substantially liquidated.

As a result of our acquisition of Starbucks Japan, we reclassified the pretax cumulative net gains in AOCI of $7.2 million related to our net investment derivative instruments used to hedge our preexisting 39.5% equity method investment in Starbucks Japan into earnings, which was included in the gain resulting from acquisition of joint venture line item on the consolidated statements of earnings. These gains offset the cumulative translation adjustment loss balance associated with our preexisting investment included in the calculation of the remeasurement gain, which is described further in Note 2, Acquisitions and Divestitures.

To mitigate the translation risk of certain balance sheet items, we enter into foreign currency swap contracts that are not designated as hedging instruments. Gains and losses from these derivatives are largely offset by the financial impact of translating foreign currency denominated payables and receivables; both are recorded in net interest income and other on our consolidated statements of earnings.

Commodities

Depending on market conditions, we enter into coffee futures contracts and collars (the combination of a purchased call option and a sold put option) to hedge a portion of anticipated cash flows under our price-to-be-fixed green coffee contracts, which are described further in Note 5, Inventories. The effective portion of the derivative's gain or loss is recorded in AOCI and is subsequently reclassified to cost of sales including occupancy costs when the hedged exposure affects net earnings.

To mitigate the price uncertainty of a portion of our future purchases of dairy products and diesel fuel, we enter into swaps, futures and collars that are not designated as hedging instruments. Gains and losses from these derivatives are recorded in net interest income and other and help offset price fluctuations on our dairy purchases and the financial impact of diesel fuel fluctuations on our shipping costs, which are included in cost of sales including occupancy costs on our consolidated statements of earnings.

66

Gains and losses on derivative contracts designated as hedging instruments included in AOCI and expected to be reclassified into earnings within 12 months, net of tax *(in millions)*:

	Net Gains/(Losses) Included in AOCI		Net Gains/(Losses) Expected to be Reclassified from AOCI into Earnings within 12 Months	Contract Remaining Maturity (Months)
	Sep 27, 2015	Sep 28, 2014		
Cash Flow Hedges:				
Interest rates	$ 30.1	$ 36.4	$ 3.5	4
Cross-currency swaps	(27.8)	—	—	111
Foreign currency - other	29.0	10.6	19.2	35
Coffee	(5.7)	(0.7)	(2.5)	12
Net Investment Hedges:				
Foreign currency	1.3	3.2	—	0

Pretax gains and losses on derivative contracts designated as hedging instruments recognized in other comprehensive income ("OCI") and reclassifications from AOCI to earnings *(in millions)*:

	Year Ended				
	Gains/(Losses) Recognized in OCI Before Reclassifications			Gains/(Losses) Reclassified from AOCI to Earnings	
	Sep 27, 2015	Sep 28, 2014		Sep 27, 2015	Sep 28, 2014
Cash Flow Hedges:					
Interest rates	$ (6.8)	$ 0.5		$ 3.2	$ 5.0
Cross-currency swaps	11.4	—		46.2	—
Foreign currency - other	52.0	24.0		26.1	8.0
Coffee	(9.0)	(0.4)		(3.5)	(13.1)
Net Investment Hedges:					
Foreign currency	4.3	25.5		7.2	—

Pretax gains and losses on derivative contracts not designated as hedging instruments recognized in earnings *(in millions)*:

	Gains/(Losses) Recognized in Earnings	
	Sep 27, 2015	Sep 28, 2014
Foreign currency	$ 27.1	$ 1.7
Coffee	(0.2)	—
Dairy	(3.8)	12.6
Diesel fuel	(9.0)	(1.0)

Notional amounts of outstanding derivative contracts *(in millions)*:

	Sep 27, 2015	Sep 28, 2014
Interest rates	$ 125	$ —
Cross-currency swaps	717	—
Foreign currency - other	577	542
Coffee	38	45
Dairy	43	24
Diesel fuel	14	17

The fair values of our derivative assets and liabilities are included in Note 4, Fair Value Measurements, and additional disclosures related to cash flow hedge gains and losses included in accumulated other comprehensive income, as well as subsequent reclassifications to earnings, are included in Note 11, Equity.

Note 4: Fair Value Measurements

Assets and Liabilities Measured at Fair Value on a Recurring Basis (in millions):

	Balance at Sep 27, 2015	Quoted Prices in Active Markets for Identical Assets (Level 1)	Significant Other Observable Inputs (Level 2)	Significant Unobservable Inputs (Level 3)
Assets:				
Cash and cash equivalents	$ 1,530.1	$ 1,530.1	$ —	$ —
Short-term investments:				
Available-for-sale securities				
Corporate debt securities	10.2	—	10.2	—
Foreign government obligations	2.0	—	2.0	—
State and local government obligations	3.3	—	3.3	—
Total available-for-sale securities	15.5	—	15.5	—
Trading securities	65.8	65.8	—	—
Total short-term investments	81.3	65.8	15.5	—
Prepaid expenses and other current assets:				
Derivative assets	50.8	—	50.8	—
Long-term investments:				
Available-for-sale securities				
Agency obligations	8.6	—	8.6	—
Corporate debt securities	121.8	—	121.8	—
Auction rate securities	5.9	—	—	5.9
Foreign government obligations	18.5	—	18.5	—
U.S. government treasury securities	104.8	104.8	—	—
State and local government obligations	9.7	—	9.7	—
Mortgage and other asset-backed securities	43.2	—	43.2	—
Total long-term investments	312.5	104.8	201.8	5.9
Other long-term assets:				
Derivative assets	54.7	—	54.7	—
Total assets	$ 2,029.4	$ 1,700.7	$ 322.8	$ 5.9
Liabilities:				
Accrued liabilities:				
Derivative liabilities	$ 19.2	$ 3.6	$ 15.6	$ —
Other long-term liabilities:				
Derivative liabilities	14.5	—	14.5	—
Total liabilities	$ 33.7	$ 3.6	$ 30.1	$ —

69

	Balance at Sep 28, 2014	Fair Value Measurements at Reporting Date Using		
		Quoted Prices in Active Markets for Identical Assets (Level 1)	Significant Other Observable Inputs (Level 2)	Significant Unobservable Inputs (Level 3)
Assets:				
Cash and cash equivalents	$ 1,708.4	$ 1,708.4	$ —	$ —
Short-term investments:				
Available-for-sale securities				
Corporate debt securities	4.9	—	4.9	—
Foreign government obligations	33.7	—	33.7	—
U.S. government treasury securities	10.9	10.9	—	—
State and local government obligations	12.7	—	12.7	—
Certificates of deposit	1.0	—	1.0	—
Total available-for-sale securities	63.2	10.9	52.3	—
Trading securities	72.2	72.2	—	—
Total short-term investments	135.4	83.1	52.3	—
Prepaid expenses and other current assets:				
Derivative assets	28.7	0.9	27.8	—
Long-term investments:				
Available-for-sale securities				
Agency obligations	8.9	—	8.9	—
Corporate debt securities	130.9	—	130.9	—
Auction rate securities	13.8	—	—	13.8
Foreign government obligations	17.4	—	17.4	—
U.S. government treasury securities	94.8	94.8	—	—
State and local government obligations	6.7	—	6.7	—
Mortgage and other asset-backed securities	45.9	—	45.9	—
Total long-term investments	318.4	94.8	209.8	13.8
Other long-term assets:				
Derivative assets	18.0	—	18.0	—
Total assets	$ 2,208.9	$ 1,887.2	$ 307.9	$ 13.8
Liabilities:				
Accrued liabilities:				
Derivative liabilities	$ 2.4	$ 0.4	$ 2.0	$ —

There were no material transfers between levels and there was no significant activity within Level 3 instruments during the periods presented. The fair values of any financial instruments presented above exclude the impact of netting assets and liabilities when a legally enforceable master netting agreement exists.

Available-for-sale Securities

Long-term investments generally mature within 4 years. Proceeds from sales of available-for-sale securities were $600.6 million, $1.5 billion, and $60.2 million for fiscal years 2015, 2014 and 2013, respectively. The increase in fiscal 2014 was due to the liquidation of a significant portion of our offshore investment portfolio in the fourth quarter of fiscal 2014 in anticipation of funding the acquisition of Starbucks Japan. Realized gains and losses on sales and maturities of available-for-sale securities were not material for fiscal years 2015, 2014, and 2013. Gross unrealized holding gains and losses on available-for-sale securities were not material as of September 27, 2015 and September 28, 2014.

Trading Securities

Trading securities include equity mutual funds and exchange-traded funds. Our trading securities portfolio approximates a portion of our liability under our Management Deferred Compensation Plan ("MDCP"), a defined contribution plan. Our MDCP liability was $98.3 million and $106.4 million as of September 27, 2015 and September 28, 2014, respectively, which is included in accrued compensation and related costs within accrued liabilities on the consolidated balance sheets. The changes in net unrealized holding gains and losses in the trading securities portfolio included in earnings for fiscal years 2015, 2014 and 2013 were a net loss of $4.5 million, and net gains of $1.2 million, and $11.7 million, respectively. Gross unrealized holding gains and losses on trading securities were not material as of September 27, 2015 and September 28, 2014.

Derivative Assets and Liabilities

Derivative assets and liabilities include foreign currency forward contracts, commodity futures contracts, collars and swaps, which are described further in Note 3, Derivative Financial Instruments.

Assets and Liabilities Measured at Fair Value on a Nonrecurring Basis

Assets and liabilities recognized or disclosed at fair value on a nonrecurring basis include items such as property, plant and equipment, goodwill and other intangible assets, equity and cost method investments, and other assets. These assets are measured at fair value if determined to be impaired. Impairment of property, plant, and equipment is included at Note 1, Summary of Significant Accounting Policies. During fiscal 2015 and 2014, there were no other material fair value adjustments.

Fair Value of Other Financial Instruments

The estimated fair value of our long-term debt based on the quoted market price (Level 2) is included at Note 9, Debt.

Note 5: Inventories *(in millions)*

	Sep 27, 2015		Sep 28, 2014	
Coffee:				
Unroasted	$	529.4	$	432.3
Roasted		279.7		238.9
Other merchandise held for sale		318.3		265.7
Packaging and other supplies		179.0		154.0
Total	$	1,306.4	$	1,090.9

Other merchandise held for sale includes, among other items, serveware and tea. Inventory levels vary due to seasonality, commodity market supply and price fluctuations.

As of September 27, 2015, we had committed to purchasing green coffee totaling $819 million under fixed-price contracts and an estimated $266 million under price-to-be-fixed contracts. As of September 27, 2015, approximately $38 million of our price-to-be-fixed contracts were effectively fixed through the use of futures contracts. Price-to-be-fixed contracts are purchase commitments whereby the quality, quantity, delivery period, and other negotiated terms are agreed upon, but the date, and therefore the price, at which the base "C" coffee commodity price component will be fixed has not yet been established. For these types of contracts, either Starbucks or the seller has the option to "fix" the base "C" coffee commodity price prior to the delivery date. Until prices are fixed, we estimate the total cost of these purchase commitments. We believe, based on relationships established with our suppliers in the past, the risk of non-delivery on such purchase commitments is remote.

Note 6: Equity and Cost Investments *(in millions)*

	Sep 27, 2015	Sep 28, 2014
Equity method investments	$ 306.4	$ 469.3
Cost method investments	45.6	45.6
Total	$ 352.0	$ 514.9

Equity Method Investments

As of September 27, 2015, we had a 50% ownership interest in each of the following international equity method investees: President Starbucks Coffee (Shanghai); Starbucks Coffee Korea Co., Ltd.; President Starbucks Coffee Corporation (Taiwan) Company Limited; and Tata Starbucks Limited (India). In addition, we had a 49% ownership interest in Starbucks Coffee España, S.L. ("Starbucks Spain"). These international entities operate licensed Starbucks® retail stores.

We also license the rights to produce and distribute Starbucks-branded products to our 50% owned joint venture, The North American Coffee Partnership with the Pepsi-Cola Company, which develops and distributes bottled Starbucks® beverages, including Frappuccino® coffee drinks, Starbucks Doubleshot® espresso drinks, Starbucks Refreshers® beverages, and Starbucks Discoveries Iced Café Favorites®.

On September 23, 2014, we entered into a two-step tender offer bid agreement to acquire the remaining 60.5% interest in Starbucks Japan, at the time a 39.5% owned equity method investment. Upon the completion of the first tender offer step in the first quarter of fiscal 2015, we obtained a controlling interest in Starbucks Japan and began consolidating its results instead of applying equity method accounting. See further discussion at Note 2, Acquisitions and Divestitures.

In the fourth quarter of fiscal 2014, we sold our 50% equity method ownership interest in our Malaysian joint venture, Berjaya Starbucks Coffee Company Sdn. Bhd., to our joint venture partner, Berjaya Food Berhad, for a total purchase price of $88.0 million. This transaction resulted in a gain of $67.8 million, which was included in net interest income and other on our consolidated statements of earnings.

In the fourth quarter of fiscal 2013, we acquired a 49% equity method ownership interest in Starbucks Spain from our licensee partner Sigla S.A. (Grupo Vips) for approximately $33 million in cash.

Our share of income and losses from our equity method investments is included in income from equity investees on our consolidated statements of earnings. Also included in this line item is our proportionate share of gross profit resulting from coffee and other product sales to, and royalty and license fee revenues generated from, equity investees. Revenues generated from these related parties were $153.4 million, $219.2 million, and $205.1 million in fiscal years 2015, 2014, and 2013, respectively. Related costs of sales were $94.5 million, $121.2 million, and $115.4 million in fiscal years 2015, 2014, and 2013, respectively. As of September 27, 2015 and September 28, 2014, there were $36.7 million and $54.9 million of accounts receivable from equity investees, respectively, on our consolidated balance sheets, primarily related to product sales and royalty revenues.

Summarized combined financial information of our equity method investees, which represent 100% of the investees' financial information *(in millions)*:

Financial Position as of	Sep 27, 2015	Sep 28, 2014
Current assets	$ 402.8	$ 701.3
Noncurrent assets	578.8	873.9
Current liabilities	490.0	615.6
Noncurrent liabilities	38.7	79.1

Results of Operations for Fiscal Year Ended	Sep 27, 2015	Sep 28, 2014	Sep 29, 2013
Net revenues	$ 2,688.0	$ 3,461.3	$ 3,018.7
Operating income	426.4	467.7	434.8
Net earnings	392.1	382.6	358.0

72

Cost Method Investments

As of September 27, 2015, we had $19 million invested in equity interests of entities that develop and operate Starbucks® licensed stores in several global markets. We have the ability to acquire additional interests in some of these cost method investees at certain intervals. Depending on our total percentage ownership interest and our ability to exercise significant influence over financial and operating policies, additional investments may require a retroactive application of the equity method of accounting. We also had a $25 million investment in the preferred stock of Square, Inc.

During the fourth quarter of fiscal 2013, we sold our 18% interest in Starbucks Coffee Argentina S.R.L. to our joint venture partner Alsea, S.A.B. de C.V., for a total purchase price of $4.4 million. This transaction resulted in a loss of $1.0 million, which was included in net interest income and other on our consolidated statements of earnings.

During the second quarter of fiscal 2013, we sold our 18% interest in Cafe Sirena S. de R.L. de CV (a Mexican limited liability company), to our controlling joint venture partner, SC de Mexico, S.A. de CV, owned by Alsea, S.A.B. de C.V., for a total purchase price of $50.3 million, which included final working capital adjustments. This transaction resulted in a gain of $35.2 million, which was included in net interest income and other on our consolidated statements of earnings.

Note 7: Supplemental Balance Sheet Information *(in millions)*

Property, Plant and Equipment, net

	Sep 27, 2015	Sep 28, 2014
Land	$ 46.6	$ 46.7
Buildings	411.5	278.1
Leasehold improvements	5,409.6	4,858.4
Store equipment	1,707.5	1,493.3
Roasting equipment	542.4	410.9
Furniture, fixtures and other	1,281.7	1,078.1
Work in progress	242.5	415.6
Property, plant and equipment, gross	9,641.8	8,581.1
Accumulated depreciation	(5,553.5)	(5,062.1)
Property, plant and equipment, net	$ 4,088.3	$ 3,519.0

Accrued Liabilities

	Sep 27, 2015	Sep 28, 2014
Accrued compensation and related costs	$ 522.3	$ 437.9
Accrued occupancy costs	137.2	119.8
Accrued taxes	259.0	272.0
Accrued dividends payable	297.0	239.8
Other	545.2	444.9
Total accrued liabilities	$ 1,760.7	$ 1,514.4

Note 8: Other Intangible Assets and Goodwill

Indefinite-Lived Intangible Assets

(in millions)	Sep 27, 2015	Sep 28, 2014
Trade names, trademarks and patents	$ 202.8	$ 197.5
Other indefinite-lived intangible assets	15.1	15.1
Total indefinite-lived intangible assets	$ 217.9	$ 212.6

Additional disclosure regarding changes in our intangible assets due to acquisitions is included at Note 2, Acquisitions and Divestitures.

Goodwill

Changes in the carrying amount of goodwill by reportable operating segment *(in millions)*:

	Americas	China/Asia Pacific	EMEA	Channel Development	All Other Segments	Total
Balance at September 29, 2013						
Goodwill prior to impairment	$ 230.2	$ 75.1	$ 62.2	$ 23.8	$ 480.2	$ 871.5
Accumulated impairment charges	(8.6)	—	—	—	—	(8.6)
Goodwill	$ 221.6	$ 75.1	$ 62.2	$ 23.8	$ 480.2	$ 862.9
Impairment	—	—	—	—	(0.8)	(0.8)
Other[1]	(2.6)	(0.2)	(3.1)	—	—	(5.9)
Balance at September 28, 2014						
Goodwill prior to impairment	$ 227.6	$ 74.9	$ 59.1	$ 23.8	$ 480.2	$ 865.6
Accumulated impairment charges	(8.6)	—	—	—	(0.8)	(9.4)
Goodwill	$ 219.0	$ 74.9	$ 59.1	$ 23.8	$ 479.4	$ 856.2
Acquisition/(divestiture)	(2.5)	815.6	—	—	—	813.1
Impairment	—	—	—	—	(0.5)	(0.5)
Other[1]	(5.3)	(86.4)	(1.7)	—	—	(93.4)
Balance at September 27, 2015						
Goodwill prior to impairment	$ 219.8	$ 804.1	$ 57.4	$ 23.8	$ 480.2	$ 1,585.3
Accumulated impairment charges	(8.6)	—	—	—	(1.3)	(9.9)
Goodwill	$ 211.2	$ 804.1	$ 57.4	$ 23.8	$ 478.9	$ 1,575.4

[1] Other is primarily comprised of changes in the goodwill balance as a result of foreign currency translation.

Finite-Lived Intangible Assets

(in millions)	Sep 27, 2015			Sep 28, 2014		
	Gross Carrying Amount	Accumulated Amortization	Net Carrying Amount	Gross Carrying Amount	Accumulated Amortization	Net Carrying Amount
Acquired and reacquired rights	$ 308.6	$ (52.5)	$ 256.1	$ 36.8	$ (10.1)	$ 26.7
Acquired trade secrets and processes	27.6	(8.2)	19.4	27.6	(5.4)	22.2
Licensing agreements	13.4	(1.1)	12.3	—	—	—
Trade names, trademarks and patents	24.5	(13.0)	11.5	21.6	(11.6)	10.0
Other finite-lived intangible assets	6.5	(3.3)	3.2	3.8	(1.8)	2.0
Total finite-lived intangible assets	$ 380.6	$ (78.1)	$ 302.5	$ 89.8	$ (28.9)	$ 60.9

Amortization expense for finite-lived intangible assets was $50.0 million, $8.7 million, and $7.7 million during fiscal 2015, 2014, and 2013, respectively.

Estimated future amortization expense as of September 27, 2015 (*in millions*):

Fiscal Year Ending		
2016	$	53.2
2017		52.9
2018		51.5
2019		51.2
2020		51.1
Thereafter		42.6
Total estimated future amortization expense	$	302.5

Additional disclosure regarding changes in our intangible assets due to acquisitions is included at Note 2, Acquisitions and Divestitures.

Note 9: Debt

Revolving Credit Facility and Commercial Paper Program

Our $750 million unsecured, revolving credit facility with various banks, of which $150 million may be used for issuances of letters of credit, is available for working capital, capital expenditures and other corporate purposes, including acquisitions and share repurchases. During the second quarter of fiscal 2015, we extended the duration of our credit facility, which is now set to mature on January 21, 2020, and amended certain facility fees and borrowing rates. Starbucks has the option, subject to negotiation and agreement with the related banks, to increase the maximum commitment amount by an additional $750 million. Borrowings under the credit facility will bear interest at a variable rate based on LIBOR, and, for U.S. dollar-denominated loans under certain circumstances, a Base Rate (as defined in the credit facility), in each case plus an applicable margin. The applicable margin is based on the better of (i) the Company's long-term credit ratings assigned by Moody's and Standard & Poor's rating agencies and (ii) the Company's fixed charge coverage ratio, pursuant to a pricing grid set forth in the credit facility. The current applicable margin is 0.565% for Eurocurrency Rate Loans and 0.00% for Base Rate Loans. The credit facility contains provisions requiring us to maintain compliance with certain covenants, including a minimum fixed charge coverage ratio, which measures our ability to cover financing expenses. As of September 27, 2015, we were in compliance with all applicable covenants. No amounts were outstanding under our credit facility as of September 27, 2015.

Under our commercial paper program, we may issue unsecured commercial paper notes up to a maximum aggregate amount outstanding at any time of $1 billion, with individual maturities that may vary, but not exceed 397 days from the date of issue. Amounts outstanding under the commercial paper program are required to be backstopped by available commitments under our credit facility discussed above. As of September 27, 2015, availability under our commercial paper program was approximately $750 million (which represents the full committed credit facility amount, as the amount of outstanding letters of credit was not material as of September 27, 2015). The proceeds from borrowings under our commercial paper program may be used for working capital needs, capital expenditures and other corporate purposes, including share repurchases, business expansion, payment of cash dividends on our common stock or the financing of possible acquisitions. In the fourth quarter of fiscal 2015, we issued and subsequently repaid commercial paper borrowings of $93 million for general corporate purposes. We had no other borrowings under our commercial paper program during fiscal 2015 or fiscal 2014, and there were no amounts outstanding as of September 27, 2015 or September 28, 2014.

Long-term Debt

In July 2015, we redeemed our $550 million of 6.250% Senior Notes (the "2017 notes") originally scheduled to mature in August 2017. The redemption resulted in a charge of $61.1 million, which is presented separately as loss on extinguishment of debt within other income and expenses on our consolidated statements of earnings. This loss primarily relates to the optional redemption payment as outlined in the 2017 notes indenture, as well as non-cash expenses related to the previously capitalized original issuance costs and accelerated amortization of the unamortized discount. In connection with the redemption, we also reclassified $2.0 million from accumulated other comprehensive income to interest expense on our consolidated statements of earnings related to remaining unrecognized losses from interest rate contracts entered into in conjunction with the 2017 notes and designated as cash flow hedges.

In June 2015, we issued additional long-term debt in an underwritten registered public offering, which consisted of $500 million of 7-year 2.700% Senior Notes (the "2022 notes") due June 2022, and $350 million of 30-year 4.300% Senior Notes (the "2045 notes") due June 2045. Interest on the 2022 and 2045 notes is payable semi-annually on June 15 and December 15 of each year, commencing on December 15, 2015.

In December 2013, we issued $400 million of 3-year 0.875% Senior Notes (the "2016 notes") due December 2016, and $350 million of 5-year 2.000% Senior Notes (the "2018 notes") due December 2018, in an underwritten registered public offering. Interest on the 2016 and 2018 notes is payable semi-annually on June 5 and December 5 of each year.

In September 2013, we issued $750 million of 10-year 3.85% Senior Notes (the "2023 notes") due October 2023, in an underwritten registered public offering. Interest on the 2023 notes is payable semi-annually on April 1 and October 1 of each year.

Components of long-term debt including the associated interest rates and related fair values *(in millions, except interest rates)*:

Issuance	Sep 27, 2015		Sep 28, 2014		Stated Interest Rate	Effective Interest Rate [1]
	Face Value	Estimated Fair Value	Face Value	Estimated Fair Value		
2016 notes	$ 400.0	$ 400	$ 400.0	$ 400	0.875%	0.941%
2017 notes	—	—	550.0	625	6.250%	—
2018 notes	350.0	354	350.0	353	2.000%	2.012%
2022 notes	500.0	503	—	—	2.700%	2.819%
2023 notes	750.0	790	750.0	786	3.850%	2.860%
2045 notes	350.0	355	—	—	4.300%	4.348%
Total	2,350.0	2,402	2,050.0	2,164		
Aggregate unamortized discount	2.5		1.7			
Total	$ 2,347.5		$ 2,048.3			

[1] Includes the effects of the amortization of any premium or discount and any gain or loss upon settlement of related treasury locks or forward-starting interest rate swaps utilized to hedge the interest rate risk prior to the debt issuance.

The indentures under which the above notes were issued also require us to maintain compliance with certain covenants, including limits on future liens and sale and leaseback transactions on certain material properties. As of September 27, 2015, we were in compliance with each of these covenants.

The following table summarizes our long-term debt maturities as of September 27, 2015 *(in millions)*:

Fiscal Year	Total
2016	$ —
2017	400.0
2018	—
2019	350.0
2020	—
Thereafter	1,600.0
Total	$ 2,350.0

Interest Expense

Interest expense, net of interest capitalized, was $70.5 million, $64.1 million, and $28.1 million in fiscal 2015, 2014 and 2013, respectively. In fiscal 2015, 2014, and 2013, $3.6 million, $6.2 million, and $10.4 million, respectively, of interest was capitalized for asset construction projects.

Note 10: Leases

Rent expense under operating lease agreements *(in millions)*:

Fiscal Year Ended	Sep 27, 2015	Sep 28, 2014	Sep 29, 2013
Minimum rent	$ 1,026.3	$ 907.4	$ 838.3
Contingent rent	111.5	66.8	56.4
Total	$ 1,137.8	$ 974.2	$ 894.7

Minimum future rental payments under non-cancelable operating leases and lease financing arrangements as of September 27, 2015 *(in millions)*:

Fiscal Year Ending	Operating Leases	Lease Financing Arrangements
2016	$ 1,032.4	$ 3.2
2017	892.5	3.2
2018	739.8	3.2
2019	624.0	3.2
2020	548.9	3.2
Thereafter	1,831.9	31.1
Total minimum lease payments	$ 5,669.5	$ 47.1

We have subleases related to certain of our operating leases. During fiscal 2015, 2014, and 2013, we recognized sublease income of $11.9 million, $13.3 million, and $9.3 million, respectively. Additionally, as of September 27, 2015, the gross carrying value of assets related to build-to-suit lease arrangements accounted for as financing leases was $66.8 million with associated accumulated depreciation of $2.5 million. We had no built-to-suit lease arrangements as of September 28, 2014.

Note 11: Equity

As discussed in Note 1, Summary of Significant Accounting Policies, on April 9, 2015, we effected a two-for-one stock split of our $0.001 par value common stock for shareholders of record as of March 30, 2015. All share data presented in this note has been retroactively adjusted to reflect this stock split.

In addition to 2.4 billion shares of authorized common stock with $0.001 par value per share, we have authorized 7.5 million shares of preferred stock, none of which was outstanding at September 27, 2015.

Included in additional paid-in capital in our consolidated statements of equity as of September 27, 2015 and September 28, 2014 is $39.4 million related to the increase in value of our share of the net assets of Starbucks Japan at the time of its initial public stock offering in fiscal 2002. Also included in additional paid-in capital as of September 27, 2015 is $1.7 million, which represents the difference between the carrying value of the remaining outstanding noncontrolling interests in Starbucks Japan prior to obtaining full ownership and the cash paid to acquire the noncontrolling interests. Refer to Note 2, Acquisitions and Divestitures, for further discussion.

We repurchased 29.0 million shares of common stock at a total cost of $1.4 billion, and 21.0 million shares at a total cost of $769.8 million for the years ended September 27, 2015 and September 28, 2014, respectively. On July 23, 2015, we announced that our Board of Directors approved an increase of 50 million shares to our ongoing share repurchase program. As of September 27, 2015, 52.7 million shares remained available for repurchase under current authorizations.

During fiscal years 2015 and 2014, our Board of Directors declared the following dividends *(in millions, except per share amounts)*:

	Dividend Per Share	Record Date	Total Amount	Payment Date
Fiscal Year 2015				
First quarter	$0.16	February 5, 2015	$240.1	February 20, 2015
Second quarter	$0.16	May 7, 2015	$240.1	May 22, 2015
Third quarter	$0.16	August 6, 2015	$239.0	August 21, 2015
Fourth quarter	$0.20	November 12, 2015	$297.0	November 27, 2015
Fiscal Year 2014:				
First quarter	$0.13	February 6, 2014	$196.4	February 21, 2014
Second quarter	$0.13	May 8, 2014	$195.5	May 23, 2014
Third quarter	$0.13	August 7, 2014	$195.3	August 22, 2014
Fourth quarter	$0.16	November 13, 2014	$239.8	November 28, 2014

Comprehensive Income

Comprehensive income includes all changes in equity during the period, except those resulting from transactions with our shareholders. Comprehensive income is comprised of net earnings and other comprehensive income. Accumulated other comprehensive income reported on our consolidated balance sheets consists of foreign currency translation adjustments and the unrealized gains and losses, net of applicable taxes, on available-for-sale securities and on derivative instruments designated and qualifying as cash flow and net investment hedges.

Changes in accumulated other comprehensive income ("AOCI") by component, for year ended September 27, 2015, net of tax:

(in millions)	Available-for-Sale Securities	Cash Flow Hedges	Net Investment Hedges	Translation Adjustment	Total
September 27, 2015					
Net gains/(losses) in AOCI, beginning of period	$ (0.4)	$ 46.3	$ 3.2	$ (23.8)	$ 25.3
Net gains/(losses) recognized in OCI before reclassifications	0.9	30.8	2.7	(185.6)	(151.2)
Net (gains)/losses reclassified from AOCI to earnings	(0.6)	(51.5)	(4.6)	14.3	(42.4)
Other comprehensive income/(loss) attributable to Starbucks	0.3	(20.7)	(1.9)	(171.3)	(193.6)
Purchase of noncontrolling interest	—	—	—	(31.1)	(31.1)
Net gains/(losses) in AOCI, end of period	$ (0.1)	$ 25.6	$ 1.3	$ (226.2)	$ (199.4)

(in millions)	Available-for-Sale Securities	Cash Flow Hedges	Net Investment Hedges	Translation Adjustment	Total
September 28, 2014					
Net gains/(losses) in AOCI, beginning of period	$ (0.5)	$ 26.8	$ (12.9)	$ 53.6	$ 67.0
Net gains/(losses) recognized in OCI before reclassifications	1.0	16.3	16.1	(77.4)	(44.0)
Net (gains)/losses reclassified from AOCI to earnings	(0.9)	3.2	—	—	2.3
Other comprehensive income/(loss) attributable to Starbucks	0.1	19.5	16.1	(77.4)	(41.7)
Net gains/(losses) in AOCI, end of period	$ (0.4)	$ 46.3	$ 3.2	$ (23.8)	$ 25.3

Impact of reclassifications from AOCI on the consolidated statements of earnings (in millions):

	Amounts Reclassified from AOCI Fiscal Year Ended		Affected Line Item in the Statements of Earnings
	Sep 27, 2015	Sep 28, 2014	
Gains/(losses) on cash flow hedges			
Interest rate hedges	$ 3.2	$ 5.0	Interest expense
Cross-currency swaps	46.2	—	Interest income and other, net
Foreign currency hedges	14.0	5.1	Revenue
Foreign currency/coffee hedges	8.6	(10.0)	Cost of sales including occupancy costs
Gains/(losses) on net investment hedges [1]	7.2	—	Gain resulting from acquisition of joint venture
Translation adjustment [2]			
Starbucks Japan	(7.2)	—	Gain resulting from acquisition of joint venture
Other	(7.1)	—	Interest income and other, net
	64.9	0.1	Total before tax
	(23.1)	(3.3)	Tax (expense)/benefit
	$ 41.8	$ (3.2)	Net of tax

[1] Release of pretax cumulative net gains in AOCI related to our net investment derivative instruments used to hedge our preexisting 39.5% equity method investment in Starbucks Japan.
[2] Release of cumulative translation adjustments to earnings upon sale or liquidation of foreign business.

Note 12: Employee Stock and Benefit Plans

We maintain several equity incentive plans under which we may grant non-qualified stock options, incentive stock options, restricted stock, restricted stock units ("RSUs"), or stock appreciation rights to employees, non-employee directors and consultants. We issue new shares of common stock upon exercise of stock options and the vesting of RSUs. We also have an employee stock purchase plan ("ESPP").

As discussed in Note 1, Summary of Significant Accounting Policies, on April 9, 2015, we effected a two-for-one stock split of our $0.001 par value common stock for shareholders of record as of March 30, 2015. All share and per-share data presented in this note has been retroactively adjusted to reflect this stock split.

As of September 27, 2015, there were 96.3 million shares of common stock available for issuance pursuant to future equity-based compensation awards and 14.3 million shares available for issuance under our ESPP.

Stock-based compensation expense recognized in the consolidated financial statements *(in millions)*:

Fiscal Year Ended	Sep 27, 2015		Sep 28, 2014		Sep 29, 2013	
Options	$	37.8	$	41.8	$	37.1
RSUs		172.0		141.4		105.2
Total stock-based compensation expense recognized in the consolidated statements of earnings	$	209.8	$	183.2	$	142.3
Total related tax benefit	$	72.3	$	63.4	$	49.8
Total capitalized stock-based compensation included in net property, plant and equipment and inventories on the consolidated balance sheets	$	1.9	$	1.9	$	1.8

Stock Option Plans

Stock options to purchase our common stock are granted at the fair value of the stock on the grant date. The majority of options become exercisable in four equal installments beginning a year from the grant date and generally expire 10 years from the grant date. Options granted to non-employee directors generally vest over one to three years. Nearly all outstanding stock options are non-qualified stock options.

The fair value of stock option awards was estimated at the grant date with the following weighted average assumptions for fiscal years 2015, 2014, and 2013:

Fiscal Year Ended	Employee Stock Options Granted During the Period					
	2015		2014		2013	
Expected term (in years)	4.2		4.5		4.8	
Expected stock price volatility	22.3%		26.8%		34.0%	
Risk-free interest rate	1.1%		1.1%		0.7%	
Expected dividend yield	1.6%		1.3%		1.6%	
Weighted average grant price	$	39.89	$	40.12	$	25.62
Estimated fair value per option granted	$	6.58	$	8.36	$	6.44

The expected term of the options represents the estimated period of time until exercise, and is based on historical experience of similar awards, giving consideration to the contractual terms, vesting schedules and expectations of future employee behavior. Expected stock price volatility is based on a combination of historical volatility of our stock and the one-year implied volatility of Starbucks traded options, for the related vesting periods. The risk-free interest rate is based on the implied yield available on U.S. Treasury zero-coupon issues with an equivalent remaining term. The dividend yield assumption is based on our anticipated cash dividend payouts. The amounts shown above for the estimated fair value per option granted are before the estimated effect of forfeitures, which reduce the amount of expense recorded in the consolidated statements of earnings.

Stock option transactions for the year ended September 27, 2015 *(in millions, except per share and contractual life amounts)*:

	Shares Subject to Options	Weighted Average Exercise Price per Share	Weighted Average Remaining Contractual Life (Years)	Aggregate Intrinsic Value
Outstanding, September 28, 2014	39.6	$ 18.93	5.8	$ 754
Granted	6.4	39.89		
Exercised	(11.3)	14.99		
Expired/forfeited	(1.1)	32.38		
Outstanding, September 27, 2015	33.6	23.81	6.0	1,150
Exercisable, September 27, 2015	21.1	16.75	4.7	872
Vested and expected to vest, September 27, 2015	32.4	23.29	5.9	1,125

The aggregate intrinsic value in the table above, which is the amount by which the market value of the underlying stock exceeded the exercise price of outstanding options, is before applicable income taxes and represents the amount optionees would have realized if all in-the-money options had been exercised on the last business day of the period indicated.

As of September 27, 2015, total unrecognized stock-based compensation expense, net of estimated forfeitures, related to nonvested options was approximately $32 million, before income taxes, and is expected to be recognized over a weighted average period of approximately 2.6 years. The total intrinsic value of options exercised was $358 million, $258 million, and $539 million during fiscal years 2015, 2014, and 2013, respectively. The total fair value of options vested was $36 million, $44 million, and $56 million during fiscal years 2015, 2014, and 2013, respectively.

RSUs

We have both time-vested and performance-based RSUs. Time-vested RSUs are awarded to eligible employees and non-employee directors and entitle the grantee to receive shares of common stock at the end of a vesting period, subject solely to the employee's continuing employment or the non-employee director's continuing service. The majority of RSUs vest in two equal annual installments beginning a year from the grant date. Our performance-based RSUs are awarded to eligible employees and entitle the grantee to receive shares of common stock if we achieve specified performance goals during the performance period and the grantee remains employed during the subsequent vesting period.

RSU transactions for the year ended September 27, 2015 *(in millions, except per share and contractual life amounts)*:

	Number of Shares	Weighted Average Grant Date Fair Value per Share	Weighted Average Remaining Contractual Life (Years)	Aggregate Intrinsic Value
Nonvested, September 28, 2014	10.8	$ 31.17	1.0	$ 407
Granted	6.7	38.56		
Vested	(5.1)	26.73		
Forfeited/canceled	(1.7)	36.10		
Nonvested, September 27, 2015	10.7	36.35	1.0	620

For fiscal 2014 and 2013, the weighted average fair value per RSU granted was $40.07 and $25.12, respectively. As of September 27, 2015, total unrecognized stock-based compensation expense related to nonvested RSUs, net of estimated forfeitures, was approximately $126 million, before income taxes, and is expected to be recognized over a weighted average period of approximately 2.3 years. The total fair value of RSUs vested was $137 million, $103 million and $104 million during fiscal years 2015, 2014, and 2013, respectively.

ESPP

Our ESPP allows eligible employees to contribute up to 10% of their base earnings toward the quarterly purchase of our common stock, subject to an annual maximum dollar amount. The purchase price is 95% of the fair market value of the stock on the last business day of the quarterly offering period. The number of shares issued under our ESPP was 0.5 million in fiscal 2015.

Deferred Compensation Plan

We have a Deferred Compensation Plan for Non-Employee Directors under which non-employee directors may, for any fiscal year, irrevocably elect to defer receipt of shares of common stock the director would have received upon vesting of restricted stock units. The number of deferred shares outstanding related to deferrals made under this plan is not material.

Defined Contribution Plans

We maintain voluntary defined contribution plans, both qualified and non-qualified, covering eligible employees as defined in the plan documents. Participating employees may elect to defer and contribute a portion of their eligible compensation to the plans up to limits stated in the plan documents, not to exceed the dollar amounts set by applicable laws.

Our matching contributions to all U.S. and non-U.S. plans were $70.9 million, $73.0 million, and $54.7 million in fiscal years 2015, 2014, and 2013, respectively.

Note 13: Income Taxes

Components of earnings/(loss) before income taxes (in millions):

Fiscal Year Ended	Sep 27, 2015	Sep 28, 2014	Sep 29, 2013		
			Total	Litigation charge	All Other
United States	$ 2,837.2	$ 2,572.4	$ (674.0)	$ (2,784.1)	$ 2,110.1
Foreign	1,065.8	587.3	444.1	—	444.1
Total earnings/(loss) before income taxes	$ 3,903.0	$ 3,159.7	$ (229.9)	$ (2,784.1)	$ 2,554.2

Provision/(benefit) for income taxes (in millions):

Fiscal Year Ended	Sep 27, 2015	Sep 28, 2014	Sep 29, 2013		
			Total	Litigation charge	All Other
Current taxes:					
U.S. federal	$ 801.0	$ 822.7	$ 616.6	$ —	$ 616.6
U.S. state and local	150.1	132.9	93.8	—	93.8
Foreign	172.2	128.8	95.9	—	95.9
Total current taxes	1,123.3	1,084.4	806.3	—	806.3
Deferred taxes:					
U.S. federal	56.5	12.0	(898.8)	(922.3)	23.5
U.S. state and local	4.0	(4.9)	(144.0)	(148.7)	4.7
Foreign	(40.1)	0.5	(2.2)	—	(2.2)
Total deferred taxes	20.4	7.6	(1,045.0)	(1,071.0)	26.0
Total income tax expense/(benefit)	$ 1,143.7	$ 1,092.0	$ (238.7)	$ (1,071.0)	$ 832.3

81

Reconciliation of the statutory U.S. federal income tax rate with our effective income tax rate:

Fiscal Year Ended	Sep 27, 2015	Sep 28, 2014	Sep 29, 2013		
			Total	Litigation charge	All Other
Statutory rate	35.0%	35.0%	35.0%	35.0%	35.0%
State income taxes, net of federal tax benefit	2.8	2.6	15.8	3.5	2.4
Benefits and taxes related to foreign operations	(2.1)	(1.9)	37.5	—	(3.4)
Domestic production activity deduction	(2.2)	(0.7)	8.1	—	(0.7)
Domestic tax credits	(0.2)	(0.2)	2.8	—	(0.3)
Charitable contributions	(0.3)	(0.4)	3.9	—	(0.3)
Gain resulting from acquisition of joint venture	(3.7)	—	—	—	—
Other, net	—	0.2	0.7	—	(0.1)
Effective tax rate	29.3%	34.6%	103.8%	38.5%	32.6%

Our effective tax rate in fiscal 2013 was significantly affected by the litigation charge we recorded as a result of the conclusion of our arbitration with Kraft. In order to provide a more meaningful analysis of tax expense and the effective tax rate, the tables above present separate reconciliations of the effect of the litigation charge. The deferred tax asset related to the litigation charge is estimated to be recovered over a period of 15 years; the deferred tax asset has been classified between current and non-current consistent with the expected recovery period for income tax reporting purposes.

U.S. income and foreign withholding taxes have not been provided on approximately $2.8 billion of cumulative undistributed earnings of foreign subsidiaries and equity investees. We intend to reinvest these earnings for the foreseeable future. If these amounts were distributed to the U.S., in the form of dividends or otherwise, we would be subject to additional U.S. income taxes, which could be material. Determination of the amount of unrecognized deferred income tax liabilities on these earnings is not practicable because of the complexities with its hypothetical calculation, and the amount of liability, if any, is dependent on circumstances existing if and when remittance occurs.

Tax effect of temporary differences and carryforwards that comprise significant portions of deferred tax assets and liabilities *(in millions)*:

		Sep 27, 2015		Sep 28, 2014
Deferred tax assets:				
Property, plant and equipment	$	121.4	$	78.5
Accrued occupancy costs		98.4		58.8
Accrued compensation and related costs		81.7		75.3
Other accrued liabilities		49.0		27.6
Asset retirement obligation asset		29.0		18.6
Stored value card liability		99.1		63.4
Asset impairments		26.2		49.5
Tax credits		20.8		20.3
Stock-based compensation		135.5		131.5
Net operating losses		93.4		104.4
Litigation charge		931.0		1,002.0
Other		104.5		77.0
Total	$	1,790.0	$	1,706.9
Valuation allowance		(143.7)		(166.8)
Total deferred tax asset, net of valuation allowance	$	1,646.3	$	1,540.1
Deferred tax liabilities:				
Property, plant and equipment		(217.5)		(148.2)
Intangible assets and goodwill		(177.3)		(92.9)
Other		(114.1)		(89.4)
Total		(508.9)		(330.5)
Net deferred tax asset	$	1,137.4	$	1,209.6
Reported as:				
Current deferred income tax assets	$	381.7	$	317.4
Long-term deferred income tax assets		828.9		903.3
Current deferred income tax liabilities (included in Accrued liabilities)		(5.4)		(4.2)
Long-term deferred income tax liabilities (included in Other long-term liabilities)		(67.8)		(6.9)
Net deferred tax asset	$	1,137.4	$	1,209.6

The valuation allowance as of September 27, 2015 and September 28, 2014 is primarily related to net operating losses and other deferred tax assets of consolidated foreign subsidiaries. The net change in the total valuation allowance was a decrease of $23.1 million and an increase of $6.3 million for fiscal 2015 and 2014, respectively.

As of September 27, 2015, we had state tax credit carryforwards of $32.0 million with an expiration date of fiscal 2024 and foreign net operating loss carryforwards of $309.5 million, the majority of which has no expiration date.

Uncertain Tax Positions

As of September 27, 2015, we had $150.4 million of gross unrecognized tax benefits of which $101.7 million, if recognized, would affect our effective tax rate. We recognized expense of $0.7 million, expense of $5.9 million, and a benefit of $0.8 million of interest and penalties in income tax expense, prior to the benefit of the federal tax deduction, for fiscal 2015, 2014 and 2013, respectively. As of September 27, 2015 and September 28, 2014, we had accrued interest and penalties of $11.3 million and $10.6 million, respectively, before the benefit of the federal tax deduction, included within other long-term liabilities on our consolidated balance sheets.

The following table summarizes the activity related to our unrecognized tax benefits *(in millions)*:

	Sep 27, 2015	Sep 28, 2014	Sep 29, 2013
Beginning balance	$ 112.7	$ 88.8	$ 75.3
Increase related to prior year tax positions	7.9	1.4	8.9
Decrease related to prior year tax positions	(0.9)	(2.2)	(9.3)
Increase related to current year tax positions	32.0	26.7	19.3
Decrease related to current year tax positions	(0.6)	(1.9)	(0.4)
Decreases related to settlements with taxing authorities	(0.7)	(0.1)	—
Decreases related to lapsing of statute of limitations	—	—	(5.0)
Ending balance	$ 150.4	$ 112.7	$ 88.8

We are currently under examination, or may be subject to examination, by various jurisdictions inside and outside the U.S. as well as U.S. state and municipal taxing jurisdictions for fiscal years 2006 through 2014. We are no longer subject to U.S. federal or state examination for years prior to fiscal year 2010, with the exception of one state and one city. We are no longer subject to examination in any material international markets prior to 2006.

There is a reasonable possibility that $31.2 million of the currently remaining unrecognized tax benefits may be recognized by the end of fiscal 2016 as a result of a lapse of the statute of limitations and expected consent from taxing authorities.

Note 14: Earnings per Share

As discussed in Note 1, Summary of Significant Accounting Policies, on April 9, 2015, we effected a two-for-one stock split of our $0.001 par value common stock for shareholders of record as of March 30, 2015. All share and per-share data presented in this note has been retroactively adjusted to reflect this stock split.

Calculation of net earnings per common share ("EPS") — basic and diluted *(in millions, except EPS)*:

Fiscal Year Ended	Sep 27, 2015	Sep 28, 2014	Sep 29, 2013
Net earnings attributable to Starbucks	$ 2,757.4	$ 2,068.1	$ 8.3
Weighted average common shares outstanding (for basic calculation)	1,495.9	1,506.3	1,498.5
Dilutive effect of outstanding common stock options and RSUs	17.5	20.0	26.0
Weighted average common and common equivalent shares outstanding (for diluted calculation)	1,513.4	1,526.3	1,524.5
EPS — basic	$ 1.84	$ 1.37	$ 0.01
EPS — diluted	$ 1.82	$ 1.35	$ 0.01

Potential dilutive shares consist of the incremental common shares issuable upon the exercise of outstanding stock options (both vested and non-vested) and unvested RSUs, calculated using the treasury stock method. The calculation of dilutive shares outstanding excludes out-of-the-money stock options (i.e., such options' exercise prices were greater than the average market price of our common shares for the period) because their inclusion would have been antidilutive. We had no out-of-the-money stock options as of September 27, 2015 and September 29, 2013, respectively. There were 5.3 million out-of-the-money stock options as of September 28, 2014.

Note 15: Commitments and Contingencies

Legal Proceedings

On November 12, 2013, the arbitrator in our arbitration with Kraft Foods Global, Inc. (now known as Kraft Foods Group, Inc.) ("Kraft") ordered Starbucks to pay Kraft $2,227.5 million in damages plus prejudgment interest and attorneys' fees. We estimated prejudgment interest, which included an accrual through the estimated payment date, and attorneys' fees to be approximately $556.6 million. As a result, we recorded a litigation charge of $2,784.1 million in our fiscal 2013 operating results.

In the first quarter of fiscal 2014, Starbucks paid all amounts due to Kraft under the arbitration, including prejudgment interest and attorneys' fees, and fully extinguished the litigation charge liability. Of the $2,784.1 million litigation charge accrued in the fourth quarter of fiscal 2013, $2,763.9 million was paid and the remainder was released as a litigation credit to reflect a reduction to our estimated prejudgment interest payable as a result of paying our obligation earlier than anticipated.

Starbucks is party to various other legal proceedings arising in the ordinary course of business, including, at times, certain employment litigation cases that have been certified as class or collective actions, but is not currently a party to any legal proceeding that management believes could have a material adverse effect on our consolidated financial position, results of operations or cash flows.

Note 16: Segment Reporting

Our chief executive officer and chief operating officer comprise the Company's Chief Operating Decision Maker function ("CODM"). Segment information is prepared on the same basis that our CODM manages the segments, evaluates financial results, and makes key operating decisions.

We have four reportable operating segments: 1) Americas, inclusive of the U.S., Canada, and Latin America; 2) China/Asia Pacific ("CAP"); 3) Europe, Middle East, and Africa ("EMEA") and 4) Channel Development.

Americas, CAP, and EMEA operations sell coffee and other beverages, complementary food, packaged coffees, single-serve coffee products and a focused selection of merchandise through company-operated stores and licensed stores. Our Americas segment is our most mature business and has achieved significant scale. Certain markets within our CAP and EMEA operations are still in the early stages of development and require a more extensive support organization, relative to their current levels of revenue and operating income, than our Americas operations. The Americas and EMEA segments also include certain foodservice accounts, primarily in Canada and the U.K.

Channel Development operations sell a selection of packaged coffees and single-serve products, as well as a selection of premium Tazo® teas globally. Channel Development operations also produce and sell a variety of ready-to-drink beverages, such as Frappuccino® coffee drinks, Starbucks Doubleshot® espresso drinks, Starbucks Refreshers® beverages and chilled multi-serve beverages. The U.S. foodservice business, which is included in the Channel Development segment, sells coffee and other related products to institutional foodservice companies.

Consolidated revenue mix by product type *(in millions)*:

Fiscal Year Ended	Sep 27, 2015		Sep 28, 2014		Sep 29, 2013	
Beverage	$ 11,115.4	58%	$ 9,458.4	58%	$ 8,674.7	58%
Food	3,085.3	16%	2,505.2	15%	2,189.8	15%
Packaged and single-serve coffees and teas	2,619.9	14%	2,370.0	14%	2,206.5	15%
Other[1]	2,342.1	12%	2,114.2	13%	1,795.8	12%
Total	$ 19,162.7	100%	$ 16,447.8	100%	$ 14,866.8	100%

[1] "Other" primarily consists of royalty and licensing revenues, beverage-related ingredients, ready-to-drink beverages and serveware, among other items.

In fiscal 2014, we moved ready-to-drink beverage revenues from the "Food" category to the "Other" category and combined packaged and single-serve teas, which were previously included in the "Other" category, with packaged and single-serve coffees, which are now categorized as "Packaged and single-serve coffees and teas." Additionally, we revised our discount allocation methodology to more precisely allocate sales discounts to the various revenue product categories. None of these changes had a material impact on the composition of our revenue mix by product type.

Information by geographic area *(in millions)*:

Fiscal Year Ended	Sep 27, 2015	Sep 28, 2014	Sep 29, 2013
Net revenues:			
United States	$ 14,123.7	$ 12,590.6	$ 11,389.6
Other countries	5,039.0	3,857.2	3,477.2
Total	$ 19,162.7	$ 16,447.8	$ 14,866.8
Long-lived assets:			
United States	$ 5,468.1	$ 5,135.8	$ 4,641.3
Other countries	2,625.3	1,448.4	1,404.0
Total	$ 8,093.4	$ 6,584.2	$ 6,045.3

No customer accounts for 10% or more of our revenues. Revenues are shown based on the geographic location of our customers. Revenues from countries other than the U.S. consist primarily of revenues from Japan, Canada, China and the U.K., which together account for approximately 76% of net revenues from other countries for fiscal 2015.

Management evaluates the performance of its operating segments based on net revenues and operating income. The accounting policies of the operating segments are the same as those described in Note 1, Summary of Significant Accounting Policies. Operating income represents earnings before other income and expenses and income taxes. Management does not evaluate the performance of its operating segments using asset measures. The identifiable assets by segment disclosed in this note are those assets specifically identifiable within each segment and include cash and cash equivalents, net property, plant and equipment, equity and cost investments, goodwill, and other intangible assets. Assets not identified by reportable operating segment below are corporate assets and are primarily comprised of cash and cash equivalents available for general corporate purposes, investments, assets of the corporate headquarters and roasting facilities, and inventory.

The table below presents financial information for our reportable operating segments and All Other Segments for the years ended September 27, 2015, September 28, 2014, and September 29, 2013.

(in millions)	Americas	China / Asia Pacific	EMEA	Channel Development	All Other Segments	Segment Total
Fiscal 2015						
Total net revenues	$ 13,293.4	$ 2,395.9	$ 1,216.7	$ 1,730.9	$ 525.8	$ 19,162.7
Depreciation and amortization expenses	522.3	150.7	52.0	2.7	16.3	744.0
Income from equity investees	—	119.6	3.1	127.2	—	249.9
Operating income/(loss)	3,223.3	500.5	168.2	653.9	(24.8)	4,521.1
Total assets	2,726.7	2,230.5	749.1	87.3	1,785.3	7,578.9
Fiscal 2014						
Total net revenues	$ 11,980.5	$ 1,129.6	$ 1,294.8	$ 1,546.0	$ 496.9	$ 16,447.8
Depreciation and amortization expenses	469.5	46.1	59.4	1.8	15.2	592.0
Income from equity investees	—	164.0	3.7	100.6	—	268.3
Operating income/(loss)	2,809.0	372.5	119.2	557.2	(26.8)	3,831.1
Total assets	2,521.4	939.8	663.0	84.6	825.2	5,034.0
Fiscal 2013						
Total net revenues	$ 11,000.8	$ 917.0	$ 1,160.0	$ 1,398.9	$ 390.1	$ 14,866.8
Depreciation and amortization expenses	429.3	33.8	55.5	1.1	11.7	531.4
Income from equity investees	2.4	152.0	0.4	96.6	—	251.4
Operating income/(loss)	2,365.2	321.2	64.2	415.5	(34.5)	3,131.6
Total assets	2,323.4	805.0	510.6	89.2	821.1	4,549.3

The following table reconciles total segment operating income in the table above to consolidated earnings/(loss) before income taxes *(in millions)*:

Fiscal Year Ended	Sep 27, 2015	Sep 28, 2014	Sep 29, 2013
Total segment operating income	$ 4,521.1	$ 3,831.1	$ 3,131.6
Unallocated corporate operating expenses [1]	(920.1)	(750.0)	(3,457.0)
Consolidated operating income/(loss)	3,601.0	3,081.1	(325.4)
Gain resulting from acquisition of joint venture	390.6	—	—
Loss on extinguishment of debt	(61.1)	—	—
Interest income and other, net	43.0	142.7	123.6
Interest expense	(70.5)	(64.1)	(28.1)
Earnings/(loss) before income taxes	$ 3,903.0	$ 3,159.7	$ (229.9)

[1] Fiscal 2013 includes a pretax charge of $2,784.1 million resulting from the litigation charge we recorded associated with the conclusion of our arbitration with Kraft.

Note 17: Selected Quarterly Financial Information *(unaudited; in millions, except EPS)*

	First Quarter	Second Quarter	Third Quarter	Fourth Quarter	Full Year
Fiscal 2015:					
Net revenues	$ 4,803.2	$ 4,563.5	$ 4,881.2	$ 4,914.8	$ 19,162.7
Operating income	915.5	777.5	938.6	969.4	3,601.0
Net earnings attributable to Starbucks	983.1	494.9	626.7	652.5	2,757.4
EPS — diluted [1]	0.65	0.33	0.41	0.43	1.82
Fiscal 2014:					
Net revenues	$ 4,239.6	$ 3,873.8	$ 4,153.7	$ 4,180.8	$ 16,447.8
Operating income	813.5	644.1	768.5	854.9	3,081.1
Net earnings attributable to Starbucks	540.7	427.0	512.6	587.9	2,068.1
EPS — diluted [1]	0.35	0.28	0.34	0.39	1.35

[1] As discussed in Note 1, Summary of Significant Accounting Policies, on April 9, 2015, we effected a two-for-one stock split of our $0.001 par value common stock for shareholders of record as of March 30, 2015. All per-share data presented in this note has been retroactively adjusted to reflect this stock split.

Note 18: Subsequent Events

Subsequent to our fiscal year end, the European Commission has concluded that decisions by the tax authorities in the Netherlands with regards to the corporate income tax paid by one of our subsidiaries did not comply with European Union rules on state aid. Based on this decision, which covers a 7-year period from fiscal 2008 to fiscal 2014, we estimate the amount of assessed past taxes to be no more than €30 million, including interest, which equates to approximately $32 million with euro converted into U.S. dollars at a reference conversion rate of 1.075 EUR to USD. The exposure amount is not material and we are currently evaluating this decision, including any impact to our fiscal 2016 tax provisions.

Management's Discussion and Analysis for Starbucks Corporation

Appendix B can be found online at the book's companion website at www.cengagebrain.com

Financial Statement Analysis Package (FSAP)

OUTPUT FROM FSAP FOR STARBUCKS CORPORATION

The Financial Statement Analysis Package (**FSAP**) that accompanies this text is a user-friendly, adaptable series of Excel®-based spreadsheet templates. FSAP enables the user to manually input financial statement data for a firm and then perform financial statement analysis, forecasting, and valuation. FSAP contains five spreadsheets: Data, Analysis, Forecasts, Forecast Development, and Valuation.

Appendix C presents the output of these spreadsheets using the data for Starbucks Corporation. The output includes the financial statement data for the years 2010–2015, the profitability and risk ratios for the years 2011–2015, financial statement forecasts, and a variety of valuation models applied to the forecasted data for Starbucks Corporation.

FSAP contains a series of User Guides that provide line-by-line instructions on how to use FSAP. You can download a blank FSAP template as well as the FSAP output for Starbucks Corporation from this book's companion website, which you'll find by going to www.cengagebrain.com and searching for this book by its author or title. FSAP data files also are available for various problems and cases in the book. The FSAP icon has been used throughout the book to denote potential applications for FSAP.

Data Spreadsheet

Analyst Name:	Wahlen, Baginski & Bradshaw					
Company Name:	Starbucks Corporation					
Year (Most recent in far right column.)	**2010**	**2011**	**2012**	**2013**	**2014**	**2015**
BALANCE SHEET DATA						
Assets:						
Cash and cash equivalents	1,164.0	1,148.1	1,188.6	2,575.7	1,708.4	1,530.1
Short-term investments	285.7	902.6	848.4	658.1	135.4	81.3
Accounts and notes receivable—net	302.7	386.5	485.9	561.4	631.0	719.0
Inventories	543.3	965.8	1,241.5	1,111.2	1,090.9	1,306.4
Prepaid expenses and other current assets	156.5	161.5	196.5	287.7	285.6	334.2
Deferred income taxes—current	304	230	239	277	317	382
Other current assets (1)						
Other current assets (2)						
Current Assets	**2,756**	**3,795**	**4,200**	**5,471**	**4,169**	**4,353**
Long-term investments	191.8	107.0	116.0	58.3	318.4	312.5
Equity and cost investments	341.5	372.3	459.9	496.5	514.9	352.0
Property, plant, and equipment—at cost	5,888.7	6,163.1	6,903.1	7,782.1	8,581.1	9,641.8
<Accumulated depreciation>	(3,472.2)	(3,808.1)	(4,244.2)	(4,581.6)	(5,062.1)	(5,553.5)
Deferred income taxes—noncurrent	195.3	156.3	97.3	967.0	903.3	828.9
Other assets	151.2	141.4	144.7	185.3	198.9	415.9
Other intangible assets	71	112	144	275	274	520
Goodwill	262	322	399	863	856	1,575
Total Assets	**6,386**	**7,360**	**8,219**	**11,517**	**10,753**	**12,446**
Liabilities and Equity:						
Accounts payable	283	540	398	492	534	684
Accrued liabilities	936	941	1,134	1,269	1,514	1,761
Notes payable and short-term debt						
Current maturities of long-term debt						
Deferred tax liabilities—current						
Insurance reserves	146	146	168	179	196	225
Stored value card liability	414	449	510	654	795	984
Accrued litigation charge				2,784		
Current Liabilities	**1,779**	**2,076**	**2,210**	**5,377**	**3,039**	**3,654**
Long-term debt	549	550	550	1,299	2,048	2,348
Long-term accrued liabilities	375	348	345	358	392	625
Deferred tax liabilities—noncurrent						
Other noncurrent liabilities (1)						
Other noncurrent liabilities (2)						
Total Liabilities	**2,704**	**2,973**	**3,105**	**7,034**	**5,479**	**6,626**

Data Spreadsheet (Continued)

Year (Most recent in far right column.)	2010	2011	2012	2013	2014	2015
Preferred stock						
Common stock + Additional paid in capital	146	41	40	283	40	43
Retained earnings <deficit>	3,471	4,297	5,046	4,130	5,207	5,975
Accum. other comprehensive income <loss>	57	46	23	67	25	(199)
<Treasury stock> and other equity adjustments						
Total Common Shareholders' Equity	**3,675**	**4,385**	**5,109**	**4,480**	**5,272**	**5,818**
Noncontrolling interests	8	2	6	2	2	2
Total Equity	**3,682**	**4,387**	**5,115**	**4,482**	**5,274**	**5,820**
Total Liabilities and Equity	**6,386**	**7,360**	**8,219**	**11,517**	**10,753**	**12,446**

INCOME STATEMENT DATA	2010	2011	2012	2013	2014	2015
Revenues	10,707	11,700	13,300	14,867	16,448	19,163
<Cost of sales and occupancy expense>	(4,459)	(4,949)	(5,813)	(6,382)	(6,859)	(7,788)
Gross Profit	**6,249**	**6,751**	**7,486**	**8,485**	**9,589**	**11,375**
<Store operating expenses>	(3,551)	(3,665)	(3,918)	(4,286)	(4,638)	(5,411)
<Other operating expenses>	(293)	(402)	(430)	(432)	(457)	(522)
<Depreciation and amortization>	(510)	(523)	(550)	(621)	(710)	(894)
<General and administrative expenses>	(570)	(636)	(801)	(938)	(991)	(1,197)
Other operating expenses (1)						
Other operating expenses (2)						
Income from equity investees	148	174	211	251	268	250
Non-recurring operating gains <losses>	(53)	30		(2,784)	20	
Operating Profit	**1,419**	**1,729**	**1,997**	**(325)**	**3,081**	**3,601**
Interest income	50	116	94	124	143	43
<Interest expense>	(33)	(33)	(33)	(28)	(64)	(71)
Income <Loss> from equity affiliates						
Other income or gains <Other expenses or losses>						330
Income before Tax	**1,437**	**1,811**	**2,059**	**(230)**	**3,160**	**3,903**
<Income tax expense>	(489)	(563)	(674)	239	(1,092)	(1,144)
Income <Loss> from discontinued operations						
Extraordinary gains <losses>						
Changes in accounting principles						
Net Income	**948**	**1,248**	**1,385**	**9**	**2,068**	**2,759**
Net income attributable to noncontrolling interests	(3)	(2)	(1)	(1)	0	(2)
Net income attributable to common shareholders	**946**	**1,246**	**1,384**	**8**	**2,068**	**2,757**
Net income (enter reported amount as a check)	946	1,246	1,384	8	2,068	2,757
Other comprehensive income items	(8)	(11)	(24)	44	(41)	(196)
Comprehensive Income	**940**	**1,237**	**1,361**	**53**	**2,026**	**2,564**

(Continued)

Data Spreadsheet (Continued)

Year (Most recent in far right column.)	2010	2011	2012	2013	2014	2015
STATEMENT OF CASH FLOWS DATA						
Net Income	948	1,248	1,385	9	2,068	2,759
Add back depreciation and amortization expenses	541	550	581	656	748	934
Add back stock-based compensation expense	114	145	154	142	183	210
Deferred income taxes	(42)	106	61	(1,046)	10	21
\<Income from equity affiliates, net of dividends\>	(17)	(33)	(49)	(56)	(44)	(42)
\<Increase\> Decrease in accounts receivable	(33)	(89)	(90)	(68)	(80)	(83)
\<Increase\> Decrease in inventories	123	(422)	(273)	153	14	(208)
\<Increase\> Decrease in prepaid expenses						
\<Increase\> Decrease in other current assets						
\<Increase\> Decrease in other noncurrent assets						
Increase \<Decrease\> in accounts payable	(4)	228	(105)	89	60	138
Increase \<Decrease\> in income taxes payable				298	310	88
Increase \<Decrease\> in other current liabilities	(19)	(82)	24	47	104	124
Increase \<Decrease\> in deferred revenues	24	36	61	140	141	170
Other addbacks to \<subtractions from\> net income	52	(52)	24	2,469	(2,912)	(412)
Other operating cash flows	17	(23)	(20)	76	5	50
Net CF from Operating Activities	**1,705**	**1,612**	**1,750**	**2,908**	**608**	**3,749**
Proceeds from sales of property, plant, and equipment						
\<Property, plant, and equipment acquired\>	(441)	(415)	(851)	(1,151)	(1,161)	(1,304)
\<Increase\> Decrease in marketable securities	(339)	(536)	48	254	258	52
Investments sold						
\<Investments acquired\>	(12)	(56)	(129)	(610)	0	(284)
Payments for acquisitions of intangible assets						
Other investment transactions	2	(13)	(42)	96	85	16
Net CF from Investing Activities	**(790)**	**(1,020)**	**(974)**	**(1,411)**	**(818)**	**(1,520)**
Increase in short-term borrowing		31	(31)			
\<Decrease in short-term borrowing\>						
Increase in long-term borrowing				715	749	238
\<Decrease in long-term borrowing\>						
Issue of capital stock	133	250	237	247	140	192
Proceeds from stock option exercises	32	89	111	137	37	57
\<Share repurchases\>	(286)	(556)	(549)	(588)	(759)	(1,436)
\<Dividend payments\>	(171)	(390)	(513)	(629)	(783)	(929)
Other financing transactions (1)	(54)	(33)	(1)	10	(7)	(379)
Other financing transactions (2)						
Net CF from Financing Activities	**(346)**	**(608)**	**(746)**	**(108)**	**(623)**	**(2,257)**
Effects of exchange rate changes on cash	(5)	(1)	10	(2)	(34)	(151)
Net Change in Cash	**564**	**(16)**	**40**	**1,387**	**(867)**	**(178)**
Cash and cash equivalents, beginning of year	600	1,164	1,148	1,189	2,576	1,708
Cash and cash equivalents, end of year	1,164	1,148	1,189	2,576	1,708	1,530

Data Spreadsheet (Continued)

Year (Most recent in far right column.)	2010	2011	2012	2013	2014	2015
SUPPLEMENTAL DATA						
Statutory tax rate	35.0%	35.0%	35.0%	35.0%	35.0%	35.0%
Average tax rate implied from income statement data	34.0%	31.1%	32.8%	103.8%	34.6%	29.3%
After-tax effects of nonrecurring and unusual items on net income	(34)	20	0	(1,810)	13	214
Depreciation expense	540	548	576	648	740	884
Preferred stock dividends (total, if any)						
Common shares outstanding	1,480	1,491	1,499	1,506	1,499	1,485
Earnings per share (basic)	0.64	0.84	0.92	0.01	1.37	1.84
Common dividends per share	0.12	0.26	0.34	0.42	0.52	0.63
Share price at fiscal year end	12.85	18.10	25.08	38.03	37.73	56.84

FINANCIAL DATA CHECKS						
Assets − Liabilities − Equity	0	0	0	0	0	0
Net Income (computed) − Net Income (reported)	0	0	0	0	0	0
Cash Changes		0	0	0	0	0

Analysis Spreadsheet

| Analyst Name: | Wahlen, Baginski & Bradshaw |
| Company Name: | Starbucks Corporation |

DATA CHECKS

Assets – Liabilities – Equity	0	0	0	0	0
Net Income (computed) – Net Income (reported)	0	0	0	0	0
Cash Changes		0	0	0	0

PROFITABILITY FACTORS:

Year	2011	2012	2013	2014	2015
RETURN ON ASSETS (based on reported amounts):					
Profit Margin for ROA	10.9%	10.6%	0.2%	12.8%	14.6%
× Asset Turnover	1.7	1.7	1.5	1.5	1.7
= Return on Assets	18.5%	18.0%	0.3%	18.9%	24.2%
RETURN ON ASSETS (excluding the effects of nonrecurring items):					
Profit Margin for ROA	10.7%	10.6%	12.4%	12.7%	13.5%
× Asset Turnover	1.7	1.7	1.5	1.5	1.7
= Return on Assets	18.2%	18.0%	18.6%	18.8%	22.3%
RETURN ON COMMON EQUITY (based on reported amounts):					
Profit Margin for ROCE	10.6%	10.4%	0.1%	12.6%	14.4%
× Asset Turnover	1.7	1.7	1.5	1.5	1.7
× Capital Structure Leverage	1.7	1.6	2.1	2.3	2.1
= Return on Common Equity	30.9%	29.2%	0.2%	42.4%	49.7%
RETURN ON COMMON EQUITY (excluding the effects of nonrecurring items):					
Profit Margin for ROCE	10.5%	10.4%	12.2%	12.5%	13.3%
× Asset Turnover	1.7	1.7	1.5	1.5	1.7
× Capital Structure Leverage	1.7	1.6	2.1	2.3	2.1
= Return on Common Equity	30.4%	29.2%	37.9%	42.1%	45.9%
OPERATING PERFORMANCE:					
Gross Profit / Revenues	57.7%	56.3%	57.1%	58.3%	59.4%
Operating Profit / Revenues	14.8%	15.0%	(2.2%)	18.7%	18.8%
Net Income / Revenues	10.6%	10.4%	0.1%	12.6%	14.4%
Comprehensive Income / Revenues	10.6%	10.2%	0.4%	12.3%	13.4%
PERSISTENT OPERATING PERFORMANCE (excluding the effects of nonrecurring items):					
Persistent Operating Profit / Revenues	14.5%	15.0%	16.5%	18.6%	18.8%
Persistent Net Income / Revenues	10.5%	10.4%	12.2%	12.5%	13.3%
GROWTH RATES:					
Revenue Growth	9.3%	13.7%	11.8%	10.6%	16.5%
Net Income Growth	31.7%	11.1%	(99.4%)	24816.9%	33.3%
Persistent Net Income Growth	25.1%	12.9%	31.4%	13.0%	23.8%

Analysis Spreadsheet (Continued)

PROFITABILITY FACTORS:

Year	2011	2012	2013	2014	2015
OPERATING CONTROL:					
Gross Profit Control Index	98.9%	97.6%	101.4%	102.2%	101.8%
Operating Profit Contol Index	111.4%	101.7%	(14.6%)	(855.9%)	100.3%
Net Profit Contol Index	120.4%	97.6%	0.6%	21238.0%	114.5%
Profit Margin Decomposition:					
Gross Profit Margin	57.7%	56.3%	57.1%	58.3%	59.4%
Operating Profit Index	25.6%	26.7%	(3.8%)	32.1%	31.7%
Leverage Index	104.8%	103.1%	70.7%	102.6%	108.4%
Tax Index	68.9%	67.2%	(3.8%)	65.4%	70.7%
Net Profit Margin	10.7%	10.4%	0.1%	12.6%	14.4%
Comprehensive Income Performance:					
Comprehensive Income Index	99.1%	98.3%	597.7%	98.0%	92.9%
Comprehensive Income Margin	10.6%	10.2%	0.4%	12.3%	13.4%

RISK FACTORS:

Year	2011	2012	2013	2014	2015
LIQUIDITY:					
Current Ratio	1.83	1.90	1.02	1.37	1.19
Quick Ratio	1.17	1.14	0.71	0.81	0.64
Operating Cash Flow to Current Liabilities	83.7%	81.7%	76.7%	14.4%	112.0%
ASSET TURNOVER:					
Cash Turnover	10.1	11.4	7.9	7.7	11.8
Days Sales Held in Cash	36.1	32.1	46.2	47.5	30.8
Accounts Receivable Turnover	34.0	30.5	28.4	27.6	28.4
Days Receivables Held	11	12	13	13	13
Inventory Turnover	6.6	5.3	5.4	6.2	6.5
Days Inventory Held	56	69	67	59	56
Accounts Payable Turnover	13.1	13.0	14.1	13.3	13.1
Days Payables Held	28	28	26	27	28
Net Working Capital Days	38	53	54	44	41
Revenues / Average Net Fixed Assets	4.9	5.3	5.1	4.9	5.0
CAPEX Index	0.8	1.5	1.8	1.6	1.5
Expected Useful Life of PPE for Depreciation	11.0	11.3	11.3	11.1	10.3
Expected Remaining Useful Life of PPE	4.3	4.6	4.9	4.8	4.6
SOLVENCY:					
Total Liabilities / Total Assets	40.4%	37.8%	61.1%	51.0%	53.2%
Total Liabilities / Total Equity	67.8%	60.7%	156.9%	103.9%	113.9%
LT Debt / LT Capital	11.1%	9.7%	22.5%	28.0%	28.7%

(Continued)

Analysis Spreadsheet (Continued)

RISK FACTORS:

Year	2011	2012	2013	2014	2015
LT Debt / Total Equity	12.5%	10.7%	29.0%	38.8%	40.3%
Operating Cash Flow to Total Liabilities	56.8%	57.6%	57.4%	9.7%	61.9%
Interest Coverage Ratio (reported amounts)	55.4	64.0	(7.2)	50.3	56.4
Interest Coverage ratio (recurring amounts)	54.5	64.0	91.9	50.0	51.7
Bankruptcy Predictors:					
Altman Z Score	8.96	10.87	6.63	9.52	10.98
Bankruptcy Probability	0.00%	0.00%	0.00%	0.00%	0.00%
Earnings Manipulation Predictors:					
Beneish Earnings Manipulation Score	(2.44)	(2.39)	(3.60)	(1.66)	(2.49)
Earnings Manipulation Probability	0.73%	0.84%	0.02%	4.88%	0.64%

DIVIDEND and STOCK MARKET-BASED RATIOS:

Year	2011	2012	2013	2014	2015
Stock Returns	42.9%	40.4%	53.3%	0.6%	52.3%
Price-Earnings Ratio (reported amounts)	21.7	27.2	3802.5	27.5	30.9
Price-Earnings Ratio (recurring amounts)	22.0	27.2	31.4	27.7	33.5
Market Value to Book Value Ratio	6.2	7.4	12.8	10.7	14.5
Common Dividends per Share	$0.26	$0.34	$0.42	$0.52	$0.63
Common Dividend Payout (% of Net Income)	(31.3%)	(37.1%)	(7577.1%)	(37.9%)	(33.7%)
Common Dividend Yield (% of Share Price)	1.4%	1.4%	1.1%	1.4%	1.1%

INCOME STATEMENT ITEMS AS A PERCENT OF REVENUES:

Year	2011	2012	2013	2014	2015
Revenues	100.0%	100.0%	100.0%	100.0%	100.0%
<Cost of sales and occupancy expense>	(42.3%)	(43.7%)	(42.9%)	(41.7%)	(40.6%)
Gross Profit	57.7%	56.3%	57.1%	58.3%	59.4%
<Store operating expenses>	(31.3%)	(29.5%)	(28.8%)	(28.2%)	(28.2%)
<Other operating expenses>	(3.4%)	(3.2%)	(2.9%)	(2.8%)	(2.7%)
<Depreciation and amortization>	(4.5%)	(4.1%)	(4.2%)	(4.3%)	(4.7%)
<General and administrative expenses>	(5.4%)	(6.0%)	(6.3%)	(6.0%)	(6.2%)
Other operating expenses (1)					
Other operating expenses (2)					
Income from equity investees	1.5%	1.6%	1.7%	1.6%	1.3%
Non-recurring operating gains <losses>	0.3%		(18.7%)	0.1%	
Operating Profit	14.8%	15.0%	(2.2%)	18.7%	18.8%
Interest income	1.0%	0.7%	0.8%	0.9%	0.2%
<Interest expense>	(0.3%)	(0.2%)	(0.2%)	(0.4%)	(0.4%)
Income <Loss> from equity affiliates					
Other income or gains <Other expenses or losses>					1.7%
Income before Tax	15.5%	15.5%	(1.5%)	19.2%	20.4%
<Income tax expense>	(4.8%)	(5.1%)	1.6%	(6.6%)	(6.0%)
Income <Loss> from discontinued operations					
Extraordinary gains <losses>					
Changes in accounting principles					

Analysis Spreadsheet (Continued)

INCOME STATEMENT ITEMS AS A PERCENT OF REVENUES:

Year	2011	2012	2013	2014	2015
Net Income	10.7%	10.4%	0.1%	12.6%	14.4%
Net income attributable to noncontrolling interests	0.0%	0.0%	0.0%	0.0%	0.0%
Net Income attributable to common shareholders	10.6%	10.4%	0.1%	12.6%	14.4%
Other comprehensive income items	(0.1%)	(0.2%)	0.3%	(0.3%)	(1.0%)
Comprehensive Income	10.6%	10.2%	0.4%	12.3%	13.4%

INCOME STATEMENT ITEMS: GROWTH RATES

Year	2011	2012	2013	2014	2015	
			YEAR TO YEAR GROWTH RATES			COMPOUND GROWTH RATE
Revenues	9.3%	13.7%	11.8%	10.6%	16.5%	12.3%
<Cost of sales and occupancy expense>	11.0%	17.5%	9.8%	7.5%	13.5%	11.8%
Gross Profit	8.0%	10.9%	13.3%	13.0%	18.6%	12.7%
<Store operating expenses>	3.2%	6.9%	9.4%	8.2%	16.7%	8.8%
<Other operating expenses>	37.1%	6.9%	0.4%	5.9%	14.2%	12.2%
<Depreciation and amortization>	2.5%	5.2%	12.9%	14.2%	26.0%	11.9%
<General and administrative expenses>	11.7%	26.0%	17.1%	5.7%	20.7%	16.0%
Other operating expenses (1)						
Other operating expenses (2)						
Income from equity investees	17.3%	21.3%	19.3%	6.7%	(6.9%)	11.0%
Non-recurring operating gains <losses>	(157.0%)	(100.0%)		(100.7%)	(100.0%)	(100.0%)
Operating Profit	21.8%	15.6%	(116.3%)	(1046.9%)	16.9%	20.5%
Interest income	130.4%	(18.6%)	30.9%	15.5%	(69.9%)	(3.1%)
<Interest expense>	1.8%	(1.8%)	(14.1%)	128.1%	10.0%	16.6%
Income <Loss> from equity affiliates						
Other income or gains <Other expenses or losses>						
Income before Tax	26.0%	13.7%	(111.2%)	(1474.4%)	23.5%	22.1%
<Income tax expense>	15.2%	19.8%	(135.4%)	(557.5%)	4.7%	18.5%
Income <Loss> from discontinued operations						
Extraordinary gains <losses>						
Changes in accounting principles						
Net Income	31.6%	11.0%	(99.4%)	23396.6%	33.4%	23.8%
Net income attributable to noncontrolling interests	(14.8%)	(60.9%)	(44.4%)	(180.0%)	(575.0%)	(6.8%)
Net Income attributable to common shareholders	31.7%	11.1%	(99.4%)	24816.9%	33.3%	23.9%
Other comprehensive income items	32.9%	116.5%	(285.6%)	(194.3%)	373.4%	88.6%
Comprehensive Income	31.6%	10.0%	(96.1%)	3752.5%	26.5%	22.2%

(Continued)

Analysis Spreadsheet (Continued)

COMMON SIZE BALANCE SHEET—AS A PERCENT OF TOTAL ASSETS

Year	2011	2012	2013	2014	2015
Assets:					
Cash and cash equivalents	15.6%	14.5%	22.4%	15.9%	12.3%
Short-term investments	12.3%	10.3%	5.7%	1.3%	0.7%
Accounts and notes receivable—net	5.3%	5.9%	4.9%	5.9%	5.8%
Inventories	13.1%	15.1%	9.6%	10.1%	10.5%
Prepaid expenses and other current assets	2.2%	2.4%	2.5%	2.7%	2.7%
Deferred income taxes—current	3.1%	2.9%	2.4%	3.0%	3.1%
Other current assets (1)					
Other current assets (2)					
Current Assets	**51.6%**	**51.1%**	**47.5%**	**38.8%**	**35.0%**
Long-term investments	1.5%	1.4%	0.5%	3.0%	2.5%
Equity and cost investments	5.1%	5.6%	4.3%	4.8%	2.8%
Property, plant, and equipment—at cost	83.7%	84.0%	67.6%	79.8%	77.5%
<Accumulated depreciation>	(51.7%)	(51.6%)	(39.8%)	(47.1%)	(44.6%)
Deferred income taxes—noncurrent	2.1%	1.2%	8.4%	8.4%	6.7%
Other assets	1.9%	1.8%	1.6%	1.8%	3.3%
Other intangible assets	1.5%	1.7%	2.4%	2.5%	4.2%
Goodwill	4.4%	4.9%	7.5%	8.0%	12.7%
Total Assets	**100.0%**	**100.0%**	**100.0%**	**100.0%**	**100.0%**
Liabilities and Equity:					
Accounts payable	7.3%	4.8%	4.3%	5.0%	5.5%
Accrued liabilities	12.8%	13.8%	11.0%	14.1%	14.1%
Notes payable and short-term debt					
Current maturities of long-term debt					
Deferred tax liabilities—current					
Insurance reserves	2.0%	2.0%	1.5%	1.8%	1.8%
Stored value card liability	6.1%	6.2%	5.7%	7.4%	7.9%
Accrued litigation charge			24.2%		
Current Liabilities	**28.2%**	**26.9%**	**46.7%**	**28.3%**	**29.4%**
Long-term debt	7.5%	6.7%	11.3%	19.0%	18.9%
Long-term accrued liabilities	4.7%	4.2%	3.1%	3.6%	5.0%
Deferred tax liabilities—noncurrent					
Other noncurrent liabilities (1)					
Other noncurrent liabilities (2)					
Total Liabilities	**40.4%**	**37.8%**	**61.1%**	**51.0%**	**53.2%**
Preferred stock					
Common stock + Additional paid in capital	0.6%	0.5%	2.5%	0.4%	0.3%
Retained earnings <deficit>	58.4%	61.4%	35.9%	48.4%	48.0%
Accum. other comprehensive income <loss>	0.6%	0.3%	0.6%	0.2%	(1.6%)
<Treasury stock> and other equity adjustments					

Analysis Spreadsheet (Continued)

COMMON SIZE BALANCE SHEET—AS A PERCENT OF TOTAL ASSETS

Year	2011	2012	2013	2014	2015
Total Common Shareholders' Equity	59.6%	62.2%	38.9%	49.0%	46.7%
Noncontrolling interests	0.0%	0.1%	0.0%	0.0%	0.0%
Total Equity	59.6%	62.2%	38.9%	49.0%	46.8%
Total Liabilities and Equity	100.0%	100.0%	100.0%	100.0%	100.0%

BALANCE SHEET ITEMS: GROWTH RATES

Year	2011	2012	2013	2014	2015	
	YEAR TO YEAR GROWTH RATES					COMPOUND GROWTH RATE
Assets:						
Cash and cash equivalents	(1.4%)	3.5%	116.7%	(33.7%)	(10.4%)	5.6%
Short-term investments	215.9%	(6.0%)	(22.4%)	(79.4%)	(40.0%)	(22.2%)
Accounts and notes receivable—net	27.7%	25.7%	15.5%	12.4%	13.9%	18.9%
Inventories	77.8%	28.5%	(10.5%)	(1.8%)	19.8%	19.2%
Prepaid expenses and other current assets	3.2%	21.7%	46.4%	(0.7%)	17.0%	16.4%
Deferred income taxes—current	(24.3%)	3.6%	16.2%	14.5%	20.3%	4.6%
Other current assets (1)						
Other current assets (2)						
Current Assets	37.7%	10.7%	30.3%	(23.8%)	4.4%	9.6%
Long-term investments	(44.2%)	8.4%	(49.7%)	446.1%	(1.9%)	(1.8%)
Equity and cost investments	9.0%	23.5%	8.0%	3.7%	(31.6%)	(43.1%)
Property, plant, and equipment—at cost	4.7%	12.0%	12.7%	10.3%	12.4%	(222.7%)
<Accumulated depreciation>	9.7%	11.5%	7.9%	10.5%	9.7%	(295.3%)
Deferred income taxes—noncurrent	(20.0%)	(37.7%)	893.8%	(6.6%)	(8.2%)	40.5%
Other assets	(6.5%)	2.3%	28.1%	7.3%	109.1%	42.5%
Other intangible assets	58.1%	28.4%	91.2%	(0.5%)	90.3%	14.7%
Goodwill	22.6%	24.1%	116.2%	(0.8%)	84.0%	(24.4%)
Total Assets	15.3%	11.7%	40.1%	(6.6%)	15.7%	14.3%
Liabilities and Equity:						
Accounts payable	91.1%	(26.3%)	23.5%	8.5%	28.2%	19.3%
Accrued liabilities	0.5%	20.5%	12.0%	19.3%	16.3%	13.5%
Notes payable and short-term debt						
Current maturities of long-term debt						
Deferred tax liabilities—current						
Insurance reserves	(0.4%)	15.2%	6.4%	9.9%	14.6%	9.0%
Stored value card liability	8.5%	13.6%	28.1%	21.5%	23.8%	18.9%
Accrued litigation charge				(100.0%)		

(Continued)

Analysis Spreadsheet (Continued)

BALANCE SHEET ITEMS: GROWTH RATES

Year	2011	2012	2013	2014	2015	COMPOUND GROWTH RATE
	YEAR TO YEAR GROWTH RATES					
Current Liabilities	**16.7%**	**6.5%**	**143.3%**	**(43.5%)**	**20.2%**	**15.5%**
Long-term debt	0.0%	0.0%	136.4%	57.6%	14.6%	33.7%
Long-term accrued liabilities	(7.3%)	(0.7%)	3.6%	9.6%	59.4%	10.8%
Deferred tax liabilities—noncurrent						
Other noncurrent liabilities (1)						
Other noncurrent liabilities (2)						
Total Liabilities	**10.0%**	**4.4%**	**126.6%**	**(22.1%)**	**20.9%**	**19.6%**
Preferred stock						
Common stock + Additional paid in capital	(71.8%)	(2.7%)	605.5%	(85.8%)	6.2%	(21.9%)
Retained earnings <deficit>	23.8%	17.4%	(18.2%)	26.1%	14.8%	11.5%
Accum. other comprehensive income <loss>	(19.1%)	(51.0%)	195.2%	(62.2%)	(888.1%)	(228.4%)
<Treasury stock> and other equity adjustments						
Total Common Shareholders' Equity	**19.3%**	**16.5%**	**(12.3%)**	**17.7%**	**10.4%**	**9.6%**
Noncontrolling interests	(68.4%)	129.2%	(61.8%)	(19.0%)	5.9%	(25.0%)
Total Equity	**19.1%**	**16.6%**	**(12.4%)**	**17.7%**	**10.4%**	**9.6%**
Total Liabilities and Equity	**15.3%**	**11.7%**	**40.1%**	**(6.6%)**	**15.7%**	**14.3%**

RETURN ON ASSETS ANALYSIS (excluding the effects of non-recurring items)

Level 1	RETURN ON ASSETS					
	2013	2014	2015			
	18.6%	18.8%	22.3%			

Level 2	PROFIT MARGIN FOR ROA			ASSET TURNOVER		
	2013	2014	2015	2013	2014	2015
	12.4%	12.7%	13.5%	1.5	1.5	1.7

Level 3	2013	2014	2015	2013	2014	2015	
Revenues	100.0%	100.0%	100.0%	28.4	27.6	28.4	Turnovers:
<Cost of sales and occupancy expense>	(42.9%)	(41.7%)	(40.6%)	5.4	6.2	6.5	Receivables Inventory
Gross Profit	57.1%	58.3%	59.4%	5.1	4.9	5.0	Fixed Assets
<Store Operating Expenses>	(28.8%)	(28.2%)	(28.2%)				
Operating Profit	(2.2%)	18.7%	18.8%				
Income before Tax	(1.5%)	19.2%	20.4%				
<Income tax expense>	1.6%	(6.6%)	(6.0%)				
Profit Margin for ROA*	12.4%	12.7%	13.5%				

*Amounts do not sum.

Analysis Spreadsheet (Continued)

RETURN ON COMMON SHAREHOLDERS' EQUITY ANALYSIS (excluding the effects of non-recurring items)

	RETURN ON COMMON SHAREHOLDERS' EQUITY		
	2013	2014	2015
	37.9%	42.1%	45.9%
PROFIT MARGIN FOR ROCE	12.2%	12.5%	13.3%
ASSET TURNOVER	1.5	1.5	1.7
CAPITAL STRUCTURE LEVERAGE	2.1	2.3	2.1

RETURN ON COMMON SHAREHOLDERS' EQUITY ANALYSIS: Alternative Approach to Disaggregation

	RETURN ON COMMON SHAREHOLDERS' EQUITY		
	2013	2014	2015
ROCE	37.9%	42.1%	45.9%
INPUT VARIABLES			
Total Revenues	$14,867	$16,448	$19,163
Net Operating Profit After Tax (NOPAT)	$ 1,817	$ 2,097	$ 2,595
Net Financing Expense After Tax	$ (1)	$ 42	$ 52
Average Net Operating Assets	$ 5,723	$ 6,552	$ 7,745
Average Financing Obligations	$ 928	$ 1,676	$ 2,200
Average Common Equity	$ 4,795	$ 4,876	$ 5,545
Profit margin for operating ROA	0.122	0.127	0.135
Net operating asset turnover	2.598	2.510	2.474
Operating ROA (NOPAT/Average NOA)	0.318	0.320	0.335
Net Borrowing Rate	(0.001)	0.025	0.024
Spread	0.318	0.295	0.312
Leverage	0.194	0.344	0.397
Leverage*Spread	0.062	0.101	0.124
ROCE = Operating ROA+Leverage*Spread	0.379	0.421	0.459

(Continued)

Analysis Spreadsheet (Continued)

STATEMENT OF CASH FLOWS: SUMMARY

Year	2011	2012	2013	2014	2015
Operating Activities:					
Net Income	1,248	1,385	9	2,068	2,759
Add back depreciation and amortization expenses	550	581	656	748	934
Net cash flows for working capital	(330)	(384)	659	550	229
Other net addbacks/subtractions	144	169	1,585	(2,758)	(173)
Net CF from Operating Activities	**1,612**	**1,750**	**2,908**	**608**	**3,749**
Investing Activities:					
Capital expenditures (net)	(415)	(851)	(1,151)	(1,161)	(1,304)
Investments	(592)	(81)	(356)	258	(232)
Other investing transactions	(13)	(42)	96	85	16
Net CF from Investing Activities	**(1,020)**	**(974)**	**(1,411)**	**(818)**	**(1,520)**
Financing Activities:					
Net proceeds from short-term borrowing	31	(31)	0	0	0
Net proceeds from long-term borrowing	0	0	715	749	238
Net proceeds from share issues and repurchases	(217)	(201)	(204)	(582)	(1,187)
Dividends	(390)	(513)	(629)	(783)	(929)
Other financing transactions	(33)	(1)	10	(7)	(379)
Net CF from Financing Activities	**(608)**	**(746)**	**(108)**	**(623)**	**(2,257)**
Effects of exchange rate changes on cash	(1)	10	(2)	(34)	(151)
Net Change in Cash	**(16)**	**40**	**1,387**	**(867)**	**(178)**

Forecasts Spreadsheet

FSAP OUTPUT: FINANCIAL STATEMENT FORECASTS

Analyst Name: Wahlen, Baginski & Bradshaw
Company Name: Starbucks Corporation

Row Format:
Actual Amounts
Common Size Percentage
Rate of Change Percentage

Row Format:
Forecast Amounts
Forecast assumption
Forecast assumption explanation

Year +6 and beyond:
Long-Run Growth Rate: 3.0%
Long-Run Growth Factor: 103.0%

	Actuals			Forecasts					
Year	2013	2014	2015	Year +1	Year +2	Year +3	Year +4	Year +5	Year +6
INCOME STATEMENT									
Revenues	14,866.8	16,447.8	19,162.7	21,678.3	23,670.5	26,294.2	29,159.4	32,286.7	33,255.3
common size	100.0%	100.0%	100.0%	13.1%	9.2%	11.1%	10.9%	10.7%	
rate of change		10.6%	16.5%	See Forecast Development worksheet for details of revenues forecasts.					
<Cost of sales and occupancy expense>	(6,382.3)	(6,858.8)	(7,787.5)	(8,653.5)	(9,390.4)	(10,336.7)	(11,358.7)	(12,461.9)	(12,835.8)
common size	(42.9%)	(41.7%)	(40.6%)	(39.9%)	(39.7%)	(39.3%)	(39.0%)	(38.6%)	
rate of change		7.5%	13.5%	See Forecast Development worksheet.					
Gross Profit	8,484.5	9,589.0	11,375.2	13,024.9	14,280.2	15,957.5	17,800.7	19,824.8	20,419.5
common size	57.1%	58.3%	59.4%	60.1%	60.3%	60.7%	61.0%	61.4%	61.4%
rate of change		13.0%	18.6%	14.5%	9.6%	11.7%	11.6%	11.4%	
<Store operating expenses>	(4,286.1)	(4,638.2)	(5,411.1)	(5,997.2)	(6,497.6)	(7,162.8)	(7,883.6)	(8,664.2)	(8,924.2)
common size	(28.8%)	(28.2%)	(28.2%)	(35.0%)	(34.8%)	(34.6%)	(34.4%)	(34.2%)	
rate of change		8.2%	16.7%	Assume slight decline in store operating expense as a percent of company-operated store revenues.					
<Other operating expenses>	(431.8)	(457.3)	(522.4)	(590.6)	(649.9)	(727.0)	(811.4)	(903.9)	(931.0)
common size	(2.9%)	(2.8%)	(2.7%)	(13.0%)	(13.0%)	(13.0%)	(13.0%)	(13.0%)	
rate of change		5.9%	14.2%	Assume steady percentage of licensed, CPG, Foodservice, and other revenues.					
<Depreciation and amortization>	(621.4)	(709.6)	(893.9)	(1,049.0)	(1,191.5)	(1,362.5)	(1,562.0)	(1,094.0)	(1,126.8)
common size	(4.2%)	(4.3%)	(4.7%)						
rate of change		14.2%	26.0%	Amounts from depreciation schedule, Forecast Development worksheet.					

(Continued)

Forecasts Spreadsheet (Continued)

| | Actuals | | | Forecasts | | | | | |
Year	2013	2014	2015	Year +1	Year +2	Year +3	Year +4	Year +5	Year +6
<General and administrative expenses>	(937.9)	(991.3)	(1,196.7)	(1,300.7)	(1,420.2)	(1,577.7)	(1,749.6)	(1,937.2)	(1,995.3)
common size	(6.3%)	(6.0%)	(6.2%)	(6.0%)	(6.0%)	(6.0%)	(6.0%)	(6.0%)	(6.0%)
rate of change		5.7%	20.7%	Assume steady state relative to revenues.					
Other operating expenses (1)	0.0	0.0	0.0	0.0	0.0	0.0	0.0	0.0	0.0
common size	0.0%	0.0%	0.0%	0.0%	0.0%	0.0%	0.0%	0.0%	0.0%
rate of change				Explain assumptions.					
Other operating expenses (2)	0.0	0.0	0.0	0.0	0.0	0.0	0.0	0.0	0.0
common size	0.0%	0.0%	0.0%	0.0%	0.0%	0.0%	0.0%	0.0%	0.0%
rate of change				Explain assumptions.					
Income from equity investees	251.4	268.3	249.9	180.4	189.4	198.9	208.8	219.3	225.9
common size	1.7%	1.6%	1.3%	50.0%	50.0%	50.0%	50.0%	50.0%	
rate of change		6.7%	(6.9%)	Assume 50% rate of return from equity investees.					
Non-recurring operating gains <losses>	(2,784.1)	20.2	0.0	0.0	0.0	0.0	0.0	0.0	0.0
common size	(18.7%)	0.1%	0.0%	0.0%	0.0%	0.0%	0.0%	0.0%	0.0%
rate of change		(100.7%)	(100.0%)	Explain assumptions.					
Operating Profit	(325.4)	3,081.1	3,601.0	4,267.7	4,710.4	5,326.4	6,002.9	7,444.8	7,668.1
common size	(2.2%)	18.7%	18.8%	19.7%	19.9%	20.3%	20.6%	23.1%	23.1%
rate of change		(1046.9%)	16.9%	18.5%	10.4%	13.1%	12.7%	24.0%	23.1%
Interest income	123.6	142.7	43.0	43.2	47.8	52.0	57.0	62.5	64.4
common size	0.8%	0.9%	0.2%	2.1%	2.1%	2.1%	2.1%	2.1%	2.1%
rate of change		15.5%	(69.9%)	Interest rate earned on average balance in cash and investment securities.					
<Interest expense>	(28.1)	(64.1)	(70.5)	(77.1)	(90.6)	(90.6)	(90.6)	(90.6)	(93.3)
common size	(0.2%)	(0.4%)	(0.4%)	(2.71%)	(2.71%)	(2.71%)	(2.71%)	(2.71%)	(2.71%)
rate of change		128.1%	10.0%	Weighted average interest rate on average balance in financial liabilities. See Forecast Development.					

Line item / metric									
Income <Loss> from equity affiliates	0.0	0.0	0.0	0.0	0.0	0.0	0.0	0.0	0.0
common size	0.0%	0.0%	0.0%	0.0%	0.0%	0.0%	0.0%	0.0%	0.0%
rate of change		0.0%	0.0%	Explain assumptions.					
Other income or gains <Other expenses or losses>	0.0	0.0	329.5	0.0	0.0	0.0	0.0	0.0	0.0
common size	0.0%	0.0%	1.7%	0.0%	0.0%	0.0%	0.0%	0.0%	0.0%
rate of change		0.0%	1.7%	Explain assumptions.					
Income before Tax	(229.9)	3,159.7	3,903.0	4,233.8	4,667.5	5,287.8	5,969.3	7,416.6	7,639.1
common size	(1.5%)	19.2%	20.4%	19.5%	19.7%	20.1%	20.5%	23.0%	23.0%
rate of change		(1474.4%)	23.5%	8.5%	10.2%	13.3%	12.9%	24.2%	23.0%
<Income tax expense>	238.7	(1,092.0)	(1,143.7)	(1,439.5)	(1,587.0)	(1,797.9)	(2,029.6)	(2,521.7)	(2,597.3)
common size	1.6%	(6.6%)	(6.0%)	(34.0%)	(34.0%)	(34.0%)	(34.0%)	(34.0%)	(34.0%)
rate of change		(557.5%)	4.7%	Effective income tax rate assumptions.					
Income <Loss> from discontinued operations	0.0	0.0	0.0	0.0	0.0	0.0	0.0	0.0	0.0
common size	0.0%	0.0%	0.0%	0.0%	0.0%	0.0%	0.0%	0.0%	0.0%
rate of change		0.0%	0.0%	Explain assumptions.					
Changes in accounting principles	0.0	0.0	0.0	0.0	0.0	0.0	0.0	0.0	0.0
common size	0.0%	0.0%	0.0%	0.0%	0.0%	0.0%	0.0%	0.0%	0.0%
rate of change		0.0%	0.0%	Explain assumptions.					
Net Income	8.8	2,067.7	2,759.3	2,794.3	3,080.6	3,490.0	3,939.8	4,895.0	5,041.8
common size	0.1%	12.6%	14.4%	12.9%	13.0%	13.3%	13.5%	15.2%	15.2%
rate of change		23396.6%	33.4%	1.3%	10.2%	13.3%	12.9%	24.2%	3.0%
Net income attributable to noncontrolling interests	(0.5)	0.4	(1.9)	0.0	0.0	0.0	0.0	0.0	0.0
common size	0.0%	0.0%	0.0%	0.0%	0.0%	0.0%	0.0%	0.0%	0.0%
rate of change		(180.0%)	(575.0%)	Assume noncontrolling interests are acquired.					

(Continued)

Forecasts Spreadsheet (Continued)

		Actuals					Forecasts			
Year	2013	2014	2015	Year +1	Year +2	Year +3	Year +4	Year +5	Year +6
Net Income attributable to common shareholders	**8.3**	**2,068.1**	**2,757.4**	**2,794.3**	**3,080.6**	**3,490.0**	**3,939.8**	**4,895.0**	**5,041.8**
common size	0.1%	12.6%	14.4%	12.9%	13.0%	13.3%	13.5%	15.2%	15.2%
rate of change		24816.9%	33.3%	1.3%	10.2%	13.3%	12.9%	24.2%	3.0%
Other comprehensive income items	**43.8**	**(41.3)**	**(195.5)**	**0.0**	**0.0**	**0.0**	**0.0**	**0.0**	**0.0**
common size	0.3%	(0.3%)	(1.0%)	0.0	0.0	0.0	0.0	0.0	
rate of change		(194.3%)	373.4%	Assume random walk, mean zero.					
Comprehensive Income	**52.6**	**2,026.4**	**2,563.8**	**2,794.3**	**3,080.6**	**3,490.0**	**3,939.8**	**4,895.0**	**5,041.8**
common size	0.4%	12.3%	13.4%	12.9%	13.0%	13.3%	13.5%	15.2%	15.2%
rate of change		3752.5%	26.5%	9.0%	10.2%	13.3%	12.9%	24.2%	3.0%

Forecasts Spreadsheet (Continued)

FSAP OUTPUT: FINANCIAL STATEMENT FORECASTS

Analyst Name:	Wahlen, Baginski & Bradshaw								
Company Name:	Starbucks Corporation								

Row Format:
Actual Amounts
common size Percent
Rate of Change Percent

Row Format:
Forecast Amounts
Forecast assumption
Forecast assumption explanation

Year +6 and beyond:
Long-Run Growth Rate: 3.0%
Long-Run Growth Factor: 103.0%

	Actuals			Forecasts					
Year	2013	2014	2015	Year +1	Year +2	Year +3	Year +4	Year +5	Year +6
BALANCE SHEET									
ASSETS:									
Cash and cash equivalents	2,575.7	1,708.4	1,530.1	1,781.8	1,945.5	2,161.2	2,396.7	2,653.7	2,733.3
common size	22.4%	15.9%	12.3%	30.0	30.0	30.0	30.0	30.0	
rate of change		(33.7%)	(10.4%)	Assume ending cash balances equal to 30 days sales.					
Short-term investments	658.1	135.4	81.3	83.7	86.3	88.8	91.5	94.2	97.1
common size	5.7%	1.3%	0.7%	3.0%	3.0%	3.0%	3.0%	3.0%	
rate of change		(79.4%)	(40.0%)	Assume 3% growth.					
Accounts and notes									
receivable—net	561.4	631.0	719.0	825.0	907.8	1,015.5	1,133.4	1,262.5	1,300.4
common size	4.9%	5.9%	5.8%	14.7%	10.0%	11.9%	11.6%	11.4%	
rate of change		12.4%	13.9%	Assume growth with licensing and CPG revenues					
Inventories	1,111.2	1,090.9	1,306.4	1,327.7	1,440.7	1,585.9	1,742.7	1,912.0	1,969.3
common size	9.6%	10.1%	10.5%	56.0	56.0	56.0	56.0	56.0	
rate of change		(1.8%)	19.8%	Assume ending inventory equals 56 days cost of goods sold.					
Prepaid expenses and	287.7	285.6	334.2	352.0	369.7	387.5	405.2	423.0	435.7
other current assets									
common size	2.5%	2.7%	2.7%	5.3%	5.0%	4.8%	4.6%	4.4%	
rate of change		(0.7%)	17.0%	Assume growth with company operated stores.					
Deferred income taxes—									
current	277.3	317.4	381.8	0.0	0.0	0.0	0.0	0.0	0.0
common size	2.4%	3.0%	3.1%	0.0%	0.0%	0.0%	0.0%	0.0%	
rate of change		14.5%	20.3%	Assume the current portion of deferred tax asets is fully realized in Year +1.					

(Continued)

Forecasts Spreadsheet (Continued)

		Actuals						Forecasts			
Year	2013	2014	2015	Year +1	Year +2	Year +3	Year +4	Year +5	Year +6		
Other current assets (1)	0.0	0.0	0.0	0.0	0.0	0.0	0.0	0.0	0.0
common size	0.0%	0.0%	0.0%	0%	0%	0%	0%	0%	
rate of change				Explain assumptions.					
Other current assets (2)	0.0	0.0	0.0	0.0	0.0	0.0	0.0	0.0	0.0
common size	0.0%	0.0%	0.0%	0%	0%	0%	0%	0%	
rate of change				Explain assumptions.					
Current Assets	5,471.4	4,168.7	4,352.8	4,370.2	4,750.0	5,238.9	5,769.5	6,345.4	6,535.8
common size	47.5%	38.8%	35.0%	34.1%	35.1%	36.1%	37.0%	36.2%	36.2%
rate of change		(23.8%)	4.4%	0.4%	8.7%	10.3%	10.1%	10.0%	3.0%
Long-term investments	58.3	318.4	312.5	321.9	331.5	341.5	351.7	362.3	373.1
common size	0.5%	3.0%	2.5%	3.0%	3.0%	3.0%	3.0%	3.0%	
rate of change		446.1%	(1.9%)	Assume steady growth at 3%.					
Equity and cost investments	496.5	514.9	352.0	369.6	388.1	407.5	427.9	449.3	462.7
common size	4.3%	4.8%	2.8%	5.0%	5.0%	5.0%	5.0%	5.0%	
rate of change		3.7%	(31.6%)	Assume steady growth at 5%.					
Property, plant, and equipment—at cost	7,782.1	8,581.1	9,641.8	11,041.8	12,541.8	14,341.8	16,441.8	18,841.8	19,407.1
common size	67.6%	79.8%	77.5%	PP&E assumptions—see schedule in forecast development.					
rate of change		10.3%	12.4%						
<Accumulated depreciation>	(4,581.6)	(5,062.1)	(5,553.5)	(6,657.7)	(7,911.9)	(9,346.0)	(10,990.2)	(12,141.8)	(12,506.1)
common size	(39.8%)	(47.1%)	(44.6%)	See depreciation schedule in forecast development worksheet.					
rate of change		10.5%	9.7%						
Deferred income taxes—noncurrent	967.0	903.3	828.9	746.0	671.4	604.3	543.8	489.5	504.1
common size	8.4%	8.4%	6.7%	(10.0%)	(10.0%)	(10.0%)	(10.0%)	(10.0%)	
rate of change		(6.6%)	(8.2%)	Assume noncurrent deferred tax assets decrease 10% per year, as tax benefits are realized.					
Other assets	185.3	198.9	415.9	436.7	458.5	481.5	505.5	530.8	546.7
common size	1.6%	1.8%	3.3%	5.0%	5.0%	5.0%	5.0%	5.0%	
rate of change		7.3%	109.1%	Assume 5% growth.					

Other intangible assets	274.8	273.5	520.4	546.4	573.7	602.4	632.5	664.2	684.1
common size	2.4%	2.5%	4.2%	Assume 5% growth.					
rate of change		(0.5%)	90.3%	5.0%	5.0%	5.0%	5.0%	5.0%	3.0%
Goodwill	862.9	856.2	1,575.4	1,654.2	1,736.9	1,823.7	1,914.9	2,010.7	2,071.0
common size	7.5%	8.0%	12.7%	Assume 5% growth.					
rate of change		(0.8%)	84.0%	5.0%	5.0%	5.0%	5.0%	5.0%	3.0%
Total Assets	11,516.7	10,752.9	12,446.2	12,829.0	13,540.1	14,495.5	15,597.5	17,552.1	18,078.6
common size	100.0%	100.0%	100.0%	100.0%	100.0%	100.0%	100.0%	100.0%	100.0%
rate of change		(6.6%)	15.7%	3.1%	5.5%	7.1%	7.6%	12.5%	3.0%
LIABILITIES:									
Accounts payable	491.7	533.7	684.2	665.5	729.0	804.1	883.4	969.0	998.0
common size	4.3%	5.0%	5.5%	Assume a 28-day payment period consistent with recent years.					
rate of change		8.5%	28.2%	28.0	28.0	28.0	28.0	28.0	28.0
Accrued liabilities	1,269.3	1,514.4	1,760.7	1,991.8	2,174.9	2,416.0	2,679.2	2,966.6	3,055.6
common size	11.0%	14.1%	14.1%	Assume growth with revenues.					
rate of change		19.3%	16.3%	13.1%	9.2%	11.1%	10.9%	10.7%	3.0%
Notes payable and short-term debt	0.0	0.0	0.0	0.0	0.0	0.0	0.0	0.0	0.0
common size	0.0%	0.0%	0.0%	Assume zero.					
rate of change		0.0%	0.0%						
Current maturities of long-term debt	0.0	0.0	0.0	400.0	350.0	0.0	0.0	0.0	0.0
common size	0.0%	0.0%	0.0%	Current maturities of long-term debt per long-term debt note (Note 9).					
rate of change		0.0%	0.0%						
Deferred tax liabilities—current	0.0	0.0	0.0	0.0	0.0	0.0	0.0	0.0	0.0
common size	0.0%	0.0%	0.0%	Explain assumptions.					
rate of change		0.0%	0.0%						
Insurance reserves	178.5	196.1	224.8	231.5	238.5	245.6	253.0	260.6	268.4
common size	1.5%	1.8%	1.8%	Assume 3% growth.					
rate of change		9.9%	14.6%	3.0%	3.0%	3.0%	3.0%	3.0%	3.0%

(Continued)

Forecasts Spreadsheet (Continued)

Year	Actuals			Forecasts						
	2013	2014	2015	Year +1	Year +2	Year +3	Year +4	Year +5	Year +6	
Stored value card liability	653.7	794.5	983.8	1,113.0	1,215.2	1,349.9	1,497.0	1,657.6	1,707.3	
common size	5.7%	7.4%	7.9%	13.1%	9.2%	11.1%	10.9%	10.7%		
rate of change		21.5%	23.8%	Assume growth with total revenues.						
Accrued litigation charge	2,784.1	0.0	0.0	0.0	0.0	0.0	0.0	0.0	0.0	
common size	24.2%	0.0%	0.0%	0.0%	0.0%	0.0%	0.0%	0.0%	0.0%	
rate of change		(100.0%)		Explain assumptions.						
Current Liabilities	5,377.3	3,038.7	3,653.5	4,401.8	4,357.6	5,165.6	5,312.6	5,853.7	6,029.3	
common size	46.7%	28.3%	29.4%	34.3%	32.2%	35.6%	34.1%	33.4%	33.4%	
rate of change		(43.5%)	20.2%	20.5%	(1.0%)	18.5%	2.8%	10.2%		
Long-term debt	1,299.4	2,048.3	2,347.5	2,947.5	3,347.5	2,997.5	3,347.5	3,347.5	3,447.9	
common size	11.3%	19.0%	18.9%	1,000.0	400.00	0.00	350.00	0.00		
rate of change		57.6%	14.6%	$1,000 new long-term debt issues in 2016; see debt maturities in Note 9.						
Long-term accrued liabilities	357.7	392.2	625.3	707.4	772.4	858.0	951.5	1,053.6	1,085.2	
common size	3.1%	3.6%	5.0%	13.1%	9.2%	11.1%	10.9%	10.7%		
rate of change		9.6%	59.4%	Assume growth with G&A expenses, which grow with revenues.						
Deferred tax liabilities—noncurrent	0.0	0.0	0.0	0.0	0.0	0.0	0.0	0.0	0.0	
common size	0.0%	0.0%	0.0%	0.0%	0.0%	0.0%	0.0%	0.0%		
rate of change				Explain assumptions.						
Other noncurrent liabilities (1)	0.0	0.0	0.0	0.0	0.0	0.0	0.0	0.0	0.0	
common size	0.0%	0.0%	0.0%	0.0%	0.0%	0.0%	0.0%	0.0%		
rate of change				Explain assumptions.						
Other noncurrent liabilities (2)	0.0	0.0	0.0	0.0	0.0	0.0	0.0	0.0	0.0	
common size	0.0%	0.0%	0.0%	0.0%	0.0%	0.0%	0.0%	0.0%		
rate of change				Explain assumptions.						
Total Liabilities	7,034.4	5,479.2	6,626.3	8,056.7	8,477.5	9,021.1	9,611.6	10,254.8	10,562.4	
common size	61.1%	51.0%	53.2%	62.8%	62.6%	62.2%	61.6%	58.4%	58.4%	
rate of change		(22.1%)	20.9%	21.6%	5.2%	6.4%	6.5%	6.7%		

SHAREHOLDERS' EQUITY:

Preferred stock	0.0	0.0	0.0	0.0	0.0	0.0	0.0	0.0	0.0
common size	0.0%	0.0%	0.0%	0.0%	0.0%	0.0%	0.0%	0.0%	0.0%
rate of change			Explain assumptions.						
Common stock +									
Additional paid in capital	282.9	40.1	42.6	43.9	46.3	49.6	53.4	60.1	61.9
common size	2.5%	0.4%	0.342%	0.342%	0.342%	0.342%	0.342%	0.342%	0.342%
rate of change		(85.8%)	6.2%	Assume steady percent of total assets.					
Retained earnings <deficit>	4,130.3	5,206.6	5,974.8	4,927.8	5,215.6	5,624.1	6,131.9	7,436.6	7,653.7
common size	35.9%	48.4%	48.0%						
rate of change		26.1%	14.8%	Add net income and subtract dividends and share repurchases; see forecast box below.					
Accum. other comprehensive income <loss>	67.0	25.3	(199.4)	(199.4)	(199.4)	(199.4)	(199.4)	(199.4)	(199.4)
common size	0.6%	0.2%	(1.6%)						
rate of change		(62.2%)	(888.1%)	0.0	0.0	0.0	0.0	0.0	0.0
				Add accumulated other comprehensive income items from income statement.					
<Treasury stock> and other equity adjustments	0.0	0.0	0.0	0.0	0.0	0.0	0.0	0.0	0.0
common size	0.0%	0.0%	0.0%	0.0%	0.0%	0.0%	0.0%	0.0%	0.0%
rate of change		0	0	0	0	0	0	0	0
				Treasury stock repurchases subtracted from retained earnings, per Starbucks.					
Total Common Shareholders' Equity	4,480.2	5,272.0	5,818.0	4,772.4	5,062.6	5,474.4	5,985.9	7,297.3	7,516.2
common size	38.9%	49.0%	46.7%	37.2%	37.4%	37.8%	38.4%	41.6%	41.6%
rate of change		17.7%	10.4%	(18.0%)	6.1%	8.1%	9.3%	21.9%	3.0%
Noncontrolling interests	2.1	1.7	1.8	0.0	0.0	0.0	0.0	0.0	0.0
common size	0.0%	0.0%	0.0%	0.0%	0.0%	0.0%	0.0%	0.0%	0.0%
rate of change		(19.0%)	5.9%	Assume noncontrolling interests are acquired.					
Total Equity	4,482.3	5,273.7	5,819.8	4,772.4	5,062.6	5,474.4	5,985.9	7,297.3	7,516.2
common size	38.9%	49.0%	46.8%	37.2%	37.4%	37.8%	38.4%	41.6%	41.6%
rate of change		17.7%	10.4%	(18.0%)	6.1%	8.1%	9.3%	21.9%	3.0%

(Continued)

Forecasts Spreadsheet (Continued)

	Actuals			Forecasts					
Year	2013	2014	2015	Year +1	Year +2	Year +3	Year +4	Year +5	Year +6
Total Liabilities and Equity	11,516.7	10,752.9	12,446.1	12,829.0	13,540.1	14,495.5	15,597.5	17,552.1	18,078.6
common size	100.0%	100.0%	100.0%	100.0%	100.0%	100.0%	100.0%	100.0%	100.0%
rate of change		(6.6%)	15.7%	3.1%	5.5%	7.1%	7.6%	12.5%	3.0%
Check figures: Balance Sheet A = L + OE?	0	0	0	0	0	0	0	0	0

Initial adjustment needed to balance the balance sheet:

	Year +1	Year +2	Year +3	Year +4	Year +5	Year +6
	(1,153.7)	16.5	(98.2)	(257.6)	(9.9)	(2,681.9)

Dividends forecasts:

	Year +1	Year +2	Year +3	Year +4	Year +5	Year +6
Common dividends:	(1,187.6)	(1,309.2)	(1,483.2)	(1,674.4)	(2,080.4)	(2,142.8)
		(42.5%)	(42.5%)	(42.5%)	(42.5%)	

Assume dividend payout of net income.

	Year +1	Year +2	Year +3	Year +4	Year +5	Year +6
Preferred dividends:	0.0	0.0	0.0	0.0	0.0	0.0
	0.0	0.0	0.0	0.0		

Enter preferred stock dividend payments, if any.

	Year +1	Year +2	Year +3	Year +4	Year +5	Year +6
Total dividends:	(1,187.6)	(1,309.2)	(1,483.2)	(1,674.4)	(2,080.4)	(2,142.8)

Total dividend forecast amounts.

Treasury Stock Purchases:

Flexible Financial Account:
Original Forecast Amounts:

	Year +1	Year +2	Year +3	Year +4	Year +5	Year +6
Treasury Stock Purchases:	(1,500.0)	(1,500.0)	(1,500.0)	(1,500.0)	(1,500.0)	
Implied adjustments:	(1,153.7)	16.5	(98.2)	(257.6)	(9.9)	(2,681.9)

Adjustment needed to balance the balance sheet, from above.

	Year +1	Year +2	Year +3	Year +4	Year +5	Year +6
Total:	(2,653.7)	(1,483.5)	(1,598.2)	(1,757.6)	(1,509.9)	(2,681.9)

Total Treasury Stock Purchase Amounts

Forecasts Spreadsheet (Continued)

FSAP OUTPUT: FINANCIAL STATEMENT FORECASTS

Analyst Name: Wahlen, Baginski & Bradshaw
Company Name: Starbucks Corporation

IMPLIED STATEMENT OF CASH FLOWS	Actuals			Forecasts				
	2014	2015	Year +1	Year +2	Year +3	Year +4	Year +5	Year +6
Net Income	2,067.7	2,759.3	2,794.3	3,080.6	3,490.0	3,939.8	4,895.0	5,041.8
Add back depreciation expense (net)	480.5	491.4	1,104.2	1,254.2	1,434.2	1,644.2	1,151.6	364.3
Add back amortization expense (net)	0.0	0.0	0.0	0.0	0.0	0.0	0.0	0.0
<Increase> Decrease in receivables—net	(69.6)	(88.0)	(106.0)	(82.8)	(107.7)	(117.9)	(129.1)	(37.9)
<Increase> Decrease in inventories	20.3	(215.5)	(21.3)	(113.1)	(145.2)	(156.8)	(169.3)	(57.4)
<Increase> Decrease in prepaid expenses	2.1	(48.6)	(17.8)	(17.8)	(17.8)	(17.8)	(17.8)	(12.7)
<Increase> Decrease in other current assets (1)	0.0	0.0	0.0	0.0	0.0	0.0	0.0	0.0
<Increase> Decrease in other current assets (2)	0.0	0.0	0.0	0.0	0.0	0.0	0.0	0.0
Increase <Decrease> in accounts payable—trade	42.0	150.5	(18.7)	63.6	75.1	79.3	85.6	29.1
Increase <Decrease> in current accrued liabilities	245.1	246.3	231.1	183.0	241.1	263.3	287.3	89.0
Increase <Decrease> in insurance reserves	17.6	28.7	6.7	6.9	7.2	7.4	7.6	7.8
Increase <Decrease> in stored value card liabilities	140.8	189.3	129.2	102.3	134.7	147.1	160.6	49.7
Increase <Decrease> in other current liabilities (2)	(2,784.1)	0.0	0.0	0.0	0.0	0.0	0.0	0.0
Net change in deferred tax assets and liabilities	23.6	10.0	464.7	74.6	67.1	60.4	54.4	(14.7)
Increase <Decrease> in long-term accrued liabilities	34.5	233.1	82.1	65.0	85.6	93.5	102.0	31.6
Increase <Decrease> in other noncurrent liabilities (1)	0.0	0.0	0.0	0.0	0.0	0.0	0.0	0.0
Increase <Decrease> in other noncurrent liabilities (2)	0.0	0.0	0.0	0.0	0.0	0.0	0.0	0.0
Net Cash Flows from Operations	**220.5**	**3,756.5**	**4,648.5**	**4,616.6**	**5,264.2**	**5,942.4**	**6,428.0**	**5,490.7**
<Increase> Decrease in property, plant, & equip. at cost	(799.0)	(1,060.7)	(1,400.0)	(1,500.0)	(1,800.0)	(2,100.0)	(2,400.0)	(565.3)
<Increase> Decrease in short-term investments	522.7	54.1	(2.4)	(2.5)	(2.6)	(2.7)	(2.7)	(2.8)
<Increase> Decrease in long-term investments	(278.5)	168.8	(27.0)	(28.1)	(29.3)	(30.6)	(31.9)	(24.3)
<Increase> Decrease in amortizable intangible assets (net)	1.3	(246.9)	(26.0)	(27.3)	(28.7)	(30.1)	(31.6)	(19.9)

(Continued)

Forecasts Spreadsheet (Continued)

	Actuals		Forecasts					
IMPLIED STATEMENT OF CASH FLOWS	2011	2012	Year +1	Year +2	Year +3	Year +4	Year +5	Year +6
<Increase> Decrease in goodwill and nonamort. intangibles	6.7	(719.2)	(78.8)	(82.7)	(86.8)	(91.2)	(95.7)	(60.3)
<Increase> Decrease in other assets	(13.6)	(217.0)	(20.8)	(21.8)	(22.9)	(24.1)	(25.3)	(15.9)
<Increase> Decrease in other noncurrent assets (2)	0.0	0.0	0.0	0.0	0.0	0.0	0.0	0.0
Net Cash Flows from Investing Activities	**(560.4)**	**(2,020.9)**	**(1,555.0)**	**(1,662.5)**	**(1,970.4)**	**(2,278.7)**	**(2,587.3)**	**(688.6)**
Increase <Decrease> in short-term debt	0.0	0.0	400.0	(400.0)	350.0	(350.0)	0.0	0.0
Increase <Decrease> in long-term debt	748.9	299.2	600.0	400.0	(350.0)	350.0	0.0	100.4
Increase <Decrease> in preferred stock	0.0	0.0	0.0	0.0	0.0	0.0	0.0	0.0
Increase <Decrease> in common stock + paid in capital	(242.8)	2.5	1.3	2.4	3.3	3.8	6.7	1.8
Increase <Decrease> in accum. OCI	(41.7)	(224.7)	0.0	0.0	0.0	0.0	0.0	0.0
Increase <Decrease> in treasury stock and other equity adjs.	0.0	0.0	0.0	0.0	0.0	0.0	0.0	0.0
Dividends and share repurchases	(991.8)	(1,989.2)	(3,841.3)	(2,792.8)	(3,081.5)	(3,432.0)	(3,590.3)	(4,824.7)
Increase <Decrease> in noncontrolling interests	0.0	(1.8)	(1.8)	0.0	0.0	0.0	0.0	0.0
Net Cash Flows from Financing Activities	**(527.4)**	**(1,914.0)**	**(2,841.7)**	**(2,790.4)**	**(3,078.2)**	**(3,428.2)**	**(3,583.6)**	**(4,722.5)**
Net Change in Cash	**(867.3)**	**(178.4)**	**251.8**	**163.7**	**215.6**	**235.5**	**257.0**	**79.6**
Check Figure:								
Net change in cash—Change in cash balance	0	0	0	0	0	0	0	0

Forecasts Spreadsheet (Continued)

APPENDIX C Financial Statement Analysis Package (FSAP) C-27

FSAP OUTPUT: FINANCIAL STATEMENT FORECASTS

Analyst Name: Wahlen, Baginski & Bradshaw
Company Name: Starbucks Corporation

	Actuals			Forecasts					
	2013	2014	2015	Year +1	Year +2	Year +3	Year +4	Year +5	Year +6
FORECAST VALIDITY CHECK DATA:									
GROWTH									
Revenue Growth Rates:	11.8%	10.6%	16.5%	13.1%	9.2%	11.1%	10.9%	10.7%	3.0%
Net Income Growth Rates:	(99.4%)	23396.6%	33.4%	1.3%	10.2%	13.3%	12.9%	24.2%	3.0%
Total Asset Growth Rates	40.1%	(6.6%)	15.7%	3.1%	5.5%	7.1%	7.6%	12.5%	3.0%
RETURN ON ASSETS (based on reported amounts):									
Profit Margin for ROA	0.2%	12.8%	14.6%	13.1%	13.3%	13.5%	13.7%	15.3%	15.3%
× Asset Turnover	1.5	1.5	1.7	1.7	1.8	1.9	1.9	1.9	1.9
= Return on Assets	0.3%	18.9%	24.2%	22.5%	23.8%	25.3%	26.6%	29.9%	28.6%
RETURN ON ASSETS (excluding the effects of nonrecurring items):									
Profit Margin for ROA	12.4%	12.7%	13.5%	13.1%	13.3%	13.5%	13.7%	15.3%	15.3%
× Asset Turnover	1.5	1.5	1.7	1.7	1.8	1.9	1.9	1.9	1.9
= Return on Assets	18.6%	18.8%	22.3%	22.5%	23.8%	25.3%	26.6%	29.9%	28.6%
RETURN ON COMMON EQUITY (based on reported amounts):									
Profit Margin for ROCE	0.1%	12.6%	14.4%	12.9%	13.0%	13.3%	13.5%	15.2%	15.2%
× Asset Turnover	1.5	1.5	1.7	1.7	1.8	1.9	1.9	1.9	1.9
× Capital Structure Leverage	2.1	2.3	2.1	2.4	2.7	2.7	2.6	2.5	2.4
= Return on Common Equity	0.2%	42.4%	49.7%	52.8%	62.6%	66.2%	68.8%	73.7%	68.1%
RETURN ON COMMON EQUITY (excluding the effects of nonrecurring items):									
Profit Margin for ROCE	12.2%	12.5%	13.3%	12.9%	13.0%	13.3%	13.5%	15.2%	15.2%
× Asset Turnover	1.5	1.5	1.7	1.7	1.8	1.9	1.9	1.9	1.9
× Capital Structure Leverage	2.1	2.3	2.1	2.4	2.7	2.7	2.6	2.5	2.4
= Return on Common Equity	37.9%	42.1%	45.9%	52.8%	62.6%	66.2%	68.8%	73.7%	68.1%

(Continued)

Forecasts Spreadsheet (Continued)

FSAP OUTPUT: FINANCIAL STATEMENT FORECASTS

Analyst Name: Wahlen, Baginski & Bradshaw
Company Name: Starbucks Corporation

	Actuals			Forecasts					
	2013	2014	2015	Year +1	Year +2	Year +3	Year +4	Year +5	Year +6
OPERATING PERFORMANCE:									
Gross Profit / Revenues	57.1%	58.3%	59.4%	60.1%	60.3%	60.7%	61.0%	61.4%	61.4%
Operating Profit Before Taxes / Revenues	(2.2%)	18.7%	18.8%	19.7%	19.9%	20.3%	20.6%	23.1%	23.1%
ASSET TURNOVER:									
Revenues / Avg. Accounts Receivable	28.4	27.6	28.4	28.1	27.3	27.3	27.1	27.0	26.0
COGS / Average Inventory	5.4	6.2	6.5	6.6	6.8	6.8	6.8	6.8	6.6
Revenues / Average Fixed Assets	5.1	4.9	5.0	2.0	1.9	1.9	1.8	1.8	1.7
LIQUIDITY:									
Current Ratio	1.0	1.4	1.2	1.0	1.1	1.0	1.1	1.1	1.1
Quick Ratio	0.7	0.8	0.6	0.6	0.7	0.6	0.7	0.7	0.7
SOLVENCY:									
Total Liabilities / Total Assets	61.1%	51.0%	53.2%	62.8%	62.6%	62.2%	61.6%	58.4%	58.4%
Total Liabilities / Total Equity	156.9%	103.9%	113.9%	168.8%	167.5%	164.8%	160.6%	140.5%	140.5%
Interest Coverage Ratio	(7.2)	50.3	56.4	55.9	52.5	59.4	66.9	82.9	82.9

Forecast Development Spreadsheet

Analyst Name: Wahlen, Baginski & Bradshaw
Company Name: Starbucks Corporation

Revenue Forecast Development

| | Actuals | | | Forecasts | | | | |
Year	2013	2014	2015	Year +1	Year +2	Year +3	Year +4	Year +5
Net Revenues (in millions):								
Company-operated stores	$ 11,802.7	$ 12,983.0	$ 15,203.2	$ 17,135.0	$ 18,671.3	$ 20,701.8	$ 22,917.5	$ 25,334.0
Licensed stores	1,351.0	1,583.5	1,856.0	2,185.0	2,454.0	2,792.6	3,162.1	3,565.0
CPG, foodservice and other	1,713.1	1,881.3	2,103.5	2,358.3	2,545.2	2,799.8	3,079.7	3,387.7
Total Net Revenues	**$14,866.8**	**$16,447.8**	**$19,162.7**	**$21,678.3**	**$23,670.5**	**$26,294.2**	**$29,159.4**	**$32,286.7**
rate of change		10.6%	16.5%	13.1%	9.2%	11.1%	10.9%	10.7%

Implied revenue growth rates.

Summary: Revenues by Segment and Type:

Starbucks: Revenue Forecasts by Segment and Type

	2013	2014	2015	Year +1	Year +2	Year +3	Year +4	Year +5
Company-operated stores	$11,802.7	$12,983.0	$15,203.2	$17,135.0	$18,671.3	$20,701.8	$22,917.5	$25,334.0
Growth rates		10.0%	17.1%	12.7%	9.0%	10.9%	10.7%	10.5%
Number of company stores	10,143	10,713	12,235	12,885	13,535	14,185	14,835	15,485
Revenues/Average Store	$ 1.007	$ 1.245	$ 1.325	$ 1.364	$ 1.413	$ 1.494	$ 1.579	$ 1.671
Revenue Growth/Average Store		23.6%	6.4%	3.0%	3.6%	5.7%	5.7%	5.8%
Licensing	$ 1,351.0	$ 1,583.5	$ 1,856.0	$ 2,185.0	$ 2,454.0	$ 2,792.6	$ 3,162.1	$ 3,565.0
Growth rates		17.2%	17.2%	17.7%	12.3%	13.8%	13.2%	12.7%
Number of licensed stores	9,624	10,653	10,808	11,958	13,108	14,258	15,408	16,558
Revenues/Average Store	$ 0.112	$ 0.156	$ 0.173	$ 0.192	$ 0.196	$ 0.204	$ 0.213	$ 0.223
Revenue Growth/Average Store		40.0%	10.7%	11.0%	2.0%	4.2%	4.5%	4.6%
CPG, Foodservice and Other	$ 1,713.1	$ 1,881.3	$ 2,103.5	$ 2,358.3	$ 2,545.2	$ 2,799.8	$ 3,079.7	$ 3,387.7
Growth rates		9.8%	11.8%	12.1%	7.9%	10.0%	10.0%	10.0%
Revenues	**$14,866.8**	**$16,447.8**	**$19,162.7**	**$21,678.3**	**$23,670.5**	**$26,294.2**	**$29,159.4**	**$32,286.7**

(Continued)

Forecast Development Spreadsheet (Continued)

Starbucks' Combined Revenue Forecasts

	Actuals:			Projections:				
Company Operated Stores:	2013	2014	2015	Year +1	Year +2	Year +3	Year +4	Year +5
Americas:	$10,038.3	$10,866.5	$11,925.6	$13,104.8	$14,440.7	$15,889.8	$17,460.7	$19,162.9
CAP:	$ 671.7	$ 859.4	$ 2,127.3	$ 2,579.0	$ 3,077.7	$ 3,633.6	$ 4,252.2	$ 4,939.6
EMEA:	$ 932.8	$ 1,013.8	$ 911.2	$ 881.6	$ 899.2	$ 917.2	$ 935.5	$ 954.2
Other Stores:	$ 159.9	$ 243.3	$ 239.1	$ 246.3	$ 253.7	$ 261.3	$ 269.1	$ 277.2
Subtotals:	$11,802.7	$12,983.0	$15,203.2	$16,811.7	$18,671.3	$20,701.8	$22,917.5	$25,334.0
The 53rd Week Effect (53/52):				1.019				
Totals:	$11,802.7	$12,983.0	$15,203.2	$17,135.0	$18,671.3	$20,701.8	$22,917.5	$25,334.0
Licensed Stores:	2013	2014	2015	Year +1	Year +2	Year +3	Year +4	Year +5
Americas:	$ 915.4	$ 1,074.9	$ 1,334.4	$ 1,495.8	$ 1,673.5	$ 1,867.2	$ 2,078.1	$ 2,307.6
CAP:	$ 245.3	$ 270.2	$ 264.4	$ 341.0	$ 430.9	$ 531.9	$ 644.8	$ 771.0
EMEA:	$ 190.3	$ 238.4	$ 257.2	$ 307.0	$ 349.5	$ 393.5	$ 439.1	$ 486.4
Subtotals:	$1,351.0	$1,583.5	$1,856.0	$2,143.8	$2,454.0	$2,792.6	$3,162.1	$3,565.0
The 53rd Week Effect (53/52):				1.019				
Totals:	$1,351.0	$1,583.5	$1,856.0	$2,185.0	$2,454.0	$2,792.6	$3,162.1	$3,565.0
CPG, Foodservice, and Other:	2013	2014	2015	Year +1	Year +2	Year +3	Year +4	Year +5
Revenues:	$ 1,713.1	$ 1,881.3	$ 2,103.5	$ 2,313.9	$ 2,545.2	$ 2,799.8	$ 3,079.7	$ 3,387.7
The 53rd Week Effect (53/52):				1.019				
Totals:	$ 1,713.1	$ 1,881.3	$ 2,103.5	$ 2,358.3	$ 2,545.2	$ 2,799.8	$ 3,079.7	$ 3,387.7
Total Net Revenues:	$14,866.8	$16,447.8	$19,162.7	$21,678.3	$23,670.5	$26,294.2	$29,159.4	$32,286.7

Forecast Development Spreadsheet (Continued)

Starbucks: Store Operating Data:

Starbucks: Revenue Forecasts by Segment and Type

Americas	2013	2014	2015	Year +1	Year +2	Year +3	Year +4	Year +5
Net new stores opened during the year:				Expectations for net new stores to be opened each year:				
Company-operated:	276	317	276	350	350	350	350	350
Licensed:	404	381	336	350	350	350	350	350
Total	**680**	**698**	**612**	**700**	**700**	**700**	**700**	**700**
Total stores:								
Company-operated:	8,078	8,395	8,671	9,021	9,371	9,721	10,071	10,421
Licensed:	5,415	5,796	6,132	6,482	6,832	7,182	7,532	7,882
Total	**13,493**	**14,191**	**14,803**	**15,503**	**16,203**	**16,903**	**17,603**	**18,303**
Revenues:								
Company-operated:	$10,038.3	$10,866.5	$11,925.6	$13,104.8	$14,440.7	$15,889.8	$17,460.7	$19,162.9
Revenues per store/year:	$ 1.264	$ 1.319	$ 1.398	$ 1.481	$ 1.570	$ 1.665	$ 1.764	$ 1.870
Growth rate:		4.4%	5.9%	6.0%	6.0%	6.0%	6.0%	6.0%
Licensed:	$ 915.4	$ 1,074.9	$ 1,334.4	$ 1,495.8	$ 1,673.5	$ 1,867.2	$ 2,078.1	$ 2,307.6
Revenues per store/year:	$ 0.176	$ 0.192	$ 0.224	$ 0.237	$ 0.251	$ 0.266	$ 0.282	$ 0.299
Growth rate:		9.2%	16.7%	6.0%	6.0%	6.0%	6.0%	6.0%

CAP	2013	2014	2015	Year +1	Year +2	Year +3	Year +4	Year +5
Net new stores opened during the year:				Expectations for net new stores to be opened each year:				
Company-operated:	239	250	1,320	300	300	300	300	300
Licensed:	349	492	(482)	600	600	600	600	600
Total	**588**	**742**	**838**	**900**	**900**	**900**	**900**	**900**
Total stores:								
Company-operated:	882	1,132	2,452	2,752	3,052	3,352	3,652	3,952
Licensed:	3,000	3,492	3,010	3,610	4,210	4,810	5,410	6,010
Total	**3,882**	**4,624**	**5,462**	**6,362**	**7,262**	**8,162**	**9,062**	**9,962**

(Continued)

Forecast Development Spreadsheet (Continued)

CAP	2013	2014	2015	Year +1	Year +2	Year +3	Year +4	Year +5
Revenues:								
Company-operated:	$671.7	$859.4	$2,127.3	$2,579.0	$3,077.7	$3,633.6	$4,252.2	$4,939.6
Revenues per store/year:	$0.881	$0.853	$0.926	$0.991	$1.061	$1.135	$1.214	$1.299
Growth rate:		(3.1%)	8.5%	7.0%	7.0%	7.0%	7.0%	7.0%
Licensed:	$245.3	$270.2	$264.4	$341.0	$430.9	$531.9	$644.8	$771.0
Revenues per store/year:	$0.087	$0.083	$0.096	$0.103	$0.110	$0.118	$0.126	$0.135
Growth rate:		(4.1%)	15.6%	7.0%	7.0%	7.0%	7.0%	7.0%

EMEA	2013	2014	2015	Year +1	Year +2	Year +3	Year +4	Year +5
Net new stores opened during the year:				Expectations for net new stores to be opened each year:				
Company-operated:	(29)	(9)	(80)	0	0	0	0	0
Licensed:	129	180	302	200	200	200	200	200
Total	**100**	**171**	**222**	**200**	**200**	**200**	**200**	**200**
Total stores:								
Company-operated:	826	817	737	737	737	737	737	737
Licensed:	1,143	1,323	1,625	1,825	2,025	2,225	2,425	2,625
Total	**1,969**	**2,140**	**2,362**	**2,562**	**2,762**	**2,962**	**3,162**	**3,362**
Revenues:								
Company-operated:	$932.8	$1,013.8	$911.2	$881.6	$899.2	$917.2	$935.5	$954.2
Revenues per store/year:	$1.110	$1.234	$1.173	$1.196	$1.220	$1.244	$1.269	$1.295
Growth rate:		11.2%	(5.0%)	2.0%	2.0%	2.0%	2.0%	2.0%
Licensed:	$190.3	$238.4	$257.2	$307.0	$349.5	$393.5	$439.1	$486.4
Revenues per store/year:	$0.176	$0.193	$0.174	$0.178	$0.182	$0.185	$0.189	$0.193
Growth rate:		9.6%	(9.8%)	2.0%	2.0%	2.0%	2.0%	2.0%

Forecast Development Spreadsheet (Continued)

Other Stores (including Teavana)	2013	2014	2015	Year +1	Year +2	Year +3	Year +4	Year +5
Net new stores opened during the year:				Expectations for net new stores to be opened each year:				
Company-operated:	343	12	6	0	0	0	0	0
Licensed:	(10)	(24)	(1)	0	0	0	0	0
Total	**333**	**(12)**	**5**	—	—	—	—	—
Other segment stores:								
Company-operated:	357	369	375	375	375	375	375	375
Licensed:	66	42	41	41	41	41	41	41
Total	**423**	**411**	**416**	**416**	**416**	**416**	**416**	**416**
Other segment store revenues:	$159.9	$243.3	$239.1	$246.3	$253.7	$261.3	$269.1	$277.2
				3%	3%	3%	3%	3%

CPG, Foodservice, and Other (including Americas, CAP, and EMEA)	2013	2014	2015	Year +1	Year +2	Year +3	Year +4	Year +5
Revenues:	$ 1,713.1	$ 1,881.3	$ 2,103.5	$ 2,313.9	$ 2,545.2	$ 2,799.8	$ 3,079.7	$ 3,387.7
Growth rates:		9.8%	11.8%	10.0%	10.0%	10.0%	10.0%	10.0%
Revenues	$14,866.8	$16,447.8	$19,162.7	$21,269.3	$23,670.5	$26,294.2	$29,159.4	$32,286.7
The 53rd week effect (53 weeks/52 weeks)				$ 409.0				
Total Revenues	$14,866.8	$16,447.8	$19,162.7	$21,678.3	$23,670.5	$26,294.2	$29,159.4	$32,286.7

Forecast Development Spreadsheet (Continued)

Forecast Development: Capital Expenditures, Property, Plant and Equipment, and Depreciation

Capital Expenditures:				CAPEX Forecasts:				
	2013	2014	2015	Year +1	Year +2	Year +3	Year +4	Year +5
CAPEX:								
PP&E Acquired	$ 1,151.2	$ 1,160.9	$ 1,303.7					
PP&E Sold	0	0	0					
Net CAPEX	**$1,151.2**	**$1,160.9**	**$1,303.7**	**$1,400.0**	**$1,500.0**	**$1,800.0**	**$2,100.0**	**$2,400.0**
Net CAPEX as a percent of:								
Gross PP&E	16.7%	14.9%	15.2%	14.5%	13.6%	14.4%	14.6%	14.6%
Revenues	7.7%	7.1%	6.8%	6.5%	6.3%	6.8%	7.2%	7.4%

Property, Plant and Equipment and Depreciation

				Property, Plant and Equipment and Depreciation Forecasts:				
PP&E at cost:	2013	2014	2015	Year +1	Year +2	Year +3	Year +4	Year +5
Beg. balance at cost:				$ 9,641.8	$ 11,041.8	$ 12,541.8	$ 14,341.8	$ 16,441.8
Add: CAPEX forecasts from above:				1,400.0	1,500.0	1,800.0	2,100.0	2,400.0
End balance at cost:	**$ 7,782.1**	**$ 8,581.1**	**$ 9,641.8**	**$11,041.8**	**$12,541.8**	**$14,341.8**	**$ 16,441.8**	**$ 18,841.8**
Accumulated Depreciation:								
Beg. Balance:				$ (5,553.5)	$ (6,657.7)	$ (7,911.9)	$ (9,346.0)	$ (10,990.2)
Subtract: Depreciation expense forecasts from below:			(1,104.2)	(1,254.2)	(1,434.2)	(1,644.2)	(1,151.6)	
End Balance:	**$(4,581.6)**	**$(5,062.1)**	**$(5,553.5)**	**$ (6,657.7)**	**$ (7,911.9)**	**$ (9,346.0)**	**$(10,990.2)**	**$(12,141.8)**
PP&E—net	**$ 3,200.5**	**$ 3,519.0**	**$ 4,088.3**	**$ 4,384.1**	**$ 4,629.9**	**$ 4,995.8**	**$ 5,451.6**	**$ 6,700.0**

Forecast Development Spreadsheet (Continued)

Depreciation Expense Forecast Development:

		Depreciation expense forecast on existing PP&E:				
Existing PP&E at cost:	$9,641.8	$ 964.2	$ 964.2	$ 964.2	$ 964.2	$ 231.6
Remaining balance to be depreciated.	$4,088.3	$3,124.1	$2,159.9	$1,195.8	$ 231.6	$ —
PP&E Purchases:		Depreciation expense forecasts on new PP&E:				
Capex Year +1	$1,400.0	$ 140.0	$ 140.0	$ 140.0	$ 140.0	$ 140.0
Capex Year +2	$1,500.0		$ 150.0	$ 150.0	$ 150.0	$ 150.0
Capex Year +3	$1,800.0			$ 180.0	$ 180.0	$ 180.0
Capex Year +4	$2,100.0				$ 210.0	$ 210.0
Capex Year +5	$2,400.0					$ 240.0
Total Depreciation Expense		**$1,104.2**	**$1,254.2**	**$1,434.2**	**$1,644.2**	**$1,151.6**
Portion Reported Separately on Income Statement (95% of total)		$1,049.0	$1,191.5	$1,362.5	$1,562.0	$1,094.0
Portion Reported within COGS on Income Statement (5% of total)		$ 55.2	$ 62.7	$ 71.7	$ 82.2	$ 57.6

Depreciation methods:

	2013	2014	2015
PPE at Cost	$7,782.1	$8,581.1	$ 9,641.8
Avg Depreciable PPE		$8,181.6	$ 9,111.5
Depreciation Expense	$ 647.9	$ 739.7	$ 883.8
Implied Avg. Useful Life in Years		11.1	10.3
Useful Life Forecast Assumption:			10.0

(in years)

APPENDIX C Financial Statement Analysis Package (FSAP)

Forecast Development Spreadsheet (Continued)

Long-Term Debt and Weighted-Average Interest Rates

Debt Issues and Maturities:	Face Value Amounts	Proportion of Total	Stated Interest Rates	Weighted Average Interest Rates
2016 Notes	$ 400.0	0.119	0.875%	0.1045%
2018 Notes	$ 350.0	0.104	2.000%	0.2090%
2021 Notes	$ 500.0	0.149	2.100%	0.3134%
2022 Notes	$ 500.0	0.149	2.700%	0.4030%
2023 Notes	$ 750.0	0.224	3.850%	0.8619%
2026 Notes	$ 500.0	0.149	2.450%	0.3657%
2045 Notes	$ 350.0	0.104	4.300%	0.4493%
Totals	$3,350.0	1.000		2.7067%

Weighted Average Interest Rate Used in Forecasts: | 2.7067%

Cost of Sales and Occupancy Costs

	2013	2014	2015	Year +1	Year +2	Year +3	Year +4	Year +5
				Cost of Sales and Occupancy Cost Projections				
Cost of Sales and Occupancy Costs:	$6,382.3	$6,858.8	$7,787.5	$8,653.5	$9,390.4	$10,336.7	$11,358.7	$12,461.9
as a percent of total revenues	42.9%	41.7%	40.6%	39.9%	39.7%	39.3%	39.0%	38.6%
Rent expense (Note 10: Leases):	$ 894.7	$ 974.2	$1,137.8	$1,282.9	$1,389.7	$ 1,501.8	$ 1,619.4	$ 1,742.8
Number of company-operated stores at fye	10,143	10,713	12,235	12,885	13,535	14,185	14,835	15,485
Average number of company-operated stores		10,428	11,474	12,560	13,210	13,860	14,510	15,160
Average annual rent per company-operated store		$ 0.093	$ 0.099	$ 0.102	$ 0.105	$ 0.108	$ 0.112	$ 0.115
Expected inflation in annual rent				3.0%	3.0%	3.0%	3.0%	3.0%
Cost of sales (net of rent expense):	$5,487.6	$5,884.6	$6,649.7	$7,370.6	$8,000.6	$ 8,834.8	$ 9,739.2	$10,719.2
as a percent of total revenues	36.9%	35.8%	34.7%	34.0%	33.8%	33.6%	33.4%	33.2%

Valuation Spreadsheet

DATA CHECKS—Estimated Value per Share

Dividend-Based Valuation	$66.10
Free Cash Flow Valuation	$66.10
Residual Income Valuation	$66.10
Residual Income Market-to-Book Valuation	$66.10
Free Cash Flow for All Debt and Equity Valuation	$65.95

Check: All Estimated Value per Share amounts should be the same, with the possible exception of the share value from the Free Cash Flow for All Debt and Equity model. See additional comments in cell L266.

FSAP OUTPUT: VALUATION MODELS

Analyst Name:	Wahlen, Baginski & Bradshaw
Company Name:	Starbucks Corporation

VALUATION PARAMETER ASSUMPTIONS

Current share price	$ 56.84		
Number of shares outstanding	1,485.1	**COST OF PREFERRED STOCK**	
Current market value	**$84,413**	Preferred stock capital	$ —
GROWTH		Preferred dividends	$ —
Long-run growth assumption used in forecasts	3.0%	**Implied yield**	**0.00%**
Long-run growth assumption used in valuation.	3.0%	**COST OF NONCONTROLLING**	
(Both long-run growth assumptions		**INTERESTS' CAPITAL**	
should be the same.)		Noncontrolling interests capital	$ —
		Earnings attributable to noncontrolling	
COST OF EQUITY CAPITAL		interests	$ —
Equity risk factor (market beta)	0.75	**Implied yield**	**0.00%**
Risk free rate	2.70%		
Market risk premium	6.0%	**WEIGHTED AVERAGE COST OF CAPITAL**	
Required rate of return on common equity	**7.20%**	Weight of equity in capital structure	0.9723
		Weight of debt in capital structure	0.0277
COST OF DEBT CAPITAL		Weight of preferred in capital structure	0.00
Debt capital	$ 2,402	Weight of noncontrolling interests in	
Cost of debt capital, before tax	2.7%	capital structure	0.00
Effective tax rate	(34.0%)	**Weighted average cost of capital**	**7.05%**
After-tax cost of debt capital	**1.79%**		

(Continued)

Valuation Spreadsheet (Continued)

FSAP OUTPUT:	VALUATION MODELS
Analyst Name:	Wahlen, Baginski & Bradshaw
Company Name:	Starbucks Corporation

	1	2	3	4	5	Continuing Value
Dividends-Based Valuation	Year +1	Year +2	Year +3	Year +4	Year +5	Year +6
Dividends Paid to Common Shareholders	1,187.6	1,309.2	1,483.2	1,674.4	2,080.4	
Less: Common Stock Issues	(1.3)	(2.4)	(3.3)	(3.8)	(6.7)	
Plus: Common Stock Repurchases	2,653.7	1,483.5	1,598.2	1,757.6	1,509.9	
Dividends to Common Equity	**3,839.9**	**2,790.4**	**3,078.2**	**3,428.2**	**3,583.6**	4,822.9
Present Value Factors	0.933	0.870	0.812	0.757	0.706	
Present Value Net Dividends	3,582.0	2,428.1	2,498.7	2,595.9	2,531.3	
Sum of Present Value Net Dividends	13,636.1					
Present Value of Continuing Value	81,112.2					
Total	94,748.3					
Adjust to Midyear Discounting	1.0360					
Total Present Value Dividends	98,159.2					
Shares Outstanding	1,485.1					
Estimated Value per Share	**$66.10**					
Current Share Price	$56.84					
Percent Difference	16%					

Valuation Spreadsheet (Continued)

FSAP OUTPUT: **VALUATION MODELS**

Analyst Name:	**Wahlen, Baginski & Bradshaw**
Company Name:	**Starbucks Corporation**

	1	2	3	4	5	Continuing Value
Free Cash Flows for Common Equity	Year +1	Year +2	Year +3	Year +4	Year +5	Year +6
Net Cash Flow from Operations	4,648.5	4,616.6	5,264.2	5,942.4	6,428.0	5,490.7
Decrease (Increase) in Cash Required for Operations	(251.8)	(163.7)	(215.6)	(235.5)	(257.0)	(79.6)
Net Cash Flow from Investing	(1,555.0)	(1,662.5)	(1,970.4)	(2,278.7)	(2,587.3)	(688.6)
Net CFs from Debt Financing	1,000.0	0.0	0.0	0.0	0.0	100.4
Net CFs into Financial Assets	0.0	0.0	0.0	0.0	0.0	0.0
Net CFs—Preferred Stock and Noncontrolling Interests	(1.8)	0.0	0.0	0.0	0.0	0.0
Free Cash Flow for Common Equity	**3,839.9**	**2,790.4**	**3,078.2**	**3,428.2**	**3,583.6**	**4,822.9**
Present Value Factors	0.933	0.870	0.812	0.757	0.706	
Present Value Free Cash Flows	3,582.0	2,428.1	2,498.7	2,595.9	2,531.3	
Sum of Present Value Free Cash Flows	13,636.1					
Present Value of Continuing Value	81,112.2					
Total	94,748.3					
Adjust to Midyear Discounting	1.036					
Total Present Value Free Cash Flows to Equity	98,159.2					
Shares Outstanding	1,485.1					
Estimated Value per Share	**$66.10**					
Current Share Price	$56.84					
Percent Difference	16%					

(Continued)

Valuation Spreadsheet (Continued)

FSAP OUTPUT:	VALUATION MODELS

Analyst Name:	Wahlen, Baginski & Bradshaw
Company Name:	Starbucks Corporation

DIVIDENDS VALUATION SENSITIVITY ANALYSIS:

		Long-Run Growth Assumptions							
	66.10	0.0%	1.0%	2.0%	2.5%	3.0%	3.5%	4.0%	5.0%
Discount	6.00%	52.05	60.26	72.57	81.36	93.09	109.50	134.12	257.23
Rates	6.50%	47.87	54.60	64.32	71.00	79.58	91.04	107.07	171.19
	6.70%	46.38	52.62	61.51	67.54	75.21	85.27	99.05	150.95
	7.00%	44.30	49.89	57.72	62.94	69.47	77.85	89.04	128.18
	7.20%	43.01	48.23	55.44	60.20	**66.10**	73.58	83.41	116.46
	7.50%	41.21	45.92	52.33	56.51	61.60	67.98	76.17	102.39
	7.70%	40.09	44.49	50.45	54.28	58.93	64.69	72.00	94.75
	8.00%	38.51	42.51	47.85	51.25	55.32	60.30	66.53	85.21
	8.50%	36.13	39.57	44.06	46.87	50.19	54.17	59.03	72.94
	9.00%	34.03	37.00	40.82	43.17	45.91	49.15	53.05	63.74
	9.50%	32.14	34.73	38.01	40.00	42.30	44.98	48.15	56.60
	10.00%	30.45	32.72	35.56	37.26	39.21	41.45	44.07	50.89
	11.00%	27.54	29.32	31.48	32.76	34.20	35.82	37.68	42.33
	12.00%	25.13	26.54	28.24	29.22	30.31	31.53	32.90	36.23

Valuation Spreadsheet (Continued)

FSAP OUTPUT:	VALUATION MODELS
Analyst Name:	Wahlen, Baginski & Bradshaw
Company Name:	Starbucks Corporation

	1	2	3	4	5	Continuing Value
RESIDUAL INCOME VALUATION	Year +1	Year +2	Year +3	Year +4	Year +5	Year +6
Comprehensive Income Available for Common Shareholders	2,794.3	3,080.6	3,490.0	3,939.8	4,895.0	5,041.8
Lagged Book Value of Common Shareholders' Equity (at t-1)	5,818.0	4,772.4	5,062.6	5,474.4	5,985.9	7,297.3
Required Earnings	418.9	343.6	364.5	394.2	431.0	525.4
Residual Income	**2,375.4**	**2,737.0**	**3,125.5**	**3,545.6**	**4,464.0**	**4,516.4**
Present Value Factors	0.933	0.870	0.812	0.757	0.706	
Present Value Residual Income	2,215.9	2,381.7	2,537.1	2,684.8	3,153.2	
Sum of Present Value Residual Income	12,972.6					
Present Value of Continuing Value	75,957.7					
Total	88,930.3					
Add: Beginning Book Value of Equity	5,818.0					
Present Value of Equity	94,748.3					
Adjust to midyear discounting	1.0360					
Total Present Value of Equity	98,159.2					
Shares Outstanding	1,485.1					
Estimated Value per Share	**$66.10**					
Current share price	$56.84					
Percent difference	16%					

(Continued)

Valuation Spreadsheet (Continued)

FSAP OUTPUT:	VALUATION MODELS

Analyst Name:	Wahlen, Baginski & Bradshaw
Company Name:	Starbucks Corporation

RESIDUAL INCOME VALUATION SENSITIVITY ANALYSIS:

		Long-Run Growth Assumptions							
	66.10	**0.0%**	**1.0%**	**2.0%**	**2.5%**	**3.0%**	**3.5%**	**4.0%**	**5.0%**
Discount	6.00%	52.05	60.26	72.57	81.36	93.09	109.50	134.12	257.23
Rates	6.50%	47.87	54.60	64.32	71.00	79.58	91.04	107.07	171.19
	6.70%	46.38	52.62	61.51	67.54	75.21	85.27	99.05	150.95
	7.00%	44.30	49.89	57.72	62.94	69.47	77.85	89.04	128.18
	7.20%	43.01	48.23	55.44	60.20	**66.10**	73.58	83.41	116.46
	7.50%	41.21	45.92	52.33	56.51	61.60	67.98	76.17	102.39
	7.70%	40.09	44.49	50.45	54.28	58.93	64.69	72.00	94.75
	8.00%	38.51	42.51	47.85	51.25	55.32	60.30	66.53	85.21
	8.50%	36.13	39.57	44.06	46.87	50.19	54.17	59.03	72.94
	9.00%	34.03	37.00	40.82	43.17	45.91	49.15	53.05	63.74
	9.50%	32.14	34.73	38.01	40.00	42.30	44.98	48.15	56.60
	10.00%	30.45	32.72	35.56	37.26	39.21	41.45	44.07	50.89
	11.00%	27.54	29.32	31.48	32.76	34.20	35.82	37.68	42.33
	12.00%	25.13	26.54	28.24	29.22	30.31	31.53	32.90	36.23

Valuation Spreadsheet (Continued)

FSAP OUTPUT: **VALUATION MODELS**

Analyst Name: Wahlen, Baginski & Bradshaw
Company Name: Starbucks Corporation

RESIDUAL INCOME VALUATION	1	2	3	4	5	Continuing Value
Market-to-Book Approach	Year +1	Year +2	Year +3	Year +4	Year +5	Year +6
Comprehensive Income Available for Common Shareholders	2,794.3	3,080.6	3,490.0	3,939.8	4,895.0	5,041.8
Book Value of Common Shareholders' Equity (at t-1)	5,318.0	4,772.4	5,062.6	5,474.4	5,985.9	7,297.3
Implied ROCE	48.0%	64.6%	68.9%	72.0%	81.8%	69.1%
Residual ROCE	40.8%	57.4%	61.7%	64.8%	74.6%	61.9%
Cumulative Growth Factor in Common Equity as of t-1	100.0%	82.0%	87.0%	94.1%	102.9%	125.4%
Residual ROCE times cumulative growth	**40.8%**	**47.0%**	**53.7%**	**60.9%**	**76.7%**	**77.6%**
Present Value Factors	0.933	0.870	0.812	0.757	0.706	
Present Value Residual ROCE Times Growth	0.381	0.409	0.436	0.461	0.542	
Sum of Present Value Residual ROCE Times Growth	2.23					
Present Value of Continuing Value	13.06					
Total Present Value Residual ROCE	15.29					
Add One for Book Value of Equity at t-1	1.0					
Sum	16.29					
Adjust to Mid-year Discounting	1.036					
Implied Market-to-Book Ratio	16.872					
Times Beginning Book Value of Equity	5,818.0					
Total Present Value of Equity	98,159.2					
Shares Outstanding	1,485.1					
Estimated Value per Share	**$66.10**					
Current Share Price	$56.84					
Percent Difference	16%					

Sensitivity analysis for the market-to-book approach should be identical to that of the residual income approach.

(Continued)

Valuation Spreadsheet (Continued)

FSAP OUTPUT: **VALUATION MODELS**

Analyst Name: Wahlen, Baginski & Bradshaw
Company Name: Starbucks Corporation

	1	2	3	4	5	Continuing Value
Free Cash Flows for All Debt and Equity	Year +1	Year +2	Year +3	Year +4	Year +5	Year +6
Net Cash Flow from Operations	4,648.5	4,616.6	5,264.2	5,942.4	6,428.0	5,490.7
Add back: Interest Expense after tax	50.9	59.8	59.8	59.8	59.8	61.6
Subtract: Interest Income after tax	0.0	0.0	0.0	0.0	0.0	0.0
Decrease (Increase) in Cash Required for Operations	(251.8)	(163.7)	(215.6)	(235.5)	(257.0)	(79.6)
Free Cash Flow from Operations	4,447.6	4,512.7	5,108.4	5,766.7	6,230.7	5,472.7
Net Cash Flow from Investing	(1,555.0)	(1,662.5)	(1,970.4)	(2,278.7)	(2,587.3)	(688.6)
Add back: Net Cash Flows into Financial Assets	0.0	0.0	0.0	0.0	0.0	0.0
Free Cash Flows—All Debt and Equity	**2,892.6**	**2,850.2**	**3,138.0**	**3,488.0**	**3,643.4**	**4,784.1**
Present Value Factors	0.934	0.873	0.815	0.761	0.711	
Present Value Free Cash Flows	2,702.1	2,487.1	2,557.9	2,656.0	2,591.6	
Sum of Present Value Free Cash Flows	12,994.7					
Present Value of Continuing Value	84,020.0					
Total Present Value Free Cash Flows to Equity and Debt	97,014.7					
Less: Value of Outstanding Debt	(2,402.0)					
Less: Value of Preferred Stock	0.0					
Plus: Value of Financial Assets	0.0					
Present Value of Equity	94,612.7					
Adjust to midyear discounting	1.0353					
Total Present Value of Equity	97,947.9					
Shares Outstanding	1,485.1					
Estimated Value per Share	**$65.95**					
Current share price	$56.84					
Percent difference	16%					

Financial Statement Ratios: Descriptive Statistics by Industry

Appendix D can be found online at the book's companion website at www.cengagebrain.com